THIS BOOK IS DEDICATED TO
MY CHILDREN
AND
GRANDCHILDREN

PREFACE TO THE FIFTH EDITION

In the prior edition of the casebook, a major reorganization of the materials was undertaken. This new Fifth Edition adheres to the general organization implemented in that prior edition: it is both a logical ordering and works well pedagogically. An interval of five years elapsed between this edition and the previous one (with one Supplement published in the intervening period). Five years in the world of anti-terrorism law is a long time, and there is a substantial body of new material included in almost all of the chapters in this edition. A brief chapter by chapter review follows.

The volume thus is divided into two main Parts, the first dealing with criminal-enforcement-against-terrorism issues in a civilian mode, and the second addressing the military processes used in anti-terrorism enforcement. With one exception, the same ordering and general subject matter of the chapters within the two Parts has been retained, although some chapter titles have been slightly modified, reflecting changes in emphasis or some content. The final chapter, titled Epilogue has been dropped from the book on the ground that it did not add enough new to merit a separate chapter. The ideas reflected in that chapter, however, surface throughout the book.

While their order remains the same, in a number of chapters, there has been a reordering and redoing of the material internal to the chapter, reflecting new developments and, sometimes, entirely new material that falls under the particular subject matter. Examples of such reordering and new material can be found in Chapter 5 dealing with electronic surveillance, the second part of Chapter 6 which deals with national security letters, and Chapter 10 which treats detention in military custody.

Chapter 1 provides an Overview that expressly takes account of the three presidential administrations that have served since the tragic attacks on September 11, 2001. Major national security speeches delivered by President Obama are quoted at some length in this chapter; they address most of the issues developed in the casebook and thereby not only provide a detailed perspective of a presidential administration but can also be viewed as a general introduction to the subject matter of the book. Changes in philosophy and approach that have occurred as a result of shifting from one President to another are also reflected, highlighted and commented upon both in this chapter and at other points in the volume.

In addressing the concept and legal and policy definitions of terrorism, Chapter 2 delves more deeply into the concept and the applicable legal definitions than in prior editions. For example, it highlights the fact that there seems to be a reluctance in the federal system to include in the elements of crimes intended to be terrorism offenses a terrorism motive, and it presents statutes and other material that can help in identifying differences between hate crimes and terrorism offenses. Important background material as to what kind of terrorism offenses are being committed around the world and in the United States is also contained in this chapter.

In the third chapter, the Supreme Court decision in Holder v. Humanitarian Law Project is placed toward the beginning of the chapter (rather than toward the end, as in the previous edition) so that students will be familiar with the Court's disposition of the mens rea and constitutional issues underlying the material support offenses, as the class progresses through the chapter. The Stewart case has been given a less central role than in previous editions. Instead, United States v. Farhane has been added and materials relating to the inchoateness feature of the material support offenses have been built around it, reflecting the increased frequency of prosecution by the government of inchoate behavior—namely, the large cohort of cases charging individuals who have tried to travel to Syria to fight on behalf of ISIS. In this chapter, also, materials relating to the action of the Secretary of State in finally removing the MEK from the list of designated Foreign Terrorist Organizations is presented along with questions about its potential significance.

Chapter 4 dealing with proactive surveillance still includes case law arising out of proactive police activity in Chicago and New York City, but cases involving similar proactive police actions in Washington, D.C. have been added to the chapter

Much new material has been added to Chapter 5, Electronic Surveillance. The second part of the chapter has been redone, particularly the materials relating to both President Bush's Terrorist Surveillance Program (TSP) and the government's obtaining of millions of telephone records from the telephone companies, while trying to obtain important information through a process of data mining. Clapper v. Amnesty International, USA, involving an effort to challenge the constitutionality of the FISA Amendments Act is one of the handful of anti-terrorism cases that have been decided by the Supreme Court. By way of contrast, a district court case, down in the trenches, United States v. Hasbajrami, is used to illustrate the issues that arise in a criminal trial when the prosecution discloses that evidence in the case had been derived from a warrantless surveillance undertaken under the authority of the FISA Amendments Act. Important provisions of the USA FREEDOM Act (as well as a summary of their import) are presented. These provisions not only modified the data mining program but also the FISA Amendments Act and the use of national security letters to obtain records (see Chapter 6). Important reports from the Privacy and Civil Liberties Oversight Board are also included.

As mentioned, the USA FREEDOM Act also contains provisions relating to national security letters, which are addressed in the second part of Chapter 6. These provisions increase the required basis for issuance of such letters while also loosening the standards that govern whether the issuance of a particular letter must be kept confidential.

New material in Chapter 7, Interrogation, includes indications that the Trump administration may change interrogation policies adopted by the Obama administration but as of the time of this writing, no firm policy changes have ben announced. The chapter also describes how a two-step approach is being currently used, mostly in shipboard interrogations of suspected terrorists who were captured abroad, in order to obtain intelligence information before giving the suspect the Miranda warnings.

Chapter 8 covers how the material witness statute and the immigration/alien laws have been used in aid of anti-terrorism enforcement. This edition also adds material on the restrictions adopted by the Trump administrations on travel to the U.S. from a handful of countries, most of them in the Middle East. This is the first major action by the Trump administration asserted to be a terrorism prevention measure.

Chapter 9,which deals with the treatment of classified information in civilian criminal trials in the U.S. district courts, was expanded in the previous edition to address issues relating to security clearance for defense counsel. It continues to provide a foundation for making comparisons between the handling of classified information in civilian and military commission trials.

Chapter 10, Military Custody, has been reorganized and contains a great deal of new, up-to-date materials including important statutes, cases and executive actions. Legislation enacted in 2012, provides express and detailed statutory authority for placing into military custody suspected terrorists with the requisite linkage to al Qaeda. As a companion to this legislation, Hedges v. Obama, a 2013 decision, is reproduced here, involving a constitutional challenge that foundered in the U.S. Court of Appeals. The chapter also brings up to the present day the controversy attached to the Guantanamo Bay detention facility—President Obama's failed effort to close the prison, with his relative success in severely paring the Gitmo population, leaving President Trump with some difficult options in trying to implement his expressed desire to send some "bad dudes" there. The President's recently issued Executive Order revoking the Obama order to close Guantanamo is noted.

The new material in Chapter 11, Military Commissions, mainly relates to the substantive crimes that can be lawfully charged in prosecutions before the commissions. A couple of cases, al-Bahlul v. United States and Hamdan v. United States, present new perspectives on the viability of criminal charges of conspiracy and material support in aid of terrorism before the military commissions. A summary of the history of the military commission cases that have been completed focuses attention on the relative efficiency of the civilian criminal trial processes and the contrasting slowness of the military process.

New material is also contained in the chapter on Targeted Killing, Chapter 12—especially regarding the process and the substantive criteria that go into making a decision to fire missiles from a drone at a particular target. Chapter 13 which deals with the use of the military in domestic enforcement includes a relevant tweet from President Trump.

The book consists of text, notes and questions as well as cases and statutory and administrative materials. Of course, an effort has been made to make the book as up-to-date and timely as possible. Whenever practicable, original official materials are used. This edition also makes extensive use, more than in previous editions, of text Notes that provide detailed and in-depth perspectives on particular topics.

The book is designed primarily for use in teaching a two or three unit advanced, specialized criminal law and procedure course on the U.S. law of anti-terrorism. Instructors will find that with great frequency the daily newspaper will have some current material on issues or topics in the book that you can effectively use in class that very day to give students a sense of the dynamic and timely nature of this area of the law.

I welcome comments from those who use the book in their courses.

I also wish to take this opportunity to acknowledge and thank Professor Gregory S. McNeal for the important contributions he made to this volume.

NORMAN ABRAMS

December, 2017

PREFACE TO THE FOURTH EDITION

This new edition is a major revamping of the casebook, in order to make it a more effective teaching tool. The book has been reorganized, streamlined, shortened and reflects a dominant theme throughout: It highlights differences in the criminal law/procedure rules applied in civilian terrorism cases and those used in ordinary crime matters as well as in military commission processes. The book is now divided into two main parts; the first deals with enforcement issues in a civilian mode; the second, using military process. Some chapters have been omitted and new chapters added. Treatment of materials from the earlier editions has in many instances been modified to emphasize the dominant theme.

The chapter dealing with Anti-terrorism Legislative Packages, for example, has not been retained. While this chapter provided a useful historical perspective on the development of U.S. terrorism statutory law pre-and post-9/11, in the current edition, it would be a digression from the main theme of the book. Further, while this material provided useful background for the students, it did not lend itself to effective use in classroom teaching. For faculty who wish to make it available to their students, permission is hereby granted to adopters of the 4th edition to reproduce copies of Chapter 2 in the 3rd edition for use in the classroom.[1]

The separate chapter dealing with Bases for Expansive Executive Authority has also been omitted; material from that chapter is reflected at other points in the book. It was thought better to deal with the government's claims of expansive authority in the specific contexts in which they were raised, for example, the Department of Justice white paper supporting the executive branch's Terrorist Surveillance Program (TSP) (which included electronic eavesdropping by the NSA on conversations between persons in the U.S. and abroad). Further, the decision not to retain the chapter is supported by the fact that the more expansive claims of presidential authority by the Bush administration have been replaced by the Obama administration's seeming exclusive reliance on the Authorization to Use Military Force (AUMF) joint resolution passed by the Congress and the laws of war.

Chapters have been added that involve devoting more material to certain subjects than was reflected in earlier editions. Thus, a separate chapter has been added that highlights the government's methods for obtaining documents, records and other physical materials in terrorism investigations through search warrants (secretly issued and enforced) and

---

[1] If you wish to reproduce this chapter for your students and a copy of the third edition is not available to you, please contact the author, Norman Abrams, at abrams@law.ucla.edu

through national security letters (the equivalent of an administrative subpoena). While there was material on these topics in previous editions, the treatment in this edition is more focused, extensive and elevated in significance through placement in a separate chapter. Similarly, the subject of targeted killing is now treated in a separate chapter in the military mode portion of the book.

As mentioned above, the dominant theme of the book is to highlight the differences between terrorism enforcement and ordinary crime enforcement as well as between civilian and military terrorism enforcement. Thus in Part One, at the outset, terrorism legislation is addressed generally, with special attention to the definitions and uses of the terrorism concept as well as to what factors make particular crimes into terrorism offenses. The focus then shifts to the frequently-prosecuted and unique material support terrorism offenses. Part One then continues with various investigative methods typically used by the government in terrorism cases and the special rules that are applicable, comparing them, along the way, with ordinary crime investigative authority. Thus, a series of chapters cover proactive surveillance[2] (e.g. involving investigation in public assemblages or through publicly available sources), electronic surveillance, obtaining records and documents through search or subpoena, and obtaining information through interrogation, irregular[3] rendition (transferring persons apprehended abroad to the U.S. or a foreign country without legal process) and detaining individuals through the use of material witness authority or authority over aliens. Part One concludes with an examination of the classified information issues that frequently arise in civilian terrorism trials; in Part Two, the same subject is addressed in the military commission setting.

The second Part of the book contains four chapters: The first two deal with detention in military custody (the issues on this subject are diverse and complex), military commissions and the rules of procedure and evidence applicable therein and the crimes subject to prosecution before the commissions. Consideration of military commission rules of procedure and evidence provides an opportunity to compare them with the rules applied in civilian terrorism trials, and the materials are designed to facilitate such comparisons.

The last two chapters in this Part (the final Epilogue chapter stands by itself) deal with the difficult issues relating to targeted killing (essentially, another military mode method of dealing with terrorists), and the use of U.S. military forces on the domestic front and the Posse Comitatus Act.

---

[2]   In the previous edition, this was termed "Political Surveillance."

[3]   In the previous edition, this was termed "Extraordinary Rendition."

While the book is designed primarily for use in teaching a specialized two or three unit advanced substantive and procedure criminal law course or seminar, the opportunity is also taken, wherever appropriate, to place the materials in the national setting of larger issues relating to enforcement against terrorism. Thus, for example, the materials include extended Notes dealing with topics such as the Obama Administration's Anti-terrorism Policies; Civil Suits challenging the Government's Enforcement Practices; and the Controversy surrounding the Proposed Closing of the Guantanamo Bay Facility. The book also includes some material on criminal charges brought by foreign governments against U.S. agents for irregular renditions perpetrated on foreign soil without permission from the foreign government.

The book consists of text, notes and questions, cases and statutory and administrative materials. Wherever practicable, original materials are utilized. In a few instances, some important statutes, for example, the Foreign Intelligence Surveillance Acts, the Classified Information Procedures Act and the Military Commissions Act are reproduced, somewhat edited, but nevertheless in quite lengthy form. This represents an author's judgment call: there are three principal options in presenting such material—1) reproduce it in the text in extenso; 2) edit the statutes severely; 3) place the extensive statutory material in an appendix, possibly with severely edited versions in the main text. The first option was chosen because the students benefit from seeing all or most of the statutory context. While the third option makes the same material available to the students, it is believed that the back and forth required between the main text and the appendix material is not conducive to efficient class discussion.

Finally, as would be expected, this new edition has been updated to include the latest Supreme Court and federal court cases, for example, review of the conviction of a lawyer for violating the material support in-aid-of-terrorist-activity statute (United States v. Stewart, 2009); a challenge to the constitutionality of the material support of-a-foreign-terrorist-organization statute (Holder v. Humanitarian Law Project, 2010); standing to challenge the constitutionality of a provision of the FISA Amendments Act of 2008 authorizing government electronic surveillance targeting non-US persons outside the United States in order to gather foreign intelligence (Amnesty International USA v. Clapper, 2011); the right of persons detained at Guantanamo to obtain habeas corpus (Boumediene v. Bush, 2008) and the right of detainees at Bagram Air Force Base in Afghanistan to obtain habeas corpus (Al-Maqaleh v. Gates, 2010); the right of an alleged wrongfully-detained material witness to obtain redress from high government officials (Ashcroft v. al-Kidd, 2011) and the standing of the father of a person targeted-to-be-killed to obtain due process for his son (Al-Aulaqi v. Obama, 2010). It also contains the latest terrorism-related statutes, for example, the FISA Amendments Act of 2008 and the Military Commissions Act of 2009; as well as Executive Orders issued by President Obama, for example, on Ensuring Lawful Interrogations, 2009, and on Periodic Review of Persons Detained at Guantanamo, 2011; and recently-promulgated internal governmental (unclassified) guidelines, for example, the FBI's Domestic Investigations and Operations Guide, 2008, and the FBI interrogation guidelines regarding Miranda warnings, 2010 (which only came to public attention in March, 2011).

I hope that those who use the book, both students and faculty, find it as fascinating a subject matter as I do. Comments are welcomed from those who use the book in their classes.

NORMAN ABRAMS

August 2011

PREFACE TO THE THIRD EDITION

There is so much that is new in the content and organization of this book that it is fair to describe it as much more than simply an updating of the previous edition.

Thus, for example, chapters have been added or expanded in significant ways:

- A new chapter on Extraordinary Rendition and Interrogation/Torture has been added, and the materials on those topics have been significantly expanded from the earlier edition.

- Government Secrecy has been elevated to chapter-level status and partnered in a single chapter with the Classified Information Procedures Act material.

- The Foreign Intelligence Surveillance Act chapter has been expanded through the addition of substantial material on the NSA eavesdropping and data mining controversies and through partnering it with the U.S. Agents Acting Abroad section.

- The coverage of the chapter that introduces the subject of the scope of Executive Authority has been expanded to include National Security and Inherent Presidential power as possible bases for the exercise of such authority.

- Most of the chapters have been expanded from what they were in the previous edition:

- The chapter on Enemy Combatant detentions has grown the most—by more than one third—reflecting the vast new material that has appeared since the previous edition. That chapter also now includes an in-depth treatment of the Padilla and al-Marri cases.

- Overall, the entire book has expanded by almost one third, reflecting the fact that new case law has been handed down in every subfield of anti-terrorism law, many new issues have arisen, much new scholarly literature has been published and numerous new statutes have been enacted.

There has also been some reorganization of the book:

- The Classified Information Procedures Act material dealing with the handling of such information in ordinary criminal trials, for example, has been moved forward in the book (from chapter 9 to chapter 6) so that it comes before, not after, the material on detention, deportation proceedings, the Combatant Status Review Tribunals, Administrative Review Tribunals and trials before Military Commissions. This move makes it possible for students to be able to compare the handling of classified information in ordinary federal criminal trials with the handling of such material in various kinds of terrorism-related adjudicatory proceedings.

- The Foreign Intelligence Surveillance Act chapter has been moved (from chapter 10 to chapter 7) so that it no longer follows but rather precedes the chapters dealing with detention and the various kinds of adjudicative special terrorism-related proceedings. Appearing just before the new chapter on Extraordinary Rendition and Interrogation/ Torture, these two chapters together provide substantial coverage of the principal kinds of governmental enforcement practices utilized in pursuing and investigating terrorists.

While some material has been compressed and treated more briefly than in the previous edition—otherwise the size of the book would have gotten out of hand—the book contains a great many new cases. Examples include, in chapter 6, United States v. Paracha, a case similar to the final Moussaoui court of appeals case; in chapter 7, United States v. Ning Wen which addresses the issues raised by the significant purpose formula under FISA; in connection with the NSA controversy, American Civil Liberties Union v. National Security Agency, which, inter alia, addresses the meaning of the legal formula of "electronic surveillance" under FISA; in chapter 8, El-Masri v. United States, a civil suit by an alleged victim of extraordinary rendition; in chapter 9, civil law suits after-the-fact challenging 1) a material witness detention, Al-Kidd v. Gonzales and 2) immigration law detentions, Iqbal v. Hasty; in chapter 10, Bismullah v. Gates, dealing with the scope of what should be provided as the record on appeal from a CSRT hearing (petition for certiorari to the Supreme Court pending); also the court of appeals decision in Boumediene v. Bush, testing the congressional withdrawal of habeas jurisdiction in alien enemy combatant/detention cases (currently pending before the Supreme Court); also the various decisions in the Jose Padilla case, including the court of appeals decision in Padilla v. Hanft and the Supreme Court's disposition of Padilla's petition for certiorari; and finally, the court of appeals panel decision in al-Marri v. Wright (awaiting decision in en banc rehearing); and in chapter 11, the Supreme Court's decision in Hamdan v. Rumsfeld.

The book also contains significant new legislative or quasi-legislative materials excerpted or described, including the Protect America Act, the RESTORE Act legislative bill, the Detainee Treatment Act, the Military Commissions Act and the Manual for Military Commissions.

The terrorism-related legal literature has also been growing at a rapid rate, and an effort has been made in certain areas to provide citations and, at appropriate junctures, new excerpted material. In addition, the book includes some key statements made by government officials—for example, the President's and the Secretary of State's public statements regarding Extraordinary Rendition. Also included are excerpts, at relevant points, from the then-Attorney General-nominee Michael Mukasey's responses to questions regarding executive authority and the torture/waterboarding controversy.

As noted in the Preface to First Edition, this volume is appropriately viewed as a specialized federal criminal law casebook, containing unique substantive criminal law and criminal procedure/criminal law administration materials that arise out of a rapidly growing, and enormously important politically and socially relevant area of the law. It is intended primarily for use in a two unit advanced course to be taught in the second or third year of law school, but the book has expanded so much in coverage that it can easily now be used to teach a three unit course. It can also be used to teach a seminar, though the book has been designed primarily for being taught in a course on Anti-terrorism Law. An abridged version of the book is also available that can be used to supplement the first year Criminal Law course or to teach a seminar or a course or seminar at the undergraduate level.

NORMAN ABRAMS

May, 2008

PREFACE TO THE SECOND EDITION

This new edition contains literally dozens of new cases and important items that have become available in the 22 months since the first edition appeared: The field continues to develop with extraordinary speed.

The organization and chapter development from the first edition—the book is divided into three principal parts—continues to make both logical and pedagogical sense, and the same choices regarding coverage, in the main, have been retained. In the natural evolution of the subject, some topics have been added or expanded. For example, the very limited amount of material in the first edition on the subject of torture and interrogation has been increased. Similarly, the availability of extensive new material on enemy combatant status now warrants treatment of that subject in a separate chapter of its own rather than as one section in a chapter dealing with other bases for extended detention.

New material has been added to every chapter in the book, and new cases in a majority of them. Some of the chapters have been substantially redone, while changes in others involve the addition of substantial new materials, including entirely new cases or the substitution of the decisions of higher courts for opinions contained in the first edition.

Without attempting to describe all of the many changes in book, here are some of the highlights:

In Chapter 2, which describes the major legislative packages dealing with terrorism enacted by the Congress, special attention is now focused on the most controversial features of the USA PATRIOT Act, which have garnered special attention from the media and civil liberties groups. Most of the controversial provisions of the Act have sunset clauses, and the issue of whether to continue them will be under consideration in the Congress at least through the remainder of 2005.

Some cases have been added to Chapter 3, which in the first edition was restricted to statutes defining terrorist offenses. Perhaps most noteworthy is the inclusion of terrorism hoax cases which, in the absence of a terrorism hoax statute, had been prosecuted under the weapons of mass destruction statute. A new hoax offense, added by the Intelligence Reform and Terrorism Prevention Act of 2004 to the panoply of federal terrorism statutes, is also reproduced in this chapter.

Chapter 4 dealing with the material support offenses has been substantially recast and expanded, and now includes coverage of 18 U.S.C. § 2339A as well as § 2339B. The Lynne Stewart prosecution, United States v. Sattar, is used as a centerpiece in the chapter.

Chapter 5 now includes some substantial law review excerpts dealing with alternatives to the Bush Administration's emphasis on the legal notion that we are "at war" and heavy reliance on the President's role as Commander-in-chief and military authority.

Chapter 6 contains new case materials dealing with goverment's use of the material witness statute and alien status to detain individuals for extended periods and highlights the question whether the government's authority in terrorism cases to detain people is broader than in other contexts.

Chapter 7 contains the new cases dealing with the authority of the military branch of the government to detain individuals as enemy combatants, including the Supreme Court decisions and the district court decisions dealing with the Guantanamo detainees as well as Padilla v. Hanft, the Padilla case, begun again in South Carolina in the wake of the Supreme Court's decision in the original case. It also now includes important material on torture and background memoranda relating to the enemy combatant versus POW issue.

Added to Chapter 8 are materials relating to the substantive crimes charged in the military commission proceedings now in process and Hamdan v. Rumsfeld, the first judicial decision arising out of those proceedings.

The focus in Chapter 9 has been broadened to take account of approaches to dealing with the treatment of classified information in judicial proceedings in addition to the Classified Information Procedures Act. Case law development since the first edition highlights and invites comparative assessment of different approaches to the problem of classified information.

Some material has been added to Chapter 10 that sharpens the focus on the use of FISA warrant authority in terrorism cases. Finally, some new case and law review material have been added to Chapters 11 and 12, which deal with political surveillance and the use of the military in domestic law enforcement, and Chapter 13, which deals with actions of U.S. agents abroad, now also includes material on legal issues relating to the use of torture in interrogations.

The pace of change in this fascinating field means, of course, that Supplements and new editions will be forthcoming on a regular basis, with short time lags between them. I hope soon also to have established a website for making available the most current materials.

NORMAN ABRAMS

April, 2005

PREFACE TO THE FIRST EDITION

The occasion for the writing of this casebook was my teaching of a Seminar on Anti-terrorism and the Law in the Fall, 2002, after being largely away from law teaching (while serving in the campus administration) for a ten year period. Once I launched into the preparation of materials for the Seminar, it did not take long to realize that the importance and intrinsic interest of the topics and the nature of the available materials make this not only an excellent subject for a course or a seminar but also an ideal candidate for casebook treatment. When I began, while I appreciated the societal importance of the subject matter, I did not realize how extraordinarily active this area of the law would become over the short span of six months, and I certainly underestimated how exciting the materials would turn out to be, when viewed against the backdrop of traditional casebook subjects.

The casebook is intended primarily for use in a two unit advanced course to be taught in the second or third year. The book can also be used in connection with a seminar on the subject of anti-terrorism enforcement. In my own teaching of the Seminar, I used less than one half of the materials, which at the time were in preliminary draft form, for the first half of the semester (the students made oral presentations in the second half). Of course, there are a variety of ways to teach a seminar, and the choice of approach will dictate how much of the book you will want to use in that context. Finally, for those who might wish to supplement the first year Criminal Law course with a substantial segment devoted to anti-terrorism criminal enforcement, assignment of selections from the book offers, I believe, a rich menu of materials from which to choose. The book may also be used at the undergraduate level for either a course or a seminar.

The casebook can be viewed as a kind of specialized federal criminal law work. It is, of course, that and much more. While the title of the book is <u>Antiterrorism and Criminal Enforcement</u>, the book develops and plays off of the tension between a criminal or law enforcement approach, on the one hand, and a wartime, military and intelligence basis, on the other. While the starting point is criminal enforcement—this is not a treatment that uses constitutional or international law or governmental relations issues as its raison—there is no way to avoid addressing these latter issues along the way. Further, the book is not restricted to a treatment of substantive criminal law issues, although it certainly includes them; nor is it restricted to process and procedure and issues of criminal enforcement administration, although it also addresses such matters. An effort has been made to adopt an approach that brings together all of these different emphases in a coherent, integrated package.

The book is divided into three principal Parts which provide the organizing basis for the development and ordering of the material. The first Part provides an overview and emphasizes criminal law-related legislation dealing with the terrorism problem. The second Part focuses on detention and adjudication-related issues, while the third Part looks at issues raised by the techniques of investigation and information-gathering used in anti-terrorism criminal enforcement.

While the selection of topics is largely defined by the subject matter, some difficult choices had to be made—for example, what kinds of investigatory and enforcement techniques to include? A case can surely be made for the inclusion of some topics that do not appear in the book—*e.g.*, profiling, interrogation rules, asset freezing, and civil suits against terrorism-supporting states. A preference not to allow the book to become too large meant that such subjects could not be included. Generally, in determining coverage, topics were chosen that were not likely to be treated in depth in other courses in the curriculum and that were directly related to criminal enforcement or a substitute for such enforcement—*e.g.*, extended detention of suspected persons.

Many of the current or recent prosecutions of terrorism cases are mentioned throughout these materials. Because it is a good idea to give students the flavor of official documents connected to such cases, copies of some documents connected to some of the most prominent prosecutions are included in an Appendix. Instructors, of course, may wish to assign this material and use it as a basis for analysis and discussion.

An effort was made to keep track of the relevant major criminal enforcement developments in the field of anti-terrorism in the year and a half since September 11. This is, of course, an extraordinarily active legal field, with developments occurring almost weekly through new judicial decisions, executive or administrative initiatives and new legislation or legislative proposals, plus enforcement activities in the field. Undoubtedly, even while this book is being published, new developments will be occurring. It will be up to the individual instructor to keep an eye out and supplement the casebook materials as needed, until those new developments can be included in a Supplement or subsequent edition.

NORMAN ABRAMS

January, 2003

ACKNOWLEDGMENTS

I wish to thank the following then-UCLA law students for their very able research and gathering of materials used in revising and updating this new edition of the casebook: Nicholas Baltaxe, Tess Curet, Brigid Mahoney, Kira Richards, Joshua Samra, Kevin Whitfield, Hannah Woerner and Benjamin Woolley. I also want to thank Tyler O'Brien for his help in proofreading page proofs of the book.

I wish to give special thanks to Tal Grietzer, UCLA Law School, for his ever-present technical brilliance in helping to prepare this volume for publication.

I would also like to thank the following individuals and organizations for the permission each has granted to reprint excerpts from their publications.

Floyd Abrams, *The First Amendment and the War Against Terrorism*, 5 U. PA. J. Const. L. 1 (2002) Copyright © (2002) By the University of Pennsylvania Journal of Constitutional Law. Reprinted by permission.

Norman Abrams, *Developments in US Anti-terrorism Law, Checks and Balances Undermined*, 4 J. INT'L CRIM. JUST. 1117 (2006) Copyright © (2006) By the Journal of International Criminal Justice. Reprinted by permission.

Norman Abrams, *The Material Support Terrorism Offenses: Perspectives Derived from the (Early) Model Penal Code*, 1 J. Nat'l Security L. & Pol'y 5, 9–11 (2005) Copyright © (2005) By the Journal of National Security Law & Policy. Reprinted by permission.

An Amnesty International Report, *USA: Below the Radar: Secret Flights to Torture and 'Disappearance'*, AI Index: Amr 51/051/2006 Amnesty International 5 April 2006, Copyright © (2006) By Amnesty International. Reprinted by permission.

Kenneth Anderson, *What To Do With Bin Laden and Al Qaeda Terrorists?: A Qualified Defense of Military Commissions and United States Policy on Detainees At Guantanamo Bay Naval Base*, 25 Harv. J.L. & Pub Pol'y 591 (2002) Copyright © (2002) By the Harvard Journal of Law & Public Policy. Reprinted by permission.

Phillip Carter, *Why Can the Army Help Cops Catch the D.C. Sniper?*, Slate, Oct. 17, 2002 Copyright © (2002) By Slate Magazine. Reprinted by permission.

Ashley J. Craw, *A Call to Arms: Civil Disorder Following Hurricane, Katrina Warrants Attack on The Posse Comitatus Act*, 14 Geo. Mason L. Rev. 829 (2007) Copyright © (2007) By the George Mason Law Review. Reprinted by permission.

Major Kirk L. Davies, *The Imposition of Martial Law In The United States*, 49 A.F. L. Rev. 67 (2000) Copyright © 2000 By the Air Force Judge Advocate General School. Reprinted by permission.

Alan M. Dershowitz, *The Torture Warrant: A Response to Professor Strauss*, 48 N.Y.L. Sch. L.Rev. 275 (2003) Copyright © 2003 By the New York Law School Law Review. Reprinted by permission.

Christian M. De Vos, *Mind, the Gap: Purpose, Pain, and the Difference between Torture and Inhuman Treatment*, 14 No. 2 Hum. Rts. Brief 4 (2007) Copyright © (2007) By the Human Rights Brief. Reprinted by permission.

John T. Elliff, *The Attorney General's Guidelines for FBI Investigations*, 69 Cornell L. Rev. 785 (1984) Copyright © (1984) By the Cornell Law Review. Reprinted by permission.

FEDERALIST SOCIETY, WHITE PAPER ON THE USA PATRIOT ACT OF 2001: CRIMINAL PROCEDURE SECTIONS (2001) Copyright © (2001) By the Federalist Society. Reprinted by permission.

George P. Fletcher, *On the Crimes Subject to Prosecution in Military Commissions*, J. Int'l Crim. Just. 39 (2007) Copyright © (2007) By the Journal of International Criminal Justice. Reprinted by permission.

George P. Fletcher, *War Crimes Proceedings in Iraq? The Bush Administration's Dilemma*, April 4, 2003, at http://writ.news.findlaw.com/commentary/20030404_fletcher.html Copyright © 2003 By FindLaw. Reprinted by permission.

Matthew Carlton Hammond, Note, *The Posse Comitatus Act: A Principle in Need of Renewal*, 75 Wash. U. L.Q. 953 (1997) Copyright © (1997) By the Washington University Law Quarterly. Reprinted by permission.

Harold Hongju Koh, *The Case Against Military Commissions*, 96 Am. J. Int'l L. 337 (2002) Reproduced with permission from 96 AJIL 337 (2002), © The American Society of International Law.

Laurie L. Levenson, *Detention, Material Witnesses and the War on Terrorism*, 35 Loy. L.A. L. Rev. 1217 (2002) Copyright © (2002) By the Loyola of Los Angeles Law Review. Reprinted by permission.

David M. Park, Note, *Re-Examining the Attorney General's Guidelines for FBI Investigations of Domestic Groups*, 39 ARIZ. L. REV. 769 (1997) Copyright © (1997) By the Arizona Board of Regents. Reprinted by permission.

Heidee Stoller, Tahlia Townsend, Rashad Hussain, and Marcia Yablon, *Developments in Law and Policy: The Costs of Post-9/11 National Security Strategy*, 22 Yale L. & Pol'y Rev. 197 (2004) Copyright © 2004 By the Yale Law & Policy Review. Reprinted by permission.

Brian Z. Tamanaha, *A Critical Review of the Classified Information Procedures Act*, 13 Am. J. Crim. L. 277 (1987) Copyright © (1987) By the American Journal of Criminal Law. Reprinted by permission.

Elllen C. Yaroshefsky, *The Slow Erosion of the Adversary System: Article III Courts, FISA, CIPA and Ethical Dilemmas*, 5 Cardozo Pub. L. Pol'y & Ethics J. 203 (2006) Copyright © (2006) By the author and Cardozo Public Law, Policy, and Ethics Journal. Reprinted by permission.

Gregory S. McNeal, Targeted Killings and Accountability, 102 Geo. L. J. 681 (2014). Copyright © 2014 By Gregory S. McNeal. Reprinted by permission.

SUMMARY OF CONTENTS

———

PART 2. IN A MILITARY MODE

TABLE OF CONTENTS

TABLE OF CASES

The principal cases are in bold type.

———

TABLE OF STATUTES

TABLE OF REGULATIONS

TABLE OF RULES

ANTI-TERRORISM AND CRIMINAL ENFORCEMENT

Fifth Edition

CHAPTER 1

OVERVIEW: TRANSITIONS
BETWEEN PRESIDENTS

■ ■ ■

The materials in this casebook focus on the U.S. Government's efforts to prevent and punish terrorism, that is, anti-terrorism. Why a book and a course on anti-terrorism? It is fair to describe it as a criminal law and procedure casebook targeted at a particular kind of criminal activity. While that is an apt general description, it hardly captures the special nature of the subject matter, its importance and intrinsic interest. Especially since September 11, 2001, the executive branch of the U.S. government has utilized or claimed authority to exercise investigative, detention and prosecutorial authority, as well as several extraordinary remedies in relation to terrorism that extends, or would extend, much beyond the governmental powers used against ordinary crime.

Congress has generally supported the executive branch's approach by enacting legislation broadening governmental authority, especially in terrorism cases. And the courts, generally, though with some exceptions, have sustained executive branch and congressional legal positions. A study of the law of anti-terrorism thus entails a detailed examination of an unusually expansive invocation of governmental power regarding criminal law and procedure issues involving terrorists and those suspected of terrorism, with special attention paid to the respective roles and responses of the three branches of government.

More specifically, a very important way in which the government has claimed the authority to act expansively in regard to terrorism is through the use of military authority and process. Accordingly, the materials in this casebook are divided into two basic Parts: Part Two is devoted to the military approach in enforcement against terrorism which triggers a complex and significant set of legal issues, while Part One covers the exercise of non-military and civilian authority in this area of the law. Even in Part One, however, our study focuses on the ways in which non-military enforcement rules relating to terrorists and those suspected of terrorism differ from civilian criminal enforcement against ordinary crime.

Thus, in Part One, we shall examine specific legal areas (e.g. the government's use of electronic surveillance against terrorism) in which, at times, the executive has made expansive claims of presidential authority, the sources of which are variously described as "to protect the national security," or "inherent presidential authority," or authority derived from the President's status as Commander-in-chief (a claim which, of course, might have been treated in the military approach reflected in Part Two). These various claims of enhanced presidential authority to address terrorism have been made in specific legal areas and sometimes, only by particular presidential administrations, and we address them in the book in the context of the particular legal areas in which the claims have been made.

On the civilian side, too, approaches or rules different from those used in ordinary criminal cases are being used in terrorism matters, often without invoking claims of expansive presidential and executive authority. Congress, for example, has enacted substantive offenses (the material support offenses) aimed at terrorism that break new ground and have the potential to be extended to ordinary crime; thus far, these offenses have not been copied for ordinary crimes. Similarly, Congress has enacted some statutes which give the FBI authority in terrorism matters that the agency does not otherwise possess. Also, as a constitutional matter, there are some existing exceptions to otherwise applicable constitutional rules that have been or might be extended to terrorism cases. An example is the FBI's promulgation of special rules regarding Miranda warnings in terrorism interrogations, which have yet to be tested in the courts.

Finally, some existing procedures, for example, relating to material witnesses and aliens, in the post-9/11 environment were adapted and used more extensively in urgent anti-terrorism investigations than would otherwise have been normal. All of these several different expansive uses of the civilian criminal legal system are addressed in Part One of the casebook.

Military detentions and prosecution in military commission proceedings addressed in Part Two are, of course, mostly different from civilian criminal process. The subject matter of this Part, for example, are: the relevant source(s) of the military's authority to act in this area, use of military detention authority in various contexts, abroad and in this country, against aliens and against U.S. citizens; the sources and details of the substantive criminal law in trials before military commissions; and the rules of procedure and evidence applied in such proceedings.

While the civil-military line is the basic boundary in the organization of the book, it is not an ironclad line, some materials located in one Part might have placed in the other, and the use of the distinction sometimes fails to come to grips with the gradations in the authority being exercised. The basic and overall approach of the book, applicable to both Parts, is to examine the nature of, and extent to which criminal enforcement against terrorism in the 21st century differs from ordinary criminal enforcement.

Of course, this overall approach calls for some familiarity, on the part of students, with the substantive law and rules governing enforcement practices applied in ordinary criminal cases. Since the book is designed for an advanced course, it is assumed that students will have previously taken the usually-required basic first year course in criminal law; this is helpful. Because special rules and approaches are often being used in terrorism cases, it is also helpful, but not a prerequisite, if students have previously taken a course in constitutional criminal procedure. While it is obviously not possible to cover in this course, all of the rules and legal doctrines used in ordinary criminal enforcement, in selected contexts—for example, in comparing the electronic surveillance rules applicable in terrorism cases and those applied for ordinary crimes—the latter rules are described in summary fashion.

While the book emphasizes the law being applied in terrorism cases, both civilian and military, and lends itself to hardnosed legal analysis, it is also and desirable to pay attention to the impact of the 9/11 trauma, relevant background considerations and developments over time, the political context and the significance of the shifts from the administration of President Bush to President Obama to President Trump. An effort is made in the book to encourage reference to, and discussion of the differences in approach depending on which administration is in power.

Indeed, the three most momentous events relating to enforcement against terrorism that have occurred since September 11, 2001, may have been the inauguration of a new President with a new administration in 2009 and 2017, and the killing of Osama Bin Laden in the spring of 2011. These events might have been expected to effect major changes in how terrorism is addressed by the federal government, but thus far, it appears that less changed in the wake of the several occurrences than might have been expected (it may be too soon to tell whether the advent of the Trump administration will lead to major changes in the U.S. approach).

There is an overriding, powerful theme reflected in questions explored in different contexts in this volume, sometimes made explicit, sometimes not—whether the particular governmental steps under consideration are necessary to preserve our security and how much and to what extent will those steps take away from us elements of our traditional civil liberties and change the very nature of our society. The purpose of this book is to make available through original and secondary sources and analytical and discussion text and questions the raw material for addressing this larger theme in an informed, balanced way—presenting, to the extent possible, relevant information on both sides of the many issues, hopefully without prejudgment or bias.

NOTE ON THE OBAMA AND TRUMP ADMINISTRATIONS' ANTI-TERRORISM POLICIES AND RELATED ACTIONS

It was anticipated by many that when Barack Obama became President in January, 2009, there would be dramatic changes in the policies and actions of the administration in regard to anti-terrorism enforcement. Potentially, the entire approach to anti-terrorism enforcement, including the use of military tribunals, designation of persons as "enemy combatants" and the like, could have changed. As it turned out, certain changes were implemented while in many instances, the same or similar policies continued to be applied. By way of introduction to our general subject, this Note gives an overview of many of the changes that were made as well as the areas in which policies similar to those of the previous administration continued. The reader may wish to refer back to this Note, in connection with various topics mentioned here, when addressing the materials in the casebook regarding those topics.

At the outset, almost immediately after the Inauguration, the Obama administration moved quickly to take certain actions. A 120 day suspension of trials before the military commissions was requested. It was announced that the so-called "black sites," long term secret detention locations in foreign countries where terrorist suspects apprehended abroad were detained and interrogated, presumably by the CIA, would be closed. The President took a step to act on his campaign promise to close the Guantanamo Bay Naval Station detention facility, by announcing that it would be closed, as soon as practicable, and not later than one year hence. Administration officials indicated that waterboarding was torture, a position that members of the Bush Administration had declined to take; the President also signed an order prohibiting the use of interrogation techniques not authorized under the standards detailed in the Army Field Manual.

Ali Saleh Kahlah al-Marri, the second person arrested in the United States to be declared an "enemy combatant" and shifted to military custody, was switched back to civilian custody for prosecution in a civilian court. A Department of Justice press release indicated that the detainees at Guantanamo would no longer be designated as "enemy combatants." And Secretary of State Clinton told the press that the administration was no longer using the phrase "war on terror."

In March, the Department of Justice released a series of legal opinions which between 2001 and 2002 had been written to provide legal advice on presidential authority, the detention and trial of individuals detained as "enemy combatants" and related matters. In April, four memoranda dealing with the legality of interrogation techniques authorized for use by the CIA were also released.

All of the foregoing actions can be viewed as involving modifications of the Bush administration's policy and approach in dealing with terrorism. But there were also actions that adhered, in the main, to the Bush approach. In March, 2009, for example, the Department of Justice filed a memorandum in court in which the government claimed a broad authority to detain the men being held in Guantanamo, basing it on the Authorization to Use Military Force joint resolution by Congress and on the laws of war. In the Jeppesen Dataplan case, see ch. 7 (involving a civil suit against an airline for providing airplanes for the government's rendition program), the government sought dismissal of the suit on the ground of the state secrets privilege—a position that the Bush administration had taken in a number of lawsuits against the government or its agents. And President Obama early in his term signed an executive order authorizing the continued "rendition" of persons suspected of terrorism to foreign countries for interrogation.

The Obama administration also adhered to the previous administration's position arguing that habeas corpus was not available to detainees at the U.S. airbase in Bagram, Afghanistan. Similarly, just as President Bush did, President Obama has continued the controversial practice of using signing statements to announce that the government will not enforce specific provisions of new legislation that are believed to be unconstitutional. President Bush engaged in this practice very frequently and in regard to terrorism-related legislation. President Obama indicated he would use this practice sparingly and not without first consulting with the Attorney General, but he then proceeded to engage in the practice in specific instances.

The administration initiated a review of the cases of the approximately 240 detainees still remaining in Guantanamo and decided that many of them could be released, that some could be prosecuted in federal court but that, significantly, the prosecution of some would continue to be in military commission trials. The administration indicated that it would propose some amendments of the rules of evidence and procedures provided for in the Military Commission Act, enacted at the behest of the Bush administration. In this connection, there were indications that there would be a cohort of detainees who could not be prosecuted (presumably either because the evidence against them had been obtained by interrogation techniques that would preclude admissibility either in court or in military commission proceedings, or was too sensitive to be used). The administration was working on legislation to authorize their indefinite detention, again a substantive position taken by the Bush administration, but without seeking express legislation dealing with the subject. Subsequently, in the National Defense Authorization Act of 2012, Congress enacted provisions that provide express legislative authority for military detention of persons like those in Guantanamo.

Over the course of its time in office and, especially during the last year, the Obama administration moved to release many of the remaining Guantanamo detainees, in aid of its intended closing of the facility, but difficulties were encountered in getting other countries to take them, and there was strong resistance in the Congress to releasing any into the United States and in closing Guantanamo. Moreover, with respect to those who continued to be incarcerated, there was congressional resistance to using U.S. prisons, the objections taking the form of "not in my state." Among other moves, a statutory provision was regularly inserted in the annual National Defense Authorization Acts that barred the use of federal funds for this purpose.

Overall, commentators and the media have noted that the substantive differences between Bush administration policies and Obama administration policies are not as great as might have been expected. The main difference seems to be in the underlying claims of authority: Bush claimed inherent authority as Commander-in-chief as one of the principal grounds for his exercise of specific powers. Obama was much more inclined to look to legislative authorization and to seek such authority from the Congress when necessary. See Charles Savage, To Critics New Policy on Terror Looks Old, N.Y. Times, July 2, 2009, A11; Peter Baker, A 'Surgical Approach' to Policy and Its Pitfalls, N.Y. Times, May 22, 2009 A1

Another feature of the Obama administration's anti-terrorism program that merits mention is the fact that a significant effort was spent to explain and justify the anti-terrorism policies that were being implemented. Hallmarks of this transparency were two major presidential addresses, delivered in May 2009 and May 2013, on the subject of national security. These addresses also serve to provide an overview and a general introduction to the subject matter of the course. Excerpts from these speeches appear below.

Excerpts from remarks by President Obama on national security, May 21, 2009, at National Archives, Washington, D.C.

THE PRESIDENT: . . .

These are extraordinary times for our country. We're confronting a historic economic crisis. We're fighting two wars. We face a range of challenges that will define the way that Americans will live in the 21st century. So there's no shortage of work to be done, or responsibilities to bear.

. . .

In the midst of all these challenges, however, my single most important responsibility as President is to keep the American people safe. It's the first thing that I think about when I wake up in the morning. It's the last thing that I think about when I go to sleep at night.

And this responsibility is only magnified in an era when an extremist ideology threatens our people, and technology gives a handful of terrorists the potential to do us great harm. We are less than eight years removed from the deadliest attack on American soil in our history. We know that al Qaeda is actively planning to attack us again. We know that this threat will be with us for a long time, and that we must use all elements of our power to defeat it.

These steps are all critical to keeping America secure. But I believe with every fiber of my being that in the long run we also cannot keep this country safe unless we enlist the power of our most fundamental values. The documents that we hold in this very hall—the Declaration of Independence, the Constitution, the Bill of Rights—these are not simply words written into aging parchment. They are the foundation of liberty and justice in this country, and a light that shines for all who seek freedom, fairness, equality, and dignity around the world.

. . .

From Europe to the Pacific, we've been the nation that has shut down torture chambers and replaced tyranny with the rule of law. That is who we are. And where terrorists offer only the injustice of disorder and destruction, America must demonstrate that our values and our institutions are more resilient than a hateful ideology.

. . .

Now let me be clear: We are indeed at war with al Qaeda and its affiliates. We do need to update our institutions to deal with this threat. But we must do so with an abiding confidence in the rule of law and due process; in checks and balances and accountability. For reasons that I will explain, the decisions that were made over the last eight years established an ad hoc legal approach for fighting terrorism that was neither effective nor sustainable—a framework that failed to rely on our legal traditions and time-tested institutions, and that failed to use our values as a compass. And that's why I took several steps upon taking office to better protect the American people.

First, I banned the use of so-called enhanced interrogation techniques by the United States of America. (Applause.)

I know some have argued that brutal methods like waterboarding were necessary to keep us safe. I could not disagree more. As Commander-in-Chief, I see the intelligence. I bear the responsibility for keeping this country safe. And I categorically reject the assertion that these are the most effective means of interrogation. (Applause.) What's more, they undermine the rule of law. They alienate us in the world. They serve as a recruitment tool for terrorists, and increase the will of our enemies to fight us, while decreasing the will of others to work with America. . . .

The second decision that I made was to order the closing of the prison camp at Guantanamo Bay. (Applause.)

For over seven years, we have detained hundreds of people at Guantanamo. During that time, the system of military commissions that were in place at Guantanamo succeeded in convicting a grand total of three suspected terrorists. Let me repeat that: three convictions in over seven years. Instead of bringing terrorists to justice, efforts at prosecution met setback after setback, cases lingered on, and in 2006 the Supreme Court invalidated the entire system. Meanwhile, over 525 detainees were released from

Guantanamo under not my administration, under the previous administration. Let me repeat that: Two-thirds of the detainees were released before I took office and ordered the closure of Guantanamo.

There is also no question that Guantanamo set back the moral authority that is America's strongest currency in the world. Instead of building a durable framework for the struggle against al Qaeda that drew upon our deeply held values and traditions, our government was defending positions that undermined the rule of law. In fact, part of the rationale for establishing Guantanamo in the first place was the misplaced notion that a prison there would be beyond the law—a proposition that the Supreme Court soundly rejected. Meanwhile, instead of serving as a tool to counter terrorism, Guantanamo became a symbol that helped al Qaeda recruit terrorists to its cause. Indeed, the existence of Guantanamo likely created more terrorists around the world than it ever detained.

. . .By any measure, the costs of keeping it open far exceed the complications involved in closing it. That's why I argued that it should be closed throughout my campaign, and that is why I ordered it closed within one year.

The third decision that I made was to order a review of all pending cases at Guantanamo. I knew when I ordered Guantanamo closed that it would be difficult and complex. There are 240 people there who have now spent years in legal limbo. In dealing with this situation, we don't have the luxury of starting from scratch. We're cleaning up something that is, quite simply, a mess—a misguided experiment that has left in its wake a flood of legal challenges that my administration is forced to deal with on a constant, almost daily basis, and it consumes the time of government

. . .

Now let me be blunt. There are no neat or easy answers here. I wish there were. But I can tell you that the wrong answer is to pretend like this problem will go away if we maintain an unsustainable status quo. As President, I refuse to allow this problem to fester. I refuse to pass it on to somebody else. It is my responsibility to solve the problem. Our security interests will not permit us to delay. Our courts won't allow it. And neither should our conscience.

. . .

Now, let me begin by disposing of one argument as plainly as I can: We are not going to release anyone if it would endanger our national security, nor will we release detainees within the United States who endanger the American people. Where demanded by justice and national security, we will seek to transfer some detainees to the same type of facilities in which we hold all manner of dangerous and violent criminals within our borders—namely, highly secure prisons that ensure the public safety.

As we make these decisions, bear in mind the following face: Nobody has ever escaped from one of our federal, supermax prisons, which hold hundreds of convicted terrorists. As Republican Lindsey Graham said, the idea that we cannot find a place to securely house 250-plus detainees within the United States is not rational.

We are currently in the process of reviewing each of the detainee cases at Guantanamo to determine the appropriate policy for dealing with them. And as we do so, we are acutely aware that under the last administration, detainees were released and, in some cases, returned to the battlefield. That's why we are doing away with the poorly planned, haphazard approach that let those detainees go in the past. Instead we are treating these cases with the care and attention that the law requires and that our security demands.

Now, going forward, these cases will fall into five distinct categories.

First, whenever feasible, we will try those who have violated American criminal laws in federal courts—courts provided for by the United States Constitution. Some have derided our federal courts as incapable of handling the trials of terrorists. They are wrong. Our courts and our juries, our citizens, are tough enough to convict terrorists. The record makes that clear. Ramzi Yousef tried to blow up the World Trade Center. He was convicted in our courts and is serving a life sentence in U.S. prisons. Zacarias Moussaoui has been identified as the 20th 9/11 hijacker. He was convicted in our courts, and he too is serving a life sentence in prison. If we can try those terrorists in our courts and hold them in our prisons, then we can do the same with detainees from Guantanamo.

Recently, we prosecuted and received a guilty plea from a detainee, al-Marri, in federal court after years of legal confusion. We're preparing to transfer another detainee to the Southern District Court of New York, where he will face trial on charges related to the 1998 bombings of our embassies in Kenya and Tanzania—bombings that killed over 200 people. Preventing this detainee from coming to our shores would prevent his trial and conviction. And after over a decade, it is time to finally see that justice is served, and that is what we intend to do. (Applause.)

The second category of cases involves detainees who violate the laws of war and are therefore best tried through military commissions. Military commissions have a history in the United States dating back to George Washington and the Revolutionary War. They are an appropriate venue for trying detainees for violations of the laws of war. They allow for the protection of sensitive sources and methods of intelligence-gathering; they allow for the safety and security of participants; and for the presentation of evidence gathered from the battlefield that cannot always be effectively presented in federal courts.

Now, some have suggested that this represents a reversal on my part. They should look at the record. In 2006, I did strongly oppose legislation proposed by the Bush administration and passed by the Congress because it failed to establish a legitimate legal framework, with the kind of meaningful due process rights for the accused that could stand up on appeal.

I said at that time, however, that I supported the use of military commissions to try detainees, provided there were several reforms, and in fact there were some bipartisan efforts to achieve those reforms. Those are the reforms that we are now making. Instead of using the flawed commissions of the last seven years, my administration is bringing our commissions in line with the rule of law. We will no longer permit the use of evidence—as evidence statements that have been obtained using cruel, inhuman, or degrading interrogation methods. We will no longer place the burden to prove that hearsay is unreliable on the opponent of the hearsay. And we will give detainees greater latitude in selecting their own counsel, and more protections if they refuse to testify. . . .

The third category of detainees includes those who have been ordered released by the courts. Now, let me repeat what I said earlier: This has nothing to do with my decision to close Guantanamo. It has to do with the rule of law. The courts have spoken. They have found that there's no legitimate reason to hold 21 of the people currently held at Guantanamo. Nineteen of these findings took place before I was sworn into office. I cannot ignore these rulings because as President, I too am bound by the law. The United States is a nation of laws and so we must abide by these rulings.

The fourth category of cases involves detainees who we have determined can be transferred safely to another country. So far, our review team has approved 50 detainees for transfer. And my administration is in ongoing discussions with a number of other countries about the transfer of detainees to their soil for detention and rehabilitation.

Now, finally, there remains the question of detainees at Guantanamo who cannot be prosecuted yet who pose a clear danger to the American people. And I have to be honest here—this is the toughest single issue that we will face. We're going to exhaust every avenue that we have to prosecute those at Guantanamo who pose a danger to our country. But even when this process is complete, there may be a number of people who cannot be prosecuted for past crimes, in some cases because evidence may be tainted, but who nonetheless pose a threat to the security of the United States. Examples of that threat include people who've received extensive explosives training at al Qaeda training camps, or commanded Taliban troops in battle, or expressed their allegiance to Osama bin Laden, or otherwise made it clear that they want to kill Americans. These are people who, in effect, remain at war with the United States.

Let me repeat: I am not going to release individuals who endanger the American people. Al Qaeda terrorists and their affiliates are at war with the United States, and those that we capture—like other prisoners of war—must be prevented from attacking us again. Having said that, we must recognize that these detention policies cannot be unbounded. They can't be based simply on what I or the executive branch decide alone. That's why my administration has begun to reshape the standards that apply to ensure that they are in line with the rule of law. We must have clear, defensible, and lawful standards for those who fall into this category. We must have fair procedures so that we don't make mistakes. We must have a thorough process of periodic review, so that any prolonged detention is carefully evaluated and justified.

I know that creating such a system poses unique challenges. And other countries have grappled with this question; now, so must we. But I want to be very clear that our goal is to construct a legitimate legal framework for the remaining Guantanamo detainees that cannot be transferred. Our goal is not to avoid a legitimate legal framework. In our constitutional system, prolonged detention should not be the decision of any one man. If and when we determine that the United States must hold individuals to keep them from carrying out an act of war, we will do so within a system that involves judicial and congressional oversight. And so, going forward, my administration will work with Congress to develop an appropriate legal regime so that our efforts are consistent with our values and our Constitution.

. . .

Now, along these same lines, my administration is also confronting challenges to what is known as the "state secrets" privilege. This is a doctrine that allows the government to challenge legal cases involving secret programs. It's been used by many past Presidents—Republican and Democrat—for many decades. And while this principle is absolutely necessary in some circumstances to protect national security, I am concerned that it has been over-used. It is also currently the subject of a wide range of lawsuits. So let me lay out some principles here. We must not protect information merely because it reveals the violation of a law or embarrassment to the government. And that's why my administration is nearing completion of a thorough review of this practice.

And we plan to embrace several principles for reform. We will apply a stricter legal test to material that can be protected under the state secrets privilege. We will not assert the privilege in court without first following our own formal process, including review by a Justice Department committee and the personal approval of the Attorney General. And each year we will voluntarily report to Congress when we have invoked the privilege and why because, as I said before, there must be proper oversight over our actions.

. . .

Now, this is what I mean when I say that we need to focus on the future. I recognize that many still have a strong desire to focus on the past. When it comes to actions of the last eight years, passions are high. Some Americans are angry; others want to re-fight debates that have been settled, in some cases debates that they have lost. I know that these debates lead directly, in some cases, to a call for a fuller accounting, perhaps through an independent commission.

I've opposed the creation of such a commission because I believe that our existing democratic institutions are strong enough to deliver accountability. The Congress can review abuses of our values, and there are ongoing inquiries by the Congress into matters like enhanced interrogation techniques. The Department of Justice and our courts can work through and punish any violations of our laws or miscarriages of justice.

. . .

Now this generation faces a great test in the specter of terrorism. And unlike the Civil War or World War II, we can't count on a surrender ceremony to bring this journey to an end. Right now, in distant training camps and in crowded cities, there are people plotting to take American lives. That will be the case a year from now, five years from now, and—in all probability—10 years from now. Neither I nor anyone can stand here today and say that there will not be another terrorist attack that takes American lives. But I can say with certainty that my administration—along with our extraordinary troops and the patriotic men and women who defend our national security—will do everything in our power to keep the American people safe. And I do know with certainty that we can defeat al Qaeda. Because the terrorists can only succeed if they swell their ranks and alienate America from our allies, and they will never be able to do that if we stay true to who we are, if we forge tough and durable approaches to fighting terrorism that are anchored in our timeless ideals. This must be our common purpose. . . .

President Obama's remarks on national security on May 23, 2013, at National Defense University, Washington, D.C.

PRESIDENT OBAMA:

. . .

. . . [F]or a moment it seemed the 21st century would be a tranquil time. And then on September 11th, 2001, we were shaken out of complacency. Thousands were taken from us as clouds of fire and metal and ash descended upon a sun-filled morning.

This was a different kind of war. No armies came to our shores, and our military was not the principal target. Instead, a group of terrorists came to kill as many civilians as they could.

And so our nation went to war. We have now been at war for well over a decade. I won't review the full history. . . .

Meanwhile, we strengthened our defenses, hardening targets, tightening transportation security, giving law enforcement new tools to prevent terror. Most of these changes were sound. Some caused inconvenience. But some, like expanded surveillance, raised difficult questions about the balance that we strike between our interests in security and our values of privacy. And in some cases, I believe we compromised our basic values—by using torture to interrogate our enemies, and detaining individuals in a way that ran counter to the rule of law.

So after I took office, we stepped up the war against al-Qaida, but we also sought to change its course.

We relentlessly targeted al-Qaida's leadership. . . . We unequivocally banned torture, affirmed our commitment to civilian courts, worked to align our policies with the rule of law and expanded our consultations with Congress.

Today Osama bin Laden is dead, and so are most of his top lieutenants. There have been no large-scale attacks on the United States, and our homeland is more secure. . . .

Now make no mistake: Our nation is still threatened by terrorists. From Benghazi to Boston, we have been tragically reminded of that truth. But we recognize that the threat has shifted and evolved from the one that came to our shores on 9/11. With a decade of experience to draw from, this is the moment to ask ourselves hard questions about the nature of today's threats and how we should confront them.

. . .

Today the core of al Qaida in Afghanistan and Pakistan is on the path to defeat. Their remaining operatives spend more time thinking about their own safety than plotting against us.

They did not direct the attacks in Benghazi or Boston. They've not carried out a successful attack on our homeland since 9/11.

Instead what we've seen is the emergence of various al-Qaida affiliates. From Yemen to Iraq, from Somalia to North Africa, the threat today is more diffuse, with al-Qaida's affiliates in the Arabian Peninsula, AQAP, the most active in plotting against our homeland. And while none of AQAP's efforts approach the scale of 9/11, they have continued to plot acts of terror, like the attempt to blow up an airplane on Christmas Day in 2009.

Unrest in the Arab world has also allowed extremists to gain a foothold in countries like Libya and Syria. But here too there are differences from 9/11. In some cases, we continue to confront state-sponsored networks like Hezbollah that engage in acts of terror to achieve political goals. Other of these groups are simply collections of local militias or extremists interested in seizing territory. And while we are vigilant for signs that these groups may pose a transnational threat, most are focused on operating in the countries and regions where they are based. And that means we'll face more localized threats like what we saw in Benghazi, or the BP oil facility in Algeria, in which local operatives—perhaps in loose affiliation with regional networks—launch periodic attacks against Western diplomats, companies and other soft targets, or resort to kidnapping and other criminal enterprises to fund their operations.

And finally, we face a real threat from radicalized individuals here in the United States.

Whether it's a shooter at a Sikh temple in Wisconsin, a plane flying into a building in Texas, or the extremists who killed 168 people at the Federal Building in Oklahoma City, America's confronted many forms of violent extremism in our history. Deranged or alienated individuals, often U.S. citizens or legal residents, can do enormous damage, particularly when inspired by larger notions of violent jihad. And that pull towards extremism appears to have led to the shooting at Fort Hood and the bombing of the Boston Marathon.

So that's the current threat. Lethal, yet less capable, al-Qaida affiliates, threats to diplomatic facilities and businesses abroad, homegrown extremists. This is the future of terrorism. We have to take these threats seriously and do all that we can to confront them. But as we shape our response, we have to recognize that the scale of this threat closely resembles the types of attacks we faced before 9/11.

In the 1980s, we lost Americans to terrorism at our embassy in Beirut, at our Marine barracks in Lebanon, on a cruise ship at sea, at a disco in Berlin, and on a Pan Am flight, Flight 103, over Lockerbie. In the 1990s, we lost Americans to terrorism at the World Trade

Center, at our military facilities in Saudi Arabia, and at our embassy in Kenya.

These attacks were all brutal. They were all deadly. And we learned that, left unchecked, these threats can grow. But if dealt with smartly and proportionally, these threats need not rise to the level that we saw on the eve of 9/11.

Moreover, we have to recognize that these threats don't arise in a vacuum. Most, though not all, of the terrorism we face is fueled by a common ideology, a belief by some extremists that Islam is in conflict with the United States and the West and that violence against Western targets, including civilians, is justified in pursuit of a larger cause. Of course, this ideology is based on a lie, for the United States is not at war with Islam. And this ideology is rejected by the vast majority of Muslims—who are the most frequent victims of terrorist attacks. Nevertheless, this ideology persists.

And in an age when ideas and images can travel the globe in an instant, our response to terrorism can't depend on military or law enforcement alone. We need all elements of national power to win a battle of wills, a battle of ideas.

So what I want to discuss here today is the components of such a comprehensive counterterrorism strategy. First, we must finish the work of defeating al-Qaida and its associated forces. . . .[W]e will work with the Afghan government to train security forces, and sustain a counterterrorism force which ensures that al-Qaida can never again establish a safe haven to launch attacks against us or our allies.

Beyond Afghanistan, we must define our effort not as a boundless global war on terror but rather as a series of persistent, targeted efforts to dismantle specific networks of violent extremists that threaten America. In many cases, this will involve partnerships with other countries. . . .

Much of our best counterterrorism cooperation results in the gathering and sharing of intelligence, the arrest and prosecution of terrorists. That's how a Somali terrorist apprehended off the coast of Yemen is now in prison in New York. That's how we worked with European allies to disrupt plots from Denmark to Germany to the United Kingdom. That's how intelligence collected with Saudi Arabia helped us stop a cargo plane from being blown up over the Atlantic. These partnerships work.

But despite our strong preference for the detention and prosecution of terrorists, sometimes this approach is foreclosed. Al-Qaida and its affiliates try to gain a foothold in some of the most distant and unforgiving places on Earth.

They take refuge in remote tribal regions. They hide in caves and walled compounds. They train in empty deserts and rugged mountains.

In some of these places, such as parts of Somalia and Yemen, the state has only the most tenuous reach into the territory. In other cases, the state lacks the capacity or will to take action.

And it's also not possible for America to simply deploy a team of special forces to capture every terrorist. Even when such an approach may be possible, there are places where it would pose profound risks to our troops and local civilians, where a terrorist compound cannot be breached without triggering a firefight—with surrounding tribal communities, for example, that pose no threat to us—times when putting U.S. boots on the ground may trigger a major international crisis.

To put it another way, our operation in Pakistan against Osama bin Laden cannot be the norm. The risks in that case were immense. The likelihood of capture, although that was our preference, was remote, given the certainty that our folks would confront resistance. The fact that we did not find ourselves confronted with civilian casualties or embroiled in a extended firefight was a testament to the meticulous planning and professionalism of our special forces, but it also depended on some luck. And it was supported by massive infrastructure in Afghanistan.

And even then, the cost to our relationship with Pakistan and the backlash among the Pakistani public over encroachment on their territory was so severe that we are just now beginning to rebuild this important partnership.

So it is in this context that the United States has taken lethal, targeted action against al-Qaida and its associated forces, including with remotely piloted aircraft commonly referred to as drones. As was true in previous armed conflicts, this new technology raises profound questions about who is targeted and why, about civilian casualties and the risk of creating new enemies, about the legality of such strikes under U.S. and international law, about accountability and morality.

So let me address these questions. To begin with, our actions are effective. Don't take my word for it. In the intelligence gathered at bin Laden's compound, we found that he wrote, we could lose the reserves to enemies' airstrikes; we cannot fight airstrikes with explosives. Other communications from al-Qaida operatives confirm this as well. Dozens of highly skilled al-Qaida commanders, trainers, bomb makers and operatives have been taken off the battlefield. Plots have been disrupted that would have targeted international aviation,

beyond politics for Congress to prevent us from closing a facility that it should—should have never been opened.

. . .

Today I once again call on Congress to lift the restrictions on detainee transfers from Gitmo. I have asked—(applause)—I have asked the Department of Defense to designate a site in the United States where we can hold military commissions.

. . .

Now, even after we take these steps, one issue will remain, which is how to deal with those Gitmo detainees who we know have participated in dangerous plots or attacks but who cannot be prosecuted, for example, because the evidence against them has been compromised or is inadmissible in a court of law. But once we commit to a process of closing Gitmo, I am confident that this legacy problem can be resolved, consistent with our commitment to the rule of law.

And I know the politics are hard. But history will cast a harsh judgment on this aspect of our fight against terrorism and those of us who fail to end it. Imagine a future 10 years from now or 20 years from now when the United States of America is still holding people who have been charged with no crime on a piece of land that is not a part of our country.

. . .

But these are tough issues, and the suggestion that we can gloss over them is wrong. . . .

So, America, we have faced down dangers far greater than al-Qaida.

. . .

Thank you very much, everybody. God bless you. May God bless the United States of America.

———————————

As of the time of this writing, the administration of President Donald Trump has not yet completed one year in office, and thus far, President Trump has not given a major address on terrorism and national security—Whether he will do so at any point in the future is unknown. So it is difficult to know exactly what steps he will take, for example, on the many issues addressed by his predecessor. Accordingly, it is too early to reach any conclusions about the details of its anti-terrorism policies and practices. Nevertheless, based on a few actions taken by his administration, and statements made by the President, both earlier as a candidate for the Presidency and since his inauguration, one can discern the general direction of some of his likely policies.

In one of the few areas where he has acted, the action is controversial, and part of the controversy relates to whether the action indeed serves national security purposes. The particular action in question is instituting a ban on immigration from specified countries, most of them predominantly Muslim countries. Initially, the ban was ruled to be unconstitutional. The ban has now been revised at least twice and has just begun to be implemented, although its legality is still being tested in the courts.

Based on President Trump's statements and those of his Attorney General, it is abundantly clear that his approach will be different from that of the prior administration. Obama wanted to close Guantanamo; Trump wants to keep it open and send "bad dudes" there. But in the meantime, while there have been a few persons captured abroad who might during the Bush administration have been sent to Guantanamo, none of the newly captured suspected terrorists has thus far been sent there.

Trump would like to prosecute individuals before the military commissions, although there is an indication that at least in the present state of matters, he recognizes that criminal trials in the federal courts are handled more efficiently than the military commission process. Soon after his inauguration, a draft of an Executive Order relating to Guantanamo and interrogation methods was leaked; the White House disclaimed knowledge of it. A few months later, there was a news report that three different versions of an Executive Order on that subject were being circulated and discussed within the administration; again, as of the time of this writing, no Executive Order on interrogation or military commission process has been issued. In January, 2018, the President did sign an Executive Order revoking the Obama mandate to close the Guantanamo facility and also indicating that captured persons could be sent there.

At a number of points in this volume, more details are provided relating to the posture and actions of the Trump administration on various anti-terrorism enforcement issues.

THE CONTENT OF SPECIFIC CHAPTERS

The book is about terrorism and begins in Part One with a) a consideration of the definition(s) of terrorism and how the concept is used in the legal system and otherwise, and b) a general overview of anti-terrorism legislation (ch. 2). It then provides an opportunity to examine in depth two conceptually-new crimes in the federal criminal code, which are now being frequently used in terrorism prosecutions (ch. 3). It also focuses on the use in anti-terrorism enforcement of special investigative approaches, e.g. proactive surveillance by both civilian and military investigative agencies (ch. 4), special rules relating to electronic surveillance (ch. 5), search authority and the use of administrative subpoenas to obtain records (ch. 6), also methods of interrogation and irregular rendition (ch. 7), the use of the material witness statute and the executive branch's authority over immigration and aliens (ch. 8), and courtroom procedures for dealing with classified information that are frequently at issue in terrorism cases (ch. 9).

On the military side in Part Two, the book examines the use of military custody as a basis for long-term detention, with reference to the detainees at the Guantanamo Bay, Cuba, detention facility but also in regard to the use of that status for two individuals who had been apprehended within the United States (ch. 10); studies the operational aspects of the military commissions, including the substantive law of crimes and rules of evidence applied in such proceedings (ch. 11); discusses the legal, policy and constitutional issues involved in the practice of targeted killing (ch. 12); and then finishes the Part Two portion of the book and the volume with an examination of the general legal framework governing the use of the military in domestic law enforcement (ch.13).

PART 1

IN A CIVILIAN MODE

■ ■ ■

CHAPTER 2

TERRORISM: INTRODUCTION TO THE CONCEPT; ENFORCEMENT ISSUES; SELECTED TERRORIST OFFENSES

■ ■ ■

A. INTRODUCTION

This book is primarily addressed to how our domestic legal system deals with individuals involved in international terrorism. The purpose of this chapter is to provide an introduction to the core concept, "terrorism," and to examine how it is defined and used in the U.S. legal system. Some of the materials in this chapter also relate to the subject of domestic terrorism in the U.S., provide a brief introduction to that subject and serve to identify differences between domestic and international terrorism.

The materials of the chapter thus focus on the legal concept of terrorism. The goal of the chapter is not only to examine the definitions—it is variously defined—but also to explore the different functions the concept serves in the legal system. Somewhat surprisingly, we learn that the concept of terrorism is not often included as part of the definition of specific federal crimes, which raises a number of questions: why is it not included more frequently? If it is not so included, what makes a crime a terrorism offense, and does it make any difference whether it is or is not such an offense? How do "terrorism" offenses, for example, differ from "hate" crimes? Also, if terrorism is not used in defining offenses, does it serve other significant "legal" functions? For example, we learn that the fact that an offense involves terrorism is a factor that can serve to enhance a convicted person's sentence under the federal Sentencing Guidelines.

General definitions of terrorism are found in various legal sources, e.g. in statutes, federal regulations, and in various federal agency policies. The definitions vary, but the differences tend to lie in details, though in some instances, these differences may be significant. There are also approaches to the concept of terrorism other than through general definitions; these, too, will be reviewed.

As mentioned, terrorism is used as a factor in policy formulations articulated by relevant government agencies. It is used as one of a variety of factors that define the investigatory jurisdiction of some government agencies, and as a basis for organizing investigating units in criminal enforcement or prosecutorial offices. Does it also affect the process and procedure applied in federal criminal trials? Terrorism is used as a concept in keeping crime statistics and as a measure of the danger level in the country. There also tends to be keen public interest in whether a particular act of violence or an attack on persons or property is an act of terrorism, or an act done with some other purpose or motive.

For each of these functions, some kind of definition of terrorism is needed. Issues of definition and the role of the concept do not arise very frequently in the case law. Consider, however, the role that the concept played in United States v. Yousef, 327 F. 3d 56 (2d Cir. 2003). The defendants were charged with various crimes arising out of a planned series of bombings of United States commercial airliners in Southeast Asia. They contended that the U.S. lacked jurisdiction to try them for certain of the charges, asserting that there was no jurisdiction under customary international law and that U.S. law is subordinate to customary international law. The reviewing court rejected this last proposition but also proceeded to conclude that even if customary international law was controlling, there was a basis for U.S. jurisdiction.

The district court had found jurisdiction under customary international law based on the universality principle.[1] The Second Circuit panel rejected this application of the universality principle, asserting that terrorism is not a crime about which there is a consensus that meets the requirements for crimes that are against the law of nations. Regarding this issue, the panel stated:

> The historical restriction of universal jurisdiction to piracy, war crimes, and crimes against humanity demonstrates that universal jurisdiction arises under customary international law only where crimes (1) are universally condemned by the

---

[1] In a footnote, the Yousef set forth a useful summary of the criminal jurisdiction requirements provided for under customary international law. While this casebook focuses primarily on U.S. domestic law, there are contexts in which international law principles become relevant, e.g., the Yousef case itself. Accordingly, students will find the following summary to be useful background:

Customary international law is comprised of those practices and customs that States view as obligatory and that are engaged in or otherwise acceded to by a preponderance of States in a uniform and consistent fashion. . . . Customary international law recognizes five bases on which a State may exercise criminal jurisdiction over a citizen or non-citizen for acts committed outside of the prosecuting State. These five well-recognized bases of criminal jurisdiction are: (1) the "objective territorial principle," which provides for jurisdiction over conduct committed outside a State's borders that has, or is intended to have, a substantial effect within its territory; (2) the "nationality principle," which provides for jurisdiction over extraterritorial acts committed by a State's own citizen; (3) the "protective principle," which provides for jurisdiction over acts committed outside the State that harm the State's interests; (4) the "passive personality principle," which provides for jurisdiction over acts that harm a State's citizens abroad; and (5) the "universality principle," which provides for jurisdiction over extraterritorial acts by a citizen or non-citizen that are so heinous as to be universally condemned by all civilized nations. . . .

community of nations, and (2) by their nature occur either outside of a State or where there is no State capable of punishing, or competent to punish, the crime (as in a time of war).

Unlike those offenses supporting universal jurisdiction under customary international law-that is, piracy, war crimes, and crimes against humanity-that now have fairly precise definitions and that have achieved universal condemnation, "terrorism" is a term as loosely deployed as it is powerfully charged. Judge Harry T. Edwards of the District of Columbia Circuit stated eighteen years ago in Tel-Oren v. Libyan Arab Republic, 233 U.S. App. D.C. 384, 726 F.2d 774 (D.C. Cir. 1984), that "while this nation unequivocally condemns all terrorist acts, that sentiment is not universal. Indeed, the nations of the world are so divisively split on the legitimacy of such aggression as to make it impossible to pinpoint an area of harmony or consensus." Id. at 795 (Edwards, J., concurring).

. . .

We regrettably are no closer now than eighteen years ago to an international consensus on the definition of terrorism or even its proscription; the mere existence of the phrase "state-sponsored terrorism" proves the absence of agreement on basic terms among a large number of States that terrorism violates public international law. Moreover, there continues to be strenuous disagreement among States about what actions do or do not constitute terrorism, nor have we shaken ourselves free of the cliche that "one man's terrorist is another man's freedom fighter.

The court proceeded in several footnotes to set forth material highlighting some specific controversies surrounding the use of the term, especially when utilized in political contexts:

For example, each side of the Israeli-Palestinian conflict charges the other with "terrorism," sentiments echoed by their allies. See, e.g., Todd S. Purdum, What Do You Mean, 'Terrorist'?, N.Y. Times, Apr. 7, 2002, Week in Review, at 1 ("If Israel sees its military campaign in the West Bank as a justifiable echo of Mr. Bush's assault on Al Qaeda, Palestinians claim affinity with the American colonists' revolt against an occupying power."). The Organization of the Islamic Conference met in Kuala Lumpur, Malaysia, in April 2002, to define terrorism; the host of the conference, Malaysian Prime Minister Mahathir Mohamad, proposed a definition of terrorism as "all attacks on civilians"; the conference's final declaration, however, stated that terrorism consists only of attacks on civilians perpetrated by non-Palestinians, stating that the Conference " 'rejects any attempt to link terrorism to the struggle of the Palestinian people in the exercise of their inalienable right to establish their independent state.' " Id. (quoting statements by Mohamad and contained in the conference's final declaration). Sentiments at the conference were far from uniform, however: The deputy foreign minister of Bosnia-Herzegovina stated that "if a person kills or harms a civilian . . . he is a terrorist" irrespective of the "race or religion" of the perpetrator and the victims. Terrorism Issue Splits Muslim Conferees, Chi. Trib., April 2, 2002, at 10 (quoting statements of Bosnian-Herzegovinian delegate to conference).

. . .

Confusion on the definition of "terrorism" abounds. See, e.g., Craig S. Smith, Debate Over Iraq Raises Fears of a Shrinking Role for NATO, N.Y. Times, Jan. 26, 2003, at L 26 (quoting Celeste A. Wallander, senior fellow at the Center for Strategic and International Studies, as stating that even among members of the North Atlantic Treaty Alliance ("NATO") there is no consensus "on how to define transnational terrorism").

Terrorism is defined variously by the perpetrators' motives, methods, targets, and victims. Motive-based definitions suffer from confusion because of the attempt to carve out an exception for assertedly legitimate armed struggle in pursuit of self-determination. For example, under one of the various United Nations resolutions addressing terrorism, armed and violent acts do not constitute "terrorism" if committed by peoples seeking self-determination in opposition to a violently enforced occupation. See, e.g., Declaration on Principles of International Law Concerning Friendly Relations Among Co-operating States in Accordance with the Charter of the United Nations, Oct. 24, 1970, G.A. Res. 2625, 25 U.N. GAOR Supp. (No. 28) at 21, U.N. Doc. A/8028 (1971), reprinted in 9 I.L.M. 1292 (1970). This attempt to distinguish "terrorists" from "freedom fighters" potentially could legitimate as non-terrorist certain groups nearly universally recognized as terrorist, including the Irish Republican Army, Hezbollah, and Hamas. . . .

By contrast, the European Convention on the Suppression of Terrorism defines terrorism solely based on the methods of violence the perpetrator employs, and explicitly removes political judgment of the acts by defining most violent acts as "non-political" (regardless of the perpetrator's claimed motive). European Convention on the

Suppression of Terrorism, Nov. 10, 1976, Europ. T.S. No. 90. Thus, in Article I, the Convention defines as terrorism any offenses, inter alia, "involving the use of a bomb, grenade, rocket, automatic firearm, or letter or parcel bomb if this use endangers persons," a definition that may fail to circumscribe the offense adequately.

The Arab Convention on the Suppression of Terrorism (Cairo, Apr. 22, 1998), reprinted in International Instruments Related to the Prevention and Suppression of International Terrorism, 152–73 (United Nations 2001), while condemning terrorism, takes a uniquely restrictive approach to defining it, stating that offenses committed against the interests of Arab states are "terrorist offenses," while offenses committed elsewhere or against other peoples or interests are not. Id. at Art. I.3 (defining "terrorist offence" as any of several defined violent actions that occur "in any of the Contracting States, or against their nationals, property or interests"). The Convention further defines as legitimate (non-terrorist) "all cases of struggle by whatever means, including armed struggle," unless such struggles "prejudice the territorial integrity of any Arab State." Id. at Art. II(a).

Compare a resolution introduced into the 114th Congress that proposed withholding United States contributions to the budget of the United Nations until the UN adopts a definition of 'international terrorism' concurrent with U.S. laws. R. 4123, 114th CONGRESS, 1st Session.

See generally Gabriel Soll, Terrorism: The Known Element No One Can Define, 11 Willamette J. Int'l L. & Disp. Resol. 123 (2004); Yonah Alexander, Terrorism in the Twenty-first Century: Threats and Responses, 12 DePaul Bus.L.J. 5 (2004), and see generally, Yonah Alexander & Edgar H. Brenner, Legal Aspects of Terrorism in the United States (2000). For more recent law review commentary, see the articles cited at the end of this chapter.

B. U.S. FEDERAL LEGAL AND POLICY DEFINITIONS OF TERRORISM

1. Federal Criminal Code Definition

Review the statutory formulations reproduced below and see what the differences are among them. Is there anything which commends one variation in preference to others? Perhaps the most significant of these statutes for our purposes is the first one reproduced below, § 2331, in Title 18, U.S.C. This provision defines the terms "international terrorism" and "domestic terrorism" as those words are used in the legislative chapter that contains most of the general terrorism statutes found in the federal criminal code. Consider, after studying the materials below how often those terms are in fact used in the legislative chapter 113B titled, Terrorism.

Title 18, U.S.C.

§ 2331. Definitions

As used in this chapter—

(1) the term "international terrorism" means activities that

(A) involve violent acts or acts dangerous to human life that are a violation of the criminal laws of the United States or of any State, or that would be a criminal violation if committed within the jurisdiction of the United States or of any State;

(B) appear to be intended

(i) to intimidate or coerce a civilian population;

(ii) to influence the policy of a government by intimidation or coercion; or

(iii) to affect the conduct of a government by mass destruction, assassination, or kidnapping; and

(C) occur primarily outside the territorial jurisdiction of the United States, or transcend national boundaries in terms of the means by which they are accomplished, the persons they appear intended to intimidate or coerce, or the locale in which their perpetrators operate or seek asylum;

. . .

(5) the term "domestic terrorism" means activities that—

(A) involve acts dangerous to human life that are a violation of the criminal laws of the United States or of any State;

(B) appear to be intended—

(i) to intimidate or coerce a civilian population;

(ii) to influence the policy of a government by intimidation or coercion; or

(iii) to affect the conduct of a government by mass destruction, assassination, or kidnapping; and

(C) occur primarily within the territorial jurisdiction of the United States.

2. DEFINITION IN IMMIGRATION LAW

Another often-referred-to statutory definitional provision is found in the Immigration and Nationality Act, § 1182, Title 8, U.S.C. This provision sets forth, inter alia, the terrorism-related grounds for excluding aliens from the United States. In that connection § 1182 contains a definition of "terrorist activity." This provision is also incorporated by reference, into certain federal criminal statutes aimed at terrorist conduct. See, for example, infra, ch. 3.

Title 8, U.S.C.

§ 1182. Inadmissible aliens

    (a)

        3.

            B.

                (iii) Terrorist activity defined.

As used in this Act, the term "terrorist activity" means any activity which is unlawful under the laws of the place where it is committed (or which, if it had been committed in the United States, would be unlawful under the laws of the United States or any State) and which involves any of the following:

    (I) The highjacking or sabotage of any conveyance (including an aircraft, or vehicle).

    (II) The seizing or detaining, and threatening to kill, injure, or continue to detain, another individual in order to compel a third person (including a governmental organization) to do or abstain from doing any act as an explicit or implicit condition for the release of the individual seized or detained.

    (III) A violent attack upon an internationally protected person (as defined in section 1116(b)(4) of title 18, United States Code) or upon the liberty of such a person.

    (IV) An assassination.

    (V) The use of any

        (a) biological agent, chemical agent, or nuclear weapon or device, or

        (b) explosive, firearm, or other weapon or dangerous device (other than for mere personal monetary gain), with intent to endanger, directly or indirectly, the safety of one or more individuals or to cause substantial damage to property.

(VI) A threat, attempt, or conspiracy to do any of the foregoing.

For a recent case applying the "terrorist activity" definition in § 1182, see Zumel v. Lynch, 803 F.3d 463 (9th Cir. 2015).

Another definitional approach, somewhat similar to § 1182, is one which uses a general definition like that in § 2331, supra, and combines it with a list of statutory offenses, with the combination of the two being the marker for terrorism. An example of this approach is found in 18 U.S.C. § 2332b, which is treated infra, this chapter.

Still another approach is one that does not try to define terrorism but rather lists offenses that are, by the nature of the harmful conduct involved in commission of the offense, deemed terrorism-related offenses. See § 2339A as an example of this listing approach. Each of the individual offenses defined in ch. 113B, which is titled, Terrorism, can, because of that title, be argued to be a terrorist offense, but as we shall see, that is a conclusion that does not necessarily follow from the use of the title. Still another category may be one which, arguably, uses a surrogate concept for the concept of terrorism—for example, the transcending national boundaries formula found in § 2332b, discussed infra.

There are formulations developed by government departments and agencies that relate to anti-terrorism activities conducted by the agency in question, or define terrorism for some other reason. Sometimes such a formulation is set forth in a statute; sometimes in an administrative regulation or policy statement. Of course, some of the administrative formulations simply cross-reference to and rely upon one of the statutory definitions discussed above.

Many government departments have responsibilities relating to anti-terrorism efforts, and a number of these have some role in criminal enforcement in aid of anti-terrorism efforts. Coordination and communication among these agencies is now the responsibility of the Homeland Security Department. At this point, we review definitions and enforcement policy statements relating to the anti-terrorism efforts of several different agencies, the State Department, the Federal Bureau of Investigation, the Department of Justice and some others.

3. THE STATE DEPARTMENT'S STATUTORY DEFINITION—REPORTS AND OTHER ACTIONS IN WHICH THE DEFINITION IS USED; THE EXTENT OF TERRORISM WORLDWIDE; FOREIGN TERRORIST ORGANIZATIONS

The main purposes of the definition of terrorism in section 2656f, Title 22, U.S.C., appears to be a) to provide a definition that can be used as the basis for the State Department's annual report on the terrorist threat worldwide; and b) to provide a basis for taking action against countries and individuals who support terrorism. This definition is also used through incorporation by reference in some criminal enforcement contexts.

Title 22, U.S.C.

§ 2656f. Annual country reports on terrorism

(a) Requirement of annual country reports on terrorism

The Secretary of State shall transmit to the Speaker of the House of Representatives and the Committee on Foreign Relations of the Senate, by April 30 of each year, a full and complete report providing—

(1) detailed assessments with respect to each foreign country

(A) in which acts of international terrorism occurred which were, in the opinion of the Secretary, of major significance;

. . .

(2) all relevant information about the activities during the preceding year of any terrorist group, and any umbrella group under which such terrorist group falls, known to be responsible for the kidnapping or death of an American citizen during the preceding five years, any terrorist group known to be financed by countries about which Congress was notified during the preceding year pursuant to section 2405(j) of the Appendix to Title 50, and any other known international terrorist group which the Secretary determines should be the subject of such report;

. . .

(d) Definitions

As used in this section

(1) the term "international terrorism" means terrorism involving citizens or the territory of more than 1 country;

(2) the term "terrorism" means premeditated, politically motivated violence perpetrated against noncombatant targets by subnational groups or clandestine agents;

. . .

Excerpts from the State Department—
Country Reports on Terrorism 2016

Country Reports on Terrorism 2016 is submitted in compliance with Title 22 of the United States Code, Section 2656f (the "Act"), which requires the Department of State to provide to Congress a full and complete annual report on terrorism for those countries and groups meeting the criteria of the Act. Beginning with the report for 2004, it replaced the previously published Patterns of Global Terrorism.

Chapter 1 of the Reports contains a Strategic Assessment, excerpts from which are reproduced below:

Chapter 1   Strategic Assessment

Although terrorist attacks and fatalities from terrorism declined globally for the second year in a row in 2016, terrorist groups continued to exploit ungoverned territory and ongoing conflict to expand their reach, and to direct and inspire attacks around the world. The Islamic State of Iraq and Syria (ISIS) remained the most potent terrorist threat to global security, with eight recognized branches and numerous undeclared networks operating beyond the group's core concentration in Iraq and Syria. Al-Qa'ida (AQ) and its regional affiliates remained a threat to the U.S. homeland and our interests abroad despite counterterrorism pressure by U.S. partners and increased international efforts to counter violent Islamist ideology and messaging. Terrorist groups supported by Iran—most prominently Hizballah—continued to threaten U.S. allies and interests even in the face of U.S.-led intensification of financial sanctions and law enforcement.

ISIS was driven out of roughly a quarter of the territory it held in Syria and Iraq at the beginning of the year through the combined efforts of Iraqi Security Forces and Syrian armed groups, enabled and supported by the 73 members of the Global Coalition to Defeat ISIS. At the same time, diplomatic efforts contributed to strengthening a broad range of travel controls that helped choke off the flow of foreign terrorist fighters to ISIS-held territory in Iraq and Syria. Along with battlefield deaths, the reduction in the flow of recruits left ISIS at its lowest battlefield strength since at least 2014. In Libya, government forces and aligned armed groups, supported by U.S. air strikes, drove ISIS out of its main Libyan stronghold in Sirte. Many ISIS fighters in Darnah and Benghazi also were driven out by the end of 2016.

ISIS attacks outside its territorial strongholds in Iraq, Syria, and Libya were an increasingly important part of its terrorism campaign in 2016. Most of these attacks took place in countries where ISIS has a declared branch, such as Afghanistan, Egypt, Saudi Arabia, and Yemen. Elsewhere around the globe, returning foreign terrorist fighters and homegrown violent extremists carried out attacks directed, assisted, or inspired by ISIS. The attacks in Brussels on March 22, carried out by the same operational cell that conducted the November 2015 Paris attacks, and attacks in Istanbul, are examples of this. Other operations outside of Iraq and Syria were conducted by individuals who were unable to travel to that region and instead conducted attacks in their home countries or regions. ISIS sought to exploit refugee and migrant flows to disguise the travel of its operatives, causing alarm but resulting in increased vigilance in many of the destination countries.

ISIS continued to commit atrocities against groups in areas under its control, including Yezidis, Christians, Shia Muslims, Sunni Muslims, Kurds, and other groups.

In 2015 and 2016, ISIS abducted, systematically raped, and abused thousands of women and children, some as young as eight years of age. Women and children were sold and enslaved, distributed to ISIS fighters as spoils of war, forced into marriage and domestic servitude, or subjected to physical and sexual abuse. ISIS established "markets" where women and children were sold with price tags attached and has published a list of rules on how to treat female slaves once captured. (For further information, refer to the Trafficking in Persons Report 2016, https://www.state.gov/j/tip/rls/tiprpt/index.htm.)

The recruitment of violent extremists through social media remained central to ISIS's terrorist campaign in 2016. The United States and its partners worked closely with social media companies and others to lawfully counter and curtail use of the internet for terrorist purposes. Due in part to these efforts, ISIS content on the internet declined 75 percent from August 2015 to August 2016, while ISIS-related traffic on Twitter declined 45 percent from mid-2014 to mid-2016. This coincided with a steep reduction in the monthly rate of official visual media releases by ISIS, from 761 in August 2015 to 194 in August 2016, according to a study published by the Combating Terrorism Center at West Point. Moreover, ISIS had 19 active media outlets at the beginning of 2017, down from at least 40 in 2015, according to another study published by the Council on Foreign Relations.

Even as ISIS attacks increased in 2016, the world experienced fewer terrorist attacks and fewer fatalities from terrorism for the second year in a row, due largely to declines in South and Central Asia and the Lake Chad Basin region of Africa. In the Lake Chad Basin, military gains by the Multinational Joint Task Force (MNJTF) and its member states against both Boko Haram and ISIS-West Africa, a Boko Haram off-shoot that emerged in 2016, helped drive down terrorist attacks and fatalities in Nigeria and elsewhere in the Lake Chad Basin region over much of the year.

Al-Qa'ida and its regional affiliates exploited the absence of credible and effective state institutions in some states and regions to remain a significant worldwide threat despite sustained pressure by the United States and its partners. Despite leadership losses, al-Qa'ida in the Arabian Peninsula (AQAP) remained a significant threat to Yemen, the region, and the United States, as ongoing conflict in Yemen hindered U.S. efforts to counter the group. Al-Qa'ida's affiliate in Syria, al-Nusrah Front, continued to exploit ongoing armed conflict to maintain a territorial safe haven in select parts of northwestern Syria. Al-Shabaab, which pledged allegiance to al-Qa'ida in 2012, continued to conduct asymmetric attacks throughout Somalia and parts of Kenya despite weakened leadership and increasing defections. In February, al-Shabaab claimed responsibility for a suicide bomb attack aboard a Daallo Airlines flight from Mogadishu that resulted in the death of the attacker, but failed to destroy the aircraft as intended. The attack demonstrated that civilian aviation targets remain a high priority for international terrorist groups despite the broad improvements in aviation security. Al-Qa'ida in the Islamic Maghreb (AQIM) and its affiliates in Mali shifted their operational emphasis from holding territory to perpetrating asymmetric attacks against government and civilian targets, including hotels in Burkina Faso and Cote d'Ivoire, as well as UN peacekeeping forces in northern Mali. Al-Qa'ida in the Indian Subcontinent (AQIS) continued to operate in South Asia, which the AQ-core has historically exploited for safe haven, and it claimed several attacks targeting religious minorities, police, secular bloggers, and publishers in Bangladesh. . . .

The use of Chemical, Biological, Radiological, or Nuclear (CBRN) materials and expertise remained a terrorist threat, as demonstrated by terrorists' stated intent to acquire, develop, and use these materials; the nature of injury and damage these

which require the FBI to be both an agency that effectively detects, investigates, and prevents crimes, and an agency that effectively protects the national security and collects intelligence.

The general objective of these Guidelines is the full utilization of all authorities and investigative methods, consistent with the Constitution and laws of the United States, to protect the United States and its people from terrorism and other threats to the national security, to protect the United States and its people from victimization by all crimes in violation of federal law, and to further the foreign intelligence objectives of the United States. At the same time, it is axiomatic that the FBI must conduct its investigations and other activities in a lawful and reasonable manner that respects liberty and privacy and avoids unnecessary intrusions into the lives of law-abiding people. The purpose of these Guidelines, therefore, is to establish consistent policy in such matters. They will enable the FBI to perform its duties with effectiveness, certainty, and confidence, and will provide the American people with a firm assurance that the FBI is acting properly under the law.

The issuance of these Guidelines represents the culmination of the historical evolution of the FBI and the policies governing its domestic operations subsequent to the September 11, 2001, terrorist attacks on the United States. Reflecting decisions and directives of the President and the Attorney General, inquiries and enactments of Congress, and the conclusions of national commissions, it was recognized that the FBI's functions needed to be expanded and better integrated to meet contemporary realities:

> [C]ontinuing coordination . . . is necessary to optimize the FBI's performance in both national security and criminal investigations . . . . [The] new reality requires first that the FBI and other agencies do a better job of gathering intelligence inside the United States, and second that we eliminate the remnants of the old "wall" between foreign intelligence and domestic law enforcement. Both tasks must be accomplished without sacrificing our domestic liberties and the rule of law, and both depend on building a very different FBI from the one we had on September 10, 2001. (Report of the Commission on the Intelligence Capabilities of the United States Regarding Weapons of Mass Destruction 466, 452 (2005).)

In line with these objectives, the FBI has reorganized and reoriented its programs and missions, and the guidelines issued by the Attorney General for FBI operations have been extensively revised over the past several years. Nevertheless, the principal directives of the Attorney General governing the FBI's conduct of criminal investigations, national security investigations, and foreign intelligence collection have persisted as separate documents involving different standards and procedures for comparable activities. These Guidelines effect a more complete integration and harmonization of standards, thereby providing the FBI and other affected Justice Department components with clearer, more consistent, and more accessible guidance for their activities, and making available to the public in a single document the basic body of rules for the FBI's domestic operations.

These Guidelines also incorporate effective oversight measures involving many Department of Justice and FBI components, which have been adopted to ensure that all FBI activities are conducted in a manner consistent with law and policy.

The broad operational areas addressed by these Guidelines are the FBI's conduct of investigative and intelligence gathering activities, including cooperation and coordination with other components and agencies in such activities, and the intelligence analysis and planning functions of the FBI.

A.　FBI responsibilities—federal crimes, threats to the national security, foreign intelligence

Part II of these Guidelines authorizes the FBI to carry out investigations to detect, obtain information about, or prevent or protect against federal crimes or threats to the national security or to collect foreign intelligence. The major subject areas of information gathering activities under these Guidelines—federal crimes, threats to the national security, and foreign intelligence— are not distinct, but rather overlap extensively. For example, an investigation relating to international terrorism will invariably crosscut these areas because international terrorism is included under these Guidelines' definition of "threat to the national security," because international terrorism subject to investigation within the United States usually involves criminal acts that violate federal law, and because information relating to international terrorism also falls within the definition of "foreign intelligence." Likewise, counterintelligence activities relating to espionage are likely to concern matters that constitute threats to the national security, that implicate violations or potential violations of federal espionage laws, and that involve information falling under the definition of "foreign intelligence."

While some distinctions in the requirements and procedures for investigations are necessary in different subject areas, the general design of these Guidelines is to take a uniform approach wherever possible, thereby promoting certainty and consistency regarding the applicable standards and facilitating compliance with those standards. Hence, these Guidelines do not require that the FBI's information gathering activities be differentially labeled as "criminal investigations," "national security investigations," or "foreign intelligence collections," or that the categories of FBI personnel who carry out investigations be segregated from each other based on the subject areas in which they operate. Rather, all of the FBI's legal authorities are available for deployment in all cases to which they apply to protect the public from crimes and threats to the national security and to further the United States' foreign intelligence objectives. In many cases, a single investigation will be supportable as an exercise of a number of these authorities—i.e., as an investigation of a federal crime or crimes, as an investigation of a threat to the national security, and/or as a collection of foreign intelligence.

1. Federal Crimes

The FBI has the authority to investigate all federal crimes that are not exclusively assigned to other agencies. . . .

2. Threats to the National Security

The FBI's authority to investigate threats to the national security derives from the executive order concerning U.S. intelligence activities, from delegations of functions by the Attorney General, and from various statutory sources. See, e.g., E.O. 12333; 50 U.S.C. 401 et seq.; 50 U.S.C. 1801 et seq. These Guidelines (Part VII.S) specifically define threats to the national security to mean: international terrorism; espionage and other intelligence activities, sabotage, and assassination, conducted by, for, or on behalf of foreign powers, organizations, or persons; foreign computer intrusion; and other matters determined by the Attorney General, consistent with Executive Order 12333 or any successor order.

Activities within the definition of "threat to the national security" that are subject to investigation under these Guidelines commonly involve violations (or potential violations) of federal criminal laws. Hence, investigations of such threats may constitute an exercise both of the FBI's criminal investigation authority and of the FBI's authority to investigate threats to the national security. As with criminal investigations generally, detecting and solving the crimes, and eventually arresting and prosecuting the perpetrators, are likely to be among the objectives of investigations relating to threats to the national security. But these investigations also often serve important purposes outside the ambit of normal criminal investigation and prosecution, by providing the basis for, and informing decisions concerning, other measures needed to protect the national security. These measures may include, for example: excluding or removing persons involved in terrorism or espionage from the United States; recruitment of double agents; freezing assets of organizations that engage in or support terrorism; securing targets of terrorism or espionage; providing threat information and warnings to other federal, state, local, and private agencies and entities; diplomatic or military actions; and actions by other intelligence agencies to counter international terrorism or other national security threats.

In line with this broad range of purposes, investigations of threats to the national security present special needs to coordinate with other Justice Department components, including particularly the Justice Department's National Security Division, and to share information and cooperate with other agencies with national security responsibilities, including other agencies of the U.S. Intelligence Community, the Department of Homeland Security, and relevant White House (including National Security Council and Homeland Security Council) agencies and entities. Various provisions in these Guidelines establish procedures and requirements to facilitate such coordination.

3.   Foreign Intelligence

As with the investigation of threats to the national security, the FBI's authority to collect foreign intelligence derives from a mixture of administrative and statutory sources. See, e.g.,

E.O. 12333; 50 U.S.C. 401 et seq.; 50 U.S.C. 1801 et seq.; 28 U.S.C. 532 note (incorporating P.L. 108-458 §§ 2001–2003). These Guidelines (Part VILE) define foreign intelligence to mean "information relating to the capabilities, intentions, or activities of foreign governments or elements thereof, foreign organizations or foreign persons, or international terrorists."

The FBI's foreign intelligence collection activities have been expanded by legislative and administrative reforms subsequent to the September 11, 2001, terrorist attacks, reflecting the FBI's role as the primary collector of foreign intelligence within the United States, and the recognized imperative that the United States' foreign intelligence collection activities become more flexible, more proactive, and more efficient in order to protect the homeland and adequately inform the United States' crucial decisions in its dealings with the rest of the world:

> The collection of information is the foundation of everything that the Intelligence Community does. While successful collection cannot ensure a good analytical product, the failure to collect information . . . turns analysis into guesswork. And as our review demonstrates, the Intelligence Community's human and technical intelligence collection agencies have collected far too little information on many of the issues we care about most. (Report of the Commission on the Intelligence Capabilities of the United States Regarding Weapons of Mass Destruction 351 (2005).)

These Guidelines accordingly provide standards and procedures for the FBI's foreign intelligence collection activities that meet current needs and realities and optimize the FBI's ability to discharge its foreign intelligence collection functions.

The authority to collect foreign intelligence extends the sphere of the FBI's information gathering activities beyond federal crimes and threats to the national security, and permits the FBI to seek information regarding a broader range of matters relating to foreign powers, organizations, or persons that may be of interest to the conduct of the United States' foreign affairs. The FBI's role is central to the effective collection of foreign intelligence within the United States because the authorized domestic activities of other intelligence agencies are more constrained than those of the FBI under applicable statutes and Executive Order 12333. In collecting foreign intelligence, the FBI will generally be guided by nationally-determined intelligence requirements, including the National Intelligence Priorities Framework and the National HUMINT Collection Directives, or any successor directives issued under the authority of the Director of National Intelligence (DNI). As provided in Part VI.F of these Guidelines, foreign intelligence requirements may also be established by the President or Intelligence Community officials designated by the President, and by the Attorney General, the Deputy Attorney General, or an official designated by the Attorney General.

The general guidance of the FBI's foreign intelligence collection activities by DNI-authorized requirements does not, however, limit the FBI's authority to conduct investigations supportable on the basis of its other authorities—to investigate federal crimes and threats to the national security—in areas in which the information sought also falls under the definition of foreign intelligence. The FBI conducts investigations of federal crimes and threats to the national security based on priorities and strategic objectives set by the Department of Justice and the FBI, independent of DNI-established foreign intelligence collection requirements.

Since the authority to collect foreign intelligence enables the FBI to obtain information pertinent to the United States' conduct of its foreign affairs, even if that information is not related to criminal activity or threats to the national security, the information so gathered may concern lawful activities. The FBI should accordingly operate openly and consensually with U.S. persons to the extent practicable when collecting foreign intelligence that does not concern criminal activities or threats to the national security.

B.   The FBI as an intelligence agency

The FBI is an intelligence agency as well as a law enforcement agency. Its basic functions accordingly extend beyond limited investigations of discrete matters, and include broader analytic and planning functions. The FBI's responsibilities in this area derive from various administrative and statutory sources. See, e.g., E.O. 12333; 28 U.S.C. 532 note (incorporating P.L. 108-458 §§ 2001–2003) and 534 note (incorporating P.L. 109-162 § 1107). Enhancement of the FBI's intelligence analysis capabilities and functions has consistently been recognized as a key priority in the legislative and administrative reform efforts following the September 11, 2001, terrorist attacks:

> [Counterterrorism] strategy should . . . encompass specific efforts to . . . enhance the depth and quality of domestic intelligence collection and analysis . . . . [T]he FBI should strengthen and improve its domestic [intelligence] capability as fully and expeditiously as possible by immediately instituting measures to . . . significantly improve strategic analytical capabilities. . . . (Joint Inquiry into Intelligence Community Activities Before and After the Terrorist Attacks of September 11, 2001, S. Rep. No. 351 & H.R. Rep. No. 792, 107th Cong., 2d Sess. 4–7 (2002) (errata print).)

> A "smart" government would integrate all sources of information to see the enemy as a whole. Integrated all-source analysis should also inform and shape strategies to collect more intelligence. . . . The importance of integrated, all-source analysis cannot be overstated. Without it, it is not

possible to "connect the dots." (Final Report of the National Commission on Terrorist Attacks Upon the United States 401, 408 (2004).)

. . .

D. WHAT MAKES AN OFFENSE A TERRORISM CRIME?

1. TERRORISM MOTIVE AS AN ELEMENT OF A FEDERAL CRIME

Over the course of the past two or three decades, many new statutes have been enacted defining new crimes that are often described as terrorism crimes. A number of these have broken new ground. Most of these statutes can be found in Title 18 of the Federal Criminal Code. Our main focus in the remainder of this chapter is on those Title 18 offenses that are specifically aimed at terrorism.

One might think that the most common reason why an offense might be labeled as a terrorism crime is that it is committed with a terrorism purpose or motive. What we mean by a terrorism purpose or motive can be derived from the definitions of terrorism that were reviewed in the previous section. While these definitions differ in certain respects, they contain common elements that arguably provide at least a general notion of the concept of terrorism as it is used in U.S. governmental statutory, regulatory and policy contexts.

Further, one might think that the most common marker for a terrorism crime would be that its definition contains as a required element that the crime be committed with a terrorism purpose or motive. What is surprising, however, is that it is difficult to find any federal crimes in the U.S. whose definitions contain as an element of the offense a terrorism purpose or motive.

There are, however, a number of offenses (but not a very large number), where a defined terrorism purpose or motive is somehow relevant in the statutory scheme even though it is not an element of the statutory crime: See, for example, 18 U.S.C. § 2332, which makes it a federal crime to kill a national of the United States outside of the U.S. To prosecute such an offense, the Attorney General or other appropriate official must first certify that such offense was intended to coerce, intimidate, or retaliate against a government or a civilian population. The requirement of a terrorism purpose is thus present, but it is not made an element of the offense. Rather, a somewhat unusual statutory prerequisite to prosecution is set up—viz., an administrative determination is to be made by a high government official that a terrorism purpose is present. The legislative history indicates that the Attorney General's certification is intended to be "final."

In somewhat similar fashion, 18 U.S.C. § 2339B makes it a federal crime to provide material support to a foreign terrorist organization (FTO) which thus makes the FTO term an element of the offense, but the designation of the organization as an FTO must have been previously made by the Secretary of State in an administrative process, and, by statute, that determination cannot be revisited in subsequent criminal trials. Accordingly, while the FTO is an element of the offense, it is not subject to dispute in the criminal trial.

Further, 18 U.S.C. § 2332b makes it a federal crime to commit various violent offenses in contexts transcending national boundaries. The caption of this section in the federal criminal code is titled, "Acts of terrorism transcending national boundaries" and the section contains, inter alia, the following provision, "the term 'Federal crime of terrorism' means an offense that—

> (A) is calculated to influence or affect the conduct of government by intimidation or coercion, or to retaliate against government conduct; and

> (B) is a violation of . . .[a long list of specified offenses]."

§ 2332b thus is labeled through its caption as involving terrorism acts and contains within its provisions a definition of Federal crime of terrorism. Nevertheless, and somewhat oddly, the offense defined in § 2332b does not contain as one of its elements that the offense be committed with a terrorism purpose or motive, nor does § 2332b contain as an element of the offense any other clear marker for a terrorism crime.

Note: §§ 2332 and 2332b are given further treatment later in this chapter while § 2339B is treated in detail in ch. 3, infra.

Does one begin to see a pattern here? True, three offenses probably do not represent a pattern, but taken together with the fact that other federal offenses generally labeled as crimes of terrorism do not contain any express language or other express link to a terrorism purpose or motive or other marker for terrorism, perhaps a pattern can be discerned: In the federal criminal system, there appears to be a reluctance to introduce as an element of a "terrorism offense" a terrorism purpose or motive, at least as those concepts have been defined in federal non-criminal statutes, regulations and policy—which leaves us with a nagging question: Why this reluctance?

The reluctance seems to be a peculiarly federal terrorism thing. Thus, many of the states make it a crime to provide material support in aid of an act of terrorism. Typically, act of terrorism is defined as a violent crime (or specified violent offenses) done with a terrorism purpose defined along the lines used in the federal definitions discussed above. In these states, the terrorism purpose thus becomes an element of the offense being charged.

See, for purposes of contrast, the comparable federal statute, § 2339A, which makes it a federal crime to provide material support in aid of a list of specific federal crimes each of which can generally (but not necessarily) be committed in a terrorism context, but none of which have a terrorism motive as an element of the offense. Once again, a federal crime aimed at terrorism does not contain as an element a requirement of a terrorism purpose or motive. In this connection, see United States v. Abu Khatallah, 151 F.Supp.3d 116, 138 (D.D.C. 2015), a case involving the prosecution of an alleged participant in the attack on the U.S. diplomatic mission in Benghazi, Libya in which the U.S. Ambassador and other U.S. personnel were killed. Excerpts from Abu Khatallah are reproduced below:

1. Whether the Material-Support Statute Applies Only to Actions that Constitute "Terrorism"

According to Abu Khatallah, the material-support statute punishes only conduct that constitutes terrorism. He contends, however, that the statute is not sufficiently definite with regard to what constitutes "terrorism" to provide fair notice of what conduct is prohibited. Because the Government charged him with "provid[ing] material support and resources to terrorists," he suggests, "[t]he absence of a specific 'terrorism' element in § 2339A renders the statute unconstitutionally vague," The Government counters that it is irrelevant whether it alleged that Abu Khatallah's actions supported terrorism or whether the material-support statute defines the term "terrorism." In its view, the reason is simple: "[T]here is no statutory requirement that [one's] actions 'qualify as terrorism' " to be guilty under § 2339A. Rather, the statute criminalizes providing "material support" with the knowledge or intent that such support will be used in preparation for, or in carrying out, a set of enumerated criminal offenses that may or may not involve terrorist activity. According to the Government, nothing in the "plain text . . . mandate[s] a showing of terrorist conduct and the federal cases do not require such proof.". Because "the government is not required to show that [a defendant's] material-support actions 'qualify as terrorism,' " it contends, the statute cannot be void for vagueness on the grounds that the term "terrorism" is imprecise or undefined.

. . .Although Abu Khatallah is correct that the material-support statute may have been designed to punish activity connected to terrorism, an association with terrorism is not an element of the crime defined by § 2339A. As the Government submits, criminal liability under § 2339A attaches regardless of any linkage to terrorism. As a result, the statute need not provide any notice of what constitutes "terrorism" to survive a void-for-vagueness challenge under the Due Process Clause.

a.   Statutory Text

Abu Khatallah argues that "the plain language of the statute . . . demonstrates that" criminal liability under "the statute requires some connection to terrorism." Reply 3. Yet the only "plain language" that Abu Khatallah points to is in the non-operative heading, which labels § 2339A as the crime of "[p]roviding material support to terrorists." 18 U.S.C. § 2339A; see also Bhd. of R.R. Trainmen v. Baltimore & O. R. Co., 331 U.S. 519, 528–29, 67 S.Ct. 1387, 91 L.Ed. 1646 (1947) ("[T]he title of a statute and the heading of a section cannot limit the plain meaning of the text."). True, "statutory titles and section headings are tools available for the resolution of a doubt about the meaning of a statute," Fla. Dep't of Rev. v. Piccadilly Cafeterias, Inc., 554 U.S. 33, 47, 128 S.Ct. 2326, 171 L.Ed.2d 203 (2008), but here the statutorily defined elements could not be clearer. To be criminally liable under § 2339A, the operative text specifies that a person must provide or conspire to provide "material support," as defined in the statute, in preparation for, or to carry out, the commission of certain enumerated offenses. The text itself contains no requirement that one's actions be connected to terrorism.

. . .

c.   Statutory Enforcement

Finally, Abu Khatallah maintains that "the government's enforcement of § 2339A also demonstrates that the statute is designed to punish [only] material support for terrorism." He asserts that "the government only uses § 2339A to prosecute material support for offenses allegedly connected to terrorism" (observing that "[a] search of the U.S. courts electronic case tracking system . . . in every federal district court reveals that in every case in which the government has charged a violation of 18 U.S.C. § 2339A, the government has alleged that the defendant provide[d] 'support to terrorists.'"). But whatever § 2339A may have been "designed to" accomplish, the Government's track record of pursuing alleged terrorists under the statute does not bear on the statutorily defined elements of the crime. Nor does the fact that "[t]he United States Attorneys' Manual lists § 2339A as one of many 'International Terrorism Statutes.'" Id. (citing U.S. Attorneys' Manual § 9-2.136).

Although the Government may have consistently used § 2339A to prosecute those that it alleges have provided "support to terrorists," apparently no court has ever required the Government to prove a specific connection to terrorism as an element of that crime. Abu Khatallah's own counsel "have found no reported decision in which a court addressed the issue presented here—that is, the failure of § 2339A to define terrorism." . . .If the Government was required to prove that a defendant's actions constituted "terrorism" in order to secure a conviction under § 2339A, it is quite odd that in so many cases no court has ever addressed "the failure of § 2339A to define terrorism." The explanation, however, is straightforward: Conviction under § 2339A does not require proof of terrorist conduct—only proof of material support in preparation for, or in carrying out, at least one of an enumerated set of violent offenses.

Because § 2339A does not include terrorist conduct as an element of criminal liability, the Court will deny Abu Khatallah's void-for-vagueness challenge that the statute provides inadequate notice of what constitutes terrorism.

For purposes of contrast with the approach typically taken in regard to terrorism crimes which do not generally include the motive of the perpetrator as an element of the crime, see the federal hate crimes statute, 18 U.S.C. § 249, which makes it a federal crime (where there is requisite connection to interstate commerce) to willfully cause bodily injury to any person because of "the actual or perceived religion, national origin, gender, sexual orientation, gender identity, or disability of any person." In the hate crimes context, there thus seems to be no federal reluctance to include the motive of the perpetrator as an element of the offense.

Is there a difference between the hate crime motive and a terrorism motive?

2. ACT OF TERRORISM OR HATE CRIME? OR BOTH?

Occasionally, cases arise in which there may be a division of opinion as to whether the case is best classified as an act of terrorism or a hate crime. In some cases might it be both? See Mark Berman, Was the Charlottesville Car Attack domestic terrorism, a hate crime, or both? Washington Post, August 14, 2017, https://www.washingtonpost.com/news/post-nation/wp/2017/08/14/was. In connection with a white supremacist protest march in Charlottesville, VA, a person with a history of neo-Nazi views drove his car into a crowd of counter-protestors, killing one person and injuring 19 others.

U.S. Attorney General Jeff Sessions was reported first to have said the car attack meets the definition of domestic terrorism and later, that it could be prosecuted as a federal hate crime. Other experts were reported to have said that the attack might straddle the line between terrorism and a hate crime; that acts like those involved here, while they might meet the definition of domestic terrorism, were not made criminal as such under the federal criminal code. Ibid. Of course, in a domestic terrorism context, other federal charges might be applicable.

Compare the incident that occurred earlier in 2017 in New York City where a white man traveled to New York from Baltimore by bus, by his own admission in order to kill blacks. He proceeded to fatally stab an African-American man whom he randomly encountered. He was charged with Murder As Act of Terrorism and Murder As a Hate Crime for the fatal stabbing. Press Release from the Office of Cyrus Vance, Jr., District Attorney, http://manhattanda.org/press-release/da-vance-james-jackson-indicted-charges-murder-first-and-second-degrees-among-other-ch.

See the definition of act of terrorism in McKinney's New York Penal Law, § 490.05:

As used in this article, the following terms shall mean and include:

1.   "Act of terrorism":

(a) . . .

(b) for purposes of subparagraph (xiii) of paragraph (a) of subdivision one of section 125.27 [ed., murder provisions] this chapter means activities that involve a violent act or acts dangerous to human life that are in violation of the criminal laws of this state and are intended to:

(i)   intimidate or coerce a civilian population;

(ii) influence the policy of a unit of government by intimidation or coercion; or

(iii) affect the conduct of a unit of government by murder, assassination or kidnapping.

Also see the definition of hate crime in McKinney's New York Penal Law § 485.05:

1.   A person commits a hate crime when he or she commits a specified offense and either:

(a) intentionally selects the person against whom the offense is committed or intended to be committed in whole or in substantial part because of a belief or perception regarding the race, color, national origin, ancestry, gender, religion, religious practice, age, disability or sexual orientation of a person, regardless of whether the belief or perception is correct, or

(b) intentionally commits the act or acts constituting the offense in whole or in substantial part because of a belief or perception regarding the race, color, national origin, ancestry, gender, religion, religious practice, age, disability or sexual orientation of a person, regardless of whether the belief or perception is correct.

Does the conduct involved in the New York City case clearly qualify as an "act of terrorism"? Clearly qualify as a "hate crime"?

3. FEDERAL CRIME OF TERRORISM AS A FEDERAL SENTENCING GUIDELINES ENHANCEMENT FACTOR

Perhaps the failure to include a terrorism motive as an element of federal "terrorism" offenses can at least partly be accounted for by a view that it is not needed as an element of the offense. Thus, even if the terrorism motive is not included as an element of the specific offense, the fact that the conduct involved constituted "terrorism" may be given legal significance in the particular criminal proceedings by virtue of the fact that there is a "terrorism" enhancement factor under the federal Sentencing Guidelines. The particular guideline in question defines terrorism by reference to the definition of "federal crime of terrorism" the definition of which is found in 18 U.S.C. § 2332b, which was referred to, supra. For an application and interpretation of this Guideline in an alleged domestic terrorism context, see, for example, United States v. Thurston, 2007 WL 1500176 (D.Ore. 2007):

> The court is asked to decide whether the sentencing enhancement for terrorism under § 3A1.4 of the United States Sentencing Guidelines applies to the defendants in the above-captioned cases, based on their convictions for conspiracy to commit arson and destruction of an energy facility of the United States and for the predicate offenses of arson, attempted arson, and destruction of an energy facility.

> . . .

> At the outset, it is important to clarify the court's role in this proceeding. The issue the court must decide is not whether the defendants are "terrorists" as the word commonly is used and understood in today's political and cultural climate.

> . . .

> Additionally, contrary to many defendants' assertions, the court is not entering into uncharted waters. As discussed in this opinion, the terrorism enhancement has been applied in several cases where the offenses of conviction caused only property

damage. While the number of decisions may not be significant, these cases provide the court with considerable guidance.

. . .

Pursuant to negotiated plea agreements, all defendants have pled guilty to one count of conspiracy to commit arson and the destruction of an energy facility in violation of 18 U.S.C. § 371. In addition to conspiracy, defendants Tubbs, Gerlach, Meyerhoff, McGowan, Savoie, Tankersley, Block, Zacher, and Paul pled guilty to numerous counts of arson and attempted arson of property used in or affecting interstate commerce in violation of 18 U.S.C. § 844(i). Defendants Tubbs and Thurston also pled guilty to arson of federal government property in violation of 18 U.S.C. § 844(f)(1), and defendants Gerlach and Meyerhoff pled guilty to the destruction of an energy facility in violation of 18 U.S.C. § 1366(a). Defendants' convictions are based on the following undisputed facts, as admitted by defendants in their plea agreements and as set forth in the Presentence Investigation Report and the government's sentencing memorandum.

Beginning in October 1996 and continuing through October 2001, defendants and other individuals formed a conspiracy to damage or destroy private and government property. Specifically, defendants conspired to commit a series of arson and other offenses on behalf of the Animal Liberation Front (ALF) and the Earth Liberation Front (ELF). The conspirators targeted federal government agencies and private parties they believed responsible for degradation of the environment, tree harvesting, and cruel treatment of animals. Eventually, the targets of arson expanded to include entities involved in genetic research.

. . .

By 2001, the conspirators had committed numerous acts of arson or attempted arson and destroyed a high voltage electrical tower across five different states. The offenses included: arson of the Dutch Girl Dairy in Eugene, Oregon in December 1995; arson and attempted arson of the United States Forest Service (USFS) Ranger Station in Detroit, Oregon in October 1996; arson of the USFS Ranger Station in Oakridge, Oregon in October 1996; arson of Cavel West Meat Packing Plant in Redmond, Oregon in July 1997; arson of the Bureau of Land Management (BLM) Wild Horse Corrals near Burns, Oregon in November 1997; arson of the United States Department of Agriculture Animal Plan Health Inspection Service and Animal Damage Control Facility in Olympia, Washington in June 1998; . . . . These actions damaged or destroyed numerous buildings and vehicles, causing tens of millions of dollars in damages.

After the arson offenses, the conspirators often sent "communiques" attributing responsibility for the particular arson to ELF or ALF and explaining the motivation for the offense. For example, a communique on behalf of ALF described the Cavel West arson in detail and accepted responsibility for destroying the "horse murdering plant." Similarly, following the fire at Childers Meat Company, a communique declared that "[a]s long as companies continue to operate and profit off of Mother Earth and Her sentient animal beings, the Animal Liberation Front will continue to target these operations and their insurance companies until they are all out of business." After the Litchfield BLM Wild Horse Corral arson, a communique was released opposing the asserted BLM policy of "round[ing] up thousands of wild horses and burros to clear public land for grazing cattle" and warning of future actions: "In the name of all that is wild we will continue to target industries and organizations that seek to profit by destroying the earth."

. . .

Defendants next argue that their convictions under 18 U.S.C. §§ 844(f)(1), 844(i), and 1366(a) cannot support imposition of the terrorism enhancement, because none of their offenses created a substantial risk of harm. Defendants contend that Congress did not intend that the enhancement apply to offenses that caused only property damage but did not cause injury or death.

. . .

However, this court is bound by the canons of statutory construction, and I find that resolution of this issue begins and ends with the plain language of the statute and Sentencing Guidelines. . . . Second, the definition of "federal crime of terrorism" does not import the element of "substantial risk of serious bodily injury" included in 18 U.S.C. § 2332b(a)(1)(A). Instead, Congress defined a "federal crimes of terrorism" as the commission of specific offenses along with the intent or desire to influence, affect, or retaliate against government conduct.

. . .

I find that a "federal crime of terrorism" under § 2332b(g)(5) does not require a substantial risk of injury.

. . .

Defendants argue that the government cannot establish the necessary motivational element to support the terrorism enhancement, because their offenses were calculated merely to gain and generate publicity rather than to influence, affect, or retaliate against government conduct. Additionally, with respect to the arson of private property, defendants maintain that they targeted those businesses with the intent to influence or affect the conduct of private parties rather than the conduct of government. . . .

The government responds that the court must look at the totality of the circumstances surrounding each arson to determine whether each offense was calculated to influence, affect, or retaliate against government conduct.

As stated during argument, the court cannot determine conclusively whether the offenses were intended to influence, affect, or retaliate against government conduct until relevant evidence is presented at the defendants' sentencing hearings. At the same time, defendants point is well taken; the definition of "federal crime of terrorism" explicitly requires an intent "to influence or affect the conduct of government by intimidation or coercion, or to retaliate against government conduct." 18 U.S.C. § 2332b(g)(5)(A) (emphasis added). Thus, the government must establish that the defendants targeted government conduct rather than the conduct of private individuals or corporations.

. . .

Note that the crimes charged in the Thurston case were not per se or inherently terrorism offenses and as mentioned supra, if the case involved terrorism, it was domestic terrorism. The primary focus of the materials in this casebook is international terrorism, but we should not be inattentive to cases of domestic terrorism, especially since instances of domestic terrorism may inform issues and interpretations of the international variety. Recall that both domestic and international terrorism are defined in 18 U.S.C. § 2331.

Apart from the particular statute at issue in the Thurston case, should the concept of terrorism be restricted to acts targeting the government, or should it also include violence directed against private institutions in order to influence their behavior, for example, large corporations.

Prior to the sentencing in the Thurston case, supra, Caroline Paul, the sister of one of the defendants, wrote an op-ed piece in The Los Angeles Times in which she argued that this was the first time terrorism sentencing enhancements were claimed when the defendants took affirmative steps to make certain that no one would be hurt. While conceding that egregious property damage was caused, she contended that it was "still just property damage." She also stated, "Could it really be true that the most powerful country in the world feels 'coerced' by a bunch of bunny huggers? Is the . . . leader of this nation being bullied by vegans?" LA Times, May 24, 2007.

Apart from the matter of statutory construction, as a matter of policy, should the notion of terrorism, or at least terrorism used as a basis for sentencing enhancement, be restricted to violent acts that cause injury to persons?

For another example of a sentencing enhancement case involving domestic terrorism, see United States v. Graham, 275 F.3d 490 (6th Cir. 2001):

> Graham and Huggett were members of a militia group called the Michigan Militia Wolverines in the early years of their marijuana cultivation business. Huggett testified that, at some point after 1995, Graham and others were expelled from the Wolverines because they were advocating violence against the government. In the summer of 1996, those individuals who had left the Wolverines formed a new militia group called the "North American Militia" ("NAM"). The purpose of the militia group was to prepare for a "war" with the government and ultimately to overthrow the government. NAM members advocated an offensive "first strike" against the government, out of fear that the government was planning an attack against them. The war was sometimes referred to as an "Armageddon." . . . Various dates for attack were selected, beginning with June 7, 1997, although each date was subsequently postponed by Carter.

> Undercover Bureau of Alcohol, Tobacco, and Firearms ("ATF") Agent Robert Stumpenhaus infiltrated NAM sometime in April 1997. Agent Stumpenhaus testified at trial that he participated in over ten meetings at Speed's and at the mall with various members of NAM. Stumpenhaus and other witnesses who testified at trial reported that among their activities, NAM collected and stockpiled weapons; held target practice and conducted paramilitary training; selected various federal and state "hard" and "soft" targets; and plotted strategy for their war. Stumpenhaus reported that Carter's strategy was to attack certain targets in Calhoun County, Michigan, and the surrounding area, create chaos, and then attempt to "hold on" for three to five days while militias in other parts of the country would rise up against the government. In preparation for their war, NAM members participated in training activities, such as going on "bivouacs;" learning "close quarters battle;" and securing a building with weapons and emptying the building of people and weapons.

Under Carter's direction, each member of the militia was assigned to a three-person "cell" which was responsible for "taking out" various "hard" and "soft" targets in a certain geographical region. Among the "hard" targets selected for attack were: (1) the intersection of Interstate 94 and U.S. Route 131 near Kalamazoo, Michigan; (2) power facilities; (3) fuel depots and gas stations; and (4) communication facilities such as a TV station in Kalamazoo, Michigan. Also mentioned as a site for attack was the nearby Fort Custer Army National Guard Post. NAM's goal was to cut off transportation, electricity, gas, and communication to the area. Among the "soft" targets identified were federal prosecutors, judges, and other federal officials as well as Senator Carl Levin of Michigan and other members of Congress. . . .

. . .

. . . .The district court concluded that Graham and his co-conspirators intended to influence and intimidate federal officers in the performance of their duties; that they conspired to possess machineguns and other weapons; and that they discussed plans to attack their targets with the weapons they had acquired, all in furtherance of the conspiracy.

Based on our review of the record, we cannot say that the district court's findings of fact are clearly erroneous.

4. PROSECUTION OF TERRORISTS AND TERRORISM-RELATED CONDUCT THROUGH CHARGES OF CRIMES THAT ARE NOT INHERENTLY CRIMES OF TERRORISM

Of course, as is illustrated in the Thurston and Graham cases supra, prosecutions of individuals for terrorism-related conduct are also frequently based on crimes that are not inherently crimes of terrorism, that is, they can be committed in non-terrorism as well as terrorism contexts. It is the context that moves such offenses into the terrorism arena. A list of the types of offenses that have been utilized in some of the terrorism cases prosecuted over the past several years covers a broad range of federal offenses.

The incidence of prosecutions for terrorism-related conduct has been growing significantly in recent years, but viewed as part of the total nationwide or total federal criminal caseload, terrorism cases continue to be a very small proportion of these totals. Of course, a single terrorism crime, successfully completed can cause catastrophic destruction and loss of life. We cannot be certain whether this growth in numbers is a trend that will continue upward or level out or actually fall in the future. We shall learn more about these issues with the passage of time.

PROBLEMS

1.   On July 4, 2002, an Egyptian citizen who was living in Irvine, California but had recently returned from a visit to Egypt pulled a gun at the El Al counter at Los Angeles International Airport, started shooting and killed two people and wounding others before he himself was killed by a security guard. The FBI investigated and, as reported in public statements, concluded it was not a terrorist act. Several newspaper articles discussed the issue. See, e.g. Joe Mathews & Henry Weinstein, A Matter for Debate: Was This a Terrorist Attack? Semantics: To the Israelis, It Seems Clear That It Was. But U.S. Government Officials, from the White House to the FBI, Take a More Cautious Approach, L.A. Times, July 6, 2002 at A17; Greg Kirkorian, LAX Shooter Motivated by Personal Woes, Probe Finds; Investigation: Federal Agents Say Egyptian Man acted Alone When He Opened Fire at El Al Counter on July 4, L.A. Times, Sept. 5, 2002 at Metro section 1. According to newspaper reports quoting government officials, the man acted alone, had no connection to any political organizations and was depressed by personal problems

Do you think that under the definition of terrorism that is applied by the FBI, supra, it arguably was anyway a terrorist act? Under any of the other definitions of terrorism presented in these materials, supra? See the materials in the next section and consider whether they affect your judgment about what constitutes terrorism in the U.S. legal system? What difference does it make whether the FBI treats it as a terrorist act or not? Might it have affected the crimes with which the perpetrator could have been charged if he had survived? Does whether the conduct is deemed terrorism have other consequences?

2.   The Foreign Intelligence Surveillance Act (FISA), discussed in Chapter 5, infra, provides authority for electronic surveillance to obtain foreign intelligence information relating to ". . . international terrorism by a foreign power or agent of a foreign power." Fourth Amendment standards different from those usually used can be applied to surveillances under the Act. The Definitions section of the Act (50 U.S.C. § 1801) uses the same definition of "international terrorism" used by the FBI. Additionally, under the Act, the definition of "foreign power" includes the following: ". . . a group engaged in international terrorism . . ."; ". . . a foreign-based political organization. . . ."

Suppose that members of a South American drug cartel who are involved in the international drug trade plan to kill a senior U.S. official working in their country in retaliation for a successful "drug bust" by the U.S. Navy on one of their vessels on the high seas. Is this activity subject to surveillance under the FISA statute?

3.   A terrorism statute enacted by the Virginia legislature in 2002 provides the death penalty for killings committed with "the intent to intimidate or coerce a civilian population or influence the policy, conduct or activities of the government . . . through intimidation or coercion." This statute was used to prosecute John Lee Malvo and John Allen Muhammad, who were accused of being the snipers who terrorized the Washington D.C. area and made demands for a 10 million dollar payment in order for them to stop the killing.

Do you think that the actions of the snipers constitute terrorism, as a general proposition? Under the Virginia statute? Does this mean that anyone who engages in an extended crime spree in Virginia involving an extortionate demand might be subject to being prosecuted under the state's terrorism statute?

4.   The deadliest mass shooting in U.S. history occurred in Las Vegas in late September, 2017. The gunman shooting from the 32nd floor of a Las Vegas Strip hotel into a crowd of 22,000 gathered for a country music concert killed 58 people and wounded over 500 others. For weeks afterwards, and still, as of the time this is being written, no one has been able to determine his motive. Absent evidence of his motive, can it be concluded that his conduct was terrorism? See Scott Shane, Shooting Tragedy that Terrorizes but without an Obvious Terrorist Motive, N.Y. Times, Oct. 3, 2017, A13.

E. INTERNATIONAL TERRORISM PROSECUTIONS SINCE 9/11

NOTE

Reproduced following this Note is an introduction to a report on international terrorism and terrorism-related conviction statistics from 9/11 through March 18, 2010, prepared by the Counterterrorism Section of the National Security Division of the Department of Justice. These statistics reflect prosecutions of terrorism and terrorism-related cases in the federal court system. The accompanying chart, not reproduced here, can be found at http://www.fas.org/irp/agency/doj/doj032610-stats.pdf. Also see Letter from the Assistant Attorney General. http://www.justice.gov/cjs/docs/terrorism-crimes-letter.html.

The question of whether persons accused of terrorism should be handled in the civilian courts or in military commission proceedings has generated much controversy since 9/11. For the most part, persons apprehended in the United States have been dealt with in the civilian system, although there have been partial exceptions. For the most part, at least until recently, persons apprehended abroad have been handled in the military system, although, again, there have been exceptions. Attorney General Holder's announcement in the fall, 2009 that it was planned to prosecute in civilian proceedings a handful of the persons detained in military custody at Guantanamo, including some directly involved in the planning that led to the 9/11 terrorist attacks served to escalate the controversy about the choice between civilian and military trials; it became a political issue. While the Attorney General did not back down from his announced choice of a civilian forum for some of the detainees, as a result of the controversy, he did decide to shift the prosecutions of the handful of persons accused of plotting the 9/11 attacks back to the military commission process. And only one Guantanamo detainee was prosecuted in federal court before the end of the Obama administration.

The fact that a large number of terrorism cases have been successfully prosecuted in the federal courts while only a few such cases have been brought to closure in the military commission system has been advanced as an argument in support of civilian handling of such cases. Accordingly, the statistics detailed below are part of the background for consideration of this issue, which is a recurring question throughout the book. We return to consideration of this issue in Part Two of the volume.

Note that the report adopts a distinction between what are termed category I and category II cases. Category I cases involve violations of federal statutes that directly relate to international terrorism. These statutes include many of the statutes that are treated or described in section F, infra.

INTRODUCTION TO NATIONAL SECURITY DIVISION STATISTICS ON UNSEALED INTERNATIONAL TERRORISM AND TERRORISM-RELATED CONVICTIONS

The National Security Division's International Terrorism and Terrorism-Related Statistics Chart tracks convictions resulting from international terrorism investigations conducted since September 11, 2001, including investigations of terrorist acts planned or committed outside the territorial jurisdiction of the United States over which Federal criminal jurisdiction exists and those within the United States involving international terrorists and terrorist groups. Convictions listed on the chart involve the use of a variety of Federal criminal statutes available to prevent, disrupt, and punish international terrorism and related criminal activity. The convictions are the product of the Department's aggressive, consistent, and coordinated national enforcement effort with respect to international terrorism that was undertaken after the September 11, 2001 terrorist attacks.

Criminal cases arising from international terrorism investigations are divided into two categories, according to the requisite level of coordination and monitoring required by the Counterterrorism Section of the National Security Division (or its predecessor section in the Criminal Division). This coordination and monitoring exists in response to the expanded Federal criminal jurisdiction over and importance of international terrorism matters and the need to ensure coherent, consistent, and effective Federal prosecutions related to such matters. Typically, multiple defendants in a case are classified in the same category.

Category I cases involve violations of federal statutes that are directly related to international terrorism and that are utilized regularly in international terrorism matters. These statutes prohibit, for example, terrorist acts abroad against United States nationals, the use of weapons of mass destruction, conspiracy to murder persons overseas, providing material support to terrorists or foreign terrorist organizations, receiving military style training from foreign terrorist organizations, and bombings of public places or government facilities. A complete list of Category I offenses is found in Appendix A.

Category II cases include defendants charged with violating a variety of other statutes where the investigation involved an identified link to international terrorism. These Category II cases include offenses such as those involving fraud, immigration, firearms, drugs, false statements, perjury, and obstruction of justice, as well as general conspiracy charges under 18 U.S.C. § 371. Prosecuting terror-related targets using Category II offenses and others is often an effective method—and sometimes the only available method—of deterring and disrupting potential terrorist planning and support activities. This approach underscores the wide variety of tools available in the U.S. criminal justice system for disrupting terror activity. Examples of Category II offenses are listed in Appendix B, and examples of Category II cases are described in Appendix C to illustrate the kinds of connections to international terrorism that are not apparent from the nature of the offenses of conviction themselves. [ed. Appendices B and C are not reproduced here.]

The chart includes the defendant's name, district, charging date, charges brought, classification category, conviction date and conviction charges. If a convicted defendant has been sentenced, the relevant date and sentence imposed is included. The chart is constantly being updated with new convictions, but currently includes only unsealed convictions from September 11, 2001 to March 18, 2010. The chart does not include defendants whose convictions remain under seal, nor does it include defendants who have been charged with a terrorism or terrorism-related offense but have not been convicted either at trial or by guilty plea. This chart does not include convictions related solely to domestic terrorism. Note that the chart maintained by the National Security Division is distinct from statistics maintained by the Bureau of Prisons to track inmates with terrorist connections. The chart lists more than 150 defendants classified in Category I and more than 240 defendants classified in Category II.

The chart is organized by conviction date, with the most recent convictions first. The earliest defendants included on the chart were identified and detained in the course of the nationwide investigation conducted after September 11, 2001, and were subsequently charged with a criminal offense. Since then, additional defendants have been added who, at the time of charging, appeared to have a connection to international terrorism, even if they were not charged with a terrorism offense. The decision to add defendants to the chart is made on a case-by-case basis by career prosecutors in the National Security Division's Counterterrorism Section, whose primary responsibility is investigating and prosecuting international and domestic terrorism cases to prevent and disrupt acts of terrorism anywhere in the world that impact on significant United States interests and persons.

Appendix A

Category I Offenses Aircraft Sabotage (18 U.S.C. § 32)

Animal Enterprise Terrorism (18 U.S.C. § 43) Crimes Against Internationally Protected Persons (18 U.S.C. §§ 112, 878, 1116, 1201(a)(4)) Use of Biological, Nuclear, Chemical or Other Weapons of Mass Destruction (18 U.S.C. §§ 175, 175b, 229, 831, 2332a)

Production, Transfer, or Possession of Variola Virus (Smallpox) (18 U.S.C. § 175c)

Participation in Nuclear and WMD Threats to the United States (18 U.S.C. § 832) Conspiracy Within the United States to Murder, Kidnap, or Maim Persons or to Damage Certain Property Overseas (18 U.S.C. § 956)

Hostage Taking (18 U.S.C. § 1203) Terrorist Attacks Against Mass Transportation Systems (18 U.S.C. § 1993) Terrorist Acts Abroad Against United States Nationals (18 U.S.C. § 2332) Terrorism Transcending National Boundaries (18 U.S.C. § 2332b)

Bombings of places of public use, Government facilities, public transportation systems and infrastructure facilities (18 U.S.C. § 2332f)

Missile Systems designed to Destroy Aircraft (18 U.S.C. § 2332g) Production, Transfer, or Possession of Radiological Dispersal Devices (18 U.S.C. § 2332h) Harboring Terrorists (18 U.S.C. § 2339) Providing Material Support to Terrorists (18 U.S.C. § 2339A) Providing Material Support to Designated Terrorist Organizations (18 U.S.C. § 2339B) Prohibition Against Financing of Terrorism (18 U.S.C. § 2339C) Receiving Military-Type Training from an FTO (18 U.S.C. § 2339D) Narco-Terrorism (21 U.S.C. § 1010A) Sabotage of Nuclear Facilities or Fuel (42 U.S.C. § 2284) Aircraft Piracy (49 U.S.C. § 46502)

Violations of IEEPA (50 U.S.C. § 1705(b)) involving E.O. 12947 (Terrorists Who Threaten to Disrupt the Middle East Peace Process); E.O. 13224 (Blocking Property and Prohibiting Transactions With Persons Who Commit, Threaten to Commit, or Support Terrorism or Global Terrorism List); and E.O. 13129 (Blocking Property and Prohibiting Transactions With the Taliban)

There is no comparable similar comprehensive report updating the number of international terrorism convictions since the report reproduced above. There are a number of different sources of data available on this subject, but the numbers are not particularly consistent. See, e.g., statements regarding such inconsistency in the Backgrounder available at the Department of Justice website, excerpts from which were reproduced supra. According to some data sources, 2012 marked a beginning of a decrease in the number of international terrorism convictions. The decrease continued for three years but beginning in 2015, the number began to increase, though slowly, each year. An example of recent international terrorism conviction numbers is provided by the Transactional Records Access Clearinghouse (TRAC), which, relying on information from the U.S. Department of Justice, reported that as of 11 months of the fiscal year, there had been 40 terrorism convictions in FY 2017, which projected out to a total of 44 for the year.

Relying on an impressionistic assessment of DOJ press releases regarding prosecutions and convictions, the number of cases also seems to be somewhat on the rise. Of course, there are differences among the cases. They include a large number of convictions of persons attempting to travel to Syria and Iraq to engage in jihad with ISIS, and a fewer number of persons plotting to engage in violent terrorist acts in the U.S., as well as a few persons charged with terrorism acts abroad. See, e.g. United States v. Khatallah, supra.

F. SELECTED TERRORISM STATUTES

1. INTRODUCTION

Chapter 113B of title 18, the federal criminal code, has the caption Terrorism attached to it so that it reads as chapter 113B Terrorism. One would expect that the crimes defined in chapter 113B would be terrorism crimes and any provisions not defining crimes would nevertheless deal with Terrorism. Largely, both of those propositions are true, but with a number of qualifications.

There are 20 provisions in chapter 113B; 11 of them define crimes. The word, terrorism is found in a number of these crime provisions but not in all of them. The first provision in the Chapter, § 2331, contains definitions of two phrases, "international terrorism" and "domestic terrorism," "as used in this chapter." As it turns out those definitions are not limited to use "in this chapter" but are also expressly invoked by other statutes or regulations for use in other contexts.

We have previously very briefly reviewed some of the chapter 113B offenses, those that refer to terrorism, but do not include a terrorism motive in their elements, namely, 2332, 2332b, and 2339A and 2339B. We address these offenses in more detail below.

There are also other provisions in chapter 113B defining crimes that do not contain any reference at all to terrorism. For example, two such offenses are § 2332a, Use of weapons of mass destruction and § 2332f, Bombings of places of public use, government facilities, public transportation systems and infrastructure facilities. Would the perpetration of either of these two offenses always involve terrorism? If so, by virtue of what, the Terrorism caption to the chapter heading? The nature of the offense? If the latter, and if you implicitly are relying on some definition of terrorism, what is that definition? If you are relying on the caption attached as a title for the chapter, should you be concerned about the fact that the Supreme Court has ruled that where captions to particular statutory provisions defining crimes set forth limitations that do not appear in the statutory language, the statutory language controls the result, not the caption. Regarding the question of whether the weapons of mass destruction offense always involves terrorism, compare § 9–2.138, United States Attorney's Manual:

> Matters involving the Weapons of Mass Destruction (WMD) statutes (18 U.S.C. §§ . . . 2332a, and 2332h), may involve international terrorism, in which case they are already covered by the policy set forth in USAM 9-2.136. Even if the matters do not involve international terrorism, however, the importance and sensitivity of these matters requires a consistent national approach . . . .

Apart from the language of the legislation defining the crimes or the nature of the crimes, there is another control on whether offenses contained in chapter 113B are restricted to terrorism contexts. Prosecution by U.S. Attorney offices around the country of many of the offenses contained in 113B requires the approval of the Counterterrorism unit in the Department of Justice. See § 9–2.136, United States Attorney's Manual.

2.   18 U.SC. § 2332. CRIMINAL PENALTIES

§ 2332. Criminal Penalties

(a) Homicide. Whoever kills a national of the United States, while such national is outside the United States, shall

(1) if the killing is murder (as defined in section 1111(a)), be fined under this title, punished by death or imprisonment for any term of years or for life, or both;

(2) if the killing is a voluntary manslaughter as defined in section 1112(a) of this title, be fined under this title or imprisoned not more than ten years, or both; and

(3) if the killing is an involuntary manslaughter as defined in section 1112(a) of this title, be fined under this title or imprisoned not more than three years, or both.

(b) Attempt or conspiracy with respect to homicide. Whoever outside the United States attempts to kill, or engages in a conspiracy to kill, a national of the United States shall

(1) in the case of an attempt to commit a killing that is a murder as defined in this chapter, be fined under this title or imprisoned not more than 20 years, or both; and

(2) in the case of a conspiracy by two or more persons to commit a killing that is a murder as defined in section 1111(a) of this title, if one or more of such persons do any overt act to effect the object of the conspiracy, be fined under this title or imprisoned for any term of years or for life, or both so fined and so imprisoned.

(c) Other conduct. Whoever outside the United States engages in physical violence

(1) with intent to cause serious bodily injury to a national of the United States; or

(2) with the result that serious bodily injury is caused to a national of the United States;

shall be fined under this title or imprisoned not more than ten years, or both.

(d) Limitation on prosecution. No prosecution for any offense described in this section shall be undertaken by the United States except on written certification of the Attorney General or the highest ranking subordinate of the Attorney General with responsibility for criminal prosecutions that, in the judgment of the certifying official, such offense was intended to coerce, intimidate, or retaliate against a government or a civilian population.

The following case involves application of subsection (d) of § 2332, supra, which is a rather unusual provision in the federal criminal code.

UNITED STATES V. YOUSEF
327 F.3d 56 (2d Cir.2003), cert. den. 540 U.S. 933 (2003)

[The facts and international criminal jurisdiction issues in the case were reproduced supra, this chapter.]

. . .

II. Conviction of Yousef Under 18 U.S.C. § 2332

Yousef argues that we should overturn his conviction on Count Fifteen because 18 U.S.C. § 2332 unconstitutionally delegates legislative power to the Attorney General of the United States. Alternatively, he contends that his conviction should be overturned because the District Court failed to charge the jury that it had to find intent to retaliate against the United States and its citizens as an element of the crime charged in Count Fifteen.

In Count Fifteen, Yousef and his co-defendants were charged with conspiring to kill United States nationals outside the United States in violation of 18 U.S.C. § 2332(b) and (d).

Under 18 U.S.C. § 2332(a) it is a crime to "kill . . . a national of the United States, while such national is outside the United States." Section 2332(b) prohibits any person outside the United States from "engaging in a conspiracy to kill . . . a national of the United States." Section 2332(d) is entitled "Limitation on prosecution" and provides:

> No prosecution for any offense described in this section shall be undertaken by the United States except on written certification of the Attorney General or the highest ranking subordinate of the Attorney General with responsibility for criminal prosecutions that, in the judgment of the certifying official, such offense was intended to coerce, intimidate, or retaliate against a government or a civilian population.

A.   Prosecutorial Discretion Under Section 2332(d)

Yousef argues that § 2332 is an unconstitutional delegation of legislative authority, because the statute authorizes the Attorney General to define what conduct constitutes an offense.

Section 2332 does not represent an unconstitutional delegation of power to the Attorney General. Indeed, § 2332(d) does not delegate any legislative power to the Attorney General. Rather, it merely sets limits on how the Attorney General can exercise his discretion to prosecute. . . . Section 2332(d) limits the Justice Department's prosecution of crimes under § 2332 to those crimes in which the defendant intended to target the Government or civilian population of the United States. Exercise of such prosecutorial discretion involves no rulemaking power on the part of the Executive Branch and, therefore, cannot constitute delegation of legislative power to the Attorney General—let alone an unlawful delegation of such power.

Even if § 2332(d) did represent a delegation of legislative power to the Attorney General, such a delegation would not be unconstitutional. It has long been the rule that Congress may delegate some of its legislative powers to the Executive Branch, so long as that delegation is made "under the limitation of a prescribed standard."

. . .

Subsection (d) provides a clearly intelligible principle to which the Attorney General must adhere-namely, to prosecute only those cases where the intent of the offense was to coerce, intimidate, or retaliate against the Government or civilian population of the United States. In sum, § 2332 does not unconstitutionally delegate legislative power to the Attorney General.

Nor does 2332 unconstitutionally remove an element of the offense from the jury. Although a criminal defendant has the right to a jury determination of every element of the crime, see Apprendi v. New Jersey, 530 U.S. 466, 477, 147 L. Ed. 2d 435, 120 S. Ct. 2348 (2000), an analysis of the text and structure of § 2332 demonstrates that subsection (d) does not comprise an element of the offenses proscribed by § 2332. First, subsection (d) follows three self-contained subsections each of which defines the elements of a distinct offense. See 18 U.S.C. § 2332(a)–(d). In particular, each subsection of (a) through (c) imposes an attendant level of intent, and none of these subsections makes reference to § 2332(d). Second, subsection (d) is expressly designated as a "limit on prosecution" rather than as an element of the offenses set forth in § 2332. We conclude, therefore, that the District Court did not err by failing to charge an intent to retaliate against the United States Government or its citizens. Even if the Court had erred in this regard, any error would have been harmless, given the overwhelming evidence that the defendants specifically intended the aircraft bombings to serve as retaliation against the United States Government and its citizens for United States foreign policy.

. . .

QUESTIONS AND NOTES

1.   Is § 2332, Title 18, United States Code, a terrorism offense? What substantive criminal conduct is covered by this offense? Note that neither the word terrorism nor any of its variants appears in the text of the offense defined in § 2332. If § 2332 is perceived as a terrorism offense, what practical or legal function does subsection (d) serve in this statutory context?

2.   Yousef is one of the only cases involving a challenge to subsection (d) of § 2332. Note that subsection (d) establishes a fact determination procedure to be conducted in the office of the Attorney General that is separate from the trial. For a discussion of the special issues posed by this provision, see Norman Abrams, Exploring Limits on the Use of Administrative Agencies in the Felony Criminal Process, 33 Israel L. Rev. 539, 542–556 (1999). Also see Brandon S. Chabner, Comment: The Omnibus Diplomatic Security and Antiterrorism Act of 1986: Prescribing and Enforcing U.S. Law Against Terrorist Violence Overseas, 37 UCLA L. Rev. 985 (1990).

3.   Does the Attorney General's certification procedure in section (d) address the question of whether the act was done with a terrorism purpose? Does the Attorney General's certification relate to an element of the offense? In the Congress, the Conference Committee Report for this legislation stated that the issue involved in the Attorney General's certification is not an element of the offense. If it were, would the procedure be constitutional? Consult Abrams, op. cit. supra note 2 at p. 542: ". . . it . . . would seem to be the type of factor that would normally be an element of the offense, that is, it addresses the purpose with which the act was done." What might be the reason(s) why

the determination of whether the conduct was engaged in with the indicated purpose was not included as one of the elements of the offense?

4. Is the matter as to which the Attorney General makes a certification jurisdictional? If it is jurisdictional, is the procedure constitutional? See Andreas F. Lowenfeld, U.S. Enforcement Abroad: The Constitution and International Law, 83 Am.J.Int'l L. 880, at 891 (1989). Also see Note: Extraterritorial Jurisdiction over Acts of Terrorism Committed Abroad: Omnibus Diplomatic Security and Antiterrorism Act of 1986, 72 Cornell L. Rev. 549 599 (1987).

5. In determining whether to initiate prosecution in an ordinary criminal case, the prosecutor makes a judgment whether the conduct involved is sufficient to constitute the offense. Is the Attorney General's certification procedure different from the usual prosecutorial determination to prosecute? Sometimes there is pre-existing policy promulgated by the prosecutor to govern the exercise of his/her discretion whether to prosecute, and the prosecutor is required to follow that policy. Is the Attorney General's certification procedure similar? Or are there important differences? Consult generally, Norman Abrams, Internal Policy: Guiding the Exercise of Prosecutorial Discretion, 19 UCLA L.Rev. 1 (1971).

6. The Yousef court rejected the constitutional challenge to § 2332 based on the nondelegation doctrine. Can you construct a different line of argument to challenge the constitutionality of the subsection (d) certification procedure?

7. In March, 2011, 14 defendants who had been seized on the high seas near the coast of Africa were indicted in the Eastern District of Virginia, for piracy (18 U.S.C. § 1651, conspiracy to commit kidnapping (18 U.S.C. § 1201), possessing, using, firearms (18 U.S.C. § 924), based on their seizing of an American yacht and holding four U.S. citizens as hostages and demanding ransom. The accused in the end killed the four hostages. The defendants were not indicted for a violation of 18 U.S.C. § 2332. Could they have been charged with a violation of that statute? For the indictment, see Case 2:11-cr-00034-MSD-DEM DOC. 3 (filed March 3, 2011, E.D. Va. Norfolk Div).

3. 18 U.S.C. § 2332a. USE OF CERTAIN WEAPONS OF MASS DESTRUCTION

§ 2332a.   Use of weapons of mass destruction

(a) Offense against a national of the United States or within the United States.—A person who, without lawful authority, uses, threatens, or attempts or conspires to use, a weapon of mass destruction—

(1) against a national of the United States while such national is outside of the United States;

(2) against any person or property within the United States, and

(A) the mail or any facility of interstate or foreign commerce is used in furtherance of the offense;

(B) such property is used in interstate or foreign commerce or in an activity that affects interstate or foreign commerce;

(C) any perpetrator travels in or causes another to travel in interstate or foreign commerce in furtherance of the offense; or

(D) the offense, or the results of the offense, affect interstate or foreign commerce, or, in the case of a threat, attempt, or conspiracy, would have affected interstate or foreign commerce;

(3) against any property that is owned, leased or used by the United States or by any department or agency of the United States, whether the property is within or outside of the United States; or

(4) against any property within the United States that is owned, leased, or used by a foreign government,

shall be imprisoned for any term of years or for life, and if death results, shall be punished by death or imprisoned for any term of years or for life.

(b) Offense by national of the United States outside of the United States.—Any national of the United States who, without lawful authority, uses, or threatens, attempts, or conspires to use, a weapon of mass destruction outside of the United States shall be imprisoned for any term of years or for life, and if death results, shall be punished by death, or by imprisonment for any term of years or for life.

(c) Definitions.—For purposes of this section—

(1) the term "national of the United States" has the meaning given in section 101(a)(22) of the Immigration and Nationality Act (8 U.S.C. 1101(a)(22));

(2) the term "weapon of mass destruction" means—

(A) any destructive device as defined in section 921 of this title;

(B) any weapon that is designed or intended to cause death or serious bodily injury through the release, dissemination, or impact of toxic or poisonous chemicals, or their precursors;

(C) any weapon involving a biological agent, toxin, or vector (as those terms are defined in section 178 of this title); or

(D) any weapon that is designed to release radiation or radioactivity at a level dangerous to human life; and

(3) the term "property" includes all real and personal property.

QUESTIONS AND NOTES

1. Note the different bases for federal criminal jurisdiction that are listed in this provision—e.g. offense against a U.S. national outside of the U.S. Compare these jurisdictional bases with the basis used in § 2332, supra.

2. Does it seem odd to you that jurisdiction over an offense involving the killing or injury of a person within the United States may require that interstate or foreign commerce be affected while the killing or injuring of U.S. nationals abroad simpliciter is a sufficient jurisdictional basis?

3. Are there other jurisdictional bases that might have been utilized in § 2332a? How far should U.S. criminal jurisdiction extend with respect to the use of weapons of mass destruction? Can you think of other categories of conduct that should be covered?

4. Note that 2332a(a) and 2332a(b) both contain the clause, "without lawful authority." What kind of situations might be covered by the "without lawful authority" language?

5. Arguing that the defendant had "threatened" to use a weapon of mass destruction, anthrax, the government used § 2332a as the basis for prosecuting a flurry of terrorist hoax incidents that occurred after the September 11, 2001 terrorist attacks. Various issues of interpretation arose as to whether 2332a applied to the facts in these cases. For example, if the "threatening" language referred to the fact that anthrax was in the building, was this a "threat to use" anthrax within the meaning of the statute? See United States v. Taylor, 2003 WL 22073040 (S.D.N.Y.)(Held: No). Is it necessary that the "threat" refer to future action? Suppose the defendant had said, "I have just dumped anthrax in your air conditioner." See United States v. Reynolds, 381 F.3d 404 (5th Cir. 2004)(Held: Yes, there is a basis for criminal liability under 2332a). Must there be a present capacity to carry out the threat?

6. Do you think that § 2332a was intended to cover hoax situations, even those involving threats relating to weapons of mass destruction. Note the penalty provided for a violation of 2332a, "any term of years or life." How would you interpret the threat provision to exclude coverage of hoaxes? Arguably, the government used § 2332a to prosecute such cases because it had no other basis for prosecution in cases like the anthrax threats, and the hoaxes were becoming a serious problem for law enforcement.

7. In December, 2004, Zameer Mohamed pleaded guilty to a federal charge of using a telephone to communicate false information about an explosive attack. LA Times, Dec. 22, 2004, B6. Mohamed was charged under 18 U.S.C. § 844, which, inter alia, covers transporting explosives and damaging property by means of fire or explosives and in § 844(e) covers making threats to use fire or explosives, knowing the same to be false, but until 2004, there was no federal provision on the books comparable to § 844(e) relating to a biological weapon like anthrax.

8. On December 17, 2004, § 1038 of Title 18 was added to the United States Code by the Intelligence Reform and Terrorism Prevention Act of 2004, which made criminal engaging "in any conduct with intent to convey false or misleading information under circumstances where such information may reasonably be believed and where such information indicates that an activity has taken, is taking, or will take place that would constitute a violation of"— [§ 1038 here lists various prohibitory statutes dealing with biological weapons, chemical weapons, nuclear devices, explosives, etc.]. § 1038 provides for a five year penalty for the basic crime with higher maxima if any one is injured or killed as a result of the conduct.

9. The enactment of § 1038 filled a gap in federal law by attempting to address in a comprehensive way the problem of hoaxes relating to threatened terrorist activity. A question that remains after enactment of § 1038 involves the fate of decisions that pre-§ 1038 had upheld the extension of section 2332a to fill a gap in federal law and to cover hoax situations. In future hoax situations, should federal prosecutors be able to charge under both § 1038 and § 2332a? This is an example of a recurring pattern in federal criminal law: A statutory offense is interpreted expansively to fill a gap in the coverage of the law (and possibly would not have been so interpreted had there not been such a gap), and later Congress enacts a specific statute to cover the situation. The case law establishing the original expansive interpretation remains on the books. It has usually been held that prosecutors can then charge under both statutes. For an example of this recurring pattern, see Norman Abrams, Sara Sun Beale and Susan Riva Klein, Federal Criminal Law and Its Enforcement, 391–393 (6th ed. 2015).

10. See United States v. Aldawsari, Case No. 5:11-MJ-017 (Filed Feb. 23, 2011, N.D. Tex.). Defendant purchased the ingredients for making an improvised explosive device (IED), and did research on the internet in aid of his plan to prepare such device and use it in some place where crowds were gathered. He was charged with an attempted violation of 18 U.S.C. § 2332a(a)(2)(A). The evidence did not reveal that anyone else was involved. Revisit this case when you study ch. 3, infra, and consider whether Aldawsari might also have been charged with a violation of 18 U.S.C. § 2339A?

4. 18 U.S.C. § 2332b. ACTS OF TERRORISM TRANSCENDING NATIONAL BOUNDARIES

§ 2332b.   Acts   of   terrorism   transcending   national boundaries

(a) Prohibited acts.

(1) Offenses. Whoever, involving conduct transcending national boundaries and in a circumstance described in subsection (b)—

(A) kills, kidnaps, maims, commits an assault resulting in serious bodily injury, or assaults with a dangerous weapon any person within the United States; or

(B) creates a substantial risk of serious bodily injury to any other person by destroying or damaging any structure, conveyance, or other real or personal property within the United States or by attempting or conspiring to destroy or damage any structure, conveyance, or other real or personal property within the United States;

in violation of the laws of any State, or the United States, shall be punished as prescribed in subsection (c).

(2) Treatment of threats, attempts and conspiracies.— Whoever threatens to commit an offense under paragraph (1), or attempts or conspires to do so, shall be punished under subsection (c).

(b) Jurisdictional bases.

(1) Circumstances. The circumstances referred to in subsection (a) are

(A) the mail or any facility of interstate or foreign commerce is used in furtherance of the offense;

(B) the offense obstructs, delays, or affects interstate or foreign commerce, or would have so obstructed, delayed, or affected interstate or foreign commerce if the offense had been consummated;

(C) the victim, or intended victim, is the United States Government, a member of the uniformed services, or any official, officer, employee, or agent of the legislative, executive, or judicial branches, or of any department or agency, of the United States;

(D) the structure, conveyance, or other real or personal property is, in whole or in part, owned, possessed, or leased to the United States, or any department or agency of the United States;

(E) the offense is committed in the territorial sea (including the airspace above and the seabed and subsoil below, and artificial islands and fixed structures erected thereon) of the United States; or

(F) the offense is committed within the special maritime and territorial jurisdiction of the United States.

(2) Co-conspirators and accessories after the fact. Jurisdiction shall exist over all principals and co-conspirators of an offense under this section, and accessories after the fact to any offense under this section, if at least one of the circumstances described in subparagraphs (A) through (F) of paragraph (1) is applicable to at least one offender.

(c) Penalties.

(1) Penalties. Whoever violates this section shall be punished

(A) for a killing, or if death results to any person from any other conduct prohibited by this section, by death, or by imprisonment for any term of years or for life;

(B) for kidnapping, by imprisonment for any term of years or for life;

(C) for maiming, by imprisonment for not more than 35 years;

(D) for assault with a dangerous weapon or assault resulting in serious bodily injury, by imprisonment for not more than 30 years;

(E) for destroying or damaging any structure, conveyance, or other real or personal property, by imprisonment for not more than 25 years;

(F) for attempting or conspiring to commit an offense, for any term of years up to the maximum punishment that would have applied had the offense been completed; and

(G) for threatening to commit an offense under this section, by imprisonment for not more than 10 years.

(2) Consecutive sentence.—Notwithstanding any other provision of law, the court shall not place on probation any person convicted of a violation of this section; nor shall the term of imprisonment imposed under this section run concurrently with any other term of imprisonment.

(d) Proof requirements.—The following shall apply to prosecutions under this section:

(1) Knowledge.—The prosecution is not required to prove knowledge by any defendant of a jurisdictional base alleged in the indictment.

(2) State law. In a prosecution under this section that is based upon the adoption of State law, only the elements of the offense under State law, and not any provisions pertaining to criminal procedure or evidence, are adopted.

(e) Extraterritorial jurisdiction. There is extraterritorial Federal jurisdiction—

(1) over any offense under subsection (a), including any threat, attempt, or conspiracy to commit such offense; and

(2) over conduct which, under section 3 [(b)(2)], renders any person an accessory after the fact to an offense under subsection (a).

(f) Investigative authority. In addition to any other investigative authority with respect to violations of this title, the Attorney General shall have primary investigative responsibility for all Federal crimes of terrorism, and any violation of section 351(e), 844(e), 844(f)(1), 956(b), 1361, 1366(b), 1366(c), 1751(e), 2152, or 2156 of this title, and the Secretary of the Treasury shall assist the Attorney General at the request of the Attorney General. Nothing in this section shall be construed to interfere with the authority of the United States Secret Service under section 3056.

(g) Definitions. As used in this section—

(1) the term "conduct transcending national boundaries" means conduct occurring outside of the United States in addition to the conduct occurring in the United States;

(2) the term "facility of interstate or foreign commerce" has the meaning given that term in section 1958(b)(2);

(3) the term "serious bodily injury" has the meaning given that term in section 1365(g)(3);

(4) the term "territorial sea of the United States" means all waters extending seaward to 12 nautical miles from the baselines of the United States, determined in accordance with international law; and

(5) the term "Federal crime of terrorism" means an offense that—

(A) is calculated to influence or affect the conduct of government by intimidation or coercion, or to retaliate against government conduct; and

(B) is a violation of

(i) section 32 (relating to destruction of aircraft or aircraft facilities), 37 (relating to violence at international airports), 81 (relating to arson within special maritime and territorial jurisdiction), 175 or 175b (relating to biological weapons), 229 (relating to chemical weapons), subsection (a), (b), (c), or (d) of section 351 (relating to congressional, cabinet, and Supreme Court assassination and kidnaping), 831 (relating to nuclear materials), 842(m) or (n) (relating to plastic explosives), 844(f)(2) or (3) (relating to arson and bombing of Government property risking or causing death), 844(i) (relating to arson and bombing of property used in interstate commerce), 930(c) (relating to killing or attempted killing during an attack on a Federal facility with a dangerous weapon), 956(a)(1) (relating to conspiracy to murder, kidnap, or maim persons abroad), 1030(a)(1) (relating to protection of computers), 1030(a)(5)(A)(i) resulting in damage as defined in 1030(a)(5)(B)(ii) through (v) (relating to protection of computers), 1114 (relating to killing or attempted killing of officers and employees of the United States), 1116 (relating to murder or manslaughter of foreign officials, official guests, or internationally protected persons), 1203 (relating to hostage taking), 1362 (relating to destruction of communication lines, stations, or systems), 1363 (relating to injury to buildings or property within special maritime and territorial jurisdiction of the United States), 1366(a) (relating to destruction of an energy facility), 1751(a), (b), (c), or (d) (relating to Presidential and Presidential staff assassination and kidnaping), 1992 (relating to wrecking trains), 1993 (relating to terrorist attacks and other acts of violence against mass transportation systems), 2155 (relating to destruction of national defense materials, premises, or utilities), 2280 (relating to violence against maritime navigation), 2281 (relating to violence against maritime fixed platforms), 2332 (relating to certain homicides and other violence against United States nationals occurring outside of the United States), 2332a (relating to use of weapons of mass destruction), 2332b (relating to acts of terrorism transcending national boundaries), 2339 (relating to harboring terrorists), 2339A (relating to providing material support to terrorists), 2339B (relating to providing material support to terrorist organizations), or 2340A (relating to torture) of this title;

(ii) section 236 (relating to sabotage of nuclear facilities or fuel) of the Atomic Energy Act of 1954 (42 U.S.C. 2284); or

(iii) section 46502 (relating to aircraft piracy), the second sentence of section 46504 (relating to assault on a flight crew with a dangerous weapon), section 46505(b)(3) or (c) (relating to explosive or incendiary devices, or endangerment of human life by means of weapons, on aircraft), section 46506 if homicide or attempted homicide is involved (relating to application of certain criminal laws to acts on aircraft), or section 60123 (b) (relating to destruction of interstate gas or hazardous liquid pipeline facility) of title 49.

QUESTIONS AND NOTES

1.   § 2332b is a very lengthy and complex statute. Because it is an important statute with a broad reach and is often used in terrorism prosecutions, it merits very careful reading and attention to its many clauses.

2.   What is the substantive scope of § 2332b? Through the breadth of the conduct covered and the number of different jurisdictional bases provided, the substantive scope of 2332b initially appears to be extremely broad. Note, however, the limiting concept for the offense to be committed: the crime must involve conduct transcending national boundaries. See subsec. (g)(1) for the definition of this phrase.

3.   Do you think that, without invoking any of the specific jurisdictional language listed in subsection (b), there might have been a basis for federal jurisdiction over conduct that occurs both outside and inside of the United States and that results in the commission of conduct prohibited under the federal criminal code or under state law? Is there a jurisdictional basis under principles of international law for the U.S. to prosecute such conduct? See United States v. Yousef, supra.

4.   The jurisdictional bases listed in subsection (b) are, of course, standard commerce power, use of the mails and federal interest jurisdictional bases. Section 2332a, discussed supra, contains a much shorter list of jurisdictional bases in its provisions. In 2332a, should the drafters have used the same bases that are used in 2332b?

5. The caption of § 2332b refers to "acts of terrorism transcending national boundaries." Does any other language in 2332b define "acts of terrorism?" Examine the substantive provisions of the section very carefully. Is there any place in the statute where the concept of terrorism or one of the definitions of terrorism appears as an element of an offense defined in any of the provisions of § 2332b?

6. The substantive offenses created by this section involve violent conduct such as killing, kidnapping, maiming and assault. § 2332b, however, contains no requirement that this conduct be committed with a terrorist purpose. Recall the caption of this section that refers to "acts of terrorism." Is there any language in this statute that would require that the killings or kidnappings, etc. that otherwise violate this provision must involve terrorism, however one defines terrorism?

7. As noted supra, this section does require that the conduct involved "transcend national boundaries." The definition of that phrase refers to conduct both outside and inside the boundaries of the United States. Is the fact, for example, that a killing involved conduct that transcended national boundaries a fact that makes it terrorism? Can you conjure up a fact situation that fits that description that would in your judgment be fairly denoted as a crime of terrorism? Can you conjure up other situations that would involve the indicated violent crime and involve conduct that transcended national boundaries that could not fairly be described as a crime involving terrorism? How adequate is the concept of "transcending national boundaries" as a marker for terrorism?

8. Note that the phrase "Federal crime of terrorism" appears in subsection (f) and is defined in subsec.(g)(5). Do you think that this phrase is intended to have the same meaning as "acts of terrorism" used in the caption to this section?

9. What does subsection (f) tell us about the function of the concept of "Federal crimes of terrorism" as used in this section? Does that function have anything to do with the substantive offenses created by this section? Does "Federal crimes of terrorism" appear anywhere else in this section (that is, apart from the definitional provision in (g)(5))? If the answer is no, is it fair to conclude therefore that the federal crime of terrorism defined in this section has no connection, or very little connection, to the substantive offense(s) created by this section?

10. In United States v. Thurston, supra, we saw one function of the definition of "Federal crime of terrorism" found in 2332b(g)(5); it is used as a sentencing enhancement factor under the Federal Sentencing Guidelines, by virtue of a provision of the Guidelines that refers to 2332b(g)(5).

11. United States v. Salim, 287 F. Supp. 2d 250 (S.D. N.Y. 2003) contains a description of the legislative history of the sentencing guideline, § 3A1.4 that refers to the definition of federal crime of terrorism in § 2332b(g)(5) and also the legislative history of § 2332b(g)(5).

That history may be summarized as follows: The legislation originally contained (as a precondition to initiating a prosecution under the section) a provision requiring certification by the Attorney General that the conduct involved a "transcending of national boundaries" activity and that it involved conduct with a terrorism-type purpose. In a subsequent version of the legislation, this certification provision was then changed to require certification that a federal crime of terrorism was involved (as that phrase is defined in this section). In this last-mentioned version of the statute, the concept of a federal crime of terrorism was also used as a basis for describing the investigative authority of the Attorney General. Then in the final version of the bill that became 2332b, the certification provision was removed from the section and the investigative authority provision was left as the only clause in 2332b in which the federal crime of terrorism definition still played a role. Meanwhile, the "transcending national boundaries" language which had also been contained in an earlier version of the certification provision was shifted from that provision to become one of the elements of the offense.

This legislative history reveals that § 2332b originally contained a certification provision similar to the one we previously considered in § 2332(d), supra. If this certification provision had remained in the final bill, the concept and definition of federal crime of terrorism would have limited the scope of application of § 2332b, albeit not as an element of the offense but rather through an administrative factfinding determination, in each case by the Attorney General. However, with the removal of the certification provision from the bill that became law, there was nothing in the specific language of 2332b that restricted its application to terrorism contexts—either through a required element of the offense or through a determination by the chief prosecutor in the federal criminal system. And so 2332b was left without any clear marker of terrorism attached to its substantive provisions.

For what reasons, might the Attorney General/certification provision have been removed by the Conference Committee from the bill that became law? This legislative history helps to explain what is otherwise a very odd combination of provisions in a single federal crime. Do you believe that the final makeup of the provisions in 2332b was likely to have been accidental or purposeful?

How likely it is that prosecutions under § 2332b will occur in non-terrorism contexts? How would you expect U.S. attorneys to want to use 2332b? Recall that a prosecution under § 2332b (as well as a number of other crimes in chapter 113B) requires approval by the Counterterrorism unit in the Department of Justice. That centralized approval process can be used to ensure that 2332b is not used to prosecute cases that by any measure do not constitute terrorism. See the Introduction to this section. If you were an Assistant U.S. Attorney, would you on your own want to limit use of the statute to terrorism cases. What might lead you to conclude that the statute should only be used in terrorism cases? Would you feel that you were legally restricted to so use the statute? In other words, how would this be different, if it would be different, from the Attorney General's certification if the certification provision had been retained in the statute?

12. Section 2332b has been utilized in some prominent terrorism prosecutions, including the persons convicted of the bombing of two U.S. embassies in Africa, and in the charges brought against Zacarias Moussaoui and John Walker Lindh.

A terrorism investigation widely reported in the press in 2009, resulted in an indictment filed in New York against a number of defendants including Najibullah Zazi. The case illustrates how a number of different terrorism offenses may be combined in a single indictment. It included a charge under § 2332b as well as under § 956 (see infra), § 2332a (see supra), and under two sections treated in ch. 3 infra, § 2339B (providing material support to a foreign terrorist organization) and § 2339D (receiving military training from a foreign terrorist organization). See United States v. Imam, 10-Cr-00019-RJD, Doc 53 (filed E.D. N.Y. 7/7/10).

5.   18 U.S.C. § 2332f. BOMBING OF PLACES OF PUBLIC USE, ETC.

§ 2332f. Bombing of places of public use, government facilities, public transportation systems and infrastructure facilities

(a)   Offenses.

(1) In general. Whoever unlawfully delivers, places, discharges, or detonates an explosive or other lethal device in, into, or against a place of public use, a state or government facility, a public transportation system, or an infrastructure facility—

(A) with the intent to cause death or serious bodily injury, or

(B) with the intent to cause extensive destruction of such a place, facility, or system, where such destruction results in or is likely to result in major economic loss,

shall be punished as prescribed in subsection (c).

(2) Attempts and conspiracies. Whoever attempts or conspires to commit an offense under paragraph (1) shall be punished as prescribed in subsection (c).

(b) Jurisdiction. There is jurisdiction over the offenses in subsection (a) if—

(1)   the offense takes place in the United States and

(A) the offense is committed against another state or a government facility of such state, including its embassy or other diplomatic or consular premises of that state;

(B) the offense is committed in an attempt to compel another state or the United States to do or abstain from doing any act;

(C) at the time the offense is committed, it is committed

(i) on board a vessel flying the flag of another state;

(ii) on board an aircraft which is registered under the laws of another state; or

(iii) on board an aircraft which is operated by the government of another state;

(D) a perpetrator is found outside the United States;

(E) a perpetrator is a national of another state or a stateless person; or

(F) a victim is a national of another state or a stateless person;

(2) the offense takes place outside the United States and

(A) a perpetrator is a national of the United States or is a stateless person whose habitual residence is in the United States;

(B) a victim is a national of the United States;

(C) a perpetrator is found in the United States;

(D) the offense is committed in an attempt to compel the United States to do or abstain from doing any act;

(E) the offense is committed against a state or government facility of the United States, including an embassy or other diplomatic or consular premises of the United States;

(F) the offense is committed on board a vessel flying the flag of the United States or an aircraft which is registered under the laws of the United States at the time the offense is committed; or

(G) the offense is committed on board an aircraft which is operated by the United States.

(c) Penalties. Whoever violates this section shall be punished as provided under section 2332a(a) of this title.

(d) Exemptions to Jurisdiction. This section does not apply to

(1) the activities of armed forces during an armed conflict, as those terms are understood under the law of war, which are governed by that law,

(2)   activities undertaken by military forces of a state in the exercise of their official duties; or

(3)   offenses committed within the United States, where the alleged offender and the victims are United States citizens and the alleged offender is found in the United States, or where jurisdiction is predicated solely on the nationality of the victims or the alleged offender and the offense has no substantial effect on interstate or foreign commerce.

(e)   Definitions. As used in this section, the term

(1)   'serious bodily injury' has the meaning given that term in section 1365(g)(3) of this title;

(2)   'national of the United States' has the meaning given that term in section 101(a)(22) of the Immigration and Nationality Act (8 U.S.C. 1101(a)(22));

(3)   'state or government facility' includes any permanent or temporary facility or conveyance that is used or occupied by representatives of a state, members of Government, the legislature or the judiciary or by officials or employees of a state or any other public authority or entity or by employees or officials of an intergovernmental organization in connection with their official duties;

(4)   'intergovernmental organization' includes international organization (as defined in section 1116(b)(5) of this title);

(5)   'infrastructure facility' means any publicly or privately owned facility providing or distributing services for the benefit of the public, such as water, sewage, energy, fuel, or communications;

(6)   'place of public use' means those parts of any building, land, street, waterway, or other location that are accessible or open to members of the public, whether continuously, periodically, or occasionally, and encompasses any commercial, business, cultural, historical, educational, religious, governmental, entertainment, recreational, or similar place that is so accessible or open to the public;

(7)   'public transportation system' means all facilities, conveyances, and instrumentalities, whether publicly or privately owned, that are used in or for publicly available services for the transportation of persons or cargo;

(8)   'explosive' has the meaning given in section 844(j) of this title insofar that it is designed, or has the capability, to cause death, serious bodily injury, or substantial material damage;

(9) 'other lethal device' means any weapon or device that is designed or has the capability to cause death, serious bodily injury, or substantial damage to property through the release, dissemination, or impact of toxic chemicals, biological agents, or toxins (as those terms are defined in section 178 of this title) or radiation or radioactive material;

(10) 'military forces of a state' means the armed forces of a state which are organized, trained, and equipped under its internal law for the primary purpose of national defense or security, and persons acting in support of those armed forces who are under their formal command, control, and responsibility;

(11) 'armed conflict' does not include internal disturbances and tensions, such as riots, isolated and sporadic acts of violence, and other acts of a similar nature; and

(12) 'state' has the same meaning as that term has under international law, and includes all political subdivisions thereof.

. . .

QUESTIONS AND NOTES

1.   Does section 2332f describe a crime of "terrorism"? A crime of "international terrorism."? If so, what feature(s) of the offense make(s) it such? What definition of terrorism are you using?

2.   The jurisdictional provisions in § 2332f(b) are complex and warrant careful study. It may be helpful in working your way through these provisions to consider the following questions:

a.   If the offense takes place in the United States, is each of the factors contained in (b)(1)A, B, C, D, E, and F, an independent basis for jurisdiction? If so, does this mean that if, let us say, a bombing of a subway station occurs in Chicago, and a perpetrator is apprehended in Canada, there is jurisdiction to prosecute him under 2332f?

b.   Similarly, in the case of the type of bombing described in a., if the perpetrator is found in Chicago and he or she is a national of a foreign country, is there jurisdiction?

c.   If in the Oklahoma City bombing perpetrated by Timothy McVeigh, one of the victims of the bombing was a tourist from Mexico, would there be jurisdiction to prosecute McVeigh under this statute? If none of the victims was a foreign person, would there be any possible basis for finding jurisdiction under this section?

d.   If a bombing of the London Underground occurs, and a perpetrator, who is a member of al Qaeda is found in New York City, would there be jurisdiction to prosecute him under this provision?

Would it make any difference if the perpetrator is a U.S. citizen, or not?

3. Refer back to the various international law theories of a basis for exercise of jurisdiction to prosecute described in United States v. Yousef, supra. How many of these theories undergird the various jurisdictional provisions of § 2332f? More specifically, if there is jurisdiction to prosecute the offender described in note 2d. supra, even if he is not a U.S. citizen, what theory of international jurisdiction might be invoked in support? Would it be relevant that an International Convention for the Suppression of Terrorist Bombing (to which the U.S. is a signatory) went into effect in May, 2001 and that it deals with the subject of terrorist bombing of public transportation systems. What would you want to know about the provisions of this Convention?

4. Note the Exemptions to Jurisdiction provision in subsection (d).

a. Would members of Al Qaeda who engage in acts covered by subsection (a) be exempted from criminal liability under this section by subsection (d)(1)? Would members of the Taliban who in military actions in Afghanistan bombed a bridge be exempted under (d)(1) or (2)? What about actions of our own military in Afghanistan?

b. No other provision of sec. 2332f, apart from the last clause of (d)(3) provides for jurisdiction based on effect on interstate or foreign commerce. Does the last clause of (d)(3) turn effect on interstate or foreign commerce into one of the jurisdictional bases for this offense?

5. For a related offense that deals with terrorist attacks against mass transportation systems, see 18 U.S.C. § 1993.

6. 18 U.S.C. § 956. CONSPIRACY TO KILL, KIDNAP, MAIM, OR INJURE PERSONS OR DAMAGE PROPERTY IN A FOREIGN COUNTRY

A statute that is often used in terrorism prosecutions, usually when combined with a charge under § 2339A, but which is not found in chapter 113B, but rather in chapter 45. Foreign Relations, is 18 U.S.C. § 956, reproduced below.

§ 956.   Conspiracy to kill, kidnap, maim, or injure persons or damage property in a foreign country

(a)(1)   Whoever, within the jurisdiction of the United States, conspires with one or more other persons, regardless of where such other person or persons are located, to commit at any place outside the United States an act that would constitute the offense of murder, kidnapping, or maiming if committed in the special maritime and territorial jurisdiction of the United States shall, if any of the conspirators commits an act within the jurisdiction of the United

States to effect any object of the conspiracy, be punished as provided in subsection (a)(2).

(2)   The punishment for an offense under subsection (a)(1) of this section is—

(A)   imprisonment for any term of years or for life if the offense is conspiracy to murder or kidnap; and

(B)   imprisonment for not more than 35 years if the offense is conspiracy to maim.

(b)   Whoever, within the jurisdiction of the United States, conspires with one or more persons, regardless of where such other person or persons are located, to damage or destroy specific property situated within a foreign country and belonging to a foreign government or to any political subdivision thereof with which the United States is at peace, or any railroad, canal, bridge, airport, airfield, or other public utility, public conveyance, or public structure, or any religious, educational, or cultural property so situated, shall, if any of the conspirators commits an act within the jurisdiction of the United States to effect any object of the conspiracy, be imprisoned not more than 25 years.

7.   NOTE ON OTHER TERRORISM-RELATED OFFENSES

18 U.S.C. § 2332e authorizes the Attorney General to request military assistance in matters involving the enforcement of § 2332a relating to weapons of mass destruction. For discussion of issues relating to the use of the military in domestic law enforcement contexts, see Chapter 13, infra.

Three additional offenses aimed at specific kinds of catastrophic offenses were enacted as part of the Intelligence Reform and Terrorism Prevention Act signed into law in December, 2004: a) 18 U.S.C. § 2332g (prohibition against producing, acquiring, transferring, using, possessing, threatening to use, etc. missile systems designed to destroy aircraft); b) 18 U.S.C. § 2332h (prohibition against producing, acquiring, transferring, using, possessing, threatening to use, etc., radiological dispersal devices, that is, any weapon that is designed or intended to release radiation or radioactivity at a level dangerous to human life); c) 18 U.S.C. § 175c (prohibition against producing, engineering, synthesizing, acquiring, transferring using, possessing and threaten to use, variola virus [a virus that can cause human smallpox]).

A major approach taken by the federal government in its enforcement efforts is also to utilize legislation which targets specific types of activities that support terrorism. Thus, 18 U.S.C. § 2332d is part of a package of provisions aimed at cutting off financial support for terrorist organizations and terrorist activity. In this instance, the criminal provision is aimed at discouraging countries that support terrorist organizations from doing so. The method of discouragement is to penalize such countries by prohibiting U.S. persons from doing business with them. This in turn is one of a series of measures designed to economically isolate such countries. The method is indirect, and the ultimate target is remote. How effective do you think such measures are likely to be? Consult generally, Stephen C. Warnecke, Note, A Preemptive Strike: Using RICO and the AEDPA to Attack the Financial Strength of International Terrorist Organizations, 78 B.U.L.Rev. 177 (1998).

A very different kind of enforcement approach is reflected in Title 18, U.S.C. § 2333, a provision that does not establish a crime but rather provides a civil remedy. Section 2333 creates a cause of action for a treble damage suit for any person injured in their person or property by an act of international terrorism. § 2333 is mentioned here even though it provides a civil remedy while the rest of the materials in this volume emphasize criminal enforcement because it provides a useful comparison to make. Query: Why should the civil remedy be limited to acts of "international terrorism?" Recall that "international terrorism" is defined for purposes of chapter 113B, Title 18, in section 2331. For some examples of suits filed under § 2333, see Smith v. Islamic Emirate of Afghanistan, 262 F.Supp.2d 217 (S.D.N.Y. 2003); Biton v. Palestinian Interim Self-Government Authority, 310 F.Supp.2d 172 (D.D.C. 2004).

G. LAW REVIEW COMMENTARY

See Jacqueline S. Hodgson, Victor Tadros, The Impossibility of Defining Terrorism, 16 New Crim. L. Rev. 494 (2013); Nick Harper, FISA's Fuzzy Line Between Domestic and International Terrorism, 81 U. Chi. L. Rev. 1123 (2014); Daniel J. Hickman, Terrorism As A Violation of the "Law of Nations:" Finally Overcoming the Definitional Problem, 29 Wis. Int'l L.J. 447 (2011); Piper Doeppe, Redefining Maritime Piracy: A Call for Legislative Action to Equate Piracy to International Terrorism in A Previously Uncertain Regulatory Environment, 14 Appalachian J.L. 97 (2014); Jenna McLaughlin, Charging Crimes As "Terrorism", 6 U. Miami Nat'l Sec. & Armed Conflict L. Rev. 101 (2016); Jared Hatch, Requiring A Nexus to National Security: Immigration, "Terrorist Activities," and Statutory Reform, 2014 B.Y.U. L. Rev. 697 (2014); Geoffrey Sant, So Banks Are Terrorists Now?: The Misuse of the Civil Suit Provision of the Anti-Terrorism Act, 45 Ariz. St. L.J. 533 (2013); Alexandra T. Stupple, Terrorism and the Animal Rights and Environmental Movements, 11 J. Animal & Nat. Resource L. 51 (2015).

CHAPTER 3

THE MATERIAL SUPPORT OFFENSES: 18 U.S.C. § 2339A, § 2339B

■ ■ ■

A. INTRODUCTION—18 U.S.C. § 2339A AND § 2339B

The materials in the previous chapter highlight the fact that many different statutory offenses can be used in prosecuting conduct relating to terrorism; many of them are fairly described as terrorism crimes while others are ordinary crimes prosecuted in a terrorism context. Note: it is common federal practice, where feasible, to include multiple charges in an indictment. In this chapter, we focus on two anti-terrorism crimes—18 U.S.C. § 2339A (providing material support in aid of terrorist offenses) and § 2339B (providing material support to a foreign terrorist organization)—which have become the most important, go-to terrorism offenses for federal prosecutors to charge (to be sure, usually along with a variety of other offenses).

Either or both of these offenses are being charged in the post-9/11 period, and especially in the past several years, more frequently than any other terrorism crimes. This is not surprising. These two offenses add up to a mini-criminal code in a bottle: They have an enormous range in the type of offense conduct to which they apply; they also have a special type of adaptability insofar as the actual conduct engaged in by a perpetrator, can be facially the most mundane, ordinary acts. And while these acts comprise substantive offenses with their own penalties, they are typically also inchoate, i.e., remote from the completion of the harmful conduct that is the essence of the crime being charged, and these offenses are chargeable even though the harmful object crime has not been committed.

There is still another reason to pay special attention to these two provisions. Some of the legal issues they generate are unusual and complicated. These are unusual criminal statutes in a number of respects.

In the following materials, the above-described characteristics of the material support offenses are featured, and specific aspects and legal issues that have arisen in the prosecution of these crimes are treated.

1. THE CURRENT STATUTES: § 2339A AND § 2339B

Title 18, U.S.C.

§ 2339A. Providing material support to terrorists

(a) **Offense.**—Whoever provides material support or resources or conceals or disguises the nature, location, source, or ownership of material support or resources, knowing or intending that they are to be used in preparation for, or in carrying out, a violation of section 32, 37, 81, 175, 229, 351, 831, 842(m) or (n), 844(f) or (i), 930(c), 956, 1091, 1114, 1116, 1203, 1361, 1362, 1363, 1366, 1751, 1992, 2155, 2156, 2280, 2281, 2332, 2332a, 2332b, 2332f, 2340A, or 2442 of this title, section 236 of the Atomic Energy Act of 1954 (42 U.S.C. 2284), section 46502 or 60123(b) of title 49, or any offense listed in section 2332b(g)(5)(B) (except for sections 2339A and 2339B) or in preparation for, or in carrying out, the concealment of an escape from the commission of any such violation, or attempts or conspires to do such an act, shall be fined under this title, imprisoned not more than 15 years, or both, and, if the death of any person results, shall be imprisoned for any term of years or for life. A violation of this section may be prosecuted in any Federal judicial district in which the underlying offense was committed, or in any other Federal judicial district as provided by law.

(b) **Definitions.**—As used in this section—

(1) the term "material support or resources" means any property, tangible or intangible, or service, including currency or monetary instruments or financial securities, financial services, lodging, training, expert advice or assistance, safehouses, false documentation or identification, communications equipment, facilities, weapons, lethal substances, explosives, personnel (1 or more individuals who may be or include oneself), and transportation, except medicine or religious materials;

(2) the term "training" means instruction or teaching designed to impart a specific skill, as opposed to general knowledge; and

(3) the term "expert advice or assistance" means advice or assistance derived from scientific, technical or other specialized knowledge.

Title 18, U.S.C.

§ 2339B.   Providing material support or resources to designated foreign terrorist organizations

(a) **Prohibited activities.—**

(1) **Unlawful conduct.—**Whoever knowingly provides material support or resources to a foreign terrorist organization, or attempts or conspires to do so, shall be fined under this title or imprisoned not more than 20 years, or both, and, if the death of any person results, shall be imprisoned for any term of years or for life. To violate this paragraph, a person must have knowledge that the organization is a designated terrorist organization (as defined in subsection (g)(6)), that the organization has engaged or engages in terrorist activity (as defined in section 212(a)(3)(B) of the Immigration and Nationality Act), or that the organization has engaged or engages in terrorism (as defined in section 140(d)(2) of the Foreign Relations Authorization Act, Fiscal Years 1988 and 1989).

. . .

(d) **Extraterritorial jurisdiction.—**

(1) **In general.—**There is jurisdiction over an offense under subsection (a) if—

(A) an offender is a national of the United States (as defined in section 101(a)(22) of the Immigration and Nationality Act (8 U.S.C. 1101(a)(22))) or an alien lawfully admitted for permanent residence in the United States (as defined in section 101(a)(20) of the Immigration and Nationality Act (8 U.S.C. 1101(a)(20)));

(B) an offender is a stateless person whose habitual residence is in the United States;

(C) after the conduct required for the offense occurs an offender is brought into or found in the United States, even if the conduct required for the offense occurs outside the United States;

(D) the offense occurs in whole or in part within the United States;

(E) the offense occurs in or affects interstate or foreign commerce; or

(F) an offender aids or abets any person over whom jurisdiction exists under this paragraph in committing an offense under subsection (a) or conspires with any person over whom jurisdiction exists under this paragraph to commit an offense under subsection (a).

(2) Extraterritorial jurisdiction.—There is extraterritorial Federal jurisdiction over an offense under this section.

. . .

(g) Definitions.—As used in this section—

. . .

(4) the term "material support or resources" has the same meaning given that term in section 2339A (including the definitions of "training" and "expert advice or assistance" in that section);

. . .

(6) the term "terrorist organization" means an organization designated as a terrorist organization under section 219 of the Immigration and Nationality Act. [ed. 8 U.S.C. 1189].

(h) Provision of personnel.—No person may be prosecuted under this section in connection with the term "personnel" unless that person has knowingly provided, attempted to provide, or conspired to provide a foreign terrorist organization with 1 or more individuals (who may be or include himself) to work under that terrorist organization's direction or control or to organize, manage, supervise, or otherwise direct the operation of that organization. Individuals who act entirely independently of the foreign terrorist organization to advance its goals or objectives shall not be considered to be working under the foreign terrorist organization's direction and control.

(i) Rule of construction.—Nothing in this section shall be construed or applied so as to abridge the exercise of rights guaranteed under the First Amendment to the Constitution of the United States.

(j) Exception.—No person may be prosecuted under this section in connection with the term "personnel", "training", or "expert advice or assistance" if the provision of that material support or resources to a foreign terrorist organization was approved by the Secretary of State with the concurrence of the Attorney General. The Secretary of State may not approve the provision of any material support that may be used to carry out terrorist activity (as defined in section 212(a)(3)(B)(iii) of the Immigration and Nationality Act).

2. NUMBER OF OFFENSES COVERED BY 2339A; RANGE OF OFFENSE CONDUCT COVERED BY §§ 2339A AND 2339B

A person with the requisite knowledge or intent who engaged in the necessary conduct may be charged with the substantive crime of providing material support in aid of the preparation to commit or the commission of any one or more of the numerous offenses listed in § 2339A(a). There are approximately three dozen offenses listed in § 2339A(a). Additionally, the long list of offenses contained in § 2332b(g)(5)(B) is expressly incorporated by reference through an express listing in the § 2339A list. The 2332 list contains more than 50 offenses, but the actual additions to the § 2339A list are about a dozen or so offenses, since the large majority of offenses listed in § 2332b(g)(5)(B) are duplicative of the crimes charged in 2339A(a). Nevertheless, more than 50 offenses combined in a single crime section may fairly be termed a mini criminal code.

In this respect, like the RICO crime, this material support offense is properly labeled a complex crime, that is, it contains within its terms the intended commission of significant additional crimes beyond that covered by the particular section of the criminal code. While the RICO offense has a very broad potential application because of the long list of crimes that may be the intended target, arguably § 2339A has a still broader application because it does not require that a criminal organization be involved. The material support can consist of almost any kind of aid.

It must also be remembered that, while a reason for the breadth of application of this offense is the large number of listed potential target offenses, none of these offenses need be committed in order for there to be criminal liability under § 2339A. Indeed in most of the prosecutions under 2339A, the main element of the prosecution is based in the mens rea of the accused—the fact that the accused knew or intended to provide material support in aid of the commission of the target offense(s), but no target offense was committed.

Similarly, § 2339B opens the door to broadly applicable criminal liability. The object of the material support under § 2339B is a (designated) foreign terrorist organization, which in 8 U.S.C. § 1189 (a)(1)(B) is defined as an organization that engages in terrorist activity or terrorism, or retains the capability and intent to engage in such actions.

Terrorist activity in turn is defined in 8 U.S.C. § 1182 (A) 3.(B) (iii) as unlawful activity that involves any of a number of different crime categories such as hijacking, seizing of people, assassination or the use of explosives or firearms other than for personal monetary gain with intent to endanger the safety of one or more individuals.

The definition of terrorism used in this context is found in 22 U.S.C. § 2656f, This definition of terrorism refers to premeditated, politically motivated violence perpetrated against noncombatant people, etc. Thus, the kinds of criminal activities that can qualify to make a foreign organization a foreign terrorist organization are very broadly described. Further, the relevant statute contains no indication of the number of instances of terrorist activity or terrorism required for the organization. Of course, the issues involved in the last three paragraphs are resolved not in the criminal prosecution of a person accused under § 2339B but rather in an administrative proceeding conducted under 8 U.S.C. § 1189, that is, the proceeding to designate an organization as a foreign terrorist organization. See infra this chapter.

3.   THE NATURE OF MATERIAL SUPPORT

a.   Categories of Conduct That Qualify as Material Support

The statute was amended to its present form in 2004, and the list of categories in the definition of material support was modified slightly. Arguably, the most significant change was to add an open-ended term like service to the list. Most of the listed categories involve facially innocent and non-dangerous conduct. Exceptions are providing weapons, lethal substances and explosives, which are not necessarily criminal but are not non-dangerous. Similarly, depending on the circumstances, providing a safehouse has suggestive overtones of non-ordinary and, possibly, criminal behavior.

b.   Material Support Acts Equal Complicitous Conduct, i.e., Acts Like Those in Which an Accomplice Might Engage

See Norman Abrams, The Material Support Terrorism Offenses: Perspectives Derived from the (Early) Model Penal Code, 1 J. Nat. Sec. L. & Policy 5, 9–11 (2005) where § 2339A and § 2339B are described as follows:

> . . . Both offenses are, in essence, specialized forms of a kind of complicity crime. Typically we define as a substantive offense conduct that involves direct commission of a harm. Normally, under modern criminal law, complicity liability is derivative from a substantive offense and is not itself defined as a separate substantive crime, though it is, of course, a basis for making a person liable for the substantive offense. Thus, a person who aids and abets others who commit a bank robbery is liable for the bank robbery, as if he or she had directly committed the robbery. Stating the matter more formally, in addition to holding criminally liable the direct perpetrators of such offenses (primary party liability), we can also hold individuals liable as accomplices

to the commission of the substantive offense if they aided or abetted the commission of the offense. . . .

Sections 2339A and 2339B are different from traditional forms of complicity liability insofar as each makes the provision of material support to the commission of offenses (directly in the case of 2339A or more indirectly in the case of 2339B), itself an independent substantive offense, with its own penalty, rather than a form of secondary liability to a substantive offense. Moreover, each is a serious offense, with a maximum penalty of 15 years [ed. now 20 years for a violation of § 2339B] or possible life imprisonment if death of a person results. . . .

Second, unlike traditional complicity, which uses a general phrase such as "aid or abet" to describe the kind of conduct that can be a basis for secondary liability, material support is defined in the statute by a listing of categories of specific kinds of conduct. . . . [T]his categorical approach to defining the actus reus of the material support offenses is a central and significant feature of these new crimes.

Third, unlike traditional complicity liability which applies to all offenses, each of these offenses is limited to terrorism-related contexts by a general description or specification of the offenses, the provision of material support for which, leads to criminal liability. As previously mentioned, under 2339A, a long list of terrorism offenses is set forth as the possible object of the material support that triggers liability. A special feature of 2339B is, the fact that the direct object of the support is not terrorism offenses themselves but rather a "terrorist organization," that is, an organization that engages in terrorist crimes.

Fourth, viewing 2339A and 2339B as forms of complicity that have been converted into substantive offenses, we should take note of the fact that unlike the basis for traditional complicity liability, under these sections, it is not required that the substantive offense for which the "accomplice" has provided "aid" must have itself have been committed.

Finally, . . . is the fact that 2339B requires knowledge and 2339A, at a minimum, requires knowledge as the requisite mens rea. Though the knowledge requirement for 2339A is more specific than for 2339B insofar as it relates to a specific offense or offenses, neither requires the kind of mens rea that most court require for complicity—a mens rea of purpose.

Two thoughts should be added to the foregoing. The first is that the fact that through § 2339B, complicitous conduct can be transformed into an independent basis for criminal liability even though the object crime is not committed, and that conduct may consist of the most mundane activities, e.g., driving someone to the bank (providing transportation) means that the essential criminality of the offense may be heavily, perhaps entirely, dependent on the adequacy of the proof of the mens rea or criminal intent. If no bank robbery or attempted robbery occurs, what was the purpose of driving them to the bank? In traditional complicity situations, the criminal nature of the mens rea is also evidenced or tends to be confirmed by the subsequent criminal conduct.

Second, as noted, the material support may be provided almost contemporaneously with the object crime or earlier, or much earlier. Because it does not typically involve any harm itself, and it is not required that the object crime be committed, it is inchoate with respect to that crime which does involve harm, and it is therefore properly characterized as an inchoate offense. That fact becomes significant since as a substantive offense, albeit one that is inchoate in nature, it can itself be the object of an attempt or conspiracy.

c. Adaptability

Both of these offenses can be applied to an endless and variable set of fact situations relating to terrorism. The combination of statutory provisions that apply both to a variety of different kinds of the conduct that the perpetrator might engage in (any of the categories of material support) and to a very large number of offenses that may be intended as the object of the support is very powerful. As you study the cases in this chapter, take note of the great variety of different kinds of conduct that have been prosecuted.

Additionally, enhancing the breadth of coverage, is the fact that some of the items listed as "material support" have been interpreted in such a way that they cover a host of other kinds of aid to or participation in terrorist activities or the activities of a foreign terrorist organization.

4. INCHOATE OFFENSE ASPECT

It follows from the description above, that many of the cases prosecuted under 2339A and 2339B do not directly involve violent actions but rather conduct early in the chronology of events that lead up to violence—for example, training in the use of explosives, or providing funds that support terrorist activities or the terrorist organization, or providing personnel, namely, oneself to assist in the activities of the terrorist organization. The material support offenses thus are frequently being used to prosecute preparatory or precursor conduct. The use of these offenses as a basis for prosecution thus has enabled the government to spread its criminal enforcement net much more widely and, intervene, nip in the bud, and then prosecute and convict individuals on their way to becoming terrorists or those who by their support increase the likelihood that the terrorists will succeed. In many instances, these offenses are also being used to add to the number of offenses charged: most terrorism-related conduct that is otherwise criminal also involves conduct that provides support either to the commission of terrorism offenses or to terrorist organizational activities.

Is this type of strategy aimed at precursor conduct a good strategy for the government to pursue? Is there any downside associated with adopting this kind of strategy? Until these offenses were enacted, the two offense categories most frequently used to prosecute inchoate or preparatory conduct were attempts and conspiracy. As you progress through these materials, consider whether and how the material support offenses are similar to, or different from, attempts and conspiracy charges. See generally, Robert M.Chesney, Beyond Conspiracy? Anticipatory Prosecution and the Challenge of Unaffiliated Terrorism, 80 S.Cal. L.Rev. 425 (2007).

5. A BIT OF HISTORY: ISSUES OF STATUTORY INTERPRETATION AND LEGISLATIVE AMENDMENTS

The crimes defined in § 2339A and § 2339B differ in a number of respects, but an essential element of each is material support must be provided and the same core definition of material support applies to both offenses. Thus, material support is defined in § 2339A(b) for purposes of § 2339A, and this definition is incorporated by reference into § 2339B by virtue of subsection (g)(4) of § 2339B.

The majority of the statutory interpretation issues that have arisen under § 2339A and § 2339B have involved construing the specific terms listed under the "material support and resources" subsection. Most of the decisions interpreting the two statutes have been handed down since September 11, 2001; most of the prosecutions under the material support statutes have been brought during this period.

A number of judicial decisions interpreting these terms triggered a legislative response that culminated in the Intelligence Reform and Terrorism Protection Act of 2004 (IRTPA), which included language that amended both § 2339A and § 2339B. The current version of these statutory provisions, reproduced supra, includes these IRTPA amendments. To fully understand the purpose and context of the amendments, however, it is useful to review both the original statutory language as well as the judicial interpretations that led to them.

In some instances, absent a familiarity with the relevant earlier judicial decision(s), the IRTPA amendments appear to be very odd and to introduce into the statute rather awkward language. In many instances, the language of the specific amendment incorporates into statutory form and in effect confirms a prior judicial interpretation. In a very few instances, the statutory amendment represents a congressional choice between conflicting judicial decisions. What might be the purpose(s) of a legislative amendment that simply incorporates into the statute a prior judicial construction of a statutory term where there is no conflict in the case law?

The pre-IRPTA language defined "material support and resources" in § 2339A as follows:

Title 18, U.S.C.

§ 2339A.   Providing material support to terrorists

> . . .

> (b) Definition.—In this section, the term "material support or resources" means currency or monetary instruments or financial securities, financial services, lodging, training, expert advice or assistance, safehouses, false documentation or identification, communications equipment, facilities, weapons, lethal substances, explosives, personnel, transportation, and other physical assets, except medicine or religious materials.

The language contained in the current version of § 2339B in subsec. (a)(1), describing the kind of knowledge required and in subsec. (h) relating to the provision of personnel was added by IRTPA and was not contained in the pre-2004 version of the statute. The parenthetical clause defining personnel, "(1 or more individuals who may be or include oneself)" was also added to § 2339A in 2004 in the subsection defining "material support."

6.   COVERAGE OF THE REMAINDER OF THIS CHAPTER

In the remainder of this chapter, we first study the only Supreme Court decision that has addressed a material support statute, Humanitarian Law Project v. Holder, which deals with application of material support terms, namely "expert assistance" and "training," in a pre-enforcement ruling under § 2339B; the HLP decision also addresses the specific intent issue and deals with first amendment and vagueness questions raised by the plaintiffs in the pre-enforcement context.

How prosecutors have used the "personnel" category of material support is examined and the inchoate uses of the material support offense are explored. The requisite mens rea elements under the two statutes are also reviewed: Is purpose or specific intent required, or is knowledge sufficient? And finally, the procedural issues that surround the administrative determination by the Secretary of State that a particular organization is a foreign terrorist organization are studied as well as the statutory preclusion of consideration of the validity of the FTO designation in a criminal prosecution under § 2339B.

B. THE HUMANITARIAN LAW PROJECT DECISION

As of the date of this writing, the Supreme Court has reviewed only one case involving one of the material support statutes, § 2339B. In Holder v. Humanitarian Law Project, reproduced below, a case addressing constitutional due process/vagueness and first amendment challenges considered in a pre-enforcement review context, the court also ruled on issues of statutory interpretation relating to several material support categories as well as the requisite mens rea under § 2339B.

HOLDER V. HUMANITARIAN LAW PROJECT
561 U.S. 1 (2010)

[ROBERTS, C.J., delivered the opinion of the Court, in which STEVENS, SCALIA, KENNEDY, THOMAS, and ALITO, JJ., joined. BREYER, J., filed a dissenting opinion, in which GINSBURG and SOTOMAYOR, JJ., joined.]

CHIEF JUSTICE ROBERTS delivered the opinion of the Court.

Congress has prohibited the provision of "material support or resources" to certain foreign organizations that engage in terrorist activity. 18 U. S. C. § 2339B(a)(1). That prohibition is based on a finding that the specified organizations "are so tainted by their criminal conduct that any contribution to such an organization facilitates that conduct." Antiterrorism and Effective Death Penalty Act of 1996 (AEDPA), § 301(a)(7), 110 Stat. 1247, note following 18 U. S. C. § 2339B (Findings and Purpose). The plaintiffs in this litigation seek to provide support to two such organizations. Plaintiffs claim that they seek to facilitate only the lawful, nonviolent purposes of those groups, and that applying the material-support law to prevent them from doing so violates the Constitution. In particular, they claim that the statute is too vague, in violation of the Fifth Amendment, and that it infringes their rights to freedom of speech and association, in violation of the First Amendment. We conclude that the material-support statute is constitutional as applied to the particular activities plaintiffs have told us they wish to pursue. We do not, however, address the resolution of more difficult cases that may arise under the statute in the future.

This litigation concerns 18 U. S. C. § 2339B, which makes it a federal crime to "knowingly provid[e] material support or resources to a foreign terrorist organization." Congress has amended the definition of "material support or resources" periodically, but at present it is defined as follows:

> "[T]he term 'material support or resources' means any property, tangible or intangible, or service, including currency or monetary instruments or financial securities, financial services, lodging, training, expert advice or assistance, safehouses, false documentation or identification, communications equipment,

facilities, weapons, lethal substances, explosives, personnel (1 or more individuals who may be or include oneself), and transportation, except medicine or religious materials." § 2339A(b)(1); see also § 2339B(g)(4).

The authority to designate an entity a "foreign terrorist organization" rests with the Secretary of State. 8 U. S. C. §§ 1189(a)(1), (d)(4). . . .

In 1997, the Secretary of State designated 30 groups as foreign terrorist organizations. See 62 Fed. Reg. 52650. Two of those groups are the Kurdistan Workers' Party (also known as the Partiya Karkeran Kurdistan, or PKK) and the Liberation Tigers of Tamil Eelam (LTTE). The PKK is an organization founded in 1974 with the aim of establishing an independent Kurdish state in southeastern Turkey. Humanitarian Law Project v. Reno, 9 F. Supp. 2d 1176, 1180–1181 (CD Cal. 1998). The LTTE is an organization founded in 1976 for the purpose of creating an independent Tamil state in Sri Lanka. 9 F. Supp. 2d, at 1182; Brief for Government 6. The District Court in this action found that the PKK and the LTTE engage in political and humanitarian activities. See 9 F. Supp. 2d, at 1180–1182. The Government has presented evidence that both groups have also committed numerous terrorist attacks, some of which have harmed American citizens. The LTTE sought judicial review of its designation as a foreign terrorist organization; the D. C. Circuit upheld that designation. See People's Mojahedin Organization of Iran v. Dept. of State, 182 F. 3d 17, 18–19, 25 (1999). The PKK did not challenge its designation.

Plaintiffs in this litigation are two U. S. citizens and six domestic organizations: the Humanitarian Law Project (HLP) (a human rights organization with consultative status to the United Nations); Ralph Fertig (the HLP's president, and a retired administrative law judge); Nagalingam Jeyalingam (a Tamil physician, born in Sri Lanka and a naturalized U. S. citizen); and five nonprofit groups dedicated to the interests of persons of Tamil descent. . . .

As relevant here, plaintiffs claimed that the material-support statute was unconstitutional on two grounds: First, it violated their freedom of speech and freedom of association under the First Amendment, because it criminalized their provision of material support to the PKK and the LTTE, without requiring the Government to prove that plaintiffs had a specific intent to further the unlawful ends of those organizations. Second, plaintiffs argued that the statute was unconstitutionally vague.

. . .

[ed. The Court here described the complicated path of the litigation in this case whereby the matter traveled up and down between the district court and the Ninth Circuit several times. In the meantime, the IRTPA statute's amendments of the material support statutes had been enacted, and ultimately, the relevant current terms of that statute were applied to the issues being litigated, first by the district court, then by the U.S. Court of Appeals. After describing the path of the litigation, the Court continued.]

In IRTPA, Congress clarified the mental state necessary to violate § 2339B, requiring knowledge of the foreign group's designation as a terrorist organization or the group's commission of terrorist acts. § 2339B(a)(1). Congress also added the term "service" to the definition of "material support or resources," § 2339A(b)(1), and defined "training" to mean "instruction or teaching designed to impart a specific skill, as opposed to general knowledge," § 2339A(b)(2). It also defined "expert advice or assistance" to mean "advice or assistance derived from scientific, technical or other specialized knowledge." § 2339A(b)(3). Finally, IRTPA clarified the scope of the term "personnel" by providing:

> "No person may be prosecuted under [§ 2339B] in connection with the term 'personnel' unless that person has knowingly provided, attempted to provide, or conspired to provide a foreign terrorist organization with 1 or more individuals (who may be or include himself) to work under that terrorist organization's direction or control or to organize, manage, supervise, or otherwise direct the operation of that organization. Individuals who act entirely independently of the foreign terrorist organization to advance its goals or objectives shall not be considered to be working under the foreign terrorist organization's direction and control." § 2339B(h).

. . .

Given the complicated 12-year history of this litigation, we pause to clarify the questions before us. Plaintiffs challenge § 2339B's prohibition on four types of material support—"training," "expert advice or assistance," "service," and "personnel." They raise three constitutional claims. First, plaintiffs claim that § 2339B violates the Due Process Clause of the Fifth Amendment because these four statutory terms are impermissibly vague. Second, plaintiffs claim that § 2339B violates their freedom of speech under the First Amendment. Third, plaintiffs claim that § 2339B violates their First Amendment freedom of association.

Plaintiffs do not challenge the above statutory terms in all their applications. Rather, plaintiffs claim that § 2339B is invalid to the extent it prohibits them from engaging in certain specified activities. With respect to the HLP and Judge Fertig, those activities are: (1) "train[ing] members of [the] PKK on how to use humanitarian and international law to peacefully resolve disputes"; (2) "engag[ing] in political advocacy on behalf of Kurds who live in Turkey"; and (3) "teach[ing] PKK members how to petition various representative bodies such as the United Nations for relief." With respect to the other plaintiffs, those activities are: (1) "train[ing] members of [the] LTTE to present claims for tsunami-related aid to mediators and international bodies"; (2) "offer[ing] their legal expertise in negotiating peace agreements between the LTTE and the Sri Lankan government"; and (3) "engag[ing] in political advocacy on behalf of Tamils who live in Sri Lanka."

. . .

One last point. Plaintiffs seek preenforcement review of a criminal statute. Before addressing the merits, we must be sure that this is a justiciable case or controversy under Article III. We conclude that it is: Plaintiffs face "a credible threat of prosecution" and "should not be required to await and undergo a criminal prosecution as the sole means of seeking relief."

. . .

Plaintiffs claim, as a threshold matter, that we should affirm the Court of Appeals without reaching any issues of constitutional law. They contend that we should interpret the material-support statute, when applied to speech, to require proof that a defendant intended to further a foreign terrorist organization's illegal activities. That interpretation, they say, would end the litigation because plaintiffs' proposed activities consist of speech, but plaintiffs do not intend to further unlawful conduct by the PKK or the LTTE.

We reject plaintiffs' interpretation of § 2339B because it is inconsistent with the text of the statute. Section 2339B(a)(1) prohibits "knowingly" providing material support. It then specifically describes the type of knowledge that is required: "To violate this paragraph, a person must have knowledge that the organization is a designated terrorist organization . . ., that the organization has engaged or engages in terrorist activity . . ., or that the organization has engaged or engages in terrorism. . . ." Congress plainly spoke to the necessary mental state for a violation of § 2339B, and it chose knowledge about the organization's connection to terrorism, not specific intent to further the organization's terrorist activities.

. . .

Finally, plaintiffs give the game away when they argue that a specific intent requirement should apply only when the material-support statute applies to speech. There is no basis whatever in the text of § 2339B to read the same provisions in that statute as requiring intent in some circumstances but not others. It is therefore clear that plaintiffs are asking us not to interpret § 2339B, but to revise it. "Although this Court will often strain to construe legislation so as to save it against constitutional attack, it must not and will not carry this to the point of perverting the purpose of a statute." Scales v. United States, 367 U. S. 203, 211 (1961).

Scales is the case on which plaintiffs most heavily rely, but it is readily distinguishable. That case involved the Smith Act, which prohibited membership in a group advocating the violent overthrow of the government. The Court held that a person could not be convicted under the statute unless he had knowledge of the group's illegal advocacy and a specific intent to bring about violent overthrow. This action is different: Section 2339B does not criminalize mere membership in a designated foreign terrorist organization. It instead prohibits providing "material support" to such a group. Nothing about Scales suggests the need for a specific intent requirement in such a case. The Court in Scales, moreover, relied on both statutory text and precedent that had interpreted closely related provisions of the Smith Act to require specific intent. Plaintiffs point to nothing similar here.

We cannot avoid the constitutional issues in this litigation through plaintiffs' proposed interpretation of § 2339B.

. . .

We turn to the question whether the material-support statute, as applied to plaintiffs, is impermissibly vague under the Due Process Clause of the Fifth Amendment. "A conviction fails to comport with due process if the statute under which it is obtained fails to provide a person of ordinary intelligence fair notice of what is prohibited, or is so standardless that it authorizes or encourages seriously discriminatory enforcement." United States v. Williams, 553 U. S. 285, 304 (2008). We consider whether a statute is vague as applied to the particular facts at issue, ... We have said that when a statute "interferes with the right of free speech or of association, a more stringent vagueness test should apply." "But 'perfect clarity and precise guidance have never been required even of regulations that restrict expressive activity.'" Williams, supra, at 304.

. . .

Under a proper analysis, plaintiffs' claims of vagueness lack merit. Plaintiffs do not argue that the material-support statute grants too much enforcement discretion to the Government. We therefore address only whether the statute "provide[s] a person of ordinary intelligence fair notice of what is prohibited."

As a general matter, the statutory terms at issue here are quite different from the sorts of terms that we have previously declared to be vague. We have in the past "struck down statutes that tied criminal culpability to whether the defendant's conduct was 'annoying' or 'indecent'—wholly subjective judgments without statutory definitions, narrowing context, or settled legal meanings." [S]ee also Papachristou v.

Jacksonville, 405 U. S. 156, n. 1 (1972) (holding vague an ordinance that punished "vagrants," defined to include "rogues and vagabonds," "persons who use juggling," and "common night walkers" (internal quotation marks omitted)). Applying the statutory terms in this action—"training," "expert advice or assistance," "service," and "personnel"—does not require similarly untethered, subjective judgments.

Congress also took care to add narrowing definitions to the material-support statute over time. These definitions increased the clarity of the statute's terms. . . .

Of course, the scope of the material-support statute may not be clear in every application. But the dispositive point here is that the statutory terms are clear in their application to plaintiffs' proposed conduct, which means that plaintiffs' vagueness challenge must fail. Even assuming that a heightened standard applies because the material-support statute potentially implicates speech, the statutory terms are not vague as applied to plaintiffs. . . .

Most of the activities in which plaintiffs seek to engage readily fall within the scope of the terms "training" and "expert advice or assistance." Plaintiffs want to "train members of [the] PKK on how to use humanitarian and international law to peacefully resolve disputes," and "teach PKK members how to petition various representative bodies such as the United Nations for relief." A person of ordinary intelligence would understand that instruction on resolving disputes through international law falls within the statute's definition of "training" because it imparts a "specific skill," not "general knowledge." § 2339A(b)(2). Plaintiffs' activities also fall comfortably within the scope of "expert advice or assistance": A reasonable person would recognize that teaching the PKK how to petition for humanitarian relief before the United Nations involves advice derived from, as the statute puts it, "specialized knowledge." § 2339A(b)(3). In fact, plaintiffs themselves have repeatedly used the terms "training" and "expert advice" throughout this litigation to describe their own proposed activities, demonstrating that these common terms readily and naturally cover plaintiffs' conduct.

Plaintiffs respond by pointing to hypothetical situations designed to test the limits of "training" and "expert advice or assistance." They argue that the statutory definitions of these terms use words of degree—like "specific," "general," and "specialized"—and that it is difficult to apply those definitions in particular cases. . . .

Whatever force these arguments might have in the abstract, they are beside the point here. . . .

Plaintiffs also contend that they want to engage in "political advocacy" on behalf of Kurds living in Turkey and Tamils living in Sri Lanka. They are concerned that such advocacy might be regarded as "material support" in the form of providing "personnel" or "service[s]," and assert that the statute is unconstitutionally vague because they cannot tell.

As for "personnel," Congress enacted a limiting definition in IRTPA that answers plaintiffs' vagueness concerns. Providing material support that constitutes "personnel" is defined as knowingly providing a person "to work under that terrorist organization's direction or control or to organize, manage, supervise, or otherwise direct the operation of that organization." § 2339B(h). The statute makes clear that "personnel" does not cover independent advocacy: "Individuals who act entirely independently of the foreign terrorist organization to advance its goals or objectives shall not be considered to be working under the foreign terrorist organization's direction and control."

"[S]ervice" similarly refers to concerted activity, not independent advocacy. See Webster's Third New International Dictionary 2075 (1993) (defining "service" to mean "the performance of work commanded or paid for by another: a servant's duty: attendance on a superior"; or "an act done for the benefit or at the command of another"). Context confirms that ordinary meaning here. The statute prohibits providing a service "to a foreign terrorist organization." § 2339B(a)(1) (emphasis added). The use of the word "to" indicates a connection between the service and the foreign group. We think a person of ordinary intelligence would understand that independently advocating for a cause is different from providing a service to a group that is advocating for that cause.

. . . The other types of material support listed in the statute, including "lodging," "weapons," "explosives," and "transportation," § 2339A(b)(1), are not forms of support that could be provided independently of a foreign terrorist organization. We interpret "service" along the same lines. Thus, any independent advocacy in which plaintiffs wish to engage is not prohibited by § 2339B. On the other hand, a person of ordinary intelligence would understand the term "service" to cover advocacy performed in coordination with, or at the direction of, a foreign terrorist organization.

Plaintiffs argue that this construction of the statute poses difficult questions of exactly how much direction or coordination is necessary for an activity to constitute a "service." . . .Plaintiffs have not provided any specific articulation of the degree to which they seek to coordinate their advocacy with the PKK and the LTTE. They have instead described the form of their intended advocacy only in the most general terms. . . .

Deciding whether activities described at such a level of generality would constitute prohibited "service[s]" under the statute would require "sheer speculation"—which means that plaintiffs cannot prevail in their preenforcement challenge. It is apparent with respect to these claims that "gradations of fact or charge would make a difference as to criminal liability," and so "adjudication of the reach and constitutionality of [the statute] must await a concrete fact situation."

. . .

We next consider whether the material-support statute, as applied to plaintiffs, violates the freedom of speech guaranteed by the First Amendment. . . .

For its part, the Government takes the foregoing too far, claiming that the only thing truly at issue in this litigation is conduct, not speech. . .

The Government is wrong that the only thing actually at issue in this litigation is conduct, . . .

Plaintiffs want to speak to the PKK and the LTTE, and whether they may do so under § 2339B depends on what they say. If plaintiffs' speech to those groups imparts a "specific skill" or communicates advice derived from "specialized knowledge"—for example, training on the use of international law or advice on petitioning the United Nations—then it is barred. On the other hand, plaintiffs' speech is not barred if it imparts only general or unspecialized knowledge.

. . .

The First Amendment issue before us is more refined than either plaintiffs or the Government would have it. It is not whether the Government may prohibit pure political speech, or may prohibit material support in the form of conduct. It is instead whether the Government may prohibit what plaintiffs want to do—provide material support to the PKK and LTTE in the form of speech.

Everyone agrees that the Government's interest in combating terrorism is an urgent objective of the highest order. Plaintiffs' complaint is that the ban on material support, applied to what they wish to do, is not "necessary to further that interest." The objective of combating terrorism does not justify prohibiting their speech, plaintiffs argue, because their support will advance only the legitimate activities of the designated terrorist organizations, not their terrorism. Id., at 51–52.

Whether foreign terrorist organizations meaningfully segregate support of their legitimate activities from support of terrorism is an empirical question. When it enacted § 2339B in 1996, Congress made specific findings regarding the serious threat posed by international terrorism. One of those findings explicitly rejects plaintiffs' contention that their support would not further the terrorist activities of the PKK and LTTE: "[F]oreign organizations that engage in terrorist activity are so tainted by their criminal conduct that any contribution to such an organization facilitates that conduct."

Plaintiffs argue that the reference to "any contribution" in this finding meant only monetary support. There is no reason to read the finding to be so limited, particularly because Congress expressly prohibited so much more than monetary support in § 2339B. Congress's use of the term "contribution" is best read to reflect a determination that any form of material support furnished "to" a foreign terrorist organization should be barred, which is precisely what the material-support statute does. Indeed, when Congress enacted § 2339B, Congress simultaneously removed an exception that had existed in § 2339A(a) (1994 ed.) for the provision of material support in the form of "humanitarian assistance to persons not directly involved in" terrorist activity. AEDPA § 323, 110 Stat. 1255; 205 F. 3d, at 1136. That repeal demonstrates that Congress considered and rejected the view that ostensibly peaceful aid would have no harmful effects.

We are convinced that Congress was justified in rejecting that view. The PKK and the LTTE are deadly groups. "The PKK's insurgency has claimed more than 22,000 lives." Declaration of Kenneth R. McKune, App. 128, ¶ 5. The LTTE has engaged in extensive suicide bombings and political assassinations, including killings of the Sri Lankan President, Security Minister, and Deputy Defense Minister. Id., at 130–132; Brief for Government 6–7. . . .

Material support meant to "promot[e] peaceable, lawful conduct," can further terrorism by foreign groups in multiple ways. "Material support" is a valuable resource by definition. Such support frees up other resources within the organization that may be put to violent ends. It also importantly helps lend legitimacy to foreign terrorist groups—legitimacy that makes it easier for those groups to persist, to recruit members, and to raise funds—all of which facilitate more terrorist attacks. "Terrorist organizations do not maintain organizational 'firewalls' that would prevent or deter . . . sharing and commingling of support and benefits." McKune Affidavit, App. 135, ¶ 11. "[I]nvestigators have revealed how terrorist groups systematically conceal their activities behind charitable, social, and political fronts." M. Levitt, Hamas: Politics, Charity, and Terrorism in the Service of Jihad 2–3 (2006). "Indeed, some designated foreign terrorist organizations use social and political components to recruit personnel to carry out terrorist operations, and to provide support to criminal terrorists and their families in aid of such operations." McKune Affidavit, App. 135, ¶ 11; Levitt, supra, at 2 ("Muddying the waters between its political activism, good works, and terrorist attacks, Hamas is able to use its overt political and charitable organizations as a financial and logistical support network for its terrorist operations").

Money is fungible, and "[w]hen foreign terrorist organizations that have a dual structure raise funds, they highlight the civilian and humanitarian ends to which such moneys could be put." McKune Affidavit,

App. 134, ¶ 9. But "there is reason to believe that foreign terrorist organizations do not maintain legitimate financial firewalls between those funds raised for civil, nonviolent activities, and those ultimately used to support violent, terrorist operations." Id., at 135, ¶ 12. . . .There is evidence that the PKK and the LTTE, in particular, have not "respected the line between humanitarian and violent activities." McKune Affidavit, App. 135, ¶ 13 (discussing PKK); see id., at 134 (LTTE).

The dissent argues that there is "no natural stopping place" for the proposition that aiding a foreign terrorist organization's lawful activity promotes the terrorist organization as a whole. But Congress has settled on just such a natural stopping place: The statute reaches only material support coordinated with or under the direction of a designated foreign terrorist organization. Independent advocacy that might be viewed as promoting the group's legitimacy is not covered.

Providing foreign terrorist groups with material support in any form also furthers terrorism by straining the United States' relationships with its allies and undermining cooperative efforts between nations to prevent terrorist attacks. We see no reason to question Congress's finding that "international cooperation is required for an effective response to terrorism, as demonstrated by the numerous multilateral conventions in force providing universal prosecutive jurisdiction over persons involved in a variety of terrorist acts, including hostage taking, murder of an internationally protected person, and aircraft piracy and sabotage." . . .

For example, the Republic of Turkey—a fellow member of NATO—is defending itself against a violent insurgency waged by the PKK. That nation and our other allies would react sharply to Americans furnishing material support to foreign groups like the PKK, and would hardly be mollified by the explanation that the support was meant only to further those groups' "legitimate" activities. From Turkey's perspective, there likely are no such activities. . . .

. . .

In analyzing whether it is possible in practice to distinguish material support for a foreign terrorist group's violent activities and its nonviolent activities, we do not rely exclusively on our own inferences drawn from the record evidence. We have before us an affidavit stating the Executive Branch's conclusion on that question. The State Department informs us that "[t]he experience and analysis of the U. S. government agencies charged with combating terrorism strongly suppor[t]" Congress's finding that all contributions to foreign terrorist organizations further their terrorism. McKune Affidavit, App. 133, ¶ 8. . . .

That evaluation of the facts by the Executive, like Congress's assessment, is entitled to deference. This litigation implicates sensitive and weighty interests of national security and foreign affairs. The PKK and the LTTE have committed terrorist acts against American citizens abroad, and the material-support statute addresses acute foreign policy concerns involving relationships with our Nation's allies. . . . It is vital in this context "not to substitute. . . our own evaluation of evidence for a reasonable evaluation by the Legislative Branch."

Our precedents, old and new, make clear that concerns of national security and foreign relations do not warrant abdication of the judicial role. We do not defer to the Government's reading of the First Amendment, even when such interests are at stake. We are one with the dissent that the Government's "authority and expertise in these matters do not automatically trump the Court's own obligation to secure the protection that the Constitution grants to individuals." But when it comes to collecting evidence and drawing factual inferences in this area, "the lack of competence on the part of the courts is marked," and respect for the Government's conclusions is appropriate.

One reason for that respect is that national security and foreign policy concerns arise in connection with efforts to confront evolving threats in an area where information can be difficult to obtain and the impact of certain conduct difficult to assess. The dissent slights these real constraints in demanding hard proof—with "detail," "specific facts," and "specific evidence"—that plaintiffs' proposed activities will support terrorist attacks. That would be a dangerous requirement. In this context, conclusions must often be based on informed judgment rather than concrete evidence, and that reality affects what we may reasonably insist on from the Government. The material-support statute is, on its face, a preventive measure—it criminalizes not terrorist attacks themselves, but aid that makes the attacks more likely to occur. The Government, when seeking to prevent imminent harms in the context of international affairs and national security, is not required to conclusively link all the pieces in the puzzle before we grant weight to its empirical conclusions. . . .

. . . In this litigation, . . .Congress and the Executive are uniquely positioned to make principled distinctions between activities that will further terrorist conduct and undermine United States foreign policy, and those that will not.

At bottom, plaintiffs simply disagree with the considered judgment of Congress and the Executive that providing material support to a designated foreign terrorist organization—even seemingly benign support—bolsters the terrorist activities of that organization. That judgment, however, is entitled to significant weight, and we have persuasive evidence before us to sustain it. Given the sensitive interests in national security and foreign affairs at stake, the political branches have adequately substantiated their determination that, to serve the Government's interest in preventing terrorism, it was necessary to prohibit providing material support in the form of training, expert advice, personnel, and services to foreign terrorist groups, even if the supporters meant to promote only the groups' nonviolent ends.

. . .

. . . [T]he dissent fails to address the real dangers at stake. It instead considers only the possible benefits of plaintiffs' proposed activities in the abstract. The dissent seems unwilling to entertain the prospect that training and advising a designated foreign terrorist organization on how to take advantage of international entities might benefit that organization in a way that facilitates its terrorist activities. In the dissent's world, such training is all to the good. Congress and the Executive, however, have concluded that we live in a different world: one in which the designated foreign terrorist organizations "are so tainted by their criminal conduct that any contribution to such an organization facilitates that conduct." . . .

All this is not to say that any future applications of the material-support statute to speech or advocacy will survive First Amendment scrutiny. It is also not to say that any other statute relating to speech and terrorism would satisfy the First Amendment. In particular, we in no way suggest that a regulation of independent speech would pass constitutional muster, even if the Government were to show that such speech benefits foreign terrorist organizations. We also do not suggest that Congress could extend the same prohibition on material support at issue here to domestic organizations. We simply hold that, in prohibiting the particular forms of support that plaintiffs seek to provide to foreign terrorist groups, § 2339B does not violate the freedom of speech.

. . .

The judgment of the United States Court of Appeals for the Ninth Circuit is affirmed in part and reversed in part, and the cases are remanded for further proceedings consistent with this opinion.

JUSTICE BREYER, with whom JUSTICES GINSBURG and SOTOMAYOR join, dissenting.

Like the Court, and substantially for the reasons it gives, I do not think this statute is unconstitutionally vague. But I cannot agree with the Court's conclusion that the Constitution permits the Government to prosecute the plaintiffs criminally for engaging in coordinated teaching and advocacy furthering the designated organizations' lawful political objectives. In my view, the Government has not met its burden of showing that an interpretation of the statute that would prohibit this speech- and association-related activity serves the Government's compelling interest in combating terrorism. And I would interpret the statute as normally placing activity of this kind outside its scope

. . .

. . . Consider the cases involving the protection the First Amendment offered those who joined the Communist Party intending only to further its peaceful activities. In those cases, this Court took account of congressional findings that the Communist Party not only advocated theoretically but also sought to put into practice the overthrow of our Government through force and violence. The Court had previously accepted Congress' determinations that the American Communist Party was a "Communist action organization" which (1) acted under the "control, direction, and discipline" of the world Communist movement, a movement that sought to employ "espionage, sabotage, terrorism, and any other means deemed necessary, to establish a Communist totalitarian dictatorship," and (2) "endeavor[ed]" to bring about "the overthrow of existing governments by . . . force if necessary." Communist Party of United States v. Subversive Activities Control Bd., 367 U. S. 1, 5–6 (1961) (internal quotation marks omitted).

Nonetheless, the Court held that the First Amendment protected an American's right to belong to that party—despite whatever "legitimating" effect membership might have had—as long as the person did not share the party's unlawful purposes. See, e.g., De Jonge, 299 U.S. 353; Scales, 367 U. S., at 228–230; Elfbrandt v. Russell, 384 U. S. 11, 17 (1966); Keyishian v. Board of Regents of Univ. of State of N. Y., 385 U. S. 589, 605–610 (1967); Robel, 389 U. S. 258 (holding that national security interests did not justify overbroad criminal prohibition on members of Communist-affiliated organizations working in any defense-related facility. . .

Nor can the Government overcome these considerations simply by narrowing the covered activities to those that involve coordinated, rather than independent, advocacy. Conversations, discussions, or logistical arrangements might well prove necessary to carry out the speech-related activities here at issue (just as conversations and discussions are a necessary part of membership in any organization). The Government does not distinguish this kind of "coordination" from any other. I am not aware of any form of words that might be used to describe "coordination" that would not, at a minimum, seriously chill not only the kind of activities the plaintiffs raise before us, but also the "independent advocacy" the Government purports to permit. And, as for the Government's willingness to distinguish independent advocacy from coordinated advocacy, the former is more likely, not less likely, to confer legitimacy than the latter. Thus, other things being equal, the distinction "coordination" makes is arbitrary in respect to furthering the statute's purposes. And a rule of law that finds the "legitimacy" argument adequate in respect to the latter would have a hard time distinguishing a statute that sought to attack the former.

. . .

In my own view, the majority's arguments stretch the concept of "fungibility" beyond constitutional limits. . . .

Moreover, the risk that those who are taught will put otherwise innocent speech or knowledge to bad use is omnipresent, at least where that risk rests on little more than (even informed) speculation. Hence to accept this kind of argument without more and to apply it to the teaching of a subject such as international human rights law is to adopt a rule of law that, contrary to the Constitution's text and First Amendment precedent, would automatically forbid the teaching of any subject in a case where national security interests conflict with the First Amendment. The Constitution does not allow all such conflicts to be decided in the Government's favor.

The majority, as I have said, cannot limit the scope of its arguments through its claim that the plaintiffs remain free to engage in the protected activity as long as it is not "coordinated." That is because there is no practical way to organize classes for a group (say, wishing to learn about human rights law) without "coordination." Nor can the majority limit the scope of its argument by pointing to some special limiting circumstance present here. That is because the only evidence the majority offers to support its general claim consists of a single reference to a book about terrorism, which the Government did not mention, and which apparently says no more than that at one time the PKK suspended its armed struggle and then returned to it.

Second, the majority discusses the plaintiffs' proposal to " 'teach PKK members how to petition various representative bodies such as the United Nations for relief.' " The majority's only argument with respect to this proposal is that the relief obtained "could readily include monetary aid," which the PKK might use to buy guns. The majority misunderstands the word "relief." In this context, as the record makes clear, the word "relief" does not refer to "money." It refers to recognition under the Geneva Conventions. . . .

Throughout, the majority emphasizes that it would defer strongly to Congress' "informed judgment." But here, there is no evidence that Congress has made such a judgment regarding the specific activities at issue in these cases. See infra, at 20–21. In any event, "whenever the fundamental rights of free speech and assembly are alleged to have been invaded, it must remain open [for judicial determination] whether there actually did exist at the time a clear danger; whether the danger, if any, was imminent; and whether the evil apprehended was one so substantial as to justify the stringent restriction interposed by the legislature." . . .

I concede that the Government's expertise in foreign affairs may warrant deference in respect to many matters, e.g., our relations with Turkey. But it remains for this Court to decide whether the Government has shown that such an interest justifies criminalizing speech activity otherwise protected by the First Amendment. And the fact that other nations may like us less for granting that protection cannot in and of itself carry the day.

Finally, I would reemphasize that neither the Government nor the majority points to any specific facts that show that the speech-related activities before us are fungible in some special way or confer some special legitimacy upon the PKK. Rather, their arguments in this respect are general and speculative. Those arguments would apply to virtually all speech-related support for a dual-purpose group's peaceful activities (irrespective of whether the speech-related activity is coordinated). Both First Amendment logic and First Amendment case law prevent us from "sacrific[ing] First Amendment protections for so speculative a gain."

. . .

For the reasons I have set forth, I believe application of the statute as the Government interprets it would gravely and without adequate justification injure interests of the kind the First Amendment protects. Thus, there is "a serious doubt" as to the statute's constitutionality. . . .

I believe that a construction that would avoid the constitutional problem is "fairly possible." In particular, I would read the statute as criminalizing First-Amendment-protected pure speech and association only when the defendant knows or intends that those activities will assist the organization's unlawful terrorist actions. Under this reading, the Government would have to show, at a minimum, that such defendants provided support that they knew was significantly likely to help the organization pursue its unlawful terrorist aims. . . .

QUESTIONS AND NOTES

1.   How much guidance does the Humanitarian Law Project (HLP) case provide? Might the plaintiffs in the case have been able to make stronger arguments on the merits of the constitutional issues if they had indeed risked criminal prosecution and been prosecuted based on specific conduct engaged in by them?

2.   Regarding the interpretation of some of the material support terms, for example, "service," the Court in HLP seems willing to add qualifiers that are not found expressly in the statutory language in order to avoid unconstitutionality. The Court, however, declines to accept plaintiffs' argument that for a similar reason a specific intent requirement should be read into the statute as the requisite mens rea. Can you explain the difference in treatment?

3.   HLP deals with issues under § 2339B. What are the implications of the Court's rulings for interpretative issues under § 2339A—for example, for interpretation of the specific kinds of material support and regarding mens rea

issues? The next two sections address issues relating to those two subjects. In studying the materials in those sections, you should keep in mind that many of the decisions, all lower federal courts (U.S. courts of appeal and district courts) were decided before the Supreme Court's decision in HLP, and some were decided before the statute was amended to its current form; most of these amendments occurred in 2004. Accordingly, a question also to keep in mind is whether the law expressed in these materials is affected by the Court's opinion in HLP.

C. SELECTED MATERIAL SUPPORT CATEGORIES: PERSONNEL, SERVICE, . . . ETC.

UNITED STATES V. ABU-JIHAAD

600 F.Supp.2d 362 (D.Conn. 2009)

MARK R. KRAVITZ, DISTRICT JUDGE.

Following a six-day trial in March 2008, a jury convicted Defendant Hassan Abu-Jihaad on two charges: (1) disclosing national defense information to those not entitled to receive it in violation of 18 U.S.C. § 793(d); and (2) providing material support to terrorists in violation of 18 U.S.C. § 2339A and § 2. The Government alleged that in 2001, while Mr. Abu-Jihaad was serving as a U.S. Navy Signalman aboard the destroyer, the U.S.S. Benfold, he disclosed classified information regarding the movement of the Fifth Fleet Battle Group, which included the aircraft carrier, the U.S.S. Constellation, to individuals in London associated with Azzam Publications, an organization that the Government alleged supported violent Islamic jihad. According to the Government, Mr. Abu-Jihaad knew or intended that the information he disclosed would be used to kill United States nationals. By its verdict, the jury agreed with the Government's assertions. Mr. Abu-Jihaad now moves for judgment of acquittal . . . .

> [ed. After stating the facts at length and assessing the evidence, Judge Kravitz denied the motion for judgment of acquittal on the charge under 18 U.S.C. § 793(d). Subsequently the defendant was sentenced to 10 years imprisonment on this charge. The judge then proceeded to consider the charge under § 2339A. He first concluded that the government's theory that the defendant had provided material support by providing "physical assets" was not sustainable.

> [Note that the government's case was entirely circumstantial; the prosecutor had presented no direct evidence that the defendant had provided the battle group information to Azzam Publications. The information was found on a computer floppy disk in 2006 and only circumstantially linked to the defendant. The government's

theory was that the defendant had provided the battle group information in the spring of 2001 prior to the sailing of the battle group. One of the items of evidence contributing to the circumstantial case was an email sent by the defendant to Azzam in which the defendant praised the earlier bombing of the navy vessel, the U.S.S. Cole as a "martyrdom operation," and derided the United States as an "infidel" and "Kuffar nation." The judge also stated, "It is also fair to read his e-mail as giving thanks to the 'mujahideen' as 'american enemies' and as the 'true champions and soldiers of Allah.' "

[The opinion then proceeded to address the question of whether the defendant had provided "personnel" within the meaning of "material support" under § 2339A.]

. . . As to "personnel," the Government argued to the jury-and the jury accepted-that by providing national defense information to Azzam, Mr. Abu-Jihaad had provided himself as "personnel." Mr. Abu-Jihaad's conviction for providing personnel presents a much closer question than the conviction for providing physical assets. . . . The task is made all the more difficult because the Second Circuit has not yet ruled on the scope of the term "personnel" in that statute, Congress amended the definition of "personnel" in § 2339B but not in § 2339A, and the case law that does exist is not entirely consistent.

Notably, all of the legislative history states that the new language added to § 2339B in 2004 was only a clarification of the definition of personnel and not a substantive change. . . .

. . .[A]s an initial matter, the Court must decide whether the amended definition of "personnel" in § 2339B applies to § 2339A as well, for even the Government concedes that if the amended definition in § 2339B applies to § 2339A, the evidence is wanting. Though the legislative history describes the definition of "personnel" in § 2339B as a mere clarification, the fact that Congress chose not to apply the more detailed definition to § 2339A causes the Court to believe that the definition Congress provided for § 2339B should not apply to § 2339A. . . . The Court must presume that Congress was aware that the definition of "personnel" was relevant to both sections, but chose to include the more detailed definition in one section and not the other. This presumption is even stronger because Congress changed the definition of "personnel" in § 2339A by adding "1 or more individuals who may be or include oneself" at the same time it added the more detailed definition of "personnel" to § 2339B. Nor is there any indication in the legislative history that Congress intended the § 2339B definition to apply to § 2339A.

Therefore, the Court is left with the language of § 2339A, which does not define either the word "provide" or "personnel." The Supreme Court has repeatedly explained that "[w]hen a word is not defined by statute, we normally construe it in accord with its ordinary or natural meaning.". Ordinarily, the term "provide" means to make available, to furnish, and to arrange for, supply, or transfer, see Random House Webster's Unabridged Dictionary (2001), and that is what the Court told the jury (without objection). . . . Furthermore, . . ., there is no reason to suppose from the language of the statute that "provides" is limited to a physical transfer or delivery of personnel:

> [S]tatutory terms are to be interpreted in their context in light of their placement and purpose in the statutory scheme. A defendant would reasonably be providing material support or resources by making these items or services available with the requisite knowledge or intent. Limiting the definition of "provides" to the physical transfer of an asset would result in a strained and untenable reading of the statute. Thus, there is no basis to limit the meaning of "provides . . . personnel" to the physical transfer of personnel, and not to include making personnel available-which is in accord with the ordinary and natural use of the term "provide," and which is consistent with its placement in the statute and the purpose of proscribing the provision of resources to be used for a prohibited purpose.

Likewise, the term "personnel" is also not defined in § 2339A. The plain meaning of that term includes "a body of persons employed by or active in an organization, service or place of work." See Random House Webster's Unabridged Dictionary (2001). In the context of § 2339A, it seems apparent that the term refers to those individuals who are provided or made available to prepare for or carry out the crimes prohibited by the statute. The individual need not be an "employee" or "quasi-employee," but there must be some form of coordination, joint action, or understanding. Entirely independent action is not sufficient to qualify as being at least "active in" an organization as required by the definition of personnel. Therefore, one who makes resources in the form of individuals (including himself) available, or furnishes individuals (including himself), for the purpose of actively preparing for or carrying out the crimes prohibited by the statute through some form of coordinated action is guilty of violating § 2339A. See, e.g., United States v. Marzook, 383 F.Supp.2d 1056, 1064 (N.D.Ill.2005) (holding that the term "personnel" includes recruiting others to join Hamas).

   . . .

Thus, the Court applies the definition of providing personnel as stated above. . . . The difficulty of applying that definition to the facts of this case arises from the Government's theory of guilt, which was that by disclosing national defense information to Azzam, Mr. Abu-Jihaad was, in effect, making himself available to terrorists for the purpose of killing U.S. nationals. That is, by providing information alone to Azzam-an act that was not directly prohibited by § 2339A-Mr. Abu-Jihaad provided personnel-that is, Mr. Abu-Jihaad himself-to Azzam, knowing that he or his assistance would be used to prepare for, or carry out, the killing of U.S. nationals.

That theory of guilt puts a strain on the language of the statute. For if the Government's argument were accepted, an individual who provided a terrorist organization with, say, weapons-perhaps by selling them at market price-would also be deemed to have provided the organization with personnel-namely, the gun dealer himself. Of course, one can imagine situations where an individual makes both himself and others available to terrorist organizations and also provides the organizations with weapons, money, or other tangible resources. But that is not invariably the case. That is, merely providing an organization with a resource, even a prohibited resource, is not necessarily the same thing as providing personnel to prepare for or carry out the prohibited purposes of the statute through some form of coordinated or joint action. For if that were the case, then much of the definition of "material support or resources" would be entirely redundant; providing weapons, explosives, or anything else on the list would also automatically constitute the provision of personnel as well.

To be sure, context and facts matter. Yet, it is context and facts that are entirely missing in this case. For we do not know how Mr. Abu-Jihaad conveyed the defense information to Azzam or what arrangements, if any, they had with each other. It could well be that Mr. Abu-Jihaad asked Azzam how he could help in supporting jihad, they told him to send defense information about the movements of the battlegroup so terrorists could attack the battlegroup, and Mr. Abu-Jihaad did as requested. In those circumstances, the Court would have little difficulty concluding that Mr. Abu-Jihaad had volunteered himself as personnel, acting in coordination with Azzam to kill U.S. nationals. On the other hand, perhaps Mr. Abu-Jihaad on a whim simply sent defense information to Azzam on one occasion, not knowing if Azzam wanted it and without any pre-disclosure or post-disclosure communication with Azzam about the information. In those circumstances, he surely provided defense information to someone not entitled to receive it, as the Court has previously found, but it would be linguistically odd to describe that lone, voluntary act as making personnel available to Azzam. . . .

The Government recognizes this gap in the evidence and seeks to get around it by pointing to a general request by Azzam to its readership in November 2000, in which it sought aid for the Taliban by requesting money, gas masks, or battlefield medical services. Of course, Azzam also exhorted its readers to assist in violent jihad. But to build a quid pro quo or understanding from these generalized requests for assistance is more than the evidence will bear, even taking all reasonable inferences in the light most favorable to the Government. In short, the evidence showed beyond a reasonable doubt that Mr. Abu-Jihaad provided classified defense information to Azzam. He may also have made himself available to assist Azzam in violent jihad. However, we simply do not know that from the evidence presented, even viewing the evidence in the light most favorable to the Government. Therefore, the Court will grant the Motion for Judgment of Acquittal on the material support charge under 18 U.S.C. § 2339A.

QUESTIONS AND NOTES

1. The defendant, Abu-Jihaad, in the principal case above, appealed his conviction under 18 U.S.C. § 793(d); the Second Circuit affirmed. The judgment of acquittal on the charge under 18 U.S.C. § 2339A was not reviewed or commented upon by the appellate court.

2. The "provide. . . personnel" category of material support on which the prosecution in Abu Jihaad was partially based has become one of the most commonly used forms of material support upon which prosecutions under both § 2339B and § 2339A can be based. Originally, the material support category of personnel in § 2339A did not include the phrase "including oneself" nor was there the "under the direction or control" language in § 2339B, but those phrases and concepts were read into the statute through judicial interpretation. See the prosecution in 2002 against John Walker Lindh, the so-called "American Taliban," which included counts alleging violations of 18 U.S.C. § 2339B. Inter alia, it was specifically alleged that Lindh continued with his Taliban fighting unit for several months "after learning that United States military forces and United States nationals had become directly engaged in support of the Northern Alliance in its military conflict with Taliban and al Qaeda forces." Pertinent excerpts from the district court's rulings on various motions made by Lindh relating to the § 2339B charge under 18 U.S.C. § 2339B appear below, United States v. Lindh, 212 F.Supp.2d 541 (E.D.Va. 2002):

> Lindh contends his conduct does not, as a matter of law, amount to providing "material support and resources," including . . . "personnel," because . . . merely enlisting in an armed force—rather than recruiting for such a force—does not constitute providing personnel. Lindh is incorrect. . . .

> . . . Lindh's conduct as a participant in the training camp and battlefield falls squarely within Section 2339B's proscription against providing support and services, including "personnel." There is little doubt, given the plain meaning of "Personnel" that Lindh provided such support and services. Citing the legislative history, Lindh contends that the term "personnel" is limited to recruitment. This contention is flatly controverted by the term's plain meaning. Indeed, under any reasonable construction of Section 2339B's statutory

language, a person who joins the armed force of a foreign terrorist organization, receives combat training from that organization, and serves in a combat unit to protect the organization and advance its goals has provided material support and resources—including, specifically, "personnel"—to that group. By any measure, Lindh provided personnel, i.e., himself, to al Qaeda . . . when he allegedly joined these organizations and engaged in a variety of conduct, including combat, to further the goals of these organizations. Thus, to provide personnel is to provide people who become affiliated with the organization and work under its direction: the individual or individuals provided could be the provider himself, or others, or both.

. . . Lindh argues. . . that he is not a member of al Qaeda's "personnel" as defined by Section 2339B. Lindh maintains that providing "personnel" to. . . . al Qaeda could in certain instances amount to nothing more than the mere act of being physically present among members of a designated organization, obtaining information and training from such members, or simply being a member. Put differently, according to Lindh, allowing a prosecution under Section 2339B for providing "personnel" to a terrorist organization presents a constitutionally unacceptable risk that a mere bystander, sympathizer, or passive member will be convicted on the basis of association alone. This argument founders on the plain meaning of the term "personnel," which means "a body of persons usu[ally] employed (as in a factory, office, or organization)," or "a body of persons employed in some service." Thus, in Section 2339B, providing "personnel" to HUM or al Qaeda necessarily means that the persons provided to the foreign terrorist organization work under the direction and control of that organization. One who is merely present with other members of the organization, but is not under the organization's direction and control, is not part of the organization's "personnel." This distinction is sound; one can become a member of a political party without also becoming part of its "personnel;" one can visit an organization's training center, or actively espouse its cause, without thereby becoming "personnel." Simply put, the term "personnel" does not extend to independent actors. Rather, it describes employees or employee-like operatives who serve the designated group and work at its command or, in Lindh's case, who provide themselves to serve the organization.

3.   It follows from cases like Walker Lindh that when Congress in 2004 incorporated into the listing of personnel in the material support definition the language "including oneself" it was simply confirming a prior judicial interpretation in statutory form; similarly, when it added to the definitions in § 2339B the phrase, "under the direction or control."

4.   Does the HLP decision with respect to providing personnel: a) overrule Abu Jihaad; b) confirm that Abu Jihaad was correctly decided; or c)

neither a) nor b)—the decision in HLP regarding providing personnel is distinguishable from the issues resolved in Abu Jihaad.

5. The court in Abu Jihaad decided that the "under the direction or control" language of § 2339B had no applicability to § 2339A and therefore it was free to interpret "personnel" for purposes of enforcement under § 2339A. Can it be argued that Congress's failure to qualify the personnel term in § 2339A with the under the direction or control language has implications for how personnel should be interpreted for purposes of § 2339A? What do you think is the explanation for the fact that Congress only applied the under the direction or control language to § 2339B and not to § 2339A?

6. As a gloss on some of the categories in the material support list in § 2339A, namely, "service," "lodging," "weapons," "explosives," and "transportation," the Court in HLP read in the idea of acts "performed in coordination with, or at the direction of, a foreign terrorist organization," stating that the listed categories "are not forms of support that could be provided independently of a foreign terrorist organization." Do you agree? Is there a difference between acts performed "in coordination with, or at the direction of, a foreign terrorist organization" and acts performed "under. . . the direction or control" of such an organization?

7. To what extent can the "provide personnel" category of material support be used as a catchall where the actual support provided is not listed in the 2339A listing? What does Abu Jihaad tell us about this issue? If personnel cannot be used in this way, what about the material support category of service? Does it have potential to be used as a catchall?

8. In Paris, in September, 2017, a mother was convicted of aiding terrorism and sentenced to two years in prison based on her having sent money to her son that aided him to join and fight on behalf of ISIS in Syria. See DW News, French mother of 'Islamic State' fighter sentenced to two years prison for financing terrorist activities http://www.dw.com/en/french-mother-of-islamic-state-fighter-sentenced-to-two-years-prison-for-financing-terrorist-activities/a-40737541. Suppose the mother lived in Los Angeles and instead of sending money, bought her son suitcases and appropriate clothing for his travel to Syria, knowing that he was going to join ISIS. Could she be successfully prosecuted under either § 2339B or § 2339A?

9. For interesting applications of the personnel category of material support with respect to both § 2339B and § 2339A, see United States v. Sattar, 314 F.Supp.2d 279 (S.D.N.Y. 2004). The district court case involved a prosecution of a lawyer who, while visiting her client in prison, assisted the translator in concealing from the guards what they were doing through various ruses (acting as if they were engaging in innocuous activities); meanwhile the translator communicated to the prisoner messages from his terrorist organization in Egypt (the prisoner was a leader of the organization) and obtained messages from the prisoner which he then arranged to be communicated to the prisoner's terrorist organization, and the lawyer herself made statements to the press that amounted to messages that would be

received by the prisoner's terrorist organization. The effect of these messages was to release the organization from a cease fire and to authorize them to renew violent terrorist acts. The trial judge in Sattar had dismissed two counts of the original indictment as unconstitutionally vague; the government filed an amended superseding indictment, and the second time around, the district court upheld this new indictment against the same claim, stating:

> Counts One and Two of the original indictment charged that Sattar, Stewart, and Yousry conspired to violate 18 U.S.C. § 2339B and committed a substantive violation of that statute by, among other means, providing themselves as "personnel" to a designated FTO . . .

> The Court dismissed Counts One and Two of the original indictment as unconstitutionally vague as applied to the conduct alleged in those counts. . . . The Court further concluded that by prohibiting the "provision" of "personnel," including oneself, to a "foreign terrorist organization," § 2339B could conceivably apply to someone engaging in advocacy on behalf of such an organization, conduct protected by the First Amendment. The Court noted that mere membership in an organization could not be prohibited without a requirement that the Government prove the defendants' specific intent to further the FTO's unlawful ends, . . . but the statute provided no means to distinguish providing oneself to an organization from mere membership in the organization.

> The S1 Indictment,[1] on the other hand, which charges a violation of 18 U.S.C. § 2339A rather than § 2339B, no longer charges Stewart and Yousry with providing themselves as personnel to an FTO, but rather with providing and conspiring to provide personnel—by making Sheikh Abdel Rahman, not themselves, available as a co-conspirator—to the conspiracy alleged in Count Two, namely the conspiracy to kill and kidnap persons in a foreign country. It also charges them with concealing and disguising the nature, location, and source of that personnel by disguising that Sheikh Abdel Rahman was a co-conspirator. These actions were allegedly done with the knowledge and intent that such personnel was to be used in preparation for, or in carrying out, the conspiracy to kill and kidnap persons in a foreign country. This is the heightened specific intent required by § 2339A.

What was missing from the allegation regarding providing personnel in the original indictment that led the court to hold this allegation to be unconstitutionally vague and violative of the First Amendment? Could the government have simply amended the providing personnel allegation without having to change its theory of the case in the superseding indictment? Why

---

[1]   [ed.] That is, the superseding indictment now before the court.

was the new theory expressed in the superseding indictment able to withstand constitutional challenge whereas the original indictment had been dismissed.

10.	In Sattar, supra, the court also upheld a conviction under 18 U.S.C. § 1001, the federal false statements statute which criminalizes the making of a material false statement within the jurisdiction of a federal agency, for example, to a federal official acting in the course of official duties. This frequently used criminal statute is not thought of particularly as a terrorism offense, but it is used frequently in national security cases and is a powerful tool for the government, oftentimes providing leverage in plea bargains and helping investigators recruit cooperating witnesses. The Intelligence Reform and Terrorism Prevention Act (IRTPA), enacted in 2004, provides for increased penalties, from five to eight years, for violations of the false statement statute stemming from domestic or international terrorism. For a subsequent opinion in the Sattar case, supra note 9, see United States v. Stewart, 590 F.3d 93 (2d Cir. 2009).

11.	In a number of instances, individuals, having traveled abroad from the U.S., for example, to Afghanistan, to receive military training to prepare them allegedly to engage in terrorist activities, were prosecuted under § 2339B on the theory that they provided "personnel," namely, themselves to a FTO. See, e.g., United States v. Goba, 220 F.Supp.2d 182 (W.D.N.Y.2002). See also United States v. Goba, 2007 WL 4404977 (W.D.N.Y. 2007) reducing Goba's sentence for providing substantial assistance to the government.

12.	In 2004, as part of IRTPA, a new offense was added to Title 18, U.S.C. § 2339D, receiving military-type training from a foreign terrorist organization. That section provides:

Title 18, U.S.C.

§ 2339D. Receiving military-type training from a foreign terrorist organization

(a)	**Offense.**—Whoever knowingly receives military-type training from or on behalf of any organization designated at the time of the training by the Secretary of State under section 219(a)(1) of the Immigration and Nationality Act as a foreign terrorist organization shall be fined under this title or imprisoned for ten years, or both. To violate this subsection, a person must have knowledge that the organization is a designated terrorist organization (as defined in subsection (c)(4)), that the organization has engaged or engages in terrorist activity (as defined in section 212 of the Immigration and Nationality Act), or that the organization has engaged or engages in terrorism (as defined in section 140(d)(2) of the Foreign Relations Authorization Act, Fiscal Years 1988 and 1989).

. . .

(c) **Definitions.**—As used in this section—

(1) the term "military-type training" includes training in means or methods that can cause death or serious bodily injury, destroy or damage property, or disrupt services to critical infrastructure, or training on the use, storage, production, or assembly of any explosive, firearm or other weapon, including any weapon of mass destruction (as defined in section 2232a(c)(2));

. . .

Accordingly, individuals who receive military training provided by a foreign terrorist organization, assuming the necessary mens rea is present, are now subject to prosecution under the new offense. Will they also continue to be subject to prosecution for such conduct under § 2339B, so that now they will have committed two offenses rather than just one? If so, this would be another example of the recurring pattern in federal criminal law—prosecution of newly-occurring criminal conduct under a general statute, and Congress then enacts a new statute targeted at the conduct.

13. Given the breadth of coverage of what can constitute "material support" under § 2339A and § 2339B, which has been achieved through the original legislation, subsequent judicial interpretations and legislative amendments, is there any type of support or aid to terrorist offenses or to foreign terrorist organizations that is not likely to be treated as "material support?" Given the apparent open-endedness of the definitional list, is the list really needed? Would it not be simpler to make the offense, "Whoever provides material support . . .," or "Whoever provides aid. . .," or even, "Whoever aids and abets . . .," without any specific listing of different kinds of support? What are the legal consequences of retaining the list or of eliminating it?

14. With respect to the questions posed in the previous note, compare the interpretative issue(s) relating to material support for a terrorist organization that were addressed in a different legal context by the court in Sesay v. Attorney General, 787 F.3d 215 (3d Cir. 2015):

Under the Immigration and Nationality Act ("INA"), an alien seeking asylum must demonstrate either (i) proof of past persecution, or (ii) a well-founded fear of future persecution in his home country "on account of race, religion, nationality, membership in a particular social group, or political opinion."

. . . Regardless of whether an alien demonstrates he is eligible for relief, he will be deemed inadmissible and ineligible for asylum or withholding of removal if he has engaged in terrorist activities, including the provision of material support for terrorist groups. 8 U.S.C. §§ 1158(b)(2)(A)(v), 1182(a)(3)(B)(i)(I), 1231(b)(3)(B), 1227(a)(4)(B).

. . .

The facts relevant here date back to early 2001, the eleventh year of what is widely recognized as a brutal civil war in Sierra Leone. . . . Sesay lived with his family in the country's capital, Freetown. One night in early 2001, three rebels from the Revolutionary United Front ("RUF") forcibly entered Sesay's home and demanded he join the RUF. When he refused, and while his parents pleaded for his safety, the rebels blindfolded him and took him away. . . .

Because Sesay was untrained in weaponry, the rebels forced him instead to provide menial assistance. Specifically, on approximately five occasions, he entered the Sierra Leone jungle with the rebels during active fighting. RUF trucks, however, had trouble traversing the jungle terrain. As a result, the rebels forced Sesay and others to carry their weapons, ammunition, drinking water, and food, and to load and unload these provisions from the trucks. Sesay complied under supervision of an armed guard.

. . .

The INA prevents an alien from receiving a grant of asylum or withholding of removal if that alien has engaged in, is engaged in, or is likely to engage in terrorism. . . . Engaging in terrorist activities, for example, includes "commit[ting] an act that the actor knows, or reasonably should know, affords material support . . . . to a terrorist organization . . . or to any member of such an organization, unless the actor can demonstrate by clear and convincing evidence that the actor did not know, and should not reasonably have known, that the organization was a terrorist organization." 8 U.S.C. § 1182(a)(3)(B)(iv)(VI).

. . .

. . . [T]he BIA and Courts of Appeals have repeatedly upheld findings that an alien's support was material, even if it was relatively low-level. See Bojnoordi v. Holder, 757 F.3d 1075, 1078 (9th Cir.2014) (upholding finding of material support because the alien "passed out flyers, wrote articles, and trained [a terrorist group's] members on the use of guns in the mountains outside Tehran, knowing that this training would further [the terrorist group's] goals"); Viegas v. Holder, 699 F.3d 798, 803 (4th Cir.2012) (upholding finding of material support because the alien "paid dues and hung posters" for a terrorist group); Barahona v. Holder, 691 F.3d 349, 351–52, 356 (4th Cir.2012) (upholding finding of material support because the alien, under threat, allowed terrorists to use his kitchen, gave them directions through the jungle, and occasionally allowed them to stay overnight); Haile, 658 F.3d at 1129 (upholding finding of material support because the alien collected funds, passed along secret documents and supplied the terrorist organization with sugar, shoes, and cigarettes); Hussain v. Mukasey, 518 F.3d 534, 538 (7th

Cir.2008) (upholding finding of material support because the alien recruited and solicited funds for a terrorist group); In Re S-K-, 23 I. & N. Dec. 936, 945–46 (BIA 2006) (upholding finding of material support because the alien contributed a total of 1,100 Singapore dollars to a terrorist group).

In the face of this case law, Sesay struggles to explain why his actions do not qualify as material support. His argument seems to be that the support he provided was so small in size that it was not "material," pursuant to the plain meaning of that word. See, e.g., Black's Law Dictionary 1124 (10th ed.2014) (defining material as "[h]aving some logical connection with the consequential facts" and "[o]f such a nature that knowledge of the item would affect a person's decision-making; significant; essential").

The BIA and Courts of Appeals have not squarely addressed whether a de minimis exception exists in the statute, although the BIA has held in a well-reasoned, not precedential opinion that assistance must be more than de minimis in order to give "material" some independent effect. See In Re: * * *, 2009 WL 9133770, at *2 (BIA July 10, 2009) (observing that even if the items taken from the alien, including "one packed lunch and the equivalent of about $4 U.S. dollars, which the terrorists expressly stated would be used to buy beer," constituted " 'support' for the terrorists, it cannot be said to be material"). We too, have held that "material" must be ascribed some meaning. See Singh-Kaur, 385 F.3d at 298 (examining Black's Law Dictionary definition of the word).

We need not define the outer boundaries of materiality today, however, because we conclude that Sesay's actions exceeded a de minimis threshold. That is, if providing food and setting up tents at religious meetings constituted material support in Singh-Kaur, 385 F.3d at 298–301, then so too does carrying weapons and ammunition for a terrorist group during a brutally violent conflict. [The court also ruled that even if the alien acted involuntarily in providing material support to a terrorist group, he was precluded from obtaining asylum or the withholding of removal,]

D. INCHOATENESS ISSUES

As mentioned in the Introduction to this chapter, the material support offenses are typically based on conduct which is inchoate with respect to its object crime, that is it takes place at a point in time prior to the commission of the object crime, and the object crime need not be committed. So what happens when another inchoate basis for criminal liability, either attempt or conspiracy, is combined with a material support offense, which itself is inchoate—that is, there are two levels of inchoateness?

UNITED STATES V. FARHANE

634 F. 3d 127 (2d Cir. 2011)

I.   Background

. . .

C.   2005: Shah and Sabir Swear Allegiance to al Qaeda and 4Attempt To Provide Material Support

For most of the time between May 2004 and May 2005, Sabir 34was out of the United States, working at a Saudi military hospital in Riyadh. On May 20, 2005, during a visit to New York, Sabir met with Saeed and Agent Soufan at Shah's Bronx apartment. Sabir told Soufan that he would soon be returning to Riyadh. He expressed interest in meeting with mujahideen operating in Saudi Arabia and agreed to provide medical assistance to any who were wounded. He suggested that he was ideally situated to provide such assistance because he would have a car in Riyadh and "carte blanche" to move freely about the city.

To ensure that Shah and Sabir were, in fact, knowingly proffering support for terrorism, Soufan stated that the purpose of "our war, . . . our jihad" is to "[e]xpel the infidels from the Arabian peninsula," and he repeatedly identified "Sheikh Osama" (in context a clear reference to Osama bin Laden) as the leader of that effort. Shah quickly agreed to the need for war to "[e]xpel the Jews and the Christians from the Arabian Peninsula," while Sabir observed that those fighting such a war were "striving in the way of Allah" and "most deserving" of his help.

To permit mujahideen needing medical assistance to contact him in Riyadh, Sabir provided Soufan with his personal and work telephone numbers. When Shah and Soufan noted that writing down this contact information might create a security risk, Sabir encoded the numbers using a code provided by Soufan.

Sabir and Shah then participated in bayat, a ritual in which each swore an oath of allegiance to al Qaeda, promising to serve as a "soldier of Islam" and to protect "brothers on the path of Jihad" and "the path of al Qaeda." The men further swore obedience to "the guardians of the pledge," whom Soufan expressly identified as "Sheikh Osama," i.e., Osama bin Laden, and his second in command, "Doctor Ayman Zawahiri."

D.   Prosecution and Conviction

Shah and Sabir were arrested on May 28, 2005, and thereafter indicted in the Southern District of New York on charges that between October 2003 and May 2005, they (1) conspired to provide material support or resources to the terrorist organization al Qaeda,; and (2) provided or attempted to provide such support. . . .

After Shah pleaded guilty on April 4, 2007, to Count One of the indictment, trial against Sabir commenced on April 24. On May 21, 2007, the jury found Sabir guilty on both the conspiratorial and substantive charges against him, and, on November 28, 2007, the district court sentenced him principally to 300 months' incarceration. This appeal followed.

II. Discussion

. . .

B. The Trial Evidence Was Sufficient To Support Sabir's Conviction

. . .

1. Count One: Conspiracy

In challenging his conviction for conspiracy to provide material support to a known terrorist organization, Sabir contends principally that the government failed to prove the existence of an agreement to violate § 2339B. We are not persuaded. . . .

Testimonial evidence established that Shah and Sabir had long voiced interest in supporting jihad and mujahideen. See, e.g., Trial Tr. at 193–96 (reporting Shah preaching jihad and support for Osama bin Laden in late 1990s at Poughkeepsie mosque); id. at 287 (recounting Sabir's 2003 conversation with mujahideen fighter inquiring how Sabir could help with jihad). It is against this background that a jury would listen to the recorded conversation of March 4, 2004, in which Shah proposed to a federal undercover agent that Shah and Sabir—close friends for 25 years—join al Qaeda as "a pair, me and a doctor," to support that organization's pursuit of jihad. More significantly, during the May 20, 2005 meeting at which Shah and Sabir formally swore allegiance and promised support to al Qaeda, Shah by providing al Qaeda members with martial arts training and Sabir by treating wounded al Qaeda members in Riyadh, Sabir acknowledged that he and Shah had talked "for a long time" about supporting jihad. Sabir plainly viewed his and Shah's actions at the May 20 meeting as part of their common agreement. When Agent Soufan observed that neither man was obligated to support al Qaeda, Sabir responded that to fail to do so would be to "abandon[ ] my brother (Shah)" with respect to "the very thing we agreed upon . . . in the first place.".

Accordingly, we identify no merit in Sabir's sufficiency challenge to his conviction for conspiracy to provide material support to a known terrorist organization.

2. Count Two: Attempt

Equally meritless is Sabir's argument that the evidence was insufficient to support his conviction for attempting to provide material support to a known foreign terrorist organization. A conviction for attempt requires proof that a defendant (a) had the intent to commit the object crime and (b) engaged in conduct amounting to a substantial step towards its commission. a. Intent

Sabir does not challenge the sufficiency of the evidence establishing his intent to provide material support to a foreign terrorist organization. Nor could he. In addition to Sabir's statements already quoted in this opinion, which constitute powerful evidence of the requisite intent, the following transcript excerpts from the May 20, 1995 meeting further support this element.

After Sabir advised that his work in a Riyadh military hospital would put him in Saudi Arabia for two years, Agent Soufan stated that Sabir could help al Qaeda "[a]s a doctor . . . as a Mujahid." Sabir not only signaled assent, he emphasized a need to "feel sure within myself that if I make a certain move, that move is going to be effective." To provide that assurance, Agent Soufan clarified how a doctor could be helpful to al Qaeda's pursuit of jihad. He stated that Osama bin Laden himself had told Soufan that "we need doctors if they are trusted." Soufan explained that "brothers" sometimes get "hurt with a bullet" during "training" and in "operation[s]. Because they cannot "go to a hospital," the organization needs "doctor brothers . . . to protect them . . . [to] keep the other brothers healthy." Sabir readily agreed to provide that support, stating, "Let me give you another number," whereupon he supplied his personal mobile telephone number, which, with Soufan's assistance, he rendered into code. Sabir understood that the purpose of the code was to conceal the fact that he was working for al Qaeda: Persons who learn the number "may not . . . understand [its] significance. . . . They may not even recognize it as a telephone number." He also understood that the coded number would be provided to a trusted al Qaeda operative, who would identify himself as "Mus'ab" when contacting Sabir on behalf of a wounded jihadist. Sabir responded to this information, "God willing."

Still later in the conversation, when Agent Soufan emphasized to Sabir that he could decline to treat mujahideen if he was not committed to al Qaeda's goals, Sabir made plain that he had no reservations about using his medical expertise to support al Qaeda: "I will [do what]ever I can do for the sake of God. . . . This is my job . . . the best I can do is to benefit those people . . . who are striving in the way of Allah. . . . [T]hese are the ones that are most deserving of the help." When Soufan further stated that it was difficult to take mujahideen to a hospital for treatment, Sabir emphasized that his military identification allowed him to travel freely around Saudi Arabia, thereby suggesting that he could go to the injured person. "[I]t's almost like carte blanche. . . . It's like you can go where you want to go with this. . . . And anybody that sees it, they don't touch you." Later, Soufan sought to confirm this understanding, stating "[t]hat ID will be very good for you . . . because you can definitely help mujahideen now," to which Sabir responded, "Yes, yes."

With evidence of his intent thus clearly established, Sabir focuses his sufficiency challenge on the "substantial step" element of attempt.

b.   Substantial Step

(1) The "Substantial Step" Requirement Expands Attempt Beyond the Common Law

The "substantial step" requirement for attempt derives from the American Law Institute's Model Penal Code, which in the early 1960s sought to "widen the ambit of attempt liability." United States v. Ivic, 700 F.2d 51, 66 (2d Cir.1983) (Friendly, J.) (citing Model Penal Code § 5.01(1)(c) (Proposed Official Draft 1962)), overruled on other grounds by National Org. for Women, Inc. v. Scheidler, 510 U.S. 249, 254–55, 262, 114 S.Ct. 798, 127 L.Ed.2d 99 (1994). Previously, at common law, attempt had been limited to conduct close to the completion of the intended crime. . . . By requiring proof only of a "substantial step" in furtherance of the intended crime, the Model Code ushered in a broader view of attempt.

This court effectively adopted the Model Code's formulation of attempt in United States v. Stallworth, 543 F.2d 1038, 1040–41 (2d Cir.1976). . . .Thus, a "substantial step" must be "something more than mere preparation, yet may be less than the last act necessary before the actual commission of the substantive crime." It is conduct " 'planned to culminate' " in the commission of the substantive crime being attempted. United States v. Ivic, 700 F.2d at 66 (quoting Model Penal Code § 5.01(c) (Proposed Official Draft 1962)).16

(2) Identifying a Substantial Step by Reference to the Crime Being Attempted

While the parameters of the substantial step requirement are simply stated, they do not always provide bright lines for application. This is not surprising; the identification of a substantial step, like the identification of attempt itself, is necessarily a matter " 'of degree,' " . . .that can vary depending on " 'the particular facts of each case' " viewed in light of the crime charged, Thus, substantial-step analysis necessarily begins with a proper understanding of the crime being attempted.

For example, in United States v. Delvecchio, 816 F.2d 859 (2d Cir.1987), a case frequently cited as illustrative of actions insufficient to demonstrate attempt, the substantive crime at issue was possession of a large quantity of heroin. We held that a substantial step to commit that crime was not established by proof that defendants had met with suppliers, agreed on terms, and provided their beeper numbers. Such evidence, at most, established a "verbal agreement," which, "without more, is insufficient as a matter of law to support an attempt[ed possession] conviction." Id. at 862. In so concluding, we noted that what was missing was any act to effect possession, such as acquisition, or attempted acquisition, of the purchase money, or travel to the agreed-on purchase site. See id.

The crime here at issue, however, is of a quite different sort. Sabir was charged with attempting to provide material support for terrorism. Whereas an attempt to possess focuses on a defendant's efforts to acquire, an attempt to provide focuses on his efforts to supply, a distinction that necessarily informs an assessment of what conduct will manifest a substantial step towards the charged objective. Thus, while an agreement to purchase drugs from a supplier is not a substantial step sufficient to convict for attempted possession, such an agreement to acquire might constitute a substantial step when the crime at issue is attempted distribution, . . .

Further important to a substantial-step assessment is an understanding of the underlying conduct proscribed by the crime being attempted. The conduct here at issue, material support to a foreign terrorist organization, is different from drug trafficking and any number of activities (e.g., murder, robbery, fraud) that are criminally proscribed because they are inherently harmful. The material support statute criminalizes a range of conduct that may not be harmful in itself but that may assist, even indirectly, organizations committed to pursuing acts of devastating harm. Thus, as the Supreme Court recently observed, the very focus of the material support statute is "preventative" in that it "criminalizes not terrorist attacks themselves, but aid that makes the attacks more likely to occur." Holder v. Humanitarian Law Project, 130 S.Ct. at 2728. Accordingly, while a substantial step to commit a robbery must be conduct planned clearly to culminate in that particular harm, a substantial step towards the provision of material support need not be planned to culminate in actual terrorist harm, but only in support—even benign support—for an organization committed to such harm.

(3) The Evidence Manifests a Substantial Step Towards the Provision of Material Support in the Form of Personnel

. . .We conclude that the evidence was sufficient to support Sabir's conviction for attempting to provide material support in the form of personnel—specifically, himself—to work for al Qaeda as a doctor on-call to treat wounded jihadists in Saudi Arabia. . . . By coming to meet with a purported al Qaeda member on May 20, 1995; by swearing an oath of allegiance to al Qaeda; by promising to be on call in Saudi Arabia to treat wounded al Qaeda members; and by providing private and work contact numbers for al Qaeda members to reach him in Saudi Arabia whenever they needed treatment, Sabir engaged in conduct planned to culminate in his supplying al Qaeda with personnel, thereby satisfying the substantial step requirement.

(4)   The Dissent's Mistaken View of the Substantial Step Requirement

(a)   Sabir Did More Than Express a Radical Idea When He Produced Himself as a Doctor Sworn To Work Under the Direction of al Qaeda

In dissent, Chief Judge Dearie asserts that by upholding Sabir's attempt conviction on the record evidence, we approve punishing a defendant for radical thoughts rather than criminal deeds. We do no such thing. Sabir's words and actions on May 20, 1995, did more than manifest radical sympathies. See United States v. Crowley, 318 F.3d at 408 (observing that substantial step requirement ensures that attempt does not punish persons "for their thoughts alone"). By attending the May 20, 2005 meeting and committing to work under al-Qaeda's direction and control as an on-call doctor, Sabir physically produced the very personnel to be provided as material support for the terrorist organization: himself. . . .

Viewed in this context, Sabir's oath of allegiance to al Qaeda evidenced more than "mere membership" in that terrorist organization. . .Sabir's purpose in swearing bayat was to formalize his promise to work as a doctor under the organization's direction and control. That is most certainly evidence of a crime: the charged crime of attempting to provide material support to terrorism in the form of personnel. See 18 U.S.C. § 2339B(h) (clarifying that what is proscribed is the provision of personnel "to work under" the "direction or control" of a terrorist organization). Further, by providing his contact numbers, Sabir took a step essential to provide al Qaeda with personnel in the form of an on-call doctor: he provided the means by which mujahideen in Riyadh could reach that doctor at any time, day or night, that they needed emergency treatment. From the totality of these facts, a reasonable jury could have concluded that on May 20, 2005, Sabir crossed the line from simply professing radical beliefs or joining a radical organization to attempting a crime, specifically, Sabir's provision of himself as personnel to work under the direction and control of al Qaeda.

(b)   The Provision of Personnel and the Subsequent Provision of Expert Services by Such Personnel Are Distinct Forms of Material Support

Chief Judge Dearie submits that the time and distance to be traveled by Sabir before he actually provided any medical treatment to al Qaeda warriors was too great to permit a jury to find that his actions constituted a substantial step towards commission of the charged crime. This mistakenly equates the provision of personnel to a terrorist organization with the subsequent provision of services by that personnel, a misapprehension that pervades the dissent and informs its conclusion that Sabir stands guilty "for an offense that he did not commit." While it may frequently be the case that a defendant who intends to provide a terrorist organization with personnel also intends for the personnel to provide the organization with services, § 2339A(b)(1) specifically recognizes "personnel" and "services"—particularly services in the form of "expert advice and assistance," such as medical treatment—as distinct types of material support. Thus, even if the provision (or attempted provision) of these two forms of material support may be simultaneous in some cases, it may not be in others. For that reason, evidence sufficient to demonstrate a substantial step towards the provision of personnel may not always be sufficient to demonstrate a substantial step towards the personnel's provision of services. Whether or not Sabir's May 20, 2005 actions were a substantial step in the provision of expert medical services to terrorists, we conclude that they were a substantial step in the provision of Sabir himself as personnel.

To illustrate, assume that, instead of offering himself as an on-call doctor to al Qaeda, Sabir had recruited a doctor who was, in all respects, identically situated to himself. Assume further that Sabir then brought that doctor to a meeting in New York where the doctor swore allegiance to al Qaeda, promised a supposed al Qaeda member that he would work as an on-call doctor for the organization, and gave the member contact numbers so that wounded jihadists in Saudi Arabia could reach the doctor when necessary. Even the dissent concedes that such evidence would be sufficient to prove Sabir "guilty of attempting to provide personnel," although the recruited doctor would not provide actual medical services until some time in the future and after he traveled from New York to Saudi Arabia. Because Sabir would be guilty of attempting to provide personnel in the circumstances hypothesized, we think it necessarily follows that he is equally guilty on the record facts. He is guilty of attempting to provide himself as personnel to al Qaeda on May 20, 2005, even if he is not yet guilty of attempting to provide medical services to that organization.

In concluding otherwise, Chief Judge Dearie submits that the recruiter in the hypothetical "has done something. He has provided a service to the organization." By contrast, he submits that Sabir "has done nothing more than conspire." We disagree. Section 2339(B) criminalizes providing personnel through self-recruitment (i.e., volunteering oneself to serve under the direction of a terrorist organization) no less than through recruitment (securing another person to serve under such direction).23 By volunteering himself as an on-call doctor for al Qaeda, Sabir rendered, or attempted to render, that organization as much of a service in producing personnel as the recruiter who solicited a doctor for that purpose. To hold otherwise would be to apply a different standard of sufficiency to the provision of personnel depending on whether the person being provided is oneself or another, a distinction for which there is no support in a statute that equally proscribes the provision of oneself or another to work under the direction of a terrorist organization.

. . .

In sum, we conclude that the totality of the evidence was more than sufficient to permit a reasonable jury to find that on May 20, 2005, Sabir took a substantial step intended to culminate in the provision of himself as personnel to work under the direction of al Qaeda. Accordingly, we uphold his convictions for both conspiring and attempting to provide material support to a foreign terrorist organization.

QUESTIONS AND NOTES

1.   See U.S. Department of Justice Press Release dated Oct. 19, 2015, https://www.justice.gov/opa/pr/suburban-chicago-man-sentenced-15-years-prison-attempting-join-jabhat-al-nusrah-syria:

> Tounisi was arrested at O'Hare International Airport in Chicago in April 2013 as he attempted to board a flight to Istanbul, Turkey. Tounisi had spent four months conducting online research related to overseas travel and violent jihad, focusing specifically on Syria and the violent Jabhat al-Nusrah terrorist organization.

> Tounisi pleaded guilty in 2015 to one count of attempting to provide material support to a foreign terrorist organization. According to his plea agreement, Tounisi in early 2013 made online contact with an individual he believed to be a recruiter for Jabhat al-Nusrah. He and the purported recruiter exchanged a series of emails, during which Tounisi shared his plan to go to Syria by way of Turkey, as well as his willingness to fight for the jihadist cause, the plea agreement states. Unbeknownst to Tounisi, the purported recruiter was actually an FBI employee.

> Tounisi, a U.S. citizen, requested an expedited passport and purchased an airline ticket for the flight from Chicago to Istanbul. He arrived at O'Hare on the evening of April 19, 2013, and was arrested after passing through security in the international terminal.

> Tounisi was sentenced to 15 years in prison, and a lifetime of supervised release.

2.   Given the facts in the previous note, consider what Tounisi actually did: He obtained an expedited passport and purchased an airline ticket for travel to Istanbul. How much of the crime he was charged with was based on his conduct and how much on what he said and planned to do, that is, intended to do? In the past couple of years, there have been in the range of three dozen federal criminal prosecutions involving facts approximating those in the Tounisi prosecution. It appears that almost all of these cases have been resolved through pleas of guilty. But see United States v. Mehanna, 735 F.3d 32 (1st Cir. 2013), infra.

3.   Might Tounisi have been guilty of the attempt offense after he ordered an expedited passport? Or after he bought the airline ticket? How far

back in the chronology leading up to the completed offense might a charge of attempted providing of material support, namely, himself, be sustainable?

4. Might Tounisi have been charged with conspiracy to violate the material support statute?

5. Does the decision in the Farhane case support the result in Tounisi and the similar cases prosecuted by the government? What are the differences, if any, between Farhane and Tounisi? Which establishes the stronger basis for criminal liability?

6. Are there any constitutional arguments that Tounisi or Farhane might have raised to contest the charges?

7. For a case in which the defendants actually traveled to Yemen in search of a training camp that would enable them to acquire training for engaging in jihaad, see United States v. Mehanna, 735 F.3d 32 (1st Cir. 2013):

> Counts 1 through 3 (the conspiracy and material support charges) were based on two separate clusters of activities. The first cluster centered on the defendant's travel to Yemen. We briefly describe that trip.
>
> On February 1, he flew from Boston to the United Arab Emirates with his associates, Kareem Abuzahra and Ahmad Abousamra. Abuzahra returned to the United States soon thereafter but the defendant and Abousamra continued on to Yemen in search of a terrorist training camp. They remained there for a week but were unable to locate a camp. The defendant then returned home, while Abousamra eventually reached Iraq.

The Mehanna case also involved an alternative theory for concluding that the defendant had provided or conspired to provide material support:

> The second cluster of activities was translation-centric. In 2005, the defendant began to translate Arab-language materials into English and post his translations on a website—at-Tibyan—that comprised an online community for those sympathetic to al-Qa'ida and Salafi-Jihadi perspectives. Website members shared opinions, videos, texts, and kindred materials in online forums. At least some offerings that the defendant translated constituted al-Qa'ida-generated media and materials supportive of al-Qa'ida and/or jihad.

8. The Mehanna case also illustrates a point touched upon briefly in note 2, supra—that material support charges generally and attempt or conspiracy combined with material support charges specifically, rely heavily on evidence that shows the criminal mens rea of the defendant(s) since the conduct is often ambiguous with respect to the criminal purpose. Thus for example, in Mehanna, the conduct proved involved travel to Yemen, and the accused defended on the ground that he was a scholar who traveled to Yemen in aid of scholarly pursuits:

The defendant argues that the only reasonable interpretation of his Yemen trip and the activities surrounding it is an innocent one: he sojourned to Yemen solely for the purpose of studying there. He describes himself as a devoted scholar of Islam and asserts that he visited Yemen, specifically, because the purest form of Arabic is spoken there. In support, he reminds us that he toured a school while in the country.

The government responded with evidence indicating the defendant's culpable state of mind:

The government's evidence of the defendant's specific intent with respect to his Yemen trip included his own actions, discussions with others, coconspirator statements, and materials that the defendant either kept on his computer or shared on the Internet. The defendant contends that this evidence, in the aggregate, showed nothing more than his participation in activities protected by the First Amendment (e.g., discussing politics and religion, consuming media related to those topics, and associating with certain individuals and groups) and, thus, could not support a finding of guilt. But the defendant is looking at the evidence through rose-colored glasses. We think it virtually unarguable that rational jurors could find that the defendant and his associates went abroad to enlist in a terrorist training camp.

On this point, the defendant's own statements are highly probative. His coconspirators testified that the defendant persistently stated his belief that engaging in jihad was "a duty upon a Muslim if he's capable of performing it," and that this duty included committing violence. The evidence further showed that, following United States intervention in Iraq, the defendant concluded "that America was at war with Islam," and saw American "soldiers as being valid targets."

Acting upon these views, the defendant and his associates—as early as 2001—discussed seeking out a terrorist training camp. Following these discussions, the defendant expressed interest in receiving military-type training in order to participate in jihad. The defendant made clear that he wished to engage in jihad if he "ever had the chance" and that he and his associates "would make a way to go." Together, they "discussed the different ways people could get into Iraq, the different training camps."

In these conversations, the defendant voiced his desire to fight against the United States military forces in Iraq. He and his associates went "in depth on details" regarding the logistics of reaching such a terrorist training camp.

Coconspirator testimony shined a bright light on the defendant's intent. This testimony made pellucid that the defendant and his comrades traveled to Yemen "for the purpose of finding a terrorist training camp" and "[e]ventually ... get[ting] into Iraq." The defendant's particular interest in Iraq was because it was "an area that was being attacked." He took the position that "there was an obligation for Muslims to stand up and fight against invasion of Iraq and the U.S. forces in Iraq."

The defendant attempts to characterize these remarks as mere political speech. The jury, however, was entitled to draw a different inference: that the defendant's comments were evidence of the formation and implementation of a scheme to go abroad, obtain training, join with al-Qa'ida, and wage war against American soldiers fighting in Iraq.

The timing of the trip and the furtiveness with which the defendant acted provide circumstantial support for this conclusion. The record contains evidence that the defendant abruptly suspended his studies in Massachusetts during the school year and kept his plans hidden from his parents. Prior to his departure, he gave his brother a bag of personal belongings and asked his brother to dispose of them. These belongings included "something about how to make a bomb."

We note that the defendant and his associates purchased round-trip airline tickets. In the travelers' own words, however, the return portions were for use "[i]f things didn't work out," as well as to avoid raising the sort of suspicion often associated with one-way ticketing. And Abuzahra testified at trial that, notwithstanding the return ticket, he did not expect to return to the United States because "[t]he purpose of . . . going was to basically fight in a war."

From this and other evidence, a rational jury could conclude that the defendant did not intend to return to the United States after leaving for Yemen. This intent dovetails with the defendant's self-proclaimed jihadi agenda and makes the purpose of the trip apparent.

. . .

E. MENS REA ISSUES UNDER §§ 2339B AND 2339A

The Supreme Court's decision in Humanitarian Law Project, supra, inter alia, addressed the mens rea required under § 2339B, concluding that neither the statute nor the Constitution required specific intent. Most earlier lower court decisions agreed, but there were some outliers including the following opinion which is one of the numerous opinions in the HLP series of lower court decisions handed down prior to the time the case reached the Supreme Court.

Note: After the issuance of the following three judge panel opinion in the Humanitarian Law Project case, a motion to rehear the matter en banc was granted, and this three judge opinion was vacated. The instruction accompanying the notice that the case was to be reheard en banc indicated that the three judge opinion was not to be cited except to the extent it was adopted by the court in the en banc opinion. 382 F. 3d 1154 (9th Cir. 2004). Despite the fact that the opinion that follows has been vacated, it is useful to review it since it helps to understand some of the amendments made to § 2339B by the IRTPA, enacted in 2004.

HUMANITARIAN LAW PROJECT V. U.S. DEPARTMENT OF JUSTICE

352 F.3d 382 (9th Cir. 2003) (vacated by 393 F.3d 902)

Appeal from the United States District Court for the Central District of California AUDREY B. COLLINS, DISTRICT JUDGE, Presiding. Before: PREGERSON, THOMAS, and RAWLINSON, CIRCUIT JUDGES. PREGERSON, CIRCUIT JUDGE.

In 1996, President Clinton signed into law the Antiterrorism and Effective Death Penalty Act of 1996 ("AEDPA"). Two provisions of AEDPA, section 302 and section 303, codified at 8 U.S.C. § 1189 and 18 U.S.C. § 2339B, authorize the Secretary of State ("Secretary") to designate an organization as a "foreign terrorist organization," and make it a crime with a maximum penalty of life in prison for a person to provide "material support or resources" [hereinafter "material support"] to a designated organization, respectively. This case addresses the question whether a criminal prosecution under 18 U.S.C. § 2339B requires the government to prove as an element of the offense that the defendant knew the organization had been designated by the Secretary as a foreign terrorist organization, or at least knew of the organization's unlawful activities leading to its designation.

Plaintiffs are legal and social service organizations and two individuals who seek to provide "material support" to the non-violent humanitarian and political activities of Kurdish and Tamil organizations the Secretary designated as "foreign terrorist organizations." Each of the plaintiffs has a history of donating money and services to support the designated organizations' humanitarian work, which assists refugees and ethnic minorities displaced by decades of conflict in securing the basic necessities for human life. Plaintiffs no longer provide such support in fear of criminal sanctions under 18 U.S.C. § 2339B.

. . .

We will, however, address plaintiffs' recently asserted Fifth Amendment due process challenge on this appeal, and hold that 18 U.S.C. § 2339B, by not requiring proof of personal guilt, raises serious Fifth Amendment due process concerns. But we conclude that there is no need to address those constitutional concerns because we construe 18 U.S.C.

§ 2339B to require proof that a person charged with violating the statute had knowledge of the organization's designation or knowledge of the unlawful activities that caused it to be so designated.

. . .

At issue in this case is 18 U.S.C. § 2339B, which makes it a crime punishable for up to life imprisonment if a person provides "material support or resources" to a designated organization:

The Kurdistan Workers Party, a.k.a., Partiya Karkeran Kurdistan ("PKK") and the Liberation Tigers of Tamil Eelam ("LTTE") have engaged in a broad range of activities, from terrorist violence to peaceful political advocacy to humanitarian aid. The plaintiffs in this case, six organizations and two United States citizens, seek to support only the humanitarian and peaceful political pursuits of the PKK and the LTTE. On October 8, 1997, the Secretary designated the PKK and LTTE, along with 28 other organizations, as foreign terrorist organizations. 62 Fed.Reg. 52,650–51 (Oct. 8, 1997). Since that date, plaintiffs have withheld their support for the non-violent humanitarian and political activities of the PKK and LTTE because they fear that they would be investigated and prosecuted criminally under 18 U.S.C. § 2339B.

. . .

As stated above, plaintiffs have raised one additional constitutional challenge to 18 U.S.C. § 2339B in their briefs to this court. . . . That challenge is that § 2339B runs afoul of the Fifth Amendment's right to due process of law because the statute does not require proof that a person charged with violating the statute had a guilty intent when he or she provided "material support" to a designated organization. Because we may, in our discretion, resolve a pure issue of law raised for the first time on appeal to this court when "injustice might otherwise result," we shall address the plaintiffs' Fifth Amendment claim.

A.

In Scales, the Supreme Court stated that:

In our jurisprudence guilt is personal, and when the imposition of punishment on a status or on conduct can only be justified by reference to the relationship of that status or conduct to other concededly criminal activity . . . that relationship must be sufficiently substantial to satisfy the concept of personal guilt in order to withstand attack under the Due Process Clause.

367 U.S. at 224–225, 81 S.Ct. 1469 The Supreme Court in Scales announced this requirement of personal guilt 42 years ago in considering the constitutionality of the Smith Act, which prohibited membership in a Communist organization or any other organization advocating the

overthrow of the government by force or violence. Congress enacted the Smith Act out of the McCarthy-era belief that the "Communist Party [was] a group bent on overthrowing the Government by force and violence . . . and establishing a totalitarian dictatorship in the United States." Id. at 281, 81 S.Ct. 1469 (Brennan, J. dissenting).

Scales established the test, stated above, to determine whether holding a person culpable for his or her relationship to an organization is consonant with due process; Scales analyzed the relationship between a person's "status or conduct" with an organization and "the underlying substantive illegal conduct in order to determine whether that relationship is indeed too tenuous to permit its use as the basis of criminal liability." The Court recognized that a person who is a merely a member of an organization does not necessarily share in the community of intent of the organization. The Court found, however, that

> [w]hatever difficulties might be thought to inhere in ascribing a course of criminal conduct to an abstract entity are certainly cured, so far as any particular defendant is concerned, by the requirement of proof that he knew that the organization engages in criminal advocacy, and that it was his purpose to further that criminal advocacy.

Thus, the Court concluded that the Smith Act satisfied the due process right to "personal guilt" because the Court read the statute to reach only " 'active' members having also a guilty knowledge and intent." In short, the Court held that the Smith Act survived a due process challenge because the Court interpreted the statute to require proof that an individual member intended to further the unlawful ends of the Communist Party.

We have applied the due process right to proof of personal guilt to cases where a person was convicted because of the link of his or her conduct to a proscribed organization.

. . .

B.

We are called upon to analyze a statute that presumes that a person acts with guilty intent whenever that person provides material support to a designated organization. In this context, Scales, . . . require[s] us to parse the purpose, intent, and acts of the person and of the designated organization.

We believe that serious due process concerns would be raised were we to accept the argument that a person who acts without knowledge of critical information about a designated organization presumably acts consistently with the intent and conduct of that designated organization. . . . The act or conduct that the statute proscribes is the act or conduct of a person providing "material support" to a designated organization that engages in both humanitarian and unlawful activities. At oral argument, the government told us that it could convict a person under § 2339B if he or she donates support to a designated organization even if he or she does not know the organization is so designated. That is, according to the government, it can convict an individual who gives money to a designated organization that solicits money at their doorstep so long as the organization identifies itself by name. It is no defense, according to the government, that the organization describes to the donor only its humanitarian work to provide basic services to support victims displaced and orphaned by conflict, or to defend the cultural and linguistic rights of ethnic minorities. And, the government further contends, it is no defense that a donor contributes money solely to support the lawful, humanitarian purposes of a designated organization. But we believe that to attribute the intent to commit unlawful acts punishable by life imprisonment to persons who acted with innocent intent—in this context, without critical information about the relevant organization—contravenes the Fifth Amendment's requirement of "personal guilt."

. . .

C.

In construing a criminal statute to determine whether Congress intended to require mens rea as an element of an offense, we have long adhered to the principle that "[t]he existence of a mens rea is the rule of, rather than the exception to, principles of Anglo-American criminal jurisprudence." This notion has deep foundations in Anglo-American common law as "indicated by Blackstone's sweeping statement that to constitute any crime there must first be a 'vicious will.'" Morissette v. United States, 342 U.S. 246, 251, 72 S.Ct. 240, 96 L.Ed. 288 (1952).

. . .

Morissette and its progeny teach us that we are to "construe [a criminal] statute in light of the fundamental principle that a person is not criminally responsible unless 'an evil-meaning mind' accompanies 'an evil-doing hand.'". . .

. . .

It "is a question of statutory construction," whether 18 U.S.C. § 2339B requires the government to prove that a person who provides "material support" to a designated organization knew of such designation or knew of the unlawful activities that caused it to be so designated. The Supreme Court has "long recognized that determining the mental state required for commission of a federal crime requires 'construction of the statute . . . and inference of the intent of Congress. " Thus, we look first to the language of the statute to determine the intent of Congress mindful that the federal judiciary "should not enlarge the reach of enacted crimes by constituting them from anything less than the incriminating components contemplated by the words used in the statute." Morissette, 342 U.S. at 263, 72 S.Ct. 240.

The language of 18 U.S.C. § 2339B does not in any way suggest that Congress intended to impose strict liability on individuals who donate "material support" to designated organizations. It is significant that Congress used the term "knowingly" to modify "provid[ing] material support or resources to a foreign terrorist organization." 18 U.S.C. § 2339B. . . . Indeed, the Supreme Court and our circuit have construed Congress' inclusion of the word "knowingly" to require proof of knowledge of the law and an intent to further the proscribed act. In Morissette, for example, the Court "used the background presumption of evil intent to conclude that the term 'knowingly' also required that the defendant have knowledge of the facts that made the taking a conversion—i.e., that the property belonged to the United States." . . .

   . . .

Applying these principles, we believe that when Congress included the term "knowingly" in § 2339B, it meant that proof that a defendant knew of the organization's designation as a terrorist organization or proof that a defendant knew of the unlawful activities that caused it to be so designated was required to convict a defendant under the statute . . .

   . . . As the government contended at oral argument, a donor to a proscribed organization could be convicted under the statute even if he or she was entirely unaware that the organization was designated as a terrorist organization. Read without a requirement that a defendant knew of the organization's designation or knew of the unlawful activities that caused it to be so designated, the statute could be used to punish moral innocents.

   . . .

   . . . [T]he maximum fifteen-year penalty under § 2339B is a severe penalty for punishing someone who acted with an innocent intent. . . . More troubling is that the statute provides for a maximum life term if "the death of any person results." 18 U.S.C. § 2339B(a). It is difficult to believe that Congress intended to impose a life sentence on a person who did not know that his or her support could go toward unlawful activities.

   . . .

D.

The Supreme Court's long-standing interpretation of the term "knowingly" directs us to read § 2339B to include a mens rea requirement. . . . Without the knowledge requirement described above, a person who simply sends a check to a school or orphanage in Tamil Eelam run by the LTTE could be convicted under the statute, even if that individual is not aware of the LTTE's designation or of any unlawful activities undertaken by the LTTE. Or, according to the government's interpretation of § 2339B, a woman who buys cookies from a bake sale outside of her grocery store to support displaced Kurdish refugees to find new homes could be held liable so long as the bake sale had a sign that said that the sale was sponsored by the PKK, without regard to her knowledge of the PKK's designation or other activities. Furthermore, the legislative history contains no indication that Congress intended to impose strict liability on persons who provide "material support" to designated organizations.

In light of the text of § 2339B, the Court's longstanding principles interpreting the word "knowingly" to indicate Congress' intent to include a mens rea requirement, and the due process concern earlier discussed, we read § 2339B to require proof of knowledge, either of an organization's designation or of the unlawful activities that caused it to be so designated. . . . Thus, to sustain a conviction under § 2339B, the government must prove beyond a reasonable doubt that the donor had knowledge that the organization was designated by the Secretary as a foreign terrorist organization or that the donor had knowledge of the organization's unlawful activities that caused it to be so designated.

    . . .

[RAWLINSON, CIRCUIT JUDGE, wrote a dissenting opinion.]

QUESTIONS AND NOTES

1.   In its original form § 2339A contained a mens rea element of "knowing or intending" that the material support being provided is to be used in the commission of specified offenses, while § 2339B contained a mens rea of "knowingly" providing material support to a foreign terrorist organization. Accordingly, both provisions established knowledge as the requisite mens rea. Neither statute expressly required a mens rea of purpose or intent. Recall the point made in the Introduction to this chapter, that traditional complicity has been interpreted by the majority of courts to require a mens rea of purpose or the equivalent.

2.   In Abrams' article on the material support offenses, quoted in the introductory materials, he offered the following explanation for why the specific categories of material support may have been listed in the statute:

> To appreciate why the statutory definition may have been drafted in the form of specific categories of support, we need to return to basic principles of accessorial liability, beginning with some quotations from an early draft of the Model Penal Code. In discussing the mens rea for complicity proposed in Tentative Draft No. 1 of the Code, the Comment stated:

The issue is whether knowingly facilitating the commission of a crime ought to be sufficient for complicity, absent a true purpose to advance the criminal end. . . .

The problem has had most attention in the federal courts where there is division of opinion as to the criterion that measures liability. The Second Circuit, speaking through Judge Learned Hand, has taken the position that the traditional definitions of complicity (aiding, abetting . . .) . . . carry an implication of purposive attitude towards it.

In this early Draft of the Model Penal Code, Professor Herbert Wechsler, the Reporter for the Code, rejected the idea that purposive aid should be an absolute prerequisite for complicity liability, instead concluding:

> . . . [W]hen a true purpose to further the crime is lacking, the draft requires that the accessorial behavior substantially facilitate commission of the crime . . . This qualification provides a basis for discrimination that should satisfy the common sense of justice."

In other words, something less than purpose, i.e. knowledge, can suffice where the aid that is provided is substantial in assisting the commission of the crime. Wechsler's innovative approach to complicity in Tentative Draft No. 1 of the Model Penal Code was not, however, accepted by the Council of the American Law Institute. Instead, the traditional approach was retained, that is, for complicity there must be a purpose to promote or facilitate the commission of the crime.

This bit of Model Penal Code history helps to put into perspective and provides us with a possible explanation for the approach taken by the drafters of §§ 2339A and 2339B. They wanted to broaden the reach of the statute since proving purpose might prove difficult in some cases where the imposition of liability might nevertheless be warranted. But a statute that simply made knowing aid a basis for serious criminal liability would be likely to meet opposition on the ground that it extended liability too far, encompassing, for example (as the same Comment to the Model Penal Code noted), the "minor employee" or "the vendor who supplies materials readily available upon the market." So it is arguable that what the drafters did— whether or not they had this in mind—was to adopt what was in fact a version of the original MPC complicity draft, basing liability on knowledge plus "substantial facilitation," but with a special twist. Rather than adopt a general formula of substantial aid or facilitation, they opted for a categorical approach to the aid/facilitation concept. On this view, "material support" is the rough equivalent of substantial facilitation but rather than use that general phrase, the concept is defined and delimited by a series of specific categories, namely, currency ... lodging, training, expert advice or assistance, ... etc.

3.   Are you persuaded by Abrams' explanation for why the material support offenses may have been constructed in this way? Consider how Abrams' theory fits with the constructions that the courts have given to the specific terms in the categorical list defining material support? If the courts had agreed with Abrams' explanation, should they have interpreted these terms differently?

4.   What are likely to be the practical consequences of the choices that the courts appear to have made in interpreting the specific terms in the categorical list defining material support? Do these choices represent sound law enforcement policy in dealing with terrorism?

5.   Taking into account the constructions given to the material support listing and the requisite mentes reae for the two material support offenses, how does the sweep of liability under these offenses compare with liability for similar conduct based on the crime of conspiracy? See Abrams article at 29–30.

6.   While the statutory language in § 2339A and § 2339B seems clearly to make a mens rea of knowledge sufficient, at least one lower court concluded that a mens rea for § 2339B of more than knowledge is constitutionally required. In United States v. Al-Arian, 308 F.Supp. 2d 1322 (M.D. Fla. 2004), the district judge read a specific intent element into § 2339B, stating:

> ... [T]he statute could likewise punish other innocent conduct, such as where a person in New York City (where the United Nations is located) gave a FTO member a ride from the airport to the United Nations before the member petitioned the United Nations. Such conduct could be punished as providing "transportation" to a FTO under Section 2339B. The end result ... is to render a substantial portion of Section 2339B unconstitutionally vague.

> But, it is not necessary to do such serious damage to the statute .... This Court concludes that it is more consistent with Congress's intent, which was to prohibit material support from FTOs to the "fullest possible basis," to imply a mens rea requirement to the "material support" element of Section 2339B(a)(1). Therefore, this Court concludes that to convict a defendant under Section 2339B(a)(1) the government must prove beyond a reasonable doubt that the defendant knew that: (a) the organization was a FTO or had committed unlawful activities that caused it to be so designated; and (b) what he was furnishing was "material support." To avoid Fifth Amendment personal guilt problems, this Court concludes that the government must show more than a defendant knew something was within a category of "material support" in order to meet (b). In order to meet (b), the government must show that the defendant knew (had a specific intent) that the support would further the illegal activities of a FTO.

This Court does not believe this burden is that great in the typical case. Often, such an intent will be easily inferred. For example, a jury could infer a specific intent to further the illegal activities of a FTO when a defendant knowingly provides weapons, explosives, or lethal substances to an organization that he knows is a FTO because of the nature of the support. Likewise, a jury could infer a specific intent when a defendant knows that the organization continues to commit illegal acts and the defendant provides funds to that organization knowing that money is fungible and, once received, the donee can use the funds for any purpose it chooses. That is, by its nature, money carries an inherent danger for furthering the illegal aims of an organization. Congress said as much when it found that FTOs were "so tainted by their criminal conduct that any contribution to such an organization facilitates that conduct."

This opinion in no way creates a safe harbor for terrorists or their supporters to try and avoid prosecution through utilization of shell "charitable organizations" or by directing money through the memo line of a check towards lawful activities. This Court believes that a jury can quickly peer through such facades when appropriate. This is especially true if other facts indicate a defendant's true intent, like where defendants or conspirators utilize codes or unusual transaction practices to transfer funds. Instead, this Court's holding works to avoid potential constitutional problems and fully accomplish congressional intent.

7. The 2004 amendments of § 2339B occurred after the opinions in the Al-Arian case, supra, were handed down, but before the trial of Al-Arian was completed. In instructions to the jury, the district court judge included a specific intent requirement, consistent with the opinion reproduced supra. Al-Arian was found not guilty on eight counts, and the jury failed to reach agreement on nine counts. Three of the not guilty verdicts involved § 2339B charges, but on the charge of conspiring to violate § 2339B, they failed to agree. Do you think that including a specific intent element in the jury instruction may have contributed to the jury verdict in the case? Are you persuaded by the judge's comment regarding the no-safe harbor-for-terrorists in the last paragraph of the Al-Arian opinion, supra?

8. Sami Al-Arian was not retried on the counts upon which the jury had disagreed. Instead, a settlement was reached with the government under the terms of which he pleaded guilty, was sentenced to a time-limited sentence and agreed to be deported at the end of serving the sentence. Press Release, Office of the U.S. Attorney, Middle Dist. of Fla., April 17, 2006. Specifically, Al-Arian was sentenced to 57 months in prison but was given credit for time already served which left a balance of 19 months. Subsequent to his release, he was subpoenaed in March, 2008, to testify before a federal grand jury in Virginia regarding an alleged "Muslim terror triangle" located in Northern Virginia. Al-Arian refused to testify. Accordingly, he was charged with criminal contempt in June, 2008 and in September, 2008, he was released on bond, subject to

house arrest. An issue in the case was whether requiring him to testify in the Virginia inquiry was precluded by the plea agreement in the Florida prosecution. The judge had scheduled a hearing in the matter in April, 2009, but the hearing was postponed. Finally in June, 2014, the government dropped the contempt case and initiated proceedings to deport Al-Arian. He was deported from the United States to Turkey in February, 2015.

9.   A substantial cohort of cases prosecuted under § 2339B has involved charges against individuals who raised funds to support foreign organizations that had been designated as FTO's. The defense that the funds were intended for the non-terrorist charitable activities wing of the organization has been generally rejected. See the Humanitarian Law Project case, supra. A case which presented a different kind of defense is United States v. Holy Land Foundation for Relief and Development, 2007 WL 1498813 (N.D.Tex. 2007):

> The defendants argue that counts 1–12 do not charge an offense under 18 U.S.C. § 2339B because those paragraphs accuse them of supporting organizations operated by or for Hamas but do not allege that the defendants supported Hamas directly. Section 2339B proscribes the knowing provision of "material support or resources to a foreign terrorist organization" as well as attempting or conspiring to provide such support if the person providing the support knows that the organization (1) is a "designated terrorist organization" that (2) has engaged or engages in "terrorist activity" or that (3) has engaged or engages in "terrorism," as those terms are defined by relevant statutes. 28 U.S.C. § 2339B(a)(1).

> Count one of the superseding indictment, in relevant part, charges the defendants with providing "material support and resources to the designated Foreign Terrorist Organization HAMAS by raising funds in the United States and elsewhere, and sending those funds to organizations and programs in the West Bank and Gaza, and elsewhere, which operated on behalf of, or under the control of, HAMAS." Similarly, counts two through twelve of the superseding indictment charge the defendants with knowingly providing or attempting to provide support to HAMAS by giving money to specific organizations "which operated on behalf of, or under the control of, HAMAS." The defendants contend this is insufficient because they did not give money directly to Hamas, and "[n]othing in the language of the statute proscribes providing material support to an organization 'acting on behalf of, or under the control of " 'a foreign terrorist organization. Defendant's Motion at 10. The court disagrees.

> The indictment charges the defendants with knowingly giving money to Hamas by giving it to organizations operated by and for Hamas. The defendants essentially ask this court to hold that it is lawful to support a terrorist organization as long as the money is funneled through a subsidiary or affiliate that has not been independently designated as a terrorist organization. Such a ruling

would completely eviscerate the statute by allowing anyone intelligent enough to launder donations to clandestinely give financial support to terrorist organizations without legal consequences. If the defendants intended that the organizations to whom they gave money should pass the money to Hamas—as the indictment alleges—then they violated the clear language of 28 U.S.C. § 2339B.

The defendants next contend that if their donations to alleged subsidiaries of Hamas violated the statute, then § 2339B is unconstitutional because "[n]othing in the language of the statute gives a person of common intelligence notice that he or she may be found guilty of violating that statute by providing humanitarian aid through organizations alleged (although not designated) to be associated with" a foreign terrorist organization. The defendants give insufficient credit to people of "common intelligence." It requires no extraordinary acumen to realize that funneling money to an organization operated by or on behalf of a specially designated terrorist organization with the intent that the money be passed on to the designated terrorist group would, at the very least, constitute an attempt to provide support or resources to the terrorist organization in contravention of § 2339B. The statute would be unconstitutional in its application to the defendants only if it sought to punish them for innocently giving money to organizations which they later learned were affiliated with Hamas. However, if the government is unable to prove that the defendants knew the groups to whom they gave money were affiliated with Hamas when they provided support, then the defendants cannot be found guilty under the terms of the statute. See 18 U.S.C. § 2339B(a)(1). Accordingly, § 2339B is not unconstitutional as applied to the defendants, and the defendants' motion to dismiss counts one through twelve of the superseding indictment is denied.

10. The government's proof in the Holy Land Foundation prosecution was aimed at showing that zakat committees in the West Bank and Gaza to which the individual defendants and the Holy Land Foundation donated money were linked to and controlled by Hamas, an organization that had been officially designated as a foreign terrorist organization and that the defendants knew this. The government's proof of the linkages between Hamas and the zakat committees was mainly based on the testimony of a former Israeli intelligence agent who was presented as an expert witness on the subject. He testified in a closed courtroom and was only identified by a first name. In the end, the jury failed to reach agreement on most of the charges (acquitting on a few), and the judge declared a mistrial. The government indicated that it would retry the case. See The Dallas Morning News, Inc., 2007–10–22.

11. In connection with issues raised by the use of a surrogate that has not itself been designated as an FTO, refer back to Chapter 2, and note the fact that in designating many middle eastern organizations and groups as FTO's, the designation and consequent listing often lists aliases used by the primary

organization/group as well as affiliates. Does this suggest that the government often has a choice between two different ways to address the problem of a surrogate or an intermediary that receives funds intended for the FTO.

12. The Holy Land case was retried. In November, 2008, the Holy Land Foundation and five of its officials and organizers were found guilty on 108 separate counts, including providing material support to a designated foreign terrorist organization, money laundering, tax fraud and various conspiracy counts. The jury also concluded that the Foundation should forfeit 12.4 million dollars related to money laundering counts on which convictions were obtained. In the second trial, the prosecution had dropped 29 counts against two of the defendants, called some new witnesses and simplified the evidence presented to the jury. In May, 2009, the five individual defendants were sentenced: the two founding members of the organization were each sentenced to 65 years in prison; another defendant was sentenced to 20 years, and two others to 15 years each. See LA Times, Nov. 25, 2008, A12 and N.Y. Times, May 28, 2009, A19. The convictions were reviewed and affirmed in United States v. El-Mezain, 664 F. 3d 467 (5th Cir. 2011).

F. ADMINISTRATIVE DESIGNATION AS A "FOREIGN TERRORIST ORGANIZATION" FOR PURPOSES OF § 2339B

The previous sections of this chapter have dealt with issues raised by criminal prosecution under §§ 2339B and 2339A—interpreting and applying the elements of those offenses. Subsection (g)(6) of § 2339B refers to a "terrorist organization" designated under section 219 of the Immigration and Nationality Act, i.e. 8 U.S.C. § 1189 as amended by the Intelligence Reform and Terrorism Prevention Act of 2004. This section establishes the procedures for designation, judicial review and revocation of the designation of an organization as a "foreign terrorist organization." This, of course, is an administrative, not a criminal process, but since it relates importantly to an element of the crime under § 2339B, it warrants careful study. Pertinent portions of the current, as revised in 2004, version of § 1189 are reproduced below.

Prior to the 2004 amendment of § 1189, the statute provided that designation as a foreign terrorist organization by the Secretary of State was for a two year period which could be renewed by the Secretary initiating a new designation action. Thus the pre-2004 process required a new proceeding every two years to continue the designation in force. This framework resulted in repeated designation procedures every two years, and, if the designated organization sought judicial review, a comparable number of review proceedings and resulting judicial opinions.

The statutory scheme as revised by the 2004 amendment modified this approach. It made a designation continuing, subject to a) a revocation proceeding initiated by the designated organization, which could only be considered if two years had passed since the previous consideration; and b) a review every five years if the designation had not been reviewed during the intervening period. The effect of the amended procedure, of course, was to cut down considerably on the number of proceedings under § 1189.

Note that the structure of the 2004 version of § 1189 deals with the procedures for revocation of a designation before it describes the procedures and standards for judicial review of a designation or a denial of a revocation. Note also that under the statute, only the designated organization can seek judicial review. Issues that have arisen upon judicial review of a designation or upon judicial review of denial of a revocation are addressed in the materials below. Note that the Secretary has the authority to revoke a designation "at any time." Revocations, and consequent delisting have not occurred very often under the statutory scheme. An important instance where the Secretary did revoke a designation is described in some detail in the materials below. Finally, take note of subsec. (a)(8) which bars collateral attack on the designation by the defendant in a criminal case. Issues raised by this provision are also considered, infra, this section.

1. THE CURRENT STATUTORY SCHEME

Title 8, U.S.C.

§ 1189. Designation of foreign terrorist organizations

    (a) Designation

        (1) In general

        The Secretary is authorized to designate an organization as a foreign terrorist organization in accordance with this subsection if the Secretary finds that—

            (A) the organization is a foreign organization;

            (B) the organization engages in terrorist activity (as defined in section 1182(a)(3)(B) of this title or terrorism (as defined in section 2656f(d)(2) of Title 22), or retains the capability and intent to engage in terrorist activity or terrorism; and

            (C) the terrorist activity or terrorism of the organization threatens the security of United States nationals or the national security of the United States.

(2) Procedure

(A) Notice

(i) To congressional leaders

Seven days before making a designation under this subsection, the Secretary shall, by classified communication, notify the Speaker and Minority Leader of the House of Representatives, the President pro tempore, Majority Leader, and Minority Leader of the Senate, and the members of the relevant committees of the House of Representatives and the Senate, in writing, of the intent to designate an organization under this subsection, together with the findings made under paragraph (1) with respect to that organization, and the factual basis therefor.

(ii) Publication in Federal Register

The Secretary shall publish the designation in the Federal Register seven days after providing the notification under clause (i).

(B) Effect of designation

(i) For purposes of section 2339B of Title 18, a designation under this subsection shall take effect upon publication under subparagraph (A)(ii).

(ii) Any designation under this subsection shall cease to have effect upon an Act of Congress disapproving such designation.

(C) Freezing of assets

Upon notification under paragraph (2)(A)(i), the Secretary of the Treasury may require United States financial institutions possessing or controlling any assets of any foreign organization included in the notification to block all financial transactions involving those assets until further directive from either the Secretary of the Treasury, Act of Congress, or order of court.

(3) Record

(A) In general

In making a designation under this subsection, the Secretary shall create an administrative record.

(B) Classified information

The Secretary may consider classified information in making a designation under this subsection. Classified information shall not be subject to disclosure for such time as it remains classified, except that such information may be disclosed to a court ex parte and in camera for purposes of judicial review under subsection (c) of this section.

(4) Period of designation

(A) In general

A designation under this subsection shall be effective for all purposes until revoked under paragraph (5) or (6) or set aside pursuant to subsection (c) of this section.

(B) Review of designation upon petition

(i) In general

The Secretary shall review the designation of a foreign terrorist organization under the procedures set forth in clauses (iii) and (iv) if the designated organization files a petition for revocation within the petition period described in clause (ii).

(ii) Petition period

For purposes of clause (i)—

(I) if the designated organization has not previously filed a petition for revocation under this subparagraph, the petition period begins 2 years after the date on which the designation was made; or

(II) if the designated organization has previously filed a petition for revocation under this subparagraph, the petition period begins 2 years after the date of the determination made under clause (iv) on that petition.

(iii) Procedures

Any foreign terrorist organization that submits a petition for revocation under this subparagraph must provide evidence in that petition that the relevant circumstances described in paragraph (1) are sufficiently different from the circumstances that were the basis for the designation such that a revocation with respect to the organization is warranted.

(iv) Determination

(I) In general

Not later than 180 days after receiving a petition for revocation submitted under this subparagraph, the Secretary shall make a determination as to such revocation.

(II) Classified information

The Secretary may consider classified information in making a determination in response to a petition for revocation. Classified information shall not be subject to disclosure for such time as it remains classified, except that such information may be disclosed to a court ex parte and in camera for purposes of judicial review under subsection (c) of this section.

(III) Publication of determination

A determination made by the Secretary under this clause shall be published in the Federal Register.

(IV) Procedures

Any revocation by the Secretary shall be made in accordance with paragraph (6).

(C) Other review of designation

(i) In general

If in a 5-year period no review has taken place under subparagraph (B), the Secretary shall review the designation of the foreign terrorist organization in order to determine whether such designation should be revoked pursuant to paragraph (6).

(ii) Procedures

If a review does not take place pursuant to subparagraph (B) in response to a petition for revocation that is filed in accordance with that subparagraph, then the review shall be conducted pursuant to procedures established by the Secretary. The results of such review and the applicable procedures shall not be reviewable in any court.

(iii) Publication of results of review

The Secretary shall publish any determination made pursuant to this subparagraph in the Federal Register.

. . .

(6) Revocation based on change in circumstances

(A) In general

The Secretary may revoke a designation made under paragraph (1) at any time, and shall revoke a designation upon completion of a review conducted pursuant to subparagraphs (B) and (C) of paragraph (4) if the Secretary finds that—

(i) the circumstances that were the basis for the designation have changed in such a manner as to warrant revocation; or

(ii) the national security of the United States warrants a revocation.

(B) Procedure

The procedural requirements of paragraphs (2) and (3) shall apply to a revocation under this paragraph. Any revocation shall take effect on the date specified in the revocation or upon publication in the Federal Register if no effective date is specified.

(7) Effect of revocation

The revocation of a designation under paragraph (5) or (6) shall not affect any action or proceeding based on conduct committed prior to the effective date of such revocation.

(8) Use of designation in trial or hearing

If a designation under this subsection has become effective under paragraph (2)(B) a defendant in a criminal action or an alien in a removal proceeding shall not be permitted to raise any question concerning the validity of the issuance of such designation as a defense or an objection at any trial or hearing.

(b) Amendments to a designation

(1) In general

The Secretary may amend a designation under this subsection if the Secretary finds that the organization has changed its name, adopted a new alias, dissolved and then reconstituted itself under a different name or names, or merged with another organization.

. . .

(4) Classified information

The Secretary may consider classified information in amending a designation in accordance with this subsection. Classified information shall not be subject to disclosure for such time as it remains classified, except that such information may be disclosed to a court ex parte and in camera for purposes of judicial review under subsection (c) of this section.

(c) Judicial review of designation

(1) In general

Not later than 30 days after publication in the Federal Register of a designation, an amended designation, or a determination in response to a petition for revocation, the designated organization may seek judicial review in the United States Court of Appeals for the District of Columbia Circuit.

(2) Basis of review

Review under this subsection shall be based solely upon the administrative record, except that the Government may submit, for ex parte and in camera review, classified information used in making the designation, amended designation, or determination in response to a petition for revocation.

(3) Scope of review

The Court shall hold unlawful and set aside a designation, amended designation, or determination in response to a petition for revocation the court finds to be—

(A) arbitrary, capricious, an abuse of discretion, or otherwise not in accordance with law;

(B) contrary to constitutional right, power, privilege, or immunity;

(C) in excess of statutory jurisdiction, authority, or limitation, or short of statutory right;

(D) lacking substantial support in the administrative record taken as a whole or in classified information submitted to the court under paragraph (2), or

(E) not in accord with the procedures required by law.

(4) Judicial review invoked

The pendency of an action for judicial review of a designation, amended designation, or determination in response to a petition for revocation shall not affect the application of this section, unless the court issues a final order setting aside the designation, amended designation, or determination in response to a petition for revocation.

(d) Definitions

As used in this section—

. . . Secretary means Secretary of State, in consultation with the Secretary of the Treasury and the Attorney General.

NOTE

Somewhat oddly, most of the case law involving judicial review of a designation sought by a foreign terrorist organization is contained in a series of cases that involve essentially the same organization, the Mojahedin-e Khalq Organization (MEK), which has been determined to have a number of aliases or alter egos, including the National Council of Resistance of Iran (NCRI) and People's Mojahedin Organization of Iran (PMOI). The culmination of the MEK series of cases was the revocation of the MEK designation by the Secretary in response to a deadline set by the U.S. Court of Appeals.

Now that the MEK is no longer a designated FTO, one wonders whether the case law on this subject will continue to develop. Of course, perhaps it is not odd that there have not been many other organizations that have sought judicial review of a designation or judicial review of a denial of revocation. See, e.g., Kahane Chai v. Department of State, 466 F.3d 125 (D.C. Cir. 2006). Organizations like al Qaeda or ISIS are not likely to come into U.S. courts to challenge a designation as an FTO. Reviewing the list of designated FTO's reproduced in Chapter 2, supra, are there other organizations on the list that might have been expected to challenge the designation?

2. JUDICIAL REVIEW OF THE SECRETARY'S DESIGNATION

What appears to have been the final judicial opinion in the series of PMOI cases is, In re: People's Mojahedin Organization of Iran, 680 F.3d 832 (D.C. Cir. 2012), reproduced below.

IN RE: PEOPLE'S MOJAHEDIN ORGANIZATION OF IRAN
680 F.3d 832 (D.C. Cir. 2012)

Before: HENDERSON and TATEL, CIRCUIT JUDGES, and WILLIAMS, SENIOR CIRCUIT JUDGE.

PER CURIAM: On July 16, 2010, we remanded this case to the Secretary (Secretary) of the United States Department of State (State Department, State), concluding that the Secretary had violated the due process rights of the petitioner, the People's Mojahedin Organization of Iran (PMOI), by maintaining its designation as a Foreign Terrorist Organization (FTO) under the Antiterrorism and Effective Death Penalty Act (AEDPA, Act), 8 U.S.C. § 1189. PMOI v. U.S. Dep't of State, 613 F.3d 220, 230–31 (D.C. Cir. 2010)(PMOI III). We instructed the Secretary to allow PMOI to "review and rebut the unclassified portions of the record on which [the Secretary] relied" in denying PMOI's petition for revocation of its FTO listing and to "indicate in her administrative summary which sources she regards as sufficiently credible that she relies on them." Id. at 230. It has been nearly two years since our remand and the Secretary has yet to issue a reviewable ruling on PMOI's petition. PMOI now seeks a writ of mandamus ordering the delisting of PMOI or, alternatively, requiring the Secretary to make a decision on PMOI's petition or our setting aside her FTO designation. For the reasons set forth below, we order the Secretary to act on PMOI's petition not later than four months from the issuance of this opinion; failing that, the petition for a writ of mandamus setting aside the FTO designation will be granted.

. . .

. . . [A]lmost four years ago, on July 15, 2008, PMOI filed a petition for revocation of the Secretary's 2003 designation.[2] In its petition, PMOI argued that, although it had engaged in terrorist actions in the past, circumstances had changed dramatically since 2003. PMOI III, 613 F.3d at 225. PMOI asserted inter alia that it had ceased its military campaign against the Iranian regime, renounced violence, surrendered its arms to U.S. forces in Iraq, cooperated with U.S. officials at Camp Ashraf (where its members operating in Iraq were consolidated), shared intelligence with the U.S. government regarding Iran's nuclear program and obtained " 'protected person' status" for all PMOI members at Camp Ashraf under the Fourth Geneva Convention. Id.[3]

On January 7, 2009, Secretary Condoleezza Rice denied PMOI's petition. See 74 Fed. Reg. 1273, 1273–74 (Jan. 12, 2009). She found that: "In considering the evidence as a whole, . . . [PMOI] ha[d] not shown that the relevant circumstances [we]re sufficiently different from the circumstances that were the basis for the 2003 [ ]designation" and that "[a]s a consequence, [PMOI] continues to be a foreign organization that engages in terrorist activity . . . or terrorism . . . or retains the capability and intent to" do so. PMOI III, 613 F.3d at 226. She noted, however, that

---

[2] The Secretary first designated the PMOI as a FTO in 1997 and made successive designations in 1999, 2001 and 2003. See Designation of Foreign Terrorist Organizations, 62 Fed. Reg. 52,650 (Oct. 8, 1997); Designation of Foreign Terrorist Organizations, 64 Fed. Reg. 55,112 (Oct. 8, 1999); Redesignation of Foreign Terrorist Organizations, 66 Fed. Reg. 51,088, 51,089 (Oct. 5, 2001); Redesignation of Foreign Terrorist Organizations, 68 Fed. Reg. 56,860, 56,861 (Oct. 2, 2003). We have upheld the successive designations. See PMOI I, 182 F.3d 17, 25; PMOI v. Dep't of State, 327 F.3d 1238, 1239 (D.C.Cir.2003) (PMOI II); Nat'l Council of Resistance of Iran v. Dep't of State, 373 F.3d 152, 154 (D.C.Cir.2004).

[3] As a result of these changed circumstances, the United Kingdom removed PMOI from its list of terrorist organizations in 2008 and the European Union followed suit in 2009. See PMOI III, 613 F.3d at 225.

changed circumstances since 2003 warranted reconsidering PMOI's FTO status in the future: "In light of the evidence submitted by [PMOI] that it has renounced terrorism and the uncertainty surrounding [PMOI's] presence in Iraq, the continued designation of [PMOI] should be reexamined by the Secretary of State in the next two years even if [PMOI] does not file a petition for revocation."

PMOI timely petitioned for review of the Secretary's decision, arguing that the determination lacked substantial support in the administrative record and that the Secretary's procedures did not provide it due process. On July 16, 2010, we granted the petition, concluding that "the Secretary failed to accord the PMOI the due process protections outlined in our previous decisions." Specifically, we held that "due process requires that the PMOI be notified of the unclassified material on which the Secretary proposes to rely and [be given] an opportunity to respond to that material before its re-designation." Because the Secretary had failed to allow PMOI access to the unclassified material before she made her decision, we remanded the case to the Secretary for her to provide PMOI that access. We also instructed the Secretary to "indicate in her administrative summary which sources she regards as sufficiently credible that she relies on them" in maintaining PMOI's designation and to "explain to which part of section 1189(a)(1)(B) the information she relies on relates."

. . .

Since our July 2010 remand, the Secretary's progress has been—to say the least—slow going. . . .

. . .

On February 27, 2012, PMOI petitioned us for the issuance of a writ of mandamus.

. . .

We believe the Secretary's delay in acting on PMOI's petition for revocation is egregious. . . .

The AEDPA provides that the Secretary "shall make a determination" on a petition of revocation "[n]ot later than 180 days after receiving [the] petition." 8 U.S.C. § 1189(a)(4)(B)(iv)(I). It has been twenty months (approximately 600 days) since our remand and the Secretary has yet to make a final, reviewable decision. . . . The Secretary's twenty-month failure to act plainly frustrates the congressional intent and cuts strongly in favor of granting PMOI's mandamus petition. The Secretary argues that because she "must make a decision in this matter while carrying out duties of the most paramount importance, addressing nearly constant emergencies," it would be "inappropriate" for us to rule that she "is not acting quickly enough on a single matter."

. . .

Here . . . the Secretary has not merely failed to meet the AEDPA's deadline or respond to the requests of the petitioner or a third party. She is failing to meet our remand mandate. And, here too, the delay has the effect of nullifying our decision while at the same time preventing PMOI from seeking judicial review. . . . We have been given no sufficient reason why the Secretary, in the last 600 days, has not been able to make a decision which the Congress gave her only 180 days to make. If the Secretary wishes to maintain PMOI's FTO status, she can do so by simply denying PMOI's petition. . . . PMOI asks us to "issue an order directing the Secretary to revoke PMOI's FTO designation" or in the alternative "requiring the Secretary to decide its revocation petition within [thirty] days and specifying that, if she does not, the designation shall be revoked." In light of the national security and foreign policy concerns underlying the designation, we decline, at this time, to revoke the FTO's designation. Instead, we order the Secretary to either deny or grant PMOI's petition not later than four months from the date this opinion issues. Once she makes her decision, it is, of course, entitled to great deference. See Islamic Am. Relief Agency v. Gonzales, 477 F.3d 728, 734 (D.C. Cir. 2007) ("[O]ur review—in [this] area at the intersection of national security, foreign policy, and administrative law—is extremely deferential."); Humanitarian Law Project v. Reno, 205 F.3d 1130, 1137 (9th Cir. 2000) (where a "regulation involves the conduct of foreign affairs, we owe the executive branch even more latitude than in the domestic context"). If she fails to take action within that period, the petition for a writ of mandamus setting aside the FTO designation will be granted.

So ordered.

QUESTIONS AND NOTES

1.   Approximately three months after the foregoing opinion was issued, the Secretary of State finally made her decision. It was announced in the following press release from the Department of State, followed by an appropriate notice in the Federal Register.

Delisting of the Mujahedin-e Khalq

Media Note

Office of the Spokesperson

Washington, DC

September 28, 2012

The Secretary of State has decided, consistent with the law, to revoke the designation of the Mujahedin-e Khalq (MEK) and its aliases as a Foreign Terrorist Organization (FTO) under the Immigration and Nationality Act and to delist the MEK as a Specially

the resulting deprivation of right would interfere with the Secretary's duty to carry out foreign policy.

To oversimplify, assume the Secretary gives notice to one of the entities that:

We are considering designating you as a foreign terrorist organization, and in addition to classified information, we will be using the following summarized administrative record. You have the right to come forward with any other evidence you may have that you are not a foreign terrorist organization.

It is not immediately apparent how the foreign policy goals of the government in general and the Secretary in particular would be inherently impaired by that notice. It is particularly difficult to discern how such a notice could interfere with the Secretary's legitimate goals were it presented to an entity such as the PMOI concerning its redesignation. We recognize, as we have recognized before, that items of classified information which do not appear dangerous or perhaps even important to judges might "make all too much sense to a foreign counterintelligence specialist who could learn much about this nation's intelligence-gathering capabilities from what these documents revealed about sources and methods." We extend that recognition to the possibility that alerting a previously undesignated organization to the impending designation as a foreign terrorist organization might work harm to this county's foreign policy goals in ways that the court would not immediately perceive. We therefore wish to make plain that we do not foreclose the possibility of the Secretary, in an appropriate case, demonstrating the necessity of withholding all notice and all opportunity to present evidence until the designation is already made. The difficulty with that in the present case is that the Secretary has made no attempt at such a showing.

We therefore hold that the Secretary must afford the limited due process available to the putative foreign terrorist organization prior to the deprivation worked by designating that entity as such with its attendant consequences, unless he can make a showing of particularized need.

. . .

To make plain . . ., those procedures which have been held to satisfy the Due Process Clause have "included notice of the action sought," along with the opportunity to effectively be heard. This, we hold, is what the Constitution requires of the Secretary in designating organizations as foreign terrorist organizations under the statute. The Secretary must afford to the entities under consideration notice that the designation is impending. Upon an adequate showing to the court, the Secretary may provide this notice after the designation where earlier notification would impinge upon the security and other foreign policy goals of the United States.

The notice must include the action sought, but need not disclose the classified information to be presented in camera and ex parte to the court under the statute. This is within the privilege and prerogative of the executive, and we do not intend to compel a breach in the security which that branch is charged to protect. However, the Secretary has shown no reason not to offer the designated entities notice of the administrative record which will in any event be filed publicly, at the very latest at the time of the court's review. We therefore require that as soon as the Secretary has reached a tentative determination that the designation is impending, the Secretary must provide notice of those unclassified items upon which he proposes to rely to the entity to be designated. There must then be some compliance with the hearing requirement of due process jurisprudence—that is, the opportunity to be heard at a meaningful time and in a meaningful manner recognized . . . .We do not suggest "that a hearing closely approximating a judicial trial is necessary.". We do, however, require that the Secretary afford to entities considered for imminent designation the opportunity to present, at least in written form, such evidence as those entities may be able to produce to rebut the administrative record or otherwise negate the proposition that they are foreign terrorist organizations.

3.   In the National Council case, supra, note 2, the court did not find that the government's argument (the foreign policy and national security nature of the evidence) for dispensing with pre-deprivation notice and opportunity to present evidence was supported by an adequate showing, while recognizing that such a showing possibly could be made in an appropriate case. What other kinds of factors, other than foreign policy and national security concerns, might support dispensing with pre-deprivation process? Consult Designation of Foreign Terrorist Organizations under the AEDPA: The National Council Court Erred in Requiring Pre-designation Process, 2002 B.Y.U.L.Rev. 675 (2002).

4.   The court in National Council, supra note 2, ordered as a remedy that "the petitioners be afforded the opportunity to file responses to the nonclassified evidence against them, to file evidence in support of their allegations that they are not terrorist organizations, and that they be afforded an opportunity to be meaningfully heard by the Secretary upon the relevant findings." In the National Council case, there was both classified and nonclassified evidence in the administrative record. Suppose that the record consisted only of classified evidence. (The language of § 1189 does not appear to preclude such a possibility.) How meaningfully would the due process right granted by the Nat'l Council court be in such a context? Is it arguable that the most important due process protection needed by an affected organization is adequate judicial review of the Secretary's finding?

5.   Section 1189 provides that classified information may be considered in deciding whether to designate an organization as a foreign terrorist organization. It does not apply the provisions of the Classified Information Procedures Act, which by its terms applies in criminal prosecutions. CIPA, which is treated in chapter 9, infra, provides that where classified information is involved, an effort should be made to provide a substitute, for example, a summary that does not disclose the confidential information, and if such efforts fail, the judge may dismiss the prosecution. Would it be appropriate or desirable to apply the CIPA, or some version of it, in § 1189 proceedings?

6.   What would you have advised the Secretary of State to do in the wake of the decision in the National Council case, supra note 2? Seek review in the Supreme Court? Provide to the organizations involved in National Council the procedural protections ordered by the court? Provide such procedural protections in all subsequent designation cases? Go back and reopen all previous designation cases and provide the prescribed procedural protections? Seek an amendment of sec. 1189 to codify by statute the procedural requirements prescribed by the court in National Council?

7.   In the aftermath of the National Council case described in note 2, supra, we inquired by telephone and fax to the State Department in two different offices as to how the Department was responding to the National Council court's decision. One State Department official, in reply to a question, indicated that they did not plan to amend § 1189 procedures as a result of the National Council decision and expressed concern about notifying terrorist groups about their designation and thus allowing them to hide their assets. Query, is the concern about the possibility that assets will be hidden a sufficient reason to provide only post-designation hearings? Should the National Council court have considered this concern in its opinion?

A more formal response was received from the Office of Legal Adviser, Law Enforcement and Intelligence, in response to a faxed inquiry:

> Your facsimile . . . was referred to me. You asked whether the Secretary of State is implementing or plans to implement the procedures outlined by the court in National Council . . ., in other cases of designating a foreign terrorist organization.

> Without waiving its right to challenge the correctness of the decision of the court in National Council . . ., the State Department has implemented such procedures where applicable. The D.C. Circuit's ruling in National Council . . . made clear, however, that the threshold question is first whether a foreign entity is present within the United States and has sufficient connections with this country to bring it within our constitutional framework. If the necessary quantum of presence and connections is missing, entities can claim no rights under the Due Process Clause. Thus, where foreign entities do not have sufficient connections with the United States such that the provisions of the Constitution could be applied to them, notice and hearings and similar procedures are not provided. See, e.g., 32

County Sovereignty Comm. v. Department of State, 292 F.3d 797, 799 (D.C.Cir. 2002).

8. What kind of presence in the U.S. is needed in order to qualify for due process protection?

9. Are there practical problems in providing notice and other procedural opportunities to the kind of organizations that are likely to be designated as foreign terrorist organizations? Consider the type of organizations that are already listed. First, all of these organizations are by definition foreign; second, many of them are also secretive and hidden. It is as if the government were obligated to provide notice to the Mafia. How does one go about it?

10. A previously mentioned issue that was considered in some of the NCRI-MEK series of cases was whether one organization was the alter ego of the other. The issue was litigated most fully in National Council of Resistance v. Department of State, 373 F.3d 152 (D.C.Cir. 2004):

> . . .NCRI submitted voluminous materials that purported to demonstrate that it was sufficiently independent of MEK that it could not be considered an alias of that organization. . . .
>
> . . .
>
> NCRI's primary argument is that the Secretary's conclusion that NCRI is an alias of MEK lacks substantial support in the administrative record. NCRI insists that it is an umbrella organization of Iranian dissident persons and groups of which MEK is only a single member, no more powerful than any other. In addressing this contention, we begin with our earlier holding in this action. In NCRI, we concluded—based on the record then presented to us—that the Secretary's designation of NCRI as an alias of MEK "does not lack substantial support and . . . is neither arbitrary, capricious, nor otherwise not in accordance with law." Although that decision is obviously not determinative of the question before us today—we are now reviewing a record that has since been supplemented both by the Government and NCRI—its holding must nevertheless inform our decision here. Logically, NCRI's challenge can succeed only if the new record materials establish its independence from MEK so that we can no longer affirm that "the Secretary, on the face of things, had enough information before [him] to come to the conclusion" that NCRI is an alias of MEK. Having reviewed the supplemented administrative record as a whole and the classified information appended to it, we conclude that NCRI has not met this burden.
>
> To explain our decision, we must first review what it means—in the very particular context of AEDPA—for one organization to be an alias of another.
>
> . . .

Just as it is silly to suppose "that Congress empowered the Secretary to designate a terrorist organization . . . only for such periods of time as it took such organization to give itself a new name, and then let it happily resume the same status it would have enjoyed had it never been designated," so too it is implausible to think that Congress permitted the Secretary to designate an FTO to cut off its support in and from the United States, but did not authorize the Secretary to prevent that FTO from marshaling all the same support via juridically separate agents subject to its control. For instance, under NCRI's conception, the Government could designate XYZ organization as an FTO in an effort to block United States support to that organization, but could not, without a separate FTO designation, ban the transfer of material support to XYZ's fundraising affiliate, FTO Fundraiser, Inc. The crabbed view of alias status advanced by NCRI is at war not only with the antiterrorism objective of AEDPA, but common sense as well.

We need not plumb all the complexities of agency law to determine when an agent, under AEDPA, is the alias of its principal. It is sufficient for our purposes to note that the requisite relationship for alias status is established at least when one organization so dominates and controls another that the latter can no longer be considered meaningfully independent from the former. . . .

We thus frame our inquiry here as whether "the Secretary, on the face of things, had enough information before [him] to come to the conclusion" that NCRI was dominated and controlled by MEK. Based on our review of the entire administrative record and the classified materials appended thereto, we find that the Secretary did have an adequate basis for his conclusion. While our determination is buttressed by classified information provided to us on an ex parte and in camera basis—the contents of which we cannot discuss—the voluminous unclassified materials contained in the administrative record by themselves and by a comfortable margin provide sufficient support for the Secretary's conclusion, given the standard of review. . . .

3. CAN THE FTO DESIGNATION BE CHALLENGED IN A CRIMINAL PROSECUTION FOR A VIOLATION OF § 2339B?

The MEK, National Council and PMOI cases, discussed in the previous subsection, all involved direct judicial review of the Secretary's decision to designate the plaintiff organization as a foreign terrorist organization. Issues relating to the designation have also arisen in criminal prosecutions of individuals or institutions charged with having provided material support to a designated FTO under 18 U.S.C. § 2339B.

United States v. Ali
799 F.3d 1008 (8th Cir. 2015)

Before Murphy, Smith, and Gruender, Circuit Judges.

Gruender, Circuit Judge.

In this consolidated appeal, we consider the criminal prosecutions that were brought against two women living in Minnesota in connection with funds sent to al Shabaab, an organization in Somalia that the United States Secretary of State had designated a foreign terrorist organization. After a jury trial, Amina Farah Ali and Hawo Mohamed Hassan were convicted on all counts. The district court sentenced Ali to 240 months in prison and Hassan to 120 months in prison. We affirm.

I. Background

Amina Farah Ali and Hawo Mohamed Hassan are naturalized citizens of the United States who live in Minnesota. Both are from Somalia. In the summer of 2008, the FBI learned that Ali had contacted members of al Shabaab, a foreign terrorist organization in Somalia. Al Shabaab had been so designated by the Secretary of State in February 2008. After a lengthy investigation, a federal grand jury returned an indictment charging (1) Ali and Hassan with one count of conspiring to provide material support to al Shabaab, see 18 U.S.C. § 2339B(a)(1); (2) Ali with twelve counts of providing material support to al Shabaab, see id.; and (3) Hassan with two counts of making a false statement, see 18 U.S.C. § 1001(a)(2).

. . .

Ali and Hassan raise two constitutional challenges to the procedure by which al Shabaab was designated a foreign terrorist organization. We review these issues de novo.

Ali and Hassan first claim that their material-support convictions violate the Due Process Clause of the Fifth Amendment. As relevant here, the material-support statute forbids "knowingly provid[ing] material support or resources to a foreign terrorist organization, or attempt[ing] or conspir[ing] to do so." 18 U.S.C. § 2339B(a)(1). The phrase "foreign terrorist organization" is a term of art that is defined in 8 U.S.C. § 1189(a)(1). Under this provision, the Secretary of State may designate an organization a foreign terrorist organization if the Secretary finds that (1) the organization is a "foreign organization"; (2) the organization engages in "terrorist activity" or "terrorism" or "retains the capability and intent to engage in terrorist activity or terrorism"; and (3) "the terrorist activity or terrorism of the organization threatens the security of United States nationals or the national security of the United States." Id. Section 1189 also provides a mechanism by which an organization can seek judicial review of its designation as a foreign terrorist organization in the United States Court of Appeals for the District of Columbia Circuit. Id.

§ 1189(c)(1). However, this ability to challenge a designation belongs to the organization, not a defendant in a criminal proceeding. Id. § 1189(a)(8).

Ali and Hassan argue that prohibiting them from challenging the Secretary of State's designation of al Shabaab as a foreign terrorist organization offends due process. Our sister circuits have rejected this argument. United States v. Hammoud, 381 F.3d 316, 331 (4th Cir.2004) (en banc), vacated on other grounds by 543 U.S. 1097, 125 S.Ct. 1051, 160 L.Ed.2d 997 (2005), reinstated in all relevant parts, 405 F.3d 1034 (4th Cir.2005) (order); United States v. Afshari, 426 F.3d 1150, 1155–59 (9th Cir.2005). For purposes of the Due Process Clause, the Supreme Court has stated that "in determining what facts must be proved beyond a reasonable doubt the . . . legislature's definition of the elements of the offense is usually dispositive." McMillan v. Pennsylvania, 477 U.S. 79, 85, 106 S.Ct. 2411, 91 L.Ed.2d 67 (1986). Under 18 U.S.C. § 2339B, "Congress has provided that the fact of an organization's designation as [a foreign terrorist organization] is an element of [the crime], but the validity of the designation is not." Hammoud, 381 F.3d at 331. Thus, like our sister circuits, we hold that it comports with due process to prohibit a criminal defendant from challenging the validity of the Secretary of State's designation of a foreign terrorist organization. See id.; Afshari, 426 F.3d at 1155–59. In reaching this conclusion, we note that an organization's designation as a foreign terrorist organization is not wholly immune from challenge. The statute provides a method by which an organization, rather than a criminal defendant, can contest the Secretary of State's designation. 8 U.S.C. § 1189(c); see Lewis v. United States, 445 U.S. 55, 65–67, 100 S.Ct. 915, 63 L.Ed.2d 198 (1980).

Ali and Hassan next contend that allowing the Secretary of State to designate foreign terrorist organizations amounts to an unconstitutional delegation of legislative power. The longstanding rule is that "Congress may delegate its legislative power if it 'lay[s] down by legislative act an intelligible principle to which the person or body authorized to [act] is directed to conform.' " South Dakota v. U.S. Dep't of Interior, 423 F.3d 790, 795 (8th Cir.2005) (alterations in original) (quoting J.W. Hampton, Jr., & Co. v. United States, 276 U.S. 394, 409, 48 S.Ct. 348, 72 L.Ed. 624 (1928)). Congress has "wide latitude in meeting the intelligible principle requirement . . . [because] 'Congress simply cannot do its job absent an ability to delegate power under broad general directives.' " Id. (quoting Mistretta v. United States, 488 U.S. 361, 372, 109 S.Ct. 647, 102 L.Ed.2d 714 (1989)). "Congress fails to give sufficient guidance in its delegations only if it 'would be impossible in a proper proceeding to ascertain whether the will of Congress has been obeyed.' " Id. at 796 (quoting Yakus v. United States, 321 U.S. 414, 426, 64 S.Ct. 660, 88 L.Ed. 834 (1944)).

The statutory scheme governing the designation of foreign terrorist organizations provides an intelligible principle. See Humanitarian Law

Project v. Reno, 205 F.3d 1130, 1137 (9th Cir.2000) (explaining that § 1189(a) "does not grant the Secretary unfettered discretion in designating the groups to which giving material support is prohibited"). As outlined above, the statute permits the Secretary to make a designation only after making three discrete findings. See 8 U.S.C. § 1189(a)(1)(A)–(C). As the Ninth Circuit has observed, "[t]he Secretary could not, under this standard, designate the International Red Cross or the International Olympic Committee as [foreign] terrorist organizations. Rather, the Secretary must have reasonable grounds to believe that an organization has engaged in terrorist acts—assassinations, bombings, hostage-taking and the like—before she can place it on the list." Humanitarian Law Project, 205 F.3d at 1137. As such, two courts have upheld § 1189(a) against a non-delegation challenge. Hammoud, 381 F.3d at 331; United States v. Taleb-Jedi, 566 F.Supp.2d 157, 172–73 (E.D.N.Y.2008) ("Congress has established detailed procedures to designate organizations as [foreign terrorist organizations] and it retains the power to revoke such a designation when made.").

Ali and Hassan ask us to chart a different course primarily due to the requirement that the Secretary of State determine that an organization "threatens the security of United States nationals or the national security of the United States." 8 U.S.C. § 1189(a)(1)(C). The term "national security," Ali and Hassan argue, is "defined without meaning." But the statute defines "national security" to mean "the national defense, foreign relations, or economic interests of the United States." Id. § 1189(d)(2). That this definition is general and broad does not an unintelligible principle make. See South Dakota, 423 F.3d at 795. Moreover, "[t]he Supreme Court has repeatedly underscored that the intelligible principle standard is relaxed for delegations in fields in which the Executive traditionally has wielded its own power." Hepting v. AT & T Corp. (In re Nat'l Sec. Agency Telecomms. Records Litig.), 671 F.3d 881, 897–98 (9th Cir.2011) (collecting cases); see Zemel v. Rusk, 381 U.S. 1, 17, 85 S.Ct. 1271, 14 L.Ed.2d 179 (1965) ("Congress—in giving the Executive authority over matters of foreign affairs—must of necessity paint with a brush broader than it customarily wields in domestic areas."). For these reasons, we hold that granting the Secretary of State the ability to designate an organization a foreign terrorist organization does not constitute an unconstitutional delegation of legislative authority.

QUESTIONS AND NOTES

1. Ali and some of cases cited therein hold that it is constitutionally permissible to bar a criminal defendant from raising as a defense at his trial on a charge of providing material support to an FTO that the FTO designation was not well-founded. This amounts to a decision that it is permissible to preclude a criminal defendant from raising as a defense the validity of a designation that provides one of the elements of the charge against him.

Consider in this connection the opinions in the following Supreme Court case dating from World War II:

> In Yakus v. United States, 321 U.S. 414 (1944), during World War II, the Emergency Price Control Act provided for review of a price regulation through a procedure for protest and review in the Emergency Court of Appeals. The applicable statute was interpreted to bar the defendant from attacking the validity of the price regulation in a criminal prosecution for violation of the regulation. The Supreme Court upheld the Act as applied against a constitutional due process challenge. Chief Justice Stone for the majority wrote:

> "[W]e are pointed to no principle of law or provision of the Constitution . . . which precludes the practice, . . . of splitting the trial for violation of an administrative regulation by committing the determination of the issue of its validity to the agency which created it, and the issue of the violation to a court which is given jurisdiction to punish violations. Such a requirement presents no novel constitutional issue. . . ."

In dissent, Justice Rutledge wrote:

> "The effect is to segregate out of the trial proper issues, whether of law or fact relating to the validity of the law for violation of which the defendants are charged, and to leave to the criminal court only the determination of whether a violation of the regulation as written actually took place. . . . On facts material to the validity of the regulation the persons charged are deprived of a full trial in the state or district where the crime occurs."

2.   Also see Adamo Wrecking Co. v. United States, 434 U.S. 275 (1978) which involved the Clean Air Act under which the Administrator of the Environmental Protection Agency was authorized to promulgate emission standards for "hazardous air pollutants." Knowing violation of an emission standard was punishable as a crime under the Act. The Act provided for judicial review of an emission standard within 30 days after promulgation and provided that the action of the Administrator was not otherwise subject to review in civil or criminal proceedings for enforcement. Adamo Wrecking was charged criminally with having knowingly violated an emission standard and tried to defend on the ground that that the purported emission standard in the matter was not an emission standard within the meaning of the Act. A majority of the Court ruled that such a defense could be raised by a criminal defendant. Justice Powell concurring said the following:

> "If the constitutional validity of sec. 307(b) of the Clean Air Act had been raised by the petitioner, I think it would have merited serious consideration . . . The Act . . . is similar to the preclusion provisions of the Emergency Price Control Act before the Court in Yakus, and petitioner may have thought the decision in that case

effectively foreclosed a due process challenge in the present case. Although I express no considered judgment, I think Yakus is at least arguably distinguishable. The statute there came before the Court during World War II, and it can be viewed as a valid exercise of the war powers of Congress . . ."

Justice Powell also stated:

"The 30 day limitation on judicial review imposed by the Clean Air Act would offer precariously little time for many affected persons even if some adequate method of notice were afforded. It also is totally unrealistic to assume that more than a fraction of the persons and entities affected by a regulation—especially small contractors scattered across the country—would have knowledge of its promulgation or familiarity with or access to the Federal Register."

3.   Justice Powell in Adamo Wrecking mentioned the fact that Yakus may be explained as having been a decision made in wartime and as an exercise of the war powers of Congress. Consider in connection with the issues raised by Justice Powell's comment the implications of the view that we are at war against al Qaeda and its affiliates. Is it relevant that § 1189 and § 2339B were originally enacted before September 11, 2001? Could the Court's ruling in Adamo Wrecking have any relevance to a prosecution under § 2339B?

CHAPTER 4

PROACTIVE SURVEILLANCE

■ ■ ■

A. INTRODUCTION

By proactive surveillance is meant surveillance and inquiries by the investigating arms of the federal government where agents make use of public or general sources of information and gather information in public venues. Such surveillance and investigation is aimed at uncovering criminal behavior or leads thereto in contexts where there is not a quantum of specific evidence akin to that which normally underlies criminal investigation. The basic inquiry is whether and to what extent there are limitations on this type of activity by law enforcement agencies, specifically the FBI, that flow from internal policies and rules, statutes or the Constitution.

There is a wide range of law enforcement activities that fall under this heading. The most controversial form of such activities involves the practice of sending undercover agents into public meetings or to join organizations, both political and other kinds, or sending agents into mosques, churches and synagogues and other places of public gathering, and surfing the net and other public information sources, all with a view to gathering information regarding possible criminal behavior. Are there government policies that authorize or control, restrict or prohibit such activities? Must the government have a specific quantum of evidence regarding suspected terrorism-related activities involving, for example, a political organization or a mosque, synagogue or church before sending an agent undercover to participate in the organization or attend services at the suspected site? Are there restrictions on what the government agents can do in these contexts?

Proactive surveillance by federal government agents usually increases significantly during wartime or during periods of social unrest or upheaval. Such surveillance during such periods of stress becomes a sensitive arena in which there are legitimate concerns about civil liberties, and there is a need to strike the proper balance between security and civil liberty. While there may be a perceived need for more proactive governmental investigative activity during such periods, there is also a concern about the chilling effect of government's intrusion into the arena of political and religious discourse and possible trenching on First Amendment freedoms.

185

The FBI is the principal agency that engages in these types of investigatory activities, and the internal rules and guidelines governing permissible FBI activities of this type are of special interest. Guidelines governing FBI surveillance and investigatory activities have been issued and revised over the years by various Attorneys General, and we examine the latest version of such guidelines. The permissibility and lawfulness of such surveillance is itself an important legal and policy issue.

There have been periods, for example, the late 1960's, when the FBI engaged in activities that went beyond possibly permissible and lawful surveillance and inquiries and that involved some clear-cut abuses. Subsequent Attorney General Guidelines not only defined the lines for permissible political surveillance but were aimed at prohibiting such abusive activities.

In addition to regulation of this area by Guidelines, Congress, on occasion, has granted authority to gather certain kinds of information that may come under the general heading of proactive surveillance as it is used in this Chapter. Thus, section 416 of the USA PATRIOT Act authorizes the Attorney General to fully implement the existing foreign-student monitoring program, and broadens the coverage of existing law to include all students at any institution of higher education or vocational school.

There are also provisions in the Homeland Security Act that are aimed at allaying concerns about too much proactive surveillance. Section 880 of the Act prohibited implementation of the TIPS program by which citizens with regular routes that brought them into contact with people were encouraged to report possible terrorism-related activities. Section 1514 of the same Act precludes the Homeland Security Act from being interpreted to authorize a national identification system or card.

In subsection B of this chapter, we examine relevant excerpts from the current Attorney General Guidelines and study features of the FBI Domestic Investigations and Operations Guidelines which implement the AG Guidelines, both of which govern the proactive surveillance practices of the FBI. In subsection C, we discuss a couple of examples of efforts to litigate issues raised by proactive surveillance practices of law enforcement agencies, with special attention to Laird v. Tatum.

B. RELEVANT FEDERAL EXECUTIVE ORDER AND GUIDELINES

There are a number of primary sources that currently govern the engaging by the FBI in what we have termed "proactive surveillance." In 1981, President Reagan promulgated Executive Order 12333, which, though having since been amended in regard to our subject in certain technical respects, is still operative 30 years later. E.O 12333 prohibits intelligence agents from joining or participating in any organization in the

United States without disclosing the person's intelligence affiliation to officials of the organization "except in accordance with procedures established. . . and approved by the Attorney General after consultation with the Director" of National Intelligence. Authorization for such participation is to be given "only if it is essential to achieving lawful purposes as determined by the head of the relevant agency." With certain limited exceptions, no such participation may be undertaken "for the purpose of influencing the activity of the organization or its members."

In September, 2008, toward the end of the Bush administration, Attorney General Mukasey issued the Attorney General's Guidelines for Domestic FBI Operations. These Guidelines consolidated and replaced various sets of guidelines issued by previous attorneys general over a period of many years.

We reproduce below excerpts from the Attorney General's Guidelines. As you examine these Guidelines, consider whether they answer such questions as: What factual basis must an FBI agent have, in connection with an inquiry in aid of trying to prevent terrorism, to surf the web for information, examine public records, attend religious services at a mosque, church or synagogue without disclosing his or her identity, join an organization without notifying the head of the organization that he/she is an FBI agent engaged in an assessment, etc.? To what extent can an agent take into account race or ethnicity in making decisions about any of the foregoing activities?

**Excerpts from The Attorney General's Guidelines
for Domestic FBI Operations (2008)**

I.

. . .

C.

. . .

4.   Undisclosed Participation in Organizations

Undisclosed participation in organizations in activities under these Guidelines shall be conducted in accordance with FBI policy approved by the Attorney General.

. . .

II.   Investigations and Intelligence Gathering

. . .

This Part authorizes different levels of information gathering activity, which afford the FBI flexibility, under appropriate standards and procedures, to adapt the methods utilized and the information sought to the nature of the matter under investigation and the character of the information supporting the need for investigation.

Assessments, authorized by Subpart A of this Part, require an authorized purpose but not any particular factual predication. For example, to carry out its central mission of preventing the commission of terrorist acts against the United States and its people, the FBI must proactively draw on available sources of information to identify terrorist threats and activities. It cannot be content to wait for leads to come in through the actions of others, but rather must be vigilant in detecting terrorist activities to the full extent permitted by law, with an eye towards early intervention and prevention of acts of terrorism before they occur. . . . The proactive investigative authority conveyed in assessments is designed for, and may be utilized by, the FBI in the discharge of these responsibilities. . . .

. . .[A]ssessments may be undertaken proactively with such objectives as detecting criminal activities; obtaining information on individuals, groups, or organizations of possible investigative interest, either because they may be involved in criminal or national security-threatening activities or because they may be targeted for attack or victimization by such activities; and identifying and assessing individuals who may have value as human sources. For example, assessment activities may involve proactively surfing the Internet to find publicly accessible websites and services through which recruitment by terrorist organizations and promotion of terrorist crimes is openly taking place. . . .

The methods authorized in assessments are generally those of relatively low intrusiveness, such as obtaining publicly available information, checking government records, and requesting information from members of the public. These Guidelines do not impose supervisory approval requirements in assessments, given the types of techniques that are authorized at this stage (e.g., perusing the Internet for publicly available information). However, FBI policy will prescribe supervisory approval requirements for certain assessments, considering such matters as the purpose of the assessment and the methods being utilized.

Beyond the proactive information gathering functions described above, assessments may be used when allegations or other information concerning crimes or threats to the national security is received or obtained, and the matter can be checked out or resolved through the relatively non-intrusive methods authorized in assessments. The checking of investigative leads in this manner can avoid the need to proceed to more formal levels of investigative activity, if the results of an assessment indicate that further investigation is not warranted.

Subpart B of this Part authorizes a second level of investigative activity, predicated investigations. The purposes or objectives of predicated investigations are essentially the same as those of assessments, but predication as provided in these Guidelines is needed—generally, allegations, reports, facts or circumstances indicative of possible criminal or national security threatening activity, or the potential for acquiring information responsive to foreign intelligence requirements—and supervisory approval must be obtained, to initiate predicated investigations. Corresponding to the stronger predication and approval requirements, all lawful methods may be used in predicated investigations. A classified directive provides further specification concerning circumstances supporting certain predicated investigations. . . .

The Attorney General Guidelines authorize as a type of investigative activity "assessments" which do not require a particular factual-predication but do require an authorized purpose. Although no particular factual predication is required, the basis of an assessment cannot be arbitrary or groundless speculation, nor can an assessment be based solely on the exercise of First Amendment protected activities or on the race, ethnicity, national origin or religion of the subject. Although difficult to define, no particular factual predication, is less than information or allegation as required for the initiation of a preliminary investigation. FBI employees who conduct assessments are responsible for assuring that assessments are not pursued for frivolous or improper purposes.

In the wake of the promulgation of the Attorney General's Guidelines in September, 2008, the FBI issued its first-ever Domestic Investigations Operations Guide (DIOG) in December, 2008. The lengthy document is essentially a single comprehensive set of internal guidelines for domestic investigations, updated, that had previously been set forth in a series of different sets of guideline documents. The 2008 DIOG was revised and updated still further in October 2011 based on comments and feedback on the 2008 version. The 2011 DIOG is available at https://vault.fbi.gov/FBI %20Domestic%20Investigations%20and%20Operations%20Guide%20%28 DIOG%29/fbi-domestic-investigations-and-operations-guide-diog-2011-version.

QUESTIONS AND NOTES

1.   The ACLU criticized the Mukasey Guidelines and the DIOG on the ground, among others, that "[u]nder the new 'assessment' authority, FBI agents can investigate anyone they choose, so long as they claim they are acting to prevent crime, protect national security, or collect foreign intelligence, with absolutely no requirement of a factual connection between their authorizing purpose and the conduct of the individuals they are investigating." Based on the Mukasey Guidelines, is this an accurate characterization of the basis on which an FBI agent can initiate an assessment?

2.   Consider the following Letter to the Editor in response to an article in the Los Angeles Times regarding the operation of the 2008 Attorney General Guidelines. Does it respond to the concern articulated by the ACLU—see note 1, supra?

To the Editor:

"F.B.I. Casts Wide Net Under Relaxed Rules for Terror Inquiries, Data Show" (news article, March 27) suggests that in late 2008, new guidelines created a relaxed standard for certain investigative activity and implies that the "relaxed" standard led to a substantial increase in assessments. In fact, the F.B.I. has long engaged in the prompt and limited checking of leads.

The 2008 Attorney General guidelines and the F.B.I.'s Domestic Investigations and Operations Guide did specify clearly for the first time how and where leads being assessed must be documented— whether the lead concerns a criminal or a national security threat. As noted in the article, previously this sort of assessment activity was not tracked.

The new guidelines and policies, together with information technology and new record-keeping systems, now allow the F.B.I. to track investigative activity at every level, including assessments, and to ascertain how many develop sufficient information to warrant the opening of an investigation.

The assessment, with its limited investigative techniques, is a valuable tool to ensure that we can "connect the dots" between disparate pieces of information to keep the country safe while still respecting the civil liberty and privacy rights of every American.

VALERIE CAPRONI
General Counsel
Federal Bureau of Investigation
Washington, March 29, 2011

3.   On July 28, 2010, newspapers reported on instances of cheating by FBI agents being tested on understanding of the Guidelines, and the story became an occasion for criticisms of the authority that the Guidelines gave, for

example, to enter mosques and otherwise focus investigations on members of religious groups. See Associated Press story, July 28, 2010, http://www.law. com/jsp/article.jsp?id=1202463982395.

4.   The notion of FBI agents cheating on tests that probed their knowledge of the Guidelines, of course, seems bizarre. What might account for it? Consider in this connection the length and detail in the relevant documents and also take into account the fact that the provisions dealing with justification and file reviews are exceedingly complex.

5.   Attorney General Ashcroft had revised the then-existing Guidelines in 2002. Brief excerpts from the Ashcroft Guidelines are reproduced below. Compare these provisions with excerpts from the 2008 Mukasey Guidelines, supra.

Excerpts from the Ashcroft Attorney General Guidelines, As revised May 30, 2002

VI. Counterterrorism Activities and Other Authorization

. . .

A.   Counterterrorism Activities

1.   Information Systems

The FBI is authorized to operate and participate in identification, tracking, and information systems for the purpose of identifying and locating terrorists, ... Systems within the scope of this paragraph may draw on and retain pertinent information from any source permitted by law, including information derived from past or ongoing investigative activities; other information collected or provided by governmental entities such as foreign intelligence information and lookout list information, publicly available information, whether obtained directly or through services or resources (whether nonprofit or commercial) that compile or analyze such information; and information voluntarily provided by private entities. . . .

2.   Visiting Public Places and Events

For the purpose of detecting or preventing terrorist activities, the FBI is authorized to visit any place and attend any event that is open to the public, on the same terms and conditions as members of the public generally. No information obtained from such visits shall be retained unless it relates to potential criminal or terrorist activity.

A.   Other Authorizations

. . . [T]he authorized law enforcement activities of the FBI include carrying out and retaining information resulting from the following activities:

1.   General Topical Research

The FBI is authorized to carry out general topical research, including conducting online searches and accessing online sites and forums as a part of such research on the same terms and conditions as members of the public generally. . . . It does not include online searches for information by individuals' names or other individual identifiers, except where such searches are incidental to topical research, such as searching to locate writings on a topic by searching under the names of the authors who write on the topic, or searching by name of a party to a case in conducting legal research.

. . .

B.   Protection of Privacy and Other Limitations

1.   General Limitations

The law enforcement activities authorized by this Part do not include maintaining files on individuals solely for the purpose of monitoring activities protected by the First Amendment or the lawful exercise of any other rights secured by the Constitution or laws of the United States.

. . .

6.   Some of the earlier history of the Attorney General Guidelines is recounted in the following two articles.

John T. Elliff, The Attorney General's Guidelines for FBI Investigations, 69 Cornell L.Rev. 785 (1984):

On March 7, 1983, Attorney General William French Smith issued new guidelines for FBI investigations in the areas of domestic security, racketeering enterprise, and general crimes. They replaced previous guidelines for FBI domestic security investigations issued in 1976 by Attorney General Edward H. Levi and guidelines for FBI racketeering enterprise and general crimes investigations issued in 1980 by Attorney General Benjamin R. Civiletti.

. . .

. . .

Before the Levi guidelines, the FBI Intelligence Division conducted internal security investigations of "subversive activities," as well as foreign counterintelligence investigations of hostile intelligence agents and international terrorists. Although internal security investigations sometimes led to criminal prosecutions for acts of violence, their scope and purposes were broader. Through the mid-1970s, FBI internal security investigations emphasized collection of extensive political intelligence on organizations and individuals espousing revolutionary, racist, or otherwise "extremist" ideological viewpoints. Before World War II, President Roosevelt asked FBI Director J. Edgar Hoover to gather intelligence about the domestic political influence of communist and fascist groups, and subsequent presidents maintained this assignment. Congress reinforced the FBI's internal security mandate with legislation such as the Smith Act of 1940 and the Voorhis Act, which punished those who advocated violent overthrow of the government, and the Internal Security Act of 1950, which required registration of Communist groups and their members and provided for detention of "dangerous" individuals in a national emergency.

During the 1960s the FBI widened the scope of its internal security investigations to include investigations of the civil rights and antiwar movements. These investigations were aimed at gathering information on Communist or "extremist" influence in the groups and acquiring advance knowledge of any disruptive demonstrations or acts of violence. The FBI went beyond investigation and employed so-called COINTELPRO operations to disrupt groups and discredit or harass individuals. When Attorney General William Saxbe released a public report on COINTELPRO in 1974, he described some of these tactics as "abhorrent in a free society."

The Levi guidelines and accompanying administrative reforms abandoned the FBI's previous internal security policies. . . . The FBI Intelligence Division devoted its attention to investigating hostile foreign intelligence operations, including Soviet efforts to influence domestic politics through the Communist Party and its front organizations.

. . .

David M. Park, Note: Re-Examining the Attorney General's Guidelines for FBI Investigations of Domestic Groups, 39 Ariz. L. Rev. 769 (1997).

When a massive fertilizer bomb destroyed the Alfred P. Murrah building in Oklahoma City on April 19, 1995, Americans found themselves confronted with a new threat to their security: domestic terrorist groups. . . .

In the aftermath of the bombing, lawmakers began searching for pro-active solutions to prevent further acts of terrorism by domestic groups. The Federal Bureau of Investigation, the nation's primary criminal investigative agency, was an important focal point in this initial search for solutions. Several politicians suggested the possibility of increasing the FBI's investigative powers. They proposed that a broadening of the FBI Guidelines, a set of rules the Bureau adopted to govern its methods of investigation, could help prevent future attacks. The idea of expanding the Guidelines, however, died a quick death. Virtually all the FBI's top officials, including Director Louis Freeh, Attorney General Janet Reno, and

Deputy Attorney General Jamie Gorelick, agreed that the current Guidelines already provided the FBI with enough power to investigate terrorist groups. They concluded an alteration of the Guidelines was unnecessary. Instead, Freeh, Reno and Gorelick announced the FBI would now begin to interpret the current version more expansively.

This announcement was not well received by civil libertarians. Many civil rights activists felt FBI activity within the current "narrow" interpretation of the Guidelines was already too invasive and certainly did not want to see these practices expanded. Activists questioned the value gained by increased FBI investigations when weighed against the loss of freedom that would surely accompany any increase in the Bureau's activities. The FBI's history of harassing non-violent political groups was another point of contention among civil rights watchdogs. Any alteration that would give the FBI greater ability to investigate domestic groups would be met with great suspicion. Additionally, civil libertarians suggested that any changes in the Guidelines or investigative procedures that granted the FBI greater authority could be constitutionally challenged.

. . .

In the wake of the Oklahoma City bombing, the FBI announced its solution to help prevent acts of domestic terrorism. Rather than ask to be granted more power, FBI officials chose to use more of the power they had already been granted by interpreting their Guidelines (the current Smith version) more expansively. In the past, the FBI had been reluctant to begin investigations of groups that advocated violence to achieve social or political objectives, unless it anticipated an imminent violation of federal law. The fact that the group may have had the ability to carry out its violent objectives was irrelevant, as long as there was no indication of an "imminent violation."

According to current Director Louis Freeh, the more expansive interpretation would now allow the FBI to begin an investigation of a group advocating violence to achieve social or political objectives somewhere short of an imminent violation of federal law, if it was apparent the group had the ability to carry out its objectives. Such a group would now fall within the Guidelines' "reasonable indication" requirement to begin an investigation.

While this appears to be a reasonable interpretation of the Guidelines, it has caused some concern among civil libertarians, who believe that such an expansive reading will lead to an impermissible infringement upon constitutional rights. They challenge this reading of the Guidelines on two grounds: the First Amendment rights of free expression and free assembly, and the Fourth Amendment protections against illegal searches and seizures.

7.　　Floyd Abrams, The First Amendment and the War Against Terrorism, 5 U. Pa. J. Const. L. 1, 6 (2002).

Let me pose another question, one that I answer the same way. It is whether FBI agents should be permitted to attend public meetings of a political or religious nature for the purpose of reporting upon what is said there. When it did so in the 1950s and 1960s, some of the worst abuses of the regime of J. Edgar Hoover occurred. The "chill" on speech was real; Hoover intended just that and achieved just that. It was a civil liberties disaster. After Hoover died, new guidelines, drafted by former Attorneys General Edward Levi and William French Smith, were adopted, effectively barring FBI agents from doing so in most circumstances. Those limits were hailed by civil libertarians—and they should have been. A quarter of a century has now passed, however, and we now face new risks. Shall we now permit, as Attorney General Ashcroft has determined, FBI surveillance of such events? If the Bureau believes that public statements made in a particular mosque, say, may be of assistance in preventing future acts of terrorism, but it is short of proof sufficient to demonstrate the likelihood of criminal behavior, should surveillance of the event be permitted? I think so. Yet when we make that trade-off, we obviously risk the very governmental overreaching and misconduct that tends to accompany any broadening of governmental powers. I have thus far cited examples that fall in the area in which I would be most inclined to give the government some greater powers. It is what we might characterize as the area of prevention of terrorism rather than punishment of it. Obviously, these areas intersect; punishment is, after all, supposed to prevent as well as to punish. But the more we move away from the surveillance mold and into that of how we treat individuals that we have already apprehended, the less willing I think we should be to move even incrementally away from the rules that have historically governed the way we treat people we have apprehended and we believe have committed grievous wrongs.

8.　　What kind of concerns might a civil libertarian have about the new guidelines? Maintaining files on people? The chilling effect of never knowing who in an organization is a government agent? The possibility that permitting fishing expeditions may lead to worse abuses?

9.　　What can the government gain from having agents join political organizations or visit places of worship? Is this a good investment of resources from a prevention or enforcement perspective?

C. LITIGATING ISSUES RAISED BY PROACTIVE SURVEILLANCE

1. PROACTIVE SURVEILLANCE BY THE U.S. MILITARY

LAIRD V. TATUM
408 U.S. 1 (1972)

BURGER, C.J., delivered the opinion of the Court, in which WHITE, BLACKMUN, POWELL, and REHNQUIST, JJ., joined. DOUGLAS, J., filed a dissenting opinion in which MARSHALL, J., joined. BRENNAN, J., filed a dissenting opinion in which STEWART and MARSHALL, JJ., joined.

MR. CHIEF JUSTICE BURGER delivered the opinion of the Court.

Respondents brought this class action in the District Court seeking declaratory and injunctive relief on their claim that their rights were being invaded by the Department of the Army's alleged "surveillance of lawful and peaceful civilian political activity." The petitioners in response described the activity as "gathering by lawful means . . . [and] maintaining and using in their intelligence activities . . . information relating to potential or actual civil disturbances [or] street demonstrations." . . . On the basis of the pleadings, the affidavits before the court, and the oral arguments advanced at the hearing, the District Court granted petitioners' motion to dismiss, holding that there was no justiciable claim for relief.

On appeal, a divided Court of Appeals reversed and ordered the case remanded for further proceedings. We granted certiorari to consider whether, as the Court of Appeals held, respondents presented a justiciable controversy in complaining of a "chilling" effect on the exercise of their First Amendment rights where such effect is allegedly caused, not by any "specific action of the Army against them, [but] only [by] the existence and operation of the intelligence gathering and distributing system, which is confined to the Army and related civilian investigative agencies." We reverse.

(1)

There is in the record a considerable amount of background information regarding the activities of which respondents complained; this information is set out primarily in the affidavits that were filed by the parties in connection with the District Court's consideration of respondents' motion for a preliminary injunction and petitioners' motion to dismiss. A brief review of that information is helpful to an understanding of the issues.

The President is authorized by 10 U. S. C. § 331 to make use of the armed forces to quell insurrection and other domestic violence if and when the conditions described in that section obtain within one of the States. Pursuant to those provisions, President Johnson ordered federal troops to assist local authorities at the time of the civil disorders in Detroit, Michigan, in the summer of 1967 and during the disturbances that followed the assassination of Dr. Martin Luther King. Prior to the Detroit disorders, the Army had a general contingency plan for providing such assistance to local authorities, but the 1967 experience led Army authorities to believe that more attention should be given to such preparatory planning. The data-gathering system here involved is said to have been established in connection with the development of more detailed and specific contingency planning designed to permit the Army, when called upon to assist local authorities, to be able to respond effectively with a minimum of force. As the Court of Appeals observed,

> "In performing this type [of] function the Army is essentially a police force or the back-up of a local police force. To quell disturbances or to prevent further disturbances the Army needs the same tools and, most importantly, the same information to which local police forces have access. Since the Army is sent into territory almost invariably unfamiliar to most soldiers and their commanders, their need for information is likely to be greater than that of the hometown policeman."

No logical argument can be made for compelling the military to use blind force. When force is employed it should be intelligently directed, and this depends upon having reliable information—in time. As Chief Justice John Marshall said of [General George] Washington, 'A general must be governed by his intelligence and must regulate his measures by his information. It is his duty to obtain correct information. . . .' So we take it as undeniable that the military, i. e., the Army, need a certain amount of information in order to perform their constitutional and statutory missions.

. . .

The system put into operation as a result of the Army's 1967 experience consisted essentially of the collection of information about public activities that were thought to have at least some potential for civil disorder, the reporting of that information to Army Intelligence headquarters at Fort Holabird, Maryland, the dissemination of these reports from headquarters to major Army posts around the country, and the storage of the reported information in a computer data bank located at Fort Holabird. The information itself was collected by a variety of means, but it is significant that the principal sources of information were the news media and publications in general circulation. Some of the information came from Army Intelligence agents who attended meetings that were open to the public and who wrote field reports describing the meetings, giving such data as the name of the sponsoring organization, the identity of speakers, the approximate number of persons in attendance, and an indication of whether any disorder occurred. And still other information was provided to the Army by civilian law enforcement agencies.

The material filed by the Government in the District Court reveals that Army Intelligence has field offices in various parts of the country; these offices are staffed in the aggregate with approximately 1,000 agents, 94% of whose time is devoted to the organization's principal mission, which is unrelated to the domestic surveillance system here involved.

By early 1970 Congress became concerned with the scope of the Army's domestic surveillance system; hearings on the matter were held before the Subcommittee on Constitutional Rights of the Senate Committee on the Judiciary. Meanwhile, the Army, in the course of a review of the system, ordered a significant reduction in its scope. For example, information referred to in the complaint as the "blacklist" and the records in the computer data bank at Fort Holabird were found unnecessary and were destroyed, along with other related records. One copy of all the material relevant to the instant suit was retained, however, because of the pendency of this litigation.

. . .

In briefs for petitioners filed with this Court, the Solicitor General has called our attention to certain directives issued by the Army and the Department of Defense subsequent to the District Court's dismissal of the action; these directives indicate that the Army's review of the needs of its domestic intelligence activities has indeed been a continuing one and that those activities have since been significantly reduced.

The District Court held a combined hearing on respondents' motion for a preliminary injunction and petitioners' motion for dismissal and thereafter announced its holding that respondents had failed to state a claim upon which relief could be granted. It was the view of the District Court that respondents failed to allege any action on the part of the Army that was unlawful in itself and further failed to allege any injury or any realistic threats to their rights growing out of the Army's actions.

In reversing, the Court of Appeals noted that respondents "have some difficulty in establishing visible injury":

> "[They] freely admit that they complain of no specific action of the Army against them. . . . There is no evidence of illegal or unlawful surveillance activities. We are not cited to any clandestine intrusion by a military agent. So far as is yet shown, the information gathered is nothing more than a good newspaper reporter would be able to gather by attendance at public meetings

and the clipping of articles from publications available on any newsstand."

The court took note of petitioners' argument "that nothing [detrimental to respondents] has been done, that nothing is contemplated to be done, and even if some action by the Army against [respondents] were possibly foreseeable, such would not present a presently justiciable controversy." With respect to this argument, the Court of Appeals had this to say:

> "This position of the [petitioners] does not accord full measure to the rather unique argument advanced by appellants [respondents]. While [respondents] do indeed argue that in the future it is possible that information relating to matters far beyond the responsibilities of the military may be misused by the military to the detriment of these civilian [respondents], yet [respondents] do not attempt to establish this as a definitely foreseeable event, or to base their complaint on this ground. Rather, [respondents] contend that the present existence of this system of gathering and distributing information, allegedly far beyond the mission requirements of the Army, constitutes an impermissible burden on [respondents] and other persons similarly situated which exercises a present inhibiting effect on their full expression and utilization of their First Amendment rights . . ."

Our examination of the record satisfies us that the Court of Appeals properly identified the issue presented, namely, whether the jurisdiction of a federal court may be invoked by a complainant who alleges that the exercise of his First Amendment rights is being chilled by the mere existence, without more, of a governmental investigative and data-gathering activity that is alleged to be broader in scope than is reasonably necessary for the accomplishment of a valid governmental purpose. We conclude, however, that, having properly identified the issue, the Court of Appeals decided that issue incorrectly.

In recent years this Court has found in a number of cases that constitutional violations may arise from the deterrent, or "chilling," effect of governmental regulations that fall short of a direct prohibition against the exercise of First Amendment rights. In none of these cases, however, did the chilling effect arise merely from the individual's knowledge that a governmental agency was engaged in certain activities or from the individual's concomitant fear that, armed with the fruits of those activities, the agency might in the future take some other and additional action detrimental to that individual. Rather, in each of these cases, the challenged exercise of governmental power was regulatory, proscriptive, or compulsory in nature, and the complainant was either presently or prospectively subject to the regulations, proscriptions, or compulsions that he was challenging.

The respondents do not meet this test; their claim, simply stated, is that they disagree with the judgments made by the Executive Branch with respect to the type and amount of information the Army needs and that the very existence of the Army's data-gathering system produces a constitutionally impermissible chilling effect upon the exercise of their First Amendment rights. That alleged "chilling" effect may perhaps be seen as arising from respondents' very perception of the system as inappropriate to the Army's role under our form of government, or as arising from respondents' beliefs that it is inherently dangerous for the military to be concerned with activities in the civilian sector, or as arising from respondents' less generalized yet speculative apprehensiveness that the Army may at some future date misuse the information in some way that would cause direct harm to respondents. Allegations of a subjective "chill" are not an adequate substitute for a claim of specific present objective harm or a threat of specific future harm; "the federal courts established pursuant to Article III of the Constitution do not render advisory opinions." United Public Workers v. Mitchell, 330 U.S. 75, 89 (1947).

Stripped to its essentials, what respondents appear to be seeking is a broad-scale investigation, conducted by themselves as private parties armed with the subpoena power of a federal district court and the power of cross-examination, to probe into the Army's intelligence gathering activities, with the district court determining at the conclusion of that investigation the extent to which those activities may or may not be appropriate to the Army's mission. The following excerpt from the opinion of the Court of Appeals suggests the broad sweep implicit in its holding:

. . .

> "[I]n the judgment of the civilian head of the Army not everything being done in the operation of this intelligence system was necessary to the performance of the military mission. If the Secretary of the Army can formulate and implement such judgment based on facts within his Departmental knowledge, the United States District Court can hear evidence, ascertain the facts, and decide what, if any, further restrictions on the complained-of activities are called for to confine the military to their legitimate sphere of activity and to protect [respondents'] allegedly infringed constitutional rights." 144 U.S.App.D.C., at 83, 444 F.2d, at 958. (Emphasis added.)

Carried to its logical end, this approach would have the federal courts as virtually continuing monitors of the wisdom and soundness of Executive action; such a role is appropriate for the Congress acting through its committees and the "power of the purse"; it is not the role of the judiciary, absent actual present or immediately threatened injury resulting from unlawful governmental action.

We, of course, intimate no view with respect to the propriety or desirability, from a policy standpoint, of the challenged activities of the Department of the Army; our conclusion is a narrow one, namely, that on this record the respondents have not presented a case for resolution by the courts.

MR. JUSTICE DOUGLAS joined by MR. JUSTICE MARSHALL, dissenting.

. . .

II

The claim that respondents have no standing to challenge the Army's surveillance of them and the other members of the class they seek to represent is too transparent for serious argument. The surveillance of the Army over the civilian sector-a part of society hitherto immune from its control-is a serious charge. It is alleged that the Army maintains files on the membership, ideology, programs, and practices of virtually every activist political group in the country, including groups such as the Southern Christian Leadership Conference, Clergy and Laymen United Against the War in Vietnam, the American Civil Liberties Union, Women's Strike for Peace, and the National Association for the Advancement of Colored People. The Army uses undercover agents to infiltrate these civilian groups and to reach into confidential files of students and other groups. The Army moves as a secret group among civilian audiences, using cameras and electronic ears for surveillance. The data it collects are distributed to civilian officials in state, federal, and local governments and to each military intelligence unit and troop command under the Army's jurisdiction (both here and abroad); and these data are stored in one or more data banks.

Those are the allegations; and the charge is that the purpose and effect of the system of surveillance is to harass and intimidate the respondents and to deter them from exercising their rights of political expression, protest, and dissent 'by invading their privacy, damaging their reputations, adversely affecting their employment and their opportunities for employment, and in other ways.' Their fear is that 'permanent reports of their activities will be maintained in the Army's data bank, and their 'profiles' will appear in the so-called 'Blaklist' and that all of this information will be released to numerous federal and state agencies upon request.'

. . .

One need not wait to sue until he loses his job or until his reputation is defamed. To withhold standing to sue until that time arrives would in practical effect immunize from judicial scrutiny all surveillance activities, regardless of their misuse and their deterrent effect. . . .

The present controversy is not a remote, imaginary conflict. Respondents were targets of the Army's surveillance. First, the surveillance was not casual but massive and comprehensive. Second, the intelligence reports were regularly and widely circulated and were exchanged with reports of the FBI, state and municipal police departments, and the CIA. Third, the Army's surveillance was not collecting material in public records but staking out teams of agents, infiltrating undercover agents, creating command posts inside meetings, posing as press photographers and newsmen, posing as TV newsmen, posing as students, and shadowing public figures.

Finally, we know from the hearings conducted by Senator Ervin that the Army has misused or abused its reporting functions. Thus, Senator Ervin concluded that reports of the Army have been 'taken from the Intelligence Command's highly inaccurate civil disturbance teletype and filed in Army dossiers on persons who have held, or were being considered for, security clearances, thus contaminating what are supposed to be investigative reports with unverified gossip and rumor. This practice directly jeopardized the employment and employment opportunities of persons seeking sensitive positions with the federal government or defense industry.'

Surveillance of civilians is none of the Army's constitutional business and Congress has not undertaken to entrust it with any such function. The fact that since this litigation started the Army's surveillance may have been cut back is not an end of the matter. Whether there has been an actual cutback or whether the announcements are merely a ruse can be determined only after a hearing in the District Court. We are advised by an amicus curiae brief filed by a group of former Army Intelligence Agents that Army surveillance of civilians is rooted in secret programs of long standing:

. . .

This case involves a cancer in our body politic. It is a measure of the disease which afflicts us. Army surveillance, like Army regimentation, is at war with the principles of the First Amendment. Those who already walk submissively will say there is no cause for alarm. But submissiveness is not our heritage. The First Amendment was designed to allow rebellion to remain as our heritage. The Constitution was designed to keep government off the backs of the people. The Bill of Rights was added to keep the precincts of belief and expression, of the press, of political and social activities free from surveillance. The Bill of Rights was designed to keep agents of government and official eavesdroppers away from assemblies of people. The aim was to allow men to be free and independent and to assert their rights against government. There can be no influence more paralyzing of that objective than Army surveillance. When an intelligence officer looks over every noncomformist's shoulder in the library, or walks invisibly by his side in a picket line, or infiltrates his club, the America once extolled as the voice of liberty heard around the world no longer is cast in the image which Jefferson and Madison designed. . . .

2.　PROACTIVE SURVEILLANCE BY A CITY POLICE DEPARTMENT AND THE FBI

ALLIANCE TO END REPRESSION V. CITY OF CHICAGO
237 F.3d 799 (7th Cir.2001)

POSNER, CIRCUIT JUDGE.

More than a quarter of a century ago a number of individuals and organizations brought suit under 42 U.S.C. § 1983 against the United States and the City of Chicago, claiming that the FBI's Chicago office and the Chicago Police Department's intelligence division were violating the plaintiffs' First Amendment rights by overly intrusive and improperly motivated investigations of alleged subversive activities. In 1981, before a trial could be held, the defendants agreed to a consent decree, which was approved by then district judge Getzendanner the following year, imposing detailed and onerous restrictions on the defendants' powers of investigation. 561 F.Supp. 537 (N.D.Ill.1982). The City has now asked the district court to modify the decree to make the restrictions that it places on the City less onerous. Fed. R. Civ. P. 60(b)(5). The district court has refused, and the City has appealed, pointing out that the decree is so strict that Judge Getzendanner said she would not have awarded the plaintiffs such draconian relief (but for the defendants' acquiescence) even if they had proved all the allegations of their complaint in a trial. 561 F.Supp. at 551.

The City argues that it has been in compliance with the decree throughout the almost two decades in which the decree has been in force and it points out that during this period the Supreme Court and this court have become ever more emphatic that the federal judiciary must endeavor to return the control of local governmental activities to local government at the earliest possible opportunity compatible with achievement of the objectives of the decree that transferred that control to the federal courts. The City also argues that the culture of local law enforcement and the character of the threats to public safety by ideologically motivated criminals have so far changed as to make much of the decree obsolete and points out that the Supreme Court has adopted a more flexible standard for the modification of decrees entered in institutional reform litigation than the Swift standard of yore. Although the federal government has not joined the City in seeking to modify the decree, the provisions applicable to the FBI are different and were interpreted by us in an earlier phase of this litigation to impose far lighter restrictions on FBI investigations than the district court had interpreted the decree to impose. Alliance to End Repression v. City of Chicago, 742 F.2d 1007 (7th Cir.1984) (en banc).

The core of the decree, which the City does not seek to modify, forbids investigations intended to interfere with or deter the exercise of the freedom of expression that the First Amendment protects, and requires the City to commission independent periodic audits of the City's compliance with the decree. The effect of these provisions is to add the threat of civil and criminal contempt to the usual sanctions for infringing civil rights and, through the requirement of the audits, to make it easier to detect such infringements. These are substantial enhancements of the ordinary deterrent effect of constitutional law. Id. at 1014–15. They annex swift and severe sanctions to the ordinary tort remedies (mainly 42 U.S.C. § 1983) for violations of that law.

The periphery of the decree, which the City considers insufficiently protective of the public safety and wishes to have lanced, comprises a dizzying array of highly specific restrictions on investigations of potential terrorists and other politically or ideologically motivated criminals. Investigations "directed toward First Amendment conduct," a defined term referring to any investigation likely to involve the collection of information about protected activity or the investigation of anyone engaged in such activity, may be conducted only for the purpose of obtaining evidence of past, present, or impending criminal conduct and only if the Chicago police already have a reasonable suspicion of such conduct. Unless "unavoidably necessary to the investigation of a reasonably suspected crime," the police may not collect information about the political group to which the target of an investigation belongs or about other members of the group or people attending the group's meetings. The investigation must terminate as soon as reasonable suspicion of criminal conduct is dispelled and upon termination all information protected by the First Amendment must be purged from the investigatory file. An investigation may not be conducted on the basis of mere advocacy of violent conduct (what the decree terms "ideological rhetoric"); only a "brief preliminary inquiry" is permitted on that basis and it must cease unless it generates a reasonable suspicion of criminal conduct. Use of undercover informants is strictly limited along with the gathering of information at rallies or other public assemblies of advocates of violence and other political extremists. There is more to the decree, and some qualifications and other nuances that we have omitted, but our summary gives the flavor.

From the 1920s to the 1970s the intelligence division of the Chicago Police Department contained a unit nicknamed the "Red Squad" which spied on, infiltrated, and harassed a wide variety of political groups that included but were not limited to left-and right-wing extremists. Most of the groups, including most of the politically extreme groups, were not only lawful, and engaged in expressive activities protected by the First Amendment, but also harmless. The motives of the Red Squad were largely political and ideological, though they included a legitimate concern with genuine threats to public order. Demonstrations against U.S. participation in the Vietnam War that climaxed in the disruption of the Democratic National Convention in Chicago in 1968, race riots in Chicago and other major cities in the same period, and the contemporaneous criminal activities of the Black Panthers, the Weathermen, and Puerto Rican separatists, all against a backdrop of acute racial and Cold War tensions, political assassinations (notably of President Kennedy, Senator Robert Kennedy, and Martin Luther King, Jr.), and communist subversion, fueled a widespread belief in the need for zealous police activity directed against political militants.

The era in which the Red Squad flourished is history, along with the Red Squad itself. The instabilities of that era have largely disappeared. Fear of communist subversion, so strong a motivator of constitutional infringements in those days, has disappeared along with the Soviet Union and the Cold War. Legal controls over the police, legal sanctions for the infringement of constitutional rights, have multiplied. The culture that created and nourished the Red Squad has evaporated. The consent decree has done its job. To this the plaintiffs reply mainly by pointing us to accusations that during the 1996 Democratic National Convention, the first to be held in Chicago since the disaster of 1968, some Chicago police officers, fearing a repetition, reverted to the old ways and harassed demonstrators. But that was at worst a temporally limited, an isolated, and very much a situation-specific lapse; in its ad hoc, unorganized, and episodic character it resembled not at all the activities of the Red Squad, which were organized, systematic, and protracted.

Mere compliance with a decree over a period of years, the plaintiffs argue, does not in itself justify the lifting of the decree.

The City in any event is asking only that the decree be modified, not that it be abrogated; and its grounds for modification go beyond a mere history of compliance. The City wants flexibility to meet new threats to the safety of Chicago's citizens. In the heyday of the Red Squad, law enforcers from J. Edgar Hoover's FBI on down to the local level in Chicago focused to an unhealthy degree on political dissidents, whose primary activity was advocacy though it sometimes spilled over into violence. Today the concern, prudent and not paranoid, is with ideologically motivated terrorism. The City does not want to resurrect the Red Squad. It wants to be able to keep tabs on incipient terrorist groups. New groups of political extremists, believers in and advocates of violence, form daily around the world. If one forms in or migrates to Chicago, the decree renders the police helpless to do anything to protect the public against the day when the group decides to commit a terrorist act. Until the group goes beyond the advocacy of violence and begins preparatory actions that might create reasonable suspicion of imminent criminal activity, the hands of the police are tied. And if the police have been forbidden to investigate until then, if the investigation cannot begin until the group is well on its way toward the commission of terrorist acts, the investigation may come too late to prevent the acts or to identify the perpetrators. If police get wind that a group of people have begun meeting and discussing the desirability of committing acts of violence in pursuit of an ideological agenda, a due regard for the public safety counsels allowing the police department to monitor the statements of the group's members, to build a file, perhaps to plant an undercover agent.

All this the First Amendment permits (unless the motives of the police are improper or the methods forbidden by the Fourth Amendment or other provisions of federal or state law, see Alliance to End Repression v. City of Chicago, supra, 742 F.2d at 1014–15, and cases cited there), but the decree forbids. The decree impedes efforts by the police to cope with the problems of today because earlier generations of police coped improperly with the problems of yesterday. Because of what the Red Squad did many years ago, today's Chicago police are fated unless the decree is modified to labor indefinitely under severe handicaps that other American police are free from. First Amendment rights are secure. But under the decree as written and interpreted, the public safety is insecure and the prerogatives of local government scorned. To continue federal judicial micromanagement of local investigations of domestic and international terrorist activities in Chicago is to undermine the federal system and to trifle with the public safety. Every consideration favors modification; the City has made a compelling case for the modification that it seeks.

Modification is not abrogation. The modified decree will leave the Chicago police under considerably greater constraints than the police forces of other cities. A violation of the constitutional rights of any person whom the Chicago police investigate will be a violation of the decree and not just of the Constitution itself and so will invite summary punishment by the exercise of the contempt power, while the requirement of outside audits will make it more difficult for the Chicago police than for their counterparts in the other big cities to commit constitutional violations undetected.

The judgment of the district court is reversed and the case remanded with instructions to make the modifications in the consent decree that the City has requested.

some extent the FBI is unavoidably under a tighter rein in Chicago than elsewhere, because of the consent decree, which applies only to Chicago. But there is no reason to magnify the disparity by looking for conflict between two sets of general language—the general principles of the decree and the general principles of the Smith Guidelines. Should they conflict in practice there will be time to force revision of the Guidelines. It would be different if the Guidelines and the decree were completely irreconcilable on their face. They are not.

    . . .

A due regard for the separation of powers, the flexibility of equity, the ambiguity of the decree, the generality of the new Justice Department guidelines, the sensitivity and importance of the subject matter, and the limitations of judicial competence argues against precipitating a premature confrontation between the judicial and executive branches in a setting where inevitably some people will say, with pardonable exaggeration, that the federal judiciary is playing fast and loose with the public safety. Fine-tuning investigative guidelines is the responsibility of the executive branch, not us. Our duty is to enforce the decree. Any actual as distinct from purely verbal threat to compliance with the decree lies in the future; we decline to anticipate that the Justice Department will so interpret the new FBI guidelines as to violate the district court's decree.

We do not depreciate the abuses of police power that led to the decree—abuses that were part of a national pattern that included such grotesque incidents as the following: after Martin Luther King was "named 'Man of the Year' by Time magazine, the FBI decided to 'take him off his pedestal,' [']reduce him completely in influence,' and select and promote its own candidate to 'assume the role of the leadership of the Negro people.'" . . . These abuses ought not be forgotten. But neither do we want to emulate the Bourbon kings, of whom it was said that they learned nothing and forgot nothing. The abuses that gave rise to this suit ended a decade ago, and much has changed since then, including the management of the Bureau, whose present director is a former federal circuit judge, and the amount of supervision of the FBI by the Attorney General, which, as the issuance of published guidelines suggests, is greater than it used to be. Also, although the number of bombings and other violent acts by domestic terrorist organizations has not risen over this period, public concern with domestic terrorism has risen—which is understandable considering the continued rise in international terrorism and the increasing lethality of the weapons available to terrorists. . . . By reading the critical sentence in the decree as prohibiting improperly motivated investigations (other parts of the decree, not in issue in this appeal, prohibit improper investigative techniques), we can reconcile the decree and the new guidelines, maintain a proper separation of powers, yet protect the First Amendment rights of the plaintiffs and the other class members.

. . . If the consent decree will bear an alternative interpretation it ought to be given one.

The order of the district court is reversed with directions to dissolve the injunction.

5. In still another incarnation of the Alliance to End Repression litigation, Judge Posner denied a claim by the class representatives of the plaintiffs in the case for more than $1 million in attorney fees for services rendered between 1994 and 2001: for services rendered in two proceedings for contempt of the original decree which failed and for opposing the modification of the decree, which opposition also failed; and for efforts to monitor the City's compliance with the decree. Alliance to End Repression v. City of Chicago, 356 F.3d 767 (7th Cir.2004).

6. The modified consent decree at issue in the Alliance to End Repression v. City of Chicago line of cases was finally dissolved with the consent of the parties, some 35 years after the litigation began. See Alliance To End Repression v. City of Chicago, 328 Fed.Appx. 339, 2009 WL 2015154 (7th Cir.). Also see ACLU v. City of Chicago, 2008 WL 4450304 (N.D. Ill.). But litigation growing out of the modified consent decree has continued, even after the dissolution of the decree, involving lawsuits alleging violation of the decree while it was still in force. See ACLU v. City of Chicago, No. 75 C 3295, 2009 WL 2409907 (N.D.Ill.).

7. Lawsuits similar to the one that led to the Chicago consent decree have been litigated in other cities. For example, in New York City, a suit similar to that involved in the Chicago series of cases has also been litigated. The city sought to be able to conduct undercover investigations of political groups where there is no evidence of criminality. In 1971, a settlement had been reached as the outcome of a lawsuit filed by the Black Panther Party, which provided that the police must obtain approval from a three person panel if they wish to conduct undercover investigations of political groups. Much later, the city sued to remove the requirement that they must first obtain permission from the panel. (Judge Charles Haight agreed to a request by the City of New York and New York Police Department to modify various restrictions on political surveillance, but he left in place a three member oversight board that can investigate specific complaints), Benjamin Weiser, Rules Eased for Surveillance of New York Groups, N.Y.Times.com, February 12, 2003).

Subsequently, in two decisions, Judge Haight modified the existing guidelines as requested by the City Police Department. See Handschu v. Special Services Division, 273 F. Supp. 2d 327 (S.D.N.Y. 2003) and 288 F. Supp. 2d 404 (S.D. N.Y. 2003). Several months later, however, he handed down the following decision in which he criticized the NYPD for the way in which a police inspector questioned persons arrested at a rally protesting the U.S.

invasion of Iraq, and as a result he modestly strengthened the consent decree. See Handschu v. Special Services Division, 288 F. Supp. 2d 411(S.D.N.Y. 2003). Subsequent litigation in the matter revolved around an underlying substantive question—whether a purpose to investigate political activity or a police purpose was involved when the police photographed or videotaped a demonstration and whether the police conduct violated NYPD Guidelines or the Constitution. See Handschu v. Special Services Division, 2008 WL 515695 (S.D. N.Y).

See also Handschu v. Special Services Division, 2007 WL 1711775 (S.D.N.Y.2007) in which Judge Haight concluded a long opinion with the following:

> . . . [V]iolations of Modified Handschu and the NYPD Guidelines must rise to a constitutional level for contempt of this Court to issue. In general injunctive relief is also available only if there is a constitutional violation; however, if it were shown that the NYPD had adopted a policy that disregards the NYPD Guidelines, the Court may exercise its continuing equitable powers in granting appropriate injunctive relief. The NYPD Guidelines only apply where the police have the purpose of investigating political activity.

In the same case, Judge Haight also opined in footnote 19:

> . . . [E]ven if the purpose of investigating political activity operates in conjunction with a permissible operational objective listed in the Order, the NYPD Guidelines are triggered and their procedures must be followed. If, for instance, an officer wished to videotape a demonstration for the purpose of deterring terrorism, he would still need to follow the procedures of the NYPD Guidelines if he also possessed the purpose of collecting information or evidence about political activity as a means of achieving his counter-terrorism goal. Merely having a counter-terrorism purpose does not get him out from under the yoke of the Guidelines where they apply. To the extent that the Note to Order 47 has not been interpreted in this fashion, but rather to suggest that the presence of a non-investigative purpose excuses the officer from application to the Intelligence Division, it would be misinforming officers about their obligations.

8.   On October 30, 2007, the Los Angeles Police Department announced a plan to map Muslim communities in Los Angeles in order to understand the Muslim community and deepen the engagement between LAPD and Muslim citizens. The commanding officer of LAPD's Counter-Terrorism Bureau indicated that the mapping was intended to lay out the geographic locations of the many different Muslim population groups around Los Angeles and take a deeper look at their history, demographics, language, culture, ethnic breakdown, socio-economic status and social interactions. The goal was to identify communities within the larger Muslim community that might be "susceptible to violent, ideologically-based extremism." The LAPD would then use an information-based approach in connection with its outreach efforts to

identify community problems and find possible solutions. See LA Times online edition, November 10, 2007. Would such a mapping of Muslim communities be permissible under the DIOG and the Mukasey Guidelines?

The proposed mapping created a strong negative reaction in the Muslim community and civil liberties groups and within two weeks after being announced, the planned mapping program was shelved, while the LAPD stated that it would continue with its outreach efforts. See MSNBC on line: US News, Crime and Courts, November 15, 2007.

9. In October, 2007, officials from several local police departments around the country, including, New York City, Kansas City, Miami-Dade and Los Angeles, testified before the Homeland Security Committee of the U.S. Senate (Joe Lieberman, Conn., Chair) reporting about programs they had begun to address and counter terrorism. For example, the Kansas City Police Department reported that its police officers were being taught about Islamic culture, concepts of Jihad, and cultivating resources in the community to assist them in identifying indications of terrorist activity.

10. In August, 2007, the New York City Police Department issued a 90 page report from its Intelligence Division entitled, "Radicalization in the West: The Home-grown Threat," analyzing what was described as a trend of radicalization that motivated unremarkable residents or citizens to become terrorism perpetrators. The report concluded that intervention at as early a point as possible was necessary to break the radicalization pattern. For a critique of the N.Y. report see the Capital Cloak blog, August 16, 2007, o-be-wise.blogspot.com/2007/08/nypd-shoots-own-foot-with-terror-report.html

11. Are the local police activities described in notes 8–10, supra, appropriate activities for the police to undertake? A threat to civil liberties? Likely to be effective approaches for police departments to take in trying to deter and prevent terrorism?

12. Litigation regarding police handling of demonstrations continued in New York City. In Washington, D.C. litigation involved restrictions imposed along the Inauguration parade route. The following two cases, one from New York City and one from Washington, both revolve around application of the law enforcement privilege.

DINLER V. CITY OF NEW YORK
607 F. 3d 923 (2d Cir. 2010)

The question presented is whether we should issue a writ of mandamus to overturn an order of the United States District Court for the Southern District of New York (Richard J. Sullivan, Judge) granting a motion to compel the production of certain sensitive intelligence reports prepared by undercover officers of the New York City Police Department ("NYPD"). In answering that question, we are called upon to examine the circumstances in which the so-called "law enforcement privilege" must yield to the needs of a party seeking discovery in a civil action.

Plaintiffs-respondents . . .are protesters and other persons who were arrested, detained, and fingerprinted after demonstrating at the 2004 Republican National Convention ("RNC") in New York City. They brought the underlying suits under 42 U.S.C. § 1983 and state law claiming that their arrest and treatment at the hands of the NYPD violated the United States Constitution and New York law.

During pretrial discovery proceedings, plaintiffs brought a motion to compel the City to produce roughly 1800 pages of confidential reports created by undercover NYPD officers who were investigating potential security threats in the months before the RNC. (Using the NYPD's parlance, we refer to these 1800 pages of reports as the "Field Reports" or simply the "Reports.") The City opposed the motion to compel by asserting, among other things, that the documents were protected from disclosure by the law enforcement privilege.

Magistrate Judge James C. Francis IV, . . . granted plaintiffs' motion to compel. The City filed objections to that decision with Judge Sullivan, and Judge Sullivan affirmed Magistrate Judge Francis's order in its entirety.

. . .

. . . [W]e hold as follows:

(a) The City has met its burden of showing that the law enforcement privilege applies to the Field Reports because the Reports, even as redacted by the District Court, contain detailed information about the NYPD's undercover "law enforcement techniques and procedures."

(b) Plaintiffs do not have a "compelling need" for the Field Reports because the Reports do not contradict, undermine, or otherwise cast doubt upon the End User Reports-the documents upon which the City will rely in defending its arrest and fingerprinting procedures.

(c) Because plaintiffs do not have a "compelling need," they have not overcome the "strong presumption" against lifting the law enforcement privilege.

(5) The City's right to a writ of mandamus is "clear and indisputable" because the District Court committed three errors that amounted to a "clear abuse of discretion," if not a "judicial usurpation of power."

(a) The District Court indisputably committed legal error when it failed to apply a strong presumption against lifting the law enforcement privilege.

(b)   The District Court indisputably committed legal error when it failed to require that plaintiffs show a compelling need for the Field Reports.

(c)   The District Court indisputably made a clearly erroneous assessment of the evidence when it found that plaintiffs' need for the Field Reports outweighed the public's interest in maintaining the integrity of the NYPD's undercover operations and the safety of NYPD officers.

For the foregoing reasons, despite the admirable care of the District Court in dealing with these sensitive and complex questions, we grant the City's petition for a writ of mandamus; we vacate the December 10, 2009 order of the District Court; and we instruct the District Court to deny plaintiffs' motion to compel the production of the Field Reports.

A.N.S.W.E.R. COALITION V. JEWELL
292 F.R.D.44 (D.DC. 2013)

OPINION AND ORDER [Footnotes omitted]

PAUL L. FRIEDMAN, DISTRICT JUDGE.

I.   BACKGROUND

Plaintiff A.N.S.W.E.R. (Act Now to Stop War and End Racism) Coalition ("ANSWER") filed this lawsuit in January 2005 to challenge certain governmental policies that have restricted ANSWER's ability to engage in expressive activity during the Presidential Inaugural Parades in Washington, D.C. One of these policies—and the only policy relevant to the matter now before the Court—is the Secret Service's prohibition on sign supports along the Inaugural Parade Route.

. . . ANSWER challenged the government's withholding of certain documents as privileged, and the Court agreed to review the disputed documents in camera. . . . ANSWER does not ask this Court, however, to review de novo every document withheld by the Secret Service. Rather, ANSWER has identified certain privilege and relevance determinations within each of Judge Kay's orders to which it specifically objects.

. . . ANSWER challenges Judge Kay's ruling that the law enforcement privilege protects the following documents from compelled disclosure: 000668, 000682, 000726, 000734–35, 000740, 000750, 000795–97.

II. DISCUSSION

[ed. Subparts A., B., C., E., and F. are omitted]

D. Documents Withheld Pursuant to the Federal Law Enforcement Privilege

The federal law enforcement privilege is a qualified privilege that allows for the nondisclosure "of information that would be contrary to the public interest in the effective functioning of law enforcement." It serves to protect "the integrity of law enforcement techniques and confidential sources, protects witnesses and law enforcement personnel, safeguards the privacy of individuals under investigation, and prevents interference with investigations." In the D.C. Circuit, the government may invoke the law enforcement privilege by presenting a formal claim of privilege by the head of the relevant law enforcement agency, after actual personal consideration by that individual, with a detailed explanation of the information withheld and the privilege's applicability to that information.

The Secret Service withheld or redacted several documents on the basis of this privilege, including portions of its Presidential Advance Manual. The Secret Service maintains that the Presidential Advance Manual contains information on "protective equipment and methodology," "protective communication means," "information regarding motorcade alignment and duties of agent personnel in motorcade," and "protective communication signal." The Secret Service asserts that the redacted portions of the powerpoint "pertain to security preparations and information regarding potential vulnerabilities regarding [the] parade route" and "the location of a law enforcement command post," and "do not pertain to the admission or prohibition of items into the Inaugural parade route."

Although the Secret Service has properly presented a formal claim of law enforcement privilege, ANSWER correctly notes that because the privilege is a qualified one, the "public interest in nondisclosure must be balanced against the need of a particular litigant for access to the privileged information." As noted by Judge Kay, the D.C. Circuit has identified the following ten factors "as illustrative of the factors the district court must consider" in balancing these interests:

> (1) the extent to which disclosure will thwart governmental processes by discouraging citizens from giving the government information; (2) the impact upon persons who have given information of having their identities disclosed; (3) the degree to which governmental self-evaluation and consequent program improvement will be chilled by disclosure; (4) whether the information sought is factual data or evaluative summary; (5) whether the party seeking discovery is an actual or potential defendant in any criminal proceeding either pending or

reasonably likely to follow from the incident in question; (6) whether the police investigation has been completed; (7) whether any interdepartmental disciplinary proceedings have arisen or may arise from the investigation; (8) whether the plaintiff's suit is nonfrivolous and brought in good faith; (9) whether the information sought is available through other discovery or from other sources[;and] (10) the importance of the information sought to the plaintiff's case.

In re Sealed Case, 856 F.2d at 272 (quoting Frankenhauser v. Rizzo, 59 F.R.D. 339, 344 (E.D.Pa.1973)).

After reviewing the withheld documents, Judge Kay found that the relevant Frankenhauser factors weigh in favor of nondisclosure. In his analysis, however, Judge Kay drew an analogy between this dispute and the facts in MacNamara v. City of New York (In re City of New York), 607 F.3d 923 (2d Cir.2010), in which the Second Circuit concluded that the law enforcement privilege protected intelligence reports prepared by undercover police officers who had investigated potential security threats prior to a political convention. ANSWER asserts that in following MacNamara, Judge Kay erroneously applied the Second Circuit's "strong presumption" against disclosure, a presumption that has never been adopted by our circuit.

ANSWER is correct that the Second Circuit's standard is distinct from the standard articulated in this circuit. In the Second Circuit, once a party has invoked the law enforcement privilege, the party opposing the privilege must overcome the "strong presumption against disclosure" by demonstrating that its suit is in good faith, the information sought is otherwise unavailable, and the party has a "compelling need" for the information. Only after the party overcomes this "strong presumption" does the Second Circuit apply the ten-factor balancing test discussed above.

By contrast, the D.C. Circuit has not recognized any strong presumption against disclosure, and the district courts in this circuit generally have conducted the balancing test, weighing the relevant Frankenhauser factors, "with an eye toward disclosure." The portion of Judge Kay's analysis that applies a "strong presumption against disclosure" therefore is erroneous.

QUESTIONS AND NOTES

1.   The court in A.N.S.W.E.R. notes that the law enforcement privilege in the D.C. Circuit is different from the standard in the Second Circuit. How do the two standards differ?

2.   Would Dinler have come out differently under the D.C. Circuit's standard? Would A.N.S.W.E.R have come out differently under the Second Circuit's standard?

CHAPTER 5

ELECTRONIC SURVEILLANCE

■ ■ ■

Among the numerous ways in which the federal government is making use of its resources in enforcement efforts against terrorism, electronic surveillance has loomed large. Obtaining judicial approval for electronic surveillance directed against ordinary crime requires that the agents have information roughly equivalent to that which would be required were they seeking judicial approval of a search warrant for physical premises. In such instances, they would be directing their efforts against an individual or individuals with probable cause to believe that a crime had been committed and the individual(s) in question had committed it.

The basis for obtaining judicial approval of electronic surveillance directed against terrorism is different; we examine the differences in this chapter. For present purposes, it is sufficient to note that the terrorism electronic surveillance "warrant" gives government agencies authority to seek terrorism intelligence, that is, information that will help to prevent future terrorism offenses and may not require focused evidence of specific criminality like a traditional search warrant.

Much of the terrorism-related electronic surveillance engaged in by the government is conducted by the FBI under the judicial approval process established by the Foreign Intelligence Surveillance Act (FISA). FISA enacted in 1978 was intended to deal with electronic surveillances conducted within the United States. Additionally, however, it was known that various kinds of electronic surveillance were conducted by the National Security Agency (NSA),without obtaining judicial approval under FISA, or otherwise. While we only have limited information about FISA surveillances, we know even less about NSA eavesdropping, which is highly classified. The general assumption, however, has been that the NSA is conducting its national security-related electronic surveillance outside of the United States.

In 2005, the New York Times reported that, without obtaining judicial approval under the FISA statute or otherwise, the NSA had been conducting terrorism-related electronic surveillance of conversations between persons in the U.S. and persons abroad, later determined to be under a program authorized by the President—the Terrorism Surveillance Program (TSP). A controversy developed in the wake of this disclosure that played out in the Congress, in the media and among scholars and that eventually led to the enactment of the FISA Amendments Act of 2008.

Meanwhile, in 2013, Edward Snowden, an employee of a private contractor which worked with government agencies on electronic surveillance matters left his employment taking with him a huge treasure trove of government classified documents relating to various electronic surveillance programs operated by the government. These documents over time have been leaked to the media.

The organization of the materials in this chapter reflects the foregoing description and history. Section A deals in detail with the FISA, largely as it is applied within the United States, and the various issues and comparisons that it engenders. Section B treats the TSP controversy and introduces some other broad-gauge electronic surveillance programs that became known during the same period. It also includes materials relating to the Bush administration's claims of presidential authority for these various programs. Section C reproduces substantial excerpts from the 2008 FISA Amendments Act which addresses the issues raised by the TSP program. Section D begins with materials that describe and critique the government's metadata mining program and how the government gains access to millions of telephone records. It contains the amended version of 50 U.S.C. § 1861 (sec. 215) and summarizes other aspects of the 2015 USA FREEDOM Act that impose restrictions on the metadata mining program and on obtaining access to the telephone records used for that program. It also references amendments added by the FISA Amendments Reauthorization Act of 2017, signed into law on January 19, 2018.

There are some common elements between the TSP that primarily focused on the acquisition of the content of communications of a target who is abroad and between persons abroad and in the U.S., on the one hand, and on large scale data mining of telephonic records on the other hand, but as mentioned above, we have, in the main, treated them separately here.

(Summaries of other provisions of the FREEDOM Act that deal with FISA Amendments Act issues or other matters are also provided at relevant points in the book.)

A. THE FOREIGN INTELLIGENCE SURVEILLANCE ACT (FISA) AND ELECTRONIC SURVEILLANCE WITHIN THE UNITED STATES

1. INTRODUCTION

Electronic surveillance of private conversations and physical searches of private premises by government agents in the United States must comply with the requirements of the Fourth Amendment. In the federal system, electronic surveillance taking place as part of an ordinary criminal investigation must also comply with relevant federal statutes. The statutory requirements establishing a warrant procedure for this type of electronic surveillance are set down in Title III of the Omnibus Crime Control and Safe Streets Act of 1968, codified at 18 U.S.C. § 2510 et seq.

In 1978, the Foreign Intelligence Surveillance Act was enacted: It gave the Attorney General a broad power to authorize, without court order, electronic surveillance to acquire foreign intelligence information if it is directed solely at communications exclusively between or among foreign powers. However, if the surveillance is directed at agents of foreign powers or is likely to acquire the contents of foreign intelligence communications involving a United States person (defined as a U.S. citizen or a permanent resident alien), the FISA established a procedure for obtaining approval by a special court, the Foreign Intelligence Surveillance Court (FISC). This warrant-type approval procedure involves the application of standards that differ from those provided in Title III, supra.

It may be useful here to pause for a moment to provide a bit of the history and background to the FISA. Until 1968, there was no federal legislation on the books providing a judicial authorization procedure for electronic surveillance by federal agents. However, beginning probably with the presidency of Franklin D. Roosevelt, some electronic surveillance without court approval was conducted by government agents under the authority of the Executive Branch, that is, the President, in aid of "national security." With the enactment of the FISA statute in 1978, it was thought that there was no longer a need for such warrantless national security electronic surveillance within the United States (apart from that which was specifically authorized under FISA).

Beginning with the Kennedy administration in the early 1960's, Congress each year had considered legislative bills proposing a judicial authorization procedure for electronic surveillance based on a probable cause standard, modeled generally after the procedure and standards used to obtain warrants for physical searches. Finally, in 1968, legislation on this subject was enacted. 18 U.S.C. §§ 2510–2522 established a judicial approval procedure for electronic surveillance in the investigation of ordinary crimes. In one of those provisions, § 2511(3), it was provided that nothing in this statute "shall limit the constitutional power of the President" to protect the national security of the United States.

Subsequently, the Supreme Court in United States v. United States District Court, 407 U.S. 297 (1972) ruled: that the government lacked the power to conduct electronic surveillance without judicial approval in "domestic security" cases; that Congress could establish standards governing electronic surveillance in such cases; and that these could differ from those applied in ordinary crime cases. The Court expressly did not address, however, whether the government could engage in surveillance of foreign governments or their agents without judicial approval.

Six years later in 1978, as described above, enactment of the FISA established procedures and standards for judicial authorization of electronic surveillance by government agents to obtain foreign intelligence information. Viewed against this historical backdrop, rather than expanding federal authority, the FISA can be seen as a statute that reined in the Executive Branch, regulating a kind of electronic eavesdropping that previously had been, on occasion, authorized by the President and had been uncontrolled by the judiciary. Viewed, however, from a different perspective—the kind of authority applied in ordinary criminal cases under Title III—the standards for authorizing electronic eavesdropping under FISA do expand federal eavesdropping authority.

2. THE FISA STATUTE

The FISA statute is found at 50 U.S.C. § 1801 et seq. Section 1803 provides for appointment by the Chief Justice of a court of eleven district judges to hear ex parte applications by the government and to approve orders for foreign intelligence electronic surveillance anywhere in the United States. Section 1803 also provides for appointment of a three judge court to review denials of applications made under the Act and for review of the decisions of that court through a petition for a writ of certiorari to the Supreme Court. The proceedings of the FISA court and the FISA reviewing court are held in secret, and the opinions of these courts are normally not published. The main provisions of the FISA statute are reproduced below.

Title 50, U.S.C.

§ 1801. Definitions

As used in this subchapter:

(a) "Foreign power" means—

(1) a foreign government or any component thereof, whether or not recognized by the United States;

(2) a faction of a foreign nation or nations, not substantially composed of United States persons;

(3) an entity that is openly acknowledged by a foreign government or governments to be directed and controlled by such foreign government or governments;

(4) a group engaged in international terrorism or activities in preparation therefor;

(5) a foreign-based political organization, not substantially composed of United States persons;

(6) an entity that is directed and controlled by a foreign government or governments; or

(7) an entity not substantially composed of United States persons that is engaged in the international proliferation of weapons of mass destruction.

(b) "Agent of a foreign power" means—

(1) any person other than a United States person, who—

(A) acts in the United States as an officer or employee of a foreign power, or as a member of a foreign power as defined in subsection (a)(4) of this section;

(B) acts for or on behalf of a foreign power which engages in clandestine intelligence activities in the United States contrary to the interests of the United States, when the circumstances of such person's presence in the United States indicate that such person may engage in such activities in the United States, or when such person knowingly aids or abets any person in the conduct of such activities or knowingly conspires with any person to engage in such activities;

(C) engages in international terrorism or activities in preparation therefore;

(D) engages in the international proliferation of weapons of mass destruction, or activities in preparation therefor; or

(E) engages in the international proliferation of weapons of mass destruction, or activities in preparation therefor for or on behalf of a foreign power; or

(2) any person who—

(A) knowingly engages in clandestine intelligence gathering activities for or on behalf of a foreign power, which activities involve or may involve a violation of the criminal statutes of the United States;

(B) pursuant to the direction of an intelligence service or network of a foreign power, knowingly engages in any other clandestine intelligence activities for or on behalf of such foreign power, which activities involve or are about to involve a violation of the criminal statutes of the United States;

(C) knowingly engages in sabotage or international terrorism, or activities that are in preparation therefor, for or on behalf of a foreign power;

(D) knowingly enters the United States under a false or fraudulent identity for or on behalf of a foreign power or, while in the United States, knowingly assumes a false or fraudulent identity for or on behalf of a foreign power; or

(E) knowingly aids or abets any person in the conduct of activities described in subparagraph (A), (B), or (C) or knowingly conspires with any person to engage in activities described in subparagraph (A), (B), or (C).

(c) "International terrorism" means activities that—

(1) involve violent acts or acts dangerous to human life that are a violation of the criminal laws of the United States or of any State, or that would be a criminal violation if committed within the jurisdiction of the United States or any State;

(2) appear to be intended—

(A) to intimidate or coerce a civilian population;

(B) to influence the policy of a government by intimidation or coercion; or

(C) to affect the conduct of a government by assassination or kidnapping; and

(3) occur totally outside the United States, or transcend national boundaries in terms of the means by which they are accomplished, the persons they appear intended to coerce or intimidate, or the locale in which their perpetrators operate or seek asylum.

(d) "Sabotage" means activities that involve a violation of chapter 105 of Title 18, or that would involve such a violation if committed against the United States.

(e) "Foreign intelligence information" means—

(1) information that relates to, and if concerning a United States person is necessary to, the ability of the United States to protect against—

(A) actual or potential attack or other grave hostile acts of a foreign power or an agent of a foreign power;

(B) sabotage, international terrorism, or the international proliferation of weapons of mass destruction by a foreign power or an agent of a foreign power; or

(C) clandestine intelligence activities by an intelligence service or network of a foreign power or by an agent of a foreign power; or

(2) information with respect to a foreign power or foreign territory that relates to, and if concerning a United States person is necessary to—

(A) the national defense or the security of the United States; or

(B) the conduct of the foreign affairs of the United States.

(f) "Electronic surveillance" means—

(1) the acquisition by an electronic, mechanical, or other surveillance device of the contents of any wire or radio communication sent by or intended to be received by a particular, known United States person who is in the United States, if the contents are acquired by intentionally targeting that United States person, under circumstances in which a person has a reasonable expectation of privacy and a warrant would be required for law enforcement purposes;

(2) the acquisition by an electronic, mechanical, or other surveillance device of the contents of any wire communication to or from a person in the United States, without the consent of any party thereto, if such acquisition occurs in the United States, but does not include the acquisition of those communications of computer trespassers that would be permissible under section 2511(2)(i) of Title 18;

(3) the intentional acquisition by an electronic, mechanical, or other surveillance device of the contents of any radio communication, under circumstances in which a person has a reasonable expectation of privacy and a warrant would be required for law enforcement purposes, and if both the sender and all intended recipients are located within the United States; or

(4) the installation or use of an electronic, mechanical, or other surveillance device in the United States for monitoring to acquire information, other than from a wire or radio communication, under circumstances in which a person has a reasonable expectation of privacy and a warrant would be required for law enforcement purposes.

(g) "Attorney General" means the Attorney General of the United States (or Acting Attorney General), the Deputy Attorney General, or, upon the designation of the Attorney General, the Assistant Attorney

General designated as the Assistant Attorney General for National Security under section 507A of title 28, United States Code.

(h) "Minimization procedures", with respect to electronic surveillance, means—

(1) specific procedures, which shall be adopted by the Attorney General, that are reasonably designed in light of the purpose and technique of the particular surveillance, to minimize the acquisition and retention, and prohibit the dissemination, of nonpublicly available information concerning unconsenting United States persons consistent with the need of the United States to obtain, produce, and disseminate foreign intelligence information;

(2) procedures that require that nonpublicly available information, which is not foreign intelligence information, as defined in subsection (e)(1) of this section, shall not be disseminated in a manner that identifies any United States person, without such person's consent, unless such person's identity is necessary to understand foreign intelligence information or assess its importance;

(3) notwithstanding paragraphs (1) and (2), procedures that allow for the retention and dissemination of information that is evidence of a crime which has been, is being, or is about to be committed and that is to be retained or disseminated for law enforcement purposes; and

(4) notwithstanding paragraphs (1), (2), and (3), with respect to any electronic surveillance approved pursuant to section 1802(a) of this title, procedures that require that no contents of any communication to which a United States person is a party shall be disclosed, disseminated, or used for any purpose or retained for longer than 72 hours unless a court order under section 1805 of this title is obtained or unless the Attorney General determines that the information indicates a threat of death or serious bodily harm to any person.

(i) "United States person" means a citizen of the United States, an alien lawfully admitted for permanent residence (as defined in section 1101(a)(20) of Title 8), an unincorporated association a substantial number of members of which are citizens of the United States or aliens lawfully admitted for permanent residence, or a corporation which is incorporated in the United States, but does not include a corporation or an association which is a foreign power, as defined in subsection (a)(1), (2), or (3) of this section.

(j) "United States", when used in a geographic sense, means all areas under the territorial sovereignty of the United States and the Trust Territory of the Pacific Islands.

(k) "Aggrieved person" means a person who is the target of an electronic surveillance or any other person whose communications or activities were subject to electronic surveillance.

(*l*) "Wire communication" means any communication while it is being carried by a wire, cable, or other like connection furnished or operated by any person engaged as a common carrier in providing or operating such facilities for the transmission of interstate or foreign communications.

(m) "Person" means any individual, including any officer or employee of the Federal Government, or any group, entity, association, corporation, or foreign power.

(n) "Contents", when used with respect to a communication, includes any information concerning the identity of the parties to such communication or the existence, substance, purport, or meaning of that communication.

(o) "State" means any State of the United States, the District of Columbia, the Commonwealth of Puerto Rico, the Trust Territory of the Pacific Islands, and any territory or possession of the United States.

(p) "Weapon of mass destruction" means—

(1) any explosive, incendiary, or poison gas device that is designed, intended, or has the capability to cause a mass casualty incident;

(2) any weapon that is designed, intended, or has the capability to cause death or serious bodily injury to a significant number of persons through the release, dissemination, or impact of toxic or poisonous chemicals or their precursors;

(3) any weapon involving a biological agent, toxin, or vector (as such terms are defined in section 178 of Title 18) that is designed, intended, or has the capability to cause death, illness, or serious bodily injury to a significant number of persons; or

(4) any weapon that is designed, intended, or has the capability to release radiation or radioactivity causing death, illness, or serious bodily injury to a significant number of persons.

§ 1802. Electronic surveillance authorization without court order; certification by Attorney General; reports to Congressional committees; transmittal under seal; duties and compensation of communication common carrier; applications; jurisdiction of court

(a)(1)   Notwithstanding any other law, the President, through the Attorney General, may authorize electronic surveillance without a court order under this subchapter to acquire foreign intelligence information for periods of up to one year if the Attorney General certifies in writing under oath that—

(A) the electronic surveillance is solely directed at—

(i) the acquisition of the contents of communications transmitted by means of communications used exclusively between or among foreign powers, as defined in section 1801(a)(1), (2), or (3) of this title; or

(ii) the acquisition of technical intelligence, other than the spoken communications of individuals, from property or premises under the open and exclusive control of a foreign power, as defined in section 1801(a)(1), (2), or (3) of this title;

(B) there is no substantial likelihood that the surveillance will acquire the contents of any communication to which a United States person is a party; and

(C) the proposed minimization procedures with respect to such surveillance meet the definition of minimization procedures under section 1801(h) of this title; and if the Attorney General reports such minimization procedures and any changes thereto to the House Permanent Select Committee on Intelligence and the Senate Select Committee on Intelligence at least thirty days prior to their effective date, unless the Attorney General determines immediate action is required and notifies the committees immediately of such minimization procedures and the reason for their becoming effective immediately.

(2) An electronic surveillance authorized by this subsection may be conducted only in accordance with the Attorney General's certification and the minimization procedures adopted by him. The Attorney General shall assess compliance with such procedures and shall report such assessments to the House Permanent Select Committee on Intelligence and the Senate

Select Committee on Intelligence under the provisions of section 1808(a) of this title.

(3) The Attorney General shall immediately transmit under seal to the court established under section 1803(a) of this title a copy of his certification. Such certification shall be maintained under security measures established by the Chief Justice with the concurrence of the Attorney General, in consultation with the Director of Central Intelligence, and shall remain sealed unless—

(A) an application for a court order with respect to the surveillance is made under sections 1801(h)(4) and 1804 of this title; or

(B) the certification is necessary to determine the legality of the surveillance under section 1806(f) of this title.

(4) With respect to electronic surveillance authorized by this subsection, the Attorney General may direct a specified communication common carrier to—

(A) furnish all information, facilities, or technical assistance necessary to accomplish the electronic surveillance in such a manner as will protect its secrecy and produce a minimum of interference with the services that such carrier is providing its customers; and

(B) maintain under security procedures approved by the Attorney General and the Director of Central Intelligence any records concerning the surveillance or the aid furnished which such carrier wishes to retain.

The Government shall compensate, at the prevailing rate, such carrier for furnishing such aid.

(b) Applications for a court order under this subchapter are authorized if the President has, by written authorization, empowered the [Attorney] General to approve applications to the court having jurisdiction under section 1803 of this title, and a judge to whom an application is made may, notwithstanding any other law, grant an order, in conformity with section 1805 of this title, approving electronic surveillance of a foreign power or an agent of a foreign power for the purpose of obtaining foreign intelligence information, except that the court shall not have jurisdiction to grant any order approving electronic surveillance directed solely as described in paragraph (1)(A) of subsection (a) of this section unless such surveillance may involve the acquisition of communications of any United States person.

§ 1803. Designation of judges

(a)   Court to hear applications and grant orders; record of denial; transmittal to court of review.

The Chief Justice of the United States shall publicly designate 11 district court judges from seven of the United States judicial circuits of whom no fewer than 3 shall reside within 20 miles of the District of Columbia who shall constitute a court which shall have jurisdiction to hear applications for and grant orders approving electronic surveillance anywhere within the United States under the procedures set forth in this Act, except that no judge designated under this subsection shall hear the same application for electronic surveillance under this Act which has been denied previously by another judge designated under this subsection. If any judge so designated denies an application for an order authorizing electronic surveillance under this Act, such judge shall provide immediately for the record a written statement of each reason for his decision and, on motion of the United States, the record shall be transmitted, under seal, to the court of review established in subsection (b).

(b)   Court of review; record, transmittal to Supreme Court.

The Chief Justice shall publicly designate three judges, one of whom shall be publicly designated as the presiding judge, from the United States district courts or courts of appeals who together shall comprise a court of review which shall have jurisdiction to review the denial of any application made under this Act. If such court determines that the application was properly denied, the court shall immediately provide for the record a written statement of each reason for its decision and, on petition of the United States for a writ of certiorari, the record shall be transmitted under seal to the Supreme Court, which shall have jurisdiction to review such decision.

(c)   Expeditious conduct of proceedings; security measures for maintenance of records.

Proceedings under this Act shall be conducted as expeditiously as possible. The record of proceedings under this Act, including applications made and orders granted, shall be maintained under security measures established by the Chief Justice in consultation with the Attorney General and the Director of Central Intelligence.

(d)   Tenure.

Each judge designated under this section shall so serve for a maximum of seven years and shall not be eligible for redesignation, except that the judges first designated under subsection (a) shall be designated for terms of from one to seven years so that one term expires each year, and that judges first designated under subsection (b) shall be designated for terms of three, five, and seven years.

§ 1804. Applications for court orders

(a) Submission by Federal officer; approval of Attorney General; contents.

Each application for an order approving electronic surveillance under this subchapter shall be made by a Federal officer in writing upon oath or affirmation to a judge having jurisdiction under section 1803 of this title. Each application shall require the approval of the Attorney General based upon his finding that it satisfies the criteria and requirements of such application as set forth in this subchapter. It shall include—

(1) the identity of the Federal officer making the application;

(2) the authority conferred on the Attorney General by the President of the United States and the approval of the Attorney General to make the application;

(3) the identity, if known, or a description of the target of the electronic surveillance;

(4) a statement of the facts and circumstances relied upon by the applicant to justify his belief that—

(A) the target of the electronic surveillance is a foreign power or an agent of a foreign power; and

(B) each of the facilities or places at which the electronic surveillance is directed is being used, or is about to be used, by a foreign power or an agent of a foreign power;

(5) a statement of the proposed minimization procedures;

(6) a detailed description of the nature of the information sought and the type of communications or activities to be subjected to the surveillance;

(7) a certification or certifications by the Assistant to the President for National Security Affairs or an executive branch official or officials designated by the President from among those executive officers employed in the area of national security or defense and appointed by the President with the advice and consent of the Senate—

(A) that the certifying official deems the information sought to be foreign intelligence information;

(B) that a significant purpose of the surveillance is to obtain foreign intelligence information;

(C) that such information cannot reasonably be obtained by normal investigative techniques;

(D) that designates the type of foreign intelligence information being sought according to the categories described in section 1801(e) of this title; and

(E) including a statement of the basis for the certification that—

(i) the information sought is the type of foreign intelligence information designated; and

(ii) such information cannot reasonably be obtained by normal investigative techniques;

(8) a statement of the means by which the surveillance will be effected and a statement whether physical entry is required to effect the surveillance;

(9) a statement of the facts concerning all previous applications that have been made to any judge under this subchapter involving any of the persons, facilities, or places specified in the application, and the action taken on each previous application;

(10) a statement of the period of time for which the electronic surveillance is required to be maintained, and if the nature of the intelligence gathering is such that the approval of the use of electronic surveillance under this subchapter should not automatically terminate when the described type of information has first been obtained, a description of facts supporting the belief that additional information of the same type will be obtained thereafter; and

(11) whenever more than one electronic, mechanical or other surveillance device is to be used with respect to a particular proposed electronic surveillance, the coverage of the devices involved and what minimization procedures apply to information acquired by each device.

(b) Exclusion of certain information respecting foreign power targets.

Whenever the target of the electronic surveillance is a foreign power, as defined in section 1801(a)(1), (2), or (3) of this title, and each of the facilities or places at which the surveillance is directed is owned, leased, or exclusively used by that foreign power, the application need not contain the information required by paragraphs (6), (7)(E), (8), and (11) of subsection (a) of this section, but shall state whether physical entry is required to effect the surveillance and shall contain such information about the surveillance techniques and communications or other information concerning United States persons likely to be obtained as may be necessary to assess the proposed minimization procedures.

. . .

§ 1805. Issuance of order

(a) Necessary findings.

Upon an application made pursuant to section 1804 of this title, the judge shall enter an ex parte order as requested or as modified approving the electronic surveillance if he finds that—

(1) the President has authorized the Attorney General to approve applications for electronic surveillance for foreign intelligence information;

(2) the application has been made by a Federal officer and approved by the Attorney General;

(3) on the basis of the facts submitted by the applicant there is probable cause to believe that—

(A) the target of the electronic surveillance is a foreign power or an agent of a foreign power: Provided, That no United States person may be considered a foreign power or an agent of a foreign power solely upon the basis of activities protected by the first amendment to the Constitution of the United States; and

(B) each of the facilities or places at which the electronic surveillance is directed is being used, or is about to be used, by a foreign power or an agent of a foreign power;

(4) the proposed minimization procedures meet the definition of minimization procedures under section 1801(h) of this title;

. . .

(b) Determination of probable cause

In determining whether or not probable cause exists for purposes of an order under subsection (a)(3), a judge may consider past activities of the target, as well as facts and circumstances relating to current or future activities of the target.

. . .

(e) Duration of order; extensions; review of circumstances under which information was acquired, retained or disseminated.

(1) An order issued under this section may approve an electronic surveillance for the period necessary to achieve its purpose, or for ninety days, whichever is less, except that

(A) an order under this section shall approve an electronic surveillance targeted against a foreign power, as defined in section 1801(a)(1), (2), or (3) of this title, for the period specified in the application or for one year, whichever is less, and

(B) an order under this chapter for a surveillance targeted against an agent of a foreign power, as defined in section 1801(b)(1)(A) of this title may be for the period specified in the application or for 120 days, whichever is less.

(2) Extensions of an order issued under this subchapter may be granted on the same basis as an original order upon an application for an extension and new findings made in the same manner as required for an original order, except that

(A) an extension of an order under this chapter for a surveillance targeted against a foreign power, as defined in section 1801(a)(5) or (6) of this title, or against a foreign power as defined in section 1801(a)(4) of this title that is not a United States person, may be for a period not to exceed one year if the judge finds probable cause to believe that no communication of any individual United States person will be acquired during the period, and

(B) an extension of an order under this chapter for a surveillance targeted against an agent of a foreign power as defined in section 1801 (b)(1)(A) of this title may be for a period not to exceed 1 year.

(3) At or before the end of the period of time for which electronic surveillance is approved by an order or an extension, the judge may assess compliance with the minimization procedures by reviewing the circumstances under which information concerning United States persons was acquired, retained, or disseminated.

(f) Emergency orders.

Notwithstanding any other provision of this subchapter, when the Attorney General reasonably determines that—

(1) an emergency situation exists with respect to the employment of electronic surveillance to obtain foreign intelligence information before an order authorizing such surveillance can with due diligence be obtained; and

(2) the factual basis for issuance of an order under this subchapter to approve such surveillance exists; he may authorize the emergency employment of electronic surveillance if a judge having jurisdiction under section 1803 of this title is informed by the Attorney General or his designee at the time of such authorization that the decision has been made to employ emergency electronic surveillance and if an application in accordance with this subchapter is made to that judge as soon as practicable, but not more than 72 hours after the Attorney General authorizes such surveillance. If the Attorney General authorizes such emergency employment of electronic surveillance, he shall require that the minimization procedures required by this subchapter for the issuance of a judicial order be followed. . .

QUESTIONS AND NOTES

1. A good description of the origins of the FISA statute and how it functions is contained in the following excerpt from a Statement for the Record, given by J. Michael McConnell, Director of National Intelligence before the U.S. Senate Judiciary Committee on September 25, 2007.

The Foreign Intelligence Surveillance Act, or FISA, is the nation's statute for conducting electronic surveillance and physical search for foreign intelligence purposes. FISA was passed in 1978, and was carefully crafted to balance the nation's need to collect foreign intelligence information with the protection of civil liberties and privacy rights. I find it helpful to remember that while today's political climate is charged with a significant degree of alarm about activities of the Executive Branch going unchecked, the late 1970's were even more intensely charged by extensively documented Government abuses. We must be ever mindful that FISA was passed in the era of Watergate and in the aftermath of the Church and Pike investigations, and therefore this foundational law has an important legacy of protecting the rights of Americans. Changes we make to this law must honor that legacy to protect Americans, both in their privacy and against foreign threats.

FISA is a complex statute, but in short it does several things. The 1978 law provided for the creation of a special court, the Foreign Intelligence Surveillance Court, which is comprised of federal district court judges who have been selected by the Chief Justice to serve. The Court's members devote a considerable amount of time and effort, over a term of seven years, serving the nation in this capacity, while at the same time fulfilling their district court responsibilities. We are grateful for their service.

The original 1978 FISA provided for Court approval of electronic surveillance operations against foreign powers and agents of foreign powers, within the United States. Congress crafted the law specifically to exclude the Intelligence Community's surveillance operations against targets outside the United States, including where those targets were in communication with Americans, so long as the U.S. side of that communication was not the real target.

FISA has a number of substantial requirements, several of which I will highlight here. A detailed application must be made by an Intelligence Community agency, such as the Federal Bureau of Investigation (FBI), through the Department of Justice, to the FISA Court. The application must be approved by the Attorney General, and certified by another high ranking national security official, such as the FBI Director. The applications that are prepared for presentation to the FISA Court contain extensive information. For example, an application that targets an agent of an international terrorist group might include detailed facts describing the target of the surveillance, the target's activities, the terrorist network in which the target is believed to be acting on behalf of, and investigative results or other intelligence information that would be relevant to the Court's findings. These applications are carefully prepared, subject to multiple layers of review for legal and factual sufficiency, and often resemble finished intelligence products.

Once the Government files its application with the Court, a judge reads the application, conducts a hearing as appropriate, and makes a number of findings, including that there is probable cause that the target of the surveillance is a foreign power or an agent of a foreign power, and that the facilities that will be targeted are used or about to be used by the target. If the judge does not find that the application meets the requirements of the statute, the judge can either request additional information from the government, or deny the application. These extensive findings, including the requirement of probable cause, are intended to apply to persons inside the United States.

It is my steadfast belief that the balance struck by Congress in 1978 was not only elegant, it was the right balance: it safeguarded privacy protection and civil liberties for those inside the United States by requiring Court approval for conducting electronic surveillance within the country, while specifically allowing the Intelligence Community to collect foreign intelligence against foreign intelligence targets located overseas. I believe that balance is the correct one, and I look forward to working with you to maintaining that balance to protect our citizens as we continue our dialogue to achieve lasting FISA modernization.

2. How does probable cause under FISA compare with traditional probable cause applied under search warrant procedures? The issues involved in this comparison are addressed in the next section.

3. The FISA statute was amended in December, 2004 by language contained in the Intelligence Reform and Terrorism Prevention Act of 2004, which added § 1801(b)(1)(C). What was the effect of this amendment on the scope of authority that the FBI had to invoke FISA in terrorism investigations? Consider in this connection also how § 1801(a)(4) and § 1801(b)(2)(C) relate to the then new provision. Did the new provision broaden the FBI's FISA terrorism authority to any significant extent? How does it relate to the idea of an agent of a foreign power?

3. COMPARING SURVEILLANCE UNDER FISA AND UNDER 18 U.S.C. § 2510 ET SEQ.

An important issue relating to FISA surveillances is how far they permit the government to depart from the "normal" Title III judicial approval requirements (18 U.S.C. § 2510 et seq.). In this connection, a detailed comparison of the probable cause, duration and informing-the-target requirements, as well as other features of both categories of surveillances, is useful.

a. The Probable Cause Requirement

a)   Before an order approving electronic surveillance can be issued under 18 U.S.C. § 2518, the judge must find that there is probable cause for belief that an individual is committing, has committed, or is about to commit a particular offense. There must also be probable cause for belief that particular communications concerning that offense will be obtained and that the facilities are being or are about to be used in connection with the commission of the offense.

b)   Under FISA, there is also a probable cause requirement, but on its face it does not require probable cause as to the commission of a crime. Rather under 50 U.S.C. § 1805, there must be probable cause that the target is a foreign power or the agent of a foreign power.

NOTE ON PROBABLE CAUSE UNDER FISA

1.   **Links to Criminality.** The issue of the extent to which the probable cause specified under 1805 relates to criminality is somewhat more complicated than at first appears. True, it relates to whether the target is a foreign power or agent of a foreign power, but how are those terms defined? Foreign power is defined to include foreign governments or government-like or -related entities. No mention of criminality here, but a foreign government can hardly claim the benefit of the probable cause requirement of the Fourth Amendment. The definition of foreign power also includes: a group engaged in international terrorism or in activities in preparation therefor. Insofar as the probable cause is that the target is such a group, the probable cause would seem to refer to a criminal behavior component.

Suppose the probable cause relates to "an agent of a foreign power." How is that phrase defined? Does it include a criminal conduct component? The definition of agent of a foreign power found in section 1801 is repeated below. It is a multi-part definition that one needs to work one's way through.

Title 50, U.S.C.

§ 1801. Definitions

. . .

(b)   "Agent of a foreign power" means—

(1)   any person other than a United States person, who—

(A)   acts in the United States as an officer or employee of a foreign power, or as a member of a foreign power as defined in subsection (a)(4) of this section;

(B)   acts for or on behalf of a foreign power which engages in clandestine intelligence activities in the United States contrary to the interests of the United States, when the circumstances of such person's presence in the United States indicate that such person may engage in such activities in the United States, or when such person knowingly aids or abets any person in the conduct of such activities or knowingly conspires with any person to engage in such activities;

(C)   engages in international terrorism or activities in preparation therefore; or

(2)   any person who—

(A)   knowingly engages in clandestine intelligence gathering activities for or on behalf of a foreign power, which activities involve or may involve a violation of the criminal statutes of the United States;

(B)   pursuant to the direction of an intelligence service or network of a foreign power, knowingly engages in any other clandestine intelligence activities for or on behalf of such foreign power, which activities involve or are about to involve a violation of the criminal statutes of the United States;

(C)   knowingly engages in sabotage or international terrorism, or activities that are in preparation therefor, for or on behalf of a foreign power;

(D)   knowingly enters the United States under a false or fraudulent identity for or on behalf of a foreign power or, while in the United States, knowingly assumes a false or fraudulent identity for or on behalf of a foreign power; or

(E) knowingly aids or abets any person in the conduct of activities described in subparagraph (A), (B), or (C) or knowingly conspires with any person to engage in activities described in subparagraph (A), (B), or (C).

Given this definition, it would seem that the phrase, "probable cause that a person is an agent of a foreign power," always requires some type of criminal conduct unless the person is so denoted because he/she is an officer or employee of a foreign power. If the person is not so labeled because an officer or employee of a foreign power, it does requires that the agent has engaged in, or be connected to some kind of criminal conduct, namely, engaging in clandestine intelligence activities that are a violation of criminal statutes or engaging in international terrorism, or having engaged in some form of identity theft.

With the December, 2004 amendment of § 1801(b)(1)(C), probable cause that an individual "engages in international terrorism or activities in preparation therefore" will suffice. While under the new language, the probable cause may relate to the conduct of an individual rather than a group, it still requires probable cause relating to terrorist activity or preparations therefore—again, it would seem to require some measure of criminal activity-related behavior. How does it compare with the probable-cause-that-an-individual-is-committing-a-crime formula under 18 U.S.C. § 2518? Section 2518 requires a specific offense and, arguably some element of temporal immediacy. Is there more of a criminal conduct element in the FISA probable cause determination than initially appeared? Is it, however, less than what is required under 2518? Section 1801 requires criminality but does not require the identification of specific statutory offenses. Overall, it seem phrased in a more general way, but it is not, as is generally thought, divorced from a connection to criminality—except where a foreign power, in the traditional sense, or one of its officers or employees, is the target.

2. **Limitation on the Scope of the Listening.** The scope of the electronic surveillance under § 2518 is delimited by the notion that there must be probable cause for a belief that particular communications concerning the offense will be obtained and that the facilities are being or are about to be used in connection with the commission of the offense. Under FISA, the scope is delimited differently. Rather the information sought must be "foreign intelligence information," which is defined as follows:

(e) "Foreign intelligence information" means—

(1) information that relates to, and if concerning a United States person is necessary to, the ability of the United States to protect against—

(A) actual or potential attack or other grave hostile acts of a foreign power or an agent of a foreign power;

(B) sabotage or international terrorism by a foreign power or an agent of a foreign power; or

(C) clandestine intelligence activities by an intelligence service or network of a foreign power or by an agent of a foreign power; or

(2) information with respect to a foreign power or foreign territory that relates to, and if concerning a United States person is necessary to—

(A) the national defense or the security of the United States; or

(B) the conduct of the foreign affairs of the United States.

The scope limitation under FISA is generally broader than under § 2518, and insofar in one of definitions uses as a reference point "the national defense or security of the United States," or "the conduct of the foreign affairs of the United States" it is much, much broader.

b. Duration of the Intercept; Time Period Within Which Target Must Be Notified About the Interception

a) Under 18 U.S.C. § 2518, the duration of the interception is limited to 30 days. Extensions can be granted by the judge but for not more than another 30 days per extension. Not later than 90 days after the period of the interception is terminated, the person named in the order approving the interception and such other parties to intercepted communications as the judge in his discretion determines, are to be provided information about the interception.

b) Under FISA, section 1805, the duration of the interception may be 90 days or 120 days, or in some circumstances as much as one year, and extensions may be for the period originally authorized or in certain cases for one year. Significantly, in what is perhaps the most significance difference between the two categories of electronic eavesdropping, there is no requirement under FISA that the persons whose communications have been intercepted be notified subsequently about the interception.

c. Other Comparisons Between FISA and 18 U.S.C. § 2518 Surveillances

The FISA permits surveillance under some circumstances even though the target has not been identified, 50 U.S.C. § 1804(a)(3), which would seem inconsistent with the Fourth Amendment requirement that the place to be searched and the person and things to be seized be described with particularity. Minimization procedures under the FISA should also be compared with those required under Title III. Also, under the FISA, if the case ripens into a criminal prosecution, the application and orders may be reviewed by the district judge in camera and ex parte, without giving the surveilled party access to them. The Attorney General also has authority under 50 U.S.C. § 1805 to issue surveillance orders in "emergency situations."

d. Statistical Comparison of FISA and Title III Electronic Surveillances

Since it first went into operation in 1979, there have been more than 14,000 applications for judicial approval of FISA surveillances. Until 2003, reportedly, no FISA application for judicial approval of a surveillance had been denied in the almost 25 year history of the Act although some had been modified. The actual number of applications between 1978 and 1995 averaged more than 500 each year. Since 1995, as reported in annual letters from the Attorney General to the Administrative Office of the Courts and to the Speaker of the House, there has been a gradual increase in the annual numbers: in 1995, 697; 1996, 839; 1997, 749; 1998, 796; 1999, 886; 2000, 1005; 2001, 932; 2002, 1228.

The letter for 2003, dated April 20, 2004, reported a significant spike in the number of applications, 1727. These include those applications for approval of searches which were solely electronic, solely physical or a combination of both electronic surveillance and physical search. For the first time, too, the report indicated that the FISA court had turned down some applications, four in all, but as a result of modification and resubmission, the court approved a total of 1724 applications. The letter also reported that the court had made substantial modifications in 79 applications.

In 2004, the number crept up to 1758 with the court approving a total of 1754. But then in 2005, the number of applications presented jumped again by more than 300 to 2074, with 2072 approved. And these numbers held steady in 2006 with 2181 applications submitted and 2176 approved; one application was reported to have been rejected in 2006. In a letter, dated May 14, 2009, sent to the chairs of the Senate and House Judiciary and Intelligence Committees, the Department of Justice reported that in calendar 2008, 2083 requests for foreign intelligence electronic and/or physical searches were approved; also that during that period, the court turned down one request and modified two others. More recently in 2015, 1456 FISA applications were approved out of 1457 applications presented. In 2016, the respective numbers were 1401 approvals out of 1485 applications presented.

At first, the foregoing numbers seem truly extraordinary—in the year, 2000, for example, an average of almost 3 applications a day and in 2003, the number jumps to almost 5 a day. And in 2006, to almost 6 a day! Can there really be so much foreign intelligence surveillance going on? These numbers are tempered somewhat, however, when one realizes that the numbers include both initial applications and applications for extensions.

There is thus a kind of double counting if one is trying to determine how many surveillances are ongoing (as opposed to how many judicial determinations have occurred). Nevertheless, the numbers are quite large.

What is the comparable number of Title III federal wiretaps? Between 1995 and 2005 the number of federal wiretaps authorized ranged from 479 to 730, averaging about 567 per year. Through, 2005, the two highest authorization years were 2004 (730) and 2005 (625). Extensions are reported separately; for example, there were 601 in 1991 and 1008 in 2001. The sheer numbers, of course, do not necessarily indicate abuse of the FISA process.

Only the foregoing type of FISA statistics are reported publicly. More extensive reports are made only to the congressional Intelligence Committees. In the period leading up to the enactment of the Intelligence Reform and Terrorism Prevention Act of 2004, a bill was introduced that would have required more information to be disclosed publicly. What came out of Congress, however, was legislation (sec. 6002 of the Intelligence Reform and Terrorism Prevention Act of 2004) that imposed more detailed reporting obligations on the Attorney General, but only in reports to the Intelligence Committees and Judiciary Committees of the two Houses of Congress.

4. ANOTHER PERSPECTIVE ON THE RELATIONSHIP BETWEEN FISA ELECTRONIC SURVEILLANCE AND ORDINARY CRIME SURVEILLANCE: THE MULTIPLE PURPOSE ISSUE

a. Background-History and the Relevant Statutory Provisions

Because FISA modifies the "normal" Fourth Amendment requirements, one way to limit its impact on privacy interests would be to restrict its use to the obtaining of "foreign intelligence information." Indeed, the original notion behind the executive branch's conducting electronic surveillance for foreign intelligence purposes without judicial authorization may have been that intelligence gathering can be done entirely separate and insulated from criminal investigation and prosecution. The notion may have been that the gathering of foreign intelligence usefully can serve many purposes that are not dependent on, or involve criminal prosecution—e.g., it can, for example: a) inform foreign policy; b) be used on occasion to expel foreign diplomats engaged in intelligence work; and c) help to protect the national security through the forestalling of plots directed against the United States.

Whatever the original conception may have been, in the early implementation of the FISA, a distinction was drawn between gathering information for intelligence purposes and gathering it for use by law enforcement for prosecution purposes (see the recounting of this history in In re Sealed Case No.'s 02–001, 02–002, 310 F.3d 717 (F.I.S.Ct.Rev. 2002)). In the statute itself, however, no hard lines were drawn. The specific language of the FISA did not bar the use by law enforcement personnel of information gathered for foreign intelligence purposes; indeed it seemed to contemplate such use, but it did single out such use for special treatment and generally did not seem to encourage it. For example, see the FISA provisions as originally enacted, 50 U.S.C. § 1806(a) and (b).

Title 50, U.S.C.

§ 1806. Use of information

(a) Compliance with minimization procedures; privileged communications; lawful purposes

Information acquired from an electronic surveillance conducted pursuant to this subchapter concerning any United States person may be used and disclosed by Federal officers and employees without the consent of the United States person only in accordance with the minimization procedures required by this subchapter. No otherwise privileged communication obtained in accordance with, or in violation of, the provisions of this subchapter shall lose its privileged character. No information acquired from an electronic surveillance pursuant to this subchapter may be used or disclosed by Federal officers or employees except for lawful purposes.

(b) Statement for disclosure

No information acquired pursuant to this subchapter shall be disclosed for law enforcement purposes unless such disclosure is accompanied by a statement that such information, or any information derived therefrom, may only be used in a criminal proceeding with the advance authorization of the Attorney General.

Provisions incorporated into the FISA post-9/11 by the USA PATRIOT Act (Public Law 107–56, 115 Stat. 272) and the Homeland Security Act (Public Law 107–296, 116 Stat. 2135) appear to have been aimed at shifting the emphasis from the discouraging of use of the information for a different purpose. These amendments appear to encourage the sharing of information between foreign intelligence personnel and law enforcement personnel. Issues of statutory interpretation are presented, however. How far do the new provisions in the FISA, added to by the USA PATRIOT Act, go in permitting the intermixing of the foreign intelligence and law enforcement functions? The USA PATRIOT Act added language that authorized the sharing by foreign intelligence personnel from their side, 50 U.S.C. § 403–5d (note the phrase "obtained as part of a criminal investigation,"), and similarly sharing by law enforcement personnel from their side, 18 U.S.C. § 2517.

Title 50, U.S.C.

§ 403–5d.   Foreign intelligence information

(1)   In general

Notwithstanding any other provision of law, it shall be lawful for foreign intelligence or counterintelligence (as defined in section 401a of this title) or foreign intelligence information obtained as part of a criminal investigation to be disclosed to any Federal law enforcement, intelligence, protective, immigration, national defense, or national security official in order to assist the official receiving that information in the performance of his official duties. Any Federal official who receives information pursuant to this provision may use that information only as necessary in the conduct of that person's official duties subject to any limitations on the unauthorized disclosure of such information.

. . .

Title 18, U.S.C.

§ 2517. Authorization for disclosure and use of intercepted wire, oral, or electronic communications

(6)   Any investigative or law enforcement officer, or attorney for the Government, who by any means authorized by this chapter, has obtained knowledge of the contents of any wire, oral, or electronic communication, or evidence derived therefrom, may disclose such contents to any other Federal law enforcement, intelligence, protective, immigration, national defense, or national security official to the extent that such contents include foreign intelligence or counterintelligence (as defined in section 3 of the National Security Act of 1947 (50 U.S.C. 401a)), or foreign intelligence information (as defined in subsection (19) of section 2510 of this title), to assist the official who is to receive that information in the performance of his official duties. Any Federal official who receives information pursuant to this provision may use that information only as necessary in the conduct of that person's official duties subject to any limitations on the unauthorized disclosure of such information.

The issues here go beyond the sharing of information, however. Ultimately the question is whether it should be permissible to undertake a foreign intelligence-type surveillance that also has a law enforcement, that is, a criminal prosecution, purpose; and whether it should be permissible to have such investigations led by law enforcement rather than foreign intelligence personnel? Those who favor these types of undertakings see no harm in them and argue that otherwise law enforcement is frustrated in their efforts to deal with terrorists and terrorist activity, and government intelligence personnel are not able to do their job properly. Those who oppose it argue that permitting the use of foreign intelligence surveillance, with its watered down standards, secrecy and lack of protection for the U.S. person is a way to get around the requirements of the Fourth Amendment; that it will lead to abuses whereby a foreign intelligence purpose will be inappropriately used to obtain judicial authorization to eavesdrop or search; and that ultimately, it establishes a slippery slope leading to the undermining of Fourth Amendment protections.

In addition to the sharing provisions quoted above, there are two other amendments added by the USA PATRIOT Act that are highly relevant to this subject. The Act added section (k) to § 1806, quoted above. Section (k) provides:

Title 50, U.S.C.

§ 1806.　Use of information

. . .

(k)　Consultation with Federal law enforcement officer

(1)　Federal officers who conduct electronic surveillance to acquire foreign intelligence information under this title may consult with Federal law enforcement officers to coordinate efforts to investigate or protect against

(A)　actual or potential attack or other grave hostile acts of a foreign power or an agent of a foreign power;

(B)　sabotage or international terrorism by a foreign power or an agent of a foreign power; or

(C)　clandestine intelligence activities by an intelligence service or network of a foreign power or by an agent of a foreign power.

(2)　Coordination authorized under paragraph (1) shall not preclude the certification required by section 1104(a)(7)(B) of this title or the entry of an order under section 1105 of this title.

In addition, an amendment was made in 50 U.S.C. § 1804 (A)(7)(B).

Title 50, U.S.C.

§ 1804.　Applications for court orders

(a)　Submission by Federal officer; approval of Attorney General; contents

Each application for an order approving electronic surveillance under this subchapter shall be made by a Federal officer in writing upon oath or affirmation to a judge having jurisdiction under section 1803 of this title. Each application shall require the approval of the Attorney General based upon his finding that it satisfies the criteria and requirements of such application as set forth in this subchapter. It shall include—

. . .

    (7)   a certification . . .

      (A) that the certifying official deems the information sought to be foreign intelligence information;

      (B) that a significant purpose of the surveillance is to obtain foreign intelligence information;

      (C) that such information cannot reasonably be obtained by normal investigative techniques;

. . .

Previously (a)(7)(B) of 50 U.S.C. § 1804 had provided that the obtaining of foreign intelligence information be "the purpose of the surveillance." That previous formulation had been interpreted to mean that the "primary purpose" of the surveillance must have been to obtain foreign intelligence information. The history of the evolution of that interpretation is set forth in the In re Sealed case.

Did changing the language from "the purpose," i.e. from the [primary] purpose, to "a significant purpose," open the door to a contention that the primary purpose of the surveillance could be a law enforcement purpose, provided only that foreign intelligence information gathering was also a significant purpose of the eavesdropping?

Further, does the language of section (k)(1) added to § 1806, as reproduced above, support the undertaking of a coordinated foreign intelligence and criminal investigation?

b.   Applying the Significant Purpose Formula

UNITED STATES V. NING WEN
477 F.3d 896 (7th Cir.2007)

Before EASTERBROOK, CHIEF JUDGE, and BAUER and EVANS, CIRCUIT JUDGES.

EASTERBROOK, CHIEF JUDGE.

A jury found Ning Wen guilty of violating the export-control laws by providing militarily useful technology to the People's Republic of China without the required license. He has been sentenced to 60 months' imprisonment. His only argument on appeal is that the district court should have suppressed evidence derived from a wiretap approved under the Foreign Intelligence Surveillance Act. After reviewing the materials in camera, the judge concluded that the intercept order was amply justified and denied this motion.

As enacted in 1978, FISA applied to interceptions the "primary purpose" of which was foreign intelligence; as amended in 2001 by the USA PATRIOT Act, the statute applies to interceptions that have international intelligence as a "significant purpose". 50 U.S.C. § 1804(a)(7)(B). The Foreign Intelligence Surveillance Court of Review has concluded that the amended statute allows domestic use of intercepted evidence as long as a "significant" international objective is in view at the intercept's inception. Sealed Case, 310 F.3d 717 (F.I.S.Ct.Rev.2002). Wen asks us to disagree with that decision and hold that evidence gathered under FISA cannot be used in domestic criminal investigations or prosecutions, even when the "domestic" crime is linked to international espionage, once that international investigation has "fizzled out" (Wen's phrase) and the investigation of domestic crime necessarily assumes primary significance.

The statutory question under the current version of the Act is whether acquiring international intelligence is a "significant purpose" of the intercept. The intercept's "primary" purpose may or may not be pertinent to the fourth amendment (we discuss that subject below) but is not pertinent to the validity of the intercept under the statute. Like the district court, we have reviewed the affidavits in camera and conclude that the statutory standards for an intercept order have been satisfied. There is no basis for suppression under FISA itself. 50 U.S.C. § 1806(e), (g).

The fourth amendment does not supply a better footing for exclusion. FISA requires each intercept to be authorized by a warrant from a federal district judge. See 50 U.S.C. § 1803(a).

. . .

The only plausible constitutional objection to the warrant actually issued would be that FISA uses a definition of "probable cause" that does not depend on whether a domestic crime has been committed. Under 50 U.S.C. § 1805(a)(3), an order may be based on probable cause to believe that the target is an agent of a foreign power and that the conversations to be intercepted concern the agent's dealings with that foreign power; the judge need not find probable cause to believe that the foreign agent probably is violating the law of this nation (although this may be implied by the findings that FISA does require).

Yet we know from the administrative-search cases that the "probable cause" of which the fourth amendment speaks is not necessarily probable cause to believe that any law is being violated. The Court held in Camara v. Municipal Court, 387 U.S. 523, 87 S.Ct. 1727, 18 L.Ed.2d 930 (1967), and See v. Seattle, 387 U.S. 541, 87 S.Ct. 1741, 18 L.Ed.2d 930 (1967), that municipal officials may not barge into homes or businesses to look for violations of the housing code; they must have warrants, which may issue on probable cause to believe that the city has adopted a reasonable system of inspections and is not targeting citizens for irregular or malicious reasons.

These principles carry over to FISA. Probable cause to believe that a foreign agent is communicating with his controllers outside our borders makes an interception reasonable. If, while conducting this surveillance, agents discover evidence of a domestic crime, they may use it to prosecute for that offense. That the agents may have known that they were likely to hear evidence of domestic crime does not make the interception less reasonable than if they were ignorant of this possibility. . . . In Horton v. California, 496 U.S. 128, 110 S.Ct. 2301, 110 L.Ed.2d 112 (1990), the Court held that evidence in plain view may be seized without a warrant even though the police expected to find it. Likewise evidence of a domestic crime, acquired during an intercept that is reasonable because it concerns traffic between a foreign state and one of its agents in the United States, may be used in a domestic prosecution whether or not the agents expected to learn about the domestic offense. It is enough that the intercept be adequately justified without regard to the possibility that evidence of domestic offenses will turn up. Interception of Wen's conversations was adequately justified under FISA's terms, so there is no constitutional obstacle to using evidence of any domestic crimes he committed. AFFIRMED

QUESTIONS AND NOTES

1. Excerpts from the opinion in a published decision of the Foreign Intelligence Court of Review identify various issues that can arise in applying the significant purpose formula. See In re Sealed Case No.'s 02–001, 02–002, 310 F.3d 717 (F.I.S.Ct.Rev. 2002):

> No committee reports accompanied the Patriot Act but the floor statements make congressional intent quite apparent. The Senate Judiciary Committee Chairman Senator Leahy acknowledged that "[p]rotection against these foreign-based threats by any lawful means is within the scope of the definition of 'foreign intelligence information,' and the use of FISA to gather evidence for the enforcement of these laws was contemplated in the enactment of FISA." 147 Cong. Rec. S11004 (Oct. 25, 2001). "This bill . . . break[s] down traditional barriers between law enforcement and foreign intelligence. This is not done just to combat international terrorism, but for any criminal investigation that overlaps a broad definition of 'foreign intelligence.'" 147 Cong. Rec. S10992 (Oct. 25, 2001) (statement of Sen. Leahy). And Senator Feinstein, a "strong support[er]," was also explicit.

>> The ultimate objective was to make it easier to collect foreign intelligence information under the Foreign Intelligence Surveillance Act, FISA. Under current law, authorities can

proceed with surveillance under FISA only if the primary purpose of the investigation is to collect foreign intelligence.

But in today's world things are not so simple. In many cases, surveillance will have two key goals—the gathering of foreign intelligence, and the gathering of evidence for a criminal prosecution. Determining which purpose is the "primary" purpose of the investigation can be difficult, and will only become more so as we coordinate our intelligence and law enforcement efforts in the war against terror.

Rather than forcing law enforcement to decide which purpose is primary—law enforcement or foreign intelligence gathering, this bill strikes a new balance. It will now require that a "significant" purpose of the investigation must be foreign intelligence gathering to proceed with surveillance under FISA. The effect of this provision will be to make it easier for law enforcement to obtain a FISA search or surveillance warrant for those cases where the subject of the surveillance is both a potential source of valuable intelligence and the potential target of a criminal prosecution. Many of the individuals involved in supporting the September 11 attacks may well fall into both of these categories.

147 Cong. Rec. S10591 (Oct. 11, 2001).

. . .

. . . [T]he Patriot Act amendments clearly disapprove the primary purpose test. And as a matter of straightforward logic, if a FISA application can be granted even if "foreign intelligence" is only a significant—not a primary—purpose, another purpose can be primary. One other legitimate purpose that could exist is to prosecute a target for a foreign intelligence crime. . . .

That leaves us with something of an analytic conundrum. On the one hand, Congress did not amend the definition of foreign intelligence information which, we have explained, includes evidence of foreign intelligence crimes. On the other hand, Congress accepted the dichotomy between foreign intelligence and law enforcement by adopting the significant purpose test. Nevertheless, it is our task to do our best to read the statute to honor congressional intent. The better reading, it seems to us, excludes from the purpose of gaining foreign intelligence information a sole objective of criminal prosecution. We therefore reject the government's argument to the contrary. Yet this may not make much practical difference. Because, as the government points out, when it commences an electronic surveillance of a foreign agent, typically it will not have decided whether to prosecute the agent (whatever may be the subjective intent of the investigators or lawyers who initiate an investigation).

So long as the government entertains a realistic option of dealing with the agent other than through criminal prosecution, it satisfies the significant purpose test.

The important point is—and here we agree with the government—the Patriot Act amendment, by using the word "significant," eliminated any justification for the FISA court to balance the relative weight the government places on criminal prosecution as compared to other counterintelligence responses. If the certification of the application's purpose articulates a broader objective than criminal prosecution—such as stopping an ongoing conspiracy—and includes other potential non-prosecutorial responses, the government meets the statutory test. Of course, if the court concluded that the government's sole objective was merely to gain evidence of past criminal conduct—even foreign intelligence crimes—to punish the agent rather than halt ongoing espionage or terrorist activity, the application should be denied.

The government claims that even prosecutions of non-foreign intelligence crimes are consistent with a purpose of gaining foreign intelligence information so long as the government's objective is to stop espionage or terrorism by putting an agent of a foreign power in prison. That interpretation transgresses the original FISA. It will be recalled that Congress intended . . . to prevent the government from targeting a foreign agent when its "true purpose" was to gain non-foreign intelligence information—such as evidence of ordinary crimes or scandals. (If the government inadvertently came upon evidence of ordinary crimes, FISA provided for the transmission of that evidence to the proper authority. 50 U.S.C. § 1801(h)(3).) It can be argued, however, that by providing that an application is to be granted if the government has only a "significant purpose" of gaining foreign intelligence information, the Patriot Act allows the government to have a primary objective of prosecuting an agent for a non-foreign intelligence crime. Yet we think that would be an anomalous reading of the amendment. For we see not the slightest indication that Congress meant to give that power to the Executive Branch. Accordingly, the manifestation of such a purpose, it seems to us, would continue to disqualify an application. That is not to deny that ordinary crimes might be inextricably intertwined with foreign intelligence crimes. For example, if a group of international terrorists were to engage in bank robberies in order to finance the manufacture of a bomb, evidence of the bank robbery should be treated just as evidence of the terrorist act itself. But the FISA process cannot be used as a device to investigate wholly unrelated ordinary crimes.

One final point; we think the government's purpose as set forth in a section 1804(a)(7)(B) certification is to be judged by the national security official's articulation and not by a FISA court inquiry into the origins of an investigation nor an examination of the personnel involved. It is up to the Director of the FBI, who typically certifies, to determine the government's national security purpose, as approved by the Attorney General or Deputy Attorney General. This is not a standard whose application the FISA court legitimately reviews by seeking to inquire into which Justice Department officials were instigators of an investigation. All Justice Department officers—including those in the FBI—are under the control of the Attorney General. If he wishes a particular investigation to be run by an officer of any division, that is his prerogative. There is nothing in FISA or the Patriot Act that suggests otherwise. That means, perforce, if the FISA court has reason to doubt that the government has any real non-prosecutorial purpose in seeking foreign intelligence information it can demand further inquiry into the certifying officer's purpose—or perhaps even the Attorney General's or Deputy Attorney General's reasons for approval. The important point is that the relevant purpose is that of those senior officials in the Executive Branch who have the responsibility of appraising the government's national security needs.

2.　　　Reportedly, government investigations of terrorist activity were energized by the decision in the In re Sealed case, supra; that prior to that decision, federal prosecutors had assumed that FISA information was off limits in criminal cases. See Glenn R. Simpson and Jess Bravin, New Powers Fuel Legal Assault on Suspected Terror Supporters, Wall Street Journal, Jan. 21, 2003.

3.　　　In an investigation of a suspected terrorist cell, the FBI obtains a FISA search warrant to search the homes of the cell members and also obtains judicial approval for electronic surveillance of these same individuals. Clearly the FBI wishes to prevent any planned terrorist attacks. But if they get evidence of planning of these attacks, they will wish also to prosecute these individuals. At some point law enforcement personnel and prosecutors concerned with prosecution will need to be brought into the picture? Does it make sense, did it ever make sense to try to build a wall between intelligence and law enforcement personnel in the context of this kind of scenario?

4.　　a.　　The FBI has information that members of a motorcycle gang involved in illegal drug trafficking who have been under law enforcement investigation have been in touch with foreign agents who the Bureau believes are plotting a terrorist action. The FBI believes that the foreign agents are exploring the possibility of importing drugs, selling them to the motorcycle gang and using the profits to help finance the terrorist plot. The Justice Department wishes to obtain judicial approval under FISA for electronic surveillance and physical searches directed against members of the motorcycle gang as well as the foreign agents. Should the FISA court approve an order authorizing the surveillance?

　　　b.　　The FBI has been investigating a drug ring. It learns that there is a new member of the ring who in the past has had ties to al

Qaeda. It requests an order under FISA approving electronic surveillance of all members of the ring. What result?

c.   A member of a terrorist group now defunct has slipped into the United States surreptitiously. The FBI wishes to obtain a judicial order under FISA to listen in to his telephone conversations. Their purpose is: a) to determine whether he is currently planning any terrorist activity; and b) to gather evidence about a past terrorist bomb planting in which they believe he was involved. What result?

5.   What does the court of review opinion in In Sealed Case, supra note 1, have to say, if anything about the propriety of a sharing of information between personnel with a law enforcement-prosecution mission and those with a foreign intelligence mission during the course of an investigation?

6.   As we learned in ch. 2, persons charged with terrorism crimes are often also charged with non-terrorism crimes. What bearing does that fact have on the In re Sealed Case's observations. Sometimes, where, for one reason or another, terrorism crimes cannot be proved against a person suspected of being a terrorist, the government will prosecute the individual for non-terrorism crimes which he has committed. Is that practice inconsistent with the court's dicta in In re Sealed Case? How would you reconcile the court's statements with the practice of prosecuting for non-terrorism crimes in order to put a suspected terrorist in prison?

7.   The Second Circuit addressed the constitutionality of the significant purpose limitation under the fourth amendment. United States v. Abu-Jihaad, 630 F.3d 102 (2d Cir.2010):

> . . . [T]he Fourth Amendment warrant requirement demands a showing of probable cause reasonable to the purpose being pursued. Thus, identification of purpose is necessary to assess the reasonableness of the probable cause standards at issue. Where multiple purposes are significant to an investigation, however, the Fourth Amendment does not require the government to identify a primary purpose or limit its ability to secure a warrant to satisfaction of the standards for that purpose. Rather, the government may secure a warrant under the probable cause standards applicable to any purpose that it pursues in good faith. Thus, we identify no constitutional defects in FISA's certification requirement of "a significant" rather than a primary "purpose . . . to obtain foreign intelligence information,

The FISA Court of Review also concluded as reasonable under the Fourth Amendment the Patriot Act's substitution of "a significant purpose" for the talismanic phrase "primary purpose." In re Sealed Case, 310 F.3d at 742–45.

8.   The In re Sealed Case, supra, triggered much law review commentary, most of it expressing concern about the watering down of Fourth Amendment protections that would result from the PATRIOT Act amendments of the FISA statute and the FISA Review Court's decision in the matter. See,

e.g., George P. Varghese, A Sense of Purpose: The Role of Law Enforcement in Foreign Intelligence Surveillance, 152 U.Pa. L.Rev. 385 (2003); Nola K. Breglio, Note: Leaving FISA Behind: The Need to Return to Warrantless Foreign Intelligence Surveillance, 113 Yale L.J. 179 (2003); David Hardin, The Fuss Over Two Small Words: The Unconstitutionality of the USA PATRIOT Act Amendments to FISA Under the Fourth Amendment, 71 Geo. Wash.L.Rev. 291 (2003); John E. Branch III, Statutory Misinterpretation: The Foreign Intelligence Court of Review's Interpretation of the "Significant Purpose" Requirement of the Foreign Intelligence Surveillance Act, 81 N.C.L.Rev. 2075 (2003).

5. CRIMINAL PROSECUTION USING FISA-DERIVED MATERIAL

UNITED STATES V. DUGGAN
743 F.2d 59 (2d Cir.1984)

KEARSE, CIRCUIT JUDGE:

The principal issues raised in this appeal by alleged agents of the Provisional Irish Republican Army ("PIRA") concern the constitutionality and proper application of the Foreign Intelligence Surveillance Act ("FISA" or the "Act"), 50 U.S.C. §§ 1801–1811 (Supp. V 1981). Defendants Andrew Duggan, Eamon Meehan, Gabriel Megahey, and Colm Meehan appeal from judgments of conviction entered in the United States District Court for the Eastern District of New York, after a jury trial before Charles P. Sifton, Judge. Duggan, Megahey, and Eamon Meehan were convicted of (a) unlicensed exportation of items on the United States Munitions List, in violation of 22 U.S.C. § 2778(b)(2) (1982) (count 2); (b) transportation of explosives in interstate commerce without a license, in violation of 18 U.S.C. § 842(a)(3)(A) (1982) (count 3); (c) transportation of explosives in interstate commerce knowing that the explosives would be used to kill, injure, or intimidate individuals, in violation of 18 U.S.C. § 844(d) (1982) (count 4); (d) transportation in interstate commerce of firearms with their serial numbers removed, in violation of 18 U.S.C. § 922(k) (1982) (count 5); (e) delivery to a common carrier of a shipment containing firearms without giving notice to the carrier of the contents of the shipment, in violation of 18 U.S.C. § 922(e) (1982) (count 6); (f) conspiracy to violate both 26 U.S.C. § 5861(d) (1982), which proscribes possession of unregistered destructive devices, and the statutes listed in counts 3 through 6, in violation of 18 U.S.C. § 371 (1982) (count 1). Colm Meehan was acquitted on the two counts involving interstate transportation of explosives (counts 3 and 4) and was convicted on all other counts. The Meehans were also convicted of possessing guns while illegal aliens, in violation of 18 U.S.C. app. § 1202(a)(5) (1982) (count 7).

On appeal, all of the defendants contend principally (1) that the district court erred in refusing to suppress evidence obtained through a wiretap pursuant to FISA on the grounds that (a) FISA is unconstitutionally broad and violates the probable cause requirement of the Fourth Amendment, and (b) the government failed to comply with FISA's prerequisites for wire surveillance; . . . .

. . . In general the evidence, presented largely through the testimony of Hanratty, videotapes of meetings between PIRA members and undercover law enforcement agents, and tape recordings of telephone conversations involving Megahey, showed defendants as part of a network of men working clandestinely on behalf of PIRA to acquire explosives, weapons, ammunition, and remote-controlled detonation devices in the United States to be exported to Northern Ireland for use in terrorist activities. Megahey, an Irish national who sought political asylum in the United States, was the leader and financier of PIRA operations in the United States. Duggan, an American citizen, was Megahey's assistant in contacting sellers of electronic equipment to be used in remote-controlled bombs and other sophisticated weaponry. Eamon Meehan, under the direction of Megahey, gathered and stored firearms and explosives; Eamon and his brother Colm—both aliens living illegally in the United States—secreted these materials in a shipment of goods bound for Northern Ireland.

. . .

1.   The Pretrial Motion to Suppress the FISA Materials

On July 27, 1982, pursuant to the provisions of FISA, 50 U.S.C. § 1806(b), the Acting Attorney General of the United States, Edward C. Schmults, authorized the use at trial of tape recordings and information obtained pursuant to the FISA surveillance of the activities of the defendants. Shortly thereafter, pursuant to 50 U.S.C. § 1806(c), the government notified the court and the defendants of its intention to introduce evidence from the FISA surveillance at trial. In the following months, the government provided the defendants with copies of all tape recordings, transcripts, surveillance logs, and pen register tapes of all telephone conversations resulting from the surveillance.

Defendants moved to suppress the fruits of the FISA surveillance on a variety of grounds. They contended that FISA surveillance violates a target's First, Fourth, and Fifth Amendment rights because it is too broad; violates the doctrine of separation of powers because it requires the courts to decide political questions; and denies due process and equal protection to aliens. In addition, defendants contended that the requirements set forth in FISA had not been met because an insufficient basis had been provided for the issuance of the surveillance order and because the government had failed to comply with FISA's "minimization" requirements. They also contended that FISA had been improperly used simply to obtain evidence of criminal activity rather than to protect the national security. Defendants asked the court to hold an evidentiary hearing to determine these issues.

The government in turn moved to have the trial court determine the propriety of the electronic surveillance on an ex parte, in camera basis pursuant to 50 U.S.C. § 1806(f). In support of this application, the government filed an Affidavit and Claim of Privilege of Acting Attorney General Schmults. The affidavit stated that the FISA applications contained sensitive information concerning United States intelligence sources and methods and other information relating to the efforts of the United States to combat international terrorism. It certified that public disclosure or an adversary hearing with respect to this information would harm the national security of the United States. An additional affidavit of the Acting Attorney General, submitted to the district court in camera, set forth in greater detail the facts upon which the claim of privilege was based. After reviewing all of these materials, Judge Sifton rejected all of defendants' FISA arguments on their merits in a thorough opinion sub nom. United States v. Megahey, 553 F.Supp. 1180 (E.D.N.Y.1982) ("Megahey"), ...

2.   The Posttrial FISA Motion

Following their convictions, defendants asserted new challenges to FISA, to wit, (1) that the surveillance was unlawful because Duggan had not been named as a target, and (2) that the trial evidence revealed that the court had been misled as to the basis for the issuance of the FISA order. The court rejected the first contention on the grounds that it was untimely raised and that there was no requirement that the government name more than one target of the surveillance. The court rejected defendants' second contention after reviewing the public and in camera documents and determining that it had not in fact been misled.

. . .

Defendants mount two types of challenge with regard to FISA. First, they contend that the Act is unconstitutional on several grounds. In addition, they contend that even if FISA is not unconstitutional, its requirements were not met in this case.

A.   The Constitutionality of FISA

Defendants contend that FISA is unconstitutional principally on the grounds that (1) it is so broad as to deprive certain persons of due process of law, (2) it violates the probable cause requirement of the Fourth Amendment, and (3) it deprives nonresident aliens of the equal protection of the law. We find no merit in these contentions.

1.   The Scope of the Act

Defendants argue that FISA is impermissibly broad in several respects. They point out that foreign intelligence information includes "information with respect . . ." The sections of the Act relied upon by the defendants to show that the Act is impermissibly broad are simply irrelevant to this case. The sections and definitions plainly applicable to Megahey are explicit, unequivocal, and clearly defined.

Nor are we impressed by defendants' argument that insofar as § 1801(e)(2) defines foreign intelligence information as information that "relates to . . . (A) the national defense or the security of the United States; or (B) the conduct of the foreign affairs of the United States" it is impermissibly vague. Section 1801(e)(1)(B) defines foreign intelligence information as "information that relates to . . . the ability of the United States to protect against . . . international terrorism by a foreign power or an agent of a foreign power." Given the information provided by Hanratty, the government plainly had a basis under this section for describing the information sought by surveillance of Megahey, self-proclaimed leader of an international terrorist group, as foreign intelligence information. Thus, even if we thought § 1801(e)(2)'s concepts of national defense, national security, or conduct of foreign affairs to be vague, which we do not, we would find therein no basis for reversing the convictions of these defendants, whose circumstances were governed by an entirely different definition.

2.   The Probable Cause Requirement of the Fourth Amendment

The Fourth Amendment provides that "no warrants shall issue, but upon probable cause. . . ." Defendants argue principally (1) that the Amendment applies to all proposed surveillances, including those in national security cases, and (2) that even if there were an exception for national security matters, it would not apply to terrorism cases where the objects of the terrorism are entirely outside of the United States. We reject these contentions.

Prior to the enactment of FISA, virtually every court that had addressed the issue had concluded that the President had the inherent power to conduct warrantless electronic surveillance to collect foreign intelligence information, and that such surveillances constituted an exception to the warrant requirement of the Fourth Amendment . . .

In Keith, the government argued that Title III of the Omnibus Crime Control and Safe Streets Act, 18 U.S.C. §§ 2510 et seq. ("Title III"), recognized the constitutional authority of the President to conduct domestic security surveillances without a warrant. The Court rejected this argument, noting that the legislative history made clear that Title III was not intended to legislate with respect to national security surveillances. The Court went on to hold that a warrant was required in Keith under the

Fourth Amendment; but the implication of its discussion was that the warrant requirement is flexible and that different standards may be compatible with the Fourth Amendment in light of the different purposes and practical considerations of domestic national security surveillances. 407 U.S. at 321–24, 92 S.Ct. at 2138–40. Thus, the Court observed that domestic security surveillance may involve different policy and practical considerations from the surveillance of "ordinary crime." The gathering of security intelligence is often long range and involves the interrelation of various sources and types of information. The exact targets of such surveillance may be more difficult to identify than in surveillance operations against many types of crime specified in Title III. Often, too, the emphasis of domestic intelligence gathering is on the prevention of unlawful activity or the enhancement of the Government's preparedness for some possible future crisis or emergency. Thus, the focus of domestic surveillance may be less precise than that directed against more conventional types of crime. . . . Different standards [for surveillance involving domestic security] may be compatible with the Fourth Amendment if they are reasonable both in relation to the legitimate need of Government for intelligence information and the protected rights of our citizens. For the warrant application may vary according to the governmental interest to be enforced and the nature of citizen rights deserving protection.

Against this background, Congress passed FISA to settle what it believed to be the unresolved question of the applicability of the Fourth Amendment warrant requirement to electronic surveillance for foreign intelligence purposes, and to "remove any doubt as to the lawfulness of such surveillance." H.R.Rep. 1283, pt. I, 95th Cong., 2d Sess. 25 (1978) ("House Report"). FISA reflects both Congress's "legislative judgment" that the court orders and other procedural safeguards laid out in the Act "are necessary to insure that electronic surveillance by the U.S. Government within this country conforms to the fundamental principles of the fourth amendment," S.Rep. No. 701, 95th Cong., 2d Sess. 13, reprinted in 1978 U.S.Code Cong. & Ad.News 3973, 3982 ("Senate Report 95–701"), and its attempt to fashion a "secure framework by which the Executive Branch may conduct legitimate electronic surveillance for foreign intelligence purposes within the context of this Nation's commitment to privacy and individual rights." S.Rep. No. 604, 95th Cong., 1st Sess. 15, reprinted in 1978 U.S.Code Cong. & Ad.News 3904, 3916 ("Senate Report 95–604"). In constructing this framework, Congress gave close scrutiny to departures from those Fourth Amendment doctrines applicable in the criminal-investigation context in order to ensure that the procedures established in [FISA] are reasonable in relation to legitimate foreign counterintelligence requirements and the protected rights of individuals. Their reasonableness depends, in part, upon an assessment of the difficulties of investigating activities planned, directed, and supported from abroad by foreign intelligence services and foreign-based terrorist groups. The differences between ordinary criminal investigations to gather evidence of specific crimes and foreign counterintelligence investigations to uncover and monitor clandestine activities have been taken into account. Other factors include the international responsibilities of the United States, the duties of the Federal Government to the States in matters involving foreign terrorism, and the need to maintain the secrecy of lawful counterintelligence sources and methods.

We regard the procedures fashioned in FISA as a constitutionally adequate balancing of the individual's Fourth Amendment rights against the nation's need to obtain foreign intelligence information. The governmental concerns are detailed in the passages quoted above from Keith and the legislative history of FISA, and those concerns make reasonable the adoption of prerequisites to surveillance that are less stringent than those precedent to the issuance of a warrant for a criminal investigation. Against this background, the Act requires that the FISA Judge find probable cause to believe that the target is a foreign power or an agent of a foreign power, and that the place at which the electronic surveillance is to be directed is being used or is about to be used by a foreign power or an agent of a foreign power; and it requires him to find that the application meets the requirements of the Act. These requirements make it reasonable to dispense with a requirement that the FISA Judge find probable cause to believe that surveillance will in fact lead to the gathering of foreign intelligence information. Further, if the target is a United States person, the Act requires the FISA Judge to determine that the executive branch's certifications pursuant to § 1804(a)(7) are not clearly erroneous in light of the application as a whole, and to find that the application properly proposes, as required by § 1801(h), to minimize the intrusion upon the target's privacy.

We conclude that these requirements provide an appropriate balance between the individual's interest in privacy and the government's need to obtain foreign intelligence information, and that FISA does not violate the probable cause requirement of the Fourth Amendment.

Nor is there any merit to defendants' contention that the national security interests of the United States are not implicated by acts of terrorism directed wholly outside the United States. The government points out that if other nations were to harbor terrorists and give them safe haven for staging terrorist activities against the United States, United States national security would be threatened. As a reciprocal matter, the United States cannot afford to give safe haven to terrorists who seek to carry out raids against other nations. Thus, international terrorism conducted from the United States, no matter where it is directed, may well have a substantial effect on United States national security and foreign policy.

. . .

B.   Compliance with the Requirements of FISA

Defendants contend that, even if FISA is constitutional, the evidence derived from the wiretap should have been suppressed because the provisions of FISA were not complied with, in that (1) the surveillance was conducted as part of a criminal investigation, rather than a national security investigation; (2) the district court erred in failing to disclose the information contained in the FISA applications and orders; and (3) Duggan, although allegedly a "target" of the FISA surveillance, was not so named in the FISA applications. We reject each of these contentions.

. . .

The Alleged Use of FISA Surveillance to Conduct a Criminal Investigation

Defendants contend that the surveillance of Megahey's telephone was not authorized by FISA because the information was sought as part of a criminal investigation. We see no grounds for concluding that the requirements of FISA were not met.

FISA permits federal officials to obtain orders authorizing electronics surveillance "for the purpose of obtaining foreign intelligence information." 50 U.S.C. § 1802(b). The requirement that foreign intelligence information be the primary objective of the surveillance is plain not only from the language of § 1802(b) but also from the requirements in § 1804 as to what the application must contain. The application must contain a certification by a designated official of the executive branch that the purpose of the surveillance is to acquire foreign intelligence information, and the certification must set forth the basis for the certifying official's belief that the information sought is the type of foreign intelligence information described. Id. § 1804(a)(7).

Once this certification is made, however, it is, under FISA, subjected to only minimal scrutiny by the courts. Congress deemed it a sufficient check in this regard to require the FISA Judge (1) to find probable cause to believe that the target of the requested surveillance is an agent of a foreign power; (2) to find that the application is complete and in proper form; and (3) when the target is a United States person, to find that the certifications are not "clearly erroneous." The FISA Judge, in reviewing the application, is not to second-guess the executive branch official's certification that the objective of the surveillance is foreign intelligence information. Further, Congress intended that, when a person affected by a FISA surveillance challenges the FISA Court's order, a reviewing court is to have no greater authority to second-guess the executive branch's certifications than has the FISA Judge. [I]n determining the legality of a surveillance . . . the trial judge . . . [is] not to make determinations which the issuing judge is not authorized to make. Where the bill specifies the scope or nature of judicial review in the consideration of an application, any review under these subsections is similarly constrained. For example, when reviewing the certifications required by [§ 1804(a)(7)], unless there is a prima facie showing of a fraudulent statement by a certifying officer, procedural regularity is the only determination to be made if a non-U.S. person is the target. . . .

We see no basis for any suggestion in the present case that the application to the FISA Court did not meet the statutory requirement for certifying that the information sought was foreign intelligence information. At the time of the FISA application, the executive branch was aware that PIRA was an international terrorist organization and that Megahey played a leadership role in PIRA activities. In such circumstances, the foreign intelligence value of a FISA wiretap on Megahey's telephone would be plain: he would likely be a prime source of information relating to PIRA membership, goals, methods, and operations. The publicly filed government affidavits in this case make clear that the FISA surveillance was instituted as part of an investigation of international terrorism. Moreover, we have reviewed the in camera submissions to the FISA Judge, and we agree with the district court's finding that "the purpose of the surveillance in this case, both initially and throughout, was to secure foreign intelligence information and was not, as [the] defendants assert, directed towards criminal investigation or the institution of a criminal prosecution." Megahey, 553 F.Supp. at 1190.

Finally, we emphasize that otherwise valid FISA surveillance is not tainted simply because the government can anticipate that the fruits of such surveillance may later be used, as allowed by § 1806(b), as evidence in a criminal trial. Congress recognized that in many cases the concerns of the government with respect to foreign intelligence will overlap those with respect to law enforcement. Thus, one Senate Report noted that [i]ntelligence and criminal law enforcement tend to merge in [the area of foreign counterintelligence investigations]. . . .

     . . .

In sum, FISA authorizes surveillance for the purpose of obtaining foreign intelligence information; the information possessed about Megahey involved international terrorism; and the fact that domestic law enforcement concerns may also have been implicated did not eliminate the government's ability to obtain a valid FISA order.

2.   The District Court's Refusal to Disclose the Substance of the FISA Applications

Defendant's contention that the district court erred in refusing to disclose the substance of the affidavits and certifications that accompanied the FISA applications need not detain us long. Section 1806(f) of FISA provides for in camera, ex parte review of the documents where the Attorney General has filed an affidavit stating that disclosure of the FISA applications and orders would harm the national security of the United States . . .

We see no error in Judge Sifton's determination that disclosure was not necessary for an accurate determination of the legality of the surveillance of Megahey. Defendants have made no showing of misrepresented facts; they do not argue that Megahey was not clearly identified as a target. They have made no other presentation warranting disclosure. Under the circumstances, Judge Sifton did not abuse his discretion.

3.   The Failure to Name Duggan as a Target of the Surveillance

Defendants contend that the fruits of the FISA surveillance should be suppressed because Duggan was not named as a target of the surveillance. The import of this argument is, apparently, that because Duggan is a United States person, the preconditions to granting an FISA order allowing surveillance of Duggan would have been more stringent than they were for surveillance of Megahey, a nonresident alien. See Part II. A. 4., supra. Defendants' motion to suppress the evidence on this ground was properly denied by the district court on the grounds that it was untimely and lacked merit.

. . .

Defendants were thus twice put on notice prior to trial that Duggan had not been named as a target and they could have advanced the Duggan-omission argument in timely fashion. Their failure to do so constituted a waiver.

If defendants' argument as to the omission of Duggan had not been waived, we would reject it on its merits. The identification requirement imposed by FISA is only that an application for surveillance identify the "target of the electronic surveillance." 50 U.S.C. § 1804(a)(3). . . .

. . .

The judgments of conviction are affirmed. The mandate shall issue forthwith.

QUESTIONS AND NOTES

1.   Duggan is an early case in which a criminal prosecution involving the use of FISA-derived material reached the federal district courts and courts of appeal. See also United States v. Nicholson, 955 F.Supp. 588 (E.D.Va.1997); United States v. Pelton, 835 F.2d 1067 (4th Cir.1987); United States v. Sarkissian, 841 F.2d 959 (9th Cir. 1988). Post-9/11, there has been an increase in the number of prosecutions in which issues growing out of the results of a FISA-authorized investigation have been raised. See, for example, United

States v. Holy Land Foundation for Relief and Development, 2007 WL 2011319 (N.D.Tex. 2007); United States v. Hassoun, 2007 WL 1068127 (S.D.Fla. 2007); United States v. Benkahla, 437 F.Supp.2d 541 (E.D.Va. 2006); United States v. Marzook, 435 F.Supp.2d 778 (N.D.Ill.2006), although in some of these cases, the FISA surveillance occurred pre-9/11. See, for example, the Marzook case, supra. We have seen the Holy Land Foundation case previously, supra, in ch. 3, and the Hassoun case, supra, is the same case in which Jose Padilla, whose saga will be treated in detail infra, Chapter 10, was one of the defendants.

See also United States v. Abu-Jihaad, 630 F.3d 102 (2d Cir. 2010).

2.   FISA proceedings are secret and ex parte. They are conducted by the special FISA court, not in a regular courtroom but in a special room through "a series of doors and secret codes," Jonathan Turley, A Shot Across the Bow From the Darkness, LA Times, August 26, 2002, B9. Accordingly, we rarely get a glimpse of the court, with neither the public nor the suspected person(s) being present or normally having access to published materials arising out of the proceedings. When criminal prosecutions relating to the FISA matter do occur, however, they provide a limited window into the earlier-occurring FISA proceedings. Duggan and similar cases provide such a window and also give a valuable perspective on how the FISA process and issues relating thereto are viewed by judges not directly involved in the FISA judicial approval process. They help us to understand how the FISA process works, and they are a vehicle for addressing the constitutional issues raised by that process.

3.   A more direct view into the FISA court process was provided in 2002 when two opinions, one from the FISA lower court and one from the FISA court of review were made public; this was a very unusual event. See In re All Matters Submitted to the Foreign Intelligence Surveillance Court ("In re FISC"), 218 F.Supp.2d 611 (Foreign Intel.Surv.Ct.2002) and In re Sealed Case No.'s 02–001, 02–002, 310 F.3d 717 (F.I.S.Ct.Rev.2002), an excerpt from which was reproduced supra.

B. THE TERRORIST SURVEILLANCE PROGRAM (TSP) CONTROVERSY AND ELECTRONIC SURVEILLANCE ABROAD

1. BACKGROUND

Sometime after September 11, 2001, President Bush approved a secret Terrorist Surveillance Program that authorized the National Security Agency (NSA) to electronically eavesdrop, without obtaining judicial approval, on international communications into and out of the United States between persons linked to al Qaeda or related terrorist organizations. The existence of the program was first disclosed in the New York Times in December 2005. Details and specifics of the TSP were not publicly disclosed, but its existence was soon confirmed by the administration. See ACLU v. National Security Agency, 493 F.3d 644 (6th Cir.2007):

> Sometime after the September 11, 2001, terrorist attacks, President Bush authorized the NSA to begin a counter-terrorism operation that has come to be known as the Terrorist Surveillance Program ("TSP"). Although the specifics remain undisclosed, it has been publicly acknowledged that the TSP includes the interception (i.e., wiretapping), without warrants, of telephone and email communications where one party to the communication is located outside the United States and the NSA has "a reasonable basis to conclude that one party to the communication is a member of al Qaeda, affiliated with al Qaeda, or a member of an organization affiliated with al Qaeda, or working in support of al Qaeda." See Press Briefing by Att'y Gen. Alberto Gonzales and Gen. Michael Hayden, Principal Deputy Dir. for Nat'l Intelligence (Dec. 19, 2005), available at http://www.whitehouse.gov/news/releases/2005/12/print/20051219–1.html (last visited July 2, 2007).[1]

---

[1] [footnote by the court] In Hepting v. AT & T Corp., the District Court for the Northern District of California collected and documented certain publicly available information, which provides some background and context for the present case:

"The New York Times disclosed the [TSP] on December 16, 2005. (James Risen and Eric Lichthlau, Bush Lets U.S. Spy on Callers Without Courts, The New York Times (Dec. 16, 2005)). The following day, President George W Bush confirmed the existence of a 'terrorist surveillance program' in his weekly radio address:

> 'In the weeks following the [September 11, 2001] terrorist attacks on our Nation, I authorized the National Security Agency, consistent with U.S. law and the Constitution, to intercept the international communications of people with known links to Al Qaeda and related terrorist organizations. Before we intercept these communications, the Government must have information that establishes a clear link to these terrorist networks.'

"[Transcript] available at http://www.whitehouse.gov/news/releases/2005/12/print/20051217.html (last visited July 19, 2006). The President also described the mechanism by which the program is authorized and reviewed:

> 'The activities I authorized are reviewed approximately every 45 days. Each review is based on a fresh intelligence assessment of terrorist threats to the continuity of our Government and the threat of catastrophic damage to our homeland. During each assessment, previous activities under the authorization are reviewed. The review includes approval by our Nation's top legal officials, including the Attorney General and the Counsel to the President. I have reauthorized this program more than 30 times since the September the 11th attacks, and I intend to do so for as long as our Nation faces a continuing threat from Al Qaeda and related groups.
>
> 'The NSA's activities under this authorization are thoroughly reviewed by the Justice Department and NSA's top legal officials, including NSA's General Counsel and Inspector General. Leaders in Congress have been briefed more than a dozen times on this authorization and the activities conducted under it. Intelligence officials involved in this activity also receive extensive training to ensure they perform their duties consistent with the letter and intent of the authorization.'

"Id.

In May, 2006, USA Today reported the existence of a second NSA program alleging that three major communications companies, BellSouth Corp., Verizon Communications Inc. and AT&T had provided millions of telephone calling records to the NSA and that the Agency used these databases not to listen in or record conversations but rather to analyze calling patterns in an effort to detect terrorist activity—a type of data mining. A fourth company, Qwest Communications International, Inc. was reported to have declined to participate in the program. Officials at BellSouth and Verizon subsequently denied providing any customer telephone records to the government. AT & T and the government neither confirmed nor denied the USA Today report.

Subsequently, and over the course of the next two years, activities occurred on a number of fronts growing out of these disclosures. In January, 2006, the Department of Justice issued a lengthy legal memorandum, referred to as a White Paper, defending the legality of the electronic surveillance conducted under the TSP.

A number of senators and representatives made public statements about the TSP, and congressional committees conducted hearings on the program and its legality, often expressing frustration about not being able to obtain sufficient information about the Program's details. See, e.g. Department of Justice Responses to the House Judiciary Committee Minority Members Joint Questions Regarding the NSA Terrorist Surveillance Program, March 24, 2006, available at http://fas.org/irp/agency/doj/fisa/doj032406.pdf. In this document, the majority of the DOJ's responses to the congressional questions declined to disclose the requested information, noting the "classified and sensitive" nature of the Program.

Lawsuits seeking to enjoin the TSP and otherwise seeking redress were filed. For an example of one such case where the district judge ruled that the Program was unconstitutional, see ACLU v. National Security Agency, 438 F.Supp.2d 754 (E.D.Mich. 2006). Subsequently, the administration reversed course to a limited extent; it had earlier rejected

---

"Attorney General Alberto Gonzales subsequently confirmed that this program intercepts 'contents of communications where . . . one party to the communication is outside the United States' and the government has 'a reasonable basis to conclude that one party to the communication is a member of al Qaeda, affiliated with al Qaeda, or a member of an organization affiliated with al Qaeda, or working in support of al Qaeda.' [Press Briefing] available at http://www.whitehouse.gov/news/releases/2005/12/print/20051219–1.html (last visited July 19, 2005). The Attorney General also noted, 'This [program] is not about wiretapping everyone. This is a very concentrated, very limited program focused at gaining information about our enemy.' Id. at 5. The President has also made a public statement, of which the court takes judicial notice, that the government's 'international activities strictly target al Qaeda and their known affiliates,' 'the government does not listen to domestic phone calls without court approval' and the government is 'not mining or trolling through the personal lives of millions of innocent Americans.' The White House, President Bush Discusses NSA Surveillance Program (May 11, 2006), [available at] http://www.whitehouse. gov/news/releases/2006/05/200605 11–1.html (last visited July 19, 2005)."
Hepting v. AT & T Corp., 439 F.Supp.2d 974, 986–87 (N.D.Cal.2006).

proposals that the TSP surveillances be brought to the FISA court for approval, but as described in ACLU v. National Security Agency, 493 F.3d 644, n. 4 (6th Cir.2007), the administration for the first time brought the FISA court into the TSP picture:

> On January 10, 2007, "a Judge of the Foreign Intelligence Surveillance Court issued orders authorizing the government to target for collection international communications into or out of the United States where there is probable cause to believe that one of the communicants is a member or agent of al Qaeda or an associated terrorist organization." Letter from Att'y Gen. Alberto Gonzales to Chair. of the Comm. on the Judiciary Patrick Leahy (Jan. 17, 2007), available at http://graphics8.nytimes.com/packages/pdf/politics/20060117gonzalesLetter.pdf (last visited July 2, 2007). According to a letter written by the Attorney General, "any electronic surveillance that was occurring as part of the [TSP] will now be conduct[ed] subject to the approval of the Foreign Intelligence Surveillance Court."

The district court order in the ACLU v. NSA case, supra, was appealed, and in July, 2007, the 6th Circuit reversed, finding that the plaintiffs did not have standing.

Lawsuits were also filed based on the alleged data mining. AT&T customers sued AT&T alleging constitutional and statutory violations and seeking damages and injunctive and declaratory relief. See, e.g., Hepting v. AT&T Corp., 439 F.Supp. 2d 974 (N.D.Cal.2006). Meanwhile, defendants throughout the country in terrorist prosecutions and in other types of cases, too, sought disclosure from the government as to whether they had been eavesdropped upon under the TSP, hoping to prove that was the case and that the eavesdropping was illegal and somehow tainted their prosecution.

Reportedly in the spring or summer of 2007, the FISA court, now newly having undertaken some kind of review of the TSP surveillances, handed down a decision that presented a problem for the government in operating the TSP program. Although the relevant judicial decision(s) was [were] secret and not published, statements by government officials indicated that the legal problem was created by the fact that what had been considered to be purely international electronic surveillances (i.e. between two parties outside of the United States), sometimes involved the communication traveling through a communications switching station within the U.S. To address this type of issue and to harden up the legal foundation for the TSP program, the administration sought new legislation toward the very end of the congressional session in the summer of 2007.

In August, 2007, Congress enacted the Protect America Act, PL 110–55, designed to address the legal problems of the TSP program. However, it was a temporary fix. The congressional action was rushed, and many of the legislators wanted to return to the subject and legislate on the subject more carefully. Accordingly, it was provided in the Act that it would sunset after 180 days, i.e., on January 31, 2008. In the next few months, there was a flurry of activity in both houses of the Congress regarding the content of the legislation that would replace the Protect America Act. A major point of controversy was whether the final legislation would contain a provision granting immunity from civil liability to the telephone companies that had cooperated with the government's TSP program. Finally, in July, 2008, the new legislation to address these issues, titled the FISA Amendments Act of 2008, was passed and signed into law. Salient provisions of this Act are reproduced, and issues relating to it are treated in section C of this chapter, infra.

2. A PERSPECTIVE ON THE TSP FROM WITHIN THE GOVERNMENT

On July 10, 2009, a report was issued titled, Unclassified Report on President's Surveillance Program. The Report had been prepared by the Inspectors General of the CIA, DOD, DOJ, NSA, and the Office of the DNI [ed. Director of National Intelligence-ODNI] and can be found at: www.fas. org/irp/eprint/psp.pdf. Excerpts from the Report are reproduced below. It appears from these excerpts that the President authorized surveillance activities that extended beyond the TSP program. The exact nature of these activities remains highly classified. The entire report merits examination.

Unclassified Report on the President's Surveillance Program

. . . Shortly thereafter, the President authorized the NSA to undertake a number of new, highly classified intelligence activities. All of these activities were authorized in a single Presidential Authorization that was periodically reauthorized.

The specific intelligence activities that were permitted by the Presidential Authorizations remain highly classified, except that beginning in December 2005 the President and other Administration officials acknowledged that these activities included the interception without a court order of certain international communications where there is "a reasonable basis to conclude that one party to the communication is a member of al-Qa'ida, affiliated with al-Qa'ida, or a member of an organization affiliated with al-Qa'ida." The President and other Administration officials referred to this publicly disclosed activity as the "Terrorist Surveillance Program," a convention we follow in this unclassified report. We refer to other intelligence activities authorized under the Presidential Authorizations as the "Other Intelligence Activities." The specific details of the Other Intelligence Activities remain highly classified, although the

Attorney General publicly acknowledged the existence of such activities in August 2007. Together, the Terrorist Surveillance Program and the Other Intelligence Activities comprise the PSP.

. . .

CONCLUSION

Pursuant to the FISA Amendments Act of 2008, the Inspectors General [ed. IGs] of the DOJ, DoD, ODNI, NSA, and CIA conducted reviews of the PSP. In this report, the classified report, and the accompanying individual reports of the participating IGs, we describe how, following the terrorist attacks of September 11, 2001, the President directed that the NSA's signals intelligence collection capabilities be used to detect and prevent acts of terrorism within the United States.

Pursuant to this authority the NSA conducted new intelligence activities, including the collection of the content of communications into and out of the United States, where one party to the communication was reasonably believed to be a member of al-Qa'ida or its affiliates. The NSA analyzed this information for dissemination as leads to the IC [ed. Intelligence Community], principally to the CIA and the FBI. As described in the IG reports, the scope of this collection authority changed over the course of the PSP.

The IG reports describe the role of each of the participating agencies in the PSP, including the NSA's management and oversight of the collection and analysis process, the CIA's and FBI's use of the PSP-derived intelligence in their counterterrorism efforts, the ODNI's involvement in the program by providing periodic threat assessments and using the program intelligence to produce analytical products, and DOJ's role in analyzing and certifying the legality of the PSP. With the exception of the NSA, the DoD had limited involvement in the PSP.

The IG reports also describe the conflicting views surrounding the legality of aspects of the PSP during 2004, the confrontation between officials from DOJ and the White House about the legal basis for parts of the program, as well as the resolution of that conflict. The ensuing transition of the PSP from presidential authority to statutory authority under FISA is also described in the IG reports.

The IGs also examined the impact of PSP information on counterterrorism efforts. Many senior IC officials believe that the PSP filled a gap in intelligence collection thought to exist under the FISA statute shortly after the al-Qa'ida terrorist attacks against the United States. Others within the IC, including FBI agents, CIA analysts and officers, and other officials had difficulty evaluating the precise contribution of the PSP to counterterrorism efforts because it was most often viewed as one source among many available analytic and intelligence-gathering tools in these efforts. The IG reports describe several examples of how PSP-derived information factored into specific investigations and operations.

Finally, the collection activities pursued under the PSP, and under FISA following the PSP's transition to that authority, involved unprecedented collection activities. We believe the retention and use by IC organizations of information collected under the PSP and FISA should be carefully monitored.

3. MATERIALS BEARING ON THE LEGALITY OF THE TSP

Sometime after the eruption of the controversy regarding the TSP program, the Department of Justice issued a memorandum, a so-called White Paper justifying the legality of the program. Excerpts from this memorandum are reproduced below.

Washington, D.C. 20530

January 19, 2006

LEGAL AUTHORITIES SUPPORTING THE ACTIVITIES OF THE NATIONAL SECURITY AGENCY DESCRIBED BY THE PRESIDENT

As the President has explained, since shortly after the attacks of September 11, 2001, he has authorized the National Security Agency ("NSA") to intercept international communications into and out of the United States of persons linked to al Qaeda or related terrorist organizations. The purpose of these intercepts is to establish an early warning system to detect and prevent another catastrophic terrorist attack on the United States. This paper addresses, in an unclassified form, the legal basis for the NSA activities described by the President ("NSA activities").

SUMMARY

. . .

The NSA activities are supported by the President's well-recognized inherent constitutional authority as Commander in Chief and sole organ for the Nation in foreign affairs to conduct warrantless surveillance of enemy forces for intelligence purposes to detect and disrupt armed attacks on the United States. The President has the chief responsibility under the Constitution to protect America from attack, and the Constitution gives the President the authority necessary to fulfill that solemn responsibility. The President has made clear that he will exercise all authority available to him, consistent with the Constitution, to protect the people of the United States.

In the specific context of the current armed conflict with al Qaeda and related terrorist organizations, Congress by statute has confirmed and supplemented the President's recognized authority under Article II of the Constitution to conduct such warrantless surveillance to prevent further catastrophic attacks on the homeland. In its first legislative response to the terrorist attacks of September 11th, Congress authorized the President to "use all necessary and appropriate force against those nations, organizations, or persons he determines planned, authorized, committed, or aided the terrorist attacks" of September 11th in order to prevent "any future acts of international terrorism against the United States." Authorization for Use of Military Force, Pub. L. No. 107–40, § 2(a), 115 Stat. 224, 224 (Sept. 18, 2001) (reported as a note to 50 U.S.C.A. § 1541) ("AUMF"). History conclusively demonstrates that warrantless communications intelligence targeted at the enemy in time of armed conflict is a traditional and fundamental incident of the use of military force authorized by the AUMF. The Supreme Court's interpretation of the AUMF in Hamdi v. Rumsfeld, 542 U.S. 507 (2004), confirms that Congress in the AUMF gave its express approval to the military conflict against al Qaeda and its allies and thereby to the President's use of all traditional and accepted incidents of force in this current military conflict—including warrantless electronic surveillance to intercept enemy communications both at home and abroad. This understanding of the AUMF demonstrates Congress's support for the President's authority to protect the Nation and, at the same time, adheres to Justice O'Connor's admonition that "a state of war is not a blank check for the President," Hamdi, 542 U.S. at 536 (plurality opinion), particularly in view of the narrow scope of the NSA activities.

The AUMF places the President at the zenith of his powers in authorizing the NSA activities. Under the tripartite framework set forth by Justice Jackson in Youngstown Sheet & Tube Co. v. Sawyer, 343 U.S. 579, 635–38 (1952) (Jackson, J., concurring), Presidential authority is analyzed to determine whether the President is acting in accordance with congressional authorization (category I), whether he acts in the absence of a grant or denial of authority by Congress (category II), or whether he uses his own authority under the Constitution to take actions incompatible with congressional measures (category III). Because of the broad authorization provided in the AUMF, the President's action here falls within category I of Justice Jackson's framework. Accordingly, the President's power in authorizing the NSA activities is at its height because he acted "pursuant to an express or implied authorization of Congress," and his power "includes all that he possesses in his own right plus all that Congress can delegate." Id. at 635.

The NSA activities are consistent with the preexisting statutory framework generally applicable to the interception of communications in the United States—the Foreign Intelligence Surveillance Act ("FISA"), as amended, 50 U.S.C. §§ 1801–1862 (2000 & Supp. II 2002), and relevant related provisions in chapter 119 of title 18.1 Although FISA generally requires judicial approval of electronic surveillance, FISA also contemplates that Congress may authorize such surveillance by a statute other than FISA. See 50 U.S.C. § 1809(a) (prohibiting any person from intentionally "engag[ing] . . . in electronic surveillance under color of law except as authorized by statute"). The AUMF, as construed by the Supreme Court in Hamdi and as confirmed by the history and tradition of armed conflict, is just such a statute. Accordingly, electronic surveillance conducted by the President pursuant to the AUMF, including the NSA activities, is fully consistent with FISA and falls within category I of Justice Jackson's framework.

Even if there were ambiguity about whether FISA, read together with the AUMF, permits the President to authorize the NSA activities, the canon of constitutional avoidance requires reading these statutes in harmony to overcome any restrictions in FISA and Title III, at least as they might otherwise apply to the congressionally authorized armed conflict with al Qaeda. Indeed, were FISA and Title III interpreted to impede the President's ability to use the traditional tool of electronic surveillance to detect and prevent future attacks by a declared enemy that has already struck at the homeland and is engaged in ongoing operations against the United States, the constitutionality of FISA, as applied to that situation, would be called into very serious doubt. In fact, if this difficult constitutional question had to be addressed, FISA would be unconstitutional as applied to this narrow context. Importantly, the FISA Court of Review itself recognized just three years ago that the President retains constitutional authority to conduct foreign surveillance apart from the FISA framework, and the President is certainly entitled, at a minimum, to rely on that judicial interpretation of the Constitution and FISA.

Finally, the NSA activities fully comply with the requirements of the Fourth Amendment. The interception of communications described by the President falls within a well-established exception to the warrant requirement and satisfies the Fourth Amendment's fundamental requirement of reasonableness. The NSA activities are thus constitutionally permissible and fully protective of civil liberties. . . .

QUESTIONS AND NOTES

1.   How many different arguments in support of the TSP program are articulated in the DOJ summary of the arguments made in the White Paper, supra?

2.   Fourteen scholars and former government officials joined in writing a letter dated January 9, 2007, to the Senate Judiciary Committee responding to the arguments made in the DOJ White Paper, characterizing the Justice Department's legal defense of the TSP program as failing "to identify any plausible legal authority for . . . [the] surveillance [program]." The letter contended:

> "[T]he AUMF cannot reasonably be construed to implicitly authorize warrantless electronic surveillance in the United States during wartime, where Congress has expressly and specifically addressed that precise questions in FISA and limited any such warrantless surveillance to the first fifteen days of war."

Regarding the DOJ claim of "inherent" presidential authority, the letter responded,

> "Congress indisputably has authority to regulate electronic surveillance within the United States as it has done in FISA. Where Congress has so regulated, the President can act in contravention of statute only if his authority is exclusive, and not subject to the check of statutory regulation."

Further, the letter argued,

> Moreover, to construe the AUMF as the DOJ suggests would itself raise serious constitutional questions under the Fourth Amendment. The Supreme Court has never upheld warrantless wiretapping within the United States. Accordingly, the principle that statutes should be construed to avoid serious constitutional questions provides an additional reason for concluding that the AUMF does not authorize the President's actions. . . ."

A Response to the Justice Department from Law Professors and Former Government Officials, January 9, 2007. See also Elizabeth B. Bazan & Jennifer K. Elsea, Congressional Research Memorandum, Presidential Authority to Conduct Warrantless Electronic Surveillance to Gather Foreign Intelligence Information, January 5, 2006.

Who has the better of the argument?

3.   Many of the critics of the TSP program argued that using FISA procedures would not have disadvantaged the TSP program electronic surveillance and would ensure judicial oversight of the surveillances in the program, where the surveillance impacted on the domestic end of a communication. Of course, the critics did not have very specific information about the TSP program. Among the issues addressed in the Department of Justice Responses to the House Judiciary Committee Minority Members Joint Questions Regarding the NSA Terrorist Surveillance Program, March 24, 2006, the DOJ said the following,

> Among the advantages offered by the Terrorist Surveillance Program compared to FISA is who makes the probable cause determination and how many layers of review must occur before surveillance begins. Under the Terrorist Surveillance Program, professional intelligence officers, who are experts on al Qaeda and its tactics (including its use of communication systems), with appropriate and rigorous oversight, make the decisions about which international communications should be intercepted. . . .

> By contrast, pursuing "prior judicial review by the FISA court" requires significantly more time. . . . [T]he Government must assemble a voluminous application, obtain the approval of the Attorney General himself and senior administrative national security officials, submit the materials to the court and await its decision. . . . [A]s a practical matter, it is necessary for NSA intelligence officers, NSA lawyers, Justice Department lawyers, and the Attorney General to review a matter before even emergency surveillance would begin. . . .

4.   Footnotes 5 and 6 in the White Paper, and a related comment in the Department of Justice's Responses to the House Judiciary Committee's Oversight Questions regarding the NSA Terrorist Surveillance Program, taken together with 18 U.S.C. § 2511(2)(f) and 50 U.S.C. § 1801(f), all of which are reproduced below, added still another complex issue to the mix in any examination of the legality of the NSA TSP program.

a.   Footnote 5 in the DOJ White Paper:

> 5   To avoid revealing details about the operation of the program, it is assumed for purposes of this paper that the activities described by the President constitute "electronic surveillance," as defined by FISA, 50 U.S.C. § 1801(f).

b.   Footnote 6 in the DOJ White Paper:

> 6   FISA's legislative history reveals that these provisions were intended to exclude certain intelligence activities conducted by the National Security Agency from the coverage of FISA. According to the report of the Senate Judiciary Committee on FISA, "this provision [ed. referencing what became the first part of section 2511(2)(f)] is designed to make clear that the

legislation does not deal with international signals intelligence activities as currently engaged in by the National Security Agency and electronic surveillance conducted outside the United States." S. Rep. No. 95–604, at 64 (1978), reprinted in 1978 U.S.C.C.A.N. 3904, 3965. The legislative history also makes clear that the definition of "electronic surveillance" was crafted for the same reason. See id. at 33–34, 1978 U.S.C.C.A.N. at 3934–36. FISA thereby "adopts the view expressed by the Attorney General during the hearings that enacting statutory controls to regulate the National Security Agency and the surveillance of Americans abroad raises problems best left to separate legislation." Id. at 64, 1978 U.S.C.C.A.N. at 3965. Such legislation placing limitations on traditional NSA activities was drafted, but never passed. See National Intelligence Reorganization and Reform Act of 1978: Hearings Before the Senate Select Committee on Intelligence, 95th Cong., 2d Sess. 999–1007 (1978) (text of unenacted legislation). And Congress understood that the NSA surveillance that it intended categorically to exclude from FISA could include the monitoring of international communications into or out of the United States of U.S. citizens. The report specifically referred to the Church Committee report for its description of the NSA's activities, S. Rep. No. 95–604, at 64 n.63, 1978 U.S.C.C.A.N. at 3965–66 n.63, which stated that "the NSA intercepts messages passing over international lines of communication, some of which have one terminal within the United States. Traveling over these lines of communication, especially those with one terminal in the United States, are messages of Americans. . . ." S. Rep. 94–755, at Book II, 308 (1976). Congress's understanding in the legislative history of FISA that such communications could be intercepted outside FISA procedures is notable.

c.   Excerpt from the DOJ Responses to the House Judiciary Committee's Oversight Questions . . .:

. . . [W]e note that the Department's legal analysis [viz. the White Paper] assumes, solely for purposes of that analysis, that the targeted interception of international communications authorized under the Terrorist Surveillance Program would constitute "electronic surveillance" as defined by FISA. As noted in our January 19 paper [viz. the White Paper], we cannot confirm whether that is actually the case without disclosing sensitive classified information.

d.   18 U.S.C. § 2511(2)(f):

§ 2511. Interception and disclosure of wire, oral, or electronic communications prohibited

(2)

. . .

(f)   Nothing contained in this chapter or chapter 121 or 206 of this title, or section 705 of the Communications Act of 1934, shall be deemed to affect the acquisition by the United States Government of foreign intelligence information from international or foreign communications, or foreign intelligence activities conducted in accordance with otherwise applicable Federal law involving a foreign electronic communications system, utilizing a means other than electronic surveillance as defined in section 101 of the Foreign Intelligence Surveillance Act of 1978, and procedures in this chapter or chapter 121 and the Foreign Intelligence Surveillance Act of 1978 shall be the exclusive means by which electronic surveillance, as defined in section 101 of such Act, and the interception of domestic wire, oral, and electronic communications may be conducted.

e.   50 U.S.C. § 1801(f) [§ 1801 is section 101 of the FISA statute— referred to in § 2511(2)(f) in note d. above].

§ 1801. Definitions

. . .

(2)

. . .

(f)   "Electronic surveillance" means—

(1)   the acquisition by an electronic, mechanical, or other surveillance device of the contents of any wire or radio communication sent by or intended to be received by a particular known United States person who is in the United States, if the contents are acquired by intentionally targeting that United States person, under circumstances in which a person has a reasonable expectation of privacy and a warrant would be required for law enforcement purposes;

(2)   the acquisition by an electronic, mechanical, or other surveillance device of the contents of any wire communication to or from a person in the United States, without the consent of any party thereto, if such acquisition occurs in the United States, but does not include the acquisition of those communications of computer trespassers that would be permissible under section 2511(2)(i) of Title 18;

(3)   the intentional acquisition by an electronic, mechanical, or other surveillance device of the contents of any

radio communication, under circumstances in which a person has a reasonable expectation of privacy and a warrant would be required for law enforcement purposes, and if both the sender and all intended recipients are located within the United States; or

(4) the installation or use of an electronic, mechanical, or other surveillance device in the United States for monitoring to acquire information, other than from a wire or radio communication, under circumstances in which a person has a reasonable expectation of privacy and a warrant would be required for law enforcement purposes.

5. What is the significance of the materials contained in note 4, supra, especially the material defining "electronic surveillance"? What is the significance of the fact that the DOJ has declined to affirm definitively whether the TSP program involves "electronic surveillance"? Do you infer from that fact that the conduct of the TSP does involve electronic surveillance? Or do you draw the contrary inference? How might it be possible that the controversial aspect of the TSP does not involve "electronic surveillance? If the TSP does not involve "electronic surveillance," what would be the legal implications of that fact?

6. Some of the issues suggested by the materials in note 4, supra, were commented upon in American Civil Liberties Union v. National Security Agency, 493 F.3d 644 (6th Cir.2007), cert. denied, 128 S.Ct. 1334 (2008):

BATCHELDER, J., delivered the judgment of the court. [A separate concurrence and dissenting opinion are not included here.]

ALICE M. BATCHELDER, CIRCUIT JUDGE.

. . .

The plaintiffs in this action include journalists, academics, and lawyers who regularly communicate with individuals located overseas, who the plaintiffs believe are the types of people the NSA suspects of being al Qaeda terrorists, affiliates, or supporters, and are therefore likely to be monitored under the TSP [Terrorist Surveillance Program]. From this suspicion, and the limited factual foundation in this case, the plaintiffs allege that they have a "well founded belief" that their communications are being tapped. According to the plaintiffs, the NSA's operation of the TSP-and the possibility of warrantless surveillance-subjects them to conditions that constitute an irreparable harm.

. . .

2. Title III

Title III of the Omnibus Crime Control and Safe Streets Act of 1968 ("Title III"), 18 U.S.C. §§ 2510–22, generally regulates the government's interception of wire, oral, and electronic communications. The first relevant question is whether Title III applies to the type of surveillance conducted by the NSA under the TSP, considering Title III's express limitations.

> Nothing contained in this [statute (i.e., Title III)] . . . shall be deemed to affect [1] the acquisition by the United States Government of foreign intelligence information from international or foreign communications, or [2] foreign intelligence activities conducted in accordance with otherwise applicable Federal law involving a foreign electronic communications system, utilizing a means other than electronic surveillance as defined in section 101 of the Foreign Intelligence Surveillance Act of 1978, and [3] procedures in this [statute (i.e., Title III)] . . . and the Foreign Intelligence Surveillance Act of 1978 shall be the exclusive means by which electronic surveillance, as defined in section 101 of such Act, and the interception of domestic wire, oral, and electronic communications may be conducted.

18 U.S.C. § 2511(2)(f).

When this statutory language is parsed into its three individual clauses, its limitations become clear. The first clause disclaims Title III applicability generally—acknowledging that Title III does not apply to "the acquisition by the United States Government of foreign intelligence information from international or foreign communications." The second clause disclaims Title III applicability specifically—recognizing that Title III does not govern "foreign intelligence activities conducted in accordance with otherwise applicable Federal law involving a foreign electronic communications system, utilizing a means other than electronic surveillance as defined in [FISA]." The final clause, which is known as the "exclusivity provision," recognizes the respective roles of Title III and FISA, by stating that the "procedures in [Title III] and [FISA] shall be the exclusive means by which electronic surveillance, as defined in section 101 of [FISA] and the interception of domestic wire, oral, and electronic communications may be conducted."

The first clause of § 2511(2)(f)—stating that Title III does not govern the acquisition of "foreign intelligence information from international or foreign communications"—expressly disclaims application of Title III to surveillance activities of the type at issue in the present case. The NSA monitors international communications for the purpose of acquiring foreign intelligence about terrorist organizations; this type of surveillance falls squarely under the disclaimer found in the first clause of § 2511(2)(f). By its own terms, then, Title III does not apply to the conduct of which the plaintiffs complain.

. . .

Because the first clause of § 2511(2)(f) expressly disclaims Title III's application to this case, it is unnecessary to construe the second and third clauses. But, it is worth acknowledging that these two clauses raise complex legal issues which cannot be resolved on the present record. The second clause explains that Title III does not apply if four factors are all satisfied: (1) the defendant is engaged in "foreign intelligence activities"; (2) the defendant is acting "in accordance with otherwise applicable Federal law"; (3) the defendant's surveillance involves a "foreign electronic communications system"; and (4) the defendant utilizes "a means other than electronic surveillance" as defined in FISA. These factors raise a host of intricate issues, such as whether the NSA's wiretapping actually involves "electronic surveillance" as defined in FISA, and whether the NSA is acting in accordance with federal law, such as the Authorization for Use of Military Force ("AUMF"), Pub.L. 107–40, § 2, 115 Stat. 224 (2001). Some of these issues involve sophisticated legal questions or complex factual questions. But, resolving these issues is unnecessary because the first clause of § 2511(2)(f) conclusively disclaims Title III's application.

It is likewise unnecessary, at this point, to delve into the numerous issues raised by the third clause, i.e., the exclusivity provision. The exclusivity provision differs from the first two clauses of § 2511(2)(f), in that it does not merely disclaim Title III's application. Instead, it states that Title III and FISA shall be the "exclusive means" by which particular types of surveillance may occur, thus prescribing the separate roles of Title III and FISA, rather than the application of Title III alone. The plaintiffs assert a statutory cause of action for the NSA's alleged violation of the exclusivity provision, which I address separately. . . . It is, therefore, unnecessary to dissect the exclusivity provision at this point in the analysis.

Because the first clause of § 2511(2)(f) states that Title III does not apply to the internationally focused surveillance activities challenged in this case, the plaintiffs have not asserted a viable cause of action under Title III.

3. FISA

The Foreign Intelligence Surveillance Act of 1978 ("FISA"), 50 U.S.C. § 1801 et seq.,—as the separate and distinct counterpart to Title III—governs the interception of electronic communications involving foreign intelligence information. See 50 U.S.C. § 1802(a)(1). FISA is fraught with detailed statutory definitions and is expressly limited, by its own terms, to situations in which the President has authorized "electronic surveillance," as defined in 50 U.S.C. § 1801(f), for the purposes of acquiring "foreign intelligence information," as defined in 50 U.S.C. § 1801(e).

First, the surveillance in question must acquire "foreign intelligence information," which includes "information that relates to . . . the ability of the United States to protect against . . . international terrorism." 50 U.S.C. § 1801(e)(1)(B). In the present case, the NSA intercepts communications in which it has a "reasonable basis to conclude that one party to the communication is a member of al Qaeda, affiliated with al Qaeda, or a member of an organization affiliated with al Qaeda, or working in support of al Qaeda." See Press Briefing by Att'y Gen. Alberto Gonzales and Gen. Michael Hayden, Principal Deputy Dir. for Nat'l Intelligence (Dec. 19, 2005), available at http://www.whitehouse.gov/news/releases/2005/12/print/20051219–1.html (last visited July 2, 2007) (emphasis added). The proclaimed purpose is to prevent future terrorist attacks, see id. ("This is a very concentrated, very limited program focused at gaining information about our enemy."), and thus the NSA's conduct satisfies this statutory requirement.

Next, the interception must occur by "electronic surveillance." According to the plaintiffs, the government's admission that it intercepts telephone and email communications—which involve electronic media and are generally considered, in common parlance, forms of electronic communications—is tantamount to admitting that the NSA engaged in "electronic surveillance" for purposes of FISA. This argument fails upon recognition that "electronic surveillance" has a very particular, detailed meaning under FISA—a legal definition that requires careful consideration of numerous factors such as the types of communications acquired, the location of the parties to the acquired communications, the location where the acquisition occurred, the location of any surveillance, device, and the reasonableness of the parties' expectation of privacy. See 50 U.S.C. § 1801(f). The plaintiffs have not shown, and cannot show, that the NSA's surveillance activities include the sort of conduct that would satisfy FISA's definition of "electronic surveillance," and the present record does not demonstrate that the NSA's conduct falls within FISA's definitions.

4. LITIGATION INVOLVING THE NSA'S TSP PROGRAM

The TSP program as a presidentially authorized program without support in legislation essentially ended in 2007, but the disclosures regarding the program led to a number of lawsuits seeking to determine whether particular individuals had been surveilled and testing the legality of the program. Generally, such legal efforts were stymied: the government, as it did in other areas of enforcement practices, challenged the standing of the plaintiffs, invoked the states secrets privilege, and generally declined to disclose on national security grounds whether particular individuals had been eavesdropped upon without a warrant under the program. A few U.S. courts of appeal and a number of district courts addressed the issues in these cases. In one instance, a district judge did reach the merits, mainly based on inadvertent and advertent disclosures by the government that indicated that electronic surveillance of the plaintiffs had taken place. Because there was no evidence that a FISA warrant had been obtained, the court concluded that the surveillance was unlawful. In re National Security Agency Telecommunications Records Litigation, 700 F.Supp 2d 1182 (N.D.Calif). After extensive litigation, the court granted the plaintiffs' motion for summary judgment. Subsequently, a verdict/settlement ensued, sub nom. Al-Haramain Islamic Foundation v. Bush, 2010 WL 5663950 in which the government was ordered to pay more than two million dollars, most of which went for attorneys' fees. Also see Al-Haramain Islamic Foundation v. Bush, 507 F.3d 1190 (9th Cir. 2007) for an earlier stage in this litigation.

As noted, civil plaintiffs and criminal defendants have made motions to order the government to disclose whether any warrantless electronic surveillance had been directed against them. In one such case, the court of appeals vacated an appeal and remanded the case to allow the district court to entertain a motion to disclose any unauthorized electronic surveillance. United States v. Al-Timimi, No. 05-4761 (4th Cir.). On November 21, 2007, the New York Times reported that following the issuance of the order in the Al-Timimi case in April 2006, the issue was "bogged down" in the trial court for 18 months during which intelligence officials made a series of classified appearances before the court; neither the defense lawyers nor the trial prosecutors were allowed to be present. The New York Times story reported that the trial judge told the prosecution that she wanted the government to arrange to give both the trial prosecutors and defense lawyers clearance to review the classified material in the case, and the judge indicated that she was prepared to order a new trial if the problem was not resolved. The story indicated that to obtain the necessary clearances relating to the NSA program might require action by the President since he "personally handled the decisions on issuing clearances for the NSA eavesdropping program." N.Y. Times, Nov. 21, 2007, A18. See also United States v. Abu Ali, 2006 WL 4483162 (E.D. Va.).

C. THE FISA AMENDMENTS ACT

The Protect America Act, hurriedly enacted in 2007 as a stopgap measure, lapsed in February, 2008. Subsequently, after difficult negotiations, the FISA Amendments Act of 2008, excerpts from which are reproduced below, was enacted in July, 2008. Some amendments to § 1881a (section 702 of the 2008 Act) were enacted in 2015 and also in 2017–18.

FISA Amendments Act of 2008

[These excerpts include subsequent amendments, for example those contained in the FISA Amendments Reauthorization Act of 2017, signed into law on January 19, 2018]

50 U.S.C.

TITLE I—FOREIGN INTELLIGENCE SURVEILLANCE

§ 1881. Definitions

(a) In general

The terms "agent of a foreign power", "Attorney General", "contents", "electronic surveillance", "foreign intelligence information", "foreign power", "person", "United States", and "United States person" have the meanings given such terms in section 1801 of this title, except as specifically provided in this subchapter.

§ 1881a. Procedures for targeting certain persons outside the United States other than United States persons

(a) Authorization

Notwithstanding any other provision of law, upon the issuance of an order in accordance with subsection (j)(3) or a determination under subsection (c)(2), the Attorney General and the Director of National Intelligence may authorize jointly, for a period of up to 1 year from the effective date of the authorization, the targeting of persons reasonably believed to be located outside the United States to acquire foreign intelligence information.

(b) Limitations

An acquisition authorized under subsection (a)—

(1) may not intentionally target any person known at the time of acquisition to be located in the United States;

(2) may not intentionally target a person reasonably believed to be located outside the United States if the purpose of such acquisition is to target a particular, known person reasonably believed to be in the United States;

(3) may not intentionally target a United States person reasonably believed to be located outside the United States;

(4) may not intentionally acquire any communication as to which the sender and all intended recipients are known at the time of the acquisition to be located in the United States;

(5) may not intentionally acquire communications that contain a reference to, but are not to or from, a target of an acquisition authorized under subsection (a), except as provided

acquisition of abouts communications, including all affidavits, procedures, exhibits, and attachments submitted therewith.

(B) The decision, order, or opinion of the Foreign Intelligence Surveillance Court approving such certification, and any pleadings, applications, or memoranda of law associated with such decision, order, or opinion.

(C) A summary of the protections in place to detect any material breach.

(D) Data or other results of modeling, simulation, or auditing of sample data demonstrating that any acquisition method involving the intentional acquisition of abouts communications shall be conducted in accordance with title VII of the Foreign Intelligence Surveillance Act of 1978 (50 U.S.C. 1881 et seq.), if such data or other results exist at the time the written notice is submitted and were provided to the Foreign Intelligence Surveillance Court.

(E) Except as provided under paragraph (4), a statement that no acquisition authorized under subsection (a) of such section 702 shall include the intentional acquisition of an abouts communication until after the end of the 30-day period described in paragraph (2)(B).

(4) EXCEPTION FOR EMERGENCY ACQUISITION.—

(A) NOTICE OF DETERMINATION.—If the Attorney General and the Director of National Intelligence make a determination pursuant to section 702(c)(2) of the Foreign Intelligence Surveillance Act of 1978 (50 U.S.C. 1881a(c)(2)) with respect to the intentional acquisition of abouts communications, the Attorney General and the Director of National Intelligence shall notify the Committee on the Judiciary and the Select Committee on Intelligence of the Senate and the Committee on the Judiciary and the Permanent Select Committee on Intelligence of the House of Representatives as soon as practicable, but not later than 7 days after the determination is made.

. . .

§ 1881b. Certain acquisitions inside the United States targeting United States persons outside the United States

(a)   Jurisdiction of the Foreign Intelligence Surveillance Court

(1)   In general

The Foreign Intelligence Surveillance Court shall have jurisdiction to review an application and to enter an order approving the targeting of a United States person reasonably believed to be located outside the United States to acquire foreign intelligence information, if the acquisition constitutes electronic surveillance or the acquisition of stored electronic communications or stored electronic data that requires an order under this chapter, and such acquisition is conducted within the United States.

(2)   Limitation

If a United States person targeted under this subsection is reasonably believed to be located in the United States during the effective period of an order issued pursuant to subsection (c), an acquisition targeting such United States person under this section shall cease unless the targeted United States person is again reasonably believed to be located outside the United States while an order issued pursuant to subsection (c) is in effect. Nothing in this section shall be construed to limit the authority of the Government to seek an order or authorization under, or otherwise engage in any activity that is authorized under, any other subchapter of this chapter.

(b)   Application

(1)   In general

Each application for an order under this section shall be made by a Federal officer in writing upon oath or affirmation to a judge having jurisdiction under subsection (a)(1). Each application shall require the approval of the Attorney General based upon the Attorney General's finding that it satisfies the criteria and requirements of such application, as set forth in this section, and shall include—

(A) the identity of the Federal officer making the application;

(B) the identity, if known, or a description of the United States person who is the target of the acquisition;

(C) a statement of the facts and circumstances relied upon to justify the applicant's belief that the United States person who is the target of the acquisition is—

(i) a person reasonably believed to be located outside the United States; and

(ii) a foreign power, an agent of a foreign power, or an officer or employee of a foreign power;

(D) a statement of proposed minimization procedures that meet the definition of minimization procedures under section 1801(h) or 1821(4) of this title, as appropriate;

(E) a description of the nature of the information sought and the type of communications or activities to be subjected to acquisition;

(F) a certification made by the Attorney General or an official specified in section 1804(a)(6) of this title that—

(i) the certifying official deems the information sought to be foreign intelligence information;

(ii) a significant purpose of the acquisition is to obtain foreign intelligence information;

(iii) such information cannot reasonably be obtained by normal investigative techniques;

(iv) designates the type of foreign intelligence information being sought according to the categories described in section 1801(e) of this title; and

(v) includes a statement of the basis for the certification that—

(I) the information sought is the type of foreign intelligence information designated; and

(II) such information cannot reasonably be obtained by normal investigative techniques;

(G) a summary statement of the means by which the acquisition will be conducted and whether physical entry is required to effect the acquisition;

(H) the identity of any electronic communication service provider necessary to effect the acquisition, provided that the application is not required to identify the specific facilities, places, premises, or property at which the acquisition authorized under this section will be directed or conducted;

(I) a statement of the facts concerning any previous applications that have been made to any judge of the Foreign Intelligence Surveillance Court involving the United States person specified in the application and the action taken on each previous application; and

(J) a statement of the period of time for which the acquisition is required to be maintained, provided that such period of time shall not exceed 90 days per application.

. . .

(6) Duration

An order approved under this subsection shall be effective for a period not to exceed 90 days and such order may be renewed for additional 90-day periods upon submission of renewal applications meeting the requirements of subsection (b).

(7) Compliance

At or prior to the end of the period of time for which an acquisition is approved by an order or extension under this section, the judge may assess compliance with the minimization procedures referred to in paragraph (1)(C) by reviewing the circumstances under which information concerning United States persons was acquired, retained, or disseminated.

(d) Emergency authorization

(1) Authority for emergency authorization

Notwithstanding any other provision of this chapter, if the Attorney General reasonably determines that—

(A) an emergency situation exists with respect to the acquisition of foreign intelligence information for which an order may be obtained under subsection (c) before an order authorizing such acquisition can with due diligence be obtained, and

(B) the factual basis for issuance of an order under this subsection to approve such acquisition exists,

the Attorney General may authorize such acquisition if a judge having jurisdiction under subsection (a)(1) is informed by the Attorney General, or a designee of the Attorney General, at the time of such authorization that the decision has been made to conduct such acquisition and if an application in accordance with this section is made to a judge of the Foreign Intelligence Surveillance Court as soon as practicable, but not more than 7 days after the Attorney General authorizes such acquisition.

(2) Minimization procedures

If the Attorney General authorizes an acquisition under paragraph (1), the Attorney General shall require that the minimization procedures referred to in subsection (c)(1)(C) for the issuance of a judicial order be followed.

(3) Termination of emergency authorization

In the absence of a judicial order approving an acquisition under paragraph (1), such acquisition shall terminate when the information sought is obtained, when the application for the order is denied, or after the expiration of 7 days from the time of authorization by the Attorney General, whichever is earliest.

(4) Use of information

If an application for approval submitted pursuant to paragraph (1) is denied, or in any other case where the acquisition is terminated and no order is issued approving the acquisition, no information obtained or evidence derived from such acquisition, except under circumstances in which the target of the acquisition is determined not to be a United States person, shall be received in evidence or otherwise disclosed in any trial, hearing, or other proceeding in or before any court, grand jury, department, office, agency, regulatory body, legislative committee, or other authority of the United States, a State, or political subdivision thereof, and no information concerning any United States person acquired from such acquisition shall subsequently be used or disclosed in any other manner by Federal officers or employees without the consent of such person, except with the approval of the Attorney General if the information indicates a threat of death or serious bodily harm to any person.

(e) Release from liability

No cause of action shall lie in any court against any electronic communication service provider for providing any information, facilities, or assistance in accordance with an order or request for emergency assistance issued pursuant to subsection (c) or (d), respectively.

. . .

§ 1881c. Other acquisitions targeting United States persons outside the United States

(a)   Jurisdiction and scope

(1)   Jurisdiction

The Foreign Intelligence Surveillance Court shall have jurisdiction to enter an order pursuant to subsection (c).

(2)   Scope

No element of the intelligence community may intentionally target, for the purpose of acquiring foreign intelligence information, a United States person reasonably believed to be located outside the United States under circumstances in which the targeted United States person has a reasonable expectation of privacy and a warrant would be required if the acquisition were conducted inside the United States for law enforcement purposes, unless a judge of the Foreign Intelligence Surveillance Court has entered an order with respect to such targeted United States person or the Attorney General has authorized an emergency acquisition pursuant to subsection (c) or (d), respectively, or any other provision of this chapter.

(3)   Limitations

(A)   Moving or misidentified targets

If a United States person targeted under this subsection is reasonably believed to be located in the United States during the effective period of an order issued pursuant to subsection (c), an acquisition targeting such United States person under this section shall cease unless the targeted United States person is again reasonably believed to be located outside the United States during the effective period of such order.

(B)   Applicability

If an acquisition for foreign intelligence purposes is to be conducted inside the United States and could be authorized under section 1881b of this title, the acquisition may only be conducted if authorized under section 1881b of this title or in accordance with another provision of this chapter other than this section.

(C)   Construction

Nothing in this paragraph shall be construed to limit the authority of the Government to seek an order or authorization under, or otherwise engage in any activity that is authorized under, any other subchapter of this chapter.

(b) Application

Each application for an order under this section shall be made by a Federal officer in writing upon oath or affirmation to a judge having jurisdiction under subsection (a)(1). Each application shall require the approval of the Attorney General based upon the Attorney General's finding that it satisfies the criteria and requirements of such application as set forth in this section and shall include—

(1) the identity of the Federal officer making the application;

(2) the identity, if known, or a description of the specific United States person who is the target of the acquisition;

(3) a statement of the facts and circumstances relied upon to justify the applicant's belief that the United States person who is the target of the acquisition is—

(A) a person reasonably believed to be located outside the United States; and

(B) a foreign power, an agent of a foreign power, or an officer or employee of a foreign power;

(4) a statement of proposed minimization procedures that meet the definition of minimization procedures under section 1801(h) or 1821(4) of this title, as appropriate;

(5) a certification made by the Attorney General, an official specified in section 1804(a)(6) of this title, or the head of an element of the intelligence community that—

(A) the certifying official deems the information sought to be foreign intelligence information; and

(B) a significant purpose of the acquisition is to obtain foreign intelligence information;

(6) a statement of the facts concerning any previous applications that have been made to any judge of the Foreign Intelligence Surveillance Court involving the United States person specified in the application and the action taken on each previous application; and

(7) a statement of the period of time for which the acquisition is required to be maintained, provided that such period of time shall not exceed 90 days per application.

(c)   Order

(1)   Findings

Upon an application made pursuant to subsection (b), the Foreign Intelligence Surveillance Court shall enter an ex parte order as requested or as modified by the Court if the Court finds that—

(A)   the application has been made by a Federal officer and approved by the Attorney General;

(B)   on the basis of the facts submitted by the applicant, for the United States person who is the target of the acquisition, there is probable cause to believe that the target is—

(i)   a person reasonably believed to be located outside the United States; and

(ii)   a foreign power, an agent of a foreign power, or an officer or employee of a foreign power;

(C)   the proposed minimization procedures, with respect to their dissemination provisions, meet the definition of minimization procedures under section 1801(h) or 1821(4) of this title, as appropriate; and

(D)   the application that has been filed contains all statements and certifications required by subsection (b) and the certification provided under subsection (b)(5) is not clearly erroneous on the basis of the information furnished under subsection (b).

(2)   Probable cause

In determining whether or not probable cause exists for purposes of paragraph (1)(B), a judge having jurisdiction under subsection (a)(1) may consider past activities of the target and facts and circumstances relating to current or future activities of the target. No United States person may be considered a foreign power, agent of a foreign power, or officer or employee of a foreign power solely upon the basis of activities protected by the first amendment to the Constitution of the United States.

An order under this paragraph shall be effective for a period not to exceed 90 days and such order may be renewed for additional 90-day periods upon submission of renewal applications meeting the requirements of subsection (b).

. . .

§ 1881e. Use of information acquired under this subchapter

(a)   Information acquired under section 1881a of this title

Information acquired from an acquisition conducted under section 1881a of this title shall be deemed to be information acquired from an electronic surveillance pursuant to subchapter I of this chapter for purposes of section 1806 of this title, except for the purposes of subsection (j) of such section.

(b)   Information acquired under section 1881b of this title

Information acquired from an acquisition conducted under section 1881b of this title shall be deemed to be information acquired from an electronic surveillance pursuant to subchapter I of this chapter for purposes of section 1806 of this title.

§ 1885a. Procedures for implementing statutory defenses

(a)   Requirement for certification

Notwithstanding any other provision of law, a civil action may not lie or be maintained in a Federal or State court against any person for providing assistance to an element of the intelligence community, and shall be promptly dismissed, if the Attorney General certifies to the district court of the United States in which such action is pending that—

(1)   any assistance by that person was provided pursuant to an order of the court established under section 1803(a) of this title directing such assistance;

(2)   any assistance by that person was provided pursuant to a certification in writing under section 2511(2)(a)(ii)(B) or 2709(b) of Title 18;

(3)   any assistance by that person was provided pursuant to a directive under section 1802(a)(4), 1805b(e), or 1881a(h) of this title directing such assistance;

(4)   in the case of a covered civil action, the assistance alleged to have been provided by the electronic communication service provider was—

(A)   in connection with an intelligence activity involving communications that was—

(i)   authorized by the President during the period beginning on September 11, 2001, and ending on January 17, 2007; and

(ii) designed to detect or prevent a terrorist attack, or activities in preparation for a terrorist attack, against the United States; and

(B) the subject of a written request or directive, or a series of written requests or directives, from the Attorney General or the head of an element of the intelligence community (or the deputy of such person) to the electronic communication service provider indicating that the activity was—

(i) authorized by the President; and

(ii) determined to be lawful; or

(5) the person did not provide the alleged assistance.

(b) Judicial review

(1) Review of certifications

A certification under subsection (a) shall be given effect unless the court finds that such certification is not supported by substantial evidence provided to the court pursuant to this section.

(2) Supplemental materials

In its review of a certification under subsection (a), the court may examine the court order, certification, written request, or directive described in subsection (a) and any relevant court order, certification, written request, or directive submitted pursuant to subsection (d).

(c) Limitations on disclosure

If the Attorney General files a declaration under section 1746 of Title 28, that disclosure of a certification made pursuant to subsection (a) or the supplemental materials provided pursuant to subsection (b) or (d) would harm the national security of the United States, the court shall—

(1) review such certification and the supplemental materials in camera and ex parte; and

(2) limit any public disclosure concerning such certification and the supplemental materials, including any public order following such in camera and ex parte review, to a statement as to whether the case is dismissed and a description of the legal standards that govern the order, without disclosing the paragraph of subsection (a) that is the basis for the certification.

(d) Role of the parties

Any plaintiff or defendant in a civil action may submit any relevant court order, certification, written request, or directive to the district court referred to in subsection (a) for review and shall be permitted to participate in the briefing or argument of any legal issue in a judicial proceeding conducted pursuant to this section, but only to the extent that such participation does not require the disclosure of classified information to such party. To the extent that classified information is relevant to the proceeding or would be revealed in the determination of an issue, the court shall review such information in camera and ex parte, and shall issue any part of the court's written order that would reveal classified information in camera and ex parte and maintain such part under seal.

. . .

CLAPPER V. AMNESTY INTERNATIONAL, USA
568 U.S. 398 (2013)

JUSTICE ALITO delivered the opinion of the Court.

Section 702 of the Foreign Intelligence Surveillance Act of 1978, 50 U.S.C. § 1881a (2006 ed., Supp. V), allows the Attorney General and the Director of National Intelligence to acquire foreign intelligence information by jointly authorizing the surveillance of individuals who are not "United States persons" and are reasonably believed to be located outside the United States. Before doing so, the Attorney General and the Director of National Intelligence normally must obtain the Foreign Intelligence Surveillance Court's approval. Respondents are United States persons whose work, they allege, requires them to engage in sensitive international communications with individuals who they believe are likely targets of surveillance under § 1881a. Respondents seek a declaration that § 1881a is unconstitutional, as well as an injunction against § 1881a-authorized surveillance. The question before us is whether respondents have Article III standing to seek this prospective relief.

Respondents assert that they can establish injury in fact because there is an objectively reasonable likelihood that their communications will be acquired under § 1881a at some point in the future. But respondents' theory of future injury is too speculative to satisfy the well-established requirement that threatened injury must be "certainly impending." And even if respondents could demonstrate that the threatened injury is certainly impending, they still would not be able to establish that this injury is fairly traceable to § 1881a. As an alternative argument, respondents contend that they are suffering present injury because the risk of § 1881a-authorized surveillance already has forced them to take costly and burdensome measures to protect the confidentiality of their international communications. But respondents cannot manufacture standing by choosing to make expenditures based on hypothetical future harm that is not certainly impending. We therefore hold that respondents lack Article III standing.

. . .

In the wake of the September 11th attacks, President George W. Bush authorized the National Security Agency (NSA) to conduct warrantless wiretapping of telephone and e-mail communications where one party to the communication was located outside the United States and a participant in "the call was reasonably believed to be a member or agent of al Qaeda or an affiliated terrorist organization," App. to Pet. for Cert. 403a. In January 2007, the FISC issued orders authorizing the Government to target international communications into or out of the United States where there was probable cause to believe that one participant to the communication was a member or agent of al Qaeda or an associated terrorist organization. App. to Pet. for Cert. 312a, 398a, 405a. These FISC orders subjected any electronic surveillance that was then occurring under the NSA's program to the approval of the FISC. Id., at 405a; see id., at 312a, 404a. After a FISC Judge subsequently narrowed the FISC's authorization of such surveillance, however, the Executive asked Congress to amend FISA so that it would provide the intelligence community with additional authority to meet the challenges of modern technology and international terrorism. Id., at 315a–318a, 331a–333a, 398a; see id., at 262a, 277a–279a, 287a.

When Congress enacted the FISA Amendments Act of 2008 (FISA Amendments Act), 122 Stat. 2436, it left much of FISA intact, but it "established a new and independent source of intelligence collection authority, beyond that granted in traditional FISA." As relevant here, § 702 of FISA, 50 U.S.C. § 1881a (2006 ed., Supp. V), which was enacted as part of the FISA Amendments Act, supplements pre-existing FISA authority by creating a new framework under which the Government may seek the FISC's authorization of certain foreign intelligence surveillance targeting the communications of non-U.S. persons located abroad. Unlike traditional FISA surveillance, § 1881a does not require the Government to demonstrate probable cause that the target of the electronic surveillance is a foreign power or agent of a foreign power. Compare § 1805(a)(2)(A), (a)(2)(B), with § 1881a(d)(1), (i)(3)(A). And, unlike traditional FISA, § 1881a does not require the Government to specify the nature and location of each of the particular facilities or places at which the electronic surveillance will occur. Compare § 1805(a)(2)(B), (c)(1) (2006 ed. and Supp. V), with § 1881a(d)(1), (g)(4), (i)(3)(A).

The present case involves a constitutional challenge to § 1881a. Surveillance under § 1881a is subject to statutory conditions, judicial authorization, congressional supervision, and compliance with the Fourth

Amendment. Section 1881a provides that, upon the issuance of an order from the Foreign Intelligence Surveillance Court, "the Attorney General and the Director of National Intelligence may authorize jointly, for a period of up to 1 year . . ., the targeting of persons reasonably believed to be located outside the United States to acquire foreign intelligence information." § 1881a(a). Surveillance under § 1881a may not be intentionally targeted at any person known to be in the United States or any U.S. person reasonably believed to be located abroad. § 1881a(b)(1)–(3); see also § 1801(i). Additionally, acquisitions under § 1881a must comport with the Fourth Amendment. § 1881a(b)(5). Moreover, surveillance under § 1881a is subject to congressional oversight and several types of Executive Branch review. See § 1881a(f)(2), (*l*).

Section 1881a mandates that the Government obtain the Foreign Intelligence Surveillance Court's approval of "targeting" procedures, "minimization" procedures, and a governmental certification regarding proposed surveillance. § 1881a(a), (c)(1), (i)(2), (i)(3). Among other things, the Government's certification must attest that (1) procedures are in place "that have been approved, have been submitted for approval, or will be submitted with the certification for approval by the [FISC] that are reasonably designed" to ensure that an acquisition is "limited to targeting persons reasonably believed to be located outside" the United States; (2) minimization procedures adequately restrict the acquisition, retention, and dissemination of nonpublic information about unconsenting U.S. persons, as appropriate; (3) guidelines have been adopted to ensure compliance with targeting limits and the Fourth Amendment; and (4) the procedures and guidelines referred to above comport with the Fourth Amendment. § 1881a(g)(2); see § 1801(h).

The Foreign Intelligence Surveillance Court's role includes determining whether the Government's certification contains the required elements. Additionally, the Court assesses whether the targeting procedures are "reasonably designed" (1) to "ensure that an acquisition . . . is limited to targeting persons reasonably believed to be located outside the United States" and (2) to "prevent the intentional acquisition of any communication as to which the sender and all intended recipients are known . . . to be located in the United States." § 1881a(i)(2)(B). The Court analyzes whether the minimization procedures "meet the definition of minimization procedures under section 1801(h) . . ., as appropriate." § 1881a(i)(2)(C). The Court also assesses whether the targeting and minimization procedures are consistent with the statute and the Fourth Amendment. See § 1881a(i)(3)(A).

Respondents are attorneys and human rights, labor, legal, and media organizations whose work allegedly requires them to engage in sensitive and sometimes privileged telephone and e-mail communications with colleagues, clients, sources, and other individuals located abroad.

Respondents believe that some of the people with whom they exchange foreign intelligence information are likely targets of surveillance under § 1881a. Specifically, respondents claim that they communicate by telephone and e-mail with people the Government "believes or believed to be associated with terrorist organizations," "people located in geographic areas that are a special focus" of the Government's counterterrorism or diplomatic efforts, and activists who oppose governments that are supported by the United States Government. App. to Pet. for Cert. 399a.

Respondents claim that § 1881a compromises their ability to locate witnesses, cultivate sources, obtain information, and communicate confidential information to their clients. Respondents also assert that they "have ceased engaging" in certain telephone and e-mail conversations. According to respondents, the threat of surveillance will compel them to travel abroad in order to have in-person conversations. In addition, respondents declare that they have undertaken "costly and burdensome measures" to protect the confidentiality of sensitive communications.

On the day when the FISA Amendments Act was enacted, respondents filed this action seeking (1) a declaration that § 1881a, on its face, violates the Fourth Amendment, the First Amendment, Article III, and separation-of-powers principles and (2) a permanent injunction against the use of § 1881a. Respondents assert what they characterize as two separate theories of Article III standing. First, they claim that there is an objectively reasonable likelihood that their communications will be acquired under § 1881a at some point in the future, thus causing them injury. Second, respondents maintain that the risk of surveillance under § 1881a is so substantial that they have been forced to take costly and burdensome measures to protect the confidentiality of their international communications; in their view, the costs they have incurred constitute present injury that is fairly traceable to § 1881a.

After both parties moved for summary judgment, the District Court held that respondents do not have standing. McConnell, 646 F.Supp.2d, at 635. On appeal, however, a panel of the Second Circuit reversed. The panel agreed with respondents' argument that they have standing due to the objectively reasonable likelihood that their communications will be intercepted at some time in the future. 638 F.3d, at 133, 134, 139. In addition, the panel held that respondents have established that they are suffering "present injuries in fact—economic and professional harms—stemming from a reasonable fear of future harmful government conduct." the Second Circuit denied rehearing en banc by an equally divided vote. 667 F.3d 163 (2011).

Because of the importance of the issue and the novel view of standing adopted by the Court of Appeals, we granted certiorari, 566 U.S. ___, 132 S.Ct. 2431, 182 L.Ed.2d 1061 (2012), and we now reverse.

. . .

To establish Article III standing, an injury must be "concrete, particularized, and actual or imminent; fairly traceable to the challenged action; and redressable by a favorable ruling." Monsanto Co. v. Geertson Seed Farms, 561 U.S. ___, ___, 130 S.Ct. 2743, 2752, 177 L.Ed.2d 461 (2010); see also Summers, supra, at 493, 129 S.Ct. 1142; Defenders of Wildlife, 504 U.S., at 560–561, 112 S.Ct. 2130. "Although imminence is concededly a somewhat elastic concept, it cannot be stretched beyond its purpose, which is to ensure that the alleged injury is not too speculative for Article III purposes—that the injury is certainly impending." . . .

. . .

Respondents assert that they can establish injury in fact that is fairly traceable to § 1881a because there is an objectively reasonable likelihood that their communications with their foreign contacts will be intercepted under § 1881a at some point in the future. This argument fails. As an initial matter, the Second Circuit's "objectively reasonable likelihood" standard is inconsistent with our requirement that "threatened injury must be certainly impending to constitute injury in fact." Furthermore, respondents' argument rests on their highly speculative fear that: (1) the Government will decide to target the communications of non-U.S. persons with whom they communicate; (2) in doing so, the Government will choose to invoke its authority under § 1881a rather than utilizing another method of surveillance; (3) the Article III judges who serve on the Foreign Intelligence Surveillance Court will conclude that the Government's proposed surveillance procedures satisfy § 1881a's many safeguards and are consistent with the Fourth Amendment; (4) the Government will succeed in intercepting the communications of respondents' contacts; and (5) respondents will be parties to the particular communications that the Government intercepts. . . .[R]espondents' theory of standing, which relies on a highly attenuated chain of possibilities, does not satisfy the requirement that threatened injury must be certainly impending. Moreover, even if respondents could demonstrate injury in fact, the second link in the above-described chain of contingencies—which amounts to mere speculation about whether surveillance would be under § 1881a or some other authority—shows that respondents cannot satisfy the requirement that any injury in fact must be fairly traceable to § 1881a.

First, it is speculative whether the Government will imminently target communications to which respondents are parties. . . . Indeed, respondents do not even allege that the Government has sought the FISC's approval for surveillance of their communications. Accordingly, respondents' theory necessarily rests on their assertion that the Government will target other individuals—namely, their foreign contacts.

Yet respondents have no actual knowledge of the Government's § 1881a targeting practices. . . .

Moreover, because § 1881a at most authorizes—but does not mandate or direct—the surveillance that respondents fear, respondents' allegations are necessarily conjectural Simply put, respondents can only speculate as to how the Attorney General and the Director of National Intelligence will exercise their discretion in determining which communications to target.[4]

. . .

Third, even if respondents could show that the Government will seek the Foreign Intelligence Surveillance Court's authorization to acquire the communications of respondents' foreign contacts under § 1881a, respondents can only speculate as to whether that court will authorize such surveillance. In the past, we have been reluctant to endorse standing theories that require guesswork as to how independent decisionmakers will exercise their judgment. . . .

We decline to abandon our usual reluctance to endorse standing theories that rest on speculation about the decisions of independent actors. . . .

Fourth, even if the Government were to obtain the Foreign Intelligence Surveillance Court's approval to target respondents' foreign contacts under § 1881a, it is unclear whether the Government would succeed in acquiring the communications of respondents' foreign contacts. And fifth, even if the Government were to conduct surveillance of respondents' foreign contacts, respondents can only speculate as to whether their own communications with their foreign contacts would be incidentally acquired.

In sum, respondents' speculative chain of possibilities does not establish that injury based on potential future surveillance is certainly impending or is fairly traceable to § 1881a.

Respondents' alternative argument—namely, that they can establish standing based on the measures that they have undertaken to avoid § 1881a-authorized surveillance—fares no better. Respondents assert that they are suffering ongoing injuries that are fairly traceable to § 1881a because the risk of surveillance under § 1881a requires them to take costly

---

[4] It was suggested at oral argument that the Government could help resolve the standing inquiry by disclosing to a court, perhaps through an in camera proceeding, (1) whether it is intercepting respondents' communications and (2) what targeting or minimization procedures it is using. This suggestion is puzzling. As an initial matter, it is respondents' burden to prove their standing by pointing to specific facts, not the Government's burden to disprove standing by revealing details of its surveillance priorities. Moreover, this type of hypothetical disclosure proceeding would allow a terrorist (or his attorney) to determine whether he is currently under U.S. surveillance simply by filing a lawsuit challenging the Government's surveillance program. Even if the terrorist's attorney were to comply with a protective order prohibiting him from sharing the Government's disclosures with his client, the court's postdisclosure decision about whether to dismiss the suit for lack of standing would surely signal to the terrorist whether his name was on the list of surveillance targets.

and burdensome measures to protect the confidentiality of their communications. Respondents claim, for instance, that the threat of surveillance sometimes compels them to avoid certain e-mail and phone conversations, to "tal[k] in generalities rather than specifics," or to travel so that they can have in-person conversations. . . .

The Second Circuit's analysis improperly allowed respondents to establish standing by asserting that they suffer present costs and burdens that are based on a fear of surveillance, so long as that fear is not "fanciful, paranoid, or otherwise unreasonable.". This improperly waters down the fundamental requirements of Article III. Respondents' contention that they have standing because they incurred certain costs as a reasonable reaction to a risk of harm is unavailing—because the harm respondents seek to avoid is not certainly impending. In other words, respondents cannot manufacture standing merely by inflicting harm on themselves based on their fears of hypothetical future harm that is not certainly impending.

If the law were otherwise, an enterprising plaintiff would be able to secure a lower standard for Article III standing simply by making an expenditure based on a nonparanoid fear. As Judge Raggi accurately noted, under the Second Circuit panel's reasoning, respondents could, "for the price of a plane ticket, . . . transform their standing burden from one requiring a showing of actual or imminent . . . interception to one requiring a showing that their subjective fear of such interception is not fanciful, irrational, or clearly unreasonable." Thus, allowing respondents to bring this action based on costs they incurred in response to a speculative threat would be tantamount to accepting a repackaged version of respondents' first failed theory of standing.

. . .

We hold that respondents lack Article III standing because they cannot demonstrate that the future injury they purportedly fear is certainly impending and because they cannot manufacture standing by incurring costs in anticipation of non-imminent harm. We therefore reverse the judgment of the Second Circuit and remand the case for further proceedings consistent with this opinion.

It is so ordered.

[JUSTICE BREYER, with whom JUSTICE GINSBURG, JUSTICE SOTOMAYOR, and JUSTICE KAGAN joined, wrote a dissenting opinion.]

QUESTIONS AND NOTES

1. Prior to Clapper, the Department of Justice (DOJ) was not providing notice to defendants that evidence obtained through use of electronic surveillance under the FISA Amendments Act was used in their prosecution. The Solicitor General made representations to the Supreme Court in oral

argument in the Clapper case inconsistent with what, reportedly, was then departmental policy. When he became aware of the inconsistency, reportedly, a policy discussion ensued in the DOJ and the policy was modified to provide for notifying defendants of the FAA generated evidence in their case. They would then have an opportunity to challenge the legality of the use of that evidence. See Jameel Jaffer and Patrick C. Toomey, "The Solicitor General Should Correct The Record In Clapper," Just Security, October 18, 2013 (available at: http://justsecurity.org/2219/solicitor-general-correct-record-clapper/).

2. A decision by the United States Foreign Intelligence Surveillance Court of Review, In re: Directives [Redacted Text] Pursuant to Section 105B of the Foreign Intelligence Surveillance Act, 551 F.3d 1004 (FISA Ct. Rev 2008), addressed constitutional issues raised by the Protect America Act. (Some of the certifications and directives under the Act's provisions continued in effect after the statute had lapsed so the case was not mooted.) Although the PAA is a different statute from the FISA Amendments Act, some of the issues are similar to those posed under the FAA. Accordingly, the case is a relevant authority on some of the constitutional issues posed by the FAA.

3. The FISA Amendments Act of 2008 has been the subject of a substantial literature.

See The FISA Amendments Act of 2008: Protecting Americans By Monitoring International Communications: Is it Reasonable? 6 Pace Int'l L. Rev. Online Companion 1; William C. Banks, Ten Questions: Responses to the Ten questions: Is the FISA Amendments Act of 2008 Good Policy? Is it Constitutional? 35 Wm. Mitchell L. Rev. 5007 (2009); Nate Olsen, Congress and the Court: Retroactive Immunity in the FISA Amendments Act and the Problem of United States v. Klein, 2009 Utah L. Rev. 1353 (2009); Jonathan D. Forgang, "The Right of the People": The NSA, The FISA Amendments Act of 2008, and Foreign Intelligence Surveillance of Americans Overseas, 78 Fordham L. Rev. 217 (2009); Elizabeth Johnson, Surveillance and Privacy Under the Obama Administration: The Foreign Intelligence Surveillance Act of 1978 Amendments Act of 2008 and the Attorney General's Guidelines for Domestic FBI Operations, 5 ISJLP 419 (2010); Zachary Keller, Big Brother's Little Helpers: Telecommunication Immunity and the FISA Amendment Act of 2008, 70 Ohio St. L.J. 1215 (2009); Stephanie Cooper Blum, What Really is at Stake with the FISA Amendments Act of 2008 and Ideas for Future Surveillance Reform, 18 B.Y. Int. L.J. 269 (2009); Recent Legislation: Electronic Surveillance—Congress Grants Telecommunications Companies Retroactive Immunity from Civil Suits for Complying with NSA Terrorist Surveillance Program.—FISA Amendments Act of 2008, Pub, L, No, 110-261, 122 Stat. 2346, 122 Harv. L. Rev. 1271 (2009); William C. Banks, Programmatic Surveillance and FISA: Of Needles and Haystacks.

Privacy and Civil Liberties Oversight Board

Report on the Surveillance Program Operated Pursuant to Section 702 [ed. 50 U.S.C. § 1881a] of the Foreign Intelligence Surveillance Act

July 2, 2014 [footnotes omitted]

[ed. Part 1 is omitted]

Part 2:

EXECUTIVE SUMMARY

I.   Overview of the Report

A.   Description and History of the Section 702 Program

Section 702 has its roots in the President's Surveillance Program developed in the immediate aftermath of the September 11th attacks. Under one aspect of that program, which came to be known as the Terrorist Surveillance Program ("TSP"), the President authorized interception of the contents of international communications from within the United States, outside of the FISA process. Following disclosures about the TSP by the press in December 2005, the government sought and obtained authorization from the Foreign Intelligence Surveillance Court ("FISA court") to conduct, under FISA, the collection that had been occurring under the TSP. Later, the government developed a statutory framework specifically designed to authorize this collection program. After the enactment and expiration of a temporary measure, the Protect America Act of 2007, Congress passed the FISA Amendments Act of 2008, which included the new Section 702 of FISA. The statute provides a procedural framework for the targeting of non-U.S. persons reasonably believed to be located outside the United States to acquire foreign intelligence information.

Section 702 permits the Attorney General and the Director of National Intelligence to jointly authorize surveillance targeting persons who are not U.S. persons, and who are reasonably believed to be located outside the United States, with the compelled assistance of electronic communication service providers, in order to acquire foreign intelligence information. Thus, the persons who may be targeted under Section 702 cannot intentionally include U.S. persons or anyone located in the United States, and the targeting must be conducted to acquire foreign intelligence information as defined in FISA. Executive branch authorizations to acquire designated types of foreign intelligence under Section 702 must be approved by the FISA court, along with procedures governing targeting decisions and the handling of information acquired.

Although U.S. persons may not be targeted under Section 702, communications of or concerning U.S. persons may be acquired in a variety of ways. An example is when a U.S. person communicates with a non-U.S. person who has been targeted, resulting in what is termed "incidental" collection. Another example is when two non-U.S. persons discuss a U.S. person. Communications of or concerning U.S. persons that are acquired in these ways may be retained and used by the government, subject to applicable rules and requirements. The communications of U.S. persons may also be collected by mistake, as when a U.S. person is erroneously targeted or in the event of a technological malfunction, resulting in "inadvertent" collection. In such cases, however, the applicable rules generally require the communications to be destroyed.

Under Section 702, the Attorney General and Director of National Intelligence make annual certifications authorizing this targeting to acquire foreign intelligence information, without specifying to the FISA court the particular non-U.S. persons who will be targeted. There is no requirement that the government demonstrate probable cause to believe that an individual targeted is an agent of a foreign power, as is generally required in the "traditional" FISA process under Title I of the statute. Instead, the Section 702 certifications identify categories of information to be collected, which must meet the statutory definition of foreign intelligence information. The certifications that have been authorized include information concerning international terrorism and other topics, such as the acquisition of weapons of mass destruction.

Section 702 requires the government to develop targeting and "minimization" procedures that must satisfy certain criteria. As part of the FISA court's review and approval of the government's annual certifications, the court must approve these procedures and determine that they meet the necessary standards. The targeting procedures govern how the executive branch determines that a particular person is reasonably believed to be a non-U.S. person located outside the United States, and that targeting this person will lead to the acquisition of foreign intelligence information. The minimization procedures cover the acquisition, retention, use, and dissemination of any non-publicly available U.S. person information acquired through the Section 702 program.

Once foreign intelligence acquisition has been authorized under Section 702, the government sends written directives to electronic communication service providers compelling their assistance in the acquisition of communications. The government identifies or "tasks" certain "selectors," such as telephone numbers or email addresses, that are associated with targeted persons, and it sends these selectors to electronic communications service providers to begin acquisition. There are two types of Section 702 acquisition: what has been referred to as "PRISM" collection and "upstream" collection.

In PRISM collection, the government sends a selector, such as an email address, to a United States-based electronic communications service provider, such as an Internet service provider ("ISP"), and the provider is compelled to give the communications sent to or from that selector to the government. PRISM collection does not include the acquisition of telephone calls. The National Security Agency ("NSA") receives all data collected through PRISM. In addition, the Central Intelligence Agency ("CIA") and the Federal Bureau of Investigation ("FBI") each receive a select portion of PRISM collection.

Upstream collection differs from PRISM collection in several respects. First, the acquisition occurs with the compelled assistance of providers that control the telecommunications "backbone" over which telephone and Internet communications transit, rather than with the compelled assistance of ISPs or similar companies. Upstream collection also includes telephone calls in addition to Internet communications. Data from upstream collection is received only by the NSA: neither the CIA nor the FBI has access to unminimized upstream data. Finally, the upstream collection of Internet communications includes two features that are not present in PRISM collection: the acquisition of so-called "about" communications and the acquisition of so-called "multiple communications transactions" ("MCTs"). An "about" communication is one in which the selector of a targeted person (such as that person's email address) is contained within the communication but the targeted person is not necessarily a participant in the communication. Rather than being "to" or "from" the selector that has been tasked, the communication may contain the selector in the body of the communication, and thus be "about" the selector. An MCT is an Internet "transaction" that contains more than one discrete communication within it. If one of the communications within an MCT is to, from, or "about" a tasked selector, and if one end of the transaction is foreign, the NSA will acquire the entire MCT through upstream collection, including other discrete communications within the MCT that do not contain the selector.

Each agency that receives communications under Section 702 has its own minimization procedures, approved by the FISA court, that govern the agency's use, retention, and dissemination of Section 702 data.11 Among other things, these procedures include rules on how the agencies may "query" the collected data. The NSA, CIA, and FBI minimization procedures all include provisions permitting these agencies to query data acquired through Section 702, using terms intended to discover or retrieve communications content or metadata that meets the criteria specified in the query. These queries may include terms that identify specific U.S. persons and can be used to retrieve the already acquired communications of specific U.S. persons. Minimization procedures set forth the standards for conducting queries. For example, the NSA's minimization procedures require that queries of Section 702-acquired information be designed so that they are "reasonably likely to return foreign intelligence information."

The minimization procedures also include data retention limits and rules outlining circumstances under which information must be purged. Apart from communications acquired by mistake, U.S. persons' communications are not typically purged or eliminated from agency databases, even when they do not contain foreign intelligence information, until the data is aged off in accordance with retention limits.

Each agency's adherence to its targeting and minimization procedures is subject to extensive oversight within the executive branch, including internal oversight within individual agencies as well as regular reviews conducted by the Department of Justice ("DOJ") and the Office of the Director of National Intelligence ("ODNI"). The Section 702 program is also subject to oversight by the FISA court, including during the annual certification process and when compliance incidents are reported to the court. Information about the operation of the program also is reported to congressional committees. Although there have been various compliance incidents over the years, many of these incidents have involved technical issues resulting from the complexity of the program, and the Board has not seen any evidence of bad faith or misconduct.

B.   Legal Analysis

The Board's legal analysis of the Section 702 program includes an evaluation of whether it comports with the terms of the statute, an evaluation of the Fourth Amendment issues raised by the program, and a discussion of the treatment of non-U.S. persons under the program.

. . . On the whole, the text of Section 702 provides the public with transparency into the legal framework for collection, and it publicly outlines the basic structure of the program. The Board concludes that PRISM collection is clearly authorized by the statute and that, with respect to the "about" collection, which occurs in the upstream component of the program, the statute can permissibly be interpreted as allowing such collection as it is currently implemented.

The Board also concludes that the core of the Section 702 program—acquiring the communications of specifically targeted foreign persons who are located outside the United States, upon a belief that those persons are likely to communicate foreign intelligence, using specific communications identifiers, subject to FISA court-approved targeting rules and multiple layers of oversight—fits within the "totality of the circumstances" standard for reasonableness under the Fourth Amendment, as that standard has been defined by the courts to date. Outside of this fundamental core, certain aspects of the Section 702 program push the program close to the line of constitutional reasonableness. Such aspects include the unknown and potentially large scope of the incidental collection of U.S. persons' communications, the use of "about" collection to acquire Internet communications that are neither to nor from the target of surveillance, and the use of queries to search for the communications of specific U.S. persons within the information that has been collected. With these concerns in mind, this Report offers a set of policy proposals designed to push the program more comfortably into the sphere of reasonableness, ensuring that the program remains tied to its constitutionally legitimate core. . .

C.   Policy Analysis

The Section 702 program has enabled the government to acquire a greater range of foreign intelligence than it otherwise would have been able to obtain—and to do so quickly and effectively. Compared with the "traditional" FISA process under Title I of the statute, Section 702 imposes significantly fewer limits on the government when it targets foreigners located abroad, permitting greater flexibility and a dramatic increase in the number of people who can realistically be targeted. The program has proven valuable in the government's efforts to combat terrorism as well as in other areas of foreign intelligence. Presently, over a quarter of the NSA's reports concerning international terrorism include information based in whole or in part on Section 702 collection, and this percentage has increased every year since the statute was enacted. Monitoring terrorist networks under Section 702 has enabled the government to learn how they operate, and to understand their priorities, strategies, and tactics. In addition, the program has led the government to identify previously unknown individuals who are involved in international terrorism, and it has played a key role in discovering and disrupting specific terrorist plots aimed at the United States and other countries.

The basic structure of the Section 702 program appropriately focuses on targeting non-U.S. persons reasonably believed to be located abroad. Yet communications of, or concerning, U.S. persons can be collected under Section 702, and certain features of the program implicate privacy concerns. These features include the potential scope of U.S. person communications that are collected, the acquisition of "about" communications, and the use of queries that employ U.S. person identifiers. . .

Overall, the Board finds that the protections contained in the Section 702 minimization procedures are reasonably designed and implemented to ward against the exploitation of information acquired under the program for illegitimate purposes. The Board has seen no trace of any such illegitimate activity associated with the program, or any attempt to intentionally circumvent legal limits. But the applicable rules potentially allow a great deal of private information about U.S. persons to be acquired by the government. The Board therefore offers a series of policy recommendations to ensure that the program appropriately balances national security with privacy and civil liberties.

II.　Recommendations

A.　Targeting and Tasking

Recommendation 1: The NSA's targeting procedures should be revised to (a) specify criteria for determining the expected foreign intelligence value of a particular target, and (b) require a written explanation of the basis for that determination sufficient to demonstrate that the targeting of each selector is likely to return foreign intelligence information relevant to the subject of one of the certifications approved by the FISA court. The NSA should implement these revised targeting procedures through revised guidance and training for analysts, specifying the criteria for the foreign intelligence determination and the kind of written explanation needed to support it. We expect that the FISA court's review of these targeting procedures in the course of the court's periodic review of Section 702 certifications will include an assessment of whether the revised procedures provide adequate guidance to ensure that targeting decisions are reasonably designed to acquire foreign intelligence information relevant to the subject of one of the certifications approved by the FISA court. Upon revision of the NSA's targeting procedures, internal agency reviews, as well as compliance audits performed by the ODNI and DOJ, should include an assessment of compliance with the foreign intelligence purpose requirement comparable to the review currently conducted of compliance with the requirement that targets are reasonably believed to be non-U.S. persons located outside the United States.

B.　U.S. Person Queries

Recommendation 2: The FBI's minimization procedures should be updated to more clearly reflect the actual practice for conducting U.S. person queries, including the frequency with which Section 702 data may be searched when making routine queries as part of FBI assessments and investigations. Further, some additional limits should be placed on the FBI's use and dissemination of Section 702 data in connection with non-foreign intelligence criminal matters.

Recommendation 3: The NSA and CIA minimization procedures should permit the agencies to query collected Section 702 data for foreign intelligence purposes using U.S. person identifiers only if the query is based upon a statement of facts showing that it is reasonably likely to return foreign intelligence information as defined in FISA. The NSA and CIA should develop written guidance for agents and analysts as to what information and documentation is needed to meet this standard, including specific examples.

C. FISA Court Role

Recommendation 4: To assist in the FISA court's consideration of the government's periodic Section 702 certification applications, the government should submit with those applications a random sample of tasking sheets and a random sample of the NSA's and CIA's U.S. person query terms, with supporting documentation. The sample size and methodology should be approved by the FISA court.

Recommendation 5: As part of the periodic certification process, the government should incorporate into its submission to the FISA court the rules for operation of the Section 702 program that have not already been included in certification orders by the FISA court, and that at present are contained in separate orders and opinions, affidavits, compliance and other letters, hearing transcripts, and mandatory reports filed by the government. To the extent that the FISA court agrees that these rules govern the operation of the Section 702 program, the FISA court should expressly incorporate them into its order approving Section 702 certifications.

D. Upstream and "About" Collection

Recommendation 6: To build on current efforts to filter upstream communications to avoid collection of purely domestic communications, the NSA and DOJ, in consultation with affected telecommunications service providers, and as appropriate, with independent experts, should periodically assess whether filtering techniques applied in upstream collection utilize the best technology consistent with program needs to ensure government acquisition of only communications that are authorized for collection and prevent the inadvertent collection of domestic communications.

Recommendation 7: The NSA periodically should review the types of communications acquired through "about" collection under Section 702, and study the extent to which it would be technically feasible to limit, as appropriate, the types of "about" collection.

E. Accountability and Transparency

Recommendation 8: To the maximum extent consistent with national security, the government should create and release, with minimal redactions, declassified versions of the FBI's and CIA's Section 702 minimization procedures, as well as the NSA's current minimization procedures.

Recommendation 9: The government should implement five measures to provide insight about the extent to which the NSA acquires and utilizes the communications involving U.S. persons and people located in the United States under the Section 702 program. Specifically, the NSA should implement processes to annually count the following: (1) the number of telephone communications acquired in which one caller is located in the United States; (2) the number of Internet communications acquired through upstream collection that originate or terminate in the United States; (3) the number of communications of or concerning U.S. persons that the NSA positively identifies as such in the routine course of its work; (4) the number of queries performed that employ U.S. person identifiers, specifically distinguishing the number of such queries that include names, titles, or other identifiers potentially associated with individuals; and (5) the number of instances in which the NSA disseminates non-public information about U.S. persons, specifically distinguishing disseminations that includes names, titles, or other identifiers potentially associated with individuals. These figures should be reported to Congress in the NSA Director's annual report and should be released publicly to the extent consistent with national security.

F.   Efficacy

Recommendation 10: The government should develop a comprehensive methodology for assessing the efficacy and relative value of counterterrorism programs.

QUESTIONS AND NOTES

1.   Note that the central distinction that appears to have been applied prior to 2007 was between surveillances that are conducted abroad of parties abroad, on the one hand, and surveillances that are conducted in the U.S., on the other, and the initial controversy that arose, when the TSP was disclosed, concerned surveillances where the international and domestic were both involved. How did the FISA Amendments Act change the perspective? What is the primary focus, the main organizing principle under the FAA? What is the difference in scope of application of 1881a on the one hand, and 1881b on the other hand? How do the sections differ with respect to authorization requirements?

2.   Is there a judicial approval requirement under 1881a as well as under 1881b? Are they the same?

3.   How do 1881b and 1881c differ? Do they both require a court order in order to lawfully engage in the type of electronic surveillance involved? Do they both apply to the targeting of a U.S. person abroad? Are both of these sections needed? How are they different, if they are different? To what extent is the distinction between them tied to the definition of "electronic surveillance"?

4.   Suppose a non-U.S. person abroad is targeted and electronically overheard with proper authorization (which section is applicable?), and that person calls someone in the United States? Can the government lawfully continue to listen in to the conversation? Does it make any difference whether the person at the U.S. end of the conversation is a U.S. person, or not?

5. Recall what was deemed controversial under the TSP program. Does the FAA authorize what was deemed by many to have been unlawful under the TSP program?

6. Language added to § 1881a in 2017–18 by the FISA Amendments Reauthorization Act deals with U.S. person queries. See subsection (f). Under what circumstances, can material obtained through sec. 702 (§ 1881a) be queried using a U.S. person query term? Does the statute impose any restrictions on, or require a specific basis for, the use of such query terms?

7. Can the FBI query material obtained through sec. 702/§ 1881a in connection with an ordinary crime investigation? Does the statute impose any limits on such queries? How would you characterize the issues raised by such queries?

8. Do you understand the PRISM collection program? The "about" collection in the upstream component?

9. How responsive is the current version of § 1881a (i.e. including the 2018 amendments) to the analysis and recommendations of the Privacy and Civil Liberties Oversight Board Report, supra, this section? Overall, does the FAA as amended handle the subject of electronic surveillance abroad in a reasonable manner? Would you draw the lines any differently? Is the FAA as amended constitutional?

10. Following Clapper, defendants subject to 702 surveillance have sought to suppress evidence gathered pursuant to 702. The Hasbajrami case below provides an example of how courts have handled the challenges, and also provides useful information regarding FISA, The Protect America Act, and the FISA Amendments Act.

UNITED STATES V. HASBAJRAMI
2016 WL 1029500 (E.D. N.Y. 2016)

JOHN GLEESON, DISTRICT JUDGE.

Defendant Agron Hasbajrami was arrested on September 6, 2011 and charged with three counts of attempting to provide material support to terrorists. He sought to suppress evidence obtained or derived from surveillance conducted pursuant to Section 702 of the FISA Amendments Act ("FAA"), codified at 50 U.S.C. § 1881a (alternatively, "702 surveillance" or "702 collection"). See Def.'s Mot. to Supp., ECF No. 92 ("Def. Br."). This memorandum explains my February 20, 2015 ruling denying the motion to suppress.

PRELIMINARY STATEMENT

Few things are more unsettling than the idea that a government is spying on its own citizens. Our country has a long history of holding our government accountable when it abuses its authority in ways that offend our Constitution's protections. . . .

The post-9/11 era has once again highlighted the tension between privacy and national security interests. The public continues to scrutinize the government's intelligence gathering techniques. But there is also no denying that in this era there are individuals and groups dedicated to inflicting grave harm on our nation, and that the intelligence gathering techniques at issue here are a critical component of our government's efforts to protect us from harm. The government has a duty to respect and protect our constitutional rights while simultaneously ensuring the nation's security. This is a difficult task. And while there has been legitimate criticism of electronic surveillance practices under the FAA—in large part because it has been shrouded in secrecy—in this case, the government conducted its national security investigation within the confines of the Fourth Amendment.

FACTUAL BACKGROUND

A.   The Criminal Investigation

An investigation by the Federal Bureau of Investigation's Joint Terrorism Task Force ("JTTF") revealed that from April 2, 2011 to August 28, 2011, Hasbajrami exchanged numerous emails with an individual he believed was associated with a terrorist organization. Gov't Unclassified Br. at 5 ("Gov't Br."). Hasbajrami sent money to the individual to support Islamic fundamentalist terrorism operations. Id. He also arranged to travel to the Federally Administered Tribal Areas ("FATA") of Pakistan to join a jihadist fighting group. Id.

On September 6, 2011, JTTF agents arrested Hasbajrami at John F. Kennedy International Airport as he was about to board a flight to Turkey en route to Pakistan. Id. A subsequent search of Hasbajrami's luggage "revealed a tent, boots, and cold-weather gear." Def. Br. at 4 (citing PSR at ¶¶ 2–3). Hasbajrami gave detailed statements regarding his offense. Id.

B.   The Government's Disclosure of its FISA Surveillance

Title I and Title III of FISA, as amended, 50 U.S.C. §§ 1801–1812 and 1821–1829, allow electronic surveillance and physical searches after obtaining a FISA warrant from the Foreign Intelligence Surveillance Court ("FISC").

On September 13, 2011, after Hasbajrami was arraigned, the government notified him that he had been subject to FISA surveillance and that it intended at trial to use information obtained or derived from that surveillance ("Title I collection") and certain physical searches ("Title III collection"). Notice, ECF No. 9. On April 12, 2012, after the government disclosed inculpatory evidence—including email communications obtained pursuant to FISA—Hasbajrami pled guilty to a single count of providing material support to terrorists. ECF No. 32. On January 8, 2013, I sentenced him principally to a 180-month term of imprisonment. ECF No. 44.

In July 2013, Hasbajrami filed a motion pursuant to 28 U.S.C. § 2255, seeking relief from his conviction and sentence on the ground that the statute under which he was convicted is unconstitutionally vague. Letter, ECF No. 61-1. Before that claim could be fully briefed and argued, the government revealed new information that eventually became the basis of the instant motion. Specifically, on February 24, 2014, the government notified Hasbajrami "that certain evidence or information, obtained or derived from Title I or III FISA collection, that the government intended to offer into evidence or otherwise use or disclose in proceedings in this case was derived from acquisition of foreign intelligence information conducted pursuant to the FAA." Supplemental Notice, ECF No. 65.

The FAA permits, subject to certain statutory requirements, the interception of electronic communications of non-U.S. persons reasonably believed to be located outside the United States in order to acquire foreign intelligence information. 50 U.S.C. § 1881a. It differs significantly from traditional FISA surveillance. To get a court order, FISA requires the government to demonstrate probable cause to believe that the "target of the electronic surveillance is a foreign power or an agent of a foreign power" and that "each of the facilities or places at which the electronic surveillance is directed is being used, or is about to be used, by a foreign power or an agent of a foreign power." 50 U.S.C. § 1805(2). By contrast, FAA surveillance does not require the government to specify the persons or places that it plans to target for surveillance. 50 U.S.C. § 1881a. Instead, the FISC may authorize surveillance under the FAA for up to one year after approving targeting and minimization procedures and receiving a government certification regarding the proposed surveillance. See 50 U.S.C. § 1881a(a), (c), and (i)(3)(A). Because the FAA does not require an individual court authorization (that is, a warrant) for each data collection, FAA-derived intelligence has been described as "warrantless wiretap" information. See, e.g., Charlie Savage, Federal Prosecutors, in a Policy Shift, Cite Warrantless Wiretaps as Evidence, N.Y. Times, Oct. 27, 2013, at A21.

C. The Withdrawal of the Guilty Plea

On October 2, 2014, I allowed Hasbajrami to withdraw his guilty plea so he could challenge the constitutionality of the FAA-derived evidence and seek its suppression. [Specifically, I allowed Hasbajrami to: [W]ithdraw his plea of guilty because I conclude that he was not sufficiently informed about the facts. Under the precise circumstances presented here, and because of a DOJ policy that transcended this case, Hasbajrami could not have made an intelligent decision about whether to plead guilty: . . .

DISCUSSION

Hasbajrami contends that the FAA surveillance violated the Fourth Amendment because it was not "confined to the collection of foreign communications by foreign actors" outside the United States. Def. Br. at 15–16. Because the government knew that the communications of U.S. persons—like Hasbajrami—inevitably would be collected, the argument goes, it was required to get a warrant. See id. Hasbajrami thus sought to suppress the FISA evidence on which the government's case was based because it was the fruit of the warrantless FAA surveillance.

For its part, the government argues that the FAA collection was constitutional because: (1) the warrant requirement is inapplicable to foreign intelligence collection targeted at foreign persons abroad, and the incidental collection of U.S. persons' communications did not trigger the warrant requirement; (2) the foreign intelligence exception to the warrant requirement applies; and (3) the FAA surveillance was reasonable under the Fourth Amendment. Accordingly, the government's argument continues, the FISC properly used the FAA-derived information in finding probable cause to support the FISA warrants, and the FISA collection was thus constitutionally sound.

. . .

2.   The Protect America Act and the FISA Amendments Act

Under FISA, the definition of "electronic surveillance" was limited to four types of domestically-focused foreign intelligence collection activities. See 50 U.S.C. § 1801(f). Because that definition did not apply to surveillance conducted outside the United States, Congress enacted the Protect America Act ("PAA") in 2007, Pub. L. No. 110–55, 121 Stat. 552 (2007), to modernize FISA in light of the "changes in communications technology" since 1978. S. Rep. No. 110–209 (Oct. 26, 2007) ("For example, in 1978, most foreign communications went through the air rather than over a wire. . . . Today, most international communications travel over a wire."). The PAA empowered the Director of National Intelligence ("DNI") and the Attorney General to authorize "the acquisition of foreign intelligence information concerning persons reasonably believed to be outside the United States." Id. § 105B(a). The PAA required the DNI and the Attorney General to certify that there were reasonable targeting procedures in place to ensure that the surveillance targeted persons reasonably believed to be outside the United States; that the minimization procedures in place satisfied FISA's requirements for such procedures; and that a significant purpose of the acquisition was to obtain foreign intelligence information. Id. § 105B(a)(1)–(5).

The PAA, however, expired in February 2008 due to a sunset provision. In response, in July 2008, Congress enacted the FAA. The provision of the FAA at issue here, Section 702, "supplements pre-existing FISA authority by creating a new framework under which the Government may seek the FISC's authorization of certain foreign intelligence surveillance targeting . . . non-U.S. persons located abroad." Clapper v. Amnesty Int'l USA, 133

S.Ct. 1138, 1144 (2013). Specifically, Section 702 (like the PAA before it) provides that upon the issuance of an order from the FISC, the Attorney General and the DNI may jointly authorize the "targeting of persons reasonably believed to be located outside the United States" for a period of up to one year to acquire "foreign intelligence information." 50 U.S.C. § 1881a(a). This includes any information "necessary to protect against the full range of foreign threats to national security, and information with respect to a foreign power that is necessary to the national defense or foreign affairs." Kris & Wilson § 17.3 (citing 50 U.S.C. §§ 1881a(a), 1801(e)). Consistent with its purpose, the statute prohibits intentionally targeting anyone located inside the United States and any United States citizens outside of the United States. 50 U.S.C. § 1881a(b)(1)–(3).

Surveillance conducted pursuant to Section 702 does not require an individualized court order for each non-U.S. person to be targeted. Rather, the FISC approves annual certifications by the Attorney General and the DNI, thereby authorizing the acquisition of foreign intelligence information by targeting non-U.S. persons reasonably believed to be located outside the United States. Id. § 1881a(a), (i)(3). The statute does not require the certifications to identify the facilities to be targeted for surveillance. Id. § 1881a(g)(4). Instead, the FISC approves the proposed targeting and minimization procedures, and if it finds that the certification contains the required elements and that those procedures are consistent with the Fourth Amendment, it issues an order authorizing the certification. See id. § 1881a(i)(3)(A).

The targeting procedures must be "reasonably designed" to ensure that the surveillance is limited to persons reasonably believed to be located outside the United States, and to "prevent the intentional acquisition of any communication as to which the sender and all intended recipients are known at the time of the acquisition to be located in the United States." Id. § 1881a(g)(2)(A)(i). Minimization procedures must also be "reasonably designed . . . to minimize the acquisition and retention, and prohibit the dissemination, of nonpublicly available information concerning unconsenting United States persons consistent with the need of the United States to obtain, produce, and disseminate foreign intelligence information." 50 U.S.C. §§ 1801(h)(1), 1821(4)(A). Thus, the targeting and minimization procedures aim to safeguard U.S. citizens against the acquisition of their communications under Section 702.

3.　Types of FAA Surveillance

There are two types of Section 702 collection: PRISM and Upstream. See PCLOB Report at 7, 33. In PRISM collection, the government identifies the user accounts it wants to monitor and sends a "selector"—a specific communications facility, such as a target's email address or telephone number—to the relevant communications service provider. Id. at 32–33. A government directive then compels the communications service provider to give it communications sent to or from that selector (i.e., the government "tasks" the selector). Id. at 33; 50 U.S.C. § 1881a(h). This type of surveillance, which intercepts "to/from" communications, can result in the interception of communications with U.S. persons if the target happens to communicate with such a person. See PCLOB Report at 33.

Upstream collection, on the other hand, involves the acquisition of communications through the compelled assistance of the providers that control the telecommunications backbone within the United States over which communications travel. Id. at 35. Like PRISM, upstream collection intercepts "to/from" communications. Id.at 37. But upstream collection is less tailored than PRISM collection; it allows the government to additionally intercept "about" communications, that is, communications that refer to, or are "about," a particular selector. Id. For example, an email in the body of which a targeted email address appears is an "about" communication, even though the targeted person is not necessarily a participant in the intercepted communication. Id. If a communication is to, from, or about a tasked selector, the NSA can acquire an entire MCT, which may contain more than one discrete communication. Id. at 39–41. Simply put, the government can collect other discrete communications that do not have anything to do with the tasked selector, which can result in the collection and querying of wholly domestic communications of non-targeted persons. Id. at 7; NSA Report at 5–6. Some have argued that the FISC erred in its approval in 2011 of "about" communications collection, instead of limiting Section 702 surveillance to communications intercepted by "to/from" collection. See, e.g., Donohue at 159; First Amended Complaint, Wikimedia Found. v. NSA, 15-CV-00662, ¶ 50 (D. Md. June 19, 2015) (equating upstream collection with allowing "a government agent [to] open every piece of mail that comes through the post to determine whether it mentions a particular word or phrase").

The government conducted the disputed surveillance in this case under the PRISM program. Gov't Cl. Br. at 54. None of the Section 702 communications used in the Title I and Title II FISA applications targeting the agent of a foreign power were "about" communications. Id. Thus, the constitutionality of upstream collection is not at issue here.

B.   The Constitutionality of Section 702 is Limited to an As Applied Challenge

As a preliminary matter, Hasbajrami asserts a facial challenge and an "as applied" challenge to the constitutionality of Section 702 collection. Def. Br. at 13–31. A facial challenge would require Hasbajrami to establish that there is no set of circumstances under which Section 702 is valid. United States v. Salerno, 481 U.S. 739, 745 (1987). Given that the government "implemented [the statute] in a defined context" in this case, I need not "speculate about the validity of the law as it might be applied in different ways or on different facts." In re Directives, 551 F.3d 1004, 1010 (FISA Ct. Rev. 2008); see also Ayotte v. Planned Parenthood of N. New England, 546 U.S. 320, 328–30 (2006) (discussing the Court's preference for as-applied challenges in an attempt to "limit the solution to the problem"); United States v. Mohamud, 2014 WL 2866749, at *13–14 (D. Oreg. June 24, 2014) (declining to consider a facial challenge under the Fourth Amendment to Section 702 collection). I therefore limit Hasbajrami's challenge to an as-applied challenge.

C.   Warrantless Surveillance Pursuant to Section 702 is Lawful Under the Fourth Amendment When It Targets Non-U.S. Persons Abroad

The Fourth Amendment protects an individual's "persons, houses, papers, and effects, against unreasonable searches and seizures." For a search or seizure to be consistent with the Fourth Amendment, it must be carried out with a valid warrant, based on probable cause, and be issued by a neutral and detached judicial officer (or fall under one of the exceptions to the warrant requirement). The central inquiry in my Fourth Amendment analysis is "the reasonableness in all the circumstances of the particular governmental invasion of a citizen's personal security." Terry v. Ohio, 392 U.S. 1, 19 (1968). Because Section 702 does not require a warrant before the government can seize the communications of non-U.S. persons abroad, the dispute before me centers on whether the search of communications between a U.S. person and individuals who are legitimate targets of Section 702 surveillance is constitutional. For the reasons that follow, I conclude that it is.

The Fourth Amendment Does Not Apply to Foreign Persons Abroad

The Fourth Amendment's protections do not "apply to activities of the United States directed against aliens in foreign territory." United States v. Verdugo-Urquidez, 494 U.S. 259, 267 (1990) (non-U.S. persons outside the United States who lack a "substantial connection" with the country do not benefit from the Fourth Amendment's protections). Accordingly, under Verdugo-Urquidez, the Fourth Amendment does not constrain the government from collecting the communications of non-U.S. individuals targeted by Section 702 surveillance. The collection at issue was directed at non-U.S. persons the government reasonably (and correctly) believed were located in foreign countries. Although Hasbajrami was a legal resident of the United States who was in the country when he communicated with one or more non-U.S. persons abroad, it was those non-U.S. persons who were the targets of Section 702 surveillance.

Defendant and amici challenge the fact that the FAA allows the government to collect these communications without establishing probable cause or finding individualized suspicion. Def. Br. at 6, 10–11; Amici Br. at

14. However, because the warrant requirement is inapplicable here, so too is the need to establish probable cause or individualized suspicion.

2. The Incidental Collection of U.S. Persons' Communications with Lawfully Targeted Non-U.S. Persons Abroad Does Not Trigger the Warrant Requirement

The real question is whether the incidental interception of U.S. persons' communications during the otherwise lawful collection of non-U.S. persons' communications is constitutional. While Section 702 does not allow intentional targeting of U.S. persons or non-U.S. persons located in the United States, 50 U.S.C. § 1881a(b)(1)–(4), it is inevitable that the government will incidentally intercept communications of persons who are not the intended targets—including, as here, U.S. persons in the United States—during the ordinary course of lawful surveillance.

Minimization and targeting procedures help protect the privacy interests of U.S. persons whose communications are incidentally intercepted. Minimization procedures mask the identities of U.S. persons whose communications the government incidentally collects. See In re Directives, 551 F.3d at 1015 (effective minimization procedures "serve . . . as a means of reducing the impact of incidental intrusions into the privacy of non-targeted United States persons"). The minimization procedures in this case required the NSA to conduct post-targeting analyses to effectuate a stop of the acquisition of communications without delay if it learned at any point that the target had either entered the United States or was in fact a U.S. person. Gov't Cl. Br. at 108.

Hasbajrami contends that the collection of U.S. persons' communications during 702 surveillance targeting non-U.S. persons abroad cannot be properly considered "incidental" because the government knows that the foreign targets will inevitably communicate with U.S. persons, Def. Br. at 11–12, and the minimization procedures permit the government to retain the communications under certain circumstances. Gov't Br. at 31 ("Such circumstances may include where the U.S. person has consented to the dissemination, the specific information about the U.S. person is already publicly available, the U.S. person's identity is necessary to understand foreign intelligence information, or the communication contains evidence of a crime and is being disseminated to law enforcement authorities." (citing PCLOB Rep. at 64–65)). However, the government notes that the same is true of Title I FISA surveillance and Title III electronic surveillance, "in which, inevitably, the government collects communications of third parties and the minimization procedures permit retention of those communications in certain circumstances." Gov't Cl. Br. at 80. . . .

3.   PRISM Collection is Reasonable Under the Fourth Amendment

"The ultimate touchstone of the Fourth Amendment is reasonableness[,]" and the requirement that the PRISM collection at issue here be reasonable applies even when the warrant requirement does not. Brigham City, Utah v. Stuart, 547 U.S. 398, 403 (2006). Thus, I must determine whether Section 702 meets the general reasonableness standard. Id. The statute aims to collect foreign intelligence information to protect national security. As discussed above, I must balance that interest with U.S. persons' privacy interests in their international communications. See Samson v. California, 547 U.S. 843, 848 (2006) (applying the totality of the circumstances test to the Fourth Amendment reasonableness inquiry). I have balanced these interests and find the intelligence gathering here is reasonable under the Fourth Amendment.

a.   The Government Has a Compelling Interest in Obtaining Foreign Intelligence Information to Protect National Security

The 702 surveillance at issue here furthered an indisputably compelling government interest. See Holder v. Humanitarian Law Project, 561 U.S. 1, 28 (2010) ("Everyone agrees that the Government's interest in combating terrorism is an urgent objective of the highest order."); Haig v. Agee, 453 U.S. 280, 307 (1981) ("It is obvious and unarguable that no governmental interest is more compelling than the security of the Nation." (internal quotation marks omitted)); see also In re Directives, 551 F.3d at 1012 (the government's national security interest in acquiring foreign intelligence information pursuant to the PAA "is of the highest order of magnitude"). The fruits of the surveillance led to the prosecution and conviction of a U.S. person who was attempting to lend support to a terrorist organization whose purpose is to inflict serious harm upon the United States.

b.   Individuals Have a Diminished Expectation of Privacy in Email Communications with Non-U.S. Persons Outside the United States

In evaluating the reasonableness of the incidental acquisition of non-targets' communications, I consider the degree to which U.S. citizens have a reasonable expectation of privacy in their email communications with non-U.S. persons abroad.

A person's expectation of privacy in email communications diminishes after sending the email because he or she assumes the risk that the recipient will share the communication with others. See United States v. Lifshitz, 369 F.3d 173, 190 (2d Cir. 2004) ("[An individual] may not . . . enjoy [ ] an expectation of privacy in transmissions over the Internet or e-mail that have already arrived at the recipient."); Guest v. Leis, 255 F.3d 325, 333 (6th Cir. 2001) (email sender loses his or her legitimate expectation of privacy in an email that has already reached the recipient). Email communications are easily forwarded to or read by other parties. But this diminished expectation of privacy in email communications does not mean the government can search every email with impunity just because the email sender communicated with a foreign person abroad.

Analogizing to traditional post-mail, the government contends that an email sender "loses any cognizable Fourth Amendment rights" in the communication once it reaches the recipient. Gov't Br. at 62; see also United States v. Gordon, 168 F.3d 1222, 1228 (10th Cir. 1999) ("[O]nce a letter is sent to someone, the sender's expectation of privacy ordinarily terminates upon delivery." (internal quotation marks omitted)). But the loss of the privacy interest in that setting typically flows from the recipient's provision of the communication to the government. This case, of course, concerns government interception of emails. Nonetheless, given that the emails here had in fact been sent to a third party, I conclude that Hasbajrami had a diminished—if not nonexistent—expectation of privacy in those communications.

c. Section 702's Safeguards and Procedures Sufficiently Protect Non-Targeted U.S. Persons' Privacy Interests

As part of my inquiry into the reasonableness of searches conducted pursuant to Section 702, I also consider the safeguards the government has employed to help protect Hasbajrami's privacy interest and to ensure that 702 surveillance is appropriately targeted at non-U.S. persons located outside the United States. Section 702 itself requires these safeguards. The government's Section 702 applications in this case included the required certifications by Executive Branch officials—the DNI and the Attorney General—that detailed the targeting and minimization procedures used to protect the privacy of U.S. and non-U.S. persons located in the United States. Gov't Cl. Br. at 49–52; 50 U.S.C. §§ 1881a(a), (g), and (i). Upon review, the FISC approved the certifications, finding that they contained the elements required by Section 702, and that the targeting and minimization procedures were consistent with the Fourth Amendment. 50 U.S.C. §§ 1881a(i)(3)(A). The Attorney General and the DNI must also periodically review the government's compliance with the minimization and targeting procedures and submit assessments to the FISC and congressional oversight committees. See 50 U.S.C. 1881a(1).

The oversight provisions of the FAA require the government to regularly report instances of non-compliance to the FISC, which can withhold approval of proposed minimization procedures or require the government to amend them to ensure that they are reasonably designed to limit the acquisition, retention, and dissemination of information concerning U.S. persons. See PCLOB Report at 76 (citing FISC Rule of Proc. 13(b)). The oversight provided by the FISC, the executive branch, and Congress work to safeguard Fourth Amendment protections, lending further support to the reasonableness of Section 702 surveillance. Cf.

collection authorities and their exercise can increase public confidence in the intelligence process and in the monumental decisions that our leaders make based on intelligence products.

In the aftermath of the Snowden disclosures, the government has released a substantial amount of information on the leaked government surveillance programs. Although there remains a deep well of distrust, these official disclosures have helped foster greater public understanding of government surveillance programs. However, to date the official disclosures relate almost exclusively to specific programs that had already been the subject of leaks, and we must be careful in citing these disclosures as object lessons for what additional transparency might be appropriate in the future.

The Board believes that the government must take the initiative and formulate longterm solutions that promote greater transparency for government surveillance policies more generally, in order to inform public debate on technology, national security, and civil liberties going beyond the current controversy. In this effort, all three branches have a role. For the executive branch, disclosures about key national security programs that involve the collection, storage and dissemination of personal information— such as the operation of the National Counterterrorism Center—show that it is possible to describe practices and policies publicly, even those that have not been otherwise leaked, without damage to national security or operational effectiveness.

With regard to the legislative process, even where classified intelligence operations are involved, the purposes and framework of a program for domestic intelligence collection should be debated in public. During the process of developing legislation, some hearings and briefings may need to be conducted in secret to ensure that policymakers fully understand the intended use of a particular authority. But the government should not base an ongoing program affecting the rights of Americans on an interpretation of a statute that is not apparent from a natural reading of the text. In the case of Section 215, the government should have made it publicly clear in the reauthorization process that it intended for Section 215 to serve as legal authority to collect data in bulk on an ongoing basis.

There is also a need for greater transparency regarding operation of the FISA court. Prospectively, we encourage the FISC judges to continue the recent practice of writing opinions with an eye to declassification, separating specific sensitive facts peculiar to the case at hand from broader legal analyses. We also believe that there is significant value in producing declassified versions of earlier opinions, and recommend that the government undertake a classification review of all significant FISC opinions and orders involving novel interpretations of law. We realize that the process of redacting opinions not drafted for public disclosure will be more difficult and will burden individuals with other pressing duties, but we believe that it is appropriate to make the effort where those opinions and orders complete the historical picture of the development of legal doctrine regarding matters within the jurisdiction of the FISA court. In addition, should the government adopt our recommendation for a Special Advocate in the FISC, the nature and extent of that advocate's role must be transparent to be effective.

It is also important to promote transparency through increased reporting to the public on the scope of surveillance programs. We urge the government to work with Internet service providers and other companies to reach agreement on standards allowing reasonable disclosures of aggregate statistics that would be meaningful without revealing sensitive government capabilities or tactics. We recommend that the government should also increase the level of detail in its unclassified reporting to Congress and the public regarding surveillance programs.

II.　Overview of the PCLOB's Recommendations

A.　Section 215 Program

Recommendation 1: The government should end its Section 215 bulk telephone records program.

The Section 215 bulk telephone records program lacks a viable legal foundation under Section 215, implicates constitutional concerns under the First and Fourth Amendments, raises serious threats to privacy and civil liberties as a policy matter, and has shown only limited value. As a result, the Board recommends that the government end the program.

Without the current Section 215 program, the government would still be able to seek telephone calling records directly from communications providers through other existing legal authorities. The Board does not recommend that the government impose data retention requirements on providers in order to facilitate any system of seeking records directly from private databases. . .

The Board also recommends against the enactment of legislation that would merely codify the existing program or any other program that collects bulk data on such a massive scale regarding individuals with no suspected ties to terrorism or criminal activity. Moreover, the Board's constitutional analysis should provide a message of caution, and as a policy matter, given the significant privacy and civil liberties interests at stake, if Congress seeks to provide legal authority for any new program, it should seek the least intrusive alternative and should not legislate to the outer bounds of its authority.

Recommendation 2: The government should immediately implement additional privacy safeguards in operating the Section 215 bulk collection program.

The Board recommends that the government immediately implement several additional privacy safeguards to mitigate the privacy impact of the present Section 215 program. The recommended changes can be implemented without any need for congressional or FISC authorization. . .

B.   FISA Court Operations

Recommendation 3: Congress should enact legislation enabling the FISC to hear independent views, in addition to the government's views, on novel and significant applications and in other matters in which a FISC judge determines that consideration of the issues would merit such additional views.

Congress should authorize the establishment of a panel of outside lawyers to serve as Special Advocates before the FISC in appropriate cases. The Presiding Judge of the FISC should select attorneys drawn from the private sector to serve on the panel. The attorneys should be capable of obtaining appropriate security clearances and would then be available to be called upon to participate in certain FISC proceedings. The decision as to whether the Special Advocate would participate in any particular matter should be left to the discretion of the FISC. . .The role of the Special Advocate, when invited by the court to participate, would be to make legal arguments addressing privacy, civil rights, and civil liberties interests. The Special Advocate would review the government's application and exercise his or her judgment about whether the proposed surveillance or collection is consistent with law or unduly affects privacy and civil liberties interests.

Recommendation 4: Congress should enact legislation to expand the opportunities for appellate review of FISC decisions by the FISCR and for review of FISCR decisions by the Supreme Court of the United States.

Providing for greater appellate review of FISC and FISCR rulings will strengthen the integrity of judicial review under FISA. Providing a role for the Special Advocate in seeking that appellate review will further increase public confidence in the integrity of the process.

Recommendation 5: The FISC should take full advantage of existing authorities to obtain technical assistance and expand opportunities for legal input from outside parties.

FISC judges should take advantage of their ability to appoint Special Masters or other technical experts to assist them in reviewing voluminous or technical materials, either in connection with initial applications or in compliance reviews. In addition, the FISC and the FISCR should develop procedures to facilitate amicus participation by third parties in cases involving questions that are of broad public interest, where it is feasible to do so consistent with national security.

C.   Promoting Transparency

Recommendation 6: To the maximum extent consistent with national security, the government should create and release with minimal redactions declassified versions of new decisions, orders and opinions by the FISC and FISCR in cases involving novel interpretations of FISA or other significant questions of law, technology or compliance.

Recommendation 7: Regarding previously written opinions, the government should perform a declassification review of decisions, orders and opinions by the FISC and FISCR that have not yet been released to the public and that involve novel interpretations of FISA or other significant questions of law, technology or compliance.

Recommendation 8: The Attorney General should regularly and publicly report information regarding the operation of the Special Advocate program recommended by the Board. This should include statistics on the frequency and nature of Special Advocate participation in FISC and FISCR proceedings.

Recommendation 9: The government should work with Internet service providers and other companies that regularly receive FISA production orders to develop rules permitting the companies to voluntarily disclose certain statistical information. In addition, the government should publicly disclose more detailed statistics to provide a more complete picture of government surveillance operations.

Recommendation 10: The Attorney General should fully inform the PCLOB of the government's activities under FISA and provide the PCLOB with copies of the detailed reports submitted under FISA to the specified committees of Congress. This should include providing the PCLOB with copies of the FISC decisions required to be produced under Section 601(a)(5).

Recommendation 11: The Board urges the government to begin developing principles and criteria for transparency.

Recommendation 12: The scope of surveillance authorities affecting Americans should be public.

In particular, the Administration should develop principles and criteria for the public articulation of the legal authorities under which it conducts surveillance affecting Americans. If the text of the statute itself is not sufficient to inform the public of the scope of asserted government authority, then the key elements of the legal opinion or other documents describing the government's legal analysis should be made public so there can be a free and open debate regarding the law's scope. This includes both original enactments such as 215's revisions and subsequent reauthorizations. While sensitive operational details regarding the conduct of government surveillance programs should remain classified, and while legal interpretations of the application of a statute in a particular case may also be secret so long as the use of that technique in a particular case is secret, the government's interpretations of statutes that provide the basis for ongoing surveillance programs affecting Americans can and should be made public.

1. THE USA FREEDOM ACT OF 2015 (USAF)

On June 2, 2015 the USA FREEDOM Act [Uniting and Strengthening America by Fulfilling Rights and Ensuring Effective Discipline Over Monitoring Act of 2015] became Public Law No: 114–23. The Act contained provisions dealing with a number of surveillance topics and, inter alia, ended the bulk collection of telephone records by the government and added greater transparency to the government's surveillance programs. Reproduced below are a. 50 U.S.C. § 1861 (sec.215) as amended by the FREEDOM Act and b. a summary of the most significant changes effected by the Act prepared by the Library of Congress's Congressional Research Service. See https://www.govtrack.us/congress/bills/114/hr2048/summary#libraryofcongress.

a. 50 U.S.C.A. § 1861

§ 1861. Access to certain business records for foreign intelligence and international terrorism investigations

(a) Application for order; conduct of investigation generally

(1) Subject to paragraph (3), the Director of the Federal Bureau of Investigation or a designee of the Director (whose rank shall be no lower than Assistant Special Agent in Charge) may make an application for an order requiring the production of any tangible things (including books, records, papers, documents, and other items) for an investigation to obtain foreign intelligence information not concerning a United States person or to protect against international terrorism or clandestine intelligence activities, provided that such investigation of a United States person is not conducted solely upon the basis of activities protected by the first amendment to the Constitution.

(2) An investigation conducted under this section shall

(A) be conducted under guidelines approved by the Attorney General under Executive Order 12333 (or a successor order); and

(B) not be conducted of a United States person solely upon the basis of activities protected by the first amendment to the Constitution of the United States.

(3) In the case of an application for an order requiring the production of library circulation records, library patron lists, book sales records, book customer lists, firearms sales records, tax return

records, educational records, or medical records containing information that would identify a person, the Director of the Federal Bureau of Investigation may delegate the authority to make such application to either the Deputy Director of the Federal Bureau of Investigation or the Executive Assistant Director for National Security (or any successor position). The Deputy Director or the Executive Assistant Director may not further delegate such authority.

(b) Recipient and contents of application. Each application under this section

(1) shall be made to—

(A) a judge of the court established by section 1803(a) of this title; or

(B) a United States Magistrate Judge under chapter 43 of Title 28, who is publicly designated by the Chief Justice of the United States to have the power to hear applications and grant orders for the production of tangible things under this section on behalf of a judge of that court; and

(2) shall include—

(A) a specific selection term to be used as the basis for the production of the tangible things sought;

(B) in the case of an application other than an application described in subparagraph (C) (including an application for the production of call detail records other than in the manner described in subparagraph (C)), a statement of facts showing that there are reasonable grounds to believe that the tangible things sought are relevant to an authorized investigation (other than a threat assessment) conducted in accordance with subsection (a)(2) to obtain foreign intelligence information not concerning a United States person or to protect against international terrorism or clandestine intelligence activities, such things being presumptively relevant to an authorized investigation if the applicant shows in the statement of the facts that they pertain to—

(i) a foreign power or an agent of a foreign power;

(ii) the activities of a suspected agent of a foreign power who is the subject of such authorized investigation; or

(iii) an individual in contact with, or known to, a suspected agent of a foreign power who is the subject of such authorized investigation;

(C) in the case of an application for the production on an ongoing basis of call detail records created before, on, or after the

(4) A denial of the application made under this subsection may be reviewed as provided in section 1803 of this title.

(d) Nondisclosure

(1) No person shall disclose to any other person that the Federal Bureau of Investigation has sought or obtained tangible things pursuant to an order issued or an emergency production required under this section, other than to

(A) those persons to whom disclosure is necessary to comply with such order or such emergency production;

(B) an attorney to obtain legal advice or assistance with respect to the production of things in response to the order or the emergency production; or

(C) other persons as permitted by the Director of the Federal Bureau of Investigation or the designee of the Director.

(2) (A) A person to whom disclosure is made pursuant to paragraph (1) shall be subject to the nondisclosure requirements applicable to a person to whom an order or emergency production is directed under this section in the same manner as such person.

(B) Any person who discloses to a person described in subparagraph (A), (B), or (C) of paragraph (1) that the Federal Bureau of Investigation has sought or obtained tangible things pursuant to an order or emergency production under this section shall notify such person of the nondisclosure requirements of this subsection.

(C) At the request of the Director of the Federal Bureau of Investigation or the designee of the Director, any person making or intending to make a disclosure under subparagraph (A) or (C) of paragraph (1) shall identify to the Director or such designee the person to whom such disclosure will be made or to whom such disclosure was made prior to the request.

. . .

(f) Judicial review of FISA orders

(1) In this subsection—

(A) the term "production order" means an order to produce any tangible thing under this section; and

(B) the term "nondisclosure order" means an order imposed under subsection (d).

(2) (A) (i) A person receiving a production order may challenge the legality of the production order or any nondisclosure order imposed

in connection with the production order by filing a petition with the pool established by section 1803(e)(1) of this title.

. . .

(C) (i) A judge considering a petition to modify or set aside a nondisclosure order may grant such petition only if the judge finds that there is no reason to believe that disclosure may endanger the national security of the United States, interfere with a criminal, counterterrorism, or counterintelligence investigation, interfere with diplomatic relations, or endanger the life or physical safety of any person.

(ii) If the judge denies a petition to modify or set aside a nondisclosure order, the recipient of such order shall be precluded for a period of 1 year from filing another such petition with respect to such nondisclosure order.

. . .

(4) Judicial proceedings under this subsection shall be concluded as expeditiously as possible. The record of proceedings, including petitions filed, orders granted, and statements of reasons for decision, shall be maintained under security measures established by the Chief Justice of the United States, in consultation with the Attorney General and the Director of National Intelligence.

(5) All petitions under this subsection shall be filed under seal. In any proceedings under this subsection, the court shall, upon request of the Government, review ex parte and in camera any Government submission, or portions thereof, which may include classified information.

(g) Minimization procedures

(1) In general. The Attorney General shall adopt, and update as appropriate, specific minimization procedures governing the retention and dissemination by the Federal Bureau of Investigation of any tangible things, or information therein, received by the Federal Bureau of Investigation in response to an order under this subchapter.

(2) Defined. In this section, the term "minimization procedures" means—

(A) specific procedures that are reasonably designed in light of the purpose and technique of an order for the production of tangible things, to minimize the retention, and prohibit the dissemination, of nonpublicly available information concerning unconsenting United States persons consistent with the need of the United States to obtain, produce, and disseminate foreign intelligence information;

(B) procedures that require that nonpublicly available information, which is not foreign intelligence information, as defined in section 1801(e)(1) of this title, shall not be disseminated in a manner that identifies any United States person, without such person's consent, unless such person's identity is necessary to understand foreign intelligence information or assess its importance; and

(C) notwithstanding subparagraphs (A) and (B), procedures that allow for the retention and dissemination of information that is evidence of a crime which has been, is being, or is about to be committed and that is to be retained or disseminated for law enforcement purposes.

(3) Rule of construction. Nothing in this subsection shall limit the authority of the court established under section 1803(a) of this title to impose additional, particularized minimization procedures with regard to the production, retention, or dissemination of nonpublicly available information concerning unconsenting United States persons, including additional, particularized procedures related to the destruction of information within a reasonable time period.

(h) Use of information. Information acquired from tangible things received by the Federal Bureau of Investigation in response to an order under this subchapter concerning any United States person may be used and disclosed by Federal officers and employees without the consent of the United States person only in accordance with the minimization procedures adopted pursuant to subsection (g). No otherwise privileged information acquired from tangible things received by the Federal Bureau of Investigation in accordance with the provisions of this subchapter shall lose its privileged character. No information acquired from tangible things received by the Federal Bureau of Investigation in response to an order under this subchapter may be used or disclosed by Federal officers or employees except for lawful purposes.

b. Congressional Research Service, Summary of the USA FREEDOM Act

TITLE I—FISA BUSINESS RECORDS REFORMS

(Sec. 101) Amends the Foreign Intelligence Surveillance Act of 1978 (FISA) to establish a new process to be followed when the Federal Bureau of Investigation (FBI) submits an application to a FISA court for an order requiring the production of business records or other tangible things for an investigation to obtain foreign intelligence information not concerning a U.S. person or to protect against international terrorism or clandestine intelligence activities. (The FBI currently uses such authority to request

FISA orders requiring telephone companies to produce telephone call records to the National Security Agency.)

Prohibits the FBI from applying for a tangible thing production order unless a specific selection term is used as the basis for the production. Maintains limitations under current law that prohibit the FBI from applying for tangible thing production orders for threat assessments.

Establishes two separate frameworks for the production of tangible things with different standards that apply based on whether the FBI's application seeks:

- production on an ongoing basis of call detail records created before, on, or after the date of the application relating to an authorized investigation to protect against international terrorism, in which case the specific selection term must specifically identify an individual, account, or personal device; or

- production of call detail records or other tangible things in any other manner, in which case the selection term must specifically identify an individual, a federal officer or employee, a group, an entity, an association, a corporation, a foreign power, an account, a physical or an electronic address, a personal device, or any other specific identifier but is prohibited from including, when not used as part of a specific identifier, a broad geographic region (including the United States, a city, county, state, zip code, or area code) or an electronic communication or remote computing service provider, unless the provider is itself a subject of an authorized investigation.

Defines "call detail record" as session identifying information (including an originating or terminating telephone number, an International Mobile Subscriber Identity number, or an International Mobile Station Equipment Identity number), a telephone calling card number, or the time or duration of a call. Excludes from such definition: (1) the contents of any communication; (2) the name, address, or financial information of a subscriber or customer; or (3) cell site location or global positioning system information.

Requires the FBI, in applications for ongoing production of call detail records for investigations to protect against international terrorism, to show: (1) reasonable grounds to believe that the call detail records are relevant to such investigation; and (2) a reasonable, articulable suspicion that the specific selection term is associated with a foreign power or an agent of a foreign power engaged in international terrorism or activities in preparation for such terrorism.

Requires a judge approving such an ongoing release of call detail records for an investigation to protect against international terrorism to:

- limit such production to a period not to exceed 180 days but allow such orders to be extended upon application, with FISA court approval;

- permit the government to require the production of an initial set of call records using the reasonable, articulable suspicion standard that the term is associated with a foreign power or an agent of a foreign power and then a subsequent set of call records using session-identifying information or a telephone calling card number identified by the specific selection term that was used to produce the initial set of records (thus limiting the government to what is commonly referred to as two "hops" of call records); and

- direct the government to adopt minimization procedures requiring prompt destruction of produced call records that are not foreign intelligence information.

Allows a FISA court to approve other categories of FBI requests for the production of call detail records or tangible things (i.e., FBI call detail record and tangible thing applications that do not seek ongoing production of call detail records created before, on, or after the date of an application relating to an authorized investigation to protect against international terrorism) without subjecting the production to: (1) the reasonable, articulable suspicion standard for an association with a foreign power or an agent of a foreign power; (2) the 180-day or the two-hop limitation; or (3) the special minimization procedures that require prompt destruction of produced records only if the order approves an ongoing production of call detail records for investigations to protect against international terrorism.

(Sec. 102) Authorizes the Attorney General to require the emergency production of tangible things without first obtaining a court order if the Attorney General: (1) reasonably determines that an emergency situation requires the production of tangible things before an order authorizing production can be obtained with due diligence, (2) reasonably determines that a factual basis exists for the issuance of such a production order, (3) informs a FISA judge of the decision to require such production at the time the emergency decision is made, and (4) makes an application to a FISA judge within seven days after the Attorney General requires such emergency production.

Terminates the authority for such emergency production of tangible things when the information sought is obtained, when the application for the order is denied, or after the expiration of seven days from the time the Attorney General begins requiring such emergency production, whichever is earliest.

Prohibits information obtained or evidence derived from such an emergency production from being received in evidence or disclosed in any proceeding in or before any court, grand jury, agency, legislative committee, or other authority of the United States, any state, or any political subdivision if: (1) the subsequent application for court approval is denied, or (2) the production is terminated and no order is issued approving the production. Bars information concerning any U.S. person acquired from such production from being used or disclosed in any other manner by federal officers or employees without the consent of such person, except with approval of the Attorney General if the information indicates a threat of death or serious bodily harm.

(Sec. 103) Requires FISA court orders approving the production of tangible things to include each specific selection term used as the basis for such production. Prohibits FISA courts from authorizing the collection of tangible things without the use of a specific selection term.

(Sec. 104) Requires a FISA court, as a condition to approving an application for a tangible thing production order, to find that the minimization procedures submitted with the application meet applicable FISA standards. Authorizes the court to impose additional minimization procedures.

Allows a nondisclosure order imposed in connection with a tangible thing production order to be challenged immediately by filing a petition for judicial review. (Currently, such a tangible thing nondisclosure order cannot be challenged until one year after the issuance of the production order.) Removes a requirement that a judge considering a petition to modify or set aside a nondisclosure order treat as conclusive a certification by the Attorney General, the Deputy Attorney General, an Assistant Attorney General, or the FBI Director that disclosure may endanger national security or interfere with diplomatic relations.

(Sec. 105) Extends liability protections to persons who provide information, facilities, or technical assistance for the production of tangible things. (Currently, liability protections are limited to persons who produce such tangible things.)

(Sec. 106) Requires the government to compensate a person for reasonable expenses incurred in producing tangible things or providing technical assistance to the government to implement production procedures.

(Sec. 108) Amends the USA PATRIOT Improvement and Reauthorization Act of 2005 to require the Inspector General of the Department of Justice to audit the effectiveness and use of FISA authority to obtain production of tangible things from 2012 to 2014, including an examination of whether minimization procedures adopted by the Attorney General adequately protect the constitutional rights of U.S. persons.

Directs the Inspector General of the Intelligence Community, for the same 2012–2014 period, to assess: (1) the importance of such information to the intelligence community; (2) the manner in which such information was collected, retained, analyzed, and disseminated; and (3) the adequacy of minimization procedures, including an assessment of any minimization procedures proposed by an element of the intelligence community that were modified or denied by the court.

Requires such Inspectors General to report to Congress regarding the results of such audit and assessment.

(Sec. 109) Requires amendments made by this Act to FISA's tangible thing requirements to take effect 180 days after enactment of this Act. Prohibits this Act from being construed to alter or eliminate the government's authority to obtain an order under the tangible things requirements of FISA as in effect prior to the effective date of such amendments during the period ending on such effective date.

(Sec. 110) Prohibits this Act from being construed to authorize the production of the contents of any electronic communication from an electronic communication service provider under such tangible thing requirements.

. . .

TITLE III—FISA ACQUISITIONS TARGETING PERSONS OUTSIDE THE UNITED STATES REFORMS

(Sec. 301) Limits the government's use of information obtained through an authorization by the Attorney General and the Director of National Intelligence (DNI) to target non-U.S. persons outside the United States if a FISA court later determines that certain targeting or minimization procedures certified to the court are unlawful.

Prohibits information obtained or evidence derived from an acquisition pursuant to a part of a targeting certification or a related minimization procedure that the court has identified as deficient concerning a U.S. person from being received in evidence or otherwise disclosed in any proceeding in or before any court, grand jury, agency, legislative committee, or other authority of the United States, any state, or any political subdivision.

Bars information concerning any U.S. person acquired pursuant to a deficient part of a certification from being used or disclosed subsequently in any other manner by federal officers or employees without the consent of the U.S. person, except with approval of the Attorney General if the information indicates a threat of death or serious bodily harm.

Allows a FISA court, if the government corrects the deficiency, to permit the use or disclosure of information obtained before the date of the correction.

TITLE IV—FOREIGN INTELLIGENCE SURVEILLANCE COURT REFORMS

(Sec. 401) Directs the presiding judges of the FISA court and the FISA court of review to jointly designate at least five individuals to serve as amicus curiae to assist in the consideration of any application for an order or review that presents a novel or significant interpretation of the law, unless the court finds that such appointment is not appropriate.

Permits FISA courts to appoint an individual or organization to serve as amicus curiae in other instances, including to provide technical expertise. Requires such amicus curiae to provide: (1) legal arguments that advance protection of individual privacy and civil liberties, or (2) other legal arguments or information related to intelligence collection or communications technology.

Allows the FISA court of review to certify a question of law to be reviewed by the Supreme Court. Permits the Supreme Court to appoint FISA amicus curiae or other persons to provide briefings or other assistance upon such a certification.

(Sec. 402) Requires the DNI to: (1) conduct a declassification review of each decision, order, or opinion issued by the FISA court or the FISA court of review that includes a significant construction or interpretation of any provision of law, including any novel or significant construction or interpretation of "specific selection term" as defined in this Act; and (2) make such decisions, orders, or opinions publicly available to the greatest extent practicable, subject to permissible redactions.

Authorizes the DNI to waive such review and public availability requirements if: (1) a waiver is necessary to protect the national security of the United States or properly classified intelligence sources or methods, and (2) an unclassified statement prepared by the Attorney General is made publicly available to summarize the significant construction or interpretation of law.

[ed. TITLE V omitted here deals with national security letter reform.]

TITLE VI—FISA TRANSPARENCY AND REPORTING REQUIREMENTS

(Sec. 601) Requires the Attorney General to expand an annual report to Congress regarding tangible thing applications to include a summary of compliance reviews and the total number of: (1) applications made for the daily production of call detail records created before, on, or after the date of an application relating to an authorized investigation to protect against international terrorism; and (2) orders approving such requests.

Directs the Attorney General to report to Congress annually regarding tangible things applications and orders in which the specific selection term does not specifically identify an individual, account, or personal device. Requires the report to indicate whether the court approving such orders has directed additional, particularized minimization procedures beyond those adopted by the Attorney General.

(Sec. 602) Directs the Administrative Office of the U.S. Courts to submit annually to Congress the number of: (1) FISA applications submitted and orders granted, modified, or denied under specified FISA authorities; and (2) appointments of an individual to serve as amicus curiae for FISA courts, including the name of each appointed individual, as well as any findings that such an appointment is not appropriate. Makes the report subject to a declassification review by the Attorney General and the DNI.

Directs the DNI to make available publicly a report that identifies, for the preceding 12-month period, the total number of: (1) FISA court orders issued for electronic surveillance, physical searches, the targeting of persons outside the United States, pen registers and trap and trace devices, call detail records, and other tangible things; and (2) national security letters issued.

Requires the DNI's reports to include the estimated number of: (1) targets of certain FISA orders, (2) search terms and queries concerning U.S. persons when the government retrieves information from electronic or wire communications obtained by targeting non-U.S. persons outside the United States, (3) unique identifiers used to communicate certain collected information, and (4) search terms concerning U.S. persons used to query a database of call detail records. Exempts certain queries by the FBI from such estimates.

(Sec. 603) Permits a person who is subject to a nondisclosure requirement accompanying a FISA order, directive, or national security letter to choose one of four methods to report publicly, on a semiannual or annual basis, the aggregate number of orders, directives, or letters with which the person was required to comply. Specifies the categories of orders, directives, and letters to be itemized or combined, the details authorized to be included with respect to contents or noncontents orders and the number of customer selectors targeted, and the ranges within which the number of orders, directives, or letters received may be reported aggregately in bands under each permitted method (i.e., reported in bands of 1000, 500, 250, or 100 depending on the chosen method).

Requires the information that may be included in certain aggregates to be delayed by 180 days, one year, or 540 days depending on the chosen reporting method and whether the nondisclosure requirements are contained in a new order or directive concerning a platform, product, or service for which the person did not previously receive an order or directive.

(Sec. 604) Expands the categories of FISA court decisions, orders, or opinions that the Attorney General is required to submit to Congress within 45 days after issuance of the decision to include: (1) a denial or modification of an application under FISA; and (2) a change of the application, or a novel application, of any FISA provision. (Currently, the Attorney General is only required to submit only decisions regarding a significant construction or interpretation of any FISA provision.)

(Sec. 605) Revises reporting requirements regarding electronic surveillance, physical searches, and tangible things to include the House Judiciary Committee as a recipient of such reports.

Requires the Attorney General to identify in an existing semiannual report each agency on behalf of which the government has applied for orders authorizing or approving the installation and use of pen registers or trap and trace devices under FISA.

TITLE VII—ENHANCED NATIONAL SECURITY PROVISIONS

(Sec. 701) Establishes procedures for a lawfully authorized targeting of a non-U.S. person previously believed to be located outside the United States to continue for a period not to exceed 72 hours from the time that the non-U.S. person is reasonably believed to be located inside the United States. Requires an element of the intelligence community, as a condition to exercising such authority, to: (1) determine that a lapse in the targeting poses a threat of death or serious bodily harm; (2) notify the Attorney General; and (3) request, as soon as practicable, the employment of emergency electronic surveillance or emergency physical search under appropriate FISA standards.

(Sec. 702) Expands the definition of "agent of a foreign power" to include a non-U.S. person who: (1) acts in the United States for or on behalf of a foreign power engaged in clandestine intelligence activities in the United States contrary to U.S. interests or as an officer, employee, or member of a foreign power, irrespective of whether the person is inside the United States; or (2) knowingly aids, abets, or conspires with any person engaging in an international proliferation of weapons of mass destruction on behalf of a foreign power or conducting activities in preparation for such proliferation.

(Sec. 704) Increases from 15 to 20 years the maximum penalty of imprisonment for providing material support or resources to a foreign terrorist organization in cases where the support does not result in the death of any person.

(Sec. 705) Amends the USA PATRIOT Improvement and Reauthorization Act of 2005 and the Intelligence Reform and Terrorism Prevention Act of 2004 to extend until December 15, 2019, FISA authorities concerning: (1) the production of business records, including call detail records and other tangible things; (2) roving electronic surveillance orders; and (3) a revised definition of "agent of a foreign power" that includes any non-U.S. persons who engage in international terrorism or preparatory activities (commonly referred to as the "lone wolf" provision). . . .

QUESTIONS AND NOTES

1. In April, 2017, the Director of National Intelligence issued a Statistical Transparency Report Regarding Use of National Security Authorities for 2016—the first of such reports to be made under the USA FREEDOM Act. The Report indicates that the NSA (acting through the FBI) obtained 40 CDR orders for 42 targets which resulted in the government receiving approximately 151 million records from providers and which were then stored in NSA facilities.

The report states that "the government counts each record separately even if the government receives the same record multiple times (whether from one provider or multiple providers). Additionally, this metric includes duplicates of unique identifiers—i.e., because the government lacks the technical ability to isolate unique identifiers, the statistic counts the number of records even if unique identifiers are repeated." Accordingly there is much double counting. Overall, however, there are fewer records than under the bulk collection program, and the data mining is better targeted. See generally, Lawfare, Caroline Lynch and Lara Flint, The USA Freedom Act Turns Two, https://www.lawfareblog.com/usa-freedom-act-turns-two.

2. How responsive to the analysis and recommendations of the Privacy and Civil Liberties Oversight Board Report, Part 1, supra this section regarding the section 215 metadata program is the amended version of § 1861 contained in the USA FREEDOM Act, supra? Civil libertarians had decried the two programs discussed in section C, above and in this section D. In 2013, prior to the enactment of the USA FREEDOM Act, a representative of the American Civil Liberties Union denounced the programs as an infringement of fundamental civil liberties: "A pox on all the three houses of government." N.Y. Times, June 7, 2013, A16. Did the USA FREEDOM Act respond to the concerns that one might have about infringement of civil liberties? How serious was the threat to civil liberties and privacy? Are the real and potential benefits worth the real and potential costs?

3. See generally, Lawfare, Benjamin Wittes, The Minimization and Targeting Procedures: An Analysis http://www.lawfareblog.com/2013/06/the-miminization-and-targeting-procedures-an-analysis/; Lawfare, Robert Chesney, Can You Understand These Data Collection Stories without Understanding the Minimization Procedures? http://www.lawfareblog.com/2013/06/minimization-procedures-data-collection/.

4.   Separate from the two programs discussed above, the NSA reportedly conducted a program involving the meta-data collection of internet traffic. The collection program began early in the Bush administration and evolved over time. It continued two years into the Obama administration and was finally ended in 2011 for "operation and resource reasons." Assumedly, the collection of such meta-data of internet traffic, like that of telephone calls, was considered not to be violative of the Fourth Amendment protections against search and seizure and expectations of privacy because it did not involve acquisition of the contents of communications.

CHAPTER 6

SEARCHES AND ADMINISTRATIVE SUBPOENAS

■ ■ ■

A. INTRODUCTION

In this chapter, we examine the different legal tools and the applicable doctrines used by the government in terrorism cases to obtain physical items or information in the form of records, documents, books and information, including computerized records, from persons who are targets of an investigation and from others who are in possession of records, etc. as well as other tangible things that have some connection to a terrorism investigation.

There are two basic types of legal tools addressed in this chapter, 1) search warrants and 2) subpoenas and subpoena-like demands or orders. Authorization for and the applicable standards and rules for, foreign intelligence search warrants for searches in the United States are contained in the Foreign Intelligence Surveillance Act (FISA); statutory provisions dealing with physical searches were added to the FISA statute in 1994; see section B below. The standards and rules applicable to such warrants should be compared with the warrants issued in ordinary criminal cases. The applicable law for searches abroad, both generally and in foreign intelligence cases—whether search warrants are required in such cases, is the subject of inquiry in section C, infra. Consider, for example, whether a search warrant equivalent to the type of provisions contained in the FISA Amendments Act of 2008 (discussed in ch. 5, supra) is needed for searches with an international feature.

The topic addressed in section D, infra is the use of a particular category of administrative subpoenas—called national security letters, to obtain records, documents, etc. useful in a terrorism investigation. Specifically, in this section the legal aspects of national security letters are addressed and should be compared with the so-called "library" provision, orders under section 215 of the USA PATRIOT Act (now 50 U.S.C. 1861), which must be issued by a judge. Both of these legal tools should be compared with administrative and judicially-authorized subpoenas used in other areas of criminal enforcement.

The chapter also provides an opportunity to compare search warrants and subpoenas, specifically administrative subpoenas, as ways of obtaining records, documents and other kinds of evidence in aid of an investigation. There are, of course, obvious differences generally between searches pursuant to a warrant and obtaining information through the use of subpoenas, and this chapter highlights the specific differences in connection with their use in terrorism-related investigations.

To cite just a few of the obvious comparisons, search warrants do not require any voluntary action on the part of the owner of the premises to be searched. Subpoenas require the person to whom the order is directed to produce the described material. Search warrants are more often than not directed against a target of the investigation. Subpoenas may be directed against either the investigatory target or a third party possessor of records, information, etc. In the case of subpoenas used in terrorism investigations, they are almost always directed against third parties. Search warrants must be approved by a judicial officer based on a specific factual finding, probable cause relating to evidence of a crime, etc. in ordinary criminal cases, and for terrorism cases, the type of finding specified in the FISA. Administrative subpoenas are issued by an executive branch official, and the necessary factual premise varies but most often it is "relevant to an investigation," a lesser standard than any form of probable cause.

B. SEARCHES WITHIN THE UNITED STATES

1. INTRODUCTION

Sections 1821–1825, Title 50, U.S.C. establish the authority to issue search warrants for foreign intelligence information. The standards and rules roughly parallel those governing electronic surveillance to obtain foreign intelligence, 50 U.S.C. §§ 1801 et seq. which were treated in ch. 5 supra. Differences between the electronic surveillance and physical search provisions generally reflect differences between physical searches and electronic surveillance. In addressing the search warrant provisions in this chapter, it is assumed that the reader has previously studied Chapter 5 so that it is not necessary again to review here the definitions previously treated in that chapter, e.g. the definitions of foreign power and agent of a foreign power, which apply equally to electronic surveillance and physical search warrants.

Excerpts from the search warrant provisions are reproduced below, followed by a series of questions regarding their scope and application. Because a requirement of secrecy generally attaches to the approval process for, and execution of, these warrants, there is little publicly available law on this subject. Even the type of limited information that has thus far become public in regard to FISA electronic surveillance (see ch. 5) has thus far generally not surfaced with respect to the FISA search warrant process. For comparison purposes, Rule 41, Federal Rules of

Criminal Procedure, which governs the issuance of search warrants in ordinary criminal cases is also reproduced here.

2.   TITLE 50, U.S.C.

§ 1821. Definitions

As used in this subchapter:

. . .

(4) "Minimization procedures" with respect to physical search, means—

(A) specific procedures, which shall be adopted by the Attorney General, that are reasonably designed in light of the purposes and technique of the particular physical search, to minimize the acquisition and retention, and prohibit the dissemination, of nonpublicly available information concerning unconsenting United States persons consistent with the need of the United States to obtain, produce, and disseminate foreign intelligence information;

(B) procedures that require that nonpublicly available information, which is not foreign intelligence information, as defined in section 1801(e)(1) of this title, shall not be disseminated in a manner that identifies any United States person, without such person's consent, unless such person's identity is necessary to understand such foreign intelligence information or assess its importance;

(C) notwithstanding subparagraphs (A) and (B), procedures that allow for the retention and dissemination of information that is evidence of a crime which has been, is being, or is about to be committed and that is to be retained or disseminated for law enforcement purposes; and

(D) notwithstanding subparagraphs (A), (B), and (C), with respect to any physical search approved pursuant to section 1822(a) of this title, procedures that require that no information, material, or property of a United States person shall be disclosed, disseminated, or used for any purpose or retained for longer than 72 hours unless a court order under section 1824 of this title is obtained or unless the Attorney General determines that the information indicates a threat of death or serious bodily harm to any person.

(5) "Physical search" means any physical intrusion within the United States into premises or property (including examination of the interior of property by technical means) that is intended to result in a seizure, reproduction, inspection, or alteration of information, material, or property, under circumstances in which a person has a reasonable expectation of privacy and a warrant would be required for law enforcement purposes, but does not include (A) "electronic surveillance", as defined in section 1801(f) of this title, or (B) the acquisition by the United States Government of foreign intelligence information from international or foreign communications, or foreign intelligence activities conducted in accordance with otherwise applicable Federal law involving a foreign electronic communications system, utilizing a means other than electronic surveillance as defined in section 1801(f) of this title.

§ 1822. Authorization of physical searches for foreign intelligence purposes

(a) Presidential authorization

(1) Notwithstanding any other provision of law, the President, acting through the Attorney General, may authorize physical searches without a court order under this subchapter to acquire foreign intelligence information for periods of up to one year if—

(A) the Attorney General certifies in writing under oath that—

(i) the physical search is solely directed at premises, information, material, or property used exclusively by, or under the open and exclusive control of, a foreign power or powers (as defined in section 1801(a)(1), (2), or (3) of this title);

(ii) there is no substantial likelihood that the physical search will involve the premises, information, material, or property of a United States person; and

(iii) the proposed minimization procedures with respect to such physical search meet the definition of minimization procedures under paragraphs (1) through (4) of section 1821(4) of this title; and

. . .

(2) A physical search authorized by this subsection may be conducted only in accordance with the certification and minimization procedures adopted by the Attorney General. The Attorney General shall assess compliance with such procedures and shall report such assessments to the Permanent Select Committee on Intelligence of the House of Representatives and the Select Committee on Intelligence of the Senate under the provisions of section 1826 of this title.

. . .

(4)(A)   With respect to physical searches authorized by this subsection, the Attorney General may direct a specified landlord, custodian, or other specified person to—

> **(i)**   furnish all information, facilities, or assistance necessary to accomplish the physical search in such a manner as will protect its secrecy and produce a minimum of interference with the services that such landlord, custodian, or other person is providing the target of the physical search; and

> **(ii)** maintain under security procedures approved by the Attorney General and the Director of National Intelligence any records concerning the search or the aid furnished that such person wishes to retain.

> **(B)** The Government shall compensate, at the prevailing rate, such landlord, custodian, or other person for furnishing such aid.

(b)   Application for order; authorization

Applications for a court order under this subchapter are authorized if the President has, by written authorization, empowered the Attorney General to approve applications to the Foreign Intelligence Surveillance Court. Notwithstanding any other provision of law, a judge of the court to whom application is made may grant an order in accordance with section 1824 of this title approving a physical search in the United States of the premises, property, information, or material of a foreign power or an agent of a foreign power for the purpose of collecting foreign intelligence information.

. . .

(d)   Court of review; record; transmittal to Supreme Court

The court of review established under section 1803(b) of this title shall have jurisdiction to review the denial of any application made under this subchapter.

. . .

§ 1823. Application for order

(a) Submission by Federal officer; approval of Attorney General; contents

Each application for an order approving a physical search under this subchapter shall be made by a Federal officer in writing upon oath or affirmation to a judge of the Foreign Intelligence Surveillance Court. Each application shall require the approval of the Attorney General based upon the Attorney General's finding that it satisfies the criteria and requirements for such application as set forth in this subchapter. Each application shall include—

(1) the identity of the Federal officer making the application;

(2) the identity, if known, or a description of the target of the search, and a description of the premises or property to be searched and of the information, material, or property to be seized, reproduced, or altered;

(3) a statement of the facts and circumstances relied upon by the applicant to justify the applicant's belief that—

(A) the target of the physical search is a foreign power or an agent of a foreign power;

(B) the premises or property to be searched contains foreign intelligence information; and

(C) the premises or property to be searched is or is about to be owned, used, possessed by, or is in transit to or from a foreign power or an agent of a foreign power;

(4) a statement of the proposed minimization procedures;

(5) a statement of the nature of the foreign intelligence sought and the manner in which the physical search is to be conducted;

(6) a certification or certifications by the Assistant to the President for National Security Affairs, [ed. other specified officials] . . .

(A) that the certifying official deems the information sought to be foreign intelligence information;

(B) that a significant purpose of the search is to obtain foreign intelligence information;

(C) that such information cannot reasonably be obtained by normal investigative techniques;

(D) that designates the type of foreign intelligence information being sought according to the categories described in section 1801(e) of this title; and

. . .

(7) where the physical search involves a search of the residence of a United States person, the Attorney General shall state what investigative techniques have previously been utilized to obtain the foreign intelligence information concerned and the degree to which these techniques resulted in acquiring such information; and

(8) a statement of the facts concerning all previous applications that have been made to any judge under this subchapter involving any of the persons, premises, or property specified in the application, and the action taken on each previous application.

. . .

(d) Personal review by Attorney General

(1)(A)   Upon written request of the Director of the Federal Bureau of Investigation, the Secretary of Defense, the Secretary of State, the Director of National Intelligence, or the Director of the Central Intelligence Agency, the Attorney General shall personally review under subsection (a) of this section an application under that subsection for a target described in section 1801(b)(2) of this title.

. . .

§ 1824. Issuance of order

. . .

(b) Determination of probable cause

In determining whether or not probable cause exists for purposes of an order under subsection (a)(2) of this section, a judge may consider past activities of the target, as well as facts and circumstances relating to current or future activities of the target.

(c) Specifications and directions of orders

An order approving a physical search under this section shall—

(1) specify—

(A) the identity, if known, or a description of the target of the physical search;

(B) the nature and location of each of the premises or property to be searched;

(C) the type of information, material, or property to be seized, altered, or reproduced;

(D) a statement of the manner in which the physical search is to be conducted and, whenever more than one physical search is authorized under the order, the authorized scope of each search and what minimization procedures shall apply to the information acquired by each search; and

(E) the period of time during which physical searches are approved; and

(2) direct—

(A) that the minimization procedures be followed;

. . .;

and

(E) that the Federal officer conducting the physical search promptly report to the court the circumstances and results of the physical search.

(d)   Duration of order; extensions; assessment of compliance

(1) An order issued under this section may approve a physical search for the period necessary to achieve its purpose, or for 90 days, whichever is less, except that (A) an order under this section shall approve a physical search targeted against a foreign power, as defined in paragraph (1), (2), or (3) of section 1801(a) of this title, for the period specified in the application or for one year, whichever is less, and (B) an order under this section for a physical search targeted against an agent of a foreign power who is not a United States person may be for the period specified in the application or for 120 days, whichever is less.

(2)   Extensions of an order issued under this subchapter may be granted on the same basis as the original order upon an application for an extension and new findings made in the same manner as required for the original order, except that an extension of an order under this chapter for a physical search targeted against a foreign power, as defined in paragraph (5), (6), or (7) of section 1801(a) of this title, or against a foreign power, as defined in section 1801(a)(4) of this title, that is not a United States person, or against an agent of a foreign power who is not a United States person, may be for a period not to exceed one year if the judge finds probable cause to believe that no property of any individual United States person will be acquired during the period.

(3) At or before the end of the period of time for which a physical search is approved by an order or an extension, or at any time after a physical search is carried out, the judge may assess compliance with the minimization procedures by reviewing the circumstances under which information concerning United States persons was acquired, retained, or disseminated.

(e)(1) Notwithstanding any other provision of this subchapter, the Attorney General may authorize the emergency employment of a physical search if the Attorney General—

(A) reasonably determines that an emergency situation exists with respect to the employment of a physical search to obtain foreign intelligence information before an order authorizing such physical search can with due diligence be obtained;

(B) reasonably determines that the factual basis for issuance of an order under this subchapter to approve such physical search exists;

(C) informs, either personally or through a designee, a judge of the Foreign Intelligence Surveillance Court at the time of such authorization that the decision has been made to employ an emergency physical search; and

(D) makes an application in accordance with this subchapter to a judge of the Foreign Intelligence Surveillance Court as soon as practicable, but not more than 7 days after the Attorney General authorizes such physical search.

(2) If the Attorney General authorizes the emergency employment of a physical search under paragraph (1), the Attorney General shall require that the minimization procedures required by this subchapter for the issuance of a judicial order be followed.

(3) In the absence of a judicial order approving such physical search, the physical search shall terminate when the information sought is obtained, when the application for the order is denied, or after the expiration of 7 days from the time of authorization by the Attorney General, whichever is earliest.

(4) A denial of the application made under this subsection may be reviewed as provided in section 1803 of this title.

(5) In the event that such application for approval is denied, or in any other case where the physical search is terminated and no order is issued approving the physical search, no information obtained or evidence derived from such physical search shall be

received in evidence or otherwise disclosed in any trial, hearing, or other proceeding in or before any court, grand jury, department, office, agency, regulatory body, legislative committee, or other authority of the United States, a State, or political subdivision thereof, and no information concerning any United States person acquired from such physical search shall subsequently be used or disclosed in any other manner by Federal officers or employees without the consent of such person, except with the approval of the Attorney General if the information indicates a threat of death or serious bodily harm to any person.

. . .

§ 1825. Use of information

. . .

(b) Notice of search and identification of property seized, altered, or reproduced

Where a physical search authorized and conducted pursuant to section 1824 of this title involves the residence of a United States person, and, at any time after the search the Attorney General determines there is no national security interest in continuing to maintain the secrecy of the search, the Attorney General shall provide notice to the United States person whose residence was searched of the fact of the search conducted pursuant to this chapter and shall identify any property of such person seized, altered, or reproduced during such search.

. . .

(f) Motion to suppress

(1) Any person against whom evidence obtained or derived from a physical search to which he is an aggrieved person is to be, or has been, introduced or otherwise used or disclosed in any trial, hearing, or other proceeding in or before any court, department, officer, agency, regulatory body, or other authority of the United States, a State, or a political subdivision thereof, may move to suppress the evidence obtained or derived from such search on the grounds that—

(A) the information was unlawfully acquired; or

(B) the physical search was not made in conformity with an order of authorization or approval.

(2) Such a motion shall be made before the trial, hearing, or other proceeding unless there was no opportunity to make such a motion or the person was not aware of the grounds of the motion.

(g)   In camera and ex parte review by district court

. . .

(j)   Notification of emergency execution of physical search; contents; postponement, suspension, or elimination

(1) If an emergency execution of a physical search is authorized under section 1824(d) of this title and a subsequent order approving the search is not obtained, the judge shall cause to be served on any United States person named in the application and on such other United States persons subject to the search as the judge may determine in his discretion it is in the interests of justice to serve, notice of—

(A) the fact of the application;

(B) the period of the search; and

(C) the fact that during the period information was or was not obtained.

(2) On an ex parte showing of good cause to the judge, the serving of the notice required by this subsection may be postponed or suspended for a period not to exceed 90 days. Thereafter, on a further ex parte showing of good cause, the court shall forego ordering the serving of the notice required under this subsection.

. . .

3.   FEDERAL RULES OF CRIMINAL PROCEDURE

Rule 41.   Search and Seizure

(a)   Scope and Definitions.

. . .

(2)   Definitions. The following definitions apply under this rule:

(A)   "Property" includes documents, books, papers, any other tangible objects, and information.

(B)   "Daytime" means the hours between 6:00 a.m. and 10:00 p.m. according to local time.

(C)   "Federal law enforcement officer" means a government agent (other than an attorney for the government) who is engaged in enforcing the criminal laws and is within any category of officers authorized by the Attorney General to request a search warrant.

(D)   "Domestic terrorism" and "international terrorism" have the meanings set out in 18 U.S.C. § 2331.

. . .

(b) Authority to Issue a Warrant. At the request of a federal law enforcement officer or an attorney for the government:

(1) a magistrate judge with authority in the district—or if none is reasonably available, a judge of a state court of record in the district—has authority to issue a warrant to search for and seize a person or property located within the district;

. . .

(3) a magistrate judge—in an investigation of domestic terrorism or international terrorism—with authority in any district in which activities related to the terrorism may have occurred has authority to issue a warrant for a person or property within or outside that district;

. . .

(c) Persons or Property Subject to Search or Seizure. A warrant may be issued for any of the following:

(1) evidence of a crime;

(2) contraband, fruits of crime, or other items illegally possessed;

(3) property designed for use, intended for use, or used in committing a crime; or

(4) a person to be arrested or a person who is unlawfully restrained.

(d) Obtaining a Warrant.

(1) In General. After receiving an affidavit or other information, a magistrate judge—or if authorized by Rule 41(b), a judge of a state court of record—must issue the warrant if there is probable cause to search for and seize a person or property or to install and use a tracking device.

. . .

(e) Issuing the Warrant.

(1) In General. The magistrate judge or a judge of a state court of record must issue the warrant to an officer authorized to execute it.

(2) Contents of the Warrant.

(A) Warrant to Search for and Seize a Person or Property. . . . . .the warrant must identify the person or property to be searched, identify any person or property to be seized, and designate the magistrate judge to whom it must be returned. The warrant must command the officer to:

(i) execute the warrant within a specified time no longer than 14 days;

(ii) execute the warrant during the daytime, unless the judge for good cause expressly authorizes execution at another time; and

(iii) return the warrant to the magistrate judge designated in the warrant.

. . .

(f) Executing and Returning the Warrant.

(1) Warrant to Search for and Seize a Person or Property.

(A) Noting the Time. The officer executing the warrant must enter on it the exact date and time it was executed.

(B) Inventory. An officer present during the execution of the warrant must prepare and verify an inventory of any property seized. The officer must do so in the presence of another officer and the person from whom, or from whose premises, the property was taken. If either one is not present, the officer must prepare and verify the inventory in the presence of at least one other credible person. . . .

(C) Receipt. The officer executing the warrant must give a copy of the warrant and a receipt for the property taken to the person from whom, or from whose premises, the property was taken or leave a copy of the warrant and receipt at the place where the officer took the property.

(D) Return. The officer executing the warrant must promptly return it—together with a copy of the inventory—to the magistrate judge designated on the warrant. The judge must, on request, give a copy of the inventory to the person from whom, or from whose premises, the property was taken and to the applicant for the warrant.

. . .

(3) Delayed Notice. Upon the government's request, a magistrate judge—or if authorized by Rule 41(b), a judge of a state court of record—may delay any notice required by this rule if the delay is authorized by statute.

(g) Motion to Return Property. A person aggrieved by an unlawful search and seizure of property or by the deprivation of property may move for the property's return. The motion must be filed in the district where the property was seized. The court must receive evidence on any factual issue necessary to decide the motion. If it grants the motion, the court must return the property to the movant, but may impose reasonable conditions to protect access to the property and its use in later proceedings.

(h) Motion to Suppress. A defendant may move to suppress evidence in the court where the trial will occur, as Rule 12 provides.

QUESTIONS AND NOTES

1.　FISA was amended in 1994 to authorize physical searches to obtain foreign intelligence under the same general criteria that applied to electronic surveillance. See United States v. Marzook, 435 F.Supp.2d 778 (N.D.Ill.2006):

> As originally drafted, FISA did not provide a protocol for obtaining permission to conduct physical searches to obtain foreign intelligence. In 1994, however, Congress amended FISA to encompass physical searches conducted for foreign intelligence purposes. Pub.L. 103–359 §§ 301–09 (1994). In essence, the government bears the same burden as that for obtaining electronic surveillance. A federal officer seeking approval of a physical search under FISA must submit an application to a FISA court, like the certification needed for electronic surveillance, . . .

2.　How does the probable cause required for a physical search under §§ 1823–24 compare with the probable cause for a search warrant for ordinary crimes?

3.　In what ways other than the probable cause element do the requirements or applicable rules for foreign intelligence physical searches differ from ordinary crime search warrants? What would you describe as the most salient difference?

4.　Under what circumstances, must the fact of a foreign intelligence search and what was obtained be disclosed to the person whose premises were searched? Is there a specified time limit within which such disclosure must be made? Compare the same issues under Rule 41, F.R.Cr.P.

5.　Is there an oddity and concern with respect to applying the same type of secrecy requirements to physical searches that are applicable to electronic surveillance "searches"? Consider, for example, the manner in which a secret foreign intelligence physical search must be conducted, leaving no trace of the fact of the search? How secret can the search be if objects are seized in the course of the search? On the other hand, suppose the purpose of the search is to gain access to the target's computer and copy information from its hard drive.

6.　Are the search warrant provisions under §§ 1823–24 applicable outside the United States? Is there a geographic limitation provision in the statute? Which provision?

7.   Suppose a physical search of the premises of a United States person is conducted outside of the United States. Do the physical search provisions of the FISA have any application? If not, what rules apply? See section C, infra.

8.   What is the bearing of the fact that the premises or privacy of a United States person would be violated by the intended physical search? Does this mean that a warrant cannot be obtained under the provisions of the FISA?

9.   Under what circumstances can a foreign intelligence search be conducted without a warrant? What conditions and requirements are applicable to such searches?

C. U.S. AGENTS ACTING ABROAD—FOURTH AMENDMENT AND RELATED ISSUES

1. INTRODUCTION

The TSP electronic surveillance controversy that was the subject of discussion in Chapter 5, which led to the enactment of the provisions of the FISA Amendments Act of 2008, involved electronic surveillance of communications between persons located outside and inside of the United States. In particular cases, it may have also involved United States persons. In Chapter 5, in the connection with such electronic surveillance, much of the focus of the materials is on the application of the relevant statutes. In this section, we primarily study whether fourth amendment protections apply to physical searches (and electronic surveillance) that take place entirely outside of the United States, but we also address other related issues. Some of the discussion harks back to, and is relevant to issues touched upon in Chapter 5.

The basic questions are, how far do U.S. constitutional protections extend? Should the extension of the reach of U.S. criminal laws carry with it application of rights protected by the U.S. Constitution? Are U.S. agents limited by the Constitution in the actions they can engage in while abroad to the same extent as in the territorial United States? Or are our agents freer to engage in actions abroad that would not be lawful if done here? Further, what kinds of factors bear on what our agents can or cannot lawfully (i.e. lawful under U.S. law) do? Does it matter whether they are working in cooperation with official personnel of the host country and/or complying with the laws of the host country? Are there limits imposed by international law that bear on these issues?

Accordingly, in this section, we address questions growing out of various kinds of actions by U.S. agents, usually FBI or CIA, acting in foreign lands. The kinds of actions by U.S. agents that are examined in this section include investigation and information-gathering of various kinds— e.g., electronic surveillance, and search and arrest. See generally, Ronald J. Sievert, War on Terrorism or Global Law Enforcement Operation?, 78

Notre Dame L.Rev. 307 (2003). Related topics are addressed in Chapter 7, infra, namely the interrogation of terrorism suspects abroad and rendition, that is, transfer of persons seized abroad to another country or to a prison facility in U.S. jurisdiction.

2. SEARCHES ABROAD—PREMISES OF A NON-U.S. PERSON; U.S. PERSON SEARCH BY NON-U.S. AGENTS

The Supreme Court addressed some of the issues raised by searches conducted abroad by U.S. agents in the following case.

UNITED STATES V. VERDUGO-URQUIDEZ
494 U.S. 259 (1990)

[CHIEF JUSTICE REHNQUIST delivered the opinion of the Court, in which WHITE, O'CONNOR, SCALIA, and KENNEDY, JJ., joined. JUSTICE KENNEDY filed a concurring opinion; JUSTICE STEVENS filed an opinion concurring in the judgment; JUSTICE BRENNAN filed a dissenting opinion, in which JUSTICE MARSHALL joined; JUSTICE BLACKMUN filed a dissenting opinion.]

CHIEF JUSTICE REHNQUIST delivered the Opinion of the Court:

The question presented by this case is whether the Fourth Amendment applies to the search and seizure by United States agents of property that is owned by a nonresident alien and located in a foreign country. We hold that it does not.

Respondent Rene Martin Verdugo-Urquidez is a citizen and resident of Mexico. He is believed by the United States Drug Enforcement Agency (DEA) to be one of the leaders of a large and violent organization in Mexico that smuggles narcotics into the United States. Based on a complaint charging respondent with various narcotics-related offenses, the Government obtained a warrant for his arrest on August 3, 1985. In January 1986, Mexican police officers, after discussions with United States marshals, apprehended Verdugo-Urquidez in Mexico and transported him to the United States Border Patrol station in Calexico, California. There, United States marshals arrested respondent and eventually moved him to a correctional center in San Diego, California, where he remains incarcerated pending trial.

Following respondent's arrest, Terry Bowen, a DEA agent assigned to the Calexico DEA office, decided to arrange for searches of Verdugo-Urquidez's Mexican residences located in Mexicali and San Felipe. Bowen believed that the searches would reveal evidence related to respondent's alleged narcotics trafficking activities and his involvement in the kidnaping and torture-murder of DEA Special Agent Enrique Camarena Salazar (for which respondent subsequently has been convicted in a separate prosecution. See United States v. Verdugo-Urquidez (C.D. Cal.,

Nov. 22, 1988)). Bowen telephoned Walter White, the Assistant Special Agent in charge of the DEA office in Mexico City, and asked him to seek authorization for the search from the Director General of the Mexican Federal Judicial Police (MFJP). After several attempts to reach high ranking Mexican officials, White eventually contacted the Director General, who authorized the searches and promised the cooperation of Mexican authorities. Thereafter, DEA agents working in concert with officers of the MFJP searched respondent's properties in Mexicali and San Felipe and seized certain documents. In particular, the search of the Mexicali residence uncovered a tally sheet, which the Government believes reflects the quantities of marijuana smuggled by Verdugo-Urquidez into the United States.

. . .

Before analyzing the scope of the Fourth Amendment, we think it significant to note that it operates in a different manner than the Fifth Amendment, which is not at issue in this case. The privilege against self-incrimination guaranteed by the Fifth Amendment is a fundamental trial right of criminal defendants. Although conduct by law enforcement officials prior to trial may ultimately impair that right, a constitutional violation occurs only at trial. The Fourth Amendment functions differently. It prohibits "unreasonable searches and seizures" whether or not the evidence is sought to be used in a criminal trial, and a violation of the Amendment is "fully accomplished" at the time of an unreasonable governmental intrusion. For purposes of this case, therefore, if there were a constitutional violation, it occurred solely in Mexico. Whether evidence obtained from respondent's Mexican residences should be excluded at trial in the United States is a remedial question separate from the existence vel non of the constitutional violation.

The Fourth Amendment provides:

> "The right of the people to be secure in their persons, houses, papers, and effects, against unreasonable searches and seizures, shall not be violated. . . ."

That text, by contrast with the Fifth and Sixth Amendments, extends its reach only to "the people." Contrary to the suggestion of amici curiae that the Framers used this phrase "simply to avoid [an] awkward rhetorical redundancy," "the people" seems to have been a term of art employed in select parts of the Constitution. The Preamble declares that the Constitution is ordained and established by "the People of the United States." The Second Amendment protects "the right of the people to keep and bear Arms," and the Ninth and Tenth Amendments provide that certain rights and powers are retained by and reserved to "the people." See also U.S. Const., Amdt. 1 ("Congress shall make no law . . . abridging . . . the right of the people peaceably to assemble") (emphasis added); Art. I,

§ 2, cl. 1 ("The House of Representatives shall be composed of Members chosen every second Year by the People of the several States") (emphasis added). While this textual exegesis is by no means conclusive, it suggests that "the people" protected by the Fourth Amendment, and by the First and Second Amendments, and to whom rights and powers are reserved in the Ninth and Tenth Amendments, refers to a class of persons who are part of a national community or who have otherwise developed sufficient connection with this country to be considered part of that community. . . . The language of these Amendments contrasts with the words "person" and "accused" used in the Fifth and Sixth Amendments regulating procedure in criminal cases.

. . .

The available historical data show . . . that the purpose of the Fourth Amendment was to protect the people of the United States against arbitrary action by their own Government; it was never suggested that the provision was intended to restrain the actions of the Federal Government against aliens outside of the United States territory.

. . .

Justice Stevens' concurrence in the judgment takes the view that even though the search took place in Mexico, it is nonetheless governed by the requirements of the Fourth Amendment because respondent was "lawfully present in the United States . . . even though he was brought and held here against his will." But this sort of presence—lawful but involuntary—is not of the sort to indicate any substantial connection with our country. The extent to which respondent might claim the protection of the Fourth Amendment if the duration of his stay in the United States were to be prolonged—by a prison sentence, for example—we need not decide. When the search of his house in Mexico took place, he had been present in the United States for only a matter of days. We do not think the applicability of the Fourth Amendment to the search of premises in Mexico should turn on the fortuitous circumstance of whether the custodian of its nonresident alien owner had or had not transported him to the United States at the time the search was made.

. . .

Not only are history and case law against respondent, but as pointed out in Johnson v. Eisentrager, 339 U.S. 763 (1950), the result of accepting his claim would have significant and deleterious consequences for the United States in conducting activities beyond its boundaries. The rule adopted by the Court of Appeals would apply not only to law enforcement operations abroad, but also to other foreign policy operations which might result in "searches or seizures." The United States frequently employs armed forces outside this country—over 200 times in our history—for the protection of American citizens or national security. Congressional

Research Service, Instances of Use of United States Armed Forces Abroad, 1798–1989 (E. Collier ed. 1989). Application of the Fourth Amendment to those circumstances could significantly disrupt the ability of the political branches to respond to foreign situations involving our national interest. Were respondent to prevail, aliens with no attachment to this country might well bring actions for damages to remedy claimed violations of the Fourth Amendment in foreign countries or in international waters. See Bivens v. Six Unknown Federal Narcotics Agents, 403 U.S. 388 (1971); cf. Tennessee v. Garner, 471 U.S. 1 (1985); Graham v. Connor, 490 U.S. 386 (1989). Perhaps a Bivens action might be unavailable in some or all of these situations due to " 'special factors counselling hesitation,' " but the Government would still be faced with case-by-case adjudications concerning the availability of such an action. And even were Bivens deemed wholly inapplicable in cases of foreign activity, that would not obviate the problems attending the application of the Fourth Amendment abroad to aliens. The Members of the Executive and Legislative Branches are sworn to uphold the Constitution, and they presumably desire to follow its commands. But the Court of Appeals' global view of its applicability would plunge them into a sea of uncertainty as to what might be reasonable in the way of searches and seizures conducted abroad. Indeed, the Court of Appeals held that absent exigent circumstances, United States agents could not effect a "search or seizure" for law enforcement purposes in a foreign country without first obtaining a warrant—which would be a dead letter outside the United States—from a magistrate in this country. Even if no warrant were required, American agents would have to articulate specific facts giving them probable cause to undertake a search or seizure if they wished to comply with the Fourth Amendment as conceived by the Court of Appeals.

We think that the text of the Fourth Amendment, its history, and our cases discussing the application of the Constitution to aliens and extraterritorially require rejection of respondent's claim. At the time of the search, he was a citizen and resident of Mexico with no voluntary attachment to the United States, and the place searched was located in Mexico. Under these circumstances, the Fourth Amendment has no application.

For better or for worse, we live in a world of nation-states in which our Government must be able to "function effectively in the company of sovereign nations." Some who violate our laws may live outside our borders under a regime quite different from that which obtains in this country. Situations threatening to important American interests may arise halfway around the globe, situations which in the view of the political branches of our Government require an American response with armed force. If there are to be restrictions on searches and seizures which occur incident to such

American action, they must be imposed by the political branches through diplomatic understanding, treaty, or legislation.

The judgment of the Court of Appeals is accordingly

Reversed.

JUSTICE KENNEDY, concurring.

I agree that no violation of the Fourth Amendment has occurred and that we must reverse the judgment of the Court of Appeals. Although some explanation of my views is appropriate given the difficulties of this case, I do not believe they depart in fundamental respects from the opinion of the Court, which I join.

. . .

The question before us then becomes what constitutional standards apply when the Government acts, in reference to an alien, within its sphere of foreign operations. . . .

The conditions and considerations of this case would make adherence to the Fourth Amendment's warrant requirement impracticable and anomalous. . . . [T]he Constitution does not require United States agents to obtain a warrant when searching the foreign home of a nonresident alien. If the search had occurred in a residence within the United States, I have little doubt that the full protections of the Fourth Amendment would apply. But that is not this case. The absence of local judges or magistrates available to issue warrants, the differing and perhaps unascertainable conceptions of reasonableness and privacy that prevail abroad, and the need to cooperate with foreign officials all indicate that the Fourth Amendment's warrant requirement should not apply in Mexico as it does in this country. For this reason, in addition to the other persuasive justifications stated by the Court, I agree that no violation of the Fourth Amendment has occurred in the case before us. The rights of a citizen, as to whom the United States has continuing obligations, are not presented by this case.

I do not mean to imply, and the Court has not decided, that persons in the position of the respondent have no constitutional protection. The United States is prosecuting a foreign national in a court established under Article III, and all of the trial proceedings are governed by the Constitution. All would agree, for instance, that the dictates of the Due Process Clause of the Fifth Amendment protect the defendant. . . . Nothing approaching a violation of due process has occurred in this case.

JUSTICE STEVENS, concurring in the judgment.

. . . I do agree, however, with the Government's submission that the search conducted by the United States agents with the approval and cooperation of the Mexican authorities was not "unreasonable" as that term is used in the first Clause of the Amendment. I do not believe the Warrant Clause has any application to searches of noncitizens' homes in foreign jurisdictions because American magistrates have no power to authorize such searches. I therefore concur in the Court's judgment.

[JUSTICES BRENNAN, BLACKMUN and MARSHALL dissented.]

QUESTIONS AND NOTES

1.   U.S. agents may be involved in electronic surveillance or a physical search outside of the United States in any of a number of different factual contexts. The U.S. agents may be active participants, either acting alone or in collaboration with local police agents, or the action may be conducted by the foreign police acting on their own.

The objects of the surveillance or search may be foreign citizens or nationals or U.S. citizens or permanent residents of the United States, or persons with some other degree of connection to the U.S. The surveillance or search may comply with the law of the foreign jurisdiction or not.

The main question that has been raised, as in the principal case, is the extent to which U.S. constitutional limitations may be applicable. The constitutional limits on police conduct embodied in the Fourth Amendment have not been held to apply to the conduct of foreign police officials acting abroad; such officials are not bound by U.S. constitutional standards. The courts of appeal that have considered the question have held that the Fourth Amendment applies to searches and unconsented-to electronic surveillances conducted abroad by U.S. government agents against U.S. citizens. See Justice Brennan dissenting in Verdugo-Urquidez (omitted in the portion of the case reproduced above).

Suppose that an electronic surveillance or a search that would be illegal under U.S. law is conducted by a foreign police official on foreign soil against a U.S. citizen and then the evidence thus obtained is turned over to FBI agents for use in a U.S. prosecution. What would you expect to be the result?

The cases have held that in this situation the U.S. agents can use the evidence and introduce it at the defendant's U.S. trial. This situation is called the "international silver platter doctrine"—the evidence is received by the U.S. agents "on a silver platter." A similar doctrine was applied regarding parallel interactions between state and federal police officials in the United States prior to the decision in Mapp v. Ohio, 367 U.S. 643 (1961).

However, if the participation of U.S. agents in the activity is so substantial as to convert the activity into a joint venture with the foreign officials, constitutional standards are applied and the evidence will be excluded at trial if those standards are violated.

A number of U.S. courts of appeal have considered joint venture issues. See, e.g., United States v. Rosenthal, 793 F.2d 1214 (11th Cir. 1986) and see United States v. Barona, 56 F.3d 1087 (9th Cir. 1995):

It is not clear, therefore, that Villabona or the other non-citizen defendants in this case are entitled to receive any Fourth Amendment protection whatsoever. Any entitlement that they may have to invoke the Fourth Amendment in the context of an extraterritorial search is by no means clear. We could hold, therefore, that Barona, Martinez, and Villabona have failed to demonstrate that, at the time of the extraterritorial search, they were "People of the United States" entitled to receive the "full panoply of rights guaranteed by our Constitution." We choose, however, not to reach the question because even if they were entitled to invoke the Fourth Amendment, their effort would be unsuccessful.

Bennett, Harris, and McCarver are all United States citizens, and thus can invoke the protection of the Fourth Amendment generally. Our cases establishing the exception as to when the Fourth Amendment can be invoked in an extraterritorial search control our analysis.

First, the district court did not clearly err in finding that the four Danish wiretaps at issue were "joint ventures." In [United States v.] Peterson, we gave weight to the fact that the DEA "was involved daily in translating and decoding intercepted transmissions as well as advising the [foreign] authorities of their relevance." 812 F.2d at 490. Similarly here, the "American Embassy" was interested in the movement of Villabona and Bennett, American agents requested the wiretaps, information obtained was immediately forwarded to them, and throughout the surveillance a Spanish to English interpreter was provided by the United States.

Because there was a joint venture, we must decide whether the search was reasonable. In determining whether the search was reasonable, we must first consult the law of the relevant foreign countries.

. . .

. . . After carefully reviewing the record, we are satisfied that Danish law was followed.

. . .

A fifth wiretap occurred in Milan, Italy. On December 9, 1987, Villabona and Bennett arrived in Milan from Copenhagen. The day before, the Danish police notified a United States special agent of this planned trip. He, in turn, telephoned a United States special agent in Milan and requested physical surveillance. The latter agent contacted Major Rabiti of the Guardia Di Finanza and requested a watch on Villabona and Bennett. Rabiti obtained authorization to wiretap their hotel room.

The district court found that this wiretap was not the product of a joint venture between United States and Italian authorities. That a United States agent told Rabiti about Villabona and Bennett did not create a "joint venture" between the United States and Italy regarding this wiretap. . . . We hold that the district court did not clearly err when it found no joint investigation surrounding the Milan wiretap, and, therefore, that Fourth Amendment principles do not apply. Because the wiretap was conducted by foreign officials without substantial United States involvement, the results are admissible.

In summary, the finding that the Milan wiretap was not a joint venture is not clearly erroneous. The finding that the Danish wiretaps were conducted pursuant to a joint venture is also not clearly erroneous, but Danish law was complied with for each Danish wiretap. None of the evidence from the wiretaps is therefore subject to exclusion under the Fourth Amendment.

2.   How much contact with the U.S. must an alien have in order to be afforded Fourth Amendment protection against searches or electronic surveillance on foreign soil by U.S agents? Do the opinions in the principal case provide an answer to this question?

3.   Because the result in these cases often turns on the fact that the defendant did not have sufficient connections with the United States, or the degree of participation of the U.S. agents was insufficient to make them joint venturers with the foreign police, the courts rarely have needed to address the question of what the applicable substantive Fourth Amendment standards are in such cases. Dissenting in the principal case, Justice Brennan argued that the same Fourth Amendment standards applicable in a domestic context should be applied in the foreign context, but the issue was not addressed by the full Court. In United States v. Peterson, 812 F.2d 486 (9th Cir. 1987), Judge Kennedy (now Justice Kennedy) stated that the law of the foreign country must be consulted as part of the determination of whether the search or surveillance was reasonable. See also United States v. Barona, supra, on the same issue.

4.   Problems

a.   Suppose that the U.S. agents are held to have been in a joint venture with the foreign police in conducting a search against a U.S. citizen on foreign soil, and therefore Fourth Amendment standards are applicable. Suppose, too, that Judge Kennedy's opinion in the Peterson case, supra, is deemed part of the controlling authority. What result if the law of the foreign jurisdiction was not followed, but the U.S. agents acting in good faith relied on assurances by their foreign counterparts that the foreign law was being followed?

b.   Suppose that there were not such assurances provided, but the suspect was suspected of being a terrorist within the meaning of FISA and the U.S. agents had enough information to have obtained a FISA warrant, but being abroad, it was not feasible to do so? See 50 U.S.C. § 1805(f).

5.   In connection with the issues discussed above, one should also take into account the fact that the United States has mutual legal assistance treaties (MLAT's) with other countries. These treaties have helped to facilitate the U.S.'s ability to obtain evidence from abroad. The MLAT's regulate such matters as searches and electronic surveillances, obtaining documents, freezing assets and maintaining evidence. The MLAT's are a fairly new development having been first entered into in the 1970's. The United States has now entered into more than 40 such bilateral agreements.

For example, the U.S. entered into a MLAT with Mexico in 1991. The treaty requires both countries to "tak[e] all appropriate measures that they have legal authority to take" to provide mutual assistance to the other in criminal matters, including executing requests for searches and seizures. It is also provided that nothing in the Treaty "empowers one party's authorities to undertake, in the territorial jurisdiction of the other, the exercise and performance of the functions or authority exclusively entrusted to the authorities of that other party by its national laws or regulations." See Eric Bentley, Jr., Toward an International Fourth Amendment: Rethinking Searches and Seizures Abroad after Verdugo-Urquidez, 27 Vand. J. Transnat'l L. 329 (1994). See also Ethan A. Nadelmann, The Role of the United States in the International Enforcement of Criminal Law, 31 Harv. Int'l L. J. 37, 62–63 (1990). DEA guidelines provide that: "DEA representatives will not engage or participate in unilateral investigative operations or other activities outside the scope of the formal or informal agreement developed between the United States and the host government unless these activities have express and explicit approval of a responsible host government official." Quoted in the Brief for the United States, United States v. Verdugo-Urquidez at 26, n. 25.

3.   SEARCH ABROAD OF THE PREMISES OF A U.S. PERSON BY U.S. AGENTS; FOREIGN INTELLIGENCE PURPOSE

IN RE TERRORIST BOMBINGS OF U.S. EMBASSIES IN EAST AFRICA—UNITED STATES V. ODEH
552 F.3d 177 (2d Cir. 2008), cert denied 558 U.S. 1137 (2010)

Before: FEINBERG, NEWMAN, and CABRANES, CIRCUIT JUDGES.

JOSÉ A. CABRANES, CIRCUIT JUDGE:

Defendant-appellant Wadih El-Hage, a citizen of the United States, challenges his conviction in the United States District Court for the Southern District of New York (LEONARD B. SAND, Judge) on numerous charges arising from his involvement in the August 7, 1998 bombings of the American Embassies in Nairobi, Kenya and Dar es Salaam, Tanzania (the "August 7 bombings"). In this opinion we consider El-Hage's challenge to the District Court's denial of his motion to suppress evidence obtained by the government from an August 1997 search of his residence in Nairobi,

Kenya and electronic surveillance of telephone lines-land-based and cellular-conducted in Kenya between August 1996 and August 1997. . . .

El-Hage contends that the District Court erred by (1) recognizing a foreign intelligence exception to the Fourth Amendment's warrant requirement, (2) concluding that the search of El-Hage's home and surveillance of his telephone lines qualified for inclusion in that exception, and (3) resolving El-Hage's motion on the basis of an ex parte review of classified materials, without affording El-Hage's counsel access to those materials or holding a suppression hearing. Because we hold that the Fourth Amendment's requirement of reasonableness-and not the Warrant Clause-governs extraterritorial searches of U.S. citizens and that the searches challenged on this appeal were reasonable, we find no error in the District Court's denial of El-Hage's suppression motion. In addition, the District Court's ex parte, in camera evaluation of evidence submitted by the government in opposition to El-Hage's suppression motion was appropriate in light of national security considerations that argued in favor of maintaining the confidentiality of that evidence. El-Hage's Fourth Amendment challenge to his conviction is therefore without merit.

American intelligence became aware of al Qaeda's presence in Kenya by mid-1996 and identified five telephone numbers used by suspected al Qaeda associates. From August 1996 through August 1997, American intelligence officials monitored these telephone lines, including two El-Hage used: a phone line in the building where El-Hage lived and his cell phone. The Attorney General of the United States then authorized intelligence operatives to target El-Hage in particular. This authorization, first issued on April 4, 1997, was renewed in July 1997. Working with Kenyan authorities, U.S. officials searched El-Hage's home in Nairobi on August 21, 1997, pursuant to a document shown to El-Hage's wife that was "identified as a Kenyan warrant authorizing a search for 'stolen property.' "
. . . El-Hage was not present during the search of his home. It is uncontested that the agents did not apply for or obtain a warrant from a U.S. court.

El-Hage filed a pretrial motion pursuant to the Fourth Amendment for the suppression of (1) evidence seized during the August 1997 search of his home in Nairobi and the fruits thereof; (2) evidence obtained through electronic surveillance of four telephone lines, including the telephone for his Nairobi residence and his Kenyan cellular phone, conducted between August 1996 and August 1997; . . . The government opposed El-Hage's motion on the ground that the Fourth Amendment's warrant requirement is inapplicable to overseas searches conducted for the purpose of gathering foreign intelligence. It also asserted that the need for an evidentiary hearing probing the basis for the Kenyan searches was outweighed by the need to maintain the confidentiality of the underlying intelligence. . . .

As a preliminary matter, we address El-Hage's objection to the District Court's resolution of his suppression motion on the basis of an in camera, ex parte review of evidence submitted by the government. El-Hage argues strenuously that without an evidentiary hearing the District Court could not properly evaluate the merits of his motion. Specifically, El-Hage contends that had he been permitted access to those materials and given an opportunity to be heard with regard to them, he would have argued that (1) the majority of the intercepted communications were unrelated to national security, (2) the government failed to limit (or "minimize") its surveillance of irrelevant communications, (3) the search of his Kenyan home was pursuant to a criminal investigation and not part of an effort to gather foreign intelligence, and (4) the surveillance was not conducted in "good faith on any level." . . . We disagree. In light of the limited factual inquiry into evidence of consequence to national security that was necessary to resolve El-Hage's motion and because the legal issues were "thoroughly briefed by the parties,", we see no error-much less an abuse of discretion-in the District Court's decision to review in camera the government's ex parte submissions.

. . .

In order to determine whether El-Hage's suppression motion was properly denied by the District Court, we must first determine whether and to what extent the Fourth Amendment's safeguards apply to overseas searches involving U.S. citizens. In United States v. Toscanino, a case involving a Fourth Amendment challenge to overseas wiretapping of a non-U.S. citizen, we observed that it was "well settled" that "the Bill of Rights has extraterritorial application to the conduct abroad of federal agents directed against United States citizens."); see also United States v. Verdugo-Urquidez, 494 U.S. 259, 283 n. 7, 110 S.Ct. 1056, 108 L.Ed.2d 222 (1990) (Brennan, J., dissenting) (recognizing "the rule, accepted by every Court of Appeals to have considered the question, that the Fourth Amendment applies to searches conducted by the United States Government against United States citizens abroad"); . . . Nevertheless, we have not yet determined the specific question of the applicability of the Fourth Amendment's Warrant Clause to overseas searches. Faced with that question now, we hold that the Fourth Amendment's warrant requirement does not govern searches conducted abroad by U.S. agents; such searches of U.S. citizens need only satisfy the Fourth Amendment's requirement of reasonableness.

. . .

The question of whether a warrant is required for overseas searches of U.S. citizens has not been decided by the Supreme Court, by our Court, or, as far as we are able to determine, by any of our sister circuits. While never addressing the question directly, the Supreme Court provided some guidance on the issue in United States v. Verdugo-Urquidez, ... With respect to the applicability of the Warrant Clause abroad, the Court expressed doubt that the clause governed any overseas searches conducted by U.S. agents, explaining that warrants issued to conduct overseas searches "would be a dead letter outside the United States." Elaborating on this observation in a concurring opinion, Justice KENNEDY concluded:

> The absence of local judges or magistrates available to issue warrants, the differing and perhaps unascertainable conceptions of reasonableness and privacy that prevail abroad, and the need to cooperate with foreign officials all indicate that the Fourth Amendment's warrant requirement should not apply in Mexico as it does in this country.

These observations and the following reasons weigh against imposing a warrant requirement on overseas searches.

First, there is nothing in our history or our precedents suggesting that U.S. officials must first obtain a warrant before conducting an overseas search. El-Hage has pointed to no authority-and we are aware of none-directly supporting the proposition that warrants are necessary for searches conducted abroad by U.S. law enforcement officers or local agents acting in collaboration with them; nor has El-Hage identified any instances in our history where a foreign search was conducted pursuant to an American search warrant. This dearth of authority is not surprising in light of the history of the Fourth Amendment and its Warrant Clause as well as the history of international affairs. . . .

    . . .

While we cannot say that the practices of foreign governments have any bearing on the constitutionality of a similar practice by our government, we find it notable that El-Hage has not pointed to any instance in which another country imposed any comparable requirements on its own law enforcement officers.

The interest served by the warrant requirement in having a "neutral and detached magistrate" evaluate the reasonableness of a search is, in part, based on separation of powers concerns-namely, the need to interpose a judicial officer between the zealous police officer ferreting out crime and the subject of the search. . . These interests are lessened in the circumstances presented here for two reasons. First, a domestic judicial officer's ability to determine the reasonableness of a search is diminished where the search occurs on foreign soil. Second, the acknowledged wide discretion afforded the executive branch in foreign affairs ought to be respected in these circumstances.

A warrant serves a further purpose in limiting the scope of the search to places described with particularity or "the persons or things to be seized" in the warrant. U.S. Const. amend. IV. In the instant case, we are satisfied that the scope of the searches at issue was not unreasonable.

Second, nothing in the history of the foreign relations of the United States would require that U.S. officials obtain warrants from foreign magistrates before conducting searches overseas or, indeed, to suppose that all other states have search and investigation rules akin to our own.

. . .The American procedure of issuing search warrants on a showing of probable cause simply does not extend throughout the globe and, pursuant to the Supreme Court's instructions, the Constitution does not condition our government's investigative powers on the practices of foreign legal regimes "quite different from that which obtains in this country."

Third, if U.S. judicial officers were to issue search warrants intended to have extraterritorial effect, such warrants would have dubious legal significance, if any, in a foreign nation. . . .

Fourth and finally, it is by no means clear that U.S. judicial officers could be authorized to issue warrants for overseas searches, . . ., although we need not resolve that issue here.

For these reasons, we hold that the Fourth Amendment's Warrant Clause has no extraterritorial application and that foreign searches of U.S. citizens conducted by U.S. agents are subject only to the Fourth Amendment's requirement of reasonableness.

The District Court's recognition of an exception to the warrant requirement for foreign intelligence searches finds support in the pre-FISA law of other circuits. See United States v. Truong Dinh Hung, 629 F.2d 908, 913 (4th Cir.1980); United States v. Buck, 548 F.2d 871, 875 (9th Cir.1977); United States v. Butenko, 494 F.2d 593, 605 (3d Cir.1974); United States v. Brown, 484 F.2d 418, 426 (5th Cir.1973). We decline to adopt this view, however, because the exception requires an inquiry into whether the "primary purpose" of the search is foreign intelligence collection. This distinction between a "primary purpose" and other purposes is inapt.

. . .

To determine whether a search is reasonable under the Fourth Amendment, we examine the "totality of the circumstances" to balance "on the one hand, the degree to which it intrudes upon an individual's privacy and, on the other, the degree to which it is needed for the promotion of legitimate governmental interests." [W]e conclude that the searches' intrusion on El-Hage's privacy was outweighed by the government's manifest need to monitor his activities as *an operative of al Qaeda because of the extreme threat al Qaeda presented, and continues to present, to national security. In light of these circumstances, the Kenyan searches were reasonable, notwithstanding El-Hage's objections, and therefore not prohibited by the Fourth Amendment.

. . .

...U.S. intelligence officers became aware of al Qaeda's presence in Kenya in the spring of 1996. At about that time, they identified five telephone lines used by suspected al Qaeda associates, one of which was located in the same building as El-Hage's Nairobi home; another was a cellular phone used by El-Hage. After these telephone lines had been monitored for several months, the Attorney General of the United States authorized surveillance specifically targeting El-Hage. That authorization was renewed four months later, and, one month after that, U.S. agents searched El-Hage's home in Nairobi. This sequence of events is indicative of a disciplined approach to gathering indisputably vital intelligence on the activities of a foreign terrorist organization. U.S. agents did not breach the privacy of El-Hage's home on a whim or on the basis of an unsubstantiated tip; rather, they monitored telephonic communications involving him for nearly a year and conducted surveillance of his activities for five months before concluding that it was necessary to search his home. In light of these findings of fact, which El-Hage has not contested as clearly erroneous, we conclude that the search, while undoubtedly intrusive on El-Hage's privacy, was restrained in execution and narrow in focus.

Balanced against this restrained and limited intrusion on El-Hage's privacy, we have the government's manifest need to investigate possible threats to national security. . . . The government had evidence establishing that El-Hage was working with al Qaeda in Kenya. On the basis of these findings of fact, we agree with the District Court that, at the time of the search of El-Hage's home, the government had a powerful need to gather additional intelligence on al Qaeda's activities in Kenya, which it had linked to El-Hage.

Balancing the search's limited intrusion on El-Hage's privacy against the manifest need of the government to monitor the activities of al Qaeda, which had been connected to El-Hage through a year of surveillance, we hold that the search of El-Hage's Nairobi residence was reasonable under the Fourth Amendment.

. . .

It cannot be denied that El-Hage suffered, while abroad, a significant invasion of privacy by virtue of the government's year-long surveillance of his telephonic communications. . . . For its part, the government does not contradict El-Hage's claims that the surveillance was broad and loosely "minimized." Instead, the government sets forth a variety of reasons justifying the breadth of the surveillance. These justifications, regardless of their merit, do not lessen the intrusion El-Hage suffered while abroad, and we accord this intrusion substantial weight in our balancing analysis.

Turning to the government's interest, we encounter again the self-evident need to investigate threats to national security presented by foreign terrorist organizations. When U.S. intelligence learned that five telephone lines were being used by suspected al Qaeda operatives, the need to monitor communications traveling on those lines was paramount, and we are loath to discount-much less disparage-the government's decision to do so.

Our balancing of these compelling, and competing, interests turns on whether the scope of the intrusion here was justified by the government's surveillance needs. We conclude that it was, for at least the following four reasons.

First, complex, wide-ranging, and decentralized organizations, such as al Qaeda, warrant sustained and intense monitoring in order to understand their features and identify their members. . . . Second, foreign intelligence gathering of the sort considered here must delve into the superficially mundane because it is not always readily apparent what information is relevant. . . .

Third, members of covert terrorist organizations, as with other sophisticated criminal enterprises, often communicate in code, or at least through ambiguous language.

. . .Fourth, because the monitored conversations were conducted in foreign languages, the task of determining relevance and identifying coded language was further complicated. . . .

Because the surveillance of suspected al Qaeda operatives must be sustained and thorough in order to be effective, we cannot conclude that the scope of the government's electronic surveillance was overbroad. While the intrusion on El-Hage's privacy was great, the need for the government to so intrude was even greater. Accordingly, the electronic surveillance, like the search of El-Hage's Nairobi residence, was reasonable under the Fourth Amendment.

In sum, because the searches at issue in this appeal were reasonable, they comport with the applicable requirement of the Fourth Amendment and, therefore, El-Hage's motion to suppress the evidence resulting from those searches was properly denied by the District Court.

. . .

QUESTIONS AND NOTES

1.   The materials in this subsection, C, prior to the Odeh case, address generally, depending on a number of different variables, the issues raised in searches involving U.S. agents that take place abroad. Odeh adds to the mix the fact that the search occurred abroad in connection with a matter involving national security/foreign intelligence concerns. Does that fact change the applicable conclusions?

2.   The Odeh case involved both physical searches and electronic surveillance. The government appeared to have had a purpose to obtain foreign intelligence information. Does the FISA statute as originally enacted have any relevance to the Odeh case? If the FISA Amendments Act of 2008 had been in force at the time of the Odeh events, would it have been relevant to the Odeh case?

3.   In resolving the issue in the case, did the court in Odeh take into account the foreign intelligence goal of the search? How did it deal with it in its opinion? Did the court give any weight to the fact that there were foreign intelligence/national security issues in the case? Stating the matter differently, how did the government argue the relevance of the foreign intelligence purpose of the investigation? Was the government's argument too narrow?

4.   As we saw in the previous subsection of this chapter, there is no statute dealing with physical searches abroad comparable to §§ 1822–25, which deal with the topic on the domestic front. Would it be useful to enact a statute that deals with physical searches abroad of the premises of U.S. persons by U.S. agents?

5.   Given the fact that the court in Odeh applied a standard of reasonableness under the fourth amendment and declined to apply the warrant clause, and that the Supreme Court denied certiorari in the matter, does it make sense to bring a warrant requirement back into such cases through enactment of a new statute?

6.   See generally, Bombed Away: How The Second Circuit Destroyed Fourth Amendment Rights Of U.S. Citizens Abroad, 2010 B.Y.U. L. Rev. 719 (2010); Streaming The International Silver Platter Doctrine: Coordinating Transnational Law Enforcement In The Age Of Global Terrorism And Technology, 49 Colum. J. Transnat'l L. 411 (2011); Corey M. Then, Note, Searches and Seizures of Americans Abroad: Re-Examining the Fourth Amendment's Warrant Clause and the Foreign Intelligence Exception Five Years After United States v. Bin Laden, 55 DUKE L.J. 1059 (2006).

D. ADMINISTRATIVE SUBPOENAS TO OBTAIN RECORDS, DOCUMENTS, ETC.—NATIONAL SECURITY LETTERS

1.   INTRODUCTION

As indicated in the Introduction to this chapter, the government can obtain records, documents and other tangibles through a search warrant process or through the issuance of what amounts to a subpoena directing a person or institution to produce specified materials in their possession. In the field of foreign intelligence or international terrorism, National Security Letters (NSLs) can be utilized to obtain records, documents and other kinds of information, usually from third party holders. NSL letters are used most frequently for this purpose. Authority to issue National

Security Letters in order to seek different kinds of records is provided under a number of statutes, see 18 U.S.C. § 2709 (electronic subscriber information); 12 U.S.C. § 3414(a)(5) (financial records); 15 U.S.C. § 1681u (credit history); 15 U.S.C. § 1681v (full credit reports); 50 U.S.C. § 436 (information concerning investigation of improper disclosure of classified information).

Section 215, codified at 50 U.S.C. § 1861, was addressed in the previous chapter in connection with its use to obtain metadata records from telephone companies. An order under this provision also can be used to demand the production of any tangible things (including books, papers, records, etc.), from individuals or institutions. Approval must be obtained from a judge of the Foreign Intelligence Surveillance Court or a special designated U.S. Magistrate. In general form, therefore, section 215 is a type of judicially approved subpoena duces tecum. Because 215 was treated in Chapter 5, it will not be reviewed here except insofar as it shares some common issues with administrative subpoenas.

National Security Letters issued under any of the listed statutes amount to administrative subpoenas which are widely utilized elsewhere in the legal system and, in some instances, in relation to, or in direct aid of criminal investigation. Note that the designated purpose of NSL subpoenas is not criminal enforcement, but rather to obtain foreign intelligence information, especially regarding terrorism. Federal agencies which have had non-NSL administrative subpoena authority include: the Drug Enforcement Agency, see 21 U.S.C. § 876; the IRS, see 26 U.S.C. § 7602; the SEC, see SEC v. Dresser Industries 628 F. 3d 1368 (D.C. Cir. 1980); the Labor Management Reporting and Disclosure Act, see Donovan v. Spadea, 757 F.2d 74 (3d Cir. 1985).

NSLs have been controversial, and have been challenged in court. A leading case involving a constitutional attack on these letters, Doe v. Mukasey, 549 F.3d 861 (2d Cir, 2008), is presented in the materials. The question is whether the letters are truly simply another kind of administrative subpoena, or whether they have some features that make them unique and involve a significant expansion of governmental powers; if so, which features. The pertinent statutes were amended in 2015, and a key issue also is whether the amendments adequately respond to the concerns that had been raised.

In order to be able to make appropriate comparisons and assessments of the NSLs, reproduced below are: a) the pre-2015 version of the most frequently used NSL authorization statute, 18 U.S.C. § 2709 as well as b) the pre-2015 provision governing judicial review for the several different NSL statutes, 18 U.S.C. § 3511; and c) by way of illustration and for purposes of comparison, an administrative subpoena available in a non-terrorism legal setting—provisions governing the issuance of administrative subpoenas used in drug enforcement investigations, 21 U.S.C. § 876–877. The 2015 revision of § 3511 is also provided.

2. AUTHORITY TO ISSUE NATIONAL SECURITY LETTERS

Title 18, U.S.C.

§ 2709. Counterintelligence access to telephone toll and transactional records [pre-2015 version]

(a) **Duty to provide.** A wire or electronic communication service provider shall comply with a request for subscriber information and toll billing records information, or electronic communication transactional records in its custody or possession made by the Director of the Federal Bureau of Investigation under subsection (b) of this section.

(b) **Required Certification.** The Director of the Federal Bureau of Investigation, or his designee in a position not lower than Deputy Assistant Director at Bureau headquarters or a Special Agent in Charge in a Bureau field office designated by the Director, may—

(1) request the name, address, length of service, and local and long distance toll billing records of a person or entity if the Director (or his designee) certifies in writing to the wire or electronic communication service provider to which the request is made that the name, address, length of service, and toll billing records sought are relevant to an authorized investigation to protect against international terrorism or clandestine intelligence activities, provided that such an investigation of a United States person is not conducted solely on the basis of activities protected by the first amendment to the Constitution of the United States; and

. . .

(c) **Prohibition of certain disclosure.—**

(1) If the Director of the Federal Bureau of Investigation, or his designee . . . certifies that otherwise there may result a danger to the national security of the United States, interference with a criminal, counterterrorism, or counterintelligence investigation, interference with diplomatic relations, or danger to the life or physical safety of any person, no wire or electronic communications service provider, or officer, employee, or agent thereof, shall disclose to any person (other than those to whom such disclosure is necessary to comply with the request or an attorney to obtain legal advice or legal assistance with respect to

the request) that the Federal Bureau of Investigation has sought or obtained access to information or records under this section.

. . .

(3) Any recipient disclosing to those persons necessary to comply with the request or to an attorney to obtain legal advice or legal assistance with respect to the request shall inform such person of any applicable nondisclosure requirement. Any person who receives a disclosure under this subsection shall be subject to the same prohibitions on disclosure under paragraph (1).

(4) At the request of the Director of the Federal Bureau of Investigation or the designee of the Director, any person making or intending to make a disclosure under this section shall identify to the Director or such designee the person to whom such disclosure will be made or to whom such disclosure was made prior to the request, except that nothing in this section shall require a person to inform the Director or such designee of the identity of an attorney to whom disclosure was made or will be made to obtain legal advice or legal assistance with respect to the request under subsection (a).

. . .

(f) Libraries.—A library (as that term is defined in section 213(1) of the Library Services and Technology Act (20 U.S.C. 9122(1)), the services of which include access to the Internet, books, journals, magazines, newspapers, or other similar forms of communication in print or digitally by patrons for their use, review, examination, or circulation, is not a wire or electronic communication service provider for purposes of this section, unless the library is providing the services defined in section 2510(15) ("electronic communication service") of this title.

3. JUDICIAL REVIEW OF NSLs [PRE-2015]

Title 18, U.S.C.

§ 3511. Judicial review of requests for information [pre-2015]

(a) The recipient of a request for records, a report, or other information under section 2709(b) of this title, section 626(a) or (b) or 627(a) of the Fair Credit Reporting Act, section 1114(a)(5)(A) of the Right to Financial Privacy Act, or section 802(a) of the National Security Act of 1947 may, in the United States district court for the district in which that person or entity does business or resides, petition for an order modifying or setting aside the request. The court may modify or set aside the request if compliance would be unreasonable, oppressive, or otherwise unlawful.

(b)

. . .

(2) If the petition is filed within one year of the request for records, a report, or other information under section 2709(b) of this title, section 626(a) or (b) or 627(a) of the Fair Credit Reporting Act, section 1114(a)(5)(A) of the Right to Financial Privacy Act, or section 802(a) of the National Security Act of 1947, the court may modify or set aside such a nondisclosure requirement if it finds that there is no reason to believe that disclosure may endanger the national security of the United States, interfere with a criminal, counterterrorism, or counterintelligence investigation, interfere with diplomatic relations, or endanger the life or physical safety of any person. If, at the time of the petition, the Attorney General, Deputy Attorney General, an Assistant Attorney General, or the Director of the Federal Bureau of Investigation, or in the case of a request by a department, agency, or instrumentality of the Federal Government other than the Department of Justice, the head or deputy head of such department, agency, or instrumentality, certifies that disclosure may endanger the national security of the United States or interfere with diplomatic relations, such certification shall be treated as conclusive unless the court finds that the certification was made in bad faith.

(3) If the petition is filed one year or more after the request for records, a report, or other information under section 2709(b) of this title, section 626(a) or (b) or 627(a) of the Fair Credit Reporting Act, section 1114(a)(5)(A) of the Right to Financial Privacy Act, or section 802(a) of the National Security Act of 1947, the Attorney General, Deputy Attorney General, an Assistant Attorney General, or the Director of the Federal Bureau of Investigation, or his designee . . . or in the case of a request by a department, agency, or instrumentality of the Federal Government other than the Federal Bureau of Investigation, the head or deputy head of such department, agency, or instrumentality, within ninety days of the filing of the petition, shall either terminate the nondisclosure requirement or re-certify that disclosure may result in a danger to the national security of the United States, interference with a criminal, counterterrorism, or counterintelligence investigation, interference with diplomatic relations, or danger to the life or physical safety of any person. In the event of re-certification, the court may modify or set aside such a nondisclosure requirement if it finds that there is no reason to believe that disclosure may endanger the national security of the United States, interfere with a criminal, counterterrorism, or

counterintelligence investigation, interfere with diplomatic relations, or endanger the life or physical safety of any person. If the recertification that disclosure may endanger the national security of the United States or interfere with diplomatic relations is made by the Attorney General, Deputy Attorney General, an Assistant Attorney General, or the Director of the Federal Bureau of Investigation, such certification shall be treated as conclusive unless the court finds that the recertification was made in bad faith. If the court denies a petition for an order modifying or setting aside a nondisclosure requirement under this paragraph, the recipient shall be precluded for a period of one year from filing another petition to modify or set aside such nondisclosure requirement.

. . .

(e) In all proceedings under this section, the court shall, upon request of the government, review ex parte and in camera any government submission or portions thereof, which may include classified information.

4. AUTHORITY TO ISSUE ADMINISTRATIVE SUBPOENAS IN DRUG-RELATED INVESTIGATIONS

Title 21, U.S.C.

§ 876.   Subpenas

(a)   Authorization of use by Attorney General

In any investigation relating to his functions under this subchapter with respect to controlled substances, listed chemicals, tableting machines, or encapsulating machines, the Attorney General may subpena witnesses, compel the attendance and testimony of witnesses, and require the production of any records (including books, papers, documents, and other tangible things which constitute or contain evidence) which the Attorney General finds relevant or material to the investigation. The attendance of witnesses and the production of records may be required from any place in any State or in any territory or other place subject to the jurisdiction of the United States at any designated place of hearing; except that a witness shall not be required to appear at any hearing more than 500 miles distant from the place where he was served with a subpena. Witnesses summoned under this section shall be paid the same fees and mileage that are paid witnesses in the courts of the United States.

. . .

§ 877.   Judicial review

All final determinations, findings, and conclusions of the Attorney General under this subchapter shall be final and conclusive decisions of the matters involved, except that any person aggrieved by a final decision of the Attorney General may obtain review of the decision in the United States Court of Appeals for the District of Columbia or for the circuit in which his principal place of business is located upon petition filed with the court and delivered to the Attorney General within thirty days after notice of the decision. Findings of fact by the Attorney General, if supported by substantial evidence, shall be conclusive.

5.   A CONSTITUTIONAL CHALLENGE TO THE NSLs AND THE JUDICIAL REVIEW PROCESS [PRE-2015]

DOE v. MUKASEY

549 F.3d 861 (2d Cir. 2008)

Before: NEWMAN, CALABRESI, and SOTOMAYOR, CIRCUIT JUDGES.

JON O. NEWMAN, CIRCUIT JUDGE:

This appeal concerns challenges to the constitutionality of statutes regulating the issuance by the Federal Bureau of Investigation ("FBI") of a type of administrative subpoena generally known as a National Security Letter ("NSL") to electronic communication service providers ("ECSPs"). See 18 U.S.C. §§ 2709, 3511 (collectively "the NSL statutes"). ECSPs are typically telephone companies or Internet service providers. An NSL, in the context of this appeal, is a request for information about specified persons or entities who are subscribers to an ECSP and about their telephone or Internet activity. Primarily at issue on this appeal are challenges to the provisions (1) prohibiting the recipient from disclosing the fact that an NSL has been received, see 18 U.S.C. § 2709(c), and (2) structuring judicial review of the nondisclosure requirement, see id. § 3511(b).

These challenges arise on an appeal by the United States from the September 7, 2007, judgment of the District Court for the Southern District of New York (Victor Marrero, District Judge), enjoining FBI officials from (1) issuing NSLs under section 2709, (2) enforcing the nondisclosure requirement of subsection 2709(c), and (3) enforcing the provisions for judicial review of the nondisclosure requirement contained in subsection 3511(b). See Doe v. Gonzales, 500 F.Supp.2d 379 (S.D.N.Y.2007) ("Doe II"). The District Court ruled that subsections 2709(c) and 3511(b) are unconstitutional on First Amendment and separation-of-powers grounds, and that subsection 2709(c) could not be severed from section 2709.

We agree that the challenged statutes do not comply with the First Amendment, although not to the extent determined by the District Court, and we also conclude that the relief ordered by the District Court is too broad. We therefore affirm in part, reverse in part, and remand for further proceedings.

Background

The parties. The Plaintiffs-Appellees are an Internet service provider (John Doe, Inc.), the provider's former president (John Doe), the American Civil Liberties Union ("ACLU"), and the American Civil Liberties Union Foundation ("ACLUF"). The Defendants-Appellants are the Attorney General, the Director of the FBI, and the General Counsel of the FBI, all sued in their official capacities.

The NSL. In February 2004, the FBI delivered the NSL at issue in this litigation to John Doe, Inc. The letter directed John Doe, Inc., "to provide the [FBI] the names, addresses, lengths of service and electronic communication transactional records, to include [other information] (not to include message content and/or subject fields) for [a specific] email address." The letter certified that the information sought was relevant to an investigation against international terrorism or clandestine intelligence activities and advised John Doe, Inc., that the law "prohibit[ed] any officer, employee or agent" of the company from "disclosing to any person that the FBI has sought or obtained access to information or records" pursuant to the NSL provisions. The letter also asked that John Doe provide the relevant information personally to a designated FBI office.

. . .

Discussion

The validity of the NSL issued to John Doe, Inc., is no longer at issue because the Government has withdrawn it, but the prohibition on disclosing receipt of the NSL remains. We therefore consider only the Government's challenges to the District Court's rulings with respect to the nondisclosure requirement, although to the extent that the nondisclosure requirement encounters valid constitutional objections, we will consider the provisions authorizing the issuance of NSLs in connection with the issue of severance.

I.   Applicable Principles

The First Amendment principles relevant to the District Court's rulings are well established, although their application to the statutory provisions at issue requires careful consideration. A judicial order "forbidding certain communications when issued in advance of the time that such communications are to occur" is generally regarded as a "prior restraint," and is "the most serious and the least tolerable infringement on First Amendment rights," "Any prior restraint on expression comes to [a court] with a heavy presumption against its constitutional validity," and "carries a heavy burden of showing justification," id. A content-based restriction is subject to review under the standard of strict scrutiny, requiring a showing that the restriction is "narrowly tailored to promote a compelling Government interest."

. . .

The national security context in which NSLs are authorized imposes on courts a significant obligation to defer to judgments of Executive Branch officials. "[C]ourts traditionally have been reluctant to intrude upon the authority of the Executive in . . . national security affairs," and the Supreme Court has acknowledged that terrorism might provide the basis for arguments "for heightened deference to the judgments of the political branches with respect to matters of national security," Zadvydas v. Davis, 533 U.S. 678, 696, 121 S.Ct. 2491, 150 L.Ed.2d 653 (2001).

. . . It is well established that courts should resolve ambiguities in statutes in a manner that avoids substantial constitutional issues.

Less clear is the authority of courts to revise a statute to overcome a constitutional defect. Of course, it is the province of the Legislative Branch to legislate. But in limited circumstances the Supreme Court has undertaken to fill in a statutory gap arising from the invalidation of a portion of a statute. . . .

. . .

Closely related to the issue of whether a court should revise a statute to avoid or overcome a constitutional defect is the issue of whether to sever the unconstitutional portion of a statute or invalidate an entire statute or even an entire statutory scheme. In general, the choice, as stated by the Supreme Court, depends on whether "the legislature [would] have preferred what is left of its statute to no statute at all." . . .

. . .

II.   The Parties' Contentions

With these principles in mind, we turn to the parties' basic contentions. From the Plaintiffs' standpoint, the nondisclosure requirement of subsection 2709(c) is a straightforward content-based prior restraint that must be tested against all the substantive and procedural limitations applicable to such an impairment of expression. In their view, the nondisclosure requirement is content-based because it proscribes disclosure of the entire category of speech concerning the fact and details of the issuance of an NSL, and it is a prior restraint in the literal sense that it is imposed before an NSL recipient has an opportunity to speak. From these premises, the Plaintiffs conclude that subsection 2709(c) is unconstitutional under strict scrutiny review because it prohibits disclosure in circumstances not narrowly tailored to a compelling governmental interest and operates as a licensing scheme without the procedural requirement of placing on the Government the burden of initiating judicial review and sustaining a burden of proof. The Plaintiffs also challenge subsection 3511(b) on the grounds that (1) the judicial review provisions do not require the Government to initiate judicial review and to sustain a burden of proof and (2) certification of certain risks by senior governmental officials is entitled to a conclusive presumption (absent bad faith). These aspects of subsection 3511(b) are alleged to violate First Amendment procedural standards and the separation of powers.

The Government responds that, to whatever extent the nondisclosure requirement can be considered a content-based prior restraint, it is subject to less rigorous scrutiny than that imposed on more typical First Amendment claimants who wish to speak or parade in public places, distribute literature, or exhibit movies. The Government points out that the nondisclosure requirement arises not to suppress a pre-existing desire to speak, but only as a result of governmental interaction with an NSL recipient. In the Government's view, the nondisclosure requirement survives a First Amendment challenge on the same rationale that has permitted secrecy requirements to be imposed on witnesses before grand juries, and judicial misconduct proceedings, and on a person or entity that acquired sensitive material through pretrial discovery

III. The Interpretation of the NSL Statutes

In assessing these contentions, we need to interpret the nondisclosure requirements before ruling on their constitutionality. [S]ubsection 2709(c) specifies what senior FBI officials must certify to trigger the nondisclosure requirement, and subsection 3511(b) specifies, in similar but not identical language, what a district court must find in order to modify or set aside such a requirement. Senior FBI officials must certify that in the absence of a nondisclosure requirement "there may result a danger to the national security of the United States, interference with a criminal, counterterrorism, or counterintelligence investigation, interference with diplomatic relations, or danger to the life or physical safety of any person." 18 U.S.C. § 2709(c)(1). Upon challenge by an NSL recipient, a district court may modify or set aside a nondisclosure requirement "if it finds that there is no reason to believe that disclosure may endanger the national security of the United States, interfere with a criminal, counterterrorism, or counterintelligence investigation, interfere with diplomatic relations, or endanger the life or physical safety of any person." Id. § 3511(b)(2).

These provisions present three issues for interpretation: (1) what is the scope of the enumerated harms? (2) what justifies a nondisclosure requirement? and (3) which side has the burden of proof?

exercise its judgment on matters of national security. Such a judgment is not to be second-guessed, but a court must receive some indication that the judgment has been soundly reached. . . .

. . . A demonstration of a reasonable likelihood of potential harm, related to international terrorism or clandestine intelligence activities, will virtually always outweigh the First Amendment interest in speaking about such a limited and particularized occurrence as the receipt of an NSL and will suffice to maintain the secrecy of the fact of such receipt.

. . .

There is not meaningful judicial review of the decision of the Executive Branch to prohibit speech if the position of the Executive Branch that speech would be harmful is "conclusive" on a reviewing court, absent only a demonstration of bad faith. To accept deference to that extraordinary degree would be to reduce strict scrutiny to no scrutiny, save only in the rarest of situations where bad faith could be shown. Under either traditional strict scrutiny or a less exacting application of that standard, some demonstration from the Executive Branch of the need for secrecy is required in order to conform the nondisclosure requirement to First Amendment standards. The fiat of a governmental official, though senior in rank and doubtless honorable in the execution of official duties, cannot displace the judicial obligation to enforce constitutional requirements. "Under no circumstances should the Judiciary become the handmaiden of the Executive."

V.   Remedy

To recapitulate our conclusions, we (1) construe subsection 2709(c) to permit a nondisclosure requirement only when senior FBI officials certify that disclosure may result in an enumerated harm that is related to "an authorized investigation to protect against international terrorism or clandestine intelligence activities," (2) construe subsections 3511(b)(2) and (b)(3) to place on the Government the burden to show that a good reason exists to expect that disclosure of receipt of an NSL will risk an enumerated harm, (3) construe subsections 3511(b)(2) and (b)(3) to mean that the Government satisfies its burden when it makes an adequate demonstration as to why disclosure in a particular case may result in an enumerated harm, (4) rule that subsections 2709(c) and 3511(b) are unconstitutional to the extent that they impose a nondisclosure requirement without placing on the Government the burden of initiating judicial review of that requirement, and (5) rule that subsections 3511(b)(2) and (b)(3) are unconstitutional to the extent that, upon such review, a governmental official's certification that disclosure may endanger the national security of the United States or interfere with diplomatic relations is treated as conclusive.

. . . We are satisfied. . . that, once the Government has initiated judicial review and prevailed on the merits, limiting an NSL recipient to annual opportunities thereafter to terminate the nondisclosure requirement does not violate First Amendment procedural requirements. The information subject to nondisclosure is extremely limited, and, once the need for secrecy—avoiding risk of harm related to international terrorism—has been shown, that need is not likely to dissipate soon.

In those instances where an NSL recipient gives notice of an intent to challenge the disclosure requirement, the Government would have several options for completing the reciprocal notice procedure by commencing such review. First, it is arguable that the Government can adapt the authority now set forth in subsection 3511(c) for the purpose of initiating judicial review. That provision authorizes the Attorney General to "invoke the aid of any [relevant] district court" in the event of "a failure to comply with a request for . . . information made to any person or entity under section 2709(b)" or other provisions authorizing NSLs. 18 U.S.C. § 3511(c). Since an NSL includes both a request for information and a direction not to disclose that the FBI has sought or obtained information, an NSL recipient's timely notice of intent to disclose, furnished in response to notice in an NSL of an opportunity to contest the nondisclosure requirement, can perhaps be considered the functional equivalent of the "failure to comply" contemplated by subsection 3511(c). Second, the Government might be able to identify some other statutory authority to invoke the equitable power of a district court to prevent a disclosure that the Government can demonstrate would risk harm to national security. Third, and as a last resort, the Government could seek explicit congressional authorization to initiate judicial review of a nondisclosure requirement that a recipient wishes to challenge. We leave it to the Government to consider how to discharge its obligation to initiate judicial review.

. . .Although the conclusive presumption clause of subsections 3511(b)(2) and (b)(3) must be stricken, we invalidate subsection 2709(c) and the remainder of subsection 3511(b) only to the extent that they fail to provide for Government-initiated judicial review. The Government can respond to this partial invalidation ruling by using the suggested reciprocal notice procedure. With this procedure in place, subsections 2709(c) and 3511(b) would survive First Amendment challenge.

. . .

We have no doubt that if Congress had understood that First Amendment considerations required the Government to initiate judicial review of a nondisclosure requirement and precluded a conclusive certification by the Attorney General, it would have wanted the remainder of the NSL statutes to remain in force. Congress would surely have wanted the Government to retain the authority to issue NSLs even if all aspects of the nondisclosure requirement of subsection 2709(c) and the judicial review provisions of section 3511(b) had been invalidated. As the Government points out, even without a nondisclosure requirement, it can protect the national interest by issuing NSLs only where it expects compliance with a request for secrecy to be honored. A fortiori, authority to issue NSLs should be preserved in view of the limiting constructions and limited invalidations we have ordered. We therefore sever the conclusive presumption language of subsection 3511(b) and leave intact the remainder of subsection 3511(b) and the entirety of section 2709 (with Government-initiated judicial review required). As a result of this ruling, we modify the District Court's injunction by limiting it to enjoining FBI officials from enforcing the nondisclosure requirement of section 2709(c) in the absence of Government-initiated judicial review.

There remains for consideration the issue of the procedure to be followed with respect to judicial review of the nondisclosure requirement with respect to the NSL issued to John Doe, Inc. Although we have ruled that the Government is obliged to initiate judicial review of a nondisclosure requirement, it would be pointless to dismiss the pending litigation and direct the Government to start anew. With judicial review already initiated in the District Court and the constitutionality of the disclosure requirement salvaged by the statutory interpretations and partial invalidations we have ordered, the sounder course is to remand so that the Government may have an opportunity to sustain its burden of proof and satisfy the constitutional standards we have outlined for maintaining the disclosure requirement. See 28 U.S.C. § 2106.

Conclusion

Accordingly, for all the foregoing reasons, subsections 2709(c) and 3511(b) are construed in conformity with this opinion and partially invalidated only to the extent set forth in this opinion, the injunction is modified as set forth in this opinion, and the judgment of the District Court is affirmed in part, reversed in part, and remanded for further proceedings consistent with this opinion.

6. THE JUDICIAL REVIEW PROVISION AS AMENDED IN 2015

Title 18, U.S.C.

§ 3511. Judicial review of requests for information

(a) The recipient of a request for records, a report, or other information under section 2709(b) of this title, section 626(a) or (b) or 627(a) of the Fair Credit Reporting Act, section 1114(a)(5)(A) of the Right to Financial Privacy Act, or section 802(a) of the National Security Act of 1947 may, in the United States district court for the district in which that person or entity does business or resides, petition for an order modifying or setting aside the request. The court may modify or set aside the request if compliance would be unreasonable, oppressive, or otherwise unlawful.

(b) Nondisclosure.—

(1) In general.—

(A) Notice.—If a recipient of a request or order for a report, records, or other information under section 2709 of this title, section 626 or 627 of the Fair Credit Reporting Act (15 U.S.C. 1681u and 1681v), section 1114 of the Right to Financial Privacy Act of 1978 (12 U.S.C. 3414), or section 802 of the National Security Act of 1947 (50 U.S.C. 3162), wishes to have a court review a nondisclosure requirement imposed in connection with the request or order, the recipient may notify the Government or file a petition for judicial review in any court described in subsection (a).

(B) Application.—Not later than 30 days after the date of receipt of a notification under subparagraph (A), the Government shall apply for an order prohibiting the disclosure of the existence or contents of the relevant request or order. An application under this subparagraph may be filed in the district court of the United States for the judicial district in which the recipient of the order is doing business or in the district court of the United States for any judicial district within which the authorized investigation that is the basis for the request is being conducted. The applicable nondisclosure requirement shall remain in effect during the pendency of proceedings relating to the requirement.

(C) Consideration.—A district court of the United States that receives a petition under subparagraph (A) or an application under subparagraph (B) should rule expeditiously, and shall, subject to paragraph (3), issue a nondisclosure order that includes conditions appropriate to the circumstances.

(2) Application contents.—An application for a nondisclosure order or extension thereof or a response to a petition filed under paragraph (1) shall include a certification from the Attorney General, Deputy Attorney General, an Assistant Attorney General, or the Director of the Federal Bureau of Investigation, or a designee in a position not lower than Deputy Assistant Director at Bureau headquarters or a Special Agent in Charge in a Bureau field office designated by the Director, or in the case of a request by a department, agency, or instrumentality of the Federal Government other than the Department of Justice, the head or deputy head of the department, agency, or instrumentality, containing a statement of specific facts indicating that the absence of a prohibition of disclosure under this subsection may result in—

    (A) a danger to the national security of the United States;

    (B) interference with a criminal, counterterrorism, or counterintelligence investigation;

    (C) interference with diplomatic relations; or

    (D) danger to the life or physical safety of any person.

    (3) Standard.—A district court of the United States shall issue a nondisclosure order or extension thereof under this subsection if the court determines that there is reason to believe that disclosure of the information subject to the nondisclosure requirement during the applicable time period may result in—

    (A) a danger to the national security of the United States;

    (B) interference with a criminal, counterterrorism, or counterintelligence investigation;

    (C) interference with diplomatic relations; or

    (D) danger to the life or physical safety of any person.

QUESTIONS AND NOTES

    1. For the disposition of the principal case, supra, on remand, see Doe v. Holder, 703 F.Supp. 2d 313 (S.D.N.Y.2010):

> Specifically, Plaintiffs contend that the Government has not provided adequate explanation to justify suppressing the Attachment as necessary to national security interests or to protect an ongoing investigation of terrorist activity. To the contrary, Plaintiffs maintain that disclosure of the Attachment would serve the public interest in understanding the type of personal records the FBI has sought to obtain through NSLs, and thus to inform congressional and public debate on the subject.

> In response, the Government submitted a Declaration (the "Declaration") of Arthur M. Cummings II ("Cummings"), Executive Assistant Director of the National Security Branch of the Federal Bureau of Investigation ("FBI"). Cummings states that the duties of his office entail supervision and control over the FBI's National Security files and records. In that capacity he declares his view that unauthorized disclosure of sensitive information contained in the NSL at issue, including the Attachment, would risk revealing sensitive information sought by the FBI in conducting national security investigations, as well as the methods and techniques used by the FBI in the course of such work. Moreover, Cummings asserts that disclosure of the Attachment may cause the target of the NSL to change behavior when dealing with internet service providers, such as by giving false information to conceal the target's true identity or intentions. Finally, Cummings declares that the effects of disclosure

of the types of information and specific items the FBI considers important in seeking to identify account holders or their computer use or access would compromise not only the current FBI investigation involving the NSL and target in this case but future probes as well, thus potentially hampering Government efforts to address national security threats.

The discrete issue now before the Court is whether the Government is justified, pursuant to §§ 2709(c) and 3511(b), in continuing to impose a nondisclosure requirement on Plaintiffs as to the Attachment. On the basis of review of the Declaration and other papers submitted by the parties, the oral argument at the Court's hearing on the matter, and the Court's ex parte conference with the Government for in camera review of the Attachment, the Court grants in part and denies in part Plaintiffs' request.

The Court concludes that some items requested in the Attachment relate to two categories of information that should be disclosed; (1) material within the scope of information that the NSL statute identifies as permissible for the FBI to obtain through use of NSLs, and (2) material that the FBI has publicly acknowledged it has previously requested by means of NSLs. These categories, insofar as specifically itemized in the Attachment, include the name, address, telephone number, account number, email address and billing information of the subscriber. The Court is not persuaded that disclosure of these two categories of information would raise a substantial risk that any of the statutorily enumerated harms would occur. Accordingly, the Court directs the Government to lift its nondisclosure requirement as it applies to those items of the Attachment.

As to the remainder of the Attachment, the Court is persuaded that the Government has demonstrated that good reason exists to believe that disclosure of the information withheld plausibly could harm an authorized ongoing investigation to protect against international terrorism or clandestine intelligence activities. Also, the Court finds that the Government has demonstrated to the satisfaction of the Court that the link between disclosure and the risk of harm is substantial. See John Doe, 549 F.3d at 881. Plaintiffs contend that there is no continuing need for nondisclosure of the entire Attachment because it would reveal only marginal information about the Government's investigation. Further, they argue that the Government's suppression justification proffered here is constitutionally deficient because: the FBI has already publicly revealed its interest in some of the types of records it has sought in this case, such as existing transaction/activity logs and email header information; disclosure of the Attachment would not impart anything about the FBI's current NSL practices; and the FBI's concerns are grounded entirely on conclusory or speculative risk of harms that might occur. The Court disagrees.

The Court is persuaded, based on Cummings's Declaration and the Government's written submissions and representations at the Court's in camera review of the Attachment, that the Government has sufficiently met its burden under § 2709(c). Specifically, the Court finds that the Government has demonstrated a reasonable likelihood that disclosure of the Attachment in its entirety could inform current targets of law enforcement investigations, including the particular target of the Government's ongoing inquiry in this action, as well as, potentially, future targets, as to certain types of records and other materials the Government seeks through national security investigations employing NSLs. The Government has made a plausible showing that public access to such information could provide knowledge about current FBI activities as well as valuable insights into the agency's investigative methods that could produce the harms the NSL statute sought to safeguard against. For instance, disclosure of the Attachment could risk providing information useful to the Government's targets of the pending investigation that could prompt changes in their behavior to prevent detection, or signal that particular targets remain under active surveillance. Thus, the Court is satisfied that the information sought by the Attachment does not entail undue impairment of First Amendment rights or other unwarranted abusive practice on the part of the FBI.

2.   To answer the question whether the NSLs expand government authority beyond what is appropriate, it is useful to compare the NSLs with another kind of administrative subpoena (in this instance, administrative subpoena authority in drug investigations), in regard to the following: a) the purpose of the issuance of the subpoena or summons; b) the factual basis or standard on which the government can act to acquire books, records, documents, etc.; c) the scope of the different legal authorizations—how broad are the categories of tangible things that can be seized or demanded; d) whether the specific person involved is the target of the investigation or a 3rd party; e) whether judicial approval must be obtained prior to the government action; f) whether an obligation of secrecy applies to the particular government action, and the nature and extent of that obligation; and g) whether the order to produce requested material is subject to judicial review and the standard of review.

3.   From a comparison of the relevant provisions, it should be apparent that the NSL does not differ significantly from the drug investigation subpoena authority with regard to the factual basis or standard on which the request or order can be issued, that is, the drug provision is a precedent from another investigatory area for using a "relevant to an investigation" standard. Stating the matter differently, why should the government be able to obtain records, etc. in a drug investigation applying a "relevant to an investigation" standard and not be able to use a similar standard in a terrorism investigation? Are

there reasons why arguably a higher standard should be applicable in a terrorism investigation than in a drug enforcement matter? Are there contrary arguments that can be offered?

4.   There do not seem to be significant differences between provisions of the drug investigation subpoena provision and § 2709 with regard to the scope of the authorization and the fact of whether the request or order is subject to judicial review (though there are significant differences with respect to the substantive limits on judicial review). The most striking difference between §§ 876–877, on the one hand, and 2709 and 3511 on the other hand is that there is no provision providing for secrecy in connection with drug investigation subpoenas issued under §§ 876 and 877. In this connection consider the following notes which are addressed to secrecy requirements under § 215, the so-called library provision, but are relevant as well to secrecy requirements under § 2709 and § 3511.

5.   One of the drafters of the PATRIOT Act, Professor Viet Dinh of Georgetown University's law school and formerly an Assistant Attorney General, was reported to have said: "There is this weird never-neverland, where the ACLU is insisting on an illogically broad reading. . . . Section 215 in and of itself is not objectionable. The thing that makes it objectionable to people is the automatic confidentiality provision." Boston Globe, March 9, 2004, p. E5. Professor Philip B. Heymann of the Harvard Law School was reported to have said, "In the area of access to records, there are always two concerns. One is that the government will use the information for the wrong purpose, particularly a political one. The other concern is . . . people are going to be inhibited in their activities. They will fear that the dirty book they take out will become a government record." N.Y. Times, February 26, 2004, p. A18.

6.   Regarding the criticisms of section 215, consider Professor Dinh's point that the real problem with 215 is the automatic confidentiality provision—that is, that persons who provide an individual's records to the government are prohibited from informing him/her. Is the secrecy mandated by the Act justified? At the time Professor Dinh made his comments, the confidentiality requirement was essentially absolute. Subsequently, 215 (as well as 2709 plus 3511) were amended into their present form, establishing provisions for judicial review by the recipient of the NSL request or 215 order and also providing a standard for continuation of the obligation of secrecy. Is 215 (as well as 2709) more acceptable now, or was the practical effect of these provisions to enable the government still to continue the obligation of confidentiality indefinitely? How do the 2015 revisions, see ch. 5, supra, change the nondisclosure calculus?

Consider the material in the next note. Is this an instance where the government's desire for secrecy, while perhaps useful and necessary in their enforcement efforts, may also make the government's enforcement program and policies more controversial and less acceptable to the public than they deserve to be? The government's penchant for secrecy and its desire to avoid judicial review of the merits of many of its controversial actions are a recurring theme in these materials.

7.   Recall Professor Heymann's point that people are inhibited in their activities by a fear that the government will keep a record of what they do. In connection with this concern, does it matter whether the provision is in fact being utilized? On the other hand, might the government make an argument that a) the evidence that a provision like 215 has not been used supports the contention that the government is not going to abuse this provision, and b) the government needs a provision like this, so that it is available to be used when an appropriate context arises.

8.   On an annual basis, the Office of the Director of National Intelligence releases a "Statistical Transparency Report Regarding Use of National Security Authorities." The report provides details about the number of surveillance orders the agency acted on. The report for calendar year 2016 provided the following details regarding the use of National Security Letters:

> The FBI is statutorily authorized to issue NSLs for specific records (as specified below) only if the information being sought is relevant to a national security investigation. NSLs may be issued for four commonly used types of records:
>
>> 1.   telephone subscriber information, toll records, and other electronic communication transactional records, see 18 U.S.C. § 2709;
>>
>> 2.   consumer-identifying information possessed by consumer8 reporting agencies (names, addresses, places of employment, institutions at which a consumer has maintained an account), see 15 U.S.C. § 1681u;
>>
>> 3.   full credit reports, see 15 U.S.C. § 1681v (only for counterterrorism, not for counterintelligence investigations); and
>>
>> 4.   financial records, see 12 U.S.C. § 3414.
>
> Counting NSLs. Today we are reporting (1) the total number of NSLs issued for all persons, and (2) the total number of requests for information (ROI) contained within those NSLs. When a single NSL contains multiple requests for information, each is considered a "request" and each request must be relevant to the same pending investigation. For example, if the government issued one NSL seeking subscriber information from one provider and that NSL identified three e-mail addresses for the provider to return records, this would count as one NSL issued and three ROIs.

9.   **The Department of Justice's Report on NSLs.** In April 2017, the Department of Justice released its Annual Foreign Intelligence Surveillance Act Report to Congress. That report, which is available online, reports on the number of requests made for certain information concerning different U.S.

persons pursuant to NSL authorities during calendar year 2016. The Department of Justice's report provides the number of individuals subject to an NSL whereas the ODNI's report provides the number of NSLs issued. Because one person may be subject to more than one NSL in an annual period, the number of NSLs issued and the number of persons subject to an NSL differs.

Why we report the number of NSL requests instead of the number of NSL targets. We are reporting the annual number of requests for multiple reasons. First, the FBI's systems are configured to comply with Congressional reporting requirements, which do not require the FBI to track the number of individuals or organizations that are the subject of an NSL. Even if the FBI systems were configured differently, it would still be difficult to identify the number of specific individuals or organizations that are the subjects of NSLs. One reason for this is that the subscriber information returned to the FBI in response to an NSL may identify, for example, one subscriber for three accounts or it may identify different subscribers for each account. In some cases this occurs because the identification information provided by the subscriber to the provider may not be true. For example, a subscriber may use a fictitious name or alias when creating the account. Thus, in many instances, the FBI never identifies the actual subscriber of a facility. In other cases, this occurs because individual subscribers may identify themselves differently for each account (e.g., inclusion of middle name, middle initial, etc.) when creating an account.

We also note that the actual number of individuals or organizations that are the subject of an NSL is different than the number of NSL requests. The FBI often issues NSLs under different legal authorities, e.g., 12 U.S.C. § 3414(a)(5), 15 U.S.C. §§ 1681u(a) and (b), 15 U.S.C. § 1681v, and 18 U.S.C. § 2709, for the same individual or organization. The FBI may also serve multiple NSLs for an individual for multiple facilities (e.g., multiple e-mail accounts, landline telephone numbers and cellular phone numbers). The number of requests, consequently, is significantly larger than the number of individuals or organizations that are the subjects of the NSLs.

NSL Statistics

National Security Letters (NSLs)	CY2013	CY2014	CY2015	CY2016
Total number of NSLs issued	19,212	16,348	12,870	**12,150**
Number of Requests for Information (ROI)	38,832	33,024	48,642	**24,801**

See 50 U.S.C. § 1873(b)(6).

10. In 2007, the Inspector General of the Department of Justice had issued a highly critical report regarding the FBI's use of NSLs, reporting that between 2003 and 2005 more than 140 thousand NSLs were issued, far more than reported in the annual reports. An unclassified version of the OIG Report, formally titled "A Review of the Federal Bureau of Investigation's Use of

National Security Letters," is available at <http://www.usdoj.gov/oig/special/s 0703b/final.pdf>, last visited Oct. 20, 2008. An unclassified version of a follow-up 2008 OIG Report, formally titled "A Review of the FBI's Use of National Security Letters: Assessment of Corrective Actions and Examination of NSL Usage in 2006," is available at <http://www.usdoj.gov/oig/special/s0803b/final. pdf>, last visited Oct. 20, 2008. As a result of these and other criticisms in the Inspector General's report, a new system of tracking and documents NSLs was instituted which was first used in 2008. See 2009 WL 1522926, 77 USLW 2726 (2009)

11. In 2010, the General Counsel of the FBI testified before a subcommittee of the House Judiciary Committee regarding the aftermath and follow-up of the 2007 Inspector General's report. Excerpts from this testimony appear below:

> Testimony of Valerie E. Caproni, General Counsel, FBI, before the
> Subcommittee on the Constitution, Civil Rights and Civil
> Liberties, House Judiciary Committee, April 14, 2010

. . .

Exigent Letters

In 2007, the OIG found that one unit at FBI Headquarters had issued over 0700 exigent letters requesting toll billing records for various telephone numbers. All of the letters stated that there were exigent circumstances but did not describe the exigency. In fact, sometimes there was no emergency. Although ECPA's emergency disclosure provision found at 18 U.S.C. § 2702(c)(4) (discussed in more detail below) does not require the FBI to provide any legal process to obtain records voluntarily from a telephone company in order to respond to a qualifying emergency, many of the letters stated that federal grand jury subpoenas had been requested for the records. In fact, no such request for grand jury subpoenas had been made, and no one intended that such a request would be made. Similarly, other exigent letters promised NSLs, which—though also legally unnecessary if there is a qualifying emergency—the agents and analysts, in fact, intended would be sent. Unfortunately, the FBI did not keep adequate records reflecting the nature of the emergencies, the telephone numbers for which records were sought, and whether the promised future process—whether legally required or not—was ever actually issued.

It should be emphasized, however, that exigent letters were not—and were never intended to be—NSLs. Rather, they appear to have been a sort of "place-holder," borne out of a misunderstanding of the import of the USA Patriot Act's amendments to ECPA. For reasons lost in the fog of history—but no doubt partially the result of the intense pace of activity in the months following the 9/11 attacks—the FBI did not adequately educate our workforce that Congress had provided a clear mechanism to obtain records in emergency situations. Although guidance was eventually provided in August 2005, the employees who had been using exigent letters for several years simply did not recognize the applicability of that guidance to their situation. In its most recent report on the issue, the OIG confirmed what the FBI acknowledged to Congress and the public in 2007: Exigent letters were sometimes used when there was no emergency and the FBI had inadequate internal controls to ensure that the promised legal process was provided. The 2010 report confirmed that these practices resulted in the FBI requesting telephone toll billing records associated with approximately 4,400 telephone numbers between 2003 and 2006.

In response to the OIG's 2007 report, in March 2007 the FBI formally barred the use of exigent letters to obtain telephone records and established detailed policies for obtaining toll billing records during an emergency situation. Since that time, employees who need to obtain ECPA-protected records on an emergency basis must do so in accordance with 18 U.S.C. § 2702. Section 2702(c)(4), which permits a carrier to provide information regarding its customers to the government "if the provider, in good faith, believes that an emergency involving danger of death or serious physical injury to any person requires disclosure without delay of information relating to the emergency." In addition to providing guidance on Section 2702 itself, we established approval and documentation requirements for requests made under this provision. As promised by Director Mueller and me in our testimony following the OIG's first report and by me in repeated briefings of congressional staff, beginning in 2007, the FBI commenced an effort to ensure that we retained only exigent letter-related telephone records for which we had a lawful basis. To that end, we dedicated significant resources to researching all of the numbers that appeared on known exigent letters and on the so-called "blanket NSLs" (discussed in more detail below). The reconciliation project team conducted a complete review, even though the disclosure of approximately half of the records at issue was not forbidden by ECPA and/or was connected to a clear emergency situation. The reconciliation project team used a conservative approach: they initially retained records for which already-existing legal process (usually an NSL or grand jury subpoena) was located. If no legal process was found, then new "corrective" NSLs were issued where ECPA allowed us to do so (i.e., the national security investigation to which the telephone records were relevant was still pending). In fact, we located or issued legal process for the overwhelming majority of the 4,400 telephone numbers. If we found no previously existing legal process and we could not legally issue new process (e.g., the case to which the records were relevant had since been closed), we would only then consider whether emergency circumstances existed at the time we requested the records. As to that group of telephone numbers, if we could not conclude that there had, in fact, been an emergency that would have qualified under section 2702, we purged the telephone records from our files and databases. These actions were fully briefed to the FBI's congressional oversight committees last year, and we appreciate the finding of the OIG that our "approach to determine which records to retain and which to purge was reasonable" (Report at 276). We are currently developing an automated system—similar in concept to the NSL system that we have briefed and demonstrated to your staffs—to generate and document emergency disclosure requests pursuant to Section 2702. Our experience with the NSL system is that it has greatly reduced non-substantive errors in NSLs, and we believe that an automated Section 2702 system would do the same. I would now like to address a few specific matters raised by the OIG's 2010 report.

Blanket NSLs The OIG's 2010 report discusses in detail 11 so-called "blanket NSLs." These blanket NSLs were not discussed with an FBI attorney prior to their preparation nor reviewed by an FBI attorney prior to their issuance. We continue to believe—as we briefed this committee in 2007—that the blanket NSLs were a good-faith but ill-conceived attempt by the Counterterrorism Division to address the backlog of numbers for which the FBI believed it had unfulfilled obligations to provide legal process as they had promised through exigent letters. The common problem with all of the blanket NSLs was that there was no electronic communication (EC) prepared describing how the information sought by the NSL was relevant to a national security investigation. Under FBI policy, such ECs are required for all NSLs. Because there was no EC, there was no documentation that connected the telephone numbers listed on the blanket NSLs to specific, pending national security investigations. As discussed above, following the 2007 report, the FBI examined each telephone number included on a blanket NSLs to determine whether there was a legal basis to retain any records obtained for the number. If we could not confirm a legal basis for retention, we purged any records we had for the number.

As noted, none of the blanket NSLs was reviewed by an FBI attorney. In March 2007, the FBI changed its policy to require attorney approval before an NSL may be issued. That policy requirement is enforced through the NSL system that automatically routes all NSLs though an attorney prior to issuance.

Other Informal Requests In addition to exigent letters and blanket NSLs, the 2010 report discusses other informal means by which the FBI Headquarters unit obtained information regarding telephone numbers. "Quick peeks" and "sneak peeks" are the terms used in the report to describe an FBI employee asking a telephone company employee to determine whether records for a telephone number existed, not what those records actually contained.

In a similar type of request, FBI employees would ask whether there was "calling activity" associated with a particular number (i.e., whether the particular telephone number was being used). Such information was conveyed to the FBI for 39 telephone numbers.

As the OIG noted, the mere existence of records or the fact that there is calling activity associated with a particular telephone number is protected by ECPA. Accordingly, we made clear in March 2007 that no telephone records may be acquired in advance of legal process, unless there is an emergency situation under Section 2702 and the emergency request procedures are followed. In addition, our Domestic Investigation Operational Guidelines (DIOG), which compiled all FBI operational policy into one document, provides an exclusive list of acceptable methods for obtaining telephone toll records.

Reporter Records The OIG's 2010 report describes three situations in which the FBI might have come into contact with protected telephone toll information of reporters. In fact, in only one case were any reporter's toll records actually provided to the FBI, and that occurred over five years ago. In that one instance, neither the substantive case agent nor any member of the investigative or prosecutorial team was aware that records had been obtained, and the FBI made no use of them. Furthermore, the only FBI employees who ever accessed the records were the analyst who initially uploaded them to our telephone records databases and an analyst involved in the exigent letter reconciliation project described above. When we learned in 2008 that we had such records, we purged them from our telephone records databases.

Although we did not use the records, Department of Justice (DOJ) regulations require attorney general approval before the issuance of grand jury subpoenas seeking toll billing records of members of the media. While no grand jury subpoena was issued in this instance, such legal process would have been the appropriate way, if at all, to obtain the records at issue given the nature of the investigation. Accordingly, when we learned that we had reporters' toll records without advance attorney general approval, we notified the reporters that their toll records had been obtained, and the Director personally called the editors of the newspapers to apologize.

Although this appears to have been an isolated incident, we issued guidance in 2008 making clear the requirements for obtaining toll records of members of the media. The DIOG similarly discusses the steps required to seek such records.

. . .

OLC Opinion

The OIG's 2010 report discusses a January 8, 2010 opinion issued by the Department of Justice's Office of Legal Counsel (OLC), which concluded that ECPA does not forbid electronic communications service providers, in certain circumstances, from disclosing certain call detail records to the FBI on a voluntary basis without legal process or a qualifying emergency under Section 2702. Many members of Congress have asked questions about this OLC opinion, which is classified. It is my understanding that this opinion has been shared with our oversight committees, including this committee, at the appropriate security level. Because of the classified nature of the OLC opinion, I cannot address it in this forum, but am available to discuss it in a secure setting. I can, however, state that the OLC opinion did not in any way factor into the FBI's flawed practice of using exigent letters between 2003 and 2006 nor did it affect in any way the records-retention decisions made by the FBI as part of the reconciliation project discussed above.

Accountability

The 2010 report notes that the OIG provided its findings to the Department of Justice's Public Integrity Section. The Public Integrity Section declined prosecution of any individuals relating to the exigent letters matter. Now that the OIG's report is complete, the FBI's Office of Professional Responsibility will have an opportunity to review the OIG's findings and determine whether any discipline of any employee is appropriate.

Conclusion

Finally, the FBI appreciates the 2010 report's recognition that FBI employees involved in this matter were attempting to advance legitimate FBI investigations, and that FBI personnel "typically requested the telephone records to pursue [their] critical counterterrorism mission" (Report at 214).

This does not excuse our failure to have in place appropriate internal controls, but it places the practices of that one FBI Headquarters unit in context: "Some of the exigent letters and other improper practices [described] in this report were used to obtain telephone records that the FBI used to evaluate some of the most serious terrorist threats posed to the United States in the last few years"

These employees were and many remain on the front lines of our fight against terrorists. At the same time, as Director Mueller has repeatedly acknowledged, we can only achieve our mission of keeping the country safe if we are trusted by all.

11.   See also In re National Security Letter, 2013 WL 1095417 (N.D. Cal.) where a district judge had also ruled that § 2709(c) and 3511(b)(2) and (b3) are

unconstitutional on a number of grounds. In the course of his opinion the district court also reported:

> Another significant factor weighs in favor of this Court resolving the facial challenge: despite evidence demonstrating that tens of thousands of NSLs are issued each year—and by the government's own estimate, 97% of them may come with a nondisclosure order— only a handful of challenges to the NSL provisions have been brought. Compare DOJ Office of Inspector General "A Review of the Federal Bureau of Investigation's Use of National Security Letters," March 2007 at 120 <http://www.usdoj.gov/oig/special/s0703b/final.pdf> (noting that in 2005, more than 47,000 NSL requests were issued) with Doe v. Gonzales, 500 F.Supp.2d 379, 405 (S.D.N.Y.2007) (finding as of 2007 that only two challenges have been made in federal court since the original enactment of the NSL statute).

CHAPTER 7

INTERROGATION AND RENDITION

∎ ∎ ∎

A. INTRODUCTION

This chapter deals with issues relating to the interrogation of terrorist suspects since September 11, 2001, during the administrations of three Presidents, George W. Bush, Barack H. Obama and Donald Trump. With respect to the last-mentioned, as of this writing, his administration is still within its first year; accordingly, those materials are based only on the actions known to have already been taken, and the portents that are currently available. The chapter also addresses issues relating to the transfer of terrorism suspects from one jurisdiction to another, through legal procedures or extra-legally. When the transfer or rendition of suspects is done extra-legally, the practice is variously labeled "extraordinary rendition," or "irregular rendition," and we mostly use the latter terminology here.

The chapter begins with a treatment of the torture controversy, that is, the issues that arose out of the use of extreme methods of interrogation under the Bush administration in the wake of the 9/11 attacks, and carries the subject through the reactive actions subsequently taken in the Obama administration and, up to this time, in the Trump administration. Accordingly, the three administrations have been used as an organizing principle for this section of the chapter. This material is of more than historical interest since there are some indications that President Trump may try to return to some of the Bush era practices. But even if its value is only historical, it is important history from which much can be learned.

The torture controversy deals with issues that arise out of the interrogation of terrorism suspects typically to obtain intelligence, not necessarily to use the information in criminal prosecutions. The more traditional legal subjects that arise out of interrogation of suspects are all based on the premise that the resulting evidence will be used in the courtroom—issues of admissibility as evidence. In subsequent subsections in this chapter, a number of different rules governing the admissibility of confessions are canvassed, including, for example, whether Miranda warning are required for interrogations that take place abroad; the extent to which these requirements vary depending on the degree of participation of U.S. agents in conducting the interrogation; application of the Quarles "public safety" exception to the Miranda warning/waiver requirements in a terrorism context; the promulgation of new FBI interrogation guidelines in reliance on the Quarles doctrine; how, assuming prosecution in a federal civilian court, the court will apply constitutional coerced confession doctrine, or stating the issue another way, how that doctrine comports with the Army Field Manual (AFM) interrogation rules; the standards applied by U.S. courts where a confession is obtained by non-U.S. agents, using allegedly coercive interrogation techniques; and finally, the use of a two-step approach to avoid the full impact of the Miranda warning/waiver doctrine.

In subsection C of this chapter, the subject of extraordinary, that is, irregular rendition, is addressed. Other methods of transfer of individuals from one country to another, such as extradition, are first considered. Government policies and opinions bearing on the legal issues and remedies available when persons are taken against their will from one country to another are reviewed. Case law involving lawsuits against the government, government officials and private companies that allegedly assisted in implementing irregular rendition is presented for discussion, as is a description of foreign prosecution of U.S. officials and agents for having engaged in irregular rendition in the foreign country.

No effort is made to treat all of these related subjects comprehensively, but rather the focus is on the special rules, if any, applicable in terrorism matters. It is assumed that students have the basic knowledge provided by a constitutional criminal procedure course, but because some students may lack this grounding, some background is provided at various points in the materials of the chapter.

Both the interrogation and rendition topics could have been placed in Part Two of book since they frequently involve, to one extent or another, the use of the military arm of the government. In effect, they lie astride the border between civilian and military process. We have chosen to treat them here, but we shall return briefly to the subject in Part Two when we address rules of admissibility in military commission trials.

B. INTERROGATION PRIMARILY TO OBTAIN TERRORISM-RELATED INTELLIGENCE: THE TORTURE CONTROVERSY

One cannot address the subject of interrogation in relation to terrorism without dealing with the subject of extreme methods of interrogation utilized by the Bush administration in the immediate aftermath of 9/11 terrorist attacks. This section deals with the many different aspects of the practices engaged in during that period and resulting controversy and issues that have continued to simmer and, occasionally, boil, through the two administrations that followed and have continued into the present.

1. THE BUSH YEARS

a. Background—The Convention Against Torture and Subsequent Legislation

In 2003 and 2004, reports and pictures of abusive treatment of prisoners in Iraq and reports of some abuse of prisoners in Guantanamo and abusive interrogation of individuals who had been transferred to "black sites" in foreign countries through extraordinary rendition made headlines and stirred up enormous controversy and soul-searching. There was a question whether abusive treatment had been authorized, condoned or fostered by actions or statements of the administration. Questions also surfaced as to the legality of using extreme methods of interrogation—questions which had been addressed internally and through originally non-public memoranda by officials in the Bush White House and in the Departments of Defense, Justice and the State Department.

The United States is a party to the Convention against Torture and Other Cruel, Inhuman and Degrading Treatment or Punishment. The Convention which went into force with respect to the United States on November 20, 1994 is implemented by federal statute in 18 U.S.C. §§ 2340 and 2340A. The signing and ratifying of the Convention against Torture is subject to a number of reservations and understandings. Thus, the Senate's advice and consent is subject to the following understanding:

> The United States understands that, in order to constitute torture, an act must be specifically intended to inflict severe physical or mental pain or suffering and that mental pain or suffering refers to prolonged mental harm caused by or resulting from: (1) the intentional infliction or threatened infliction of severe physical pain or suffering; (2) the administration or application, or threatened administration or application, of mind altering substances or other procedures calculated to disrupt profoundly the senses or the personality; (3) the threat of imminent death; or (4) the threat that another person will imminently be subjected to death, severe physical pain or suffering, or the administration or application of mind altering substances or other procedures calculated to disrupt profoundly the senses or personality.

The definition of torture adopted by the Congress in 18 U.S.C. § 2340 largely tracks the definition of torture in the U.S. understanding attached to the Torture Convention.

Title 18, U.S.C.

§ 2340. As used in this chapter—

(1) "torture" means an act committed by a person acting under the color of law specifically intended to inflict severe physical or mental pain or suffering (other than pain or suffering incidental to lawful sanctions) upon another person within his custody or physical control;

(2) "severe mental pain or suffering" means the prolonged mental harm caused by or resulting from—

(A) the intentional infliction or threatened infliction of severe physical pain or suffering;

(B) the administration or application, or threatened administration or application, of mind-altering substances or other procedures calculated to disrupt profoundly the senses or the personality;

(C) the threat of imminent death; or

(D) the threat that another person will imminently be subjected to death, severe physical pain or suffering, or the administration or application of mind-altering substances or other procedures calculated to disrupt profoundly the senses or personality; and

(3) "United States" means the several States of the United States, the District of Columbia, and the commonwealths, territories, and possessions of the United States.

§ 2340A.   Torture

(a) Offense.—Whoever outside the United States commits or attempts to commit torture shall be fined under this title or imprisoned not more than 20 years, or both, and if death results to any person from conduct prohibited by this subsection, shall be punished by death or imprisoned for any term of years or for life.

(b) Jurisdiction.—There is jurisdiction over the activity prohibited in subsection (a) if—

(1) the alleged offender is a national of the United States; or

(2) the alleged offender is present in the United States, irrespective of the nationality of the victim or alleged offender.

(c) Conspiracy.—A person who conspires to commit an offense under this section shall be subject to the same penalties (other than the penalty of death) as the penalties prescribed for the offense, the commission of which was the object of the conspiracy.

Further, the Convention not only bans torture but also prohibits "cruel, inhuman or degrading treatment or punishment." With respect to this latter prohibition, the Senate's advice and consent is subject to the following reservation: That the United States considers itself bound by the obligation under Article 16 to prevent "cruel, inhuman or degrading treatment or punishment," only insofar as the term "cruel, inhuman or degrading treatment or punishment" means the cruel, unusual and inhumane treatment or punishment prohibited by the Fifth, Eighth, and/or Fourteenth Amendments to the Constitution of the United States.

Whereas in the wake of the ratification of the Convention, the U.S. in 1994, enacted statutory provisions criminalizing torture, legislation prohibiting cruel, inhuman or degrading treatment by U.S. officials was not passed until 2005, see infra, and this latter statute is not in the form of a criminal provision. What can viewed as follow-up legislation dealing with rules governing interrogation is contained in the National Defense Authorization bill of 2016. See infra, the Obama years. As it turned out, a distinction between torture, on the one hand, and cruel, inhuman, or degrading treatment, on the other hand, was a key element in the legal strategy of the Bush administration relating to the use of extreme methods of interrogation in the wake of the 9/11 attacks.

b. Memoranda and Statements of Officials in the Bush Administration Regarding the Legality of Enhanced Methods of Interrogation

Beginning in the early fall, 2002, within the Bush administration, the treatment of the prisoners seized in Afghanistan and in Iraq and what techniques could be used in interrogating them were the subject of a series of high level memoranda in the Departments of Justice and Defense:

1) In a memorandum dated August 1, 2002 (usually referred to as the Bybee memorandum), Memorandum from Jay S. Bybee, Department of Justice, Office of Legal Counsel to Alberto R. Gonzales, Counsel to the President, Standards of Conduct for Interrogation under 18 U.S.C. §§ 2340–2340A (Aug. 1, 2002), the Office of Legal Counsel in the Department of Justice responded to a request from Alberto R. Gonzales, then Counsel to the President and later, Attorney General, to comment on the definition of torture under § 2340, Title 18, U.S.C. Pertinent conclusions in this memorandum included the following:

> We conclude that for an act to constitute torture as defined in Section 2340, it must inflict pain that is difficult to endure. Physical pain amounting to torture must be equivalent in intensity to the pain accompanying serious physical injury, such as organ failure, impairment of bodily function, or even death. For purely mental pain or suffering to amount to torture under

Section 2340, it must result in significant psychological harm of significant duration, e.g., lasting for months or even years. We conclude that the mental harm also must result from one of the predicate acts listed in the statute, namely: threats of imminent death; threats of infliction of the kind of pain that would amount to physical torture; infliction of such physical pain as a means of psychological torture; use of drugs or other procedures designed to deeply disrupt the senses, or fundamentally alter an individual's personality; or threatening to do any of these things to a third party. . . . We conclude that the statute, taken as a whole makes plain that it prohibits only extreme acts.

2)   In the Department of Defense, an October 11, 2002 Legal Brief on Proposed Counter-Resistance Strategies stated: "To ensure the security of the United States and its Allies, more aggressive interrogation techniques than the ones presently used, such as the methods proposed in the attached recommendation, may be required in order to obtain information from detainees that are resisting interrogation efforts and are suspected of having significant information essential to national security." The Brief went on to discuss the legal issues relating to interrogation techniques under international and domestic law and characterized the legality of certain techniques as follows:

With regard to Category II methods, the use of stress positions such as the proposed standing for four hours, the use of isolation for up to thirty days, and interrogating the detainee in an environment other than the standard interrogation booth are all legally permissible so long as no severe physical pain is inflicted and prolonged mental harm intended, and because there is a legitimate governmental objective in obtaining the information necessary. . . .

The deprivation of light and auditory stimuli, the placement of a hood over the detainee's head during transportation and questioning, and the use of 20 hour interrogations are all legally permissible so long as there is an important governmental objective. . . .

With respect to the Category III advanced counter-resistance strategies, the use of scenarios designed to convince the detainee that death or severely painful consequences are imminent is not illegal for the same aforementioned reasons that there is a compelling governmental interest and it is not done intentionally to cause prolonged harm. However, caution should be utilized with this technique because the torture statute specifically mentions making death threats as an example of inflicting mental pain and suffering. Exposure to cold weather or water is permissible with appropriate medical monitoring. The use of a wet towel to induce the misperception of suffocation would be permissible if not done with the specific intent to cause prolonged mental harm, and absent medical evidence that it would. . . .

3) In an action memo, dated November 27, 2002, from William J. Haynes II, General Counsel of the Defense Department to the Secretary of Defense, it was recommended that only Category I and II techniques be used to aid in interrogating detainees at Guantanamo Bay, with the addition of one of the techniques in the more aggressive Category III, namely, "use of mild, non-injurious physical contact such as grabbing, poking in the chest with the finger, and light pushing." The recommendation was approved by Secretary Rumsfeld on December 2, 2002, but he also attached a handwritten note that stated: "However, I stand for 8–10 hours a day. Why is standing limited to 4 hours?"

4) On January 15, 2003, Secretary of Defense Rumsfeld sent a memo rescinding the approval of Category I and II techniques (along with the thumb poking Category III technique). The memo also indicated that specific requests to use I or II techniques should be forwarded to him, that humane treatment of detainees should continue regardless of the techniques used, and that an attached memo to the General Counsel was setting in motion a study to be completed in 15 days.

5) In a Draft Pentagon Working Group Report on Detainee Interrogations in the Global War on Terrorism, dated March 6, 2003, originally revealed in an exclusive story by Wall Street Journal reporter Jesse Bravin, it was stated that "the Torture Convention prohibits torture only as defined in the U.S. Understanding, and prohibits "cruel, inhuman, and degrading treatment and punishment" only to the extent of the U.S. Reservation relating to the U.S. Constitution." The Report also extensively discussed the fact that criminal liability could not be imposed under § 2340A, absent specific intent to inflict severe pain.

6) On December 30, 2004, a memorandum was made public that had been sent earlier from the Acting Assistant Attorney General for the Office of Legal Counsel to Deputy Attorney General James B. Comey. See Memorandum from Daniel Levin, Acting Asst. Att'y Gen., to James B. Comey, Deputy Att'y Gen., Legal Standards Applicable Under 18 U.S.C. §§ 2340–2340A (Dec. 30, 2004). The memorandum included the following statements:

> Torture is abhorrent both to American law and values and to international norms. . . .

> Questions have since been raised, both by this Office and by others, about the appropriateness and relevance of the non-statutory discussion in the August 2002 Memorandum [ed. See 1) above], and also about various aspects of the statutory analysis,

in particular the statement that "severe" pain under the statute was limited to pain "equivalent in intensity to the pain accompanying serious physical injury, such as organ failure, impairment of bodily function, or even death." . . .

This Memorandum supersedes the August 2002 Memorandum in its entirety. Because the discussion in that memorandum concerning the President's Commander-in-Chief power and the potential defenses to liability was—and remains— unnecessary, it has been eliminated from the analysis that follows. Consideration of the bounds of any such authority would be inconsistent with the President's unequivocal directive that United States personnel not engage in torture.

7)   As indicated in 6). above, the President had issued a directive that U.S. personnel not engage in torture. Of course, the application of the prohibition depended on how torture was defined.

8)   Subsequently, on April 16, 2009, the Department of Justice released the four legal memoranda prepared in 2002 and in 2005, directed to John Rizzo, General Counsel of the CIA. These were the memoranda designed to provide legal advice to the CIA with regard to the use of various interrogation techniques in questioning high value al Qaeda detainees. Each of the memoranda had examined the use of specific techniques—the memos went into excruciating detail on a variety of different techniques (reaching conclusions such as, e.g., "The waterboard does not . . . inflict 'severe pain or suffering,' " Bybee Memo to Rizzo, Aug. 1, 2002).

In fact, there had been earlier leaks or release of other memoranda including perhaps the most controversial, the so-called Bybee Memorandum, which has been described in 1) above.

The official release of these four memoranda, all at once, ignited a firestorm of controversy in the media that continued for some time—about extremely harsh interrogation practices under the Bush administration and the lawyers and other officials involved in approving and authorizing them. Much attention focused on the practice of waterboarding—inducing in the person being interrogated a sense of drowning and suffocation by pouring water over the nose and mouth when in a reclined position. Information was disclosed that waterboarding had been used to obtain information from three of the "high value" detainees and that this technique had been used on some of them a great many times. News reports in 2007, however, had indicated that the Director of the CIA had in the previous year taken waterboarding off the list of techniques approved for use. It is noteworthy that throughout all of this period, as far as can be determined, officials of the Bush administration never stated that waterboarding was torture, or that during their administration detained persons had been tortured.

It seems clear that the afore-listed memoranda that were prepared during this period were designed to: a) provide some guidance to the interrogators in the field as to methods that they could use; and b) to provide legal advice intended to protect the agents from being subsequently prosecuted for having engaged in torture. Thus, some of the memoranda set the threshold for torture very high so that extreme methods of interrogation were being authorized as not involving torture. In this connection, a distinction was thus drawn between torture (criminal conduct) and cruel, inhuman or degrading treatment (not a basis for criminal prosecution),

c. A Comment on the Standards of Torture and Cruel, Inhuman or Degrading Treatment

See Christian M. De Vos, Mind, the Gap: Purpose, Pain, and the Difference between Torture and Inhuman Treatment, 14 No. 2 Hum. Rts. Brief 4 (2007):

> Condemnation of torture is universal and its prohibition forms not only part of customary international law, but has joined that narrow category of crimes so egregious as to demand universal criminal jurisdiction. Yet despite the considerable progress made towards outlawing torture, there is a frequent and growing tendency to circumvent the law against it by drawing ever finer distinctions between its depravities and the "lesser" acts of what is commonly known as cruel, inhuman, or degrading treatment (CIDT), which is also prohibited but not criminalized as extensively as torture. Perhaps most emblematic of such circumvention has been the Bush administration's policies toward torture and inhuman treatment in the wake of its putative "War on Terror," which this article adopts as its case study. In so doing, it examines how the now infamous torture memos produced by the Department of Justice's Office of Legal Counsel exploited the "gap" between torture and CIDT by focusing almost exclusively on the severity of treatment and the degree of pain suffered . . .: it ignores important jurisprudential developments emphasizing the principal distinction between the two. Even more troubling, however, is the perverted effect this approach has had on debates over torture itself, making it too often the centerpiece of discussion at the cost of "lesser," but more common abuses, such as CIDT.

> . . .

> A new assault on the legal regime prohibiting torture and inhuman treatment began shortly after September 11, 2001, when the "United States and an increasing number of other

governments ... adopted a legal position which, while acknowledging the absolute nature of the prohibition on torture, [put] the absolute nature of the prohibition on CIDT in question." Most emblematic of this attempt was the authoring of a 2002 Department of Justice memorandum (Bybee Memo) by the Office of Legal Counsel for Alberto Gonzales, then Counsel to President Bush and now U.S. Attorney General. Principally authored by Deputy Assistant Attorney General John Yoo, the Bybee Memo provided a detailed legal analysis of Section 2340 of the United States Criminal Code, which was implemented as part of U.S. obligations to criminalize torture after ratifying CAT [Convention against Torture] in 1992. Section 2340A makes it a criminal offense for any persons outside of the U.S. to commit (or attempt to commit) an act of torture, while § 2340, tracking the language of Article 1 of CAT, defines such an act as one "committed by a person acting under the color of law specifically intended to inflict severe physical or mental pain or suffering (other than pain or suffering that is incidental to lawful sanctions) upon another person within his custody or physical control." Significantly, the statutes do not criminalize inhuman treatment. Rather, it was the U.S. position prior to ratifying CAT that the "vagueness of the phrase [cruel, inhuman, and degrading] could not be construed to bar acts not prohibited by the U.S. Constitution." As a result, the government declared that it only considered itself bound by the obligation to prevent CIDT "insofar as the term ... means the cruel, unusual, and inhumane treatment or punishment prohibited by the Fifth, Eighth, and/or Fourteenth Amendments."

While there is much to criticize in the Bybee Memo, especially noteworthy is the extremely high threshold for torture it set forth, defined as:

> [I]ntense pain or suffering of the kind that is equivalent to the pain that would be associated with serious physical injury so severe that death, organ failure, or permanent damage resulting in a loss of significant body function will likely result.

Additionally, with respect to psychological torture, the memo opined that:

> Severe mental pain requires suffering not just at the moment of infliction but it also requires lasting psychological harm, such as seen in mental disorders like post-traumatic stress disorder ... Because the acts inflicting torture are extreme, there is a significant range of acts that might

constitute cruel, inhuman, or degrading treatment or punishment but fail to rise to the level of torture.

Essentially, the Bybee Memo stood for the proposition that the "key statutory phrase in the definition of torture" is whether it causes severe pain or suffering.

This rationale, in turn, served as the legal basis for the now infamous interrogation techniques applied to suspected terrorists at the Guantanamo Bay facilities and, undoubtedly, in Afghanistan and Iraq as well. Indeed, by December 2002, former Defense Secretary Donald Rumsfeld had authorized the use of aggressive interrogation techniques (a menu of nineteen "counter-resistance techniques," in the administration's parlance) that tested the very limits of the Bybee Memo, including the use of stress positions for up to four hours, interrogations for up to twenty hours, solitary detention for up to thirty days, forced grooming, removal of all comfort items (including the Koran and toilet paper), hooding, the removal of clothing, forced shaving of facial hair, auditory/environmental manipulation, and "mild non-injurious physical contact."

The extent of the abuse perpetuated by these techniques is still unknown, but will certainly continue to be scrutinized . . . .Indeed, the findings of the U.S. government itself underscore the primacy the Bybee Memo attached to severity as a means of distinguishing between torture and inhuman treatment. An official investigation into the case of Mohammed al-Qahtani, suspected of being the "20th hijacker" in the September 11th attacks, is illustrative. In response to concerns raised by FBI agents as to the interrogation techniques used on al-Qahtani, military investigators began reviewing his case and found that:

> [D]etainee No. 063 was forced to wear a bra. He had a thong placed on his head. He was massaged by a female interrogator who straddled him like a lap dancer. He was told that his mother and sisters were whores. He was told that other detainees knew he was gay. He was forced to dance with a male interrogator. He was strip-searched in front of women. He was led on a leash and forced to perform dog tricks. He was doused with water. He was prevented from praying. He was forced to watch as an interrogator squatted over the Koran.

In July 2005, the Army's internal investigation determined that Major General Geoffrey Miller—then commander of the detention facilities at Guantanamo (and later Iraq's Abu Ghraib prison)—had failed to adequately monitor the interrogation of al-

Qahtani but determined that "technically, no torture occurred." Similarly, then Secretary of Defense Donald Rumsfeld stated prior to the Army's investigation, "My impression is that what has been charged thus far is abuse, which I believe technically is different from torture . . . I don't know if . . . it is correct to say . . . that torture has taken place, or that there's been a conviction for torture. And therefore I'm not going to address the torture word."

It took two years and the public horror of Abu Ghraib for the Bybee Memo, which only came to light after being leaked to the press, to be formally withdrawn and replaced with a new memorandum prepared by Acting Assistant Attorney General Daniel Levin (Levin Memo). The Levin Memo asserts that it "supersedes the August 2002 Memorandum in its entirety" and repudiates some of the more extreme aspects of the Bybee Memo's interpretation of torture. Unfortunately, however, it retains the Bybee Memo's core distinction between torture and CIDT, i.e., that the decisive criterion for distinguishing between the two is the severity of pain or suffering inflicted on a victim. The memo notes, in part, that "[d]rawing distinctions among gradations of pain (for example, severe, mild, moderate, substantial, extreme, intense, excruciating, or agonizing) is obviously not an easy task" but such distinctions nevertheless form the heart of its analysis. Notably, this approach remains significantly out of step with international law and the later jurisprudence of both the European Court and the Committee against Torture.

Note that an effort was made to draw a sharp legal distinction between torture and cruel, inhuman or degrading treatment with the enactment of the Military Commissions Act of 2006. The relevant provisions are discussed infra, Chapter 11.

d. Can Torture Ever Be: a) Justified; b) Lawful? The Ticking Bomb Debate

Consider the following views. What factors need to be taken into account or need to be known in choosing among them?

1) "I am generally against torture as a normative matter, and I would like to see its use minimized. . . . I think that if we ever confronted an actual case of imminent mass terrorism that could be prevented by the infliction of torture, we would use torture (even lethal torture). . . .

". . . I pose the issue as follows: If torture is in fact being and/or would in fact be used in an actual ticking bomb mass terrorism case, would it be normatively better or worse to have such torture regulated by some kind of warrant. . . ." See Alan M.

Dershowitz, The Torture Warrant: A Response to Professor Strauss, 48 N.Y. L. Sch. L.Rev. 275 (2003).

2) "Dershowitz believes that the occasions for the use of torture should be regularized—by requiring a judicial warrant. . . . But he overlooks an argument for leaving such things to executive discretion. If rules are promulgated permitting torture in defined circumstances, some officials are bound to want to explore the outer bounds of the rules. Better to leave in place the formal and customary prohibitions, but with the understanding that that they will not be enforced in extreme circumstances." Richard A. Posner, The Best Offense, The New Republic, Sept. 2, 2002, 28, quoted in Dershowitz, op. cit. supra 1) at 279.

3) "We would articulate the Posner approach somewhat differently and with a slightly different rationale. Better to leave in place the customary prohibitions which make torture a crime, thus warning the police that if they torture they are opening themselves up to criminal penalties. Despite that warning, in the most extreme emergency, the police are highly likely to disregard the warning and do what they think is necessary, taking the risk of criminal sanctions later. This approach helps to ensure that the narrowest possible interpretation will be given to the emergency that leads the police to engage in torture, that is, where the police instinct for self-preservation overcomes their fear of criminal sanctions that might be imposed subsequently." Norman Abrams, Terrorism Prosecutions in Federal Court: Exceptions to Constitutional Evidence Rules and the Development of a Cabined Exception for Coerced Confessions, 4 Nat. Security L. J. 58, n. 122 (2012).

e. The Detainee Treatment Act of 2005

In December, 2005, the Detainee Treatment Act of 2005 was passed by the House of Representatives and the Senate and signed into law by President Bush. Inter alia, it included an amendment proposed by Senator John McCain. This was the first piece of federal legislation in the post-9/11 period to attempt to regulate the processes of interrogation of terrorists. Subsequently, the Military Commission Acts of 2006 and 2009, a Presidential Executive Order (during the administration of President Obama) and additional legislation, the NDAA of 2016, were promulgated, all containing provisions relating to interrogation and statements obtained therefrom. These additional pieces of legislation are all either described or reproduced infra, this volume. When your reach these materials, be prepared to compare these various legislative (or quasi-legislative) approaches to interrogation issues.

SEC. 1001. SHORT TITLE.

This title may be cited as the 'Detainee Treatment Act of 2005'.

SEC. 1002. UNIFORM STANDARDS FOR THE INTERROGATION OF PERSONS UNDER THE DETENTION OF THE DEPARTMENT OF DEFENSE.

(a) In General—No person in the custody or under the effective control of the Department of Defense or under detention in a Department of Defense facility shall be subject to any treatment or technique of interrogation not authorized by and listed in the United States Army Field Manual on Intelligence Interrogation.

(b) Applicability—Subsection (a) shall not apply with respect to any person in the custody or under the effective control of the Department of Defense pursuant to a criminal law or immigration law of the United States.

(c) Construction—Nothing in this section shall be construed to affect the rights under the United States Constitution of any person in the custody or under the physical jurisdiction of the United States.

SEC. 1003. PROHIBITION ON CRUEL, INHUMAN, OR DEGRADING TREATMENT OR PUNISHMENT OF PERSONS UNDER CUSTODY OR CONTROL OF THE UNITED STATES GOVERNMENT.

(a) In General—No individual in the custody or under the physical control of the United States Government, regardless of nationality or physical location, shall be subject to cruel, inhuman, or degrading treatment or punishment.

(b) Construction—Nothing in this section shall be construed to impose any geographical limitation on the applicability of the prohibition against cruel, inhuman, or degrading treatment or punishment under this section.

(c) Limitation on Supersedure—The provisions of this section shall not be superseded, except by a provision of law enacted after the date of the enactment of this Act which specifically repeals, modifies, or supersedes the provisions of this section.

(d) Cruel, Inhuman, or Degrading Treatment or Punishment Defined—In this section, the term 'cruel, inhuman, or degrading treatment or punishment' means the cruel, unusual, and inhumane treatment or punishment prohibited by the Fifth, Eighth, and Fourteenth Amendments to the Constitution of the United States, as defined in the United States Reservations, Declarations and Understandings to the United Nations Convention Against Torture and Other Forms of Cruel, Inhuman or Degrading Treatment or Punishment done at New York, December 10, 1984.

SEC. 1004. PROTECTION OF UNITED STATES GOVERNMENT PERSONNEL ENGAGED IN AUTHORIZED INTERROGATIONS.

(a) Protection of United States Government Personnel—In any civil action or criminal prosecution against an officer, employee, member of the Armed Forces, or other agent of the United States Government who is a United States person, arising out of the officer, employee, member of the Armed Forces, or other agent's engaging in specific operational practices, that involve detention and interrogation of aliens who the President or his designees have determined are believed to be engaged in or associated with international terrorist activity that poses a serious, continuing threat to the United States, its interests, or its allies, and that were officially authorized and determined to be lawful at the time that they were conducted, it shall be a defense that such officer, employee, member of the Armed Forces, or other agent did not know that the practices were unlawful and a person of ordinary sense and understanding would not know the practices were unlawful. Good faith reliance on advice of counsel should be an important factor, among others, to consider in assessing whether a person of ordinary sense and understanding would have known the practices to be unlawful. Nothing in this section shall be construed to limit or extinguish any defense or protection otherwise available to any person or entity from suit, civil or criminal liability, or damages, or to provide immunity from prosecution for any criminal offense by the proper authorities.

(b) Counsel—The United States Government may provide or employ counsel, and pay counsel fees, court costs, bail, and other expenses incident to the representation of an officer, employee, member of the Armed Forces, or other agent described in subsection (a), with respect to any civil action or criminal prosecution arising out of practices described in that subsection, under the same conditions, and to the same extent, to which such services and payments are authorized under section 1037 of title 10, United States Code.

f. Legal Literature

The reports of torture in Iraq and Guantanamo and the government memoranda on the subject triggered a significant amount of discussion and debate in the law journals. See, e.g., Linda Carter, Torture and the War on Terror: The Need for Consistent Definitions and Legal Remedies, 6 J.Nat'l Security L.&Pol'y. 291 (2012); Julianne Harper, Defining Torture: Bridging the Gap between Rhetoric and Reality, 49 Santa Clara L.Rev. 893 (2009); John Alan Cohan, Torture and the Necessity Doctrine, 41 VAL. U. L. REV. 1587 (2007); Henry Shue, Torture in Dreamland: Disposing of the Ticking

Time Bomb, 37 CASE W. RES. J. INT'L L. 231 (2005); M. Cherif Bassiouni, The Institutionalization of Torture under the Bush Administration, 37 CASE W. RES. J. INT'L L. 389 (2005); John Duberstein, Excluding Torture: a Comparison of the British and American Approaches to Evidence Obtained by Third Party Torture, 32 N.C.J. INT'L L. & COM. REG. 159 (2006); John Radsan, A Better Model for Interrogating High-Level Terrorists, 79 TEMP. L. REV. 1227 (2006); AMERICAN CIVIL LIBERTIES UNION [ACLU], ENDURING ABUSE: TORTURE AND CRUEL TREATMENT BY THE UNITED STATES AT HOME AND ABROAD (2006). Also see Marcy Strauss, Torture, 48 N.Y.L. Sch. L.Rev. 201 (2003) and Alan M. Dershowitz, The Torture Warrant: A Response to Professor Strauss, 48 N.Y.L. Sch. L.Rev. 275 (2003).

2. THE OBAMA YEARS

a. Looking Forward, ... and Backward; the Senate Select Committee on Intelligence Study

There was strong criticism of the legal analyses in the Bush administration memoranda by a number of legal scholars, and there were calls by some human rights advocates for criminal prosecution of the interrogators who engaged in the extreme methods and of the authors of the legal memoranda. In response, President Obama announced that the interrogators who relied on these legal opinions would not be investigated or prosecuted if they had stayed within the parameters of the legal advice in the memoranda. He indicated that the Justice Department would make the decisions on whether others should be prosecuted, but his comments emphasized that we should be looking forward. (In 2009, Attorney General Holder opened a criminal investigation into the interrogation of certain detainees and then closed it in 2012, without any prosecutions.) Despite this background, some have continued to advocate for prosecution of those involved.

The targets of the investigation, however, have not been without their defenders who suggested that the authors were acting in good faith under intense pressure in the post-9/11 climate, and that the Bybee memorandum caused no long-term legal damage because it was withdrawn and redrafted.

There were also calls to investigate the CIA program. The Senate Select Committee on Intelligence under the leadership of Senator Dianne Feinstein (D. California) in 2009 undertook to conduct an investigation and prepared a lengthy, detailed three volume report (6700 pages long with 38,000 footnotes) titled, Committee Study of the Central Intelligence Agency's Detention and Interrogation Program. The Study was completed and approved in 2012. Portions were declassified in 2014, including a 499 page Executive Summary. The Study was highly critical of almost every aspect of the CIA detention and interrogation program, concluding, inter alia, that:

1.   The CIA's "enhanced interrogation techniques" were not effective.

2.   The CIA provided extensive inaccurate information about the operation of the program and its effectiveness to policymakers and the public.

3.   The CIA's management of the program was inadequate and deeply flawed.

4.   The CIA program was far more brutal than the CIA represented to policymakers and the American public.

In response, the minority Republican members of the Senate Committee issued statements highly critical of the methodology and various aspects of the Study, concluding that the Study itself was flawed. They disagreed with the Study's conclusions that the interrogation methods used were ineffective and argued that the interrogations had produced actionable intelligence. In turn, the Chair of the Committee issued statements responding to these criticisms. The Executive Summary and key findings of the Study and various post-study comments can be found at: https://www.intelligence.senate.gov/press/committee-releases-study-cias-detention-and-interrogation-program.

For another report on the treatment of the detainees, see International Committee of the Red Cross: Report on the Treatment of Fourteen "High Value" Detainees in CIA Custody.

b.   Interrogation Practices Under the Army Field Manual

As one of his first acts after taking office, President Obama issued an Executive Order that effectively prohibited the use of the interrogation techniques that had triggered the torture controversy, by requiring that the interrogation rules set forth in the Army Field Manual, as revised in 2006, be followed.

After much discussion within and without the Department of Defense, including consideration of having two sets of standards for military interrogations, one classified and one unclassified, in September 2006, a revised Army Field Manual on Interrogation, FM 2–22.3 (FM 34–52), was issued. Inter alia, this Manual serves as the sole set of standards and rules governing the interrogation of prisoners by the military. The Manual contains provisions prohibiting certain interrogation techniques and permitting others. Illustrative provisions are set forth below.

5–74.   All captured or detained personnel, regardless of status, shall be treated humanely, and in accordance with the Detainee Treatment Act of 2005 and DOD Directive 2310.1E, "Department of Defense Detainee Program," and no person in the custody or under the control of DOD, regardless of nationality or physical location, shall be subject to torture or cruel, inhuman, or degrading treatment or punishment, in accordance with and as defined in US law. . . .

Use of torture is not only illegal but also it is a poor technique that yields unreliable results, may damage subsequent collection efforts, and can induce the source to say what he thinks the HUMINT collector wants to hear. Use of torture can also have many possible negative consequences at national and international levels.

All prisoners and detainees, regardless of status, will be treated humanely. Cruel, inhuman and degrading treatment is prohibited. The Detainee Treatment Act of 2005 defines "cruel, inhuman or degrading treatment" as the cruel unusual, and inhumane treatment or punishment prohibited by the Fifth, Eighth, and Fourteenth Amendments to the U.S. Constitution. This definition refers to an extensive body of law developed by the courts of the United States to determine when, under various circumstances, treatment of individuals would be inconsistent with American constitutional standards related to concepts of dignity, civilization, humanity, decency and fundamental fairness. All DOD procedures for treatment of prisoners and detainees have been reviewed and are consistent with these standards, as well as our obligations under international law as interpreted by the United States.

. . .

The following actions will not be approved and cannot be condoned in any circumstances: forcing an individual to perform or simulate sexual acts or to pose in a sexual manner; exposing an individual to outrageously lewd and sexually provocative behavior; intentionally damaging or destroying an individual's religious articles.

5–75. If used in conjunction with intelligence interrogations, prohibited actions include, but are not limited to—

Forcing the detainee to be naked, perform sexual acts, or pose in a sexual manner.

Placing hoods or sacks over the head of a detainee; using duct tape over the eyes.

Applying beatings, electric shock, burns, or other forms of physical pain.

"Waterboarding."

Using military working dogs.

Inducing hypothermia or heat injury.

Conducting mock executions.

Depriving the detainee of necessary food, water, or medical care.

. . .

CAUTION: Although no single comprehensive source defines impermissible coercion, certain acts are clearly prohibited. Certain prohibited physical coercion may be obvious, such as physically abusing the subject of the screening or interrogation. Other forms of impermissible coercion may be more subtle, and may include threats to turn the individual over to others to be abused; subjecting the individual to impermissible humiliating or degrading treatment; implying harm to the individual or his property. Other prohibited actions include implying a deprivation of applicable protections guaranteed by law because of a failure to cooperate; threatening to separate parents from their children; or forcing a protected person to guide US forces in a dangerous area. Where there is doubt, you should consult your supervisor or servicing judge advocate.

Many standard interrogation techniques not involving physical means are permitted under the AFM with few limitations. Thus the AFM authorizes: playing on the emotions of the detainee—love, hate, fear; offering incentives to provide information; exploiting the detainees weak self-esteem and ego strength; offering to protect the detainee from things he fears; impressing on him the futility of resisting or inducing the idea that the interrogator knows everything.

Distinguishing between acceptable and unacceptable practices under the AFM relating to religion illustrates the sometimes difficult line drawing that may need to be done regarding acceptable interrogation practices. Thus, the AFM states:

Although it is acceptable to use religion in all interrogation approaches, even to express doubts about a religion, an interrogator is not permitted to denigrate a religion's symbols (for example, a Koran, prayer rug, icon, or religious statue) or violate a religion's tenets, except where appropriate for health, safety, and security reasons.

Under the AFM, many forms of deception are permissible. An interrogator may:

use ruses of war to build rapport with interrogation sources, and this may include posing or "passing himself off" as someone other than a military interrogator [or an interrogator from another country].

But the AFM does impose some specific restrictions on deceptions. The interrogator must not pose as—

A doctor, medic, or any other type of medical personnel.

Any member of the International Committee of the Red Cross (ICRC) or its affiliates. Such a ruse is a violation of US treaty obligations.

A chaplain or clergyman.

A journalist.

A member of the US Congress.[1]

c.   The Obama Executive Order Adopting the AFM Guidelines

On January 22, 2009, the use of extreme interrogation methods in terrorism investigations in an armed conflict against persons in custody was prohibited, government-wide, and an effort was made to leave the torture controversy relating to the post-9/11 extreme interrogations behind (although still to be argued about and still alive for those who wished that interrogators and others should be prosecuted, or the facts pursued before a kind of truth commission). On that date, newly inaugurated President Obama signed Executive Order 13491 reproduced below:

EXECUTIVE ORDER—ENSURING LAWFUL INTERROGATIONS

By the authority vested in me by the Constitution and the laws of the United States of America, in order to improve the effectiveness of human intelligence gathering, to promote the safe, lawful, and humane treatment of individuals in United States custody and of United States personnel who are detained in armed conflicts, to ensure compliance with the treaty obligations of the United States, including the Geneva Conventions, and to take care that the laws of the United States are faithfully executed, I hereby order as follows:

Section 1.   Revocation. Executive Order 13440 of July 20, 2007, is revoked. All executive directives, orders, and regulations inconsistent with this order, including but not limited to those issued to or by the Central Intelligence Agency (CIA) from September 11, 2001, to January 20, 2009, concerning detention or the interrogation of detained individuals, are revoked to the extent of their inconsistency with this order. Heads of departments and agencies shall take all necessary steps to ensure that all directives, orders, and regulations of their respective departments or agencies are consistent with this

---

[1]   U.S. Dep't of the Army, Field Manual 2-22.3, Human Intelligence Collector Operations (Sept. 2006).

order. Upon request, the Attorney General shall provide guidance about which directives, orders, and regulations are inconsistent with this order.

Sec. 2. Definitions. As used in this order:

. . .

(c) "Common Article 3" means Article 3 of each of the Geneva Conventions.

(d) "Convention Against Torture" means the Convention Against Torture and Other Cruel, Inhuman or Degrading Treatment or Punishment, December 10, 1984, 1465 U.N.T.S. 85, S. Treaty Doc. No. 100 20 (1988).

(e) "Geneva Conventions" means:

(i) the Convention for the Amelioration of the Condition of the Wounded and Sick in Armed Forces in the Field, August 12, 1949 (6 UST 3114);

(ii) the Convention for the Amelioration of the Condition of Wounded, Sick and Shipwrecked Members of Armed Forces at Sea, August 12, 1949 (6 UST 3217);

(iii) the Convention Relative to the Treatment of Prisoners of War, August 12, 1949 (6 UST 3316); and

(iv) the Convention Relative to the Protection of Civilian Persons in Time of War, August 12, 1949 (6 UST 3516).

(f) "Treated humanely," "violence to life and person," "murder of all kinds," "mutilation," "cruel treatment," "torture," "outrages upon personal dignity," and "humiliating and degrading treatment" refer to, and have the same meaning as, those same terms in Common Article 3.

(g) The terms "detention facilities" and "detention facility" in section 4(a) of this order do not refer to facilities used only to hold people on a short-term, transitory basis.

Sec. 3. Standards and Practices for Interrogation of Individuals in the Custody or Control of the United States in Armed Conflicts.

(a) Common Article 3 Standards as a Minimum Baseline. Consistent with the requirements of the Federal torture statute, 18 U.S.C. 2340 2340A, section 1003 of the Detainee Treatment Act of 2005, 42 U.S.C. 2000dd, the Convention Against Torture, Common Article 3, and other laws regulating the treatment and interrogation of individuals detained in any armed conflict, such persons shall in all circumstances be treated humanely and shall not be subjected to violence to life and person (including murder of all kinds, mutilation, cruel treatment, and torture), nor to outrages upon personal dignity (including humiliating and degrading treatment), whenever such individuals are in the custody or under the effective control of an officer, employee, or other agent of the United States Government or detained within a facility owned, operated, or controlled by a department or agency of the United States.

(b) Interrogation Techniques and Interrogation-Related Treatment. Effective immediately, an individual in the custody or under the effective control of an officer, employee, or other agent of the United States Government, or detained within a facility owned, operated, or controlled by a department or agency of the United States, in any armed conflict, shall not be subjected to any interrogation technique or approach, or any treatment related to interrogation, that is not authorized by and listed in Army Field Manual 2 22.3 (Manual). Interrogation techniques, approaches, and treatments described in the Manual shall be implemented strictly in accord with the principles, processes, conditions, and limitations the Manual prescribes. Where processes required by the Manual, such as a requirement of approval by specified Department of Defense officials, are inapposite to a department or an agency other than the Department of Defense, such a department or agency shall use processes that are substantially equivalent to the processes the Manual prescribes for the Department of Defense. Nothing in this section shall preclude the Federal Bureau of Investigation, or other Federal law enforcement agencies, from continuing to use authorized, non-coercive techniques of interrogation that are designed to elicit voluntary statements and do not involve the use of force, threats, or promises.

(c) Interpretations of Common Article 3 and the Army Field Manual. From this day forward, unless the Attorney General with appropriate consultation provides further guidance, officers, employees, and other agents of the United States Government may, in conducting interrogations, act in reliance upon Army Field Manual 2 22.3, but may not, in conducting interrogations, rely upon any interpretation of the law governing interrogation—including interpretations of Federal criminal laws, the Convention Against Torture, Common Article 3, Army Field Manual 2 22.3, and its predecessor document, Army Field Manual 34 52 issued by the Department of Justice between September 11, 2001, and January 20, 2009.

Sec. 4. Prohibition of Certain Detention Facilities, and Red Cross Access to Detained Individuals.

(a) CIA Detention. The CIA shall close as expeditiously as possible any detention facilities that it currently operates and shall not operate any such detention facility in the future.

(b) International Committee of the Red Cross Access to Detained Individuals. All departments and agencies of the Federal Government shall provide the International Committee of the Red Cross with notification of, and timely access to, any individual detained in any armed conflict in the custody or under the effective control of an officer, employee, or other agent of the United States Government or detained within a facility owned, operated, or controlled by a department or agency of the United States Government, consistent with Department of Defense regulations and policies.

Sec. 5. Special Interagency Task Force on Interrogation and Transfer Policies.

(a) Establishment of Special Interagency Task Force. There shall be established a Special Task Force on Interrogation and Transfer Policies (Special Task Force) to review interrogation and transfer policies.

. . .

Subsequently, Attorney General Holder issued the following statement:

Washington, D.C. August 24, 2009

WASHINGTON—Attorney General Eric Holder today announced that the Special Task Force on Interrogations and Transfer Policies, which was created pursuant to Executive Order 13491 on Jan. 22, 2009, has proposed that the Obama Administration establish a specialized interrogation group to bring together officials from law enforcement, the U.S. Intelligence Community, and the Department of Defense to conduct interrogations in a manner that will strengthen national security consistent with the rule of law.

The Task Force also made policy recommendations with respect to scenarios in which the United States moves or facilitates the movement of a person from one country to another or from U.S. custody to the custody of another country to ensure that U.S. practices in such transfers comply with U.S. law, policy and international obligations and do not result in the transfer of individuals to face torture.

"The new policies proposed by the Task Force will allow us to draw the best personnel from across the government to conduct interrogations that will yield valuable intelligence and strengthen our national security," said Attorney General Holder. "There is no tension between strengthening our national security and meeting our commitment to the rule of law, and these new policies will accomplish both."

Interrogations

After extensively consulting with representatives of the Armed Forces, the relevant agencies in the Intelligence Community, and some of the nation's most experienced and skilled interrogators, the Task Force concluded that the Army Field Manual provides appropriate guidance on interrogation for military interrogators and that no additional or different guidance was necessary for other agencies. These conclusions rested on the Task Force's unanimous assessment, including that of the Intelligence Community, that the practices and techniques identified by the Army Field Manual or currently used by law enforcement provide adequate and effective means of conducting interrogations.

The Task Force concluded, however, that the United States could improve its ability to interrogate the most dangerous terrorists by forming a specialized interrogation group, or High-Value Detainee Interrogation Group (HIG), that would bring together the most effective and experienced interrogators and support personnel from across the Intelligence Community, the Department of Defense and law enforcement. The creation of the HIG would build upon a proposal developed by the Intelligence Science Board.

To accomplish that goal, the Task Force recommended that the HIG should coordinate the deployment of mobile teams of experienced interrogators, analysts, subject matter experts and linguists to conduct interrogations of high-value terrorists if the United States obtains the ability to interrogate them. The primary goal of this elite interrogation group would be gathering intelligence to prevent terrorist attacks and otherwise to protect national security. Advance planning and interagency coordination prior to interrogations would also allow the United States, where appropriate, to preserve the option of gathering information to be used in potential criminal investigations and prosecutions.

The Task Force recommended that the specialized interrogation group be administratively housed within the Federal Bureau of Investigation, with its principal function being intelligence gathering, rather than law enforcement. Moreover, the Task Force recommended that the group be subject to policy guidance and oversight coordinated by the National Security Council.

The Task Force also recommended that this specialized interrogation group develop a set of best practices and disseminate these for training purposes among agencies that conduct interrogations. In addition, the Task Force recommended that a scientific research program for interrogation be established to study the comparative effectiveness of interrogation approaches and techniques, with the goal of identifying the existing techniques that are most effective and developing new lawful techniques to improve intelligence interrogations.

QUESTIONS AND NOTES

1. Additional excerpts from Attorney General Holder's statement, supra, regarding the creation of a Special Task Force on Interrogations and Transfer Policy (i.e. irregular rendition) are presented infra.

2. A key provision in the Executive Order, supra, is sec. 3(b), which extends the applicability of the Army Field Manual (AFM) interrogation rules and requirements to anyone "in the custody, or under the effective control of an officer, employee, or other agent of the United States Government, or detained within a facility owned, operated, or controlled by a department or agency of the United States, in any armed conflict, . . ." But also see the proviso relating to the FBI and other federal law enforcement agencies at the end of sec. 3(b). What is the purpose of the proviso? Are there reasons why the FBI and other federal law enforcement agencies should be treated differently under the Executive Order? Under the Executive Order, which agencies of the federal government are likely to be impacted by the requirement to follow the terms of the AFM?

3. Problems: Consider whether the AFM interrogation provisions must be followed in connection with the interrogations of the following individuals.

a. In 2011, a member of al Qaeda is apprehended on an international air flight with a bomb in his possession which he managed to smuggle past the security inspection. He is transferred to a U.S. aircraft carrier on the high seas and interrogated there.

b. Same case as a. but the individual is brought to New York City for interrogation.

c. A small group of al Qaeda sympathizers who are legal residents of the United States are apprehended by the FBI in New York City. There is evidence that they have been planning to plant a series of bombs in the New York subway in retaliation for the killing of Osama Bin Laden by U.S. forces.

d. Same case as c. except that the members of the group have no connection or association with al Qaeda. They are Muslims who believe that the U.S. government has been attacking Muslims worldwide, and they plan to plant bombs in the New York subway as a form of retaliation.

4.   The adoption of the Army Field Manual interrogation guidelines in 2006 and the issuance in 2009 of the Executive Order quoted above, shifted the ground rules for the interrogation of terror suspects by establishing a list of prohibited as well as permitted techniques and methods of interrogation. As a result of the torture controversy, the attention of most scholars and others had been on extreme methods of interrogation, but the change in approach now enabled a focus on ground rules for interrogation at the other end of the spectrum: what kinds of techniques are permissible?

5.   During the early years of the first term of the Obama administration, plans were announced to prosecute some of the high value Guantanamo detainees in federal court in New York City. The announcement triggered controversy and eventually the plans were abandoned, but subsequently at least one low level Guantanamo detainee and others apprehended abroad more recently have been prosecuted in federal court. Adopting the Army Field Manual interrogation rules while, at the same time, beginning to prosecute detainees from Guantanamo and others seized abroad in federal court poses the question whether interrogation statements obtained using the AFM interrogation rules meet constitutional standards of admissibility applied in the civilian courts. Issues raised by this question are addressed infra in this chapter. Further, additional interrogation issues triggered by the many different factual variations that arise in practice are also examined.

d.   The NDAA of 2016 and the AFM Interrogation Rules

On November 25, 2015, the National Defense Authorization Act of 2016 (NDAA) was signed into law. Section 1045 of this Act hardened into legislation the provisions relating to the application of the Army Field Manual interrogation rules and requirements that had previously been contained in Executive Order 13491, supra. But compare the language relating to the FBI and other agencies contained in section 1045, below, with the wording in sec. 3(b) of the Executive Order, supra. Are the differences significant?

How significant is it that the requirement that the terms of the AFM be followed by most government agencies is now enshrined in statutory form rather than in an Executive Order?

NDAA of 2016

Sec. 1045

(a)

. . .

    (5) INTERROGATION   BY   FEDERAL   LAW ENFORCEMENT.—The limitations in this subsection shall not apply to officers, employees, or agents of the Federal Bureau of Investigation, the Department of Homeland Security, or other Federal law enforcement entities.

3. THE FIRST YEAR OF THE TRUMP ADMINISTRATION

As of the time of this writing, it is still relatively early in the time of the Trump administration, and not that much has been done to definitively determine how the Trump administration will address interrogation issues and what policies it will follow in this regard. Similar questions arise with respect to the related subject of the detention policies that will be followed. For example, at some point during the Trump administration will suspected terrorists apprehended abroad be sent to Guantanamo? Issues relating to this question are addressed in Part 2 of this volume.

Meanwhile, there is only a limited amount of information and materials available to provide guidance in trying to determine what interrogation policies are being or will be followed during the Trump administration. Sources that are available include: a) statements made by Donald Trump as a candidate and since he became President; b) a draft Executive Order that leaked but which the White House denied was a White House draft; and c) available information about some interrogation processes that have taken place since President Trump took office. (An Executive Order dealing with detention of terrorists was issued on January 30, 2018.)

a. President Trump's Statements Regarding Confessions and Torture

As a candidate, Donald Trump stated on numerous occasions that as President he would authorize use of waterboarding and even more extreme methods of interrogation. When challenged on the ground that such techniques are unlawful, for example, he would subsequently state that he would not authorize anything that was illegal—that he would not order a military officer to disobey the law; that as president he would be bound by laws just like all Americans. See https://www.cbsnews.com/news/donald-trump-vows-to-strengthen-laws-to-allow-torture-waterboarding-election-2016/.

Shortly after his inauguration, President Trump said he was open to using waterboarding because he believes "absolutely" that it works, that he has consulted experts who have told him that it works, but that he would rely on the counsel of the Director of the CIA and the Secretary of Defense in regard to these issues. See, e.g., http://www.cnn.com/2017/01/25/politics/donald-trump-waterboarding-torture/index.html.

Thus far, however, with the first year of his administration coming to a close, there are no indications that there has been a resumption of the use of extreme methods of interrogation, or that as President, he has issued any orders authorizing such a resumption. The only sign that action along these lines might occur is the leaked draft Executive Order described in the next subsection. There is a question, however, whether all of the talk of resuming waterboarding and other methods amounting to torture may be having harmful effects. See generally, James Risen and Sheri Fink, Trump's Talk on Torture Adds to Global Anxiety, N.Y. Times, January 6, 2017, A13.

b. The Draft Executive Order Dealing with Interrogation, Detention and Blacksites

The afore-mentioned draft Executive Order was titled, Detention and Interrogation of Enemy Combatants. Among other Executive Orders to be revoked under its terms, it provided for revocation of E.O. 13491, the Obama Executive Order applying the rules set forth in the Army Field Manual provisions to most government agencies. It contained two sections expressly dealing with interrogation. In sec. 5, it called for

> "review of the interrogation policies set forth in the Army Field Manual. . . and shall make such modifications in and additions to those policies as consistent with the law, for the safe, lawful and effective interrogation of enemy combatants captured. . . ."

In sec. 7, it called for a Policy Review and Recommendations Concerning a Program of Interrogation Operated by the Central Intelligence Agency. It called for named relevant officials to review the current intelligence needs of the United States and for them to recommend:

> . . . whether to reinitiate a program of interrogation of high value alien terrorists to be operated outside the United States and whether such programs should include the use of detention facilities operated by the Central Intelligence Agency [and]. . .any legislative proposals that would be necessary to protect our national security and to permit the resumption of an effective and lawful interrogation program.

The draft would seem to be aimed at reversing the actions of the Obama administration relating to interrogation methods and to implement the positions of the minority members of the Feinstein Select Intelligence Committee report. While it did not speak in terms of reinstating the extreme methods of interrogation used during the early Bush years post-9/11, it was widely interpreted as aimed at accomplishing exactly that. It has been pointed out, however, that such steps could no longer be accomplished by Executive Order alone, since the NDAA of 2016 had incorporated the requirements of the Army Field Manual into statutory law. Interestingly, none of those who commented on the draft Executive Order mentioned the fact that even apart from the provisions of the NDAA of 2016, torture abroad was made criminal by 18 U.S.C. §§ 2340 and 2340A and that a Presidential order to reinstate the use of torture would be ordering the performance of criminal acts. (Of course, this calls to mind the efforts during the Bush administration to avoid the risk of criminal prosecution by setting a very high threshold for torture by drawing a distinction between torture and cruel, inhuman or degrading treatment.) Finally, of course, it must be remembered that this was only a draft of an Executive Order, and the White House had announced that the draft had not come from the White House.

c.　Interrogation Practices During the Trump Administration

A couple of instances have occurred since President Trump took office in which the same type of two-step interrogation process used to question terrorist suspects captured abroad during the Obama administration has continued to be utilized. See infra this section. But it is too early, and these instances are too few to draw any firm general conclusions as to whether interrogation practices will change during the Trump presidency.

d.　More Looking Backward

1)　The Possibility of International Prosecutions Arising out of the Interrogation of the Afghanistan Armed Conflict Detainees

The prosecutor for the International Criminal Court at the Hague announced in November, 2017 that she was requesting permission to open a formal investigation of possible war crimes committed in the Afghanistan armed conflict and to Afghan prisoners. If the Court grants the requested permission, it could eventually lead to indictments against Americans for various alleged actions, including CIA agents for using extreme methods of interrogation of Afghan prisoners at various foreign sites. The U.S. does not accept the Court's jurisdiction: Accordingly, how it would respond to indictments of its citizens for the conduct engaged in by any military personnel or other U.S. operatives is not clear. See Rick Gladstone and Marlise Simons, High Court May Charge U.S. Forces with Torture, N.Y. Times, A7, Nov. 4, 2017.

While the possibility of international prosecutions mainly would relate to Bush era interrogations and other actions, the fact that it arises during the Trump administration is significant. If prosecutions do result, it will pose challenges for that administration. The fact of the prosecutions or even the risk of international indictments being handed down in the future could also, of course, influence the Trump administration with respect to the possible resumption of extreme methods of interrogation and other related actions.

2) Lawsuits Against Private Contractors—Psychologists Who Aided in the Use of Extreme Methods of Interrogation

In 2015, a lawsuit was filed by two former detainees at CIA "black sites" abroad and the family of a third who died in custody against two psychologists who, as private contractors engaged by the CIA, were alleged to have helped set up and operate the CIA interrogation program for several years. At one point in the litigation the Trump administration invoked executive privilege to prevent several government officials from having to give testimony. See James Risen, Sheri Fink and Charlie Savage, State Secrets Privilege Invoked to Block Testimony in CIA Torture Case, N.Y. Times, March 9, 2017, A20. On at least two occasions, the judge in the case declined to grant the government's motion to dismiss the case and in July, 2017, the judge denied motions for summary judgment. See Sheri Fink, Lawsuit Advances in CIA Torture Case, N.Y. Times, January 28, 2017, A10. Through the taking of depositions from the psychologists, some information about the methods of interrogation used was obtained. See Sheri Fink and James Risen, Suit Gives New Details of Brutal Interrogations, N.Y. Times, June 22, 2017, A1. In August 2017, the case was settled without a full trial being held; the terms of the settlement were not revealed. See Sheri Fink, Ex-Detainees Reach Settlement with 2 Psychologists in CIA Torture Case, N.Y. Times, August 18, 2017, A12.

Generally, lawsuits filed by former detainees to obtain redress for their seizure, detention and extreme interrogation have not been successful principally because the courts have accepted the invocation of the state secrets and executive privileges to block testimony. The success in obtaining a settlement from the government in the suit against the two psychologists, above, is thus a rare occurrence, but note that by settling the case, the government was able to avoid a detailed investigation in court of the interrogation methods that had been used in the early period post-9/11.

C. INTERROGATION OF TERRORIST SUSPECTS PRIMARILY TO OBTAIN EVIDENCE TO BE USED IN CRIMINAL PROSECUTIONS: LEGAL ISSUES

Issues of admissibility of the results of interrogating terrorist suspects in criminal prosecutions in U.S. district court can arise in a variety of factual circumstances that may affect the legal response to the question of admissibility. The interrogation may occur abroad in many different kinds of settings. It may be conducted entirely by foreign police, prosecutors or military personnel. Or the interrogation may be conducted abroad by FBI agents or other U.S. personnel, or jointly with foreign officials. And the suspect being interrogated may be a U.S. citizen, U.S. person (e.g. resident alien of the U.S) or a non-resident alien. And the legal doctrines applicable and applied in the particular circumstances may involve coerced confession/voluntariness doctrine, Fifth Amendment Miranda issues or other constitutional or statutory issues, for example, right to counsel or prompt arraignment.

Generally, the legal issues addressed in this section are issues that have arisen or are likely to arise especially in terrorism prosecutions, although they could arise as well in non-terrorism cases. For example, restrictions on, exceptions to, or avoidance of, the requirements of the Miranda doctrine are treated herein because they are of a type that have arisen or are likely to arise in terrorism cases.

1. COERCED CONFESSION/VOLUNTARINESS ISSUES: ABROAD; NON-U.S. INTERROGATORS

UNITED STATES V. ABU ALI
528 F.3d 210 (4th Cir. 2008)

[Affirmed in part reversed in part, and remanded by published opinion. JUDGE WILKINSON, JUDGE MOTZ, and JUDGE TRAXLER wrote a joint opinion in this case. JUDGE WILKINSON and JUDGE TRAXLER join the opinion in its entirety. JUDGE MOTZ joins the opinion with the exception of footnote 5 and Section VII [ed. not reproduced here], as to which she has written a dissenting statement and opinion.]

WILKINSON, MOTZ, and TRAXLER, CIRCUIT JUDGES:

Ahmed Omar Abu Ali was convicted by a jury of nine criminal counts arising from his affiliation with an al-Qaeda terrorist cell located in Medina, Saudi Arabia, and its plans to carry out a number of terrorist acts in this country. He was sentenced by the district court to 360 months imprisonment and 360 months of supervised release following imprisonment. Abu Ali appeals his convictions and the government cross-appeals his sentence. For the following reasons, we affirm the conviction, but we vacate and remand for purposes of resentencing.

Unlike some others suspected of terrorist acts and designs upon the United States, Abu Ali was formally charged and tried according to the customary processes of the criminal justice system. Persons of good will may disagree over the precise extent to which the formal criminal justice process must be utilized when those suspected of participation in terrorist cells and networks are involved. There should be no disagreement, however, that the criminal justice system does retain an important place in the ongoing effort to deter and punish terrorist acts without the sacrifice of American constitutional norms and bedrock values. As will be apparent herein, the criminal justice system is not without those attributes of adaptation that will permit it to function in the post-9/11 world. These adaptations, however, need not and must not come at the expense of the requirement that an accused receive a fundamentally fair trial. In this case, we are satisfied that Abu Ali received a fair trial, though not a perfect one, and that the criminal justice system performed those functions which the Constitution envisioned for it. The three of us unanimously express our conviction that this is so in this opinion, which we have jointly authored.

Some differences do exist, however, among the panel members. Judge Wilkinson and Judge Traxler join in the opinion in its entirety. Judge Motz dissents (in footnote 6) from the majority's holding that the interrogation of Abu Ali on June 15, 2003, did not constitute a joint venture between law enforcement officers of Saudi Arabia and those of the United States. Judge Motz likewise dissents from Section VII of the panel's opinion, which directs that the case be remanded to the district court for the purposes of resentencing.

I.

A.

Abu Ali is an American citizen. He was born in Texas and raised in Falls Church, Virginia by his mother and father, the latter of whom was employed at the Royal Embassy of Saudi Arabia in Washington, D.C. After graduating from the Saudi Islamic Academy in Virginia, Abu Ali studied for one semester at the University of Maryland and then enrolled in the Institute in Virginia to study Islamic Sciences.

In September 2002, at the age of 21, Abu Ali left his home in Falls Church, Virginia and traveled to Saudi Arabia to study at the Islamic University in Medina. Within a few months of his arrival in Medina, Abu Ali contacted Moeith al-Qahtani ("al-Qahtani"). Abu Ali and al-Qahtani had become friends two years earlier when Abu Ali attended an Islamic summer study session in Saudi Arabia and, upon his return to Saudi Arabia, Abu Ali renewed the friendship. The two "often talked about jihad" and, in November 2002, al-Qahtani introduced Abu Ali to Sultan Jubran

Sultan al-Qahtani ("Sultan Jubran"), who was also known by the name of "Ali." Sultan Jubran had been a mujahid soldier during the United States bombing of Tora Bora in Afghanistan (a major battle between al-Qaeda/Taliban forces and United States forces during the Afghanistan invasion) and, when introduced to Abu Ali, was second-in-command of an al-Qaeda cell in Medina. Abu Ali "accepted and liked the idea" of meeting the "mujahid brother." After their introduction, he and Sultan Jubran also talked "about the virtues of jihad" and exchanged cell phone numbers to keep in touch.

In the ensuing months, Abu Ali and Sultan Jubran continued their discussions. . . . Shortly thereafter, Sultan Jubran did contact Abu Ali and the two men met again in Jiddah, Saudi Arabia, which is just to the south of Medina. At this meeting, Sultan Jubran urged Abu Ali to engage in jihad against America. According to Abu Ali, Sultan Jubran "told me that they had something to do" and "asked [me] to be ready to join them in working against America." Abu Ali "immediately accepted, because of my hatred of the [United States] for what I felt was its support of Israel against the Palestinian people, and because I was originally from Jerusalem."

Later, Sultan Jubran advised Abu Ali that Abu Ali would soon be meeting "the person in charge of the organization." According to Abu Ali, Sultan Jubran "explained to me that I was one of them now, and that I could speak in the name of al-Qaeda." A few days later, Sultan Jubran arranged a meeting between himself, Abu Ali, and Ali Abd alRahman al-Faq'asi al-Ghamdi ("al-Faq'asi"), the leader or "brother in charge" of the al-Qaeda terrorist cell in Medina, who was also known by the name of "Adil."

Abu Ali and al-Faq'asi met a number of times thereafter to discuss the Medina cell's plans for jihad. More specifically, al-Faq'asi advised Abu Ali that an assignment was planned inside the United States and the two men discussed and considered a number of alternatives for terrorist attacks within the United States. According to Abu Ali, al-Faq'asi "presented me with two ideas, based on the fact that I was a [United States] citizen and that I had not engaged in jihad before." "The first idea was to carry out a major operation that he would arrange." The second was "that I would go to the [United States], settle down, find work, lead a normal life, blend into American society and marry a Christian," which would allow him to "plan successive operations inside the [United States] for which . . . al-Faq'asi would send individuals to carry out." In other words, Abu Ali, who was a United States citizen able to return at will and move freely about in the country, would marry a Christian woman, live an overtly normal life to deflect attention, establish a sleeper cell within this country, and prepare for operation instructions and additional operatives to assist.

After this introduction to al-Faq'asi, Abu Ali "became directly connected" to the leader of the cell and "stopped seeing or hearing from

Sultan" Jubran. However, he "continued to meet . . . al-Faq'asi in various places" and "discuss [ed] how to carry out the assignment in the [United States]." According to Abu Ali, he met with al-Faq'asi on six separate occasions to plan such terrorist operations within the United States. In the course of these meetings, Abu Ali suggested assassinations or kidnappings of members of the United States Senate, the United States Army, and the Bush Administration, a plan to rescue the prisoners at Guantanamo Bay, and plans to blow up American warplanes on United States bases and at United States ports, similar to the USS Cole operation. Al-Faq'asi suggested an operation similar to the 9/11 bombings, but which would originate in planes departing from Britain or Australia for Canada in order to circumvent the requirements of a United States visa to enter the country, and plans to assassinate President Bush. With regard to the presidential assassination, Abu Ali suggested two possibilities: an assassination plot involving at least three snipers to fire upon the President while in public or a martyr operation conducted while the President was out greeting the public.

In the course of these plans and discussions, Al-Faq'asi requested that Abu Ali move out of the dormitory where he lived and advised Abu Ali that a "suitable residence" would be found where he "could be trained on manufacturing explosives, information gathering, and forgery." Abu Ali went with al-Faq'asi to live in a villa in the al-Iskan neighborhood in Medina for training. Using the name "Ashraf," Abu Ali was trained by a man called "Ahmad" on how to assemble and disassemble the Kalashnikov machine gun, five of which were located in the villa along with ammunition. . . .

In addition to training, the al-Faq'asi Medina cell provided Abu Ali with finances and equipment. He was given money to buy a laptop computer, a cell phone, and books, as well as written materials on security and methods of concealment. He was also given a USB memory chip that included a clip taken during the bombing of Afghanistan which contained the voices of American pilots, and tasked with translating the recording into Arabic.

　　. . .

　　. . . [O]n May 12, 2003, al-Qaeda carried out a number of suicide bombings in Riyadh, killing approximately 34 people including 9 Americans. That night, Abu Ali and the other cell members performed guard duty at the cell's safehouses. After the bombings, Abu Ali and a number of the others moved to a second villa in an al-Iskan neighborhood where they stayed for three days, although Abu Ali did not spend the night in the villa with the others. According to Abu Ali, the villa contained "a dimly-lit room that contained wires and cell phones, . . . machine guns, ammunition, a pistol and a hand grenade." Later, the group moved back to the farm, where Abu Ali continued his training in explosives and forgery. He received lessons from Majid (Mohammad Salem al-Ghamdi) on forging and removing seals, altering photos, and removing visas, and received lessons from al-Faq'asi on explosives, making explosives, and compounds. Another man, Umar al-Hakmi, provided lessons on fuses and wiring.

On May 26 and 27, 2003, authorities with the Saudi Mabahith received orders to raid several suspected terrorist safe houses in Medina, including the safe house in the Al-Azhari villa where Abu Ali had received training. Among the evidence retrieved during the search of one safe house was an English translation of an American pilot's radio transmission and a paper with Abu Ali's additional alias names of "Hani" and "Hanimohawk" written on it. The authorities also recovered a number of automatic rifles and guns, ammunition, fertilizer, hand grenades, cell phones which were being converted to explosives, as well as computers, cameras, walkie-talkies, and laminating equipment for identification cards. A number of members of the al-Faq'asi terrorist cell were arrested during the raids, including al-Ghamdi, who had trained Abu Ali, and Sheikh Nasser, who had given Abu Ali the blessing for the presidential assassination. Al-Faq'asi and Sultan Jubran, disguised in women's clothing, escaped.

During subsequent questioning by the Saudi authorities, al-Ghamdi informed the Mabahith that one of their members was a student at the University of Medina of either American or European background who went by the alias "Reda" or "Ashraf." Further investigative efforts resulted in the photo identification of Abu Ali as the American or European member of the cell.

On June 8, 2003, Abu Ali was arrested by the Mabahith at the Islamic University in Medina and his dormitory room was searched. Among the items found there were a GPS device, jihad literature, a walkie talkie, a United States passport, a Jordanian passport and identification card, a Nokia cellular telephone, a telephone notebook containing al-Qahtani's name, and literature on jihad. Abu Ali was then flown from Medina to Riyadh, where he was interrogated by the Mabahith. Although he initially denied involvement with the al-Faq'asi cell, he confessed when the Mabahith officers addressed him with his alias names of "Reda" and "Ashraf." Specifically, Abu Ali confessed to his affiliation with al-Qaeda and, in particular, the Medina cell headed by al-Faq'asi. According to Abu Ali, he joined the al-Qaeda cell "to prepare and train for an operation inside the [United States]," including an "intention to prepare and train to kill the [United States] President." In addition to written confessions, the Mabahith obtained a videotaped confession in which Abu Ali admitted his affiliation with the Medina cell and its plans to conduct terrorist operations within the United States, including the plan to assassinate President Bush and to destroy airliners destined to this country.

Following Abu Ali's arrest by the Saudi authorities, the FBI was notified of his suspected involvement in the al-Qaeda cell in Saudi Arabia and advised that the cell was planning on conducting terrorism operations in the United States. Although the FBI requested access to Abu Ali, the Mabahith denied the request. On June 15, 2003, the Mabahith allowed the FBI to supply proposed questions, but later rejected the list and the breadth of the inquiry sought. Ultimately, the Mabahith only agreed to ask Abu Ali six of those questions and to allow the FBI officers to observe his responses through a one-way mirror. Abu Ali was asked whether he was tasked to assassinate the President (as had been reported by the Mabahith to the FBI), when he arrived in Saudi Arabia, whether he knew of any planned terrorist attacks against American, Saudi, or Western interests, whether he was recruited by any terrorist organization, whether he had used false passports, and the nature of his father's position in the Embassy. Other than consular contact, the United States was denied all access to Abu Ali until September of 2003.

In the meantime, on June 16, 2003, the FBI obtained and executed a search warrant at Abu Ali's home in Virginia. Among the items found there, the agents discovered a printout of the buddy list of email addresses from MSN Hotmail account Ahmedabuali@hotmail.com, which contained an address of abumuslim99@hotmail.com for al-Qahtani, an address book containing the name of al-Qahtani, a two-page article praising the 9/11 attacks in this country, a handguns magazine addressed to Abu Ali which contained a feature article on methods for the concealed carrying of handguns, and an email message from an unknown individual to Abu Ali discussing opportunities for Muslim fighters in the conflict between Muslim rebels and Russians in Chechnya.

B.

On February 3, 2005, a federal grand jury returned an indictment against Abu Ali. The Saudi officials surrendered Abu Ali to United States authorities and he was flown back to the United States on February 21, 2005. . . In the superseding indictment, Abu Ali was charged with the following offenses: Conspiracy to Provide Material Support and Resources to a Designated Foreign Terrorist Organization (al-Qaeda), in violation of 18 U.S.C.A. § 2339B (Count 1); Providing Material Support and Resources to a Designated Foreign Terrorist Organization (al-Qaeda), in violation of 18 U.S.C.A. § 2339B (Count 2); Conspiracy to Provide Material Support to Terrorists, in violation of 18 U.S.C.A. § 2339A (Count 3); Providing Material Support to Terrorists, in violation of 18 U.S.C.A. § 2339A (Count 4); Contribution of Services to al-Qaeda, in violation of 50 U.S.C.A. § 1705(b), 31 C.F.R. § 595.204 (Count 5); Receipt of Funds and Services from al-Qaeda, 50 U.S.C.A. § 1705(b), 31 C.F.R. § 595.204 (Count 6); Conspiracy to Assassinate the President of the United States, 18 U.S.C. § 1751 (Count 7); Conspiracy to Commit Aircraft Piracy, 49 U.S.C.A.

§ 46502(a)(2) (Count 8); and Conspiracy to Destroy Aircraft, 18 U.S.C.A. § 32(b)(4) (Count 9).

On November 22, 2005, Abu Ali was convicted of all charges. He was subsequently sentenced to 360 months imprisonment to be followed by a term of 360 months of supervised release. Abu Ali appeals his convictions and his sentence on a number of grounds and the government cross-appeals the sentence.

. . .

Abu Ali next claims that all of his statements and confessions while in Saudi custody should have been suppressed as involuntary. The district court rejected this argument, finding that the government had "demonstrated by a 'preponderance of the evidence' that any incriminating statements" made by Abu Ali while in Saudi custody in June and July, 2003, were "voluntary" and so admissible at trial.

When Miranda warnings are unnecessary, as in the case of an interrogation by foreign officials, we assess the voluntariness of a defendant's statements by asking whether the confession is "the product of an essentially free and unconstrained choice by its maker." If it is, "it may be used against him." But, if the defendant's "will has been overborne and his capacity for self-determination critically impaired, the use of his confession offends due process." The government acknowledges that "[t]he crucial inquiry is whether [Abu Ali's] will has been 'overborne,'" and maintains that it was not; Abu Ali, of course, contends that it was.

In evaluating whether a defendant's will has been overborne, courts must assess the totality of the circumstances, taking into account characteristics of the accused, and details of the interrogation. . .: "the youth of the accused, his lack of education, or his low intelligence, the lack of any advice to the accused of his constitutional rights, the length of detention, the repeated and prolonged nature of the questioning, and the use of physical punishment such as the deprivation of food or sleep." We review a trial court's legal conclusion as to the voluntariness of an accused's statements de novo, but its "findings of fact on the circumstances surrounding the confession" for clear error. We particularly defer to a district court's credibility determinations, for "it is the role of the district court to observe witnesses and weigh their credibility during a pre-trial motion to suppress.".

In this case, after hearing nearly fourteen days of testimony, the court issued a 113-page opinion describing and analyzing the testimony of over 20 witnesses, including Abu Ali, his Saudi captors, FBI agents, and American consular officials who met with Abu Ali during his detention in Saudi Arabia, as well as psychiatrists, other doctors, and nurses. The court evaluated the demeanor and testimony of these witnesses, and then made extensive findings of fact as to the credibility of the witnesses, including

Abu Ali, and the conditions of Abu Ali's confinement and interrogation. We need only briefly summarize these factual findings here.

Initially, the court properly recognized that "torture, and evidence obtained thereby, have no place in the American system of justice." But, based on its evaluations of "the credibility of the witnesses," and "the quality of the evidence presented," the district court found itself "left with lingering questions concerning the credibility of Mr. Abu Ali and his claim that he was tortured," The court credited the testimony of the Saudi Arresting Officer and the Lieutenant Colonel (the Warden at the Medina detention facility where Abu Ali was held for two days following his arrest) that no Saudi official used coercive interrogation techniques on Abu Ali. The court found that the Lieutenant Colonel's testimony that Abu Ali was never abused was believable while Abu Ali's contrary testimony "raise[d] questions that bear on the defendant's credibility."

In addition, the court relied on the testimony of two other Saudi officials, the Brigadier General and the Captain, that the interrogation of Abu Ali in Riyadh "was conducted in the absence of threats or torture." The court found "implausible" Abu Ali's "claim about having been whipped" during the early period of his detention because several Saudi and American witnesses who observed him during this period reported behavior "that do[es] not coincide with how a recently beaten person would behave." Moreover, the court found that "[s]ome aspects" of Abu Ali's testimony "just do not flow logically," and observed that "during his testimony, there were times where Mr. Abu Ali seemed to deflect the question," Finally, the court considered, but found deficiencies in, the testimony of Abu Ali's medical experts who supported his torture claim, crediting instead the testimony of the government's experts that Abu Ali showed no physical or psychological signs of mistreatment.

The district court largely rested its legal conclusion that Abu Ali's statements were voluntary on its factual findings concerning his claims of torture and abuse. Our thorough review of the record provides no basis for finding clear error in any of those findings. This, however, does not end our inquiry. We must evaluate the voluntariness of Abu Ali's confessions de novo, looking to the totality of the circumstances to determine whether his will was "overborne."

In making this evaluation, we consider that Abu Ali was not provided the legal protections—including prompt presentment and Miranda warnings—that the Constitution requires be provided to suspects by United States law enforcement officers. Saudi Arabia is a sovereign nation with its own legal system, and the failure to provide Abu Ali these protections does not, in and of itself, require exclusion of the statements Abu Ali made in Saudi custody. At the same time, we do consider the absence of these protections as one factor in the totality of circumstances in evaluating whether Abu Ali made his statements voluntarily.

In making this voluntariness determination, we also look to the district court's factual findings as to Abu Ali's personal characteristics, and the conditions of his confinement. The court noted that Abu Ali "is an intelligent, well-educated man with a rich and graphic vocabulary," and found him "intelligent, capable, and articulate," It is undisputed that Abu Ali attended school in Saudi Arabia, and he does not allege any religious, cultural, or linguistic difficulties in dealing with his Saudi interrogators. Indeed, he responded to his interrogators' questions in Arabic, and the district court found that the Saudi officers provided him with a prayer rug and Koran among other accommodations. For these reasons, Abu Ali's personal characteristics did not render him particularly susceptible to coercion or pressure.

In addition, the district court rejected Abu Ali's testimony that the Saudis subjected him to coercive conditions of confinement. Instead, the court found believable the testimony of Saudi officers that they confined Abu Ali under reasonable conditions, including provision of three meals a day, and a cell with a bed, blanket and pillow. The court further found believable Saudi testimony that Saudi authorities did not question Abu Ali during his initial detention in Medina, and noted that Abu Ali's own description of the Riyadh interrogation suggested that he was not questioned in Medina.

Saudi authorities did question Abu Ali after transporting him to Riyadh on June 10, 2003. But, the district court credited their testimony that "Abu Ali was granted breaks, access to food, water, a bathroom, and refreshments during breaks in questioning," and that they did not attempt to deprive him of sleep. The court further found believable testimony from Saudi authorities that during just the second session of questioning, on June 11th, Abu Ali "began his lengthy and detailed confession." Abu Ali's extensive written responses to questions, beginning June 11, 2003—his second day in Riyadh—support this finding. Although the questioning of Abu Ali lasted many days, that he began to confess in great detail on just the second day of interrogation indicates that his will was not overborne by prolonged questioning.

After consideration of all of the evidence and the extensive factual findings made by the district court, we conclude that Abu Ali's statements were voluntary. Abu Ali was intelligent, articulate, and comfortable with the language and culture of the country in which he was detained and questioned. The district court found, based upon copious record evidence, that he was not tortured, abused, threatened, held in cruel conditions, or subjected to coercive interrogations. On the basis of the totality of these circumstances, we conclude that Abu Ali's statements were "the product of an essentially free and unconstrained choice."

QUESTIONS AND NOTES

1. Was it significant for the result in the case that Abu Ali is a U.S. citizen? Was it significant that the interrogators in Abu Ali were not U.S. personnel?

2. The court in Abu Ali ruled that the failure to give him Miranda warnings was not a violation of his rights, but that if U.S. agents had been joint venturers with the Saudis in the interrogation, the failure to give Miranda warnings would have violated his rights. A majority of the panel, in a portion not reproduced here, concluded that on the facts there was no joint venture between the U.S. agents and the Saudis in conducting the interrogation. What facts bear on the issue?

3. The issue presented in the excerpt from the principal case reproduced here is whether Abu Ali's confession to the Saudi interrogators was coerced. If it was, the confession would have been inadmissible. What standard does the court apply in determining whether his confession was coerced? Do you think the court applied the same standard of voluntariness that it would have applied to an interrogation conducted by U.S. agents? Should it be the same standard?

4. Compare with Abu Ali, the decision in United States v. Karake, 443 F.Supp.2d 8 (D.D.C. 2006). Rwandan nationals and members of the Liberation Army of Rwanda (ALIR), were charged with murder, conspiracy to commit murder, and using a firearm during a crime of violence in connection with the killings of two United States tourists in Uganda. In a motion to suppress hearing the district court held that the defendants, statements were inadmissible: the statements to Rwandan officials were involuntary; the taint of the earlier involuntary statements was not attenuated in connection with the statements made by the defendants to U.S. officials; any waiver of Miranda rights was not voluntary.

> Except for Nyaminani's two earliest statements, all of the statements at issue were made while defendants were housed at what the Rwandans have referred to as a military "barracks," known as Kami, located outside the Rwandan capital of Kigali. Kami Camp, approximately 200 acres in size, houses between 90 and 120 Rwandan soldiers. According to Captain Alex Kibingo, who was in charge of Kami during the relevant time period, the camp was used to store military equipment such as uniforms, guns and bullets. Kami also served as a detention center for Rwandan soldiers who were subject to disciplinary action and captured ALIR soldiers prior to their transport to repatriation camps in Rwanda's Ruhengeri province. Most, but not all, of the statements obtained by Rwandan officials out of the presence of Americans were taken at Kami by Kibingo. Defendants were transported from Kami to the Rwandan

National Police Headquarters at Kacyiru ("Police Headquarters" or "Kacyiru") for all of the interrogations in which American investigators participated.

. . .

While the Court has thoroughly explained its reasons for rejecting Kibingo's testimony and for its finding that defendants' statements were the product of coercion, there is one further observation that convinces the Court of the correctness of its credibility determinations and its ultimate finding of involuntariness. Over the course of the defendants' detention at Kami, an unmistakable pattern continually repeated itself. Each defendant initially denied his involvement at Bwindi, but was then held incommunicado at Kami until Kibingo extracted statements that he believed were wanted either by his superiors or the Americans and were needed in order to solve the murders, close the investigation, or support a prosecution. With the exception of Nyaminani, the Rwandans did not even inform the U.S. investigators that they had a suspect in custody until they were informed that a defendant had confessed, and each initial confession was obtained only by Kibingo while no one else was present. He would then deliver the information to his superiors who, in turn, several days later, would contact Kayumba, at which point Bachmann would conduct an interrogation. If the defendant provided less information than was expected, as happened with respect to each defendant, he was returned to Kami and subjected to further interrogation and mistreatment. Only after Kibingo announced to the Rwandans that he had obtained further information, was the defendant returned to the Americans for more questioning.

5.   Miranda v. Arizona was decided in 1966. Since that decision, the U.S. Supreme Court has handed down relatively few coerced confession decisions, whereas prior to Miranda, the Court decided many such cases. See, e.g., the following statement quoted by the United States v. Odeh court, see infra, commenting on the relationship between Miranda and the fall-off in coerced confession decisions:

. . . [A]s the Supreme Court has observed, "cases in which a defendant can make a colorable argument that a self-incriminating statement was 'compelled' despite the fact that the law enforcement authorities adhered to the dictates of Miranda are rare."

Rather, the focus, when Miranda warnings have been given and the suspect waives and responds to questions, tends to be on a different voluntariness issue—whether the waiver was voluntary. The very fact of the warnings and waiver makes it more difficult for the suspect to succeed with a claim that the confession itself was involuntary.

Of course, if in future terrorism/intelligence interrogations, Miranda warnings (and consequent waivers) are not given, in reliance on exigent circumstances under the FBI guidelines, supra, the insulating effect of the Miranda warnings will not be present. In such cases, it will be as if we are thrust back into a pre-Miranda period where the entire focus was on whether the statements obtained were coerced within the meaning of the applicable constitutional principles.

6.   In a series of decisions in the decade of the 1950's and early 60's that preceded the Miranda decision, the Supreme Court increasingly had found confessions to have been coerced in situations that did not involve physical brutality or the use of extreme methods of questioning. Thus, for example, the Supreme Court took into account: whether the confession was obtained by threats, for example, to prosecute a loved one, or to take away custody of the suspect's children;[2] the fact that the police refused to allow the suspect to call his wife until he gave a statement;[3] whether some forms of deception were used, for example, a false friend technique where the police officer, a childhood friend of the suspect, told him that his calling him had got him in trouble and put his job at risk;[4] and the fact the interrogator concealed the fact that he was a psychiatrist, leading the suspect to believe he was an ordinary physician who was there to treat his sinus condition.[5]

7.   Recall the interrogation rules set forth in the Army Field Manual, supra, especially the guidelines for interrogation methods that are permitted. How do the AFM permitted methods compare with the police techniques described in the previous paragraph which the Supreme Court has held contributed to the determination that the confessions thereby obtained were coerced? Will use of the AFM-approved interrogation methods comply with constitutional coerced confession standards applied by the federal courts? For a proposal suggesting recognition of a public safety/intelligence exception to coerced confession doctrine, (along the lines of the Quarles exception to the Miranda requirements, see infra) see Norman Abrams, Terrorism Prosecutions in Federal Court: Exceptions to Constitutional Evidence Rules and the Development of a Cabined Exception for Coerced Confessions, 4 Nat. Security J. 58 (2012).

2. MIRANDA WARNINGS/WAIVER ISSUES

a. Restrictions on Applicability of Miranda Abroad

Can a non-resident alien with no connection to the U.S. who was interrogated abroad by U.S. agents or with the participation of U.S. agents

---

[2]   See, e.g., Lynumn v. Illinois, 372 U.S. 528 (1963). Also see Rogers v. Richmond, 365 U.S. 534 (1961).

[3]   See Haynes v. Washington, 373 U.S. 503 (1963).

[4]   See Spano v. New York, 360 U.S. 315 (1959).

[5]   See Leyra v. Denno, 347 U.S. 556 (1954).

claim the benefit of Fifth Amendment protections in a federal criminal prosecution in this country? Consider the following case:

IN RE TERRORIST BOMBINGS OF U.S. EMBASSIES IN EAST AFRICA—UNITED STATES V. ODEH

552 F.3d 177 (2d Cir. 2008), certiorari denied, Odeh v. U.S., 556 U.S. 1283 (2009)

Before: FEINBERG, NEWMAN, and CABRANES, CIRCUIT JUDGES.

JOSÉ A. CABRANES, CIRCUIT JUDGE:

Defendants-appellants Mohamed Rashed Daoud Al-'Owhali and Mohamed Sadeek Odeh challenge their convictions in the United States District Court for the Southern District of New York (LEONARD B. SAND, Judge) on numerous charges arising from their involvement in the August 7, 1998 bombings of the American Embassies in Nairobi, Kenya and Dar es Salaam, Tanzania (the "August 7 bombings"). In this opinion we consider their challenges to the District Court's rulings that denied, for the most part, their respective motions to suppress statements each of them made overseas to U.S. and non-U.S. officials. . . .

Al-'Owhali and Odeh contend that neither the "Advice of Rights" form ("AOR") that they received nor the subsequent oral warnings of an Assistant United States Attorney ("AUSA") satisfied Miranda v. Arizona. In addition, Al-'Owhali asserts that the conditions of his confinement made his statements involuntary and therefore inadmissible under the Fifth Amendment. . . .

As explained in greater detail below, all of these claims lack merit. The AUSA's oral warnings fulfilled, and the AOR substantially complied with, the government's obligations, insofar as it had any, under Miranda, and the admission of Al-'Owhali's and Odeh's statements did not otherwise run afoul of the Fifth Amendment.

A.   Factual Overview

1.   Al-'Owhali

Al-'Owhali was detained on August 12, 1998 by Kenyan authorities in "an arrest [that] was valid under Kenyan law." United States v. Bin Laden, 132 F.Supp.2d 168, 173 (S.D.N.Y.2001). Within one hour of his arrest, Al-'Owhali was transported to Kenyan police headquarters in Nairobi and interrogated by two members of the Joint Terrorist Task Force-an FBI Special Agent and a New York City police detective-operating out of New York City and two officers of Kenya's national police. The New York police detective presented Al-'Owhali with an Advice of Rights form often used by U.S. law enforcement when operating overseas. The AOR, written in English, read in its entirety as follows:

We are representatives of the United States Government. Under our laws, you have certain rights. Before we ask you any questions, we want to be sure that you understand those rights.

You do not have to speak to us or answer any questions. Even if you have already spoken to the Kenyan authorities, you do not have to speak to us now.

If you do speak with us, anything that you say may be used against you in a court in the United States or elsewhere.

In the United States, you would have the right to talk to a lawyer to get advice before we ask you any questions and you could have a lawyer with you during questioning. In the United States, if you could not afford a lawyer, one would be appointed for you, if you wish, before any questioning.

Because we are not in the United States, we cannot ensure that you will have a lawyer appointed for you before any questioning.

If you decide to speak with us now, without a lawyer present, you will still have the right to stop answering questions at any time.

You should also understand that if you decide not to speak with us, that fact cannot be used as evidence against you in a court in the United States.

I have read this statement of my rights and I understand what my rights are. I am willing to make a statement and answer questions. I do not want a lawyer at this time. I understand and know what I am doing. No promises or threats have been made to me and no pressure or coercion of any kind has been used against me.

Al-'Owhali told the American law enforcement agents that he could not read English and had a limited understanding of spoken English. Accordingly, the police detective "read the AOR aloud in English, going slowly and checking for visual signs of comprehension. Al-'Owhali appeared to [the detective to] understand, replied that he understood when asked, and signed his alias at the bottom of the AOR in Arabic when requested to do so." A one-hour interrogation ensued, in which Al-'Owhali responded in "broken English."

Finding their ability to communicate with Al-'Owhali limited by the end of that hour, the agents decided to continue Al-'Owhali's interrogation with the assistance of an interpreter. The special agent began this interview by reading the AOR in English, which the interpreter translated into Arabic. Id. Al-'Owhali stated that he "understood that the warning was the same one as from the morning session," "understood his rights as described therein," and "agreed to answer questions." Al-'Owhali was then interviewed for about three hours and, thereafter, was questioned on eight other days: . . .[4] At the start of each of the interviews on August 13, 14, 17 and 21, the agents showed Al-'Owhali the signed AOR, asked whether he remembered his rights, and whether he would continue to answer their questions. Al-'Owhali consented on each occasion. Until August 21, he denied any involvement in the embassy bombings.

During the August 21 interview, the U.S. agents described the inculpatory evidence they had gathered on Al-'Owhali, and "[a]fter acknowledging that the agents 'knew everything,' Al-'Owhali said that he would tell the truth about his involvement in the bombing if he could be tried in the United States." He explained that the reason he wanted to stand trial in the United States was "because the United States was his enemy, not Kenya."

. . .

2.   Odeh

On August 7, 1998, Pakistani immigration officials detained Odeh, following his arrival at the Karachi airport on a flight from Kenya, on the ground that he used a false passport. . . . he was held in Pakistani custody until August 14, during which time he was interrogated by Pakistani officials. Id. On August 14, Odeh was transported to Nairobi, Kenya, and transferred from Pakistani custody to Kenyan custody. The next day, he was interrogated by two special agents of the FBI, an AUSA, and three Kenyan police officers. Odeh communicated with his interrogators, without difficulty, entirely in English. The U.S. officials explained to Odeh that whether or not he spoke with Pakistani authorities during his detention in Karachi had no bearing on his decision to speak to them. "Thereafter, when Odeh raised the issue of his admissions to the Pakistani authorities, he was told that the Americans did not know or care about what had transpired in Pakistan." One of the FBI special agents read Odeh an AOR similar in all material respects to the one read to Al-'Owhali. . . .

. . .

As the FBI special agent read the AOR, Odeh asked about the availability of a lawyer but did not specifically request one. After further discussion of the AOR and Odeh's willingness to speak to U.S. officials, the interview temporarily ceased so that the AUSA could investigate whether Kenyan counsel was available to Odeh.

Believing that Odeh lacked financial resources, the AUSA inquired into the availability of appointed-but not privately retained-Kenyan counsel. A "high-ranking" Kenyan law enforcement officer informed the AUSA that under Kenyan law, appointed counsel was not provided at the investigative stage and it was their "practice to continue questioning a

---

[4]   The interviews lasted between two and four hours, with the exception of the interviews on August 22 and August 25, which lasted seven and nine hours respectively.

person who requests an appointed attorney." The AUSA informed Odeh of what he had learned from the Kenyan police officer, verified that Odeh had not already retained an attorney, and then orally informed him of his rights under Miranda:

Odeh was told that he had the right to remain silent and that invocation of the right to silence could not be used against him in court. He was also told that if he did speak to the American officials, statements that he made could be used against him. With respect to the right to counsel, AUSA [redacted] told Odeh that he was entitled to have an attorney present and to have an attorney appointed if he could not afford one. However, AUSA [redacted] informed Odeh that no American attorney was currently available to represent him in Kenya. AUSA [redacted] emphasized that Odeh was "the boss" with respect to answering questions without an attorney present.

The AUSA explained that Odeh could (1) exercise his right to remain silent; (2) invoke his right to have an attorney present, in which case the Americans would leave the room and he could then decide whether or not to speak with the Kenyan police; or (3) speak to both the American and Kenyan authorities without the presence of an attorney. . . Odeh suggested a fourth possibility: "speaking with the American officials outside the presence of the Kenyans." While the U.S. and Kenyan authorities were investigating the viability of Odeh's proposal, Odeh changed his mind and decided to speak to both the U.S. and Kenyan officials. Odeh then signed the AOR. Odeh never stated a desire to hire an attorney, and "[i]n fact, he asked the officials what would happen if he subsequently decided that he did not want to speak without a lawyer present." In response, the AUSA "informed him that he always had the right to stop talking with the American officials."

After signing the AOR on August 15, Odeh was interviewed for about seven hours. During the interrogation the next day, the AUSA again informed Odeh that he had the right to the presence of an attorney at the interview, even though no American attorney was available, and that if Odeh wanted an attorney, the Americans would not interrogate him. Odeh expressed his willingness to answer questions and did not request an attorney, but he did make inquiries into the status of property confiscated upon his arrest. Odeh was interrogated on a daily basis from approximately 9:00 a.m. to 6:00 p.m. until he was taken to the United States on August 27, 1998. During these sessions, "Odeh admitted that he was a member of al Qaeda but denied any participation in (or foreknowledge of) the embassy bombings." When Odeh was transferred to American custody on August 27, he was given the standard Miranda warnings.

B. Al-'Owhali's and Odeh's Challenges to the Denial of their Motions to Suppress Inculpatory Statements

. . .

2. The Applicability of the Fifth Amendment and Miranda to the Admission at Trial of Inculpatory Statements Made in Foreign Custody to U.S. Agents

Like the District Court, we conclude that the admissibility at trial of statements made to U.S. agents by foreign nationals held in foreign custody is governed by the Fifth Amendment. Indeed, the government does not argue otherwise. Although we need not decide whether we agree with the District Court as to all aspects of its ruling on the Fifth Amendment and Miranda, it suffices to hold, as described in greater detail below, that insofar as Miranda might apply to interrogations conducted overseas, that decision is satisfied when a U.S. agent informs a foreign detainee of his rights under the U.S. Constitution when questioned overseas.

We note that U.S. agents acting overseas need not become experts in foreign criminal procedure in order to comply with Miranda; nor need they advocate for the appointment of local counsel on a foreign suspect's behalf. While doing so may provide additional grounds for finding that any statements obtained in the course of interrogations were made voluntarily, it is not required by either the Fifth Amendment or Miranda. If the suspect chooses to make a knowing and voluntary waiver of his rights after a warning adapted to the circumstances of questioning overseas and chooses to speak with a U.S. agent, then neither the Fifth Amendment nor Miranda will bar the admission of his statement at trial.

. . . While a violation of the Fourth Amendment's prohibition of unreasonable searches and seizures occurs at the time of the search or seizure, regardless of whether unlawfully obtained evidence is ever offered at trial, a violation of the Fifth Amendment's right against self-incrimination occurs only when a compelled statement is offered at trial against the defendant. . . For this reason, it naturally follows that, regardless of the origin—i.e., domestic or foreign—of a statement, it cannot be admitted at trial in the United States if the statement was "compelled.". Similarly, it does not matter whether the defendant is a U.S. citizen or a foreign national: "no person" tried in the civilian courts of the United States can be compelled "to be a witness against himself."

. . .

Accordingly, we hold that foreign nationals interrogated overseas but tried in the civilian courts of the United States are protected by the Fifth Amendment's self-incrimination clause.

. . .

Having determined that the Fifth Amendment right against self-incrimination governs the admissibility at trial of statements made overseas, we turn to the related question of Miranda's applicability to overseas interrogations conducted by U.S. agents. The Supreme Court has not ruled on this particular question, but it has held that the framework established by "Miranda . . . govern[s] the admissibility of statements made during custodial interrogation in both state and federal courts." Dickerson v. United States, 530 U.S. 428, 432, 120 S.Ct. 2326, 147 L.Ed.2d 405 (2000). Proceeding on the assumption that the Miranda framework generally governs the admissibility of statements obtained overseas by U.S. agents, we conclude that the application of that framework to overseas interrogations may differ from its domestic application, depending on local circumstances, in keeping with the context-specific nature of the Miranda rule.

In Dickerson, the Supreme Court explained that the Miranda "warning/waiver" framework arose from the risk "that the coercion inherent in custodial interrogation blurs the line between voluntary and involuntary statements, and thus heightens the risk that an individual will not be 'accorded his privilege under the Fifth Amendment . . . not to be compelled to incriminate himself.' ". . . In response, the Court set forth "constitutional guidelines" conditioning the admissibility of statements obtained in custodial interrogations on whether a suspect had been warned that he:

"has the right to remain silent, that anything he says can be used against him in a court of law, that he has the right to the presence of an attorney, and that if he cannot afford an attorney one will be appointed for him prior to any questioning if he so desires."

Undergirding these guidelines are two objectives: "trustworthiness and deterrence." . . . Thus, courts suppress un-warned statements, even those that may otherwise be voluntary and trustworthy, in order to deter future misconduct by law enforcement agents.

Recognizing that the threat of suppression in U.S. courts for failure to comply with Miranda holds little sway over foreign authorities, we have declined to suppress un-warned statements obtained overseas by foreign officials. . . . Instead of applying Miranda in such cases, we have required that "[w]henever a court is asked to rule upon the admissibility of a statement made to a foreign police officer, the court must consider the totality of the circumstances to determine whether the statement was voluntary. If the court finds the statement involuntary, it must exclude this because of its inherent unreliability."

When U.S. law enforcement agents or officials are involved in overseas interrogation, however, the deterrence rationale retains its force. In such circumstances, the twin goals of ensuring trustworthiness and deterring misconduct might compel the application of Miranda. We suggested as much in Yousef, 327 F.3d at 56. In Yousef, we observed that "statements taken by foreign police in the absence of Miranda warnings are admissible if voluntary," subject to two exceptions. One of these exceptions-the so-called "joint venture doctrine"-appears to have been "implicitly adopted" by our Court, even though we have "failed to define its precise contours."[18] Pursuant to this exception, "statements elicited during overseas interrogation by foreign police in the absence of Miranda warnings must be suppressed whenever United States law enforcement agents actively participate in questioning conducted by foreign authorities." .... In light of these precedents, we proceed on the assumption that the Miranda "warning/waiver" framework generally governs the admissibility in our domestic courts of custodial statements obtained by U.S. officials from individuals during their detention under the authority of foreign governments.[19]

Even if we were to conclude, rather than assume, that Miranda applies to overseas interrogations involving U.S. agents, that would not mean that U.S. agents must recite verbatim the familiar Miranda warnings to those detained in foreign lands.

. . .

As . . . decisions demonstrate, where Miranda has been applied to overseas interrogations by U.S. agents, it has been so applied in a flexible fashion to accommodate the exigencies of local conditions. This context-specific approach is wholly consistent with our reading of the Supreme Court decisions construing the Miranda framework, and we now apply that approach to the facts of this case.[20]

. . .

In cases where a suspect has no entitlement to counsel under the law of the foreign land, it would be misleading to inform him falsely that he was guaranteed the presence or appointment of an attorney-and Miranda does not require the provision of false assurances.

---

[18] The other exception noted by the Yousef Court pertains to "statements obtained under circumstances that 'shock the judicial conscience.' "

[19] Our recognition that Miranda might apply to foreign detainees held overseas should in no way impair the ability of the U.S. government to gather foreign intelligence. First, Miranda's "public safety" exception, see New York v. Quarles, 467 U.S. 649, 104 S.Ct. 2626, 81 L.Ed.2d 550 (1984), would likely apply overseas with no less force than it does domestically. When exigent circumstances compel an un-warned interrogation in order to protect the public, Miranda would not impair the government's ability to obtain that information. Second, we emphasize that the Miranda framework governs only the admission of custodial statements at U.S. trials. Insofar as U.S. agents do not seek to introduce statements obtained through overseas custodial interrogations at U.S. trials, Miranda's strictures would not apply.

[20] Because we conclude that, assuming they apply, the strictures of Miranda were satisfied in this case, we leave for another day the question of whether the Miranda "warning/waiver" framework governs the admissibility of statements obtained by U.S. agents in the course of custodial interrogations conducted overseas.

The warning at issue here was candid: It explained the rights provided by the U.S. Constitution, while recognizing that, because defendants were detained outside the United States, U.S. law did not govern the terms of their detention or interrogation. Rather than indicating that defendants had no right to appointed counsel, the AOR stated that defendants may have to look to local law for the effectuation of those rights. Indeed, the facts presented by Odeh's case bear this out. Upon hearing the AOR's warnings, Odeh did not assume that counsel was unavailable; instead, he inquired whether counsel was available under Kenyan law. For these reasons, we do not equate the language of the AOR with a statement that counsel was unavailable. Instead, we read that language as a candid acknowledgment of the possible disparity between rights established by the U.S. Constitution, on the one hand, and the availability of counsel and entitlement to the assistance of counsel under the law of the detaining authority, on the other.

The District Court compensated for this potential disparity between U.S. constitutional rights and the rights that obtain overseas by requiring U.S. agents to study local criminal procedure and urge local officials to provide suspects with counsel, if requested, so as to "replicate" the rights that they would have in the United States. We do not agree that Miranda requires such efforts.

. . . In other words, Miranda requires government agents to be the conduits of information to detained suspects-both as to (1) their rights under the U.S. Constitution to the presence and appointment of counsel at custodial interrogations and (2) the procedures through which they might be able to vindicate those rights under local law. It does not compel the police to serve as advocates for detainees before local authorities, endeavoring to expand the rights and privileges available under local law. This is not to say that if, after being informed of his Miranda rights, a detainee insists on the immediate appointment of counsel as a condition of making a statement, the U.S. officials are barred from attempting to expedite the provision of counsel. Quite the contrary; doing so is perfectly consistent with Miranda, but it is not required.

Because compliance with Miranda does not require law enforcement to advocate on behalf of suspects detained in the United States, we see no basis for adopting a different rule for detainees held overseas by foreign powers. It is true that the rights of foreign detainees to the presence and appointment of counsel will depend on foreign law, but, as noted above, Miranda does not require the provision of legal services. It requires only that, until legal services are either provided or waived, no interrogation take place. At the request of foreign detainees or on their own initiative, U.S. agents are free to describe the procedures by which attorneys are made available in foreign countries, so long as they make an honest, good faith effort to provide accurate information. Foreign detainees may, of course, insist that they receive local counsel or U.S. counsel as a condition of making a statement. In response, U.S. agents may, in their discretion, appeal to local authorities to appoint counsel or even obtain U.S. counsel for them. Alternatively, foreign detainees may determine that, in light of the difficulty of obtaining or unavailability of counsel under local law, it is in their best interests to waive their right to counsel and make a statement to U.S. agents.

We are aware that, as defendants urge, foreign detainees may run the risk of refusing to speak to U.S. officials only to find themselves forced to speak to their foreign jailors. This would be so, however, even if U.S. agents made efforts to secure counsel on their behalf and those efforts proved fruitless. The risk of being forced to speak to their foreign jailors would also exist, moreover, if U.S. agents were not involved at all. Of course, statements obtained under these circumstances could not be admitted in a U.S. trial if the situation indicated that the statements were made involuntarily.

Our decision not to impose additional duties on U.S. agents operating overseas is animated, in part, by our recognition that it is only through the cooperation of local authorities that U.S. agents obtain access to foreign detainees. We have no desire to strain that spirit of cooperation by compelling U.S. agents to press foreign governments for the provision of legal rights not recognized by their criminal justice systems.

. . .

Although we do not find the advice of rights concerning counsel as deficient as did the District Court, we think the wording that was used created a needless risk of misunderstanding by stating, albeit accurately, what the right to counsel would have been had the interrogation occurred in the United States. An advice of rights should state only what rights are available, not what rights would be available if circumstances were different. This does not mean that U.S. agents need to determine what rights are in fact available under local law. All they need to say is that counsel rights depend on local law, and that U.S. agents will afford the accused whatever rights are available under local law. Thus, an AOR used hereafter might usefully advise as to counsel rights in the following language:

Whether you can retain a lawyer, or have a lawyer appointed for you, and whether you can consult with a lawyer and have a lawyer present during questioning are matters that depend on local law, and we cannot advise you on such matters. If local authorities permit you to obtain counsel (retained or appointed) and to consult with a lawyer at this time, you may attempt to obtain and consult with an attorney before speaking with us. Similarly, if local authorities permit you to have a lawyer present during questioning by local authorities, your lawyer may attend any questioning by us.

For these reasons, we conclude that the AOR substantially complied with whatever Miranda requirements were applicable, but we need not rule definitively on the matter because of the adequacy of the subsequent oral warning, and because the error, if any, in excluding the statements obtained prior to the oral warning benefitted defendants and was therefore harmless.

. . .

   c.   Defendants' Waiver of their Miranda Rights and their Subsequent Statements

Al-'Owhali and Odeh contend that the conditions of their confinement made their Miranda waivers and subsequent statements involuntary. Al-'Owhali urges that his "secret and relentless interrogation . . . over a ten day period of incommunicado and solitary confinement in a Kenyan prison" renders all of the statements he made during his incarceration, including his Miranda waiver, involuntary. According to Al-'Owhali, his "only chance to escape this prolonged isolation and interrogation, and to have an attorney to consult, was to confess his involvement in the bombing, which would enable him to go to America, where he would have an attorney.". Similarly, Odeh argues that his "choice was not really between remaining silent or talking, but between talking to the Kenyans alone or talking to them and the Americans." The circumstances in which he made this choice were "disturbing," in his view, because he agreed to make a statement only after having been left alone with Kenyan police officers, whom he accuses of having a "reputation . . . for torture." With respect to whether the waiver was knowing under the Miranda framework, Odeh argues that it was not because he did not "underst[and] that he had the option of delaying the interrogation for even a day or two in order to obtain counsel" and "was not provided with the option of speaking with the Jordanian consulate, or the chance to consult with his wife."

. . .

We "will affirm a district court's conclusion that a defendant knowingly and voluntarily waived his constitutional rights if any reasonable view of the evidence supports it." . . . [A]s the Supreme Court has observed, "cases in which a defendant can make a colorable argument that a self-incriminating statement was 'compelled' despite the fact that the law enforcement authorities adhered to the dictates of Miranda are rare."

   i.   The Miranda Waivers

. . . We . . . conclude that the Miranda waivers of Al-'Owhali and Odeh were executed voluntarily.

Turning to the question of whether the waivers were executed knowingly, we observe that only Odeh challenges the District Court's ruling on this score. The District Court found:

Odeh told the Americans that he was comfortable speaking English and that he would ask clarifying questions if he did not understand his rights or anything else the agents said. At no time did Odeh indicate that he was experiencing comprehension problems during the interview sessions. Furthermore, AUSA [redacted] explained to Odeh his Miranda rights with a tremendous degree of conscientiousness, precision, and detail. Odeh himself asked AUSA [redacted] a number of follow-up questions concerning his rights, thereby revealing Odeh's grasp of the salient issues. Because Odeh fully appreciated the fact that he was the "boss" as to whether he would accede to questioning by Americans, we find Odeh's waiver to be knowing and intelligent.

. . .

We therefore conclude that both Al-'Owhali and Odeh knowingly and voluntarily executed valid Miranda waivers.

ii.   The Voluntariness of the Statements

We now consider the question of whether the circumstances of Al-'Owhali and Odeh's confinement rendered their statements involuntary. In order to do so, "we must examine the totality of the circumstances. Specifically, these circumstances include 1) the accused's characteristics, 2) the conditions of the interrogation, and 3) the conduct of the police."

. . . [T]he District Court found that Al-'Owhali had a basic understanding of spoken English, received two years of university-level education, and was familiar with political and world events. . . With respect to the conditions of his confinement, the District Court found that Al-'Owhali was held in "incommunicado detention" for fourteen days, at first in a ten-by-eleven foot cell and then in an eight-by-eight foot cell, and during this time, he received medical attention "as needed." The District Court noted "[a] photograph of Al-'Owhali in his cell, taken at some point during his U.S. interrogation in Kenya, show[ing] him smiling and striking a triumphant pose." The District Court described the interrogation sessions, which were "intermittent and reasonable in duration," as follows:

Al-'Owhali was never in handcuffs during any of his interviews in Kenya. All interviews were held in a library-like room fitted with tables and chairs. Frequent breaks were taken to allow Al-'Owhali to use the restroom, pray, and eat. Prayer breaks lasted for about 15 minutes. Bottled water was provided upon request; food was often provided by the agents. No threats were made by the U.S. agents, nor were any promises made.

The District Court also took note of the "evidence that Al-'Owhali regarded his sessions with [an FBI agent] as a cat-and-mouse game between trained professionals."

We have no reason to doubt the District Court's conclusion that Al-'Owhali was "a well-educated and intelligent individual . . . [whose] demeanor before the Americans was one indicative of confidence, not of intimidation." Likewise, there is no evidence in the record suggesting that the conduct of Al-'Owhali's interrogators was oppressive; quite the contrary: they permitted breaks, provided food and water, limited the duration of the sessions, and never placed him in restraints. Indeed, Al-'Owhali does not appear to argue otherwise, as his challenge to the voluntariness of his statements centers primarily on the circumstances of his incommunicado detention in Kenya. The District Court found the conditions of his confinement, "although non-ideal . . . far from oppressive." Id. Al-'Owhali argues, however, that the length of time he was held in detention imposed "terrible psychological and coercive pressures" on him. Al-'Owhali

Without minimizing in any way the potentially coercive effects of incommunicado detention lasting for fourteen days, we must consider this fact as only one data point-albeit a significant one-in our totality-of-the-circumstances analysis.[24] . . . Weighing against the potentially coercive circumstances of Al-'Owhali's confinement are the District Court's careful findings of fact regarding Al-'Owhali's personal characteristics (his education, his knowledge of English and current events, and his demeanor) and the restrained conduct of his interrogators (who never resorted to threats, promises, or coercion to obtain information from him, and who informed him of his rights from the very beginning). In addition, we must consider the District Court's conclusion that

> what truly motivated Al-'Owhali to inculpate himself was his own overriding desire that he be tried in the United States. As he declared to the U.S. agents interviewing him, it was the United States which was his enemy, not Kenya. Particularly significant is the fact that the suggestion that he be tried in America was initiated entirely by Al-'Owhali. And when Al-'Owhali was dissatisfied by the less-than-firm assurances offered in the first DOU, he demanded that AUSA [redacted] do better.

Taking into account the totality of the circumstances, as we must, we cannot conclude that, because Al-'Owhali was detained incommunicado for fourteen days, the statements he made after waiving his Miranda rights were involuntary. . . .

---

[24] As noted earlier, incommunicado detention describes detention without contact with the outside world and is not to be confused with solitary confinement.

Odeh does not argue explicitly that his post-warning statements were made involuntarily. . . . The only question that concerns us in this regard is whether, unlike Al-'Owhali, Odeh's fourteen-day incommunicado detention rendered involuntary his post-warning statements. We conclude that it did not.

. . . [W]e conclude that, in light of the District Court's findings regarding Odeh's personal characteristics, the absence of oppressive interrogation methods, and his decision to speak with U.S. officials immediately upon encountering them, Odeh's post-warning statements cannot be attributed to the coercive effects of his incommunicado detention.

. . . To summarize, we hold:

(1) The inculpatory statements of Al-'Owhali and Odeh that were obtained overseas by U.S. agents were properly admitted at trial because (a) the oral warnings of the federal prosecutor satisfied, and the "Advice of Rights" form signed by defendants substantially complied with, the government's obligations, insofar as it had any, under Miranda v. Arizona, and (b) the statements were not obtained involuntarily from defendants in violation of the Fifth Amendment;

. . .

For these reasons, and for those set forth in In re Terrorist Bombings of U.S. Embassies in East Africa, 552 F.3d 93 (2d Cir.2008), the judgments of conviction entered by the District Court against Al-'Owhali and Odeh are affirmed in all respects.

QUESTIONS AND NOTES

1. For a summary of the case law on the issues addressed in the principal case, supra, see, for example, United States v. Chan Hok Shek, 2010 WL 4694448 (D.Mass):

> Neither the Supreme Court nor the First Circuit has considered whether the Fifth Amendment's Miranda requirements apply to interrogations of aliens conducted by U.S. agents on foreign soil. At least one federal appeals court has directly addressed this question and concluded that the privilege does apply. See In re Terrorist Bombings of U.S. Embassies in E. Africa, 552 F.3d 177, 199 (2d Cir. 2008) (noting that a violation of the Fifth Amendment's privilege against self-incrimination takes place when the unlawfully obtained statement is offered at trial, not at the point at which the statement was elicited, and, therefore, no foreign defendant "tried in the civilian courts of the United States can be compelled to be a witness against himself"); see also United States v. Heller, 625 F.2d 594, 599 (5th Cir. 1980) (Kravitch, J.) (noting that "if American officials participated in the foreign search or interrogation, or if the foreign authorities were acting as agents for their American counterparts, the exclusionary

rule should be invoked"). However, other circuits have held that "non-resident aliens who have insufficient contacts with the United States are not entitled to Fifth Amendment protections." See, e.g., Jifry v. FAA, 370 F.3d 1174, 1182, 361 U.S. App. D.C. 450 (D.C. Cir. 2004); see also People's Mojahedin Org. of Iran v. U.S. Dep't of State, 182 F.3d 17, 22, 337 U.S. App. D.C. 106 (D.C. Cir. 1999) ("A foreign entity without property or presence in this country has no constitutional rights, under the due process clause or otherwise."). It is therefore unclear whether the Fifth Amendment's privilege against self-incrimination attaches when U.S. agents question a foreign national and non-U.S. resident outside of U.S. territory. However, while I view the analysis in In re Terrorist Bombings as compelling, I need not reach that issue here in order to rule on the motion to suppress because Chan was not "in custody" and, therefore, the agents were not obligated to give him Miranda warnings.

2. Recall the rules applied in a search and seizure context abroad as described in the material in Chapter 6, supra. Should the fifth amendment interrogation rules be different? Does the Odeh analysis follow from the fact where there is a factual basis for a fifth amendment violation it does not actually legally occur until the statements involved are offered into evidence in a trial in the U.S.? Must there be a legal basis for the claim that the police conduct at the earlier point in time violated applicable constitutional standards? Is there such, if the person involved was not entitled to the protection of the U.S. Constitution? Note that the Odeh court did not actually decide the fifth amendment issue but only "assumed" that conclusion for purposes of its analysis.

3. See footnote 19 in Odeh, supra. It is one of the first times that a court recognized the possible application of the "public safety" exception to the Miranda warning/waiver requirements in a terrorism/intelligence context. We address the relevant issues in subsection b, infra. In subsection c, we then consider an approach that enables the government to obtain intelligence information while also being able to obtain evidence for use in prosecution without violating the Miranda requirements.

4. See generally, Mark A. Godsey, The New Frontier of Constitutional Confession Law—The International Arena: Exploring the Admissibility of Confessions Taken by U.S. Investigators from Non-Americans Abroad, 91 Geo. L.J. 851 (2003); Adam Shedd, The Fifth Amendment Privilege Against Self-Incrimination—Does It Exist Extra-territorially? 77 Tul.L.Rev. 767 (2003).

b. The Exigent Circumstances/Public Safety Exception to the Miranda Warning/Waiver Requirements as Applied in Terrorism Contexts

1) *The Quarles Decision*

In New York v. Quarles, 467 U.S. 649 (1984), a majority of the Supreme Court carved out a public safety exception to the Miranda requirements in a situation where there was immediate need for the police to learn where the suspect had gotten rid of a gun. The police, having apprehended the suspect in a supermarket, asked him, without giving him Miranda warnings, where the gun was (the suspect was wearing an empty shoulder holster), and the suspect responded, "The gun is over there." The Court ruled that the suspect's statement was admissible because of "concern for public safety."

2) *Application of the Public Safety Exception in Terrorism Cases*

The exception was applied in a terrorism case in United States v. Khalil, 214 F. 3d 111 (2d Cir. 2000). The fact situation, arguably, involved the same type of immediate exigency as was involved in Quarles itself:

> The officers peeked into the black bag and saw wiring. Technicians thereafter examined the bag's contents; they found pipe bombs, observed that a switch on one of the bombs had been flipped, and were concerned that the bomb would explode before they could disarm it. Other officers went to the hospital and questioned Abu Mezer that morning as to how many bombs there were, how many switches were on each bomb, which wires should be cut to disarm the bombs, and whether there were any timers. Abu Mezer answered all of these questions, stating that he had made five bombs, that they contained gunpowder, and that each would explode when its four switches were flipped. Abu Mezer was also asked whether he had planned to kill himself in the explosion, to which he responded simply, " 'Poof.' " . . .

> . . .

> [T]he [trial] court ruled that the "public safety" exception, . . . made interrogation permissible without Miranda warnings. Abu Mezer challenges that ruling only insofar as the court failed to suppress his response to the question whether he had intended to kill himself in detonating the bombs, his response having been simply, "Poof." He contends that that question was unrelated to the matter of public safety. We are inclined to disagree, given that Abu Mezer's vision as to whether or not he would survive his

attempt to detonate the bomb had the potential for shedding light on the bomb's stability.

See also United States v. Rahimi, 2017 WL 4652068 (S.D.N.Y.).

The commission of a major domestic terrorism event, the bombs detonated at the Boston Marathon, in April, 2013, triggered arguments in the press about whether the surviving suspect in the case, Dzhokhar Tsarnaev, should have been read his Miranda rights as early in the interrogation process as they were given. Reportedly, the FBI, treating the matter as involving the public safety exception and proceeding under the relevant Guidelines, see below, interrogated Tsarnaev for a period of time without providing the Miranda warnings. Tsarnaev was initially charged on Sunday, April 21, 2013, and the magistrate before whom the charges were filed came to the hospital where Tsarnaev was being treated on Monday, April 22 for his first appearance "in court." In the course of the proceedings in the hospital room, the magistrate read the Miranda warnings to him. Reportedly, Tsarnaev stopped talking to the investigators after being advised of his rights. Wall Street Journal, April 26, 2013, A6.

Note that a suspect is required under the Federal Rules of Criminal Procedure to be brought before a magistrate "without unnecessary delay." In this instance, the magistrate, by coming to the hospital to convene the court, determined when the first appearance in court occurred. If Tsarnaev had not been in the hospital but in the local jail, as a practical matter who would have determined when he was brought before the magistrate? Do the FBI Guidelines, below, imply a public safety exception to the "without unnecessary delay" requirement? See generally, Norman Abrams, Terrorism Prosecutions in Federal Court: Exceptions to Constitutional Evidence Rules and the Development of a Cabined Exception for Coerced Confessions, 4 Harv.Nat.Sec.J. 58 (2012).

Meanwhile, some Republican lawmakers, including Senators John McCain and Lindsey Graham, had called for Tsarnaev, a naturalized U.S. citizen, to be treated as an enemy combatant under the laws of war and interrogated without giving him Miranda warnings or legal counsel. N.Y. Times, April 21, 2013, p. 14. For consideration of the type of issues that would be raised thereby, see ch. 10, infra.

3) The FBI Guidelines

The public safety exception has been relied upon for an extension beyond the kind of immediate exigency situations involved in Quarles and Khalil. Specifically, in March 2011, the New York Times reported about an FBI internal memorandum, dated October, 2010, setting forth guidelines for interrogation of operational terrorists within the United States which, arguably, extends the public safety exception beyond immediately-exigent circumstances.

conclusion that the warnings preceding Abu Khattalah's second set of interviews functioned effectively.

To start, while the questioning in the intelligence interviews was comprehensive and detailed, the overlapping content between the two interrogations was much more limited than in Seibert. The intelligence interviews covered a broader list of topics than the law enforcement interviews, consistent with their respective aims. More to the point, the Benghazi embassy attack was the focus of only one of the seven intelligence interviews, while it was the primary focus of all six law enforcement interviews. Because the FBI's interviews were focused on one topic as opposed to many, the discussion of the attack was much more exhaustive than in the intelligence interviews. The intelligence interviews left much "unsaid" for the FBI interviews.

There was also a significant break in time and at least some change in circumstances between the two interviews: Abu Khatallah had two days entirely free of interviews, and during that break, he began receiving an extra daily meal and more regular shower privileges. . . . cf. Seibert, 542 U.S. at 616, 124 S.Ct. 2601 ("[P]ause of only fifteen to twenty minutes" for a cigarette break was insufficient). The furniture in the interrogation pod was rearranged, new wallpaper was posted, and a green tablecloth and pictures were added to distinguish the setting. And two FBI agents who Abu Khatallah had not met previously, with the help of a different interpreter, conducted the law enforcement interviews.

Finally, unlike the police officer in Seibert who created an impression of a "continuum" by repeatedly referring to the unwarned interview during the warned portion the FBI agents here began the interviews by clearly distinguishing them from the intelligence interviews that had come before. Agent Clarke prefaced the interviews by telling Abu Khatallah "[y]ou are not compelled to speak with us today just because you have already spoken with others in the past. If you decide to talk today, it is essential for you to know that anything you say could be used against you in U.S. courts." The FBI agents also did not reference any information from the prior interviews, nor could they have, as they did not know what was discussed. . . . Moreover, before the FBI agents began their interviews on June 21, 2014, they told Abu Khatallah that he was under arrest because of his involvement in the attack on the American Mission in Benghazi—something the intelligence team had not done.

Abu Khatallah contends that the second round of interviews can only be seen as a continuum of the first because the differences between them were insignificant given that he had no sense of time or location, and that most of the circumstances surrounding the interrogation remained unchanged. He stresses that he had no meaningful contact with anyone other than his interrogators, that all of his interviews were conducted in identically shaped pods by two agents and an interpreter, and that he was always escorted to interrogations by DOD guards while handcuffed and blindfolded. While it is true that hanging a few pictures on a wall or covering a table with a tablecloth would not have been very meaningful by themselves, these minor changes must be viewed along with the other factors distinguishing the two sets of interrogations. All in all, the two-day break, the change in personnel and focus of the interviews, the autonomy Abu Khatallah had in refusing to answer certain questions, and the repeated advisory that his prior statements would likely not be admissible, all support a finding that "a reasonable person in [Abu Khatallah's] shoes" would have understood that he retained a choice about continuing to talk. Accordingly, the Miranda warnings were effective.

C.   Whether Abu Khatallah's Miranda Waivers Were Otherwise Knowing and Voluntary

Abu Khatallah further contends that he did not voluntarily waive his Miranda rights. A defendant waives his Miranda rights if "the waiver is made voluntarily, knowingly and intelligently." A waiver is voluntary if "it was the product of a free and deliberate choice rather than intimidation, coercion, or deception." Generally speaking, the Miranda voluntariness standard is the same as that used in evaluating the voluntariness of statements under the Due Process Clause. See Colorado v. Connelly, 479 U.S. 157, 169, 107 S.Ct. 515, 93 L.Ed.2d 473 (1986). A waiver is knowing and intelligent if it was "made with a full awareness of both the nature of the right being abandoned and the consequences of the decision to abandon it." Burbine, 475 U.S. at 421, 106 S.Ct. 1135. That said, "[t]he Constitution does not require that a criminal suspect know and understand every possible consequence of a waiver." Colorado v. Spring, 479 U.S. 564, 574, 107 S.Ct. 851, 93 L.Ed.2d 954 (1987).

Evaluating whether there was a valid waiver is context-specific: It depends "upon the particular facts and circumstances surrounding the case, including the background, experience, and conduct of the accused." The government carries the burden to establish a valid waiver by a preponderance of the evidence, although that burden may be met with various types of evidence. For instance, the government has no constitutional obligation to make or produce audio or visual recordings of interrogation sessions.

Considering the totality of the circumstances, the Court finds that Abu Khatallah's Miranda waivers were "made voluntarily, knowingly and intelligently.". The waivers were voluntary because the conditions Abu Khatallah experienced prior to waiving his rights were not coercive, and did not in any way prevent his waivers from being "the product of a free and deliberate choice.". No threats or promises were made to induce the waivers, and Abu Khatallah was physically unrestrained before, during, and after each waiver was made, The waivers were elicited by an unarmed team of FBI personnel—an Arabic interpreter, and two agents dressed in civilian clothes—with no DOD guards present. They were in every instance preceded by a health and welfare check, which ensured that Abu Khatallah was well-rested, engaged, and alert. And Abu Khatallah was treated humanely and courteously: He was given breaks every hour or two, and offered snacks and refreshments. The sheer number of times Abu Khatallah waived his Miranda rights—once in writing and twice verbally on each typical interview day—is further evidence of the waivers' voluntariness.

Abu Khatallah argues that his waivers were involuntary due to his treatment in the days prior to the law enforcement interrogation, when he "was forcefully abducted and transported to an American warship [and then] held incommunicado and interrogated for five days before any attempt was made to advise him of his rights.". But Abu Khatallah's treatment during the intelligence phase of the interrogations was similarly humane and non-coercive, and as the Court has already found, that prior interrogation was insufficient to undermine the Miranda waivers' validity. As for the capture operation: While it was obviously forceful and resulted in some minor bruising and lacerations. Abu Khatallah's apprehension occurred six days before he waived his Miranda rights, and his physical condition had improved markedly during that time. Besides, courts have generally upheld the validity of Miranda waivers even in circumstances where defendants were injured during arrest. . . .

Abu Khatallah separately contends that his prior "expos[ure] to tyrannical, intolerant, and abusive government authorities" in Libya would have led him to "reasonably believe[ ] that in order to survive, he needed to comply with interrogators. If anything, though, Abu Khatallah's treatment by U.S. officials during the six days leading up to his first Miranda waiver would have cast in stark relief his prior experience as a Libyan detainee. For instance, where Abu Khatallah was "beaten for the first few days" of his imprisonment at Abu Salim prison, he was read Article III of the Geneva Conventions in his first hours onboard the USS New York, and continued to be treated in a manner consistent with those guarantees. After nearly a week of humane treatment, it would not have been reasonable for him to believe that waiving his Miranda rights was necessary to avoid abuse, let alone crucial for his survival.

The Court likewise finds that Abu Khatallah waived his Miranda rights knowingly and intelligently. On no fewer than fifteen occasions, he was advised of his Miranda rights in Arabic—six times in writing, and nine times verbally. Without exception, he indicated either verbally or in writing that he understood those rights and wished to waive them. As Abu Khatallah identifies no defects in the Government's advice-of-rights form, or in the content of the verbal Miranda warnings, these facts alone could end the inquiry. But Abu Khatallah's conduct and demeanor provide additional evidence that he comprehended the rights he was waiving. For example, the fact that he made a special notation at the bottom of each written waiver—to the effect that he wished to waive his right to an attorney presently but reserve that right for the future—provides strong evidence that the waiver was knowing. And as Special Agent Clarke testified, Abu Khatallah's eyes followed the Arabic text on the advice-of-rights form as his rights were being read aloud, and he was "alert" and "engaged" with the law enforcement agents throughout, see id. at 588.

Abu Khatallah nevertheless insists that his waiver was unknowing, pointing primarily to his "lack of education" and lack of familiarity with U.S. legal culture. One flaw with this argument is that Abu Khatallah is not as unsophisticated as his arguments would suggest: He received nine years of formal schooling (not none), and he has given numerous interviews to Western media outlets, touching on topics such as civilian versus military courts, Even setting those facts aside, however, Abu Khatallah's status as a foreign national is but one relevant factor in evaluating whether his Miranda waiver was knowing and intelligent, and courts have found waivers to be valid under similar circumstances. . . .

The Court therefore finds that Abu Khatallah "voluntarily, knowingly and intelligently" waived his Miranda rights. Burbine, 475 U.S. at 421, 106 S.Ct. 1135.

E. Whether Abu Khatallah's Custodial Statements Were Voluntary

Finally, Abu Khatallah contends that the statements he made to law enforcement agents were not voluntary and thus cannot be used against him at trial. The voluntariness inquiry "examines 'whether a defendant's will was overborne' by the circumstances surrounding the giving of a confession." Dickerson v. United States, 530 U.S. 428, 434, 120 S.Ct. 2326, 147 L.Ed.2d 405 (2000) (quoting Schneckloth v. Bustamonte, 412 U.S. 218, 226, 93 S.Ct. 2041, 36 L.Ed.2d 854 (1973)). In evaluating voluntariness, a court should assess "the totality of all the surrounding circumstances—both the characteristics of the accused and the details of the interrogation." Schneckloth, 412 U.S. at 226, 93 S.Ct. 2041. Relevant considerations include "the youth of the accused, his lack of education, his low intelligence, the lack of any advice to the accused of his constitutional rights, the length of detention, the repeated and prolonged nature of the questioning, and the use of physical punishment such as the deprivation of food or sleep." "[T]he prosecution must prove at least by a preponderance of the evidence that the confession was voluntary." Lego v. Twomey, 404 U.S. 477, 489, 92 S.Ct. 619, 30 L.Ed.2d 618 (1972).

All cases finding confessions involuntary "have contained a substantial element of coercive police conduct." Colorado v. Connelly, 479 U.S. 157, 164, 107 S.Ct. 515, 93 L.Ed.2d 473 (1986). Accordingly, without "police conduct causally related to the confession, there is simply no basis for concluding that any state actor has deprived a criminal defendant of due process of law." Id. The paradigmatic cases of involuntariness involve tactics such as physical beatings, see Brown v. Mississippi, 297 U.S. 278, 56 S.Ct. 461, 80 L.Ed. 682 (1936), and the use of drugs akin to truth serums, see Townsend v. Sain, 372 U.S. 293, 83 S.Ct. 745, 9 L.Ed.2d 770 (1963). By contrast, confessions have been found voluntary even when elicited after extended interrogation, see United States v. Van Metre, 150 F.3d 339, 348 (4th Cir. 1998), under basic physical restraint (e.g., handcuffs), see United States v. Cardenas, 410 F.3d 287, 295 (5th Cir. 2005), or due to officers' promises of help or leniency, see United States v. Stokes, 631 F.3d 802, 808 (6th Cir. 2011).

The Court previously found that Abu Khatallah waived his Miranda rights voluntarily. . . . The facts bearing on that finding are also relevant here, and they compel the same conclusion. To summarize: Abu Khatallah was treated respectfully and humanely while in custody; he was not subject to threats or promises of any kind; and his interview sessions were broken up frequently with time for meals, rest, and prayer. Two significant considerations not relevant to the Miranda-waiver voluntariness inquiry may be added to this list. First, Abu Khatallah sometimes chose not to answer the questions posed to him, which would strongly suggest that the answers he did provide were freely given. And second, the Government's frequent "administration of proper Miranda warnings, followed by a written waiver of the rights described in those warnings," indicates that Abu Khatallah's "decision to speak [was] not compelled." For all of these reasons, the Court finds that Abu Khatallah's statements were voluntarily given.

For similar reasons, the Court finds that Abu Khatallah's intelligence interview statements—while inadmissible in the Government's case-in-chief because not Mirandized—were nevertheless voluntary and thus are admissible for impeachment purposes, subject to objections on other grounds. [See Classified Insert 5.]

III. Conclusion

For the foregoing reasons, the Court will deny Abu Khatallah's Motion to Suppress in its entirety. A separate Order accompanies this Memorandum Opinion.

. . .

[Supplement to this Memorandum Opinion with inserts containing classified information has been filed with a Department of Justice Classified Information Security Officer ("CISO") for possible declassification or for filing in redacted form on the public docket.]

QUESTIONS AND NOTES

1. On November 28, 2017, Abu Khatallah was convicted in a trial in U.S. District Court in Washington, D.C. on four counts and acquitted on 14 others including multiple counts of murder. The four counts on which he was convicted were providing material support for terrorist offenses, conspiracy to provide material support, destroying property at the mission and carrying a semiautomatic weapon during a crime of violence. As of the time of this writing, he had not yet been sentenced. The maximum sentence applicable is life imprisonment. See Adam Goldman and Charlie Savage, Mixed Verdict for Libyan in Trial over Benghazi Attacks, N.Y. Times, Nov.29, 2017, A9.

2. The two step interrogation process, often on shipboard, currently seems to be the approach of choice when a terrorism suspect is captured abroad, and the plan is to prosecute the individual in federal court. In part, this development may be a result of the fact that during President Obama's administration, a policy decision was made not to send terrorists seized abroad to Guantanamo. While President Trump has expressed a view supportive of sending such individuals to Guantanamo and for prosecution before military commissions, in fact the Obama practice appears to be continuing to be used for a number of pragmatic reasons. See infra, ch. 10. There have been a number of recent cases, in addition to Abu Khatallah, in which the two step process has been used:

     a. A terrorism suspected named, Ahmed Abdulkadir Warsame, may have been the first in which a terrorism suspect captured abroad was transported to a U.S. ship, and interrogated on shipboard, in this case, for an extended period. After being captured, he was questioned for over the course of a two month period in a two step process. A Somali seized from a fishing boat in April, 2011, he was suspected of aiding al Qaeda's affiliate in Yemen and al Shabaah, a Somali FTO. See Norman Abrams, Responses to the Five Questions, 38 William Mitchell Law Review, 1597, 1601(2012). Subsequently Warsame secretly pled guilty and began cooperating with authorities, providing useful information. Because of his guilty plea, the two step process used in his case was not tested in court. See Benjamin Weiser, Terrorist Has Cooperated With U.S. Since Secret Guilty Plea in 2011, Papers Show, March 25, 2013 http://www.nytimes.com/2013/03/26/nyregion/since-2011-guilty-plea-somali-terrorist-has-cooperated-with-authorities.html.

     b. A terrorism suspect named Mohamed Ibrahim Ahmed was also interrogated using the two step process. See Benjamin Weiser, Hearing on Terror Suspect Explores Miranda Warning, Dec. 12, 2011, http://www.nytimes.com/2011/12/13/nyregion/us-terror-hearing-explores-use-of-miranda-warning.html. The record in the case contained an email sent by an FBI agent in which before the second step interview and the giving of the Miranda warnings began, he suggested that if the suspect would not waive, they could continue the "dirty interview," that is, the unMirandized interrogation to obtain intelligence.

c.　　Also see Benjamin Weiser and Charlie Savage, How the U.S. Is Interrogating a Qaeda Suspect, Oct. 7, 2013, http://www.ny times.com/2013/10/08/world/africa/q-and-a-on-interrogation-of-libyan-suspect.html in which an alleged computer specialist for al Qaeda, Abu Anas al-Libi, was captured in Libya and interrogated on shipboard and subsequently was indicted in U.S. district court. He died in a U.S. hospital before he could be tried. For a description of the history of Abu Anas al-Libi, see https://en.wikipedia.org/wiki/Abu_Anas_al-Libi.

d.　　See United States v. Khweis, 2017 WL 2385355 (E.D. Va. June 1, 2017), discussed in Abu Khatallah supra; Khweis, a U.S. citizen had recently came to the Middle East and was captured in Kurdistan. Legal issues in his case were complicated by the fact that he had been in Kurdish custody and the Kurds also have had an interest in prosecuting him. Also see United States v. Harun, 232 F.Supp.3d 282 (E.D. N.Y. 2017), where the defendant initially was in Italian custody; the court rejected defendant's claim that a two step analysis under Siebert should be applied.

e.　　See the case of Mustafa al-Imam, who like Abu Khatallah was alleged to have been involved in the attack on the U.S. diplomatic mission in Benghazi. On Oct. 29, 2017, he was captured by a U.S. military team sent into Libya, and, reportedly, was subsequently interrogated on shipboard in a two-step process. See Pete Williams, Second Benghazi Suspect Appears in Court, NBC News, Nov. 3, 2017, https://www.nbcnews.com/politics/national-security/second-benghazi-suspect-appears-court-n817406. Given the date of the capture and his court appearance, the two step interrogation process appears to have been conducted on a more abbreviated schedule than in the Abu Khatallah case. Also contrast the two month shipboard interrogation of Ahmed Warsame, supra this note. Abu Khatallah was tried first, see note 1, supra, and al-Imam's trial, as of the date of this writing, is expected to follow soon thereafter. See Adam Goldman and Charlie Savage, Mixed Verdict for Libyan in Trial over Benghazi Attacks, N.Y. Times, Nov.29, 2017, A9.

f.　　Finally, as of this writing, there is the pending case in which the U.S. is reported to have in custody a U.S. citizen captured in Iraq suspected of being an ISIS fighter. U.S. authorities have refused to identify him and thus far have not given him access to a lawyer, although the International Red Cross has been given access to him. The ACLU has been trying to act on his behalf, but there is a question regarding their standing to act. Because he has not been identified, it is not feasible for any relatives to act on his behalf in seeking habeas corpus to test the legality of the current continuing detention.

Reportedly, the government faces a dilemma: 1) he is a U.S. citizen; 2) they do not have enough admissible evidence to prosecute him. News reports indicate that he was interrogated under the two step process, but after he was given Miranda warnings in the second step, he declined to answer any further questions. It has been suggested that placing a U.S. citizen, an ISIS fighter, in indefinite detention in Guantanamo or elsewhere would pose a number of legal issues that the government at present probably does not wish to have tested in court. See ch. 10, infra. See Eric Schmitt and Charlie Savage, American Held as ISIS Suspect, Creating Quandary for Trump Administration, N.Y. Times, Oct. 7, 2017, A8.

3. How much do we know about how the first step of the interrogation, seeking intelligence in the foregoing cases, was conducted? Note that it is labelled in the Abu Khatallah case as "classified." This is a situation where the suspect is aware of at least the external circumstances of the interrogation. What are the likely reasons for classifying information about the interrogation? The court's opinion in Abu Khatallah does contain a few sentences that tell us a bit about the circumstances of the intelligence interrogation, but overall, not very much. We can assume that no enhanced or extreme methods of interrogation as described in the first section of this chapter were used. These were prohibited by President Obama's Executive Order 13491 and statutory language in the NDAA of 2016. See supra. While during the early days of the Trump administration, the draft of an Executive Order that would reverse E.O. 13491 was leaked, see supra, this Executive Order has not been issued and there are no present indications that it will be promulgated. Even were it adopted, it would not repeal the related provision of the NDAA of 2016. Accordingly, the interrogators seeking intelligence in the principal case and in the cases described in note 2, supra, would have been limited by law to using the interrogation techniques permitted under the Army Field Manual, and to abide by the prohibitions of the AFM. But query, in all of the cases in reviewed in note 2, supra, might the specific circumstances of the first interrogation to obtain intelligence bear on the question of whether the first interrogation somehow contaminated the second? If so, how can that issue be addressed if the first step interrogation is classified?

4. Compare the two stepped interrogations that occurred in Missouri v. Siebert and in the Abu Khatallah case. Of course, in the Siebert case, the court concluded that the accused's statements had been improperly admitted at his trial. In Abu Khatallah, applying both the plurality and Justice Kennedy approaches in Siebert, the court reached the opposite conclusion. There are, of course, a number of differences and a separation between, the two interrogations in each of the cases, and the court in Abu Khatallah reviewed them. It can be argued that the most salient difference is the fact that in Abu Khatallah each interrogation had a different purpose—1) the first, to obtain intelligence and 2) the second, a law enforcement purpose, that is, to obtain evidence to use in court. What is the significance of the difference in purpose of each interrogation? For example, is it likely to make a difference in the type

of questions asked? In what kind of information the interrogator is seeking? In whether the interrogator has an incentive (perhaps unconscious) to shape the information being provided toward a particular goal? See generally, Norman Abrams, Confrontation and Hearsay Issues in Federal Court Terrorism Prosecutions of Gitmo Detainees: Moussaoui and Paracha as Harbingers, 75 Brooklyn L.Rev. 1067 (2010).

5. We saw earlier what can be viewed as a slightly different type and ordering of a two step process interrogation process, namely, one that might occur under the FBI Guidelines promulgated to deal with the public safety/Quarles exception to the Miranda rules. Under the Guidelines, invocation of the Miranda requirements is not required at the beginning of an interrogation conducted in exigent public safety circumstances, but under some circumstances, arguably when there is an intelligence need, the interrogation may continue beyond the period called for by the exigency. What use can be made of the information obtained during this "second step"?

6. The NDAA of 2010 contained a provision prohibiting members of the Armed Forces or employees of the Department of Defense from giving Miranda warnings to foreign nationals detained as enemy belligerents outside of the United States in DOD facilities. See section 1040, NDAA of 2010. This prohibition does not apply to officials of the Department of Justice. Ibid. How does this provision bear on the two step approach to interrogation considered in this subsection? See ch. 10, infra.

D. RENDITION

1. INTRODUCTION

In the early post-9/11 years, the U.S. government with some frequency apprehended suspected terrorists outside of the United States and detained and interrogated them. Some continued to be detained and interrogated for a period at so-called "black sites" operated by the CIA in a number of countries. Others were transferred to the Guantanamo Bay detention facility, and still others were reportedly transferred to other countries where they were imprisoned and further interrogated, and some were eventually released. We have limited detailed information about these practices and the particular cases, variously termed extraordinary or irregular rendition, that is, the surreptitious transfer of individuals against their will, often without the official permission of the country in which the travel begins and without going through traditional legal process such as extradition or ordinary rendition where the first country cooperates with sending the individual to another country. A recent decision, United States v. Abu Khatallah (see excerpts from the case, infra; excerpts from the same case dealing with the interrogation process are reproduced, supra) provides a detailed window into how currently the U.S military can act to capture a suspected al Qaeda or ISIS terrorist in a foreign country and, ultimately, transfer him to the United States for prosecution. Earlier cases sometimes involved the seizing of a person by CIA agents, sometimes with the cooperation of the intelligence agents of the host country.

In some of these earlier cases, the target of seizure by U.S. personnel was prosecuted in U.S. proceedings. Because U.S. courts generally rule that in a criminal case, the court will not inquire into how the defendant was brought before the court, whether by unlawful means, questions of alleged irregularity of the rendition process have generally not been litigated in criminal cases. While some civil lawsuits have been subsequently filed by alleged victims of such rendition practices seeking redress, the government has, through invocation of various legal doctrines, generally been able to avoid judicial consideration of the propriety of the government's actions. Generally, the courts have not reached the merits of the plaintiffs' cases.

One consequence of this situation is that our information regarding these practices is limited; most of what we "know" has come from the allegations of the "victims" in civil suits they brought, and some unofficial investigations. But see the excerpts from Abu Khatallah, infra. We have, accordingly, included here material regarding some of the civil lawsuits that have been filed because they contain relevant information, limited as it is. In addition, in a couple of instances, a foreign government has brought a prosecution against U.S. officials, accusing them of having participated in illegal rendition actions in their country, and we have included some information about these cases, too. Finally, some efforts have been made to obtain information through freedom of information lawsuits and by committees of the Congress, but these have not been very successful. But see the Select Committee report relating to interrogation practices described, supra.

When persons suspected of crimes violative of U.S. law, including terrorists, are apprehended abroad, and the government wishes to bring them to the United States for trial, interrogation or detention, there are a number of traditional, lawful ways in which such removal can be effected. This chapter begins with a review of these traditional ways as background for consideration of the practice of irregular or extraordinary rendition.

The normal way in which individuals who have been apprehended in a foreign country are brought to the United States to be prosecuted is through the legal procedure of extradition which is governed by treaties between various foreign countries and the United States.

A second possibility is that the individual waives extradition and is voluntarily transferred to the U.S. See, e.g., Hong Kong Terror Suspects Agree to Extradition to U.S., LA Times, January 6, 2002, at A4.

A third possibility is that police of the foreign jurisdiction turn the individual over to U.S. officials informally for transportation back to the U.S. For example, the individual might be put on an airliner and into the custody of U.S. agents who would then transport the person to the United States. Compare the handing over of Verdugo-Urquidez to U.S. agents as described by Chief Justice Rehnquist, supra, ch. 6.

A fourth possibility is reflected in a type of sting operation involving apprehension in international waters, such as that described below in an excerpt from United States v. Yunis, 924 F.2d 1086 (D.C.Cir.1991):

> An American investigation identified Yunis as the probable leader of the hijackers and prompted U.S. civilian and military agencies, led by the Federal Bureau of Investigation (FBI), to plan Yunis' arrest. After obtaining an arrest warrant, the FBI put "Operation Goldenrod" into effect in September 1987. Undercover FBI agents lured Yunis onto a yacht in the eastern Mediterranean Sea with promises of a drug deal, and arrested him once the vessel entered international waters. The agents transferred Yunis to a United States Navy munitions ship and interrogated him for several days as the vessel steamed toward a second rendezvous, this time with a Navy aircraft carrier. Yunis was flown to Andrews Air Force Base from the aircraft carrier, and taken from there to Washington, D.C.

A fifth possibility, as mentioned above, involves forcibly kidnapping or seizing the person in a foreign country, by non-military personnel (viz., the CIA, etc.) or military forces, with or without, the cooperation or acquiescence of officials of the host country. This type of fact situation led to the Supreme Court's decision in United States v. Alvarez-Machain, 504 U.S. 655 (1992). It also led to the criminal prosecution in Italy of CIA agents and other U.S. officials, which is described infra.

In the instances of irregular rendition, how is the suspect transported to the new destination, be it the United States or elsewhere? In the instances of seizure by military personnel, military transportation, ship or air, has often been used. What about seizure by non-military personnel, a practice that was used with some frequency during the Bush administration, post 9/11? See the Wash. Post, December 27, 2004, p. A01, reporting on a mysterious Gulfstream V turbojet that was purportedly being used by the CIA to carry out "renditions," transporting suspected terrorists to various countries, with one of the suspected purposes, "to transfer captives to countries that use harsh interrogation methods outlawed in the United States." Query, is the type of transfer that was used in the Abu Khatallah case, infra, fairly called irregular rendition?

Among the early actions of the Obama administration was to close down CIA "black" sites in foreign countries where some prisoners were detained and interrogated. See the Executive Order issued on January 22, 2009, infra. While it closed these sites, the Obama administration did not stop the practice of seizing suspected terrorists abroad. A draft Executive

Order leaked during the early days of the Trump administration (but disowned by the White House) also contains provisions relevant to this topic. See draft Executive Order, Detention and Interrogation of Enemy Combatants, sec. 7:

> The Director of National Intelligence, in consultation with the Attorney General, the Director of the Central Intelligence Agency, and other senior national security officers as appropriate, shall review the current intelligence needs of the United States in the fight against radical Islamism and shall:
>
> > (a) recommend to the President whether to reinitiate a program of interrogation of high value alien terrorists to be operated outside the United States and whether such program shall include the use of detention facilities operated by the Central Intelligence Agency (CIA).
>
> . . .

See White House draft order calls for review on use of CIA 'black site' prisons overseas https://www.washingtonpost.com/world/national-security/white-house-draft-order-calls-for-review-on-use-of-cia-black-sites-overseas/2017/01/25/e4318970-e310-11e6-a547-5fb9411d332c_story.html?utm_term=.e29c8514afeb.

We begin treatment of the subject with the Supreme Court's decision in a case involving a kidnapping to bring a person to the U.S. where there was also an extradition treaty between the two concerned countries.

2. KIDNAPPING OR MILITARY CAPTURE IN LIEU OF EXTRADITION; EXTRADITION TREATIES

UNITED STATES V. ALVAREZ-MACHAIN
504 U.S. 655 (1992)

[REHNQUIST, C.J., delivered the opinion of the Court, in which WHITE, SCALIA, KENNEDY, SOUTER, and THOMAS, JJ., joined. STEVENS, J., filed a dissenting opinion, in which BLACKMUN and O'CONNOR, JJ., joined]

CHIEF JUSTICE REHNQUIST delivered the opinion of the Court.

The issue in this case is whether a criminal defendant, abducted to the United States from a nation with which it has an extradition treaty, thereby acquires a defense to the jurisdiction of this country's courts. We hold that he does not, and that he may be tried in federal district court for violations of the criminal law of the United States.

Respondent, Humberto Alvarez-Machain, is a citizen and resident of Mexico. He was indicted for participating in the kidnap and murder of United States Drug Enforcement Administration (DEA) special agent

Enrique Camarena-Salazar and a Mexican pilot working with Camarena, Alfredo Zavala-Avelar. The DEA believes that respondent, a medical doctor, participated in the murder by prolonging Agent Camarena's life so that others could further torture and interrogate him. On April 2, 1990, respondent was forcibly kidnaped from his medical office in Guadalajara, Mexico, to be flown by private plane to El Paso, Texas, where he was arrested by DEA officials. The District Court concluded that DEA agents were responsible for respondent's abduction, although they were not personally involved in it. United States v. Caro-Quintero, 745 F.Supp. 599, 602–604, 609 (C.D.Cal.1990).[2]

Respondent moved to dismiss the indictment, claiming that his abduction constituted outrageous governmental conduct, and that the District Court lacked jurisdiction to try him because he was abducted in violation of the extradition treaty between the United States and Mexico. Extradition Treaty, May 4, 1978, [1979] United States-United Mexican States, 31 U.S.T. 5059, T.I.A.S. No. 9656 (Extradition Treaty or Treaty). The District Court rejected the outrageous governmental conduct claim, but held that it lacked jurisdiction to try respondent because his abduction violated the Extradition Treaty. The District Court discharged respondent and ordered that he be repatriated to Mexico. 745 F.Supp. at 614.

The Court of Appeals affirmed the dismissal of the indictment and the repatriation of respondent, relying on its decision in United States v. Verdugo-Urquidez, 939 F.2d 1341 (C.A.9 1991), cert. pending, No. 91–670, 946 F.2d 1466 (1991). In Verdugo, the Court of Appeals held that the forcible abduction of a Mexican national with the authorization or participation of the United States violated the Extradition Treaty between the United States and Mexico. Although the Treaty does not expressly prohibit such abductions, the Court of Appeals held that the "purpose" of the Treaty was violated by a forcible abduction, 939 F.2d at 1350, which, along with a formal protest by the offended nation, would give a defendant the right to invoke the Treaty violation to defeat jurisdiction of the District Court to try him. The Court of Appeals further held that the proper remedy for such a violation would be dismissal of the indictment and repatriation of the defendant to Mexico.

. . .

We granted certiorari, and now reverse.

Although we have never before addressed the precise issue raised in the present case, we have previously considered proceedings in claimed violation of an extradition treaty and proceedings against a defendant

---

[2]   Apparently, DEA officials had attempted to gain respondent's presence in the United States through informal negotiations with Mexican officials, but were unsuccessful. DEA officials then, through a contact in Mexico, offered to pay a reward and expenses in return for the delivery of respondent to the United States. United States v. Caro-Quintero, 745 F.Supp. at 602–604.

brought before a court by means of a forcible abduction. We addressed the former issue in United States v. Rauscher, 119 U.S. 407, 30 L.Ed. 425, 7 S.Ct. 234 (1886); more precisely, the issue whether the Webster-Ashburton Treaty of 1842, 8 Stat. 576, which governed extraditions between England and the United States, prohibited the prosecution of defendant Rauscher for a crime other than the crime for which he had been extradited. Whether this prohibition, known as the doctrine of specialty, was an intended part of the treaty had been disputed between the two nations for some time. Rauscher, 119 U.S. at 411. Justice Miller delivered the opinion of the Court, which carefully examined the terms and history of the treaty; the practice of nations in regards to extradition treaties; the case law from the States; and the writings of commentators, and reached the following conclusion:

> "[A] person who has been brought within the jurisdiction of the court by virtue of proceedings under an extradition treaty, can only be tried for one of the offences described in that treaty, and for the offence with which he is charged in the proceedings for his extradition, until a reasonable time and opportunity have been given him, after his release or trial upon such charge, to return to the country from whose asylum he had been forcibly taken under those proceedings." Id., at 430 (emphasis added).

. . . Unlike the case before us today, the defendant in Rauscher had been brought to the United States by way of an extradition treaty; there was no issue of a forcible abduction.

In Ker v. Illinois, 119 U.S. 436, 30 L.Ed. 421, 7 S.Ct. 225 (1886), also written by Justice Miller and decided the same day as Rauscher, we addressed the issue of a defendant brought before the court by way of a forcible abduction. Frederick Ker had been tried and convicted in an Illinois court for larceny; his presence before the court was procured by means of forcible abduction from Peru. A messenger was sent to Lima with the proper warrant to demand Ker by virtue of the extradition treaty between Peru and the United States. The messenger, however, disdained reliance on the treaty processes, and instead forcibly kidnaped Ker and brought him to the United States. We distinguished Ker's case from Rauscher, on the basis that Ker was not brought into the United States by virtue of the extradition treaty between the United States and Peru, and rejected Ker's argument that he had a right under the extradition treaty to be returned to this country only in accordance with its terms. We rejected Ker's due process argument more broadly, holding in line with "the highest authorities" that "such forcible abduction is no sufficient reason why the party should not answer when brought within the jurisdiction of the court which has the right to try him for such an offence, and presents no valid objection to his trial in such court." Ker, supra, at 444.

. . .

In Frisbie v. Collins, 342 U.S. 519, 96 L.Ed. 541, 72 S.Ct. 509, rehearing denied, 343 U.S. 937, 96 L.Ed. 1344, 72 S.Ct. 768 (1952), we applied the rule in Ker to a case in which the defendant had been kidnaped in Chicago by Michigan officers and brought to trial in Michigan. We upheld the conviction over objections based on the Due Process Clause and the federal Kidnaping Act and stated:

> "This Court has never departed from the rule announced in [Ker] that the power of a court to try a person for crime is not impaired by the fact that he had been brought within the court's jurisdiction by reason of a 'forcible abduction.' No persuasive reasons are now presented to justify overruling this line of cases. They rest on the sound basis that due process of law is satisfied when one present in court is convicted of crime after having been fairly apprized of the charges against him and after a fair trial in accordance with constitutional procedural safeguards. There is nothing in the Constitution that requires a court to permit a guilty person rightfully convicted to escape justice because he was brought to trial against his will." Frisbie, supra, at 522.

The only differences between Ker and the present case are that Ker was decided on the premise that there was no governmental involvement in the abduction, 119 U.S. at 443; and Peru, from which Ker was abducted, did not object to his prosecution. Respondent finds these differences to be dispositive, as did the Court of Appeals in Verdugo, contending that they show that respondent's prosecution, like the prosecution of Rauscher, violates the implied terms of a valid extradition treaty. The Government, on the other hand, argues that Rauscher stands as an "exception" to the rule in Ker only when an extradition treaty is invoked, and the terms of the treaty provide that its breach will limit the jurisdiction of a court. Therefore, our first inquiry must be whether the abduction of respondent from Mexico violated the Extradition Treaty between the United States and Mexico. If we conclude that the Treaty does not prohibit respondent's abduction, the rule in Ker applies, and the court need not inquire as to how respondent came before it.

In construing a treaty, as in construing a statute, we first look to its terms to determine its meaning. The Treaty says nothing about the obligations of the United States and Mexico to refrain from forcible abductions of people from the territory of the other nation, or the consequences under the Treaty if such an abduction occurs. Respondent submits that Article 22(1) of the Treaty, which states that it "shall apply to offenses specified in Article 2 [including murder] committed before and after this Treaty enters into force," evidences an intent to make application of the Treaty mandatory for those offenses. However, the more natural conclusion is that Article 22 was included to ensure that the Treaty was applied to extraditions requested after the Treaty went into force, regardless of when the crime of extradition occurred.

More critical to respondent's argument is Article 9 of the Treaty, which provides:

> "1. Neither Contracting Party shall be bound to deliver up its own nationals, but the executive authority of the requested Party shall, if not prevented by the laws of that Party, have the power to deliver them up if, in its discretion, it be deemed proper to do so.

> "2. If extradition is not granted pursuant to paragraph 1 of this Article, the requested Party shall submit the case to its competent authorities for the purpose of prosecution, provided that Party has jurisdiction over the offense."

According to respondent, Article 9 embodies the terms of the bargain which the United States struck: If the United States wishes to prosecute a Mexican national, it may request that individual's extradition. Upon a request from the United States, Mexico may either extradite the individual or submit the case to the proper authorities for prosecution in Mexico. In this way, respondent reasons, each nation preserved its right to choose whether its nationals would be tried in its own courts or by the courts of the other nation. This preservation of rights would be frustrated if either nation were free to abduct nationals of the other nation for the purposes of prosecution. More broadly, respondent reasons, as did the Court of Appeals, that all the processes and restrictions on the obligation to extradite established by the Treaty would make no sense if either nation were free to resort to forcible kidnaping to gain the presence of an individual for prosecution in a manner not contemplated by the Treaty.

We do not read the Treaty in such a fashion. Article 9 does not purport to specify the only way in which one country may gain custody of a national of the other country for the purposes of prosecution. In the absence of an extradition treaty, nations are under no obligation to surrender those in their country to foreign authorities for prosecution. . . . Extradition treaties exist so as to impose mutual obligations to surrender individuals in certain defined sets of circumstances, following established procedures. See 1 J. Moore, A Treatise on Extradition and Interstate Rendition § 72 (1891). The Treaty thus provides a mechanism which would not otherwise exist, requiring, under certain circumstances, the United States and Mexico to extradite individuals to the other country, and establishing the procedures to be followed when the Treaty is invoked.

The history of negotiation and practice under the Treaty also fails to show that abductions outside of the Treaty constitute a violation of the Treaty. As the Solicitor General notes, the Mexican Government was made aware, as early as 1906, of the Ker doctrine, and the United States' position that it applied to forcible abductions made outside of the terms of the United States-Mexico Extradition Treaty.[11] Nonetheless, the current version of the Treaty, signed in 1978, does not attempt to establish a rule that would in any way curtail the effect of Ker.[12] Moreover, although language which would grant individuals exactly the right sought by respondent had been considered and drafted as early as 1935 by a prominent group of legal scholars sponsored by the faculty of Harvard Law School, no such clause appears in the current Treaty.[13]

Thus, the language of the Treaty, in the context of its history, does not support the proposition that the Treaty prohibits abductions outside of its terms. The remaining question, therefore, is whether the Treaty should be interpreted so as to include an implied term prohibiting prosecution where the defendant's presence is obtained by means other than those established by the Treaty. . . .

Respondent contends that the Treaty must be interpreted against the backdrop of customary international law, and that international abductions are "so clearly prohibited in international law" that there was no reason to include such a clause in the Treaty itself. The international censure of international abductions is further evidenced, according to respondent, by the United Nations Charter and the Charter of the Organization of American States. Respondent does not argue that these sources of international law provide an independent basis for the right respondent asserts not to be tried in the United States, but rather that they should inform the interpretation of the Treaty terms.

The Court of Appeals deemed it essential, in order for the individual defendant to assert a right under the Treaty, that the affected foreign government had registered a protest. ("In the kidnapping case there must

---

[11] In correspondence between the United States and Mexico growing out of the 1905 Martinez incident, in which a Mexican national was abducted from Mexico and brought to the United States for trial, the Mexican Charge wrote to the Secretary of State protesting that as Martinez' arrest was made outside of the procedures established in the extradition treaty, "the action pending against the man can not rest [on] any legal foundation." Letter of Balbino Davalos to Secretary of State, reprinted in Papers Relating to the Foreign Relations of the United States, H. R. Doc. No. 1, 59th Cong., 2d Sess., pt. 2, p. 1121 (1906). The Secretary of State responded that the exact issue raised by the Martinez incident had been decided by Ker, and that the remedy open to the Mexican Government, namely, a request to the United States for extradition of Martinez' abductor, had been granted by the United States. Letter of Robert Bacon to Mexican Charge, reprinted in Papers Relating to the Foreign Relations of the United States, H. R. Doc. No. 1, supra, at 1121–1122.

[12] The parties did expressly include the doctrine of specialty in Article 17 of the Treaty, notwithstanding the judicial recognition of it in United States v. Rauscher, 119 U.S. 407, 30 L.Ed. 425, 7 S.Ct. 234 (1886). 31 U.S. T., at 5071–5072.

[13] In Article 16 of the Draft Convention on Jurisdiction with Respect to Crime, the Advisory Committee of the Research in International Law proposed:

"In exercising jurisdiction under this Convention, no State shall prosecute or punish any person who has been brought within its territory or a place subject to its authority by recourse to measures in violation of international law or international convention without first obtaining the consent of the State or States whose rights have been violated by such measures." Harvard Research in International Law, 29 Am. J. Int'l L. 442 (Supp. 1935).

be a formal protest from the offended government after the kidnapping"). Respondent agrees that the right exercised by the individual is derivative of the nation's right under the Treaty, since nations are authorized, notwithstanding the terms of an extradition treaty, to voluntarily render an individual to the other country on terms completely outside of those provided in the treaty. The formal protest, therefore, ensures that the "offended" nation actually objects to the abduction and has not in some way voluntarily rendered the individual for prosecution. Thus the Extradition Treaty only prohibits gaining the defendant's presence by means other than those set forth in the Treaty when the nation from which the defendant was abducted objects.

This argument seems to us inconsistent with the remainder of respondent's argument. The Extradition Treaty has the force of law, and if, as respondent asserts, it is self-executing, it would appear that a court must enforce it on behalf of an individual regardless of the offensiveness of the practice of one nation to the other nation. In Rauscher, the Court noted that Great Britain had taken the position in other cases that the Webster-Ashburton Treaty included the doctrine of specialty, but no importance was attached to whether or not Great Britain had protested the prosecution of Rauscher for the crime of cruel and unusual punishment as opposed to murder. More fundamentally, the difficulty with the support respondent garners from international law is that none of it relates to the practice of nations in relation to extradition treaties. In Rauscher, we implied a term in the Webster-Ashburton Treaty because of the practice of nations with regard to extradition treaties. In the instant case, respondent would imply terms in the Extradition Treaty from the practice of nations with regards to international law more generally. Respondent would have us find that the Treaty acts as a prohibition against a violation of the general principle of international law that one government may not "exercise its police power in the territory of another state." There are many actions which could be taken by a nation that would violate this principle, including waging war, but it cannot seriously be contended that an invasion of the United States by Mexico would violate the terms of the Extradition Treaty between the two nations.

In sum, to infer from this Treaty and its terms that it prohibits all means of gaining the presence of an individual outside of its terms goes beyond established precedent and practice. In Rauscher, the implication of a doctrine of specialty into the terms of the Webster-Ashburton Treaty, which, by its terms, required the presentation of evidence establishing probable cause of the crime of extradition before extradition was required, was a small step to take. By contrast, to imply from the terms of this Treaty that it prohibits obtaining the presence of an individual by means outside of the procedures the Treaty establishes requires a much larger inferential leap, with only the most general of international law principles to support it. The general principles cited by respondent simply fail to persuade us that we should imply in the United States-Mexico Extradition Treaty a term prohibiting international abductions.

Respondent and his amici may be correct that respondent's abduction was "shocking," and that it may be in violation of general international law principles. Mexico has protested the abduction of respondent through diplomatic notes, and the decision of whether respondent should be returned to Mexico, as a matter outside of the Treaty, is a matter for the Executive Branch.[16] We conclude, however, that respondent's abduction was not in violation of the Extradition Treaty between the United States and Mexico, and therefore the rule of Ker v. Illinois is fully applicable to this case. The fact of respondent's forcible abduction does not therefore prohibit his trial in a court in the United States for violations of the criminal laws of the United States.

The judgment of the Court of Appeals is therefore reversed, and the case is remanded for further proceedings consistent with this opinion.

So ordered.

QUESTIONS AND NOTES

1.   Three years before the decision in the Alvarez-Machain case, the Office of Legal Counsel in the Department of Justice issued the following opinion, 13 U.S. Op. Off. Legal Counsel 163, 1989 WL 595835 (O.L.C.):

Office of Legal Counsel

U.S. Department of Justice

AUTHORITY OF THE FEDERAL BUREAU OF INVESTIGATION TO OVERRIDE

INTERNATIONAL LAW IN EXTRATERRITORIAL LAW ENFORCEMENT ACTIVITIES

June 21, 1989

At the direction of the President or the Attorney General, the FBI may use its statutory authority to investigate and arrest individuals for violating United States law, even if the FBI's actions contravene customary international law. The President, acting through the Attorney General, has the inherent constitutional authority to deploy the FBI to investigate and arrest individuals for violating United States law, even if those actions contravene customary international law. Extraterritorial law enforcement activities that are authorized by domestic law are not barred even if they contravene unexecuted treaties or treaty provisions, such as

---

[16] The Mexican Government has also requested from the United States the extradition of two individuals it suspects of having abducted respondent in Mexico, on charges of kidnapping. App. 39–66. . . .

Article 2(4) of the United Nations Charter. An arrest that is inconsistent with international or foreign law does not violate the Fourth Amendment.

This memorandum responds to the request of the Federal Bureau of Investigation ("FBI") that we reconsider our 1980 opinion that the FBI has no authority under 28 U.S.C. § 533(1) to apprehend and abduct a fugitive residing in a foreign state when those actions would be contrary to customary international law. Extraterritorial Apprehension by the Federal Bureau of Investigation, 4B Op. O.L.C. 543 (1980) (the "1980 Opinion" or "Opinion"). After undertaking a comprehensive review of the applicable law, we conclude that the 1980 Opinion erred in ruling that the FBI does not have legal authority to carry out extraterritorial law enforcement activities that contravene customary international law.

First, we conclude that, with appropriate direction, the FBI may use its broad statutory authority under 28 U.S.C. § 533(1) and 18 U.S.C. § 3052 to investigate and arrest individuals for violations of United States law even if those investigations and arrests are not consistent with international law. Second, we conclude that the President, acting through the Attorney General, has inherent constitutional authority to order the FBI to investigate and arrest individuals in a manner that departs from international law. The international law that may be abridged in this manner includes not only customary international law but also Article 2(4) of the U.N. Charter and other unexecuted treaties or treaty provisions that have not become part of the domestic law of the United States. Finally, we reaffirm the conclusion of the 1980 Opinion that an arrest departing from international law does not violate the Fourth Amendment, and we further conclude that an arrest in violation of foreign law does not abridge the Fourth Amendment.

We caution that this memorandum addresses only whether the FBI has the legal authority to carry out law enforcement operations that contravene international law. It does not address the serious policy considerations that may weigh against carrying out such operations.

The 1980 Opinion addressed the legal implications of a proposed operation in which FBI agents would forcibly apprehend a fugitive in a foreign country that would not consent to the apprehension. That Opinion acknowledges that 28 U.S.C. § 533(1), the statute authorizing FBI investigations, contains no explicit geographical restrictions. It also refers to a previous opinion issued by this Office that concluded that the statute's general authorization to detect and prosecute crimes against the United States appears broad enough to include such law enforcement activity no matter where it is undertaken. The 1980 Opinion asserts, however, that customary and other international law limits the reach of section 533(1). Under customary international law, as viewed by the 1980 Opinion, it is considered an invasion of sovereignty for one country to carry out law enforcement activities within another country without that country's consent. Thus, the Opinion concludes that section 533(1) authorizes extraterritorial apprehension of a fugitive only where the apprehension is approved by the asylum state.

The Opinion supports this conclusion with "two distinct but related lines of analysis." Id. at 552. First, citing The Schooner Exchange v. McFaddon, 11 U.S. (7 Cranch) 116, 136 (1812) (Marshall, C.J.), the Opinion concludes that the authority of the United States outside its territory is limited by the sovereignty of other nations. The Opinion does not explain the juridical source of this limitation on the authority of the United States. In The Schooner Exchange, however, Chief Justice Marshall relies on customary international law for many of his conclusions, and this part of the 1980 Opinion appears to suggest that customary international law imposes absolute jurisdictional limitations on the United States' lawmaking authority.

Second, the Opinion implicitly relies on the principle of statutory construction that statutes should be construed, when possible, so as to avoid conflict with international law. The Opinion notes that a statute imposing a duty ordinarily is construed to authorize all reasonable and necessary means of executing that duty. The Opinion concludes that although the law enforcement methods at issue may be necessary to carry out the FBI agents' duties under section 533(1), those methods are "unreasonable" and hence, unauthorized, if executed in violation of international law. Thus, the Opinion concludes that without asylum state consent, "the FBI is acting outside the bounds of its statutory authority when it makes an apprehension of the type proposed here—either because § 533 could not contemplate a violation of international law or because the powers of the FBI are delimited by those of the enabling sovereign." Id. at 553.

The 1980 Opinion's impact on the ability of the United States to execute necessary law enforcement operations may be significant. The reasoning of the 1980 Opinion would seem to apply to a broad range of law enforcement activities other than forcible apprehension. United States law enforcement agents frequently are required to travel to foreign countries to conduct investigative activities or to meet foreign informants. Formal consent cannot always be obtained from the foreign government, and indeed, in many cases to seek such consent would endanger both the agents and their investigation. Although such activities are less intrusive than forcible apprehension and removal of the fugitive, under the 1980 Opinion they nonetheless may be viewed as encroachments on the asylum state's sovereignty and hence, violations of international law, if not authorized by that state. . . . Thus, the 1980 Opinion has the potential to preclude the United States not only from apprehending fugitives in foreign countries, but also from engaging in a variety of more routine law enforcement activities. The United States is facing increasingly serious threats to its domestic security from both international terrorist groups and narcotics traffickers. While targeting the United States and United States citizens, these criminal organizations frequently operate from foreign sanctuaries. Unfortunately, some foreign governments have failed to take effective steps to protect the United States from these predations, and some foreign governments actually act in complicity with these groups. Accordingly, the extraterritorial enforcement of United States laws is becoming increasingly important to the nation's ability to protect its own vital national interests.

2. To what extent might the OLC opinion in the previous note, as well as the majority opinion in the principal case have laid the foundation for the current practices of irregular rendition. Compare with the OLC opinion in the preceding note, footnote 21 from Justice Stevens' dissenting opinion in Alvarez-Machain:

When Abraham Sofaer, Legal Adviser of the State Department, was questioned at a congressional hearing, he resisted the notion that such seizures were acceptable: " 'Can you imagine us going into Paris and seizing some person we regard as a terrorist . . .? [H]ow would we feel if some foreign nation—let us take the United Kingdom—came over here and seized some terrorist suspect in New York City, or Boston, or Philadelphia, . . . because we refused through the normal channels of international, legal communications, to extradite that individual?' " Bill To Authorize Prosecution of Terrorists and Others Who Attack U.S. Government Employees and Citizens Abroad: Hearing before the Subcommittee on Security and Terrorism of the Senate Committee on the Judiciary, 99th Cong., 1st Sess., 63 (1985).

3. See Arar v. United States, 585 F.3d 559 (2d Cir. 2010):

The United States Department of State records that, between 1993 and 2001, "rendition" provided the means for obtaining custody of ten suspected terrorists and "extradition" applied to another four suspects. See U.S. Dep't of State, Patterns of Global Terrorism 2001, App. D: Extraditions and Renditions of Terrorists to the United States. Accordingly, the rendition of suspected terrorists outside the mechanisms established by extradition treaties-so-called extraordinary rendition-had been employed as a means of combating terrorists for nearly a decade prior to the events giving rise to this litigation. See John B. Bellinger III, Legal Adviser, U.S. Dep't of State, Letter to the Editor, Wall St. J., July 5, 2006, at A25 (discussing the renditions of suspected terrorists Ramzi Yousef and Mir Aimal Kansi to the United States and the rendition of Illich

Ramirez Sanchez, also known as "Carlos the Jackal," by French authorities from the Sudan to France, "which was subsequently upheld by the European Commission on Human Rights"), reprinted in Digest of United States Practice in International Law 162–63 (Sally J. Cummings ed., 2006); see also Remarks of Condoleezza Rice, U.S. Sec'y of State (Dec. 5, 2005) ("For decades, the United States and other countries have used 'renditions' to transport terrorist suspects from the country where they were captured to their home country or to other countries where they can be questioned, held, or brought to justice."), in Digest of United States Practice in International Law 100, 102 (Sally J. Cummings ed., 2005).

4.   United States v. Toscanino, 500 F.2d 267 (2d Cir.1974) is usually cited for the proposition that an abduction in which U.S. agents are involved and accompanying conduct that shocks the conscience are grounds for taking into account how the defendant came before the court and for dismissing the prosecution. The court in Toscanino described the defendant's claim and offer of proof as follows:

> He alleged that he had been kidnapped from his home in Montevideo, Uruguay, and brought into the Eastern District only after he had been detained for three weeks of interrogation accompanied by physical torture in Brazil. He offered to prove the following:

> > "On or about January 6, 1973 Francisco Toscanino was lured from his home in Montevideo, Uruguay by a telephone call. This call had been placed by or at the direction of Hugo Campos Hermedia. Hermedia was at that time and still is a member of the police in Montevideo, Uruguay. In this effort, however, and those that will follow in this offer, Hermedia was acting ultra vires in that he was the paid agent of the United States government . . .

> > ". . . The telephone call ruse succeeded in bringing Toscanino and his wife, seven months pregnant at the time, to an area near a deserted bowling alley in the City of Montevideo. Upon their arrival there Hermedia together with six associates abducted Toscanino. This was accomplished in full view of Toscanino's terrified wife by knocking him unconscious with a gun and throwing him into the rear seat of Hermedia's car. Thereupon Toscanino, bound and blindfolded, was driven to the Uruguayan-Brazilian border by a circuitous route . . .

> > "At one point during the long trip to the Brazilian border discussion was had among Toscanino's captors as to changing the license plates of the abductor's car in order to avoid detection by the Uruguayan authorities. At another point the abductor's car was abruptly brought to a halt, and Toscanino was ordered to get out. He was brought to an apparently secluded place and

told to lie perfectly still or he would be shot then and there. Although his blindfold prevented him from seeing, Toscanino could feel the barrel of the gun against his head and could hear the rumbling noises of what appeared to be an Uruguayan military convoy. A short time after the noise of the convoy had died away, Toscanino was placed in another vehicle and whisked to the border. There by pre-arrangement and again at the connivance of the United States government, the car was met by a group of Brazilians who took custody of the body of Francisco Toscanino.

"At no time had there been any formal or informal request on the part of the United States of the government of Uruguay for the extradition of Francisco Toscanino nor was there any legal basis to justify this rank criminal enterprise. In fact, the Uruguayan government claims that it had no prior knowledge of the kidnapping nor did it consent thereto and had indeed condemned this kind of apprehension as alien to its laws.

"Once in the custody of Brazilians, Toscanino was brought to Porto Alegre where he was held incommunicado for eleven hours. His requests to consult with counsel, the Italian Consulate, and his family were all denied. During this time he was denied all food and water.

"Later that same day Toscanino was brought to Brasilia. . . . For seventeen days Toscanino was incessantly tortured and interrogated. Throughout this entire period the United States government and the United States Attorney for the Eastern District of New York prosecuting this case was aware of the interrogation and did in fact receive reports as to its progress. Furthermore, during this period of torture and interrogation a member of the United States Department of Justice, Bureau of Narcotics and Dangerous Drugs was present at one or more intervals and actually participated in portions of the interrogation. . . . [Toscanino's] captors denied him sleep and all forms of nourishment for days at a time. Nourishment was provided intravenously in a manner precisely equal to an amount necessary to keep him alive. Reminiscent of the horror stories told by our military men who returned from Korea and China, Toscanino was forced to walk up and down a hallway for seven or eight hours at a time. When he could no longer stand he was kicked and beaten but all in a manner contrived to punish without scarring. When he would not answer, his fingers were pinched with metal pliers. Alcohol was flushed into his eyes and nose and other fluids . . . were forced up his anal passage. Incredibly, these agents of the United States government attached electrodes to Toscanino's earlobes, toes, and genitals. Jarring jolts of electricity were shot throughout his body, rendering him unconscious for indeterminate periods of time but again leaving no physical scars.

"Finally on or about January 25, 1973 Toscanino was brought to Rio de Janeiro where he was drugged by Brazilian-American agents and placed on Pan American Airways Flight #202 destined for the waiting arms of the United States government. On or about January 26, 1973 he woke in the United States, was arrested on the aircraft, and was brought immediately to Thomas Puccio, Assistant United States Attorney."

. . .

The government prosecutor neither affirmed nor denied these allegations but claimed they were immaterial to the district court's power to proceed.

5.　　Defendants in many subsequent cases of abduction have tried to invoke the so-called Toscanino "exception" to the Ker-Frisbie doctrine so as to divest the court of jurisdiction. Typically, these claims are rejected. See, e.g. United States v. Bridgewater, 175 F.Supp.2d 141 (D.Puerto Rico 2001): "There was no threat, no torture, no struggle, no violence, and no physical or verbal abuse."

6.　　The United States has extradition treaties with approximately 100 different countries.

7.　　Given the Ker-Frisbie doctrine and the apparent ease with which the United States in the past, acting through intermediaries or using its own personnel, has been able through subterfuge or force been able to bring a suspect to the United States, one may wonder why extradition is still frequently used. In fact, in a significant number of cases, terrorism suspects have been extradited or brought to the United States through ordinary rendition, that is, the foreign country having surrendered the prisoner to United States agents.

8.　　In June, 2014, a U.S. military team engaged in a successful operation to seize a suspected terrorist, Abu Khatallah, a person thought to have been a leader of the attack on the U.S. mission in Benghazi, Libya that resulted in the death of the U.S. Ambassador and three others. Excerpts from a judicial opinion in the case ruling on motions relating to his interrogation on shipboard are reproduced supra, this chapter. Here, extensive excerpts are presented from the same judicial opinion that deal with the details of his capture, issues relating to the choice of the method to transfer him to the United States and how they were resolved and other transfer-related questions. Abu Khatallah, 2017 WL 3534989 (D. D.C.):

[These excerpts present an unusually detailed window into the procedures and practices utilized in this instance of arguably "irregular rendition." Is this truly a case of rendition or should instances of apprehension and transfer by military authorities be put in a different category?]

The operation to capture Abu Khatallah followed nearly a year of planning across multiple U.S. government agencies. U.S. officials seriously considered two options in bringing Abu Khatallah to the United States after his capture: transport by aircraft, and transport by boat. The former option involved what is known as a foreign transfer-of-custody ("FTOC") request: Abu Khatallah would be taken to a third country and then flown across the Atlantic Ocean. The latter required transporting Abu Khatallah aboard the USS New York, a San Antonio-class amphibious warship.

. . .

The FBI ultimately planned for an operation that would allow for both transport options across the Atlantic. About five weeks prior to the operation, the FBI described the plan in internal e-mails as follows: The FBI would arrest Abu Khatallah in Libya and transfer him to a naval vessel in international waters. The vessel would then travel westward across the Mediterranean Sea for two to four days. During this time, intelligence agents would conduct non-Mirandized interrogations of Abu Khatallah as the State Department simultaneously contacted countries regarding the possibility of an FTOC request. FBI agents would then board the ship following the conclusion of the intelligence interrogations. If a third country agreed to an FTOC request, the ship would proceed to that country. If no country agreed, it would continue through the Mediterranean and across the Atlantic.

U.S. officials harbored serious doubts about the viability of the FTOC alternative for two reasons. First, the United States needed permission from a third country in order to conduct an FTOC, as it necessarily involved an intrusion upon the territorial sovereignty of another country. Given the site of the arrest, the State Department could have requested permission from countries in Europe, North Africa, and the Middle East. Officials were skeptical, however, that European countries would agree to such a request given the potential application of the death penalty to Abu Khatallah. Countries in North Africa and the Middle East were also doubtful participants given the potential domestic backlash they could face from cooperating with the United States on an anti-terrorism operation. And State Department officials were averse to making a request that was likely to be denied given the possible diplomatic ramifications. As Mr. Siberell put it, "When we make a request of a government, we do not want to put that government in the position of saying no to us on a very difficult issue. That may have some costs more broadly in the relationship. "As you and I discussed, there are costs to making requests and I'd prefer not to throw a bunch of spaghetti against the wall."). Given these concerns, the State Department believed that making an FTOC request would be "difficult" and "a hard one for [foreign] governments to accept."

The second reason that U.S. officials doubted the viability of flying Abu Khatallah through a third country concerned the timing of the request. The relevant officials concluded they would not be able to make an FTOC request of another country until after Abu Khatallah had been captured. As one Justice Department official involved in the deliberations testified, contacting a third country with this request prior to the operation would have entailed "a high security risk." An FBI official explained that a belated request was necessary because there was no guarantee that the third country would have kept the request confidential. The FBI was concerned that either the Libyan Government or various rebel groups inside Libya would learn of the operation beforehand, which "would significantly increase the risk to the mission and the possibility of failure of the operation." With any FTOC request on hold until after the operation began, the FBI focused much of its planning on transporting Khatallah across the Atlantic by ship. ("[The Department of Defense] has tasked [us] with developing [a plan] for transportation back to U.S. via opportune naval vessels. While everyone understands this is not the preferred [plan], it is the only one which the planners can start working on.").

The FBI nonetheless believed that "an FTOC out of a third country would have been the preferred and most likely course of action if [it] could [have been brought] to bear." It began laying the groundwork for this option in the fall of 2013, in conjunction with the planned apprehension of another terror suspect in Libya, Abu Anas al-Libi. The FBI developed an informal list of about a dozen countries that might help facilitate the FTOC, although even this informal list betrayed skepticism about the viability of this option. ("Truly believe though that given the media surrounding [the Benghazi attack] that the list of countries being willing to help on this would be very small . . . . [I]f all say no . . . we are stuck with the Trans Atlantic boat movement option.").

D.   The Capture Operation

FBI Agent "Johnson" described the planning and execution of Abu Khatallah's capture at the evidentiary hearing. An eight-member team began training for the operation in April 2014. The team, which included an FBI agent and a military translator trained as an Arabic linguist, departed the United States in early June. On June 9, 2014, they flew by helicopter from a base in Southern Europe to the USS New York, as it was travelling eastward in the Mediterranean toward the Libyan coast. All team members were armed with pistols and dressed in civilian clothing that was intended to blend in with the environment. In addition to their side arms, half the team carried backpacks containing assault-style weapons. The team divided itself among the villa's four rooms and waited for Abu Khatallah to arrive.

The team planned for one of Abu Khatallah's acquaintances to lead him to the villa. When Abu Khatallah and his acquaintance entered the villa, they were immediately swarmed. . . .

The capture team then led a handcuffed—but mobile—Abu Khatallah into the bathroom, where Agent Johnson, through the Arabic linguist, identified himself as a member of the U.S. government. He told Abu Khatallah that he was in government custody and would be taken to the United States. He also asked Abu Khatallah to identify himself, whether he was armed, and if anybody knew his current whereabouts. Abu Khatallah responded by stating his name and confirming that he was not armed and that no one knew where he was. The capture team had decided not to identify themselves to Abu Khatallah earlier because they felt this was the safest way to apprehend him. In the bathroom with the lights on, Johnson observed a gash on Abu Khatallah's head and signs of bruising and swelling around his eyes, but he was unable to say precisely how Abu Khatallah had sustained those injuries. No one on the capture team was injured. A member of the capture team with medical training gave Abu Khatallah a cursory medical examination to make sure he was able to travel and not suffering from any significant injuries. The entire apprehension—from Abu Khatallah's entrance into the villa until the conversation in the bathroom—lasted approximately eleven minutes.

Ten minutes later, after the team had cleaned the villa, it escorted Abu Khatallah about 500 meters to the shore, where a boat with another FBI agent on board was waiting. Abu Khatallah was in handcuffs, the front of his face was obscured by a blindfold, his ears were covered, and he was gagged. Two team members guided him by the arms. Before boarding the vessel, the agents switched Abu Khatallah's handcuffs to the front and outfitted him with a life preserver so that he would be able to tread water in case he fell overboard. At roughly 10:30 p.m., the boat departed the Libyan coast, and after ten minutes at sea, it pulled alongside a larger boat. Abu Khatallah was lifted into the second vessel, which then proceeded toward the USS New York. During the two-hour journey to the USS New York, Agent Johnson removed Abu Khatallah's gag because he was no longer within shouting distance of the shore, and a medic examined him. The medic checked Abu Khatallah's vital signs and informed Agent Johnson that he was fit to continue. Abu Khatallah reportedly repeated the phrase "God, why me" during the journey. Upon arriving at the USS New York, the boat pulled alongside the ship's rear cargo door, and the medic placed a harness around himself and Abu Khatallah, and they were hoisted approximately ten to twelve feet to the ship's berth. . . .

The capture team's efforts were supported by a team on board the USS New York, who helped ready the ship for Abu Khatallah's arrival. Special Agent Robert Story, a supervisor in the FBI's counterterrorism division and a member of the support team, testified concerning Abu Khatallah's treatment and living conditions on the ship. Agent Story was tapped for the team in May 2014 and boarded the USS New York on June 9, 2014. While awaiting Abu Khatallah's capture, the team erected a detention facility in an open area within the ship's rear interior that consisted of four mobile pods in a row. The pods measured roughly 8 feet in length by 7 feet in width by 8 feet in height and were designated as either living quarters (pods "D1" and "D2") or interrogation rooms (pods "I1" or "I2"). A larger, adjacent pod served as the latrine ("L"). Id. The pods were ventilated and screened off from the rest of the ship so that they could not be viewed from the sides or above. Id.; Gov't Ex. 405A–E. Abu Khatallah would live in pod D1 for the duration of the ship's journey. An arrow on the wall of the pod pointed west towards Mecca and for the initial phase of his transit he was provided a blanket, a Quran, and a prayer rug.

Agent Story was responsible for processing Abu Khatallah as soon as he boarded the USS New York. Story, along with two Department of Defense ("DOD") guards and with the assistance of an Arabic linguist, verbally instructed Abu Khatallah and physically guided him to the detention facility. Abu Khatallah's hearing restraint was removed but his handcuffs and blindfold remained in place, which would be the general protocol whenever he was moved between pods. Abu Khatallah followed all instructions, and Agent Story described him as "compliant" and "very calm." Upon reaching the detention facility, Abu Khatallah was searched and taken to pod D2 for initial processing.

Once inside the processing pod, Abu Khatallah's blindfold, ear coverings, and handcuffs were removed. Staff Sergeant Dylan Lee Peterson—a member of the DOD guard force that provided security on board the ship—testified that he read Abu Khatallah the provisions of Article III of the Geneva Conventions, pausing throughout so that the interpreter could repeat the provisions in Arabic. Abu Khatallah was told, for example, that he would be "treated humanely, without any adverse distinction founded on race, color, religion or faith, sex, birth or wealth, or any other similar criteria," and that U.S. personnel would not engage in "violence to life and person, in particular murder of all kinds, mutilation, cruel treatment and torture." Written versions of those guarantees in both English and Arabic were also posted on the wall of the pod, where they remained for the duration of the trip.

Further processing included photographing Abu Khatallah in the clothes he arrived in and conducting a medical screening. The ship's physician, Dr. Brad Smith, performed an initial medical exam and treated Abu Khatallah throughout his journey on the USS New

York. (Abu Khatallah's medical records). Dr. Smith characterized Abu Khatallah's head injury as a "subcutaneous laceration," and he closed the wound with three staples after applying local anaesthetic. He also examined Abu Khatallah's left hand, which showed signs of swelling and bruising around the fourth finger. Dr. Smith took x-rays of Abu Khatallah's hand and jaw, which were negative. At the end of the exam, Dr. Smith informed Abu Khatallah that he would be "seeing him again on a daily basis" and would remove the staples later.

The DOD guards were present throughout the initial processing and medical examination, and they attended to Abu Khatallah's general care and handling while on the ship. They gave him a set of rules, which included instructions to use one-word requests such as "water" and "bathroom," and directed him to "notify the staff" if he felt "abused." The guards kept a written log of all of Abu Khatallah's movements, including his visits to the latrine, the medical unit, and the interrogation pod. Each time Abu Khatallah was transported from one place on the ship to another, he was handcuffed, and his ears and eyes were covered. The logs also reflect brief checks on Abu Khatallah that occurred every two hours: The guards would peer through a window in the door of his cell "to make sure he was moving, awake, [and] alive."

. . .

U.S. officials also seriously considered making an FTOC request of G-21, a country in Europe. About a month prior to the operation, an FBI legal attaché stationed in that country had asked his counterpart in G-21 about assisting with an FTOC, in general terms. According to Bryan Paarmann, G-21 was apparently "extremely receptive to the FTOC idea." Id. As he later testified, however, G-21 was not aware of the specifics of the operation—particularly the identity of the arrestee being transferred. Because G-21 had previously refused an FTOC request for Abu Anas al-Libi, "it was decided that G-21 would be unlikely to say yes given the specifics of Abu Khatallah." The United States therefore did not make an official FTOC request of G-21.

. . .

Captain Brunette explained that the ship is a San Antonio-class amphibious warship that is powered by four diesel engines. As the USS New York proceeded toward the Mediterranean, its crew noticed a fuel dilution problem in one of the engines. The crew began running a series of tests on the engine on June 5, 2014. On or about June 9, the crew realized that they were unable to solve the problem on their own, and decided to shut the engine down until a diesel engine inspector could travel to the ship to assist them. The engine inspector arrived on the ship via helicopter on June 19, after Abu Khatallah had boarded, as it neared the Strait of Gibraltar headed toward the Atlantic. At the direction of the inspector, the crew ran additional tests for several days and resolved the issue on June 25.

The USS New York experienced additional difficulties in another engine on June 23, as it ventured toward the United States. As tests were being run on the first problem engine, the diesel engine inspector noticed that one of the ship's other engines was operating with high vacuum pressure. Captain Brunette described this as a "very serious condition" that could "render that entire engine completely useless." The ship's crew deliberated and determined that there was no way to conduct the necessary repairs at sea. The engine therefore had to be shut down until the ship reached the mainland United States.

The upshot of these mechanical issues was that two of the USS New York's four engines were shut down at the same time for a period of about 50 hours. As a result, the ship had to slow considerably during that time. Id. The ship is "governed by directives that define how fast [it] should or should not transit" at any given time. These directives take into account fuel efficiency, "wear and tear" on the engines, and the body of water in which the ship is traveling. They provide that the USS New York should travel at about sixteen knots in the Atlantic, and at about fourteen knots in the Mediterranean. The ship's maximum speed depends on how many of the ship's four engines are fully functional. During the time that two of the ship's engines were inoperable—from about June 23 to June 25—the ship was limited to thirteen knots. After the first troublesome engine was restored on June 25, Captain Burnette ordered the USS New York to travel at eighteen knots for the remainder of its voyage to the United States—above the recommended speed provided for in the ship's directives.

. . .

Abu Khatallah moved to dismiss all but one of the counts, arguing that most of the charged statutes could not be applied to conduct undertaken outside the United States. The Court largely denied Abu Khatallah's motion in a December 2015 Memorandum Opinion, reserving judgment on two counts until it could receive additional briefing. See 151 F.Supp.3d 116 (D.D.C. 2015). The Court denied his motion with respect to those remaining two counts in a separate Memorandum Opinion on March 2, 2016. See 168 F.Supp.3d 210 (D.D.C. 2016). Abu Khatallah moved to suppress the statements he made to government officials on board the USS New York on November 15, 2016. The Court held an evidentiary hearing from May 10 to May 18, 2017, at which 15 witnesses testified, and heard oral argument on the motion on June 6, 2017.

II. Discussion

A. Whether the Government Violated Abu Khatallah's Right to Prompt Presentment

Abu Khatallah first moves to suppress the statements he gave to FBI agents on board the USS New York on the ground that the Government violated his right to prompt presentment before a neutral magistrate. Given the extraordinary facts of this case, which present numerous concerns that were not present in the Supreme Court's leading prompt-presentment cases, the Court will begin by reviewing the history and general principles of the presentment requirement.

1. The Right to Prompt Presentment: Background and General Principles

. . .

At the federal level, the right to prompt presentment was codified across several statutes by the mid-twentieth century—none of which provided an exclusionary rule or any other sort of enforcement mechanism. Id. The Supreme Court first confronted this issue in McNabb. In that case, federal agents arrested a small clan of Tennessee mountaineers on murder charges and interrogated them for several days. McNabb, 318 U.S. at 333–36, 63 S.Ct. 608. No lawyer was present, nor were the suspects advised of any of their rights. Id. The agents brought the suspects before a magistrate only after securing confessions that were essential to their subsequent convictions. Id. at 338, 63 S.Ct. 608. The Supreme Court reversed the convictions, explaining that "a conviction resting on evidence secured through such a flagrant disregard of the procedure which Congress has commanded cannot be allowed to stand." Id. at 345, 63 S.Ct. 608. The Court also noted that the purpose of the presentment requirement was to "avoid all the evil implications of secret interrogation of persons accused of crime." Id. at 344, 63 S.Ct. 608.

Federal Rule of Criminal Procedure 5, promulgated several years after McNabb, provides that "[a] person making an arrest outside the United States must take the defendant without unnecessary delay before a magistrate judge, unless a statute provides otherwise." Fed. R. Crim. P. 5(a)(1)(B).10 This rule "pulled the several statutory presentment provisions together in one place." Corley, 556 U.S. at 307, 129 S.Ct. 1558. But like its predecessors, Rule 5 failed to specify a remedy for violations of the presentment requirement. The Supreme Court nonetheless reaffirmed the McNabb exclusionary rule with two important clarifications. First, in Upshaw v. United States, it held that McNabb required the exclusion of incriminating statements even if those statements were voluntarily made by the defendant. 335 U.S. 410, 413, 69 S.Ct. 170,

93 L.Ed. 100 (1948). Second, in Mallory v. United States, the Supreme Court held that even short delays in presentment—i.e., delays of several hours—can violate an arrestee's presentment rights if the arresting officers caused the delay in order to interrogate the arrestee. 354 U.S. 449, 455–56, 77 S.Ct. 1356, 1 L.Ed.2d 1479 (1957). The principle that emerged from these cases is referred to as the McNabb-Mallory rule, which "generally renders inadmissible confessions made during periods of detention that violate the prompt presentment requirement of Rule 5(a)." Corley, 556 U.S. at 309, 129 S.Ct. 1558 (internal quotation marks omitted).

Congress narrowed the scope of the McNabb-Mallory rule in 1968 by enacting 18 U.S.C. § 3501(c). See id. Section 3501(c) creates a six-hour grace period immediately following an arrest, and provides that any incriminating statements made in that period "shall not be inadmissible solely because of delay in [presentment]." 18 U.S.C. § 3501(c). Under § 3501(c), statements made during a presentment delay of more than six hours are inadmissible unless "[the delay] beyond such six-hour period is found by the trial judge to be reasonable considering the means of transportation and the distance to be traveled to the nearest available . . . magistrate judge." Id. The Supreme Court has thus restated the McNabb-Mallory rule in light of § 3501(c) as a two-part test:

Under the rule as revised by § 3501(c), a district court with a suppression claim must find whether the defendant confessed within six hours of arrest (unless a longer delay was 'reasonable considering the means of transportation and the distance to be traveled to the nearest available magistrate"). [1] If the confession came within that period, it is admissible, subject to other Rules of Evidence, so long as it was made voluntarily and the weight to be given it is left to the jury. [2] If the confession occurred before presentment and beyond six hours, however, the court must decide whether delaying that long was unreasonable or unnecessary under the McNabb-Mallory cases, and if it was, the confession is to be suppressed.

As for what constitutes an "unreasonable or unnecessary [delay] under the McNabb-Mallory cases," a court does not assess reasonableness simply by "watching the clock." Muschette v. United States, 322 F.2d 989, 992 (D.C. Cir. 1963), vacated on other grounds, 378 U.S. 569, 84 S.Ct. 1927, 12 L.Ed.2d 1039 (1964). It must look instead to the cause of any delay. See id. "[D]elay for the purpose of interrogation is the epitome of 'unnecessary delay' " and is inherently unreasonable. Corley, 556 U.S. at 309, 129 S.Ct. 1558 (citing Mallory, 354 U.S. at 455–56, 77 S.Ct. 1356). After all, the McNabb-Mallory rule arose from the Supreme Court's desire to deter police from engaging in extensive prearraignment detentions in order to further interrogate a defendant. United States v. Garcia-Hernandez, 569 F.3d 1100, 1106 (9th Cir. 2009).

Beyond this, however, courts "have been careful not to overextend McNabb-Mallory's prophylactic rule in cases where there was a reasonable delay unrelated to any prolonged interrogation of the arrestee." . . .

2. Applying the McNabb-Mallory Rule to Overseas Arrests

The principle that reasonableness turns on the cause of any delay, rather than the length of the delay alone, applies with equal force to arrests made outside the United States. Crucially, "[t]he prompt presentment requirement does not require a magistrate to be available twenty-four hours a day, and the government is not required to take the fastest possible route to the courthouse—just a reasonable one." Boche-Perez, 755 F.3d at 338; . . . .This is particularly relevant for overseas arrests, as the distance between the site of arrest and the nearest magistrate often leads to unavoidable delays in presentment.

Consistent with this principle, a number of federal courts have found extensive presentment delays to be reasonable under the circumstances presented. For example, in United States v. Odom, 526 F.2d 339 (5th Cir. 1976), the U.S. Coast Guard stopped a small boat in international waters between Cuba and Mexico during a routine patrol. After determining that the vessel was registered in the United States, Coast Guard officials conducted a safety and documentation inspection, which led to the discovery of a large amount of marijuana. Id. at 341. The defendants were arrested and placed on board the Coast Guard ship. During the vessel's five-day return journey to Florida, DEA agents arrived on the boat via helicopter. Id. The arrestees waived their Miranda rights and were interrogated on the boat for several days before being presented before a magistrate in Florida. Id. Citing the "unique circumstances in [the] case," the Fifth Circuit declined to suppress the statements made on board the vessel under the McNabb-Mallory rule. See id. at 343.

Other federal courts have upheld even longer delays in presentment. See, e.g., United States v. Zakharov, 468 F.3d 1171, 1179 (9th Cir. 2006) (16-day presentment delay found reasonable where defendants were brought by boat 1,620 nautical miles from international waters near southern Mexico to San Diego); United States v. Cheme-Ibarra, No. 14-cr-3305, slip op. at 12 (S.D. Cal. June 6, 2016) (16-day presentment delay found reasonable where defendants were brought by boat 2,500 nautical miles from international waters near Panama to San Diego); United States v. Gonzales-Corredor, No. 12-cr-2550 (S.D. Cal. Dec. 13, 2012) (19-day delay in presentment found reasonable where defendants were brought by boat several thousand miles from the eastern Pacific Ocean to San Diego); United States v. Greyshock, 719 F.Supp. 927, 932–33 (D. Haw. 1989) (9-day presentment delay found reasonable where defendants were brought by boat 900 miles from international waters in the Pacific to Honolulu, Hawaii).

As Abu Khatallah rightly points out, the above cases are distinguishable insofar as the arrests were not planned in advance. However, the D.C. Circuit's ruling in United States v. Yunis, 859 F.2d 953 (D.C. Cir. 1988), illustrates the application of McNabb-Mallory to overseas arrests that occurred following extensive planning. In Yunis, the FBI arrested the defendant, a Lebanese citizen, for his alleged involvement in the 1985 hijacking of a commercial airplane. Id. at 954–55. The FBI planned the capture and arrest in concert with other federal agencies. Id. at 955. Agents lured the defendant to a yacht in the eastern Mediterranean, where they arrested him and brought him onboard a nearby U.S. Navy ship. Id. The ship then traveled westward across the Mediterranean until it rendezvoused with an aircraft carrier, where Yunis was put on a plane and flown to the United States to be arraigned. Id. The journey across the Mediterranean took four days, during which time FBI agents repeatedly interrogated Yunis and procured incriminating statements from him. Id. at 955–57.

In Yunis, alternative modes of transportation "were never seriously considered [by the government] only because their defects were readily apparent." Id. at 968 (internal quotation marks omitted). For example, the government declined to fly Yunis directly from a Mediterranean country because of possible "extradition problems." Id. at 968. The government also rejected the option of hiring a commercial sea plane to fly Yunis across the Mediterranean "because no American companies had planes in the region, and, in any event, the inclusion of civilians . . . posed security and other risks." Id. (internal citations omitted). Still, the district court found that the government had "purposely created the delay between arrest and arraignment" and "deliberately scheduled a four-day voyage across the Mediterranean to allow the FBI sufficient time to interview and secure a statement from [the defendant]." Id. (quoting United States v. Yunis, 681 F.Supp. 909, 927 (D.D.C. 1988)). The D.C. Circuit reversed this factual finding as clearly erroneous, and further held that the district court erred as a matter of law in finding that the presentment delay was unreasonable on the ground that it was not "as short as it could have been." Id.

The D.C. Circuit also noted that "a principal concern of the McNabb-Mallory rule [was] absent from Yunis' case." Id. at 969. In the vast majority of criminal cases, the police have no warrant for an arrest. Id. In these cases, "[a]n arraignment is thus essential 'so that the issue of probable cause may be promptly determined by a neutral magistrate.'" Id. at 969 (quoting Mallory, 354 U.S. at 454, 77 S.Ct. 1356). But becuase there was an arrest warrant in Yunis, "there [was] no possibility that the government pursued an investigatory arrest, delaying the arraignment so that it could obtain a confession that would then supply the probable cause." Id. (internal quotation marks omitted). The D.C. Circuit reiterated this point several years later in Salamanca:

> [The defendant's] argument that there was an unreasonable delay is also weakened by the fact that he was arrested pursuant to a warrant. One of the primary rationales for a prompt appearance before a magistrate is to resolve the issue of probable cause, which had already been resolved when the warrant was issued. See Yunis, 859 F.2d at 969.

3.   Application of McNabb-Mallory to Abu Khatallah's Motion to Suppress

The Court now turns to Abu Khatallah's contention that his statements to FBI agents on board the USS New York must be suppressed on prompt-presentment grounds. As noted, there was a thirteen-day delay between Abu Khatallah's arrest and his presentment before a magistrate judge in Washington, D.C.—well beyond the six-hour safe harbor provided for in 18 U.S.C. § 3501(c). But as both the text of § 3501(c) and the above-cited cases indicate, the length of the delay cannot be considered in isolation. Rather, "the court must decide whether delaying that long was unreasonable or unnecessary under the McNabb-Mallory cases, and if it was, the [statements are] to be suppressed." Abu Khatallah argues that the Government transported him aboard the USS New York in order to maximize interrogation time, and that it never undertook a serious effort to fly him to the United States by way of another country in the region. The Government's conduct, in his view, reflected "a deliberate strategy approved at the highest levels of government and engineered to create the illusion that there were no other alternatives to a two-week delay.".

Yet the record supports no such conclusion. To the contrary, it demonstrates that transporting Abu Khatallah by air through an FTOC to a third country was an integral part of the Government's planning in the months leading up to Abu Khatallah's capture. For example, U.S. officials discussed that option nearly a year in advance as they planned the capture of another suspected terrorist in Libya. These discussions refer to a trans-Atlantic voyage by boat as "an option of last resort," and reflect the view that "an FTOC out of a third country would have been the preferred and most likely course of action if [it] could [have been] brought to bear,"

And while the officials who oversaw the operation may have made an FTOC request of only a single country after considering more than a dozen, they have offered reasoned grounds for such restraint. As the State Department's Acting Coordinator for Counterterrorism, Justin Siberell, credibly testified, there are diplomatic costs to even making an FTOC request. The decision to do so therefore "need[ed] to be a very considered judgment." Countries in Europe were not approached because none were likely to agree to an FTOC for a defendant facing the death penalty. As Deputy Assistant Attorney General Bruce Swartz testified, "[e]very European Union member state and the European Union itself will refuse to allow extradition for an individual charged with the death penalty, or transit through their territory of such an individual without an assurance that the death penalty will not be imposed." Mr. Swartz explained further that making a futile FTOC request for Abu Khatallah to a European Union member state would have been "extremely harmful" and "not . . . an ask that would be appropriate for us to make under those circumstances."

Countries south of the Mediterranean, too, were taken off the table because of the potential for political backlash. Mr. Siberell explained:

> [S]ome countries will view [the FTOC of Abu Khatallah] as a particularly sensitive matter insofar as they may perceive that they would themselves be implicated in the operation . . . . [M]any governments, who although are prepared to address these threats within their own borders and do so aggressively, do so quietly and do not want their actions necessarily to be known publicly. So to associate themselves with our actions in this case . . . could [have] open[ed] themselves to threats.

In light of these domestic political realities, the view of the State Department was that an FTOC through these coutnries would be "difficult" and a "hard one for [them] to accept." Notwithstanding these concerns, the State Department made a request of Country G-24, a nation south of the Mediterranean that U.S. officials believed would be the most likely to assist given its history of cooperation with the United States on similar operations. When Country G-24 denied the FTOC request, the State Department exercised its considered judgment not to approach other countries, concluding that any additional requests would carry undue diplomatic costs and were unlikely to be successful. The Court finds nothing in the record that would cause it to second guess that determination.

Abu Khatallah dismisses the government's consideration of FTOC options as "merely a ruse.". But his supporting evidence does not bear the weight he places on it. . . .

Abu Khatallah also contends that the decision by U.S. officials to delay contacting a third country about an FTOC until after the operation was underway was purposefully designed to "mak[e] the chances of success remote." The record, however, supports the Government's position that the belated request was reasonably justified by security concerns. As DOJ and FBI officials testified, an earlier request would have risked disclosure of the operation—potentially to Libyan rebel groups—which in turn would have significantly increased the risk of the operation and the safety of those involved in the capture. Mr. Siberell credibly testified that "the same factors that were considered after the fact would likely have been considered prior to the operation," thus leading to the same result. On these facts, the Court finds it reasonable for the State Department to have delayed making an FTOC request until after Abu Khatallah's arrest.

. . .

Abu Khatallah also suggests that the Government could have flown him back to the United States without the help of a third country, as it did in Yunis. He specifically contends that the Government "could have flown a V-22 Osprey which could be refueled in mid-air, to an aircraft carrier in the region which [did have] planes that [could] fly trans-Atlantic." Id. The record, however, casts significant doubt on the feasibility of such an option in this case. As Mr. Swartz of DOJ testified, there were no aircraft carriers in the region. The captain of the USS New York, moreover, confirmed that the nearest aircraft carrier, the USS George H.W. Bush, was in the Arabian Gulf. He also explained why it would not have been possible to fly Abu Khatallah to that carrier:

> Q: [W]hen you took Mr. Khatallah on board . . . could you have used your Osprey or any other aircraft . . . capable of landing or taking off from your ship to transport Mr. Khatallah to the USS Bush, which was in the northern Arabian Gulf?
>
> A: No . . . there would be no way to fly that distance. That's approximately 3,000 miles. If you tried to stay over water, you would have to go over the Suez Canal, which is Egyptian air space. You could not do it.
>
> Q: Well, hypothetically speaking, if you had been able to get Mr. Khatallah to the USS George H.W. Bush, would it have been [able] to bring him back to the United States without stopping in a third country?
>
> A: No . . . . There are only [three] types of aircraft that we transport passengers to and from ships . . . [T]here's no way to fly with [their] range all the way back to the continental United States.
>
> Q: Let me ask you, if we can't take Mr. Khatallah to the aircraft carrier, would it have made operational sense to bring the aircraft carrier to him?
>
> A: In my opinion, no . . . It's approximately a 3,000 mile transit [and] would take several days to get to where the USS New York was operating . . . . I don't think it [would have made]

operational sense to do that. Also, the U.S.S. George H.W. Bush and her strike group were executing operations in the northern Arabian Gulf. That's why they were there . . . I don't think it would have made sense to call off those operations to be able to come transport an individual.

Id. at 1000:6–1003:3. Given the absence of evidence in the record to contradict this testimony, the Court finds that the Government's decision to refrain from using an aircraft carrier did not violate Abu Khatallah's right to a prompt presentment. After all, "the government is not required to take the fastest possible route to the courthouse—just a reasonable one." Boche-Perez, 755 F.3d at 338. In this instance, it strikes the Court as eminently reasonable for the Government not to divert military resources being used elsewhere in order to expedite Abu Khatallah's presentment.

Finally, Abu Khatallah points to the fact that the USS New York was not traveling at its maximum speed across the Atlantic, arguing that "[t]here is at least some indication that the true reason was to conduct additional interrogation.". Again, however, the record does not support that conclusion. As the ship's captain testified, the USS New York encountered problems with two of its engines that required it to reduce its speed to 13 knots for approximately 50 hours. Abu Khatallah has not identified any evidence suggesting that the Government deliberately caused the delay in order to prolong his interrogation. And after the ship's crew restored one of the engines, the ship proceeded at eighteen knots—above its recommended speed. In addition to recounting these engine difficulties, Captain Burnette testified that the USS New York was not traveling at its maximum speed even when doing so would have been theoretically possible, as it would have risked damage to ship's engines. Accordingly, the Court finds that the added time caused by the ship's reduced speeds did not render the delay between Abu Khatallah's arrest and presentment unreasonable. See Yunis, 859 F.2d at 969 (ship's failure to cruise at maximum speed did not violate prompt presentment right).

On this factual record, the Court declines to suppress Abu Khatallah's statements on prompt-presentment grounds. The thirteen-day delay was reasonable given the distance between the site of the arrest and the nearest available magistrate, as well as the means of transportation chosen. The Government has offered sound law enforcement and national security rationales for not making any FTOC requests prior to Abu Khatallah's capture, and legitimate diplomatic reasons for making only a single FTOC request thereafter. It was also reasonable for the Government not to have diverted an aircraft carrier from ongoing military operations in order to expedite Abu Khatallah's presentment. The Court thus finds that the Government's decision to transport Abu Khatallah by ship was reasonable, and not motivated by a desire to prolong his interrogation.

It also bears repeating that two of the primary concerns of the McNabb-Mallory rule—the need to quickly secure a probable cause determination and the need to promptly advise an arrestee of his or her rights—were not present in this case. Like in Yunis, a warrant was issued prior to the arrest. As a result, "there is no possibility that the government pursued an 'investigatory arrest,' delaying the arraignment so that it could obtain a confession that would then supply the probable cause." Yunis, 859 F.2d at 969. The record also indicates that Abu Khatallah was advised of his Miranda rights and voluntarily waived them. See infra Part II.B.

Notwithstanding the Court's conclusion on the presentment issue, it is worth underscoring that "each case involving the McNabb rule must . . . be decided without resort to a semanticism that obscures the facts out of which it arises." United States v. Leviton, 193 F.2d 848, 854 (2d Cir. 1951). Every case will be different. The McNabb-Mallory framework is not a "stiff formula" that mechanically permits a prolonged presentment delay in all cases where a defendant is apprehended overseas, or where the government's justifications for delay are buoyed by national security or diplomatic concerns. Id. In this particular case, however, the record supports the reasonableness of the delay in presenting Abu Khatallah before a magistrate.

. . .

9. What kinds of considerations might influence United States authorities not to go through standard legal channels and use extradition to bring a suspect to the United States? Does the Ker-Frisbie doctrine, in effect, encourage the use of kidnapping, sting operations, or military actions to bring suspects to the United States? Should some mechanism be adopted to discourage such practices? What about the possible extradition of the kidnappers back to the country from which the suspect was taken? See footnotes 11 and 16 in the Alvarez-Machain case, supra. What are the implications of using military operations to seize the suspected terrorist, as in the Abu Khatallah case, supra.

10. Some countries are reluctant to extradite or engage in ordinary rendition regarding individuals who may be subject to the death penalty in connection with the crimes for which they are being extradited. Similarly, In June, 2002, a related issue surfaced in connection with the prosecution of Zacarias Moussaoui. Both France and Germany indicated reluctance to provide information and evidence to the United States relating to Moussaoui as long as Moussaoui might be subject to the death penalty as an outcome of the prosecution. See Hugh Williamson, Schroeder Sees Way Out of Evidence Dispute, Financial Times, London, June 12, 2002 (reporting that Germany's Chancellor said that he expects Berlin and Washington to find a "common

position" regarding the matter of Germany supplying the U.S. with evidence that could be used in the prosecution of Moussaoui.).

11. Another reason why some foreign countries may be reluctant to transfer a captured suspected terrorist to the U.S. is concern that the individual will be sent to Guantanamo and dealt with through military commission process. In cases where the foreign capturer of the suspected terrorist has this type of concern, it can impose as a condition of the transfer that the individual not be sent to Guantanamo. As a result of such cases, a number of individuals captured abroad have been sent to New York for prosecution in civilian criminal proceedings even under Donald Trump, a President who has expressed a preference for sending suspected terrorists to Guantanamo. Are there other reasons why the Trump administration might decide to send persons to New York rather than Guantanamo despite the President's expressed preference?

12. Following the decision in United States v. Alvarez-Machain, the prosecution went to trial. At the close of the government's case, the District Court granted the defendant's motion for a judgment of acquittal. Subsequently, Alvarez filed a civil action which ended up again in the Supreme Court. The issue before the Court was highly technical involving application of the Federal Tort Claims Act and the Alien Tort Statute which deals with civil actions by aliens for a tort committed in violation of the law of nations or a U.S. treaty. The Court concluded that he was not entitled to a remedy under either statute. Sosa v. Alvarez-Machain, 542 U.S. 692 (2004).

13. See Jacques Semmelman, Due Process, International Law, and Jurisdiction over Criminal Defendants Abducted Extraterritorially: The Ker-Frisbie Doctrine Reexamined, 30 Colum. J. Transnat'l L. 513 (1992); Malvina Halberstam, In Defense of the Supreme Court Decision in Alvarez-Machain, 86 Am. J. Int'l L. 736 (1992). For a case involving a forcible abduction in Pakistan by FBI agents of a person charged with the killing of CIA employees, see Kasi v. Angelone, 300 F.3d 487 (4th Cir.2002).

3. LAWSUITS BROUGHT BY ALLEGED VICTIMS OF EXTRAORDINARY RENDITION

ARAR V. ASHCROFT

585 F. 3d 559 (2d Cir. 2009) (en banc), cert. denied 560 U.S. 978 (2010)

[Before JACOBS, CHIEF JUDGE, MCLAUGHLIN, CALABRESI, CABRANES, POOLER, SACK, SOTOMAYOR,[6] PARKER, RAGGI, WESLEY, HALL, and LIVINGSTON, CIRCUIT JUDGES. KATZMANN, CIRCUIT JUDGE, took no part in the consideration or decision of the case.

---

[6] The Honorable Sonia Sotomayor, who was originally a member of the in banc panel and who participated in oral argument, was elevated to the Supreme Court on August 8, 2009.

JACOBS, C.J., filed the majority opinion in which MCLAUGHLIN, CABRANES, RAGGI, WESLEY, HALL, and LIVINGSTON, JJ., joined.

SACK, J., filed a dissenting opinion in which CALABRESI, POOLER, and PARKER, JJ., joined. PARKER, J., filed a dissenting opinion in which CALABRESI, POOLER, and SACK, JJ., joined. POOLER, J., filed a dissenting opinion in which CALABRESI, SACK, and PARKER, JJ., joined.

CALABRESI, J., filed a dissenting opinion in which POOLER, SACK, and PARKER, JJ., joined.]

DENNIS JACOBS, CHIEF JUDGE:

Maher Arar appeals from a judgment of the United States District Court for the Eastern District of New York (Trager, J.) dismissing his complaint against the Attorney General of the United States, the Secretary of Homeland Security, the Director of the Federal Bureau of Investigation, and others, including senior immigration officials. Arar alleges that he was detained while changing planes at Kennedy Airport in New York (based on a warning from Canadian authorities that he was a member of Al Qaeda), mistreated for twelve days while in United States custody, and then removed to Syria via Jordan pursuant to an inter-governmental understanding that he would be detained and interrogated under torture by Syrian officials. The complaint alleges a violation of the Torture Victim Protection Act ("TVPA") and of his Fifth Amendment substantive due process rights arising from the conditions of his detention in the United States, the denial of his access to counsel and to the courts while in the United States, and his detention and torture in Syria.

The district court dismissed the complaint (with leave to re-plead only as to the conditions of detention in the United States and his access to counsel and the courts during that period) and Arar timely appealed (without undertaking to amend). Arar v. Ashcroft, 414 F.Supp.2d 250 (E.D.N.Y.2006). A three-judge panel of this Court unanimously held that: (1) the District Court had personal jurisdiction over Thompson, Ashcroft, and Mueller; (2) Arar failed to state a claim under the TVPA; and (3) Arar failed to establish subject matter jurisdiction over his request for a declaratory judgment. Arar v. Ashcroft, 532 F.3d 157 (2d Cir.2008). A majority of the panel also dismissed Arar's Bivens claims, with one member of the panel dissenting. Id. The Court voted to rehear the appeal in banc. We now affirm.

We have no trouble affirming the district court's conclusions that Arar sufficiently alleged personal jurisdiction over the defendants who challenged it, and that Arar lacks standing to seek declaratory relief. We do not reach issues of qualified immunity or the state secrets privilege. As to the TVPA, we agree with the unanimous position of the panel that Arar insufficiently pleaded that the alleged conduct of United States officials was done under color of foreign law. We agree with the district court that

Arar insufficiently pleaded his claim regarding detention in the United States, a ruling that has been reinforced by the subsequent authority of Bell Atlantic Corp. v. Twombly, 550 U.S. 544, 570 (2007). Our attention is therefore focused on whether Arar's claims for detention and torture in Syria can be asserted under Bivens v. Six Unknown Named Agents of Federal Bureau of Narcotics, 403 U.S. 388, 91 S.Ct. 1999, 29 L.Ed.2d 619 (1971) ("Bivens").

To decide the Bivens issue, we must determine whether Arar's claims invoke Bivens in a new context; and, if so, whether an alternative remedial scheme was available to Arar, or whether (in the absence of affirmative action by Congress) " 'special factors counsel[ ] hesitation.' This opinion holds that "extraordinary rendition" is a context new to Bivens claims, but avoids any categorical ruling on alternative remedies-because the dominant holding of this opinion is that, in the context of extraordinary rendition, hesitation is warranted by special factors. We therefore affirm.

. . .

Our ruling does not preclude judicial review and oversight in this context. But if a civil remedy in damages is to be created for harms suffered in the context of extraordinary rendition, it must be created by Congress, which alone has the institutional competence to set parameters, delineate safe harbors, and specify relief. If Congress chooses to legislate on this subject, then judicial review of such legislation would be available.

Applying our understanding of Supreme Court precedent, we decline to create, on our own, a new cause of action against officers and employees of the federal government. Rather, we conclude that, when a case presents the intractable "special factors" apparent here, it is for the Executive in the first instance to decide how to implement extraordinary rendition, and for the elected members of Congress-and not for us as judges-to decide whether an individual may seek compensation from government officers and employees directly, or from the government, for a constitutional violation. Administrations past and present have reserved the right to employ rendition, see David Johnston, U.S. Says Rendition to Continue, but with More Oversight, N.Y. Times, Aug. 24, 2009, and notwithstanding prolonged public debate, Congress has not prohibited the practice, imposed limits on its use, or created a cause of action for those who allege they have suffered constitutional injury as a consequence.

I

Arar's complaint sets forth the following factual allegations.

Arar is a dual citizen of Syria, where he was born and raised, and of Canada, to which his family immigrated when he was 17.

While on vacation in Tunisia in September 2002, Arar was called back to work in Montreal. His itinerary called for stops in Zurich and New York.

Arar landed at Kennedy Airport around noon on September 26. Between planes, Arar presented his Canadian passport to an immigration official who, after checking Arar's credentials, asked Arar to wait nearby. About two hours later, Arar was fingerprinted and his bags searched. Between 4 p.m. and 9 p.m., Arar was interviewed by an agent from the Federal Bureau of Investigation ("FBI"), who asked (inter alia) about his relationships with certain individuals who were suspected of terrorist ties. Arar admitted knowing at least one of them, but denied being a member of a terrorist group. Following the FBI interview, Arar was questioned by an official from the Immigration and Nationalization Service ("INS") for three more hours; he continued to deny terrorist affiliations.

Arar spent the night alone in a room at the airport. The next morning (September 27) he was questioned by FBI agents from approximately 9 a.m. until 2 p.m.; the agents asked him about Osama Bin Laden, Iraq, Palestine, and other things. That evening, Arar was given an opportunity to return voluntarily to Syria. He refused, citing a fear of torture, and asked instead to go to Canada or Switzerland. Later that evening, he was transferred to the Metropolitan Detention Center ("MDC") in Brooklyn, where he remained until October 8.

On October 1, the INS initiated removal proceedings, and served Arar with a document stating that he was inadmissible because he belonged to a terrorist organization. Later that day, he called his mother-in-law in Ottawa-his prior requests to place calls and speak to a lawyer having been denied or ignored. His family retained a lawyer to represent him and contacted the Canadian Consulate in New York.

A Canadian consular official visited Arar on October 3. The next day, immigration officers asked Arar to designate in writing the country to which he would want to be removed. He designated Canada. On the evening of October 5, Arar met with his attorney. The following evening, a Sunday, Arar was again questioned by INS officials. The INS District Director in New York left a voicemail message on the office phone of Arar's attorney that the interview would take place, but the attorney did not receive the message in time to attend. Arar was told that she chose not to attend. In days following, the attorney was given false information about Arar's whereabouts.

On October 8, 2002, Arar learned that the INS had: (1) ordered his removal to Syria, (2) made a (required) finding that such removal would be consistent with Article 3 of the Convention Against Torture ("CAT"), and (3) barred him from re-entering the United States for five years. He was found inadmissible to the United States on the basis of 8 U.S.C. § 1182(a)(3)(B)(i)(V), which provides that any alien who "is a member of a terrorist organization" is inadmissible to the United States. The finding was based on Arar's association with a suspected terrorist and other (classified) information. Thereafter, Defendant J. Scott Blackman, an INS Regional Director, made a determination that Arar was clearly and unequivocally a member of Al Qaeda and inadmissible to the United States. A "Final Notice of Inadmissibility," dated October 8, and signed by Defendant Deputy Attorney General Larry Thompson, stated that Arar's removal to Syria would be consistent with the CAT, notwithstanding Arar's articulated fear of torture.

Later that day, Arar was taken to New Jersey, whence he flew in a small jet to Washington, D.C., and then to Amman, Jordan. When he arrived in Amman on October 9, he was handed over to Jordanian authorities who treated him roughly and then delivered him to the custody of Syrian officials, who detained him at a Syrian Military Intelligence facility. Arar was in Syria for a year, the first ten months in an underground cell six feet by three, and seven feet high. He was interrogated for twelve days on his arrival in Syria, and in that period was beaten on his palms, hips, and lower back with a two-inch-thick electric cable and with bare hands. Arar alleges that United States officials conspired to send him to Syria for the purpose of interrogation under torture, and directed the interrogations from abroad by providing Syria with Arar's dossier, dictating questions for the Syrians to ask him, and receiving intelligence learned from the interviews.

On October 20, 2002, Canadian Embassy officials inquired of Syria as to Arar's whereabouts. The next day, Syria confirmed to Canada that Arar was in its custody; that same day, interrogation ceased. Arar remained in Syria, however, receiving visits from Canadian consular officials. On August 14, 2003, Arar defied his captors by telling the Canadians that he had been tortured and was confined to a small underground cell. Five days later, after signing a confession that he had trained as a terrorist in Afghanistan, Arar was moved to various locations. On October 5, 2003, Arar was released to the custody of a Canadian embassy official in Damascus, and was flown to Ottawa the next day.

. . .

In Bivens v. Six Unknown Named Agents of Federal Bureau of Narcotics, 403 U.S. 388, 91 S.Ct. 1999, 29 L.Ed.2d 619 (1971), the Supreme Court "recognized for the first time an implied private action for damages against federal officers alleged to have violated a citizen's constitutional rights." The plaintiff in Bivens had been subjected to an unlawful, warrantless search which resulted in his arrest. The Supreme Court allowed him to state a cause of action for money damages directly under the Fourth Amendment, thereby giving rise to a judicially-created remedy stemming directly from the Constitution itself.

The purpose of the Bivens remedy "is to deter individual federal officers from committing constitutional violations." Malesko, 534 U.S. at

70, 122 S.Ct. 515. So a Bivens action is brought against individuals, and any damages are payable by the offending officers. Notwithstanding the potential breadth of claims that would serve that objective, the Supreme Court has warned that the Bivens remedy is an extraordinary thing that should rarely if ever be applied in "new contexts...

This case requires us to examine whether allowing this Bivens action to proceed would extend Bivens to a new "context," and if so, whether such an extension is advisable.

"Context" is not defined in the case law. At a sufficiently high level of generality, any claim can be analogized to some other claim for which a Bivens action is afforded, just as at a sufficiently high level of particularity, every case has points of distinction. We construe the word "context" as it is commonly used in law: to reflect a potentially recurring scenario that has similar legal and factual components.

The context of this case is international rendition, specifically, "extraordinary rendition." Extraordinary rendition is treated as a distinct phenomenon in international law. See supra note 1. Indeed, law review articles that affirmatively advocate the creation of a remedy in cases like Arar's recognize "extraordinary rendition" as the context. See, e.g., Peter Johnston, Note, Leaving the Invisible Universe: Why All Victims of Extraordinary Rendition Need a Cause of Action Against the United States, 16 J.L. & Pol'y 357, 363 (2007). More particularly, the context of extraordinary rendition in Arar's case is the complicity or cooperation of United States government officials in the delivery of a non-citizen to a foreign country for torture (or with the expectation that torture will take place). This is a "new context": no court has previously afforded a Bivens remedy for extraordinary rendition.

Once we have identified the context as "new," we must decide whether to recognize a Bivens remedy in that environment of fact and law. The Supreme Court tells us that this is a two-part inquiry. In order to determine whether to recognize a Bivens remedy in a new context, we must consider: whether there is an alternative remedial scheme available to the plaintiff; and whether " 'special factors counsel[ ] hesitation' " in creating a Bivens remedy. Wilkie, 551 U.S. at 550, 127 S.Ct. 2588 (quoting Bush, 462 U.S. at 378, 103 S.Ct. 2404).

. . .

There are several possible alternative remedial schemes here. . . . In the end, we need not decide whether an alternative remedial scheme was available because, "even in the absence of an alternative [remedial scheme], a Bivens remedy is a subject of judgment . . . [in which] courts must . . . pay particular heed . . . to any special factors counselling hesitation before authorizing a new kind of federal litigation." Such special factors are clearly present in the new context of this case, and they sternly counsel hesitation.

. . .

When the Bivens cause of action was created in 1971, the Supreme Court explained that such a remedy could be afforded because that "case involve[d] no special factors counselling hesitation in the absence of affirmative action by Congress." . . . Among the "special factors" that have "counsel[ed] hesitation" and thereby foreclosed a Bivens remedy are: military concerns,; separation of powers, the comprehensiveness of available statutory schemes, national security concerns, and foreign policy considerations, ...Two principles emerge from this review of case law:

- "Special factors" is an embracing category, not easily defined; but it is limited in terms to factors that provoke "hesitation." While special factors should be substantial enough to justify the absence of a damages remedy for a wrong, no account is taken of countervailing factors that might counsel alacrity or activism, and none has ever been cited by the Supreme Court as a reason for affording a Bivens remedy where it would not otherwise exist.

- The only relevant threshold-that a factor "counsels hesitation"-is remarkably low. It is at the opposite end of the continuum from the unflagging duty to exercise jurisdiction. . . .

. . .

Although this action is cast in terms of a claim for money damages against the defendants in their individual capacities, it operates as a constitutional challenge to policies promulgated by the executive. Our federal system of checks and balances provides means to consider allegedly unconstitutional executive policy, but a private action for money damages against individual policymakers is not one of them. . . . Here, we need not decide categorically whether a Bivens action can lie against policymakers because in the context of extraordinary rendition, such an action would have the natural tendency to affect diplomacy, foreign policy, and the security of the nation, and that fact counsels hesitation. Our holding need be no broader.

. . .

The Executive has practiced rendition since at least 1995. . . .A suit seeking a damages remedy against senior officials who implement such a policy is in critical respects a suit against the government as to which the government has not waived sovereign immunity. Such a suit unavoidably influences government policy, probes government secrets, invades government interests, enmeshes government lawyers, and thereby elicits government funds for settlement. (Canada has already paid Arar $10 million.)

It is a substantial understatement to say that one must hesitate before extending Bivens into such a context. A suit seeking a damages remedy against senior officials who implement an extraordinary rendition policy would enmesh the courts ineluctably in an assessment of the validity and rationale of that policy and its implementation in this particular case, matters that directly affect significant diplomatic and national security concerns. It is clear from the face of the complaint that Arar explicitly targets the "policy" of extraordinary rendition; he cites the policy twice in his complaint, and submits documents and media reports concerning the practice. His claim cannot proceed without inquiry into the perceived need for the policy, the threats to which it responds, the substance and sources of the intelligence used to formulate it, and the propriety of adopting specific responses to particular threats in light of apparent geopolitical circumstances and our relations with foreign countries.

The Supreme Court has expressly counseled that matters touching upon foreign policy and national security fall within "an area of executive action 'in which courts have long been hesitant to intrude'" absent congressional authorization.

. . .

Absent clear congressional authorization, the judicial review of extraordinary rendition would offend the separation of powers and inhibit this country's foreign policy. It does not matter for our purposes whether such consequences would flow from innocent interference or from deliberate manipulation. These concerns must counsel hesitation in creating a new damages remedy that Congress has not seen fit to authorize.

. . .

The extraordinary rendition context involves exchanges among the ministries and agencies of foreign countries on diplomatic, security, and intelligence issues. . . . Even the probing of these matters entails the risk that other countries will become less willing to cooperate with the United States in sharing intelligence resources to counter terrorism. "At its core," as the panel opinion observed, "this suit arises from the Executive Branch's alleged determination that (a) Arar was affiliated with Al Qaeda, and therefore a threat to national security, and (b) his removal to Syria was appropriate in light of U.S. diplomatic and national security interests." To determine the basis for Arar's alleged designation as an Al Qaeda member and his subsequent removal to Syria, the district court would have to consider what was done by the national security apparatus of at least three foreign countries, as well as that of the United States. Indeed, the Canadian government-which appears to have provided the intelligence that United States officials were acting upon when they detained Arar-paid

Arar compensation for its role in the events surrounding this lawsuit, but has also asserted the need for Canada itself to maintain the confidentiality of certain classified materials related to Arar's claims.

. . .

Allegations of conspiracy among government agencies that must often work in secret inevitably implicate a lot of classified material that cannot be introduced into the public record. Allowing Arar's claims to proceed would very likely mean that some documents or information sought by Arar would be redacted, reviewed in camera, and otherwise concealed from the public. Concealment does not bespeak wrongdoing: in such matters, it is just as important to conceal what has not been done. Nevertheless, these measures would excite suspicion and speculation as to the true nature and depth of the supposed conspiracy, and as to the scope and depth of judicial oversight. Indeed, after an inquiry at oral argument as to whether classified materials relating to Arar's claims could be made available for review in camera, Arar objected to the supplementation of the record with material he could not see. See Letter from David Cole, Counsel for Maher Arar (Dec. 23, 2008). After pointing out that such materials are unnecessary to the adjudication of a motion on the pleadings (where the allegations of the complaint must be accepted as true), Arar protested that any materials submitted ex parte and in camera would not be subject to adversarial testing and that consideration of such documents would be "presumptively unconstitutional" since they would result in a decision "on the basis of secret information available to only one side of the dispute."

The court's reliance on information that cannot be introduced into the public record is likely to be a common feature of any Bivens actions arising in the context of alleged extraordinary rendition. This should provoke hesitation, given the strong preference in the Anglo-American legal tradition for open court proceedings, . . .

Granted, there are circumstances in which a court may close proceedings to which a public right of access presumptively attaches. . . . And the problems posed by the need to consider classified material are unavoidable in some criminal prosecutions and in other cases where we have a duty, imposed by Congress, to exercise jurisdiction. But this is not such a circumstance or such a case. The preference for open rather than clandestine court proceedings is a special factor that counsels hesitation in extending Bivens to the extraordinary rendition context.

. . .

A government report states that this case involves assurances received from other governments in connection with the determination that Arar's removal to Syria would be consistent with Article 3 of the CAT. Office of Inspector General, Dep't of Homeland Sec., (Unclassified) The Removal of a Canadian Citizen to Syria 5, 22, 26–27 (2008). This case is not unique in that respect. Cases in the context of extraordinary rendition are very likely to present serious questions relating to private diplomatic assurances from foreign countries received by federal officials, and this feature of such claims opens the door to graymail.

. . .

The regulations promulgated pursuant to the FARRA explicitly authorize the removal of an alien to a foreign country following receipt from that country of sufficiently reliable assurances that the alien will not be tortured. See 8 C.F.R. § 208.18(c). Should we decide to extend Bivens into the extraordinary rendition context, resolution of these actions will require us to determine whether any such assurances were received from the country of rendition and whether the relevant defendants relied upon them in good faith in removing the alien at issue.

Any analysis of these questions would necessarily involve us in an inquiry into the work of foreign governments and several federal agencies, the nature of certain classified information, and the extent of secret diplomatic relationships. An investigation into the existence and content of such assurances would potentially embarrass our government through inadvertent or deliberate disclosure of information harmful to our own and other states. Given the general allocation of authority over foreign relations to the political branches and the decidedly limited experience and knowledge of the federal judiciary regarding such matters, such an investigation would also implicate grave concerns about the separation of powers and our institutional competence. See, e.g., Kiyemba v. Obama, 561 F.3d 509, 515 (D.C.Cir.2009) ("[S]eparation of powers principles . . . preclude the courts from second-guessing the Executive's assessment of the likelihood a detainee will be tortured by a foreign sovereign."). These considerations strongly counsel hesitation in acknowledging a Bivens remedy in this context.

. . .

As emphasized above, Arar invokes Bivens to challenge policies promulgated and pursued by the executive branch, not simply isolated actions of individual federal employees. Such an extension of Bivens is without precedent and implicates questions of separation of powers as well as sovereign immunity. This, by itself, counsels hesitation; there is further reason to hesitate where, as in this case, the challenged government policies are the subject of classified communications: a possibility that such suits will make the government "vulnerable to 'graymail,' i.e., individual lawsuits brought to induce the [government] to settle a case (or prevent its filing) out of fear that any effort to litigate the action would reveal classified information that may undermine ongoing covert operations," or otherwise compromise foreign policy efforts. We cast no aspersions on Arar, or his lawyers; this dynamic inheres in any case where there is a risk that a defendant might "disclose classified information in the course of a trial." This is an endemic risk in cases (however few) which involve a claim like Arar's.

The risk of graymail is itself a special factor which counsels hesitation in creating a Bivens remedy. There would be hesitation enough in an ordinary graymail case, i.e., where the tactic is employed against the government, which can trade settlement cash (or the dismissal of criminal charges) for secrecy. But the graymail risk in a Bivens rendition case is uniquely troublesome. The interest in protecting military, diplomatic, and intelligence secrets is located (as always) in the government; yet a Bivens claim, by definition, is never pleaded against the government. So in a Bivens case, there is a dissociation between the holder of the non-disclosure interest (the government, which cannot be sued directly under Bivens) and the person with the incentive to disclose (the defendant, who cannot waive, but will be liable for any damages assessed). In a rendition case, the Bivens plaintiff could in effect pressure the individual defendants until the government cries uncle. Thus any Bivens action involving extraordinary rendition would inevitably suck the government into the case to protect its considerable interests, and-if disclosure is ordered-to appeal, or to suffer the disclosure, or to pay.

This pressure on the government to pay a settlement has (at least) two further perverse effects. First, a payment from the Treasury tends to obviate any payment or contribution by the individual defendants. Yet, "[Bivens] is concerned solely with deterring the unconstitutional acts of individual officers" by extracting payment from individual wrongdoers. When the government elects to settle a Bivens case which is susceptible to graymail, the individual wrongdoer pays nothing and the deterrent effect is lost. Second, the individual defendant in such a case has no incentive to resist discovery that imperils government interests; rather, discovery induces the government to settle. So in the extraordinary rendition context, there is a risk (or likelihood) that the government effectively becomes the real defendant in interest, and the named defendants become proxies that the government cannot control. . . .

In the end, a Bivens action based on rendition is-in all but name-a claim against the government. It is not for nothing that Canada (the government, not an individual officer of it) paid Arar $10 million dollars.

. . .

In the small number of contexts in which courts have implied a Bivens remedy, it has often been easy to identify both the line between constitutional and unconstitutional conduct, and the alternative course which officers should have pursued. The guard who beat a prisoner should not have beaten him; the agent who searched without a warrant should have gotten one; and the immigration officer who subjected an alien to multiple strip searches without cause should have left the alien in his clothes. This distinction may or may not amount to a special factor counseling hesitation in the implication of a Bivens remedy. But it is surely remarkable that the context of extraordinary rendition is so different, involving as it does a complex and rapidly changing legal framework beset with critical legal judgments that have not yet been made, as well as policy choices that are by no means easily reached.

Consider: should the officers here have let Arar go on his way and board his flight to Montreal? Canada was evidently unwilling to receive him; it was, after all, Canadian authorities who identified Arar as a terrorist (or did something that led their government to apologize publicly to Arar and pay him $10 million).

Should a person identified as a terrorist by his own country be allowed to board his plane and go on to his destination? Surely, that would raise questions as to what duty is owed to the other passengers and the crew.

Or should a suspected terrorist en route to Canada have been released on the Canadian border-over which he could re-enter the United States virtually at will? Or should he have been sent back whence his plane came, or to some third country? Should those governments be told that Canada thinks he is a terrorist? If so, what country would take him?

Or should the suspected terrorist have been sent to Guantanamo Bay or-if no other country would take him-kept in the United States with the prospect of release into the general population? See Zadvydas v. Davis, 533 U.S. 678, 699–700, 121 S.Ct. 2491, 150 L.Ed.2d 653 (2001).

None of this is to say that extraordinary rendition is or should be a favored policy choice. At the same time, the officials required to decide these vexed issues are "subject to the pull of competing obligations." Given the ample reasons for pause already discussed, we need not and do not rely on this consideration in concluding that it is inappropriate to extend Bivens to this context. Still, Congress is the appropriate branch of government to decide under what circumstances (if any) these kinds of policy decisions-which are directly related to the security of the population and the foreign affairs of the country-should be subjected to the influence of litigation brought by aliens.

. . .

All of these special factors notwithstanding, we cannot ignore that, as the panel dissent put it, "there is a long history of judicial review of Executive and Legislative decisions related to the conduct of foreign relations and national security." Where does that leave us? We recognize our limited competence, authority, and jurisdiction to make rules or set parameters to govern the practice called rendition. By the same token, we can easily locate that competence, expertise, and responsibility elsewhere:

in Congress. Congress may be content for the Executive Branch to exercise these powers without judicial check. But if Congress wishes to create a remedy for individuals like Arar, it can enact legislation that includes enumerated eligibility parameters, delineated safe harbors, defined review processes, and specific relief to be afforded. Once Congress has performed this task, then the courts in a proper case will be able to review the statute and provide judicial oversight to the "Executive and Legislative decisions [which have been made with regard] to the conduct of foreign relations and national security."

. . .

For the reasons stated above, the judgment of the District Court is affirmed. The panel opinion is hereby vacated.

QUESTIONS AND NOTES

1.   A case from the 4th circuit containing factual allegations similar to Arar and decided on state secret grounds is El-Masri v. United States, 479 F.3d 296 (4th Cir.2007), cert. denied 128 S.Ct. 373 (2007). A three-judge panel of the U.S. Court of Appeals affirmed the trial court's dismissal of the case, stating:

On December 6, 2005, El-Masri, a German citizen of Lebanese descent, filed his Complaint in this case, alleging, in substance, as follows: on December 31, 2003, while travelling in Macedonia, he was detained by Macedonian law enforcement officials; after twenty-three days in Macedonian custody, he was handed over to CIA operatives, who flew him to a CIA-operated detention facility near Kabul, Afghanistan; he was held in this CIA facility until May 28, 2004, when he was transported to Albania and released in a remote area; and Albanian officials then picked him up and took him to an airport in Tirana, Albania, from which he travelled to his home in Germany. The Complaint asserted that El-Masri had not only been held against his will, but had also been mistreated in a number of other ways during his detention, including being beaten, drugged, bound, and blindfolded during transport; confined in a small, unsanitary cell; interrogated several times; and consistently prevented from communicating with anyone outside the detention facility, including his family or the German government. El-Masri alleged that his detention and interrogation were carried out pursuant to an unlawful policy and practice devised and implemented by defendant Tenet known as "extraordinary rendition": the clandestine abduction and detention outside the United States of persons suspected of involvement in terrorist activities, and their subsequent interrogation using methods impermissible under U.S. and international laws.

According to the Complaint, the corporate defendants provided the CIA with an aircraft and crew to transport El-Masri to

Afghanistan, pursuant to an agreement with Director Tenet, and they either knew or reasonably should have known that "Mr. El-Masri would be subjected to prolonged arbitrary detention, torture and cruel, inhuman, or degrading treatment in violation of federal and international laws during his transport to Afghanistan and while he was detained and interrogated there." El-Masri also alleges that CIA officials "believed early on that they had the wrong person," and that Director Tenet was notified in April 2004 that "the CIA had detained the wrong person" in El-Masri.

The Complaint alleged three separate causes of action. The first claim was against Director Tenet and the unknown CIA employees, pursuant to Bivens v. Six Unknown Named Agents of Federal Bureau of Narcotics, 403 U.S. 388, 91 S.Ct. 1999, 29 L.Ed.2d 619 (1971), for violations of El-Masri's Fifth Amendment right to due process. Specifically, El-Masri contends that Tenet and the defendant CIA employees contravened the Due Process Clause's prohibition against subjecting anyone held in United States custody to treatment that shocks the conscience or depriving a person of liberty in the absence of legal process. El-Masri's second cause of action was initiated pursuant to the Alien Tort Statute (the "ATS"), and alleged that each of the defendants had contravened the international legal norm against prolonged arbitrary detention. The third cause of action was also asserted under the ATS, and maintained that each defendant had violated international legal norms prohibiting cruel, inhuman, or degrading treatment.

. . .

The effect of a successful interposition of the state secrets privilege by the United States will vary from case to case. If a proceeding involving state secrets can be fairly litigated without resort to the privileged information, it may continue. But if " 'the circumstances make clear that sensitive military secrets will be so central to the subject matter of the litigation that any attempt to proceed will threaten disclosure of the privileged matters,' dismissal is the proper remedy." The Supreme Court has recognized that some matters are so pervaded by state secrets as to be incapable of judicial resolution once the privilege has been invoked.

. . .

El-Masri also contends that, instead of dismissing his Complaint, the district court should have employed some procedure under which state secrets would have been revealed to him, his counsel, and the court, but withheld from the public. Specifically, he suggests that the court ought to have received all the state secrets evidence in camera and under seal, provided his counsel access to it pursuant to a nondisclosure agreement (after arranging for necessary security clearances), and then conducted an in camera trial. We need not dwell long on El-Masri's proposal in this regard, for it is expressly foreclosed by Reynolds, the Supreme Court decision that controls this entire field of inquiry. Reynolds plainly held that when "the occasion for the privilege is appropriate, . . . the court should not jeopardize the security which the privilege is meant to protect by insisting upon an examination of the evidence, even by the judge alone, in chambers." 345 U.S. at 10, 73 S.Ct. 528. El-Masri's assertion that the district court erred in not compelling the disclosure of state secrets to him and his lawyers is thus without merit.

In addition to his analysis under the controlling legal principles, El-Masri presents a sharp attack on what he views as the dire constitutional and policy consequences of dismissing his Complaint. He maintains that the district court's ruling, if affirmed, would enable the Executive to unilaterally avoid judicial scrutiny merely by asserting that state secrets are at stake in a given matter. More broadly, he questions the very application of the state secrets doctrine in matters where "egregious executive misconduct" is alleged, contending that, in such circumstances, the courts' "constitutional duty to review executive action" should trump the procedural protections traditionally accorded state secrets.

Contrary to El-Masri's assertion, the state secrets doctrine does not represent a surrender of judicial control over access to the courts. As we have explained, it is the court, not the Executive, that determines whether the state secrets privilege has been properly invoked. In order to successfully claim the state secrets privilege, the Executive must satisfy the court that disclosure of the information sought to be protected would expose matters that, in the interest of national security, ought to remain secret. Similarly, in order to win dismissal of an action on state secrets grounds, the Executive must persuade the court that state secrets are so central to the action that it cannot be fairly litigated without threatening their disclosure. The state secrets privilege cannot be successfully interposed, nor can it lead to dismissal of an action, based merely on the Executive's assertion that the pertinent standard has been met.

In this matter, the reasons for the United States' claim of the state secrets privilege and its motion to dismiss were explained largely in the Classified Declaration, which sets forth in detail the nature of the information that the Executive seeks to protect and explains why its disclosure would be detrimental to national security. We have reviewed the Classified Declaration, as did the district court, and the extensive information it contains is crucial to our decision in this matter. El-Masri's contention that his Complaint was dismissed based on the Executive's "unilateral assert[ion] of a need for secrecy" is entirely unfounded. It is no doubt frustrating to El-Masri that many of the specific reasons for the dismissal of his Complaint are classified. An inherent feature of the state secrets privilege, however, is that the party against whom it is asserted will often not be privy to the information that the Executive seeks to protect. That El-Masri is unfamiliar with the Classified Declaration's explanation for the privilege claim does not imply, as he would have it, that no such explanation was required, or that the district court's ruling was simply an unthinking ratification of a conclusory demand by the executive branch.

. . .

As we have observed in the past, the successful interposition of the state secrets privilege imposes a heavy burden on the party against whom the privilege is asserted. That party loses access to evidence that he needs to prosecute his action and, if privileged state secrets are sufficiently central to the matter, may lose his cause of action altogether. Moreover, a plaintiff suffers this reversal not through any fault of his own, but because his personal interest in pursuing his civil claim is subordinated to the collective interest in national security. See id. ("[T]here can be no doubt that, in limited circumstances like these, the fundamental principle of access to court must bow to the fact that a nation without sound intelligence is a nation at risk.").[7] In view of these considerations, we recognize the gravity of our conclusion that El-Masri must be denied a judicial forum for his Complaint, and reiterate our past observations that dismissal on state secrets grounds is appropriate only in a narrow category of disputes. Nonetheless, we think it plain that the matter before us falls squarely within that narrow class, and we are unable to find merit in El-Masri's assertion to the contrary.

Pursuant to the foregoing, we affirm the Order of the district court.

2. Another case, this time from the 9th circuit, where the court also based its decision on the state secrets doctrine is Mohamed v. Jeppesen Dataplan, Inc., 614 F.3d 1070 (9th Cir. 2010), cert. denied, 131 S.Ct. 2442 (2011) (like the Arar case, decided en banc):

---

[7] It should be unnecessary for us to point out that the Executive's authority to protect confidential military and intelligence information is much broader in civil matters than in criminal prosecutions. The Supreme Court explained this principle in Reynolds, observing:

Respondents have cited us to those cases in the criminal field, where it has been held that the Government can invoke its evidentiary privileges only at the price of letting the defendant go free. The rationale of the criminal cases is that, since the Government which prosecutes an accused also has the duty to see that justice is done, it is unconscionable to allow it to undertake prosecution and then invoke its governmental privileges to deprive the accused of anything which might be material to his defense. Such rationale has no application in a civil forum where the Government is not the moving party, but is a defendant only on terms to which it has consented. 345 U.S. at 12, 73 S.Ct. 528.

El-Masri's reliance on our decision in United States v. Moussaoui, 382 F.3d 453 (4th Cir.2004), in which we required the United States to grant a criminal defendant substantial access to enemy-combatant witnesses whose very identities were highly classified, is thus misplaced.

This case requires us to address the difficult balance the state secrets doctrine strikes between fundamental principles of our liberty, including justice, transparency, accountability and national security. Although as judges we strive to honor all of these principles, there are times when exceptional circumstances create an irreconcilable conflict between them. On those rare occasions, we are bound to follow the Supreme Court's admonition that "even the most compelling necessity cannot overcome the claim of privilege if the court is ultimately satisfied that [state] secrets are at stake." United States v. Reynolds, 345 U.S. 1, 11, 73 S.Ct. 528, 97 L.Ed. 727 (1953). After much deliberation, we reluctantly conclude this is such a case, and the plaintiffs' action must be dismissed. Accordingly, we affirm the judgment of the district court.

I. Background

We begin with the factual . . . history relevant to this appeal. In doing so, we largely draw upon the three-judge panel's language in Mohamed v. Jeppesen Dataplan, Inc., 579 F.3d 943, 949–52 (9th Cir.) (Jeppesen I), rehearing en banc granted, 586 F.3d 1108 (9th Cir.2009). We emphasize that this factual background is based only on the allegations of plaintiffs' complaint, which at this stage in the litigation we construe "in the light most favorable to the plaintiff[s], taking all [their] allegations as true and drawing all reasonable inferences from the complaint in [their] favor." Doe v. United States, 419 F.3d 1058, 1062 (9th Cir.2005). Whether plaintiffs' allegations are in fact true has not been decided in this litigation, and, given the sensitive nature of the allegations, nothing we say in this opinion should be understood otherwise.

A. Factual Background

1. The Extraordinary Rendition Program

Plaintiffs allege that the Central Intelligence Agency ("CIA"), working in concert with other government agencies and officials of foreign governments, operated an extraordinary rendition program to gather intelligence by apprehending foreign nationals suspected of involvement in terrorist activities and transferring them in secret to foreign countries for detention and interrogation by United States or foreign officials. According to plaintiffs, this program has allowed agents of the U.S. government "to employ interrogation methods that would [otherwise have been] prohibited under federal or international law." Relying on documents in the public domain, plaintiffs, all foreign nationals, claim they were each processed through the extraordinary rendition program. They also make the following individual allegations.

Plaintiff Ahmed Agiza, an Egyptian national who had been seeking asylum in Sweden, was captured by Swedish authorities, allegedly transferred to American custody and flown to Egypt. In Egypt, he claims he was held for five weeks "in a squalid, windowless, and frigid cell," where he was "severely and repeatedly beaten" and subjected to electric shock through electrodes attached to his ear lobes, nipples and genitals. Agiza was held in detention for two and a half years, after which he was given a six-hour trial before a military court, convicted and sentenced to 15 years in Egyptian prison. According to plaintiffs, "[v]irtually every aspect of Agiza's rendition, including his torture in Egypt, has been publicly acknowledged by the Swedish government."

Plaintiff Abou Elkassim Britel, a 40-year-old Italian citizen of Moroccan origin, was arrested and detained in Pakistan on immigration charges. After several months in Pakistani detention, Britel was allegedly transferred to the custody of American officials. These officials dressed Britel in a diaper and a torn t-shirt and shackled and blindfolded him for a flight to Morocco. Once in Morocco, he says he was detained incommunicado by Moroccan security services at the Temara prison, where he was beaten, deprived of sleep and food and threatened with sexual torture, including sodomy with a bottle and castration. After being released and re-detained, Britel says he was coerced into signing a false confession, convicted of terrorism-related charges and sentenced to 15 years in a Moroccan prison.

Plaintiff Binyam Mohamed, a 28-year-old Ethiopian citizen and legal resident of the United Kingdom, was arrested in Pakistan on immigration charges. Mohamed was allegedly flown to Morocco under conditions similar to those described above, where he claims he was transferred to the custody of Moroccan security agents. These Moroccan authorities allegedly subjected Mohamed to "severe physical and psychological torture," including routinely beating him and breaking his bones. He says they cut him with a scalpel all over his body, including on his penis, and poured "hot stinging liquid" into the open wounds. He was blindfolded and handcuffed while being made "to listen to extremely loud music day and night." After 18 months in Moroccan custody, Mohamed was allegedly transferred back to American custody and flown to Afghanistan. He claims he was detained there in a CIA "dark prison" where he was kept in "near permanent darkness" and subjected to loud noise, such as the recorded screams of women and children, 24 hours a day. Mohamed was fed sparingly and irregularly and in four months he lost between 40 and 60 pounds. Eventually, Mohamed was transferred to the U.S. military prison at Guantanamo Bay, Cuba, where he remained for nearly five years. He was released and returned to the United Kingdom during the pendency of this appeal.

Plaintiff Bisher al-Rawi, a 39-year-old Iraqi citizen and legal resident of the United Kingdom, was arrested in Gambia while traveling on legitimate business. Like the other plaintiffs, al-Rawi claims he was put in a diaper and shackles and placed on an airplane, where he was flown to Afghanistan. He says he was detained in the same "dark prison" as Mohamed and loud noises were played 24 hours per day to deprive him of sleep. Al-Rawi alleges he was eventually transferred to Bagram Air Base, where he was "subjected to humiliation, degradation, and physical and psychological torture by U.S. officials," including being beaten, deprived of sleep and threatened with death. Al-Rawi was eventually transferred to Guantanamo; in preparation for the flight, he says he was "shackled and handcuffed in excruciating pain" as a result of his beatings. Al-Rawi was eventually released from Guantanamo and returned to the United Kingdom.

Plaintiff Farag Ahmad Bashmilah, a 38-year-old Yemeni citizen, says he was apprehended by agents of the Jordanian government while he was visiting Jordan to assist his ailing mother. After a brief detention during which he was "subject[ed] to severe physical and psychological abuse," Bashmilah claims he was given over to agents of the U.S. government, who flew him to Afghanistan in similar fashion as the other plaintiffs. Once in Afghanistan, Bashmilah says he was placed in solitary confinement, in 24-hour darkness, where he was deprived of sleep and shackled in painful positions. He was subsequently moved to another cell where he was subjected to 24-hour light and loud noise. Depressed by his conditions, Bashmilah attempted suicide three times. Later, Bashmilah claims he was transferred by airplane to an unknown CIA "black site" prison, where he "suffered sensory manipulation through constant exposure to white noise, alternating with deafeningly loud music" and 24-hour light. Bashmilah alleges he was transferred once more to Yemen, where he was tried and convicted of a trivial crime, sentenced to time served abroad and released.

2. Jeppesen's Alleged Involvement in the Rendition Program

Plaintiffs contend that publicly available information establishes that defendant Jeppesen Dataplan, Inc., a U.S. corporation, provided flight planning and logistical support services to the aircraft and crew on all of the flights transporting each of the five plaintiffs among the various locations where they were detained and allegedly subjected to torture. The complaint asserts "Jeppesen played an integral role in the forced" abductions and detentions and "provided direct and substantial services to the United States for its so-called 'extraordinary rendition' program," thereby "enabling the clandestine and forcible transportation of terrorism suspects to secret overseas detention facilities." It also alleges that Jeppesen provided this assistance with actual or constructive "knowledge of the objectives of the rendition program," including knowledge that the plaintiffs "would be subjected to forced disappearance, detention, and torture" by U.S. and foreign government officials.

. . .

While the appeal was pending Barack Obama succeeded George W. Bush as President of the United States. On September 23, 2009, the Obama administration announced new policies for invoking the state secrets privilege, effective October 1, 2009, in a memorandum from the Attorney General. See Memorandum from the Attorney Gen. to the Heads of Executive Dep'ts and Agencies on Policies and Procedures Governing Invocation of the State Secrets Privilege (Sept. 23, 2009) ("Holder Memo"), http://www.justice.gov/opa/documents/ state-secret-privileges.pdf. The government certified both in its briefs and at oral argument before the en banc court that officials at the "highest levels of the Department of Justice" of the new administration had reviewed the assertion of privilege in this case and determined that it was appropriate under the newly announced policies. See Redacted, Unclassified Br. for U.S. on Reh'g En Banc ("U.S. Br.") 3.

. . .

Here, further litigation presents an unacceptable risk of disclosure of state secrets no matter what legal or factual theories Jeppesen would choose to advance during a defense. Whether or not Jeppesen provided logistical support in connection with the extraordinary rendition and interrogation programs, there is precious little Jeppesen could say about its relevant conduct and knowledge without revealing information about how the United States government does or does not conduct covert operations. Our conclusion holds no matter what protective procedures the district court might employ. Adversarial litigation, including pretrial discovery of documents and witnesses and the presentation of documents and testimony at trial, is inherently complex and unpredictable. Although district courts are well equipped to wall off isolated secrets from disclosure, the challenge is exponentially greater in exceptional cases like this one, where the relevant secrets are difficult or impossible to isolate and even efforts to define a boundary between privileged and unprivileged evidence would risk disclosure by implication. In these rare circumstances, the risk of disclosure that further proceedings would create cannot be averted through the use of devices such as protective orders or restrictions on testimony.

Dismissal at the pleading stage under Reynolds is a drastic result and should not be readily granted. We are not persuaded, however, by the dissent's views that the state secrets privilege can never be "asserted during the pleading stage to excise entire allegations," or that the government must be required "to make its claims of state secrets with regard to specific items of evidence or groups of such items as their use is sought in the lawsuit."

. . .

Although we are necessarily precluded from explaining precisely why this case cannot be litigated without risking disclosure of state secrets, or the nature of the harm to national security that we are convinced would result from further litigation, we are able to offer a few observations.

First, we recognize that plaintiffs have proffered hundreds of pages of publicly available documents, many catalogued in the dissent's Appendix, that they say corroborate some of their allegations concerning Jeppesen's alleged participation in aspects of the extraordinary rendition program. As the government has acknowledged, its claim of privilege does not extend to public documents. Accordingly, we do not hold that any of the documents plaintiffs have submitted are subject to the privilege; rather, we conclude that even assuming plaintiffs could establish their entire case solely through nonprivileged evidence-unlikely as that may be-any effort by Jeppesen to defend would unjustifiably risk disclosure of state secrets. . . .

Second, we do not hold that the existence of the extraordinary rendition program is itself a state secret. The program has been publicly acknowledged by numerous government officials including the President of the United States. Even if its mere existence may once have been a "matter[ ] which, in the interest of national security, should not be divulged," it is not a state secret now. Reynolds, 345 U.S. at 10, 73 S.Ct. 528; . . .Nonetheless, partial disclosure of the existence and even some aspects of the extraordinary rendition program does not preclude other details from remaining state secrets if their disclosure would risk grave harm to national security. . . .

Third, we acknowledge the government's certification at oral argument that its assertion of the state secrets privilege comports with the revised standards set forth in the current administration's September 23, 2009 memorandum, adopted several years after the government first invoked the privilege in this case. Those standards require the responsible agency to show that "assertion of the privilege is necessary to protect information the unauthorized disclosure of which reasonably could be expected to cause significant harm to the national defense or foreign relations." Holder Memo, supra, at 1. They also mandate that the Department of Justice "will not defend an invocation of the privilege in order to: (i) conceal violations of the law, inefficiency, or administrative error; (ii) prevent embarrassment to a person, organization, or agency of the United States government; (iii) restrain competition; or (iv) prevent or delay the release of information the release of which would not reasonably be expected to cause significant harm to national security." That certification here is consistent with our independent conclusion, having reviewed the government's public and classified declarations, that the government is not invoking the privilege to avoid embarrassment or to escape scrutiny of its recent controversial transfer and interrogation policies, rather than to protect legitimate national security concerns.

V.   Other Remedies

Our holding today is not intended to foreclose-or to pre-judge-possible nonjudicial relief, should it be warranted for any of the plaintiffs. Denial of a judicial forum based on the state secrets doctrine poses concerns at both individual and structural levels. For the individual plaintiffs in this action, our decision forecloses at least one set of judicial remedies, and deprives them of the opportunity to prove their alleged mistreatment and obtain damages. At a structural level, terminating the case eliminates further judicial review in this civil litigation, one important check on alleged abuse by government officials and putative contractors. Other remedies may partially mitigate these concerns, however, although we recognize each of these options brings with it its own set of concerns and uncertainties.

First, that the judicial branch may have deferred to the executive branch's claim of privilege in the interest of national security does not preclude the government from honoring the fundamental principles of justice. The government, having access to the secret information, can determine whether plaintiffs' claims have merit and whether misjudgments or mistakes were made that violated plaintiffs' human rights. Should that be the case, the government may be able to find ways to remedy such alleged harms while still maintaining the secrecy national security demands. For instance, the government made reparations to Japanese Latin Americans abducted from Latin America for internment in the United States during World War II.

Second, Congress has the authority to investigate alleged wrongdoing and restrain excesses by the executive branch. . . .

Third, Congress also has the power to enact private bills. . . . Because as a general matter the federal courts are better equipped to handle claims, Congress can refer the case to the Court of Federal Claims to make a recommendation before deciding whether to enact a private bill,. . . . although Congress alone will make the ultimate decision. When national security interests deny alleged victims of wrongful governmental action meaningful access to a judicial forum, private bills may be an appropriate alternative remedy. . . .

Fourth, Congress has the authority to enact remedial legislation authorizing appropriate causes of action and procedures to address claims like those presented here. . . .

VI. Conclusion

We, like the dissent, emphasize that it should be a rare case when the state secrets doctrine leads to dismissal at the outset of a case. Nonetheless, there are such cases. . ., those where the mandate for dismissal is apparent even under the more searching examination required by Reynolds. This is one of those rare cases.

For all the reasons the dissent articulates-including the impact on human rights, the importance of constitutional protections and the constraints of a judge-made doctrine-we do not reach our decision lightly or without close and skeptical scrutiny of the record and the government's case for secrecy and dismissal. . . . We also acknowledge that this case presents a painful conflict between human rights and national security. As judges, we have tried our best to evaluate the competing claims of plaintiffs and the government and resolve that conflict according to the principles governing the state secrets doctrine set forth by the United States Supreme Court.

For the reasons stated, we hold that the government's valid assertion of the state secrets privilege warrants dismissal of the litigation, and affirm the judgment of the district court. The government shall bear all parties' costs on appeal.

3.　　Footnote 8 in Jeppesen Dataplan, omitted in the excerpts from the case reproduced supra, states the following:

. . . [S]kepticism is all the more justified in cases that allege serious government wrongdoing. Such allegations heighten the risk that government officials may be motivated to invoke the state secrets doctrine not only by their obligation to protect national security but also by a desire to protect themselves or their associates from scrutiny

4.　　Note that the Supreme Court denied certiorari in all three of the cases presented above, Arar, El-Masri and Jeppesen Dataplan. Note also that these cases came from three different circuits, and in two, the circuit court decision was en banc. What significance do you attach to these facts?

5.　　Following up on the Executive Order issued by President Obama on January 22, 2009, which, inter alia, appointed a Task Force to make recommendation about the United States' use of transfer (i.e. rendition), on August 24, 2009, Attorney General Holder reported on the recommendations of the Task Force:

Transfers

The Task Force also made policy recommendations with respect to scenarios in which the United States moves or facilitates the movement of a person from one country to another or from U.S. custody to the custody of another country to ensure that U.S. practices in such transfers comply with U.S. law, policy and international obligations and do not result in the transfer of individuals to face torture. In keeping with the broad language of the Executive Order, the Task Force considered seven types of transfers conducted by the U.S. government: extradition, transfers pursuant to immigration proceedings, transfers pursuant to the Geneva Conventions, transfers from Guantanamo Bay, military transfers within or from Afghanistan, military transfers within or from Iraq, and transfers pursuant to intelligence authorities.

When the United States transfers individuals to other countries, it may rely on assurances from the receiving country. The Task Force made several recommendations aimed at clarifying and strengthening U.S. procedures for obtaining and evaluating those assurances. These included a recommendation that the State Department be involved in evaluating assurances in all cases and a recommendation that the Inspector Generals of the Departments of State, Defense, and Homeland Security prepare annually a coordinated report on transfers conducted by each of their agencies in reliance on assurances.

The Task Force also made several recommendations aimed at improving the United States' ability to monitor the treatment of individuals transferred to other countries. These include a recommendation that agencies obtaining assurances from foreign countries insist on a monitoring mechanism, or otherwise establish a monitoring mechanism, to ensure consistent, private access to the individual who has been transferred, with minimal advance notice to the detaining government.

The Task Force also made a series of recommendations that are specific to immigration proceedings and military transfer scenarios. In addition, the Task Force made classified recommendations that are designed to ensure that, should the Intelligence Community participate in or otherwise support a transfer, any affected individuals are subjected to proper treatment.

Background Information

The Task Force on Interrogations and Transfer Policies is chaired by the Attorney General, with the Director of National Intelligence and the Secretary of Defense serving as Co-Vice-Chairs. Other members of the Task Force are the Secretaries of State and Homeland Security, the Director of the Central Intelligence Agency, and the Chairman of the Joint Chiefs of Staff. Each of these officials appointed senior-level representatives to serve on a working-level task force to complete the work of the Executive Order.

The Executive Order directed the Task Force to study and evaluate "whether the interrogation practices and techniques in Army Field Manual 2-22.3, when employed by departments and agencies outside the military, provide an appropriate means of acquiring the intelligence necessary to protect the Nation, and, if warranted, to recommend any additional or different guidance for other departments or agencies."

The Task Force was also directed to study and evaluate "the practices of transferring individuals to other nations in order to ensure that such practices comply with the domestic laws, international obligations, and policies of the United States and do not result in the transfer of individuals to other nations to face torture or otherwise for the purpose, or with the effect, of undermining or circumventing the commitments or obligations of the United States to ensure the humane treatment of individuals in its custody and control.

4. CRIMINAL CHARGES BY FOREIGN GOVERNMENTS AGAINST U.S. AGENTS WHO ALLEGEDLY PERPETRATED IRREGULAR RENDITION TRANSFERS

In January, 2007, prosecutors in Munich, Germany issued arrest warrants against 10 CIA agents based on their alleged role in the kidnapping of Khaled El-Masri, a German national, and transporting him to Afghanistan for interrogation.

SPIEGEL ONLINE—June 25, 2007, 02:56 PM, in an article by John Goetz, Marcel Rosenbach and Holger Stark, URL:http://www.spiegel.de/international/germany/0,1518,490514,00.html, it was reported that the issuance of the arrest warrants was straining German-American relations; that the prosecutors in Munich were pushing to have the agents extradited to Germany so that they could stand trial; and that the German government has the authority by statute to stop any prosecution of the U.S. agents but realizes that to do so would cause a strong public reaction.

A similar scenario developed in Italy, where Italian prosecutors had charged 26 U.S. agents with kidnapping a radical imam known as Abu Omar on a Milan street in 2003 and taking him to Cairo, where he says he was tortured. In an article by Craig Whitlock, Washington Post Foreign Service, February 1, 1007, AO1, European law enforcement authorities were said to have acknowledged that it was high unlikely that any U.S. agents would be apprehended or extradited from the United States but that diplomatic relations between the concerned countries were being strained. Regarding the German-U.S. issue, a member of a parliamentary committee investigating the matter was quoted:

This policy of rendition has to be stopped, "said Johannes Jung, a member of the Social Democratic Party." It's totally out of control, and the U.S. needs to rethink its policy in this regard. We couldn't imagine that this policy of rendition could really be true, but we have learned that it is true.

Italy authorizes prosecutions in absentia and none of the U.S. defendants were present when the trial of the 26 American defendants, some of whom were identified only by aliases and some Italian officials was begun in June, 2007. The U.S. government refused to cooperate with the prosecution. The trial was quickly interrupted when the Italian government tried to squelch the prosecution asserting that the prosecutor had violated state secrecy laws in gathering evidence. The issue of whether such secrecy laws were violated was then brought to the Italian Constitutional Court for resolution. See Ian Fisher and Elisabetta Povoledo, At issue in Italian trial: Are renditions a crime?, International Herald Tribune, June 8, 2007, p. 1, 2007 WLNR 10702717.

Subsequently, the Italian Constitutional Court's decision allowed the trial to proceed but with certain restrictions. On November 4, 2009, the Italian judge convicted 23 Americans, including the CIA base chief at the time. Three other Americans were not convicted based on their diplomatic immunity. Since the American defendants were tried in absentia, after the conviction, they became fugitives, which restricts their ability to travel, certainly to Italy and, also, to other European countries. See N.Y. Times, November 5, 2009, A14. The Times reported that most of the defendants have already left the CIA, with the exception of one of the defendants. The convictions of the 23 Americans were reported to have been upheld by Italy's highest criminal court, "paving the way for possible extradition requests by Italy." LA Times, Sept. 20, 2012, A5. Subsequently, on April 5. 2013, the President of Italy pardoned one of the 23 defendants, a U.S. Air Force Colonel, reportedly the only one of the 23 who was not a CIA employee. The office of the Italian President "said that he hoped that the pardoning. . . would ease a 'delicate' situation between the two allies. . . ." N.Y. Times, April 6, 2013, A5.

In 2015, the legal battles relating to this prosecution continued. One of the defendants convicted in absentia for family reasons moved to Portugal. Subsequently, a move to extradite her to Italy was upheld by the Portuguese Supreme Court in April 2016, and her lawyer stated that he would appeal the decision to the Portuguese Constitutional Court. In February, 2017, she was detained in Lisbon and ten days later was scheduled to be extradited to Milan, Italy. Just before she was transferred, the President of Italy commuted her sentence to three years, which opened up the possibility of an alternative punishment not involving serving prison time. See Raphael Minder, In Portugal, Court Backs CIA Agent's Extradition, N.Y. Times,. April 12, 2016, A10; Elisabetta Povoledo, Sentence Reduced for Ex-CIA Officer Sought by Italy, N.Y. Times, March 1, 2017, A3.

5. AN UNOFFICIAL, NONGOVERNMENTAL REPORT ABOUT THE PRACTICE OF EXTRAORDINARY RENDITION

Compare with how the transfer was handled in the Abu Khatallah case, excerpts from which are reproduced, supra, the following description of the practices allegedly engaged in by the Bush administration during the post 9/11 period. What conclusions do you draw, having made this comparison?

Excerpts from a report by Amnesty International, USA, Report, United States of America, Below the Radar: Secret Flights to Torture and "Disappearance" (April 5, 2006)

Amnesty International uses the term "rendition" to describe the transfer of individuals from one country to another, by means that bypass all judicial and administrative due process. In the "war on terror" context, the practice is mainly—although not exclusively—initiated by the USA, and carried out with the collaboration, complicity or acquiescence of other governments. The most widely known manifestation of rendition is the secret transfer of terror suspects into the custody of other states— including Egypt, Jordan and Syria—where physical and psychological brutality feature prominently in interrogations. The rendition network's aim is to use whatever means necessary to gather intelligence, and to keep detainees away from any judicial oversight.

However, the rendition network also serves to transfer people into US custody, where they may end up in Guantánamo Bay in Cuba, detention centres in Iraq or Afghanistan, or in secret facilities known as "black sites" run by the USA's Central Intelligence Agency (CIA). In a number of cases, individuals have been transferred in and out of US custody several times. Muhammad Saad Iqbal Madni, for instance, was arrested by Indonesian intelligence agents in January 2002, allegedly on the instructions of the CIA, who flew him from Jakarta to Egypt, where he "disappeared" and was rumoured to have died under interrogation. In fact, he had been secretly returned to Afghanistan via Pakistan in April 2002 and held there for 11 months before being sent to Guantánamo Bay in March 2003. It was more than a year later that fellow detainees, who said he had been "driven mad" by his treatment, managed to get word of his existence to their lawyers.

Rendition is sometimes presented simply as an efficient means of transporting terror suspects from one place to another without red tape. Such benign characterizations conceal the truth about a system that puts the victim beyond the protection of the law, and sets the perpetrator above it.

Renditions involve multiple layers of human rights violations. Most victims of rendition were arrested and detained illegally in the first place: some were abducted; others were denied access to any legal process, including the ability to challenge the decision to transfer them because of the risk of torture. There is also a close link between renditions and enforced disappearances. Many of those who have been illegally detained in one country and illegally transported to another have subsequently "disappeared", including dozens who have "disappeared" in US custody. Every one of the victims of rendition interviewed by Amnesty International has described incidents of torture and other ill-treatment.

Because of the secrecy surrounding the practice of rendition, and because many of the victims have "disappeared", it is difficult to estimate the scope of the programme. In many countries, families are reluctant to report their relatives as missing, for fear that intelligence officials will turn their attention on them. Amnesty International has spoken to several people who have given credible accounts of rendition, but are unwilling to make their names or the circumstances of their arrests and transfers known. Some cases come to light when the victim is released or given access to a lawyer, although neither event is a common occurrence in the life of a rendition victim. The number of cases currently appears to be in the hundreds: Egypt's Prime Minister noted in 2005 that the USA had transferred some 60–70 detainees to Egypt alone, and a former CIA agent with experience in the region believes that hundreds of detainees have been sent by the USA to prisons in the Middle East. The USA has acknowledged the capture of about 30 "high value" detainees whose whereabouts remain unknown, and the CIA is reportedly investigating some three dozen additional cases of "erroneous rendition", in which people were detained based on flawed evidence or confusion over names.

However, this is a minimum estimate. Rendition, like "disappearance", is designed to evade public and judicial scrutiny, to hide the identity of the perpetrators and the fate of the victims.

. . .

Amnesty International makes the following recommendations as immediate and essential steps towards putting an end to the rendition programme and its associated practices, including enforced disappearance, torture and incommunicado and secret detention.

Recommendations to all governments:

No renditions

—Do not render or otherwise transfer to the custody of another state anyone suspected or accused of security offences unless the transfer is carried out under judicial supervision and in full observance of due legal process.

—Ensure that anyone subject to transfer has the right to challenge its legality before an independent tribunal, and that they have access to an independent lawyer and an effective right of appeal.

—Do not receive into custody anyone suspected or accused of security offences unless the transfer is carried out under judicial supervision and in full observance of due legal process.

—Information on the numbers, nationalities and current whereabouts of all terror suspects rendered, extradited or otherwise transferred into custody from abroad should be publicly available. Full personal details should be promptly supplied to the families and lawyers of the detainees, and to the International Committee of the Red Cross (ICRC).

—Bring all such detainees before a judicial authority within 24 hours of entry into custody.

—Ensure that detainees have prompt access to legal counsel and to family members, and that lawyers and family members are kept informed of the detainee's whereabouts.

—Ensure that detainees who are not nationals of the detaining country have access to diplomatic or other representatives of their country of nationality or former habitual residence.

No "disappearances", no secret detention

—End immediately the practices of incommunicado and secret detention wherever and under whatever agency it occurs.

—Hold detainees only in officially recognized places of detention with access to family, legal counsel and courts.

—Ensure that those responsible for "disappearances" are brought to justice, and that victims and families receive restitution, compensation and rehabilitation.

—Investigate any allegations that their territory hosts or has hosted secret detention facilities, and make public the results of such investigations.

No torture or other ill-treatment

—Ensure that interrogations are carried out in accordance with international standards, in particular without any use of torture or other cruel, inhuman or degrading treatment.

—Investigate all complaints and reports of torture or other ill-treatment promptly, impartially and effectively, using an agency independent of the alleged perpetrators, and ensure that anyone found responsible is brought to justice.

—Ensure that victims of torture obtain prompt reparation from the state including restitution, fair and adequate financial compensation and appropriate medical care and rehabilitation.

No diplomatic assurances

—Prohibit the return or transfer of people to places where they are at risk of torture or other ill-treatment.

—Do not require or accept "diplomatic assurances" or similar bilateral agreements to justify renditions or any other form of involuntary transfers of individuals to countries where there is a risk of torture or other ill-treatment.

No renditions flights

—Identify to the aviation authorities any plane or helicopter used to carry out the missions of the intelligence services as a state aircraft, even if the aircraft in question is chartered from a private company.

—Ensure that airports and airspace are not used to support and facilitate renditions or rendition flights.

—Maintain and update a register of aircraft operators whose planes have been implicated in rendition flights, and require them to provide detailed information before allowing them landing or flyover rights. Such information should include: the full flight plan of the aircraft, including onward stops and full itinerary, the full names and nationalities of all passengers on board, and the purposes of their travel.

—If any passengers are listed as prisoners or detainees, more detailed information about their status and the status of their flight should be required, including their destination and the legal basis for their transfer.

—Refuse access to airspace and airfields if requested information is not provided.

—If there are grounds to believe that an aircraft is being used in connection with renditions or other human rights violations, board the plane or require it to land for inspection.

—If such inspection indicates that the flight is being used for the unlawful transfer of people, or other human rights violations, the flight should be held until the lawfulness or otherwise of its purpose can be established, and appropriate law enforcement action taken.

Additional recommendations to the US government

—Ensure that anyone held in US custody in any part of the world can exercise the right to legal representation and to a fair and transparent legal process.

—Disclose the location and status of the detention centres where Muhammad Abdullah Salah al-Assad, Muhammad Faraj Ahmed Bashmilah and Salah Nasser Salim 'Ali Qaru were held between October 2003 and May 2005.

—Disclose the identities and whereabouts of all others held in secret locations and their legal status, and invite the ICRC to have full and regular access to all those detained.

—Release all detainees in US custody at undisclosed locations unless they are to be charged with internationally recognizable criminal offences and brought to trial promptly and fairly, in full accordance with relevant international standards, and without recourse to the death penalty.

—Promptly and thoroughly investigate all allegations of "disappearance", and bring those suspected of having committed, ordered or authorized a "disappearance" before the competent civil authorities for prosecution and trial.

Recommendations to private aircraft operators and leasing agents

—Ensure that the company is aware of the end use of any aircraft it is leasing or operating.

—Do not lease or otherwise allow the operation of any aircraft where there is reason to believe it might be used in human rights violations, including rendition or associated operations.

—Develop an explicit human rights policy, ensuring that it complies with the UN Norms on the Responsibilities of

Transnational Corporations and Other Business Enterprises with Regard to Human Rights.

6. IRREGULAR RENDITION LITERATURE

Alex Turner, Extraordinary Results in Extraordinary Rendition, 69 SMU L. Rev. 559 (2016); V. Noah Gimbel, Has the Rendition Program Disappeared, FPIF June 16, 2011, http://www.fpif.org/articles/has_the_rendition_program_disappeared; Daniel L. Pines, Rendition Operations, Does U.S. Law Impose Any Restrictions, 42 Loy. U. Chi. L.J.); 523 (2011); John Radsan, A More Regular Process for Irregular Rendition, 37 Seton Hall L.Rev. 1 (2006); Beth Henderson, From Justice to Torture: the Dramatic Evolution of U.S.-sponsored Renditions, Temple Int. and Comp. L.J. 189 (Spring 2006); Michael v. Sage, The Exploitation of Legal Loopholes in the Name of National Security: A Case Study on Extraordinary Rendition, Cal.Western Int. L.J. (Fall 2006); Leila Nadya Sadat, Extraordinary Rendition, Torture, and other Nightmares from the War on Terror, Geo.Wash. Law Rev. 1200 (August 2007); John Yoo, Transferring Terrorists, 79 Notre Dame L. Rev. 1183, 1221–22 (2004) (discussing the President's authority and discretion over the liberty of captured enemy prisoners); David Weissbrodt and Amy Bergquist, Extraordinary Rendition and the Humanitarian Law of War and Occupation, Va.J. of Int.L.Assoc. 295 (2007); David Weissbrodt and Amy Bergquist, Extraordinary Rendition and the Torture Convention, Va.J. Int. L.Assoc. 585 (Summer 2006).

CHAPTER 8

MATERIAL WITNESS AND IMMIGRATION DETENTION

■ ■ ■

A. INTRODUCTION

The previous four chapters each explored investigatory tools and approaches used by the federal government in enforcement against terrorism. This chapter similarly examines the use of the material witness statute and the power to detain aliens under the immigration laws which are traditionally used to ensure availability of individuals for proceedings and in aid of investigation. The power to detain an individual for an extended period is a potent weapon of enforcement, however, that goes much beyond its use simply to ensure availability or for investigation. To be sure, a period of extended detention provides an opportunity to interrogate and obtain information—to be used against the person being detained or to assist in the apprehension and prosecution of others. Detention extended long enough, may also viewed as an effective means to take the person out of action and incapacitate and prevent the commission of crimes. Extended detention also can serve as a kind of sanction, albeit without the sanctioned person having had a trial or having been convicted. The length of detention, the conditions under which a person is detained and what goes on during the detention have implications for the issue of whether the detention amounts to punishment.

The length, conditions and what goes on during incarceration are also relevant to the legality of any interrogation that takes place. Issues relating to the interrogation of detainees by U.S. agents or by surrogates were directly considered in Chapter 7, but they remain highly relevant to the matters considered in this chapter.

The power to detain for an extended period without notifying relatives or providing access to the detainee and without providing a hearing before a judicial officer or charging the individual is one of the hallmarks of a totalitarian regime in which the people live in fear.

There are a number of different legal bases for detaining people in the United States, in addition to the detention imposed as the result of conviction of crime. Post-arrest, prior-to-charge detention that does not have any other basis is usually limited in length. Post-charge, pre-trial detention can be quite lengthy if the accused is denied bail or cannot make the bail that is set. The use of preventive detention pending trial, on the ground that the accused is dangerous, is a relatively recent development in the federal system based on specific statutory authorization. See United States v. Salerno, 481 U.S. 739 (1987). Also see 18 U.S.C. § 3142 (e) and (f), and section 6952 of the Intelligence Reform and Terrorism Prevention Act of 2004 (extending the presumption of preventive detention in a certain category of cases to additional offenses).

There are special categories of persons subject to lawful extended detention, for example, under some circumstances, juveniles, sex offenders, and persons suffering from mental illness, but such instances are not directly relevant to the anti-terrorist enforcement effort, though in addressing legal issues in detention cases, the courts often look to such categories as either precedents or as cases to be distinguished. See, e.g., Zadvydas v. Davis, infra this chapter.

Another basis for a detention that is not based on a criminal conviction that can last in certain circumstances up to one year, or possibly two, is the citing for contempt and detaining of a recalcitrant witness who refuses to testify before the grand jury, for the period during which the grand jury sits.

A major area of detention related to the fight against terrorism is detention in military custody on the ground that we are at war and enemy combatants can be detained for the duration of the conflict. That is a major subject of study in this volume and is treated in depth in Part Two, Chapter 10 infra.

Following the traumatic events of September 11, 2001, federal agents, in aid of trying to prevent another terrorist act and investigating possible terrorist plots, arrested and detained over 1000 individuals, many of whom remained under detention for an extended period, in some cases for more than a year. Generally, either of two legal justifications was invoked for these detentions. One basis was that individuals were being held as material witnesses. The second, more frequently invoked basis, where it could be used, was that the individuals were aliens and had committed immigration law violations and could be held pending disposition of the alleged violations.

The focus in section B below is on the first of these justifications for extended detention, namely, holding a person as a material witness, even though charges have not yet been filed against anyone. In section C, below, the detention of aliens based upon immigration law violations is addressed. In both sections, the legality of using these legal justifications in aid of the investigation and prevention of terrorism is explored. Further, legislative provisions that are expressly aimed at the detention of aliens on the ground that they are suspected terrorists are reviewed. Finally, in section D, a different approach to the use of immigration law as a terrorism prevention method, invoked by President Trump, early in his time in office, is examined—limiting entry to the United States from specified countries which are asserted not to have adequate systems for vetting persons coming to the U.S. This approach has been challenged in the courts on the ground that it is a veiled way to apply a religious basis for admission to the U.S. since it is aimed primarily at countries that are predominantly Muslim. While this material departs from the detention subject matter of the chapter, it is closely tied to the fact that the immigration laws detention approach, post 9/11, not surprisingly, was used against Muslims. It can be said that the immigration/detention approach is a micro method of terrorism investigation and prevention while alien exclusion is a macro method. What are the strengths and weaknesses of each approach?

Issues relating to the widespread use of these two bases for extended detention and the use of executive branch authority over aliens' entry to the U.S. have been and are being litigated in a number of legal contexts. One of the initial legal efforts involved the attempt by a number of public interest groups to obtain detailed information about the detentions under both the material witness and immigration laws. The Department of Justice declined, however, to provide information about who was being detained, where these individuals were being detained and how many persons were being detained.

In response, lawsuits were filed under the Freedom of Information Act to obtain such information. The issues were eventually considered by the U.S. Court of Appeals for the District of Columbia, which generally ruled against requiring the government to release the information. Center for National Security Studies v. U.S. Department of Justice, 331 F.3d 918 (D.C.Cir. 2003), cert. denied 540 U.S. 1101 (2004).

B. MATERIAL WITNESS DETENTION

1. INTRODUCTION

The early litigation testing the government's use of the material witness statute post 9/11 involved direct challenges by the detained person to the legality and the incidents of the detention, see In re Material Witness Warrant, 213 F.Supp.2d 287 (S.D.N.Y.2002), or to a criminal prosecution that was argued to be the fruit of an illegal detention, see United States v. Awadallah, 349 F.3d 42 (2d Cir. 2003). The Awadallah case is reproduced infra. Subsequently, the legal issues involved in these uses of the material witness statute were also litigated in a civil lawsuit brought against government officials by a person who had been detained as a material witness alleging that the material witness statute, as it was being invoked under government policy, was being misused. See Ashcroft v. al-Kidd, infra.

The federal material witness statute is 18 U.S.C. § 3144.

Title 18, U.S.C.

§ 3144. Release or detention of a material witness

If it appears from an affidavit filed by a party that the testimony of a person is material in a criminal proceeding, and if it is shown that it may become impracticable to secure the presence of the person by subpoena, a judicial officer may order the arrest of the person and treat the person in accordance with the provisions of section 3142 of this title. No material witness may be detained because of inability to comply with any condition of release if the testimony of such witness can adequately be secured by deposition, and if further detention is not necessary to prevent a failure of justice. Release of a material witness may be delayed for a reasonable period of time until the deposition of the witness can be taken pursuant to the Federal Rules of Criminal Procedure.

Also see Rule 46 of the Federal Rules of Criminal Procedure:

Rule 46. Release from Custody; Supervising Detention

(a)   Before Trial. The provisions of 18 U.S.C. §§ 3142 and 3144 govern pretrial release.

. . .

(h)   Supervising Detention Pending Trial.

(1) In General. To eliminate unnecessary detention, the court must supervise the detention within the district of any defendants awaiting trial and of any persons held as material witnesses.

(2) Reports. An attorney for the government must report biweekly to the court, listing each material witness held in custody for more than 10 days pending indictment, arraignment, or trial. For each material witness listed in the report, an attorney for the government must state why the witness should not be released with or without a deposition being taken under Rule 15(a).

QUESTIONS AND NOTES

1.   Under certain conditions, section 3144 authorizes the arrest and detention of a person whose testimony is material in a criminal proceeding:

a.   An affidavit must be filed by the government alleging that the testimony of the person to be detained is "material in a criminal proceeding."

b.   A showing must be made that it is impractical to secure the presence of the person by subpoena.

c.   If the testimony of the material witness can be adequately secured by deposition and if detention is not necessary to prevent a failure of justice, he/she may not be detained.

2.   The basic showing that needs to be made is that the testimony of the witness is material in a criminal proceeding. The government has taken the position that individuals can be held as material witnesses even if a relevant criminal prosecution has not been initiated, provided that the grand jury was sitting and investigating criminal matters. The government's theory is that the grand jury proceeding is a "criminal proceeding" within the meaning of section 3144.

Acceptance of the government's theory (see the Awadallah case below) seems to permit the government to hold the individual at least for the period in which the instant grand jury continues to sit. Compare the case of a witness called before the grand jury to testify who refuses to do so, is held in contempt and is subject to being detained for the duration of the period in which that grand jury sits.

3.   The material witness provision, 18 U.S.C. § 3144 refers to § 3142, which deals with conditions of release and hearing requirements for defendants. § 3142 is discussed in Awadallah, infra.

4.   Rule 46 of the Federal Rules of Criminal Procedure deals with material witness matters. An amendment of Rule 46 promulgated in 2002 is relevant to the issue of whether a grand jury proceeding is a criminal proceeding within the meaning of § 3144. See the discussion in Awadallah, below.

2.   DIRECT CHALLENGE TO MATERIAL WITNESS DETENTION

UNITED STATES V. AWADALLAH

349 F.3d 42 (2d Cir.2003), cert. denied, Awadallah v. United States, 543 U.S. 1056 (2005)

Before: JACOBS and STRAUB, CIRCUIT JUDGES, and CARMAN, CHIEF JUDGE. JUDGE STRAUB concurs in the opinion except as to Part II.C.3, and has filed a separate concurrence.

JACOBS, CIRCUIT JUDGE.

This appeal, which arises from the government's investigation of the September 11, 2001 terrorist attacks, presents questions about the scope of the federal material witness statute and the government's powers of arrest and detention thereunder. See 18 U.S.C. § 3144. The district court (Scheindlin, J.) ruled that the statute cannot be applied constitutionally to a grand jury witness such as the defendant-appellee, Osama Awadallah, and dismissed the perjury indictment against him as fruit of an illegal detention. . . . We conclude that these rulings must be reversed and the indictment reinstated. . . .

In the days immediately following September 11, 2001, the United States Attorney for the Southern District of New York initiated a grand jury investigation into the terrorist attacks. Investigators quickly identified Nawaf Al-Hazmi and Khalid Al-Mihdhar as two of the hijackers on American Airlines Flight 77, which crashed into the Pentagon. The Justice Department released the identities of all nineteen hijackers on Friday, September 14, 2001, and news media around the country publicized their names and photographs the following day. A search of the car Al-Hazmi abandoned at Dulles Airport in Virginia produced a piece of paper with the notation, "Osama 589-5316." Federal agents tracked this number to a San Diego address at which the defendant, Osama Awadallah, had lived approximately eighteen months earlier. Al-Hazmi and Al-Mihdhar also had lived in the San Diego vicinity around that time. The district court made extensive factual findings concerning the ensuing events of September 20 and 21, 2001. See United States v. Awadallah, 202 F.Supp.2d 82, 85–96 (S.D.N.Y.2002) ("Awadallah IV"). With two minor exceptions, the court credited Awadallah's testimony over that of the FBI agents. . . . However, the government "has elected not to appeal Judge Scheindlin's credibility findings and does not contest them here." For purposes of this appeal, then, the government accepts and relies on the facts found by the district court, as does Awadallah. Our recitation of the facts conforms to the district court's findings. . . .

Throughout the questioning . . ., the FBI agents in San Diego had been in contact with an Assistant United States Attorney ("AUSA") in New York. At approximately 2:00 p.m. Eastern time, the AUSA instructed the agents to arrest Awadallah as a material witness. The agents handcuffed Awadallah and took him to the San Diego correctional center for booking. Meanwhile, prosecutors and agents in New York prepared an application for a material witness warrant. In the supporting affidavit, FBI Special Agent Ryan Plunkett recounted how the FBI found the phone number in Al-Hazmi's car, Awadallah's admission that he knew Al-Hazmi, and the results of the agents' searches, including the "box-cutter" and the photographs of bin Laden. Agent Plunkett stated that it might become difficult to secure Awadallah's grand jury testimony because he had extensive family ties in Jordan and might be a flight risk. The affidavit did not say when Awadallah said he had last seen Al-Hazmi (over a year earlier); that Awadallah had moved eighteen months earlier from the address associated with the phone number; that Awadallah had used the "box-cutter" recently to install a new carpet in his apartment; that Awadallah had been (ostensibly) cooperative with the FBI agents in San Diego; or that Awadallah had three brothers who lived in San Diego, one of whom was an American citizen. Also, the affidavit stated that the "box-cutter" had been found in Awadallah's apartment when, in fact, it had been found in his inoperative second car. Shortly before 6:00 p.m. Eastern time, Agent Plunkett and an AUSA presented the material witness warrant application to Chief Judge Mukasey of the United States District Court for the Southern District of New York. Based solely on the contents of Agent Plunkett's affidavit, Chief Judge Mukasey issued a warrant to arrest Awadallah as a material witness pursuant to 18 U.S.C. § 3144. The court was unaware that Awadallah had already been arrested as a material witness three hours earlier.

On September 25, 2001, Awadallah appeared before a Magistrate Judge Ruben B. Brooks in the Southern District of California, who declined to release him on bail and ordered that he be removed to New York. On October 2, 2001, the day after he arrived in New York, Awadallah appeared before Chief Judge Mukasey for a second bail hearing. Chief Judge Mukasey also declined to release Awadallah on bail, finding his continued detention to be "reasonable under the circumstances."

During the period of his detention, Awadallah spent time in four prisons as he was transferred to the New York correctional center by way of Oklahoma City. He alleges that he received harsh and improper treatment during this period. Because these allegations of abuse and mistreatment were immaterial to the issues before the district court, Judge Scheindlin expressly declined to make "findings of fact on disputed issues regarding the conditions of confinement. . . ." On October 10, 2001, twenty days after his arrest as a material witness, Awadallah testified before the grand jury in the Southern District of New York. The prosecutor questioned him for most of the day. In the course of his testimony, Awadallah denied knowing anyone named Khalid Al-Mihdhar or Khalid. . . . On October 15, 2001, when Awadallah again appeared before the grand jury, he stated that his recollection of Khalid's name had been refreshed by his October 10 testimony and that the disputed writing in the exam booklet was in fact his own. However, he did not admit to making false statements in his first grand jury appearance.

The United States Attorney for the Southern District of New York filed charges against Awadallah on two counts of making false statements to the grand jury in violation of 18 U.S.C. § 1623: falsely denying that he knew Khalid Al-Mihdhar (Count One); and falsely denying that the handwriting in the exam booklet was his own (Count Two).

On November 27, 2001, the district court (Scheindlin, J.) granted Awadallah's bail application. He satisfied the bail conditions and was released approximately two weeks later. In December 2001, Awadallah moved to dismiss the indictment. . . .

On April 30, 2002, after an evidentiary hearing and further briefing, the district court issued two orders dismissing the indictment against Awadallah. In Awadallah III, the court ruled that the federal material witness statute, 18 U.S.C. § 3144, did not apply to grand jury witnesses. 202 F.Supp.2d at 61–79. This ruling evidently was made without briefing or argument. The court held that Awadallah's arrest and detention were therefore unlawful. . . . Judge Scheindlin ruled that Awadallah's perjured grand jury testimony had to be suppressed as fruit of this illegal arrest and detention. . . .

The government filed a timely notice of appeal. . . . Awadallah remains free on bail at this time.

We consider the issues presented on appeal in the order in which the district court developed them: (1) whether the federal material witness statute, 18 U.S.C. § 3144, may be applied to grand jury witnesses like Awadallah; . . .

The first issue presented is whether the federal material witness statute, 18 U.S.C. § 3144, allows the arrest and detention of grand jury witnesses. In Awadallah III, the district court determined that it did not. Shortly thereafter, however, on July 11, 2002, Chief Judge Mukasey issued an opinion in an unrelated case that declined to follow the reasoning and holding of Awadallah III. Specifically, Judge Mukasey held that 18 U.S.C. § 3144 applies to grand jury witnesses. See In re Material Witness Warrant, 213 F.Supp.2d 287, 288 (S.D.N.Y.2002). Thus there is now a split of authority within the Circuit on this question.

. . . Both parties to this appeal, as well as the amici, persuasively urge us to decide whether § 3144 may properly be applied to grand jury witnesses. The issue is squarely presented, has been fully briefed, and will tend to evade review in future cases where the detention is brief or matters take a different procedural course.

18 U.S.C. § 3144 . . . is cast in terms of a material witness in "a criminal proceeding." The decisive question here is whether that term encompasses proceedings before a grand jury. Based on its study of the statutory wording, context, legislative history, and case law, the district court held that "Section 3144 only allows the detention of material witnesses in the pretrial (as opposed to the grand jury) context." We have found no other decision that has arrived at this conclusion.

The only prior case that squarely considered the issue held that 18 U.S.C. § 3149, the precursor to today's material witness statute, allowed detention of grand jury witnesses. See Bacon v. United States, 449 F.2d 933, 936–41 (9th Cir.1971). The Ninth Circuit conceded that "[t]he term 'criminal proceeding,' absent a clear context, [was] ambiguous," but held that the relevant statutes and Federal Rules of Criminal Procedure, "[t]aken as a whole," were "clearly broad enough in scope to encompass grand jury investigations".

Other courts, including this one, have assumed that the material witness statute authorizes detention of grand jury witnesses. . . .

Two judges have also declined to follow the district court's ruling in this case. In In re Material Witness Warrant, 213 F.Supp.2d 287 (S.D.N.Y.2002), Chief Judge Mukasey "decline[d] to follow the reasoning and holding in Awadallah," holding instead:

> Given the broad language of the statute, its legislative history . . ., the substantial body of case law indicating that there is no constitutional impediment to detention of grand jury witnesses, and the unquestioned application of the statute to grand jury witnesses over a period of decades before Awadallah, to perceive a Congressional intention that grand jury witnesses be excluded from the reach of section 3144 is to perceive something that is not there.

[S]ee also In re Grand Jury Material Witness Detention, 271 F.Supp.2d 1266, 1268 (D.Or.2003) (concluding that "a grand jury proceeding constitutes a 'criminal proceeding,' as the term is used in § 3144"). Having the benefit of thorough opinions on both sides of the question, we conclude that the district court's ruling in this case must be reversed.

. . .

As noted above, § 3144 applies to witnesses whose testimony is material in "a criminal proceeding." 18 U.S.C. § 3144. "Criminal proceeding" is a broad and capacious term, and there is good reason to conclude that it includes a grand jury proceeding. First, it has long been recognized that "[t]he word 'proceeding' is not a technical one, and is aptly used by courts to designate an inquiry before a grand jury." Second, the term "criminal proceeding" has been construed in other statutes to encompass grand jury proceedings. . . .

Notwithstanding this support for the general view that "criminal proceedings" encompass grand jury proceedings, however, we cannot say that the statutory wording alone compels that conclusion. Black's Law Dictionary defines a "criminal proceeding" as "[a] proceeding instituted to determine a person's guilt or innocence or to set a convicted person's punishment; a criminal hearing or trial." Black's Law Dictionary 1221 (7th ed.1999). It defines a "grand jury" as "[a] body of . . . people . . . who, in ex parte proceedings, decide whether to issue indictments. If the grand jury decides that evidence is strong enough to hold a suspect for trial, it returns a bill of indictment . . . charging the suspect with a specific crime." Defined this way, a grand jury proceeding is not a "proceeding instituted to determine a person's guilt or innocence or to set a convicted person's punishment," but rather a proceeding to "decide whether to issue indictments." . . . A grand jury proceeding is certainly a stage of criminal justice; and it is certainly a proceeding. As a proceeding, it is certainly not civil, administrative, arbitral, commercial, social, or any type of proceeding other than (or as much as) criminal. Even so, the dictionary entries could suggest that grand jury proceedings lie outside the scope of § 3144.

. . .

The statutory context does not allay all uncertainty. Under § 3144, a judge "may order the arrest of the person and treat the person in accordance with the provisions of section 3142 of this title." 18 U.S.C. § 3144. Section 3142, which sets conditions for the "[r]elease or detention of a defendant pending trial," uses terms not normally associated with grand juries. It provides: Upon the appearance before a judicial officer of a person charged with an offense, the judicial officer shall issue an order that, pending trial, the person be—(1) released on personal recognizance or upon execution of an unsecured appearance bond . . .; (2) released on a condition or combination of conditions . . .; (3) temporarily detained to permit revocation of conditional release, deportation, or exclusion . . .; or (4) detained. . . .

By its own terms, § 3142 applies during the post-indictment ("a person charged with an offense") and pretrial ("pending trial") phase of criminal prosecution. The section also goes on to identify factors to be considered "in determining whether there are conditions of release that will reasonably assure the appearance of the person as required and the safety of any other person and the community." 18 U.S.C. § 3142(g). Two of the four listed considerations have little bearing on the situation of an individual detained as a material witness in a grand jury proceeding. See 18 U.S.C. § 3142(g)(1) ("[t]he nature and circumstances of the offense charged"); id. § 3142(g)(2) ("the weight of the evidence against the person"). For these reasons, we must look beyond the text of § 3144 to discern the meaning of "criminal proceeding."

The legislative history of § 3144 makes clear Congress's intent to include grand jury proceedings within the definition of "criminal proceeding." Congress enacted § 3144 in its current form as part of the Bail Reform Act of 1984. See Pub.L. No. 98–473, 98 Stat. 1837, 1976–81 (1984). Its language is nearly identical to the text of its predecessor statute, 18 U.S.C. § 1349 (1966), which the Ninth Circuit construed to encompass grand juries. See Bacon, 449 F.2d at 939–41. . . .

The most telling piece of legislative history appears in the Senate Judiciary Committee Report that accompanied the 1984 enactment of § 3144. The Report stated that, "[i]f a person's testimony is material in any criminal proceeding, and if it is shown that it may become impracticable to secure his presence by subpoena, the government is authorized to take such person into custody." S.Rep. No. 98–225, at 28 (1983), reprinted in 1984 U.S.C.C.A.N. 3182, 3211. A footnote to this statement advised categorically that "[a] grand jury investigation is a 'criminal proceeding' within the meaning of this section. Bacon v. United States, 449 F.2d 933 (9th Cir.1971)." Id. at 25 n. 88, 1984 U.S.C.C.A.N. at 3208. The approving citation to Bacon by the Senate Committee with responsibility for this bill is as indicative as the text of the footnote. . . .

In surveying legislative history we have repeatedly stated that the authoritative source for finding the Legislature's intent lies in the Committee Reports on the bill, which "represen[t] the considered and collective understanding of those Congressmen involved in drafting and studying proposed legislation."

Here, the Senate committee report states in so many words the intent to include grand jury proceedings within the ambit of the statute—an intent that is consistent with the statute's language, even if not compelled by it.

This statement of congressional intent is particularly telling, because the Bail Reform Act of 1984 reenacted the provisions of the former § 3149 in nearly identical language. "Congress is presumed to be aware of an administrative or judicial interpretation of a statute and to adopt that interpretation when it re-enacts a statute without change." . . .

Awadallah and an amicus party supporting his position argue that this principle of ratification by reenactment is inapplicable because there was no "settled judicial interpretation" of the term "criminal proceeding" when § 3144 was enacted in 1984. We disagree. The Senate report stated that "[a] grand jury investigation is a 'criminal proceeding' within the meaning of this section." S.Rep. No. 98–225, at 25 n. 88 (1983), 1984 U.S.C.C.A.N. at 3208 (emphasis added). As of 1984, a single court had expressly considered whether the term "criminal proceeding" within the meaning of the federal material witness statute included grand jury proceedings—and it had held that it did. . . . When Congress enacted § 3144—and until the district court ruled otherwise in this case—there was a settled view that a grand jury proceeding is a "criminal proceeding" for purposes of the material witness statute. We therefore conclude that a grand jury proceeding is a "criminal proceeding" for purposes of § 3144.

. . .

As a threshold matter, the detention of material witnesses for the purpose of securing grand jury testimony has withstood constitutional challenge.

. . . [W]e see no serious constitutional problem that would warrant the exclusion of grand jury proceedings from the scope of § 3144.

. . .

The essential purpose of the proscriptions in the Fourth Amendment is to impose a standard of "reasonableness" upon the exercise of discretion by government officials, including law enforcement agents, in order "to safeguard the privacy and security of individuals against arbitrary invasions. . . ." Thus, the permissibility of a particular law enforcement practice is judged by balancing its intrusion on the individual's Fourth Amendment interests against its promotion of legitimate governmental interests.

. . . Thus we must consider both "the nature and quality of the intrusion on the individual's Fourth Amendment interests" and "the importance of the governmental interests alleged to justify the intrusion." . . . In its balancing analysis, the district court found that "[t]he only legitimate reason to detain a grand jury witness is to aid in 'an ex parte investigation to determine whether a crime has been committed and whether criminal proceedings should be instituted against any person.'" . . . This is no small interest. . . . The district court noted (and we agree) that it would be improper for the government to use § 3144 for other ends, such as the detention of persons suspected of criminal activity for which probable cause has not yet been established. However, the district court made no finding (and we see no evidence to suggest) that the government arrested Awadallah for any purpose other than to secure information material to a grand jury investigation. Moreover, that grand jury was investigating the September 11 terrorist attacks. The particular governmental interests at stake therefore were the indictment and successful prosecution of terrorists whose attack, if committed by a sovereign, would have been tantamount to war, and the discovery of the conspirators' means, contacts, and operations in order to forestall future attacks.

On the other side of the balance, the district court found in essence that § 3144 was not calibrated to minimize the intrusion on the liberty of a grand jury witness. According to the district court, several procedural safeguards available to trial witnesses are not afforded in the grand jury context. We agree with the district court, of course, that arrest and detention are significant infringements on liberty, but we conclude that § 3144 sufficiently limits that infringement and reasonably balances it against the government's countervailing interests.

The first procedural safeguard to be considered is § 3144's provision that "[n]o material witness may be detained because of inability to comply with any condition of release if the testimony of such witness can adequately be secured by deposition, and if further detention is not necessary to prevent a failure of justice." 18 U.S.C. § 3144 (emphasis added). The district court agreed with the government that this deposition provision does not apply to grand jury witnesses. The government's altered position on appeal is that "Congress intended depositions to be available as a less restrictive alternative to detaining a grand jury witness." Such a pivot by the government on appeal is awkward, but we accept the government's explanation that it was persuaded by Chief Judge Mukasey's view in In re Material Witness Warrant, 213 F.Supp.2d at 296.

We conclude that the deposition mechanism is available for grand jury witnesses detained under § 3144. At the time of Awadallah's detention, the Federal Rule of Criminal Procedure that governs depositions provided:

If a witness is detained pursuant to [§ 3144], the court on written motion of the witness and upon notice to the parties may direct that the witness' deposition be taken. After the deposition has been subscribed the court may discharge the witness.

The district court is thereby authorized to order a deposition and to release the witness once it has been taken. Awadallah and the NYCDL argue that this provision cannot apply to grand jury witnesses because there can be no "party" or "trial" prior to indictment. The prosecutor and the witness may broadly be deemed parties, however, in the sense that each has interests to advance or protect before the grand jury. Thus, the rule governing the issuance of subpoenas—which indisputably applies during grand jury proceedings—refers to "the party requesting" a subpoena. Fed.R.Crim.P. 17(a).

The district court found the deposition provision inapplicable in the grand jury context in part because a conventional deposition is inconsistent with the procedural and evidentiary rules of a grand jury hearing. . . . [T]he district court may set additional conditions for the conduct of a deposition. Compare Fed.R.Crim.P. 15(d) (1987) ("[s]ubject to such additional conditions as the court shall provide"), with Fed.R.Crim.P. 15(e) (2003) ("[u]nless these rules or a court order provides otherwise"). The court thus can limit the deposition according to grand jury protocol, for example by limiting the witness's right to have counsel present during the deposition or by permitting the use of hearsay.

Rule 46 of the Federal Rules of Criminal Procedure, which governs detention and release, further supports the view that depositions are available to grand jury witnesses detained under § 3144. The version of Rule 46 in effect at the time of Awadallah's detention provided that "[t]he attorney for the government shall make a biweekly report to the court listing each defendant and witness who has been held in custody pending indictment, arraignment or trial for a period in excess of ten days," and as to "each witness so listed," state "the reasons why such witness should not be released with or without the taking of a deposition pursuant to Rule 15(a)." Fed.R.Crim.P. 46(g) (1993) (emphasis added). The new version of the rule, which omits the reference to defendants, is even more explicit:

An attorney for the government must report biweekly to the court, listing each material witness held in custody for more than 10 days pending indictment, arraignment, or trial. For each material witness listed in the report, an attorney for the government must state why the witness should not be released with or without a deposition being taken under Rule 15(a).

Fed. R. Crim. P. 46(h)(2) (2003).

Both versions of the rule expressly contemplate the deposition of a "witness held in custody . . . pending indictment." It follows that the deposition mechanism of § 3144 is a safeguard available to grand jury witnesses.

The second procedural safeguard at issue is § 3144's express invocation of the bail and release provisions set forth in 18 U.S.C. § 3142. Section 3144 directs that "a judicial officer may . . . treat the [detained] person in accordance with the provisions of section 3142 of this title." 18 U.S.C. § 3144. As noted above, § 3142 sets conditions for the "[r]elease or detention of a defendant pending trial," as follows:

Upon the appearance before a judicial officer of a person charged with an offense, the judicial officer shall issue an order that, pending trial, the person be—(1) released on personal recognizance or upon execution of an unsecured appearance bond . . .; (2) released on a condition or combination of conditions . . .; (3) temporarily detained to permit revocation of conditional release, deportation, or exclusion . . .; or (4) detained. . . . 18 U.S.C. § 3142(a).

As the district court observed, some of the terms used in § 3142—namely, "a person charged with an offense" and "pending trial"—do not comport with the structure of grand jury proceedings. However, we do not deduce (as the district court did) that "it is plain that section 3142 cannot apply to grand jury proceedings." We agree with Chief Judge Mukasey that the provisions of § 3142 govern insofar as they are applicable in the grand jury setting:

[T]he common sense reading of section 3144 is that it refers to section 3142 only insofar as that section is applicable to witnesses, in making available such alternatives to incarceration as release on bail or on conditions, in suggesting standards such as risk of flight, likelihood that the person will appear, and danger to the community, and in providing for a detention hearing. Not every provision of section 3142 applies to witnesses, but some do, and those govern. In re Material Witness Warrant, 213 F.Supp.2d at 295.

Thus, a person detained as a material witness in a grand jury investigation may obtain a hearing on the propriety of his continued detention and the conditions, if any, which will allow his release.

The district court also observed that the closed nature of a grand jury investigation limits the court's ability to assess the materiality of a witness's testimony. This may be true at the margins, because the materiality of the testimony given by a trial witness can be assessed on the basis of the indictment, discovery materials, and trial evidence, whereas grand jury secrecy requires the judge to rely largely on the prosecutor's representations about the scope of the investigation and the materiality of the witness's testimony. However, as Chief Judge Mukasey observed, "courts make similar determinations all the time, based on sealed submissions, when deciding whether a subpoena calls for relevant information, whether such information is privileged, and the like." Moreover, "the hypothesized difficulty of the materiality decision can be just as great, or greater, when a court must determine if a trial witness must be detained, because the decision likely will have to be made before the trial begins and thus before it is possible to fit the witness's testimony into the grid of other evidence." The materiality determination called for by § 3144 lies within the district court's competence.

Finally, Awadallah and the NYCDL argue that § 3144 provides no limit on how long a grand jury witness may be detained, whereas the detention of a trial witness is implicitly limited (or speeded) by the time limits on prosecution contained in the Speedy Trial Act, 18 U.S.C. § 3161 et seq. However, the Speedy Trial Act permits delay for various reasons, see 18 U.S.C. § 3161(h), which may have the collateral effect of extending the detention of a material witness; and nothing in the Speedy Trial Act requires a court to consider the effect of a continuance or delay on a detained witness. The Act therefore provides cold comfort to a detained trial witness.

While § 3144 contains no express time limit, the statute and related rules require close institutional attention to the propriety and duration of detentions: "[n]o material witness may be detained because of inability to comply with any condition of release if the testimony of such witness can adequately be secured by deposition, and if further detention is not necessary to prevent a failure of justice." 18 U.S.C. § 3144. The court must "treat the person in accordance with the provisions of section 3142," which provides a mechanism for release. And release may be delayed only "for a reasonable period of time until the deposition of the witness can be taken pursuant to the Federal Rules of Criminal Procedure." Perhaps most important, Rule 46 requires the government to make a "biweekly report" to the court listing each material witness held in custody for more than ten days and justifying the continued detention of each witness. Fed.R.Crim.P. 46(g) (1993); see also Fed.R.Crim.P. 46(h)(2) (2003). These measures tend to ensure that material witnesses are detained no longer than necessary.

In light of the foregoing analysis, we must ask whether Awadallah was properly detained when he was held for several weeks without being allowed to give his deposition and obtain release. Such a detention constitutes a significant intrusion on liberty, since a material witness can be arrested with little or no notice, transported across the country, and detained for several days or weeks. Under the circumstances of this case, however, we are satisfied that Awadallah's detention was not unreasonably prolonged. . . .

As indicated above, the deposition mechanism invoked in § 3144 is available to grand jury witnesses, but it is not required in every instance. Section 3144 requires release after deposition only if "the testimony of such witness can adequately be secured by deposition" and "further detention is not necessary to prevent a failure of justice." 18 U.S.C. § 3144 (emphasis added). Similarly, § 3142 provides that a person may be detained if, "after a hearing . . ., the judicial officer finds that no condition or combination of conditions will reasonably assure the appearance of the person as required and the safety of any other person and the community." 18 U.S.C. § 3142(e).

The procedural history demonstrates that Awadallah received adequate process to ensure that the duration of his detention was reasonable. Awadallah was arrested on Friday, September 21, 2001. He first appeared before a magistrate judge in San Diego for a bail hearing on Monday, September 24. That hearing was adjourned until the following day in order for Awadallah's counsel to obtain a translator. When Awadallah appeared before the magistrate judge the next day, the court received testimony from his witnesses and heard argument from counsel. Awadallah's attorney argued, among other things, that a deposition should be taken pursuant to § 3144. The court found that, under § 3142, there were no conditions of release that would reasonably assure Awadallah's appearance before the grand jury. The court denied bail and ordered that Awadallah be removed to New York. The government transported Awadallah across the country, and he arrived in New York on Monday, October 1. The next day, he appeared for a second bail hearing before Chief Judge Mukasey in the Southern District of New York. Chief Judge Mukasey also declined to release Awadallah from detention, finding that, "given the facts alleged in the application[,] he may well have incentive to leave," and that "[t]here is no way to prevent him from leaving, no effective way, unless he is detained." The court found that his continued detention was "reasonable under the circumstances." During this hearing, the government informed the court that the grand jury met only on Mondays and Wednesdays, that the following Monday was a holiday, and that the next opportunity to present Awadallah to the grand jury would be Wednesday, October 10. The court therefore set October 11 as a control date for further hearings.

When Awadallah appeared before the grand jury on Wednesday, October 10, he made statements that resulted in perjury charges being filed against him. He testified before the grand jury a second time on Monday,

October 15, and he was arrested on the perjury charges on Friday, October 19. All told, Awadallah spent 20 days in detention as a material witness before testifying before the grand jury and uttering the allegedly perjurious statements. The undisputed facts establish that he received two bail hearings pursuant to § 3142 within days of his arrest, and that the judges in both hearings found his continued detention to be both reasonable and necessary. Under these circumstances, Awadallah's detention as a material witness was a scrupulous and constitutional use of the federal material witness statute.

QUESTIONS AND NOTES

1.   Note that the district court judge in Awadallah had ruled in favor of the detained person, but that there was a contrary district court ruling in another case that held that a grand jury proceeding was a criminal proceeding within the meaning of the material witness statute. In re Material Witness, 213 F.Supp.2d 287 (S.D.N.Y.2002). It is worth mentioning that the district judge in the latter case, Michael B. Mukasey, subsequently served, toward the end of the Bush administration, as Attorney General of the United States. The court of appeals in Awadallah relied heavily on Judge Mukasey's opinion below in the unrelated case.

2.   The issue of whether a grand jury proceeding is a criminal proceeding within the meaning of the material witness statute is addressed in some detail by the Awadallah court as an issue of statutory interpretation. Inter alia, the court relies on a judicial precedent and a legislative committee citation approval of that same precedent. The court also relies on the language of and an amendment of Rule 46 of the Federal Rules of Criminal Procedure. Can the language of Rule 46 that was in effect at the time of Awadallah's detention be read in a different way than the court's reading?

3.   Note that the court of appeals in Awadallah, relying on Judge Mukasey's reasoning in his district court opinion in another case rejects arguments based on the awkward fit between applying the material witness statute at the grand jury stage and the language of 18 U.S.C. § 3142, which is made applicable to material witnesses by § 3144, the material witness statute.

4.   Recall that arrest as a material witness is only authorized when a showing has been made that it is impractical to secure the presence of the witness by subpoena; and if the testimony can be secured by deposition, a person cannot be detained. How does the court of appeals treat these issues in the Awadallah case?

5.   What are the practical implications of the use of the material witness statute even in the absence of a criminal charge having been filed against anyone? Does it mean that the material witness statute can be invoked in a much wider range of cases? Does it mean that there are increased risks of abuse of the statute, that is, that it can more easily be used for purposes other

than those for which the statute was intended? Of course, that raises the question: What are the true purposes of the material witness statute?

6.   The exact number of persons who were held as material witnesses in the immediate aftermath of the 9/11 attacks has not been made public. In 2002, the Washington Post reported that "at least 44 persons" have been detained under this heading since September 11, 2001. Washington Post, November 24, 2002, p. AO1. Consistent with that number is an estimate of 40 to 50 persons while another source concludes that at least 70 individuals were detained, all male and all but one Muslim. See Donald Q. Cochran, Material Witness Detention in a Post-9/11 World: Mission Creep or Fresh Start? 18 Geo.Mason L.Rev. 1, at n. 51 and 52 (2010).

7.   In the district court opinion in Center for National Security Studies v. U.S. DOJ, 215 F.Supp. 2d 94, 106 (D.D.C. 2002), Judge Kessler stated:

> The Government's reliance on grand jury secrecy rules to justify withholding the identities of material witnesses is fundamentally wrong as a matter of law. First, on its face, Fed. R. Crim. P. 6(e) does not bar disclosure of the identities of persons detained as material witnesses. Fed. R. Crim. P. 6(e) (2) prohibits disclosure of "matters occurring before the grand jury." Fed. R. Crim. P. 6(e) (6) provides that "records, orders and subpoenas relating to grand jury proceedings shall be kept under seal to the extent and for such time as is necessary to prevent disclosure of matters occurring before a grand jury."

Compare, however, Judge Mukasey's view expressed in footnote 1 in the In re Material Witness Warrant, 213 F.Supp. 2d 287, 288 (S.D.N.Y. 2002):

> The witness who has filed the current motion was taken into custody pursuant to a warrant issued in aid of a grand jury subpoena, and the docket and the record of all appearances in this matter have been sealed as proceedings ancillary to grand jury proceedings. See Fed. R. Crim. P. 6(e)(2), (5) and (6) (setting forth general rule of secrecy and rules for closing of hearings and sealing of records). Accordingly, neither the witness's name nor any identifying facts about him or this matter are set forth in this opinion, except to the extent necessary to treat the legal issues presented.

Judge Mukasey, however, was also reported to have given a talk at the Brooklyn Law School in which he mentioned the subject of secrecy surrounding the detention of a person as a material witness, indicating that the material witnesses were not being held "incommunicado," and that "[a]lthough the court proceedings were sealed . . . the lawyers for the witnesses were free to talk about the cases or not, as they chose." Washington Post, November 24, 2002, p. AO1. The same article suggests that there is confusion among lawyers about what they can and cannot reveal. Ibid.

Can you reconcile the Kessler and Mukasey view (as he expressed it in In re Material Witness Warrant case) about the relevance of grand jury secrecy to material witness status in these matters? Is it an implication of the Mukasey view that government can keep secret the identities of any persons taken into custody as material witnesses on the theory that their testimony before a grand jury is needed? Regarding this question, see The Center for National Security Studies case, supra, this note, which was appealed to the U.S. Court of Appeals for the D.C. Circuit, 331 F.3d 918 (D.C.Circuit, 2003). That court revisited the Rule 6(e) exemption and observed:

> Finally, the government invokes Exemption 3, which exempts from disclosure matters that are "specifically exempted from disclosure by statute . . ., provided that such statute . . . requires that the matters be withheld from the public in such a manner as to leave no discretion on the issue." 5 U.S.C. § 552(b)(3). According to the government, Exemption 3, which encompasses Federal Rule of Criminal Procedure 6(e)'s prohibition on the disclosure of "matters occurring before the grand jury," see Fund for Constitutional Gov't v. Nat'l Archives & Records Serv., 656 F.2d 856, 867–68 (D.C.Cir.1981), excuses it from disclosing the names of detainees held on material witness warrants, since "each of these warrants was issued to procure a witness's testimony before a grand jury," Reynolds Second Supp. Decl. ¶ 4. As such, the government contends that Exemption 3 provides a ground for nondisclosure independent of Exemption 7.

> Rule 6(e) forbids disclosure of "not only what has occurred and what is occurring, but also what is likely to occur" before a grand jury, including disclosure of witnesses' identities. In re Motions of Dow Jones & Co., 142 F.3d 496, 500 (D.C.Cir.1998). Therefore, the names of persons detained on material witness warrants who have actually testified before grand juries are unquestionably exempt from disclosure. The government, however, insists that Exemption 3 also covers the names of material witness detainees who have neither testified before grand juries nor are scheduled to do so, as well as the names of detainees who were released without ever having testified, because all of these detainees were originally detained in order to "procure [their] testimony before a grand jury." Reynolds Second Supp. Decl. ¶ 4.

> Saying that the material witness detainees were held in order to secure their testimony is quite different from saying that their testimony is "likely to occur" before a grand jury. Indeed, the record indicates that at least seven material witnesses have been released without testifying before a grand jury, so in their cases, it seems more accurate to say that their testimony is quite unlikely to occur before a grand jury. See Indiana Men Ordered to Testify to Return to Evansville, ASSOC. PRESS, Oct. 25, 2001. Furthermore, although current detainees may be, on the whole, somewhat more likely to testify before grand juries, their testimony is not necessarily "likely to occur" for purposes of Rule 6(e). We have said that the "likely to occur" language must be read sensibly: It does not authorize the

government to draw "a veil of secrecy . . . over all matters occurring in the world that happen to be investigated by a grand jury." In re Sealed Case, 192 F.3d 995, 1001–02 (D.C.Cir.1999) (internal quotation marks and citation omitted). Accordingly, we have made clear that Rule 6(e) covers "testimony about to be presented to a grand jury" (emphasis added)—hence the "likely to occur" language—but does not cover government investigations that merely parallel grand jury investigations. Id. at 1002–03. Because the government fails to show that all material witness detainees are likely to testify before grand juries, it may not, on this record, withhold their names under Rule 6(e). To hold otherwise would convert this circuit's carefully crafted standard into an absolute rule that would permit the government to keep secret the name of any witness whom it ever thought might testify at a grand jury proceeding, or who might testify at some indefinite point in the future. Neither Rule 6(e) nor the law of this circuit justifies that result.

8.   It has also been suggested that a built-in safeguard in connection with the detaining of a person as a material witness is the fact that a judge always supervises the matter, although it has been reported that some former prosecutors do not believe that judges offer much supervision in such matters. Washington Post, November 24, 2002, p. AO1.

9.   Awadallah was subsequently tried on the perjury charge that had been filed arising out of his grand jury testimony. He was acquitted in November, 2006. See N.Y. Times online ed. November 17, 2006.

10.   Sometimes arresting a person as a material witness is a temporizing action, while the prosecutor gathers enough evidence to charge the individual with a crime. See Laurie E. Levenson, 35 Loy. L.A. L.Rev. 1217, 1222 (2002). Some well-known defendants originally detained as material witnesses and then later charged with a crime include Zacarias Moussauoi and Jose Padilla. Padilla was originally detained as a material witness, and then the government switched his status to that of an "enemy combatant" in military custody, and still later, he was transferred back to civilian custody and indicted and prosecuted in a federal criminal trial. In this last-mentioned proceeding, he moved to suppress physical evidence on the ground that there had not been probable cause for his original detention as a material witness.

3.   CIVIL LAWSUIT ALLEGING ILLEGAL DETENTION AS A MATERIAL WITNESS

ASHCROFT V. AL-KIDD
563 U.S. 731 (2011)

[SCALIA, J., delivered the opinion of the Court, in which ROBERTS, C.J., and KENNEDY, THOMAS, and ALITO, JJ., joined. KENNEDY, J., filed a concurring opinion, in which GINSBURG, BREYER, and SOTOMAYOR, JJ., joined as to

Part I. GINSBURG, J., filed an opinion concurring in the judgment, in which BREYER and SOTOMAYOR, JJ., joined. SOTOMAYOR, J., filed an opinion concurring in the judgment, in which GINSBURG and BREYER, JJ., joined. KAGAN, J., took no part in the consideration or decision of the case.]

JUSTICE SCALIA delivered the opinion of the Court.

We decide whether a former Attorney General enjoys immunity from suit for allegedly authorizing federal prosecutors to obtain valid material-witness warrants for detention of terrorism suspects whom they would otherwise lack probable cause to arrest.

I

The federal material-witness statute authorizes judges to "order the arrest of [a] person" whose testimony "is material in a criminal proceeding . . . if it is shown that it may become impracticable to secure the presence of the person by subpoena." 18 U.S.C. § 3144. Material witnesses enjoy the same constitutional right to pretrial release as other federal detainees, and federal law requires release if their testimony "can adequately be secured by deposition, and if further detention is not necessary to prevent a failure of justice." Ibid.

Because this case arises from a motion to dismiss, we accept as true the factual allegations in Abdullah al-Kidd's complaint. The complaint alleges that, in the aftermath of the September 11th terrorist attacks, then-Attorney General John Ashcroft authorized federal prosecutors and law enforcement officials to use the material-witness statute to detain individuals with suspected ties to terrorist organizations. It is alleged that federal officials had no intention of calling most of these individuals as witnesses, and that they were detained, at Ashcroft's direction, because federal officials suspected them of supporting terrorism but lacked sufficient evidence to charge them with a crime.

It is alleged that this pretextual detention policy led to the material-witness arrest of al-Kidd, a native-born United States citizen. FBI agents apprehended him in March 2003 as he checked in for a flight to Saudi Arabia. Two days earlier, federal officials had informed a Magistrate Judge that, if al-Kidd boarded his flight, they believed information "crucial" to the prosecution of Sami Omar al-Hussayen would be lost. al-Kidd remained in federal custody for 16 days and on supervised release until al-Hussayen's trial concluded 14 months later. Prosecutors never called him as a witness.

In March 2005, al-Kidd filed this Bivens action, see Bivens v. Six Unknown Fed. Narcotics Agents, 403 U.S. 388, 91 S.Ct. 1999, 29 L.Ed.2d 619 (1971) to challenge the constitutionality of Ashcroft's alleged policy; he also asserted several other claims not relevant here against Ashcroft and others. Ashcroft filed a motion to dismiss based on absolute and qualified immunity, which the District Court denied. A divided panel of the United

States Court of Appeals for the Ninth Circuit affirmed, holding that the Fourth Amendment prohibits pretextual arrests absent probable cause of criminal wrongdoing, and that Ashcroft could not claim qualified or absolute immunity.

Judge Bea dissented, 580 F.3d, at 981, and eight judges dissented from the denial of rehearing en banc, see 598 F.3d 1129, 1137, 1142 (C.A.9 2010). We granted certiorari.

II

Qualified immunity shields federal and state officials from money damages unless a plaintiff pleads facts showing (1) that the official violated a statutory or constitutional right, and (2) that the right was "clearly established" at the time of the challenged conduct. . . .

. . .When . . . a Court of Appeals does address both prongs of qualified-immunity analysis, we have discretion to correct its errors at each step. Although not necessary to reverse an erroneous judgment, doing so ensures that courts do not insulate constitutional decisions at the frontiers of the law from our review or inadvertently undermine the values qualified immunity seeks to promote. The former occurs when the constitutional-law question is wrongly decided; the latter when what is not clearly established is held to be so. In this case, the Court of Appeals' analysis at both steps of the qualified-immunity inquiry needs correction.

A

The Fourth Amendment protects "[t]he right of the people to be secure in their persons, houses, papers, and effects, against unreasonable searches and seizures." An arrest, of course, qualifies as a "seizure" of a "person" under this provision, Dunaway v. New York, 442 U.S. 200 (1979), and so must be reasonable under the circumstances. Al-Kidd does not assert that Government officials would have acted unreasonably if they had used a material-witness warrant to arrest him for the purpose of securing his testimony for trial. He contests, however (and the Court of Appeals here rejected), the reasonableness of using the warrant to detain him as a suspected criminal.

Fourth Amendment reasonableness "is predominantly an objective inquiry." Edmond, 121 S.Ct. 447. We ask whether "the circumstances, viewed objectively, justify [the challenged] action." If so, that action was reasonable " whatever the subjective intent" motivating the relevant officials. Whren v. United States, 517 U.S. 806, 814, 116 S.Ct. 1769, 135 L.Ed.2d 89 (1996). This approach recognizes that the Fourth Amendment regulates conduct rather than thoughts, and it promotes evenhanded, uniform enforcement of the law.

Two "limited exception[s]" to this rule are our special-needs and administrative-search cases, where "actual motivations" do matter. A judicial warrant and probable cause are not needed where the search or seizure is justified by "special needs, beyond the normal need for law enforcement," such as the need to deter drug use in public schools, or the need to assure that railroad employees engaged in train operations are not under the influence of drugs or alcohol; and where the search or seizure is in execution of an administrative warrant authorizing, for example, an inspection of fire-damaged premises to determine the cause, an inspection of residential premises to assure compliance with a housing code, Camara v. Municipal Court of City and County of San Francisco, 387 U.S. 523, 535–538, 87 S.Ct. 1727, 18 L.Ed.2d 930 (1967). But those exceptions do not apply where the officer's purpose is not to attend to the special needs or to the investigation for which the administrative inspection is justified. See Whren, supra, at 811–812, 116 S.Ct. 1769. The Government seeks to justify the present arrest on the basis of a properly issued judicial warrant—so that the special-needs and administrative-inspection cases cannot be the basis for a purpose inquiry here.

Apart from those cases, we have almost uniformly rejected invitations to probe subjective intent. There is one category of exception, upon which the Court of Appeals principally relied. In Edmond, 531 U.S. 32, 121 S.Ct. 447, 148 L.Ed.2d 333, we held that the Fourth Amendment could not condone suspicionless vehicle checkpoints set up for the purpose of detecting illegal narcotics. Although we had previously approved vehicle checkpoints set up for the purpose of keeping off the road unlicensed drivers, and for the purpose of interdicting those who illegally cross the border, we found the drug-detection purpose in Edmond invalidating because it was "ultimately indistinguishable from the general interest in crime control," 531 U.S., at 44, 121 S.Ct. 447. In the Court of Appeals' view, Edmond established that " 'programmatic purpose' is relevant to Fourth Amendment analysis of programs of seizures without probable cause." 580 F.3d, at 968.

That was mistaken. It was not the absence of probable cause that triggered the invalidating-purpose inquiry in Edmond. To the contrary, Edmond explicitly said that it would approve checkpoint stops for "general crime control purposes" that were based upon merely "some quantum of individualized suspicion.". Purpose was relevant in Edmond because "programmatic purposes may be relevant to the validity of Fourth Amendment intrusions undertaken pursuant to a general scheme without individualized suspicion,"

Needless to say, warrantless, "suspicionless intrusions pursuant to a general scheme," are far removed from the facts of this case. A warrant issued by a neutral Magistrate Judge authorized al-Kidd's arrest. The affidavit accompanying the warrant application (as al-Kidd concedes) gave individualized reasons to believe that he was a material witness and that he would soon disappear. The existence of a judicial warrant based on individualized suspicion takes this case outside the domain of not only our special-needs and administrative-search cases, but of Edmond as well.

A warrant based on individualized suspicion in fact grants more protection against the malevolent and the incompetent than existed in most of our cases eschewing inquiries into intent. In Whren, 517 U.S., at 813, 116 S.Ct. 1769, we declined to probe the motives behind seizures supported by probable cause but lacking a warrant approved by a detached magistrate. We review even some suspicionless searches for objective reasonableness. If concerns about improper motives and pretext do not justify subjective inquiries in those less protective contexts, we see no reason to adopt that inquiry here.

Al-Kidd would read our cases more narrowly. He asserts that Whren establishes that we ignore subjective intent only when there exists "probable cause to believe that a violation of law has occurred,"—which was not the case here. That is a distortion of Whren. Our unanimous opinion held that we would not look behind an objectively reasonable traffic stop to determine whether racial profiling or a desire to investigate other potential crimes was the real motive. In the course of our analysis, we dismissed Whren's reliance on our inventory-search and administrative-inspection cases by explaining that those cases do not "endors[e] the principle that ulterior motives can invalidate police conduct that is justifiable on the basis of probable cause to believe that a violation of law has occurred," But to say that ulterior motives do not invalidate a search that is legitimate because of probable cause to believe a crime has occurred is not to say that it does invalidate all searches that are legitimate for other reasons.

"[O]nly an undiscerning reader," would think otherwise. . . .

Because al-Kidd concedes that individualized suspicion supported the issuance of the material-witness arrest warrant; and does not assert that his arrest would have been unconstitutional absent the alleged pretextual use of the warrant; we find no Fourth Amendment violation. Efficient[4] and evenhanded application of the law demands that we look to whether the arrest is objectively justified, rather than to the motive of the arresting officer.

B

A Government official's conduct violates clearly established law when, at the time of the challenged conduct, "[t]he contours of [a] right [are] sufficiently clear" that every "reasonable official would have understood

---

[4]   We may note in passing that al-Kidd alleges that the Attorney General authorized the use of material-witness warrants for detention of suspected terrorists, but not that he forbade the use of those warrants to detain material witnesses. Which means that if al-Kidd's inquiry into actual motive is accepted, mere determination that the Attorney General promulgated the alleged policy would not alone decide the case. Al-Kidd would also have to prove that the officials who sought his material-arrest warrant were motivated by Ashcroft's policy, not by a desire to call al-Kidd as a witness.

that what he is doing violates that right." We do not require a case directly on point, but existing precedent must have placed the statutory or constitutional question beyond debate. The constitutional question in this case falls far short of that threshold.

At the time of al-Kidd's arrest, not a single judicial opinion had held that pretext could render an objectively reasonable arrest pursuant to a material-witness warrant unconstitutional. A district-court opinion had suggested, in a footnoted dictum devoid of supporting citation, that using such a warrant for preventive detention of suspects "is an illegitimate use of the statute"—implying (we accept for the sake of argument) that the detention would therefore be unconstitutional. . . Even a district judge's ipse dixit of a holding is not "controlling authority" in any jurisdiction, much less in the entire United States; and his ipse dixit of a footnoted dictum falls far short of what is necessary absent controlling authority: a robust "consensus of cases of persuasive authority."

. . .

While featuring a District Court's footnoted dictum, the Court of Appeals made no mention of this Court's affirmation in Edmond of the "predominan[t]" rule that reasonableness is an objective inquiry. Nor did it mention Whren's statements that subjective intent mattered in a very limited subset of our Fourth Amendment cases; . . . .The Court of Appeals seems to have cherry-picked the aspects of our opinions that gave colorable support to the proposition that the unconstitutionality of the action here was clearly established.

Qualified immunity gives government officials breathing room to make reasonable but mistaken judgments about open legal questions. When properly applied, it protects "all but the plainly incompetent or those who knowingly violate the law." Ashcroft deserves neither label, not least because eight Court of Appeals judges agreed with his judgment in a case of first impression. He deserves qualified immunity even assuming—contrafactually—that his alleged detention policy violated the Fourth Amendment.

* * *

We hold that an objectively reasonable arrest and detention of a material witness pursuant to a validly obtained warrant cannot be challenged as unconstitutional on the basis of allegations that the arresting authority had an improper motive. Because Ashcroft did not violate clearly established law, we need not address the more difficult question whether he enjoys absolute immunity. The judgment of the Court of Appeals is reversed, and the case is remanded for further proceedings consistent with this opinion.

It is so ordered.

JUSTICE KAGAN took no part in the consideration or decision of this case.

QUESTIONS AND NOTES

1.   In a companion case to the lower court decisions in the principal case, al-Kidd v. Gonzales, 2006 WL 5429570, an amicus brief was filed, excerpts from which are reproduced below:

al-Kidd v. Ashcroft, 2007 WL 2786867

Brief of Amici Curiae Former Federal Prosecutors and Others in Support of Plaintiff-Appellee and in Support of Affirmance

. . .

STATEMENT OF INTEREST OF AMICI CURIAE

Amici curiae, identified in the Appendix, are former federal prosecutors and others who have worked prominently on issues related to the prosecution of federal crimes. We submit this brief amici curiae, with the consent of the parties, in support of Plaintiff-Appellee Abdullah al-Kidd's opposition to Defendant-Appellant John Ashcroft's appeal and affirmance of the District Court's denial of Appellant's motion to dismiss.

Collectively, amici have had decades of experience in federal criminal prosecution, including prosecution of domestic and international terrorism. All but four amici are former federal prosecutors, some of whom worked in the U.S. Department of Justice, and the other four amici are former presidents of the American Bar Association. Amici are therefore familiar with both the protocols and historical practices of the Department of Justice regarding the detention and treatment of material witnesses by federal prosecutors. Amici submit this brief to ensure a fair presentation of the practical issues presented by this matter.

INTRODUCTION

Based on personal experience, amici have a unique appreciation of the value of the federal material witness statute. If used properly, the statute is an indispensable law enforcement tool, permitting prosecutors to secure essential testimony when material witnesses are unwilling to testify. Yet amici are also aware of the dangers inherent in arresting and detaining individuals who are, in the eyes of the law, innocent. Great care must be taken to ensure that persons arrested and detained as material witnesses are treated throughout any arrest and detention as witnesses, unless and until probable cause exists to classify them otherwise.

Under the Department of Justice's explicit policy of using the federal material witness statute as a means of preventively arresting and detaining terrorism suspects, the critical distinction between material witnesses and criminal suspects has been blurred, and care has not been taken to ensure the protection of the particular constitutional rights of material witnesses. Because constitutional violations under this policy were foreseeable—if not expected—Appellant is not entitled to immunity, and the district court properly denied his motion to dismiss on immunity grounds.

SUMMARY OF THE ARGUMENT

While the language of the federal material witness statute is broad, federal prosecutors understand that constitutional limitations must guide the application of the statute. The arrest and detention of an individual as a material witness is no less an invasion of that individual's constitutional security and liberty interests than an arrest and detention on a criminal charge. Thus, the arrest of a material witness must be based on probable cause that the witness's testimony is material and that it would be impracticable to secure it by subpoena, and the conditions of a material witness's detention must be commensurate with his status as a witness.

In the case of Plaintiff-Appellee Abdullah al-Kidd, the material witness statute was not applied within these constitutional bounds: according to his complaint—the allegations of which are deemed to be true for this appeal—al-Kidd's arrest lacked probable cause because he was not an unwilling witness or a flight risk, and the harsh conditions of al-Kidd's detention amounted to punishment in violation of his due process rights.

Al-Kidd's legal action was properly allowed to proceed against Appellant, former Attorney General John Ashcroft, because the unconstitutional application of the statute in al-Kidd's case was not an aberrance, attributable to individual error by a federal prosecutor. Rather, it and the numerous other reported abuses of the federal material witness statute were the foreseeable consequences of an explicit policy regarding the application of the federal material witness statute, implemented by then-Attorney General Ashcroft. As part of a larger national security policy of preventively arresting and detaining terrorism suspects, Appellant instructed federal prosecutors, as well as the FBI and others, to use the federal material witness statute to arrest and detain persons purportedly connected to terrorism. This policy was expressly designed to secure indefinite detention of persons whom the government lacked probable cause to arrest and detain as criminal suspects, through "aggressive" application of the material witness statute. Fidelity to the specific legal requirements for detaining a person as a material witness were not addressed in these policy statements. Moreover, once detained, persons arrested as material witnesses in the anti-terrorism effort were treated not like witnesses, but like the most dangerous of criminal suspects.

Because the constitutional violations alleged by al-Kidd constituted foreseeable harm arising from Appellant's national security policy, Appellant is not immune from al-Kidd's suit. Appellant is not entitled to absolute prosecutorial immunity as his policy was implemented pursuant to his investigatory and national security functions, not pursuant to a pure prosecutorial function. Nor is Appellant entitled to qualified immunity, as his policy led to foreseeable violations of clearly established constitutional rights. Amici do not address the question of the district court's jurisdiction.

Amici therefore request that this Court affirm the decision of the district court denying Appellant's motion to dismiss on immunity grounds.

2.   Does Justice Scalia decide whether the alleged pretextual use of the material witness statute against al-Kidd is constitutional? Whether the material witness statute is consistent with the fourth amendment? Is his opinion premised on the notion that the material witness warrant was properly issued as far as the factual basis for its issuance? What specific issues did his opinion address and resolve?

3.   The amici brief, supra note 1, makes the following statement about the basis for issuance of a material witness warrant:

Thus, the arrest of a material witness must be based on probable cause that the witness's testimony is material and that it would be impracticable to secure it by subpoena, and the conditions of a material witness's detention must be commensurate with his status as a witness.

Does Justice Scalia characterize the basis for issuance of a material witness warrant differently?

4.   a.   Is it a misuse of the material witness statute to hold individuals because the government wants to be certain, that at least for the period of the detention, they are not free to engage in terrorist acts? Is this a proper basis on which to invoke the material witness statute? What does Awadallah say about that practice? What does al-kidd say?

b.   Some have suggested that the use of statutes like the material witness law to detain individuals for extended periods can be used to coerce information. See, e.g., Christian Science Monitor, June 19, 2002, p. 1. Is this an improper reason to detain an individual under the material witness statute? Compare the use of a contempt citation and detention of a person who declines to answer questions before the grand jury. Is the use of the material witness statute for this purpose different?

5.   See Laurie E. Levenson, 35 Loy. L.A. L.Rev. 1217, 1222 (2002):

When America adopted into its laws the power to detain material witnesses, the focus of the law was on having an individual available to testify in a criminal proceeding. Although they were being detained, material witnesses were conceptually different from defendants who were incarcerated. Material witnesses were to be held because they could assist the criminal justice system in convicting those who pose a danger; they themselves were not considered a threat.

With the War on Terrorism, the legal seas have changed. The designation of material witness has often become a temporary moniker to identify an individual who will soon bear the status of defendant. Consider, for example, the initial designation of Terry Lynn Nichols as a material witness in the bombing of the Murrah Federal Building in Oklahoma City. When Nichols challenged the material witness warrant, the authorities simply substituted it with a criminal complaint charging malicious destruction of government property. Given the breadth of our conspiracy laws, it is not difficult to find a sufficient link to charge a person who has intimate knowledge regarding a crime as a co-conspirator to that crime.

Similarly, it has not been difficult for prosecutors in terrorism cases to convert material witnesses into defendants. One standard technique is to question the witness before the grand jury, knowing that the individual is unlikely to cooperate fully. When the detainee withholds information or lies to the grand jury, charges of perjury or obstruction of justice can be substituted for the material witness warrant.

Material witness laws provide the government with the perfect avenue to jail those it considers dangerous. It is preventive detention. . . . [T]he Attorney General has indicated he still considers material witness warrants as a viable investigative tool. The government uses these laws to round up people because of what it expects them to do, rather than what it can prove they have done.

6.   Consider the characterization of the use of the material witness statute in the following excerpts from Heidee Stoller, Tahlia Townsend, Rashad Hussain, and Marcia Yablon, Developments in Law and Policy: The Costs of Post-9/11 National Security Strategy, 22 Yale L. & Pol'y Rev. 197, 199, 201–202, 205–206, 208–209 (2004).

Material witness detentions are controversial because they involve the extreme step of imprisoning individuals who have not been charged with committing any crime. The more usual procedure is to issue a subpoena to compel testimony, and only to imprison the witness once she has failed to comply with the subpoena.

. . . [I]t is often much easier to satisfy the probable cause requirement when arresting someone as a material witness for a grand jury proceeding than when taking her into custody as a criminal suspect. Whereas a suspected criminal may not be arrested until a judge has satisfied herself that the evidence of criminal activity is sufficient to establish probable cause, individuals who are suspected of having information material to a grand jury investigation and who may be deemed a flight risk (such as immigrants, those who cannot afford bail, and those with few ties to a community) can be subjected to arrest and detention solely on the basis of a statement from a law enforcement official.

. . . A report by the U.S. Department of Justice (DOJ) Office of the Inspector General has intensified concerns that the material witness warrant is being used in just such a pretextual manner to detain individuals for preventive or coercive purposes. According to the Inspector General's report, a DOJ official indicated that "the Department's official policy was to "use whatever means legally available' to detain a person linked to the terrorists who might present a threat and to make sure that no one else was killed." A senior DOJ official, discussing the "hold until cleared" policy in a document entitled "Maintaining Custody of Terrorism Suspects," stated:

> The Department of Justice . . . is utilizing several tools to ensure that we maintain in custody all individuals suspected of being involved in the September 11 attacks without violating the rights of any person. If a person is legally present in this country, the person may be held only if federal or local law enforcement is pursuing criminal charges against him or pursuant to a material witness warrant.

These findings, along with statements by Attorney General Ashcroft and former Assistant Attorney General for the Office of Legal Policy Viet Dinh, raise the specter of a new DOJ policy under which, in the absence of evidence to sustain criminal or immigration charges, the material witness statute is to be used as a "tool" of preventive detention, allowing the DOJ to hold those suspected of connection with terrorist activity until their names have been cleared by the FBI. The fact that at least twenty of the individuals detained never testified before a grand jury prior to their release further supports the idea that these detentions may have diverged from their stated purpose of securing testimony.

The application of the law since September 11 has aroused controversy for at least three additional reasons, namely that all of the individuals arrested pursuant to these material witness warrants have been detained for appearance before a grand jury rather than as trial witnesses; more than fifty percent of the material witnesses detained in connection with the September 11 terrorist attacks were held for longer than a month, and several were detained longer than ninety days; and harsh conditions of confinement have been documented in a number of the cases.

untimely. Haddad v. Ashcroft, Sixth Cir. No. 03–3852 (July 11, 2003) (order). Subsequently the plaintiff was deported from the United States. The government now moves to remand to the district court with instructions to vacate and dismiss the complaint as moot. There has been no response.

Because a final order of removal has been entered and effectuated, the conditions of the plaintiff's pre-removal detention are no longer at issue. . . . When a matter becomes moot on appeal, the proper course is to vacate the district court's decision and remand with instructions to dismiss the complaint.

Therefore, these appeals are REMANDED to the district court with instructions to vacate the orders of September 17 and October 7, 2002, and to dismiss the underlying complaint.

QUESTIONS AND NOTES

1. New Jersey Media ruled that across the board closure of special interest deportation hearings is not violative of the First Amendment. Detroit Free Press, on the other hand, requires open hearings but permits them to be closed when sensitive information or other national security concerns require it. How much different in their practical effects are the two contrary decisions?

2. How persuasive are the national security justifications for closing special interest deportation proceedings that are listed in the New Jersey Media case?

3. IS INDEFINITE, OPEN-ENDED DETENTION POSSIBLE IN CONNECTION WITH EFFORTS TO REMOVE AN INDIVIDUAL FROM THE UNITED STATES?

In the following case, the Supreme Court addressed the question of how long an alien as to whom removal had been ordered could be detained if removal could not be effected, if, for example, the government could not find a country willing to accept the person. While not directly involving a terrorism-related matter, the case generally bears on preventive detention issues that have implications for terrorism enforcement. Also, the majority opinion in the case contains dicta that directly touch upon the application of preventive detention to terrorists.

ZADVYDAS V. DAVIS

533 U.S. 678 (2001)

JUDGES: BREYER, J., delivered the opinion of the Court, in which STEVENS, O'CONNOR, SOUTER, and GINSBURG, JJ., joined. SCALIA, J., filed a dissenting opinion, in which THOMAS, J., joined. KENNEDY, J., filed a dissenting opinion, in which REHNQUIST, C.J., joined, and in which SCALIA and THOMAS, JJ., joined as to Part I.

JUSTICE BREYER delivered the opinion of the Court.

When an alien has been found to be unlawfully present in the United States and a final order of removal has been entered, the Government ordinarily secures the alien's removal during a subsequent 90-day statutory "removal period," during which time the alien normally is held in custody.

A special statute authorizes further detention if the Government fails to remove the alien during those 90 days. It says:

> "An alien ordered removed [1] who is inadmissible . . . [2] [or] removable [as a result of violations of status requirements or entry conditions, violations of criminal law, or reasons of security or foreign policy] or [3] who has been determined by the Attorney General to be a risk to the community or unlikely to comply with the order of removal, may be detained beyond the removal period and, if released, shall be subject to [certain] terms of supervision. . . ." 8 U.S.C. § 1231(a)(6) (1994 ed., Supp. V).

In these cases, we must decide whether this post-removal-period statute authorizes the Attorney General to detain a removable alien indefinitely beyond the removal period or only for a period reasonably necessary to secure the alien's removal. We deal here with aliens who were admitted to the United States but subsequently ordered removed. Aliens who have not yet gained initial admission to this country would present a very different question. Based on our conclusion that indefinite detention of aliens in the former category would raise serious constitutional concerns, we construe the statute to contain an implicit "reasonable time" limitation, the application of which is subject to federal court review.

The post-removal-period detention statute is one of a related set of statutes and regulations that govern detention during and after removal proceedings. While removal proceedings are in progress, most aliens may be released on bond or paroled. 66 Stat. 204, as added and amended, 110 Stat. 3009–585, 8 U.S.C. §§ 1226 (a)(2), (c) (1994 ed., Supp. V). After entry of a final removal order and during the 90-day removal period, however, aliens must be held in custody. § 1231(a)(2). Subsequently, as the post-removal-period statute provides, the Government "may" continue to detain an alien who still remains here or release that alien under supervision. § 1231(a)(6).

. . .

We consider two separate instances of detention. The first concerns Kestutis Zadvydas, a resident alien who was born, apparently of Lithuanian parents, in a displaced persons camp in Germany in 1948.

When he was eight years old, Zadvydas immigrated to the United States with his parents and other family members, and he has lived here ever since.

Zadvydas has a long criminal record, involving drug crimes, attempted robbery, attempted burglary, and theft. He has a history of flight, from both criminal and deportation proceedings. Most recently, he was convicted of possessing, with intent to distribute, cocaine; sentenced to 16 years' imprisonment; released on parole after two years; taken into INS custody; and, in 1994, ordered deported to Germany. See 8 U.S.C. § 1251(a)(2) (1988 ed., Supp. V) (delineating crimes that make alien deportable).

In 1994, Germany told the INS that it would not accept Zadvydas because he was not a German citizen. Shortly thereafter, Lithuania refused to accept Zadvydas because he was neither a Lithuanian citizen nor a permanent resident. In 1996, the INS asked the Dominican Republic (Zadvydas' wife's country) to accept him, but this effort proved unsuccessful. In 1998, Lithuania rejected, as inadequately documented, Zadvydas' effort to obtain Lithuanian citizenship based on his parents' citizenship; Zadvydas' reapplication is apparently still pending.

The INS kept Zadvydas in custody after expiration of the removal period. In September 1995, Zadvydas filed a petition for a writ of habeas corpus under 28 U.S.C. § 2241 challenging his continued detention. In October 1997, a Federal District Court granted that writ and ordered him released under supervision. In its view, the Government would never succeed in its efforts to remove Zadvydas from the United States, leading to his permanent confinement, contrary to the Constitution. The Fifth Circuit reversed this decision. Zadvydas v. Underdown, 185 F.3d 279 (1999). It concluded that Zadvydas' detention did not violate the Constitution because eventual deportation was not "impossible," good faith efforts to remove him from the United States continued, and his detention was subject to periodic administrative review. The Fifth Circuit stayed its mandate pending potential review in this Court.

The second case is that of Kim Ho Ma. Ma was born in Cambodia in 1977. When he was two, his family fled, taking him to refugee camps in Thailand and the Philippines and eventually to the United States, where he has lived as a resident alien since the age of seven. In 1995, at age 17, Ma was involved in a gang-related shooting, convicted of manslaughter, and sentenced to 38 months' imprisonment. He served two years, after which he was released into INS custody.

In light of his conviction of an "aggravated felony," Ma was ordered removed. See 8 U.S.C. §§ 1101(a)(43)(F) (defining certain violent crimes as aggravated felonies), 1227(a)(2)(A)(iii) (1994 ed., Supp. IV) (aliens convicted of aggravated felonies are deportable). The 90-day removal period expired in early 1999, but the INS continued to keep Ma in custody, because, in light of his former gang membership, the nature of his crime, and his planned participation in a prison hunger strike, it was "unable to conclude that Mr. Ma would remain nonviolent and not violate the conditions of release."

In 1999 Ma filed a petition for a writ of habeas corpus under 28 U.S.C. § 2241. A panel of five judges in the Federal District Court for the Western District of Washington, considering Ma's and about 100 similar cases together, issued a joint order holding that the Constitution forbids post-removal-period detention unless there is "a realistic chance that [the] alien will be deported" (thereby permitting classification of the detention as "in aid of deportation"). The District Court then held an evidentiary hearing, decided that there was no "realistic chance" that Cambodia (which has no repatriation treaty with the United States) would accept Ma, and ordered Ma released.

The Ninth Circuit affirmed Ma's release. Kim Ho Ma v. Reno, 208 F.3d 815 (2000). It concluded, based in part on constitutional concerns, that the statute did not authorize detention for more than a "reasonable time" beyond the 90-day period authorized for removal. And, given the lack of a repatriation agreement with Cambodia, that time had expired upon passage of the 90 days. Zadvydas asked us to review the decision of the Fifth Circuit authorizing his continued detention. The Government asked us to review the decision of the Ninth Circuit forbidding Ma's continued detention. We granted writs in both cases, agreeing to consider both statutory and related constitutional questions.

. . .

The post-removal-period detention statute applies to certain categories of aliens who have been ordered removed, namely inadmissible aliens, criminal aliens, aliens who have violated their nonimmigrant status conditions, and aliens removable for certain national security or foreign relations reasons, as well as any alien "who has been determined by the Attorney General to be a risk to the community or unlikely to comply with the order of removal." 8 U.S.C. § 1231(a)(6) (1994 ed., Supp. V). . . . It says that an alien who falls into one of these categories "may be detained beyond the removal period and, if released, shall be subject to [certain] terms of supervision."

The Government argues that the statute means what it literally says. It sets no "limit on the length of time beyond the removal period that an alien who falls within one of the Section 1231(a)(6) categories may be detained." Hence, "whether to continue to detain such an alien and, if so, in what circumstances and for how long" is up to the Attorney General, not up to the courts.

. . .

A statute permitting indefinite detention of an alien would raise a serious constitutional problem. The Fifth Amendment's Due Process Clause forbids the Government to "deprive" any "person . . . of . . . liberty . . . without due process of law." Freedom from imprisonment—from government custody, detention, or other forms of physical restraint—lies at the heart of the liberty that Clause protects, see Foucha v. Louisiana, 504 U.S. 71, 80, 112 S. Ct. 1780, 118 L. Ed. 2d 437 (1992). And this Court has said that government detention violates that Clause unless the detention is ordered in a criminal proceeding with adequate procedural protections, see United States v. Salerno, 481 U.S. 739, 107 S. Ct. 2095, 746, 95 L. Ed. 2d 697 (1987), or, in certain special and "narrow" non-punitive "circumstances," Foucha, supra, at 80, where a special justification, such as harm-threatening mental illness, outweighs the "individual's constitutionally protected interest in avoiding physical restraint." Kansas v. Hendricks, 521 U.S. 346, 117 S. Ct. 2072, 356, 138 L. Ed. 2d 501 (1997).

The proceedings at issue here are civil, not criminal, and we assume that they are nonpunitive in purpose and effect. There is no sufficiently strong special justification here for indefinite civil detention—at least as administered under this statute. The statute, says the Government, has two regulatory goals: "ensuring the appearance of aliens at future immigration proceedings" and "preventing danger to the community." Brief for Respondents in No. 99–7791, p. 24. But by definition the first justification—preventing flight—is weak or nonexistent where removal seems a remote possibility at best. . . .

The second justification—protecting the community—does not necessarily diminish in force over time. But we have upheld preventive detention based on dangerousness only when limited to specially dangerous individuals and subject to strong procedural protections. Compare Hendricks, supra, at 368 (upholding scheme that imposes detention upon "a small segment of particularly dangerous individuals" and provides "strict procedural safeguards") and Salerno, supra, at 747, 750–752 (in upholding pretrial detention, stressing "stringent time limitations," the fact that detention is reserved for the "most serious of crimes," the requirement of proof of dangerousness by clear and convincing evidence, and the presence of judicial safeguards), with Foucha, supra, at 81–83 (striking down insanity-related detention system that placed burden on detainee to prove nondangerousness). In cases in which preventive detention is of potentially indefinite duration, we have also demanded that the dangerousness rationale be accompanied by some other special circumstance, such as mental illness, that helps to create the danger. See Hendricks, supra, at 358, 368.

The civil confinement here at issue is not limited, but potentially permanent. Cf. Salerno, supra, at 747 (noting that "maximum length of pretrial detention is limited" by "stringent" requirements). . . . The provision authorizing detention does not apply narrowly to "a small segment of particularly dangerous individuals," Hendricks, supra, at 368, say suspected terrorists, but broadly to aliens ordered removed for many and various reasons, including tourist visa violations cf. Hendricks, 521 U.S. at 357–358 (only individuals with "past sexually violent behavior and a present mental condition that creates a likelihood of such conduct in the future" may be detained). And, once the flight risk justification evaporates, the only special circumstance present is the alien's removable status itself, which bears no relation to a detainee's dangerousness.

Moreover, the sole procedural protections available to the alien are found in administrative proceedings, where the alien bears the burden of proving he is not dangerous, without (in the Government's view) significant later judicial review. . . . This Court has suggested, however, that the Constitution may well preclude granting "an administrative body the unreviewable authority to make determinations implicating fundamental rights." . . . The serious constitutional problem arising out of a statute that, in these circumstances, permits an indefinite, perhaps permanent, deprivation of human liberty without any such protection is obvious.

The Government argues that, from a constitutional perspective, alien status itself can justify indefinite detention, and points to Shaughnessy v. United States ex rel. Mezei, 345 U.S. 206, 73 S. Ct. 625, 97 L. Ed. 956 (1953), as support. That case involved a once lawfully admitted alien who left the United States, returned after a trip abroad, was refused admission, and was left on Ellis Island, indefinitely detained there because the Government could not find another country to accept him. The Court held that Mezei's detention did not violate the Constitution. Id. at 215–216.

Although Mezei, like the present cases, involves indefinite detention, it differs from the present cases in a critical respect. As the Court emphasized, the alien's extended departure from the United States required him to seek entry into this country once again. His presence on Ellis Island did not count as entry into the United States. Hence, he was "treated," for constitutional purposes, "as if stopped at the border." And that made all the difference.

. . .

In light of this critical distinction between Mezei and the present cases, Mezei does not offer the Government significant support, and we need not consider the aliens' claim that subsequent developments have undermined Mezei's legal authority.

The Government also looks for support to cases holding that Congress has "plenary power" to create immigration law, and that the judicial branch must defer to executive and legislative branch decisionmaking in that area. . . . But that power is subject to important constitutional limitations. . . . Rather, the issue we address is whether aliens that the Government finds itself unable to remove are to be condemned to an indefinite term of imprisonment within the United States.

. . .

Nor do the cases before us require us to consider the political branches' authority to control entry into the United States. Hence we leave no "unprotected spot in the Nation's armor." Neither do we consider terrorism or other special circumstances where special arguments might be made for forms of preventive detention and for heightened deference to the judgments of the political branches with respect to matters of national security. The sole foreign policy consideration the Government mentions here is the concern lest courts interfere with "sensitive" repatriation negotiations. But neither the Government nor the dissents explain how a habeas court's efforts to determine the likelihood of repatriation, if handled with appropriate sensitivity, could make a significant difference in this respect.

Finally, the Government argues that, whatever liberty interest the aliens possess, it is "greatly diminished" by their lack of a legal right to "live at large in this country." . . . The choice, however, is not between imprisonment and the alien "living at large." . . .

Despite this constitutional problem, if "Congress has made its intent" in the statute "clear, 'we must give effect to that intent.'" . . . We cannot find here, however, any clear indication of congressional intent to grant the Attorney General the power to hold indefinitely in confinement an alien ordered removed. And that is so whether protecting the community from dangerous aliens is a primary or (as we believe) secondary statutory purpose. After all, the provision is part of a statute that has as its basic purpose effectuating an alien's removal. Why should we assume that Congress saw the alien's dangerousness as unrelated to this purpose?

. . .

The Government points to similar related statutes that require detention of criminal aliens during removal proceedings and the removal period, and argues that these show that mandatory detention is the rule while discretionary release is the narrow exception. But the statute before us applies not only to terrorists and criminals, but also to ordinary visa violators, and, more importantly, post-removal-period detention, unlike detention pending a determination of removability or during the subsequent 90-day removal period, has no obvious termination point.

In early 1996, Congress explicitly expanded the group of aliens subject to mandatory detention, eliminating provisions that permitted release of criminal aliens who had at one time been lawfully admitted to the United States. Antiterrorism and Effective Death Penalty Act of 1996, § 439(c),

110 Stat. 1277. And later that year Congress enacted the present law, which liberalizes pre-existing law by shortening the removal period from six months to 90 days, mandates detention of certain criminal aliens during the removal proceedings and for the subsequent 90-day removal period, and adds the post-removal-period provision here at issue. Illegal Immigration Reform and Immigrant Responsibility Act of 1996, Div. C, §§ 303, 305, 110 Stat. 3009–585, 3009–598 to 3009–599; 8 U.S.C. §§ 1226(c), 1231(a) (1994 ed., Supp. V).

We have found nothing in the history of these statutes that clearly demonstrates a congressional intent to authorize indefinite, perhaps permanent, detention. Consequently, interpreting the statute to avoid a serious constitutional threat, we conclude that, once removal is no longer reasonably foreseeable, continued detention is no longer authorized by statute.

The Government seems to argue that, even under our interpretation of the statute, a federal habeas court would have to accept the Government's view about whether the implicit statutory limitation is satisfied in a particular case, conducting little or no independent review of the matter. In our view, that is not so.

In answering that basic question, the habeas court must ask whether the detention in question exceeds a period reasonably necessary to secure removal. It should measure reasonableness primarily in terms of the statute's basic purpose, namely assuring the alien's presence at the moment of removal. Thus, if removal is not reasonably foreseeable, the court should hold continued detention unreasonable and no longer authorized by statute. In that case, of course, the alien's release may and should be conditioned on any of the various forms of supervised release that are appropriate in the circumstances, and the alien may no doubt be returned to custody upon a violation of those conditions. . . . And if removal is reasonably foreseeable, the habeas court should consider the risk of the alien's committing further crimes as a factor potentially justifying confinement within that reasonable removal period.

We recognize, as the Government points out, that review must take appropriate account of the greater immigration-related expertise of the Executive Branch, of the serious administrative needs and concerns inherent in the necessarily extensive INS efforts to enforce this complex statute, and the Nation's need to "speak with one voice" in immigration matters. But we believe that courts can take appropriate account of such matters without abdicating their legal responsibility to review the lawfulness of an alien's continued detention.

. . .

We realize that recognizing this necessary Executive leeway will often call for difficult judgments. In order to limit the occasions when courts will need to make them, we think it practically necessary to recognize some presumptively reasonable period of detention.

. . .

While an argument can be made for confining any presumption to 90 days, we doubt that when Congress shortened the removal period to 90 days in 1996 it believed that all reasonably foreseeable removals could be accomplished in that time. We do have reason to believe, however, that Congress previously doubted the constitutionality of detention for more than six months. . . . Consequently, for the sake of uniform administration in the federal courts, we recognize that period. After this 6-month period, once the alien provides good reason to believe that there is no significant likelihood of removal in the reasonably foreseeable future, the Government must respond with evidence sufficient to rebut that showing. And for detention to remain reasonable, as the period of prior post-removal confinement grows, what counts as the "reasonably foreseeable future" conversely would have to shrink. This 6-month presumption, of course, does not mean that every alien not removed must be released after six months. To the contrary, an alien may be held in confinement until it has been determined that there is no significant likelihood of removal in the reasonably foreseeable future.

. . . [W]e vacate the decisions below and remand both cases for further proceedings consistent with this opinion.

It is so ordered.

QUESTIONS AND NOTES

1.   On the one hand, Zadvydas provides some comfort for those who are concerned that the government is detaining people for too long based on too little evidence. The case establishes that indefinite, open-ended detention is impermissible for persons ordered to be removed from the U.S in circumstances where no country will accept them. Zadvydas thus is a strong statement against detention that extends too long, even for alien criminals.

2.   On the other hand, Zadvydas several times seems to recognize that the detention of terrorists may be a possible exception to the restriction on indefinite detention. How many times does Justice Breyer mention the matter of detaining terrorists? Does the court majority clearly opine on the question of extended detention of terrorists? What do you read into the majority's mention of terrorists in this context? Are the Court's statements mentioning terrorists restricted to alien terrorists?

3.   In the wake of the Zadvydas decision, Congress enacted legislation as part of the USA PATRIOT Act that provided that aliens whose removal is unlikely in the reasonably foreseeable future and whose release "will threaten the security of the United States or the safety of the community or any person"

may be detained subject to the detention being reviewed every six months. 8 U.S.C. § 1226a(a)(6). The full § 1226a is reproduced infra.

4.   Following the decision in Zadvydas, the question of how to deal with aliens who had not yet been admitted into this country but ended up in U.S. custody and were otherwise in the same situation as Zadvydas came before the Supreme Court in Clark v. Martinez, 543 U.S. 371 (2005). Were aliens who had never been admitted to this country to be treated the same as the aliens in Zadvydas? Justice Scalia opined as follows:

> The dissent's belief that Zadvydas compels this result rests primarily on that case's statement that "aliens who have not yet gained initial admission to this country would present a very different question." This mistakes the reservation of a question with its answer. . . . The opinion in that case considered whether § 1231(a)(6) permitted the Government to detain removable aliens indefinitely; relying on ambiguities in the statutory text and the canon that statutes should be interpreted to avoid constitutional doubts, the opinion held that it did not. Despite the dissent's repeated claims that § 1231(a)(6) could not be given a different reading for inadmissible aliens, the Court refused to decide that question—the question we answer today. It is indeed different from the question decided in Zadvydas, but because the statutory text provides for no distinction between admitted and nonadmitted aliens, we find that it results in the same answer.[4]

> . . .

> The Zadvydas dissent . . . concluded that the release of "Mariel Cubans and other illegal, inadmissible aliens . . . would seem a necessary consequence of the majority's construction of the statute." Tellingly, the Zadvydas majority did not negate either charge.

> The Government, joined by the dissent, argues that the statutory purpose and the constitutional concerns that influenced our statutory construction in Zadvydas are not present for aliens, such as Martinez and Benitez, who have not been admitted to the United States. Be that as it may, it cannot justify giving the same detention provision a different meaning when such aliens are involved.

> . . .

> The Government fears that the security of our borders will be compromised if it must release into the country inadmissible aliens

---

[4]   The dissent is quite wrong in saying, . . . that the Zadvydas Court's belief that § 1231(a)(6) did not apply to all aliens is evidenced by its statement that it did not "consider terrorism or other special circumstances where special arrangements might be made for forms of preventive detention," The Court's interpretation of § 1231(a)(6) did not affect the detention of alien terrorists for the simple reason that sustained detention of alien terrorists is a "special arrangement" authorized by a different statutory provision, 8 U.S.C. § 1537(b)(2)(C).

who cannot be removed. If that is so, Congress can attend to it.[8] But for this Court to sanction indefinite detention in the face of Zadvydas would establish within our jurisprudence, beyond the power of Congress to remedy, the dangerous principle that judges can give the same statutory text different meanings in different cases.

Since the Government has suggested no reason why the period of time reasonably necessary to effect removal is longer for an inadmissible alien, the 6-month presumptive detention period we prescribed in Zadvydas applies. Both Martinez and Benitez were detained well beyond six months after their removal orders became final. The Government having brought forward nothing to indicate that a substantial likelihood of removal subsists despite the passage of six months (indeed, it concedes that it is no longer even involved in repatriation negotiations with Cuba); and the District Court in each case having determined that removal to Cuba is not reasonably foreseeable; the petitions for habeas corpus should have been granted. Accordingly, we affirm the judgment of the Ninth Circuit, reverse the judgment of the Eleventh Circuit, and remand both cases for proceedings consistent with this opinion.

5.   The issue of continuing detention during the course of removal proceedings recently returned to the Supreme Court. In Jennnings v. Rodriguez, 583 U.S.___, 138 S.Ct. 830 (decided, Feb. 27, 2018), the Court ruled that interpreting three provisions of U.S. immigration law, detained aliens do not have a right to periodic bond hearings during the applicable proceedings. The court of appeals below had misapplied the constitutional avoidance canon of construction in concluding that detained aliens had such a statutory right to periodic bond hearings. The Court distinguished Zadvydas. The Court also took note of the fact that its decision in Demore v. Kim, 538 U.S. 510 (2003) had distinguished one of the statutory provisions involved in the instant case from the statute in the Zadvydas case, concluding that it authorized detention until the conclusion of removal proceedings.

---

[8]   That Congress has the capacity to do so is demonstrated by its reaction to our decision in Zadvydas. Less than four months after the release of our opinion, Congress enacted a statute which expressly authorized continued detention, for a period of six months beyond the removal period (and renewable indefinitely), of any alien (1) whose removal is not reasonably foreseeable and (2) who presents a national security threat or has been involved in terrorist activities. Uniting and Strengthening America by Providing Appropriate Tools Required to Intercept and Obstruct Terrorism Act of 2001 (USA PATRIOT Act, § 412(a), 115 Stat. 350 (enacted Oct. 26, 2001) (codified at 8 U.S.C. § 1226a(a)(6) (2000 ed., Supp. II)).

4. CIVIL SUITS BY ALIENS OF MIDDLE EASTERN ORIGIN SEEKING REDRESS FOR CONDITIONS OF POST-9/11 DETENTIONS

ASHCROFT V. IQBAL
556 U.S. 662 (2009)

JUSTICE KENNEDY delivered the opinion of the Court.

Respondent Javaid Iqbal is a citizen of Pakistan and a Muslim. In the wake of the September 11, 2001, terrorist attacks he was arrested in the United States on criminal charges and detained by federal officials. Respondent claims he was deprived of various constitutional protections while in federal custody. To redress the alleged deprivations, respondent filed a complaint against numerous federal officials, including John Ashcroft, the former Attorney General of the United States, and Robert Mueller, the Director of the Federal Bureau of Investigation (FBI). Ashcroft and Mueller are the petitioners in the case now before us. As to these two petitioners, the complaint alleges that they adopted an unconstitutional policy that subjected respondent to harsh conditions of confinement on account of his race, religion, or national origin.

In the District Court petitioners raised the defense of qualified immunity and moved to dismiss the suit, contending the complaint was not sufficient to state a claim against them. The District Court denied the motion to dismiss, concluding the complaint was sufficient to state a claim despite petitioners' official status at the times in question. . . .

Respondent's account of his prison ordeal could, if proved, demonstrate unconstitutional misconduct by some governmental actors. But the allegations and pleadings with respect to these actors are not before us here. This case instead turns on a narrower question: Did respondent, as the plaintiff in the District Court, plead factual matter that, if taken as true, states a claim that petitioners deprived him of his clearly established constitutional rights. We hold respondent's pleadings are insufficient.

Following the 2001 attacks, the FBI and other entities within the Department of Justice began an investigation of vast reach to identify the assailants and prevent them from attacking anew. The FBI dedicated more than 4,000 special agents and 3,000 support personnel to the endeavor. By September 18 "the FBI had received more than 96,000 tips or potential leads from the public." Dept. of Justice, Office of Inspector General, The September 11 Detainees: A Review of the Treatment of Aliens Held on Immigration Charges in Connection with the Investigation of the September 11 Attacks 1, 11–12 (Apr.2003) (hereinafter OIG Report), http://www.usdoj.gov/oig/special/0306/full.pdf?bcsi_scan_61073EC0F74759AD=0

&bcsi_scan_filename=full.pdf (as visited May 14, 2009, and available in Clerk of Court's case file).

In the ensuing months the FBI questioned more than 1,000 people with suspected links to the attacks in particular or to terrorism in general. Of those individuals, some 762 were held on immigration charges; and a 184-member subset of that group was deemed to be "of 'high interest' " to the investigation. The high-interest detainees were held under restrictive conditions designed to prevent them from communicating with the general prison population or the outside world.

Respondent was one of the detainees. According to his complaint, in November 2001 agents of the FBI and Immigration and Naturalization Service arrested him on charges of fraud in relation to identification documents and conspiracy to defraud the United States. Iqbal v. Hasty, 490 F.3d 143, 147–148 (C.A.2 2007). Pending trial for those crimes, respondent was housed at the Metropolitan Detention Center (MDC) in Brooklyn, New York. Respondent was designated a person "of high interest" to the September 11 investigation and in January 2002 was placed in a section of the MDC known as the Administrative Maximum Special Housing Unit (ADMAX SHU). As the facility's name indicates, the ADMAX SHU incorporates the maximum security conditions allowable under Federal Bureau of Prison regulations. ADMAX SHU detainees were kept in lockdown 23 hours a day, spending the remaining hour outside their cells in handcuffs and leg irons accompanied by a four-officer escort.

Respondent pleaded guilty to the criminal charges, served a term of imprisonment, and was removed to his native Pakistan. He then filed a Bivens action in the United States District Court for the Eastern District of New York against 34 current and former federal officials and 19 "John Doe" federal corrections officers. See Bivens v. Six Unknown Fed. Narcotics Agents, 403 U.S. 388, 91 S.Ct. 1999, 29 L.Ed.2d 619 (1971). The defendants range from the correctional officers who had day-to-day contact with respondent during the term of his confinement, to the wardens of the MDC facility, all the way to petitioners-officials who were at the highest level of the federal law enforcement hierarchy.

The 21-cause-of-action complaint does not challenge respondent's arrest or his confinement in the MDC's general prison population. Rather, it concentrates on his treatment while confined to the ADMAX SHU. The complaint sets forth various claims against defendants who are not before us. For instance, the complaint alleges that respondent's jailors "kicked him in the stomach, punched him in the face, and dragged him across" his cell without justification, subjected him to serial strip and body-cavity searches when he posed no safety risk to himself or others, and refused to let him and other Muslims pray because there would be "[n]o prayers for terrorists,"

The allegations against petitioners are the only ones relevant here. The complaint contends that petitioners designated respondent a person of high interest on account of his race, religion, or national origin, in contravention of the First and Fifth Amendments to the Constitution. The complaint alleges that "the [FBI], under the direction of Defendant Mueller, arrested and detained thousands of Arab Muslim men . . . as part of its investigation of the events of September 11." It further alleges that "[t]he policy of holding post-September-11th detainees in highly restrictive conditions of confinement until they were 'cleared' by the FBI was approved by Defendants Ashcroft and Mueller in discussions in the weeks after September 11, 2001." Lastly, the complaint posits that petitioners "each knew of, condoned, and willfully and maliciously agreed to subject" respondent to harsh conditions of confinement "as a matter of policy, solely on account of [his] religion, race, and/or national origin and for no legitimate penological interest.". The pleading names Ashcroft as the "principal architect" of the policy, and identifies Mueller as "instrumental in [its] adoption, promulgation, and implementation."

Petitioners moved to dismiss the complaint for failure to state sufficient allegations to show their own involvement in clearly established unconstitutional conduct. The District Court denied their motion. Accepting all of the allegations in respondent's complaint as true, the court held that "it cannot be said that there [is] no set of facts on which [respondent] would be entitled to relief as against" petitioners. . . .

The Court of Appeals . . . held respondent's pleading adequate to allege petitioners' personal involvement in discriminatory decisions which, if true, violated clearly established constitutional law.

Judge CABRANES concurred. He agreed that the majority's "discussion of the relevant pleading standards reflect[ed] the uneasy compromise . . . between a qualified immunity privilege rooted in the need to preserve the effectiveness of government as contemplated by our constitutional structure and the pleading requirements of Rule 8(a) of the Federal Rules of Civil Procedure." Judge CABRANES nonetheless expressed concern at the prospect of subjecting high-ranking Government officials—entitled to assert the defense of qualified immunity and charged with responding to "a national and international security emergency unprecedented in the history of the American Republic"—to the burdens of discovery on the basis of a complaint as nonspecific as respondent's. Reluctant to vindicate that concern as a member of the Court of Appeals, Judge CABRANES urged this Court to address the appropriate pleading standard "at the earliest opportunity." We granted certiorari, 554 U.S. ___ (2008), and now reverse.

. . .

. . . [W]e conclude that the Court of Appeals had jurisdiction to hear petitioners' appeal. The District Court's order denying petitioners' motion to dismiss turned on an issue of law and rejected the defense of qualified immunity. It was therefore a final decision "subject to immediate appeal." Respondent says that "a qualified immunity appeal based solely on the complaint's failure to state a claim, and not on the ultimate issues relevant to the qualified immunity defense itself, is not a proper subject of interlocutory jurisdiction."

In other words, respondent contends the Court of Appeals had jurisdiction to determine whether his complaint avers a clearly established constitutional violation but that it lacked jurisdiction to pass on the sufficiency of his pleadings. Our opinions, however, make clear that appellate jurisdiction is not so strictly confined.

. . .

. . . Here. . . we begin by taking note of the elements a plaintiff must plead to state a claim of unconstitutional discrimination against officials entitled to assert the defense of qualified immunity.

In Bivens—proceeding on the theory that a right suggests a remedy— this Court "recognized for the first time an implied private action for damages against federal officers alleged to have violated a citizen's constitutional rights." Because implied causes of action are disfavored, the Court has been reluctant to extend Bivens liability "to any new context or new category of defendants." That reluctance might well have disposed of respondent's First Amendment claim of religious discrimination. For while we have allowed a Bivens action to redress a violation of the equal protection component of the Due Process Clause of the Fifth Amendment, we have not found an implied damages remedy under the Free Exercise Clause. Indeed, we have declined to extend Bivens to a claim sounding in the First Amendment. Petitioners do not press this argument, however, so we assume, without deciding, that respondent's First Amendment claim is actionable under Bivens.

In the limited settings where Bivens does apply, the implied cause of action is the "federal analog to suits brought against state officials under Rev. Stat. § 1979, 42 U.S.C. § 1983." Based on the rules our precedents establish, respondent correctly concedes that Government officials may not be held liable for the unconstitutional conduct of their subordinates under a theory of respondeat superior. ("[I]t is undisputed that supervisory Bivens liability cannot be established solely on a theory of respondeat superior"). . . . Because vicarious liability is inapplicable to Bivens and § 1983 suits, a plaintiff must plead that each Government-official defendant, through the official's own individual actions, has violated the Constitution.

The factors necessary to establish a Bivens violation will vary with the constitutional provision at issue. Where the claim is invidious discrimination in contravention of the First and Fifth Amendments, our decisions make clear that the plaintiff must plead and prove that the defendant acted with discriminatory purpose. Church of Lukumi Babalu Aye, Inc. v. Hialeah, 508 U.S. 520, 540–541, 113 S.Ct. 2217, 124 L.Ed.2d 472 (1993) (First Amendment); Washington v. Davis, 426 U.S. 229, 240, 96 S.Ct. 2040, 48 L.Ed.2d 597 (1976) (Fifth Amendment). Under extant precedent purposeful discrimination requires more than "intent as volition or intent as awareness of consequences." Personnel Administrator of Mass. v. Feeney, 442 U.S. 256, 279, 99 S.Ct. 2282, 60 L.Ed.2d 870 (1979). It instead involves a decisionmaker's undertaking a course of action " 'because of,' not merely 'in spite of,' [the action's] adverse effects upon an identifiable group." It follows that, to state a claim based on a violation of a clearly established right, respondent must plead sufficient factual matter to show that petitioners adopted and implemented the detention policies at issue not for a neutral, investigative reason but for the purpose of discriminating on account of race, religion, or national origin.

Respondent disagrees. He argues that, under a theory of "supervisory liability," petitioners can be liable for "knowledge and acquiescence in their subordinates' use of discriminatory criteria to make classification decisions among detainees." That is to say, respondent believes a supervisor's mere knowledge of his subordinate's discriminatory purpose amounts to the supervisor's violating the Constitution. We reject this argument. Respondent's conception of "supervisory liability" is inconsistent with his accurate stipulation that petitioners may not be held accountable for the misdeeds of their agents. In a § 1983 suit or a Bivens action—where masters do not answer for the torts of their servants—the term "supervisory liability" is a misnomer. Absent vicarious liability, each Government official, his or her title notwithstanding, is only liable for his or her own misconduct. In the context of determining whether there is a violation of clearly established right to overcome qualified immunity, purpose rather than knowledge is required to impose Bivens liability on the subordinate for unconstitutional discrimination; the same holds true for an official charged with violations arising from his or her superintendent responsibilities.

We turn to respondent's complaint. . . .

. . .

We begin our analysis by identifying the allegations in the complaint that are not entitled to the assumption of truth. Respondent pleads that petitioners "knew of, condoned, and willfully and maliciously agreed to subject [him]" to harsh conditions of confinement "as a matter of policy, solely on account of [his] religion, race, and/or national origin and for no legitimate penological interest.". The complaint alleges that Ashcroft was the "principal architect" of this invidious policy, and that Mueller was "instrumental" in adopting and executing it. These bare assertions, . . .

amount to nothing more than a "formulaic recitation of the elements" of a constitutional discrimination claim, namely, that petitioners adopted a policy " 'because of,' not merely 'in spite of,' its adverse effects upon an identifiable group." As such, the allegations are conclusory and not entitled to be assumed true. To be clear, we do not reject these bald allegations on the ground that they are unrealistic or nonsensical. . . . It is the conclusory nature of respondent's allegations, rather than their extravagantly fanciful nature, that disentitles them to the presumption of truth.

We next consider the factual allegations in respondent's complaint to determine if they plausibly suggest an entitlement to relief. The complaint alleges that "the [FBI], under the direction of Defendant MUELLER, arrested and detained thousands of Arab Muslim men . . . as part of its investigation of the events of September 11.". It further claims that "[t]he policy of holding post-September-11th detainees in highly restrictive conditions of confinement until they were 'cleared' by the FBI was approved by Defendants ASHCROFT and MUELLER in discussions in the weeks after September 11, 2001." Taken as true, these allegations are consistent with petitioners' purposefully designating detainees "of high interest" because of their race, religion, or national origin. But given more likely explanations, they do not plausibly establish this purpose.

The September 11 attacks were perpetrated by 19 Arab Muslim hijackers who counted themselves members in good standing of al Qaeda, an Islamic fundamentalist group. Al Qaeda was headed by another Arab Muslim—Osama bin Laden—and composed in large part of his Arab Muslim disciples. It should come as no surprise that a legitimate policy directing law enforcement to arrest and detain individuals because of their suspected link to the attacks would produce a disparate, incidental impact on Arab Muslims, even though the purpose of the policy was to target neither Arabs nor Muslims. On the facts respondent alleges the arrests Mueller oversaw were likely lawful and justified by his nondiscriminatory intent to detain aliens who were illegally present in the United States and who had potential connections to those who committed terrorist acts. As between that "obvious alternative explanation" for the arrests, and the purposeful, invidious discrimination respondent asks us to infer, discrimination is not a plausible conclusion.

But even if the complaint's well-pleaded facts give rise to a plausible inference that respondent's arrest was the result of unconstitutional discrimination, that inference alone would not entitle respondent to relief. It is important to recall that respondent's complaint challenges neither the constitutionality of his arrest nor his initial detention in the MDC. Respondent's constitutional claims against petitioners rest solely on their ostensible "policy of holding post-September-11th detainees" in the ADMAX SHU once they were categorized as "of high interest." To prevail on that theory, the complaint must contain facts plausibly showing that petitioners purposefully adopted a policy of classifying post-September-11 detainees as "of high interest" because of their race, religion, or national origin.

This the complaint fails to do. Though respondent alleges that various other defendants, who are not before us, may have labeled him a person of "of high interest" for impermissible reasons, his only factual allegation against petitioners accuses them of adopting a policy approving "restrictive conditions of confinement" for post-September-11 detainees until they were " 'cleared' by the FBI." Accepting the truth of that allegation, the complaint does not show, or even intimate, that petitioners purposefully housed detainees in the ADMAX SHU due to their race, religion, or national origin. All it plausibly suggests is that the Nation's top law enforcement officers, in the aftermath of a devastating terrorist attack, sought to keep suspected terrorists in the most secure conditions available until the suspects could be cleared of terrorist activity. Respondent does not argue, nor can he, that such a motive would violate petitioners' constitutional obligations. He would need to allege more by way of factual content to "nudg[e]" his claim of purposeful discrimination "across the line from conceivable to plausible."

. . . [R]espondent's complaint does not contain any factual allegation sufficient to plausibly suggest petitioners' discriminatory state of mind. His pleadings thus do not meet the standard necessary to comply with Rule 8.

It is important to note, however, that we express no opinion concerning the sufficiency of respondent's complaint against the defendants who are not before us. Respondent's account of his prison ordeal alleges serious official misconduct that we need not address here. Our decision is limited to the determination that respondent's complaint does not entitle him to relief from petitioners.

. . .

. . . The basic thrust of the qualified-immunity doctrine is to free officials from the concerns of litigation, including "avoidance of disruptive discovery." There are serious and legitimate reasons for this. If a Government official is to devote time to his or her duties, and to the formulation of sound and responsible policies, it is counterproductive to require the substantial diversion that is attendant to participating in litigation and making informed decisions as to how it should proceed. Litigation, though necessary to ensure that officials comply with the law, exacts heavy costs in terms of efficiency and expenditure of valuable time and resources that might otherwise be directed to the proper execution of the work of the Government. The costs of diversion are only magnified when Government officials are charged with responding to, as Judge CABRANES aptly put it, "a national and international security emergency unprecedented in the history of the American Republic."

It is no answer to these concerns to say that discovery for petitioners can be deferred while pretrial proceedings continue for other defendants. It is quite likely that, when discovery as to the other parties proceeds, it would prove necessary for petitioners and their counsel to participate in the process to ensure the case does not develop in a misleading or slanted way that causes prejudice to their position. Even if petitioners are not yet themselves subject to discovery orders, then, they would not be free from the burdens of discovery.

We decline respondent's invitation to relax the pleading requirements on the ground that the Court of Appeals promises petitioners minimally intrusive discovery. That promise provides especially cold comfort in this pleading context, where we are impelled to give real content to the concept of qualified immunity for high-level officials who must be neither deterred nor detracted from the vigorous performance of their duties. Because respondent's complaint is deficient under Rule 8, he is not entitled to discovery, cabined or otherwise.

We hold that respondent's complaint fails to plead sufficient facts to state a claim for purposeful and unlawful discrimination against petitioners. The Court of Appeals should decide in the first instance whether to remand to the District Court so that respondent can seek leave to amend his deficient complaint.

The judgment of the Court of Appeals is reversed, and the case is remanded for further proceedings consistent with this opinion.

[JUSTICE SOUTER, with whom JUSTICE STEVENS, JUSTICE GINSBURG, and JUSTICE BREYER joined, filed a dissenting opinion. JUSTICE BREYER also wrote a dissenting opinion.]

5. STATUTORY DETENTION AND REMOVAL PROVISIONS DIRECTED SPECIFICALLY TOWARD TERRORISTS UNDER THE USA PATRIOT ACT AND OTHER IMMIGRATION LAW PROVISIONS

The USA PATRIOT Act (P.L. 107–56, Oct. 26, 2001) added Section 1226a to Title 8, United States Code, which contains the codified parts of the Immigration and Nationality Act of 1952. It adds another tool to the array of immigration law provisions that can be used in alien terrorist cases. See footnote 8 in Clark v. Martinez, supra, and reconsider the dicta in Zadvydas v. Davis, supra.

Title 8, U.S.C.

§ 1226a. Mandatory detention of suspected terrorists; habeas corpus; judicial review

(a) Detention of terrorist aliens.

(1) Custody.—The Attorney General shall take into custody any alien who is certified under paragraph (3).

(2) Release.—Except as provided in paragraphs (5) and (6), the Attorney General shall maintain custody of such an alien until the alien is removed from the United States. Except as provided in paragraph (6), such custody shall be maintained irrespective of any relief from removal for which the alien may be eligible, or any relief from removal granted the alien, until the Attorney General determines that the alien is no longer an alien who may be certified under paragraph (3). If the alien is finally determined not to be removable, detention pursuant to this subsection shall terminate.

(3) Certification.—The Attorney General may certify an alien under this paragraph if the Attorney General has reasonable grounds to believe that the alien—

(A) is described in section 212(a)(3)(A)(i), 212(a)(3)(A)(iii), 212(a)(3)(B), 237(a)(4)(A)(i), 237(a)(4)(A)(iii), or 237(a)(4)(B) [8 USC §§ 1182(a)(3)(A)(i), 1182(a)(3)(A)(iii), 1182(a)(3)(B), 1227(a)(4)(A)(i), 1227(a)(4)(A)(iii), or 1227(a)(4)(B)]; or

(B) is engaged in any other activity that endangers the national security of the United States.

(4) Nondelegation.—The Attorney General may delegate the authority provided under paragraph (3) only to the Deputy Attorney General. The Deputy Attorney General may not delegate such authority.

(5) Commencement of proceedings.—The Attorney General shall place an alien detained under paragraph (1) in removal proceedings, or shall charge the alien with a criminal offense, not later than 7 days after the commencement of such detention. If the requirement of the preceding sentence is not satisfied, the Attorney General shall release the alien.

(6) Limitation on indefinite detention.—An alien detained solely under paragraph (1) who has not been removed under section 241(a)(1)(A) [8 USC § 1231(a)(1)(A)], and whose removal is unlikely in the reasonably foreseeable future, may be detained for additional periods of up to six months only if the release of the

(c) Chief judge

(1) Designation

The Chief Justice shall publicly designate one of the judges of the removal court to be the chief judge of the removal court.

(2) Responsibilities

The chief judge shall—

(A) promulgate rules to facilitate the functioning of the removal court; and

(B) assign the consideration of cases to the various judges on the removal court.

(d) Expeditious and confidential nature of proceedings

The provisions of section 103(c) of the Foreign Intelligence Surveillance Act of 1978 (50 U.S.C. § 1803(c)) shall apply to removal proceedings in the same manner as they apply to proceedings under that Act (50 U.S.C. 1801 et seq.).

(e) Establishment of panel of special attorneys

The removal court shall provide for the designation of a panel of attorneys each of whom—

(1) has a security clearance which affords the attorney access to classified information, and

(2) has agreed to represent permanent resident aliens with respect to classified information under section 1534(e)(3) of this title in accordance with (and subject to the penalties under) this subchapter.

§ 1533. Removal court procedure

(a) Application

(1) In general

In any case in which the Attorney General has classified information that an alien is an alien terrorist, the Attorney General may seek removal of the alien under this subchapter by filing an application with the removal court that contains—

(A) the identity of the attorney in the Department of Justice making the application;

(B) a certification by the Attorney General or the Deputy Attorney General that the application satisfies the criteria and requirements of this section;

(C) the identity of the alien for whom authorization for the removal proceeding is sought; and

(D) a statement of the facts and circumstances relied on by the Department of Justice to establish probable cause that—

(i) the alien is an alien terrorist;

(ii) the alien is physically present in the United States; and

(iii) with respect to such alien, removal under subchapter II of this chapter would pose a risk to the national security of the United States.

(2) Filing

An application under this section shall be submitted ex parte and in camera, and shall be filed under seal with the removal court.

(b) Right to dismiss

The Attorney General may dismiss a removal action under this subchapter at any stage of the proceeding.

(c) Consideration of application

(1) Basis for decision

In determining whether to grant an application under this section, a single judge of the removal court may consider, ex parte and in camera, in addition to the information contained in the application—

(A) other information, including classified information, presented under oath or affirmation; and

(B) testimony received in any hearing on the application, of which a verbatim record shall be kept.

(2) Approval of order

The judge shall issue an order granting the application, if the judge finds that there is probable cause to believe that—

(A) the alien who is the subject of the application has been correctly identified and is an alien terrorist present in the United States; and

(B) removal under subchapter II of this chapter would pose a risk to the national security of the United States.

(3) Denial of order

If the judge denies the order requested in the application, the judge shall prepare a written statement of the reasons for the denial, taking all necessary precautions not to disclose any classified information contained in the Government's application.

(d) Exclusive provisions

If an order is issued under this section granting an application, the rights of the alien regarding removal and expulsion shall be governed solely by this subchapter, and except as they are specifically referenced in this subchapter, no other provisions of this chapter shall be applicable.

§ 1534. Removal hearing

(a) In general

(1) Expeditious hearing

In any case in which an application for an order is approved under section 1533(c)(2) of this title, a removal hearing shall be conducted under this section as expeditiously as practicable for the purpose of determining whether the alien to whom the order pertains should be removed from the United States on the grounds that the alien is an alien terrorist.

(2) Public hearing

The removal hearing shall be open to the public.

. . .

§ 1535. Appeals

. . .

(e) Appeal of detention order

. . .

(2) No review of continued detention. The determinations and actions of the Attorney General pursuant to section 507(b)(2)(C) [8 USCS § 1537(b)(2)(C)] shall not be subject to judicial review, including application for a writ of habeas corpus, except for a claim by the alien that continued detention violates the alien's rights under the Constitution. Jurisdiction over any such challenge shall lie exclusively in the United States Court of Appeals for the District of Columbia Circuit.

. . .

§ 1537. Custody and release after removal hearing

. . .

(b) Custody and removal

(1) Custody. If the judge decides that an alien shall be removed, the alien shall be detained pending the outcome of any appeal. After the conclusion of any judicial review thereof which affirms the removal order, the Attorney General shall retain the alien in custody and remove the alien to a country specified under paragraph (2).

(2) Removal

(A) In general. The removal of an alien shall be to any country which the alien shall designate if such designation does not, in the judgment of the Attorney General, in consultation with the Secretary of State, impair the obligation of the United States under any treaty (including a treaty pertaining to extradition) or otherwise adversely affect the foreign policy of the United States.

(B) Alternate countries. If the alien refuses to designate a country to which the alien wishes to be removed or if the Attorney General, in consultation with the Secretary of State, determines that removal of the alien to the country so designated would impair a treaty obligation or adversely affect United States foreign policy, the Attorney General shall cause the alien to be removed to any country willing to receive such alien.

(C) Continued detention. If no country is willing to receive such an alien, the Attorney General may, notwithstanding any other provision of law, retain the alien in custody. The Attorney General, in coordination with the Secretary of State, shall make periodic efforts to reach agreement with other countries to accept such an alien and at least every 6 months shall provide to the attorney representing the alien at the removal hearing a written report on the Attorney General's efforts. Any alien in custody pursuant to this subparagraph shall be released from custody solely at the discretion of the Attorney General and subject to such conditions as the Attorney General shall deem appropriate.

§ 1227. General classes of deportable aliens

(a) Classes of deportable aliens

Any alien (including an alien crewman) in and admitted to the United States shall, upon the order of the Attorney General, be removed if the alien is within one or more of the following classes of deportable aliens:

. . .

(4) Security and related grounds

(A) In general

Any alien who has engaged, is engaged, or at any time after admission engages in—

(i) any activity to violate any law of the United States relating to espionage or sabotage or to violate or evade any law prohibiting the export from the United States of goods, technology, or sensitive information,

(ii) any other criminal activity which endangers public safety or national security, or

(iii) any activity a purpose of which is the opposition to, or the control or overthrow of, the Government of the United States by force, violence, or other unlawful means, is deportable.

(B) Terrorist activities

Any alien who has engaged, is engaged, or at any time after admission engages in any terrorist activity (as defined in section 1182(a)(3)(B)(iii) of this title) is deportable.

QUESTIONS AND NOTES

1.   Neither § 1226a nor the special removal court provisions appear to have as yet been utilized against alien suspected terrorists.

2.   See generally, Juliet P. Stumpf, The Implausible Alien: Iqbal and the influence of Immigration Law, 14 Lewis & Clark L. Rev. 231 (2010); Susan M. Akram & Maritza Karmely, Immigration and Constitutional Consequences of Post-9/11 Policies Involving Arabs and Muslims in the United States: Is Alienage a Distinction without a Difference?, 38 U.C. DAVIS L. REV. 609 (2005).

3.   In 2011, by Executive Order, the Obama administration adopted rules for reviewing the status of persons detained for extended periods at Guantanamo. See infra, ch. 10.

6. THE TRUMP TRAVEL BAN

As of the time of this writing, the only major anti-terrorism measure put into effect by the Trump administration has been Executive Order 13780, dated March 6, 2017 and an implementing Presidential Proclamation, dated September 2017 that had the effect of banning or restricting travel from certain listed countries. The rationale of this ban was that these countries did not do enough or did not provide enough information to demonstrate that they were doing enough to vet travelers so as to prevent dangerous individuals from entering the U.S. This Executive Order is reproduced below.

As noted in section 1 h of the Executive Order, "Recent history shows that some of those who have entered the United States through our immigration system have proved to be threats to our national security." The rationale is thus that this broad brush action is an effort in terrorism prevention. It differs from the types of anti-terrorism actions studied in this volume which, for the most part, are targeted at terrorists or suspected terrorists. The travel ban sweeps more broadly since it bans most travelers from the listed countries; it inevitably bans the innocent and non-dangerous along with those who present risks.

But it was not easy to get to point where the ban was effective. The first version of an Executive Order on this subject created chaos at airports and was legally vulnerable. Critics were able quickly to obtain injunctions against its enforcement. This Order was modified and strengthened and eventually became the March 6th Order. Finally, in early December 2017, the Supreme Court allowed the Order to go into effect while the lawsuits challenging it continued. This recent history is recounted in more detail, infra.

a. The Executive Orders and Proclamation

EXECUTIVE ORDER 13780

The White House

Office of the Press Secretary

For Immediate Release

March 06, 2017

Executive Order Protecting The Nation From Foreign Terrorist Entry Into The United States

EXECUTIVE ORDER

PROTECTING THE NATION FROM FOREIGN TERRORIST ENTRY INTO THE UNITED STATES

By the authority vested in me as President by the Constitution and the laws of the United States of America, including the Immigration and Nationality Act (INA), 8 U.S.C. 1101 et seq., and section 301 of title 3, United States Code, and to protect the Nation from terrorist activities by foreign nationals admitted to the United States, it is hereby ordered as follows:

Section 1.   Policy and Purpose. (a) It is the policy of the United States to protect its citizens from terrorist attacks, including those committed by foreign nationals. The screening and vetting protocols and procedures associated with the visa-issuance process and the United States Refugee Admissions Program (USRAP) play a crucial role in detecting foreign nationals who may commit, aid, or support acts of terrorism and in preventing those individuals from entering the United States. It is therefore the policy of the United States to improve the screening and vetting protocols and procedures associated with the visa-issuance process and the USRAP.

(b) On January 27, 2017, to implement this policy, I issued Executive Order 13769 (Protecting the Nation from Foreign Terrorist Entry into the United States).

(i) Among other actions, Executive Order 13769 suspended for 90 days the entry of certain aliens from seven countries: Iran, Iraq, Libya, Somalia, Sudan, Syria, and Yemen. These are countries that had already been identified as presenting heightened concerns about terrorism and travel to the United States. Specifically, the suspension applied to countries referred to in, or designated under, section 217(a)(12) of the INA, 8 U.S.C. 1187(a)(12), in which Congress restricted use of the Visa Waiver Program for nationals of, and aliens recently present in, (A) Iraq or Syria, (B) any country designated by the Secretary of State as a state sponsor of terrorism (currently Iran, Syria, and Sudan), and (C) any other country designated as a country of concern by the Secretary of Homeland Security, in consultation with the Secretary of State and the Director of National Intelligence. In 2016, the Secretary of Homeland Security designated Libya, Somalia, and Yemen as additional countries of concern for travel purposes, based on consideration of three statutory factors related to terrorism and national security: "(I) whether the presence of an alien in the country or area increases the likelihood that the alien is a credible threat to the national security of the United States; (II) whether a foreign terrorist organization has a significant presence in the country or area; and (III) whether the country or area is a safe haven for terrorists." 8 U.S.C. 1187(a)(12)(D)(ii). Additionally, Members of Congress have expressed concerns about screening and vetting procedures following recent terrorist attacks in this country and in Europe.

(ii) In ordering the temporary suspension of entry described in subsection (b)(i) of this section, I exercised my authority under Article II of the Constitution and under section 212(f) of the INA, which provides in relevant part: "Whenever the President finds that the entry of any aliens or of any class of aliens into the United States would be detrimental to the interests of the United States, he may by proclamation, and for such period as he shall deem necessary, suspend the entry of all aliens or any class of aliens as immigrants or nonimmigrants, or impose on the entry of aliens any restrictions he may deem to be appropriate." 8 U.S.C. 1182(f). Under these authorities, I determined that, for a brief period of 90 days, while existing screening and vetting procedures were under review, the entry into the United States of certain aliens from the seven identified countries—each afflicted by terrorism in a manner that compromised the ability of the United States to rely on normal decision-making procedures about travel to the United States—would be detrimental to the interests of the United States. Nonetheless, I permitted the Secretary of State and the Secretary of Homeland Security to grant case-by-case waivers when they determined that it was in the national interest to do so.

(iii) Executive Order 13769 also suspended the USRAP for 120 days. Terrorist groups have sought to infiltrate several nations through refugee programs. Accordingly, I temporarily suspended the USRAP pending a review of our procedures for screening and vetting refugees. Nonetheless, I permitted the Secretary of State and the Secretary of Homeland Security to jointly grant case-by-case waivers when they determined that it was in the national interest to do so.

(iv) Executive Order 13769 did not provide a basis for discriminating for or against members of any particular religion. While that order allowed for prioritization of refugee claims from members of persecuted religious minority groups, that priority applied to refugees from every nation, including those in which Islam is a minority religion, and it applied to minority sects within a religion. That order was not motivated by animus toward any religion, but was instead intended to protect the ability of religious minorities— whoever they are and wherever they reside—to avail themselves of the USRAP in light of their particular challenges and circumstances.

(c)   The implementation of Executive Order 13769 has been delayed by litigation. Most significantly, enforcement of critical provisions of that order has been temporarily halted by court orders that apply nationwide and extend even to foreign nationals with no prior or substantial connection to the United States. On February 9, 2017, the United States Court of Appeals for the Ninth Circuit declined to stay or narrow one such order pending the outcome of further judicial proceedings, while noting that the "political branches are far better equipped to make appropriate distinctions" about who should be covered by a suspension of entry or of refugee admissions.

(d)   Nationals from the countries previously identified under section 217(a)(12) of the INA warrant additional scrutiny in connection with our immigration policies because the conditions in these countries present heightened threats. Each of these countries is a state sponsor of terrorism, has been significantly compromised by terrorist organizations, or contains active conflict zones. Any of these circumstances diminishes the foreign government's willingness or ability to share or validate important information about individuals seeking to travel to the United States. Moreover, the significant presence in each of these countries of terrorist organizations, their members, and others exposed to those organizations increases the chance that conditions will be exploited to enable terrorist operatives or sympathizers to travel to the United States. Finally, once foreign nationals from these countries are admitted to the United States, it is often difficult to remove them, because many of these countries typically delay issuing, or refuse to issue, travel documents.

(e)   The following are brief descriptions, taken in part from the Department of State's Country Reports on Terrorism 2015 (June 2016), of some of the conditions in six of the previously designated countries that demonstrate why their nationals continue to present heightened risks to the security of the United States:

(i)   Iran. Iran has been designated as a state sponsor of terrorism since 1984 and continues to support various terrorist groups, including Hizballah, Hamas, and terrorist groups in Iraq. Iran has also been linked to support for al-Qa'ida and has permitted al-Qa'ida to transport funds and fighters through Iran to Syria and South Asia. Iran does not cooperate with the United States in counterterrorism efforts.

(ii) Libya. Libya is an active combat zone, with hostilities between the internationally recognized government and its rivals. In many parts of the country, security and law enforcement functions are provided by armed militias rather than state institutions. Violent extremist groups, including the Islamic State of Iraq and Syria (ISIS), have exploited these conditions to expand their presence in the country. The Libyan government provides some cooperation with the United States' counterterrorism efforts, but it is unable to secure thousands of miles of its land and maritime borders, enabling the illicit flow of weapons, migrants, and foreign terrorist fighters. The United States Embassy in Libya suspended its operations in 2014.

(iii) Somalia. Portions of Somalia have been terrorist safe havens. Al-Shabaab, an al-Qa'ida-affiliated terrorist group, has operated in the country for years and continues to plan and mount operations within Somalia and in neighboring countries. Somalia has porous borders, and most countries do not recognize Somali identity documents. The Somali government cooperates with the United States in some counterterrorism operations but does not have the capacity to sustain military pressure on or to investigate suspected terrorists.

(iv) Sudan. Sudan has been designated as a state sponsor of terrorism since 1993 because of its support for international terrorist groups, including Hizballah and Hamas. Historically, Sudan provided safe havens for al-Qa'ida and other terrorist groups to meet and train. Although Sudan's support to al-Qa'ida has ceased and it provides some cooperation with the United States' counterterrorism efforts, elements of core al-Qa'ida and ISIS-linked terrorist groups remain active in the country.

(v)   Syria. Syria has been designated as a state sponsor of terrorism since 1979. The Syrian government is engaged in an ongoing military conflict against ISIS and others for control of portions of the country. At the same time, Syria continues to support other terrorist groups. It has allowed or encouraged extremists to pass through its territory to enter Iraq. ISIS continues to attract foreign fighters to Syria and to use its base in Syria to plot or encourage attacks around the globe, including in the United States. The United States Embassy in Syria suspended its operations in 2012. Syria does not cooperate with the United States' counterterrorism efforts.

(vi) Yemen. Yemen is the site of an ongoing conflict between the incumbent government and the Houthi-led opposition. Both ISIS and a second group, al-Qa'ida in the Arabian Peninsula (AQAP), have exploited this conflict to expand their presence in Yemen and to carry out hundreds of attacks. Weapons and other materials smuggled across Yemen's porous borders are used to finance AQAP and other terrorist activities. In 2015, the United States Embassy in Yemen suspended its operations, and embassy staff were relocated out of the country. Yemen has been supportive of, but has not been able to cooperate fully with, the United States in counterterrorism efforts.

(f)   In light of the conditions in these six countries, until the assessment of current screening and vetting procedures required by section 2 of this order is completed, the risk of erroneously permitting entry of a national of one of these countries who intends to commit terrorist acts or otherwise harm the national security of the United States is unacceptably high. Accordingly, while that assessment is ongoing, I am imposing a temporary pause on the entry of nationals from Iran, Libya, Somalia, Sudan, Syria, and Yemen, subject to categorical exceptions and case-by-case waivers, as described in section 3 of this order.

(g)   Iraq presents a special case. Portions of Iraq remain active combat zones. Since 2014, ISIS has had dominant influence over significant territory in northern and central Iraq. Although that influence has been significantly reduced due to the efforts and sacrifices of the Iraqi government and armed forces, working along with a United States-led coalition, the ongoing conflict has impacted the Iraqi government's capacity to secure its borders and to identify fraudulent travel documents. Nevertheless, the close cooperative relationship between the United States and the democratically elected Iraqi government, the strong United States diplomatic presence in Iraq, the significant presence of United States forces in Iraq, and Iraq's commitment to combat ISIS justify different treatment for Iraq. In particular, those Iraqi government forces that have fought to regain more than half of the territory previously dominated by ISIS have shown steadfast determination and earned enduring respect as they battle an armed group that is the common enemy of Iraq and the United States. In addition, since Executive Order 13769 was issued, the Iraqi government has expressly undertaken steps to enhance travel documentation, information sharing, and the return of Iraqi nationals subject to final orders of removal. Decisions about issuance of visas or granting admission to Iraqi nationals should be subjected to additional scrutiny to determine if applicants have connections with ISIS or other terrorist organizations, or otherwise pose a risk to either national security or public safety.

(h) Recent history shows that some of those who have entered the United States through our immigration system have proved to be threats to our national security. Since 2001, hundreds of persons born abroad have been convicted of terrorism-related crimes in the United States. They have included not just persons who came here legally on visas but also individuals who first entered the country as refugees. For example, in January 2013, two Iraqi nationals admitted to the United States as refugees in 2009 were sentenced to 40 years and to life in prison, respectively, for multiple terrorism-related offenses. And in October 2014, a native of Somalia who had been brought to the United States as a child refugee and later became a naturalized United States citizen was sentenced to 30 years in prison for attempting to use a weapon of mass destruction as part of a plot to detonate a bomb at a crowded Christmas-tree-lighting ceremony in Portland, Oregon. The Attorney General has reported to me that more than 300 persons who entered the United States as refugees are currently the subjects of counterterrorism investigations by the Federal Bureau of Investigation.

(i) Given the foregoing, the entry into the United States of foreign nationals who may commit, aid, or support acts of terrorism remains a matter of grave concern. In light of the Ninth Circuit's observation that the political branches are better suited to determine the appropriate scope of any suspensions than are the courts, and in order to avoid spending additional time pursuing litigation, I am revoking Executive Order 13769 and replacing it with this order, which expressly excludes from the suspensions categories of aliens that have prompted judicial concerns and which clarifies or refines the approach to certain other issues or categories of affected aliens.

Sec. 2. Temporary Suspension of Entry for Nationals of Countries of Particular Concern During Review Period. (a) The Secretary of Homeland Security, in consultation with the

Secretary of State and the Director of National Intelligence, shall conduct a worldwide review to identify whether, and if so what, additional information will be needed from each foreign country to adjudicate an application by a national of that country for a visa, admission, or other benefit under the INA (adjudications) in order to determine that the individual is not a security or public-safety threat. The Secretary of Homeland Security may conclude that certain information is needed from particular countries even if it is not needed from every country.

(b) The Secretary of Homeland Security, in consultation with the Secretary of State and the Director of National Intelligence, shall submit to the President a report on the results of the worldwide review described in subsection (a) of this section, including the Secretary of Homeland Security's determination of the information needed from each country for adjudications and a list of countries that do not provide adequate information, within 20 days of the effective date of this order. The Secretary of Homeland Security shall provide a copy of the report to the Secretary of State, the Attorney General, and the Director of National Intelligence.

(c) To temporarily reduce investigative burdens on relevant agencies during the review period described in subsection (a) of this section, to ensure the proper review and maximum utilization of available resources for the screening and vetting of foreign nationals, to ensure that adequate standards are established to prevent infiltration by foreign terrorists, and in light of the national security concerns referenced in section 1 of this order, I hereby proclaim, pursuant to sections 212(f) and 215(a) of the INA, 8 U.S.C. 1182(f) and 1185(a), that the unrestricted entry into the United States of nationals of Iran, Libya, Somalia, Sudan, Syria, and Yemen would be detrimental to the interests of the United States. I therefore direct that the entry into the United States of nationals of those six countries be suspended for 90 days from the effective date of this order, subject to the limitations, waivers, and exceptions set forth in sections 3 and 12 of this order.

(d) Upon submission of the report described in subsection (b) of this section regarding the information needed from each country for adjudications, the Secretary of State shall request that all foreign governments that do not supply such information regarding their nationals begin providing it within 50 days of notification.

(e) After the period described in subsection (d) of this section expires, the Secretary of Homeland Security, in consultation with the Secretary of State and the Attorney General, shall submit to the President a list of countries recommended for inclusion in a Presidential proclamation that would prohibit the entry of appropriate categories of foreign nationals of countries that have not provided the information requested until they do so or until the Secretary of Homeland Security certifies that the country has an adequate plan to do so, or has adequately shared information through other means. The Secretary of State, the Attorney General, or the Secretary of Homeland Security may also submit to the President the names of additional countries for which any of them recommends other lawful restrictions or limitations deemed necessary for the security or welfare of the United States.

(f) At any point after the submission of the list described in subsection (e) of this section, the Secretary of Homeland Security, in consultation with the Secretary of State and the Attorney General, may submit to the President the names of any additional countries recommended for similar treatment, as well as the names of any countries that they recommend should be removed from the scope of a proclamation described in subsection (e) of this section.

(g) The Secretary of State and the Secretary of Homeland Security shall submit to the President a joint report on the progress in implementing this order within 60 days of the effective date of this order, a second report within 90 days of the effective date of this order, a third report within 120 days of the effective date of this order, and a fourth report within 150 days of the effective date of this order.

Sec. 3. Scope and Implementation of Suspension.

(a) Scope. Subject to the exceptions set forth in subsection (b) of this section and any waiver under subsection (c) of this section, the suspension of entry pursuant to section 2 of this order shall apply only to foreign nationals of the designated countries who:

(i) are outside the United States on the effective date of this order;

(ii) did not have a valid visa at 5:00 p.m., eastern standard time on January 27, 2017; and

(iii) do not have a valid visa on the effective date of this order.

(b) Exceptions. The suspension of entry pursuant to section 2 of this order shall not apply to:

(i)   any lawful permanent resident of the United States;

(ii)   any foreign national who is admitted to or paroled into the United States on or after the effective date of this order;

(iii) any foreign national who has a document other than a visa, valid on the effective date of this order or issued on any date thereafter, that permits him or her to travel to the United States and seek entry or admission, such as an advance parole document;

(iv)   any dual national of a country designated under section 2 of this order when the individual is traveling on a passport issued by a non-designated country;

(v)   any foreign national traveling on a diplomatic or diplomatic-type visa, North Atlantic Treaty Organization visa, C-2 visa for travel to the United Nations, or G-1, G-2, G-3, or G-4 visa; or

(vi)   any foreign national who has been granted asylum; any refugee who has already been admitted to the United States; or any individual who has been granted withholding of removal, advance parole, or protection under the Convention Against Torture.

(c) Waivers. Notwithstanding the suspension of entry pursuant to section 2 of this order, a consular officer, or, as appropriate, the Commissioner, U.S. Customs and Border Protection (CBP), or the Commissioner's delegee, may, in the consular officer's or the CBP official's discretion, decide on a case-by-case basis to authorize the issuance of a visa to, or to permit the entry of, a foreign national for whom entry is otherwise suspended if the foreign national has demonstrated to the officer's satisfaction that denying entry during the suspension period would cause undue hardship, and that his or her entry would not pose a threat to national security and would be in the national interest. Unless otherwise specified by the Secretary of Homeland Security, any waiver issued by a consular officer as part of the visa issuance process will be effective both for the issuance of a visa and any subsequent entry on that visa, but will leave all other requirements for admission or entry unchanged. Case-by-case waivers could be appropriate in circumstances such as the following:

(i)   the foreign national has previously been admitted to the United States for a continuous period of work, study, or other long-term activity, is outside the United States on the effective date of this order, seeks to reenter the United States to resume that activity, and the denial of reentry during the suspension period would impair that activity;

(ii) the foreign national has previously established significant contacts with the United States but is outside the United States on the effective date of this order for work, study, or other lawful activity;

(iii) the foreign national seeks to enter the United States for significant business or professional obligations and the denial of entry during the suspension period would impair those obligations;

(iv) the foreign national seeks to enter the United States to visit or reside with a close family member (e.g., a spouse, child, or parent) who is a United States citizen, lawful permanent resident, or alien lawfully admitted on a valid nonimmigrant visa, and the denial of entry during the suspension period would cause undue hardship;

(v) the foreign national is an infant, a young child or adoptee, an individual needing urgent medical care, or someone whose entry is otherwise justified by the special circumstances of the case;

(vi) the foreign national has been employed by, or on behalf of, the United States Government (or is an eligible dependent of such an employee) and the employee can document that he or she has provided faithful and valuable service to the United States Government;

(vii) the foreign national is traveling for purposes related to an international organization designated under the International Organizations Immunities Act (IOIA), 22 U.S.C. 288 et seq., traveling for purposes of conducting meetings or business with the United States Government, or traveling to conduct business on behalf of an international organization not designated under the IOIA;

(viii) the foreign national is a landed Canadian immigrant who applies for a visa at a location within Canada; or

(ix) the foreign national is traveling as a United States Government-sponsored exchange visitor.

Sec. 4.   Additional Inquiries Related to Nationals of Iraq. An application by any Iraqi national for a visa, admission, or other immigration benefit should be subjected to thorough review, including, as appropriate, consultation with a designee of the Secretary of Defense and use of the additional information that has been obtained in the context of the close U.S.-Iraqi security partnership, since Executive Order 13769 was issued, concerning individuals suspected of ties to ISIS or other terrorist organizations and individuals coming from territories controlled or formerly controlled by ISIS. Such review shall include consideration of whether the applicant has connections with ISIS or other terrorist organizations or with territory that is or has been under the dominant influence of ISIS, as well as any other information bearing on whether the applicant may be a threat to commit acts of terrorism or otherwise threaten the national security or public safety of the United States.

Sec. 5. Implementing Uniform Screening and Vetting Standards for All Immigration Programs. (a) The Secretary of State, the Attorney General, the Secretary of Homeland Security, and the Director of National Intelligence shall implement a program, as part of the process for adjudications, to identify individuals who seek to enter the United States on a fraudulent basis, who support terrorism, violent extremism, acts of violence toward any group or class of people within the United States, or who present a risk of causing harm subsequent to their entry. This program shall include the development of a uniform baseline for screening and vetting standards and procedures, such as in-person interviews; a database of identity documents proffered by applicants to ensure that duplicate documents are not used by multiple applicants; amended application forms that include questions aimed at identifying fraudulent answers and malicious intent; a mechanism to ensure that applicants are who they claim to be; a mechanism to assess whether applicants may commit, aid, or support any kind of violent, criminal, or terrorist acts after entering the United States; and any other appropriate means for ensuring the proper collection of all information necessary for a rigorous evaluation of all grounds of inadmissibility or grounds for the denial of other immigration benefits.

(b) The Secretary of Homeland Security, in conjunction with the Secretary of State, the Attorney General, and the Director of National Intelligence, shall submit to the President an initial report on the progress of the program described in subsection (a) of this section within 60 days of the effective date of this order, a second report within 100 days of the effective date of this order, and a third report within 200 days of the effective date of this order.

Sec. 6. Realignment of the U.S. Refugee Admissions Program for Fiscal Year 2017. (a) The Secretary of State shall suspend travel of refugees into the United States under the USRAP, and the Secretary of Homeland Security shall suspend decisions on applications for refugee status, for 120 days after the effective date of this order, subject to waivers pursuant to subsection (c) of this section. During the 120-day period, the Secretary of State, in conjunction with the Secretary of Homeland Security and in consultation with the Director of National Intelligence, shall review the USRAP application and adjudication processes to determine what additional procedures should be used to ensure that individuals seeking admission as refugees do not pose a threat to the security and welfare of the United States, and shall implement such additional procedures. The suspension described in this subsection shall not apply to refugee applicants who, before the effective date of this order, have been formally scheduled for transit by the Department of State. The Secretary of State shall resume travel of refugees into the United States under the USRAP 120 days after the effective date of this order, and the Secretary of Homeland Security shall resume making decisions on applications for refugee status only for stateless persons and nationals of countries for which the Secretary of State, the Secretary of Homeland Security, and the Director of National Intelligence have jointly determined that the additional procedures implemented pursuant to this subsection are adequate to ensure the security and welfare of the United States.

(b) Pursuant to section 212(f) of the INA, I hereby proclaim that the entry of more than 50,000 refugees in fiscal year 2017 would be detrimental to the interests of the United States, and thus suspend any entries in excess of that number until such time as I determine that additional entries would be in the national interest.

(c) Notwithstanding the temporary suspension imposed pursuant to subsection (a) of this section, the Secretary of State and the Secretary of Homeland Security may jointly determine to admit individuals to the United States as refugees on a case-by-case basis, in their discretion, but only so long as they determine that the entry of such individuals as refugees is in the national interest and does not pose a threat to the security or welfare of the United States, including in circumstances such as the following: the individual's entry would enable the United States to conform its conduct to a preexisting international agreement or arrangement, or the denial of entry would cause undue hardship.

(d) It is the policy of the executive branch that, to the extent permitted by law and as practicable, State and local jurisdictions be granted a role in the process of determining the placement or settlement in their jurisdictions of aliens eligible to be admitted to the United States as refugees. To that end, the Secretary of State shall examine existing law to determine the extent to which, consistent with applicable law, State and local jurisdictions may have greater involvement in the process of determining the placement or resettlement of refugees in their jurisdictions, and shall devise a proposal to lawfully promote such involvement.

Sec. 7.   Rescission of Exercise of Authority Relating to the Terrorism Grounds of Inadmissibility. The Secretary of State and the Secretary of Homeland Security shall, in consultation with the Attorney General, consider rescinding the exercises of authority permitted by section 212(d)(3)(B) of the INA, 8 U.S.C. 1182(d)(3)(B), relating to the terrorism grounds of inadmissibility, as well as any related implementing directives or guidance.

Sec. 8.   Expedited Completion of the Biometric Entry-Exit Tracking System. (a) The Secretary of Homeland Security shall expedite the completion and implementation of a biometric entry exit tracking system for in-scope travelers to the United States, as recommended by the National Commission on Terrorist Attacks Upon the United States.

(b) The Secretary of Homeland Security shall submit to the President periodic reports on the progress of the directive set forth in subsection (a) of this section. The initial report shall be submitted within 100 days of the effective date of this order, a second report shall be submitted within 200 days of the effective date of this order, and a third report shall be submitted within 365 days of the effective date of this order. The Secretary of Homeland Security shall submit further reports every 180 days thereafter until the system is fully deployed and operational.

Sec. 9.   Visa Interview Security. (a) The Secretary of State shall immediately suspend the Visa Interview Waiver Program and ensure compliance with section 222 of the INA, 8 U.S.C. 1202, which requires that all individuals seeking a nonimmigrant visa undergo an in-person interview, subject to specific statutory exceptions. This suspension shall not apply to any foreign national traveling on a diplomatic or diplomatic-type visa, North Atlantic Treaty Organization visa, C-2 visa for travel to the United Nations, or G-1, G-2, G-3, or G-4 visa; traveling for purposes related to an international organization designated under the

IOIA; or traveling for purposes of conducting meetings or business with the United States Government.

(b) To the extent permitted by law and subject to the availability of appropriations, the Secretary of State shall immediately expand the Consular Fellows Program, including by substantially increasing the number of Fellows, lengthening or making permanent the period of service, and making language training at the Foreign Service Institute available to Fellows for assignment to posts outside of their area of core linguistic ability, to ensure that nonimmigrant visa-interview wait times are not unduly affected.

Sec. 10. Visa Validity Reciprocity. The Secretary of State shall review all nonimmigrant visa reciprocity agreements and arrangements to ensure that they are, with respect to each visa classification, truly reciprocal insofar as practicable with respect to validity period and fees, as required by sections 221(c) and 281 of the INA, 8 U.S.C. 1201(c) and 1351, and other treatment. If another country does not treat United States nationals seeking nonimmigrant visas in a truly reciprocal manner, the Secretary of State shall adjust the visa validity period, fee schedule, or other treatment to match the treatment of United States nationals by that foreign country, to the extent practicable.

Sec. 11. Transparency and Data Collection. (a) To be more transparent with the American people and to implement more effectively policies and practices that serve the national interest, the Secretary of Homeland Security, in consultation with the Attorney General, shall, consistent with applicable law and national security, collect and make publicly available the following information:

(i) information regarding the number of foreign nationals in the United States who have been charged with terrorism-related offenses while in the United States; convicted of terrorism-related offenses while in the United States; or removed from the United States based on terrorism-related activity, affiliation with or provision of material support to a terrorism-related organization, or any other national-security-related reasons;

(ii) information regarding the number of foreign nationals in the United States who have been radicalized after entry into the United States and who have engaged in terrorism-related acts, or who have provided material support to terrorism-related organizations in countries that pose a threat to the United States;

(iii) information regarding the number and types of acts of gender-based violence against women, including so-called "honor killings," in the United States by foreign nationals; and

(iv) any other information relevant to public safety and security as determined by the Secretary of Homeland Security or the Attorney General, including information on the immigration status of foreign nationals charged with major offenses.

(b) The Secretary of Homeland Security shall release the initial report under subsection (a) of this section within 180 days of the effective date of this order and shall include information for the period from September 11, 2001, until the date of the initial report. Subsequent reports shall be issued every 180 days thereafter and reflect the period since the previous report.

Sec. 12. Enforcement. (a) The Secretary of State and the Secretary of Homeland Security shall consult with appropriate domestic and international partners, including countries and organizations, to ensure efficient, effective, and appropriate implementation of the actions directed in this order.

(b) In implementing this order, the Secretary of State and the Secretary of Homeland Security shall comply with all applicable laws and regulations, including, as appropriate, those providing an opportunity for individuals to claim a fear of persecution or torture, such as the credible fear determination for aliens covered by section 235(b)(1)(A) of the INA, 8 U.S.C. 1225(b)(1)(A).

(c) No immigrant or nonimmigrant visa issued before the effective date of this order shall be revoked pursuant to this order.

(d) Any individual whose visa was marked revoked or marked canceled as a result of Executive Order 13769 shall be entitled to a travel document confirming that the individual is permitted to travel to the United States and seek entry. Any prior cancellation or revocation of a visa that was solely pursuant to Executive Order 13769 shall not be the basis of inadmissibility for any future determination about entry or admissibility.

(e) This order shall not apply to an individual who has been granted asylum, to a refugee who has already been admitted to the United States, or to an individual granted withholding of removal or protection under the Convention Against Torture. Nothing in this order shall be construed to limit the ability of an individual to seek asylum, withholding of removal, or protection under the Convention Against Torture, consistent with the laws of the United States.

Sec. 13. Revocation. Executive Order 13769 of January 27, 2017, is revoked as of the effective date of this order.

Sec. 14. Effective Date. This order is effective at 12:01 a.m., eastern daylight time on March 16, 2017.

Sec. 15. Severability. (a) If any provision of this order, or the application of any provision to any person or circumstance, is held to be invalid, the remainder of this order and the application of its other provisions to any other persons or circumstances shall not be affected thereby.

(b) If any provision of this order, or the application of any provision to any person or circumstance, is held to be invalid because of the lack of certain procedural requirements, the relevant executive branch officials shall implement those procedural requirements.

Sec. 16. General Provisions. (a) Nothing in this order shall be construed to impair or otherwise affect:

(i) the authority granted by law to an executive department or agency, or the head thereof; or

(ii) the functions of the Director of the Office of Management and Budget relating to budgetary, administrative, or legislative proposals.

(b) This order shall be implemented consistent with applicable law and subject to the availability of appropriations.

(c) This order is not intended to, and does not, create any right or benefit, substantive or procedural, enforceable at law or in equity by any party against the United States, its departments, agencies, or entities, its officers, employees, or agents, or any other person.

DONALD J. TRUMP

THE WHITE HOUSE,

March 6, 2017.

b. Post-Issuance of the March 6th Executive Order: The Recent History

1) The Executive Order presented above was challenged in courts throughout the United States, with challenges reaching the U.S. Supreme Court. On October 5, 2017, the Clerk of the U.S. Supreme Court issued an

order requesting the parties address whether a subsequent proclamation and modification of the Order above rendered the appeals moot.

According to the U.S. Department of Justice:

On September 24, the President issued a Proclamation summarizing the completed review and notice process, as well as his findings and corresponding determinations. Proclamation No. 9645, 82 Fed. Reg. 45,161 (Sept. 27, 2017). The Proclamation describes how, as part of the government's review, the Secretary of Homeland Security, in consultation with the Secretary of State and the Director of National Intelligence, determined the information needed from or about foreign governments to enable the United States to assess its ability to make informed decisions about foreign nationals applying for visas. That information had three components: (1) identity-management information, to assess "whether the country issues electronic passports embedded with data to enable confirmation of identity, reports lost and stolen passports to appropriate entities, and makes available upon request identity-related information not included in its passports"; (2) national-security and public-safety information, to determine "whether the country makes available * * * known or suspected terrorist and criminal-history information upon request, whether the country provides passport and national-identity document exemplars, and whether the country impedes the United States Government's receipt of information"; and (3) a national-security and public-safety risk assessment, including such factors as "whether the country is a known or potential terrorist safe haven, whether it is a participant in the Visa Waiver Program * * * that meets all of [the program's] requirements, and whether it regularly fails to receive its nationals subject to final orders of removal from the United States." § 1(c).

After developing these criteria, the Department of Homeland Security, in coordination with the Department of State, collected data on and evaluated every foreign country. Based on the specified criteria, the Secretary of Homeland Security identified 16 countries as "inadequate." § 1(e). Another 31 countries were classified as "at risk" of becoming "inadequate." Ibid. These preliminary results were submitted to the President on July 9, as the Order directed. § 1(c). The Department of State then conducted a 50-day engagement period to encourage all foreign governments to improve their performance. These diplomatic efforts yielded significant gains: for example, 29 countries produced travel-document exemplars to combat fraud, and 11 countries agreed to share information on known or suspected terrorists. § 1(f3). After the engagement period ended, the

Secretary of Homeland Security submitted a report to the President, per Section 2(e), recommending entry restrictions on certain nationals from seven countries (Chad, Iran, Libya, North Korea, Syria, Venezuela, and Yemen) that continue to be "inadequate" in providing information to the United States. § 1(h)(ii). The Secretary also determined that Iraq did not meet the United States' requirements, but in lieu of entry restrictions, recommended additional scrutiny of Iraqi nationals seeking entry because of the United States' close cooperative relationship with Iraq, the strong United States diplomatic presence in Iraq, the significant presence of United States forces in Iraq, and Iraq's commitment to combatting the Islamic State of Iraq and Syria (ISIS). § 1(g). The Secretary also recommended entry restrictions on nationals of Somalia. Although Somalia generally satisfies the information-sharing criteria, the Secretary found that the Somali government's inability to effectively and consistently cooperate, as well as the terrorist threat that emanates from its territory, present special circumstances warranting limitations on entry. § 1(i).

Pursuant to the President's broad authority under Article II of the Constitution and federal statutes, including 8 U.S.C. 1182(f) and 1185(a)(1), and based on extensive consultation with his Cabinet, the President issued a Proclamation on September 24, 2017 consistent with the Secretary of Homeland Security's recommendations. The Proclamation imposes a different set of restrictions than Section 2(c) of the Order, and it applies to a different set of countries. Unlike the Order, the Proclamation imposes no restrictions on Sudan, but it does impose restrictions on Chad, North Korea, and Venezuela. The restrictions are tailored for each country to take account of U.S. goals for foreign policy, national security, and counterterrorism, as well as individualized assessments of the country's conditions and capabilities. Thus, for countries that refuse to cooperate regularly with the United States (Iran, North Korea, and Syria), the Proclamation suspends entry of persons seeking both immigrant and nonimmigrant visas; for countries that are valuable terrorism partners but nonetheless have information-sharing deficiencies (Chad, Libya, and Yemen), it suspends entry only of persons seeking immigrant visas and business, tourist, and business/tourist nonimmigrant visas; for Somalia, it suspends entry of persons seeking immigrant visas and requires additional scrutiny of nationals seeking nonimmigrant visas; and for Venezuela, it suspends entry of "officials of government agencies of Venezuela involved in screening and vetting procedures" and "their immediate family members" on nonimmigrant business and tourist visas. § 2. The Proclamation also exempts certain categories of foreign nationals from the suspensions and provides that the limitations on entry are subject to case-by-case waivers in accordance with guidance implemented by the Departments of State and Homeland Security. § 3.

For each country, the Proclamation is designed "to encourage cooperation" and to "protect the United States until such time as improvements occur." § 1(h)(i). To that end, it requires an ongoing review process to determine whether the limitations imposed should be continued, terminated, modified, or supplemented. § 4. The suspensions on entry were effective immediately for foreign nationals who previously were restricted under the Order and this Court's June 26 stay, and they will be effective October 18 for all other covered persons. § 7.

Section 2(c)'s 90-day entry suspension ended on September 24. Section 6(b)'s refugee cap ended on September 30. As a result, the preliminary injunction in IRAP against Section 2(c) is now without effect, as are the portions of the preliminary injunction in Hawaii against Sections 2(c) and 6(b). Thus, these appeals of the injunctions are moot.

The Court should vacate both of the lower courts' judgments as moot. The appeal of the Fourth Circuit's judgment is now moot in full, as is the Ninth Circuit appeal concerning Sections 2(c) and 6(b). For the only portion of the Ninth Circuit's judgment still at issue—regarding the global refugee suspension in Section 6(a)—no respondent has a justiciable claim, and in any event the global suspension will expire in less than three weeks. At a minimum, once Section 6(a) expires on October 24, this Court should vacate the judgments and remand with instructions to dismiss the complaints. To the extent the Court concludes that any part of either appeal is not moot, the case should be reset for argument, and the judgments of the courts of appeals should be reversed.

See, Supplemental Brief of Petitioners (10/5/17), available at: http://www.scotusblog.com/wp-content/uploads/2017/10/16-1436-16-1540-tssb.pdf.

2) The parties challenging the mooting of their appeal disagreed, writing:

The "voluntary cessation of a challenged practice" does not moot a controversy unless and until the Government makes it "absolutely clear that the allegedly wrongful behavior could not reasonably be expected to recur." Friends of the Earth, Inc. v. Laidlaw Envtl. Servs. (TOC), Inc., 528 U.S. 167, 189 (2000) (internal quotation marks omitted). Here, the Government has not even ceased to implement all of the challenged portions of

Executive Order No. 13,780 ("EO-2"), as the refugee bar in Section 6(a) remains in place. But even if Section 6(a) is permitted to expire on October 24, the Government cannot come close to meeting its "heavy burden" to demonstrate that the bans will not be revived. Id. The Government has previously informed this Court that the President is free to revise the "temporal scope" of EO-2 whenever he wishes. Pet. Br. 37. And the President himself has expressed his desire to return to a "much tougher version" of the bans.1 Indeed, by issuing EO-3, he has already reinstated many of the exclusions imposed by Section 2(c) of EO-2. The controversy therefore is not moot, and the Court can and should review the existing challenge to EO-2.

Nonetheless, if the Court determines that it is not prudent to resolve the important questions presented in this posture, the writ of certiorari should be dismissed as improvidently granted. The Court has often taken this course where the statute or order under review is altered during the pendency of the case. And because challenges to EO-3 are already underway in the lower courts, the Court will soon have another opportunity to determine the legality of the President's actions in the context of the new order.

No matter which course it takes, this Court should not vacate the decisions below. Because the case is not moot, there is no justification for vacatur. And even if this Court were to conclude that the case is moot, vacatur would be inappropriate. Any mootness would be entirely the consequence of the Government's voluntary actions—in managing the timing of the bans, in declining to seek a swift hearing on the merits, and in rebottling its old ban in a new order. It would be profoundly inequitable to permit the Government to use these maneuvers to obtain the very relief it sought on the merits: vacatur of the injunctions.

Supplemental Brief of Respondents (10/5/17), Available at: http://www.scotusblog.com/wp-content/uploads/2017/10/16-1540-bssb-Hawaii.pdf.

3) On October 24, 2017 the Supreme Court remanded to the 4th Circuit Court of Appeals consolidated challenges originating in the 4th and 9th Circuits, with orders to dismiss the challenge to Executive Order 13780 as moot.

4) On December 4, 2017 the Supreme Court allowed a third version of the Trump Administration's travel ban to go into effect while legal challenges proceeded. See Adam Liptak, The New York Times, Supreme Court Allows Trump Travel Ban to Take Effect, December 4, 2017, available at: https://www.nytimes.com/2017/12/04/us/politics/trump-travel-ban-supreme-court.html.

CHAPTER 9

CLASSIFIED INFORMATION IN CIVILIAN TERRORISM TRIALS

■ ■ ■

A. INTRODUCTION—THE CLASSIFIED INFORMATION PROCEDURES ACT

The Classified Information Procedures Act (CIPA) which addresses the handling of classified materials in federal criminal prosecutions is the main focus of this chapter. Previous chapters have dealt primarily with terrorism crimes and with pre-trial investigation and enforcement methods; this is the first time we have ventured into the processes of the trial itself. Moreover, we are not here addressing all of the many incidents of criminal trials in terrorism cases, such as the rules of evidence and procedure. (In previous chapters, we have touched upon issues that have evidentiary implications—e.g. rules governing the admissibility of interrogation statements.)

The subject of the handling of classified information has been singled out here because a) although they are not unique to terrorism prosecutions, classified information issues are likely to arise in almost every terrorism trial; b) students are unlikely to have encountered these issues in other courses in the curriculum; and c) it provides a foundation for comparing the handling of classified materials in civilian terrorism trials with how they are treated in military commission proceedings, which will be described infra Part Two, ch. 11.

Why does classified information play such an important central role in U.S. district court terrorism cases? These prosecutions are often developed through intelligence information that the government is reluctant to reveal for fear of compromising sources or methods of obtaining the information, or where the information itself has a national security dimension. As the number of terrorism prosecutions has increased in the past decade, it has become important for lawyers and judges working in the terrorism enforcement process or those who wish to know something about the workings of that process to gain some familiarity with the CIPA and the handling of classified information in federal criminal trials. (During an earlier time, CIPA issues arose mainly in the prosecution of spies or cases involving leaks of information or the prosecution of federal employees for criminal behavior.)

The purpose of CIPA is to strike a balance between protecting the rights of a criminal defendant to know the evidence being used against him or her and the government's need to protect against disclosure of certain types of confidential information that the government is unwilling to disclose or have disclosed publicly.

Prior to the enactment of CIPA in 1980, the government often found itself in a dilemma—either disclose classified information that the government believed should not be disclosed, or face dismissal of the prosecution on the ground that the right of the defendant to access information needed for his/her defense was being denied. A defendant's putting the government in this kind of bind came to be known as the use of "graymail" (i.e. give me the information or else face dismissal of the prosecution, or, alternatively, I shall disclose the information if you prosecute me). The CIPA was intended to address and soften this tension in a way that adequately protected the rights of the criminal defendant while reducing the frequency with which the government is faced with the difficult choice whether to disclose the underlying information or give up the prosecution. An important question that you should consider in light of the materials in this chapter is the extent to which the CIPA resolved the underlying tension in this area.

We shall not delve here into all of the nooks and crannies of CIPA law, but rather shall only focus on several salient features that tend to arise in terrorism cases. We shall also take note of the extent to which practices have developed for dealing with classified information that are outside of the CIPA framework. This is a subject where developments and adjustments have occurred in practice for dealing with classified information issues that go beyond the written law.

Where classified information is relevant to issues in the case, CIPA makes provision for several possible alternative remedies, the most frequently utilized of which is providing a summary as a substitute for the information itself. Inter alia, we examine issues relating to the use of a summary as a means of resolving the recurring dilemma; the extent to which in camera, or in camera and ex parte, proceedings may be used under CIPA; and the use of security clearance for participants in the process as a means to resolve some of the dilemmas posed by the need to use classified information in a criminal case.

One view of CIPA is that it tracks Rule 16 of the Federal Rules of Criminal Procedure, which deals with criminal discovery by the defendant, and simply adds the use of a summary-as-a-substitute to the possible remedies in criminal discovery. To the extent that CIPA operates in a discovery context, this observation is essentially correct. However, CIPA issues can arise in contexts other than criminal discovery by the defendant. For example, CIPA issues can be raised when a criminal defendant proposes to disclose at trial classified information to which he already has access, although this scenario is not very likely in terrorism trials. CIPA issues can also arise at the instance of the government when the prosecutor anticipates that a discovery request for classified information will be made by the defendant. Similarly, the government itself may wish to use at trial information that is classified, and in order to do so, may propose to introduce a summary under the terms of CIPA. The context in which the CIPA issue is raised and who wishes to introduce the classified information or a substitute may affect the disposition of the matter.

B. THE CLASSIFIED INFORMATION PROCEDURES ACT

An excerpted text of CIPA (the full text of which can be found at 18 U.S.C. App. 3, §§ 1–16) is set forth below.

Title 18, U.S.C.

APPENDIX 3.

CLASSIFIED INFORMATION PROCEDURES ACT

Public Law 96–456 (94 Stat. 2025), Oct. 15, 1980

§ 1. Definitions

(a) "Classified information", as used in this Act, means any information or material that has been determined by the United States Government pursuant to an Executive order, statute, or regulation, to require protection against unauthorized disclosure for reasons of national security and any restricted data, as defined in paragraph r. of section 11 of the Atomic Energy Act of 1954 (42 U.S.C. 2014(y)).

(b) "National security", as used in this Act, means the national defense and foreign relations of the United States.

§ 2. Pretrial Conference

At any time after the filing of the indictment or information, any party may move for a pretrial conference to consider matters relating to classified information that may arise in connection with the prosecution. Following such motion, or on its own motion, the court shall promptly hold a pretrial conference to establish the timing of requests for discovery, the provision of notice required by section 5 of this Act, and the initiation of the procedure established by section 6 of this Act. In addition, at the pretrial conference the court may consider any matters which relate to classified information or which may promote a fair and expeditious trial. No admission made by the defendant or by any attorney for the defendant at such a conference may be used against the defendant unless the admission is in writing and is signed by the defendant and by the attorney for the defendant.

§ 3. Protective Orders

Upon motion of the United States, the court shall issue an order to protect against the disclosure of any classified information disclosed by the United States to any defendant in any criminal case in a district court of the United States.

§ 4. Discovery of classified information by defendants

The court, upon a sufficient showing, may authorize the United States to delete specified items of classified information from documents to be made available to the defendant through discovery under the Federal Rules of Criminal Procedure, to substitute a summary of the information for such classified documents, or to substitute a statement admitting relevant facts that the classified information would tend to prove. The court may permit the United States to make a request for such authorization in the form of a written statement to be inspected by the court alone. If the court enters an order granting relief following such an ex parte showing, the entire text of the statement of the United States shall be sealed and preserved in the records of the court to be made available to the appellate court in the event of an appeal.

§ 5. Notice of defendant's intention to disclose classified information

(a) Notice by defendant

If a defendant reasonably expects to disclose or to cause the disclosure of classified information in any manner in connection with any trial or pretrial proceeding involving the criminal prosecution of such defendant, the defendant shall, within the time specified by the court or, where no time is specified, within thirty days prior to trial, notify the attorney for the United States and the court in writing. Such notice shall include a brief description of the classified information. Whenever a defendant learns of additional classified information he reasonably expects to disclose at any such proceeding, he shall notify the attorney for the United States and the court in writing as soon as possible thereafter and shall include a brief description of the classified information. No defendant shall disclose any information known or believed to be classified in connection with a trial or pretrial proceeding until notice has been given under this subsection and until the United States has been afforded a reasonable opportunity to seek a determination pursuant to the procedure set forth in section 6 of this Act, and until the time for the United States to appeal such determination under section 7 has expired or any appeal under section 7 by the United States is decided.

(b) Failure to comply

If the defendant fails to comply with the requirements of subsection (a) the court may preclude disclosure of any classified information not made the subject of notification and may prohibit the examination by the defendant of any witness with respect to any such information.

§ 6. Procedure for cases involving classified information

(a) Motion for hearing

Within the time specified by the court for the filing of a motion under this section, the United States may request the court to conduct a hearing to make all determinations concerning the use, relevance, or admissibility of classified information that would otherwise be made during the trial or pretrial proceeding. Upon such a request, the court shall conduct such a hearing. Any hearing held pursuant to this subsection (or any portion of such hearing specified in the request of the Attorney General) shall be held in camera if the Attorney General certifies to the court in such petition that a public proceeding may result in the disclosure of classified information. As to each item of classified information, the court shall set forth in writing the basis for its determination. Where the United States' motion under this subsection is filed prior to the trial or pretrial proceeding, the court shall rule prior to the commencement of the relevant proceeding.

(b) Notice

(1) Before any hearing is conducted pursuant to a request by the United States under subsection (a), the United States shall provide the defendant with notice of the classified information that is at issue. Such notice shall identify the specific classified information at issue whenever that information previously has been made available to the defendant by the United States. When the United States has not previously made the information available to the defendant in connection with the case, the information may be described by generic category, in such form as the court may approve, rather than by identification of the specific information of concern to the United States.

(2) Whenever the United States requests a hearing under subsection (a), the court, upon request of the defendant, may order the United States to provide the defendant, prior to trial, such details as to the portion of the indictment or information at issue in the hearing as are needed to give the defendant fair notice to prepare for the hearing.

(c) Alternative procedure for disclosure of classified information

(1) Upon any determination by the court authorizing the disclosure of specific classified information under the procedures established by this section, the United States may move that, in lieu of the disclosure of such specific classified information, the court order—

(A) the substitution for such classified information of a statement admitting relevant facts that the specific classified information would tend to prove; or

(B) the substitution for such classified information of a summary of the specific classified information.

The court shall grant such a motion of the United States if it finds that the statement or summary will provide the defendant with substantially the same ability to make his defense as would disclosure of the specific classified information. The court shall hold a hearing on any motion under this section. Any such hearing shall be held in camera at the request of the Attorney General.

(2) The United States may, in connection with a motion under paragraph (1), submit to the court an affidavit of the Attorney General certifying that disclosure of classified information would cause identifiable damage to the national security of the United States and explaining the basis for the classification of such information. If so requested by the United States, the court shall examine such affidavit in camera and ex parte.

(d) Sealing of records of in camera hearings

If at the close of an in camera hearing under this Act (or any portion of a hearing under this Act that is held in camera) the court determines that the classified information at issue may not be disclosed or elicited at the trial or pretrial proceeding, the record of such in camera hearing shall be sealed and preserved by the court for use in the event of an appeal. The defendant may seek reconsideration of the court's determination prior to or during trial.

(e) Prohibition on disclosure of classified information by defendant, relief for defendant when United States opposes disclosure

(1) Whenever the court denies a motion by the United States that it issue an order under subsection (c) and the United States files with the court an affidavit of the Attorney General objecting to disclosure of the classified information at issue, the court shall order that the defendant not disclose or cause the disclosure of such information.

(2) Whenever a defendant is prevented by an order under paragraph (1) from disclosing or causing the disclosure of classified information, the court shall dismiss the indictment or information; except that, when the court determines that the interests of justice would not be served by dismissal of the indictment or information, the court shall order such other action, in lieu of dismissing the indictment or information, as the court determines is appropriate. Such action may include, but need not be limited to—

(A) dismissing specified counts of the indictment or information;

(B) finding against the United States on any issue as to which the excluded classified information relates; or

(C) striking or precluding all or part of the testimony of a witness.

An order under this paragraph shall not take effect until the court has afforded the United States an opportunity to appeal such order under section 7, and thereafter to withdraw its objection to the disclosure of the classified information at issue.

(f) Reciprocity

Whenever the court determines pursuant to subsection (a) that classified information may be disclosed in connection with a trial or pretrial proceeding, the court shall, unless the interests of fairness do not so require, order the United States to provide the defendant with the information it expects to use to rebut the classified information. The court may place the United States under a continuing duty to disclose such rebuttal information. If the United States fails to comply with its obligation under this subsection, the court may exclude any evidence not made the subject of a required disclosure and may prohibit the examination by the United States of any witness with respect to such information.

§ 7. Interlocutory appeal

(a) An interlocutory appeal by the United States taken before or after the defendant has been placed in jeopardy shall lie to a court of appeals from a decision or order of a district court in a criminal case authorizing the disclosure of classified information, imposing sanctions for nondisclosure of classified information, or refusing a protective order sought by the United States to prevent the disclosure of classified information.

(b) An appeal taken pursuant to this section either before or during trial shall be expedited by the court of appeals. Prior to trial, an appeal shall be taken within ten days after the decision or order appealed from and the trial shall not commence until the appeal is resolved. . . .

§ 8. Introduction of classified information

(a) Classification status

Writings, recordings, and photographs containing classified information may be admitted into evidence without change in their classification status.

(b) Precautions by court

The court, in order to prevent unnecessary disclosure of classified information involved in any criminal proceeding, may order admission into evidence of only part of a writing, recording, or photograph, or may order admission into evidence of the whole writing, recording, or photograph with excision of some or all of the classified information contained therein, unless the whole ought in fairness be considered.

(c) Taking of testimony

During the examination of a witness in any criminal proceeding, the United States may object to any question or line of inquiry that may require the witness to disclose classified information not previously found to be admissible. Following such an objection, the court shall take such suitable action to determine whether the response is admissible as will safeguard against the compromise of any classified information. Such action may include requiring the United States to provide the court with a proffer of the witness' response to the question or line of inquiry and requiring the defendant to provide the court with a proffer of the nature of the information he seeks to elicit.

§ 9. Security procedures

(a) Within one hundred and twenty days of the date of the enactment of this Act, the Chief Justice of the United States, in consultation with the Attorney General, the Director of Central Intelligence, and the Secretary of Defense, shall prescribe rules establishing procedures for the protection against unauthorized disclosure of any classified information in the custody of the United States district courts, courts of appeal, or Supreme Court. Such rules, and any changes in such rules, shall be submitted to the appropriate committees of Congress and shall become effective forty-five days after such submission.

(b) Until such time as rules under subsection (a) first become effective, the Federal courts shall in each case involving classified information adopt procedures to protect against the unauthorized disclosure of such information.

§ 10.   Identification of information related to national defense

In any prosecution in which the United States must establish that material relates to the national defense or constitutes classified information, the United States shall notify the defendant, within the time before trial specified by the court, of the portions of the material that it reasonably expects to rely upon to establish the national defense or classified information element of the offense.

. . .

§ 12.   Attorney General guidelines

(a)   Within one hundred and eighty days of enactment of this Act, the Attorney General shall issue guidelines specifying the factors to be used by the Department of Justice in rendering a decision whether to prosecute a violation of Federal law in which, in the judgment of the Attorney General, there is a possibility that classified information will be revealed. Such guidelines shall be transmitted to the appropriate committees of Congress.

(b)   When the Department of Justice decides not to prosecute a violation of Federal law pursuant to subsection (a), an appropriate official of the Department of Justice shall prepare written findings detailing the reasons for the decision not to prosecute. The findings shall include—

(1)   the intelligence information which the Department of Justice officials believe might be disclosed,

(2)   the purpose for which the information might be disclosed,

(3)   the probability that the information would be disclosed, and

(4)   the possible consequences such disclosure would have on the national security.

. . .

C. ADJUDGING THE ADEQUACY OF SUBSTITUTIONS FOR CLASSIFIED INFORMATION

Under the terms of CIPA, a summary may be substituted for the classified information when it provides "substantially the same ability to make [a] . . . defense" as the original information. If defense counsel is trying to introduce classified information in the hands of the government, which she has not ever had access to, she may have a difficult task in challenging the adequacy of the summary offered as a substitute, even given that standard. The inquiry regarding adequacy is conducted in camera. Query, is it also ex parte?

UNITED STATES V. REZAQ

134 F.3d 1121 (D.C.Cir. 1998)

Before WALD, SENTELLE and HENDERSON, CIRCUIT JUDGES.

WALD, CIRCUIT JUDGE:

Omar Mohammed Ali Rezaq appeals his conviction on one count of aircraft piracy under 49 U.S.C. App. § 1472(n) (1994). In 1985, Rezaq hijacked an Air Egypt flight shortly after takeoff from Athens, and ordered it to fly to Malta. On arrival, Rezaq shot a number of passengers, killing two of them, before he was apprehended. Rezaq pleaded guilty to murder charges in Malta, served seven years in prison, and was released in February 1993. Shortly afterwards, he was taken into custody in Nigeria by United States authorities and brought to the United States for trial . . .

I. Background

Rezaq did not deny committing the hijacking at trial, relying instead on the defenses of insanity and obedience to military orders. Thus, the following account of the hijacking was not contested at Rezaq's trial.

Rezaq is Palestinian, and was, at the time of the hijacking, a member of a Palestinian terrorist organization, which planned and ordered the hijacking. On the evening of November 23, 1985, Rezaq boarded Air Egypt Flight 648 in Athens. He was accompanied by two other hijackers; one of his confederates, named Salem, was the leader of the operation, and the name of the other is unknown. Shortly after the plane took off, the three produced weapons, announced that they were seizing the plane, and demanded that the captain fly it to Malta. A gun battle ensued between the hijackers and an Egyptian plainclothes sky marshal stationed on the plane, as a result of which Salem was killed and the sky marshal was wounded.

Rezaq then took charge of the hijacking. After the plane arrived in Malta, he separated the Israeli and American passengers from the others, and moved them to the front of the plane. He released a number of Egyptian and Filipino female passengers, as well as two wounded flight attendants. He then demanded that the aircraft be refueled; when the authorities refused, he announced that he would shoot a passenger every fifteen minutes until his demand was met.

Rezaq carried out his threat. He first shot Israeli national Tamar Artzi. Although he shot her twice, once in the head, she survived. Fifteen minutes later, he shot her companion, Nitzan Mendelson, also an Israeli; Ms. Mendelson died of her injuries nine days later. Rezaq then shot Patrick

Baker, an American, but only succeeded in grazing his head. Two or three hours later, Rezaq shot Scarlett Rogenkamp—a United States citizen and an employee of the United States Air Force—in the head, killing her. Some time later, he shot Jackie Pflug, also an American, in the head, injuring her very seriously. Rezaq shot his victims near the front door of the plane, and either threw them or let them fall onto the tarmac; this may explain why three of the five were able to survive, either by escaping (Artzi and Baker), or by feigning death (Pflug).

In the evening of November 24th—about a day after the hijacking began—Egyptian commandos stormed the plane. The operation seems to have been a singularly incompetent one. The commandos fired indiscriminately, and set off an explosive device of some kind, as a result of which the aircraft burst into flames. Fifty-seven passengers were killed, as was the third hijacker. Rezaq was injured, and was taken, with a multitude of injured passengers, to a hospital. There, he was identified as the hijacker by passengers, members of the crew, and several of his victims.

The authorities in Malta charged Rezaq with murder, attempted murder, and hostage taking. He pled guilty, and was sentenced to 25 years' imprisonment. For reasons unclear, Maltese authorities released him some seven years later, in February 1993, and allowed him to board a plane to Ghana. Rezaq's itinerary was to carry him from there to Nigeria, and then to Ethiopia, and finally to Sudan. Ghanaian officials detained Rezaq for several months, but eventually allowed him to proceed to Nigeria. When Rezaq's plane landed in Nigeria, Nigerian authorities placed him in the custody of FBI agents, who transported him on a waiting aircraft to the United States.

Rezaq was indicted and tried for air piracy in the District Court for the District of Columbia. At trial, Rezaq invoked the defenses of insanity and obedience to military orders. In support of his insanity defense, Rezaq presented evidence that he suffered from post-traumatic stress disorder ("PTSD"). As witnesses, he called several members of his own family and three psychiatric experts; Rezaq himself also testified at length. Rezaq asserted that his PTSD sprang from numerous traumatic events he had experienced, first in the Jordanian refugee camp in which he spent much of his youth, and later in Lebanon, where he was active in Palestinian revolutionary organizations from 1978 to 1985. The Lebanese experiences he described included witnessing the killing of hundreds of refugees by Israeli forces in Beirut in 1982; witnessing the killings of the populations of entire villages; and nearly being killed in a car bombing. Rezaq's family testified that when he left Jordan he was normal, friendly, and extroverted, but that when he returned from Lebanon he was pale, inattentive, prone to nightmares, antisocial, and had lost his sense of humor. Rezaq's psychiatric experts said that these changes in behavior were symptomatic of PTSD, and, based on their examination of Rezaq and on the testimony of other witnesses, they concluded that Rezaq was suffering from PTSD when he committed the hijacking in November 1985. The United States presented two psychiatric experts of its own, who testified that Rezaq's symptoms were not as intense as those usually associated with PTSD, and that Rezaq was able to reason and make judgments normally at the time he hijacked the plane.

The jury did not credit Rezaq's defenses, and found him guilty of the one count with which he was charged, aircraft piracy in violation of 49 U.S.C. App. § 1472(n) (1994). At the time of Rezaq's prosecution, that section provided (it has since been amended):

> (1) Whoever aboard an aircraft in flight outside the special aircraft jurisdiction of the United States commits an "offense," as defined in the Convention for the Suppression of Unlawful Seizure of Aircraft, and is afterward found in the United States shall be punished—

>> (A) by imprisonment for not less than 20 years; or

>> (B) if the death of another person results from the commission or attempted commission of the offense, by death or by imprisonment for life.

> (2) A person commits 'an offense,' as defined in the Convention for the Suppression of Unlawful Seizure of Aircraft, when, while aboard an aircraft in flight, he—

>> (A) unlawfully, by force or threat thereof, or by any other form of intimidation, seizes, or exercises control of, that aircraft, or attempts to perform any such act; or

49 U.S.C.App. § 1472(n) (1994). Because death resulted from Rezaq's commission of the offense, § 1472(n)(1)(B) applied, and the district court sentenced Rezaq to life imprisonment. (The United States had not sought the death sentence.) The district court also ordered Rezaq to pay a total of $254,000 in restitution, an amount which it found to represent the financial cost to the victims of his crime.

. . .

When classified materials may be relevant to criminal proceedings, the Classified Information Procedures Act ("CIPA"), 18 U.S.C. App. III (1994), provides procedures designed to protect the rights of the defendant while minimizing the associated harm to national security. In the course of preparing for trial, the United States identified a number of arguably discoverable classified materials, and obtained permission from the district court to file an ex parte, in camera motion for a protective order. After reviewing this motion and the accompanying documents, the district court ordered the United States to prepare an index listing the contents of each document, whether it believed the document to be subject to discovery, and why. This document, too, was submitted ex parte and in camera; the district court subjected this document to detailed review, and prepared a list of the materials that it considered discoverable.

Under CIPA, the court may allow the United States to disclose "a statement admitting relevant facts that the classified information would tend to prove," in lieu of disclosing the information itself. 18 U.S.C. App. III § 4 (1994). The United States sought, and obtained, permission to substitute admissions for all of the documents that the district court had identified as discoverable. The district court reviewed the United States's proposed substitutions, and concluded that they fairly stated the relevant elements of the classified documents. The substitutions were then disclosed to Rezaq's attorney.

Rezaq's request on appeal is very limited. He does not ask us to review the district court's determination as to which documents were discoverable in the first instance. Instead, he asks only that we review the documents that the district court found to be discoverable, and decide whether the summaries that the court furnished to him were as helpful to his defense as the original documents would have been. He is particularly concerned that the summaries may have omitted important information, or that the process of transforming the documents into desiccated statements of material fact might have hampered the "evidentiary richness and narrative integrity" of the defense he was able to present.

We found in Yunis that a defendant seeking classified information is not entitled to receive it "on a mere showing of theoretical relevance," but "is entitled only to information that is at least 'helpful to the defense of the accused.'" 867 F.2d at 623 (quoting Roviaro v. United States, 353 U.S. 53, 60–61, 77 S.Ct. 623, 627–28, 1 L.Ed.2d 639 (1957)). This principle applies to sub-elements of individual documents; if some portion or aspect of a document is classified, a defendant is entitled to receive it only if it may be helpful to his defense. A court applying this rule should, of course, err on the side of protecting the interests of the defendant. In some cases, a court might legitimately conclude that it is necessary to place a fact in context in order to ensure that the jury is able to give it its full weight. For instance, it might be appropriate in some circumstances to attribute a statement to its source, or to phrase it as a quotation.

The district court's substitution decisions turned on the relevance of the facts contained in the discoverable documents, and are therefore reviewed, like other relevance decisions under CIPA, for abuse of discretion. See United States v. Yunis, 867 F.2d 617, 625 (D.C.Cir.1989). We are obliged to consider the district court's substitution decisions very carefully, as Rezaq's counsel is unable to consult the original documents, and so cannot present arguments on his client's behalf. We have accordingly conducted a detailed in camera comparison of the originals of the discoverable documents with the summaries approved by the district court. We find that the district court did a commendable job of discharging its obligations under CIPA, and in particular that its orders protected Rezaq's rights very effectively despite the fact that Rezaq's attorney was unable to participate in the CIPA proceedings. No information was omitted from the substitutions that might have been helpful to Rezaq's defense, and the discoverable documents had no unclassified features that might have been disclosed to Rezaq.

QUESTIONS AND NOTES

1.   As mentioned in Rezaq, before reaching the question of whether the substituted summary is adequate, the court must determine whether the underlying classified information is admissible and therefore discoverable: the standard of admissibility is whether the evidence is relevant and helpful to the defense.

2.   A case that should be compared with Rezaq is United States v. Fernandez, 913 F.2d 148 (4th Cir. 1990), a prosecution of a former CIA station chief for having made false statements to a body investigating the diversion of arms transfers, intended for Iran, to Nicaraguan resistance forces known as Contras (the Iran-Contra scandal). The summaries of classified documents prepared by the government were deemed not adequate to enable the defendant to make his defenses. The U.S. court of appeals affirmed the decision of the district court, dismissing the case with prejudice after the Attorney General filed an affidavit under § 6(e)(1) of CIPA prohibiting the disclosure of classified evidence that the district court had previously ruled to be relevant and admissible.

3.   The Fernandez court's opinion addressing the adequacy of the substitutions is lengthy and very detailed. The flavor and amount of detail differs considerably from that of the Rezaq opinion. There are a number of things that might account for this difference. Might one of the factors be the fact that Rezaq involved an ex parte determination where the judge made his ruling essentially without any input from the defendant's counsel, while in Fernandez, the issues were addressed in an adversary proceeding? Why was the issue in Fernandez able to be addressed in an adversary hearing while Rezaq involved an ex parte proceeding? What accounts for this procedural difference? Rezaq proceeded under sec. 4 of CIPA while Fernandez proceeded under sec. 6. Sec. 4 provides for an in camera ex parte proceeding while sec. 6 in subsec. (a) provides for an in camera hearing. (Compare, however, sec. 6(c)(2).)

4.   Note, too, that Fernandez was a former CIA station chief who had earlier probably had full access to the documents involved and was generally familiar with them. Given that likelihood, why was the government so insistent on not permitting the introduction of the original documents into evidence? We must assume that this was an instance where it was not a

concern about disclosing the information to the defendant, but rather disclosing it to the jury, and, ultimately, to the public.

5.   Consider the differences between the ex parte in camera and the in camera proceedings in light of the following excerpt from Brian Z. Tamanaha, A Critical Review of the Classified Information Procedures Act, 13 Am.J.Crim.L. 277, 307–308 (1987):

> . . . [T]he creation of substitutions is the only feature unique to CIPA which effectively inhibits graymail. Substitutions are also powerful weapons for the prosecution with a high potential for abuse. They are used where the defendant's right to a fair trial most directly conflicts with the government's need to protect national security information. . . .
>
> The standard in section 6(c) that substitutions are not permissible unless substantially equivalent to the nondisclosed information, was included in fairness to the defendant. Likewise, to ensure that substitutions did not violate constitutional requirements, Congress provides in section 6 that substitutions may be approved only after a full adversary hearing in which the defendant has access to all the underlying documents.
>
> Not all substitutions, however, are created with the protection contained in section 6. Section 4 of CIPA allows the government to submit an ex parte request for the substitution of discoverable information in lieu of producing the actual documents. Since the substitution is formulated and approved ex parte, the defendant cannot oppose it and never has access to the underlying documents. The defendant has no way of knowing whether the substitution contains all the discoverable information, or whether it correctly states this information. . . .
>
> More troublesome, section 4 threatens to swallow the protections contained in section 6. To circumvent the adversary hearing in section 6, where the defendant has access to all the underlying information and is able to contest the adequacy of each substitution, the government may simply produce all or most of the discoverable information in the form of ex parte approved substitutions. Nothing in CIPA prohibits this approach and, indeed, a prosecutor would be remiss if this strategy were not adopted because it significantly reduces the amount of classified information that will be disclosed to the defendant. Following this strategy, the only substitutions subject to the adversary process will be those containing information already possessed by the defendant independent of discovery. Relevant classified information not possessed by the defendant may be substituted without input from the defense.
>
> Congress was aware that substitutions are approved ex parte in section 4 and not in section 6. The rationale for this different

treatment is that 'since the government is seeking to withhold classified information from the defendant, an adversary hearing with defense knowledge would defeat the very purpose of the discovery rules.'

D. CLASSIFIED INFORMATION AND THE RIGHT OF CONFRONTATION

UNITED STATES V. ABU ALI

528 F 3d 210 (4th Cir. 2008)

[For a detailed statement of the facts in this case, see the same case reproduced in ch. 7 on Interrogation and Irregular Rendition.]

VI.

Abu Ali also challenges the district court's handling of certain classified information under the provisions of the Classified Information Procedures Act ("CIPA"), 18 U.S.C.App. 3, §§ 1–16 (West 2000 & Supp.2007).[13] Abu Ali's primary contention is that the district court violated his Sixth Amendment Confrontation Clause rights by admitting as evidence unredacted versions of two classified documents that Abu Ali had only been permitted to view in a redacted form, and by refusing to allow Abu Ali and his lead trial counsel to attend and participate in the hearings conducted under CIPA to discuss the classified evidence.

A.

The Sixth Amendment guarantees that "[i]n all criminal prosecutions, the accused shall enjoy . . . the right to be confronted with the witnesses against him." U.S. Const. amend. VI. Its "main and essential purpose . . . is to secure for the opponent the opportunity of cross-examination.". . . . Thus, while this is not the ordinary case, we think the criminal defendant's right to confront witnesses necessarily encompasses his right to also see any documentary evidence that such witnesses offer at trial as evidence to support a conviction. . . .

A defendant's right to see the evidence that is tendered against him during trial, however, does not necessarily equate to a right to have classified information disclosed to him prior to trial. Evidentiary privileges may serve as valid bases to block the disclosure of certain types of evidence, and the validity of such privileges may be tested by in camera and ex parte proceedings before the court "for the limited purpose of determining whether the asserted privilege is genuinely applicable." As a general rule, "[i]f the court finds that the claimed privilege does not apply, then the other side must be given access to the information." If the court finds that the

---

[13] These issues were separately raised via classified briefs and argued in closed proceedings before this panel.

privilege does apply, then it may preclude access to the information. But neither scenario results in the conviction of a defendant "based upon evidence he was never permitted to see and to rebut."

In the area of national security and the government's privilege to protect classified information from public disclosure, we look to CIPA for appropriate procedures. . . .

. . .CIPA establishes procedures to protect classified information from public disclosure, including disclosure to a defendant and his counsel if they do not possess the requisite security clearance. Prior to CIPA, "the government had no method of evaluating such disclosure claims before trial actually began" and "[o]ftentimes . . . would abandon prosecution rather than risk possible disclosure of classified information." "CIPA establishes procedures for making decisions about the use of such information."

B.

Classified information, as defined by CIPA, includes "any information or material that has been determined by the United States Government pursuant to an Executive order, statute, or regulation, to require protection against unauthorized disclosure for reasons of national security." . . .

. . . CIPA vests district courts with wide latitude to deal with thorny problems of national security in the context of criminal proceedings. When evaluating the governmental privilege in classified information which CIPA serves to protect, however, district courts must ultimately balance this "public interest in protecting the information against the individual's right to prepare his defense." . . .Specifically,[t]he trial court is required to balance the public interest in nondisclosure against the defendant's right to prepare a defense. A decision on disclosure of such information must depend on the "particular circumstances of each case, taking into consideration the crime charged, the possible defenses, the possible significance of the [evidence,] and other relevant factors."

If the district court determines that the information "is helpful to the defense of an accused, or is essential to a fair determination of a cause," it must be admitted. . . ("There is no question that the Government cannot invoke national security concerns as a means of depriving [the defendant] of a fair trial.").

. . .Ultimately, as these cases make clear, the appropriate procedure is for the district court to order production of the evidence or witness and leave to the Government the choice of whether to comply with that order. If the Government refuses to produce the information at issue-as it may properly do—the result is ordinarily dismissal.

. . .The "district court may order disclosure only when the information is at least essential to the defense, necessary to [the] defense, and neither merely cumulative nor corroborative, nor speculative." But if the necessary showing is made and "no adequate substitution can be found, the government must decide whether it will [continue to] prohibit the disclosure of the classified information; if it does so, the district court must impose a sanction, which is presumptively dismissal of the indictment." In sum, CIPA "enjoins district courts to seek a solution that neither disadvantages the defendant nor penalizes the government (and the public) for protecting classified information that may be vital to national security."

C.

With these principles in mind, we turn first to Abu Ali's Confrontation Clause challenge to the government's introduction at trial of two unredacted, classified documents that memorialized communications between Sultan Jubran and Abu Ali in the days following the May 2003 safe house raids conducted by the Saudi officials in Medina, as well as to his exclusion from the CIPA proceedings in which these communications were discussed.

1.

We begin with some additional background facts. After Abu Ali was indicted, Attorney Khurrum Wahid and Attorney Ashraf Nubani appeared to represent him. However, because one failed to apply for security clearance and the other was not approved by the Department of Justice, neither attorney was authorized to view the classified documents. On September 8, 2005, the district court, informed that the case would involve national security interests and CIPA proceedings and anticipating Abu Ali's need for an attorney with the proper security clearance, appointed Attorney Nina J. Ginsberg to act as CIPA-cleared counsel for Abu Ali. On October 14, 2005, the government first produced unredacted copies of the classified documents to Ms. Ginsberg and informed her that it intended to introduce the documents as evidence at trial. However, the government advised Ms. Ginsberg that it would proceed under CIPA to seek "certain limitations on public disclosure that will be necessary to prevent the revelation of extremely sensitive national security information."

Three days later, the government provided Abu Ali's uncleared defense counsel with slightly redacted copies of the classified documents, which it described as "newly declassified communications between the defendant and Sultan Jubran Sultan al-Qahtani occurring on May 27, 2003, and June 6, 2003," in their Arabic versions and with English translations, and advised counsel of the government's "inten[t] to offer these communications into evidence at trial as proof that the defendant provided material support to al-Qaeda." The first declassified document was dated May 27, 2003, and read as follows:

> Peace, How are you and how is your family? I hope they are good. I heard the news about the children's sickness. I wish them

a speedy recovery, God willing. Anyway, please keep in touch. Greetings to the group, Hani.

The government intended to demonstrate that "Hani" was a known alias of Abu Ali and that "news about the children's sickness" was a coded reference to the raids conducted by the Mabahith and the arrest of the Medina cell members. The second declassified document was dated June 6, 2003, and read as follows:

> To my brother, Peace to you with God's mercy and blessings. Thank God, I am fine. I was saved from the accident by a great miracle. I ask God that I would be thankful to Him. I have no idea about the others. However, according to what one doctor mentioned, 'Adil was not with them, thank God. The important thing is to get yourself ready for the medical checkup because you may have an appointment soon. Therefore, you must keep yourself ready by refraining from eating high fat meals and otherwise.

With regard to this communication, the government intended to demonstrate that the term "accident" was also a coded reference to the safe house raids. According to the government's theory, Sultan Jubran was advising Abu Ali that he did not know which cell members had escaped and which were captured, but that he and al-Faq'asi (a/k/a "Adil"), had escaped, and warning that Abu Ali might also be at risk.

A comparison of the classified and unclassified documents reveals that the declassified versions provided the dates, the opening salutations, the entire substance of the communications, and the closings, and had only been lightly redacted to omit certain identifying and forensic information.

On October 19, 2005, the government filed an in camera, ex parte motion pursuant to § 4 of CIPA, seeking a protective order prohibiting testimony and lines of questioning that would lead to the disclosure of the classified information during the trial. See 18 U.S.C.App. 3 § 4. The government advised that the classified portions of the communications could not be provided to Abu Ali and his uncleared counsel because they contained highly sensitive information which, if confirmed in a public setting, would divulge information detrimental to national security interests. The district court granted the government's motion by in camera, ex parte, sealed order. However, the district court ruled that the United States could use the "silent witness rule" to disclose the classified information to the jury at trial.[18]

---

[18] The "silent witness" rule was described in United States v. Zettl, 835 F.2d 1059, 1063 (4th Cir.1987), as follows.

[T]he witness would not disclose the information from the classified document in open court. Instead, the witness would have a copy of the classified document before him. The court, counsel and the jury would also have copies of the classified document. The witness would refer to specific places in the document in response to questioning. The jury would

Abu Ali immediately responded with a motion that the government declassify the documents in their entirety or be ordered to provide the dates on which the communications were obtained by the government and the manner in which they were obtained. The stated purpose of the request, however, was not to contest that Abu Ali was a party to the communications, but to enable Abu Ali to ascertain whether the government had discovered the existence of the communications prior to Abu Ali's arrest by the Saudi officials. If so, Abu Ali sought to rely upon this fact to demonstrate that each confession he made to the Saudi officials was the product of a joint venture with American law enforcement and, therefore, inadmissible.

On October 21, 2005, the district court conducted an in camera CIPA hearing to consider Abu Ali's motion. Abu Ali was not present at the hearing, but was represented by his CIPA-cleared counsel, who objected to the exclusion of her client and his other uncleared counsel, but did not specifically object to the use of the declassified version of the document or to the use of the "silent witness" procedure. With regard to the joint venture issue, the government advised the court that the communications were obtained prior to Abu Ali's arrest by the Saudi officials, but that they were obtained "based on intelligence collecting by the United States government with no involvement whatsoever of Saudi authorities." The district court found that the communications were discovered independently from the Saudi government's investigation and, therefore, were not the product of a joint venture. The district court also concluded that the declassified, redacted version of the documents provided to Abu Ali "me[t] the defense's need for access to the information."

After trial commenced, Abu Ali moved the court pursuant to § 5 of CIPA to allow uncleared counsel to question the two government witnesses slated to introduce the substance of the classified communications into evidence "about their role in extracting, sharing, transferring, and handling [the] communications." See 18 U.S.C.App. 3 § 5. The first witness was the compliance manager and custodian of records for the legal department of the communications carrier involved and the person tasked with the duty of responding to orders issued by the Foreign Intelligence Surveillance Act ("FISA") Court. The second was a Special Agent with the FBI, who received the information from the compliance manager. Because this line of questioning would lead to the disclosure of the classified information, the government opposed the motion. On November 9, 2005, the district court held another in camera hearing with CIPA-cleared defense counsel present but in the absence of Abu Ali and his uncleared

---

then refer to the particular part of the document as the witness answered. By this method, the classified information would not be made public at trial but the defense would be able to present that classified information to the jury.

Id.

bolstering the claim that the United States was acting in joint venture with the Saudis when Abu Ali was interrogated and confessed to the crimes upon which he now stands convicted. With regard to the redaction of the forensic information, Abu Ali's CIPA-cleared counsel was provided with all classified information and afforded the unfettered opportunity to challenge the government witnesses regarding the information. Yet no showing was made then or now that disclosure of the redacted information was necessary to ensure that Abu Ali obtained a fair trial and no request was made to have that information evaluated by outside forensic experts with appropriate clearance.

Abu Ali's eleventh-hour argument that the government cannot demonstrate harmless error because he was prohibited from developing evidence of an alibi at the time of the communications or to otherwise contest that he was, in actuality, a party to them is unpersuasive for the same reasons. At no point prior to or during the trial did Abu Ali contest that he was a party to the declassified communications provided to him or attempt to formulate any such alibi, his CIPA-cleared counsel made no request that the identifying information be evaluated, and Abu Ali admitted that he had communicated with Sultan Jubran after the Medina safe houses were raided. Thus, the information that had been redacted from the declassified version was largely cumulative to Abu Ali's own confessions and the evidence discovered during the safe house raids, which were presented to the jury.

In sum, while the district court violated Abu Ali's Sixth Amendment right to confront the evidence against him by submitting the unredacted versions of the documents, instead of the redacted substitute versions, to the jury as evidence at trial, we are satisfied that the error was harmless beyond a reasonable doubt.

QUESTIONS AND NOTES

1.   The CIPA issues in Abu Ali are somewhat unusual. First, there is the fact that one of his attorneys did not apply for security clearance and the other was not able to obtain security clearance and the fact that the court therefore appointed an attorney for him who had security clearance. Cleared counsel represented him in aspects of the case where clearance was necessary. These are not unheard-of circumstances, but probably not commonplace. Issues arising out of the need for security clearance for counsel are addressed in more detail infra this chapter. Does the use of security cleared counsel in terrorism prosecutions have a potential to generally resolve the dilemma posed by the use of classified information in such cases? Is there a problem where counsel for the defendant, or as in the principal case, one of defendant's counsel, has access to relevant and material classified information that the defendant himself is not able to see?

2. Second, there is the use of the "silent witness" procedure. Normally, what is contemplated when this procedure is used? Who does not gain access to the classified information at issue? The court? Defense counsel? The defendant? The jury? The public including the press? Wherein did the trial court err in the use of the silent witness procedure in this case?

3. An important proposition comes out of the appellate court's conclusion that the right of confrontation was violated in this case? What is it?

4. What does Abu Ali tell us about the following issues? Would it violate the confrontation clause to have examination or cross-examination of a witness conducted in an in camera hearing (i.e. before the judge) by cleared counsel but not in the presence of the jury? Would it violate the confrontation clause to have evidence that the jury has seen available to defendant's cleared counsel but not to defendant himself?

5. The court was upset by the failure of uncleared counsel to object to the court's decision to allow the jury to see evidence that defendant was not given access to while objecting to the fact that they had been prevented from having access to the redacted, classified portions of the documents at issue and from being able to introduce them publicly at the trial. How serious was this failure?

E. CLASSIFIED INFORMATION AND THE RIGHT TO COMPULSORY PROCESS OF WITNESSES

UNITED STATES V. MOUSSAOUI

382 F. 3d 453 (4th Cir. 2004), cert. denied, Moussaoui v.
United States, 544 U.S. 931 (2005)

Before WILKINS, CHIEF JUDGE, and WILLIAMS and GREGORY, CIRCUIT JUDGES.

[Affirmed in part, vacated in part, and remanded by published opinion. CHIEF JUDGE WILKINS announced the judgment of the court and wrote an opinion, in which JUDGE WILLIAMS concurs, and in which JUDGE GREGORY concurs except as to Part V.C. JUDGE WILLIAMS wrote a concurring opinion. JUDGE GREGORY wrote an opinion concurring in part and dissenting in part.]

WILKINS, CHIEF JUDGE.

The Government appeals a series of rulings by the district court granting Appellee Zacarias Moussaoui access to certain individuals ("the enemy combatant witnesses" or "the witnesses") for the purpose of deposing them pursuant to Federal Rule of Criminal Procedure 15; rejecting the Government's proposed substitutions for the depositions; and imposing sanctions for the Government's refusal to produce the witnesses. We are presented with questions of grave significance—questions that test the commitment of this nation to an independent judiciary, to the constitutional guarantee of a fair trial even to one accused of the most heinous of crimes, and to the protection of our citizens against additional terrorist attacks. These questions do not admit of easy answers.

For the reasons set forth below, we reject the Government's claim that the district court exceeded its authority in granting Moussaoui access to the witnesses. We affirm the conclusion of the district court that the enemy combatant witnesses could provide material, favorable testimony on Moussaoui's behalf, and we agree with the district court that the Government's proposed substitutions for the witnesses' deposition testimony are inadequate. However, we reverse the district court insofar as it held that it is not possible to craft adequate substitutions, and we remand with instructions for the district court and the parties to craft substitutions under certain guidelines. Finally, we vacate the order imposing sanctions on the Government.

I.

A. Background Information

. . .

Moussaoui was arrested for an immigration violation in mid-August 2001 and, in December of that year, was indicted on several charges of conspiracy related to the September 11 attacks. In July 2002, the Government filed a superceding indictment charging Moussaoui with six offenses: conspiracy to commit acts of terrorism transcending national boundaries, see 18 U.S.C.A. § 2332b(a)(2), (c) (West 2000); conspiracy to commit aircraft piracy, see 49 U.S.C.A. § 46502(a)(1)(A), (a)(2)(B) (West 1997); conspiracy to destroy aircraft, see 18 U.S.C.A. §§ 32(a)(7), 34 (West 2000); conspiracy to use weapons of mass destruction, see 18 U.S.C.A. § 2332a(a) (West 2000 & Supp.2003); conspiracy to murder United States employees, see 18 U.S.C.A. §§ 1114, 1117 (West 2000 & Supp.2003), and conspiracy to destroy property, see 18 U.S.C.A. § 844(f), (i), (n) (West 2000 & Supp.2003). The Government seeks the death penalty on the first four of these charges.

According to the allegations of the indictment, Moussaoui was present at an al Qaeda training camp in April 1998. The indictment further alleges that Moussaoui arrived in the United States in late February 2001 and thereafter began flight lessons in Norman, Oklahoma. Other allegations in the indictment highlight similarities between Moussaoui's conduct and the conduct of the September 11 hijackers. Each of the four death-eligible counts of the indictment alleges that the actions of Moussaoui and his coconspirators "result [ed] in the deaths of thousands of persons on September 11, 2001."

. . .

Simultaneously with its prosecution of Moussaoui, the Executive Branch has been engaged in ongoing efforts to eradicate al Qaeda and to capture its leader, Usama bin Laden. These efforts have resulted in the capture of numerous members of al Qaeda, including the witnesses at issue here: [Redacted] ("Witness A"), [Redacted] ("Witness B"), [Redacted] and [Redacted] ("Witness C"), [Redacted]

Witness A was captured [Redacted]. Shortly thereafter, Moussaoui (who at that time was representing himself in the district court) moved for access to Witness A, asserting that the witness would be an important part of his defense. Moussaoui's motion was supported by then-standby counsel, who filed a motion seeking pretrial access to Witness A and a writ of habeas corpus ad testificandum to obtain Witness A's trial testimony. The Government opposed this request.

The district court conducted a hearing, after which it issued an oral ruling granting access to Witness A ("the January 30 order"). The court subsequently issued a memorandum opinion explaining its ruling in greater detail. The district court concluded that Witness A could offer material testimony in Moussaoui's defense; in particular, the court determined that Witness A had extensive knowledge of the September 11 plot and that his testimony would support Moussaoui's claim that he was not involved in the attacks. At a minimum, the court observed, Witness A's testimony could support an argument that Moussaoui should not receive the death penalty if convicted.

The district court acknowledged that Witness A is a national security asset and therefore denied standby counsel's request for unmonitored pretrial access and declined to order his production at trial. The court also determined, however, that the Government's national security interest must yield to Moussaoui's right to a fair trial. Accordingly, the court ordered that Witness A's testimony be preserved by means of a Rule 15 deposition. See Fed.R.Crim.P. 15(a)(1) (providing that court may order deposition of witness to preserve testimony for trial "because of exceptional circumstances and in the interest of justice"). In an attempt to minimize the effect of its order on national security, the district court ordered that certain precautions be taken. Specifically, the court directed that the deposition would be taken by remote video, with Witness A in an undisclosed location and Moussaoui, standby counsel, and counsel for the Government in the presence of the district court, [Redacted]

While the Government's appeal of the January 30 order was pending before this court, we remanded for the purpose of allowing the district court to determine whether any substitution existed that would place Moussaoui in substantially the same position as would a deposition. On remand, both the Government and standby counsel offered proposed substitutions for

Witness A's deposition testimony.[5] The district court rejected the Government's proposed substitutions, reasoning that (a) the information in the [Redacted] reports was unreliable, and (b) the substitutions themselves were flawed in numerous respects. Believing itself bound to consider only the Government's proposed substitutions, the district court did not review the substitutions offered by standby counsel.

The proceedings on remand complete, we conducted oral argument on June 3, 2003. Upon receiving the mandate of this court, the district court entered an order directing the Government to inform the court whether it would comply with the January 30 order. On July 14, 2003, the Government filed a pleading indicating that it would refuse to provide access to Witness A for the purpose of conducting a deposition.

On August 29, the district court entered an order ("the August 29 order") granting access to Witnesses B and C for purposes of conducting Rule 15 depositions of those witnesses. The order imposed the same conditions as those applicable to Witness A. . . . Following the rejection of its proposed substitutions, the Government informed the court that it would not comply with the August 29 order.

The district court then directed the parties to submit briefs concerning the appropriate sanction to be imposed for the Government's refusal to comply with the January 30 and August 29 orders. Standby counsel sought dismissal but alternatively asked the district court to dismiss the death notice. The Government filed a responsive pleading stating that "[t]o present the issue most efficiently to the Court of Appeals, and because [the Classified Information Procedures Act] prescribes dismissal as the presumptive action a district court must take in these circumstances, we do not oppose standby counsel's suggestion that the appropriate action in this case is to dismiss the indictment.". (asserting that "dismissal of the indictment . . . is the surest route for ensuring that the questions at issue here can promptly be presented to the Fourth Circuit").

Noting that "[t]he unprecedented investment of both human and material resources in this case mandates the careful consideration of some sanction other than dismissal," the district court rejected the parties' claims that the indictment should be dismissed. Rather, the court dismissed the death notice, reasoning that Moussaoui had adequately demonstrated that the witnesses could provide testimony that, if believed,

---

[5]   These substitutions were derived as follows. Those responsible [Redacted] have recorded the witnesses' answers to questions in [Redacted] reports. These highly classified reports are intended for use in the military and intelligence communities; they were not prepared with this litigation in mind. Portions of the [Redacted] reports concerning Moussaoui and the September 11 attacks have been excerpted and set forth in documents prepared for purposes of this litigation. These documents, deemed [Redacted] summaries" by the parties and the district court, have been provided to defense counsel in conformance with the Government's obligations under Brady v. Maryland, 373 U.S. 83, 83 S.Ct. 1194, 10 L.Ed.2d 215 (1963). The proposed substitutions are based on the [Redacted] summaries.

might preclude a jury from finding Moussaoui eligible for the death penalty. Further, because proof of Moussaoui's involvement in the September 11 attacks was not necessary to a conviction, and because the witnesses' testimony, if believed, could exonerate Moussaoui of involvement in those attacks, the district court prohibited the Government "from making any argument, or offering any evidence, suggesting that the defendant had any involvement in, or knowledge of, the September 11 attacks.". In conjunction with this ruling, the district court denied the Government's motions to admit into evidence cockpit voice recordings made on September 11; video footage of the collapse of the World Trade Center towards; and photographs of the victims of the attacks.

The Government appealed, attacking multiple aspects of the rulings of the district court.

C.   Events Leading to Issuance of this Amended Opinion

We issued our decision on April 22, 2004. See United States v. Moussaoui, 365 F.3d 292 (4th Cir.2004). Moussaoui thereafter timely filed a petition for rehearing and suggestion for rehearing en banc (the Petition). On May 12, the Government submitted a letter to the court purporting to "clarify certain factual matters." Letter to Deputy Clerk from United States Attorney at 1 (May 12, 2004) [hereinafter "Letter"]. In particular, the Government referred to pages 50–51 of the classified slip opinion, where the court stated:

[Redacted]

In response to the emphasized portion of the above quotation, the Government stated that

members of the prosecution team, including FBI Special Agents assigned to the September 11 and other related investigations, [Redacted] have provided [Redacted] information [Redacted] consistent with the [Redacted] desire to maximize their own efforts to obtain actionable information [Redacted]

Letter at 2. The Government went on to note, however, that "[a]ny information or suggested areas of inquiry that have been shared [Redacted] have been used, like information from numerous other sources, at the sole discretion [Redacted]" Id. at 3. The Government asserted that [Redacted] Id.

Based in part on the revelations in the May 12 letter, we directed the Government to file a response to the Petition. In particular, we directed the Government to provide answers to the following questions:

(1) Why was the information in the May 12 Letter not provided to this court or the district court prior to May 12?

(2) [Redacted]

(3) [Redacted]

(4) [Redacted] provided inculpatory of exculpatory information regarding Moussaoui?

(5) In light of the information contained in the Letter and any other pertinent developments, would it now be appropriate to submit written questions to any of the enemy combatant witnesses?

(6) What restrictions would apply to such a process and how should it be conducted?

(7) If access is granted by written questions, is the Compulsory Process Clause satisfied?

(8) If access is granted by written questions, what effect, if any, would Crawford v. Washington, [541] U.S. [36], 124 S.Ct. 1354, 158 L.Ed.2d 177 (2004), have on such a process?

(9) If circumstances have changed such that submission of written questions is now possible, when did the circumstances change and why was neither this court nor the district court so informed at that time?

See United States v. Moussaoui, 365 F.3d 292 (4th Cir.2004) (order directing response to petition for rehearing and suggestion for rehearing en banc). Underlying this order were concerns among the panel members that members of the prosecution team may have [Redacted] rendered the witnesses' statements less reliable.

The Government filed its response (the Response), supplemented by a classified joint appendix and a classified ex parte appendix, on May 19. Moussaoui filed a reply on May 24, in which, inter alia, he raised concerns [Redacted].

We conducted a sealed oral argument regarding the petition for rehearing on June 3, 2004. During a discussion [Redacted] the panel asked the Government to provide documentation [Redacted]. On June 16, the Government filed an ex parte document responding to this request.

Additional Facts Contained in the Government's Submissions in Response to the Petition

1. Agent Zebley and the PENTTBOM Team

The FBI team investigating the terrorist attacks of September 11, 2001 is known as "the PENTTBOM team." The Government considers these investigators to be part of the prosecution team. See Letter at 2.

. . .

The classified joint appendix submitted by the Government with the Response includes [Redacted]

2. Oral Communications

[Redacted]

3. Written Communications

[Redacted]

4. Intelligence Community Use of Information

[Redacted][12] [Redacted] the intelligence community is interested only in obtaining information that has foreign intelligence value; the intelligence community is not concerned with obtaining information to aid in the prosecution of Moussaoui. [Redacted] not create special [Redacted] reports for use by the prosecution, rather, the prosecution and the PESTTBOM team receive the same reports that are distributed to the intelligence community at large. Information is included in these reports only if [Redacted] the information to have foreign intelligence value.[14]

II.

. . .

III.

With respect to the merits, the Government first argues that the district court erred in ordering the production of the enemy combatant witnesses for the purpose of deposing them. Within the context of this argument, the Government makes two related claims. First, the Government asserts that because the witnesses are noncitizens outside the territorial boundaries of the United States, there is no means by which the district court can compel their appearance on Moussaoui's behalf. Second,

---

[12] After the Petition was filed, news articles indicated that the National Commission on Terrorist Attacks Upon the United States ("the 9/11 Commission") had submitted questions to be asked of unidentified al Qaeda detainees. See Philip Shenon, "Accord Near for 9/11 Panel to Question Qaeda Leaders," N.Y. Times, May 12, 2004, at A20 (reporting a statement by the 9/11 Commission that it was "close to an agreement with the Bush administration that would allow the panel to submit questions to captured Qaeda leaders who are believed to have been involved in planning the attacks"); see also Associated Press, "Vice Chairman Expects Responses to Written Questions Soon" (May 13, 2004), available at www.msnbc.msn.com/id/4972789 (stating that "[t]he Sept. 11 commission has submitted written questions about the 2001 attacks to al-Qaida detainees and expects to receive responses soon"). [Redacted] see Nat'l Comm'n on Terrorist Attacks upon the United States, Staff Statement No. 16, at 1 (released June 16, 2004) (stating that Commission had no "direct access" to al Qaeda members but rather relied on written materials).

[14] The Government's submissions indicate that those responsible for [Redacted] the witnesses record and pass on only information [Redacted] to have foreign intelligence value. Consequently, it is at least possible, albeit unlikely, that one of the witnesses has imparted significant exculpatory information related to Moussaoui that has not been included [Redacted] If so, there may be a due process problem under Brady v. Maryland, 373 U.S. 83, 83 S.Ct. 1194, 10 L.Ed.2d 215 (1963). See United States v. Perdomo, 929 F.2d 967, 971 (3d Cir.1991) (stating that prosecution is obligated under Brady to disclose all exculpatory information "in the possession of some arm of the state"). We need not consider this question, however, as there is no evidence before us that the Government possesses exculpatory material that has not been disclosed to the defense.

the Government maintains that even if the district court has the power to reach the witnesses, its exercise of that power is curtailed by the reality that the witnesses are in military custody in time of war, and thus requiring them to be produced would violate constitutional principles of separation of powers. We address these arguments seriatim.

. . .

The Government maintains that because the enemy combatant witnesses are foreign nationals outside the boundaries of the United States, they are beyond the process power of the district court and, hence, unavailable to Moussaoui.

The Government's argument rests primarily on the well established and undisputed principle that the process power of the district court does not extend to foreign nationals abroad. . . . This is not the controlling principle, however.

The Government's argument overlooks the critical fact that the enemy combatant witnesses are [Redacted] of the United States Government. Therefore, we are concerned not with the ability of the district court to issue a subpoena to the witnesses, but rather with its power to issue a writ of habeas corpus ad testificandum ("testimonial writ") to the witnesses' custodian.

In determining whether a district court possesses the power to serve a writ of habeas corpus, the critical principle is that the writ is served not upon the prisoner, but upon the custodian. . . . Therefore, the relevant question is not whether the district court can serve the witnesses, but rather whether the court can serve the custodian.[16]

. . .

The Government next argues that even if the district court would otherwise have the power to order the production of the witnesses, the January 30 and August 29 orders are improper because they infringe on the Executive's warmaking authority, in violation of separation of powers principles.

---

[16] At oral argument, the Government described the capture of the enemy combatant witnesses as "a windfall" from which Moussaoui should not be entitled to benefit. We agree with the Government's premise; there can be no doubt that, were it not for the capture of these witnesses, Moussaoui could have no hope of obtaining their testimony. It does not follow, however, that this fortuity should not inure to Moussaoui's benefit. Indeed, the Government acknowledged that if the witnesses were brought to the United States for reasons unrelated to Moussaoui's prosecution, the district court would have the power to order their production. We are unable to discern why Moussaoui should be entitled to the benefit of the second windfall but not the first.

We also think that the Government's "windfall" argument mistakenly focuses on the ability of the district court to serve process on the witnesses, rather than on the custodian. The district court has never had—and does not now have—the power to serve process on the witnesses. But, as explained in Part III,B, the district court has always had the power to serve process on the custodian, [Redacted]

. . .

Stated in its simplest terms, the separation of powers doctrine prohibits each branch of the government from "intrud[ing] upon the central prerogatives of another." Such an intrusion occurs when one branch arrogates to itself powers constitutionally assigned to another branch or when the otherwise legitimate actions of one branch impair the functions of another. See

This is not a case involving arrogation of the powers or duties of another branch. The district court orders requiring production of the enemy combatant witnesses involved the resolution of questions properly—indeed, exclusively—reserved to the judiciary. Therefore, if there is a separation of powers problem at all, it arises only from the burden the actions of the district court place on the Executive's performance of its duties. The Supreme Court has explained on several occasions that determining whether a judicial act places impermissible burdens on another branch of government requires balancing the competing interests. See, e.g., Nixon v. Admin'r of Gen. Servs., 433 U.S. 425, 443, 97 S.Ct. 2777, 53 L.Ed.2d 867 (1977). In a case concerning the extent of the President's executive immunity, the Supreme Court noted that "[c]ourts traditionally have recognized the President's constitutional responsibilities and status as factors counseling judicial deference and restraint." Nixon v. Fitzgerald, 457 U.S. 731, 753, 102 S.Ct. 2690, 73 L.Ed.2d 349 (1982). The Court continued,

It is settled law that the separation-of-powers doctrine does not bar every exercise of jurisdiction over the President of the United States. But our cases also have established that a court, before exercising jurisdiction, must balance the constitutional weight of the interest to be served against the dangers of intrusion on the authority and functions of the Executive Branch.

C. Balancing

1. The Burden on the Government

The Constitution charges the Congress and the Executive with the making and conduct of war. . . . It is not an exaggeration to state that the effective performance of these duties is essential to our continued existence as a sovereign nation. Indeed, "no governmental interest is more compelling than the security of the Nation." . . .Thus, "[i]n accordance with [the] constitutional text, the Supreme Court has shown great deference to the political branches when called upon to decide cases implicating sensitive matters of foreign policy, national security, or military affairs.

The Government alleges—and we accept as true—that [Redacted] the enemy combatant witnesses is critical to the ongoing effort to combat terrorism by al Qaeda. The witnesses are [Redacted] al Qaeda operatives who have extensive knowledge concerning not just the September 11 attacks, but also other past attacks, future operations, and the structure, personnel, and tactics of al Qaeda. Their value as intelligence sources can hardly be overstated. And, we must defer to the Government's assertion that interruption [Redacted] of these witnesses will have devastating effects on the ability to gather information from them. Cf. CIA v. Sims, 471 U.S. 159, 176, 105 S.Ct. 1881, 85 L.Ed.2d 173 (1985) (noting that "whether an intelligence source will be harmed if his identity is revealed will often require complex political, historical, and psychological judgments" that courts are poorly equipped to make). [Redacted] it is not unreasonable to suppose that interruption [Redacted] could result in the loss of information that might prevent future terrorist attacks.

The Government also asserts that production of the witnesses would burden the Executive's ability to conduct foreign relations. . . . The Government claims that if the Executive's assurances of confidentiality can be abrogated by the judiciary, the vital ability to obtain the cooperation of other governments will be devastated. The Government also reminds us of the bolstering effect production of the witnesses might have on our enemies.

A basic consideration in habeas corpus practice is that the prisoner will be produced before the court. . . . To grant the writ to these prisoners might mean that our army must transport them across the seas for hearing. This would require allocation of shipping space, guarding personnel, billeting and rations. . . . The writ, since it is held to be a matter of right, would be equally available to enemies during active hostilities as in the present twilight between war and peace. Such trials would hamper the war effort and bring aid and comfort to the enemy. They would diminish the prestige of our commanders, not only with enemies but with wavering neutrals. It would be difficult to devise more effective fettering of a field commander than to allow the very enemies he is ordered to reduce to submission to call him to account in his own civil courts and divert his efforts and attention from the military offensive abroad to the legal defensive at home. Nor is it unlikely that the result of such enemy litigiousness would be a conflict between judicial and military opinion highly comforting to enemies of the United States.

In summary, the burdens that would arise from production of the enemy combatant witnesses are substantial.

2. Moussaoui's Interest

The importance of the Sixth Amendment right to compulsory process is not subject to question—it is integral to our adversarial criminal justice system:

The need to develop all relevant facts in the adversary system is both fundamental and comprehensive. The ends of criminal justice would be defeated if judgments were to be founded on a partial or speculative presentation of the facts. The vary integrity of the judicial system and public confidence in the system depend on full disclosure of all the facts, within the framework of the rules of evidence. To ensure that justice is done, it is imperative to the function of the courts that compulsory process be available for the production of evidence needed either by the prosecution or by the defense.

To state the matter more succinctly, "[f]ew rights are more fundamental than that of an accused to present witnesses in his own defense."

The compulsory process right does not attach to any witness the defendant wishes to call, however. Rather, a defendant must demonstrate that the witness he desires to have produced would testify "in his favor,". Thus, in order to assess Moussaoui's interest, we must determine whether the enemy combatant witnesses could provide testimony material to Moussaoui's defense.[20]

. . .

Because Moussaoui has not had—and will not receive—direct access to any of the witnesses, he cannot be required to show materiality with the degree of specificity that applies in the ordinary case. Rather, it is sufficient if Moussaoui can make a "plausible showing" of materiality. (noting that a defendant who has not interviewed a potential witness may demonstrate materiality by relating "the events to which a witness might testify[ ] and the relevance of those events to the crime charged"). However, in determining whether Moussaoui has made a plausible showing, we must bear in mind that Moussaoui does have access to the [Redacted] summaries.

Before considering whether Moussaoui has made the necessary showing with respect to each witness, we pause to consider some general arguments raised by the Government concerning materiality. First, the Government maintains that Moussaoui can demonstrate materiality only by relying on admissible evidence. We agree with the Government to a certain extent—Moussaoui should not be allowed to rely on obviously inadmissible statements (e.g., statements resting on a witness' belief rather than his personal knowledge). . . . However, because many rulings on admissibility—particularly those relating to relevance—can only be decided in the context of a trial, most of the witnesses' statements cannot

---

[20] We adhere to our prior ruling that CIPA does not apply because the January 30 and August 29 orders of the district court are not covered by either of the potentially relevant provisions of CIPA: § 4 (concerning deletion of classified information from documents to be turned over to the defendant during discovery) or § 6 (concerning the disclosure of classified information by the defense during pretrial or trial proceedings). See Moussaoui I, 333 F.3d at 514–15. Like the district court, however, we believe that CIPA provides a useful framework for considering the questions raised by Moussaoui's request for access to the enemy combatant witnesses.

meaningfully be assessed for admissibility at this time. Moreover, statements that may not be admissible at the guilt phase may be admissible during the penalty phase, with its more relaxed evidentiary standards.

Second, the Government maintains that Moussaoui cannot establish materiality unless he can prove that the witnesses would not invoke their Fifth Amendment rights against self-incrimination. We have previously indicated, however, that a court should not assume that a potential witness will invoke the Fifth Amendment. . . .

Additionally, the Government argues that even if the witnesses' testimony would tend to exonerate Moussaoui of involvement in the September 11 attacks, such testimony would not be material because the conspiracies with which Moussaoui is charged are broader than September 11. Thus, the Government argues, Moussaoui can be convicted even if he lacked any prior knowledge of September 11. This argument ignores the principle that the scope of an alleged conspiracy is a jury question, and the possibility that Moussaoui may assert that the conspiracy culminating in the September 11 attacks was distinct from any conspiracy in which he was involved. Moreover, even if the jury accepts the Government's claims regarding the scope of the charged conspiracy, testimony regarding Moussaoui's non-involvement in September 11 is critical to the penalty phase. If Moussaoui had no involvement in or knowledge of September 11, it is entirely possible that he would not be found eligible for the death penalty.

We now consider the rulings of the district court regarding the ability of each witness to provide material testimony in Moussaoui's favor.

a. Witness A

The district court did not err in concluding that Witnese A could offer material evidence on Moussaoui's behalf. Redacted] Several statements by Witness A tend to exculpate Moussaoui. [Redacted] to undermine the theory (which the Government may or may not intend to advance at trial) that Moussaoui was to pilot a fifth plane into the White House. [Redacted] This statement is significant in light of other evidence [Redacted] This is consistent with Moussaoui's claim that he was to be part of a post-September 11 operation.

The Government argues that Witness A's statements are actually incriminatory of Moussaoui. It is true that Witness A has made some statements that arguably implicate Moussaoui in the September 11 attacks. [Redacted] On balance, however, Moussaoui has made a sufficient showing that evidence from Witness A would be more helpful than hurtful, or at least that we cannot have confidence in the outcome of the trial without Witness A's evidence.

b. Witness B

There can be no question that Witness B could provide material evidence on behalf of Moussaoui. [Redacted] Witness B [Redacted] has indicated that Moussaoui's operational knowledge was limited, a fact that is clearly of exculpatory value as to both guilt and penalty. [Redacted] Thus, of all three witnesses, Witness B is of the greatest exculpatory value.

c. Witness C

[Redacted]

The district court determined that Witness C could provide material evidence because he could support Moussaoui's contention that he was not involved in the September 11 attacks. We agree with the district court that a jury might reasonably infer, from Witness C [Redacted] that Moussaoui was not involved in September 11. We therefore conclude that Moussaoui has made a plausible showing that Witness C would, if available, be a favorable witness.

3. Balancing

Having considered the burden alleged by the Government and the right claimed by Moussaoui, we now turn to the question of whether the district court should have refrained from acting in light of the national security interests asserted by the Government. The question is not unique; the Supreme Court has addressed similar matters on numerous occasions. In all cases of this type—cases falling into "what might loosely be called the area of constitutionally guaranteed access to evidence," . . .Ultimately, as these cases make clear, the appropriate procedure is for the district court to order production of the evidence or witness and leave to the Government the choice of whether to comply with that order. If the government refuses to produce the information at issue—as it may properly do—the result is ordinarily dismissal.

. . .

In addition to the pronouncements of the Supreme Court in this area, we are also mindful of Congress' judgment, expressed in CIPA, that the Executive's interest in protecting classified information does not overcome a defendant's right to present his case. Under CIPA, once the district court determines that an item of classified information is relevant and material, that item must be admitted unless the government provides an adequate substitution. . . . If no adequate substitution can be found, the government must decide whether it will prohibit the disclosure of the classified information; if it does so, the district court must impose a sanction, which is presumptively dismissal of the indictment.

In view of these authorities, it is clear that when an evidentiary privilege—even one that involves national security—is asserted by the

Government in the context of its prosecution of a criminal offense, the "balancing" we must conduct is primarily, if not solely, an examination of whether the district court correctly determined that the information the Government seeks to withhold is material to the defense. We have determined that the enemy combatant witnesses can offer material testimony that is essential to Moussaoui's defense, and we therefore affirm the January 30 and August 29 orders, Thus, the choice is the Government's whether to comply with those orders or suffer a sanction.

V.

As noted previously, the Government has stated that it will not produce the enemy combatant witnesses for depositions (or, we presume, for any other purpose related to this litigation). We are thus left in the following situation: the district court has the power to order production of the enemy combatant witnesses and has properly determined that they could offer material testimony on Moussaoui's behalf, but the Government has refused to produce the witnesses. Under such circumstances, dismissal of the indictment is the usual course. Like the district court, however, we believe that a more measured approach is required. Additionally, we emphasize that no punitive sanction is warranted here because the Government has rightfully exercised its prerogative to protect national security interests by refusing to produce the witnesses.[26]

Although, as explained above, this is not a CIPA case, that act nevertheless provides useful guidance in determining the nature of the remedies that may be available. Under CIPA, dismissal of an indictment is authorized only if the government has failed to produce an adequate substitute for the classified information, and the interests of justice would not be served by imposition of a lesser sanction, CIPA thus enjoins district courts to seek a solution that neither disadvantages the defendant nor penalizes the government (and the public) for protecting classified information that may be vital to national security.

A similar approach is appropriate here. Under such an approach, the first question is whether there is any appropriate substitution for the witnesses' testimony. Because we conclude, for the reasons set forth below, that appropriate substitutions are available, we need not consider any other remedy.

A. Standard

CIPA provides that the government may avoid the disclosure of classified information by proposing a substitute for the information, which

---

[26] We emphasize that by all appearances, the Government's refusal to produce the witnesses is done in the utmost good faith. The Government is charged not only with the task of bringing wrongdoers to justice, but also with the grave responsibility of protecting the lives of the citizenry. The choice the Government has made is not without consequences, but those consequences are not punitive in nature.

the district court must accept if it "will provide the defendant with substantially the same ability to make his defense as would disclosure of the specific classified information." . . .

B.   Substitutions proposed by the Government

The Government proposed substitutions for the witnesses' deposition testimony in the form of a series of statements derived from the [Redacted] summaries.[27] The district court rejected all proposed substitutions as inadequate. The ruling of the district court was based on its conclusions regarding the inherent inadequacy of the substitutions and its findings regarding the specific failings of the Government's proposals. For the reasons set forth below, we reject the ruling of the district court that any substitution for the witnesses' testimony would be inadequate. We agree, however, with the assessment that the particular proposals submitted by the Government are inadequate in their current form.

First, the district court deemed the substitutions inherently inadequate because the [Redacted] reports, from which the substitutions were ultimately derived, were unreliable.[29] This was so, the court reasoned, because the witnesses' [Redacted] The district court also complained that it cannot be determined whether the [Redacted] reports accurately reflect the witnesses' statements [Redacted][30] The court further commented that the lack of quotation marks in the [Redacted] reports made it impossible to determine whether a given statement is a verbatim recording or [Redacted].

The conclusion of the district court that the proposed substitutions are inherently inadequate is tantamount to a declaration that there could be no adequate substitution for the witnesses' deposition testimony. We reject this conclusion. The answer to the concerns of the district court regarding the accuracy of the [Redacted] reports is that those who are [Redacted] the witnesses have a profound interest in obtaining accurate information from the witnesses and in reporting that information accurately to those who can use it to prevent acts of terrorism and to capture other al Qaeda

---

[27] In the case of Witness A, the proposed substitutions were submitted in narrative form rather than as excerpts from the [Redacted] summaries. The substitutions for Witnesses B and C more closely tracked the language of the [Redacted] summaries.

[29] The court also deemed the substitutions inadequate because the use of substitutions would deprive Moussaoui of the ability to question the witnesses regarding matters that do not appear in the [Redacted] reports. In essence, the district court appears to have concluded that the substitutions are inadequate because they are not the same thing as a deposition. However, we have already determined that a proposed substitution need not provide Moussaoui with all the benefits of a deposition in order to be adequate.

[30] The district court did not complain that the [Redacted] summaries do not accurately summarize the [Redacted] reports. At the hearing concerning the Government's proposed substitutions for Witness A's testimony, the court commented that it had been "impressed with the accuracy" of the [Redacted] summaries.

operatives. These considerations provide sufficient indicia of reliability to alleviate the concerns of the district court.

Next, the district court noted that the substitutions do not indicate that they are summaries of statements made over the course of several months. We agree with the district court that in order to adequately protect Moussaoui's right to a fair trial, the jury must be made aware of certain information concerning the substitutions. The particular content of any instruction to the jury regarding the substitutions lies within the discretion of the district court. However, at the very least the jury should be informed that the substitutions are derived from reports [Redacted] of the witnesses. The instructions must account for the fact that members of the prosecution team have provided information and suggested [Redacted] The jury should also be instructed that the statements were obtained under circumstances that support a conclusion that the statements are reliable.[31]

We reject the suggestion of the district court that the Government acted improperly in attempting to organize the information presented in the substitutions. Counsel rarely, if ever, present information to the jury in the order they received it during pretrial investigations. Indeed, organizing and distilling voluminous information for comprehensible presentation to a jury is a hallmark of effective advocacy. In short, while there may be problems with the manner in which the Government organized the substitutions, the fact that the Government has attempted such organization is not a mark against it.

The district court identified particular problems with the proposed substitutions for Witness A's testimony. For example, the court noted that the proposed substitutions failed to include exculpatory information provided by Witness A and incorporated at least one incriminatory inference not supplied by Witness A's statements.[Redacted] Our own review of the proposed substitutions for the testimony of Witnesses B and C reveals similar problems.[Redacted] These problems, however, may be remedied as described below.

C. Instructions for the District Court

1. Submission of Questions by Moussaoui

The Government's submissions in response to the Petition make clear that members of the prosecution team, [Redacted] have had some input

---

[31] Nothing in the Government's submissions in connection with the Petition contradicts our conclusion that those [Redacted] the witnesses have a profound interest in obtaining truthful information. To the contrary, we are even more persuaded that the [Redacted] process is carefully designed to elicit truthful and accurate information from the witnesses.

We emphasize that we have never held, nor do we new hold, that the witnesses' statements are in fact truthful, and the jury should not be so instructed. Instead, the jury should be informed that the circumstances were designed to elicit truthful statements from the witnesses. We offer no opinion regarding whether this instruction may include information regarding [Redacted]

[Redacted] the enemy combatant witnesses. Our review of the circumstances of this access indicates that the input by the prosecution team into the [Redacted] process has worked no unfairness on Moussaoui. Nevertheless, in order to provide Moussaoui with the fullest possible range of information from the witnesses, we direct the district court to provide Moussaoui with an opportunity to [Redacted] for [Redacted] discretionary use [Redacted] of the witnesses.[34]

2. Substitutions

For the reasons set forth above, we conclude that the district court erred in ruling that any substitution for the witnesses' testimony is inherently inadequate to the extent it is derived from the [Redacted] reports. To the contrary, we hold that the [Redacted] summaries (which, as the district court determined, accurately recapitulate the [Redacted] reports) provide an adequate basis for the creation of written statements that may be submitted to the jury in lieu of the witnesses' deposition testimony.

The compiling of substitutions is a task best suited to the district court, given its greater familiarity with the facts of the case and its authority to manage the presentation of evidence.[35] Nevertheless, we think it is appropriate to provide some guidance to the court and the parties.

First, the circumstances of this case—most notably, the fact that the substitutions may very well support Moussaoui's defense—dictate that the compiling of substitutions be an interactive process among the parties and the district court. Second, we think that accuracy and fairness are best achieved by compiling substitutions that use the exact language of the [Redacted] summaries to the greatest extent possible. We believe that the best means of achieving both of these objectives is for defense counsel to identify particular portions of the [Redacted] summaries that Moussaoui may want to admit into evidence at trial. The Government may then offer any objections and argue that additional portions must be included in the interest of completeness, as discussed below. If the substitutions are to be admitted at all (we leave open the possibility that Moussaoui may decide not to use the substitutions in his defense), they may be admitted only by Moussaoui. Based on defense counsel's submissions and the Government's

---

[34] During the hearing regarding the Petition, defense counsel expressed concern over whether [Redacted] would result in the disclosure of trial strategy to the Government. The Government, in its June 16 filing, informs us that measures can be taken to avoid such disclosures. We leave the particulars of any such process to the discretion of the district court. At an absolute minimum, however, whatever process is adopted must ensure that the prosecution team is not privy to [Redacted] propounded by the defense, just as the defense was unaware or [Redacted] propounded by the prosecution team.

[35] We note that the district court will not be drafting original language for submission to the jury. Instead, as we discuss further in the text, Moussaoui will designate portions of the [Redacted] summaries for submission; the Government will raise objections and cross-designate portions of the summaries it believes are required by the rule of completeness; and the district court will make rulings as necessary to compile an appropriate set of substitutions.

objections, the district court could then compile an appropriate set of substitutions. We leave to the discretion of the district court the question of whether to rule on the admissibility of a particular substitution (e.g., whether a substitution is relevant) at trial or during pre-trial proceedings.

As previously indicated, the jury must be provided with certain information regarding the substitutions. While we leave the particulars of the instructions to the district court, the jury must be informed, at a minimum, that the substitutions are what the witnesses would say if called to testify; that the substitutions are derived from statements obtained under conditions that provide circumstantial guarantees of reliability; that the substitutions contain statements obtained over the course of weeks or months; that members of the prosecution team have contributed to [Redacted] the witnesses; and, if applicable, that Moussaoui has [Redacted] to the witnesses.

. . .

b.   CIPA

On rehearing, both parties acknowledged our holding that CIPA does not apply here but indicated their belief that once the district court has approved substitutions for the witnesses' testimony, CIPA comes into play, with the result that the Government may object to the disclosure of the classified information in the substitutions and request that the district court adopt an alternative form of evidence. We disagree.

It must be remembered that the substitution process we here order is a replacement for the testimony of the enemy combatant witnesses. Because the Government will not allow Moussaoui to have contact with the witnesses, we must provide a remedy adequate to protect Moussaoui's constitutional rights. Here, that remedy is substitutions. Once Moussaoui has selected the portions of the [Redacted] summaries he wishes to submit to the jury and the Government has been given an opportunity to be heard, the district court will compile the substitutions, using such additional language as may be necessary to aid the understanding of the jury. Once this process is complete, the matter is at an end—there are to be no additional or supplementary proceedings under CIPA regarding the substitutions.

VI.

In summary, the judgment of the court is as follows. The January 30 and August 29 orders are affirmed, as is the rejection of the Government's proposed substitutions by the district court. The order imposing sanctions on the Government is vacated, and the case is remanded for the compiling of substitutions for the deposition testimony of the enemy combatant witnesses.

QUESTIONS AND NOTES

1.   Note how much material is officially redacted (wherever the word, Redacted appears in brackets) from the Moussaoui opinion. At certain points, the redactions make portions of the opinion incomprehensible. Is there any solution to this problem? On the face of it, do some of the redactions also seem rather odd because they appear to redact material the content of which seems to be obvious. What concerns, if any, should we have about significant redactions in published appellate opinions?

2.   In Abu Ali, supra, in connection with the introduction of the substitutions, the court found a violation of the confrontation clause. Is there a confrontation issue in regard to the substitutions in the Moussaoui case? Is there a hearsay problem in Moussaoui?

3.   For a characterization of the substitutions and a discussion of the legal implications of the Moussaoui opinion, see Norman Abrams, Confrontation/Hearsay and Compulsory Process Issues in Post-Gitmo Federal Court Terrorism Prosecutions: Moussaoui and Paracha as Harbingers, 75 Brooklyn L.Rev. 1067 (2010):

> The substitutions approved in principal by the court had unique features. They were summaries, but of what? The witnesses were not subjected to depositions. Rather 1) detailed statements from the putative three witnesses [hereinafter declarants], labeled by the court as A, B and C, had been obtained, apparently through interrogation, by government agents seeking intelligence that could be used in preventing future terrorist actions and apprehending other terrorists. . . .

> The statements thus obtained from A, B, and C had then been "recorded" in "highly classified" 2) reports which had been prepared for "use in the military and intelligence communities; they were not prepared with this litigation in mind."

> Portions of the reports were then "excerpted and set forth in documents prepared for purposes of this litigation" which were labelled 3) summaries. The summaries were provided to defense counsel. 4) Finally, the substitutions to be offered into evidence were prepared from the summaries. These consisted of the summaries of statements that had been obtained over the course of several months but were not identical to the summaries since in preparing the substitutions, the government had reorganized the information.

> It is apparent from the foregoing that there are multiple levels of hearsay involved in the substitutions that were being considered by the court, with A, B, and C being the declarants at level 1), supra, and the declarants involved in levels 2–4 being unknown government agents or employees.

4. On what grounds did the Moussaoui court conclude that the substitutions in the case were reliable? Are there any flaws in the court's reasoning?

5. As decided in the Moussaoui opinion, reproduced above, the Fourth Circuit remanded so that the district court, working with the parties, could revise the substitutions in lieu of requiring that the enemy combatant witnesses be produced. After the Supreme Court denied certiorari, Moussaoui pled guilty, apparently ending the case. Later, however, he moved to withdraw his plea of guilty. See United States v. Moussaoui, 591 F 3d 263 (4th Cir. 2010) where the fourth circuit reaffirmed the details of its earlier opinion. Further, the apparent effect of the earlier guilty plea had been to cut short the process of revising the substitutions. However, it turns out that the revision of the substitutions, in fact, took place. Thus in the 2010 Moussaoui circuit opinion, the court stated in footnote 18:

> 18 Finally, we note that the CIPA process actually continued after the guilty plea in preparation for the sentencing proceeding, and the exculpatory, classified information was made available for Moussaoui's use in an appropriate form. Moussaoui thereafter testified, confirmed his guilt to the offenses as charged, and contradicted the supposed exculpatory statements of the ECWs as they related to his intended participation in the 9/11 strikes. . . .

The adequacy of the substitutions thus prepared by the district court was not, however, subjected to any further appellate review (other than the appellate court's statement, "was made available for Moussaoui's use in an appropriate form," supra). The Fourth Circuit did not otherwise address the adequacy of the final version of the substitutions prepared by the district court, given Moussaoui's guilty plea, nor was further review of the case sought in the Supreme Court.

6. A district court in New York followed and used essentially Moussaoui-type instructions in a similar context. See United States v. Paracha, 2006 WL 12768 (S.D.N.Y. 2006). The United States Court of Appeals for the Second Circuit then affirmed Paracha's conviction in an unpublished opinion, United States v. Paracha, 2008 U.S.App. Lexis 12937, which contains the following paragraph:

> Paracha contends that his Sixth Amendment rights to compulsory process and confrontation of witnesses were violated by the government's discussion in summation of declassified summaries of interviews with witnesses not present at trial. We disagree. The government did not exceed the boundaries of the district court's limiting instructions—as the district court found, the government's reference to the summaries during its summation was not inculpatory but rather made for the purpose of trying to persuade the jury that, were the statements to be believed, they did not undermine the government's case—and Paracha waived any claim that his right to compulsory process was violated by the court's "compromise"

solution of allowing the defense to introduce the summaries in lieu of live testimony.

F. SECURITY CLEARANCE FOR COUNSEL

QUESTIONS AND NOTES

1.   No express language in CIPA indicates that defense counsel are required to obtain security clearance, nor that if they wish to gain access to classified materials relating to the case at hand that they can request that they be permitted to go through security clearance. However, as the materials in this section indicate, the use of security clearance for counsel has become an almost ever-present occurrence in terrorism prosecutions.

2.   What provisions of CIPA, if any, address the issue of security clearance? See sec. 9 of the Act, supra, pursuant to which the Chief Justice issued the following rules:

SECURITY PROCEDURES ESTABLISHED PURSUANT TO PUB.L. 96–456, 94 STAT. 2025, BY THE CHIEF JUSTICE OF THE UNITED STATES FOR THE PROTECTION OF CLASSIFIED INFORMATION

1.   Purpose. The purpose of these procedures is to meet the requirements of Section 9(a) of the Classified Information Procedures Act of 1980, Pub.L. 96–456, 94 Stat. 2025, which in pertinent part provides that:

> ". . . [T]he Chief Justice of the United States, in consultation with the Attorney General, the Director of Central Intelligence, and the Secretary of Defense, shall prescribe rules establishing procedures for the protection against unauthorized disclosure of any classified information in the custody of the United States district courts, courts of appeal, or Supreme Court. . . ."

These procedures apply in all proceedings in criminal cases involving classified information, and appeals therefrom, before the United States district courts, the courts of appeal and the Supreme Court.

2.   Court Security Officer. In any proceeding in a criminal case or appeal therefrom in which classified information is within, or reasonably expected to be within, the custody of the court, the court shall designate a court security officer. The Attorney General or the Department of Justice Security Officer, with the concurrence of the head of the agency or agencies from which the classified information originates, or their representatives, shall recommend to the court persons qualified to serve as court security officer. The court security officer shall be selected from among those persons so recommended.

The court security officer shall be an individual with demonstrated competence in security matters, and shall, prior to designation, have been certified to the court in writing by the Department of Justice Security Officer as cleared for the level and category of classified information that will be involved. The court security officer may be an employee of the Executive Branch of the Government detailed to the court for this purpose. One or more alternate court security officers, who have been recommended and cleared in the manner specified above, may be designated by the court as required. The court security officer shall be responsible to the court for document, physical, personnel and communications security, and shall take measures reasonably necessary to fulfill these responsibilities. The court security officer shall notify the court and the Department of Justice Security Officer of any actual, attempted, or potential violation of security procedures.

3.   Secure Quarters. Any in camera proceeding—including a pretrial conference, motion hearing, or appellate hearing—concerning the use, relevance, or admissibility of classified information, shall be held in secure quarters recommended by the court security officer and approved by the court.

The secure quarters shall be located within the Federal courthouse, unless it is determined that none of the quarters available in the courthouse meets, or can reasonably be made equivalent to, security requirements of the Executive Branch applicable to the level and category of classified information involved. In that event, the court shall designate the facilities of another United States Government agency, recommended by the court security officer, which is located within the vicinity of the courthouse, as the site of the proceedings.

The court security officer shall make necessary arrangements to ensure that the applicable Executive Branch standards are met and shall conduct or arrange for such inspection of the quarters as may be necessary. The court security officer shall, in consultation with the United States Marshal, arrange for the installation of security devices and take such other measures as may be necessary to protect against any unauthorized access to classified information. All of the aforementioned activity shall be conducted in a manner which does not interfere with the orderly proceedings of the court. Prior to any hearing or other proceeding, the court security officer shall certify in writing to the court that the quarters are secure.

4.   Personnel Security—Court Personnel. No person appointed by the court or designated for service therein shall be given access to any classified information in the custody of the court, unless such person has received a security clearance as provided herein and unless access to such information is necessary for the performance of an official function. A security clearance for justices and judges is not

required, but such clearance shall be provided upon the request of any judicial officer who desires to be cleared.

The court shall inform the court security officer or the attorney for the government of the names of court personnel who may require access to classified information. That person shall then notify the Department of Justice Security Officer, who shall promptly make arrangements to obtain any necessary security clearances and shall approve such clearances under standards of the Executive Branch applicable to the level and category of classified information involved. The Department of Justice Security Officer shall advise the court in writing when the necessary security clearances have been obtained.

If security clearances cannot be obtained promptly, personnel in the Executive Branch having the necessary clearances may be temporarily assigned to assist the court. If a proceeding is required to be recorded and an official court reporter having the necessary security clearance is unavailable, the court may request the court security officer or the attorney for the government to have a cleared reporter from the Executive Branch designated to act as reporter in the proceedings. The reporter so designated shall take the oath of office as prescribed by 28 U.S.C. § 753(a).

Justices, judges and cleared court personnel shall not disclose classified information to anyone who does not have a security clearance and who does not require the information in the discharge of an official function. However, nothing contained in these procedures shall preclude a judge from discharging his official duties, including giving appropriate instructions to the jury. Any problem of security involving court personnel or persons acting for the court shall be referred to the court for appropriate action.

5. Persons Acting for the Defendant. The government may obtain information by any lawful means concerning the trustworthiness of persons associated with the defense and may bring such information to the attention of the court for the court's consideration in framing an appropriate protective order pursuant to Section 3 of the Act.

6. Jury. Nothing contained in these procedures shall be construed to require an investigation or security clearance of the members of the jury or interfere with the functions of a jury, including access to classified information introduced as evidence in the trial of a case.

After a verdict has been rendered by a jury, the trial judge should consider a government request for a cautionary instruction to jurors regarding the release or disclosure of classified information contained in documents they have reviewed during the trial.

UNITED STATES V. BIN LADEN

58 F.Supp.2d 113 (S.D.N.Y. 1999)

SAND, DISTRICT JUDGE.

The sixth superseding indictment in this case charges fifteen Defendants with numerous crimes arising from, among other things, the August 1998 bombings of the United States' embassies in Nairobi, Kenya, and Dar es Salaam, Tanzania, as well with subsequent attempts to hinder the investigation into those crimes. Five of the Defendants are presently in the custody of the Bureau of Prisons: Mamdouh Mahmud Salim, Ali Mohamed ("Mohamed"), Wadih El Hage ("El Hage"), Mohamed Sadeek Odeh ("Odeh"), and Mohamed Rashed Daoud Al-Owhali.

The Government has asked that the Court file a protective order containing the following language:

> 5.   No defendant, counsel for a defendant, employee of counsel for a defendant, defense witness, or Courtroom personnel required by the Court for its assistance, shall have access to any classified information involved in this case unless that person shall first have:
>
> > (a)   received approval from either the Government or the Court for access to the particular classified information in question . . .; and
> >
> > (b)   . . . agree[d] to comply with the term[s] of this Order.
>
> 6.   For the purpose of establishing security clearances necessary for access to classified information that may be involved in the pre-trial preparation or trial or appeal of this case, Standard Form 86, "Questionnaire for National Security Positions," attached releases, and full fingerprints shall be completed and submitted to the CSO forthwith by all defense counsel, persons whose assistance the defense reasonably requires and by such [C]ourtroom personnel as the Court requires for its assistance.

The Department of Justice ("DOJ") regulations governing the clearance application process contain the following provisions:

> (b)   Eligibility for access to classified information is limited to United States citizens for whom an appropriate investigation of their personal and professional history affirmatively indicated loyalty to the United States, strength of character, trustworthiness, honesty, reliability, discretion, and sound judgment, as well as freedom from conflicting allegiances and potential for coercion, and willingness and ability to abide by

regulations governing the use, handling, and protection of classified information. . . .

(c) The Department of Justice does not discriminate on the basis of race, color, religion, sex, national origin, disability, or sexual orientation in granting access to classified information. However, the Department may investigate and consider any matter that relates to the determination of whether access is clearly consistent with the interests of national security. No negative inferences concerning the standards for access may be raised solely on the basis of the sexual orientation of the employee or mental health counseling.

28 C.F.R. § 17.41 (1998).

The proposed security clearance procedure would be supervised by a Court-appointed Court Security Officer ("CSO") who (1) "would serve as an officer of this [C]ourt in implementing and enforcing the terms of the proposed protective order" and (2) would "not be a member of the prosecution team in this case."

The Government has also indicated that the CSO would be required to maintain the confidentiality of materials relating to any clearance application and that the DOJ's recommendation with respect to any such application would be furnished only to the Court and the particular applicant. The regulations governing the clearance procedures provide for appeal within DOJ, see Exec.Order No. 12968, 60 Fed.Reg. 40,245, at Part 5 (1995), and any applicant who received an adverse recommendation could ultimately raise ex parte objections with the Court, which would be the final arbiter of all clearance questions. See generally United States v. Musa, 833 F.Supp. 752, 755–57 (E.D.Mo.1993) (providing a detailed description of procedures used in a case involving classified information, albeit one in which the Government did not request clearance of counsel).

Defendant Odeh filed a motion objecting to the proposed protective order insofar as it requires his counsel to obtain clearance before viewing classified information. Defendants Mohamed and El Hage subsequently joined this motion at oral argument. The Moving Defendants argue that the Court lacks the authority to require clearance of counsel and that, even if the Court were to possess such authority, exercising it would violate their Sixth Amendment rights. At oral argument on June 22, 1999, counsel for Defendant Odeh moved to intervene in the proceedings "for the limited purposes of asserting defense counsel's independent constitutional rights on this issue

We begin with three basic propositions. First, pursuant to Federal Rule of Criminal Procedure 16(d)(1), which governs the use of protective orders with respect to discovery in criminal cases, the Court "may at any time order that the discovery or inspection be denied, restricted, or deferred, or make such other order as is appropriate."

Second, pursuant to Section 3 of the Classified Information Procedures Act ("CIPA"), Pub.L. No. 96–456, 94 Stat. 2025 (1980), codified at 18 U.S.C. app. 3 § 3, the Court has the authority to "issue an order to protect against the disclosure of any classified information disclosed by the United States to any defendant in any criminal case in a district court of the United States."

Third, pursuant to Security Procedures Chief Justice Burger promulgated under Section 9 of CIPA, "[t]he government may obtain information by any lawful means concerning the trustworthiness of persons associated with the defense and may bring such information to the attention of the court for the court's consideration in framing an appropriate protective order pursuant to Section 3 of the Act."

The Court is therefore empowered to take information regarding the background of Defense counsel in this case, gleaned from an investigation conducted by the United States Attorney's Office, and consider that information in framing a protective order that attempts to prevent disclosure of confidential information. The Moving Defendants have argued, however, that the rules do not allow the Court to direct Defense counsel to participate in any clearance process and, in addition, that use of such a compulsory procedure would be both unconstitutional and undesirable.

We are therefore presented with three questions. (1) Do the rules governing cases involving classified information permit the Court to direct counsel to apply for security clearance? (2) Is it constitutional to require counsel to utilize a process in which DOJ makes an initial recommendation as to clearance applications but that leaves final authority to resolve all clearance matters with the Court? (3) If use of this procedure is in fact permissible, should the Court direct counsel for the Moving Defendants to submit to it or, in the alternative, should the Court allow counsel to "opt out" and therefore force the United States Attorney's Office to conduct its own investigation into each attorney's background and to furnish that background information to the Court, pursuant to Section 5 of the Chief Justice's Security Procedures? There is a remarkable paucity of case law addressing these questions and they certainly appear to be matters of first impression within this Circuit.

The Moving Defendants argue that the legislative history of CIPA and the circumstances surrounding Chief Justice Burger's promulgation of the Security Procedures create an inference that neither Congress nor the Chief Justice vested the Court with the authority to compel Defense counsel to undergo a DOJ-initiated security clearance procedure. We think the sounder reading of the available material indicates that although neither Congress nor the Chief Justice sought to impose a mandatory clearance requirement in all cases involving classified information, they did not attempt to foreclose resort to such a requirement in all circumstances.

CIPA and the accompanying Security Procedures create a system by which the trial court has wide latitude to impose reasonable restrictions likely to prevent the unauthorized disclosure of classified information. See, e.g., S.Rep. 96–823 (1980), reprint in 1980 U.S.C.C.A.N. 4294 ("The details of each [protective] order are fashioned by the trial judge according to the circumstances of the particular case" . . . and "under what conditions the materials may be reviewed"). . . .

The text and structure of both CIPA and the Security Procedures therefore create a presumption that the Court possesses the authority to require Defense counsel to seek security clearance before the Court will provide them with access to classified materials. Even conceding that the history surrounding enactment of these provisions is at times murky, there is simply little to support the contention that Congress or the Chief Justice acted to prohibit the courts from utilizing a clearance requirement in every circumstance. . . .

We recognize that this position may appear to be at odds with the result in United States v. Jolliff, 548 F.Supp. 232 (D.Md.1981), which stated that "Section 5 [of CIPA] does not provide the Court with authority to make submission to a security clearance requirement a prerequisite to representation of a defendant in a case involving classified information." Id. at 233. . . .

The Government distinguishes . . . [this case] on the ground that. . . . [this analysis is] limited to Section 5 of CIPA and make[s] no reference to Section 3. We find the Government's reading . . . persuasive. We also note that the relevant clause from Jolliff may well be obiter dictum as the Government apparently did not request clearance in that case.

Even if we were to read Jolliff . . . as holding that CIPA does not permit any clearance requirement, however, we would depart from their analyses. We simply see no indication that Congress or the Chief Justice aimed to preclude resort to compulsory clearance of counsel in all circumstances. To the contrary, both CIPA and the Security Procedures consistently leave the most sensitive questions surrounding classified information to be resolved in the sound discretion of the District Courts. We therefore conclude that our authority under the Federal Rules of Criminal Procedure, CIPA, and the Chief Justice's Security Procedures encompasses a power to require counsel to seek security clearance.

We must also evaluate whether it is consistent with the Federal Constitution to impose a clearance requirement on Defense counsel in this case. The Moving Defendants have asserted that imposition of a mandatory

DOJ-initiated clearance procedure violates their rights under the Sixth Amendment. Our starting point must be the Supreme Court's conclusion that the Sixth Amendment does not promise a defendant his choice of counsel but rather aims to guarantee that each criminal defendant receives an effective advocate.

In essence, the Moving Defendants' argument boils down to the claim that any DOJ-initiated security clearance procedure necessarily vests the Government with veto power over the Moving Defendants' choice of counsel and that the philosophy behind such a system is fundamentally inimical to the adversarial process. Although we agree that it would be flatly unconstitutional to grant the Government an unfettered ability to remove any Defendant's counsel, the facts of this case are a great distance from the parade of horribles raised by the Moving Defendants.

First, the facts do not indicate that the Government unduly delayed before requesting this procedure, such as might allow for an inference that the Government's true motivation was to harass or otherwise interfere with the Moving Defendants' pretrial preparations. The Moving Defendants argue forcefully that the Government erred by failing to advise counsel prior to appointment, or immediately thereafter, of the likely need to seek clearance. We do not believe that the Government's conduct gives rise to a concern that the clearance requirement is designed to interfere with any counsel's ability to meaningfully represent his client.

On November 3, 1998, at the parties' first meeting, the Government advised Defense counsel "of the realistic probability that there would be classified information in the case, and that prudence dictated that they obtain security clearances to be permitted to receive such information." Two days later, the Government submitted a letter to the Court, which was also sent to counsel for each of the Defendants, summarizing the substance of this meeting. This letter contains the following passage:

> The Government advised defense counsel that it is anticipated that during the litigation and trial of this matter the Government and defense counsel will have to deal with classified material in some manner. . . . The Government also suggested that while it is too early to have a specific conversation about how classified information may become pertinent to the litigation of this case, defense counsel may wish to apply (through the FBI) for security clearances which take some time to obtain. . . . [T]he Government will do whatever it can to assist in the expedited processing of security clearances for any defense counsel (or staff of the Court) seeking to obtain clearances. Given that past experience has shown that CIPA litigation can be time-consuming, it is respectfully suggested that any defense counsel

who intend to seek a clearance do so promptly to avoid delay down the road when the issues crystallize.

. . .

We believe that the Government's notifications to counsel were sufficiently prompt to eliminate any inference of purposeful delay. The Moving Defendants assert that their counsel had already invested significant time in the case by the November 3 meeting, but the litigation was plainly in its infancy at that time and we see no reason to believe that the Government's request was aimed to disrupt established relationships between counsel and their clients.

In sum, the magnitude of the Government's investigation, the limited work Defense counsel had yet performed on behalf of their clients, and the fact that the Government advised Defense counsel about the need for clearance at the parties' first face-to-face meeting in early November, all serve to eliminate any inference that the Government purposefully delayed in requesting clearances to force a change of counsel mid-stream or for the purpose of harassment. We are simply not faced with a situation in which an eleventh hour request appears designed to disrupt counsels' preparations or to drive them from this litigation.

Second, we think the Moving Defendants overstate the danger that one of their attorneys might be arbitrarily dismissed at the behest of the prosecution. The CSO will be an officer of the Court, rather than a member of the prosecution, and will be prohibited from sharing any information regarding clearance applications, including their outcomes, with members of the prosecution.

Further, in the unlikely event that DOJ officials recommend that the Court deny any counsel's application for clearance, this result would be appealable both within the DOJ as well as directly to the Court. The Court will of course remain the ultimate arbiter of disputes surrounding the security clearance applications and will be available to insure both proper respect for counsels' confidentiality and that no applications are denied for improper reasons. See, e.g., United States v. Musa, 833 F.Supp. 752, 756–57 (E.D.Mo.1993) (stating that if "the CSO should determine that any person should not obtain a security clearance," the Court will "conduct an ex parte hearing to determine" that person's eligibility to see classified materials, that "[o]nly the CSO and defense counsel will be heard on this issue," and that "the prosecution will not be notified of the hearing or allowed to participate in it"). Although we recognize the Moving Defendants' concern that the Government not be given the unfettered power to disqualify their present counsel, we think the procedures governing the clearance process, when combined with the Court's vigilance in responding to questions of potential abuse in the application process, will be sufficient to protect the Moving Defendants' rights.

The exceptional facts of this case decidedly warrant some inquiry into counsels' backgrounds to minimize the risk of the unauthorized disclosure of classified information. Counsel for the Moving Defendants conceded as much at oral argument. We note that the exceptional facts alleged in the indictment also require clearance of Court personnel and members of the Government who will come into contact with classified information. The circumstances precipitating CIPA's enactment make it abundantly clear that it is easier and more effective to prevent the release of classified information in advance than to attempt to undo the damage of unauthorized disclosures after the fact.

. . .

The concerns are heightened in this case because the Government's investigation is ongoing, which increases the possibility that unauthorized disclosures might place additional lives in danger. In addition, the Government has alleged that the Defendants are part of a conspiracy whose members have previously gained access to unfiled court documents and forwarded those documents to other members of the conspiracy. The case therefore involves special circumstances warranting particular control over the flow of classified information, such as have already prompted the Court to impose restrictive conditions of confinement on the Defendants and which formed the basis of the protective order that the Court entered in December 1998.

Our insistence that every person who comes into contact with classified information in this litigation undergo some objective evaluation is, of course, no commentary on the reputations of the Defense counsel in this case. The fact remains that it is practically impossible to remedy the damage of an unauthorized disclosure ex post and we refuse to await the possibility of repairing what in this case might be a particularly disastrous security breach when reasonable measures could have prevented the disclosure altogether. We believe it is appropriate to require some form of clearance on the facts we have before us.

Having concluded that a clearance requirement is warranted, we must decide whether to utilize the DOJ-initiated clearance procedure or the alternative course discussed previously, by which the United States Attorney's Office would investigate counsel for the Moving Defendants and advise the Court of the results. The issue therefore is not "whether?" but "by whom?" the inquiry will be conducted. The Government suggests that it be done initially by the CSO, without involvement by the prosecution.[4]

---

[4] The parties dispute the significance of the court's actions in another classified information case in the Eastern District of New York, United States v. Pappas, which are apparently unreported save for a Second Circuit decision that does not address the issues that presently concern us. See 94 F.3d 795 (2d Cir.1996). In Pappas, all defense counsel apparently sought clearance but the CSO expressed concern about one application. The Court thereafter entered a modified protective order granting that counsel access to at least some of the materials, albeit on

Counsel for one of the Moving Defendants has suggested that it be conducted by the United States Attorney's Office without counsels' cooperation and with a report to be made in the first instance to the Court.

Aside from the Moving Defendants' philosophical objection to the DOJ-initiated procedure on the ground that it requires their counsel to participate actively in certain phases of the review, we see not a single advantage to any investigation conducted by the United States Attorney's Office. Such an inquiry would certainly be more time-consuming and expensive than the DOJ-initiated procedure and would, in all likelihood, prove more intrusive and fundamentally inconsistent with the adversarial process.

Moreover, given that it presently takes DOJ more than two months to process clearance applications, we can only surmise how long it would take the United States Attorney's Office, which does not have the same expertise in that particular area, to conduct an equally probing investigation without the underlying individual's consent. It is inescapable that such a system would require a far lengthier investigation, during which time counsel for the Moving Defendants would of course be precluded from viewing classified information.

In addition, this approach would force the Court to make clearance determinations in the first instance without the reasoned judgment of the Department of Justice, the agency with the greatest expertise in this area. We find it entirely preferable to allow experts in clearance matters—who will be bound by strict rules of confidentiality—to consider each counsel's application initially rather than to resort to a system whereby the Court and the United States Attorney's Office are forced to act as amateur sleuths. In the likely event that counsels' clearance applications are unremarkable, the DOJ-initiated procedure offers the very real possibility that the fewest possible individuals will learn anything whatsoever about counsels' backgrounds.

Given the nature of the potential classified information and the special circumstances surrounding this case, we conclude that counsel must submit to the DOJ-initiated security clearance procedure should they wish to have access to classified information. Accordingly, the Moving Defendants' motion is denied.

The request to intervene by counsel for Defendant Odeh is sparsely briefed on both sides. Defendant Odeh's original brief only alluded to counsel's personal rights and counsel made no formal request to intervene until oral argument, after all briefs had been filed. Our research has not revealed any reported case, either from within this Circuit or elsewhere, in

---

a restricted basis. In the event that similar circumstances arise here, the Court will consider entering an amended protective order. Until that time, however, Defense counsel who wish to have access to classified information must seek clearance.

which a court entertained a request similar to that proffered by counsel to Defendant Odeh.

Here, by contrast, counsel has asserted his own privacy rights. The Supreme Court has referred to two analytically distinct privacy interests: "[o]ne is the individual interest in avoiding disclosure of personal matters, and another is the interest in independence in making certain kinds of important decisions." Whalen v. Roe, 429 U.S. 589, 599–600, 97 S.Ct. 869, 51 L.Ed.2d 64 (1977) (footnote omitted). The former right, which the Second Circuit has characterized "as a right to 'confidentiality,'" Doe v. City of New York, 15 F.3d 264, 267 (2d Cir.1994), is implicated here because counsel objects to being required to disclose private information. We therefore do not quarrel with counsel's assertion that, if permitted to intervene, he could assert some valid interest in not being forced to reveal certain personal information.

The presence of a valid interest, however, does not terminate our inquiry. See, e.g., Nixon v. Administrator of Gen. Servs., 433 U.S. 425, 458, 97 S.Ct. 2777, 53 L.Ed.2d 867 (1977). The Second Circuit has explained that claims for violation of a privacy right, such as that asserted by counsel, should be examined using intermediate scrutiny. See Barry v. City of New York, 712 F.2d 1554, 1559 (2d Cir.1983). Under this level of review, the Court balances the competing interests of counsel and the Government and must uphold the policy if it is "substantially related to an important governmental objective," Clark v. Jeter, 486 U.S. 456, 461, 108 S.Ct. 1910, 100 L.Ed.2d 465 (1988), or, in Second Circuit parlance, if the policy "is designed to further a substantial governmental interest and does not land very wide of any reasonable mark in making its classifications."

Here, there is plainly a substantial governmental objective in guarding against the unauthorized disclosure of classified information, this interest manifestly outweighs counsel's desire not to disclose personal information needed to conduct a thorough background check, and the clearance procedure presents a reasonable method for effecting the Government's legitimate goals.

Counsel has simply provided no authority, and we are aware of none, that would sustain his objections with respect to the clearance procedure. Any faithful balancing of the relevant interests must end with the conclusion that counsel's own privacy rights are outweighed by the Government's right to protect highly classified information, the unauthorized disclosure of which could cause irreparable harm to our national security. Accordingly, counsel's motion to intervene is denied.

QUESTIONS AND NOTES

1.   United States v. Al-Arian, 267 F. Supp.2d 1258 (M.D. Fla. 2003):

At the status conference, co-counsel for Al-Arian contended that this Court would violate their constitutional rights to privacy if it required them to submit forms and obtain a security clearance as part of their representation of Al-Arian. As an initial matter, this Court would note that the government has indicated in nearly every hearing since this case began that a majority of the telephone recordings were classified. Moreover, the government, the magistrate judge presiding over this case, and even this Court have repeatedly told defense counsel that they should go ahead and apply for security clearances to prevent delay of this case. Al-Arian's counsel never raised an objection nor a concern about obtaining a security clearance.[21] Now three months after their appointment, for the first time, they raise this issue.

This Court does not dispute that counsel will disclose personal matters as a result of completing the security clearance packet and the subsequent investigation.[22] This Court does not take issue with counsel's assertion that they have a privacy interest in avoiding disclosure of personal matters

The Eleventh Circuit and the former Fifth Circuit have held, however, that the fact that a privacy interest is implicated does not end the inquiry. Instead, these courts have held that the constitutional right to confidentiality is overcome if the government has a legitimate interest that outweighs the individual's privacy interest.

In this case, counsel's right to confidentiality is weighed against the United States' interest in protecting classified information. This Court cannot think of a more compelling or substantial interest that the United States possesses than protection of classified information. The Supreme Court of the United States has stated that without adequate procedures to protect classified information the United States will suffer irreparable harm without the ability to seek redress. See Snepp v. United States, 444 U.S. 507, 512–15, 62 L.Ed.2d 704, 100 S.Ct. 763 (1980) (per curiam). Requiring lawyers and their staffs to submit to a security clearance procedure to protect classified information outweighs an individual's privacy interest. Most recently, the Southern District of New York similarly concluded, applying a higher standard (intermediate scrutiny), that

---

21 Indeed, if co-counsel felt so strongly about obtaining a security clearance, one has to wonder why they would accept the court appointment to this case. It should have been obvious to counsel that a security clearance was likely to be required and they should have refused appointment.

22 This Court would note for the record that it is requiring its whole staff to undergo this procedure also.

CHAPTER 10

DETENTION IN MILITARY CUSTODY

■ ■ ■

A. INTRODUCTION

The military detention of terrorist suspects, the subject of this chapter, raises a wide range of issues—e.g. what is the relevant source of legal authority to detain militarily; is the legal authority constitutionally based or is there statutory authority; does the authority extend to U.S. citizens as well as non-U.S. citizens; what is the standard for deciding whether a suspected terrorist can be held in military detention; does it extend to persons arrested in the U.S. as well as persons captured abroad; does the authority to militarily detain apply to all terrorists or only a subset? what kind of process must be provided in deciding whether a person can be militarily detained; is there a right of habeas corpus; how long can detention go on; must there be some periodic review of a detainee's status; must the detention be tied to and preliminary to criminal prosecution? Detaining persons in military custody is closely tied to the question whether we are "at war," or engaged in an armed conflict, and if so, with whom? What are the criteria for determining whether we are at war?

The matters treated in the chapter include: the AUMF, the Authorization to Use Military Force, passed by the Congress in the immediate wake of the terrorist attack on September 11, 2011, and whether it is currently an adequate source of legal authority for the type of cases that are arising; and the labeling as enemy combatants of two persons arrested in the United States; their cases are treated in some depth here. The chapter also deals extensively with the detention in Guantanamo of persons seized abroad and their right to habeas corpus review in U.S. courts as well as the administrative process developed in the military for determining their status. Disposition of those still detained at Guantanamo, efforts to close that facility and relevant changes in policy from the administrations of Bush, Obama and Trump are also addressed.

B. LEGAL BASIS FOR EXTENDED MILITARY DETENTION; PROCESS DUE DETAINEES MILITARILY DETAINED IN THE UNITED STATES

1. THE AUMF

Within a week after the attacks that occurred on September 11, 2001, at the behest of the administration, Congress passed the following Joint Resolution, S.J. Res. 23, 107th Cong., 115 Stat. 224 (2001), authorizing the use of military force, and subsequently generally referred to as the AUMF, which was signed by the President on September 18, 2001:

Public Law 107–40

107th Congress

Joint Resolution

To authorize the use of United States Armed Forces against those responsible for the recent attacks launched against the United States.

Whereas, on September 11, 2001, acts of treacherous violence were committed against the United States and its citizens; and

Whereas, such acts render it both necessary and appropriate that the United States exercise its rights to self-defense and to protect United States citizens both at home and abroad; and

Whereas, in light of the threat to the national security and foreign policy of the United States posed by these grave acts of violence; and

Whereas, such acts continue to pose an unusual and extraordinary threat to the national security and foreign policy of the United States; and

Whereas, the President has authority under the Constitution to take action to deter and prevent acts of international terrorism against the United States: Now, therefore, be it

Resolved by the Senate and House of Representatives of the United States of America in Congress assembled,

SECTION 1.   SHORT TITLE.

This joint resolution may be cited as the "Authorization for Use of Military Force."

SECTION 2.   AUTHORIZATION FOR USE OF UNITED STATES ARMED FORCES.

(a) IN GENERAL.—That the President is authorized to use all necessary and appropriate force against those nations, organizations, or persons he determines planned, authorized, committed, or aided the terrorist attacks that occurred on September 11, 2001, or harbored such organizations or persons, in order to prevent any future acts of international terrorism against the United States by such nations, organizations or persons.

(b) WAR POWERS RESOLUTION REQUIREMENTS.—

(1) SPECIFIC STATUTORY AUTHORIZATION.— Consistent with section 8(a)(1) of the War Powers Resolution, the Congress declares that this section is intended to constitute specific statutory authorization within the meaning of section 5(b) of the War Powers Resolution.

(2) APPLICABILITY OF OTHER REQUIREMENTS.— Nothing in this resolution supersedes any requirement of the War Powers Resolution.

Approved September 18, 2001.

A NOTE ON THE AUMF

As of the date of this writing, the Authorization to Use Military Force signed by the President on September 18, 2011 is the, or a, source of legal authority for President to use military force against "those nations, organizations, or persons he determines planned, authorized, committed, or aided the terrorist attacks that occurred on September 11, 2001, or harbored such organizations or persons. . . ." Al Qaeda is not mentioned by name in the formulation, perhaps because at the time the Joint Resolution was passed, al Qaeda's role had not been confirmed. Subsequently, because al Qaeda was determined to have been responsible for the attacks and all of those who were identified as participating were persons associated with al Qaeda, the AUMF has been viewed as authorizing the use of military force against al Qaeda and its affiliates and individual members. . . .

The Bush administration interpreted the executive branch's authority in the fight against international terrorism very broadly relying on the AUMF, the President's authority as commander-in-chief and the notion of inherent presidential authority. Note that the last of the Whereas clauses in the preamble to the AUMF stated,

Whereas, the President has authority under the Constitution to take action to deter and prevent acts of international terrorism against the United States. . . .

This expansive interpretation was relied upon to support a number of controversial actions that were subsequently undertaken by the Bush administration, for example, in connection with the NSA electronic surveillance controversy, see ch. 5 supra. Some of the views advanced by lawyers working in the Bush administration at the time regarding presidential authority are controversial and have been rejected by many constitutional law scholars.

The Obama administration did not take as expansive a view as did the Bush administration of the President's inherent authority and as Commander-in-Chief. The decisive moment may have been the filing of a memorandum on March 13, 2009 in the In re Guantanamo Bay Detainee Litigation, Misc. No. 08-442 (TFH), regarding the government's authority to detain the persons held at Guantanamo. In this memorandum, rather than relying, in part, on inherent and commander-in-chief authority (which had been expressly relied upon for example, in approving the Military Order, see immediately below), the government relied exclusively on "the detention authority conferred by the AUMF" as informed by the laws of war. Note that the premise underlying this legal position is that the President's authority to take military action in this realm is limited by congressional legislation and may be modified or repealed by the Congress.

Presently, concerns relating to the scope of presidential authority under the AUMF have focused on a different issue. While there are still branches of al Qaeda operating, and military actions relating to them can easily be justified under the AUMF, a major focus of U.S. military action and its incidents in the past few years has been against ISIS, Islamic State of Iraq and Syria, also called ISIL, Islamic State of Iraq and the Levant. See Clint Watts, ISIS and al Qaeda Race to the Bottom, Foreign Affairs, November 23, 2015, https://www.foreignaffairs.com/articles/2015-11-23/isis-and-al-qaeda-race-bottom, referring to the fact that al Qaeda and ISIS "broke up in 2013" and thereafter were in competition. See also Insite Blog on Terrorism and Extremism, Assessing the ISIS–al-Qaeda Split: Introduction, http://news.siteintelgroup.com/blog/index.php/about-us/21-jihad/4388-assessing-the-isis-al-qaeda-split-introduction.

Is it significant whether ISIS broke off from al Qaeda or is simply another terrorist organization that is in competition with al Qaeda but never was part of al Qaeda? The U.S. government appears to have relied upon the fact that ISIS was once a part of al Qaeda and then broke away to argue that the authority to act against al Qaeda applies as well to ISIS. But evidence that that claim is shaky can be found in the fact that the Obama administration itself at one point sent a proposal to Congress to adopt a limited authorization to use military force against ISIS that would also have left the 2001 AUMF untouched. See Jim Acosta and Jeremy Diamond, Obama ISIS Fight Request Sent to Congress, CNN, February 12, 2015, http://www.cnn.com/2015/02/11/politics/isis-aumf-white-house-congress/index.html. That limited authorization was not acted upon by the Congress. Meanwhile other proposals to repeal or amend the 2001 AUMF have periodically been circulated in the Congress. See, e.g., Karoun Demirjian, New AUMF proposals to combat ISIS revive debate, but may not resolve differences, Power Post, December 10, 2015, https://www.washingtonpost.com/news/powerpost/wp/2015/12/10/new-aumf-proposals-to-combat-isis-revive-debate-but-may-not-resolve-differences/?utm_term=.8cc32 45a6a76. None of these proposals has been enacted.

Accordingly, the issue of whether the authority provided by the AUMF extends to the armed conflict with ISIS has neither been clarified by legislation nor, thus far, resolved by adjudication. Nor, as we shall see further along in these materials, does it appear that the government has been looking for opportunities to test the issue in court.

Is the AUMF a Declaration of War, or the legal equivalent? How is it treated by the courts? See, for example, Hamdi v. Rumsfeld, infra, this section.

We shall have occasion to return to the issues of legal authority under the AUMF as we address specific questions of authority to act against terrorists that are raised throughout this volume.

2. THE MILITARY ORDER ISSUED BY THE PRESIDENT

On November 13, 2001, two months after September 11, 2001, President Bush issued a Military Order that provided for the detention of certain categories of persons involved in acts of international terrorism and prosecuting them before military commissions. In issuing the Order, the government again expressly relied on the inherent authority of the President, his authority as Commander in Chief of the Armed Forces, and the afore-mentioned congressional Authorization for Use of Military Force (AUMF)) (Public Law 107–40, 115 Stat. 224), and also on two long-standing legislative provisions 10 U.S.C. §§ 821 and 836 which are reproduced in Chapter 11, infra.

Notice

Detention, Treatment, and Trial of Certain Non-Citizens in the War Against Terrorism.

66 Fed. Reg. 57833.

By the authority vested in me as President and as Commander in Chief of the Armed Forces of the United States by the Constitution and the laws of the United States of America, including the Authorization for Use of Military Force Joint Resolution (Public Law 107–40, 115 Stat. 224) and sections 821 and 836 of title 10, United States Code, it is hereby ordered as follows:

Sec. 1. Findings.

(a) International terrorists, including members of al Qaida, have carried out attacks on United States diplomatic and military personnel and facilities abroad and on citizens and property within the United States on a scale that has created a state of armed conflict that requires the use of the United States Armed Forces.

(b) In light of grave acts of terrorism and threats of terrorism, including the terrorist attacks on September 11, 2001, on the headquarters of the United States Department of Defense in the national capital region, on the World Trade Center in New

York, and on civilian aircraft such as in Pennsylvania, I proclaimed a national emergency on September 14, 2001 (Proc. 7463, Declaration of National Emergency by Reason of Certain Terrorist Attacks).

(c) Individuals acting alone and in concert involved in international terrorism possess both the capability and the intention to undertake further terrorist attacks against the United States that, if not detected and prevented, will cause mass deaths, mass injuries, and massive destruction of property, and may place at risk the continuity of the operations of the United States Government.

(d) The ability of the United States to protect the United States and its citizens, and to help its allies and other cooperating nations protect their nations and their citizens, from such further terrorist attacks depends in significant part upon using the United States Armed Forces to identify terrorists and those who support them, to disrupt their activities, and to eliminate their ability to conduct or support such attacks.

(e) To protect the United States and its citizens, and for the effective conduct of military operations and prevention of terrorist attacks, it is necessary for individuals subject to this order pursuant to section 2 hereof to be detained, and, when tried, to be tried for violations of the laws of war and other applicable laws by military tribunals.

(f) Given the danger to the safety of the United States and the nature of international terrorism, and to the extent provided by and under this order, I find consistent with section 836 of title 10, United States Code, that it is not practicable to apply in military commissions under this order the principles of law and the rules of evidence generally recognized in the trial of criminal cases in the United States district courts.

(g) Having fully considered the magnitude of the potential deaths, injuries, and property destruction that would result from potential acts of terrorism against the United States, and the probability that such acts will occur, I have determined that an extraordinary emergency exists for national defense purposes, that this emergency constitutes an urgent and compelling government interest, and that issuance of this order is necessary to meet the emergency.

Sec. 2. Definition and Policy.

(a) The term "individual subject to this order" shall mean any individual who is not a United States citizen with respect to whom I determine from time to time in writing that:

(1) there is reason to believe that such individual, at the relevant times,

(i)   is or was a member of the organization known as al Qaida;

(ii) has engaged in, aided or abetted, or conspired to commit, acts of international terrorism, or acts in preparation therefor, that have caused, threaten to cause, or have as their aim to cause, injury to or adverse effects on the United States, its citizens, national security, foreign policy, or economy; or

(iii) has knowingly harbored one or more individuals described in subparagraphs (i) or (ii) of subsection 2(a)(1) of this order; and

(2) it is in the interest of the United States that such individual be subject to this order.

(b) It is the policy of the United States that the Secretary of Defense shall take all necessary measures to ensure that any individual subject to this order is detained in accordance with section 3, and, if the individual is to be tried, that such individual is tried only in accordance with section 4.

(c) It is further the policy of the United States that any individual subject to this order who is not already under the control of the Secretary of Defense but who is under the control of any other officer or agent of the United States or any State shall, upon delivery of a copy of such written determination to such officer or agent, forthwith be placed under the control of the Secretary of Defense.

Sec. 3. Detention Authority of the Secretary of Defense. Any individual subject to this order shall be—

(a) detained at an appropriate location designated by the Secretary of Defense outside or within the United States;

(b) treated humanely, without any adverse distinction based on race, color, religion, gender, birth, wealth, or any similar criteria;

(c) afforded adequate food, drinking water, shelter, clothing, and medical treatment;

(d) allowed the free exercise of religion consistent with the requirements of such detention; and

(e) detained in accordance with such other conditions as the Secretary of Defense may prescribe.

Sec. 4. Authority of the Secretary of Defense Regarding Trials of Individuals Subject to this Order.

(a) Any individual subject to this order shall, when tried, be tried by military commission for any and all offenses triable by military commission that such individual is alleged to have committed, and may be punished in accordance with the penalties provided under applicable law, including life imprisonment or death.

(b) As a military function and in light of the findings in section 1, including subsection (f) thereof, the Secretary of Defense shall issue such orders and regulations, including orders for the appointment of one or more military commissions, as may be necessary to carry out subsection (a) of this section.

(c) Orders and regulations issued under subsection (b) of this section shall include, but not be limited to, rules for the conduct of the proceedings of military commissions, including pretrial, trial, and post-trial procedures, modes of proof, issuance of process, and qualifications of attorneys, which shall at a minimum provide for—

(1) military commissions to sit at any time and any place, consistent with such guidance regarding time and place as the Secretary of Defense may provide;

(2) a full and fair trial, with the military commission sitting as the triers of both fact and law;

(3) admission of such evidence as would, in the opinion of the presiding officer of the military commission (or instead, if any other member of the commission so requests at the time the presiding officer renders that opinion, the opinion of the commission rendered at that time by a majority of the commission), have probative value to a reasonable person;

(4) in a manner consistent with the protection of information classified or classifiable under Executive Order 12958 of April 17, 1995, as amended, or any successor Executive Order, protected by statute or rule from unauthorized disclosure, or otherwise protected by law, (A) the handling of, admission into evidence of, and access to materials and information, and (B) the conduct, closure of, and access to proceedings;

(5) conduct of the prosecution by one or more attorneys designated by the Secretary of Defense and conduct of the defense by attorneys for the individual subject to this order;

(6) conviction only upon the concurrence of two-thirds of the members of the commission present at the time of the vote, a majority being present;

(7) sentencing only upon the concurrence of two-thirds of the members of the commission present at the time of the vote, a majority being present; and

(8) submission of the record of the trial, including any conviction or sentence, for review and final decision by me or by the Secretary of Defense if so designated by me for that purpose.

Sec. 5. Obligation of Other Agencies to Assist the Secretary of Defense.

Departments, agencies, entities, and officers of the United States shall, to the maximum extent permitted by law, provide to the Secretary of Defense such assistance as he may request to implement this order.

Sec. 6. Additional Authorities of the Secretary of Defense.

(a) As a military function and in light of the findings in section 1, the Secretary of Defense shall issue such orders and regulations as may be necessary to carry out any of the provisions of this order.

(b) The Secretary of Defense may perform any of his functions or duties, and may exercise any of the powers provided to him under this order (other than under section 4(c)(8) hereof) in accordance with section 113(d) of title 10, United States Code.

Sec. 7. Relationship to Other Law and Forums.

(a) Nothing in this order shall be construed to—

(1) authorize the disclosure of state secrets to any person not otherwise authorized to have access to them;

(2) limit the authority of the President as Commander in Chief of the Armed Forces or the power of the President to grant reprieves and pardons; or

(3) limit the lawful authority of the Secretary of Defense, any military commander, or any other officer or agent of the United States or of any State to detain or try any person who is not an individual subject to this order.

(b) With respect to any individual subject to this order—

(1) military tribunals shall have exclusive jurisdiction with respect to offenses by the individual; and

(2) the individual shall not be privileged to seek any remedy or maintain any proceeding, directly or indirectly, or to have any such remedy or proceeding sought on the individual's behalf, in

    (i) any court of the United States, or any State thereof,

    (ii) any court of any foreign nation, or

    (iii) any international tribunal.

(c) This order is not intended to and does not create any right, benefit, or privilege, substantive or procedural, enforceable at law or equity by any party, against the United States, its departments, agencies, or other entities, its officers or employees, or any other person.

(d) For purposes of this order, the term "State" includes any State, district, territory, or possession of the United States.

(e) I reserve the authority to direct the Secretary of Defense, atany time hereafter, to transfer to a governmental authority control of any individual subject to this order. Nothing in this order shall be construed to limit the authority of any such governmental authority to prosecute any individual for whom control is transferred.

Sec. 8. Publication.

This order shall be published in the Federal Register.

GEORGE W. BUSH

THE WHITE HOUSE,

November 13, 2001

A NOTE ON THE PRESIDENT'S MILITARY ORDER

The Military Order promulgated by the President about two months after the passage of the AUMF has a number of features that merit attention. It makes even clearer reliance, in this quasi-legislative context, on the constitutional authority of the President as well as his role as Commander-in-chief, in addition to relying on legislative actions by the Congress. It also makes clear that "individuals subject to this order" are persons who are members of al Qaeda or persons who engage in international terrorism that adversely affects U.S. interests. The order also only applies to persons who are not U.S. citizens. Does this use of military authority extend to international terrorists apart from those linked to al Qaeda? How does it relate to the enemy specified in the AUMF?

The Military Order provided authority for two sets of actions, detention of "individuals subject to this order" and trial by military commission of offenses committed by individuals subject to this order. It established general parameters for these military commission trials, and subsequently-issued

be not to the lack of certainty regarding the date on which the conflict will end, but to the substantial prospect of perpetual detention. We recognize that the national security underpinnings of the "war on terror," although crucially important, are broad and malleable. As the Government concedes, "given its unconventional nature, the current conflict is unlikely to end with a formal cease-fire agreement." The prospect Hamdi raises is therefore not far-fetched. If the Government does not consider this unconventional war won for two generations, and if it maintains during that time that Hamdi might, if released, rejoin forces fighting against the United States, then the position it has taken throughout the litigation of this case suggests that Hamdi's detention could last for the rest of his life.

It is a clearly established principle of the law of war that detention may last no longer than active hostilities. See Article 118 of the Geneva Convention (III) Relative to the Treatment of Prisoners of War, Aug. 12, 1949, [1955] 6 U.S.T. 3316, 3406, T.I.A.S. No. 3364 ("Prisoners of war shall be released and repatriated without delay after the cessation of active hostilities"). See also . . . Paust, Judicial Power to Determine the Status and Rights of Persons Detained without Trial, 44 Harv. Int'l L.J. 503, 510–511 (2003) (prisoners of war "can be detained during an armed conflict, but the detaining country must release and repatriate them 'without delay after the cessation of active hostilities,' unless they are being lawfully prosecuted or have been lawfully convicted of crimes and are serving sentences". . . .

Hamdi contends that the AUMF does not authorize indefinite or perpetual detention. Certainly, we agree that indefinite detention for the purpose of interrogation is not authorized. Further, we understand Congress' grant of authority for the use of "necessary and appropriate force" to include the authority to detain for the duration of the relevant conflict, and our understanding is based on longstanding law-of-war principles. If the practical circumstances of a given conflict are entirely unlike those of the conflicts that informed the development of the law of war, that understanding may unravel. But that is not the situation we face as of this date. Active combat operations against Taliban fighters apparently are ongoing in Afghanistan. . . . The United States may detain, for the duration of these hostilities, individuals legitimately determined to be Taliban combatants who "engaged in an armed conflict against the United States." If the record establishes that United States troops are still involved in active combat in Afghanistan, those detentions are part of the exercise of "necessary and appropriate force," and therefore are authorized by the AUMF.

Ex parte Milligan, 4 Wall. 2, 125, 18 L.Ed. 281 (1866), does not undermine our holding about the Government's authority to seize enemy combatants, as we define that term today. In that case, the Court made repeated reference to the fact that its inquiry into whether the military tribunal had jurisdiction to try and punish Milligan turned in large part on the fact that Milligan was not a prisoner of war, but a resident of Indiana arrested while at home there. That fact was central to its conclusion. Had Milligan been captured while he was assisting Confederate soldiers by carrying a rifle against Union troops on a Confederate battlefield, the holding of the Court might well have been different. The Court's repeated explanations that Milligan was not a prisoner of war suggest that had these different circumstances been present he could have been detained under military authority for the duration of the conflict, whether or not he was a citizen.[1]

. . .

Quirin was a unanimous opinion. It both postdates and clarifies Milligan, providing us with the most apposite precedent that we have on the question of whether citizens may be detained in such circumstances. Brushing aside such precedent—particularly when doing so gives rise to a host of new questions never dealt with by this Court—is unjustified and unwise.

. . .

III

Even in cases in which the detention of enemy combatants is legally authorized, there remains the question of what process is constitutionally due to a citizen who disputes his enemy-combatant status. Hamdi argues that he is owed a meaningful and timely hearing and that "extra-judicial detention [that] begins and ends with the submission of an affidavit based on third-hand hearsay" does not comport with the Fifth and Fourteenth Amendments. The Government counters that any more process than was provided below would be both unworkable and "constitutionally intolerable." Our resolution of this dispute requires a careful examination both of the writ of habeas corpus, which Hamdi now seeks to employ as a mechanism of judicial review, and of the Due Process Clause, which informs the procedural contours of that mechanism in this instance.

A

Though they reach radically different conclusions on the process that ought to attend the present proceeding, the parties begin on common ground. All agree that, absent suspension, the writ of habeas corpus remains available to every individual detained within the United States. U.S. Const., Art. I, § 9, cl. 2 ("The Privilege of the Writ of Habeas Corpus shall not be suspended, unless when in Cases of Rebellion or Invasion the

---

[1]   Here the basis asserted for detention by the military is that Hamdi was carrying a weapon against American troops on a foreign battlefield; that is, that he was an enemy combatant. The legal category of enemy combatant has not been elaborated upon in great detail. The permissible bounds of the category will be defined by the lower courts as subsequent cases are presented to them.

public Safety may require it")... . At all other times, it has remained a critical check on the Executive, ensuring that it does not detain individuals except in accordance with law.... All agree suspension of the writ has not occurred here. Thus, it is undisputed that Hamdi was properly before an Article III court to challenge his detention under 28 U.S.C. § 2241. Further, all agree that § 2241 and its companion provisions provide at least a skeletal outline of the procedures to be afforded a petitioner in federal habeas review. Most notably, § 2243 provides that "the person detained may, under oath, deny any of the facts set forth in the return or allege any other material facts," and § 2246 allows the taking of evidence in habeas proceedings by deposition, affidavit, or interrogatories.

The simple outline of § 2241 makes clear both that Congress envisioned that habeas petitioners would have some opportunity to present and rebut facts and that courts in cases like this retain some ability to vary the ways in which they do so as mandated by due process. The Government recognizes the basic procedural protections required by the habeas statute, but asks us to hold that, given both the flexibility of the habeas mechanism and the circumstances presented in this case, the presentation of the Mobbs Declaration to the habeas court completed the required factual development. It suggests two separate reasons for its position that no further process is due.

B

First, the Government urges the adoption of the Fourth Circuit's holding below—that because it is "undisputed" that Hamdi's seizure took place in a combat zone, the habeas determination can be made purely as a matter of law, with no further hearing or factfinding necessary. This argument is easily rejected. As the dissenters from the denial of rehearing en banc noted, the circumstances surrounding Hamdi's seizure cannot in any way be characterized as "undisputed," as "those circumstances are neither conceded in fact, nor susceptible to concession in law, because Hamdi has not been permitted to speak for himself or even through counsel as to those circumstances." Further, the "facts" that constitute the alleged concession are insufficient to support Hamdi's detention. Under the definition of enemy combatant that we accept today as falling within the scope of Congress' authorization, Hamdi would need to be "part of or supporting forces hostile to the United States or coalition partners" and "engaged in an armed conflict against the United States" to justify his detention in the United States for the duration of the relevant conflict. The habeas petition states only that "[w]hen seized by the United States Government, Mr. Hamdi resided in Afghanistan." An assertion that one resided in a country in which combat operations are taking place is not a concession that one was "captured in a zone of active combat operations in a foreign theater of war," and certainly is not a concession that one was "part of or supporting forces hostile to the United States or coalition partners" and "engaged in an armed conflict against the United States." Accordingly, we reject any argument that Hamdi has made concessions that eliminate any right to further process.

C

The Government's second argument requires closer consideration. This is the argument that further factual exploration is unwarranted and inappropriate in light of the extraordinary constitutional interests at stake. Under the Government's most extreme rendition of this argument, "[r]espect for separation of powers and the limited institutional capabilities of courts in matters of military decision-making in connection with an ongoing conflict" ought to eliminate entirely any individual process, restricting the courts to investigating only whether legal authorization exists for the broader detention scheme. At most, the Government argues, courts should review its determination that a citizen is an enemy combatant under a very deferential "some evidence" standard. Id., at 34 ("Under the some evidence standard, the focus is exclusively on the factual basis supplied by the Executive to support its own determination") (citing Superintendent, Mass. Correctional Institution at Walpole v. Hill, 472 U.S. 445, 455–457, 105 S.Ct. 2768, 86 L.Ed.2d 356 (1985) (explaining that the some evidence standard "does not require" a "weighing of the evidence," but rather calls for assessing "whether there is any evidence in the record that could support the conclusion")). Under this review, a court would assume the accuracy of the Government's articulated basis for Hamdi's detention, as set forth in the Mobbs Declaration, and assess only whether that articulated basis was a legitimate one. . . .

In response, Hamdi emphasizes that this Court consistently has recognized that an individual challenging his detention may not be held at the will of the Executive without recourse to some proceeding before a neutral tribunal to determine whether the Executive's asserted justifications for that detention have basis in fact and warrant in law. . . . He argues that the Fourth Circuit inappropriately "ceded power to the Executive during wartime to define the conduct for which a citizen may be detained, judge whether that citizen has engaged in the proscribed conduct, and imprison that citizen indefinitely," and that due process demands that he receive a hearing in which he may challenge the Mobbs Declaration and adduce his own counter evidence. The District Court, agreeing with Hamdi, apparently believed that the appropriate process would approach the process that accompanies a criminal trial. It therefore disapproved of the hearsay nature of the Mobbs Declaration and anticipated quite extensive discovery of various military affairs. Anything less, it concluded, would not be "meaningful judicial review."

Both of these positions highlight legitimate concerns. And both emphasize the tension that often exists between the autonomy that the

Government asserts is necessary in order to pursue effectively a particular goal and the process that a citizen contends he is due before he is deprived of a constitutional right. The ordinary mechanism that we use for balancing such serious competing interests, and for determining the procedures that are necessary to ensure that a citizen is not "deprived of life, liberty, or property, without due process of law," is the test that we articulated in Mathews v. Eldridge, 424 U.S. 319, 96 S.Ct. 893, 47 L.Ed.2d 18 (1976). . . . Mathews dictates that the process due in any given instance is determined by weighing "the private interest that will be affected by the official action" against the Government's asserted interest, "including the function involved" and the burdens the Government would face in providing greater process. . . . The Mathews calculus then contemplates a judicious balancing of these concerns, through an analysis of "the risk of an erroneous deprivation" of the private interest if the process were reduced and the "probable value, if any, of additional or substitute safeguards." We take each of these steps in turn.

It is beyond question that substantial interests lie on both sides of the scale in this case. Hamdi's "private interest . . . affected by the official action," is the most elemental of liberty interests—the interest in being free from physical detention by one's own government. . . .

Nor is the weight on this side of the Mathews scale offset by the circumstances of war or the accusation of treasonous behavior, for "[i]t is clear that commitment for any purpose constitutes a significant deprivation of liberty that requires due process protection,". . . . Moreover, as critical as the Government's interest may be in detaining those who actually pose an immediate threat to the national security of the United States during ongoing international conflict, history and common sense teach us that an unchecked system of detention carries the potential to become a means for oppression and abuse of others who do not present that sort of threat. . . . We reaffirm today the fundamental nature of a citizen's right to be free from involuntary confinement by his own government without due process of law, and we weigh the opposing governmental interests against the curtailment of liberty that such confinement entails.

On the other side of the scale are the weighty and sensitive governmental interests in ensuring that those who have in fact fought with the enemy during a war do not return to battle against the United States. As discussed above, . . . the law of war and the realities of combat may render such detentions both necessary and appropriate, and our due process analysis need not blink at those realities. Without doubt, our Constitution recognizes that core strategic matters of warmaking belong in the hands of those who are best positioned and most politically accountable for making them. Department of Navy v. Egan, 484 U.S. 518, 530, 108 S.Ct. 818, 98 L.Ed.2d 918 (1988) (noting the reluctance of the courts "to intrude upon the authority of the Executive in military and national security affairs"); Youngstown Sheet & Tube Co. v. Sawyer, 343 U.S. 579, 587, 72 S.Ct. 863, 96 L.Ed. 1153 (1952) (acknowledging "broad powers in military commanders engaged in day-to-day fighting in a theater of war").

The Government also argues at some length that its interests in reducing the process available to alleged enemy combatants are heightened by the practical difficulties that would accompany a system of trial-like process. In its view, military officers who are engaged in the serious work of waging battle would be unnecessarily and dangerously distracted by litigation half a world away, and discovery into military operations would both intrude on the sensitive secrets of national defense and result in a futile search for evidence buried under the rubble of war. To the extent that these burdens are triggered by heightened procedures, they are properly taken into account in our due process analysis.

Striking the proper constitutional balance here is of great importance to the Nation during this period of ongoing combat. But it is equally vital that our calculus not give short shrift to the values that this country holds dear or to the privilege that is American citizenship. It is during our most challenging and uncertain moments that our Nation's commitment to due process is most severely tested; and it is in those times that we must preserve our commitment at home to the principles for which we fight abroad. . . .

With due recognition of these competing concerns, we believe that neither the process proposed by the Government nor the process apparently envisioned by the District Court below strikes the proper constitutional balance when a United States citizen is detained in the United States as an enemy combatant. That is, "the risk of erroneous deprivation" of a detainee's liberty interest is unacceptably high under the Government's proposed rule, while some of the "additional or substitute procedural safeguards" suggested by the District Court are unwarranted in light of their limited "probable value" and the burdens they may impose on the military in such cases.

We therefore hold that a citizen-detainee seeking to challenge his classification as an enemy combatant must receive notice of the factual basis for his classification, and a fair opportunity to rebut the Government's factual assertions before a neutral decisionmaker. . . . These essential constitutional promises may not be eroded.

At the same time, the exigencies of the circumstances may demand that, aside from these core elements, enemy combatant proceedings may be tailored to alleviate their uncommon potential to burden the Executive at a time of ongoing military conflict. Hearsay, for example, may need to be accepted as the most reliable available evidence from the Government in such a proceeding. Likewise, the Constitution would not be offended by a presumption in favor of the Government's evidence, so long as that presumption remained a rebuttable one and fair opportunity for rebuttal were provided. Thus, once the Government puts forth credible evidence that the habeas petitioner meets the enemy-combatant criteria, the onus could shift to the petitioner to rebut that evidence with more persuasive evidence that he falls outside the criteria. A burden-shifting scheme of this sort would meet the goal of ensuring that the errant tourist, embedded journalist, or local aid worker has a chance to prove military error while giving due regard to the Executive once it has put forth meaningful support for its conclusion that the detainee is in fact an enemy combatant.

We think it unlikely that this basic process will have the dire impact on the central functions of warmaking that the Government forecasts. The parties agree that initial captures on the battlefield need not receive the process we have discussed here; that process is due only when the determination is made to continue to hold those who have been seized. The Government has made clear in its briefing that documentation regarding battlefield detainees already is kept in the ordinary course of military affairs. Any factfinding imposition created by requiring a knowledgeable affiant to summarize these records to an independent tribunal is a minimal one. Likewise, arguments that military officers ought not have to wage war under the threat of litigation lose much of their steam when factual disputes at enemy-combatant hearings are limited to the alleged combatant's acts. This focus meddles little, if at all, in the strategy or conduct of war, inquiring only into the appropriateness of continuing to detain an individual claimed to have taken up arms against the United States. While we accord the greatest respect and consideration to the judgments of military authorities in matters relating to the actual prosecution of a war, and recognize that the scope of that discretion necessarily is wide, it does not infringe on the core role of the military for the courts to exercise their own time-honored and constitutionally mandated roles of reviewing and resolving claims like those presented here.

In sum, while the full protections that accompany challenges to detentions in other settings may prove unworkable and inappropriate in the enemy-combatant setting, the threats to military operations posed by a basic system of independent review are not so weighty as to trump a citizen's core rights to challenge meaningfully the Government's case and to be heard by an impartial adjudicator.

D

In so holding, we necessarily reject the Government's assertion that separation of powers principles mandate a heavily circumscribed role for the courts in such circumstances. Indeed, the position that the courts must forgo any examination of the individual case and focus exclusively on the legality of the broader detention scheme cannot be mandated by any reasonable view of separation of powers, as this approach serves only to condense power into a single branch of government. We have long since made clear that a state of war is not a blank check for the President when it comes to the rights of the Nation's citizens. Youngstown Sheet & Tube, 343 U.S., at 587, 72 S.Ct. 863. Whatever power the United States Constitution envisions for the Executive in its exchanges with other nations or with enemy organizations in times of conflict, it most assuredly envisions a role for all three branches when individual liberties are at stake. . . . Likewise, we have made clear that, unless Congress acts to suspend it, the Great Writ of habeas corpus allows the Judicial Branch to play a necessary role in maintaining this delicate balance of governance, serving as an important judicial check on the Executive's discretion in the realm of detentions. . . . Thus, while we do not question that our due process assessment must pay keen attention to the particular burdens faced by the Executive in the context of military action, it would turn our system of checks and balances on its head to suggest that a citizen could not make his way to court with a challenge to the factual basis for his detention by his government, simply because the Executive opposes making available such a challenge. Absent suspension of the writ by Congress, a citizen detained as an enemy combatant is entitled to this process.

Because we conclude that due process demands some system for a citizen detainee to refute his classification, the proposed "some evidence" standard is inadequate. Any process in which the Executive's factual assertions go wholly unchallenged or are simply presumed correct without any opportunity for the alleged combatant to demonstrate otherwise falls constitutionally short. As the Government itself has recognized, we have utilized the "some evidence" standard in the past as a standard of review, not as a standard of proof. . . . This standard therefore is ill suited to the situation in which a habeas petitioner has received no prior proceedings before any tribunal and had no prior opportunity to rebut the Executive's factual assertions before a neutral decisionmaker.

Today we are faced only with such a case. Aside from unspecified "screening" processes, and military interrogations in which the Government suggests Hamdi could have contested his classification, Hamdi has received no process. An interrogation by one's captor, however effective an intelligence-gathering tool, hardly constitutes a constitutionally adequate factfinding before a neutral decisionmaker. . . . Plainly, the "process" Hamdi has received is not that to which he is entitled under the Due Process Clause.

There remains the possibility that the standards we have articulated could be met by an appropriately authorized and properly constituted military tribunal. Indeed, it is notable that military regulations already provide for such process in related instances, dictating that tribunals be made available to determine the status of enemy detainees who assert prisoner-of-war status under the Geneva Convention. See Enemy Prisoners of War, Retained Personnel, Civilian Internees and Other Detainees, Army Regulation 190–8, § 1–6 (1997). In the absence of such process, however, a court that receives a petition for a writ of habeas corpus from an alleged enemy combatant must itself ensure that the minimum requirements of due process are achieved. Both courts below recognized as much, focusing their energies on the question of whether Hamdi was due an opportunity to rebut the Government's case against him. The Government, too, proceeded on this assumption, presenting its affidavit and then seeking that it be evaluated under a deferential standard of review based on burdens that it alleged would accompany any greater process. As we have discussed, a habeas court in a case such as this may accept affidavit evidence like that contained in the Mobbs Declaration, so long as it also permits the alleged combatant to present his own factual case to rebut the Government's return. We anticipate that a District Court would proceed with the caution that we have indicated is necessary in this setting, engaging in a factfinding process that is both prudent and incremental. We have no reason to doubt that courts faced with these sensitive matters will pay proper heed both to the matters of national security that might arise in an individual case and to the constitutional limitations safeguarding essential liberties that remain vibrant even in times of security concerns.

IV

Hamdi asks us to hold that the Fourth Circuit also erred by denying him immediate access to counsel upon his detention and by disposing of the case without permitting him to meet with an attorney. Since our grant of certiorari in this case, Hamdi has been appointed counsel, with whom he has met for consultation purposes on several occasions, and with whom he is now being granted unmonitored meetings. He unquestionably has the right to access to counsel in connection with the proceedings on remand. No further consideration of this issue is necessary at this stage of the case.

. . .

The judgment of the United States Court of Appeals for the Fourth Circuit is vacated, and the case is remanded for further proceedings.

It is so ordered.

JUSTICE SOUTER, with whom JUSTICE GINSBURG joins, concurring in part, dissenting in part, and concurring in the judgment.

. . .

IV

Because I find Hamdi's detention forbidden by § 4001(a) and unauthorized by the Force Resolution, I would not reach any questions of what process he may be due in litigating disputed issues in a proceeding under the habeas statute or prior to the habeas enquiry itself. For me, it suffices that the Government has failed to justify holding him in the absence of a further Act of Congress, criminal charges, a showing that the detention conforms to the laws of war, or a demonstration that § 4001(a) is unconstitutional. I would therefore vacate the judgment of the Court of Appeals and remand for proceedings consistent with this view.

Since this disposition does not command a majority of the Court, however, the need to give practical effect to the conclusions of eight members of the Court rejecting the Government's position calls for me to join with the plurality in ordering remand on terms closest to those I would impose. Although I think litigation of Hamdi's status as an enemy combatant is unnecessary, the terms of the plurality's remand will allow Hamdi to offer evidence that he is not an enemy combatant, and he should at the least have the benefit of that opportunity.

It should go without saying that in joining with the plurality to produce a judgment, I do not adopt the plurality's resolution of constitutional issues that I would not reach. It is not that I could disagree with the plurality's determinations (given the plurality's view of the Force Resolution) that someone in Hamdi's position is entitled at a minimum to notice of the Government's claimed factual basis for holding him, and to a fair chance to rebut it before a neutral decision maker . . .; nor, of course, could I disagree with the plurality's affirmation of Hamdi's right to counsel,. . . . On the other hand, I do not mean to imply agreement that the Government could claim an evidentiary presumption casting the burden of rebuttal on Hamdi, or that an opportunity to litigate before a military tribunal might obviate or truncate enquiry by a court on habeas. . . .

Subject to these qualifications, I join with the plurality in a judgment of the Court vacating the Fourth Circuit's judgment and remanding the case.

JUSTICE SCALIA, with whom JUSTICE STEVENS joins, dissenting.

. . . This case brings into conflict the competing demands of national security and our citizens' constitutional right to personal liberty. Although I share the Court's evident unease as it seeks to reconcile the two, I do not agree with its resolution.

Where the Government accuses a citizen of waging war against it, our constitutional tradition has been to prosecute him in federal court for treason or some other crime. Where the exigencies of war prevent that, the Constitution's Suspension Clause, Art. I, § 9, cl. 2, allows Congress to relax the usual protections temporarily. Absent suspension, however, the Executive's assertion of military exigency has not been thought sufficient to permit detention without charge. No one contends that the congressional Authorization for Use of Military Force, on which the Government relies to justify its actions here, is an implementation of the Suspension Clause. Accordingly, I would reverse the decision below.

. . .

Many think it not only inevitable but entirely proper that liberty give way to security in times of national crisis—that, at the extremes of military exigency, inter arma silent leges. Whatever the general merits of the view that war silences law or modulates its voice, that view has no place in the interpretation and application of a Constitution designed precisely to confront war and, in a manner that accords with democratic principles, to accommodate it. Because the Court has proceeded to meet the current emergency in a manner the Constitution does not envision, I respectfully dissent.

JUSTICE THOMAS, dissenting.

The Executive Branch, acting pursuant to the powers vested in the President by the Constitution and with explicit congressional approval, has determined that Yaser Hamdi is an enemy combatant and should be detained. This detention falls squarely within the Federal Government's war powers, and we lack the expertise and capacity to second-guess that decision. As such, petitioners' habeas challenge should fail, and there is no reason to remand the case. The plurality reaches a contrary conclusion by failing adequately to consider basic principles of the constitutional structure as it relates to national security and foreign affairs and by using the balancing scheme of Mathews v. Eldridge, 424 U.S. 319, 96 S.Ct. 893, 47 L.Ed.2d 18 (1976). I do not think that the Federal Government's war powers can be balanced away by this Court. Arguably, Congress could provide for additional procedural protections, but until it does, we have no right to insist upon them. But even if I were to agree with the general approach the plurality takes, I could not accept the particulars. The plurality utterly fails to account for the Government's compelling interests and for our own institutional inability to weigh competing concerns correctly. I respectfully dissent.

QUESTIONS AND NOTES

1. Writing for a plurality of the Court, what legal basis did Justice O'Connor articulate for the extended detention of Hamdi? To what extent were the legal grounds based on the AUMF? On the fact that Hamdi had been seized on the battlefield? On the fact that he fit within the definition of an enemy combatant? On the fact that the war with the Taliban was still going on? On the fact that we were at war with al Qaeda? What will be the legal effect when the U.S. withdraws its forces from Afghanistan? Will the legal basis for detaining individuals seized in the war against the Taliban disappear? Are we at war with al Qaeda?

2.   In the aftermath of the Supreme Court's decision in the Hamdi case, the government and Hamdi reached a negotiated settlement. (The Supreme Court opinion was handed down on June 28, 2004; the settlement was finalized on September 17, 2004.) Under the terms of the settlement, Hamdi was released and transported to Saudi Arabia; the U.S. agreed to make no request that he be detained by the Saudis; he agreed that he would not engage in any combat activities against the U.S. nor engage in terrorism or aid or affiliate with al Qaeda, the Taliban or any terrorist organization, and he would inform Saudi officials and the U.S. embassy if he were solicited to engage in such activities; he also agreed to renounce his U.S. nationality; he agreed not to travel outside of the Saudi Arabian kingdom for a period of five years, never to travel to Afghanistan, Iraq, Israel, Pakistan, Syria, the West Bank or the Gaza Strip, nor to travel to the United States for ten years and then only having obtained express permission from named high U.S. government officials, and for 15 years to notify the U.S. Embassy of any plans to travel outside of Saudi Arabia. Hamdi also agreed that if he failed to fulfill the conditions of the agreement, he was subject to being detained immediately "insofar as consistent with the law of armed conflict." Finally, the settlement provided for dismissal of the action, Hamdi v. Rumsfeld, with prejudice.

3.   Consider the significance of the Hamdi settlement. Should the government have entered into the settlement prior to the Supreme Court decision in the case? Are there any terms that you consider inappropriate? Any terms that might have been added? How easy or difficult is it likely to be to enforce the terms, if Hamdi does not abide by them?

4.   Following announcement of the settlement in the Hamdi case, lawyers for John Walker Lindh filed a request for clemency. LA Times, Sept. 29, 2004, p.A1. Lindh had been wounded in the fighting in Afghanistan and pled guilty to supplying services to the Taliban and carrying firearms and destructive devices. He received a 20 year sentence. Both Lindh and Hamdi were seized in the same general area of Afghanistan. Both are American citizens. Does the Hamdi settlement warrant granting clemency to Lindh?

5.   In Ex parte Quirin, 317 U.S. 1 (1942), the Supreme Court made the following statements distinguishing between lawful and unlawful combatants (the Quirin case is reproduced in Chapter 11, infra):

> Our Government, by thus defining lawful belligerents entitled to be treated as By universal agreement and practice the law of war draws a distinction between the armed forces and the peaceful populations of belligerent nations and also between those who are lawful and unlawful combatants. Lawful combatants are subject to capture and detention as prisoners of war by opposing military forces. Unlawful combatants are likewise subject to capture and detention, but in addition they are subject to trial and punishment by military tribunals for acts which render their belligerency unlawful. The spy who secretly and without uniform passes the military lines of a belligerent in time of war, seeking to gather military information and

communicate it to the enemy, or an enemy combatant who without uniform comes secretly through the lines for the purpose of waging war by destruction of life or property, are familiar examples of belligerents who are generally deemed not to be entitled to the status of prisoners of war, but to be offenders against the law of war subject to trial and punishment by military tribunals. . . .

. . .

Our Government, by thus defining lawful belligerents entitled to be treated as. prisoners of war, has recognized that there is a class of unlawful belligerents not entitled to that privilege, including those who though combatants do not wear 'fixed and distinctive emblems'.

. . .

Citizenship in the United States of an enemy belligerent does not relieve him from the consequences of a belligerency which is unlawful because in violation of the law of war. Citizens who associate themselves with the military arm of the enemy government, and with its aid, guidance and direction enter this country bent on hostile acts are enemy belligerents within the meaning of the Hague Convention and the law of war. . . .

6.   Review carefully the positions taken in each of the opinions in the Hamdi case and the lineup of the various justices in support of each position. How many justices supported the government's position in the case? How many justices would have released Hamdi? How many justices were of the view that the preferred outcome was that which actually occurred?

7.   Does the Hamdi case authorize indefinite detention of terrorist detainees? Does it establish ground rules for the kind of process that needs to be afforded in cases of extended or indefinite detention?

8.   Two other terrorism-related cases were decided the same day as Hamdi. In one, Rasul v. Bush, 542 U.S. 466 (2004), the court addressed whether the Guantanamo detainees had a statutory right to habeas corpus. The question of what are the habeas corpus rights of the Gitmo detainees, is treated infra. The third case was Rumsfeld v. Padilla, 542 U.S. 426 (2004) which is described in the next section.

NOTE ON THE IMMEDIATE LEGAL BACKGROUND OF THE "STATUS AS AN ENEMY COMBATANT" ISSUE

The legal basis on which Yaser Hamdi was being held in military custody was that he was an enemy combatant. See footnote 1 in the plurality opinion in Hamdi indicating that that legal category "has not been elaborated upon in great detail. The permissible bounds of the category will be defined by the lower courts as subsequent cases are presented to them." Issues relating to the definition of enemy combatant and related legal categories arose both before the decision in Hamdi and often since. It is an issue touched upon throughout this volume. See, for example, sections 1021 and 1022 of the NDAA of 2012, infra this chapter, and the issue presented in the combatant status review tribunals and before the courts considering issues in the habeas corpus actions filed by Guantanamo detainees.

It is helpful to review the background of the development of a legal response by the U.S. government to questions about the treatment, status and disposition of persons captured in military actions undertaken in the wake of and related to the 9/11 attacks. Early in 2002, the issue of what status to accord to al Qaeda and Taliban captives was being debated in the Department of Justice and the Department of State. White House memos and letters from that period reveal the nature of the debate. On February 1, 2002, Attorney General Ashcroft sent a letter to the President describing "two basic theories" that supported the conclusion that Taliban combatants are not legally entitled to Geneva Convention protections as prisoners of war: a) Afghanistan was a failed state; as such the treaty's protections do not apply because it has lost its status as party to the treaty able to fulfill its obligations; b) if during the relevant times Afghanistan was a party to the treaty, Taliban combatants were not entitled to Geneva Convention III prisoner of war status because they were unlawful combatants. The letter went on to detail the risks of adopting the one theory or the other, namely, under theory a) no court would subsequently entertain charges that U.S. officials had violated the War Crimes Act through a violation of the Geneva Convention, whereas theory b) would not "accord American officials the same protection from legal consequences."

A week before, on January 25, 2002, a draft memorandum for the President had been prepared by the Alberto Gonzales, then Counsel to the President (later Attorney General) noting that on January 18, 2002, he had advised the President that the Department of Justice had issued a formal legal opinion concluding that the Geneva Convention III on the Treatment of Prisoners (GPW) does not apply to the conflict with al Qaeda; also that there are reasonable grounds for concluding that the Convention does not apply to the Taliban; and noting that the President had decided that the Convention does not apply and that al Qaeda and Taliban detainees are not POWs under the Convention. This was a key early presidential decision made regarding the legal status of the Guantanamo detainees. The January 25 memorandum went on to relate that the Secretary of State had requested that the President reconsider that decision and that the Legal Adviser to the State Department had reached conclusions different from the Department of Justice. In this memorandum, Mr. Gonzales presented arguments in support of reconsideration and reversal of the decision that the GPW does not apply to either al Qaeda or the Taliban as well as the arguments opposed. Some of the arguments presented for reversing the decision were as follows:

> The United States could not invoke the GPW if enemy forces threatened to mistreat . . . U.S. or coalition forces captured during operations in Afghanistan, or if they denied Red Cross access or other POW privileges.

. . .

Our position would likely provoke widespread condemnation among our allies and in some domestic quarters, even if we make clear that we will comply with the core humanitarian principles of the treaty as a matter of policy.

. . .

Other countries may be less inclined to turn over terrorists or provide legal assistance to us if we do not recognize a legal obligation to comply with the GPW.

A determination that GPW does not apply to al Qaeda and the Taliban could undermine U.S. military culture which emphasizes maintaining the highest standards of conduct in combat, and could introduce an element of uncertainty in the status of adversaries.

Mr. Gonzalez then stated his belief that "on balance" these arguments were unpersuasive and presented responses to them:

. . . [Y]our [i.e. the President's] policy of providing humane treatment to enemy detainees gives us the credibility to insist on like treatment for our soldiers.

. . . [O]ur adversaries in several recent conflicts have not been deterred by GPW in their mistreatment of captured U.S. personnel, and terrorists will not follow GPW in any event.

. . .

The statement that other nations would criticize the U.S. because we have determined that GPW does not apply is undoubtedly true. . . . [W]e can facilitate cooperation with other nations by reassuring them that we fully support GPW where it is applicable and by acknowledging that in this conflict the U.S. continues to respect other recognized standards.

. . .

[T]he argument based on military culture fails to recognize that our military remain bound to apply the principles of GPW because that is what you [i.e. the President] have directed them to do.

In July 2004, the Government adopted the following definition of enemy combatant, which was applied to foreign nationals held at Guantanamo:

[A]n individual who was part of or supporting Taliban or al Qaeda forces, or associated forces that are engaged in hostilities against the United States or its coalition partners. This includes any person who has committed a belligerent act or has directly supported hostilities in aid of enemy armed forces.

See Deputy Secretary of Defense Paul Wolfowitz, Memorandum for the Secretary of the Navy, Order Establishing Combatant Status

Review Tribunal (July 7, 2004) cited in Khalid v. Bush, 355 F.Supp.2d 311 (D.D.C. 2005).

How does the definition described in the previous paragraph compare with the related definitions found in the AUMF, the President's Military Order and the definitions used in section 1021 and 1022 of the NDAA of 2012, infra this chapter?

A primary element in the legal background against which the presidential decision, described above, was made is the Geneva Convention III. Relevant provisions are reproduced in the Appendix.

Numerous questions are raised by the administration's position on the prisoner of war versus enemy combatant issue. Insofar as the provisions of the Geneva Convention, supra, are deemed relevant, the Bush administration apparently relied on the four-part test of Article 4A.2., supra. This test includes in the category of prisoners of war, those members of militia or organized resistance forces who have serve under a commander, with a "fixed distinctive sign recognizable at a distance", who carry "arms openly," and who observe the laws of war in their conduct. The administration argues, inter alia, that members of the al Qaeda and the Taliban do not wear uniforms or the equivalent; therefore they do not qualify for prisoner of war status. Accordingly, the issue of whether prisoner of war status is warranted under the terms of the Convention should vary depending on the specific group of captives.

Consider what difference it would have made if Geneva Convention-prisoner of war status had been recognized for the detainees? Among other things, it would have made it difficult for the government to interrogate and, possibly, obtain information from them, given the terms of Article 1.7 of the Convention. The Convention also contemplates repatriation at the end of hostilities. While both the Bush and Obama administrations have released a large majority of the detainees to their home countries or to another country, both the Bush administration and the Obama administration have contemplated extended, even indefinite, detention for some of them.

Finally, consider the following quotation with respect to the most confounding question regarding the detainees—how long may they be held?

However, even if the detainees were not covered by the Third Geneva Convention, a person may not be held forever without charges or trial. At some point, in some manner, . . . the question of indefinite and possibly permanent detention without trial must eventually arise. . . . Moreover, one could argue—decisively, in my view—that as long as operations are carried out against Al Qaeda, the organization whose destruction is one of the war aims of the United States, the United States is perfectly entitled . . . to detain fighters whom it determines to be a security risk. . . . It probably could not do so with respect to an endless and essentially metaphorical 'war on terrorism' dealing with targets wholly unrelated to Al Qaeda—a war which might indeed have no end—but it is certainly entitled to do so with fighters . . . connected even loosely with Al Qaeda, wherever they may be.

> Kenneth Anderson, What to Do with Bin Laden and Al Qaeda Terrorists? A Qualified Defense of Military Commissions and United States Policy on Detainees at Guantanamo Bay Naval Base, 25 Harv. J.L. & Pub Pol'y 591, 625–626 (2002).

4. MILITARY CUSTODY FOR PERSONS ARRESTED IN THE UNITED STATES—CITIZEN AND NON-CITIZEN: THE JOSE PADILLA AND ALI SALEH KAHLAH AL-MARRI CASES

Early in the post-9/11 period, on different occasions, the government arrested two persons in the United States as material witnesses, thereafter declared them to be enemy combatants under the authority of the AUMF, shifted them into military custody and sent them to a naval brig in Charleston, S.C.(It is worth noting neither one was sent to Guantanamo.) The trail of litigation in both cases is treated below.

The first of these cases involved Jose Padilla, an American citizen arrested at Chicago's O'Hare Airport, originally as a material witness in connection with an alleged plot to detonate a dirty bomb (i.e. an explosive device sheathed in radioactive material). Subsequently, President Bush issued an order declaring Padilla an enemy combatant, and he was transferred to military jurisdiction and detained in a military brig. From that point forward, he was denied access to counsel and had no contact with anyone on the outside. His attorney, retained earlier when he was still in material witness status, filed suit on his behalf in New York against the Secretary of Defense. The case eventually reached the Supreme Court in Rumsfeld v. Padilla, 542 U.S. 426 (2004). The Supreme Court reversed the court of appeals decision, 352 F.3d 695 (2d Cir. 2003), which in turn had reversed the district court decision.

In the Supreme Court, a majority of the justices concluded that the Secretary of Defense was not the proper respondent in the case; the appropriate respondent was the commander of the naval brig where Padilla was being detained. Further, the district court in the Southern District of New York did not have jurisdiction over the commander of the brig. Accordingly, the court of appeals decision was reversed, and the case was dismissed "without prejudice." The Court majority (Rehnquist, C.J. joined by Justices O'Connor, Scalia, Kennedy and Thomas) did not reach the merits of whether the President had authority to detain Padilla militarily. The four dissenting justices (Stevens J. joined by Justices Souter, Ginsburg and Breyer) voted to uphold the district court's jurisdiction and, reaching the merits, stated:

Whether respondent is entitled to immediate release is a question that reasonable jurists may answer in different ways.[8] There is, however, only one possible answer to the question whether he is entitled to a hearing on the justification for his detention.[9]

At stake in this case is nothing less than the essence of a free society. Even more important than the method of selecting the people's rulers and their successors is the character of the constraints imposed on the Executive by the rule of law. Unconstrained Executive detention for the purpose of investigating and preventing subversive activity is the hallmark of the Star Chamber.[10] Access to counsel for the purpose of protecting the citizen from official mistakes and mistreatment is the hallmark of due process.

Executive detention of subversive citizens, like detention of enemy soldiers to keep them off the battlefield, may sometimes be justified to prevent persons from launching or becoming missiles of destruction. It may not, however, be justified by the naked interest in using unlawful procedures to extract information. Incommunicado detention for months on end is such a procedure. Whether the information so procured is more or less reliable than that acquired by more extreme forms of torture is of no consequence. For if this Nation is to remain true to the ideals symbolized by its flag, it must not wield the tools of tyrants even to resist an assault by the forces of tyranny. . . .

Justice Stevens also wrote in a footnote in his dissent in Padilla that the relevant statutes do not authorize protracted, incommunicado detention of an American citizen, Might the government's protracted detention of Padilla possibly be justified on the ground that he was involved in plans to detonate a "dirty bomb"; that his detention was necessary to keep him from launching a "missile of destruction"?

---

8   Consistent with the judgment of the Court of Appeals, I believe that the Non-Detention Act, 18 U.S.C. § 4001(a), prohibits—and the Authorization for Use of Military Force Joint Resolution, 115 Stat. 224, adopted on September 18, 2001, does not authorize—the protracted, incommunicado detention of American citizens arrested in the United States.

9   Respondent's custodian has been remarkably candid about the Government's motive in detaining respondent: " '[O]ur interest really in his case is not law enforcement, it is not punishment because he was a terrorist or working with the terrorists. Our interest at the moment is to try and find out everything he knows so that hopefully we can stop other terrorist acts.' " 233 F.Supp.2d 564, 573–574 (S.D.N.Y.2002) (quoting News Briefing, Dept. of Defense (June 12, 2002), 2002 WL 22026773).

10   See Watts v. Indiana, 338 U.S. 49, 54, 69 S.Ct. 1347, 93 L.Ed. 1801 (1949) (opinion of Frankfurter, J.). "There is torture of mind as well as body; the will is as much affected by fear as by force. And there comes a point where this Court should not be ignorant as judges of what we know as men." Id., at 52, 69 S.Ct. 1347.

Arguably, the issues that arise when an alleged terrorist is apprehended in the United States and is treated by the government as an unlawful enemy combatant diverge from those issues that are raised by the cases of the detainees who were captured on the battlefield in Afghanistan (or seized elsewhere in the world) and removed to the Guantanamo Bay prison facility. Of course, Hamdi was seized on the battlefield and initially detained at Guantanamo but later removed to a South Carolina naval brig when it was discovered that he was a U.S. citizen, while all of the other Guantanamo detainees are aliens. And Padilla is the prototype case of a U.S. citizen arrested in the U.S. and then treated as an enemy combatant, while another case to be treated below, that of Ali Saleh Kahlah al-Marri, presents another variation—a person legally in the United States but not a U.S. citizen who is arrested and, like Padilla, then declared to be an enemy combatant and detained in military custody.

We address below legal issues relating to the detention of Padilla and al Marri. We then proceed to consider various issues that have arisen regarding the detainees at Guantanamo including their habeas corpus rights, the kind of hearings held to determine whether their continuing detention is warranted and whether the Guantanamo Bay facility should continue to remain open.

Soon after the Supreme Court's decision in Rumsfeld v. Padilla, supra, in July, 2004, Padilla filed a new habeas corpus action in the U.S. District Court for the District of South Carolina against the commander of the brig in which he was being detained. Padilla moved for summary judgment, and the district court ruled in favor of Padilla. That decision was reversed by the U.S. Court of Appeals for the Fourth Circuit in the following opinion.

PADILLA V. HANFT

423 F.3d 386 (4th Cir.2005)

Before LUTTIG, MICHAEL, and TRAXLER, CIRCUIT JUDGES.

JUDGE LUTTIG wrote the opinion for the Court, in which JUDGE MICHAEL and JUDGE TRAXLER joined.

LUTTIG, CIRCUIT JUDGE.

Appellee Jose Padilla, a United States citizen, associated with forces hostile to the United States in Afghanistan and took up arms against United States forces in that country in our war against al Qaeda. Upon his escape to Pakistan from the battlefield in Afghanistan, Padilla was recruited, trained, funded, and equipped by al Qaeda leaders to continue prosecution of the war in the United States by blowing up apartment buildings in this country. Padilla flew to the United States on May 8, 2002, to begin carrying out his assignment, but was arrested by civilian law enforcement authorities upon his arrival at O'Hare International Airport in Chicago.

Thereafter, in a letter to the Secretary of Defense, the President of the United States personally designated Padilla an "enemy combatant" against this country, stating that the United States is "at war" with al Qaeda, that "Mr. Padilla engaged in conduct that constituted hostile and war-like acts, including conduct in preparation for acts of international terrorism that had the aim to cause injury to or adverse effects on the United States," and that "Mr. Padilla represents a continuing, present and grave danger to the national security of the United States." Having determined that "detention of Mr. Padilla is necessary to prevent him from aiding al Qaeda in its efforts to attack the United States or its armed forces, other governmental personnel, or citizens," the President directed the Secretary of Defense to take Padilla into military custody, in which custody Padilla has remained ever since. The full text of the President's memorandum to the Secretary of Defense reads as follows:

THE WHITE HOUSE WASHINGTON

FOR OFFICIAL USE ONLY

TO THE SECRETARY OF DEFENSE:

Based on the information available to me from all sources,

REDACTED

In accordance with the Constitution and consistent with the laws of the United States, including the Authorization for Use of Military Force Joint Resolution (Public Law 107–40);

I, GEORGE W. BUSH, as President of the United States and Commander in Chief of the U.S. armed forces, hereby DETERMINE for the United States of America that:

(1) Jose Padilla, who is under the control of the Department of Justice and who is a U.S. citizen, is, and at the time he entered the United States in May 2002 was, an enemy combatant;

(2) Mr. Padilla is closely associated with al Qaeda, an international terrorist organization with which the United States is at war;

(3) Mr. Padilla engaged in conduct that constituted hostile and war-like acts, including conduct in preparation for acts of international terrorism that had the aim to cause injury to or adverse effects on the United States;

(4) Mr. Padilla possesses intelligence, including intelligence about personnel and activities of al Qaeda, that,

if communicated to the U.S., would aid U.S. efforts to prevent attacks by al Qaeda on the United States or its armed forces, other governmental personnel, or citizens;

(5) Mr. Padilla represents a continuing, present and grave danger to the national security of the United States, and detention of Mr. Padilla is necessary to prevent him from aiding al Qaeda in its efforts to attack the United States or its armed forces, other governmental personnel, or citizens;

(6) it is in the interest of the United States that the Secretary of Defense detain Mr. Padilla as an enemy combatant; and

(7) it is REDACTED consistent with U.S. law and the laws of war for the Secretary of Defense to detain Mr. Padilla as enemy combatant.

Accordingly, you are directed to receive Mr. Padilla from the Department of Justice and to detain him as an enemy combatant.

DATE: June 9, 2002

Signature

/George Bush/

The exceedingly important question before us is whether the President of the United States possesses the authority to detain militarily a citizen of this country who is closely associated with al Qaeda, an entity with which the United States is at war; who took up arms on behalf of that enemy and against our country in a foreign combat zone of that war; and who thereafter traveled to the United States for the avowed purpose of further prosecuting that war on American soil, against American citizens and targets.

We conclude that the President does possess such authority pursuant to the Authorization for Use of Military Force Joint Resolution enacted by Congress in the wake of the attacks on the United States of September 11, 2001. Accordingly, the judgment of the district court is reversed.

Al Qaeda operatives recruited Jose Padilla, a United States citizen, to train for jihad in Afghanistan in February 2000, while Padilla was on a religious pilgrimage to Saudi Arabia.[1] Subsequently, Padilla met with al Qaeda operatives in Afghanistan, received explosives training in an al Qaeda-affiliated camp, and served as an armed guard at what he understood to be a Taliban outpost. When United States military operations began in Afghanistan, Padilla and other al Qaeda operatives

---

[1] For purposes of Padilla's summary judgment motion, the parties have stipulated to the facts as set forth by the government. J.A. 30–31. It is only on these facts that we consider whether the President has the authority to detain Padilla.

moved from safehouse to safehouse to evade bombing or capture. Padilla was, on the facts with which we are presented, "armed and present in a combat zone during armed conflict between al Qaeda/Taliban forces and the armed forces of the United States."

Padilla eventually escaped to Pakistan, armed with an assault rifle. Once in Pakistan, Padilla met with Khalid Sheikh Mohammad, a senior al Qaeda operations planner, who directed Padilla to travel to the United States for the purpose of blowing up apartment buildings, in continued prosecution of al Qaeda's war of terror against the United States. After receiving further training, as well as cash, travel documents, and communication devices, Padilla flew to the United States in order to carry out his accepted assignment.

Upon arrival at Chicago's O'Hare International Airport on May 8, 2002, Padilla was detained by FBI agents, who interviewed and eventually arrested him pursuant to a material witness warrant issued by the district court for the Southern District of New York in conjunction with a grand jury investigation of the September 11 attacks. Padilla was transported to New York, where he was held at a civilian correctional facility until, on June 9, 2002, the President designated him an "enemy combatant" against the United States and directed the Secretary of Defense to take him into military custody. Since his delivery into the custody of military authorities, Padilla has been detained at a naval brig in South Carolina.

On June 11, 2002, Padilla filed a petition for a writ of habeas corpus in the Southern District of New York, claiming that his detention violated the Constitution. The Supreme Court of the United States ultimately ordered Padilla's petition dismissed without prejudice, holding that his petition was improperly filed in the Southern District of New York. Rumsfeld v. Padilla, 542 U.S. 426, 124 S.Ct. 2711, 2727, 159 L.Ed.2d 513 (2004). And on July 2, 2004, Padilla filed the present petition for a writ of habeas corpus in the District of South Carolina.

The district court subsequently held that the President lacks the authority to detain Padilla, that Padilla's detention is in violation of the Constitution and laws of the United States, and that Padilla therefore must either be criminally charged or released. This appeal followed. We expedited consideration of this appeal at the request of the parties, hearing argument in the case on July 19, 2005.

The Authorization for Use of Military Force Joint Resolution (AUMF), upon which the President explicitly relied in his order that Padilla be detained by the military and upon which the government chiefly relies in support of the President's authority to detain Padilla, was enacted by Congress in the immediate aftermath of the September 11, 2001, terrorist attacks on the United States. It provides as follows:

[T]he President is authorized to use all necessary and appropriate force against those nations, organizations, or persons he determines planned, authorized, committed, or aided the terrorist attacks that occurred on September 11, 2001, or harbored such organizations or persons, in order to prevent any future acts of international terrorism against the United States by such nations, organizations or persons.

Pub.L. No. 107–40, § 2(a), 115 Stat. 224 (September 18, 2001). The Supreme Court has already once interpreted this Joint Resolution in the context of a military detention by the President. In Hamdi v. Rumsfeld, the Supreme Court held, on the facts alleged by the government, that the AUMF authorized the military detention of Yaser Esam Hamdi, an American citizen who fought alongside Taliban forces in Afghanistan, was captured by United States allies on a battlefield there, and was detained in the United States by the military.[2] The narrow question, addressed by the Court in Hamdi was whether the Executive has the authority to detain citizens who qualify as enemy combatants, defined for purposes of that case as individual[s] who . . . [were] part of or supporting forces hostile to the United States or coalition partners in Afghanistan and who engaged in an armed conflict against the United States there. The controlling plurality of the Court answered that narrow question in the affirmative, concluding, based upon longstanding law-of-war principles, that Hamdi's detention was necessary and appropriate within the meaning of the AUMF because [t]he capture and detention of lawful combatants and the capture, detention, and trial of unlawful combatants, by universal agreement and practice, are important incident[s] of war. The rationale for this law-of-war principle, Justice O'Connor explained for the plurality, is that detention to prevent a combatant's return to the battlefield is a fundamental incident of waging war.

As the AUMF authorized Hamdi's detention by the President, so also does it authorize Padilla's detention. Under the facts as presented here, Padilla unquestionably qualifies as an "enemy combatant" as that term was defined for purposes of the controlling opinion in Hamdi. Indeed, under the definition of "enemy combatant" employed in Hamdi, we can discern no difference in principle between Hamdi and Padilla. Like Hamdi, Padilla associated with forces hostile to the United States in Afghanistan. Compare J.A. 19–23 (detailing Padilla's association with al Qaeda in Afghanistan and Pakistan), with Hamdi, 124 S.Ct. at 2637 (describing Hamdi's affiliation with the Taliban in Afghanistan). And, like Hamdi, Padilla took up arms against United States forces in that country in the same way and to the same extent as did Hamdi. Compare J.A. 21 (averring that Padilla was "armed and present in a combat zone during armed

---

[2]   Having concluded that detention was authorized on the facts alleged by the government, the Court in Hamdi remanded the case for a hearing to determine, pursuant to the due process requirements set forth in its opinion, whether those alleged facts were true.

conflict between al Qaeda/Taliban forces and the armed forces of the United States"), and (alleging that Padilla was "armed with an assault rifle" as he escaped to Pakistan), with Hamdi, 124 S.Ct. at 2642, n. 1 (noting that the asserted basis for detaining Hamdi was that he "carr[ied] a weapon against American troops on a foreign battlefield"), and id. at 2637 (quoting Mobbs Affidavit that Hamdi had " 'surrender[ed] his Kalishnikov assault rifle' " to Northern Alliance forces (alteration in original)). Because, like Hamdi, Padilla is an enemy combatant, and because his detention is no less necessary than was Hamdi's in order to prevent his return to the battlefield, the President is authorized by the AUMF to detain Padilla as a fundamental incident to the conduct of war.

Our conclusion that the AUMF as interpreted by the Supreme Court in Hamdi authorizes the President's detention of Padilla as an enemy combatant is reinforced by the Supreme Court's decision in Ex parte Quirin, on which the plurality in Hamdi itself heavily relied. In Quirin, the Court held that Congress had authorized the military trial of Haupt, a United States citizen who entered the country with orders from the Nazis to blow up domestic war facilities but was captured before he could execute those orders. The Court reasoned that Haupt's citizenship was no bar to his military trial as an unlawful enemy belligerent, concluding that "[c]itizens who associate themselves with the military arm of the enemy government, and with its aid, guidance and direction enter this country bent on hostile acts, are enemy belligerents within the meaning of . . . the law of war."

Like Haupt, Padilla associated with the military arm of the enemy, and with its aid, guidance, and direction entered this country bent on committing hostile acts on American soil. J.A. 22–23. Padilla thus falls within Quirin's definition of enemy belligerent, as well as within the definition of the equivalent term accepted by the plurality in Hamdi. Compare Quirin, 317 U.S. at 37–38, 63 S.Ct. 2 (holding that [c]itizens who associate themselves with the military arm of the enemy government, and with its aid, guidance and direction enter this country bent on hostile acts, are enemy belligerents within the meaning of . . . the law of war), with Hamdi, 124 S.Ct. at 2639 (accepting for purposes of the case the government's definition of enemy combatants as those who were part of or supporting forces hostile to the United States or coalition partners' in Afghanistan and who engaged in an armed conflict against the United States' there).

We understand the plurality's reasoning in Hamdi to be that the AUMF authorizes the President to detain all those who qualify as enemy combatants within the meaning of the laws of war, such power being universally accepted under the laws of war as necessary in order to prevent the return of combatants to the battlefield during conflict. Given that Padilla qualifies as an enemy combatant under both the definition adopted by the Court in Quirin and the definition accepted by the controlling opinion in Hamdi, his military detention as an enemy combatant by the President is unquestionably authorized by the AUMF as a fundamental incident to the President's prosecution of the war against al Qaeda in Afghanistan.[3]

Padilla marshals essentially four arguments for the conclusion that his detention is unlawful. None of them ultimately is persuasive.

Recognizing the hurdle to his position represented by the Supreme Court's decision in Hamdi, Padilla principally argues that his case does not fall within the narrow circumstances considered by the Court in that case because, although he too stood alongside Taliban forces in Afghanistan, he was seized on American soil, whereas Hamdi was captured on a foreign battlefield. In other words, Padilla maintains that capture on a foreign battlefield was one of the narrow circumstances to which the plurality in Hamdi confined its opinion. We disagree. When the plurality articulated the narrow question before it, it referred simply to the permissibility of detaining an individual who . . . was part of or supporting forces hostile to the United States or coalition partners in Afghanistan and who engaged in an armed conflict against the United States' there. Nowhere in its framing of the narrow question presented did the plurality even mention the locus of capture.

The actual reasoning that the plurality thereafter employed is consistent with the question having been framed so as to render locus of capture irrelevant. That reasoning was that Hamdi's detention was an exercise of necessary and appropriate force within the meaning of the AUMF because detention to prevent a combatant's return to the battlefield is a fundamental incident of waging war. This reasoning simply does not admit of a distinction between an enemy combatant captured abroad and detained in the United States, such as Hamdi, and an enemy combatant who escaped capture abroad but was ultimately captured domestically and detained in the United States, such as Padilla. As we previously explained, Padilla poses the same threat of returning to the battlefield as Hamdi posed at the time of the Supreme Court's adjudication of Hamdi's petition. Padilla's detention is thus necessary and appropriate to the same extent as was Hamdi's.

Padilla directs us to a passage from the plurality's opinion in Hamdi in which, when responding to the dissent, the plurality charged that the dissent ignore[d] the context of th[e] case: a United States citizen captured in a foreign combat zone. Padilla argues that this passage proves that capture on a foreign battlefield was one of the factual circumstances by

---

[3] Under Hamdi, the power to detain that is authorized under the AUMF is not a power to detain indefinitely. Detention is limited to the duration of the hostilities as to which the detention is authorized. Because the United States remains engaged in the conflict with al Qaeda in Afghanistan, Padilla's detention has not exceeded in duration that authorized by the AUMF.

which the Court's opinion was limited. If this language stood alone, Padilla's argument as to the limitation of Hamdi at least would have more force, though to acknowledge that foreign battlefield capture was part of the context of the case still is not to say (at least not necessarily) that the locus of capture was essential to the Court's reasoning. However, this language simply cannot bear the weight that Padilla would have it bear when it is considered against the backdrop of both the quite different limitations that were expressly imposed by the Court through its framing of the question presented, and the actual reasoning that was employed by the Court in reaching its conclusion, which reasoning was consistent with the question having been framed so as to render an enemy combatant's point of capture irrelevant to the President's power to detain. In short, the plurality carefully limited its opinion, but not in a way that leaves room for argument that the President's power to detain one who has associated with the enemy and taken up arms against the United States in a foreign combat zone varies depending upon the geographic location where that enemy combatant happens to be captured.

Our conclusion that the reasoning in Hamdi does not support a distinction based on the locus of capture is buttressed by the plurality's analysis of Quirin. Although at issue in Quirin was the authority of the President to subject a United States citizen who was also an enemy combatant to military trial, the plurality in Hamdi went to lengths to observe that Haupt, who had been captured domestically, could instead have been permissibly detained for the duration of hostilities. That analysis strongly suggests, if it does not confirm, that the plurality did not regard the locus of capture (within or without the United States) as relevant to the President's authority to detain an enemy combatant who is also a citizen, and that it believed that the detention of such a combatant is not more or less a necessary incident of the President's power to wage war depending upon the locus of eventual capture.

Given the lack of any reference to locus of capture in the plurality's articulation of the narrow question before it, the absence of any basis in Hamdi's reasoning for a distinction between foreign and domestic capture of one who has both associated with the enemy and taken up arms against the United States on behalf of that enemy in a foreign combat zone, and the plurality's understanding of and reliance upon Quirin as a precedent that would permit the detention of an enemy combatant who had been captured domestically, we simply cannot ascribe to the rejoinder to Justice Scalia the significance, much less the dispositive significance, that Padilla urges.[4]

---

[4]   Padilla also argues that the locus of capture should be legally relevant to the scope of the AUMF's authorization because there is a higher probability of an erroneous determination that one is an enemy combatant when the seizure occurs on American soil. It is far from clear that this is actually the case. In any event, Padilla's argument confuses the scope of the President's power

Padilla also argues, and the district court held, that Padilla's military detention is neither necessary nor appropriate because he is amenable to criminal prosecution. Related to this argument, Padilla attempts to distinguish Quirin from his case on the grounds that he has simply been detained, unlike Haupt who was charged and tried in Quirin. Neither the argument nor the attempted distinction is convincing.

As to the fact that Padilla can be prosecuted, the availability of criminal process does not distinguish him from Hamdi. If the mere availability of criminal prosecution rendered detention unnecessary within the meaning of the AUMF, then Hamdi's detention would have been unnecessary and therefore unauthorized, since he too was detained in the United States and amenable to criminal prosecution. We are convinced, in any event, that the availability of criminal process cannot be determinative of the power to detain, if for no other reason than that criminal prosecution may well not achieve the very purpose for which detention is authorized in the first place—the prevention of return to the field of battle. Equally important, in many instances criminal prosecution would impede the Executive in its efforts to gather intelligence from the detainee and to restrict the detainee's communication with confederates so as to ensure that the detainee does not pose a continuing threat to national security even as he is confined—impediments that would render military detention not only an appropriate, but also the necessary, course of action to be taken in the interest of national security.

The district court acknowledged the need to defer to the President's determination that Padilla's detention is necessary and appropriate in the interest of national security. However, we believe that the district court ultimately accorded insufficient deference to that determination, effectively imposing upon the President the equivalent of a least-restrictive-means test. To subject to such exacting scrutiny the President's determination that criminal prosecution would not adequately protect the Nation's security at a very minimum fails to accord the President the deference that is his when he acts pursuant to a broad delegation of authority from Congress, such as the AUMF.

As for Padilla's attempted distinction of Quirin on the grounds that, unlike Haupt, he has never been charged and tried by the military, the plurality in Hamdi rejected as immaterial the distinction between detention and trial (apparently regarding the former as a lesser imposition than the latter), noting that "nothing in Quirin suggests that [Haupt's United States] citizenship would have precluded his mere detention for the duration of the relevant hostilities."

---

to detain enemy combatants under the AUMF with the process for establishing that a detainee is in fact an enemy combatant. Hamdi itself provides process to guard against the erroneous detention of non-enemy combatants.

Padilla, citing Ex parte Endo, 323 U.S. 283, 65 S.Ct. 208, 89 L.Ed. 243 (1944), and relying upon Quirin, next argues that only a clear statement from Congress can authorize his detention, and that the AUMF is not itself, and does not contain, such a clear statement.

In Endo, the Court did state that, when asked to find implied powers in a wartime statute, it must assume that "the law makers intended to place no greater restraint on the citizen than was clearly and unmistakably indicated by the language [the law makers] used." The Court almost immediately thereafter observed, however, that the "fact that the Act" at issue was "silent on detention [did] not of course mean that any power to detain [was] lacking," an observation that proves that the Court did not adopt or even apply in that case a "clear statement" rule of the kind for which Padilla argues.

Padilla contends that Quirin also supports the existence of a clear statement rule. However, in no place in Quirin did the Court even purport to establish a clear statement rule. In its opinion, the Court did note that Congress had "explicitly" authorized Haupt's military trial. . . . In fact, to the extent that Quirin can be understood to have addressed the need for a clear statement of authority from Congress at all, the rule would appear the opposite:

[T]he detention and trial of petitioners—ordered by the President in the declared exercise of his powers as Commander in Chief of the Army in time of war and of grave public danger—are not to be set aside by the courts without the clear conviction that they are in conflict with the Constitution or laws of Congress constitutionally enacted.

Of course, even were a clear statement by Congress required, the AUMF constitutes such a clear statement according to the Supreme Court. In Hamdi, stating that "it [was] of no moment that the AUMF does not use specific language of detention," the plurality held that the AUMF "clearly and unmistakably authorized" Hamdi's detention. Nothing in the AUMF permits us to conclude that the Joint Resolution clearly and unmistakably authorized Hamdi's detention but not Padilla's. To the contrary, read in light of its purpose clause ("in order to prevent any future acts of international terrorism against the United States") and its preamble (stating that the acts of 9/11 "render it both necessary and appropriate . . . to protect United States citizens both at home and abroad"), the AUMF applies even more clearly and unmistakably to Padilla than to Hamdi. Padilla, after all, in addition to supporting hostile forces in Afghanistan and taking up arms against our troops on a battlefield in that country like Hamdi, also came to the United States in order to commit future acts of terrorism against American citizens and targets.

These facts unquestionably establish that Padilla poses the requisite threat of return to battle in the ongoing armed conflict between the United

States and al Qaeda in Afghanistan, and that his detention is authorized as a "fundamental incident of waging war," in order "to prevent a combatant's return to the battlefield," Congress "clearly and unmistakably," authorized such detention when, in the AUMF, it "permitt[ed] the use of 'necessary and appropriate force,'" to prevent other attacks like those of September 11, 2001.

. . .

The Congress of the United States, in the Authorization for Use of Military Force Joint Resolution, provided the President all powers necessary and appropriate to protect American citizens from terrorist acts by those who attacked the United States on September 11, 2001. As would be expected, and as the Supreme Court has held, those powers include the power to detain identified and committed enemies such as Padilla, who associated with al Qaeda and the Taliban regime, who took up arms against this Nation in its war against these enemies, and who entered the United States for the avowed purpose of further prosecuting that war by attacking American citizens and targets on our own soil—a power without which, Congress understood, the President could well be unable to protect American citizens from the very kind of savage attack that occurred four years ago almost to the day.

The detention of petitioner being fully authorized by Act of Congress, the judgment of the district court that the detention of petitioner by the President of the United States is without support in law is hereby reversed.

REVERSED.

Following the court of appeals decision, supra, the Padilla saga continued. He sought certiorari review in the Supreme Court. Justice Kennedy's opinion below concurring in the denial of certiorari details what happened next.

PADILLA V. HANFT

547 U.S. 1062 (2006)

Case below, 423 F.3d 386.

Petition for writ of certiorari to the United States Court of Appeals for the Fourth Circuit denied.

The petition for a writ of certiorari is denied. JUSTICE SOUTER and JUSTICE BREYER would grant the petition for a writ of certiorari.

JUSTICE KENNEDY, with whom THE CHIEF JUSTICE and JUSTICE STEVENS join, concurring in the denial of certiorari.

The Court's decision to deny the petition for writ of certiorari is, in my view, a proper exercise of its discretion in light of the circumstances of the case. The history of petitioner Jose Padilla's detention, however, does require this brief explanatory statement.

Padilla is a United States citizen. Acting pursuant to a material witness warrant issued by the United States District Court for the Southern District of New York, federal agents apprehended Padilla at Chicago's O'Hare International Airport on May 8, 2002. He was transported to New York, and on May 22 he moved to vacate the warrant. On June 9, while that motion was pending, the President issued an order to the Secretary of Defense designating Padilla an enemy combatant and ordering his military detention. The District Court, notified of this action by the Government's ex parte motion, vacated the material witness warrant.

Padilla was taken to the Consolidated Naval Brig in Charleston, South Carolina. On June 11, Padilla's counsel filed a habeas corpus petition in the Southern District of New York challenging the military detention. The District Court denied the petition, but the Court of Appeals for the Second Circuit reversed and ordered the issuance of a writ directing Padilla's release. This Court granted certiorari and ordered dismissal of the habeas corpus petition without prejudice, holding that the District Court for the Southern District of New York was not the appropriate court to consider it. See Rumsfeld v. Padilla, 542 U.S. 426, 124 S.Ct. 2711, 159 L.Ed.2d 513 (2004).

The present case arises from Padilla's subsequent habeas corpus petition, filed in the United States District Court for the District of South Carolina on July 2, 2004. Padilla requested that he be released immediately or else charged with a crime. The District Court granted the petition on February 28, 2005, but the Court of Appeals for the Fourth Circuit reversed that judgment on September 9, 2005. Padilla then filed the instant petition for writ of certiorari.

After Padilla sought certiorari in this Court, the Government obtained an indictment charging him with various federal crimes. The President ordered that Padilla be released from military custody and transferred to the control of the Attorney General to face criminal charges. The Government filed a motion for approval of Padilla's transfer in the Court of Appeals for the Fourth Circuit. The Court of Appeals denied the motion, but this Court granted the Government's subsequent application respecting the transfer. Hanft v. Padilla, 546 U.S. 1084, 126 S.Ct. 978, 163 L.Ed.2d 721 (2006). The Government also filed a brief in opposition to certiorari, arguing, among other things, that Padilla's petition should be denied as moot.

The Government's mootness argument is based on the premise that Padilla, now having been charged with crimes and released from military custody, has received the principal relief he sought. Padilla responds that his case was not mooted by the Government's voluntary actions because there remains a possibility that he will be redesignated and redetained as an enemy combatant.

Whatever the ultimate merits of the parties' mootness arguments, there are strong prudential considerations disfavoring the exercise of the Court's certiorari power. Even if the Court were to rule in Padilla's favor, his present custody status would be unaffected. Padilla is scheduled to be tried on criminal charges. Any consideration of what rights he might be able to assert if he were returned to military custody would be hypothetical, and to no effect, at this stage of the proceedings.

In light of the previous changes in his custody status and the fact that nearly four years have passed since he first was detained, Padilla, it must be acknowledged, has a continuing concern that his status might be altered again. That concern, however, can be addressed if the necessity arises. Padilla is now being held pursuant to the control and supervision of the United States District Court for the Southern District of Florida, pending trial of the criminal case. In the course of its supervision over Padilla's custody and trial the District Court will be obliged to afford him the protection, including the right to a speedy trial, guaranteed to all federal criminal defendants. See, e.g., U.S. Const., Amdt. 6; 18 U.S.C. § 3161. Were the Government to seek to change the status or conditions of Padilla's custody, that court would be in a position to rule quickly on any responsive filings submitted by Padilla. In such an event, the District Court, as well as other courts of competent jurisdiction, should act promptly to ensure that the office and purposes of the writ of habeas corpus are not compromised. Padilla, moreover, retains the option of seeking a writ of habeas corpus in this Court. See this Court's Rule 20; 28 U.S.C. §§ 1651(a), 2241.

That Padilla's claims raise fundamental issues respecting the separation of powers, including consideration of the role and function of the courts, also counsels against addressing those claims when the course of legal proceedings has made them, at least for now, hypothetical. This is especially true given that Padilla's current custody is part of the relief he sought, and that its lawfulness is uncontested.

These are the reasons for my vote to deny certiorari.

JUSTICE GINSBURG, dissenting from the denial of certiorari.

This case, here for the second time, raises a question "of profound importance to the Nation," Rumsfeld v. Padilla, 542 U.S. 426, 455, 124 S.Ct. 2711, 159 L.Ed.2d 513 (2004) (STEVENS, J., dissenting): Does the President have authority to imprison indefinitely a United States citizen arrested on United States soil distant from a zone of combat, based on an Executive declaration that the citizen was, at the time of his arrest, an "enemy combatant"? It is a question the Court heard, and should have decided, two years ago. Nothing the Government has yet done purports to retract the assertion of Executive power Padilla protests.

Although the Government has recently lodged charges against Padilla in a civilian court, nothing prevents the Executive from returning to the road it earlier constructed and defended. A party's voluntary cessation does not make a case less capable of repetition or less evasive of review. See Spencer v. Kemna, 523 U.S. 1, 17, 118 S.Ct. 978, 140 L.Ed.2d 43 (1998) (the capable-of-repetition exception to mootness applies where "(1) the challenged action [is] in its duration too short to be fully litigated prior to cessation or expiration, and (2) there [is] a reasonable expectation that the same complaining party [will] be subject to the same action again" (emphasis added)) (citations and internal quotation marks omitted); cf. United States v. Concentrated Phosphate Export Assn., Inc., 393 U.S. 199, 203, 89 S.Ct. 361, 21 L.Ed.2d 344 (1968) (party whose actions threaten to moot a case must make "absolutely clear that the allegedly wrongful behavior could not reasonably be expected to recur"); United States v. W. T. Grant Co., 345 U.S. 629, 632–633, 73 S.Ct. 894, 97 L.Ed. 1303 (1953) (voluntary cessation of illegal activity will not render case moot unless there is "no reasonable expectation that the wrong will be repeated". See also Lane v. Williams, 455 U.S. 624, 633–634, 102 S.Ct. 1322, 71 L.Ed.2d 508 (1982) (applying "capable of repetition, yet evading review" in a habeas case. Satisfied that this case is not moot, I would grant the petition for certiorari.

NOTE ON STRATEGIC CONSIDERATIONS IN THE CIVILIAN CRIMINAL PROSECUTION OF JOSE PADILLA

Padilla was arrested in 2002 as a material witness, two months later labeled an enemy combatant, held in military custody for three years, then transferred back to civilian custody and indicted on terrorism charges based on evidence obtained before he was placed in military custody. The challenge for counsel was how to test in court the way in which the government had proceeded and the conditions under which he was detained. In United States v. Padilla, below, Padilla moved to dismiss the indictment based on alleged "outrageous government conduct" relating to the conditions of his military detention and interrogation. Might Padilla also have made a claim of a speedy trial violation based on the length of the military detention that intervened between his original arrest by civilian authorities and later transfer back to civilian authorities for prosecution. Compare United States v. Ghailani, 733 F.3d 29 (2d Cir. 2013), where the accused was indicted in federal court while a fugitive; then subsequently captured and interrogated by CIA agents over the course of a two year period; then sent to Guantanamo where a prosecution before a military commission was initiated and then suspended as part of a suspension of military commission proceedings by President Obama. Five years after his capture, a prosecution was initiated in the U. S. District Court in New York based on the original indictment. Defendant's claim of a speedy trial violation was rejected in a lengthy opinion.

UNITED STATES V. PADILLA
2007 WL 1079090 (S.D.Fla. 2007)

MARCIA G. COOKE, UNITED STATES DISTRICT JUDGE.

This cause came before the Court upon defendant Jose Padilla's Motion to Dismiss for Outrageous Government Conduct filed on October 5, 2006. The government filed its Response on November 13, 2006 and defendant Padilla filed his Reply on December 1, 2006. This Court has reviewed these pleadings, and finds as follows:

. . .

Padilla filed the instant motion to dismiss the indictment for outrageous government conduct on October 5, 2006. In his motion, Mr. Padilla argues that the conditions of his military detention and interrogation while at the Naval Brig "shock[ ] the conscience" in violation of his due process rights. Padilla claims that the mistreatment he allegedly suffered while at the Naval Brig divests the government of its jurisdiction to prosecute him for the crimes charged in the indictment. Mr. Padilla's allegations with regard to his mistreatment stem exclusively from his time at the Naval Brig. Padilla makes no allegations regarding outrageous government conduct prior to his arrest, during the course of his arrest or during his civilian custodial detention in connection with the crimes charged in the indictment. Mr. Padilla also makes no claim of prosecutorial misconduct related to the government's efforts to try this case. For the reasons addressed in this Order, Defendant Padilla's Motion to Dismiss [the Indictment] for Outrageous Government Conduct is denied.

In United States v. Russell, 411 U.S. 423 (1973), the Court noted, in dicta, that it "may some day be presented with a situation in which the conduct of law enforcement agents is so outrageous that due process principles would absolutely bar the government from invoking judicial process to obtain a conviction." The Russell court ultimately found that the governmental conduct at issue did not rise to this level, and cited the defendant's predisposition to commit the crime charged as fatal to his entrapment claim.

. . .

Regardless of whether courts choose to recognize, yet not apply the doctrine, or reject the doctrine outright, the question comes up almost exclusively within the context of government involvement in the defendant's crime and entrapment. Since the doctrine has never been effectively applied in any context, courts have had difficulty ascertaining its precise contours, if any. Interpreting the austere dicta in Russell, courts have attempted to delineate precisely when governmental involvement in the crime charged is so substantial and objectionable, that it should be deemed "outrageous."

. . .

In its Response to Mr. Padilla's Motion to Dismiss [the Indictment] for Outrageous Government Conduct the government argues that the "motion fails as a matter of law." In order to assess whether Padilla's motion is legally insufficient, this Court must accept its allegations as true, and determine whether he has stated a cognizable claim. Thus, while this Court has not held a hearing, nor made any findings with regard to Padilla's claims of abuse and torture at the Naval Brig, for the sake of this Order, this Court will accept Padilla's allegations as true.

In his pleadings, Padilla fails to cite any cases where charges were dismissed for outrageous government conduct. While failure to provide evidence of the claim's application is by no means fatal to Padilla's motion, it bears testament to the claim's severely narrow scope. Furthermore, the case law that Padilla does cite is predominantly comprised of cases where the doctrine is considered in the context of governmental participation in the crime charged and entrapment.[6] In fact, many cases that defendant cites expressly state that the only instance where the claim may be properly invoked is within this governmental participation context.

. . .

In one of the few cases cited by defendant where the outrageous governmental conduct stems from something other than governmental participation in the charged crime, the court is careful to delineate the appropriate contours of the claim. In United States v. Boone, 437 F.3d 829, 841–42 (8th Cir.2006), the defendant argued that the attempted murder charge against her should have been dismissed due to the outrageous government conduct of an FBI agent. Defendant claimed that she was threatened, intimidated, verbally abused, and subjected to other inappropriate conduct by the FBI agent during the investigation of the

---

[6] In Defendant's Reply, Mr. Padilla refutes the government's assertion that the circuits have not been willing to consider outrageous government conduct claims by citing to a litany of cases where the appellate courts have recognized the doctrine. However, Padilla fails to acknowledge that in the cited string of cases, the claim arises almost exclusively in the context of governmental participation in the crime charged and entrapment. This factor significantly distinguishes these cases from Padilla's case. In the cited cases, the allegedly objectionable governmental conduct occurred during the commission of the offense that the defendant was seeking to dismiss from the indictment. In Padilla's case, however, he is seeking to have criminal charges dismissed because of governmental actions perpetrated after the commission of the charged crimes. Furthermore, the objectionable governmental action did not occur during the course of his detainment for the criminal charges he is currently attempting to dismiss. Rather, the allegedly outrageous governmental conduct occurred during an independent military detainment in connection with his enemy combatant status.

crime and the subsequent arrest. The court held "the rule that outrageous government conduct can foreclose criminal charges has been applied by our court almost exclusively to situations involving entrapment, where law enforcement officers have sought to create crimes in order to lure a defendant into illegal activity that she was not otherwise ready and willing to commit." The court concluded that since defendant "has not even alleged that any government official had engaged in such conduct [in the case at bar, defendant] has not shown any due process bar to her attempted murder conviction."

Mr. Padilla's failure to cite case law where outrageous government conduct claims are premised upon post-arrest abuse of the defendant is of no small moment. In Boone, the Eighth Circuit echoed the holdings of its sister circuits by articulating that in order to invoke an outrageous government conduct claim, the government need first involve itself in the criminal scheme along with the defendant. This makes practical sense since the claim itself is borne out of due process concerns. Thus, a law enforcement officer may be behaving "outrageously" in certain instances where her over-involvement in a criminal enterprise "violates fundamental fairness" or is "shocking to the universal sense of justice." On these occasions, due process concerns could preclude prosecution of the very claim in which the governmental agent was overzealously embroiled. Thus, courts have noted, that in the rarest of circumstances, if it was impossible to extract the objectionable governmental conduct from the crime, the prosecution may need to be stymied.

Mr. Padilla's claim does not present this scenario. Padilla claims that his charges should be dismissed due to outrageous governmental conduct perpetrated after the commission of his alleged crimes. Padilla seeks this relief despite the fact that the objectionable conduct occurred during his military detention in connection with his enemy combatant status. Padilla's argument contains numerous legal infirmities.

First, the fact that the governmental conduct occurred at a time and place removed from the crimes charged makes the remedy Padilla is seeking considerably more attenuated and arbitrary. Short of resorting to a "two wrongs make a right" judicial process, it is difficult for this Court to ascertain how the remedy sought emanates from the infirmity defendant describes. This is considerably distinguishable from a government entrapment scenario, where the crime that the defendant is charged with is the crux of the outrageous government conduct claim.[7]

---

[7] An indictment may also be dismissed upon a sufficient showing of prejudice within the prosecutorial misconduct context. See United States v. Accetturo, 858 F.2d 679 (11th Cir.1988). Prosecutorial misconduct is analogous to claims of outrageous government conduct premised on entrapment or government participation in the defendant's crime. In both instances, government action has prejudiced defendant with respect to the charges he is attempting to dismiss. Conversely, Mr. Padilla's claim focuses on governmental conduct that is not necessarily related to

Second, the outrageous conduct occurred while Padilla was under military control at the Naval Brig in Charleston, South Carolina. At this time, Padilla was being held under Presidential orders in connection with his enemy combatant status and had not been charged with the crimes he is currently facing. This further attenuates Padilla's outrageous government conduct claim. Even if Padilla's due process rights were violated while being held at the Naval Brig as an enemy combatant, he fails to explain how this violation should result in the dismissal of distinct crimes that he was not charged with at that point.[8]

Third, Mr. Padilla fails to explain why suppressing governmental use of any evidence obtained from him at the Naval Brig is insufficient for purposes of this trial. In his motion, Padilla acknowledges that the government has already averred not to seek introduction of any of the Naval Brig evidence at trial.[9] Despite summarily rejecting this remedy as "clearly inadequate," Padilla fails to support this contention or explain why his requested remedy is more appropriate.[10] In fact, in his motion, Padilla relies heavily on United States v. Toscanino, 500 F.2d 267 (2d Cir.1974), a case where the Second Circuit sanctions this very approach. Padilla's Motion concedes that "the court in Toscanino noted that many cases involving due process violations center on unlawful government acquisition of evidence and that, in those instances, the proper remedy would be the exclusion of the tainted evidence."

. . .

For the reasons set forth above, it is hereby:

Ordered and adjudged that Defendant Padilla's Motion to Dismiss for Outrageous Government Conduct filed on October 5, 2006 is denied.

---

the charges he is facing and does not prejudice him in this prosecution. Although the pleadings cite to cases covering prosecutorial misconduct, Mr. Padilla has made no claim to this effect.

[8]   Taken to its logical extreme, this rationale would effectively provide a defendant with amnesty for any uncharged crime so long as the government violated that defendant's due process rights at some prior point. This erroneous recitation clearly misconstrues the law regarding the outrageous government conduct doctrine as well as defendant's due process rights.

[9]   Counsel for the government has stated to this Court in a number of contexts that the Naval Brig events are irrelevant to this criminal prosecution. The government has even sought to exclude all references to events at the Naval Brig. See Government's Motion In Limine to Exclude Evidence and Argument Regarding the Circumstances of Defendant Padilla's Pre-Indictment Detention as an Unlawful Enemy Combatant. However, the government has not agreed to absolutely preclude referencing Naval Brig events at trial. The government has stated, that should Mr. Padilla testify at trial, Padilla's Naval Brig statements may be offered as impeachment evidence. The Court has yet to rule on the government's motion to exclude Naval Brig evidence at trial. However, should any Naval Brig statements be introduced at trial, for impeachment or otherwise, the circumstances surrounding the making of the statements may be relevant and hence admissible.

[10]   This Court's holding does not imply that this is Mr. Padilla's only remedy with regard to any alleged mistreatment at the Naval Brig, only that it is the most appropriate remedy within the framework of this prosecution. Mr. Padilla is free to institute a Bivens action, an action for monetary damages or any other form of redress that he is legally entitled to pursue.

NOTE ON THE OUTCOME OF THE PADILLA CASE

As detailed in United States v. Padilla, supra, after being returned to the custody of civilian authorities, Padilla was indicted in Miami, Florida along with four other defendants on three counts: "Conspiracy to Murder, Kidnap, and Maim Persons in a Foreign Country"; "Conspiracy to Provide Material Support to Terrorists" and providing "Material Support to Terrorists". On August 15, 2007, he was convicted on all counts, the jury having taken little more than a day to reach its verdict. Padilla, age 37, was initially sentenced to 17 years and four months. The judge said that she took into consideration the harsh treatment he had undergone while detained as an enemy combatant in military custody. The prosecutor had sought a life sentence. Washington Post, January 23, 2008, A03. The government appealed the sentence and the court of appeals reversed, concluding that the trial judge erred when she gave Padilla credit for the time served in detention and she failed to account for his "heightened risk of dangerousness" as a result of his al Qaeda training and his numerous previous arrests. Upon remand, Padilla was resentenced to a 21 year term of imprisonment. See https://www.npr.org/sections/thetwo-way/2014/09/09/347127580/jose-padilla-gets-4-years-added-to-his-2007-sentence.

NOTE ON THE CASE OF ALI SALEH KAHLAH AL-MARRI

Another detainee, in a situation similar to Padilla's, was arrested in the United States by civilian authorities and then declared to be an enemy combatant and transferred to military custody, but in this instance he was a non-U.S. citizen. Ali Saleh Kahlah al-Marri, like Padilla, was originally arrested as a material witness, indicted on civilian criminal charges and subsequently, again like Padilla, declared by Presidential order to be an enemy combatant. He was detained for four years in military custody and sought habeas corpus review. The fourth circuit eventually decided his petition en banc in Al-Marri v. Pucciarelli, 534 F.3d 213 (4th Cir. 2008) where the court ruled as follows:

> The parties present two principal issues for our consideration: (1) assuming the Government's allegations about al-Marri are true, whether Congress has empowered the President to detain al-Marri as an enemy combatant; and (2) assuming Congress has empowered the President to detain al-Marri as an enemy combatant provided the Government's allegations against him are true, whether al-Marri has been afforded sufficient process to challenge his designation as an enemy combatant.

> Having considered the briefs and arguments of the parties, the en banc court now holds: (1) by a 5 to 4 vote (Chief Judge Williams and Judges Wilkinson, Niemeyer, Traxler, and Duncan voting in the affirmative; Judges Michael, Motz, King, and Gregory voting in the negative), that, if the Government's allegations about al-Marri are true, Congress has empowered the President to detain him as an enemy combatant; and (2) by a 5 to 4 vote (Judges Michael, Motz,

Traxler, King, and Gregory voting in the affirmative; Chief Judge Williams and Judges Wilkinson, Niemeyer, and Duncan voting in the negative), that, assuming Congress has empowered the President to detain al-Marri as an enemy combatant provided the Government's allegations against him are true, al-Marri has not been afforded sufficient process to challenge his designation as an enemy combatant.

Al-Marri's subsequent petition for certiorari to the Supreme Court was granted. Before the Supreme Court could review the case on the merits, however, the Department of Justice moved to transfer al-Marri from military to civilian custody. The Supreme Court granted the application, vacated the decision in al-Marri v. Pucciarelli, supra, and ordered a dismissal of the appeal as moot. Al-Marri v. Spagone, 129 S.Ct. 1545 (March 6, 2009).

After he was transferred to civilian custody, al-Marri was indicted in the Central District of Illinois on two counts, conspiracy to provide material support to a foreign terrorist organization and providing material support to a foreign terrorist organization. On April 29, 2009, al-Marri pled guilty to one count of conspiring to provide material support to a foreign terrorist organization. He was sentenced to eight years in prison. He was released from prison in January, 2015 and returned to Qatar. See Benjamin Wittes, Thoughts on the al-Marri Release, https://www.lawfareblog.com/thoughts-al-marri-release. Suppose that al-Marri had not pled guilty. What kind of issues might the government have encountered in seeking to obtain a conviction?

For an in-depth treatment of the al-Marri case (as well as many of the other related issues and decisions then facing the Obama administration), see Jane Mayer, Reporter at Large, The Hard Cases, The New Yorker, Feb. 23, 2009.

There are some parallels in the way that the government handled the cases of Jose Padilla and Ali Saleh Kahlah al-Marri. Are the cases similar? What are the differences, if any?

NOTE ON LEGISLATION AUTHORIZING MILITARY DETENTION—§§ 1021–1022, NDAA OF 2012

In regard to the subject of detention in military custody, the National Defense Authorization Act for 2012 contains the following provisions (sections 1021–1023) authorizing a kind of law of war detention; it is not, by its terms, restricted to Guantanamo detainees. As detailed below, these provisions quickly became the subject of controversy and litigation.

National Defense Authorization Act, 2012

SEC. 1021. AFFIRMATION OF AUTHORITY OF THE ARMED FORCES OF THE UNITED STATES TO DETAIN COVERED PERSONS PURSUANT TO THE AUTHORIZATION FOR USE OF MILITARY FORCE.

(a) IN GENERAL.—Congress affirms that the authority of the President to use all necessary and appropriate force pursuant to the Authorization for Use of Military Force (Public Law 107–40; 50 U.S.C. 1541 note) includes the authority for the Armed Forces of the United States to detain covered persons (as defined in subsection (b)) pending disposition under the law of war.

(b) COVERED PERSONS.—A covered person under this section is any person as follows:

(1) A person who planned, authorized, committed, or aided the terrorist attacks that occurred on September 11, 2001, or harbored those responsible for those attacks.

(2) A person who was a part of or substantially supported al-Qaeda, the Taliban, or associated forces that are engaged in hostilities against the United States or its coalition partners, including any person who has committed a belligerent act or has directly supported such hostilities in aid of such enemy forces.

(c) DISPOSITION UNDER LAW OF WAR.—The disposition of a person under the law of war as described in subsection (a) may include the following:

(1) Detention under the law of war without trial until the end of the hostilities authorized by the Authorization for Use of Military Force.

(2) Trial under chapter 47A of title 10, United States Code (as amended by the Military Commissions Act of 2009 (title XVIII of Public Law 111–84)).

(3) Transfer for trial by an alternative court or competent tribunal having lawful jurisdiction.

(4) Transfer to the custody or control of the person's country of origin, any other foreign country, or any other foreign entity.

(d) CONSTRUCTION.—Nothing in this section is intended to limit or expand the authority of the President or the scope of the Authorization for Use of Military Force.

(e) AUTHORITIES.—Nothing in this section shall be construed to affect existing law or authorities relating to the detention of United States citizens, lawful resident aliens of the United States, or any other persons who are captured or arrested in the United States.

(f) REQUIREMENT FOR BRIEFINGS OF CONGRESS.—The Secretary of Defense shall regularly brief Congress regarding the application of the authority described in this section, including the organizations, entities, and individuals considered to be "covered persons" for purposes of subsection (b)(2).

SEC. 1022. MILITARY CUSTODY FOR FOREIGN AL-QAEDA TERRORISTS.

(a) CUSTODY PENDING DISPOSITION UNDER LAW OF WAR.—

(1) IN GENERAL.—Except as provided in paragraph (4), the Armed Forces of the United States shall hold a person described in paragraph (2) who is captured in the course of hostilities authorized by the Authorization for Use of Military Force (Public Law 107–40) in military custody pending disposition under the law of war.

(2) COVERED PERSONS.—The requirement in paragraph (1) shall apply to any person whose detention is authorized under section 1021 who is determined—

(A) to be a member of, or part of, al-Qaeda or an associated force that acts in coordination with or pursuant to the direction of al-Qaeda; and (B) to have participated in the course of planning or carrying out an attack or attempted attack against the United States or its coalition partners.

(3) DISPOSITION UNDER LAW OF WAR.—For purposes of this subsection, the disposition of a person under the law of war has the meaning given in section 1021(c), except that no transfer otherwise described in paragraph (4) of that section shall be made unless consistent with the requirements of section 1028.

(4) WAIVER FOR NATIONAL SECURITY.—The President may waive the requirement of paragraph (1) if the President submits to Congress a certification in writing that such a waiver is in the national security interests of the United States.

(b) APPLICABILITY TO UNITED STATES CITIZENS AND LAWFUL RESIDENT ALIENS.—

(1) UNITED STATES CITIZENS.—The requirement to detain a person in military custody under this section does not extend to citizens of the United States.

(2) LAWFUL RESIDENT ALIENS.—The requirement to detain a person in military custody under this section does not extend to a lawful resident alien of the United States on the basis of conduct taking place within the United States, except to the extent permitted by the Constitution of the United States.

(c)   IMPLEMENTATION PROCEDURES.—

(1)   IN GENERAL.—Not later than 60 days after the date of the enactment of this Act, the President shall issue, and submit to Congress, procedures for implementing this section. . . .

In the wake of, and possibly in response to the controversy precipitated by the signing into law of sections 1021 and 1022 of the NDAA of 2012, on February 28, 2012, President Obama issued a Presidential Policy Directive relating to section 1022, supra. An accompanying Fact Sheet issued by the White House stated that, "Section 1022 does not apply to U.S. citizens, and the President has decided to waive its application to lawful permanent residents arrested in the United States."

Responding to some of the same concerns reflected in the White House Presidential Policy Directive/Fact Sheet, supra, two Senators, Feinstein and Lee, proposed an amendment, sec. 1033 (see below) to the NDAA for the following year, 2013. The Feinstein/Lee amendment, sec. 1033, was included in the bill passed by the Senate, but this section was deleted in the conference committee.

SEC. 1033. PROCEDURES FOR PERIODIC DETENTION REVIEW OF INDIVIDUALS DETAINED AT UNITED STATES NAVAL STATION, GUANTANAMO BAY, CUBA

Section 4001 of title 18, United States Code, is amended—

(1)   by redesignating subsection (b) as subsection (c); and

(2)   by inserting after subsection (a) the following:

(b)(1)   An authorization to use military force, a declaration of war, or any similar authority shall not authorize the detention without charge or trial of a citizen or lawful permanent resident of the United States apprehended in the United States, unless an Act of Congress expressly authorizes such detention.

'(2) Paragraph (1) applies to an authorization to use military force, a declaration of war, or any similar authority enacted before, on, or after the date of the enactment of the National Defense Authorization Act For Fiscal Year 2013.

'(3) Paragraph (1) shall not be construed to authorize the detention of a citizen of the United States, a lawful permanent resident of the United States, or any other person who is apprehended in the United States.'.

After sec. 1033 was deleted in the conference committee, another section, sec.1029, see below, was substituted and included in the final legislation that was enacted.

SEC. 1029. RIGHTS UNAFFECTED.

Nothing in the Authorization for Use of Military Force (Public Law 107–40; 50 U.S.C. 1541 note) or the National Defense Authorization Act for Fiscal Year 2012 (Public Law 112–81) shall be construed to deny the availability of the writ of habeas corpus or to deny any Constitutional rights in a court ordained or established by or under Article III of the Constitution to any person inside the United States who would be entitled to the availability of such writ or to such rights in the absence of such laws.

During the spring, 2012, a group of activists and writers filed a lawsuit challenging the constitutionality of section 1021 of the NDAA of 2012, supra. In Hedges v. Obama, 2012 WL 1721124 (S.D. N.Y. 2012), the district judge issued a preliminary injunction against enforcement of section 1021. In a subsequent opinion, 2012 WL 2044565, the court rejected the government's contention that the injunction issued by the court applied only to the parties to the lawsuit.

The Government appealed the Hedges district court decision to the Second Circuit. The excerpted opinion is reproduced below.

HEDGES V. OBAMA
724 F.3d 170 (2d Cir. 2013)

Before KEARSE and LOHIER, CIRCUIT JUDGES, and KAPLAN, DISTRICT JUDGE.

LEWIS A. KAPLAN, DISTRICT JUDGE.

On September 11, 2001, the al-Qaeda terrorist network attacked multiple targets in the United States with hijacked commercial airliners, killing approximately 3,000 people. A week later, Congress enacted the Authorization for Use of Military Force (the "AUMF"), which empowered President Bush to use all necessary and appropriate force against those nations, organizations, and persons responsible for the attacks and those who harbored such organizations or persons.

Nearly twelve years later, the hostilities continue. Presidents Bush and Obama have asserted the right to place certain individuals in military detention, without trial, in furtherance of their authorized use of force. Substantial litigation has ensued over the scope of presidential military detention authority—that is, whom did Congress authorize the President to detain when it passed the AUMF?

On December 31, 2011, President Obama signed into law the National Defense Authorization Act for Fiscal Year 2012. Section 1021 of that statute, which fits on a single page, is Congress' first—and, to date, only— foray into providing further clarity on that question. Of particular importance for our purposes, Section 1021(b)(2) appears to permit the President to detain anyone who was part of, or has substantially supported, al-Qaeda, the Taliban, or associated forces.

The controversy over Section 1021 was immediate. The government contends that Section 1021 simply reaffirms authority that the government already had under the AUMF, suggesting at times that the statute does next to nothing at all. Plaintiffs take a different view. They are journalists and activists who allegedly fear that the government may construe their work as having substantially supported al-Qaeda, the Taliban, or associated forces. They contend that Section 1021 is a dramatic expansion of the President's military detention authority, supposedly authorizing the military, for the first time, to detain American citizens on American soil. As one group of amici has noted, "[r]arely has a short statute been subject to more radically different interpretations than Section 1021."

Plaintiffs brought this action shortly after the statute was enacted. They sought an injunction barring enforcement of Section 1021 and a declaration that it violates, among other things, their rights under the First and Fifth Amendments to the United States Constitution. The district court agreed and entered a permanent injunction restraining detention pursuant to Section 1021(b)(2). It is that decision that we review here.

We conclude that plaintiffs lack standing to seek preenforcement review of Section 1021 and vacate the permanent injunction. The American citizen plaintiffs lack standing because Section 1021 says nothing at all about the President's authority to detain American citizens. And while Section 1021 does have a real bearing on those who are neither citizens nor lawful resident aliens and who are apprehended abroad, the non-citizen plaintiffs also have failed to establish standing because they have not shown a sufficient threat that the government will detain them under Section 1021. Accordingly, we do not address the merits of plaintiffs' constitutional claims.

[Judge Kaplan here reviewed the judicial history of detention authority under the AUMF, beginning with Hamdi and running through the post-Boumediene habeas cases treatment of that issue. He also reviewed the legislative history of section 1021 and then continued.]

. . .

Four plaintiffs submitted evidence that was considered by the district court and that is relevant to this appeal: two American citizens, Hedges and Alexa O'Brien and two non-citizens, Birgitta Jonsdottir and Kai Wargalla. FN101 They are journalists or members of advocacy organizations who assert that they fear that their work makes them subject to indefinite detention under Section 1021. The government submitted no evidence.

. . .

The district court granted the preliminary injunction by opinion filed May 16, 2012. It concluded that each plaintiff had an actual fear of detention under Section 1021 and that this fear was reasonable. In reaching this latter conclusion, the court relied in significant part on the government's initial refusal to represent that the plaintiffs' activities would not subject them to detention under Section 1021. It rejected the government's contention that Section 1021 was just an "affirmation" of the AUMF that did nothing new. Determining further that the expressive conduct of each plaintiff had been chilled and that each had incurred concrete costs as a reasonable consequence of this fear, the court concluded that each plaintiff had standing to challenge Section 1021. It held that plaintiffs had shown a likelihood of success on claims that Section 1021 violated the First Amendment and was impermissibly vague in violation of the Fifth Amendment. Finally, it concluded that the other relevant factors supported preliminary injunctive relief.

The government moved for reconsideration on May 25, 2012, clarifying its position by stating that, "[a]s a matter of law, individuals who engage in the independent journalistic activities or independent public advocacy described in plaintiffs' affidavits and testimony, without more, are not subject to law of war detention as affirmed by section 1021(a)–(c), solely on the basis of such independent journalistic activities or independent public advocacy." By agreement of the parties, the court proceeded directly to permanent injunction proceedings (thus mooting the motion for reconsideration) and took no new evidence for purposes of the permanent injunction.

Concluding that the government's "newly espoused position" did not alter its previous conclusion as to plaintiffs' standing, the court, on September 12, 2012, "permanently enjoin[ed] enforcement of § 1021(b)(2) in any manner, as to any person," generally affirming but also significantly expanding its prior analysis. It further held that "[m]ilitary detention based on allegations of 'substantially supporting' or 'directly supporting' the Taliban, al-Qaeda, or associated forces, is not encompassed within the AUMF and is enjoined by this Order regarding § 1021(b)(2)."

This appeal followed. We granted a temporary stay of the district court's order on September 17, 2012, and then granted a stay pending appeal on October 2, 2012.

II. Discussion

. . .

The parties raise a number of important and difficult questions, but we need not reach most of them. We consider here only plaintiffs' standing under Article III of the Constitution. . . .

B. The Proper Construction of Section 1021

We deal first with the meaning of Section 1021.

. . .

"As with any question of statutory interpretation, we begin by examining the text of the statute."

. . .

The AUMF authorized the President to "use all necessary and appropriate force against those nations, organizations, or persons he determines planned, authorized, committed, or aided the terrorist attacks that occurred on September 11, 2001, or harbored such organizations or persons." Section 1021(a) "affirms" that the AUMF authority includes the detention of a "covered person[ ]," which under Section 1021(b) means (1) a "person who planned, authorized, committed, or aided the terrorist attacks that occurred on September 11, 2001, or harbored those responsible for those attacks" or (2) a "person who was a part of or substantially supported al-Qaeda, the Taliban, or associated forces that are engaged in hostilities against the United States or its coalition partners, including any person who has committed a belligerent act or has directly supported such hostilities in aid of such enemy forces."

At first blush, Section 1021 may seem curious, if not contradictory. While Section 1021(b)(1) mimics language in the AUMF, Section 1021(b)(2) adds language absent from the AUMF. Yet Section 1021(a) states that it only "affirms" authority included under the AUMF, and Section 1021(d) indicates that Section 1021 is not "intended to limit or expand the authority of the President or the scope of the [AUMF]."

Fortunately, this apparent contradiction—that Section 1021 merely affirms AUMF authority even while it adds language not used in the AUMF—is readily resolved. It is true that the language regarding persons who "planned, authorized, committed, or aided" the 9/11 attacks (or harbored those who did) is identical in the AUMF and Section 1021(b)(1). The AUMF, however, does not merely define persons who may be detained, as does Section 1021(b). Instead, it provides the President authority to use "force" against the "nations, organizations, or persons" responsible for 9/11.FN124 Section 1021(b)(1) (read with Section 1021(a)) affirms that the AUMF authority to use force against the persons responsible for 9/11 includes a power to detain such persons. But it does not speak to what additional detention authority, if any, is included in the President's separate AUMF authority to use force against the organizations responsible for 9/11.

This is where Section 1021(b)(2), a provision concerned with the organizations responsible for 9/11—al-Qaeda and the Taliban—plays a role. Section 1021(b)(2) naturally is understood to affirm that the general AUMF authority to use force against these organizations includes the more specific authority to detain those who were part of, or those who substantially supported, these organizations or associated forces. Because one obviously cannot "detain" an organization, one must explain how the authority to use force against an organization translates into detention authority. Hence, it is not surprising that Section 1021(b)(2) contains language that does not appear in the AUMF, notwithstanding Section 1021(d). Plaintiffs create a false dilemma when they suggest that either Section 1021 expands the AUMF detention authority or it serves no purpose.

. . .

Indeed, there are perfectly sensible and legitimate reasons for Congress to have affirmed the nature of AUMF authority in this way. To the extent that reasonable minds might have differed—and in fact very much did differ—over whether the administration could detain those who were part of or substantially supported al-Qaeda, the Taliban, and associated forces under the AUMF authority to use force against the "organizations" responsible for 9/11, Section 1021(b)(2) eliminates any confusion on that particular point. At the same time, Section 1021(d) ensures that Congress' clarification may not properly be read to suggest that the President did not have this authority previously—a suggestion that might have called into question prior detentions. This does not necessarily make the section a " 'legislative attempt at an ex post facto "fix" . . . to try to ratify past detentions which may have occurred under an overly-broad interpretation of the AUMF,' " as plaintiffs contend. Rather, it is simply the 112th Congress' express resolution of a previously debated question about the scope of AUMF authority.

It remains to consider what effect Section 1021(e) has on this understanding. That provision states that "[n]othing in this section shall be construed to affect existing law or authorities relating to the detention of United States citizens, lawful resident aliens of the United States, or any other persons who are captured or arrested in the United States." Although this provision may appear superficially similar to Section 1021(d), nuances in the text and the legislative history make clear that Section 1021(e) actually is a significantly different provision.

As discussed above, in stating that Section 1021 is not intended to limit or expand the scope of the detention authority under the AUMF, Section 1021(d) mostly made a statement about the original AUMF—that is, it indicated that the specific power to detain those who were part of or who substantially supported the enumerated forces had been implicit in the more generally phrased AUMF. By contrast, in saying that Section 1021 shall not be construed to affect "existing law or authorities" relating to citizens, lawful resident aliens, or any other persons captured or arrested in the United States, Section 1021(e) expressly disclaims any statement about existing authority. Rather, it states only a limitation about how

Section 1021 may be construed to affect that existing authority, whatever that existing authority may be.

This understanding is reinforced by the legislative history. As discussed above, Senator Feinstein and others feared that Section 1021 would greatly expand the power of the government with particular reference to the authority to detain American citizens captured domestically. Senator Feinstein explained that she did not believe the government had such authority while Senators Graham and Levin, perhaps among others, believed that the government already did. Thus, Section 1021(e) was introduced specifically to effect a "truce" that ensured that—as to those covered by Section 1021(e)—courts would decide detention authority based not on Section 1021(b), but on what the law previously had provided in the absence of that enactment. This is not to say that Section 1021(e) specifically "exempts" these individuals from the President's AUMF detention authority, in the sense that Section 1022 expressly exempts United States citizens from its requirements. Rather, Section 1021(e) provides that Section 1021 just does not speak—one way or the other—to the government's authority to detain citizens, lawful resident aliens, or any other persons captured or arrested in the United States.[134]

We thus conclude, consistent with the text and buttressed in part by the legislative history, that Section 1021 means this: With respect to individuals who are not citizens, are not lawful resident aliens, and are not captured or arrested within the United States, the President's AUMF authority includes the authority to detain those responsible for 9/11 as well as those who were a part of, or substantially supported, al-Qaeda, the Taliban, or associated forces that are engaged in hostilities against the United States or its coalition partners—a detention authority that Section 1021 concludes was granted by the original AUMF. But with respect to citizens, lawful resident aliens, or individuals captured or arrested in the United States, Section 1021 simply says nothing at all.

We recognize that Section 1021 perhaps could have been drafted in a way that would have made this clearer and that the absence of any

---

[134]   To the extent that the text of Section 1021(e) may not make explicit whether "captured or arrested in the United States" is meant to modify only "any other persons" rather than modifying also "United States citizens" and "lawful resident aliens of the United States," we conclude that the former reading is correct. First, because commas follow "United States citizens" and "lawful resident aliens of the United States" but not "any other persons," under the rule of the last antecedent we read the limiting phrase as modifying only the term immediately preceding it, unless a contrary intention is apparent. Second, the alternative reading would render superfluous Congress' references to citizens and lawful resident aliens—Congress could have much more simply referred to "persons captured or arrested in the United States." Finally, legislative history provides no reason to conclude otherwise. Although Senator Feinstein suggested that her principal concern was the detention of American citizens apprehended on American soil, she and other senators expressed concern about the detention of American citizens generally, see, e.g., 157 Cong. Rec. S7,943–01, S7,953 (daily ed. Nov. 29, 2011) (statement of Sen. Leahy), and the amendment was described in such terms, see 157 Cong. Rec. S8,094–03, S8,124 (daily ed. Dec. 1, 2011) (statements of Sen. Levin and Sen. Graham).

reference to American citizens in Section 1021(b) led the district court astray in this case. Perhaps the last-minute inclusion of Section 1021(e) as an amendment introduced on the floor of the Senate explains the somewhat awkward construction. But that is neither here nor there. It is only our construction, just described, that properly gives effect to the text of all of the parts of Section 1021 and thus reflects congressional intent.

. . .

With this understanding of Section 1021, we may dispose of the claims of the citizen plaintiffs, Hedges and O'Brien. As discussed above, Section 1021 says nothing at all about the authority of the government to detain citizens. There simply is no threat whatsoever that they could be detained pursuant to that section. While it is true that Section 1021(e) does not foreclose the possibility that previously "existing law" may permit the detention of American citizens in some circumstances—a possibility that Hamdi clearly envisioned in any event—Section 1021 cannot itself be challenged as unconstitutional by citizens on the grounds advanced by plaintiffs because as to them it neither adds to nor subtracts from whatever authority would have existed in its absence. For similar reasons, plaintiffs cannot show that any detention Hedges and O'Brien may fear would be redressable by the relief they seek, an injunction of Section 1021.

. . .

The claims of Jonsdottir and Wargalla stand differently. Whereas Section 1021 says nothing about the government's authority to detain citizens, it does have real meaning regarding the authority to detain individuals who are not citizens or lawful resident aliens and are apprehended abroad.FN139 It provides that such individuals may be detained until the end of hostilities if they were part of or substantially supported al-Qaeda, the Taliban, or associated forces. To be sure, Section 1021 in substance provides also that this authority was implicit in the original AUMF. But, as discussed above, that the 112th Congress in passing Section 1021 expressed such a view does not mean that Section 1021 itself is a nullity. It is not immediately apparent on the face of the AUMF alone that the President had the authority to detain those who substantially supported al-Qaeda, and indeed many federal judges had concluded otherwise prior to Section 1021's passage. Hence, Section 1021(b)(2) sets forth an interpretation of the AUMF that had not previously been codified by Congress. Where a statute codifies an interpretation of an earlier law that is subject to reasonable dispute, the interpretive statute itself may affect the rights of persons under the earlier law.

As the standing inquiry as to these two plaintiffs is more involved, we discuss the relevant facts and applicable law in detail.

Jonsdottir is a citizen of Iceland and a member of its parliament. She is an activist and spokesperson for a number of groups, including

WikiLeaks, an organization famous for releasing troves of classified information of the United States government to the public. In early 2010, Jonsdottir helped WikiLeaks produce the video Collateral Murder, which allegedly depicts an American helicopter opening fire on unarmed individuals in Iraq. She testified that, around the same time, she had been working with people around the world, including some at WikiLeaks, to create a safe haven for freedom of information in Iceland. Jonsdottir testified that Collateral Murder made WikiLeaks known to the world shortly before its release later in 2010 of the Afghan and Iraq war logs and a substantial number of State Department cables—classified information allegedly leaked to WikiLeaks by one Bradley Manning. Jonsdottir further testified that she is aware that Manning has been charged by the United States government for aiding the enemy on the ground that he knew the classified information he provided to WikiLeaks would end up in the hands of al-Qaeda. She testified that a number of American politicians have called WikiLeaks a terrorist organization and that the government has been considering criminal charges against the organization and its founder, Julian Assange. As part of this investigation, she has received a subpoena from a federal grand jury for content from her Twitter account. She has received a number of invitations to speak in the United States, but will not travel here—thereby forgoing contacts and compensation—because of the subpoena and her fears of detention under Section 1021.

Wargalla, a German citizen, is an organizer and activist based in London, and is associated with the organizations Revolution Truth, Occupy London, and Justice for Assange UK. She testified that Occupy London has been listed as a terrorist group by the City of London police department. Moreover, she testified that she has been a supporter of WikiLeaks since 2010 as it was releasing the classified information noted above. Since January 2011, she has organized rallies, demonstrations, and protests on behalf of Assange and Manning. She testified that she has met Assange, who is familiar with her support, and has had contact with other employees of WikiLeaks. Wargalla testified that her fears of detention under Section 1021 have made it nearly impossible to pursue her everyday work.

The district court found that both Jonsdottir and Wargalla had an actual fear of detention under Section 1021 and had incurred costs and other present injuries due to this fear.FN141

. . .

We have no occasion to disturb the factual findings of the district court, which are well-supported by the record, or to question the truth of the factual testimony of the plaintiffs, which the district court found credible. Rather, we are faced only with a question of law: whether the non-citizen plaintiffs' fears of enforcement, as well as any present costs they have incurred as a result of those fears, establish their standing to bring this challenge.

. . .

Plaintiffs never articulate a precise theory on which they fear detention under Section 1021(b)(2)—that is, in what sense the government may conclude that they were a "part of or substantially supported al-Qaeda, the Taliban, or associated forces that are engaged in hostilities against the United States or its coalition partners." The strongest argument would seem to be a contention that the work of Jonsdottir and Wargalla substantially, if indirectly, supports al-Qaeda and the Taliban as the term "support" is understood colloquially. The record demonstrates a number of ways in which the government has concluded, or would have a basis to conclude, that WikiLeaks has provided some support to al-Qaeda and the Taliban. This includes the evidence that the government is prosecuting Manning for aiding the enemy by his releases to WikiLeaks and news articles in the record or cited by the Jonsdottir declaration reporting on the immense amount of classified information that WikiLeaks made public, much of which is related specifically to the government's military efforts against al-Qaeda and the Taliban. One perhaps might fear that Jonsdottir's and Wargalla's efforts on behalf of WikiLeaks could be construed as making them indirect supporters of al-Qaeda and the Taliban as well.

. . .

The government rejoins that the term "substantial support" cannot be construed so in this particular context. Rather, it contends that the term must be understood—and limited—by reference to who would be detainable in analogous circumstances under the laws of war. It points to (1) the Hamdi plurality's limitation of the duration of the detention authority it recognized based on the laws of war, (2) the March 2009 Memo's repeated invocation of law-of-war limiting principles and the legislative history suggesting that Section 1021 was meant to codify the interpretation that the Memo set forth, (3) Section 1021(d), to the extent that Hamdi and the administration suggested that the laws of war inform AUMF authority, as bearing on how broadly "substantial support" may be construed, and (4) the references to "law of war" in Section 1021 itself, albeit not in Section 1021(b)(2). The government then contends that individuals like Jonsdottir and Wargalla are civilians who are not detainable under these law-of-war principles and so cannot reasonably fear detention under Section 1021.

In these circumstances, we are faced with a somewhat peculiar situation. The government has invited us to resolve standing in this case by codifying, as a matter of law, the meaningful limits it has placed on itself in its interpretation of Section 1021. We decline the government's invitation to do so. Thus, we express no view regarding whether the laws of war inform and limit detention authority under Section 1021(b)(2) or whether such principles would foreclose the detention of individuals like Jonsdottir and Wargalla. This issue presents important questions about the scope of the government's detention authority under the AUMF, and we are wary of allowing a preenforcement standing inquiry to become the vehicle by which a court addresses these matters unless it is necessary. Because we conclude that standing is absent in any event, we will assume without deciding that Section 1021(b)(2) covers Jonsdottir and Wargalla in light of their stated activities.

We next consider whether there is a sufficient threat of enforcement even given this assumption.

. . .

The question is the extent to which such a presumption is applicable here. The district court concluded that it was, reasoning that Section 1021 "is equivalent to a criminal statute" because "the possibility of being placed in indefinite military detention is the equivalent of a criminal penalty." Certainly we agree that military detention until the termination of hostilities would be severe and that the prospect of such detention can be "as inhibiting of speech as can trepidation in the face of threatened criminal prosecution." FN171 But that is a separate question from whether it is appropriate to presume that Section 1021 will be enforced as would any criminal or civil punitive statute.

On this point, there are several important differences between Section 1021 and a typical statute imposing criminal or civil penalties. Section 1021 is not a law enforcement statute, but an affirmation of the President's military authority. As discussed above, it applies only to individuals who are not citizens, are not lawful resident aliens, and are apprehended outside the United States. It thus speaks entirely to the authority of the President in the context of military force, national security, and foreign affairs, areas in which the President generally enjoys "unique responsibility" and "broad discretion." The Supreme Court has recognized that "Congress cannot anticipate and legislate with regard to every possible action the President may find it necessary to take" in the fields of national security and foreign affairs. As a result, "Congress—in giving the Executive authority over matters of foreign affairs—must of necessity paint with a brush broader than that it customarily wields in domestic areas."

Moreover, Section 1021 "at most authorizes—but does not mandate or direct"—the detention that plaintiffs fear. To be sure, the executive branch enjoys prosecutorial discretion with regard to traditional punitive statutes. Congress generally does not mandate or direct criminal prosecution or civil enforcement. But we can distinguish between Congress, on the one hand, proscribing a certain act and then leaving it to the President to enforce the law under his constitutional duty to "take Care that the Laws be faithfully executed" and Congress, on the other hand, authorizing the President to use a certain kind of military force against non-citizens abroad.

Consequently, there is a world of difference between assuming that a state executive will enforce a statute imposing civil penalties for certain campaign finance violations—or even that the executive branch will enforce a federal criminal statute barring provision of material support to terrorists—and assuming that the President will detain any non-citizen abroad that Congress authorizes him to detain under the AUMF. Clapper further supports this understanding, as it made clear that plaintiffs cannot establish standing on the basis of speculation about how the government may choose to utilize its authority to engage in foreign surveillance. In short, while it generally may be appropriate to presume for standing purposes that the government will enforce the law against a plaintiff covered by a traditional punitive statute, such a presumption carries less force with regard to a statute concerned entirely with the President's authority to use military force against non-citizens abroad. Thus, in the circumstances of this case, Jonsdottir and Wargalla must show more than that the statute covers their conduct to establish preenforcement standing.

We need not quantify precisely what more is required because Jonsdottir and Wargalla have shown nothing further here. Indeed, they have not established a basis for concluding that enforcement against them is even remotely likely. We reach this conclusion independent of the government's litigation position on appeal that plaintiffs are "in no danger whatsoever" of being detained on the basis of their stated activities.

. . .

. . . [P]laintiffs bear the burden of establishing standing. Whether Section 1021 can or will alter executive practice, particularly with regard to individuals like them, is purely a matter of speculation. The fact remains that—despite the executive at least nominally asserting the authority to detain on the basis of "support" since the 2004 CSRT enemy combatant definition, and on the basis of "substantial support" since the March 2009 Memo, and despite the D.C. Circuit recognizing the lawfulness of detention at least on the basis of "purposeful and material support" since 2010— plaintiffs have provided no basis for believing that the government will place Jonsdottir and Wargalla in military detention for their supposed substantial support. In all the circumstances, plaintiffs have not shown a sufficient threat of enforcement to establish standing. Moreover, they cannot "manufacture standing" based on any present injuries incurred due to their expressed fears.

Nothing in this decision should be confused as deference to the political branches because the case involves national security and foreign affairs.

We adhere to the principle that courts have a vigorous and meaningful role to play in assessing the propriety of military detention, as the Supreme Court has made clear in cases from Hamdi to Boumediene. We hold only that a court first must satisfy itself that the case comports with the "irreducible constitutional minimum" of Article III standing. This inquiry is rooted in fundamental separation-of-powers principles and must be "especially rigorous" where, as here, the merits of the dispute require the court to "decide whether an action taken by one of the other two branches of the Federal Government was unconstitutional." Section 1021 is concerned entirely with the military authority of the President with respect to non-citizens abroad—a context in which Congress provides the President broad authority to exercise with considerable discretion. Particularly after Clapper, plaintiffs must show more than that they fall within the ambit of this authority to establish the sufficient threat of enforcement necessary for Article III standing. They have failed to do so here.

. . .

In sum, Hedges and O'Brien do not have Article III standing to challenge the statute because Section 1021 simply says nothing about the government's authority to detain citizens. While Section 1021 does have meaningful effect regarding the authority to detain individuals who are not citizens or lawful resident aliens and are apprehended abroad, Jonsdottir and Wargalla have not established standing on this record. We vacate the permanent injunction and remand for further proceedings consistent with this opinion.

QUESTIONS AND NOTES

1.   The Presidential Policy Directive issued on February 28, 2012 in regard to the NDAA of 2012, applied only to section 1022. How is section 1022 different from 1021? Taking into account Judge Kaplan's opinion in Hedges v. Obama, supra, what would have been the effect of the Feinstein/Lee amendment, sec. 1033, supra, if it had been enacted?

2.   Suppose secs. 1021 and 1022 had been enacted prior to the arrest and subsequent military detention of Jose Padilla, see supra. In light of Hedges v. Obama, supra, would the government's authority to detain Padilla in military custody have been affected by these provisions? Would these provisions have any bearing on the authority of the government to detain al Marri in military custody?

3.   See generally, The Power to Detain: Detention of Terrorism Suspects after 9/11, 38 Yale J. Int'l L. 123 (2013); Creating a More Meaningful Detention Statute: Lessons Learned from Hedges v. Obama, 81 Fordham L.Rev. 2853 (2013).

C. THE DETAINEES AT GUANTANAMO; LEGAL PROCEEDINGS INVOLVING THE DETAINEES; DISPOSITION OF THE DETAINEES; DISPOSITION OF GUANTANAMO UNDER OBAMA, UNDER TRUMP

During the Bush administration, and in the aftermath of 9/11, at its peak, approximately 780 men were detained at the Guantanamo Bay detention facility, most of them having been captured in Afghanistan but many also having been seized elsewhere. The countries of origin of these individuals varied, but they were mostly middle eastern countries, e.g., Saudi Arabia and Yemen. During the period between 2002 and January, 2009 when Barack Obama ascended to the presidency, the Bush administration released a majority of these detainees, most of them after some sort of legal process—see below. Insofar as some them returned to terrorism-related activities, controversy attached to their release, but the numbers of those who had resumed such activity were disputed.

By the beginning of the Obama administration, over 500 detainees had been transferred or released from Guantanamo and 242 men were still detained there. One of President Obama's first acts was to order closure of Guantanamo within a year. As it turned out, his plan to close the facility was unsuccessful, and Guantanamo still remains open today. Meanwhile Donald Trump has succeeded to the Presidency, and given the statements that he has made about keeping Guantanamo open and steps he has taken, there seems little or no likelihood of closing this detention facility in the near term. Issues relating to the attempt to close Guantanamo will be described below. While Obama was unsuccessful in closing the facility, he did make strenuous efforts to reduce the detainee population, especially in the final year of his Presidency. At the time of this writing, the number of detainees at Guantanamo stands at 41, and again, given President Trump's statements and actions, it seems unlikely that that number will get any lower in the near term. More information will be provided below about the detainees in this group.

A substantial number of legal issues have arisen relating to the detainees: whether they have a right to access U.S. courts; what kinds of substantive rights, if any, are U.S. courts required to afford them, and the related question, what kind of procedural protections are they entitled to in administrative proceedings to determine their status or whether they can continue to be detained; ultimately, how long can their detention continue; and how long will Guantanamo be kept open? These and related questions are addressed below

Over the course of the sixteen years that the post-9/11 Guantanamo Bay detention facility has been in existence, there have been at least five different specific types of legal processes to which Guantanamo detainees have been subjected or that have been available for them to make use of: some of these existed for a relatively short period of time and then were, as a practical matter, replaced by another type of proceeding that performed the same general function; some are traditional legal proceedings; some of the proceedings are judicial, some administrative; and the procedural and evidentiary rules used in each type of proceeding differ. There have been several Supreme Court decisions relating to these legal processes, a couple of which were examined above; the others will be discussed in the materials that follow in this chapter and in the next.

The different kinds of proceedings are Combatant Status Review Tribunals (CSRT), to determine in the first instance whether there is an adequate factual and legal basis for detaining the individual; Administrative Review Boards (ARB), a system of annual reviews of the status of the individual following up after the CSRT process—to determine whether each detainee is still dangerous or still could provide intelligence; Habeas Corpus actions in federal court; Periodic Review Boards, established by an Executive Order issued by President Obama and providing for a review similar to the ARB process, but with clear standards and procedures and different intervals for the reviews; and criminal prosecution before military commissions. The first four of these are treated in the materials that follow in this chapter, while Chapter 11, infra, is devoted to the subject of military commission prosecutions.

1. COMBATANT STATUS REVIEW TRIBUNALS (CSRT)

The CSRT process were created largely in response to and in the shadow of the Supreme Court's opinion in Hamdi v. Rumsfeld, supra. (Prior to the decision in Hamdi, the government had been working on establishing a formal review procedure for all of the Guantanamo detainees, and, indeed, had informally reviewed and released a couple of hundred detainees to their home countries.) The issue in the CSRT review was whether or not the particular detainee is an enemy combatant, which status provided a legal basis for detaining the person. So the issue in that proceeding involved a legal question, which turned on determining past and current facts.

The CSRT hearings were heard by three-person boards of military officers. A military officer who acted as a representative, not as his attorney or advocate, was made available to each of the detainees whose case was reviewed by a CSRT. (Some of the detainees were later represented by counsel in connection with subsequent habeas corpus actions—see below. Each detainee was given a written document with those accusations that did not reveal classified information that bore on the question of the detainee's status as an enemy combatant. The CSRT, however, could consider information not contained in the document that was provided to the detainee, that is, classified information, and there was very often such information available to the tribunal. At the hearing, the detainee was allowed to testify, and his family and home nation were allowed to submit written testimony. Reportedly, almost half the detainees refused to participate in the proceedings.

Following completion of a CSRT hearing, the hearing procedure was reviewed administratively to make sure that it was conducted properly and then sent to an Admiral who had delegated authority to make the final decision in these cases. Enactment of the Detainee Treatment Act in 2005 subjected the CSRT determinations to a limited form of judicial review in the U.S. Court of Appeals for the District of Columbia, as described infra in the opinion in Boumediene v. Bush.

Determination in a CSRT hearing that a detainee was not an enemy combatant resulted in a decision to release the individual and efforts by the State Department to return him to his home country, or if that was inappropriate, to another country. Determination that he was an enemy combatant resulted in continued detention and subsequent annual review in the ARB procedure.

In all, the Office for the Administrative Review of the Detention of Enemy Combatants (OARDEC) held 572 tribunals between July 30, 2004 and June 15, 2007. The tribunals determined that 534 detainees were properly classified as enemy combatants and 38 detainees were found no longer to be classified as enemy combatants.

In March, 2007, the Defense Department reported that in 2006, 111 detainees had been either released or transferred from Guantanamo, resulting in a cumulative total of approximately 390 releases and transfers since 2002. At the time, the number of detainees at Guantanamo was approximately 385, of which more than 80 had been designated for release or transfer, pending discussions with other nations.

Prior to the creation of the CSRT procedure, approximately 200 detainees had been released. Special Department of Defense Briefing conducted by Gordon England, Secretary of the Navy, Federal News Service, December 20, 2004.

The CSRT procedure is described in detail in Boumediene v. Bush, infra, where one of the issues was whether the CSRT sufficed as a substitute for habeas corpus review. The legal effect of the decision in Boumediene was to make available habeas corpus in the federal courts as a means for the detainees to challenge their detention as enemy combatants.

2. ADMINISTRATIVE REVIEW TRIBUNALS (ARB)

The issue in the ARB review was whether the individual (who had previously gone through a CSRT proceeding and had been determined to be an enemy combatant and therefore detainable) continued to be a threat or had intelligence information which would be of value. As an outcome of the ARB proceeding, any of three dispositions was possible: release of the detainee and transportation to his home country; transfer of the detainee to his home country with conditions as negotiated with that country; or continued detention at Guantanamo. The recommendations of the ARB'S were reviewed by the Secretary of the Navy. See generally, Special Department of Defense Briefing conducted by Gordon England, Secretary of the Navy, Federal News Service, December 20, 2004. In April, 2006, a report regarding Administrative Review Tribunal (ARB) hearings held annually indicated that in the second round of such hearings, 55 detainees were determined to be eligible for transfer; 273 continued to be detained.

3. AVAILABILITY TO GUANTANAMO DETAINEES OF HABEAS CORPUS IN U.S. COURTS

Yaser Hamdi sought his freedom through a writ of habeas corpus in a U.S. court, but Hamdi was a U.S. citizen then detained in a naval brig in the United States. Do aliens detained at the Guantanamo Bay detention facility, a base leased by the U.S. from Cuba, or at other U.S. bases abroad, have a right to access U.S. courts seeking their freedom through a writ of habeas corpus? The Supreme Court in Rasul v. Bush, 542 U.S. 466 (2004) initially ruled on that issue, holding that U.S. courts had jurisdiction under existing legislation to hear actions filed by foreign national detainees who had been captured abroad in connection with hostilities and housed at Guantanamo and who were challenging the legal basis for their detention. Subsequently, Congress passed legislation providing for limited review of certain administrative determinations concerning the detainees' status but expressly withdrawing jurisdiction from the federal courts to hear their habeas actions. Subsequently, the detainees sought habeas relief in the federal courts challenging the constitutionality of the statutory withdrawal of habeas jurisdiction.

BOUMEDIENE V. BUSH
553 U.S. 723 (2008)

[KENNEDY, J., delivered the opinion of the Court, in which STEVENS, SOUTER, GINSBURG, and BREYER, JJ., joined. SOUTER, J., filed a concurring opinion, in which GINSBURG and BREYER, JJ., joined. ROBERTS, C. J., filed a dissenting opinion, in which SCALIA, THOMAS, and ALITO, JJ., joined. SCALIA, J., filed a dissenting opinion, in which ROBERTS, C. J., and THOMAS and ALITO, JJ., joined.]

JUSTICE KENNEDY delivered the opinion of the Court.

Petitioners are aliens designated as enemy combatants and detained at the United States Naval Station at Guantanamo Bay, Cuba. There are others detained there, also aliens, who are not parties to this suit.

Petitioners present a question not resolved by our earlier cases relating to the detention of aliens at Guantanamo: whether they have the constitutional privilege of habeas corpus, a privilege not to be withdrawn except in conformance with the Suspension Clause, Art. I, § 9, cl. 2. We hold these petitioners do have the habeas corpus privilege. Congress has enacted a statute, the Detainee Treatment Act of 2005 (DTA), 119 Stat. 2739, that provides certain procedures for review of the detainees' status. We hold that those procedures are not an adequate and effective substitute for habeas corpus. Therefore § 7 of the Military Commissions Act of 2006 (MCA), 28 U. S. C. A. § 2241(e) (Supp. 2007), operates as an unconstitutional suspension of the writ. We do not address whether the President has authority to detain these petitioners nor do we hold that the writ must issue. These and other questions regarding the legality of the detention are to be resolved in the first instance by the District Court.

I

Under the Authorization for Use of Military Force (AUMF), § 2(a), 115 Stat. 224, note following 50 U. S. C. § 1541 (2000 ed., Supp. V), the President is authorized "to use all necessary and appropriate force against those nations, organizations, or persons he determines planned, authorized, committed, or aided the terrorist attacks that occurred on September 11, 2001, or harbored such organizations or persons, in order to prevent any future acts of international terrorism against the United States by such nations, organizations or persons."

In Hamdi v. Rumsfeld, 542 U. S. 507 (2004), five Members of the Court recognized that detention of individuals who fought against the United States in Afghanistan "for the duration of the particular conflict in which they were captured, is so fundamental and accepted an incident to war as to be an exercise of the 'necessary and appropriate force' Congress has authorized the President to use." Id., at 518 (plurality opinion of O'Connor, J.), id., at 588–589 (Thomas, J., dissenting). After Hamdi, the Deputy Secretary of Defense established Combatant Status Review Tribunals (CSRTs) to determine whether individuals detained at Guantanamo were "enemy combatants," as the Department defines that term. A later memorandum established procedures to implement the CSRTs. The Government maintains these procedures were designed to comply with the due process requirements identified by the plurality in Hamdi.

Interpreting the AUMF, the Department of Defense ordered the detention of these petitioners, and they were transferred to Guantanamo. Some of these individuals were apprehended on the battlefield in

Afghanistan, others in places as far away from there as Bosnia and Gambia. All are foreign nationals, but none is a citizen of a nation now at war with the United States. Each denies he is a member of the al Qaeda terrorist network that carried out the September 11 attacks or of the Taliban regime that provided sanctuary for al Qaeda. Each petitioner appeared before a separate CSRT; was determined to be an enemy combatant; and has sought a writ of habeas corpus in the United States District Court for the District of Columbia.

. . .

After Rasul, petitioners' cases were consolidated and entertained in two separate proceedings. In the first set of cases, Judge RICHARD J. LEON granted the Government's motion to dismiss, holding that the detainees had no rights that could be vindicated in a habeas corpus action. In the second set of cases Judge JOYCE HENS GREEN reached the opposite conclusion, holding the detainees had rights under the Due Process Clause of the Fifth Amendment. See Khalid v. Bush, 355 F. Supp. 2d 311, 314 (DC 2005); In re Guantanamo Detainee Cases, 355 F. Supp. 2d 443, 464 (DC 2005).

While appeals were pending from the District Court decisions, Congress passed the DTA. Subsection (e) of § 1005 of the DTA amended 28 U. S. C. § 2241 to provide that "no court, justice, or judge shall have jurisdiction to hear or consider . . . an application for a writ of habeas corpus filed by or on behalf of an alien detained by the Department of Defense at Guantanamo Bay, Cuba." 119 Stat. 2742. Section 1005 further provides that the Court of Appeals for the District of Columbia Circuit shall have "exclusive" jurisdiction to review decisions of the CSRTs. Ibid.

. . .

Petitioners' cases were consolidated on appeal, and the parties filed supplemental briefs in light of our decision in Hamdan [v. Rumsfeld, 548 U.S. 557 (2006)]. The Court of Appeals' ruling, 476 F. 3d 981 (CADC 2007), is the subject of our present review and today's decision.

The Court of Appeals concluded that MCA § 7 must be read to strip from it, and all federal courts, jurisdiction to consider petitioners' habeas corpus applications, id., at 987; that petitioners are not entitled to the privilege of the writ or the protections of the Suspension Clause, id., at 990–991; and, as a result, that it was unnecessary to consider whether Congress provided an adequate and effective substitute for habeas corpus in the DTA.

We granted certiorari.

II

As a threshold matter, we must decide whether MCA § 7 denies the federal courts jurisdiction to hear habeas corpus actions pending at the time of its enactment. We hold the statute does deny that jurisdiction, so that, if the statute is valid, petitioners' cases must be dismissed.

. . .

If this ongoing dialogue between and among the branches of Government is to be respected, we cannot ignore that the MCA was a direct response to Hamdan's holding that the DTA's jurisdiction-stripping provision had no application to pending cases. The Court of Appeals was correct to take note of the legislative history when construing the statute, . . .; and we agree with its conclusion that the MCA deprives the federal courts of jurisdiction to entertain the habeas corpus actions now before us.

III

In deciding the constitutional questions now presented we must determine whether petitioners are barred from seeking the writ or invoking the protections of the Suspension Clause either because of their status, i.e., petitioners' designation by the Executive Branch as enemy combatants, or their physical location, i.e., their presence at Guantanamo Bay. The Government contends that noncitizens designated as enemy combatants and detained in territory located outside our Nation's borders have no constitutional rights and no privilege of habeas corpus. Petitioners contend they do have cognizable constitutional rights and that Congress, in seeking to eliminate recourse to habeas corpus as a means to assert those rights, acted in violation of the Suspension Clause.

We begin with a brief account of the history and origins of the writ. Our account proceeds from two propositions. First, protection for the privilege of habeas corpus was one of the few safeguards of liberty specified in a Constitution that, at the outset, had no Bill of Rights. In the system conceived by the Framers the writ had a centrality that must inform proper interpretation of the Suspension Clause. Second, to the extent there were settled precedents or legal commentaries in 1789 regarding the extraterritorial scope of the writ or its application to enemy aliens, those authorities can be instructive for the present cases.

A

The Framers viewed freedom from unlawful restraint as a fundamental precept of liberty, and they understood the writ of habeas corpus as a vital instrument to secure that freedom. Experience taught, however, that the common-law writ all too often had been insufficient to guard against the abuse of monarchial power. That history counseled the necessity for specific language in the Constitution to secure the writ and ensure its place in our legal system.

. . .

Post-1789 habeas developments in England, though not bearing upon the Framers' intent, do verify their foresight. Those later events would underscore the need for structural barriers against arbitrary suspensions of the writ. Just as the writ had been vulnerable to executive and parliamentary encroachment on both sides of the Atlantic before the American Revolution, despite the Habeas Corpus Act of 1679, the writ was suspended with frequency in England during times of political unrest after 1789. . . .

In our own system the Suspension Clause is designed to protect against these cyclical abuses. The Clause protects the rights of the detained by a means consistent with the essential design of the Constitution. It ensures that, except during periods of formal suspension, the Judiciary will have a time-tested device, the writ, to maintain the "delicate balance of governance" that is itself the surest safeguard of liberty. The Clause protects the rights of the detained by affirming the duty and authority of the Judiciary to call the jailer to account. . . . The separation-of-powers doctrine, and the history that influenced its design, therefore must inform the reach and purpose of the Suspension Clause.

B

The broad historical narrative of the writ and its function is central to our analysis, but we seek guidance as well from founding-era authorities addressing the specific question before us: whether foreign nationals, apprehended and detained in distant countries during a time of serious threats to our Nation's security, may assert the privilege of the writ and seek its protection. The Court has been careful not to foreclose the possibility that the protections of the Suspension Clause have expanded along with post-1789 developments that define the present scope of the writ. . . . But the analysis may begin with precedents as of 1789, for the Court has said that "at the absolute minimum" the Clause protects the writ as it existed when the Constitution was drafted and ratified.

. . .

We know that at common law a petitioner's status as an alien was not a categorical bar to habeas corpus relief. . . . We know as well that common-law courts entertained habeas petitions brought by enemy aliens detained in England-"entertained" at least in the sense that the courts held hearings to determine the threshold question of entitlement to the writ. . . .

. . . To the extent these authorities suggest the common-law courts abstained altogether from matters involving prisoners of war, there was greater justification for doing so in the context of declared wars with other nation states. Judicial intervention might have complicated the military's ability to negotiate exchange of prisoners with the enemy, a wartime practice well known to the Framers. . . .

We find the evidence as to the geographic scope of the writ at common law informative, but, again, not dispositive. Petitioners argue the site of their detention is analogous to two territories outside of England to which the writ did run: the so-called "exempt jurisdictions," like the Channel Islands; and (in former times) India. There are critical differences between these places and Guantanamo, however.

. . .

In the end a categorical or formal conception of sovereignty does not provide a comprehensive or altogether satisfactory explanation for the general understanding that prevailed when Lord Mansfield considered issuance of the writ outside England. In 1759 the writ did not run to Scotland but did run to Ireland, even though, at that point, Scotland and England had merged under the rule of a single sovereign, whereas the Crowns of Great Britain and Ireland remained separate (at least in theory). . . .But there was at least one major difference between Scotland's and Ireland's relationship with England during this period that might explain why the writ ran to Ireland but not to Scotland. English law did not generally apply in Scotland (even after the Act of Union) but it did apply in Ireland. . . . This distinction, and not formal notions of sovereignty, may well explain why the writ did not run to Scotland (and Hanover) but would run to Ireland.

The prudential barriers that may have prevented the English courts from issuing the writ to Scotland and Hanover are not relevant here. We have no reason to believe an order from a federal court would be disobeyed at Guantanamo. No Cuban court has jurisdiction to hear these petitioners' claims, and no law other than the laws of the United States applies at the naval station. The modern-day relations between the United States and Guantanamo thus differ in important respects from the 18th-century relations between England and the kingdoms of Scotland and Hanover. This is reason enough for us to discount the relevance of the Government's analogy.

Each side in the present matter argues that the very lack of a precedent on point supports its position. The Government points out there is no evidence that a court sitting in England granted habeas relief to an enemy alien detained abroad; petitioners respond there is no evidence that a court refused to do so for lack of jurisdiction.

Both arguments are premised, however, upon the assumption that the historical record is complete and that the common law, if properly understood, yields a definite answer to the questions before us. There are reasons to doubt both assumptions. Recent scholarship points to the inherent shortcomings in the historical record. . . . And given the unique status of Guantanamo Bay and the particular dangers of terrorism in the modern age, the common-law courts simply may not have confronted cases with close parallels to this one. We decline, therefore, to infer too much, one way or the other, from the lack of historical evidence on point. . . .

IV

Drawing from its position that at common law the writ ran only to territories over which the Crown was sovereign, the Government says the Suspension Clause affords petitioners no rights because the United States does not claim sovereignty over the place of detention.

Guantanamo Bay is not formally part of the United States. See DTA § 1005(g), 119 Stat. 2743. And under the terms of the lease between the United States and Cuba, Cuba retains "ultimate sovereignty" over the territory while the United States exercises "complete jurisdiction and control." See Lease of Lands for Coaling and Naval Stations, Feb. 23, 1903, U. S.-Cuba, Art. III, T. S. No. 418 (hereinafter 1903 Lease Agreement); Rasul, 542 U. S., at 471. Under the terms of the 1934 Treaty, however, Cuba effectively has no rights as a sovereign until the parties agree to modification of the 1903 Lease Agreement or the United States abandons the base. See Treaty Defining Relations with Cuba, May 29, 1934, U. S.-Cuba, Art. III, 48 Stat. 1683, T. S. No. 866.

The United States contends, nevertheless, that Guantanamo is not within its sovereign control. This was the Government's position well before the events of September 11, 2001. And in other contexts the Court has held that questions of sovereignty are for the political branches to decide. . . . Even if this were a treaty interpretation case that did not involve a political question, the President's construction of the lease agreement would be entitled to great respect. . . .

We therefore do not question the Government's position that Cuba, not the United States, maintains sovereignty, in the legal and technical sense of the term, over Guantanamo Bay. But this does not end the analysis. Our cases do not hold it is improper for us to inquire into the objective degree of control the Nation asserts over foreign territory. . . . As we did in Rasul, however, we take notice of the obvious and uncontested fact that the United States, by virtue of its complete jurisdiction and control over the base, maintains de facto sovereignty over this territory.

Were we to hold that the present cases turn on the political question doctrine, we would be required first to accept the Government's premise that de jure sovereignty is the touchstone of habeas corpus jurisdiction. This premise, however, is unfounded. For the reasons indicated above, the history of common-law habeas corpus provides scant support for this proposition; and, for the reasons indicated below, that position would be inconsistent with our precedents and contrary to fundamental separation-of-powers principles.

A

The Court has discussed the issue of the Constitution's extraterritorial application on many occasions. These decisions undermine the Government's argument that, at least as applied to noncitizens, the Constitution necessarily stops where de jure sovereignty ends

. . .

Practical considerations weighed heavily as well in Johnson v. Eisentrager, 339 U. S. 763 (1950), where the Court addressed whether habeas corpus jurisdiction extended to enemy aliens who had been convicted of violating the laws of war. The prisoners were detained at Landsberg Prison in Germany during the Allied Powers' postwar occupation. The Court stressed the difficulties of ordering the Government to produce the prisoners in a habeas corpus proceeding. It "would require allocation of shipping space, guarding personnel, billeting and rations" and would damage the prestige of military commanders at a sensitive time. In considering these factors the Court sought to balance the constraints of military occupation with constitutional necessities. [S]ee Rasul, 542 U. S., at 475–476 (discussing the factors relevant to Eisentrager's constitutional holding); 542 U. S., at 486 (Kennedy, J., concurring in judgment) (same).

. . .

. . . [B]ecause the United States lacked both de jure sovereignty and plenary control over Landsberg Prison, it is far from clear that the Eisentrager Court used the term sovereignty only in the narrow technical sense and not to connote the degree of control the military asserted over the facility. The Justices who decided Eisentrager would have understood sovereignty as a multifaceted concept. . . . Even if we assume the Eisentrager Court considered the United States' lack of formal legal sovereignty over Landsberg Prison as the decisive factor in that case, its holding is not inconsistent with a functional approach to questions of extraterritoriality. The formal legal status of a given territory affects, at least to some extent, the political branches' control over that territory. De jure sovereignty is a factor that bears upon which constitutional guarantees apply there.

. . .

B

The Government's formal sovereignty-based test raises troubling separation-of-powers concerns as well. The political history of Guantanamo illustrates the deficiencies of this approach. . . . The necessary implication of the argument is that by surrendering formal sovereignty over any unincorporated territory to a third party, while at the same time entering into a lease that grants total control over the territory back to the United

States, it would be possible for the political branches to govern without legal constraint.

Our basic charter cannot be contracted away like this. The Constitution grants Congress and the President the power to acquire, dispose of, and govern territory, not the power to decide when and where its terms apply. . . . Abstaining from questions involving formal sovereignty and territorial governance is one thing. To hold the political branches have the power to switch the Constitution on or off at will is quite another. The former position reflects this Court's recognition that certain matters requiring political judgments are best left to the political branches. The latter would permit a striking anomaly in our tripartite system of government, leading to a regime in which Congress and the President, not this Court, say "what the law is." Marbury v. Madison, 1 Cranch 137, 177 (1803).

These concerns have particular bearing upon the Suspension Clause question in the cases now before us, for the writ of habeas corpus is itself an indispensable mechanism for monitoring the separation of powers. The test for determining the scope of this provision must not be subject to manipulation by those whose power it is designed to restrain.

C

As we recognized in Rasul, 542 U. S., at 476; id., at 487 (Kennedy, J., concurring in judgment), the outlines of a framework for determining the reach of the Suspension Clause are suggested by the factors the Court relied upon in Eisentrager. In addition to the practical concerns discussed above, the Eisentrager Court found relevant that each petitioner:

"(a) is an enemy alien; (b) has never been or resided in the United States; (c) was captured outside of our territory and there held in military custody as a prisoner of war; (d) was tried and convicted by a Military Commission sitting outside the United States; (e) for offenses against laws of war committed outside the United States; (f) and is at all times imprisoned outside the United States." 339 U. S., at 777.

Based on this language from Eisentrager, and the reasoning in our other extraterritoriality opinions, we conclude that at least three factors are relevant in determining the reach of the Suspension Clause: (1) the citizenship and status of the detainee and the adequacy of the process through which that status determination was made; (2) the nature of the sites where apprehension and then detention took place; and (3) the practical obstacles inherent in resolving the prisoner's entitlement to the writ.

Applying this framework, we note at the onset that the status of these detainees is a matter of dispute. The petitioners, like those in Eisentrager, are not American citizens. But the petitioners in Eisentrager did not contest, it seems, the Court's assertion that they were "enemy alien[s]." In the instant cases, by contrast, the detainees deny they are enemy combatants. They have been afforded some process in CSRT proceedings to determine their status; but, unlike in Eisentrager, there has been no trial by military commission for violations of the laws of war. The difference is not trivial. The records from the Eisentrager trials suggest that, well before the petitioners brought their case to this Court, there had been a rigorous adversarial process to test the legality of their detention. . . .

In comparison the procedural protections afforded to the detainees in the CSRT hearings are far more limited, and, we conclude, fall well short of the procedures and adversarial mechanisms that would eliminate the need for habeas corpus review. Although the detainee is assigned a "Personal Representative" to assist him during CSRT proceedings, the Secretary of the Navy's memorandum makes clear that person is not the detainee's lawyer or even his "advocate." The Government's evidence is accorded a presumption of validity. The detainee is allowed to present "reasonably available" evidence, but his ability to rebut the Government's evidence against him is limited by the circumstances of his confinement and his lack of counsel at this stage. And although the detainee can seek review of his status determination in the Court of Appeals, that review process cannot cure all defects in the earlier proceedings. See Part V, infra.

As to the second factor relevant to this analysis, the detainees here are similarly situated to the Eisentrager petitioners in that the sites of their apprehension and detention are technically outside the sovereign territory of the United States. As noted earlier, this is a factor that weighs against finding they have rights under the Suspension Clause. But there are critical differences between Landsberg Prison, circa 1950, and the United States Naval Station at Guantanamo Bay in 2008. Unlike its present control over the naval station, the United States' control over the prison in Germany was neither absolute nor indefinite. Like all parts of occupied Germany, the prison was under the jurisdiction of the combined Allied Forces. . . . The Allies had not planned a long-term occupation of Germany, nor did they intend to displace all German institutions even during the period of occupation. . . . Guantanamo Bay, on the other hand, is no transient possession. In every practical sense Guantanamo is not abroad; it is within the constant jurisdiction of the United States

As to the third factor, we recognize, as the Court did in Eisentrager, that there are costs to holding the Suspension Clause applicable in a case of military detention abroad. Habeas corpus proceedings may require expenditure of funds by the Government and may divert the attention of military personnel from other pressing tasks. While we are sensitive to these concerns, we do not find them dispositive. Compliance with any judicial process requires some incremental expenditure of resources. . . The Government presents no credible arguments that the military mission at

Guantanamo would be compromised if habeas corpus courts had jurisdiction to hear the detainees' claims. And in light of the plenary control the United States asserts over the base, none are apparent to us.

The situation in Eisentrager was far different, given the historical context and nature of the military's mission in post-War Germany. . . . In addition to supervising massive reconstruction and aid efforts the American forces stationed in Germany faced potential security threats from a defeated enemy. In retrospect the post-War occupation may seem uneventful. But at the time Eisentrager was decided, the Court was right to be concerned about judicial interference with the military's efforts to contain "enemy elements, guerilla fighters, and 'were-wolves.'"

Similar threats are not apparent here; nor does the Government argue that they are. The United States Naval Station at Guantanamo Bay consists of 45 square miles of land and water. The base has been used, at various points, to house migrants and refugees temporarily. At present, however, other than the detainees themselves, the only long-term residents are American military personnel, their families, and a small number of workers. See History of Guantanamo Bay online at https://www.cnic.navy. mil/Guantanamo/AboutGTMO/gtmohistorygeneral/gtmohistgeneral. The detainees have been deemed enemies of the United States. At present, dangerous as they may be if released, they are contained in a secure prison facility located on an isolated and heavily fortified military base.

There is no indication, furthermore, that adjudicating a habeas corpus petition would cause friction with the host government. No Cuban court has jurisdiction over American military personnel at Guantanamo or the enemy combatants detained there. While obligated to abide by the terms of the lease, the United States is, for all practical purposes, answerable to no other sovereign for its acts on the base. Were that not the case, or if the detention facility were located in an active theater of war, arguments that issuing the writ would be "impracticable or anomalous" would have more weight. Under the facts presented here, however, there are few practical barriers to the running of the writ. To the extent barriers arise, habeas corpus procedures likely can be modified to address them. See Part VI-B, infra.

It is true that before today the Court has never held that noncitizens detained by our Government in territory over which another country maintains de jure sovereignty have any rights under our Constitution. But the cases before us lack any precise historical parallel. They involve individuals detained by executive order for the duration of a conflict that, if measured from September 11, 2001, to the present, is already among the longest wars in American history. . . . The detainees, moreover, are held in a territory that, while technically not part of the United States, is under the complete and total control of our Government. Under these circumstances the lack of a precedent on point is no barrier to our holding.

We hold that Art. I, § 9, cl. 2, of the Constitution has full effect at Guantanamo Bay. If the privilege of habeas corpus is to be denied to the detainees now before us, Congress must act in accordance with the requirements of the Suspension Clause. Cf. Hamdi, 542 U. S., at 564 (Scalia, J., dissenting) ("[I]ndefinite imprisonment on reasonable suspicion is not an available option of treatment for those accused of aiding the enemy, absent a suspension of the writ"). This Court may not impose a de facto suspension by abstaining from these controversies. . . . The MCA does not purport to be a formal suspension of the writ; and the Government, in its submissions to us, has not argued that it is. Petitioners, therefore, are entitled to the privilege of habeas corpus to challenge the legality of their detention.

V

In light of this holding the question becomes whether the statute stripping jurisdiction to issue the writ avoids the Suspension Clause mandate because Congress has provided adequate substitute procedures for habeas corpus. The Government submits there has been compliance with the Suspension Clause because the DTA review process in the Court of Appeals, see DTA § 1005(e), provides an adequate substitute. Congress has granted that court jurisdiction to consider

"(i) whether the status determination of the [CSRT] . . . was consistent with the standards and procedures specified by the Secretary of Defense . . . and (ii) to the extent the Constitution and laws of the United States are applicable, whether the use of such standards and procedures to make the determination is consistent with the Constitution and laws of the United States." § 1005(e)(2)(C), 119 Stat. 2742.

The Court of Appeals, having decided that the writ does not run to the detainees in any event, found it unnecessary to consider whether an adequate substitute has been provided. In the ordinary course we would remand to the Court of Appeals to consider this question in the first instance. . . Departure from the rule is appropriate in "exceptional" circumstances.

The gravity of the separation-of-powers issues raised by these cases and the fact that these detainees have been denied meaningful access to a judicial forum for a period of years render these cases exceptional. The parties before us have addressed the adequacy issue. While we would have found it informative to consider the reasoning of the Court of Appeals on this point, we must weigh that against the harms petitioners may endure from additional delay. And, given there are few precedents addressing what features an adequate substitute for habeas corpus must contain, in all likelihood a remand simply would delay ultimate resolution of the issue by this Court.

We do have the benefit of the Court of Appeals' construction of key provisions of the DTA. When we granted certiorari in these cases, we noted "it would be of material assistance to consult any decision" in the parallel DTA review proceedings pending in the Court of Appeals, specifically any rulings in the matter of Bismullah v. Gates. 551 U. S. ___ (2007). Although the Court of Appeals has yet to complete a DTA review proceeding, the three-judge panel in Bismullah has issued an interim order giving guidance as to what evidence can be made part of the record on review and what access the detainees can have to counsel and to classified information. See 501 F. 3d 178 (CADC) (Bismullah I), reh'g denied, 503 F. 3d 137 (CADC 2007) (Bismullah II). In that matter the full court denied the Government's motion for rehearing en banc, see Bismullah v. Gates, 514 F. 3d 1291 (CADC 2008) (Bismullah III). The order denying rehearing was accompanied by five separate statements from members of the court, which offer differing views as to scope of the judicial review Congress intended these detainees to have. Ibid.

Under the circumstances we believe the costs of further delay substantially outweigh any benefits of remanding to the Court of Appeals to consider the issue it did not address in these cases.

A

Our case law does not contain extensive discussion of standards defining suspension of the writ or of circumstances under which suspension has occurred. This simply confirms the care Congress has taken throughout our Nation's history to preserve the writ and its function. Indeed, most of the major legislative enactments pertaining to habeas corpus have acted not to contract the writ's protection but to expand it or to hasten resolution of prisoners' claims. . . .

There are exceptions, of course. . . .

. . . [H]ere we confront statutes, the DTA and the MCA, that were intended to circumscribe habeas review. . . .

. . . [T]he DTA's jurisdictional grant is quite limited. The Court of Appeals has jurisdiction not to inquire into the legality of the detention generally but only to assess whether the CSRT complied with the "standards and procedures specified by the Secretary of Defense" and whether those standards and procedures are lawful. DTA § 1005(e)(2)(C), 119 Stat. 2742. If Congress had envisioned DTA review as coextensive with traditional habeas corpus, it would not have drafted the statute in this manner. . . .[M]oreover, there has been no effort to preserve habeas corpus review as an avenue of last resort. No saving clause exists in either the

MCA or the DTA. And MCA § 7 eliminates habeas review for these petitioners.

The differences between the DTA and the habeas statute that would govern in MCA § 7's absence, 28 U. S. C. § 2241 (2000 ed. and Supp. V), are likewise telling. In § 2241 (2000 ed.) Congress confirmed the authority of "any justice" or "circuit judge" to issue the writ. That statute accommodates the necessity for factfinding that will arise in some cases by allowing the appellate judge or Justice to transfer the case to a district court of competent jurisdiction, whose institutional capacity for factfinding is superior to his or her own. See 28 U. S. C. § 2241(b). By granting the Court of Appeals "exclusive" jurisdiction over petitioners' cases, see DTA § 1005(e)(2)(A), 119 Stat. 2742, Congress has foreclosed that option. This choice indicates Congress intended the Court of Appeals to have a more limited role in enemy combatant status determinations than a district court has in habeas corpus proceedings. The DTA should be interpreted to accord some latitude to the Court of Appeals to fashion procedures necessary to make its review function a meaningful one, but, if congressional intent is to be respected, the procedures adopted cannot be as extensive or as protective of the rights of the detainees as they would be in a § 2241 proceeding. Otherwise there would have been no, or very little, purpose for enacting the DTA.

To the extent any doubt remains about Congress' intent, the legislative history confirms what the plain text strongly suggests: In passing the DTA Congress did not intend to create a process that differs from traditional habeas corpus process in name only. It intended to create a more limited procedure. . . . It is against this background that we must interpret the DTA and assess its adequacy as a substitute for habeas corpus. . . .

B

We do not endeavor to offer a comprehensive summary of the requisites for an adequate substitute for habeas corpus. We do consider it uncontroversial, however, that the privilege of habeas corpus entitles the prisoner to a meaningful opportunity to demonstrate that he is being held pursuant to "the erroneous application or interpretation" of relevant law. St. Cyr, 533 U. S., at 302. And the habeas court must have the power to order the conditional release of an individual unlawfully detained-though release need not be the exclusive remedy and is not the appropriate one in every case in which the writ is granted. . . . These are the easily identified attributes of any constitutionally adequate habeas corpus proceeding. But, depending on the circumstances, more may be required.

Indeed, common-law habeas corpus was, above all, an adaptable remedy. Its precise application and scope changed depending upon the circumstances. . . . It appears the common-law habeas court's role was most extensive in cases of pretrial and noncriminal detention, where there had been little or no previous judicial review of the cause for detention. . . .

There is evidence from 19th-century American sources indicating that, even in States that accorded strong res judicata effect to prior adjudications, habeas courts in this country routinely allowed prisoners to introduce exculpatory evidence that was either unknown or previously unavailable to the prisoner. . . .

The idea that the necessary scope of habeas review in part depends upon the rigor of any earlier proceedings accords with our test for procedural adequacy in the due process context. . . . This principle has an established foundation in habeas corpus jurisprudence as well, ...

. . .

Where a person is detained by executive order, rather than, say, after being tried and convicted in a court, the need for collateral review is most pressing. A criminal conviction in the usual course occurs after a judicial hearing before a tribunal disinterested in the outcome and committed to procedures designed to ensure its own independence. These dynamics are not inherent in executive detention orders or executive review procedures. In this context the need for habeas corpus is more urgent. The intended duration of the detention and the reasons for it bear upon the precise scope of the inquiry. Habeas corpus proceedings need not resemble a criminal trial, even when the detention is by executive order. But the writ must be effective. The habeas court must have sufficient authority to conduct a meaningful review of both the cause for detention and the Executive's power to detain.

To determine the necessary scope of habeas corpus review, therefore, we must assess the CSRT process, the mechanism through which petitioners' designation as enemy combatants became final. Whether one characterizes the CSRT process as direct review of the Executive's battlefield determination that the detainee is an enemy combatant-as the parties have and as we do-or as the first step in the collateral review of a battlefield determination makes no difference in a proper analysis of whether the procedures Congress put in place are an adequate substitute for habeas corpus. What matters is the sum total of procedural protections afforded to the detainee at all stages, direct and collateral.

Petitioners identify what they see as myriad deficiencies in the CSRTs. The most relevant for our purposes are the constraints upon the detainee's ability to rebut the factual basis for the Government's assertion that he is an enemy combatant. As already noted, see Part IV-C, supra, at the CSRT stage the detainee has limited means to find or present evidence to challenge the Government's case against him. He does not have the assistance of counsel and may not be aware of the most critical allegations that the Government relied upon to order his detention. . . . the detainee can access only the "unclassified portion of the Government Information". The detainee can confront witnesses that testify during the CSRT proceedings. But given that there are in effect no limits on the admission of hearsay evidence—the only requirement is that the tribunal deem the evidence "relevant and helpful,"—the detainee's opportunity to question witnesses is likely to be more theoretical than real.

The Government defends the CSRT process, arguing that it was designed to conform to the procedures suggested by the plurality in Hamdi. Setting aside the fact that the relevant language in Hamdi did not garner a majority of the Court, it does not control the matter at hand. None of the parties in Hamdi argued there had been a suspension of the writ. Nor could they. The § 2241 habeas corpus process remained in place, ... Accordingly, the plurality concentrated on whether the Executive had the authority to detain and, if so, what rights the detainee had under the Due Process Clause. True, there are places in the Hamdi plurality opinion where it is difficult to tell where its extrapolation of § 2241 ends and its analysis of the petitioner's Due Process rights begins. But the Court had no occasion to define the necessary scope of habeas review, for Suspension Clause purposes, in the context of enemy combatant detentions. The closest the plurality came to doing so was in discussing whether, in light of separation-of-powers concerns, § 2241 should be construed to forbid the District Court from inquiring beyond the affidavit Hamdi's custodian provided in answer to the detainee's habeas petition. The plurality answered this question with an emphatic "no."

Even if we were to assume that the CSRTs satisfy due process standards, it would not end our inquiry. Habeas corpus is a collateral process that exists, in Justice HOLMES' words, to "cu[t] through all forms and g[o] to the very tissue of the structure. It comes in from the outside, not in subordination to the proceedings, and although every form may have been preserved opens the inquiry whether they have been more than an empty shell." Frank v. Mangum, 237 U. S. 309, 346 (1915) (dissenting opinion). Even when the procedures authorizing detention are structurally sound, the Suspension Clause remains applicable and the writ relevant. . .

Although we make no judgment as to whether the CSRTs, as currently constituted, satisfy due process standards, we agree with petitioners that, even when all the parties involved in this process act with diligence and in good faith, there is considerable risk of error in the tribunal's findings of fact. This is a risk inherent in any process that, in the words of the former Chief Judge of the Court of Appeals, is "closed and accusatorial." See Bismullah III, 514 F. 3d, at 1296 (GINSBURG, C. J., concurring in denial of rehearing en banc). And given that the consequence of error may be detention of persons for the duration of hostilities that may last a generation or more, this is a risk too significant to ignore.

For the writ of habeas corpus, or its substitute, to function as an effective and proper remedy in this context, the court that conducts the habeas proceeding must have the means to correct errors that occurred during the CSRT proceedings. This includes some authority to assess the sufficiency of the Government's evidence against the detainee. It also must have the authority to admit and consider relevant exculpatory evidence that was not introduced during the earlier proceeding. Federal habeas petitioners long have had the means to supplement the record on review, even in the postconviction habeas setting. . . . Here that opportunity is constitutionally required.

. . .

The extent of the showing required of the Government in these cases is a matter to be determined. We need not explore it further at this stage. We do hold that when the judicial power to issue habeas corpus properly is invoked the judicial officer must have adequate authority to make a determination in light of the relevant law and facts and to formulate and issue appropriate orders for relief, including, if necessary, an order directing the prisoner's release.

C

We now consider whether the DTA allows the Court of Appeals to conduct a proceeding meeting these standards. . . .

. . .

By foreclosing consideration of evidence not presented or reasonably available to the detainee at the CSRT proceedings, the DTA disadvantages the detainee by limiting the scope of collateral review to a record that may not be accurate or complete. In other contexts, e.g., in post-trial habeas cases where the prisoner already has had a full and fair opportunity to develop the factual predicate of his claims, similar limitations on the scope of habeas review may be appropriate. . . . In this context, however, where the underlying detention proceedings lack the necessary adversarial character, the detainee cannot be held responsible for all deficiencies in the record.

The Government does not make the alternative argument that the DTA allows for the introduction of previously unavailable exculpatory evidence on appeal. It does point out, however, that if a detainee obtains such evidence, he can request that the Deputy Secretary of Defense convene a new CSRT. See Supp. Brief for Respondents 4. Whatever the merits of this procedure, it is an insufficient replacement for the factual review these detainees are entitled to receive through habeas corpus. The Deputy Secretary's determination whether to initiate new proceedings is wholly a discretionary one. . . .

We do not imply DTA review would be a constitutionally sufficient replacement for habeas corpus but for these limitations on the detainee's ability to present exculpatory evidence. For even if it were possible, as a textual matter, to read into the statute each of the necessary procedures we have identified, we could not overlook the cumulative effect of our doing so. To hold that the detainees at Guantanamo may, under the DTA, challenge the President's legal authority to detain them, contest the CSRT's findings of fact, supplement the record on review with exculpatory evidence, and request an order of release would come close to reinstating the § 2241 habeas corpus process Congress sought to deny them. The language of the statute, read in light of Congress' reasons for enacting it, cannot bear this interpretation. Petitioners have met their burden of establishing that the DTA review process is, on its face, an inadequate substitute for habeas corpus.

. . .

VI

A

In light of our conclusion that there is no jurisdictional bar to the District Court's entertaining petitioners' claims the question remains whether there are prudential barriers to habeas corpus review under these circumstances.

The Government argues petitioners must seek review of their CSRT determinations in the Court of Appeals before they can proceed with their habeas corpus actions in the District Court. As noted earlier, in other contexts and for prudential reasons this Court has required exhaustion of alternative remedies before a prisoner can seek federal habeas relief. . . .

The real risks, the real threats, of terrorist attacks are constant and not likely soon to abate. The ways to disrupt our life and laws are so many and unforeseen that the Court should not attempt even some general catalogue of crises that might occur. Certain principles are apparent, however. Practical considerations and exigent circumstances inform the definition and reach of the law's writs, including habeas corpus. The cases and our tradition reflect this precept.

In cases involving foreign citizens detained abroad by the Executive, it likely would be both an impractical and unprecedented extension of judicial power to assume that habeas corpus would be available at the moment the prisoner is taken into custody. If and when habeas corpus jurisdiction applies, as it does in these cases, then proper deference can be accorded to reasonable procedures for screening and initial detention under lawful and proper conditions of confinement and treatment for a reasonable period of time. Domestic exigencies, furthermore, might also impose such onerous burdens on the Government that here, too, the Judicial Branch would be required to devise sensible rules for staying habeas corpus proceedings until the Government can comply with its requirements in a responsible way. Cf. Ex parte Milligan, 4 Wall., at 127 ("If, in foreign invasion or civil war, the courts are actually closed, and it is impossible to administer criminal justice according to law, then, on the theatre of active military operations, where war really prevails, there is a necessity to furnish a substitute for the civil authority, thus overthrown, to preserve the safety of the army and society; and as no power is left but the military, it is allowed to govern by martial rule until the laws can have their free course"). Here, as is true with detainees apprehended abroad, a relevant consideration in determining the courts' role is whether there are suitable alternative processes in place to protect against the arbitrary exercise of governmental power.

The cases before us, however, do not involve detainees who have been held for a short period of time while awaiting their CSRT determinations. Were that the case, or were it probable that the Court of Appeals could complete a prompt review of their applications, the case for requiring temporary abstention or exhaustion of alternative remedies would be much stronger. These qualifications no longer pertain here. In some of these cases six years have elapsed without the judicial oversight that habeas corpus or an adequate substitute demands. And there has been no showing that the Executive faces such onerous burdens that it cannot respond to habeas corpus actions. To require these detainees to complete DTA review before proceeding with their habeas corpus actions would be to require additional months, if not years, of delay. The first DTA review applications were filed over a year ago, but no decisions on the merits have been issued. While some delay in fashioning new procedures is unavoidable, the costs of delay can no longer be borne by those who are held in custody. The detainees in these cases are entitled to a prompt habeas corpus hearing.

Our decision today holds only that the petitioners before us are entitled to seek the writ; that the DTA review procedures are an inadequate substitute for habeas corpus; and that the petitioners in these cases need not exhaust the review procedures in the Court of Appeals before proceeding with their habeas actions in the District Court. The only law we identify as unconstitutional is MCA § 7, 28 U. S. C. A. § 2241(e) (Supp. 2007). Accordingly, both the DTA and the CSRT process remain intact. Our holding with regard to exhaustion should not be read to imply that a habeas court should intervene the moment an enemy combatant steps foot in a territory where the writ runs. The Executive is entitled to a reasonable period of time to determine a detainee's status before a court entertains that detainee's habeas corpus petition. The CSRT process is the mechanism Congress and the President set up to deal with these issues. Except in cases of undue delay, federal courts should refrain from entertaining an enemy combatant's habeas corpus petition at least until after the Department, acting via the CSRT, has had a chance to review his status.

B

Although we hold that the DTA is not an adequate and effective substitute for habeas corpus, it does not follow that a habeas corpus court may disregard the dangers the detention in these cases was intended to prevent. . . . Certain accommodations can be made to reduce the burden habeas corpus proceedings will place on the military without impermissibly diluting the protections of the writ.

In the DTA Congress sought to consolidate review of petitioners' claims in the Court of Appeals. Channeling future cases to one district court would no doubt reduce administrative burdens on the Government. This is a legitimate objective that might be advanced even without an amendment to § 2241. If, in a future case, a detainee files a habeas petition in another judicial district in which a proper respondent can be served, see Rumsfeld v. Padilla, 542 U. S. 426, 435–436 (2004), the Government can move for change of venue to the court that will hear these petitioners' cases,

. . .

Another of Congress' reasons for vesting exclusive jurisdiction in the Court of Appeals, perhaps, was to avoid the widespread dissemination of classified information. The Government has raised similar concerns here and elsewhere. See Brief for Respondents 55–56; Bismullah Pet. 30. We make no attempt to anticipate all of the evidentiary and access-to-counsel issues that will arise during the course of the detainees' habeas corpus proceedings. We recognize, however, that the Government has a legitimate interest in protecting sources and methods of intelligence gathering; and we expect that the District Court will use its discretion to accommodate this interest to the greatest extent possible. Cf. United States v. Reynolds, 345 U. S. 1, 10 (1953) (recognizing an evidentiary privilege in a civil damages case where "there is a reasonable danger that compulsion of the evidence will expose military matters which, in the interest of national security, should not be divulged").

These and the other remaining questions are within the expertise and competence of the District Court to address in the first instance.

. . .

Our opinion does not undermine the Executive's powers as Commander in Chief. On the contrary, the exercise of those powers is vindicated, not eroded, when confirmed by the Judicial Branch. Within the Constitution's separation-of-powers structure, few exercises of judicial power are as legitimate or as necessary as the responsibility to hear challenges to the authority of the Executive to imprison a person. Some of these petitioners have been in custody for six years with no definitive judicial determination as to the legality of their detention. Their access to the writ is a necessity to determine the lawfulness of their status, even if, in the end, they do not obtain the relief they seek.

Because our Nation's past military conflicts have been of limited duration, it has been possible to leave the outer boundaries of war powers undefined. If, as some fear, terrorism continues to pose dangerous threats to us for years to come, the Court might not have this luxury. This result is not inevitable, however. The political branches, consistent with their independent obligations to interpret and uphold the Constitution, can engage in a genuine debate about how best to preserve constitutional values while protecting the Nation from terrorism. Cf. Hamdan, 548 U. S., at 636 (Breyer, J., concurring) ("[J]udicial insistence upon that consultation does not weaken our Nation's ability to deal with danger. To the contrary, that insistence strengthens the Nation's ability to determine-through democratic means-how best to do so").

It bears repeating that our opinion does not address the content of the law that governs petitioners' detention. That is a matter yet to be determined. We hold that petitioners may invoke the fundamental procedural protections of habeas corpus. The laws and Constitution are designed to survive, and remain in force, in extraordinary times. Liberty and security can be reconciled; and in our system they are reconciled within the framework of the law. The Framers decided that habeas corpus, a right of first importance, must be a part of that framework, a part of that law.

The determination by the Court of Appeals that the Suspension Clause and its protections are inapplicable to petitioners was in error. The judgment of the Court of Appeals is reversed. The cases are remanded to the Court of Appeals with instructions that it remand the cases to the District Court for proceedings consistent with this opinion.

It is so ordered.

[JUSTICE SOUTER, with whom JUSTICE GINSBURG and JUSTICE BREYER joined wrote a separate concurring opinion.]

CHIEF JUSTICE ROBERTS, with whom JUSTICE SCALIA, JUSTICE THOMAS, and JUSTICE ALITO join, dissenting.

Today the Court strikes down as inadequate the most generous set of procedural protections ever afforded aliens detained by this country as enemy combatants. The political branches crafted these procedures amidst an ongoing military conflict, after much careful investigation and thorough debate. The Court rejects them today out of hand, without bothering to say what due process rights the detainees possess, without explaining how the statute fails to vindicate those rights, and before a single petitioner has even attempted to avail himself of the law's operation. And to what effect? The majority merely replaces a review system designed by the people's representatives with a set of shapeless procedures to be defined by federal courts at some future date. One cannot help but think, after surveying the modest practical results of the majority's ambitious opinion, that this decision is not really about the detainees at all, but about control of federal policy regarding enemy combatants.

. . .

If the CSRT procedures meet the minimal due process requirements outlined in Hamdi, and if an Article III court is available to ensure that these procedures are followed in future cases, . . . there is no need to reach the Suspension Clause question. Detainees will have received all the process the Constitution could possibly require, whether that process is called "habeas" or something else. The question of the writ's reach need not be addressed.

This is why the Court should have required petitioners to exhaust their remedies under the statute. . . . Because the majority refuses to assess whether the CSRTs comport with the Constitution, it ends up razing a system of collateral review that it admits may in fact satisfy the Due Process Clause and be "structurally sound." But if the collateral review procedures Congress has provided-CSRT review coupled with Article III scrutiny-are sound, interference by a federal habeas court may be entirely unnecessary.

The only way to know is to require petitioners to use the alternative procedures Congress designed. Mandating that the petitioners exhaust their statutory remedies "is in no sense a suspension of the writ of habeas corpus. It is merely a deferment of resort to the writ until other corrective procedures are shown to be futile."

. . .

II

The majority's overreaching is particularly egregious given the weakness of its objections to the DTA. Simply put, the Court's opinion fails on its own terms. The majority strikes down the statute because it is not an "adequate substitute" for habeas review, . . . but fails to show what rights the detainees have that cannot be vindicated by the DTA system.

Because the central purpose of habeas corpus is to test the legality of executive detention, the writ requires most fundamentally an Article III court able to hear the prisoner's claims and, when necessary, order release. . . . The only issue in dispute is the process the Guantanamo prisoners are entitled to use to test the legality of their detention. Hamdi concluded that American citizens detained as enemy combatants are entitled to only limited process, and that much of that process could be supplied by a military tribunal, with review to follow in an Article III court.

That is precisely the system we have here. It is adequate to vindicate whatever due process rights petitioners may have.

A

The Court reaches the opposite conclusion partly because it misreads the statute. The majority appears not to understand how the review system it invalidates actually works-specifically, how CSRT review and review by the D. C. Circuit fit together. After briefly acknowledging in its recitation of the facts that the Government designed the CSRTs "to comply with the due process requirements identified by the plurality in Hamdi," the Court proceeds to dismiss the tribunal proceedings as no more than a suspect method used by the Executive for determining the status of the detainees in the first instance. This leads the Court to treat the review the DTA provides in the D. C. Circuit as the only opportunity detainees have to challenge their status determination.

. . .

III

For all its eloquence about the detainees' right to the writ, the Court makes no effort to elaborate how exactly the remedy it prescribes will differ from the procedural protections detainees enjoy under the DTA. The Court objects to the detainees' limited access to witnesses and classified material, but proposes no alternatives of its own. Indeed, it simply ignores the many difficult questions its holding presents. What, for example, will become of the CSRT process? The majority says federal courts should generally refrain from entertaining detainee challenges until after the petitioner's CSRT proceeding has finished. ("[e]xcept in cases of undue delay"). But to what deference, if any, is that CSRT determination entitled?

. . .

The majority rests its decision on abstract and hypothetical concerns. Step back and consider what, in the real world, Congress and the Executive have actually granted aliens captured by our Armed Forces overseas and found to be enemy combatants:

The right to hear the bases of the charges against them, including a summary of any classified evidence.

The ability to challenge the bases of their detention before military tribunals modeled after Geneva Convention procedures. Some 38 detainees have been released as a result of this process.

The right, before the CSRT, to testify, introduce evidence, call witnesses, question those the Government calls, and secure release, if and when appropriate.

The right to the aid of a personal representative in arranging and presenting their cases before a CSRT.

Before the D. C. Circuit, the right to employ counsel, challenge the factual record, contest the lower tribunal's legal determinations, ensure compliance with the Constitution and laws, and secure release, if any errors below establish their entitlement to such relief.

In sum, the DTA satisfies the majority's own criteria for assessing adequacy. This statutory scheme provides the combatants held at Guantanamo greater procedural protections than have ever been afforded alleged enemy detainees-whether citizens or aliens-in our national history.

. . .

So who has won? Not the detainees. The Court's analysis leaves them with only the prospect of further litigation to determine the content of their new habeas right, followed by further litigation to resolve their particular cases, followed by further litigation before the D. C. Circuit-where they could have started had they invoked the DTA procedure. Not Congress, whose attempt to "determine-through democratic means-how best" to balance the security of the American people with the detainees' liberty interests, see Hamdan v. Rumsfeld, 548 U. S. 557, 636 (2006) (Breyer, J., concurring), has been unceremoniously brushed aside. Not the Great Writ, whose majesty is hardly enhanced by its extension to a jurisdictionally quirky outpost, with no tangible benefit to anyone. Not the rule of law, unless by that is meant the rule of lawyers, who will now arguably have a greater role than military and intelligence officials in shaping policy for alien enemy combatants. And certainly not the American people, who today lose a bit more control over the conduct of this Nation's foreign policy to unelected, politically unaccountable judges.

I respectfully dissent.

QUESTIONS AND NOTES

1.   The original strategy of the Bush administration in establishing the detention facility at Guantanamo Bay in connection with post-9/11 anti-terrorism efforts probably assumed that the fact that the facility was offshore and not in territory owned by the United States would make it easier to argue: a) that U.S. civilian law and, specifically, most constitutional protections, were inapplicable to persons detained there; and b) persons detained there had no right to access U.S. courts. As we have seen in Boumediene v. Bush, supra, the Supreme Court ruled that the Guantanamo detainees had a constitutional right to obtain habeas corpus review of the legality of their detention. It remained to be seen whether the courts would apply other constitutional protections to the Guantanamo detainees.

2.   Boumediene having established that Guantanamo detainees had a right to challenge their detention in federal court, opened the door to the filing of a large number of habeas corpus actions. Materials related to the body of law thereby created is the subject of materials below.

3. On March 7, 2011, President Obama issued an Executive Order creating Periodic Review Boards and prescribing procedures for determining through periodic proceedings whether a detainee continued to be a significant threat to the security of the United States. The Periodic Review process thereby established can be viewed as a successor to the Administrative Review Board (ARB) process described supra, albeit now better defined in an Executive Order, and it very quickly became an important avenue for reviewing and, in a number of cases, authorizing the release and transfer of, detainees still remaining in Guantanamo. The Periodic Review Process and the outcomes of cases reviewed in that process are described infra.

4. In Boumediene, the Supreme Court concluded that the CSRT process was not an adequate substitute for habeas corpus review in an Article III court, even when combined with the judicial review established under the DTA of 2005. What were the weaknesses of the CSRT process? How does the process afforded in habeas review differ? Consider the following list of infirmities of the CSRT process? Does the habeas review process supply or strengthen these elements? Are there any other weaknesses of the CSRT process that you can add to the list?

In the CSRT process:

    a.   the detainee was not represented by a lawyer;

    b.   the detainee did not have access to the classified information relied upon by the decisionmaker or a substitute that meets the standards of the Classified Information Procedures Act;

    c.   the process was not a true adversary process;

    d.   Until December 2005, there was no appeal to an Article III court;

    e.   Since December 2005, judicial review became available, but it was circumscribed.

5. In the wake of the Boumediene decision, a further issue arose— whether an implication of that decision is that habeas corpus relief should be available to individuals detained in a facility even further afield from the U.S. than Guantanamo Bay. That issue is addressed below.

AL-MAQALEH V. GATES

605 F.3d 84 (D.C. Cir. 2010)

SENTELLE, CHIEF JUDGE:

Three detainees at Bagram Air Force Base in Afghanistan petitioned the district court for habeas corpus relief from their confinement by the United States military. Appellants (collectively "the United States" or "the government") moved to dismiss for lack of jurisdiction based on § 7(a) of the Military Commissions Act of 2006, Pub.L. No. 109–366, 120 Stat. 2600 (2006) ("MCA"). The district court agreed with the United States that § 7(a) of the MCA purported to deprive the court of jurisdiction, but held that this section could not constitutionally be applied to deprive the court of jurisdiction under the Supreme Court's test articulated in Boumediene v. Bush, 553 U.S. 723, 128 S.Ct. 2229, 171 L.Ed.2d 41 (2008). The court therefore denied the motion to dismiss but certified the three habeas cases for interlocutory appeal under 28 U.S.C. § 1292(b). Pursuant to that certification, the government filed a petition to this court for interlocutory appeal. We granted the petition and now consider the jurisdictional question. Upon review, and applying the Supreme Court decision in Boumediene, we determine that the district court did not have jurisdiction to consider the petitions for habeas corpus. We therefore reverse the order of the district court and order that the petitions be dismissed.

. . .

All three petitioners are being held as unlawful enemy combatants at the Bagram Theater Internment Facility on the Bagram Airfield Military Base in Afghanistan. Petitioner Fadi Al-Maqaleh is a Yemeni citizen who alleges he was taken into custody in 2003. While Al-Maqaleh's petition asserts "on information and belief" that he was captured beyond Afghan borders, a sworn declaration from Colonel James W. Gray, Commander of Detention Operations, states that Al-Maqaleh was captured in Zabul, Afghanistan. Redha Al-Najar is a Tunisian citizen who alleges he was captured in Pakistan in 2002. Amin Al-Bakri is a Yemeni citizen who alleges he was captured in Thailand in 2002. Both Al-Najar and Al-Bakri allege they were first held in some other unknown location before being moved to Bagram.

. . .

Bagram Airfield Military Base is the largest military facility in Afghanistan occupied by United States and coalition forces. The United States entered into an "Accommodation Consignment Agreement for Lands and Facilities at Bagram Airfield" with the Islamic Republic of Afghanistan in 2006, which "consigns all facilities and land located at Bagram Airfield . . . owned by [Afghanistan,] or Parwan Province, or private individuals, or others, for use by the United States and coalition forces for military purposes." (Accommodation and Consignment Agreement for Lands and Facilities at Bagram Airfield Between the Islamic Republic of Afghanistan and the United States of America) The Agreement refers to Afghanistan as the "host nation" and the United States "as the lessee." The leasehold created by the agreement is to continue "until the United States or its successors determine that the premises are no longer required for its use."

Afghanistan remains a theater of active military combat. The United States and coalition forces conduct "an ongoing military campaign against al Qaeda, the Taliban regime, and their affiliates and supporters in Afghanistan." These operations are conducted in part from Bagram

Airfield. Bagram has been subject to repeated attacks from the Taliban and al Qaeda, including a March 2009 suicide bombing striking the gates of the facility, and Taliban rocket attacks in June of 2009 resulting in death and injury to United States service members and other personnel.

While the United States provides overall security to Bagram, numerous other nations have compounds on the base. Some of the other nations control access to their respective compounds. The troops of the other nations are present at Bagram both as part of the American-led military coalition in Afghanistan and as members of the International Security Assistance Force (ISAF) of the North Atlantic Treaty Organization. The mission of the ISAF is to support the Afghan government in the maintenance of security in Afghanistan. . . . According to the United States, as of February 1, 2010, approximately 38,000 non-United States troops were serving in Afghanistan as part of the ISAF, representing 42 other countries.

. . .

Appellees in this action, three detainees at Bagram, filed habeas petitions against the President of the United States and the Secretary of Defense in the district court. The government moved to dismiss for lack of jurisdiction, relying principally upon § 7(a) of the Military Commissions Act of 2006. After the change in presidential administrations on January 22, 2009, the court invited the government to express any change in its position on the jurisdictional question. The government informed the district court that it "adheres to its previously articulated position."

The district court, recognizing that the issue of whether the court had jurisdiction presented a controlling question of law as to which there were substantial grounds for difference of opinion, certified the question for interlocutory appeal under 28 U.S.C. § 1292(b). We accepted the case for interlocutory review, bringing the jurisdictional issue before us in the present appeal.

. . .

. . .[T]he Court [in Boumediene] concluded that "at least three factors are relevant in determining the reach of the Suspension Clause." Those three factors, which we must apply today in answering the . . . question as to detainees at Bagram, are:

> (1) the citizenship and status of the detainee and the adequacy of the process through which that status determination was made; (2) the nature of the sites where apprehension and then detention took place; and (3) the practical obstacles inherent in resolving the prisoner's entitlement to the writ.

Applying these factors to the detainees at Guantanamo, the Court [in Boumediene] held that the petitioners had the protection of the Suspension Clause.

. . .

Our duty, as explained above, is to determine the reach of the right to habeas corpus and therefore of the Suspension Clause to the factual context underlying the petitions we consider in the present appeal. In doing so, we are controlled by the Supreme Court's interpretation of the Constitution in Eisentrager as construed and explained in the Court's more recent opinion in Boumediene. This is not an easy task, as illustrated by the thorough and careful opinion of the district court. While we are properly respectful of the district court's careful undertaking of this difficult task, as we review rulings on motions to dismiss . . .de novo, we reexamine the issue and ultimately reach a different conclusion.

At the outset, we note that each of the parties has asserted both an extreme understanding of the law after Boumediene and a more nuanced set of arguments upon which each relies in anticipation of the possible rejection of the bright-line arguments. The United States would like us to hold that the Boumediene analysis has no application beyond territories that are, like Guantanamo, outside the de jure sovereignty of the United States but are subject to its de facto sovereignty. As the government puts it in its reply brief, "[t]he real question before this Court, therefore, is whether Bagram may be considered effectively part of the United States in light of the nature and history of the U.S. presence there." We disagree.

Relying upon three independent reasons, the Court in Boumediene expressly repudiated the argument of the United States in that case to the effect "that the Eisentrager Court adopted a formalistic, sovereignty-based test for determining the reach of the Suspension Clause." . . .The Boumediene Court explicitly did "not accept the idea that . . . the [sovereignty discussion] from Eisentrager is the only authoritative language in the opinion and that all the rest is dicta. The Court's further determinations, based on practical considerations, were integral to Part II of its opinion and came before the decision announced its holding.". Second, the Court rejected the Government's reading of Eisentrager because the meaning of the word "sovereignty" in the Eisentrager opinion was not limited to the "narrow technical sense" of the word and could be read "to connote the degree of control the military asserted over the facility." . . .

True, the second factor articulated in Boumediene for rejecting the government's reading of Eisentrager might apply differently in this case because of differences in the levels of control over the military facilities. But we must keep in mind that the second factor is only one of the three reasons offered by the Boumediene Court for the rejection of "a formalistic, sovereignty-based test for determining the reach of the Suspension

Clause.".. Whatever the force of the second reason offered by the Court in Boumediene, the first and third reasons make it plain that the Court's understanding of Eisentrager, and therefore of the reach of the Suspension Clause, was based not on a formalistic attachment to sovereignty, but on a consideration of practical factors as well. We note that the very fact that the Boumediene Court set forth the three-factor test outlined above parallels the Eisentrager Court's further reasoning addressed by the Boumediene Court in its rejection of the bright-line de jure sovereignty argument before it. That is, had the Boumediene Court intended to limit its understanding of the reach of the Suspension Clause to territories over which the United States exercised de facto sovereignty, it would have had no need to outline the factors to be considered either generally or in the detail which it in fact adopted. We therefore reject the proposition that Boumediene adopted a bright-line test with the effect of substituting de facto for de jure in the otherwise rejected interpretation of Eisentrager.

For similar reasons, we reject the most extreme position offered by the petitioners. At various points, the petitioners seem to be arguing that the fact of United States control of Bagram under the lease of the military base is sufficient to trigger the extraterritorial application of the Suspension Clause, or at least satisfy the second factor of the three set forth in Boumediene. Again, we reject this extreme understanding. Such an interpretation would seem to create the potential for the extraterritorial extension of the Suspension Clause to noncitizens held in any United States military facility in the world, and perhaps to an undeterminable number of other United States-leased facilities as well. Significantly, the court engaged in an extended dialog with counsel for the petitioners in which we repeatedly sought some limiting principle that would distinguish Bagram from any other military installation. Counsel was able to produce no such distinction. Again, such an extended application is not a tenable interpretation of Boumediene. If it were the Supreme Court's intention to declare such a sweeping application, it would surely have said so. Just as we reject the extreme argument of the United States that would render most of the decision in Boumediene dicta, we reject the first line of argument offered by petitioners. Having rejected the bright-line arguments of both parties, we must proceed to their more nuanced arguments, and reach a conclusion based on the application of the Supreme Court's enumerated factors to the case before us.

The first of the enumerated factors is "the citizenship and status of the detainee and the adequacy of the process through which that status determination was made." Citizenship is, of course, an important factor in determining the constitutional rights of persons before the court. It is well established that there are "constitutional decisions of [the Supreme] Court expressly according differing protection to aliens than to citizens." United States v. Verdugo-Urquidez, 494 U.S. at 273, 110 S.Ct. 1056. However, clearly the alien citizenship of the petitioners in this case does not weigh against their claim to protection of the right of habeas corpus under the Suspension Clause. So far as citizenship is concerned, they differ in no material respect from the petitioners at Guantanamo who prevailed in Boumediene. As to status, the petitioners before us are held as enemy aliens. But so were the Boumediene petitioners. While the Eisentrager petitioners were in a weaker position by having the status of war criminals, that is immaterial to the question before us. This question is governed by Boumediene and the status of the petitioners before us again is the same as the Guantanamo detainees, so this factor supports their argument for the extension of the availability of the writ.

So far as the adequacy of the process through which that status determination was made, the petitioners are in a stronger position for the availability of the writ than were either the Eisentrager or Boumediene petitioners. As the Supreme Court noted, the Boumediene petitioners were in a very different posture than those in Eisentrager in that "there ha[d] been no trial by military commission for violations of the laws of war." Unlike the Boumediene petitioners or those before us, "[t]he Eisentrager petitioners were charged by a bill of particulars that made detailed factual allegations against them." The Eisentrager detainees were "entitled to representation by counsel, allowed to introduce evidence on their own behalf, and permitted to cross-examine the prosecution's witnesses" in an adversarial proceeding. The status of the Boumediene petitioners was determined by Combatant Status Review Tribunals (CSRTs) affording far less protection. Under the CSRT proceeding, the detainee, rather than being represented by an attorney, was advised by a "Personal Representative" who was "not the detainee's lawyer or even his 'advocate.'" The CSRT proceeding was less protective than the military tribunal procedures in Eisentrager in other particulars as well, and the Supreme Court clearly stated that "[t]he difference is not trivial."

The status of the Bagram detainees is determined not by a Combatant Status Review Tribunal but by an "Unlawful Enemy Combatant Review Board" (UECRB). As the district court correctly noted, proceedings before the UECRB afford even less protection to the rights of detainees in the determination of status than was the case with the CSRT.[4] Therefore, as the district court noted, "while the important adequacy of process factor strongly supported the extension of the Suspension Clause and habeas rights in Boumediene, it even more strongly favors petitioners here." Therefore, examining only the first of the Supreme Court's three enumerated factors, petitioners have made a strong argument that the

---

[4] The Government argues that in our analysis of this first factor, we should consider new procedures that it has put into place at Bagram in the past few months for evaluating the continued detention of individuals. But we will decide this case based on the procedures that have been in place, not on the new procedures that are being implemented only now when the case is before the Court of Appeals.

right to habeas relief and the Suspension Clause apply in Bagram as in Guantanamo. However, we do not stop with the first factor.

The second factor, "the nature of the sites where apprehension and then detention took place," weighs heavily in favor of the United States. Like all petitioners in both Eisentrager and Boumediene, the petitioners here were apprehended abroad. While this in itself would appear to weigh against the extension of the writ, it obviously would not be sufficient, otherwise Boumediene would not have been decided as it was. However, the nature of the place where the detention takes place weighs more strongly in favor of the position argued by the United States and against the extension of habeas jurisdiction than was the case in either Boumediene or Eisentrager. In the first place, while de facto sovereignty is not determinative, for the reasons discussed above, the very fact that it was the subject of much discussion in Boumediene makes it obvious that it is not without relevance. As the Supreme Court set forth, Guantanamo Bay is "a territory that, while technically not part of the United States, is under the complete and total control of our Government." While it is true that the United States holds a leasehold interest in Bagram, and held a leasehold interest in Guantanamo, the surrounding circumstances are hardly the same. The United States has maintained its total control of Guantanamo Bay for over a century, even in the face of a hostile government maintaining de jure sovereignty over the property. In Bagram, while the United States has options as to duration of the lease agreement, there is no indication of any intent to occupy the base with permanence, nor is there hostility on the part of the "host" country. Therefore, the notion that de facto sovereignty extends to Bagram is no more real than would have been the same claim with respect to Landsberg in the Eisentrager case. While it is certainly realistic to assert that the United States has de facto sovereignty over Guantanamo, the same simply is not true with respect to Bagram. Though the site of detention analysis weighs in favor of the United States and against the petitioners, it is not determinative.

But we hold that the third factor, that is "the practical obstacles inherent in resolving the prisoner's entitlement to the writ," particularly when considered along with the second factor, weighs overwhelmingly in favor of the position of the United States. It is undisputed that Bagram, indeed the entire nation of Afghanistan, remains a theater of war. Not only does this suggest that the detention at Bagram is more like the detention at Landsberg than Guantanamo, the position of the United States is even stronger in this case than it was in Eisentrager. As the Supreme Court recognized in Boumediene, even though the active hostilities in the European theater had "c[o]me to an end," at the time of the Eisentrager decision, many of the problems of a theater of war remained:

> In addition to supervising massive reconstruction and aid efforts the American forces stationed in Germany faced potential

security threats from a defeated enemy. In retrospect the post-War occupation may seem uneventful. But at the time Eisentrager was decided, the Court was right to be concerned about judicial interference with the military's efforts to contain "enemy elements, guerilla fighters, and 'were-wolves.' " 128 S.Ct. at 2261 (quoting Eisentrager, 339 U.S. at 784, 70 S.Ct. 936).

In ruling for the extension of the writ to Guantanamo, the Supreme Court expressly noted that "[s]imilar threats are not apparent here." In the case before us, similar, if not greater, threats are indeed apparent. The United States asserts, and petitioners cannot credibly dispute, that all of the attributes of a facility exposed to the vagaries of war are present in Bagram. The Supreme Court expressly stated in Boumediene that at Guantanamo, "[w]hile obligated to abide by the terms of the lease, the United States is, for all practical purposes, answerable to no other sovereign for its acts on the base. Were that not the case, or if the detention facility were located in an active theater of war, arguments that issuing the writ would be 'impractical or anomalous' would have more weight." Id. at 2261–62 (emphasis added). . . .We therefore conclude that under both Eisentrager and Boumediene, the writ does not extend to the Bagram confinement in an active theater of war in a territory under neither the de facto nor de jure sovereignty of the United States and within the territory of another de jure sovereign.

We are supported in this conclusion by the rationale of Eisentrager, which was not only not overruled, but reinforced by the language and reasoning just referenced from Boumediene. As we referenced in the background discussion of this opinion, we set forth more fully now concerns expressed by the Supreme Court in reaching its decision in Eisentrager:

> Such trials would hamper the war effort and bring aid and comfort to the enemy. They would diminish the prestige of our commanders, not only with enemies but with wavering neutrals. It would be difficult to devise more effective fettering of a field commander than to allow the very enemies he is ordered to reduce to submission to call him to account in his own civil courts and divert his efforts and attention from the military offensive abroad to the legal defensive at home. Nor is it unlikely that the result of such enemy litigiousness would be a conflict between judicial and military opinion highly comforting to enemies of the United States. Eisentrager, 339 U.S. at 779, 70 S.Ct. 936.

Those factors are more relevant to the situation at Bagram than they were at Landsberg. While it is true, as the Supreme Court noted in Boumediene, that the United States forces in Germany in 1950 faced the possibility of unrest and guerilla warfare, operations in the European theater had ended with the surrender of Germany and Italy years earlier.

Bagram remains in a theater of war. We cannot, consistent with Eisentrager as elucidated by Boumediene, hold that the right to the writ of habeas corpus and the constitutional protections of the Suspension Clause extend to Bagram detention facility in Afghanistan, and we therefore must reverse the decision of the district court denying the motion of the United States to dismiss the petitions.

We do not ignore the arguments of the detainees that the United States chose the place of detention and might be able "to evade judicial review of Executive detention decisions by transferring detainees into active conflict zones, thereby granting the Executive the power to switch the Constitution on or off at will." However, that is not what happened here. Indeed, without dismissing the legitimacy or sincerity of appellees' concerns, we doubt that this fact goes to either the second or third of the Supreme Court's enumerated factors. We need make no determination on the importance of this possibility, given that it remains only a possibility; its resolution can await a case in which the claim is a reality rather than a speculation. In so stating, we note that the Supreme Court did not dictate that the three enumerated factors are exhaustive. It only told us that "at least three factors" are relevant. Perhaps such manipulation by the Executive might constitute an additional factor in some case in which it is in fact present. However, the notion that the United States deliberately confined the detainees in the theater of war rather than at, for example, Guantanamo, is not only unsupported by the evidence, it is not supported by reason. To have made such a deliberate decision to "turn off the Constitution" would have required the military commanders or other Executive officials making the situs determination to anticipate the complex litigation history set forth above and predict the Boumediene decision long before it came down.

Also supportive of our decision that the third factor weighs heavily in favor of the United States, as the district court recognized, is the fact that the detention is within the sovereign territory of another nation, which itself creates practical difficulties. Indeed, it was on this factor that the district court relied in dismissing the fourth petition, which was filed by an Afghan citizen detainee. While that factor certainly weighed more heavily with respect to an Afghan citizen, it is not without force with respect to detainees who are alien to both the United States and Afghanistan. The United States holds the detainees pursuant to a cooperative arrangement with Afghanistan on territory as to which Afghanistan is sovereign. While we cannot say that extending our constitutional protections to the detainees would be in any way disruptive of that relationship, neither can we say with certainty what the reaction of the Afghan government would be.

In sum, taken together, the second and especially the third factors compel us to hold that the petitions should have been dismissed.

. . .

For the reasons set forth above, we hold that the jurisdiction of the courts to afford the right to habeas relief and the protection of the Suspension Clause does not extend to aliens held in Executive detention in the Bagram detention facility in the Afghan theater of war. We therefore reverse the order of the district court denying the motion for dismissal of the United States and order that the petitions be dismissed for lack of jurisdiction.

NOTE

Following on the principal decision in Al-Maqaleh v. Gates, supra, a series of lawsuits were brought by detainees at Bagram Air Base claiming new evidence that warranted reopening the question of whether under the Boumediene test habeas corpus review in U.S. courts was available to them. The same petitioner as in the principal case brought such a suit, Al-Maqaleh v. Gates, 899 F.Supp.2d 10 (D.D.C. 2012). Also see, e.g., Wahid v. Gates, 876 F.Supp.2d 15 (D.D.C. 2012); Hamidullah v. Obama, 899 F.Supp.2d 3 (D.D.C. 2012); Amanatullah v. Obama 904 F.Supp.2d 45 (D.D.C. 2012). In each case, in similar opinions the court rejected the claims. Of some interest, was the following argument made by a petitioner similar to a claim considered in Boumediene:

> Amanatullah also suggests that the government was employing Bagram as a detention site to deliberately evade judicial review, which, he argues, should influence the court's jurisdictional analysis. In support of this theory, he relies on several news articles, government documents obtained under FOIA, and several "Wikileaks documents." He also points to declarations by Col. Lawrence B. Wilkerson (Ret.) and Glenn Carle, a retired high-ranking CIA officer.

The court responded to the argument as follows:

> This argument fails for several reasons. First, this Court agrees with Judge Bates' skepticism regarding the petitioner's assumption that the question of "purposeful evasion" is or should be part of the Boumediene jurisdictional analysis. Such a theory of jurisdiction seems to lack any limiting principle and would threaten to "create universal habeas jurisdiction"—something plainly at odds with the careful balancing of the Boumediene test. See Al Maqaleh III, 899 F.Supp.2d at 23, at 10. Moreover, even if "purposeful evasion" were a factor in the jurisdictional analysis, Amanatullah has not offered sufficient "new" evidence that would allow this Court to depart from the conclusion of the Court of Appeals in Al Maqaleh II. [ed. Al-Maqaleh v. Gates, 605 F.3d 84 (D.C. Cir. 2010)]. Most (if not all) of Amanatullah's "new" evidence purporting to support this theory had been publicly available when they presented their case to the Court of Appeals in Al Maqaleh II and thus may not lead this court to depart

from the conclusion that court reached. Finally, this Court also notes, as did Judge Bates, that the facts are "not as one-sided as petitioners represent," since some detainees (including high-value ones) were transferred to Guantanamo after Rasul v. Bush, 542 U.S. 466, 124 S.Ct. 2686, 159 L.Ed.2d 548 (2004) (the 2004 case that petitioner argues triggered the purposeful evasion). See Al Maqaleh III, 899 F.Supp.2d at 23, at 10. Thus, again, Amanatullah has failed to introduce evidence that would lead this Court to depart from the analysis of Al Maqaleh II.

All of this litigation has now been overtaken by events. Various news reports about how many detainees were housed at Bagram had been conflicting. For example, in November 2011, it was reported that there were 3000 detainees held there see https://www.cbsnews.com/news/bagram-the-other-guantanamo/. In June, 2011, 1700. See https://www.salon.com/2011/06/04/bagram_obama_gitmo/. Whatever the actual total, the number was being reduced significantly through transfers between 2011 and 2014. In December 2014, it was reported that the U.S. Department of Defense said that it had closed the Air Base prison facility on December 10, 2014. It was also announced that the Government of Afghanistan would be responsible for all detention facilities from January 1, 2015. See http://www.nydailynews.com/news/world/u-s-closes-afghan-bagram-prison-no-detainees-held-article-1.2042422; Sudarsan Raghavan, US Closes Last Detainee Site in Afghanistan as Troop Pullout Advances, Washington Post, Dec. 11, 2014, https://www.washingtonpost.com/world/united-states-closes-last-detainee-site-in-afghanistan-as-troop-pullout-advances/2014/12/11/e238f10a-8140-11e4-9f38-95a187e4c1f7_story.html?utm_term=.be55042cbfd5.

4.   POST-BOUMEDIENE HABEAS CORPUS REVIEWS

Following the Supreme Court's decision in Boumediene v. Bush, not surprisingly, numerous habeas corpus actions were filed by individuals detained at Guantanamo. This section generally describes the legal issues that have arisen in these cases and provides general information about the disposition of the cases. Examining this case law reveals a very complex picture of outcomes at the district court and court of appeals levels.

Overall, this picture can be summarized through three generalizations. The first is that the district courts, which do the basic factfinding in the habeas process often ruled in favor of the detainee petitioners, more often as it turned out than did the U.S. Court of Appeals. The second is that while a number of detainees were released as the outcome of the habeas process, generally they became eligible for release when the district court ruled in their favor and the government did not appeal, that is, when the government did not oppose the release. In those cases where the government appealed to the U.S. Court of Appeals for the District of Columbia, seeking to overturn a decision below in favor of the detainee, the court of appeals ruled fairly consistently in favor of the government, sometimes returning the case for further proceedings to the district court. The third generalization is that, having decided the Boumediene case, over the course of the next decade, the Supreme Court declined to intervene in, or otherwise oversee, the disposition of the individual habeas cases.

But there is much more to the picture than that. Detainee releases approved by President Obama's Guantánamo Review Task Force which issued its report in 2010, those accomplished through the habeas corpus reviews and others through the periodic reviews (discussed in the next section), all in combination, became paths to release and transfer from the detention facility for a majority of the remaining Guantanamo detainees. And some detainees were even transferred whose habeas actions were denied and who had not been approved for transfer in the periodic review process. Further, a fact that may have improved the prospect for release and transfer of most of the detainees was President Obama's wish to close Guantanamo, which very likely served as an impetus to reduce the number of detainees to the lowest possible number. Those who remained in Guantanamo were being, or were going to be, prosecuted, or were hardcore detainees who could not be prosecuted, whom the government thought were too dangerous to release.

The overall result of Obama's move to reduce the number of detainees to the lowest possible number has been to bring that number down to 41 individuals, at the time of this writing. Of course, President Trump has promised to send more suspected terrorists to Guantanamo, but thus far, in the few instances where that possibility existed, he has not done so, probably deterred or prevented by certain factors to be discussed further, infra. Issues relating to the possibility of closing Guantanamo or, alternatively, a resumption of sending more suspected terrorists there are treated infra.

A number of different sources kept unofficial score cards on the results of the habeas reviews from 2008 until recently, reporting, for example, on the number of habeas cases where the detainee was ordered freed, or in which habeas relief was denied, and the number of cases where persons ordered freed, were actually released and transferred, etc. Such information was included in the previous edition of this casebook. Currently, however, since the various processes have all wound down, there seems to be little value in reporting the intermediate data that resulted in the final number of 41. For those who wish to see such score card-type information or insightful commentary on the habeas process, see, e.g., Larkin Reynolds, The Harvard Law School National Security Research Committee, Benjamin Wittes, and Robert M. Chesney, The Emerging Law of Detention 2.0: The Guantánamo Habeas Cases as Lawmaking, May 12, 2011 https://www.brookings.edu/research/the-emerging-law-of-detention-2-0-the-guantanamo-habeas-cases-as-lawmaking/; Linda Greenhouse, Mirror of Guantanamo, N.Y. Times, Dec. 11, 2013, Human Rights First, Guantanamo by the Numbers, March 23, 2017, https://www.humanrightsfirst.org/sites/default/files/gtmo-by-the-numbers.pdf; Worthington, Andy (June 2011). "Guantánamo Habeas Results: The Definitive List". Andy Worthington. Retrieved September 29, 2011. http://www.andyworthington.co.uk/guantanamo-habeas-results-the-definitive-list/. It is still useful to review the legal issues that were addressed and the body of doctrine in the case law that comprises the detainee habeas litigation.

The following is one of the often-cited U.S. court of appeals decisions that ruled on some of the evidentiary and procedural issues in the detainee habeas corpus litigation.

BENSAYAH V. OBAMA
610 F.3d 718 (D.C. Cir. 2010)

Opinion for the Court filed by CIRCUIT JUDGE GINSBURG.

GINSBURG, CIRCUIT JUDGE:

Belkacem Bensayah petitioned the district court for a writ of habeas corpus in order to challenge his detention at the Naval Station at Guantanamo Bay, Cuba. The district court denied his petition, holding the Government had shown by a preponderance of the evidence that Bensayah was being held lawfully pursuant to the Authorization for Use of Military Force (AUMF), because he had provided "support" to al Qaeda. On appeal the Government has eschewed reliance upon certain evidence the district court had considered and has abandoned its position that Bensayah's detention is lawful because of the support he rendered to al Qaeda; instead it argues only that his detention is lawful because he was "part of" that organization-a contention the district court did not reach.

We agree with the Government that its authority under the AUMF extends to the detention of individuals who are functionally part of al Qaeda. The evidence upon which the district court relied in concluding Bensayah supported al Qaeda is insufficient, however, to show he was part of that organization. We therefore remand this case for the district court to determine whether, considering all reliable evidence, Bensayah was functionally part of al Qaeda.

. . .

Bensayah, an Algerian citizen, was arrested by the Bosnian police on immigration charges in late 2001. He was later told that he and five other Algerian men arrested in Bosnia were suspected of plotting to attack the United States Embassy in Sarajevo. Because the ensuing three-month investigation failed to uncover evidence sufficient to continue the detention of the six men, the Supreme Court of the Federation of Bosnia and

Herzogovina ordered that they be released. The men were then turned over to the United States Government and transported to the U.S. Naval Station at Guantanamo Bay, where they have been detained since January 2002.

. . .

In August 2008 the district court entered a case management order (CMO) establishing the procedures that would govern this case. See CMO, Boumediene v. Bush, No. 04-1166(RJL) (D.D.C. Aug. 27, 2008). The CMO placed upon the Government the burden of establishing, by a preponderance of the evidence, the lawfulness of the petitioner's detention. The Government was required to submit a return stating the factual and legal bases for detaining that prisoner, who was then required to file a traverse stating the relevant facts in support of his petition and a rebuttal of the Government's legal justification for his detention. The CMO allowed discovery only "by leave of the Court for good cause shown," and required that requests for discovery

> (1) be narrowly tailored; (2) specify why the request is likely to produce evidence both relevant and material to the petitioner's case; (3) specify the nature of the request . . .; and (4) explain why the burden on the Government to produce such evidence is neither unfairly disruptive nor unduly burdensome.

It also required the Government to provide to the petitioner any exculpatory evidence "contained in the material reviewed in developing the return for the petitioner [ ] and in preparation for the hearing for the petitioner."

The Government claimed authority to detain the six men pursuant both to the AUMF and to the President's inherent powers as Commander in Chief. It argued each of the six men was lawfully detained as an "enemy combatant," which the district court had in an earlier order defined as

> an individual who was part of or supporting Taliban or al Qaeda forces, or associated forces that are engaged in hostilities against the United States or its coalition partners. This includes any person who has committed a belligerent act or has directly supported hostilities in aid of enemy armed forces.

Boumediene v. Bush, 583 F.Supp.2d 133, 135 (2008). The Government contended all six men were lawfully detained because they had planned to travel to Afghanistan in late 2001 in order to take up arms against the United States and allied forces. It also contended Bensayah's detention was lawful because he was a member of and a travel facilitator for al Qaeda. The only direct evidence the Government offered in support of its contentions about Bensayah was contained in a classified document [redacted] from an unnamed source and in certain other pieces of evidence it claimed corroborated that document.

The district court granted habeas to each petitioner other than Bensayah, holding the Government had failed to show by a preponderance of the evidence that they had planned to travel to Afghanistan to fight against the United States. Boumediene, 579 F.Supp.2d at 197–98. Because the Government did not sufficiently establish the reliability of the allegations in the classified document about those petitioners, the court refused to credit those allegations.

The district court denied Bensayah's petition because it determined "the Government has met its burden by providing additional evidence that sufficiently corroborates its allegations from this unnamed source that Bensayah is an al-Qaida facilitator. The corroborative evidence provided by the Government is of three sorts: (1) evidence linking Bensayah to al Qaeda, and specifically to a "senior al-Qaida facilitator"; (2) evidence of Bensayah's history of travel "between and among countries using false passports in multiple names"; and (3) evidence creating "sufficient doubt as to Bensayah's credibility."

Having deemed the allegations about Bensayah in the classified document reliable, the district court held "the Government has established by a preponderance of the evidence that it is more likely than not . . . Bensayah not only planned to take up arms against the United States but also [planned to] facilitate the travel of unnamed others to do the same." The court further held such planning and facilitating "amounts to 'support' within the meaning of the 'enemy combatant' definition governing this case." Because it held Bensayah's detention was lawful based upon his support of al Qaeda, the court did not go on to consider whether he was a "member" of al Qaeda or whether his detention was lawful on the alternative ground that he was "part of" that organization.

There have been three developments since the district court's decision. First, the Government has eschewed reliance upon a portion of the evidence that the "senior al-Qaida facilitator" with whom Bensayah allegedly had contact was in fact a senior al Qaeda facilitator. Second, the Government has changed its position concerning the source and scope of its authority to detain Bensayah. Whereas the Government had previously claimed authority to detain Bensayah based upon both the AUMF and the President's constitutional authority as Commander in Chief, it now relies solely upon the AUMF. Third, the Government has abandoned its argument that Bensayah is being detained lawfully because of the support he rendered to al Qaeda-the sole basis upon which the district court denied Bensayah's petition. The Government now contends that Bensayah's detention is lawful only because he was "part of" al Qaeda.

   . . .

Some but not all Bensayah's many arguments on appeal were mooted when the Government abandoned its theory that Bensayah's detention is lawful because he rendered support to al Qaeda. As for matters of procedure, Bensayah still challenges the district court's (1) reliance upon the preponderance of the evidence standard, (2) refusal to require the Government to search for reasonably available exculpatory evidence in its possession, (3) denial of his discovery requests, and (4) admission of the Government's "rebuttal" evidence. As for matters of substance, Bensayah still argues the district court erred in (1) adopting an overbroad definition of the Executive's detention authority, and (2) crediting "inadequately corroborated raw intelligence." Even if that evidence is credited, he argues (3) it is insufficient to establish his detention is lawful.

We review de novo the district court's conclusions of law, including its ultimate denial of a writ of habeas corpus. We review its factual determinations for clear error, and its evidentiary rulings for abuse of discretion, Whether a detainee was "part of" al Qaeda is a mixed question of law and fact. Awad v. Obama, No. 09-5351, slip op. at 17 (June 2, 2010). "That is, whether a detainee's alleged conduct . . . justifies his detention under the AUMF is a legal question. The question whether the [G]overnment has proven that conduct . . . is a factual question that we review for clear error." Barhoumi v. Obama, No. 09-5383, slip op. at 12–13 (June 11, 2010)).

. . .

In Boumediene the Supreme Court held detainees at Guantanamo Bay are entitled to "the fundamental procedural protections of habeas corpus," but did not expand upon which procedural protections are "fundamental." It left open, for instance, the standard of proof the Government must meet in order to defeat a petition for habeas corpus. ("The extent of the showing required of the Government in these cases is a matter to be determined"). Bensayah argues that because he is liable to be held "for the duration of hostilities that may last a generation or more," requiring the Government to prove the lawfulness of his detention by a mere preponderance of the evidence is inappropriate. He contends the district court should have required the Government to prove its case beyond a reasonable doubt, or at least by clear and convincing evidence. This argument has been overtaken by events, for we have recently held a standard of proof higher than a preponderance of the evidence is not a "fundamental procedural protection" of habeas required by Boumediene. Awad, slip op. at 18 ("A preponderance of the evidence standard satisfies constitutional requirements in considering a habeas petition from a detainee held pursuant to the AUMF"); Al-Bihani v. Obama, 590 F.3d 866, 878 (2010) ("Our narrow charge is to determine whether a preponderance standard is unconstitutional. Absent more specific and relevant guidance, we find no indication that it is.").

The CMO requires the Government to

> provide on an ongoing basis any evidence contained in the material [it] reviewed in developing the return for the petitioner, and in preparation for the hearing for the petitioner, that tends materially to undermine the Government's theory as to the lawfulness of the petitioner's detention.

Bensayah argues the district court abused its discretion by imposing upon the Government an impermissibly narrow obligation to disclose exculpatory evidence. He maintains the Government must search all "reasonably available" information and disclose not only information that "tends materially to undermine the Government's theory as to the lawfulness of the petitioner's detention" but also information that "undermines the reliability of other purportedly inculpatory evidence" or "names potential witnesses capable of providing material evidence."

Bensayah does not contend the disclosure requirement imposed by the district court is in any way unconstitutional. Nor has he shown that broader disclosure is required by any opinion of the Supreme Court or of this court. He cites Bismullah v. Gates, 503 F.3d 137, 138–39 (D.C.Cir.2007), for the proposition that the Government must search all "reasonably available" information, but that decision was compelled by the terms of a statutory scheme not at issue here. He cites Al Odah, 559 F.3d at 546, for the proposition that evidence may be material even if it is not directly exculpatory. The CMO is not, however, in tension with Al Odah. Information that undermines the reliability of other materials, e.g., inculpatory evidence, also tends "materially to undermine the Government's theory as to the lawfulness of the petitioner's detention" and hence must be disclosed by the Government. We therefore agree with the Government that the standard for disclosure ordered by the district court, coupled with the opportunity to make specific discovery requests, is consistent with the Supreme Court's directive in Boumediene that a detainee be provided with the opportunity to challenge "the sufficiency of the Government's evidence" and to "supplement the record on review" with additional "exculpatory evidence."

Bensayah's primary concern seems to be that the disclosure requirement allows the Government to withhold exculpatory evidence because personnel from other agencies will pass only inculpatory evidence on to the attorneys actually "developing the return" and "preparing for the hearing." That practice is not permissible, however, under the current disclosure requirement. Any information that has been strategically filtered out of the record in order to withhold exculpatory evidence is plainly "material reviewed in developing the return"-and hence subject to the disclosure requirement-even if the individual doing the filtering works for a Government agency other than the Department of Justice.

Bensayah next argues that the district court erred by placing upon him the burden of explaining why each of his discovery requests would be neither "unfairly disruptive [nor] unduly burdensome to the Government." The district court did not abuse its discretion in structuring discovery this way. The Supreme Court specifically recognized the district court's discretion to accommodate the Government's legitimate interest in protecting sources and intelligence-gathering methods, acknowledging that "[c]ertain accommodations can be made to reduce the burden habeas corpus proceedings will place on the military without impermissibly diluting the protections of the writ.". It is not necessary to address Bensayah's specific discovery requests relating to [redacted] because, as explained below, we hold this exhibit may not be relied upon by the district court on remand in the absence of additional corroborative evidence. Any discovery requests pertaining to new corroborative evidence should be decided by the district court in the first instance. Finally, we find no merit in Bensayah's claims the district court abused its discretion in denying his request for discovery into the treatment of [redacted] or in allowing the Government to present "rebuttal" evidence.

. . .

The Government asserts the authority to detain Bensayah pursuant to the AUMF, in which the Congress authorized the President

> to use all necessary and appropriate force against those nations, organizations, or persons he determines planned, authorized, committed, or aided the terrorist attacks that occurred on September 11, 2001, or harbored such organizations or persons, in order to prevent any future acts of international terrorism against the United States by such nations, organizations or persons.

As mentioned before, the Government contends it may lawfully detain an individual if he is "part of" al Qaeda. Bensayah objects to this formulation, but we have made clear elsewhere that the AUMF authorizes the Executive to detain, at the least, any individual who is functionally part of al Qaeda. Barhoumi, slip op. at 29 (detainee "was 'part of an al-Qaida-associated force and therefore properly detained pursuant to the AUMF"); Awad, slip op. at 19 ("Once [a petitioner is shown to be] 'part of al Qaeda . . . the requirements of the AUMF [are] satisfied"); Al-Bihani, 590 F.3d at 872–74.

Although it is clear al Qaeda has, or at least at one time had, a particular organizational structure, see The 9/11 Commission Report: Final Report of the National Commission on Terrorist Attacks upon the United States 56 (2004) ("[Al Qaeda's] structure included as its operating arms an intelligence component, a military committee, a financial committee, a political committee, and a committee in charge of media affairs and propaganda"), the details of its structure are generally unknown, see Audrey Kurth Cronin, Congressional Research Service Report for Congress: Al Qaeda After the Iraq Conflict (2003) ("There is a great deal that remains unknown or debatable about the specific nature, size, structure and reach of [al Qaeda]"), but it is thought to be somewhat amorphous, Kenneth Katzman, Congressional Research Service Report for Congress: Al Qaeda: Profile and Threat Assessment (2005) ("Al Qaeda has always been more a coalition of different groups than a unified structure, many argue, and it has been this diversity that gives Al Qaeda global reach"). As a result, it is impossible to provide an exhaustive list of criteria for determining whether an individual is "part of" al Qaeda. That determination must be made on a case-by-case basis by using a functional rather than a formal approach and by focusing upon the actions of the individual in relation to the organization. That an individual operates within al Qaeda's formal command structure is surely sufficient but is not necessary to show he is "part of" the organization; there may be other indicia that a particular individual is sufficiently involved with the organization to be deemed part of it, see Awad, slip op. at 19 ("there are ways other than making a 'command structure' showing to prove that a detainee is 'part of' al Qaeda"), but the purely independent conduct of a freelancer is not enough.

As the district court noted, a [redacted] is the only evidence directly suggesting that Bensayah is an al Qaeda facilitator. That document, [redacted], contains the warning "INFORMATION REPORT, NOT FINALLY EVAULATED INTELLIGENCE." [redacted]

[redacted] contains a number of allegations about Bensayah. It states:

[redacted]

[redacted]

[redacted]

[redacted]

The district court, quoting Parhat v. Gates, 532 F.3d 834, 847 (D.C.Cir.2008), correctly stated that it must "evaluate the raw evidence, finding it to be sufficiently reliable and sufficiently probative to demonstrate the truth of the asserted proposition with the requisite degree of certainty." See Barhoumi, slip op. at 21 ("we agree . . . Parhat sets the guideposts for our inquiry into the reliability of the . . . evidence [in a detainee's habeas case]"). Although the district court found [redacted] contains some inherent indicia of reliability, viz., [redacted] uncertainty about the source of the document and about how the information therein was gathered led the court to conclude [redacted] is not by itself reliable.

In Parhat we made clear that the reliability of evidence can be determined not only by looking at the evidence alone but, alternatively, by considering "sufficient additional information ... permit[ting the factfinder] to assess its reliability." Here the district court, after looking at additional information, concluded "there is sufficient corroborating evidence in the record to credit and rely upon the [ ] assertions made in [redacted] about Bensayah." The evidence in question is of three sorts: (1) evidence linking Bensayah to al Qaeda, and specifically to, [redacted], allegedly a "senior al-Qaida operative and facilitator"; (2) evidence of Bensayah's travel plans and travel history; and (3) evidence raising "questions ... about Bensayah's whereabouts in the early 1990s," which evidence created "sufficient doubt as to Bensayah's credibility."

Bensayah argues the district court clearly erred by finding [redacted] reliable. He contends the [redacted] upon which the district court relied were categorically insufficient to corroborate [redacted]. We disagree with Bensayah's broad contention that two pieces of evidence, each unreliable when viewed alone, cannot ever corroborate each other. ... We agree, however, with his alternative argument that even if the additional evidence relied upon by the district court in this case is itself reliable, it is not sufficiently corroborative to support reliance upon the statements concerning Bensayah in [redacted].

. . .

The district court found [redacted] were corroborated by Bensayah's "connections" to al Qaeda, viz., (1) Bensayah was directly linked to [redacted], allegedly a "senior al-Qaida operative and facilitator," and (2) [redacted].

Evidence linking Bensayah to [redacted] included [redacted]. The district court found the Government "has put forth more than sufficient credible evidence that [redacted] was a senior al-Qaida operative and facilitator." Since the district court's decision, however, the Government has eschewed reliance upon much of that evidence; it now maintains the other evidence upon which the district court relied is sufficient to link [redacted] to al Qaeda. In an order denying a Rule 60(b) motion filed by Bensayah, the district court indicated it would have concluded [redacted] was sufficiently corroborated to be relied upon, even "putting aside completely any evidence linking Bensayah to [redacted].

Assuming, as the Government contends, [redacted] was connected to al Qaeda, the evidence linking Bensayah to [redacted][1] and al Qaeda does not, by itself or together with the other evidence discussed below, corroborate [redacted] sufficiently so that it can be relied upon. The Government presented no direct evidence of actual communication between Bensayah and any al Qaeda member, much less evidence suggesting Bensayah communicated with [redacted] or anyone else in order

---

[1] [redacted]

to facilitate travel by an al Qaeda member. Indeed, the district court determined the record did not support the allegations in [redacted] concerning the only individuals named therein whose travel Bensayah allegedly planned to facilitate.

. . .

The district court found the assertions in [redacted] were corroborated by evidence that Bensayah (1) [redacted], and (2) had "experience in obtaining and traveling in and out of numerous countries on fraudulent passports." Bensayah admits to having used multiple travel documents, "some of which were in an assumed name," but maintains he traveled under fraudulent documents in order to avoid being sent back to Algeria, "where he reasonably feared persecution." He presented "unrebutted declarations" that "mere possession and use of false travel documents is neither proof of involvement with terrorism nor evidence of facilitation of travel by others." We agree. That Bensayah had experience with fraudulent travel documents [redacted] is not sufficiently corroborative of [redacted] that Bensayah was a travel facilitator for al Qaeda or anyone else. As noted in the prior paragraph, the district court determined the Government had failed to show that Bensayah's co-petitioners planned to travel to Afghanistan in order to engage U.S. forces. Therefore, Bensayah could not have been facilitating their travel for that purpose.

. . .

The district court found "serious questions [had] been raised about Bensayah's whereabouts in the early 1990s." This finding at most undermines Bensayah's own credibility; no account of his whereabouts ties him to al Qaeda or suggests he facilitated anyone's travel during that time. These "questions" in no way demonstrate that Bensayah had ties to and facilitated travel for al Qaeda in 2001.

* * *

Because the evidence, viewed in isolation or together, is insufficiently corroborative of [redacted], the district court on remand may not, in the absence of additional corroborative evidence not already considered, rely upon that exhibit in determining whether Bensayah was part of al Qaeda.

. . .

The Government argues it is authorized by the AUMF to detain Bensayah solely on the ground he was functionally a member or "part of" al Qaeda. The evidence upon which the district court relied in concluding Bensayah "supported" al Qaeda is insufficient, however, to show he was part of that organization. Accordingly, we reverse the judgment of the district court and remand the case for the district court to hear such evidence as the parties may submit and to decide in the first instance whether Bensayah was functionally part of al Qaeda.

NOTE

See Bensayah v. Obama, 2014 WL 395693 (Feb. 3, 2014, D. D.C.) in which the following was reported:

> On December 5, 2013, Bensayah was transferred from Guantanamo to the custody of the Government of Algeria, effectively mooting his habeas request. See Petitioner's Unopposed Mot. for Vacatur of the District Court's Judgment as to Mr. Bensayah and for Remand with Instructions to Dismiss his Case as Moot at 2, Bensayah v. Obama, No. 08–5537 (D.C.Cir.2013). Bensayah promptly filed an unopposed motion with the Court of Appeals requesting vacatur of this Court's judgment and remand of the case with instructions to dismiss it as moot. On January 9, 2014, the Court of Appeals granted Bensayah's motion, vacating this Court's judgment, and remanding with instructions to dismiss the case as moot.

> Thus, for the foregoing reasons, and in accordance with the January 9, 2014 Order of our Court of Appeals, it is hereby

> **ORDERED** that petitioner's case is **DISMISSED** as moot.

The following case contains the district court's assessment of detailed facts bearing on whether the petitioner should be released. It also involves application by the district court of a number of different legal rules and standards utilized in the detainee habeas actions, some of which were decided upon in Bensayah, supra. The case provides a useful introduction to the type of issues that were litigated in the detainee habeas cases in the District of Columbia following on the decision in Boumediene, and how the courts handled them.

SHAWALI KHAN V. OBAMA

2014 WL 4843907 (Sept. 2, 2014, D.D.C.)

MEMORANDUM OPINION

BATES, J.

Shawali Khan, a citizen of Afghanistan, has been in United States custody since mid-November 2002, and has been detained at the United States Naval Base at Guantánamo Bay, Cuba since early 2003. Contending that he was unlawfully detained under the September 18, 2001 Authorization for Use of Military Force ("AUMF"), Pub.L. No. 107–40, 115 Stat. 224 (2001). Khan filed a petition for a writ of habeas corpus in 2008. After several years of discovery, briefing, and a three-day evidentiary hearing, this Court denied Khan's petition, concluding that it was more likely than not that Khan was "part of" Hezb-i-Islami Gulbuddin ("HIG"), an "associated force" of the Taliban and al-Qaeda in hostilities against the

United States and its coalition partners and, hence, that Khan was lawfully detained under the AUMF. The D.C. Circuit affirmed.

Now before the Court is Khan's motion for post-judgment relief under Federal Rule of Civil Procedure 60(b). Khan argues that subsequent developments have weakened the government's case for detention and that, therefore, the Court should vacate its prior judgment and reopen these proceedings. Although the government's case for Khan's detention has been weakened slightly by recent developments, it remains more likely than not that Khan was "part of" forces associated with the Taliban and al-Qaeda at the time of his capture. In addition, Khan's motion fails to clear the high bar required to obtain post-judgment relief under Rule 60(b). For these reasons. Khan's detention remains lawful, and his motion will be denied.

BACKGROUND

I.　Factual Background

It is undisputed that Shawali Khan is a citizen of Afghanistan, who, at the time he was captured in November 2002, was living in the Kandahar region and managing a small oil shop. Other than that, the parties disagree on almost every relevant fact in this case. So, the Court will offer a broad summary of the factual narratives offered by each side.

A.　The government's narrative; Khan was a member of so HIG cell.

According to the government: Khan's connections to HIG date back to the time of the Soviet invasion of Afghanistan in the 1980s. Khan v. Obama, 655 F.3d 20, 21 (D.C.Cir.2011) ("Khan III"); see also Khan v. Obama, 646 F.Supp.2d 6, 17 (D-D.C.2009) ("Khan I") (Khan "was active in HIG during jihad against the former Soviet Union"). Khan allegedly worked as a radio operator in a unit commanded by his uncle, Zabit Jalil, fighting with the mujahideen in the anti-Soviet jihad Khan III, 655 F.3d at 21. After KIG's founder, leader, and namesake, Gulbiddin Hekmatyar, returned to Afghanistan from his exile in Iran after September 11, 2001, HIG joined forces with al-Qaeda and the Taliban to fight United States and coalition forces operating in Afghanistan. See id.; see also May 13, 2010 Hr'g Tr. 108:15–17 (Testimony of Prof. Brian Williams) ("[P]ost 9/11, when you have this burying of the hatchet between the Taliban .... and HIG, you also have the sort of burying of the hatchet with Bin Laden and al-Qaeda."). Around that same time period, as reported by various U.S. intelligence collectors, a handful of Afghan informants described a small HIG terrorist cell operating in the Kandahar region of southern Afghanistan. Khan III, 655 F.3d at 21.

Informant A1 reported that the HIG cell was led by Khan's uncle, Zabit Jalil; that it had already successfully carried out attacks on U.S. and coalition forces near the Kandahar airfield; and that additional attacks were still in their planning phases. See Evidentiary Hr'g, Gov't's Ex. 18 (IIR 6 044 0249 03), at 1–4; Evidentiary Hr'g, Gov't's Ex. 19 (IIR 6 044 0266 03), at 1–4. Specifically, the HIG cell planted explosives on roads frequented by U.S. military vehicles—apparently, "even the little children" in Afghanistan know how to spot them, IIR 6 044 0249 03 at 2—then detonated the explosives remotely in a specific "binary" pattern. Informant A described how the cell would stagger the explosions to maximize American casualties:

> When the Americans are close enough to the kill zone, the first explosion is detonated. . . . The intent of the first explosion is to cause injury and disable the vehicle. This act will force other Americans to investigate the scene and help evacuate the wounded. When a large enough crowd has gathered around the disabled vehicle and wounded personnel, a second, more powerful explosion is detonated. . . . The purpose of the second explosion is to kill the wounded and those who are trying to help them

Informant A provided U.S. intelligence collectors with the precise radio frequencies used by the HIG cell to detonate the pair of explosions, see id. [redacted] as welt as the specific type of explosive that would be used: "a Chinese or Russian antitank mine approximately 12 inches in diameter" connected to an "electric blasting cap" that is in turn "attached to the radio-controlled electronic detonator," Evidentiary Hr'g, Gov't's Ex. 20 (IIR 6 044 0267 03) at 3. Informant A specifically named petitioner, Shawali Khan, as the group's communicator, reporting that Khan facilitated radio contact amongst the cell's members. IIR 6 044 0266 03, at 3.

A second informant, Informant B, also named Khan as a member of the Kandahar HIG cell, describing Khan as "a go-between and a facilitator." Evidentiary Hr'g, Gov't's Ex, 17 (IIR 6 044 0025 03), at 3. He claimed that Khan "use[d] [his] oil shop to conduct meetings and as a contact point with other members within the cell." Id. Finally, a third informant, Informant C, offered additional specifics about the HIG cell's future plans to carry out attacks: apparently, "mines ha[d] already been emplaced" at two specific locations, but "they ha[d] not been armed with a remote detonation device" yet. Evidentiary Hr'g, Gov't's Ex. 21 (IIR 6 044 0300 03), at 5.

In November of 2002, the U.S. military decided to capture Khan and neutralize the HIG cell. Relying on Informant A to identify Khan's likely whereabouts on a particular date and time, American forces successfully carried out an operation to capture Khan. Evidentiary Hr'g, Gov't's Ex. 1, Decl. of [redacted] at ¶¶ 45–46.2 After arresting Khan, and searching his oil shop and his home, U.S. forces recovered several pieces of incriminating physical evidence, [redacted] The documents were mostly written in

Arabic, and included several notebooks about assassination, surveillance, counterfeiting, and the use and maintenance of automatic weapons, and a book of poems authored by a high-level al-Qaeda leader. See generally Evidentiary Hr'g, Gov't's Ex. 59, AFGP-2003-000483 (Harmony Database Entry); Evidentiary Hr'g, Gov't's Ex. 60, AFGP-2003-000483 (Original); Evidentiary Hr'g, Gov't's Ex. 62 AFGP-2003-000484 (Translation); Evidentiary Hr'g, Gov't's Ex. 68, AFGP-2003-000540 (Original). [redacted]

After Khan's capture, Informant B reported that Khan's uncle, Zabit Jalil—a long-time HIG commander and the leader of the Kandahar HIG cell—called a meeting with his HIG colleagues in Pakistan, explaining Ms desire to replace the entire Kandahar cell, which he felt had been compromised as a result of Khan's capture. See Evidentiary Hr'g, Gov't's Ex. 23 (IIR 6 044 0433 03) at 1–2 (Nov. 22, 2002). And, for the two months following Khan's capture, improvised explosive device attacks in the area stopped completely. Evidentiary Hr'g, Gov't's Ex. 2, Decl. of [redacted] ¶ 15(d).

B.   Khan's narrative: Khan is an innocent shopkeeper.

Primarily, Khan challenges the reliability of the government's evidence, rather than offering his own, alternative narrative. Bot, to the extent he offers his own version of events, Khan claims to be an innocent shopkeeper, wrongfully accused by corrupt Afghans who offered lies about him to U.S. forces in return for money. Regarding the physical evidence recovered at Ms oil shop and his home, Khan has offered some shifting explanations, but primarily claims that he both (1) [ed. did] not know the items were (e.g., [redacted] he couldn't read the jihadist training materials because he speaks Pashto, not Arabic), and (2) they did not belong to him (e.g., they were recovered by chance during some looting he did of local businesses or homes abandoned by Arabs fleeing the region).

II.   Procedural Background

In Boumediene v. Bush, the United States Supreme Court held that aliens detained as enemy combatants at the United Stales Naval Base at Guantánamo Bay, Cuba "are entitled to the privilege of habeas corpus to challenge the legality of their detention." 553 U.S. 723, 771, 128 S.Ct. 2229, 171 L.Ed.2d 41 (2008). Khan filed a petition for a writ of habeas corpus two weeks after Boumediene issued, on June 25, 2008. See Khan's Pet. [ECF No. 1]. In his petition, Khan alleged that he was "detained without lawful basis," and asked to be released.

. . .

After considering all of the evidence in the record, the Court denied Khan's habeas petition on September 3, 2010, The Court relied heavily on sworn declarations from members of the intelligence team who had authored intelligence reports tying Khan to the HIG cell, which the Court held "provide [d] the information necessary to assess the sources' reliability under the principles accepted in the intelligence community." Khan v. Obama, 741 F.Supp.2d 1, 13 (D.D.C.2010) ("Khan II"). Having rectified the primary concern raised by the Court in its opinion denying Khan's motion for judgment on the record—that is, the reliability of a handful of highly incriminating intelligence documents—the Court focused its decision "on a few key pieces of evidence, which the Court finds reliable and which clearly establish Khan was a 'part of HIG when he was captured in 2002." Id. al 4.

The D.C. Circuit affirmed in a unanimous opinion, "[f]inding no error" in what it described as this Court's "careful consideration of the evidence." Khan III, 655 F.3d at 21. The D.C. Circuit, just as this Court had done, focused heavily on a handful of "heavily redacted intelligence reports that describe items recovered in searches of [Khan's] properties." Id. at 30. The D.C. Circuit found "[t]hose reports highly incriminating, both because of the nature of the items themselves and because their presence on Khan's properties further corroborates the informants' description of Khan's role in the Kandahar HIG cell." Id. The D.C. Circuit also explicitly affirmed this Court's "finding that HIG was associated with al Qaeda and the Taliban in late 2002." Id. at 33.

. . .

To further complicate things, during briefing on Khan's Rule 60(b) motion, the government filed a "notice that [it is] no longer relying on statements made by Petitioner Shawali Khan during custodial interrogations, or during his Administrative Review Board ('ARB') proceedings, to justify his detention." Gov't's Oct. 12, 2011 Notice of Withdrawal of Reliance on Pet'r's Statements [ECF No. 250]. That same day, the government filed an ex parte submission, "provid[ing] the Court with additional information regarding Respondents' decision to withdraw reliance on statements made by Petitioner Shawali Khan." Gov't's Oct. 12, 2011 Notice of Ex Parts Filing [ECF No. 251].

. . .

LEGAL STANDARDS

. . .

II. Evidentiary Issues

Pursuant to the Case Management Order in this action, "[t]he government bears the burden of proving by a preponderance of the evidence that the petitioner's detention is lawful." Feb. 20, 2009 Case Management Order, § II.A; accord Al-Adahi v. Obama, 613 F.3d 1102, 1105 (D.C.Cir.2010); Awad v. Obama, 608 F.3d), 10–11 (D.C.Cir.2010). That standard " 'simply requires the trier of fact to believe that the existence of a fact is more probable than its nonexistence before he may find in favor of the party who has the burden to persuade the judge of the fact's existence.' "

Concrete Pipe Sc Prods, of Cal., Inc. v. Constr. Laborers Pension Trust for S. Cal., 508 U.S. 602, 622, 113 S.Ct. 2264, 124 L.Ed.2d 539 (1993).

The evidence on which the government relies to justify Khan's detention is "atypical of evidence usually presented in federal actions." Abdah v. Obama, 709 F.Supp.2d 25, 27 (D.D.C.2010). In particular, the government presents a variety of documents "produced and used by government intelligence agencies." Id. This evidence includes Intelligence Information Reports ("IIRs"), [redacted] and Form 40s ("FM40s"). IIRs are Department of Defense documents reporting information obtained from human intelligence sources by the Defense Intelligence Agency and the military's intelligence services. See Evidentiary Hr'g, Gov't's Ex. 11 (Decl. of [redacted] at 6. FM40s are law enforcement documents that record "investigation activity, such as witness interviews," and "record information relevant to how a crime was committed as well as the logical and factual basis for any deductions about guilt." Id. at 7. [redacted]

Although many of these documents contain hearsay, hearsay is always admissible in Guantánamo habeas cases. See Al-Bihani, 590 F.3d at 879. The Court must determine, however, "what probative weight to ascribe to whatever indicia of reliability [the hearsay evidence] exhibits." Id. Hence, " '[t]he fact finder must evaluate the raw evidence," resolving whether it is "sufficiently reliable and sufficiently probative to demonstrate the truth of the asserted proposition with the requisite degree of certainty.' " Parhat v. Gates, 532 F.3d 834, 847 (D.C.Cir.2008) (quoting Concrete Pipe, 508 U.S. at 622)). The parties therefore must present hearsay evidence "in a form, or with sufficient additional information, that permits the . . . court to assess its reliability." Id. at 849.

Under Parhat, then, the Court first considers whether a particular piece of evidence itself possesses "sufficient hallmarks of reliability," and whether it is corroborated by other reliable evidence. See Khan I, 646 F.Supp.2d at 13; see also Parhat, 532 F.3d at 849 ("There may well be other forms in which the government can submit information that will permit an appropriate assessment of the information's reliability while protecting the anonymity of a highly sensitive source."); Rugendorf v. United States, 376 U.S. 528, 533, 84 S.Ct. 825, 11 L.Ed.2d 887 (1964) (affidavit in support of a search warrant containing hearsay from a confidential source may be reliable "so long as there was a substantial basis for crediting the hearsay"); United States v. Laws, 808 F.2d 92, 100–03 (D.C.Cir.1986) (one informant's hearsay statement can corroborate another informant's hearsay statement). The Court then determines "whether the evidence is in fact sufficiently reliable to be used as a justification for detention." Khan I, 646 F, Supp.2d at 12. "[I]f courts cannot assess reliability, then the evidence in question is inherently unreliable and may not be relied upon to justify detention." Id.

. . .

ANALYSIS

Because Khan challenges a final judgment, he faces a higher bar to obtain relief than he did when the Court first considered his habeas petition. For that reason, the Court could deny his motion for failure to present the sort of "extraordinary circumstances" needed to justify relief under Rule 60(b); for failure to raise some of his arguments in a timely fashion; and for failure to demonstrate that some of his evidence is, in fact, "newly discovered"—even without determining whether it is more likely than not, on the state of the current record, that be is legally detainable under the AUMF. The Court will address all of those defects in Khan's motion, which significantly limit Khan's ability to obtain post-judgment relief. But, because Khan alleges that he is an innocent man who has been unlawfully detained at Guantanamo Bay for over a decade, and because the government's evidence in this case has never been overwhelming, the Court also believes it appropriate to conduct a somewhat more searching inquiry into the current slate of the remaining evidence in this case. Nevertheless, after conducting this (essentially, de novo) review of the evidentiary record, the Court is still convinced that it is more likely than not that Khan was "part of" a force associated with the al-Qaeda and the Taliban at the time of his capture. For all these reasons, Khan's motion will be denied.

I.   Post-Judgment Developments Do Not Undermine The Conclusion That It Is More Likely Than Not That Khap Is Lawfully Detained Under The AUMF.

Since entering judgment in this case, several new developments have undermined the government's case for detention. Most importantly, the government abandoned all reliance on Khan's statements, as memorialized by interrogation reports submitted as part of the government's case-in-chief. In addition, [redacted] argues Khan, contradicts some key facts in the government's case, and thus casts doubt upon the credibility of all of the intelligence collectors, whose declarations have been relied upon heavily in this case (by both this Court and the D.C. Circuit). Ultimately, although these developments have, undoubtedly, made this a closer case, ft is still more likely than not that Khan was "part of" an associated force of the Taliban and al-Qaeda at the time of his capture.

A.   The Court need not revisit its prior conclusion that HIG is an "associated force" of the Taliban and al-Qaeda.

There is no allegation that Khan was "part of" the Taliban or al-Qaeda at the time of his capture—only that he was a member of a small HIG cell. So in order to detain him, the government must demonstrate a link between HIG and the Taliban or al-Qaeda, existing at the time of Khan's capture. See Al-Bihani, 590 F.3d at 872 (allowing detention of an individual who "engaged in hostilities . . . against the United States," who "purposefully and materially supported hostilities against the United States or its coalition partners," or who "is part of the Taliban, al-Qaida, or associated forces").

Once again, "[t]he Court does not assess whether HIG is an 'associated force' of al-Qaida or the Taliban on a blank slate." Khan II, 741 F.Supp.2d at 8. This issue was heavily disputed at the evidentiary hearing in May 2010. The government presented evidence that—despite past disagreements—HIG had "buried the hatchet" with the Taliban and al-Qaeda after September 11, 2001 and the start of Operation Enduring Freedom, and began a cooperative campaign to target U.S. and coalition forces in the region. See, e.g., Evidentiary Hr'g, Gov't's Ex. 13 (Decl. of [redacted] at 1 [redacted] id. at 2 [redacted] On the other hand, Khan offered testimony from Professor Brian Williams, his expert on Afghan warlords, who testified that it wag unlikely that HIG would be operating in the Kandahar region of Afghanistan at the relevant time period. See, e.g., Evidentiary Hr'g, Pet'r's Ex. 8 (Decl. of Brian Williams), at 8 ("The odds are against Hekmatyar having followers in distant Kandahar so soon after his return from exile."); May 13, 2010 Hr'g Tr. 118:10–12 ("I don't want to say that there's no way Hekmaryar could be there, but 1 will say that it strikes me as strange, improbable, unlikely.").

Considering all of this evidence, the Court concluded that "HIG was an 'associated force' of al-Qaida and the Taliban at the time of Khan's capture in late 2002." Khan II, 741 F.Supp.2d at 8; accord Khan I, 646 F.Supp.2d at 19. . . .

In his Rule 60(b) motion, Khan does not explicitly challenge the conclusion that HIG is properly considered an "associated force" of the Taliban and al-Qaeda. None of the "new" evidence he puts forth relates to HIG's relationship with the Taliban or al-Qaeda. And this Court did not rely on Khan's statements, now withdrawn from the government's case, in any significant way in issuing its previous decisions on this issue. Nor did the D.C. Circuit. Accordingly, the conclusion that HIG is an "associated force" of the Taliban and al-Qaeda stands unchallenged. Hence, the government need only show that it is more likely than not that Khan was "part of" HIG at the time of his capture in order to lawfully detain him. See Al-Bihani, 590 F.3d at 872.

B. Even without Khan's statements, sufficient evidence supports the conclusion that Khan was "part of" HIG at the time of his capture.

The most significant development since the entry of judgment in this Court, and the D.C. Circuit's affirmance of that judgment, is the government's decision to abandon any reliance on Khan's statements (that is, with the exception of Khan's testimony at the merits hearing). Those statements were relied upon by the government for many years, and were specifically advanced by the government at the merits hearing as part of the case for Khan's detention. But, as discussed below, although Khan's statements generally supported the conclusion that Khan was detainable under the AUMF, those (mostly incriminating) statements were not central to the analysis in this Court or in the D.C. Circuit. Even without them, other evidence in the record supports the conclusion that it is more likely than not that Khan was an HIG operative—not an innocent shopkeeper.

1. Intelligence reports describe highly incriminating physical evidence recovered at Khan's properties.

"As framed over the course of these proceedings, this case now centers on a few key pieces of evidence" that are highly incriminating. Khan II, 741 F.Supp.2d at 4. Chief among them: intelligence reports describing physical evidence recovered at Khan's properties, which is not just incriminating on its own, but also corroborates other incriminating reports from Afghan informants.

[redacted] Needless to the say, the odds of this exact [redacted] appearing by chance in two places at once—first, in a description from an informant about Khan's involvement in an HIG cell; second, on [redacted] found at a search incident to Khan's arrest—approach zero. And although there may be, theoretically, alternative possible explanations—for example, that Khan was set up as a part of some elaborate conspiracy—it is much more likely than not that Khan was in possession [redacted] for the reason offered by the government and its informants: Khan was part of an HIG cell, planning attacks on U.S. and coalition forces by means of a radio-controlled, binary explosive device. As the Court explained once before, "[t]he government's narrative ... corroborates itself—that [redacted] recovered from Khan's properties renders reliable [Informant A's] report [redacted] and vice versa." Khan II, 741 F.Supp.2d at 18.

Even setting aside [redacted] other physical evidence recovered by U.S. forces is also incriminating. For example, finding [redacted] on Khan's property is, once again, highly supportive of the conclusion (hat Khan was a member of an HIG cell, specializing in explosive attacks on U.S. and coalition personnel.

None of this evidence depends on Khan's statements. To be sure, the Court did cite a December 17, 2002 interrogation report—in which Khan admitted [redacted] (he offered somewhat implausible explanations [redacted]—as additional corroboration of the government's arguments tying Khan to this evidence. See Khan II, 741 F.Supp.2d at 17 ("The Court concludes, however, that it need not rely on the four corners of the interrogation summary to determine its reliability—the other evidence in the record corroborates Khan's admission [redacted] But the evidence itself is still highly incriminating, and is still reliable enough for current purposes, see infra Section I.B.3, even without Khan's statements.

2. Intelligence documents detail incriminating reports from several informants.

Several informants pointed to Khan as a key member of an HIG cell that targeted U.S. and coalition forces in and around Kandahar. Informant A "identified two members of the cell—Shawali Khan and Noor Agha—and indicated that Khan served as a communicator between Noor Agha, the cell's facilitator, and other cell members." Khan II, 741 F.Supp.2d at 9. Informant A also told U.S. intelligence collectors that the HIG cell was "planning an attack against Americans through the use of radio-controlled binary explosive devices." IIR 6 044 0249 03 at 1. He also brought the intelligence collectors one of the binary detonators, id. at 4—apparently a highly unusual gesture—suggesting Informant A's reliability and trustworthiness, see Decl. of [redacted] ¶ 43 ("It was extremely unusual for a source to provide such evidence to back up his statements. This type of action is a sign of above average reliability.").

Informant B offered similar incriminating information about Khan. This source related that "Shah ((Wali)) [Khan] is a go-between and a facilitator within a Hezb-i-Islami, Gulbuddin operations cell," who "delivered a radio-controlled binary detonation device and two blasting caps to art [?] operative working within his organization." IIR 6 044 0025 03, at 3. Finally, Informant C offered corroborative information about the HIG cell generally, its operations in Kandahar, and its plans to attack U.S. and coalition forces. See, e.g., IIR 6 044 0300 03, at 6–7 ("The information and methods of operation in this report confirms, in part, the information reported in IIR 6044 0249 03.").

None of this evidence relies on Khan's statements, in any way.

3. The key evidence is reliable, even without Khan's statements.

At the heart of this case, and all its iterations before this Court and the D.C. Circuit, is the question of the reliability of the incriminating intelligence reports and informant tips discussed above. It is upon this evidence that the government's case for detention primarily rests. In Khan I, this Court held that, "standing alone," the incriminating intelligence reports bore "none of the hallmarks of reliability that the intelligence community itself looks to in assessing the reliability of raw, human intelligence." Khan I, 646 F.Supp.2d at 14. But after full discovery, in Khan II the Court held that detailed, sworn declarations from members of the intelligence team that prepared the intelligence reports assuaged the Court's concerns. See Khan II, 741 F.Supp.2d at 13 ("These declarations provide the information necessary to assess the sources' reliability under the principles accepted in the intelligence community.").

This conclusion was based on the detailed and persuasive accounts from the intelligence team as to the procedures and methods they used to ensure they were working with reliable information. For example, with respect to Informant A, the intelligence team knew that be bad direct access to the information he was providing, because he was a member of the HIG cell. See Decl. of [redacted] at ¶ 37. But, for that very same reason, the intelligence collectors initially were "wary because [they] would not easily trust a man that had already attacked U.S. forces and planned to do so again." Id. ¶ 38. As their meetings continued, the intelligence collectors "became more and more confident that [Informant A] was providing extremely reliable information. He spoke to [the collectors] voluntarily and in a spontaneous and detailed way, and to the extent [the collectors] were able to make a determination, the intelligence [Informant A] provided was accurate." Id.; see also id. ¶ 41 ("Our Team was able to independently verify much of the information he provided."). The intelligence team ultimately "concluded that [Informant A's] information was sufficiently reliable to plan the operation for Khan's capture based on it." Khan II, 741 F.Supp.2d at 13 (citing Decl. of [redacted] at ¶ 45). This Court remains of the view that "[i]ntelligence collectors in the field, facing dangerous life-or-death situations, would not . . . act on the basis of information they felt was unreliable," id.—and that is strong support for the reliability of the key evidence in this case.

The D.C. Circuit agreed, affirming this Court's conclusion that the key evidence against Khan was sufficiently reliable, pointing to much of the same information. . . .

The question, then, is whether the absence of Khan's statements requires a reassessment of that conclusion. It does not. Khan's statements had little to do with this Court's or the D.C. Circuit's assessments that the key evidence in this case survived scrutiny under the Parhat standard. Indeed, Khan's motion attacks the reliability of this evidence on other grounds—for example, newly discovered factual inconsistencies that allegedly bear on the intelligence collectors' credibility, see infra, Sections I.C, I.D—but does not challenge the legal conclusion that there are sufficient indicia of reliability on the face of these reports to satisfy the Parhat standard. To be sure, many of Khan's statements did offer additional corroboration of the government's case. But those statements were only supportive of the conclusion that the reports were reliable—they were not necessary (or even significant) to that conclusion. Hence, the Court reaffirms its prior conclusion, affirmed by the D.C. Circuit, that "the key pieces of evidence deployed by the government are reliable." Khan II, 741 F.Supp.2d at 17; see also Khan III, 655 F.3d at 30 ("We find no error in the district court's determination that [the intelligence reports] were reliable.").

4.   No evidence in the record supports Khan's theory of the case.

Khan's primary arguments are directed to challenging the reliability of the evidence upon which the government relies. But, ultimately, he does offer his own narrative: that he was an innocent shopkeeper, set up by corrupt Afghans (possibly due to his uncle's ties to HIG), seeking bounty payments from the U.S. military. Previously, the Court explained that it "does not find credible Khan's insistence that he was merely managing a small petrol shop at the lime of his capture." Khan II, 741 F.Supp.2d at 18. And on the specific issue of cash bounties, sworn testimony from the intelligence collectors strongly contradicts Khan's theory. See, e.g., Decl. of [redacted], at ¶ 47 ("I do not recall providing any compensation to [Informant A]"); id. ¶ 63 ("I am not aware of any information that suggests a bounty was paid in regards to Shawali Khan's capture."); Decl. of [redacted] at ¶ 16 ("[Informant A] would not accept compensation from me in exchange his assistance. He was paid by HIG so he was not desperate for money and it was my assessment that he provided information to my Team, in part, to make amends for the attack that resulted in the death of some of his tribesmen."); . . . .

In response, Khan offers nothing. In other words, the record still contains no credible evidence to support the theory that Khan was set up as a part of some elaborate conspiracy that duped the U.S. military. And, in addition to all of the evidence supporting the government's narrative that Khan was part of an HIG cell, and the declarations from intelligence collectors refuting Khan's bounty theory, some evidence in the record affirmatively undermines Khan's conspiracy theory.

The government's belated decision to forego all reliance on Khan's statements—which statements previously had been affirmatively advanced by the government in its written briefs and at the evidentiary hearing—is certainly the most significant post-judgment development in this case. And its timing is quite unfortunate. Nevertheless, after a de novo consideration of the remaining evidence in the record, the Court is confident that the absence of Kban's statements does not undermine its previous conclusion, affirmed by the D.C. Circuit, that it is more likely than not that Khan is lawfully detained under the AUMF.

. . .

D. Evidence that Khan did not understand Arabic does not significantly undermine the Court's conclusions.

[redacted] second piece of exculpatory information: that Khan likely was not able to read or write Arabic Khan argues that this bolsters his credibility, relying on [redacted]

[redacted]

[redacted] Khan has insisted that these materials—which included several notebooks about [redacted] the use and maintenance automatic weapons, and a book of poems authored by a high-level al-Qaeda leader—

did not belong to him, and that he had collected them after looting the homes and businesses of Arabs fleeing Afghanistan.

Khan is correct that this information is exculpatory: it bolsters the credibility of Khan's assertion that he had these materials for reasons other than terrorist affiliations. But, ultimately, it docs not tip the overall evidentiary balance in Khan's favor, for two reasons. The first is that the Court has never placed any significant reliance on these materials. Indeed, they were hardly mentioned in Khao II or in the D.C. Circuit opinion affirming it. This evidence was simply not necessary to the ultimate conclusion that it was more likely than not that Khan was a "pan of" HIG, in light of the other, stronger evidence in the record, [redacted] and the several (and consistent) incriminating reports from government informants.

The second reason is that, even if Khan could not read Arabic, finding jihadist training materials in his home is still generally supportive—albeit just slightly—of the government's narrative. To be sure, this evidence is less compelling—perhaps much less compelling—if Khan could not understand the text in the documents. But that does not drain them of all evidentiary significance—it remains possible (indeed, perhaps even likely, given the other evidence in the record) that Khan had these materials because of his terrorist connections. So even though they are less probative now than when the government thought that Khan could read Arabic, that does not mean this evidence is valueless.

In sum, these materials have never played a significant role in the Court's analysis of the overall evidentiary picture in this case. And any marginal value of this evidence to the government's case has now been undermined by the new information about Khan's language skills. But the overall picture remains the same: it is more likely than not that Khan was "part of" HIG at the time of his capture. [redacted] Khan's lack [of] Arabic proficiency does not undermine that conclusion.

. . . .

CONCLUSION

This Court and the D.C. Circuit have already held that Khan is lawfully detained under the AUMB, because it is more likely than not he was "part of" an associated force of the Taliban and al-Qaeda at the time of his capture in mid-November 2002. None of the post-judgment developments raised by Khan are sufficient to undermine that conclusion— let alone to justify the extraordinary relief of reopening a final judgment. Hence, upon consideration of the parties' submissions, the extensive evidentiary record in this case, applicable law, and the entire record herein. Khan's motion for post-judgment relief will be denied. A separate Order has issued on this date.

QUESTIONS AND NOTES

1.   An unofficial source indicates that Shawali Khan was released from Guantanamo in December 2014, three months after the decision in the principal case. See Andy Worthington, The Definitive Prisoner List (Part 5), No. 899, http://www.andyworthington.co.uk/guantanamo-the-definitive-prisoner-list-part-5/. His name does not appear on the list of 41 detainees that, as of the date of this writing, still remain in Guantanamo.

2.   The legal issues needing resolution that arose in the Guantanamo detainee post-Boumediene habeas cases, included the following:

        a.   What is (are) the legal standard(s) applied in determining the legality of the detention?

        b.   What is (are) the source(s) of legal authority relied upon by the government as the basis for the detention?

        c.   What is the burden of proof applied in these cases?

        d.   Who has the burden of persuasion?

        e.   What is the detainee's right to discovery?

        f.   How is classified information handled?

        g.   What rule regarding the admissibility of hearsay is applied and how is it implemented?

        h.   What rule regarding the admissibility of confessions, allegedly coerced is applied?

        i.   What is the scope of appellate review of a district court habeas decision?

3.   The Bensayah case, supra, provides answers or information regarding the answers to questions 2.a–f, supra. What does the case tell us about each of these questions. Regarding questions 2.g, 2.h and 2.i., see the notes below.

4.   Regarding reliance on hearsay evidence: Compare Bihani v. Obama, 590 F.3d 866, 879 (D.C. Cir. 2010) ("[T]he question a habeas court must ask when presented with hearsay is not whether it is admissible-it is always admissible-but what probative weight to ascribe to whatever indicia of reliability it exhibits.") with Awad v. Obama, 608 F.3d 1, 7 (D.C. Cir. 2010) ("We have already held that hearsay evidence is admissible in this type of habeas proceeding if the hearsay is reliable," citing Bihani). For a habeas decision determining the reliability of a specific item of hearsay evidence, see Barhoumi v. Obama, 2010 WL 2553540 (D.C. Cir.)

5.   Regarding the treatment of allegedly coerced statements in the habeas hearings, see, e.g., Salahi v. Obama, 2010 WL 1443543 (D.D.C.):

        There is ample evidence in this record that Salahi was subjected to extensive and severe mistreatment at Guantanamo from mid-June 2003 to September 2003, Salahi's position is that every incriminating statement he made while in custody must therefore be disregarded. Salahi made most, if not all, of the statements that the government seeks to use against him during the mistreatment or during the 2 years following it.

The government acknowledges that Salahi's abusive treatment could diminish the reliability of some of his statements. But abuse and coercive interrogation methods do not throw a blanket over every statement, no matter when given, or to whom, or under what circumstances. Allegations of mistreatment certainly taint petitioner's statements, raising questions about their reliability. But at some point—after the passage of time and intervening events, and considering the circumstances—the taint of abuse and coercion may be attenuated enough for a witness's statements to be considered reliable—there must certainly be a "clean break" between the mistreatment and any such statement. Here, it is the government's burden to demonstrate that a particular statement was not the product of coercion, and that it has other indicia of reliability.

The government submits that the only statements of Salahi's on which it relies were made after a clean break, and after the passage of enough time to attenuate any taint, and that they are corroborated by documentary evidence and the statements of other persons (some of them detainees). Salahi attacks corroborating statements as unreliable hearsay, or subject to the same coercive tactics described above, or both. My approach here, . . .has been to formally "receive" all the evidence offered by either side, and to give it the weight I believe it deserves. . . .

The government had to adduce evidence—which is different from intelligence—showing that it was more likely than not that Salahi was "part of" al-Qaida. To do so, it had to show that the support Salahi undoubtedly did provide from time to time was provided within al-Qaida's command structure. The government has not done so. The government has shown that Salahi was an al-Qaida sympathizer—perhaps a "fellow traveler"; that he was in touch with al-Qaida members; and that from time to time, before his capture, he provided sporadic support to members of al-Qaida.

The government's problem is that its proof that Salahi gave material support to terrorists is so attenuated, or so tainted by coercion and mistreatment, or so classified, that it cannot support a successful criminal prosecution. Nevertheless, the government wants to hold Salahi indefinitely, because of its concern that he might renew his oath to al-Qaida and become a terrorist upon his release. That concern may indeed be well-founded. Salahi fought with al-Qaida in Afghanistan (twenty years ago), associated with at least a half-dozen known al-Qaida members and terrorists, and somehow found and lived among or with al-Qaida cell members in Montreal. But a habeas court may not permit a man to be held indefinitely upon suspicion, or because of the government's prediction that he may do unlawful acts in the future—any more than a habeas court may rely upon its prediction that a man will not be dangerous in the future and order his release if he was lawfully detained in the first place. The question, upon which the government had the burden of proof, was whether, at the time of his capture, Salahi was a "part of al-Qaida. On the record before me, I cannot find that he was.

6.   The government appealed from the district court's decision in the Salahi case, supra note 5. See Salahi v. Obama, 625 F.3d 745 (D.C. Cir. 2010):

This case is more than merely the latest installment in a series of Guantanamo habeas appeals. The United States seeks to detain Mohammedou Ould Salahi on the grounds that he was "part of" al-Qaida not because he fought with al-Qaida or its allies against the United States, but rather because he swore an oath of allegiance to the organization, associated with its members, and helped it in various ways, including hosting its leaders and referring aspiring jihadists to a known al-Qaida operative. After an evidentiary hearing at which Salahi testified, the district court found that although Salahi "was an al-Qaida sympathizer" who "was in touch with al-Qaida members" and provided them with "sporadic support," the government had failed to show that he was in fact "part of" al-Qaida at the time of his capture. The district court thus granted the writ and ordered Salahi released. Since then, however, this Court has issued three opinions—Al-Adahi v. Obama, 613 F.3d 1102 (D.C.Cir.2010); Bensayah v. Obama, 610 F.3d 718 (D.C.Cir.2010); and Awad v. Obama, 608 F.3d 1 (D.C.Cir.2010)—that cast serious doubt on the district court's approach to determining whether an individual is "part of" al-Qaida. We agree with the government that we must therefore vacate the district court's judgment, but because that court, lacking the benefit of these recent cases, left unresolved key factual questions necessary for us to determine as a matter of law whether Salahi was " part of" al-Qaida when captured, we remand for further proceedings consistent with this opinion.

. . .

As the government points out, the district court's approach is inconsistent with our recent decisions in Awad and Bensayah, which were issued after the district court granted Salahi's habeas petition. These decisions make clear that the determination of whether an individual is "part of" al-Qaida "must be made on a case-by-case basis by using a functional rather than a formal approach and by focusing upon the actions of the individual in relation to the organization." Bensayah, 610 F.3d at 725. Evidence that an individual operated within al-Qaida's command structure is "sufficient but is not necessary to show he is 'part of' the organization." Id.; see also Awad,

608 F.3d at 11. "[T]here may be other indicia that a particular individual [was] sufficiently involved with the organization to be deemed part of it." Bensayah, 610 F.3d at 725. For example, since petitioner in Awad joined and was accepted by al-Qaida fighters who were engaged in hostilities against Afghan and allied forces, he could properly be considered "part of" al-Qaida even if he never formally received or executed any orders. See Awad, 608 F.3d at 3–4, 11.

As we explained in Bensayah, however, "the purely independent conduct of a freelancer is not enough" to establish that an individual is "part of" al-Qaida. 610 F.3d at 725. Thus, as government counsel conceded at oral argument, the government's failure to prove that an individual was acting under orders from al-Qaida may be relevant to the question of whether the individual was "part of" the organization when captured. See Oral Arg. Tr. at 20:17–21:5. Consider this very case. Unlike petitioner in Awad, who affiliated with al-Qaida fighters engaged in active hostilities against U.S. allies in Afghanistan, Salahi is not accused of participating in military action against the United States. Instead, the government claims that Salahi was "part of" al-Qaida because he swore bayat and thereafter provided various services to the organization, including recruiting, hosting leaders, transferring money, etc. Under these circumstances, whether Salahi performed such services pursuant to al-Qaida orders may well be relevant to determining if he was "part of" al-Qaida or was instead engaged in the "purely independent conduct of a freelancer." Bensayah, 610 F.3d at 725. The problem with the district court's decision is that it treats the absence of evidence that Salahi received and executed orders as dispositive. See Salahi, 710 F.Supp.2d at 5–6, 11–12, 15–16. The decision therefore cannot survive Awad and Bensayah.

The government urges us to reverse and direct the district court to deny Salahi's habeas petition. Although we agree that Awad and Bensayah require that we vacate the district court's judgment, we think the better course is to remand for further proceedings consistent with those opinions. Because the district court, lacking the guidance of these later decisions, looked primarily for evidence that Salahi participated in al-Qaida's command structure, it did not make definitive findings regarding certain key facts necessary for us to determine as a matter of law whether Salahi was in fact "part of" al-Qaida when captured. See Barhoumi, 609 F.3d at 423 (noting that whether the facts found by the district court are sufficient to establish that an individual was "part of" al-Qaida is a legal question that we review de novo). For example, does the government's evidence support the inference that even if Salahi was not acting under express orders, he nonetheless had a tacit understanding with al-Qaida operatives that he would refer prospective jihadists to the organization? See Salahi, 710 F.Supp.2d at 10–12. Has the government presented sufficient evidence for the court to make findings regarding what Salahi said to bin al-Shibh during their "discussion of jihad and Afghanistan"? Id. at 11. Did al-Qaida operatives ask Salahi to assist the organization with telecommunications projects in Sudan, Afghanistan, or Pakistan? See id. at 12–13.Did Salahi provide any assistance to al-Qaida in planning denial-of-service computer attacks, even if those attacks never came to fruition? See id. at 13. May the court infer from Salahi's numerous ties to known al-Qaida operatives that he remained a trusted member of the organization? See id. at 16 ("Salahi . . . associated with at least a half-dozen known al-Qaida members and terrorists[ ] and somehow found and lived among or with al-Qaida cell members in Montreal."); cf. Awad, 608 F.3d at 3 (noting that the al-Qaida fighters Awad joined "treated [him] as one of their own"). With answers to questions like these, which may require additional testimony, the district court will be able to determine in the first instance whether Salahi was or was not "sufficiently involved with [al-Qaida] to be deemed part of it." Bensayah, 610 F.3d at 725.

A final note: since we are remanding for further factual findings, we think it appropriate to reiterate this Court's admonition in Al-Adahi, also decided after the district court issued its decision in this case, that a court considering a Guantanamo detainee's habeas petition must view the evidence collectively rather than in isolation. 613 F.3d at 1105–06. Merely because a particular piece of evidence is insufficient, standing alone, to prove a particular point does not mean that the evidence "may be tossed aside and the next [piece of evidence] may be evaluated as if the first did not exist." Id. at 1105. The evidence must be considered in its entirety in determining whether the government has satisfied its burden of proof.

. . .

The President seeks to detain Salahi on the grounds that he was "part of" al-Qaida at the time he was captured. Because additional fact-finding is required to resolve that issue under this circuit's evolving case law, we vacate and remand for further proceedings consistent with this opinion.

So ordered.

7. In the fall of 2015, Salahi, see notes 5 and 6, supra, made a motion in the district court for an order to show cause that if granted would have required the Department of Defense to promptly provide to him a hearing before a Periodic Review Board. His motion was denied. Salahi v. Obama, 2015 WL 9216557 (Dec. 17 2015, D. D.C.). According to an unofficial source Salahi was released from Guantanamo in October, 2016. See Andy Worthington, Prisoners: Who's Still Held? https://www.closeguantanamo.org/Prisoners.

8. Regarding the handling of classified information in the habeas hearings, note the significant number of redactions in the Bensayah and Khan opinions, supra, which makes it difficult for the reader to determine the factual underpinnings for some of the court's rulings. This results from the government's reliance on classified information in the course of the hearing. See generally Chapter 9, supra, which deals with the Classified Information Procedures Act (CIPA), which is applicable only in criminal proceedings, not habeas cases. The habeas courts have, however, tended to look to the CIPA for general guidance on the handling of classified information.

9. Counsel in Bensayah obtained security clearance, and they generally had access to the classified information in the case, but could not share this information with their detainee-clients. See Odah v. United States, 559 F. 3d 539 (D.C. Cir. 2009), holding that in a habeas action the government must provide classified information that is relevant and material to detainee's counsel who has obtained security clearance but may also consider the use of alternative means such as substitutions. Regarding the problems associated with this type of situation, see, generally, Chapter 9, supra. Final arguments in Bensayah were held in closed sessions. Because of the need to refer to classified information, neither the detainee-petitioners nor members of the public were present at these sessions.

10. In Bensayah, the government also proposed to provide the court with additional material on an ex parte basis, so-called "black box" material that was sufficiently sensitive that it could not even be shared with security-cleared counsel for the detainees who vigorously opposed the government's proposal.

11. One of the five detainees whose release was ordered by the district court was Lakhdar Boumediene, the lead petitioner in Boumediene v. Bush.

12. Early in his administration, President Obama appointed an investigating body called the Guantanamo Review Task Force to review the status of all of the individuals then detained at Guantanamo. The Task Force completed and reported on its review of the detainees at Guantanamo in January, 2010. The Executive Summary of the Report stated:

> The decisions reached on the 240 detainees subject to the review are as follows:
>
> - **126 detainees** were approved for transfer. To date, 44 of these detainees have been transferred from Guantanamo to countries outside the United States.
>
> - **44 detainees** over the course of the review were referred for prosecution either in federal court or a military commission, and **36 of these detainees** remain the subject of active cases or investigations. The Attorney General has announced that the government will pursue prosecutions against six of these detainees in federal court and will pursue prosecutions against six others in military commissions.

- **48 detainees** were determined to be too dangerous to transfer but not feasible for prosecution. They will remain in detention pursuant to the government's authority under the Authorization for Use of Military Force passed by Congress in response to the attacks of September 11, 2001. Detainees may challenge the legality of their detention in federal court and will periodically receive further review within the Executive Branch

5. THE PERIODIC REVIEW BOARD PROCESS

QUESTIONS AND NOTES

1.   On March 7, 2011, the White House issued a press release reporting, inter alia, on the renewal of military commission prosecutions, again reporting on the fact that many of the detainees would be prosecuted in Article III courts and that an Executive Order was being issued providing for periodic review of detainees who continue to be held without prosecution. The press release appears immediately below. The Executive Order is reproduced in note 2, infra.

THE WHITE HOUSE

Office of the Press Secretary

For Immediate Release March 7, 2011

FACT SHEET: NEW ACTIONS ON GUANTANAMO AND DETAINEE POLICY

In a speech nearly two years ago at the National Archives, the President advanced a four-part approach to closing the detention facility at Guantanamo Bay, keeping our country safe, and upholding the law: (1) to bring detainees to justice in prosecutions in either federal civilian courts or in reformed military commissions, (2) to comply with court-ordered releases of detainees, (3) to transfer detainees from Guantanamo whenever it is possible to do so safely and humanely, and (4) when neither prosecution nor other legal options are available, to hold these individuals in lawful military detention. He affirmed that "whenever feasible, we will try those who have violated American criminal laws in federal courts."

The Administration remains committed to closing the detention facility at Guantanamo Bay, and to maintain a lawful, sustainable and principled regime for the handling of detainees there, consistent with the full range of U.S. national security interests. In keeping with the strategy we laid out, we are proceeding today with the following actions:

Resumption of Military Commissions

The Secretary of Defense will issue an order rescinding his prior suspension on the swearing and referring of new charges in the military commissions. New charges in military commissions have been suspended since the President announced his review of detainee policy, shortly after taking office.

The Administration, working on a bipartisan basis with members of Congress, has successfully enacted key reforms, such as a ban on the use of statements taken as a result of cruel, inhuman or degrading treatment, and a better system for handling classified information. With these and other reforms, military commissions, along with prosecutions of suspected terrorists in civilian courts, are an available and important tool in combating international terrorists that fall within their jurisdiction while upholding the rule of law.

Executive Order on Periodic Review

In the Archives speech, the President recognized there are certain Guantanamo detainees who have not been charged, convicted, or designated for transfer, but must continue to be detained because they "in effect, remain at war with the United States." For this category of detainees, the President stated: "We must have a thorough process of periodic review, so that any prolonged detention is carefully evaluated and justified."

Today, the President issued an Executive Order establishing such a process for these detainees. A copy of the order is attached.

The periodic review established by this order will help to ensure that individuals who we have determined will be subject to long-term detention continue to be detained only when lawful and necessary to protect against a significant threat to the security of the United States. If a final determination is made that a detainee no longer constitutes a significant threat to our security, the Executive Order provides that the Secretaries of State and Defense are to identify a suitable transfer location outside the United States, consistent with the national security and foreign policy interests of the United States and applicable law. As the President has stated before, no Guantanamo detainee will be released into the United States.

We are grateful to all of our allies and partners who have worked with the Administration to implement the transfers undertaken thus far in a secure and humane manner, especially those who have resettled detainees from third countries. Our friends and allies should know that we remain determined in our efforts and that, with their continued assistance, we intend to complete the difficult challenge of closing Guantanamo.

Continued Commitment to Article III Trials

Pursuant to the President's order to close Guantanamo, this Administration instituted the most thorough review process ever applied to the detainees held there. Among other things, for the first time, we consolidated all information available to the federal government about these individuals. That information was carefully examined by some of our government's most experienced prosecutors, a process that resulted in the referral of 36 individuals for potential prosecution. Since the time of those referrals, the Departments of Justice and Defense, with the advice of career military and civilian prosecutors, have been working to bring these defendants to justice, securing convictions in a number of cases and evaluating others to determine which system—military or civilian—is most appropriate based on the nature of the evidence and traditional principles of prosecution.

In recent months, some in Congress have sought to undermine this process. In December, Congress enacted restrictions on the prosecution of Guantanamo detainees in Federal courts. The Administration opposes these restrictions as a dangerous and unprecedented challenge to Executive authority to select the most effective means available to bring terrorists to justice and safeguard our security. The Executive Branch possesses the information and expertise necessary to make the best judgment about where a particular prosecution should proceed, and Congress's intrusion upon this function is inconsistent with the long-standing and appropriate allocation of authority between the Executive and Legislative branches.

Time and again, our Federal courts have delivered swift justice and severe punishment to those who seek to attack us. In the last two years alone, federal prosecutors have convicted numerous defendants charged with terrorism offenses, including those who plotted to bomb the New York subway system; attempted to detonate a bomb in Times Square; and conspired in murderous attacks on our embassies abroad. These prosecutions have generated invaluable intelligence about our enemies, permitted us to incapacitate and detain dangerous terrorists, and vindicated the interests of victims—all while reaffirming our commitment to the rule of law. Spanning multiple administrations, Republican and Democratic, our Federal courts have proven to be one of our most effective counterterrorism tools, and should not be restricted in any circumstances.

Military commissions should proceed in cases where it has been determined appropriate to do so. Because there are situations, however, in which our federal courts are a more appropriate forum for trying particular individuals, we will seek repeal of the restrictions imposed by Congress, so that we can move forward in the forum that is, in our judgment, most in line with our national security interests and the interests of justice.

We will continue to vigorously defend the authority of the Executive to make these well-informed prosecution decisions, both with respect to those detainees in our custody at Guantanamo and those we may apprehend in the future. A one-size-fits-all policy for the prosecution of suspected terrorists, whether for past or future cases, undermines our Nation's counterterrorism efforts and harms our national security.

. . .

2. Executive Order 13567, reproduced below established periodic review of detainees who continue in detention without being prosecuted criminally. Compare this process with the prior CSRT process, with the process provided in the post-Boumediene habeas actions and with the earlier Administrative Review Boards (described earlier in this chapter).

For Immediate Release March 7, 2011

EXECUTIVE ORDER

_____,

PERIODIC REVIEW OF INDIVIDUALS DETAINED AT GUANTÁNAMO BAY NAVAL STATION PURSUANT TO THE AUTHORIZATION FOR USE OF MILITARY FORCE

By the authority vested in me as President by the Constitution and the laws of the United States of America, including the Authorization for Use of Military Force of September 2001 (AUMF), Public Law 107–40, and in order to ensure that military detention of individuals now held at the U.S. Naval Station, Guantánamo Bay, Cuba (Guantánamo), who were subject to the interagency review under section 4 of Executive Order 13492 of January 22, 2009, continues to be carefully evaluated and justified, consistent with the national security and foreign policy interests of the United States and the interests of justice, I hereby order as follows:

Section 1. Scope and Purpose. (a) The periodic review described in section 3 of this order applies only to those detainees held at Guantánamo on the date of this order, whom the interagency review established by Executive Order 13492 has (i) designated for continued law of war detention; or (ii) referred for prosecution, except for those detainees against whom charges are pending or a judgment of conviction has been entered.

(b) This order is intended solely to establish, as a discretionary matter, a process to review on a periodic basis the executive branch's continued, discretionary exercise of existing detention authority in individual cases. It does not create any additional or separate source of detention authority, and it does not affect the scope of detention authority under existing law. Detainees at Guantánamo have the constitutional privilege of the writ of habeas corpus, and nothing in this order is intended to affect the jurisdiction of Federal courts to determine the legality of their detention.

(c) In the event detainees covered by this order are transferred from Guantánamo to another U.S. detention facility where they remain in law of war detention, this order shall continue to apply to them.

Sec. 2.　Standard for Continued Detention. Continued law of war detention is warranted for a detainee subject to the periodic review in section 3 of this order if it is necessary to protect against a significant threat to the security of the United States.

Sec. 3.　Periodic Review. The Secretary of Defense shall coordinate a process of periodic review of continued law of war detention for each detainee described in section 1(a) of this order. In consultation with the Attorney General, the Secretary of Defense shall issue implementing guidelines governing the process, consistent with the following requirements:

(a)　Initial Review. For each detainee, an initial review shall commence as soon as possible but no later than 1 year from the date of this order. The initial review will consist of a hearing before a Periodic Review Board (PRB). The review and hearing shall follow a process that includes the following requirements:

(1)　Each detainee shall be provided, in writing and in a language the detainee understands, with advance notice of the PRB review and an unclassified summary of the factors and information the PRB will consider in evaluating whether the detainee meets the standard set forth in section 2 of this order. The written summary shall be sufficiently comprehensive to provide adequate notice to the detainee of the reasons for continued detention.

(2)　The detainee shall be assisted in proceedings before the PRB by a Government-provided personal representative (representative) who possesses the security clearances necessary for access to the information described in subsection (a)(4) of this section. The representative shall advocate on behalf of the detainee before the PRB and shall be responsible for challenging the Government's information and introducing information on behalf of the detainee. In addition to the representative, the detainee may be assisted in proceedings before the PRB by private counsel, at no expense to the Government.

(3)　The detainee shall be permitted to (i) present to the PRB a written or oral statement; (ii) introduce relevant information, including written declarations; (iii) answer any questions posed by the PRB; and (iv) call witnesses who are reasonably available and willing to provide information that is relevant and material to the standard set forth in section 2 of this order.

(4)　The Secretary of Defense, in coordination with other relevant Government agencies, shall compile and provide to the PRB all information in the detainee disposition recommendations produced by the Task Force established under Executive Order 13492 that is relevant to the determination whether the standard in section 2 of this order has been met and on which the Government seeks to rely for that determination. In addition, the Secretary of Defense, in coordination with other relevant Government agencies, shall compile any additional information relevant to that determination, and on which the Government seeks to rely for that determination, that has become available since the conclusion of the Executive Order 13492 review. All mitigating information relevant to that determination must be provided to the PRB.

(5) The information provided in subsection (a)(4) of this section shall be provided to the detainee's representative. In exceptional circumstances where it is necessary to protect national security, including intelligence sources and methods, the PRB may determine that the representative must receive a sufficient substitute or summary, rather than the underlying information. If the detainee is represented by private counsel, the information provided in subsection (a)(4) of this section shall be provided to such counsel unless the Government determines that the need to protect national security, including intelligence sources and methods, or law enforcement or privilege concerns, requires the Government to provide counsel with a sufficient substitute or summary of the information. A sufficient substitute or summary must provide a meaningful opportunity to assist the detainee during the review process.

(6) The PRB shall conduct a hearing to consider the information described in subsection (a)(4) of this section, and other relevant information provided by the detainee or the detainee's representative or counsel, to determine whether the standard in section 2 of this order is met. The PRB shall consider the reliability of any information provided to it in making its determination.

(7) The PRB shall make a prompt determination, by consensus and in writing, as to whether the detainee's continued detention is warranted under the standard in section 2 of this order. If the PRB determines that the standard is not met, the PRB shall also recommend any conditions that relate to the detainee's transfer. The PRB shall provide a written summary of any final determination in unclassified form to the detainee, in a language the detainee understands, within 30 days of the determination when practicable.

(8) The Secretary of Defense shall establish a secretariat to administer the PRB review and hearing process. The Director of National Intelligence shall assist in preparing the unclassified notice and the substitutes or summaries described above. Other executive departments and agencies shall assist in the process of providing the PRB with information required for the review processes detailed in this order.

(b) Subsequent Full Review. The continued detention of each detainee shall be subject to subsequent full reviews and hearings by the PRB on a triennial basis. Each subsequent review shall employ the procedures set forth in section 3(a) of this order.

(c) File Reviews. The continued detention of each detainee shall also be subject to a file review every 6 months in the intervening years between full reviews. This file review will be conducted by the PRB and shall consist of a review of any relevant new information related to the detainee compiled by the Secretary of Defense, in coordination with other relevant agencies, since the last review and, as appropriate, information considered during any prior PRB review. The detainee shall be permitted to make a written submission in connection with each file review. If, during the file review, a significant question is raised as to whether the detainee's continued detention is warranted under the standard in section 2 of this order, the PRB will promptly convene a full review pursuant to the standards in section 3(a) of this order.

(d) Review of PRB Determinations. The Review Committee (Committee), as defined in section 9(d) of this order, shall conduct a review if (i) a member of the Committee seeks review of a PRB determination within 30 days of that determination; or (ii) consensus within the PRB cannot be reached.

Sec. 4. Effect of Determination to Transfer. (a) If a final determination is made that a detainee does not meet the standard in section 2 of this order, the Secretaries of State and Defense shall be responsible for ensuring that vigorous efforts are undertaken to identify a suitable transfer location for any such detainee, outside of the United States, consistent with the national security and foreign policy interests of the United States and the commitment set forth in section 2242(a) of the Foreign Affairs Reform and Restructuring Act of 1998 (Public Law 105–277).

(b) The Secretary of State, in consultation with the Secretary of Defense, shall be responsible for obtaining appropriate security and humane treatment assurances regarding any detainee to be transferred to another country, and for determining, after consultation with members of the Committee, that it is appropriate to proceed with the transfer.

(c) The Secretary of State shall evaluate humane treatment assurances in all cases, consistent with the recommendations of the Special Task Force on Interrogation and Transfer Policies established by Executive Order 13491 of January 22, 2009.

Sec. 5. Annual Committee Review. (a) The Committee shall conduct an annual review of sufficiency and efficacy of transfer efforts, including:

(1) the status of transfer efforts for any detainee who has been subject to the periodic review under section 3 of this order, whose continued detention has been determined not to be warranted, and who has not been transferred more than 6 months after the date of such determination;

(2) the status of transfer efforts for any detainee whose petition for a writ of habeas corpus has been granted by a U.S. Federal court with no pending appeal and who has not been transferred;

(3) the status of transfer efforts for any detainee who has been designated for transfer or conditional detention by the Executive Order 13492 review and who has not been transferred; and

(4) the security and other conditions in the countries to which detainees might be transferred, including a review of any suspension of transfers to a particular country, in order to determine whether further steps to facilitate transfers are appropriate or to provide a recommendation to the President regarding whether continuation of any such suspension is warranted.

(b) After completion of the initial reviews under section 3(a) of this order, and at least once every 4 years thereafter, the Committee shall review whether a continued law of war detention policy remains consistent with the interests of the United States, including national security interests.

Sec. 6. Continuing Obligation of the Departments of Justice and Defense to Assess Feasibility of Prosecution. As to each detainee whom the interagency review established by Executive Order 13492 has designated for continued law of war detention, the Attorney General and the Secretary of Defense shall continue to assess whether prosecution of the detainee is feasible and in the national security interests of the United States, and shall refer detainees for prosecution, as appropriate.

Sec. 7. Obligation of Other Departments and Agencies to Assist the Secretary of Defense. All departments, agencies, entities, and officers of the United States, to the maximum extent permitted by law, shall provide the Secretary of Defense such assistance as may be requested to implement this order.

Sec. 8. Legality of Detention. The process established under this order does not address the legality of any detainee's law of war detention. If, at any time during the periodic review process established in this order, material information calls into question the legality of detention, the matter will be referred immediately to the Secretary of Defense and the Attorney General for appropriate action.

Sec. 9. Definitions. (a) "Law of War Detention" means: detention authorized by the Congress under the AUMF, as informed by the laws of war.

(b) "Periodic Review Board" means: a board composed of senior officials tasked with fulfilling the functions described in section 3 of this order, one appointed by each of the following departments and offices: the Departments of State, Defense, Justice, and Homeland Security, as well as the Offices of the Director of National Intelligence and the Chairman of the Joint Chiefs of Staff.

(c) "Conditional Detention" means: the status of those detainees designated by the Executive Order 13492 review as eligible for transfer if one of the following conditions is satisfied: (1) the security situation improves in Yemen; (2) an appropriate rehabilitation program becomes available; or (3) an appropriate third-country resettlement option becomes available.

(d) "Review Committee" means: a committee composed of the Secretary of State, the Secretary of Defense, the Attorney General, the Secretary of Homeland Security, the Director of National Intelligence, and the Chairman of the Joint Chiefs of Staff.

Sec. 10. General Provisions. (a) Nothing in this order shall prejudice the authority of the Secretary of Defense or any other official to determine the disposition of any detainee not covered by this order.

(b) This order shall be implemented subject to the availability of necessary appropriations and consistent with applicable law including: the Convention Against Torture; Common Article 3 of the Geneva Conventions; the Detainee Treatment Act of 2005; and other laws relating to the transfer, treatment, and interrogation of individuals detained in an armed conflict.

(c) This order is not intended to, and does not, create any right or benefit, substantive or procedural, enforceable at law or in equity by any party against the United States, its departments, agencies, or entities, its officers, employees, or agents, or any other person.

(d) Nothing in this order, and no determination made under this order, shall be construed as grounds for release of detainees covered by this order into the United States.

BARACK OBAMA

THE WHITE HOUSE,

March 7, 2011.

3. On May 9, 2012, the Deputy Secretary of Defense issued Implementing Guidelines for the PRB process. Directive-Type Memorandum (DTM) 12-005, "Implementing Guidelines for Periodic Review of Detainees Held at Guantanamo Bay per Executive Order 13567." The Guidelines flesh out the procedures of the Periodic Review Boards and address a number of issues that would be likely to arise in those proceedings. Of special interest, the Guidelines provide much more detail on what can be taken into account in

addressing the "continuing significant threat" standard used to determine whether a detainee may be released. Attachment 3, Periodic Review Procedures and Process:

. . .

3.　STANDARD. Continued law of war detention is warranted for a detainee subject to periodic review if such detention is necessary to protect against a continuing significant threat to the security of the United States. In making that assessment, the PRB may review all relevant materials including information from the final Task Force assessments produced pursuant to Reference (k); the work product of a prior PRB; or any relevant intelligence produced subsequent to either. Application of this standard is specifically not intended to require a reexamination of the underlying materials that supported the work products of either Reference (k) or a prior PRB and is not intended to create a requirement that each PRB conduct a zero-based review of all original source materials concerning a detainee. In assessing whether a detainee continues to meet this standard, the PRB may consider:

a.　Baseline threat information included in Reference (k), including but not limited to:

(1)　The extent to which the detainee was involved in or facilitated terrorist activities, including the extent to which the detainee may have planned or participated in specific terrorist attacks.

(2)　The detainee's conduct when acting as part of, or substantially supporting, Taliban or al-Qa'ida forces or associated forces that are engaged in hostilities against the United States or its coalition partners.

(3)　The level of knowledge, skills, or training possessed by the detainee that has been or could be used for terrorist purposes, including:

(a)　Training or ability to plan, lead, finance, organize, or execute acts of terrorism.

(b)　Training or ability to facilitate the movement or training of terrorists.

(c)　Any specialized training or operational experience (e.g., training in paramilitary tactics, explosives, or weapons of mass casualty).

(4)　The nature and extent of the detainee's ties with individual terrorists, terrorist organizations, terrorist support networks, or other extremists.

b. Information pertaining to the detainee's potential threat if transferred or released, including but not limited to the factors listed in paragraph 3.a. of this attachment, and:

(1) Information pertaining to the likelihood that the detainee intends to or is likely to engage in terrorist activities upon his transfer or release.

(2) Information pertaining to the likelihood that the detainee will reestablish ties with al-Qa'ida, the Taliban, or associated forces that are engaged in hostilities against the United States or its coalition partners, and information pertaining to whether the group the detainee was part of at the time of capture is now defunct.

(3) The potential destination country for the detainee, with specific regard to:

(a) The presence of terrorist groups, instability, or other factors in that country that could negatively influence the detainee's potential to engage in terrorist activities upon transfer.

(b) The likelihood of family, tribal, or government rehabilitation or support for the detainee.

(c) The availability and credibility of measures by the receiving government to mitigate substantially the assessed threat posed by the detainee, including information regarding past detainee transfers to that country, if applicable.

(4) The likelihood the detainee may be subject to trial by military commission, or any other law enforcement interest in the detainee.

(5) The detainee's conduct in custody, including behavior, habits, traits, rehabilitation efforts, and whether the detainee was considered a danger to other detainees or other individuals.

(6) The detainee's physical and psychological condition.

(7) Any other relevant factors bearing on the threat the individual's transfer or release may pose to the United States, its citizens, and/or its interests.

(8) Any other relevant information bearing on the national security and foreign policy interests of the United States or the interests of justice.

[ed. Reference (k) cited in the Guidelines is Reference (k) Executive Order 13492, "Review and Disposition of Individuals Detained at the

Guantanamo Bay Naval Base and Closure of Detention Facilities," January 22, 2009.]

4. One other piece of legislation relevant to the PRB topic is the NDAA of 2012, section 1023 which provides as follows:

SEC. 1023. PROCEDURES FOR PERIODIC DETENTION REVIEW OF INDIVIDUALS DETAINED AT UNITED STATES NAVAL STATION, GUANTANAMO BAY, CUBA.

(a) PROCEDURES REQUIRED.—Not later than 180 days after the date of the enactment of this Act, the Secretary of Defense shall submit to the appropriate committees of Congress a report setting forth procedures for implementing the periodic review process required by Executive Order No. 13567 for individuals detained at United States Naval Station, Guantanamo Bay, Cuba, pursuant to the Authorization for Use of Military Force (Public Law 107–40; 50 U.S.C. 1541 note).

(b) COVERED MATTERS.—The procedures submitted under subsection (a) shall, at a minimum—

(1) clarify that the purpose of the periodic review process is not to determine the legality of any detainee's law of war detention, but to make discretionary determinations whether or not a detainee represents a continuing threat to the security of the United States;

(2) clarify that the Secretary of Defense is responsible for any final decision to release or transfer an individual detained in military custody at United States Naval Station, Guantanamo Bay, Cuba, pursuant to the Executive Order referred to in subsection (a), and that in making such a final decision, the Secretary shall consider the recommendation of a periodic review board or review committee established pursuant to such Executive Order, but shall not be bound by any such recommendation;

(3) clarify that the periodic review process applies to any individual who is detained as an unprivileged enemy belligerent at United States Naval Station, Guantanamo Bay, Cuba, at any time; and

(4) ensure that appropriate consideration is given to factors addressing the need for continued detention of the detainee, including—

(A) the likelihood the detainee will resume terrorist activity if transferred or released;

(B) the likelihood the detainee will reestablish ties with al-Qaeda, the Taliban, or associated forces that are engaged in hostilities against the United States or its coalition partners if transferred or released;

(C) the likelihood of family, tribal, or government rehabilitation or support for the detainee if transferred or released;

(D) the likelihood the detainee may be subject to trial by military commission; and

(E) any law enforcement interest in the detainee.

5. The PRB review process finally began functioning in November 2013 approximately 2 and 1/2 years after the issuance of the authorizing Executive Order. About two out of every three detainees who were reviewed were approved for release through this process. Many, however, who were approved for release waited for lengthy periods, some, for years, before they were actually released, usually due to the difficulties in finding an appropriate destination. For example, there were many Yemenis among the detainees and the government was unwilling to send them back to Yemen because of the unstable conditions in that country. Overall, about 64 detainees received hearings before Periodic Review Boards. As of the date of this writing, no detainee has been given a follow-up triennial review as provided for in the Executive Order.

6. The U.S government consistently has claimed the authority to detain a number of the remaining detainees at Guantanamo for a prolonged period, possibly indefinitely, subject only to the Periodic Review process, on the ground that we are at war with al Qaeda and affiliated terrorist groups, and detention of enemy combatants is permissible for the duration of the conflict. See Justice O'Connor's opinion for a plurality of the Court in the Hamdi case, supra this chapter. And President Obama included that possibility in his several national security addresses. See ch. 1, supra. While Justice O'Connor in Hamdi seemed to express concern about the possibility of indefinite detention, in effect, a life term, she failed either to reject or accept its constitutionality.

During the Obama administration, some government officials also claimed an even more startling authority, namely, for some of the detainees who have been prosecuted and served their sentences, or who have even been acquitted (!), afterwards, for the government to be able to return them to prolonged, indefinite military detention. See Norman Abrams, Addressing the Guantanamo "Legacy Problem": Bringing Law-of-War Prolonged Military Detention and Criminal Prosecution into Closer Alignment, 7 J. Nat. Sec. L. and Pol'cy 527, fns. 95 and 96 (2014). No instance of the exercise of such claimed authority has, as yet, arisen. Should such an exercise of authority be ruled constitutional? For a detailed treatment of the issues raised by these claims of authority, and a set of proposals for regulating and imposing, on a principled basis, some kind of limits on the possibility of such prolonged detentions while still protecting the national security, see Norman Abrams, Addressing the Guantanamo "Legacy Problem", op.cit.supra.

7. Given the currently applicable statutes, does the government have authority to release and transfer detainees from Guantanamo without judicial

consideration in a habeas corpus action or having made a release determination through the Periodic Review Board process. On June 11, 2014 The House Armed Services Committee held a hearing about the transfer of five senior Taliban commanders out of Guantanamo, in exchange for the release of U.S. prisoner of war, Sergeant Bowie Bergdahl. The transfer implicated Section 1035 of the 2014 NDAA, which provides for release only through periodic review, habeas corpus review or after the Secretary of Defense has made a set of detailed findings as provided for in section 1035. This section also contains a requirement of giving the appropriate committees of the Congress notice 30 days before releasing the detainee. The statutorily required notice was not given in connection with the exchange of Sergeant Bergdahl for the Taliban commanders.

It was reported that Department of Defense General Counsel Stephen Preston testified at the hearing that the Office of Legal Counsel in the Department of Justice informed him that non-compliance was lawful because section1035 intruded on the President's constitutional powers as Commander in Chief. Preston testified that where the exercise of the President's constitutional authority is in conflict with a statute, and where the President has a duty to protect members of the Armed Forces, the requirements of the statute must yield to the President's constitutional authority. Secretary of Defense Hagel was reported to have said that the administration believed the notice provision was constitutional and the administration planned to comply with it in normal circumstances. See Jack Goldsmith, Lawfare Blog, June 12, 2014 "Two Legal Takeaways from Yesterday's HASC Hearing."

6. THE OBAMA ORDER TO CLOSE THE GUANTANAMO BAY FACILITY. WHAT WILL THE TRUMP ADMINISTRATION DO WITH NEWLY APPREHENDED SUSPECTED TERRORISTS?

QUESTIONS AND NOTES

1.   As recounted above, the decision in Boumediene opened the door to habeas corpus actions filed by Guantanamo detainees, and meanwhile, the Periodic Review process was activated. During this same period, another complex scenario was also occurring in relation to the Guantanamo Bay facility. President Obama had pledged to close Guantanamo within a year of his assuming office. As it turned out, there was strong opposition, mainly from Republicans in the Congress: a) to closing Guantanamo, b) to transferring the remaining detainees to a prison on the mainland U.S., (at one point, the Obama administration reportedly planned to purchase a currently unused state prison facility in Illinois for this purpose) and c) to prosecuting any Guantanamo detainees in U.S. district courts (which followed, as a consequence, of prohibiting transfer to the mainland.

Congress proceeded to block by legislative means any plan to transfer the remaining Guantanamo detainees to the mainland U.S. By similar provisions incorporated in the annual enactments of the National Defense Authorization Act, the Congress barred the use of federal funds authorized under each Act for either the transfer of Guantanamo detainees to the mainland U.S. or for constructing or modifying facilities on the mainland for that purpose. See, e.g., NDAA of 2014, secs. 1033, 1034; and NDAA of 2015, secs. 1032, 1033.

2.   President Obama on a number of occasions and in different settings strongly protested against these legislative restrictions on his freedom of action in regard to the detainees and Guantanamo, suggesting that they violated the separation of powers. See, for example, his signing statement issued in connection with his signing the NDAA for 2013:

THE WHITE HOUSE

Office of the Press Secretary

For Immediate Release January 2, 2013

STATEMENT BY THE PRESIDENT

Today I have signed into law H.R. 4310, the "National Defense Authorization Act for Fiscal Year 2013." I have approved this annual defense authorization legislation, as I have in previous years, because it authorizes essential support for service members and their families, renews vital national security programs, and helps ensure that the United States will continue to have the strongest military in the world.

Even though I support the vast majority of the provisions contained in this Act, which is comprised of hundreds of sections spanning more than 680 pages of text, I do not agree with them all. Our Constitution does not afford the President the opportunity to approve or reject statutory sections one by one. I am empowered either to sign the bill, or reject it, as a whole. In this case, though I continue to oppose certain sections of the Act, the need to renew critical defense authorities and funding was too great to ignore.

. . .

Sections 1022, 1027 and 1028 continue unwise funding restrictions that curtail options available to the executive branch. Section 1027 renews the bar against using appropriated funds for fiscal year 2012 to transfer Guantanamo detainees into the United States for any purpose. I continue to oppose this provision, which substitutes the Congress's blanket political determination for careful and fact-based determinations, made by counterterrorism and law enforcement professionals, of when and where to prosecute Guantanamo detainees. For decades, Republican and Democratic administrations have successfully prosecuted hundreds of terrorists in Federal court. Those prosecutions are a legitimate, effective, and powerful tool in our efforts to protect the Nation, and in certain cases may be the only legally available process for trying detainees.

Removing that tool from the executive branch undermines our national security. Moreover, this provision would, under certain circumstances, violate constitutional separation of powers principles.

Section 1028 fundamentally maintains the unwarranted restrictions on the executive branch's authority to transfer detainees to a foreign country. This provision hinders the Executive's ability to carry out its military, national security, and foreign relations activities and would, under certain circumstances, violate constitutional separation of powers principles. The executive branch must have the flexibility to act swiftly in conducting negotiations with foreign countries regarding the circumstances of detainee transfers. The Congress designed these sections, and has here renewed them once more, in order to foreclose my ability to shut down the Guantanamo Bay detention facility. I continue to believe that operating the facility weakens our national security by wasting resources, damaging our relationships with key allies, and strengthening our enemies. My Administration will interpret these provisions as consistent with existing and future determinations by the agencies of the Executive responsible for detainee transfers. And, in the event that these statutory restrictions operate in a manner that violates constitutional separation of powers principles, my Administration will implement them in a manner that avoids the constitutional conflict.

. . .

BARACK OBAMA

THE WHITE HOUSE,

January 2, 2013.

3.   Given its goal of closing the island facility, during its eight years in office the Obama administration sent no newly apprehended suspected terrorists to Guantanamo. To be sure, the numbers of those apprehended during this period were very small. Nevertheless, most of those, as previously recounted in Chapter 7 and this chapter, were detained on shipboard for varying but not unduly long periods, were interrogated there, and then were brought to the mainland for criminal prosecution in civilian courts. Happily, for the Obama administration, during the years of his Presidency, no instance occurred where a terrorist suspect was apprehended abroad and it was determined that he was too dangerous to release but could not be prosecuted. Such a case, of course, would pose the question: Where can he be detained? The Trump administration may be faced with such a case, as of the time of this writing. The case involves a captured U.S. citizen who fought with ISIS, but, apparently, cannot be prosecuted because he is refusing to answer questions after having been given the Miranda warnings. See a report on the case in ch. 7, supra. The practice of using U.S. ships for initial detention of persons

apprehended abroad has triggered interest and possible concern on the part of the Congress.

Section 1024 of the NDAA of 2013 was the result:

NDAA OF 2013

Sec. 1024.

Notice and report on use of naval vessels for detention of individuals captured outside Afghanistan pursuant to the Authorization for Use of Military Force

(a) Notice to Congress. Not later than 30 days after first detaining an individual pursuant to the Authorization for Use of Military Force (Public Law 107–40; 50 U.S.C. 1541 note) on a naval vessel outside the United States, the Secretary of Defense shall submit to the Committees on Armed Services of the Senate and House of Representatives notice of the detention. In the case of such an individual who is transferred or released before the submittal of the notice of the individual's detention, the Secretary shall also submit to such Committees notice of the transfer or release.

(b) Report.

(1) In general

Not later than 90 days after the date of the enactment of this Act, the Secretary of Defense shall submit to the Committees on Armed Services of the Senate and House of Representatives a report on the use of naval vessels for the detention outside the United States of any individual who is detained pursuant to the Authorization for Use of Military Force (Public Law 107–40; 50 U.S.C. 1541 note). Such report shall include—

(A) procedures and any limitations on detaining such individuals at sea on board United States naval vessels;

(B) an assessment of any force protection issues associated with detaining such individuals on such vessels;

(C) an assessment of the likely effect of such detentions on the original mission of such naval vessels; and

(D) any restrictions on long-term detention of individuals on United States naval vessels.

(2) Form of report

The report required under paragraph (1) may be submitted in classified form.

4. The following testimony from hearings before the Senate Armed Services Committee on June 28, 2011 relating to the nominations of Admiral McRaven as the new SOCOM commander and General Allen as the new

commander in Afghanistan provides some perspectives of those who were charged with responsibility for what was, at the time, a newly evolving policy:

SENATOR GRAHAM: . . . If you caught someone tomorrow in Yemen, Somalia, you name the theater, outside of Afghanistan, where would you detain that person?

ADMIRAL MCRAVEN: Sir, right now, as you're well aware, that is always a difficult issue for us. When we conduct an operation outside the major theaters of war in Iraq or Afghanistan, we put forth— we—. . .No two cases seem to be alike. As you know, there are certain individuals that are under the AUMF, the use of military force, and those are easier to deal with than folks that may not have been under the authority for AUMF. In many cases, we will put them on a naval vessel and we will hold them until we can either get a case to prosecute them in U.S. court or. . .

. . .

SENATOR GRAHAM: What's the longest we can keep somebody on the ship?

ADMIRAL MCRAVEN: Sir, I think it depends on whether or not we think we can prosecute that individual in a U.S. court or we can return him to a third party country.

SENATOR GRAHAM: What if you can't do either one of those?

ADMIRAL MCRAVEN: Sir, it— again, if we can't do either one of those, then we'll release that individual and that becomes the— the unenviable option, but it is an option.

. . .

SENATOR LEVIN: Finally, Admiral. . . you made reference to a couple I think that are on a ship, something like that. Is there any legal prohibition against them being tried before an Article 3 court or before a military commission?

ADMIRAL MCRAVEN: Sir, again, it depends on the individual case, and I'd be more than happy to discuss the cases that we've dealt with.

SENATOR LEVIN: Well, no, not. . .specific cases so much as is there any legal prohibition, assuming it's planned. . .having those people tried either before an Article 3 court, if they've committed a crime against the United States, or if they've committed a crime of war, by being tried by a U.S. military commission?

ADMIRAL MCRAVEN: Sir, not to my knowledge, there is no prohibition.

. . .

SENATOR AYOTTE: . . . .I wanted to follow up, General Allen, on the question of detention. If we were to, for example, capture someone like Ayman al-Zawahri in Yemen, for example, outside of Afghanistan, could we detain him in Afghanistan at the detention facilities there?

GENERAL ALLEN: We would not recommend that.

SENATOR AYOTTE: And why is that?

GENERAL ALLEN: Because Afghanistan is a sovereign country.

SENATOR AYOTTE: So we're not going to use the detention facilities, for example, in Afghanistan to detain terrorists who are captured outside the territory of Afghanistan?

GENERAL ALLEN: It's not our intention.

SENATOR AYOTTE: And following up, Admiral, with respect to detention, if we, for example, were to capture al-Zawahiri and— capture and not kill him but hold him for purposes of gathering intelligence and detaining him long term, because we felt we needed to under the law of war, where would we hold him?

ADMIRAL MCRAVEN: Yes, ma'am, I think that is a policy question that I'm really not in a position to answer. From a practical military standpoint, obviously we can hold— hold Zawahiri or Anwar al-Awlaki or anybody else in a number of places, from a practical standpoint. It becomes a policy issue and a sovereignty issue for various countries. And as General Allen said, we have looked a number of times at whether or not we would do that in Afghanistan, but owing to the nature of the sovereignty of Afghanistan and the concern about the potential backlash from the Afghan government, we have recommended not to do that.

SENATOR AYOTTE: And, Admiral, would it not be helpful 10 years into the war on terror to have a long-term detention and interrogation facility that would be secure for individuals where we need to gather further intelligence?

ADMIRAL MCRAVEN: Ma'am, I believe it would be very helpful.

SENATOR AYOTTE: And as far as you understand it, is Guantanamo Bay still off the table in terms of being used for that type of facility?

ADMIRAL MCRAVEN: As far as I understand it, it is, yes, ma'am.

5.   During this period, as previously recounted, in lieu of the fact that it had failed to close Guantanamo, the Obama administration was strongly motivated to reduce the number of detainees at Guantanamo to as low a

number as possible through the periodic review process and transfers. The final four transfers of the Obama administration occurred the day before the new President was inaugurated. The remaining number of detainees, 41, was composed of a few waiting to be transferred, those who were being prosecuted or had been convicted of crimes and those who could not be prosecuted but were deemed too dangerous to release.

6. With the transition to the Trump administration, the government's attitude toward Guantanamo, of course, changed. As a candidate, Trump had promised to send some "bad dudes" there, and he made similar statements after he became President. Attorney General Sessions had made statements supporting the use of Guantanamo for detainees, referring to it as "a very fine place." See Charlie Savage, Sessions Says Guantanamo is 'Fine Place' for Suspects, N.Y. Times, March 10, 2017, A14. And prominent members of Congress had also spoken in favor of continuing to use Guantanamo for suspected terrorists.

7. In Chapter 7, supra, a leaked draft Executive Order (disclaimed by the Trump White House) was discussed that would have reversed the Obama order to close the facility. In August 2017, the New York Times reported that the Trump administration is "making a fresh start at drafting an executive order on handling terrorism detainees" and the relevant government agencies were being asked to consider three versions of a draft Executive Order on the subject. See Charlie Savage and Adam Goldman, Administration to Renew Discussions on Sending More Detainees to Guantanamo, N.Y. Times, Aug. 19, 2017, A15. Finally on January 30, 2018, President Trump signed a new Executive Order relating to Guantanamo. See note 9, infra.

8. Despite the statements and actions described in the previous notes, as of the date of this writing, almost one year into the Trump administration, no person apprehended since the Trump administration took office, has been sent to Guantanamo. See ch. 7, supra, for a description of a few cases of persons captured abroad who were detained for a time on shipboard, interrogated and then brought to the U.S. mainland for prosecution in federal court. Despite the statements and promises to send terrorist suspects to Guantanamo, there were numerous obstacles to doing so that would need to be overcome.

a. Authority to send terrorist suspects to Guantanamo has been derived from the post-9/11 AUMF, which is linked to those who perpetrated the 9/11 attacks and are connected to al Qaeda. Similarly, sections 1021 and 1022 of the NDAA of 2012, which provides statutory authority to place individuals in military custody, is also linked to the AUMF basis for legal authority. Accordingly, terrorist suspects who do not have those linkages could not be placed in military custody and sent to Guantanamo, unless Congress were to broaden the basis for legal authority beyond what is provided in the AUMF. Congress thus far has not seen fit to do so.

1) Accordingly, it has been suggested that Abu Khatallah whose case is discussed supra, Chapter 7, and was convicted in

U.S. district court of crimes involving the attack on the Benghazi diplomatic mission could not have been sent to Guantanamo.

2) There appears to be a reluctance of Trump administration officials to send any newly apprehended ISIS fighters to Guantanamo because of uncertainty about whether the ISIS connection to al Qaeda is sufficient to bring them under authority provided by the AUMF, and the government apparently has been reluctant to test the issue.

b. Overall, as the battlefield action against ISIS winds down, there will be fewer potential detainees from that group. Sending to Guantanamo persons in the U.S. who have links to ISIS and are apprehended in the United States planning or committing terrorist acts would be controversial and would pose legal issues akin to those involving Padilla or al Marri, as discussed at the beginning of this chapter.

c. In instances where other countries capture terrorist suspects and might otherwise transfer them to the custody of the U.S., many of those countries have made it a condition of the transfer that the individual not be sent to Guantanamo.

d. Sending suspected terrorists to Guantanamo has been tied to the prospect of criminal prosecution in a military commission trial. As discussed in the next chapter, the military commission trials have not been an efficiently operating process. The link between detention at Guantanamo and military commission prosecution has thus been weakened, which has strengthened the case for prosecution in a U.S. district court.

9. While the larger issue of whether Guantanamo should be closed does not seem to have been the subject of debate within the Trump administration, it nevertheless merits attention. An important original reason why the Bush administration established Guantanamo was the legal view that the off-shore leased nature of the facility would mean that detainees would not have the benefit of constitutional protections and access to U.S. courts. The decision in the Boumediene case undermined that particular rationale. Are there other persuasive reasons for keeping Guantanamo open and using it to detain terrorist suspects? What is the case for closing it? On January 30, 2018, President Trump issued an Executive Order on Protecting America Through Lawful Detention of Terrorists. The key features of this Order include: 1) revocation of President Obama's Order issued on January 22, 2009 ordering closure of the Guantanamo Bay detention facility; 2) a statement that the United States may transport additional detainees to the facility; 3) application of the periodic review process to any new detainees transferred to Guantanamo; 4) a statement that nothing in this order shall affect existing law or authorities relating to U.S. citizens "or any persons who are captured or arrested in the United States."

CHAPTER 11

MILITARY COMMISSIONS AND THE CHOICE BETWEEN CRIMINAL PROSECUTION IN THE FEDERAL COURTS OR MILITARY COMMISSION TRIALS

■ ■ ■

A. INTRODUCTION

The military prosecution of terrorist suspects raises many issues parallel to those discussed in the previous chapter. In fact, of course, military detention in Guantanamo and criminal prosecution before military commissions are closely linked. Witness to this observation is the fact that through the issuance of the Military Order in the immediate aftermath of the 9/11 attacks, President Bush authorized both military detention of terrorists and the creation of military commissions to prosecute those who had a role in the attacks or who were involved in al Qaeda. The use of military commissions in wartime to prosecute enemy fighters for conduct that violates the law of war has numerous precedents in the history of this country.

Accordingly, this chapter deals with: the President's legal authority to establish military commissions, in light of the historical precedents, relevant statutes and the Constitution; the response by the U.S. Supreme Court in Hamdan v. Rumsfeld to a challenge to the specific exercise of executive authority by President Bush in establishing the commissions, procedures and evidentiary rules for commission trials; the procedures and evidence rules legislated by the Congress in response to the Hamdan decision; the crimes legislated by the Congress for prosecution before the commissions and their status in the courts; and the choice between prosecuting suspected terrorists before the military commissions, or pursuing them with criminal charges in United States district courts.

B. LEGAL AUTHORITY

1. THE QUIRIN CASE

A foundational case for the establishment of military commissions for the trial of "unlawful enemy combatants" is Ex Parte Quirin, a case involving the trial and execution of Nazi saboteurs toward the beginning of World War II.

EX PARTE QUIRIN
317 U.S. 1 (1942)

MR. CHIEF JUSTICE STONE delivered the opinion of the Court.

These cases are brought here by petitioners' several applications for leave to file petitions for habeas corpus in this Court, and by their petitions for certiorari to review orders of the District Court for the District of Columbia, which denied their applications for leave to file petitions for habeas corpus in that court.

The question for decision is whether the detention of petitioners by respondent for trial by Military Commission, appointed by Order of the President of July 2, 1942, on charges preferred against them purporting to set out their violations of the law of war and of the Articles of War, is in conformity to the laws and Constitution of the United States.

After denial of their applications by the District Court, 47 F.Supp. 431, petitioners asked leave to file petitions for habeas corpus in this Court. In view of the public importance of the questions raised by their petitions and of the duty which rests on the courts, in time of war as well as in time of peace, to preserve unimpaired the constitutional safeguards of civil liberty, and because in our opinion the public interest required that we consider and decide those questions without any avoidable delay, we directed that petitioners' applications be set down for full oral argument at a special term of this Court, convened on July 29, 1942. The applications for leave to file the petitions were presented in open court on that day and were heard on the petitions, the answers to them of respondent, a stipulation of facts by counsel, and the record of the testimony given before the Commission.

While the argument was proceeding before us, petitioners perfected their appeals from the orders of the District Court to the United States Court of Appeals for the District of Columbia and thereupon filed with this Court petitions for certiorari to the Court of Appeals before judgment, pursuant to Section 240(a) of the Judicial Code, 28 U.S.C. § 347(a). We granted certiorari before judgment for the reasons which moved us to convene the special term of Court. In accordance with the stipulation of counsel we treat the record, briefs and arguments in the habeas corpus proceedings in this Court as the record, briefs and arguments upon the writs of certiorari.

On July 31, 1942, after hearing argument of counsel and after full consideration of all questions raised, this Court affirmed the orders of the District Court and denied petitioners' applications for leave to file petitions for habeas corpus. By per curiam opinion, . . . we announced the decision of the Court, and that the full opinion in the causes would be prepared and filed with the Clerk.

The following facts appear from the petitions or are stipulated. Except as noted they are undisputed.

All the petitioners were born in Germany; all have lived in the United States. All returned to Germany between 1933 and 1941. All except petitioner Haupt are admittedly citizens of the German Reich, with which the United States is at war. Haupt came to this country with his parents when he was five years old; it is contended that he became a citizen of the United States by virtue of the naturalization of his parents during his minority and that he has not since lost his citizenship. The Government, however, takes the position that on attaining his majority he elected to maintain German allegiance and citizenship or in any case that he has by his conduct renounced or abandoned his United States citizenship. See Perkins v. Elg, 307 U.S. 325, 334, 59 S.Ct. 884, 889, 83 L.Ed. 1320; United States ex rel. Rojak v. Marshall, D.C., 34 F.2d 219; United States ex rel. Scimeca v. Husband, 2 Cir., 6 F.2d 957, 958; 8 U.S.C. § 801, and compare 8 U.S.C. § 808. For reasons presently to be stated we do not find it necessary to resolve these contentions.

After the declaration of war between the United States and the German Reich, petitioners received training at a sabotage school near Berlin, Germany, where they were instructed in the use of explosives and in methods of secret writing. Thereafter petitioners, with a German citizen, Dasch, proceeded from Germany to a seaport in Occupied France, where petitioners Burger, Heinck and Quirin, together with Dasch, boarded a German submarine which proceeded across the Atlantic to Amagansett Beach on Long Island, New York. The four were there landed from the submarine in the hours of darkness, on or about June 13, 1942, carrying with them a supply of explosives, fuses and incendiary and timing devices. While landing they wore German Marine Infantry uniforms or parts of uniforms. Immediately after landing they buried their uniforms and the other articles mentioned and proceeded in civilian dress to New York City.

The remaining four petitioners at the same French port boarded another German submarine, which carried them across the Atlantic to Ponte Vedra Beach, Florida. On or about June 17, 1942, they came ashore during the hours of darkness wearing caps of the German Marine Infantry and carrying with them a supply of explosives, fuses, and incendiary and timing devices. They immediately buried their caps and the other articles mentioned and proceeded in civilian dress to Jacksonville, Florida, and thence to various points in the United States. All were taken into custody in New York or Chicago by agents of the Federal Bureau of Investigation. All had received instructions in Germany from an officer of the German High Command to destroy war industries and war facilities in the United

States, for which they or their relatives in Germany were to receive salary payments from the German Government. They also had been paid by the German Government during their course of training at the sabotage school and had received substantial sums in United States currency, which were in their possession when arrested. The currency had been handed to them by an officer of the German High Command, who had instructed them to wear their German uniforms while landing in the United States.

The President, as President and Commander in Chief of the Army and Navy, by Order of July 2, 1942, appointed a Military Commission and directed it to try petitioners for offenses against the law of war and the Articles of War, and prescribed regulations for the procedure on the trial and for review of the record of the trial and of any judgment or sentence of the Commission. On the same day, by Proclamation, the President declared that 'all persons who are subjects, citizens or residents of any nation at war with the United States or who give obedience to or act under the direction of any such nation, and who during time of war enter or attempt to enter the United States ... through coastal or boundary defenses, and are charged with committing or attempting or preparing to commit sabotage, espionage, hostile or warlike acts, or violations of the law of war, shall be subject to the law of war and to the jurisdiction of military tribunals'.

The Proclamation also stated in terms that all such persons were denied access to the courts.

Pursuant to direction of the Attorney General, the Federal Bureau of Investigation surrendered custody of petitioners to respondent, Provost Marshal of the Military District of Washington, who was directed by the Secretary of War to receive and keep them in custody, and who thereafter held petitioners for trial before the Commission.

On July 3, 1942, the Judge Advocate General's Department of the Army prepared and lodged with the Commission the following charges against petitioners, supported by specifications:

    1.   Violation of the law of war.

    2.   Violation of Article 81 of the Articles of War, defining the offense of relieving or attempting to relieve, or corresponding with or giving intelligence to, the enemy.

    3.   Violation of Article 82, defining the offense of spying.

    4.   Conspiracy to commit the offenses alleged in charges 1, 2 and 3.

The Commission met on July 8, 1942, and proceeded with the trial, which continued in progress while the causes were pending in this Court. On July 27th, before petitioners' applications to the District Court, all the evidence for the prosecution and the defense had been taken by the

Commission and the case had been closed except for arguments of counsel. It is conceded that ever since petitioners' arrest the state and federal courts in Florida, New York, and the District of Columbia, and in the states in which each of the petitioners was arrested or detained, have been open and functioning normally.

. . .

Petitioners' main contention is that the President is without any statutory or constitutional authority to order the petitioners to be tried by military tribunal for offenses with which they are charged; that in consequence they are entitled to be tried in the civil courts with the safeguards, including trial by jury, which the Fifth and Sixth Amendments guarantee to all persons charged in such courts with criminal offenses. In any case it is urged that the President's Order, in prescribing the procedure of the Commission and the method for review of its findings and sentence, and the proceedings of the Commission under the Order, conflict with Articles of War adopted by Congress—particularly Articles 38, 43, 46, 50 1/2 and 70—and are illegal and void.

The Government challenges each of these propositions. But regardless of their merits, it also insists that petitioners must be denied access to the courts, both because they are enemy aliens or have entered our territory as enemy belligerents, and because the President's Proclamation undertakes in terms to deny such access to the class of persons defined by the Proclamation, which aptly describes the character and conduct of petitioners. It is urged that if they are enemy aliens or if the Proclamation has force no court may afford the petitioners a hearing. But there is certainly nothing in the Proclamation to preclude access to the courts for determining its applicability to the particular case. And neither the Proclamation nor the fact that they are enemy aliens forecloses consideration by the courts of petitioners' contentions that the Constitution and laws of the United States constitutionally enacted forbid their trial by military commission. As announced in our per curiam opinion we have resolved those questions by our conclusion that the Commission has jurisdiction to try the charge preferred against petitioners. There is therefore no occasion to decide contentions of the parties unrelated to this issue. We pass at once to the consideration of the basis of the Commission's authority.

We are not here concerned with any question of the guilt or innocence of petitioners. Constitutional safeguards for the protection of all who are charged with offenses are not to be disregarded in order to inflict merited punishment on some who are guilty. Ex parte Milligan, 4 Wall. 119, 132, 18 L.Ed. 281; Tumey v. Ohio, 273 U.S. 510, 535, 47 S.Ct. 437, 445, 71 L.Ed. 749, 50 A.L.R. 1243; Hill v. Texas, 316 U.S. 400, 62 S.Ct. 1159, 1161, 1162, 86 L.Ed. 1559. But the detention and trial of petitioners—ordered by the

President in the declared exercise of his powers as Commander in Chief of the Army in time of war and of grave public danger—are not to be set aside by the courts without the clear conviction that they are in conflict with the Constitution or laws of Congress constitutionally enacted.

Congress and the President, like the courts, possess no power not derived from the Constitution. But one of the objects of the Constitution, as declared by its preamble, is to 'provide for the common defence'. As a means to that end the Constitution gives to Congress the power to 'provide for the common Defence', Art. I, § 8, cl. 1; 'To raise and support Armies', 'To provide and maintain a Navy', Art. I, § 8, cls. 12, 13; and 'To make Rules for the Government and Regulation of the land and naval Forces', Art. I, § 8, cl. 14. Congress is given authority 'To declare War, grant Letters of Marque and Reprisal, and make Rules concerning Captures on Land and Water', Art. I, § 8, cl. 11; and 'To define and punish Piracies and Felonies committed on the high Seas, and Offenses against the Law of Nations', Art. I, § 8, cl. 10. And finally the Constitution authorizes Congress 'To make all Laws which shall be necessary and proper for carrying into Execution the foregoing Powers, and all other Powers vested by this Constitution in the Government of the United States, or in any Department or Officer thereof.' Art. I, § 8, cl. 18.

The Constitution confers on the President the 'executive Power', Art II, § 1, cl. 1, and imposes on him the duty to 'take Care that the Laws be faithfully executed'. Art. II, § 3. It makes him the Commander in Chief of the Army and Navy, Art. II, § 2, cl. 1, and empowers him to appoint and commission officers of the United States. Art. II, § 3, cl. 1.

The Constitution thus invests the President as Commander in Chief with the power to wage war which Congress has declared, and to carry into effect all laws passed by Congress for the conduct of war and for the government and regulation of the Armed Forces, and all laws defining and punishing offences against the law of nations, including those which pertain to the conduct of war.

By the Articles of War, 10 U.S.C. §§ 1471–1593, Congress has provided rules for the government of the Army. It has provided for the trial and punishment, by courts martial, of violations of the Articles by members of the armed forces and by specified classes of persons associated or serving with the Army. Arts. 1, 2. But the Articles also recognize the 'military commission' appointed by military command as an appropriate tribunal for the trial and punishment of offenses against the law of war not ordinarily tried by court martial. See Arts. 12, 15. Articles 38 and 46 authorize the President, with certain limitations, to prescribe the procedure for military commissions. Articles 81 and 82 authorize trial, either by court martial or military commission, of those charged with relieving, harboring or corresponding with the enemy and those charged with spying. And Article

15 declares that 'the provisions of these articles conferring jurisdiction upon courts-martial shall not be construed as depriving military commissions . . . or other military tribunals of concurrent jurisdiction in respect of offenders or offenses that by statute or by the law of war may be triable by such military commissions . . . or other military tribunals'. Article 2 includes among those persons subject to military law the personnel of our own military establishment. But this, as Article 12 provides, does not exclude from that class 'any other person who by the law of war is subject to trial by military tribunals' and who under Article 12 may be tried by court martial or under Article 15 by military commission.

Similarly the Espionage Act of 1917, which authorizes trial in the district courts of certain offenses that tend to interfere with the prosecution of war, provides that nothing contained in the act 'shall be deemed to limit the jurisdiction of the general courts-martial, military commissions, or naval courts-martial'. 50 U.S.C. § 38.

From the very beginning of its history this Court has recognized and applied the law of war as including that part of the law of nations which prescribes, for the conduct of war, the status, rights and duties of enemy nations as well as of enemy individuals. By the Articles of War, and especially Article 15, Congress has explicitly provided, so far as it may constitutionally do so, that military tribunals shall have jurisdiction to try offenders or offenses against the law of war in appropriate cases. Congress, in addition to making rules for the government of our Armed Forces, has thus exercised its authority to define and punish offenses against the law of nations by sanctioning, within constitutional limitations, the jurisdiction of military commissions to try persons for offenses which, according to the rules and precepts of the law of nations, and more particularly the law of war, are cognizable by such tribunals. And the President, as Commander in Chief, by his Proclamation in time of war has invoked that law. By his Order creating the present Commission he has undertaken to exercise the authority conferred upon him by Congress, and also such authority as the Constitution itself gives the Commander in Chief, to direct the performance of those functions which may constitutionally be performed by the military arm of the nation in time of war.

An important incident to the conduct of war is the adoption of measures by the military command not only to repel and defeat the enemy, but to seize and subject to disciplinary measures those enemies who in their attempt to thwart or impede our military effort have violated the law of war. It is unnecessary for present purposes to determine to what extent the President as Commander in Chief has constitutional power to create military commissions without the support of Congressional legislation. For here Congress has authorized trial of offenses against the law of war before such commissions. We are concerned only with the question whether it is within the constitutional power of the national government to place petitioners upon trial before a military commission for the offenses with which they are charged. We must therefore first inquire whether any of the acts charged is an offense against the law of war cognizable before a military tribunal, and if so whether the Constitution prohibits the trial. We may assume that there are acts regarded in other countries, or by some writers on international law, as offenses against the law of war which would not be triable by military tribunal here, either because they are not recognized by our courts as violations of the law of war or because they are of that class of offenses constitutionally triable only by a jury. It was upon such grounds that the Court denied the right to proceed by military tribunal in Ex parte Milligan, supra. But as we shall show, these petitioners were charged with an offense against the law of war which the Constitution does not require to be tried by jury.

It is no objection that Congress in providing for the trial of such offenses has not itself undertaken to codify that branch of international law or to mark its precise boundaries, or to enumerate or define by statute all the acts which that law condemns. An Act of Congress punishing 'the crime of piracy as defined by the law of nations' is an appropriate exercise of its constitutional authority, Art. I, § 8, cl. 10, 'to define and punish' the offense since it has adopted by reference the sufficiently precise definition of international law. United States v. Smith, 5 Wheat. 153, 5 L.Ed. 57; see The Marianna Flora, 11 Wheat. 1, 40, 41, 6 L.Ed. 405; United States v. The Malek Adhel, 2 How. 210, 232, 11 L.Ed. 239; The Ambrose Light, D.C., 25 F. 408, 423, 428; 18 U.S.C. § 481. Similarly by the reference in the 15th Article of War to 'offenders or offenses that . . . by the law of war may be triable by such military commissions', Congress has incorporated by reference, as within the jurisdiction of military commissions, all offenses which are defined as such by the law of war (compare Dynes v. Hoover, 20 How. 65, 82, 15 L.Ed. 838), and which may constitutionally be included within that jurisdiction. Congress had the choice of crystallizing in permanent form and in minute detail every offense against the law of war, or of adopting the system of common law applied by military tribunals so far as it should be recognized and deemed applicable by the courts. It chose the latter course.

By universal agreement and practice the law of war draws a distinction between the armed forces and the peaceful populations of belligerent nations and also between those who are lawful and unlawful combatants. Lawful combatants are subject to capture and detention as prisoners of war by opposing military forces. Unlawful combatants are likewise subject to capture and detention, but in addition they are subject to trial and punishment by military tribunals for acts which render their belligerency unlawful. The spy who secretly and without uniform passes the military lines of a belligerent in time of war, seeking to gather military information and communicate it to the enemy, or an enemy combatant who without uniform comes secretly through the lines for the purpose of waging war by destruction of life or property, are familiar examples of belligerents who are generally deemed not to be entitled to the status of prisoners of war, but to be offenders against the law of war subject to trial and punishment by military tribunals. See Winthrop, Military Law, 2d Ed., pp. 1196–1197, 1219–1221; Instructions for the Government of Armies of the United States in the Field, approved by the President, General Order No. 100, April 24, 1863, sections IV and V.

Such was the practice of our own military authorities before the adoption of the Constitution, and during the Mexican and Civil Wars.

. . .

Our Government, by thus defining lawful belligerents entitled to be treated as prisoners of war, has recognized that there is a class of unlawful belligerents not entitled to that privilege, including those who though combatants do not wear 'fixed and distinctive emblems'. And by Article 15 of the Articles of War Congress has made provision for their trial and punishment by military commission, according to 'the law of war'.

By a long course of practical administrative construction by its military authorities, our Government has likewise recognized that those who during time of war pass surreptitiously from enemy territory into our own, discarding their uniforms upon entry, for the commission of hostile acts involving destruction of life or property, have the status of unlawful combatants punishable as such by military commission. This precept of the law of war has been so recognized in practice both here and abroad, and has so generally been accepted as valid by authorities on international law that we think it must be regarded as a rule or principle of the law of war recognized by this Government. . . .

Specification 1 of the First charge is sufficient to charge all the petitioners with the offense of unlawful belligerency, trial of which is within the jurisdiction of the Commission, and the admitted facts affirmatively show that the charge is not merely colorable or without foundation.

Specification 1 states that petitioners 'being enemies of the United States and acting for . . . the German Reich, a belligerent enemy nation, secretly and covertly passed, in civilian dress, contrary to the law of war, through the military and naval lines and defenses of the United States . . . and went behind such lines, contrary to the law of war, in civilian dress . . . for the purpose of committing . . . hostile acts, and, in particular, to destroy certain war industries, war utilities and war materials within the United States'.

This specification so plainly alleges violation of the law of war as to require but brief discussion of petitioners' contentions. As we have seen, entry upon our territory in time of war by enemy belligerents, including those acting under the direction of the armed forces of the enemy, for the purpose of destroying property used or useful in prosecuting the war, is a hostile and war-like act. It subjects those who participate in it without uniform to the punishment prescribed by the law of war for unlawful belligerents. It is without significance that petitioners were not alleged to have borne conventional weapons or that their proposed hostile acts did not necessarily contemplate collision with the Armed Forces of the United States. Paragraphs 351 and 352 of the Rules of Land Warfare, already referred to, plainly contemplate that the hostile acts and purposes for which unlawful belligerents may be punished are not limited to assaults on the Armed Forces of the United States. Modern warfare is directed at the destruction of enemy war supplies and the implements of their production and transportation quite as much as at the armed forces. Every consideration which makes the unlawful belligerent punishable is equally applicable whether his objective is the one or the other. The law of war cannot rightly treat those agents of enemy armies who enter our territory, armed with explosives intended for the destruction of war industries and supplies, as any the less belligerent enemies than are agents similarly entering for the purpose of destroying fortified places or our Armed Forces. By passing our boundaries for such purposes without uniform or other emblem signifying their belligerent status, or by discarding that means of identification after entry, such enemies become unlawful belligerents subject to trial and punishment.

Citizenship in the United States of an enemy belligerent does not relieve him from the consequences of a belligerency which is unlawful because in violation of the law of war. Citizens who associate themselves with the military arm of the enemy government, and with its aid, guidance and direction enter this country bent on hostile acts are enemy belligerents within the meaning of the Hague Convention and the law of war. Cf. Gates v. Goodloe, 101 U.S. 612, 615, 617, 618, 25 L.Ed. 895. It is as an enemy belligerent that petitioner Haupt is charged with entering the United States, and unlawful belligerency is the gravamen of the offense of which he is accused.

Nor are petitioners any the less belligerents if, as they argue, they have not actually committed or attempted to commit any act of depredation or entered the theatre or zone of active military operations. The argument leaves out of account the nature of the offense which the Government charges and which the Act of Congress, by incorporating the law of war, punishes. It is that each petitioner, in circumstances which gave him the status of an enemy belligerent, passed our military and naval lines and defenses or went behind those lines, in civilian dress and with hostile purpose. The offense was complete when with that purpose they entered— or, having so entered, they remained upon—our territory in time of war without uniform or other appropriate means of identification. For that reason, even when committed by a citizen, the offense is distinct from the crime of treason defined in Article III, § 3 of the Constitution, since the absence of uniform essential to one is irrelevant to the other.

But petitioners insist that even if the offenses with which they are charged are offenses against the law of war, their trial is subject to the requirement of the Fifth Amendment that no person shall be held to answer for a capital or otherwise infamous crime unless on a presentment or indictment of a grand jury, and that such trials by Article III, § 2, and the Sixth Amendment must be by jury in a civil court. Before the Amendments, § 2 of Article III, the Judiciary Article, had provided: 'The Trial of all Crimes, except in Cases of Impeachment, shall be by Jury', and had directed that 'such Trial shall be held in the State where the said Crimes shall have been committed'.

Presentment by a grand jury and trial by a jury of the vicinage where the crime was committed were at the time of the adoption of the Constitution familiar parts of the machinery for criminal trials in the civil courts. But they were procedures unknown to military tribunals, which are not courts in the sense of the Judiciary Article, Ex parte Vallandigham, 1 Wall. 243, 17 L.Ed. 589; In re Vidal, 179 U.S. 126, 21 S.Ct. 48, 45 L.Ed. 118; cf. Williams v. United States, 289 U.S. 553, 53 S.Ct. 751, 77 L.Ed. 1372, and which in the natural course of events are usually called upon to function under conditions precluding resort to such procedures. As this Court has often recognized, it was not the purpose or effect of § 2 of Article III, read in the light of the common law, to enlarge the then existing right to a jury trial. The object was to preserve unimpaired trial by jury in all those cases in which it had been recognized by the common law and in all cases of a like nature as they might arise in the future, District of Columbia v. Colts, 282 U.S. 63, 51 S.Ct. 52, 75 L.Ed. 177, but not to bring within the sweep of the guaranty those cases in which it was then well understood that a jury trial could not be demanded as of right.

. . .

In the light of this long-continued and consistent interpretation we must conclude that § 2 of Article III and the Fifth and Sixth Amendments cannot be taken to have extended the right to demand a jury to trials by military commission, or to have required that offenses against the law of war not triable by jury at common law be tried only in the civil courts.

. . .

Section 2 of the Act of Congress of April 10, 1806, 2 Stat. 371, derived from the Resolution of the Continental Congress of August 21, 1776, imposed the death penalty on alien spies 'according to the law and usage of nations, by sentence of a general court martial'. This enactment must be regarded as a contemporary construction of both Article III, § 2, and the

Amendments as not foreclosing trial by military tribunals, without a jury, of offenses against the law of war committed by enemies not in or associated with our Armed Forces. It is a construction of the Constitution which has been followed since the founding of our government, and is now continued in the 82nd Article of War. Such a construction is entitled to the greatest respect. Stuart v. Laird, 1 Cranch, 299, 309, 2 L.Ed. 115; Field v. Clark, 143 U.S. 649, 691, 12 S.Ct. 495, 504, 36 L.Ed. 294; United States v. Curtiss-Wright Corp., 299 U.S. 304, 328, 57 S.Ct. 216, 224, 81 L.Ed. 255. It has not hitherto been challenged, and so far as we are advised it has never been suggested in the very extensive literature of the subject that an alien spy, in time of war, could not be tried by military tribunal without a jury.

The exception from the Amendments of 'cases arising in the land or naval forces' was not aimed at trials by military tribunals, without a jury, of such offenses against the law of war. Its objective was quite different— to authorize the trial by court martial of the members of our Armed Forces for all that class of crimes which under the Fifth and Sixth Amendments might otherwise have been deemed triable in the civil courts. The cases mentioned in the exception are not restricted to those involving offenses against the law of war alone, but extend to trial of all offenses, including crimes which were of the class traditionally triable by jury at common law.

Since the Amendments, like § 2 of Article III, do not preclude all trials of offenses against the law of war by military commission without a jury when the offenders are aliens not members of our Armed Forces, it is plain that they present no greater obstacle to the trial in like manner of citizen enemies who have violated the law of war applicable to enemies. Under the original statute authorizing trial of alien spies by military tribunals, the offenders were outside the constitutional guaranty of trial by jury, not because they were aliens but only because they had violated the law of war by committing offenses constitutionally triable by military tribunal.

We cannot say that Congress in preparing the Fifth and Sixth Amendments intended to extend trial by jury to the cases of alien or citizen offenders against the law of war otherwise triable by military commission, while withholding it from members of our own armed forces charged with infractions of the Articles of War punishable by death. It is equally inadmissible to construe the Amendments—whose primary purpose was to continue unimpaired presentment by grand jury and trial by petit jury in all those cases in which they had been customary—as either abolishing all trials by military tribunals, save those of the personnel of our own armed forces, or what in effect comes to the same thing, as imposing on all such tribunals the necessity of proceeding against unlawful enemy belligerents only on presentment and trial by jury. We conclude that the Fifth and Sixth Amendments did not restrict whatever authority was conferred by the Constitution to try offenses against the law of war by military commission, and that petitioners, charged with such an offense not required to be tried by jury at common law, were lawfully placed on trial by the Commission without a jury.

Petitioners, and especially petitioner Haupt, stress the pronouncement of this Court in the Milligan case, 4 Wall. page 121, 18 L.Ed. 281, that the law of war 'can never be applied to citizens in states which have upheld the authority of the government, and where the courts are open and their process unobstructed'.

Elsewhere in its opinion, 4 Wall. at pages 118, 121, 122, and 131, 18 L.Ed. 281, the Court was at pains to point out that Milligan, a citizen twenty years resident in Indiana, who had never been a resident of any of the states in rebellion, was not an enemy belligerent either entitled to the status of a prisoner of war or subject to the penalties imposed upon unlawful belligerents. We construe the Court's statement as to the inapplicability of the law of war to Milligan's case as having particular reference to the facts before it. From them the Court concluded that Milligan, not being a part of or associated with the armed forces of the enemy, was a non-belligerent, not subject to the law of war save as—in circumstances found not there to be present and not involved here— martial law might be constitutionally established.

The Court's opinion is inapplicable to the case presented by the present record. We have no occasion now to define with meticulous care the ultimate boundaries of the jurisdiction of military tribunals to try persons according to the law of war. It is enough that petitioners here, upon the conceded facts, were plainly within those boundaries, and were held in good faith for trial by military commission, charged with being enemies who, with the purpose of destroying war materials and utilities, entered or after entry remained in our territory without uniform—an offense against the law of war. We hold only that those particular acts constitute an offense against the law of war which the Constitution authorizes to be tried by military commission.

. . .

Accordingly, we conclude that Charge I, on which petitioners were detained for trial by the Military Commission, alleged an offense which the President is authorized to order tried by military commission; that his Order convening the Commission was a lawful order and that the Commission was lawfully constituted; that the petitioners were held in lawful custody and did not show cause for their discharge. It follows that the orders of the District Court should be affirmed, and that leave to file petitions for habeas corpus in this Court should be denied.

MR. JUSTICE MURPHY took no part in the consideration or decision of these cases.

Orders of District Court affirmed and leave to file petitions for habeas corpus in the Supreme Court denied.

2. THE PRESIDENT'S MILITARY ORDER AND RELATED PROVISIONS REDUX

In Chapter 10, the Authorization to Use Military Force (AUMF) and the President's Military Order issued on November 13, 2001 were reproduced because they provide the legal basis for detaining individuals in military custody. The Military Order also provides presidential authority for the establishment of, and trial by "military commission" of certain categories of persons involved in acts of international terrorism. As reported in Chapter 10, in issuing the Order, the government expressly relied on the President's authority as Commander in Chief of the Armed Forces; on the Joint Resolution of the Congress, (Authorization for Use of Military Force Joint Resolution) (Public Law 107–40, 115 Stat. 224), and on two long-standing legislative provisions 10 U.S.C. §§ 821 and 836. Excerpts from the Military Order that deal with, or are relevant to military commissions matters are again reproduced here as well as the two relevant legislative provisions. Also see Hamdan v. Rumsfeld, infra sec. 3, this chapter, which ruled that the procedures and structure of the military commissions as established lacked power to proceed because in violation of the Uniform Code of Military Justice and the Geneva Conventions.

NOTICE: DETENTION, TREATMENT, AND TRIAL OF CERTAIN NON-CITIZENS IN THE WAR AGAINST TERRORISM.
66 Fed. Reg. 57833

By the authority vested in me as President and as Commander in Chief of the Armed Forces of the United States by the Constitution and the laws of the United States of America, including the Authorization for Use of Military Force Joint Resolution (Public Law 107–40, 115 Stat. 224) and sections 821 and 836 of title 10, United States Code, it is hereby ordered as follows:

Section 1. Findings.

(a) International terrorists, including members of al Qaida, have carried out attacks on United States diplomatic and military personnel and facilities abroad and on citizens and property within the United States on a scale that has created a state of armed conflict that requires the use of the United States Armed Forces.

(b) In light of grave acts of terrorism and threats of terrorism, including the terrorist attacks on September 11, 2001, on the headquarters of the United States Department of Defense in the national capital region, on the World Trade Center in New York, and on civilian aircraft such as in

Pennsylvania, I proclaimed a national emergency on September 14, 2001 (Proc. 7463, Declaration of National Emergency by Reason of Certain Terrorist Attacks).

(c) Individuals acting alone and in concert involved in international terrorism possess both the capability and the intention to undertake further terrorist attacks against the United States that, if not detected and prevented, will cause mass deaths, mass injuries, and massive destruction of property, and may place at risk the continuity of the operations of the United States Government.

(d) The ability of the United States to protect the United States and its citizens, and to help its allies and other cooperating nations protect their nations and their citizens, from such further terrorist attacks depends in significant part upon using the United States Armed Forces to identify terrorists and those who support them, to disrupt their activities, and to eliminate their ability to conduct or support such attacks.

(e) To protect the United States and its citizens, and for the effective conduct of military operations and prevention of terrorist attacks, it is necessary for individuals subject to this order pursuant to section 2 hereof to be detained, and, when tried, to be tried for violations of the laws of war and other applicable laws by military tribunals.

(f) Given the danger to the safety of the United States and the nature of international terrorism, and to the extent provided by and under this order, I find consistent with section 836 of title 10, United States Code, that it is not practicable to apply in military commissions under this order the principles of law and the rules of evidence generally recognized in the trial of criminal cases in the United States district courts.

(g) Having fully considered the magnitude of the potential deaths, injuries, and property destruction that would result from potential acts of terrorism against the United States, and the probability that such acts will occur, I have determined that an extraordinary emergency exists for national defense purposes, that this emergency constitutes an urgent and compelling government interest, and that issuance of this order is necessary to meet the emergency.

Sec. 2. Definition and Policy.

(a) The term "individual subject to this order" shall mean any individual who is not a United States citizen with respect to whom I determine from time to time in writing that:

    (1) there is reason to believe that such individual, at the relevant times,

        (i) is or was a member of the organization known as al Qaida;

(ii) has engaged in, aided or abetted, or conspired to commit, acts of international terrorism, or acts in preparation therefor, that have caused, threaten to cause, or have as their aim to cause, injury to or adverse effects on the United States, its citizens, national security, foreign policy, or economy; or

(iii) has knowingly harbored one or more individuals described in subparagraphs (i) or (ii) of subsection 2(a)(1) of this order; and

(2) it is in the interest of the United States that such individual be subject to this order.

(b) It is the policy of the United States that the Secretary of Defense shall take all necessary measures to ensure that any individual subject to this order . . . if the individual is to be tried, that such individual is tried only in accordance with section 4.

. . .

Sec. 4. Authority of the Secretary of Defense Regarding Trials of Individuals Subject to this Order.

(a) Any individual subject to this order shall, when tried, be tried by military commission for any and all offenses triable by military commission that such individual is alleged to have committed, and may be punished in accordance with the penalties provided under applicable law, including life imprisonment or death.

(b) As a military function and in light of the findings in section 1, including subsection (f) thereof, the Secretary of Defense shall issue such orders and regulations, including orders for the appointment of one or more military commissions, as may be necessary to carry out subsection (a) of this section.

(c) Orders and regulations issued under subsection (b) of this section shall include, but not be limited to, rules for the conduct of the proceedings of military commissions, including pretrial, trial, and post-trial procedures, modes of proof, issuance of process, and qualifications of attorneys, which shall at a minimum provide for—

(1) military commissions to sit at any time and any place, consistent with such guidance regarding time and place as the Secretary of Defense may provide;

(2) a full and fair trial, with the military commission sitting as the triers of both fact and law;

(3) admission of such evidence as would, in the opinion of the presiding officer of the military commission (or instead, if any other member of the commission so requests at the time the presiding officer renders that opinion, the opinion of the commission rendered at that

time by a majority of the commission), have probative value to a reasonable person;

(4) in a manner consistent with the protection of information classified or classifiable under Executive Order 12958 of April 17, 1995, as amended, or any successor Executive Order, protected by statute or rule from unauthorized disclosure, or otherwise protected by law, (A) the handling of, admission into evidence of, and access to materials and information, and (B) the conduct, closure of, and access to proceedings;

(5) conduct of the prosecution by one or more attorneys designated by the Secretary of Defense and conduct of the defense by attorneys for the individual subject to this order;

(6) conviction only upon the concurrence of two-thirds of the members of the commission present at the time of the vote, a majority being present;

(7) sentencing only upon the concurrence of two-thirds of the members of the commission present at the time of the vote, a majority being present; and

(8) submission of the record of the trial, including any conviction or sentence, for review and final decision by me or by the Secretary of Defense if so designated by me for that purpose.

Sec. 6. Additional Authorities of the Secretary of Defense.

(a) As a military function and in light of the findings in section 1, the Secretary of Defense shall issue such orders and regulations as may be necessary to carry out any of the provisions of this order.

(b) The Secretary of Defense may perform any of his functions or duties, and may exercise any of the powers provided to him under this order (other than under section 4(c)(8) hereof) in accordance with section 113(d) of title 10, United States Code.

Sec. 7. Relationship to Other Law and Forums.

(a) Nothing in this order shall be construed to—

(1) authorize the disclosure of state secrets to any person not otherwise authorized to have access to them;

(2) limit the authority of the President as Commander in Chief of the Armed Forces or the power of the President to grant reprieves and pardons; or

(3) limit the lawful authority of the Secretary of Defense, any military commander, or any other officer or agent of the United States or of any State to detain or try any person who is not an individual subject to this order.

(b) With respect to any individual subject to this order—

(1) military tribunals shall have exclusive jurisdiction with respect to offenses by the individual; and

(2) the individual shall not be privileged to seek any remedy or maintain any proceeding, directly or indirectly, or to have any such remedy or proceeding sought on the individual's behalf, in

      (i) any court of the United States, or any State thereof,

      (ii) any court of any foreign nation, or

      (iii) any international tribunal.

. . .

TITLE 10—UNITED STATES CODE (ARMED FORCES) SUBTITLE A—GENERAL MILITARY LAW PART II— PERSONNEL CHAPTER 47—UNIFORM CODE OF MILITARY JUSTICE—SUBCHAPTER IV— COURT-MARTIAL JURISDICTION

Section 821. Art. 21. Jurisdiction of courts-martial not exclusive

The provisions of this chapter conferring jurisdiction upon courts-martial do not deprive military commissions, provost courts, or other military tribunals of concurrent jurisdiction with respect to offenders or offenses that by statute or by the law of war may be tried by military commissions, provost courts, or other military tribunals.

Section 836. Art. 36. President may prescribe rules

(a) Pretrial, trial, and post-trial procedures, including modes of proof, for cases arising under this chapter triable in courts-martial, military commissions and other military tribunals, and procedures for courts of inquiry, may be prescribed by the President by regulations which shall, so far as he considers practicable, apply the principles of law and the rules of evidence generally recognized in the trial of criminal cases in the United States district courts, but which may not be contrary to or inconsistent with this chapter.

(b) All rules and regulations made under this article shall be uniform insofar as practicable.

QUESTIONS AND NOTES

1. The issuance of the Presidential Military Order generated a great deal of commentary, both in law reviews and the general media. Much of the commentary attacked the Order as being either an unconstitutional or unwise assertion of authority by the President. The main constitutional argument made against the Order was that the President did not have the authority to

issue the order without congressional authorization. The response of the administration and the administration's defenders was that the President had such authority as Commander in Chief. If further congressional authorization was needed, the post-Sept. 11 Joint Resolution (Public Law 107–40) and the two long-standing Title 10 sections, supra, provided such authority. The government also cited the decision of the Supreme Court in Ex parte Quirin, 317 U.S. 1 (1942).

2.   Does Quirin provide adequate support for the issuance of the Military Order by the President? Following the issuance of the Military Order, the legal literature filled with scholarly debate about the question of presidential power to authorize the establishment of military commissions. See, e.g., Neal K. Katyal and Laurence H. Tribe, Waging War, Deciding Guilt: Trying the Military Tribunals, 111 Yale L.J. 1259, 1269–1270 (2002); Curtis A. Bradley and Jack L. Goldsmith, The Constitutional Validity of Military Commissions, 5 Green Bag 2d 249, 252, Spring 2002; Ruth Wedgwood, Agora: Military Commissions: Al Qaeda, Terrorism, and Military Commissions, 96 Am J. Int'l L. 328 (2002); Jonathan J. Paust, Antiterrorism Military Commissions: Courting Illegality, 23 Michigan Mich. J. Int'l L. 1, 5–9 (2001); Harold Hongju Koh, The Case against Military Commissions, 96 Am. J. Int'l L 337, 339–342 (2002).

3.   Criticisms were also directed against the prospect of prosecution before military commissions, reflecting concerns about the lack of procedural protections." See, e.g., Koh, supra note 1, at 340:

> These specific legal deficiencies stand atop a much broader rule-of-law concern. International law permits the United States to redress the unprovoked killing of thousands on September 11, 2001, by itself engaging in an armed attack upon the Al Qaeda perpetrators. But should those culprits be captured, the United States must try, not lynch, them to promote four legal values higher than vengeance: holding them accountable for their crimes against humanity; telling the world the truth about those crimes; reaffirming that such acts violate all norms of civilized society; and demonstrating that law-abiding societies, unlike terrorists, respect human rights by channeling retribution into criminal punishment for even the most heinous outlaws.

> The Military Order undermines each of these values. . . .

See also George P. Fletcher, The Military Tribunal Order: On Justice and War: Contradictions in the Proposed Military Tribunals, 25 Harv. J.L. & Pub. Pol'y 635, 639 (2002).

4.   Many of the criticisms and scholarly concerns (but certainly not all) were responded to when the Department of Defense in March, 2002, issued regulations under the authority of the Military Order, titled Military Commissions Order No. 1, as supplemented by subsequent amendments, that spelled out in some detail the procedures to be followed in hearings before the

commissions. These original regulations were published at http://www.defense link.mil/news/Mar2002/d20020321ord.pdf.

3. THE HAMDAN CASE

HAMDAN V. RUMSFELD
548 U.S. 557 (2006)

[The opinion of the Court and the concurring opinions are reproduced here. The dissenting opinions have been omitted.]

ON WRIT OF CERTIORARI TO THE UNITED STATES COURT OF APPEALS FOR THE DISTRICT OF COLUMBIA CIRCUIT

JUSTICE STEVENS announced the judgment of the Court and delivered the opinion of the Court with respect to Parts I through IV, Parts VI through VI-D-iii, Part VI-D-v, and Part VII, and an opinion with respect to Parts V and VI-D-iv, in which JUSTICE SOUTER, JUSTICE GINSBURG, and JUSTICE BREYER join.

Petitioner Salim Ahmed Hamdan, a Yemeni national, is in custody at an American prison in Guantanamo Bay, Cuba. In November 2001, during hostilities between the United States and the Taliban (which then governed Afghanistan), Hamdan was captured by militia forces and turned over to the U.S. military. In June 2002, he was transported to Guantanamo Bay. Over a year later, the President deemed him eligible for trial by military commission for then-unspecified crimes. After another year had passed, Hamdan was charged with one count of conspiracy "to commit . . . offenses triable by military commission."

Hamdan filed petitions for writs of habeas corpus and mandamus to challenge the Executive Branch's intended means of prosecuting this charge. He concedes that a court-martial constituted in accordance with the Uniform Code of Military Justice (UCMJ), 10 U.S.C. § 801 et seq. (2000 ed. and Supp. III), would have authority to try him. His objection is that the military commission the President has convened lacks such authority, for two principal reasons: First, neither congressional Act nor the common law of war supports trial by this commission for the crime of conspiracy— an offense that, Hamdan says, is not a violation of the law of war. Second, Hamdan contends, the procedures that the President has adopted to try him violate the most basic tenets of military and international law, including the principle that a defendant must be permitted to see and hear the evidence against him.

The District Court granted Hamdan's request for a writ of habeas corpus. 344 F. Supp. 2d 152 (DC 2004). The Court of Appeals for the District of Columbia Circuit reversed. 415 F. 3d 33 (2005). Recognizing, as we did over a half-century ago, that trial by military commission is an extraordinary measure raising important questions about the balance of powers in our constitutional structure, Ex parte Quirin, 317 U.S. 1, 19 (1942), we granted certiorari

For the reasons that follow, we conclude that the military commission convened to try Hamdan lacks power to proceed because its structure and procedures violate both the UCMJ and the Geneva Conventions. Four of us also conclude, see Part V, infra, that the offense with which Hamdan has been charged is not an "offens[e] that by . . . the law of war may be tried by military commissions." 10 U.S.C. § 821.

On September 11, 2001, agents of the al Qaeda terrorist organization hijacked commercial airplanes and attacked the World Trade Center in New York City and the national headquarters of the Department of Defense in Arlington, Virginia. Americans will never forget the devastation wrought by these acts. Nearly 3,000 civilians were killed.

Congress responded by adopting a Joint Resolution authorizing the President to "use all necessary and appropriate force against those nations, organizations, or persons he determines planned, authorized, committed, or aided the terrorist attacks . . . in order to prevent any future acts of international terrorism against the United States by such nations, organizations or persons." Authorization for Use of Military Force (AUMF), 115 Stat. 224, note following 50 U.S.C. § 1541 (2000 ed., Supp. III). Acting pursuant to the AUMF, and having determined that the Taliban regime had supported al Qaeda, the President ordered the Armed Forces of the United States to invade Afghanistan. In the ensuing hostilities, hundreds of individuals, Hamdan among them, were captured and eventually detained at Guantanamo Bay.

On November 13, 2001, while the United States was still engaged in active combat with the Taliban, the President issued a comprehensive military order intended to govern the "Detention, Treatment, and Trial of Certain Non-Citizens in the War Against Terrorism," 66 Fed. Reg. 57833 (hereinafter November 13 Order or Order). Those subject to the November 13 Order include any noncitizen for whom the President determines "there is reason to believe" that he or she (1) "is or was" a member of al Qaeda or (2) has engaged or participated in terrorist activities aimed at or harmful to the United States. Id., at 57834. Any such individual "shall, when tried, be tried by military commission for any and all offenses triable by military commission that such individual is alleged to have committed, and may be punished in accordance with the penalties provided under applicable law, including imprisonment or death." Ibid. The November 13 Order vested in the Secretary of Defense the power to appoint military commissions to try individuals subject to the Order, but that power has since been delegated to John D. Altenberg, Jr., a retired Army major general and longtime military lawyer who has been designated "Appointing Authority for Military Commissions."

On July 3, 2003, the President announced his determination that Hamdan and five other detainees at Guantanamo Bay were subject to the November 13 Order and thus triable by military commission. In December 2003, military counsel was appointed to represent Hamdan. Two months later, counsel filed demands for charges and for a speedy trial pursuant to Article 10 of the UCMJ, 10 U.S.C. § 810. On February 23, 2004, the legal adviser to the Appointing Authority denied the applications, ruling that Hamdan was not entitled to any of the protections of the UCMJ. Not until July 13, 2004, after Hamdan had commenced this action in the United States District Court for the Western District of Washington, did the Government finally charge him with the offense for which, a year earlier, he had been deemed eligible for trial by military commission.

The charging document, which is unsigned, contains 13 numbered paragraphs. The first two paragraphs recite the asserted bases for the military commission's jurisdiction—namely, the November 13 Order and the President's July 3, 2003, declaration that Hamdan is eligible for trial by military commission. The next nine paragraphs, collectively entitled "General Allegations," describe al Qaeda's activities from its inception in 1989 through 2001 and identify Osama bin Laden as the group's leader. Hamdan is not mentioned in these paragraphs.

Only the final two paragraphs, entitled "Charge: Conspiracy," contain allegations against Hamdan. Paragraph 12 charges that "from on or about February 1996 to on or about November 24, 2001," Hamdan "willfully and knowingly joined an enterprise of persons who shared a common criminal purpose and conspired and agreed with [named members of al Qaeda] to commit the following offenses triable by military commission: attacking civilians; attacking civilian objects; murder by an unprivileged belligerent; and terrorism." App. to Pet. for Cert. 65a. There is no allegation that Hamdan had any command responsibilities, played a leadership role, or participated in the planning of any activity.

Paragraph 13 lists four "overt acts" that Hamdan is alleged to have committed sometime between 1996 and November 2001 in furtherance of the "enterprise and conspiracy": (1) he acted as Osama bin Laden's "bodyguard and personal driver," "believ[ing]" all the while that bin Laden "and his associates were involved in" terrorist acts prior to and including the attacks of September 11, 2001; (2) he arranged for transportation of, and actually transported, weapons used by al Qaeda members and by bin Laden's bodyguards (Hamdan among them); (3) he "drove or accompanied [O]sama bin Laden to various al Qaida-sponsored training camps, press conferences, or lectures," at which bin Laden encouraged attacks against

Americans; and (4) he received weapons training at al Qaeda-sponsored camps. Id., at 65a–67a.

. . .

On November 7, 2005, we granted certiorari to decide whether the military commission convened to try Hamdan has authority to do so, and whether Hamdan may rely on the Geneva Conventions in these proceedings.

. . .

As the Court of Appeals here recognized, Quirin "provides a compelling historical precedent for the power of civilian courts to entertain challenges that seek to interrupt the processes of military commissions." The circumstances of this case, like those in Quirin, simply do not implicate the "obligations of comity" that, under appropriate circumstances, justify abstention.

Finally, the Government has identified no other "important countervailing interest" that would permit federal courts to depart from their general "duty to exercise the jurisdiction that is conferred upon them by Congress." To the contrary, Hamdan and the Government both have a compelling interest in knowing in advance whether Hamdan may be tried by a military commission that arguably is without any basis in law and operates free from many of the procedural rules prescribed by Congress for courts-martial—rules intended to safeguard the accused and ensure the reliability of any conviction. While we certainly do not foreclose the possibility that abstention may be appropriate in some cases seeking review of ongoing military commission proceedings (such as military commissions convened on the battlefield), the foregoing discussion makes clear that, under our precedent, abstention is not justified here. We therefore proceed to consider the merits of Hamdan's challenge.

IV

The military commission, a tribunal neither mentioned in the Constitution nor created by statute, was born of military necessity. See W. Winthrop, Military Law and Precedents 831 (rev. 2d ed. 1920) (hereinafter Winthrop). Though foreshadowed in some respects by earlier tribunals like the Board of General Officers that General Washington convened to try British Major John André for spying during the Revolutionary War, the commission "as such" was inaugurated in 1847. Id., at 832; G. Davis, A Treatise on the Military Law of the United States 308 (2d ed. 1909) (hereinafter Davis). As commander of occupied Mexican territory, and having available to him no other tribunal, General Winfield Scott that year ordered the establishment of both " 'military commissions' " to try ordinary crimes committed in the occupied territory and a "council of war" to try offenses against the law of war. Winthrop 832 (emphases in original).

When the exigencies of war next gave rise to a need for use of military commissions, during the Civil War, the dual system favored by General Scott was not adopted. Instead, a single tribunal often took jurisdiction over ordinary crimes, war crimes, and breaches of military orders alike. As further discussed below, each aspect of that seemingly broad jurisdiction was in fact supported by a separate military exigency. Generally, though, the need for military commissions during this period—as during the Mexican War—was driven largely by the then very limited jurisdiction of courts-martial: "The occasion for the military commission arises principally from the fact that the jurisdiction of the court-martial proper, in our law, is restricted by statute almost exclusively to members of the military force and to certain specific offences defined in a written code." Id., at 831 (emphasis in original).

Exigency alone, of course, will not justify the establishment and use of penal tribunals not contemplated by Article I, § 8 and Article III, § 1 of the Constitution unless some other part of that document authorizes a response to the felt need. See Ex parte Milligan, 4 Wall. 2, 121 (1866) ("Certainly no part of the judicial power of the country was conferred on [military commissions]"); . . . And that authority, if it exists, can derive only from the powers granted jointly to the President and Congress in time of war. See id., at 26–29; In re Yamashita, 327 U.S. 1, 11 (1946).

The Constitution makes the President the "Commander in Chief" of the Armed Forces, Art. II, § 2, cl. 1, but vests in Congress the powers to "declare War . . . and make Rules concerning Captures on Land and Water," Art. I, § 8, cl. 11, to "raise and support Armies," id., cl. 12, to "define and punish . . . Offences against the Law of Nations," id., cl. 10, and "To make Rules for the Government and Regulation of the land and naval Forces," id., cl. 14. The interplay between these powers was described by Chief Justice Chase in the seminal case of Ex parte Milligan:

"The power to make the necessary laws is in Congress; the power to execute in the President. Both powers imply many subordinate and auxiliary powers. Each includes all authorities essential to its due exercise. But neither can the President, in war more than in peace, intrude upon the proper authority of Congress, nor Congress upon the proper authority of the President. . . . Congress cannot direct the conduct of campaigns, nor can the President, or any commander under him, without the sanction of Congress, institute tribunals for the trial and punishment of offences, either of soldiers or civilians, unless in cases of a controlling necessity, which justifies what it compels, or at least insures acts of indemnity from the justice of the legislature." 4 Wall., at 139–140.

Whether Chief Justice Chase was correct in suggesting that the President may constitutionally convene military commissions "without the sanction of Congress" in cases of "controlling necessity" is a question this

Court has not answered definitively, and need not answer today. For we held in Quirin that Congress had, through Article of War 15, sanctioned the use of military commissions in such circumstances. 317 U.S., at 28 ("By the Articles of War, and especially Article 15, Congress has explicitly provided, so far as it may constitutionally do so, that military tribunals shall have jurisdiction to try offenders or offenses against the law of war in appropriate cases"). Article 21 of the UCMJ, the language of which is substantially identical to the old Article 15 and was preserved by Congress after World War II, reads as follows:

"Jurisdiction of courts-martial not exclusive.

"The provisions of this code conferring jurisdiction upon courts-martial shall not be construed as depriving military commissions, provost courts, or other military tribunals of concurrent jurisdiction in respect of offenders or offenses that by statute or by the law of war may be tried by such military commissions, provost courts, or other military tribunals." 64 Stat. 115.

We have no occasion to revisit Quirin's controversial characterization of Article of War 15 as congressional authorization for military commissions. Contrary to the Government's assertion, however, even Quirin did not view the authorization as a sweeping mandate for the President to "invoke military commissions when he deems them necessary." Rather, the Quirin Court recognized that Congress had simply preserved what power, under the Constitution and the common law of war, the President had had before 1916 to convene military commissions—with the express condition that the President and those under his command comply with the law of war. That much is evidenced by the Court's inquiry, following its conclusion that Congress had authorized military commissions, into whether the law of war had indeed been complied with in that case. See ibid.

The Government would have us dispense with the inquiry that the Quirin Court undertook and find in either the AUMF or the DTA specific, overriding authorization for the very commission that has been convened to try Hamdan. Neither of these congressional Acts, however, expands the President's authority to convene military commissions. First, while we assume that the AUMF activated the President's war powers, see Hamdi v. Rumsfeld, 542 U.S. 507 (2004) (plurality opinion), and that those powers include the authority to convene military commissions in appropriate circumstances, see id., at 518; Quirin, 317 U.S., at 28–29; see also Yamashita, 327 U.S., at 11, there is nothing in the text or legislative history of the AUMF even hinting that Congress intended to expand or alter the authorization set forth in Article 21 of the UCMJ.

Likewise, the DTA cannot be read to authorize this commission. Although the DTA, unlike either Article 21 or the AUMF, was enacted after the President had convened Hamdan's commission, it contains no language authorizing that tribunal or any other at Guantanamo Bay. The DTA obviously "recognize[s]" the existence of the Guantanamo Bay commissions in the weakest sense, Brief for Respondents 15, because it references some of the military orders governing them and creates limited judicial review of their "final decision[s]," DTA § 1005(e)(3), 119 Stat. 2743. But the statute also pointedly reserves judgment on whether "the Constitution and laws of the United States are applicable" in reviewing such decisions and whether, if they are, the "standards and procedures" used to try Hamdan and other detainees actually violate the "Constitution and laws." Ibid.

Together, the UCMJ, the AUMF, and the DTA at most acknowledge a general Presidential authority to convene military commissions in circumstances where justified under the "Constitution and laws," including the law of war. Absent a more specific congressional authorization, the task of this Court is, as it was in Quirin, to decide whether Hamdan's military commission is so justified. It is to that inquiry we now turn.

V

The common law governing military commissions may be gleaned from past practice and what sparse legal precedent exists. Commissions historically have been used in three situations. See Bradley & Goldsmith, Congressional Authorization and the War on Terrorism, 118 Harv. L. Rev. 2048, 2132–2133 (2005); . . . First, they have substituted for civilian courts at times and in places where martial law has been declared. . . . Second, commissions have been established to try civilians "as part of a temporary military government over occupied enemy territory or territory regained from an enemy where civilian government cannot and does not function." . . . Illustrative of this second kind of commission is the one that was established, with jurisdiction to apply the German Criminal Code, in occupied Germany following the end of World War II.

The third type of commission, convened as an "incident to the conduct of war" when there is a need "to seize and subject to disciplinary measures those enemies who in their attempt to thwart or impede our military effort have violated the law of war," Quirin, 317 U.S., at 28–29, has been described as "utterly different" from the other two. Bickers, Military Commissions are Constitutionally Sound: A Response to Professors Katyal and Tribe, 34 Tex. Tech. L. Rev. 899, 902 (2002–2003). Not only is its jurisdiction limited to offenses cognizable during time of war, but its role is primarily a factfinding one—to determine, typically on the battlefield itself, whether the defendant has violated the law of war. The last time the U.S. Armed Forces used the law-of-war military commission was during World War II. In Quirin, this Court sanctioned President Roosevelt's use of such a tribunal to try Nazi saboteurs captured on American soil during the War. And in Yamashita, we held that a military commission had jurisdiction to try a Japanese commander for failing to prevent troops under his command from committing atrocities in the Philippines.

Quirin is the model the Government invokes most frequently to defend the commission convened to try Hamdan. That is both appropriate and unsurprising. Since Guantanamo Bay is neither enemy-occupied territory nor under martial law, the law-of-war commission is the only model available. At the same time, no more robust model of executive power exists; Quirin represents the high-water mark of military power to try enemy combatants for war crimes.

The classic treatise penned by Colonel William Winthrop, whom we have called "the 'Blackstone of Military Law,'" Reid v. Covert, 354 U.S. 1, 19, n. 38 (1957) (plurality opinion), describes at least four preconditions for exercise of jurisdiction by a tribunal of the type convened to try Hamdan. First, "[a] military commission, (except where otherwise authorized by statute), can legally assume jurisdiction only of offenses committed within the field of the command of the convening commander." Winthrop 836. The "field of command" in these circumstances means the "theatre of war." Second, the offense charged "must have been committed within the period of the war." No jurisdiction exists to try offenses "committed either before or after the war." Third, a military commission not established pursuant to martial law or an occupation may try only "[i]ndividuals of the enemy's army who have been guilty of illegitimate warfare or other offences in violation of the laws of war" and members of one's own army "who, in time of war, become chargeable with crimes or offences not cognizable, or triable, by the criminal courts or under the Articles of war." Finally, a law-of-war commission has jurisdiction to try only two kinds of offense: "Violations of the laws and usages of war cognizable by military tribunals only," and "[b]reaches of military orders or regulations for which offenders are not legally triable by court-martial under the Articles of war."

All parties agree that Colonel Winthrop's treatise accurately describes the common law governing military commissions, and that the jurisdictional limitations he identifies were incorporated in Article of War 15 and, later, Article 21 of the UCMJ. It also is undisputed that Hamdan's commission lacks jurisdiction to try him unless the charge "properly set[s] forth, not only the details of the act charged, but the circumstances conferring jurisdiction." Id., at 842 (emphasis in original). The question is whether the preconditions designed to ensure that a military necessity exists to justify the use of this extraordinary tribunal have been satisfied here.

The charge against Hamdan, described in detail in Part I, supra, alleges a conspiracy extending over a number of years, from 1996 to

November 2001. All but two months of that more than 5-year-long period preceded the attacks of September 11, 2001, and the enactment of the AUMF—the Act of Congress on which the Government relies for exercise of its war powers and thus for its authority to convene military commissions. Neither the purported agreement with Osama bin Laden and others to commit war crimes, nor a single overt act, is alleged to have occurred in a theater of war or on any specified date after September 11, 2001. None of the overt acts that Hamdan is alleged to have committed violates the law of war.

These facts alone cast doubt on the legality of the charge and, hence, the commission; as Winthrop makes plain, the offense alleged must have been committed both in a theater of war and during, not before, the relevant conflict. But the deficiencies in the time and place allegations also underscore—indeed are symptomatic of—the most serious defect of this charge: The offense it alleges is not triable by law-of-war military commission. See Yamashita, 327 U.S., at 13 ("Neither congressional action nor the military orders constituting the commission authorized it to place petitioner on trial unless the charge proffered against him is of a violation of the law of war").

There is no suggestion that Congress has, in exercise of its constitutional authority to "define and punish . . . Offences against the Law of Nations," U.S. Const., Art. I, § 8, cl. 10, positively identified "conspiracy" as a war crime. As we explained in Quirin, that is not necessarily fatal to the Government's claim of authority to try the alleged offense by military commission; Congress, through Article 21 of the UCMJ, has "incorporated by reference" the common law of war, which may render triable by military commission certain offenses not defined by statute. When, however, neither the elements of the offense nor the range of permissible punishments is defined by statute or treaty, the precedent must be plain and unambiguous. To demand any less would be to risk concentrating in military hands a degree of adjudicative and punitive power in excess of that contemplated either by statute or by the Constitution. . . .

This high standard was met in Quirin; the violation there alleged was, by "universal agreement and practice" both in this country and internationally, recognized as an offense against the law of war. . . .

At a minimum, the Government must make a substantial showing that the crime for which it seeks to try a defendant by military commission is acknowledged to be an offense against the law of war. That burden is far from satisfied here. The crime of "conspiracy" has rarely if ever been tried as such in this country by any law-of-war military commission not exercising some other form of jurisdiction, and does not appear in either the Geneva Conventions or the Hague Conventions—the major treaties on the law of war. Winthrop explains that under the common law governing military commissions, it is not enough to intend to violate the law of war and commit overt acts in furtherance of that intention unless the overt acts either are themselves offenses against the law of war or constitute steps sufficiently substantial to qualify as an attempt. See Winthrop 841

The Government cites three sources that it says show otherwise. First, it points out that the Nazi saboteurs in Quirin were charged with conspiracy. Second, it observes that Winthrop at one point in his treatise identifies conspiracy as an offense "prosecuted by military commissions." Finally, it notes that another military historian, Charles Roscoe Howland, lists conspiracy " 'to violate the laws of war by destroying life or property in aid of the enemy' " as an offense that was tried as a violation of the law of war during the Civil War. On close analysis, however, these sources at best lend little support to the Government's position and at worst undermine it. By any measure, they fail to satisfy the high standard of clarity required to justify the use of a military commission.

That the defendants in Quirin were charged with conspiracy is not persuasive, since the Court declined to address whether the offense actually qualified as a violation of the law of war—let alone one triable by military commission. The Quirin defendants were charged with the following offenses:

"[I.]　Violation of the law of war.

"[II.]　Violation of Article 81 of the Articles of War, defining the offense of relieving or attempting to relieve, or corresponding with or giving intelligence to, the enemy.

"[III.]　Violation of Article 82, defining the offense of spying.

"[IV.]　Conspiracy to commit the offenses alleged in charges [I, II, and III]." 317 U.S., at 23.

The Government, defending its charge, argued that the conspiracy alleged "constitute[d] an additional violation of the law of war." The saboteurs disagreed; they maintained that "[t]he charge of conspiracy can not stand if the other charges fall." The Court, however, declined to resolve the dispute. It concluded, first, that the specification supporting Charge I adequately alleged a "violation of the law of war" that was not "merely colorable or without foundation." The facts the Court deemed sufficient for this purpose were that the defendants, admitted enemy combatants, entered upon U.S. territory in time of war without uniform "for the purpose of destroying property used or useful in prosecuting the war." That act was "a hostile and warlike" one. The Court was careful in its decision to identify an overt, "complete" act. Responding to the argument that the saboteurs had "not actually committed or attempted to commit any act of depredation or entered the theatre or zone of active military operations" and therefore had not violated the law of war, the Court responded that they had actually "passed our military and naval lines and defenses or went behind those lines, in civilian dress and with hostile purpose." "The offense was complete when with that purpose they entered—or, having so entered, they remained upon—our territory in time of war without uniform or other appropriate means of identification."

Turning to the other charges alleged, the Court explained that "[s]ince the first specification of Charge I sets forth a violation of the law of war, we have no occasion to pass on the adequacy of the second specification of Charge I, or to construe the 81st and 82nd Articles of War for the purpose of ascertaining whether the specifications under Charges II and III allege violations of those Articles or whether if so construed they are constitutional." No mention was made at all of Charge IV—the conspiracy charge.

If anything, Quirin supports Hamdan's argument that conspiracy is not a violation of the law of war. Not only did the Court pointedly omit any discussion of the conspiracy charge, but its analysis of Charge I placed special emphasis on the completion of an offense; it took seriously the saboteurs' argument that there can be no violation of a law of war—at least not one triable by military commission—without the actual commission of or attempt to commit a "hostile and warlike act."

That limitation makes eminent sense when one considers the necessity from whence this kind of military commission grew: The need to dispense swift justice, often in the form of execution, to illegal belligerents captured on the battlefield. . . . The same urgency would not have been felt vis—vis enemies who had done little more than agree to violate the laws of war. Cf. 31 Op. Atty. Gen. 356, 357, 361 (1918) (opining that a German spy could not be tried by military commission because, having been apprehended before entering "any camp, fortification or other military premises of the United States," he had "committed [his offenses] outside of the field of military operations"). The Quirin Court acknowledged as much when it described the President's authority to use law-of-war military commissions as the power to "seize and subject to disciplinary measures those enemies who in their attempt to thwart or impede our military effort have violated the law of war."

Winthrop and Howland are only superficially more helpful to the Government. Howland, granted, lists "conspiracy by two or more to violate the laws of war by destroying life or property in aid of the enemy" as one of over 20 "offenses against the laws and usages of war" "passed upon and punished by military commissions." Howland 1071. But while the records of cases that Howland cites following his list of offenses against the law of war support inclusion of the other offenses mentioned, they provide no support for the inclusion of conspiracy as a violation of the law of war. Winthrop, apparently recognizing as much, excludes conspiracy of any kind from his own list of offenses against the law of war. See Winthrop 839–840. . .

Finally, international sources confirm that the crime charged here is not a recognized violation of the law of war. . . . The International Military Tribunal at Nuremberg, over the prosecution's objections, pointedly refused to recognize as a violation of the law of war conspiracy to commit war crimes, . . . and convicted only Hitler's most senior associates of conspiracy to wage aggressive war, see S. Pomorski, Conspiracy and Criminal Organization, in the Nuremberg Trial and International Law 213, 233–235 (G. Ginsburgs & V. Kudriavtsev eds. 1990). As one prominent figure from the Nuremberg trials has explained, members of the Tribunal objected to recognition of conspiracy as a violation of the law of war on the ground that "[t]he Anglo-American concept of conspiracy was not part of European legal systems and arguably not an element of the internationally recognized laws of war." T. Taylor, Anatomy of the Nuremberg Trials: A Personal Memoir 36 (1992); . . . .

In sum, the sources that the Government and Justice Thomas rely upon to show that conspiracy to violate the law of war is itself a violation of the law of war in fact demonstrate quite the opposite. Far from making the requisite substantial showing, the Government has failed even to offer a "merely colorable" case for inclusion of conspiracy among those offenses cognizable by law-of-war military commission. Because the charge does not support the commission's jurisdiction, the commission lacks authority to try Hamdan.

The charge's shortcomings are not merely formal, but are indicative of a broader inability on the Executive's part here to satisfy the most basic precondition—at least in the absence of specific congressional authorization—for establishment of military commissions: military necessity. Hamdan's tribunal was appointed not by a military commander in the field of battle, but by a retired major general stationed away from any active hostilities. Hamdan is charged not with an overt act for which he was caught redhanded in a theater of war and which military efficiency demands be tried expeditiously, but with an agreement the inception of which long predated the attacks of September 11, 2001 and the AUMF. That may well be a crime, but it is not an offense that "by the law of war may be tried by military commissio[n]." 10 U.S.C. § 821. None of the overt acts alleged to have been committed in furtherance of the agreement is itself a war crime, or even necessarily occurred during time of, or in a theater of, war. Any urgent need for imposition or execution of judgment is utterly belied by the record; Hamdan was arrested in November 2001 and he was not charged until mid-2004. These simply are not the circumstances in which, by any stretch of the historical evidence or this Court's precedents, a military commission established by Executive Order under the authority of Article 21 of the UCMJ may lawfully try a person and subject him to punishment.

VI

Whether or not the Government has charged Hamdan with an offense against the law of war cognizable by military commission, the commission lacks power to proceed. The UCMJ conditions the President's use of military commissions on compliance not only with the American common law of war, but also with the rest of the UCMJ itself, insofar as applicable, and with the "rules and precepts of the law of nations," Quirin, 317 U.S., at 28—including, inter alia, the four Geneva Conventions signed in 1949. See Yamashita, 327 U.S., at 20–21, 23–24. The procedures that the Government has decreed will govern Hamdan's trial by commission violate these laws.

A

The commission's procedures are set forth in Commission Order No. 1, which was amended most recently on August 31, 2005—after Hamdan's trial had already begun. Every commission established pursuant to Commission Order No. 1 must have a presiding officer and at least three other members, all of whom must be commissioned officers. § 4(A)(1). The presiding officer's job is to rule on questions of law and other evidentiary and interlocutory issues; the other members make findings and, if applicable, sentencing decisions. § 4(A)(5). The accused is entitled to appointed military counsel and may hire civilian counsel at his own expense so long as such counsel is a U.S. citizen with security clearance "at the level SECRET or higher." §§ 4(C)(2)–(3).

The accused also is entitled to a copy of the charge(s) against him, both in English and his own language (if different), to a presumption of innocence, and to certain other rights typically afforded criminal defendants in civilian courts and courts-martial. See §§ 5(A)–(P). These rights are subject, however, to one glaring condition: The accused and his civilian counsel may be excluded from, and precluded from ever learning what evidence was presented during, any part of the proceeding that either the Appointing Authority or the presiding officer decides to "close." Grounds for such closure "include the protection of information classified or classifiable . . .; information protected by law or rule from unauthorized disclosure; the physical safety of participants in Commission proceedings, including prospective witnesses; intelligence and law enforcement sources, methods, or activities; and other national security interests." § 6(B)(3). Appointed military defense counsel must be privy to these closed sessions, but may, at the presiding officer's discretion, be forbidden to reveal to his or her client what took place therein. Ibid.

Another striking feature of the rules governing Hamdan's commission is that they permit the admission of any evidence that, in the opinion of the presiding officer, "would have probative value to a reasonable person." § 6(D)(1). Under this test, not only is testimonial hearsay and evidence obtained through coercion fully admissible, but neither live testimony nor witnesses' written statements need be sworn. See §§ 6(D)(2)(b), (3). Moreover, the accused and his civilian counsel may be denied access to evidence in the form of "protected information" (which includes classified information as well as "information protected by law or rule from unauthorized disclosure" and "information concerning other national security interests," §§ 6(B)(3), 6(D)(5)(a)(v)), so long as the presiding officer concludes that the evidence is "probative" under § 6(D)(1) and that its admission without the accused's knowledge would not "result in the denial of a full and fair trial." § 6(D)(5)(b). Finally, a presiding officer's determination that evidence "would not have probative value to a reasonable person" may be overridden by a majority of the other commission members. § 6(D)(1).

Once all the evidence is in, the commission members (not including the presiding officer) must vote on the accused's guilt. A two-thirds vote will suffice for both a verdict of guilty and for imposition of any sentence not including death (the imposition of which requires a unanimous vote). § 6(F). Any appeal is taken to a three-member review panel composed of military officers and designated by the Secretary of Defense, only one member of which need have experience as a judge. § 6(H)(4). The review panel is directed to "disregard any variance from procedures specified in this Order or elsewhere that would not materially have affected the outcome of the trial before the Commission." Ibid. Once the panel makes its recommendation to the Secretary of Defense, the Secretary can either remand for further proceedings or forward the record to the President with his recommendation as to final disposition. § 6(H)(5). The President then, unless he has delegated the task to the Secretary, makes the "final decision." § 6(H)(6). He may change the commission's findings or sentence only in a manner favorable to the accused. Ibid.

B

Hamdan raises both general and particular objections to the procedures set forth in Commission Order No. 1. His general objection is that the procedures' admitted deviation from those governing courts-martial itself renders the commission illegal. Chief among his particular objections are that he may, under the Commission Order, be convicted based on evidence he has not seen or heard, and that any evidence admitted against him need not comply with the admissibility or relevance rules typically applicable in criminal trials and court-martial proceedings.

The Government objects to our consideration of any procedural challenge at this stage . . . .

First, because Hamdan apparently is not subject to the death penalty (at least as matters now stand) and may receive a sentence shorter than 10 years' imprisonment, he has no automatic right to review of the commission's "final decision" before a federal court under the DTA. See § 1005(e)(3), 119 Stat. 2743. Second, contrary to the Government's assertion, there is a "basis to presume" that the procedures employed during Hamdan's trial will violate the law: The procedures are described with particularity in Commission Order No. 1, and implementation of some of them has already occurred. One of Hamdan's complaints is that he will be, and indeed already has been, excluded from his own trial. See Reply Brief for Petitioner 12; App. to Pet. for Cert. 45a. Under these circumstances, review of the procedures in advance of a "final decision"— the timing of which is left entirely to the discretion of the President under the DTA—is appropriate. We turn, then, to consider the merits of Hamdan's procedural challenge.

C

In part because the difference between military commissions and courts-martial originally was a difference of jurisdiction alone, and in part to protect against abuse and ensure evenhandedness under the pressures of war, the procedures governing trials by military commission historically have been the same as those governing courts-martial. See, e.g., 1 The War of the Rebellion 248 (2d series 1894) (General Order 1 issued during the Civil War required military commissions to "be constituted in a similar manner and their proceedings be conducted according to the same general rules as courts-martial in order to prevent abuses which might otherwise arise"). Accounts of commentators from Winthrop through General Crowder—who drafted Article of War 15 and whose views have been deemed "authoritative" by this Court, Madsen, 343 U.S., at 353—confirm as much. As recently as the Korean and Vietnam wars, during which use of military commissions was contemplated but never made, the principle of procedural parity was espoused as a background assumption. See Paust, Antiterrorism Military Commissions: Courting Illegality, 23 Mich. J. Int'l L. 1, 3–5 (2001–2002).

There is a glaring historical exception to this general rule. The procedures and evidentiary rules used to try General Yamashita near the end of World War II deviated in significant respects from those then governing courts-martial. See 327 U.S. 1. The force of that precedent, however, has been seriously undermined by post-World War II developments.

Yamashita, from late 1944 until September 1945, was Commanding General of the Fourteenth Army Group of the Imperial Japanese Army, which had exercised control over the Philippine Islands. On September 3, 1945, after American forces regained control of the Philippines, Yamashita surrendered. Three weeks later, he was charged with violations of the law of war. A few weeks after that, he was arraigned before a military commission convened in the Philippines. He pleaded not guilty, and his trial lasted for two months. On December 7, 1945, Yamashita was convicted and sentenced to hang. This Court upheld the denial of his petition for a writ of habeas corpus.

The procedures and rules of evidence employed during Yamashita's trial departed so far from those used in courts-martial that they generated an unusually long and vociferous critique from two Members of this Court. See id., at 41–81 (Rutledge, J., joined by Murphy, J., dissenting). Among the dissenters' primary concerns was that the commission had free rein to consider all evidence "which in the commission's opinion 'would be of assistance in proving or disproving the charge,' without any of the usual modes of authentication."

The majority, however, did not pass on the merits of Yamashita's procedural challenges because it concluded that his status disentitled him to any protection under the Articles of War (specifically, those set forth in Article 38, which would become Article 36 of the UCMJ) or the Geneva Convention of 1929, 47 Stat. 2021 (1929 Geneva Convention). The Court explained that Yamashita was neither a "person made subject to the Articles of War by Article 2" thereof, 327 U.S., at 20, nor a protected prisoner of war being tried for crimes committed during his detention, id., at 21.

At least partially in response to subsequent criticism of General Yamashita's trial, the UCMJ's codification of the Articles of War after World War II expanded the category of persons subject thereto to include defendants in Yamashita's (and Hamdan's) position, and the Third Geneva Convention of 1949 extended prisoner-of-war protections to individuals tried for crimes committed before their capture. See 3 Int'l Comm. of Red Cross, Commentary: Geneva Convention Relative to the Treatment of Prisoners of War 413 (1960) (hereinafter GCIII Commentary) (explaining that Article 85, which extends the Convention's protections to "[p]risoners of war prosecuted under the laws of the Detaining Power for acts committed prior to capture," was adopted in response to judicial interpretations of the 1929 Convention, including this Court's decision in Yamashita). The most notorious exception to the principle of uniformity, then, has been stripped of its precedential value.

The uniformity principle is not an inflexible one; it does not preclude all departures from the procedures dictated for use by courts-martial. But any departure must be tailored to the exigency that necessitates it. See Winthrop 835, n. 81. That understanding is reflected in Article 36 of the UCMJ, which provides:

"(a) The procedure, including modes of proof, in cases before courts-martial, courts of inquiry, military commissions, and other military tribunals may be prescribed by the President by regulations which shall, so far as he considers practicable, apply the principles of law and the rules of evidence generally recognized in the trial of criminal cases in the United States district courts, but which may not be contrary to or inconsistent with this chapter.

"(b) All rules and regulations made under this article shall be uniform insofar as practicable and shall be reported to Congress." 70A Stat. 50.

Article 36 places two restrictions on the President's power to promulgate rules of procedure for courts-martial and military commissions alike. First, no procedural rule he adopts may be "contrary to or inconsistent with" the UCMJ—however practical it may seem. Second, the rules adopted must be "uniform insofar as practicable." That is, the rules applied to military commissions must be the same as those applied to courts-martial unless such uniformity proves impracticable.

Hamdan argues that Commission Order No. 1 violates both of these restrictions; he maintains that the procedures described in the Commission Order are inconsistent with the UCMJ and that the Government has offered no explanation for their deviation from the procedures governing courts-martial, which are set forth in the Manual for Courts-Martial, United States (2005 ed.) (Manual for Courts-Martial). Among the inconsistencies Hamdan identifies is that between § 6 of the Commission Order, which permits exclusion of the accused from proceedings and denial of his access to evidence in certain circumstances, and the UCMJ's requirement that "[a]ll . . . proceedings" other than votes and deliberations by courts-martial "shall be made a part of the record and shall be in the presence of the accused." 10 U.S.C.A. § 839(c) (Supp. 2006). Hamdan also observes that the Commission Order dispenses with virtually all evidentiary rules applicable in courts-martial.

The Government has three responses. First, it argues, only 9 of the UCMJ's 158 Articles—the ones that expressly mention "military commissions" actually apply to commissions, and Commission Order No. 1 sets forth no procedure that is "contrary to or inconsistent with" those 9 provisions. Second, the Government contends, military commissions would be of no use if the President were hamstrung by those provisions of the UCMJ that govern courts-martial. Finally, the President's determination that "the danger to the safety of the United States and the nature of international terrorism" renders it impracticable "to apply in military commissions . . . the principles of law and rules of evidence generally recognized in the trial of criminal cases in the United States district courts," November 13 Order § 1(f), is, in the Government's view, explanation enough for any deviation from court-martial procedures. See Brief for Respondents 43–47, and n. 22.

Hamdan has the better of this argument. Without reaching the question whether any provision of Commission Order No. 1 is strictly "contrary to or inconsistent with" other provisions of the UCMJ, we conclude that the "practicability" determination the President has made is insufficient to justify variances from the procedures governing courts-martial. Subsection (b) of Article 36 was added after World War II, and requires a different showing of impracticability from the one required by subsection (a). Subsection (a) requires that the rules the President promulgates for courts-martial, provost courts, and military commissions alike conform to those that govern procedures in Article III courts, "so far as he considers practicable." 10 U.S.C. § 836(a) (emphasis added). Subsection (b), by contrast, demands that the rules applied in courts-martial, provost courts, and military commissions—whether or not they conform with the Federal Rules of Evidence—be "uniform insofar as practicable." § 836(b) (emphasis added). Under the latter provision, then, the rules set forth in the Manual for Courts-Martial must apply to military commissions unless impracticable.

The President here has determined, pursuant to subsection (a), that it is impracticable to apply the rules and principles of law that govern "the trial of criminal cases in the United States district courts," § 836(a), to Hamdan's commission. We assume that complete deference is owed that determination. The President has not, however, made a similar official determination that it is impracticable to apply the rules for courts-martial. And even if subsection (b)'s requirements may be satisfied without such an official determination, the requirements of that subsection are not satisfied here.

Nothing in the record before us demonstrates that it would be impracticable to apply court-martial rules in this case. There is no suggestion, for example, of any logistical difficulty in securing properly sworn and authenticated evidence or in applying the usual principles of relevance and admissibility. Assuming arguendo that the reasons articulated in the President's Article 36(a) determination ought to be considered in evaluating the impracticability of applying court-martial rules, the only reason offered in support of that determination is the danger posed by international terrorism. Without for one moment underestimating that danger, it is not evident to us why it should require, in the case of Hamdan's trial, any variance from the rules that govern courts-martial.

The absence of any showing of impracticability is particularly disturbing when considered in light of the clear and admitted failure to apply one of the most fundamental protections afforded not just by the Manual for Courts-Martial but also by the UCMJ itself: the right to be present. See 10 U.S.C.A. § 839(c) (Supp. 2006). Whether or not that departure technically is "contrary to or inconsistent with" the terms of the UCMJ, 10 U.S.C. § 836(a), the jettisoning of so basic a right cannot lightly be excused as "practicable."

Under the circumstances, then, the rules applicable in courts-martial must apply. Since it is undisputed that Commission Order No. 1 deviates in many significant respects from those rules, it necessarily violates Article 36(b).

The Government's objection that requiring compliance with the court-martial rules imposes an undue burden both ignores the plain meaning of Article 36(b) and misunderstands the purpose and the history of military commissions. The military commission was not born of a desire to dispense a more summary form of justice than is afforded by courts-martial; it developed, rather, as a tribunal of necessity to be employed when courts-martial lacked jurisdiction over either the accused or the subject matter. See Winthrop 831. Exigency lent the commission its legitimacy, but did not further justify the wholesale jettisoning of procedural protections. That history explains why the military commission's procedures typically have been the ones used by courts-martial. That the jurisdiction of the two tribunals today may sometimes overlap, see Madsen, 343 U.S., at 354, does not detract from the force of this history; Article 21 did not transform the military commission "from a tribunal of true exigency into a more convenient adjudicatory tool. Article 36, confirming as much, strikes a careful balance between uniform procedure and the need to accommodate exigencies that may sometimes arise in a theater of war. That Article not having been complied with here, the rules specified for Hamdan's trial are illegal.

D

The procedures adopted to try Hamdan also violate the Geneva Conventions. . . .

i

The Court of Appeals relied on Johnson v. Eisentrager, 339 U.S. 763 (1950), to hold that Hamdan could not invoke the Geneva Conventions to challenge the Government's plan to prosecute him in accordance with Commission Order No. 1. Eisentrager involved a challenge by 21 German nationals to their 1945 convictions for war crimes by a military tribunal convened in Nanking, China, and to their subsequent imprisonment in occupied Germany. The petitioners argued, inter alia, that the 1929 Geneva Convention rendered illegal some of the procedures employed during their trials, which they said deviated impermissibly from the procedures used by courts-martial to try American soldiers. We rejected that claim on the merits because the petitioners (unlike Hamdan here) had failed to identify any prejudicial disparity "between the Commission that tried [them] and those that would try an offending soldier of the American forces of like rank," and in any event could claim no protection, under the 1929 Convention, during trials for crimes that occurred before their confinement as prisoners of war.

Buried in a footnote of the opinion, however, is this curious statement suggesting that the Court lacked power even to consider the merits of the Geneva Convention argument:

> "We are not holding that these prisoners have no right which the military authorities are bound to respect. The United States, by the Geneva Convention of July 27, 1929, 47 Stat. 2021, concluded with forty-six other countries, including the German Reich, an agreement upon the treatment to be accorded captives. These prisoners claim to be and are entitled to its protection. It is, however, the obvious scheme of the Agreement that responsibility for observance and enforcement of these rights is upon political and military authorities. Rights of alien enemies are vindicated under it only through protests and intervention of protecting powers as the rights of our citizens against foreign governments are vindicated only by Presidential intervention." Id., at 789, n. 14.

The Court of Appeals, on the strength of this footnote, held that "the 1949 Geneva Convention does not confer upon Hamdan a right to enforce its provisions in court." 415 F. 3d, at 40.

Whatever else might be said about the Eisentrager footnote, it does not control this case. We may assume that "the obvious scheme" of the 1949 Conventions is identical in all relevant respects to that of the 1929 Convention, and even that that scheme would, absent some other provision of law, preclude Hamdan's invocation of the Convention's provisions as an independent source of law binding the Government's actions and furnishing petitioner with any enforceable right. For, regardless of the nature of the rights conferred on Hamdan, they are, as the Government does not dispute, part of the law of war. See Hamdi, 542 U.S., at 520–521 (plurality opinion). And compliance with the law of war is the condition upon which the authority set forth in Article 21 is granted.

ii

For the Court of Appeals, acknowledgment of that condition was no bar to Hamdan's trial by commission. As an alternative to its holding that Hamdan could not invoke the Geneva Conventions at all, the Court of Appeals concluded that the Conventions did not in any event apply to the armed conflict during which Hamdan was captured. The court accepted the Executive's assertions that Hamdan was captured in connection with the

United States' war with al Qaeda and that that war is distinct from the war with the Taliban in Afghanistan. It further reasoned that the war with al Qaeda evades the reach of the Geneva Conventions. See 415 F. 3d, at 41–42. We, like Judge Williams, disagree with the latter conclusion.

The conflict with al Qaeda is not, according to the Government, a conflict to which the full protections afforded detainees under the 1949 Geneva Conventions apply because Article 2 of those Conventions (which appears in all four Conventions) renders the full protections applicable only to "all cases of declared war or of any other armed conflict which may arise between two or more of the High Contracting Parties." 6 U.S.T., at 3318. Since Hamdan was captured and detained incident to the conflict with al Qaeda and not the conflict with the Taliban, and since al Qaeda, unlike Afghanistan, is not a "High Contracting Party"—i.e., a signatory of the Conventions, the protections of those Conventions are not, it is argued, applicable to Hamdan.

We need not decide the merits of this argument because there is at least one provision of the Geneva Conventions that applies here even if the relevant conflict is not one between signatories. Article 3, often referred to as Common Article 3 because, like Article 2, it appears in all four Geneva Conventions, provides that in a "conflict not of an international character occurring in the territory of one of the High Contracting Parties, each Party to the conflict shall be bound to apply, as a minimum," certain provisions protecting "[p]ersons taking no active part in the hostilities, including members of armed forces who have laid down their arms and those placed hors de combat by . . . detention." One such provision prohibits "the passing of sentences and the carrying out of executions without previous judgment pronounced by a regularly constituted court affording all the judicial guarantees which are recognized as indispensable by civilized peoples." Ibid.

The Court of Appeals thought, and the Government asserts, that Common Article 3 does not apply to Hamdan because the conflict with al Qaeda, being " 'international in scope,' " does not qualify as a " 'conflict not of an international character.' " 415 F. 3d, at 41. That reasoning is erroneous. The term "conflict not of an international character" is used here in contradistinction to a conflict between nations. So much is demonstrated by the "fundamental logic [of] the Convention's provisions on its application." Id., at 44 (Williams, J., concurring). Common Article 2 provides that "the present Convention shall apply to all cases of declared war or of any other armed conflict which may arise between two or more of the High Contracting Parties." 6 U.S.T., at 3318 (Art. 2, ¶ 1). High Contracting Parties (signatories) also must abide by all terms of the Conventions vis—vis one another even if one party to the conflict is a nonsignatory "Power," and must so abide vis—vis the nonsignatory if "the latter accepts and applies" those terms. Ibid. (Art. 2, ¶ 3). Common Article

3, by contrast, affords some minimal protection, falling short of full protection under the Conventions, to individuals associated with neither a signatory nor even a nonsignatory "Power" who are involved in a conflict "in the territory of" a signatory. The latter kind of conflict is distinguishable from the conflict described in Common Article 2 chiefly because it does not involve a clash between nations (whether signatories or not). In context, then, the phrase "not of an international character" bears its literal meaning. See, e.g., J. Bentham, Introduction to the Principles of Morals and Legislation 6, 296 (J. Burns & H. Hart eds. 1970) (using the term "international law" as a "new though not inexpressive appellation" meaning "betwixt nation and nation"; defining "international" to include "mutual transactions between sovereigns as such"); Commentary on the Additional Protocols to the Geneva Conventions of 12 August 1949, p. 1351 (1987) ("[A] non-international armed conflict is distinct from an international armed conflict because of the legal status of the entities opposing each other").

Although the official commentaries accompanying Common Article 3 indicate that an important purpose of the provision was to furnish minimal protection to rebels involved in one kind of "conflict not of an international character," i.e., a civil war, see GCIII Commentary 36–37, the commentaries also make clear "that the scope of the Article must be as wide as possible," id., at 36. In fact, limiting language that would have rendered Common Article 3 applicable "especially [to] cases of civil war, colonial conflicts, or wars of religion," was omitted from the final version of the Article, which coupled broader scope of application with a narrower range of rights than did earlier proposed iterations. See GCIII Commentary 42–43.

iii

Common Article 3, then, is applicable here and, as indicated above, requires that Hamdan be tried by a "regularly constituted court affording all the judicial guarantees which are recognized as indispensable by civilized peoples." 6 U.S.T., at 3320 (Art. 3, ¶ 1(d)). While the term "regularly constituted court" is not specifically defined in either Common Article 3 or its accompanying commentary, other sources disclose its core meaning. The commentary accompanying a provision of the Fourth Geneva Convention, for example, defines " 'regularly constituted' " tribunals to include "ordinary military courts" and "definitely exclud[e] all special tribunals." GCIV Commentary 340 (defining the term "properly constituted" in Article 66, which the commentary treats as identical to "regularly constituted"); . . . .

The Government offers only a cursory defense of Hamdan's military commission in light of Common Article 3. See Brief for Respondents 49–50. As Justice Kennedy explains, that defense fails because "[t]he regular military courts in our system are the courts-martial established by congressional statutes." At a minimum, a military commission "can be 'regularly constituted' by the standards of our military justice system only if some practical need explains deviations from court-martial practice." As we have explained, see Part VI-C, supra, no such need has been demonstrated here.

iv

Inextricably intertwined with the question of regular constitution is the evaluation of the procedures governing the tribunal and whether they afford "all the judicial guarantees which are recognized as indispensable by civilized peoples." 6 U.S.T., at 3320 (Art. 3, ¶ 1(d)). Like the phrase "regularly constituted court," this phrase is not defined in the text of the Geneva Conventions. But it must be understood to incorporate at least the barest of those trial protections that have been recognized by customary international law. Many of these are described in Article 75 of Protocol I to the Geneva Conventions of 1949, adopted in 1977 (Protocol I). Although the United States declined to ratify Protocol I, its objections were not to Article 75 thereof. Indeed, it appears that the Government "regard[s] the provisions of Article 75 as an articulation of safeguards to which all persons in the hands of an enemy are entitled." Taft, The Law of Armed Conflict After 9/11: Some Salient Features, 28 Yale J. Int'l L. 319, 322 (2003). Among the rights set forth in Article 75 is the "right to be tried in [one's] presence." Protocol I, Art. 75(4)(e).

We agree with Justice Kennedy that the procedures adopted to try Hamdan deviate from those governing courts-martial in ways not justified by any "evident practical need," post, at 11, and for that reason, at least, fail to afford the requisite guarantees. We add only that, as noted in Part VI-A, supra, various provisions of Commission Order No. 1 dispense with the principles, articulated in Article 75 and indisputably part of the customary international law, that an accused must, absent disruptive conduct or consent, be present for his trial and must be privy to the evidence against him. See §§ 6(B)(3), (D). That the Government has a compelling interest in denying Hamdan access to certain sensitive information is not doubted. But, at least absent express statutory provision to the contrary, information used to convict a person of a crime must be disclosed to him.

v

Common Article 3 obviously tolerates a great degree of flexibility in trying individuals captured during armed conflict; its requirements are general ones, crafted to accommodate a wide variety of legal systems. But requirements they are nonetheless. The commission that the President has convened to try Hamdan does not meet those requirements.

VII

We have assumed, as we must, that the allegations made in the Government's charge against Hamdan are true. We have assumed, moreover, the truth of the message implicit in that charge—viz., that Hamdan is a dangerous individual whose beliefs, if acted upon, would cause great harm and even death to innocent civilians, and who would act upon those beliefs if given the opportunity. It bears emphasizing that Hamdan does not challenge, and we do not today address, the Government's power to detain him for the duration of active hostilities in order to prevent such harm. But in undertaking to try Hamdan and subject him to criminal punishment, the Executive is bound to comply with the Rule of Law that prevails in this jurisdiction.

The judgment of the Court of Appeals is reversed, and the case is remanded for further proceedings.

It is so ordered.

THE CHIEF JUSTICE took no part in the consideration or decision of this case.

JUSTICE BREYER, with whom JUSTICE KENNEDY, JUSTICE SOUTER, and JUSTICE GINSBURG join, concurring.

The dissenters say that today's decision would "sorely hamper the President's ability to confront and defeat a new and deadly enemy." (opinion of Thomas, J.). They suggest that it undermines our Nation's ability to "preven[t] future attacks" of the grievous sort that we have already suffered. That claim leads me to state briefly what I believe the majority sets forth both explicitly and implicitly at greater length. The Court's conclusion ultimately rests upon a single ground: Congress has not issued the Executive a "blank check." Cf. Hamdi v. Rumsfeld, 542 U.S. 507, 536 (2004) (plurality opinion). Indeed, Congress has denied the President the legislative authority to create military commissions of the kind at issue here. Nothing prevents the President from returning to Congress to seek the authority he believes necessary.

Where, as here, no emergency prevents consultation with Congress, judicial insistence upon that consultation does not weaken our Nation's ability to deal with danger. To the contrary, that insistence strengthens the Nation's ability to determine—through democratic means—how best to do so. The Constitution places its faith in those democratic means. Our Court today simply does the same.

JUSTICE KENNEDY, with whom JUSTICE SOUTER, JUSTICE GINSBURG, and JUSTICE BREYER join as to Parts I and II, concurring in part.

Military Commission Order No. 1, which governs the military commission established to try petitioner Salim Hamdan for war crimes, exceeds limits that certain statutes, duly enacted by Congress, have placed on the President's authority to convene military courts. This is not a case, then, where the Executive can assert some unilateral authority to fill a void left by congressional inaction. It is a case where Congress, in the proper exercise of its powers as an independent branch of government, and as part of a long tradition of legislative involvement in matters of military justice, has considered the subject of military tribunals and set limits on the President's authority. Where a statute provides the conditions for the exercise of governmental power, its requirements are the result of a deliberative and reflective process engaging both of the political branches. Respect for laws derived from the customary operation of the Executive and Legislative Branches gives some assurance of stability in time of crisis. The Constitution is best preserved by reliance on standards tested over time and insulated from the pressures of the moment.

These principles seem vindicated here, for a case that may be of extraordinary importance is resolved by ordinary rules. The rules of most relevance here are those pertaining to the authority of Congress and the interpretation of its enactments.

It seems appropriate to recite these rather fundamental points because the Court refers, as it should in its exposition of the case, to the requirement of the Geneva Conventions of 1949 that military tribunals be "regularly constituted"—a requirement that controls here, if for no other reason, because Congress requires that military commissions like the ones at issue conform to the "law of war," 10 U.S.C. § 821. Whatever the substance and content of the term "regularly constituted" as interpreted in this and any later cases, there seems little doubt that it relies upon the importance of standards deliberated upon and chosen in advance of crisis, under a system where the single power of the Executive is checked by other constitutional mechanisms. All of which returns us to the point of beginning—that domestic statutes control this case. If Congress, after due consideration, deems it appropriate to change the controlling statutes, in conformance with the Constitution and other laws, it has the power and prerogative to do so.

I join the Court's opinion, save Parts V and VI-D-iv. To state my reasons for this reservation, and to show my agreement with the remainder of the Court's analysis by identifying particular deficiencies in the military commissions at issue, this separate opinion seems appropriate.

I

Trial by military commission raises separation-of-powers concerns of the highest order. Located within a single branch, these courts carry the risk that offenses will be defined, prosecuted, and adjudicated by executive officials without independent review. Concentration of power puts personal liberty in peril of arbitrary action by officials, an incursion the

These structural differences between the military commissions and courts-martial—the concentration of functions, including legal decisionmaking, in a single executive official; the less rigorous standards for composition of the tribunal; and the creation of special review procedures in place of institutions created and regulated by Congress—remove safeguards that are important to the fairness of the proceedings and the independence of the court. Congress has prescribed these guarantees for courts-martial; and no evident practical need explains the departures here. For these reasons the commission cannot be considered regularly constituted under United States law and thus does not satisfy Congress' requirement that military commissions conform to the law of war.

Apart from these structural issues, moreover, the basic procedures for the commissions deviate from procedures for courts-martial, in violation of § 836(b). As the Court explains, ante, the Military Commission Order abandons the detailed Military Rules of Evidence, which are modeled on the Federal Rules of Evidence in conformity with § 836(a)'s requirement of presumptive compliance with district-court rules.

Instead, the order imposes just one evidentiary rule: "Evidence shall be admitted if . . . the evidence would have probative value to a reasonable person," MCO No. 1, § 6(D)(1). Although it is true some military commissions applied an amorphous evidence standard in the past, see, e.g., 1 Law Reports 117–118 (discussing World War II military commission orders); Exec. Order No. 9185, 7 Fed. Reg. 5103 (1942) (order convening military commission to try Nazi saboteurs), the evidentiary rules for those commissions were adopted before Congress enacted the uniformity requirement of 10 U.S.C. § 836(b) as part of the UCMJ, see Act of May 5, 1950, ch. 169, 64 Stat. 107, 120, 149. And while some flexibility may be necessary to permit trial of battlefield captives like Hamdan, military statutes and rules already provide for introduction of deposition testimony for absent witnesses, 10 U.S.C. § 849(d); R. C. M. 702, and use of classified information, Military Rule Evid. 505. Indeed, the deposition—testimony provision specifically mentions military commissions and thus is one of the provisions the Government concedes must be followed by the commission at issue. That provision authorizes admission of deposition testimony only if the witness is absent for specified reasons, § 849(d)—a requirement that makes no sense if military commissions may consider all probative evidence. Whether or not this conflict renders the rules at issue "contrary to or inconsistent with" the UCMJ under § 836(a), it creates a uniformity problem under § 836(b).

The rule here could permit admission of multiple hearsay and other forms of evidence generally prohibited on grounds of unreliability. Indeed, the commission regulations specifically contemplate admission of unsworn written statements, MCO No. 1, § 6(D)(3); and they make no provision for exclusion of coerced declarations save those "established to have been made as a result of torture," MCI No. 10, § 3(A) (Mar. 24, 2006), available at www.defenselink.mil/news/Mar2006/d20060327MCI10.pdf; cf. Military Rule Evid. 304(c)(3) (generally barring use of statements obtained "through the use of coercion, unlawful influence, or unlawful inducement"); 10 U.S.C. § 831(d) (same). Besides, even if evidence is deemed nonprobative by the presiding officer at Hamdan's trial, the military-commission members still may view it. In another departure from court-martial practice the military commission members may object to the presiding officer's evidence rulings and determine themselves, by majority vote, whether to admit the evidence. MCO No. 1, § 6(D)(1); cf. R. C. M. 801(a)(4), (e)(1) (providing that the military judge at a court-martial determines all questions of law).

As the Court explains, the Government has made no demonstration of practical need for these special rules and procedures, either in this particular case or as to the military commissions in general; nor is any such need self-evident. For all the Government's regulations and submissions reveal, it would be feasible for most, if not all, of the conventional military evidence rules and procedures to be followed.

In sum, as presently structured, Hamdan's military commission exceeds the bounds Congress has placed on the President's authority in §§ 836 and 821 of the UCMJ. Because Congress has prescribed these limits, Congress can change them, requiring a new analysis consistent with the Constitution and other governing laws. At this time, however, we must apply the standards Congress has provided. By those standards the military commission is deficient.

III

In light of the conclusion that the military commission here is unauthorized under the UCMJ, I see no need to consider several further issues addressed in the plurality opinion by Justice Stevens and the dissent by Justice Thomas.

First, I would not decide whether Common Article 3's standard—a "regularly constituted court affording all the judicial guarantees which are recognized as indispensable by civilized peoples," 6 U.S.T., at 3320 (¶ (1)(d))—necessarily requires that the accused have the right to be present at all stages of a criminal trial. As Justice Stevens explains, Military Commission Order No. 1 authorizes exclusion of the accused from the proceedings if the presiding officer determines that, among other things, protection of classified information so requires. See §§ 6(B)(3), (D)(5); Justice Stevens observes that these regulations create the possibility of a conviction and sentence based on evidence Hamdan has not seen or heard—a possibility the plurality is correct to consider troubling. . . .

As the dissent by Justice Thomas points out, however, the regulations bar the presiding officer from admitting secret evidence if doing so would deprive the accused of a "full and fair trial." MCO No. 1, § 6(D)(5)(b); [t]his fairness determination, moreover, is unambiguously subject to judicial review under the DTA. See § 1005(e)(3)(D)(i), 119 Stat. 2743 (allowing review of compliance with the "standards and procedures" in Military Commission Order No. 1). The evidentiary proceedings at Hamdan's trial have yet to commence, and it remains to be seen whether he will suffer any prejudicial exclusion.

There should be reluctance, furthermore, to reach unnecessarily the question whether, as the plurality seems to conclude, Article 75 of Protocol I to the Geneva Conventions is binding law notwithstanding the earlier decision by our Government not to accede to the Protocol. For all these reasons, and without detracting from the importance of the right of presence, I would rely on other deficiencies noted here and in the opinion by the Court—deficiencies that relate to the structure and procedure of the commission and that inevitably will affect the proceedings—as the basis for finding the military commissions lack authorization under 10 U.S.C. § 836 and fail to be regularly constituted under Common Article 3 and § 821.

I likewise see no need to address the validity of the conspiracy charge against Hamdan—an issue addressed at length in Part V of Justice Stevens' opinion and in Part II-C of Justice Thomas' dissent. In light of the conclusion that the military commissions at issue are unauthorized Congress may choose to provide further guidance in this area. Congress, not the Court, is the branch in the better position to undertake the "sensitive task of establishing a principle not inconsistent with the national interest or international justice." Banco Nacional de Cuba v. Sabbatino, 376 U. S. 398, 428 (1964).

Finally, for the same reason, I express no view on the merits of other limitations on military commissions described as elements of the common law of war in Part V of Justice Stevens' opinion.

With these observations I join the Court's opinion with the exception of Parts V and VI-D-iv.

[ROBERTS, C.J. took no part in the consideration or decision of the case. JUSTICES SCALIA, THOMAS and ALITO each filed dissenting opinions joined variously by the other two dissenting justices.]

C. THE RESPONSE TO HAMDAN— CONGRESSIONAL ENACTMENT OF THE MILITARY COMMISSIONS ACT OF 2006, AND LATER, THE MILITARY COMMISSIONS ACT OF 2009

1. INTRODUCTION

In Hamdan, a number of the Justices had indicated that in establishing the military commissions, the President had acted without legislative authority. Congress responded quickly by enacting the Military Commissions Act (MCA) in the early fall, 2006. The MCA of 2006 contained provisions authorizing the establishment of military commissions by the President and generally prescribed procedures and some rules of evidence, as well as related matters. The Act also listed and defined offenses that are triable before the commissions. [The Act also withdrew habeas corpus jurisdiction and provided for an exclusive route for judicial review of decisions of the military commissions. These latter provisions were addressed by the Supreme Court in the Boumediene case supra, Chapter 10.] Subsequently, in 2009, at the instance of the Obama administration, the Military Commissions Act of 2009 was enacted, which amended the 2006 Act in a number of important respects. The provisions below are from the MCA of 2009.

[Note: In 2010, a revised Manual for Military Commissions was issued; it, of course, tracks the statute, but also contains more detailed provisions, including, for example, a very detailed set of rules of evidence. It was further revised in 2012. See http://www.mc.mil/Portals/0/pdfs/2012Manual ForMilitaryCommissions.pdf.]

The portion of the provisions of the MCA of 2009, reproduced below are intended to provide an overall sense of the structure of the commissions and their operating ground rules These provisions, for example, provide a window into the composition of the military commissions; how representatives for the prosecution and defense are provided; decision-making processes; basic procedures; and certain important rules of evidence. The provisions in the 2009 MCA describing and defining the crimes that may be charged in commissions proceedings are also reproduced below.

Among the provisions of the 2009 Act, certain key provisions mainly dealing with issues of evidentiary admissibility are reproduced in bold type in section 3 so that they can be easily located among the many provisions reproduced. The substance and impact of these particular provisions are addressed in section 2, below. Separate consideration of these bolded provisions helps in making comparisons between the military commissions process and trials in civilian federal court. The bolded provisions deal with such subjects as the admissibility of evidence seized without a warrant, the applicability of the Miranda warnings, and rules regarding confessions, hearsay and classified information.

Because it is assumed that even in the Trump administration, and later presidential administrations, some enemy combatant cases will be prosecuted in military commission trials and some in federal district court, it is useful to understand the extent to which the two processes are similar and the ways in which they differ.

In connection with consideration of some of the selected items in section 2 below, a brief review is presented about how the provisions dealing with each particular subject have been changed and evolved through the various amendments of Military Commissions Order No. 1 and through enactments of the MCA of 2006 and now the 2009 Act—that is, how the current rules are different from earlier versions of the military commission process. The differences between the military commissions process and federal district court trials are much less today than when these military commissions were first authorized in 2001. Each successive set of amendments and rule changes has moved the military commissions process closer to the rules applicable in ordinary federal criminal trials. But differences still remain. As you move through these materials, you should ask yourself: What are the remaining differences? How important are they?

2. THE APPROACH TAKEN IN THE MILITARY COMMISSION ACTS TO SELECTED EVIDENCE TOPICS

In enacting the Military Commissions Act of 2009, supra, which amended the MCA of 2006, Congress, inter alia, enacted or amended provisions dealing with selected subjects such as search and seizure, coerced confessions, hearsay and classified information. Additionally, in the same legislative act containing the 2009 MCA, namely the 2010 National Defense Appropriations Act, Congress also separately enacted provisions dealing with the applicability of the Miranda warning requirements. As mentioned, supra, the relevant provisions are highlighted by printing them in bold typeface in the set of excerpts from the 2009 MCA reproduced in section 3, below.

a. Search and Seizure—Exclusionary Rule

Sec. 949a (b)(3)(A), bolded in subsection 3, below, contains the relevant provision which authorizes the Secretary of Defense to make the exclusionary rule inapplicable in military commission proceedings where the evidence was seized outside of the United States without a warrant or without authority. The 2009 MCA narrowed the 2006 MCA rule by restricting the inapplicability of the exclusionary rule that the Secretary could authorize to situations involving evidence seized outside of the United States.

b. Miranda Warnings

In the National Defense Authorization Act for 2010, separate from the Military Commissions Act amendments, which were in the same legislative package, Congress legislated the following prohibition on Department of Defense employees giving Miranda warnings to foreign nationals captured or detained outside the United States as enemy belligerents. The prohibition, by its terms, does not apply to persons in the custody of the Department of Justice or to employees of the Department of Justice, namely, the FBI.

SEC. 1040. NO MIRANDA WARNINGS FOR AL QAEDA TERRORISTS.

(a) No Miranda Warnings—

(1) IN GENERAL—Absent a court order requiring the reading of such statements, no member of the Armed Forces and no official or employee of the Department of Defense or a component of the intelligence community (other than the Department of Justice) may read to a foreign national who is captured or detained outside the United States as an enemy belligerent and is in the custody or under the effective control of the Department of Defense or otherwise under detention in a Department of Defense facility the statement required by Miranda v. Arizona (384 U.S. 436 (1966)), or otherwise inform such an individual of any rights that the individual may or may not have to counsel or to remain silent consistent with Miranda v. Arizona (384 U.S. 436 (1966)).

(2) NONAPPLICABILITY TO DEPARTMENT OF JUSTICE—This subsection shall not apply to the Department of Justice.

(3) DEFINITIONS—In this subsection:

(A) The term 'foreign national' means an individual who is not a citizen or national of the United States.

(B) The term 'enemy belligerent' includes a privileged belligerent against the United States and an unprivileged enemy belligerent, as those terms are defined in section 948a of title 10, United States Code, as amended by section 1802 of this Act.

(b) Report Required on Notification of Detainees of Rights Under Miranda v. Arizona—Not later than 90 days after the date of the enactment of this Act, the Secretary of Defense shall submit to the congressional defense committees a report on how the reading of rights under Miranda v. Arizona (384 U.S. 436 (1966)) to individuals detained by the United States in Afghanistan may affect—

> (1) the tactical questioning of detainees at the point of capture by United States Armed Forces deployed in support of Operation Enduring Freedom;

> (2) post-capture theater-level interrogations and intelligence-gathering activities conducted as part of Operation Enduring Freedom;

> (3) the overall counterinsurgency strategy and objectives of the United States for Operation Enduring Freedom;

> (4) United States military operations and objectives in Afghanistan; and

> (5) potential risks to members of the Armed Forces operating in Afghanistan.

Section 1040 deals with DOD employees and the inapplicability of Miranda warnings to foreign national prisoners abroad. This leaves open the question of whether FBI agents are required to give Miranda warnings abroad to foreign nationals. We have considered this issue and related questions in Chapter 7, in connection with United States v. Odeh.

c. Confessions

The main set of provisions dealing with allegedly coerced confessions is found in section 948r of the 2009 MCA, reproduced in bold typeface below. Section 949a (b)(3)(B) also deals with the subject by referencing 948r.

Section 948r makes inadmissible statements obtained through torture or cruel, inhuman or degrading treatment (CIDT), thereby amending the approach taken in the 2006 statute. The 2006 MCA had distinguished between those two categories of statements, ruling statements obtained by torture inadmissible under all circumstances and the CIDT statements admissible if obtained prior to December 2005, but inadmissible if obtained after that date.

The justification for drawing that distinction was that the Detainee Treatment Act was enacted in December 2005, and the DTA was the first statutory prohibition on cruel, inhuman or degrading treatment of persons detained by U.S. agents. Distinguishing between statements obtained prior to December 2005 and those taken after that date can be viewed as part of a strategy on the part of the Bush administration to try to retain admissibility for interrogation statements obtained through the use of rather extreme interrogation methods in the early years following 9/11.

Recall that, as developed in Chapter 7, supra, lawyers for the Bush administration had written memoranda concluding that certain extreme methods of interrogation, e.g., waterboarding, were not torture; under this approach, they were able to use the category of cruel, inhuman or degrading treatment as a safe harbor, at least until December 2005.

But the 2006 MCA did, for the first time, raise some significant barriers to the admissibility of confessions compared with the prior applicable provisions , namely the Military Commission Order No. 1 and its various amendments. Under those provisions, confessions were admissible if of sufficient reliability and probative value.

The 2009 statute also introduces the notion of voluntariness for determining the admissibility of confessions that are not barred by the torture or CIDT barriers. The statute thus, for the first time begins to link up with constitutional law doctrine applicable to confessions in federal criminal prosecutions, but the linkage is not complete. The statute does not expressly incorporate by reference the Supreme Court's case law on this subject. Rather, it develops its own definitional terms, which, surely overlap somewhat with, but in the end, may or may not accord exactly with doctrine developed in the Supreme Court cases. 948r incorporates considerations relating to military circumstances and seems to make a special point of including as relevant lapse of time between interrogation sessions and changes in who is doing the questioning as factors affecting admissibility.

One conclusion that can be drawn from the foregoing is that military commissions confessions law has evolved significantly so that it now is quite similar to the constitutional law applied to allegedly coerced confessions in federal district court proceedings. What remains to be seen is whether the courts, especially the Supreme Court will apply to military commission trials the same coerced confession doctrine applicable in ordinary federal criminal prosecutions, and if not, whether it will deem the standards enacted in section 948r to be consistent with the Constitution.

d.   Hearsay

The provisions in the 2009 MCA dealing with hearsay are found in section 949a (b)(3)(D) et seq, in bold typeface below. Several things should be noted about these provisions. They are essentially procedural, requiring notice to the opposing party and describing factors that should be taken into account by the military judge in determining whether to admit the evidence. Note that not all hearsay is subject to these procedures, only hearsay that would not otherwise be admissible under the rules of evidence applicable in courts martial proceedings—that is, the traditional rules of evidence with all of the hearsay exceptions. The Manual for Military Commissions adopts a definition for hearsay in rule 801 borrowing the language from the Federal Rules of Evidence.

The principal change from the 2006 MCA provisions is that the 2006 statute puts the burden on the opponent of the hearsay evidence whereas the 2009 MCA puts the burden where it would be most appropriate to put it. . .on the proponent.

Under the pre-2006 applicable law, the President's Military Order and the Military Commissions Order No. 1 with its amendments, there were no special provisions or procedures for dealing with hearsay; it was admissible if deemed to have probative value to a reasonable person.

e. Classified Information

The provisions in the 2009 MCA dealing with classified information are found in sections 949p-1 through 949p-7; they are quite extensive, and, accordingly, only a few salient provisions have been highlighted by bolding the typeface. The provisions in the 2009 statute largely track the provisions of the Classified Information Procedures Act (CIPA), which were studied in Chapter 9.

Perhaps, the largest degree of change in the applicable rules for military commissions has occurred in the odyssey and evolution of the provisions for dealing with classified information. Under the early approach taken in the Military Commissions Order No. 1, the accused was given detailed defense counsel, that is, an assigned officer, and might also have a civilian defense counsel. The presiding officer had broad powers to deal with classified information, with no applicable standard limiting his authority. His authority extended even to excluding the accused and the civilian counsel, but not detailed defense counsel from the courtroom. Classified evidence could be considered by the judges even though not available to the accused or civilian defense counsel but it could not be admitted into evidence for consideration by the Commission if not presented to detailed defense counsel.

The early approach thus relied upon drawing a distinction between civilian and detailed defense counsel and allowing for the exclusion of the accused from the courtroom (and also civilian defense counsel) for the classified portion of the proceedings. It was this aspect of the military commission process that a plurality of the Supreme Court criticized in their Hamdan opinion.

The 2006 MCA, responding to the Hamdan opinion, largely adopted the CIPA approach but without providing expressly for the possibility of dismissal of the proceeding or setting forth a standard that substituted evidence must meet. The 2009 provisions track CIPA in this respect: the test that substitutions must meet is to provide the accused with substantially the same ability to make his defense, and if that standard cannot be met, the possible remedies include dismissal of charges.

3. THE MCA OF 2009: GENERAL PROVISIONS, PROCEDURES AND EVIDENCE RULES

SUBCHAPTER I—GENERAL PROVISIONS

"**Sec. 948a. Definitions**

"In this chapter:

"(1) ALIEN.—The term "alien" means an individual who is not a citizen of the United States.

"(2) CLASSIFIED INFORMATION.—The term "classified information" means the following:

"(A) Any information or material that has been determined by the United States Government pursuant to statute, Executive order, or regulation to require protection against unauthorized disclosure for reasons of national security.

"(B) Any restricted data, as that term is defined in section 11 y. of the Atomic Energy Act of 1954 (42 U.S.C. 2014(y)).

"(3) COALITION PARTNER.—The term "coalition partner", with respect to hostilities engaged in by the United States, means any State or armed force directly engaged along with the United States in such hostilities or providing direct operational support to the United States in connection with such hostilities.

"(4) GENEVA CONVENTION RELATIVE TO THE TREATMENT OF PRISONERS OF WAR.—The term "Geneva Convention Relative to the Treatment of Prisoners of War" means the Convention Relative to the Treatment of Prisoners of War, done at Geneva August 12, 1949 (6 UST 3316).

"(5) GENEVA CONVENTIONS.—The term "Geneva Conventions" means the international conventions signed at Geneva on August 12, 1949.

"(6) PRIVILEGED BELLIGERENT.—The term "privileged belligerent" means an individual belonging to one of the eight categories enumerated in Article 4 of the Geneva Convention Relative to the Treatment of Prisoners of War.

"(7) UNPRIVILEGED ENEMY BELLIGERENT.—The term "unprivileged enemy belligerent" means an individual (other than a privileged belligerent) who—

"(A) has engaged in hostilities against the United States or its coalition partners;

"(B) has purposefully and materially supported hostilities against the United States or its coalition partners; or

"(C) was a part of al Qaeda at the time of the alleged offense under this chapter.

"(8) NATIONAL SECURITY.—The term "national security" means the national defense and foreign relations of the United States.

"(9) HOSTILITIES.—The term "hostilities" means any conflict subject to the laws of war.

"Sec. 948b. Military commissions generally

"(a) Purpose.—This chapter establishes procedures governing the use of military commissions to try alien unprivileged enemy belligerents for violations of the law of war and other offenses triable by military commission.

"(b) Authority for Military Commissions Under This Chapter.— The President is authorized to establish military commissions under this chapter for offenses triable by military commission as provided in this chapter.

"(c) Construction of Provisions.—The procedures for military commissions set forth in this chapter are based upon the procedures for trial by general courts-martial under chapter 47 of this title (the Uniform Code of Military Justice). Chapter 47 of this title does not, by its terms, apply to trial by military commission except as specifically provided therein or in this chapter, and many of the provisions of chapter 47 of this title are by their terms inapplicable to military commissions. The judicial construction and application of chapter 47 of this title, while instructive, is therefore not of its own force binding on military commissions established under this chapter.

"(d) Inapplicability of Certain Provisions.—

"(1) The following provisions of this title shall not apply to trial by military commission under this chapter:

"(A) Section 810 (article 10 of the Uniform Code of Military Justice), relating to speedy trial, including any rule of courts-martial relating to speedy trial.

"(B) Sections 831(a), (b), and (d) (articles 31(a), (b), and (d) of the Uniform Code of Military Justice), relating to compulsory self-incrimination.

"(C) Section 832 (article 32 of the Uniform Code of Military Justice), relating to pretrial investigation.

"(2) Other provisions of chapter 47 of this title shall apply to trial by military commission under this chapter only to the extent provided by the terms of such provisions or by this chapter.

"(e) Geneva Conventions Not Establishing Private Right of Action.—No alien unprivileged enemy belligerent subject to trial by military commission under this chapter may invoke the Geneva Conventions as a basis for a private right of action.

"Sec. 948c. Persons subject to military commissions

"Any alien unprivileged enemy belligerent is subject to trial by military commission as set forth in this chapter.

"Sec. 948d. Jurisdiction of military commissions

"A military commission under this chapter shall have jurisdiction to try persons subject to this chapter for any offense made punishable by this chapter, sections 904 and 906 of this title (articles 104 and 106 of the Uniform Code of Military Justice), or the law of war, whether such offense was committed before, on, or after September 11, 2001, and may, under such limitations as the President may prescribe, adjudge any punishment not forbidden by this chapter, including the penalty of death when specifically authorized under this chapter. A military commission is a competent tribunal to make a finding sufficient for jurisdiction.

"SUBCHAPTER II—COMPOSITION OF MILITARY COMMISSIONS

. . .

Sec. 948i. Who may serve on military commissions

"(a) In General.—Any commissioned officer of the armed forces on active duty is eligible to serve on a military commission under this chapter, including commissioned officers of the reserve components of the armed forces on active duty, commissioned officers of the National Guard on active duty in Federal service, or retired commissioned officers recalled to active duty.

"(b) Detail of Members.—When convening a military commission under this chapter, the convening authority shall detail as members thereof such members of the armed forces eligible under subsection (a) who, in the opinion of the convening authority, are best qualified for the duty by reason of age, education, training, experience, length of service, and judicial temperament. No member of an armed force is eligible to serve as a member of a military commission when such member is the accuser or a witness for the prosecution or has acted as an investigator or counsel in the same case.

"(c) Excuse of Members.—Before a military commission under this chapter is assembled for the trial of a case, the convening authority may excuse a member from participating in the case.

"Sec. 948j.　Military judge of a military commission

"(a) Detail of Military Judge.—A military judge shall be detailed to each military commission under this chapter. The Secretary of Defense shall prescribe regulations providing for the manner in which military judges are so detailed to military commissions. The military judge shall preside over each military commission to which such military judge has been detailed.

"(b) Eligibility.—A military judge shall be a commissioned officer of the armed forces who is a member of the bar of a Federal court, or a member of the bar of the highest court of a State, and who is certified to be qualified for duty under section 826 of this title (article 26 of the Uniform Code of Military Justice) as a military judge of general courts-martial by the Judge Advocate General of the armed force . . . .

"(f) Prohibition on Evaluation of Fitness by Convening Authority.—The convening authority of a military commission under this chapter may not prepare or review any report concerning the effectiveness, fitness, or efficiency of a military judge detailed to the military commission which relates to such judge's performance of duty as a military judge on the military commission.

"Sec. 948k.　Detail of trial counsel and defense counsel

"(a) Detail of Counsel Generally.—

"(1) Trial counsel and military defense counsel shall be detailed for each military commission under this chapter.

"(2) Assistant trial counsel and assistant and associate defense counsel may be detailed for a military commission under this chapter.

"(3) Military defense counsel for a military commission under this chapter shall be detailed as soon as practicable.

"(4) The Secretary of Defense shall prescribe regulations providing for the manner in which trial counsel and military defense counsel are detailed for military commissions under this chapter and for the persons who are authorized to detail such counsel for such military commissions.

"(b) Trial Counsel.—Subject to subsection (e), a trial counsel detailed for a military commission under this chapter shall be—

"(1) a judge advocate (as that term is defined in section 801 of this title (article 1 of the Uniform Code of Military Justice)) who is—

"(A) a graduate of an accredited law school or a member of the bar of a Federal court or of the highest court of a State; and

"(B) certified as competent to perform duties as trial counsel before general courts-martial by the Judge Advocate General of the armed force of which such judge advocate is a member; or

"(2) a civilian who is—

"(A) a member of the bar of a Federal court or of the highest court of a State; and

"(B) otherwise qualified to practice before the military commission pursuant to regulations prescribed by the Secretary of Defense.

"(c) Defense Counsel.—

"(1) Subject to subsection (e), a military defense counsel detailed for a military commission under this chapter shall be a judge advocate (as so defined) who is—

"(A) a graduate of an accredited law school or a member of the bar of a Federal court or of the highest court of a State; and

"(B) certified as competent to perform duties as defense counsel before general courts-martial by the Judge Advocate General of the armed force of which such judge advocate is a member.

"(2) The Secretary of Defense shall prescribe regulations for the appointment and performance of defense counsel in capital cases under this chapter.

"(d) Chief Prosecutor; Chief Defense Counsel.—

"(1) The Chief Prosecutor in a military commission under this chapter shall meet the requirements set forth in subsection (b)(1).

"(2) The Chief Defense Counsel in a military commission under this chapter shall meet the requirements set forth in subsection (c)(1).

. . .

"Sec. 948m. Number of members; excuse of members; absent and additional members

"(a) Number of Members.—

"(1) Except as provided in paragraph (2), a military commission under this chapter shall have at least five members.

"(2) In a case in which the accused before a military commission under this chapter may be sentenced to a penalty of death, the military commission shall have the number of members prescribed by section 949m(c) of this title.

"(b) Excuse of Members.—No member of a military commission under this chapter may be absent or excused after the military commission has been assembled for the trial of a case unless excused—

"(1) as a result of challenge;

"(2) by the military judge for physical disability or other good cause; or

"(3) by order of the convening authority for good cause.

"(c) Absent and Additional Members.—Whenever a military commission under this chapter is reduced below the number of members required by subsection (a), the trial may not proceed unless the convening authority details new members sufficient to provide not less than such number. The trial may proceed with the new members present after the recorded evidence previously introduced before the members has been read to the military commission in the presence of the military judge, the accused (except as provided in section 949d of this title), and counsel for both sides.

"SUBCHAPTER III—PRE-TRIAL PROCEDURE

. . .

"Sec. 948r. Exclusion of statements obtained by torture or cruel, inhuman, or degrading treatment; prohibition of self-incrimination; admission of other statements of the accused

"(a) Exclusion of Statements Obtain by Torture or Cruel, Inhuman, or Degrading Treatment.—No statement obtained by the use of torture or by cruel, inhuman, or degrading treatment (as defined by section 1003 of the Detainee Treatment Act of 2005 (42 U.S.C. 2000dd)), whether or not under color of law, shall be admissible in a military commission under this chapter, except against a person accused of torture or such treatment as evidence that the statement was made.

"(b) Self-incrimination Prohibited.—No person shall be required to testify against himself or herself at a proceeding of a military commission under this chapter.

"(c) Other Statements of the Accused.—A statement of the accused may be admitted in evidence in a military commission under this chapter only if the military judge finds—

"(1) that the totality of the circumstances renders the statement reliable and possessing sufficient probative value; and

"(2) that—

"(A) the statement was made incident to lawful conduct during military operations at the point of capture or during closely related active combat engagement, and the interests of justice would best be served by admission of the statement into evidence; or

"(B) the statement was voluntarily given.

"(d) Determination of Voluntariness.—In determining for purposes of subsection (c)(2)(B) whether a statement was voluntarily given, the military judge shall consider the totality of the circumstances, including, as appropriate, the following:

"(1) The details of the taking of the statement, accounting for the circumstances of the conduct of military and intelligence operations during hostilities.

"(2) The characteristics of the accused, such as military training, age, and education level.

"(3) The lapse of time, change of place, or change in identity of the questioners between the statement sought to be admitted and any prior questioning of the accused.

"SUBCHAPTER IV—TRIAL PROCEDURE

. . .Sec. 949a.   Rules

"(a) Procedures and Rules of Evidence.—Pretrial, trial, and post-trial procedures, including elements and modes of proof, for cases triable by military commission under this chapter may be prescribed by the Secretary of Defense. Such procedures may not be contrary to or inconsistent with this chapter. Except as otherwise provided in this chapter or chapter 47 of this title, the procedures and rules of evidence applicable in trials by general courts-martial of the United States shall apply in trials by military commission under this chapter.

"(b) Exceptions.—

"(1) In trials by military commission under this chapter, the Secretary of Defense, in consultation with the Attorney General, may make such exceptions in the applicability of the procedures and rules of evidence otherwise applicable in general courts-martial as may be required by the unique circumstances of the conduct of military and intelligence operations during hostilities or by other practical need consistent with this chapter.

"(2) Notwithstanding any exceptions authorized by paragraph (1), the procedures and rules of evidence in trials by military commission under this chapter shall include, at a minimum, the following rights of the accused:

"(A) To present evidence in the accused's defense, to cross-examine the witnesses who testify against the accused, and to examine and respond to all evidence admitted against the accused on the issue of guilt or innocence and for sentencing, as provided for by this chapter.

"(B) To be present at all sessions of the military commission (other than those for deliberations or voting), except when excluded under section 949d of this title.

"(C)

"(i) When none of the charges preferred against the accused are capital, to be represented before a military commission by civilian counsel if provided at no expense to the Government, and by either the defense counsel detailed or the military counsel of the accused's own selection, if reasonably available.

"(ii) When any of the charges preferred against the accused are capital, to be represented before a military commission in accordance with clause (i) and, to the greatest extent practicable, by at least one additional counsel who is learned in applicable law relating to capital cases and who, if necessary, may be a civilian and compensated in accordance with regulations prescribed by the Secretary of Defense.

"(D) To self-representation, if the accused knowingly and competently waives the assistance of counsel, subject to the provisions of paragraph (4).

"(E) To the suppression of evidence that is not reliable or probative.

"(F) To the suppression of evidence the probative value of which is substantially outweighed by—

"(i) the danger of unfair prejudice, confusion of the issues, or misleading the members; or

"(ii) considerations of undue delay, waste of time, or needless presentation of cumulative evidence.

"(3) In making exceptions in the applicability in trials by military commission under this chapter from the procedures and rules otherwise applicable in general courts-martial, the Secretary of Defense may provide the following:

"(A) Evidence seized outside the United States shall not be excluded from trial by military commission on the grounds that the evidence was not seized pursuant to a search warrant or authorization.

"(B) A statement of the accused that is otherwise admissible shall not be excluded from trial by military commission on grounds of alleged coercion or compulsory self-incrimination so long as the evidence complies with the provisions of section 948r of this title.

"(C) Evidence shall be admitted as authentic so long as—

"(i) the military judge of the military commission determines that there is sufficient evidence that the evidence is what it is claimed to be; and

"(ii) the military judge instructs the members that they may consider any issue as to authentication or identification of evidence in determining the weight, if any, to be given to the evidence.

"(D) Hearsay evidence not otherwise admissible under the rules of evidence applicable in trial by general courts-martial may be admitted in a trial by military commission only if—

"(i) the proponent of the evidence makes known to the adverse party, sufficiently in advance to provide the adverse party with a fair opportunity to meet the evidence, the proponent's intention to offer the evidence, and the particulars of the evidence (including information on the circumstances under which the evidence was obtained); and

"(ii) the military judge, after taking into account all of the circumstances surrounding the taking of the statement, including the degree to which the statement is corroborated, the indicia of reliability within the statement itself, and whether the will of the declarant was overborne, determines that—

"(I) the statement is offered as evidence of a material fact;

"(II) the statement is probative on the point for which it is offered;

"(III) direct testimony from the witness is not available as a practical matter, taking into consideration the physical location of the witness, the unique circumstances of military and intelligence operations during hostilities, and the adverse impacts on military or intelligence operations that would likely result from the production of the witness; and

"(IV) the general purposes of the rules of evidence and the interests of justice will best be served by admission of the statement into evidence.

"(4)

"(A) The accused in a military commission under this chapter who exercises the right to self-representation under paragraph (2)(D) shall conform the accused's deportment and the conduct of the defense to the rules of evidence, procedure, and decorum applicable to trials by military commission.

"(B) Failure of the accused to conform to the rules described in subparagraph (A) may result in a partial or total revocation by the military judge of the right of self-representation under paragraph (2)(D). In such case, the military counsel of the accused or an appropriately authorized civilian counsel shall perform the functions necessary for the defense.

"(c) Delegation of Authority To Prescribe Regulations.—The Secretary of Defense may delegate the authority of the Secretary to prescribe regulations under this chapter.

"(d) Notice to Congress of Modification of Rules.—Not later than 60 days before the date on which any proposed modification of the rules in effect for military commissions under this chapter goes into effect, the Secretary of Defense shall submit to the Committee on Armed Services of the Senate and the Committee on Armed Services of the House of Representatives a report describing the proposed modification.

. . .

"Sec. 949c. Duties of trial counsel and defense counsel

"(a) Trial Counsel.—The trial counsel of a military commission under this chapter shall prosecute in the name of the United States.

"(b) Defense Counsel.—

"(1) The accused shall be represented in the accused's defense before a military commission under this chapter as provided in this subsection.

"(2) The accused may be represented by military counsel detailed under section 948k of this title or by military counsel of the accused's own selection, if reasonably available.

"(3) The accused may be represented by civilian counsel if retained by the accused, provided that such civilian counsel—

"(A) is a United States citizen;

"(B) is admitted to the practice of law in a State, district, or possession of the United States, or before a Federal court;

"(C) has not been the subject of any sanction of disciplinary action by any court, bar, or other competent governmental authority for relevant misconduct;

"(D) has been determined to be eligible for access to information classified at the level Secret or higher; and

"(E) has signed a written agreement to comply with all applicable regulations or instructions for counsel, including any rules of court for conduct during the proceedings.

"(4) If the accused is represented by civilian counsel, military counsel shall act as associate counsel.

"(5) The accused is not entitled to be represented by more than one military counsel. However, the person authorized under regulations prescribed under section 948k of this title to detail counsel, in such person's sole discretion, may detail additional military counsel to represent the accused.

"(6) Defense counsel may cross-examine each witness for the prosecution who testifies before a military commission under this chapter.

"(7) Civilian defense counsel shall protect any classified information received during the course of representation of the accused in accordance with all applicable law governing the protection of classified information, and may not divulge such information to any person not authorized to receive it.

"Sec. 949d. Sessions

"(a) Sessions Without Presence of Members.—

"(1) At any time after the service of charges which have been referred for trial by military commission under this chapter, the military judge may call the military commission into session without the presence of the members for the purpose of—

"(A) hearing and determining motions raising defenses or objections which are capable of determination without trial of the issues raised by a plea of not guilty;

"(B) hearing and ruling upon any matter which may be ruled upon by the military judge under this chapter, whether or not the matter is appropriate for later consideration or decision by the members;

"(C) if permitted by regulations prescribed by the Secretary of Defense, receiving the pleas of the accused; and

"(D) performing any other procedural function which may be performed by the military judge under this chapter or under rules prescribed pursuant to section 949a of this title and which does not require the presence of the members.

"(2) Except as provided in subsections (b), (c), and (d), any proceedings under paragraph (1) shall be conducted in the presence of the accused, defense counsel, and trial counsel, and shall be made part of the record.

"(b) Deliberation or Vote of Members.—When the members of a military commission under this chapter deliberate or vote, only the members may be present.

"(c) Closure of Proceedings.—

"(1) The military judge may close to the public all or part of the proceedings of a military commission under this chapter.

"(2) The military judge may close to the public all or a portion of the proceedings under paragraph (1) only upon

making a specific finding that such closure is necessary to—

"(A) protect information the disclosure of which could reasonably be expected to cause damage to the national security, including intelligence or law enforcement sources, methods, or activities; or

"(B) ensure the physical safety of individuals.

"(3) A finding under paragraph (2) may be based upon a presentation, including a presentation ex parte or in camera, by either trial counsel or defense counsel.

"(d) Exclusion of Accused From Certain Proceedings.—The military judge may exclude the accused from any portion of a proceeding upon a determination that, after being warned by the military judge, the accused persists in conduct that justifies exclusion from the courtroom—d

"(1) to ensure the physical safety of individuals; or

"(2) to prevent disruption of the proceedings by the accused.

". . .

"Sec. 949j. Opportunity to obtain witnesses and other evidence

"(a) In General.—

"(1) Defense counsel in a military commission under this chapter shall have a reasonable opportunity to obtain witnesses and other evidence as provided in regulations prescribed by the Secretary of Defense. The opportunity to obtain witnesses and evidence shall be comparable to the opportunity available to a criminal defendant in a court of the United States under article III of the Constitution.

"(2) Process issued in military commissions under this chapter to compel witnesses to appear and testify and to compel the production of other evidence—

"(A) shall be similar to that which courts of the United States having criminal jurisdiction may lawfully issue; and

"(B) shall run to any place where the United States shall have jurisdiction thereof.

"(b) Disclosure of Exculpatory Evidence.—

"(1) As soon as practicable, trial counsel in a military commission under this chapter shall disclose to the defense the existence of any evidence that reasonably tends to—

"(A) negate the guilt of the accused of an offense charged; or

"(B) reduce the degree of guilt of the accused with respect to an offense charged.

"(2) The trial counsel shall, as soon as practicable, disclose to the defense the existence of evidence that reasonably tends to impeach the credibility of a witness whom the government intends to call at trial.

"(3) The trial counsel shall, as soon as practicable upon a finding of guilt, disclose to the defense the existence of evidence that is not subject to paragraph (1) or paragraph (2) but that reasonably may be viewed as mitigation evidence at sentencing.

"(4) The disclosure obligations under this subsection encompass evidence that is known or reasonably should be known to any government officials who participated in the investigation and prosecution of the case against the defendant.

"Sec. 949k. Defense of lack of mental responsibility

"(a) Affirmative Defense.—It is an affirmative defense in a trial by military commission under this chapter that, at the time of the commission of the acts constituting the offense, the accused, as a result of a severe mental disease or defect, was unable to appreciate the nature and quality or the wrongfulness of the acts. Mental disease or defect does not otherwise constitute a defense.

"(b) Burden of Proof.—The accused in a military commission under this chapter has the burden of proving the defense of lack of mental responsibility by clear and convincing evidence.

"(c) Findings Following Assertion of Defense.—Whenever lack of mental responsibility of the accused with respect to an offense is properly at issue in a military commission under this chapter, the military judge shall instruct the members as to the defense of lack of mental responsibility under this section and shall charge the members to find the accused—

"(1) guilty;

"(2) not guilty; or

"(3) subject to subsection (d), not guilty by reason of lack of mental responsibility.

"(d) Majority Vote Required for Finding.—The accused shall be found not guilty by reason of lack of mental responsibility under subsection (c)(3) only if a majority of the members present at the time the vote is taken determines that the defense of lack of mental responsibility has been established.

"Sec. 949*l*.   Voting and rulings

"(a) Vote by Secret Written Ballot.—Voting by members of a military commission under this chapter on the findings and on the sentence shall be by secret written ballot.

"(b) Rulings.—

"(1) The military judge in a military commission under this chapter shall rule upon all questions of law, including the admissibility of evidence and all interlocutory questions arising during the proceedings.

"(2) Any ruling made by the military judge upon a question of law or an interlocutory question (other than the factual issue of mental responsibility of the accused) is conclusive and constitutes the ruling of the military commission. However, a military judge may change such a ruling at any time during the trial.

"(c) Instructions Prior to Vote.—Before a vote is taken of the findings of a military commission under this chapter, the military judge shall, in the presence of the accused and counsel, instruct the members as to the elements of the offense and charge the members—

"(1) that the accused must be presumed to be innocent until the accused's guilt is established by legal and competent evidence beyond a reasonable doubt;

"(2) that in the case being considered, if there is a reasonable doubt as to the guilt of the accused, the doubt must be resolved in favor of the accused and the accused must be acquitted;

"(3) that, if there is reasonable doubt as to the degree of guilt, the finding must be in a lower degree as to which there is no reasonable doubt; and

"(4) that the burden of proof to establish the guilt of the accused beyond a reasonable doubt is upon the United States.

"Sec. 949m. Number of votes required

"(a) Conviction.—No person may be convicted by a military commission under this chapter of any offense, except as provided in section 949i(b) of this title or by concurrence of two-thirds of the members present at the time the vote is taken.

"(b) Sentences.—

"(1) Except as provided in paragraphs (2) and (3), sentences shall be determined by a military commission by the concurrence of two-thirds of the members present at the time the vote is taken.

"(2) No person may be sentenced to death by a military commission, except insofar as—

"(A) the penalty of death has been expressly authorized under this chapter, chapter 47 of this title, or the law of war for an offense of which the accused has been found guilty;

"(B) trial counsel expressly sought the penalty of death by filing an appropriate notice in advance of trial;

"(C) the accused was convicted of the offense by the concurrence of all the members present at the time the vote is taken; and

"(D) all members present at the time the vote was taken concurred in the sentence of death.

"(3) No person may be sentenced to life imprisonment, or to confinement for more than 10 years, by a military commission under this chapter except by the concurrence of three-fourths of the members present at the time the vote is taken.

"(c) Number of Members Required for Penalty of Death.—

"(1) Except as provided in paragraph (2), in a case in which the penalty of death is sought, the number of members of the military commission under this chapter shall be not less than 12 members.

"(2) In any case described in paragraph (1) in which 12 members are not reasonably available for a military commission because of physical conditions or military exigencies, the convening authority shall specify a lesser number of members for the military commission (but not fewer than 9 members), and the military commission may be assembled, and the trial held, with not less than the number of members so specified. In any such case, the convening authority shall make a detailed written statement, to be appended to the record, stating why a greater number of members were not reasonably available.

. . .

"Sec. 949*o*. Record of trial

. . .

"(b) Complete Record Required.—A complete record of the proceedings and testimony shall be prepared in every military commission under this chapter.

"(c) Provision of Copy to Accused.—A copy of the record of the proceedings of the military commission under this chapter shall be given the accused as soon as it is authenticated. If the record contains classified information, or a classified annex, the accused shall receive a redacted version of the record consistent with the requirements of subchapter V of this chapter. **Defense counsel shall have access to the unredacted record, as provided in regulations prescribed by the Secretary of Defense.**

"SUBCHAPTER V—CLASSIFIED INFORMATION PROCEDURES

. . .

"Sec. 949p–1.   Protection   of   classified   information: applicability of subchapter

"(a) Protection of Classified Information.—Classified information shall be protected and is privileged from disclosure if disclosure would be detrimental to the national security. Under no circumstances may a military judge order the release of classified information to any person not authorized to receive such information.

"(b) Access to Evidence.—Any information admitted into evidence pursuant to any rule, procedure, or order by the military judge shall be provided to the accused.

"(c) Declassification.—Trial counsel shall work with the original classification authorities for evidence that may be used at trial to ensure that such evidence is declassified to the maximum extent possible, consistent with the requirements of national security. A decision not to declassify evidence under this section shall not be subject to review by a military commission or upon appeal.

"(d) Construction of Provisions.—The judicial construction of the Classified Information Procedures Act (18 U.S.C. App.) shall be authoritative in the interpretation of this subchapter, except to the extent that such construction is inconsistent with the specific requirements of this chapter.

"Sec. 949p–2.   Pretrial conference

"(a) Motion.—At any time after service of charges, any party may move for a pretrial conference to consider matters relating to classified information that may arise in connection with the prosecution.

"(b) Conference.—Following a motion under subsection (a), or sua sponte, the military judge shall promptly hold a pretrial conference. Upon request by either party, the court shall hold such conference ex parte to the extent necessary to protect classified information from disclosure, in accordance with the practice of the Federal courts under the Classified Information Procedures Act (18 U.S.C. App.).

"(c) Matters To Be Established at Pretrial Conference.—

"(1) TIMING OF SUBSEQUENT ACTIONS.—At the pretrial conference, the military judge shall establish the timing of—

"(A) requests for discovery;

"(B) the provision of notice required by section 949p-5 of this title; and

"(C) the initiation of the procedure established by section 949p-6 of this title.

"(2) OTHER MATTERS.—At the pretrial conference, the military judge may also consider any matter—

"(A) which relates to classified information; or

"(B) which may promote a fair and expeditious trial.

"(d) Effect of Admissions by Accused at Pretrial Conference.—No admission made by the accused or by any counsel for the accused at a pretrial conference under this section may be used against the accused unless the admission is in writing and is signed by the accused and by the counsel for the accused.

"Sec. 949p–3.   Protective orders

"Upon motion of the trial counsel, the military judge shall issue an order to protect against the disclosure of any classified information that has been disclosed by the United States to any accused in any military commission under this chapter or that has otherwise been provided to, or obtained by, any such accused in any such military commission.

"Sec. 949p–4.   Discovery of, and access to, classified information by the accused

"(a) Limitations on Discovery or Access by the Accused.—

"(1) DECLARATIONS BY THE UNITED STATES OF DAMAGE TO NATIONAL SECURITY.—In any case before a military commission in which the United States seeks to delete, withhold, or otherwise obtain other relief with respect to the discovery of or access to any classified information, the trial counsel shall submit a declaration invoking the United States' classified information privilege and setting forth the damage to the national security that the discovery of or access to such information reasonably could be expected to cause. The declaration shall be signed by a knowledgeable United States official possessing authority to classify information.

"(2) STANDARD FOR AUTHORIZATION OF DISCOVERY OR ACCESS.—Upon the submission of a declaration under paragraph (1), the military judge may not authorize the discovery of or access to such classified information unless the military judge determines that such classified information would be noncumulative, relevant, and helpful to a legally cognizable defense, rebuttal of the prosecution's case, or to sentencing, in accordance with standards generally applicable to discovery of or access to classified information in Federal criminal cases. If the discovery of or access to such classified information is authorized, it shall be addressed in accordance with the requirements of subsection (b).

"(b) Discovery of Classified Information.—

"(1) SUBSTITUTIONS AND OTHER RELIEF.—The military judge, in assessing the accused's discovery of or access to classified information under this section, may authorize the United States—

"(A) to delete or withhold specified items of classified information;

"(B) to substitute a summary for classified information; or

"(C) to substitute a statement admitting relevant facts that the classified information or material would tend to prove.

"(2) EX PARTE PRESENTATIONS.—The military judge shall permit the trial counsel to make a request for an authorization under paragraph (1) in the form of an ex parte presentation to the extent necessary to protect classified information, in accordance with the practice of the Federal courts under the Classified Information Procedures Act (18 U.S.C. App.). If the military judge enters an order granting relief following such an ex parte showing, the entire presentation (including the text of any written submission, verbatim transcript of the ex parte oral conference or hearing, and any exhibits received by the court as part of the ex parte presentation) shall be sealed and preserved in the records of the military commission to be made available to the appellate court in the event of an appeal.

"(3) ACTION BY MILITARY JUDGE.—The military judge shall grant the request of the trial counsel to substitute a summary or to substitute a statement admitting relevant facts, or to provide other relief in accordance with paragraph (1), if the military judge finds that the summary, statement, or other relief would provide the accused with substantially the same ability to make a defense as would discovery of or access to the specific classified information.

"(c) Reconsideration.—An order of a military judge authorizing a request of the trial counsel to substitute, summarize, withhold, or prevent access to classified information under this section is not subject to a motion for reconsideration by the accused, if such order was entered pursuant to an ex parte showing under this section.

" . . .

"Sec. 949p–6.   Procedure for cases involving classified information

"(a) Motion for Hearing.—

"(1) REQUEST FOR HEARING.—Within the time specified by the military judge for the filing of a motion under this section, either party may request the military judge to conduct a hearing to make all determinations concerning the use, relevance, or admissibility of classified information that would otherwise be made during the trial or pretrial proceeding.

"(2) CONDUCT OF HEARING.—Upon a request by either party under paragraph (1), the military judge shall conduct such a hearing and shall rule prior to conducting any further proceedings.

"(3) IN CAMERA HEARING UPON DECLARATION TO COURT BY APPROPRIATE OFFICIAL OF RISK OF DISCLOSURE OF CLASSIFIED INFORMATION.—Any hearing held pursuant to this subsection (or any portion of such hearing specified in the request of a knowledgeable United States official) shall be held in camera if a knowledgeable United States official possessing authority to classify information submits to the military judge a declaration that a public proceeding may result in the disclosure of classified information. **Classified information is not subject to disclosure under this section unless the information is relevant and necessary to an**

element of the offense or a legally cognizable defense and is otherwise admissible in evidence.

"(4) MILITARY JUDGE TO MAKE DETERMINATIONS IN WRITING.—As to each item of classified information, the military judge shall set forth in writing the basis for the determination.

"(b) Notice and Use of Classified Information by the Government.—

"(1) NOTICE TO ACCUSED.—Before any hearing is conducted pursuant to a request by the trial counsel under subsection (a), trial counsel shall provide the accused with notice of the classified information that is at issue. Such notice shall identify the specific classified information at issue whenever that information previously has been made available to the accused by the United States. When the United States has not previously made the information available to the accused in connection with the case the information may be described by generic category, in such forms as the military judge may approve, rather than by identification of the specific information of concern to the United States.

"(2) ORDER BY MILITARY JUDGE UPON REQUEST OF ACCUSED.—Whenever the trial counsel requests a hearing under subsection (a), the military judge, upon request of the accused, may order the trial counsel to provide the accused, prior to trial, such details as to the portion of the charge or specification at issue in the hearing as are needed to give the accused fair notice to prepare for the hearing.

"(c) Substitutions.—

"(1) IN CAMERA PRETRIAL HEARING.—Upon request of the trial counsel pursuant to the Military Commission Rules of Evidence, and in accordance with the security procedures established by the military judge, the military judge shall conduct a classified in camera pretrial hearing concerning the admissibility of classified information.

"(2) PROTECTION OF SOURCES, METHODS, AND ACTIVITIES BY WHICH EVIDENCE ACQUIRED.—**When trial counsel seeks to introduce evidence before a military commission under this chapter and the Executive branch has classified the sources, methods, or activities by which the United States acquired the evidence, the military judge shall permit trial counsel to introduce the evidence, including a substituted evidentiary foundation pursuant to the procedures described in subsection (d), while** protecting from disclosure information identifying those sources, methods, or activities, if—

"(A) the evidence is otherwise admissible; and

"(B) the military judge finds that—

"(i) the evidence is reliable; and

"(ii) the redaction is consistent with affording the accused a fair trial.

"(d) Alternative Procedure for Disclosure of Classified Information.—

"(1) MOTION BY THE UNITED STATES.—Upon any determination by the military judge authorizing the disclosure of specific classified information under the procedures established by this section, the trial counsel may move that, in lieu of the disclosure of such specific classified information, the military judge order—

"(A) the substitution for such classified information of a statement admitting relevant facts that the specific classified information would tend to prove;

"(B) the substitution for such classified information of a summary of the specific classified information; or

"(C) any other procedure or redaction limiting the disclosure of specific classified information.

"(2) ACTION ON MOTION.—The military judge shall grant such a motion of the trial counsel if the military judge finds that the statement, summary, or other procedure or redaction will provide the defendant with substantially the same ability to make his defense as would disclosure of the specific classified information.

"(3) HEARING ON MOTION.—The military judge shall hold a hearing on any motion under this subsection. Any such hearing shall be held in camera at the request of a knowledgeable United States official possessing authority to classify information.

"(4) SUBMISSION OF STATEMENT OF DAMAGE TO NATIONAL SECURITY IF DISCLOSURE ORDERED.—The trial counsel may, in connection with a motion under paragraph (1), submit to the military judge a declaration signed by a knowledgeable United States official possessing authority to classify information certifying that disclosure of classified information would cause identifiable damage to the national security of the United States and explaining the basis for the classification of such information. If so requested by the trial counsel, the military judge shall examine such declaration during an ex parte presentation.

"(e) Sealing of Records of in Camera Hearings.—If at the close of an in camera hearing under this section (or any portion of a hearing under this section that is held in camera), the military judge determines that the classified information at issue may not be disclosed or elicited at the trial or pretrial proceeding, the record of such in camera hearing shall be sealed and preserved for use in the event of an appeal. The accused may seek reconsideration of the military judge's determination prior to or during trial.

"(f) Prohibition on Disclosure of Classified Information by the Accused; Relief for Accused When the United States Opposes Disclosure.—

"(1) ORDER TO PREVENT DISCLOSURE BY ACCUSED.—Whenever the military judge denies a motion by the trial counsel that the judge issue an order under subsection (a), (c), or (d) and the trial counsel files with the military judge a declaration signed by a knowledgeable United States official possessing authority to classify information objecting to disclosure of the classified information at issue, the military judge shall order that the accused not disclose or cause the disclosure of such information.

"(2) RESULT OF ORDER UNDER PARAGRAPH (1).—Whenever an accused is prevented by an order under paragraph (1) from disclosing or causing the disclosure of classified information, the military judge shall dismiss the case, except that, when the military judge determines that the interests of justice would not be served by dismissal of the case, the military judge shall order such other action, in lieu of dismissing the charge or specification, as the military judge determines is appropriate. Such action may include, but need not be limited to, the following:

"(A) Dismissing specified charges or specifications.

"(B) Finding against the United States on any issue as to which the excluded classified information relates.

"(C) Striking or precluding all or part of the testimony of a witness.

"(3) TIME FOR THE UNITED STATES TO SEEK INTERLOCUTORY APPEAL.—An order under paragraph (2) shall not take effect until the military judge has afforded the United States—

"(A) an opportunity to appeal such order under section 950d of this title; and

"(B) an opportunity thereafter to withdraw its objection to the disclosure of the classified information at issue.

"(g) Reciprocity.—

"(1) DISCLOSURE OF REBUTTAL INFORMATION.— Whenever the military judge determines that classified information may be disclosed in connection with a trial or pretrial proceeding, the military judge shall, unless the interests of fairness do not so require, order the United States to provide the accused with the information it expects to use to rebut the classified information. The military judge may place the United States under a continuing duty to disclose such rebuttal information.

"(2) SANCTION FOR FAILURE TO COMPLY.—If the United States fails to comply with its obligation under this subsection, the military judge—

"(A) may exclude any evidence not made the subject of a required disclosure; and

"(B) may prohibit the examination by the United States of any witness with respect to such information.

"Sec. 949p–7.   Introduction of classified information into evidence

"(a) Preservation of Classification Status.—Writings, recordings, and photographs containing classified information may be admitted into evidence in proceedings of military commissions under this chapter without change in their classification status.

"(b) Precautions by Military Judges.—

"(1) PRECAUTIONS IN ADMITTING CLASSIFIED INFORMATION INTO EVIDENCE.—The military judge in a trial by military commission, in order to prevent unnecessary disclosure of classified information, may order admission into evidence of only part of a writing, recording, or photograph, or may order admission into evidence of the whole writing, recording, or photograph with excision of some or all of the classified information contained therein, unless the whole ought in fairness be considered.

"(2) CLASSIFIED INFORMATION KEPT UNDER SEAL.—The military judge shall allow classified information offered or accepted into evidence to remain under seal during the trial, even if such evidence is disclosed in the military commission, and may, upon motion by the United States, seal exhibits containing classified information for any period after trial as necessary to prevent a disclosure of classified information when a knowledgeable United States official possessing authority to classify information submits to the military judge a declaration setting forth the damage to the national security that the disclosure of such information reasonably could be expected to cause.

"(c) Taking of Testimony.—

"(1) OBJECTION BY TRIAL COUNSEL.—During the examination of a witness, trial counsel may object to any question or line of inquiry that may require the witness to disclose classified information not previously found to be admissible.

"(2) ACTION BY MILITARY JUDGE.—Following an objection under paragraph (1), the military judge shall take such suitable action to determine whether the response is admissible as will safeguard against the compromise of any classified information. Such action may include requiring trial counsel to provide the military judge with a proffer of the witness' response to the question or line of inquiry and requiring the accused to provide the military judge with a proffer of the nature of the information sought to be elicited by the accused. Upon request, the military judge may accept an ex parte proffer by trial counsel to the extent necessary to protect classified information from disclosure, in accordance with the practice of the Federal courts under the Classified Information Procedures Act (18 U.S.C. App.).

"(d) Disclosure at Trial of Certain Statements Previously Made by a Witness.—

"(1) MOTION FOR PRODUCTION OF STATEMENTS IN POSSESSION OF THE UNITED STATES.—After a witness called by the trial counsel has testified on direct examination, the military judge, on motion of the accused, may order production of statements of the witness in the possession of the United States which relate to the subject matter as to which the witness has testified. This paragraph does not preclude discovery or assertion of a privilege otherwise authorized.

"(2) INVOCATION OF PRIVILEGE BY THE UNITED STATES.—If the United States invokes a privilege, the trial counsel may provide the prior statements of the witness to the military judge during an ex parte presentation to the extent necessary to protect classified information from disclosure, in accordance with the practice of the Federal courts under the Classified Information Procedures Act (18 U.S.C. App.).

"(3) ACTION BY MILITARY JUDGE ON MOTION.—If the military judge finds that disclosure of any portion of the statement identified by the United States as classified would be detrimental to the national security in the degree to warrant classification under the applicable Executive Order, statute, or regulation, that such portion of the statement is consistent with the testimony of the witness, and that the disclosure of such portion is not necessary to afford the accused a fair trial, the military judge shall excise that portion from the statement. If the military judge finds that such portion of the statement is inconsistent with the testimony of the witness or that its disclosure is necessary to afford the accused a fair trial, the military judge, shall, upon the request of the trial counsel, review alternatives to disclosure in accordance with section 949p-6(d) of this title.

"§ 950f. Review by United States Court of Military Commission Review

"(a) ESTABLISHMENT.—There is a court of record to be known as the 'United States Court of Military Commission Review' (in this section referred to as the 'Court'). The Court shall consist of one or more panels, each composed of not less than three appellate military judges. For the purpose of reviewing decisions of military commissions under this chapter, the Court may sit in panels or as a whole, in accordance with rules prescribed by the Secretary of Defense.

"(b) JUDGES.—

"(1) Judges on the Court shall be assigned or appointed in a manner consistent with the provisions of this subsection.

"(2) The Secretary of Defense may assign persons who are appellate military judges to be judges on the Court. Any judge so assigned shall be a commissioned officer of the armed forces, and shall meet the qualifications for military judges prescribed by section 948j(b) of this title.

"(3) The President may appoint, by and with the advice and consent of the Senate, additional judges to the United States Court of Military Commission Review.

"(4) No person may serve as a judge on the Court in any case in which that person acted as a military judge, counsel, or reviewing official.

. . .

"(c) CASES TO BE REVIEWED nder regulations of the Secretary, review the record in each case that is referred to the Court by the convening authority under section 950c of this title with respect to any matter properly raised by the accused.

"(d) STANDARD AND SCOPE OF REVIEW.—In a case reviewed by the Court under this section, the Court may act only with respect to the findings and sentence as approved by the convening authority. The Court may affirm only such findings of guilty, and the sentence or such part or amount of the sentence, as the Court finds correct in law and fact and determines, on the basis of the entire record, should be approved. In considering the record, the Court may weigh the evidence, judge the credibility of witnesses, and determine controverted questions of fact, recognizing that the military commission saw and heard the witnesses.

. . . .

"§ 950g. Review by United States Court of Appeals for the District of Columbia Circuit; writ of certiorari to Supreme Court

"(a) EXCLUSIVE APPELLATE JURISDICTION.—Except as provided in subsection (b), the United States Court of Appeals for the District of Columbia Circuit shall have exclusive jurisdiction to determine the validity of a final judgment rendered by a military commission (as approved by the convening authority and, where applicable, the United States Court of Military Commission Review) under this chapter.

H. R. 2647–415

"(b) EXHAUSTION OF OTHER APPEALS.—The United States Court of Appeals for the District of Columbia Circuit may not review a final judgment described in subsection (a) until all other appeals under this chapter have been waived or exhausted.

. . .

"(d) SCOPE AND NATURE OF REVIEW.—The United States Court of Appeals for the District of Columbia Circuit may act under this section only with respect to the findings and sentence as approved by the convening authority and as affirmed or set aside as incorrect in law by the United States Court of Military Commission Review, and shall take action only with respect to matters of law, including the sufficiency of the evidence to support the verdict.

"(e) REVIEW BY SUPREME COURT.—The Supreme Court may review by writ of certiorari pursuant to section 1254 of title 28 the final judgment of the United States Court of Appeals for the District of Columbia Circuit under this section.

. . .

4. THE MCA OF 2009: DEFINITION OF OFFENSES

Sec. 950p. Definitions; construction of certain offenses; common circumstances

'(a) Definitions—In this subchapter:

'(1) The term 'military objective' means combatants and those objects during hostilities which, by their nature, location, purpose, or use, effectively contribute to the war-fighting or war-sustaining capability of an opposing force and whose total or partial destruction, capture, or neutralization would constitute a definite military advantage to the attacker under the circumstances at the time of an attack.

'(2) The term 'protected person' means any person entitled to protection under one or more of the Geneva Conventions, including civilians not taking an active part in hostilities, military personnel placed out of combat by sickness, wounds, or detention, and military medical or religious personnel.

'(3) The term 'protected property' means any property specifically protected by the law of war, including buildings dedicated to religion, education, art, science, or charitable purposes, historic monuments, hospitals, and places where the sick and wounded are collected, but only if and to the extent such property is not being used for military purposes or is not otherwise a military objective. The term includes objects properly identified by one of the distinctive emblems of the Geneva Conventions, but does not include civilian property that is a military objective.

'(b) Construction of Certain Offenses—The intent required for offenses under paragraphs (1), (2), (3), (4), and (12) of section 950t of this title precludes the applicability of such offenses with regard to collateral damage or to death, damage, or injury incident to a lawful attack.

'(c) Common Circumstances—An offense specified in this subchapter is triable by military commission under this chapter only if the offense is committed in the context of and associated with hostilities.

'(d) Effect—The provisions of this subchapter codify offenses that have traditionally been triable by military commission. This chapter does not establish new crimes that did not exist before the date of the enactment of this subchapter, as amended by the National Defense Authorization Act for Fiscal Year 2010, but rather codifies those crimes for trial by military commission. Because the provisions of this subchapter codify offenses that have traditionally been triable under the law of war or otherwise triable by military commission, this subchapter does not preclude trial for offenses that occurred before the date of the enactment of this subchapter, as so amended.

'Sec. 950q. Principals

'Any person punishable under this chapter who—

'(1) commits an offense punishable by this chapter, or aids, abets, counsels, commands, or procures its commission;

'(2) causes an act to be done which if directly performed by him would be punishable by this chapter; or

'(3) is a superior commander who, with regard to acts punishable by this chapter, knew, had reason to know, or should have known, that a subordinate was about to commit such acts or had done so and who failed to take the necessary and reasonable measures to prevent such acts or to punish the perpetrators thereof,

is a principal.

'Sec. 950r. Accessory after the fact

'Any person subject to this chapter who, knowing that an offense punishable by this chapter has been committed, receives, comforts, or assists the offender in order to hinder or prevent his apprehension, trial, or punishment shall be punished as a military commission under this chapter may direct.

'Sec. 950s. Conviction of lesser offenses

'An accused may be found guilty of an offense necessarily included in the offense charged or of an attempt to commit either the offense charged or an attempt to commit either the offense charged or an offense necessarily included therein.

'Sec. 950t. Crimes triable by military commission

'The following offenses shall be triable by military commission under this chapter at any time without limitation:

'(1) MURDER OF PROTECTED PERSONS—Any person subject to this chapter who intentionally kills one or more protected persons shall be punished by death or such other punishment as a military commission under this chapter may direct.

'(2) ATTACKING CIVILIANS—Any person subject to this chapter who intentionally engages in an attack upon a civilian population as such, or individual civilians not taking active part in hostilities, shall be punished, if death results to one or more of the victims, by death or such other punishment as a military commission under this chapter may direct, and, if death does not result to any of the victims, by such punishment, other than death, as a military commission under this chapter may direct.

'(3) ATTACKING CIVILIAN OBJECTS—Any person subject to this chapter who intentionally engages in an attack upon a civilian object that is not a military objective shall be punished as a military commission under this chapter may direct.

'(4) ATTACKING PROTECTED PROPERTY—Any person subject to this chapter who intentionally engages in an attack upon protected property shall be punished as a military commission under this chapter may direct.

'(5) PILLAGING—Any person subject to this chapter who intentionally and in the absence of military necessity appropriates or seizes property for private or personal use, without the consent of a person with authority to permit such appropriation or seizure, shall be punished as a military commission under this chapter may direct.

'(6) DENYING QUARTER—Any person subject to this chapter who, with effective command or control over subordinate groups, declares, orders, or otherwise indicates to those groups that there shall be no survivors or surrender accepted, with the intent to threaten an adversary or to conduct hostilities such that there would be no survivors or surrender accepted, shall be punished as a military commission under this chapter may direct.

'(7) TAKING HOSTAGES—Any person subject to this chapter who, having knowingly seized or detained one or more persons, threatens to kill, injure, or continue to detain such person or persons with the intent of compelling any nation, person other than the hostage, or group of persons to act or refrain from acting as an explicit or implicit condition for the safety or release of such person or persons, shall be punished, if death results to one or more of the victims, by death or such other punishment as a military commission under this chapter may direct, and, if death does not result to any of the victims, by such punishment, other than death, as a military commission under this chapter may direct.

'(8) EMPLOYING POISON OR SIMILAR WEAPONS—Any person subject to this chapter who intentionally, as a method of warfare, employs a substance or weapon that releases a substance that causes death or serious and lasting damage to health in the ordinary course of events, through its asphyxiating, bacteriological, or toxic properties, shall be punished, if death results to one or more of the victims, by death or such other punishment as a military commission under this chapter may direct, and, if death does not result to any of the victims, by such punishment, other than death, as a military commission under this chapter may direct.

'(9) USING PROTECTED PERSONS AS A SHIELD—Any person subject to this chapter who positions, or otherwise takes advantage of, a protected person with the intent to shield a military objective from attack. or to shield, favor, or impede military operations, shall be punished, if death results to one or more of the victims, by death or such other punishment as a military commission under this chapter may direct, and, if death does not result to any of the victims, by such punishment, other than death, as a military commission under this chapter may direct.

'(10) USING PROTECTED PROPERTY AS A SHIELD—Any person subject to this chapter who positions, or otherwise takes advantage of the location of, protected property with the intent to shield a military objective from attack, or to shield, favor, or impede military operations, shall be punished as a military commission under this chapter may direct.

'(11) TORTURE—

'(A) OFFENSE—Any person subject to this chapter who commits an act specifically intended to inflict severe physical or mental pain or suffering (other than pain or suffering incidental to lawful sanctions) upon another person within his custody or physical control for the purpose of obtaining information or a confession, punishment, intimidation, coercion, or any reason based on discrimination of any kind, shall be punished, if death results to one or more of the victims, by death or such other punishment as a military commission under this chapter may direct, and, if death does not result to any of the victims, by such punishment, other than death, as a military commission under this chapter may direct.

'(B) SEVERE MENTAL PAIN OR SUFFERING DEFINED— In this paragraph, the term 'severe mental pain or suffering' has the meaning given that term in section 2340(2) of title 18.

'(12) CRUEL OR INHUMAN TREATMENT—Any person subject to this chapter who subjects another person in their custody or under their physical control, regardless of nationality or physical location, to cruel or inhuman treatment that constitutes a grave breach of common Article 3 of the Geneva Conventions shall be punished, if death results to the victim, by death or such other punishment as a military commission under this chapter may direct, and, if death does not result to the victim, by such punishment, other than death, as a military commission under this chapter may direct.

'(13) INTENTIONALLY CAUSING SERIOUS BODILY INJURY—

'(A) OFFENSE—Any person subject to this chapter who intentionally causes serious bodily injury to one or more persons, including privileged belligerents, in violation of the law of war shall be punished, if death results to one or more of the victims, by death or such other punishment as a military commission under this chapter may direct, and, if death does not result to any of the victims, by such punishment, other than death, as a military commission under this chapter may direct.

'(B) SERIOUS BODILY INJURY DEFINED—In this paragraph, the term 'serious bodily injury' means bodily injury which involves—

'(i) a substantial risk of death;

'(ii) extreme physical pain;

'(iii) protracted and obvious disfigurement; or

'(iv) protracted loss or impairment of the function of a bodily member, organ, or mental faculty.

'(14) MUTILATING OR MAIMING—Any person subject to this chapter who intentionally injures one or more protected persons by disfiguring the person or persons by any mutilation of the person or persons, or by permanently disabling any member, limb, or organ of the body of the person or persons, without any legitimate medical or dental purpose, shall be punished, if death results to one or more of the victims, by death or such other punishment as a military commission under this chapter may direct, and, if death does not result to any of the victims, by such punishment, other than death, as a military commission under this chapter may direct.

'(15) MURDER IN VIOLATION OF THE LAW OF WAR—Any person subject to this chapter who intentionally kills one or more persons, including privileged belligerents, in violation of the law of war shall be punished by death or such other punishment as a military commission under this chapter may direct.

'(16) DESTRUCTION OF PROPERTY IN VIOLATION OF THE LAW OF WAR—Any person subject to this chapter who intentionally destroys property belonging to another person in violation of the law of war shall punished as a military commission under this chapter may direct.

'(17) USING TREACHERY OR PERFIDY—Any person subject to this chapter who, after inviting the confidence or belief of one or more persons that they were entitled to, or obliged to accord, protection under the law of war, intentionally makes use of that confidence or belief in killing, injuring, or capturing such person or persons shall be punished, if death results to one or more of the victims, by death or such other punishment as a military commission under this chapter may direct, and, if death does not result to any of the victims, by such punishment, other than death, as a military commission under this chapter may direct.

'(18) IMPROPERLY USING A FLAG OF TRUCE—Any person subject to this chapter who uses a flag of truce to feign an intention to negotiate, surrender, or otherwise suspend hostilities when there is no such intention shall be punished as a military commission under this chapter may direct.

'(19) IMPROPERLY USING A DISTINCTIVE EMBLEM—Any person subject to this chapter who intentionally uses a distinctive emblem recognized by the law of war for combatant purposes in a manner prohibited by the law of war shall be punished as a military commission under this chapter may direct.

'(20) INTENTIONALLY MISTREATING A DEAD BODY—Any person subject to this chapter who intentionally mistreats the body of a dead person, without justification by legitimate military necessary, shall be punished as a military commission under this chapter may direct.

'(21) RAPE—Any person subject to this chapter who forcibly or with coercion or threat of force wrongfully invades the body of a person by penetrating, however slightly, the anal or genital opening of the victim with any part of the body of the accused, or with any foreign object, shall be punished as a military commission under this chapter may direct.

'(22) SEXUAL ASSAULT OR ABUSE—Any person subject to this chapter who forcibly or with coercion or threat of force engages in sexual contact with one or more persons, or causes one or more persons to engage in sexual contact, shall be punished as a military commission under this chapter may direct

'(23) HIJACKING OR HAZARDING A VESSEL OR AIRCRAFT—Any person subject to this chapter who intentionally seizes, exercises unauthorized control over, or endangers the safe navigation of a vessel or aircraft that is not a legitimate military objective shall be punished, if death results to one or more of the victims, by death or such other punishment as a military commission under this chapter may direct, and, if death does not result to any of the victims, by such punishment, other than death, as a military commission under this chapter may direct.

'(24) TERRORISM—Any person subject to this chapter who intentionally kills or inflicts great bodily harm on one or more protected persons, or intentionally engages in an act that evinces a wanton disregard for human life, in a manner calculated to influence or affect the conduct of government or civilian population by intimidation or coercion, or to retaliate against government conduct, shall be punished, if death results to one or more of the victims, by death or such other punishment as a military commission under this chapter may direct, and, if death does not result to any of the victims, by such punishment, other than death, as a military commission under this chapter may direct.

'(25) PROVIDING MATERIAL SUPPORT FOR TERRORISM—

'(A) OFFENSE—Any person subject to this chapter who provides material support or resources, knowing or intending that they are to be used in preparation for, or in carrying out, an act of terrorism (as set forth in paragraph (24) of this section), or who intentionally provides material support or resources to an international terrorist organization engaged in hostilities against the United States, knowing that such organization has engaged or engages in terrorism (as so set forth), shall be punished as a military commission under this chapter may direct.

'(B) MATERIAL SUPPORT OR RESOURCES DEFINED— In this paragraph, the term 'material support or resources' has the meaning given that term in section 2339A(b) of title 18.

'(26) WRONGFULLY AIDING THE ENEMY—Any person subject to this chapter who, in breach of an allegiance or duty to the United States, knowingly and intentionally aids an enemy of the United States, or one of the co-belligerents of the enemy, shall be punished as a military commission under this chapter may direct.

'(27) SPYING—Any person subject to this chapter who, in violation of the law of war and with intent or reason to believe that it is to be used to the injury of the United States or to the advantage of a foreign power, collects or attempts to collect information by clandestine means or while acting under false pretenses, for the purpose of conveying such information to an enemy of the United States, or one of the co-belligerents of the enemy, shall be punished by death or such other punishment as a military commission under this chapter may direct.

'(28) ATTEMPTS—

'(A) IN GENERAL—Any person subject to this chapter who attempts to commit any offense punishable by this chapter shall be punished as a military commission under this chapter may direct.

'(B) SCOPE OF OFFENSE—An act, done with specific intent to commit an offense under this chapter, amounting to more than mere preparation and tending, even though failing, to effect its commission, is an attempt to commit that offense.

'(C) EFFECT OF CONSUMMATION—Any person subject to this chapter may be convicted of an attempt to commit an offense although it appears on the trial that the offense was consummated.

'(29) CONSPIRACY—Any person subject to this chapter who conspires to commit one or more substantive offenses triable by military commission under this subchapter, and who knowingly does any overt act to effect the object of the conspiracy, shall be punished, if death results to one or more of the victims, by death or such other punishment as a military commission under this chapter may direct, and, if death does not result to any of the victims, by such punishment, other than death, as a military commission under this chapter may direct.

'(30) SOLICITATION—Any person subject to this chapter who solicits or advises another or others to commit one or more substantive offenses triable by military commission under this chapter shall, if the offense solicited or advised is attempted or committed, be punished with the punishment provided for the commission of the offense, but, if the offense solicited or advised is not committed or attempted, shall be punished as a military commission under this chapter may direct.

'(31) CONTEMPT—A military commission under this chapter may punish for contempt any person who uses any menacing word, sign, or gesture in its presence, or who disturbs its proceedings by any riot or disorder.

'(32) PERJURY AND OBSTRUCTION OF JUSTICE—A military commission under this chapter may try offenses and impose such punishment as the military commission may direct for perjury, false testimony, or obstruction of justice related to the military commission.'.

D. A SUMMARY HISTORY OF THE POST-9/11 MILITARY COMMISSIONS PROSECUTIONS

Prior to the decision of the Supreme Court in Hamdan v. Rumsfeld, supra, the military commissions operated under the terms of President Bush's post-9/11 Military Order authorizing establishment of the military commissions and also, inter alia, under the terms of Military Commissions Order No. 1, supplemented by amendments which contained detailed provisions regarding the procedures to be used in military commission proceedings.

Prior to the Hamdan decision, 10 individuals had been charged with offenses to be tried before the military commissions. In January, 2007, at a Department of Defense press briefing, it was reported that in addition to the 10 cases that had been initiated, there were 14 cases in various stages of preparation, and that there were potentially viable charges for violations of law of war in the range of 60 to 80 cases.

The charges variously included conspiracy to commit various offenses including attacking civilians, murder by an unprivileged belligerent, and terrorism. Proceedings against some of those charged had been conducted in the late summer and early fall, 2004. News reports regarding these proceedings reported that "officials acknowledge that the process is in turmoil." N.Y. Times, Sept. 26, 2004, Pt. I, 26. Among other problems, some of the trial panel's members were successfully challenged for bias or conflict of interest, and the translation system was inadequate. Ibid.

The Supreme Court's decision in Hamdan v. Rumsfeld and the subsequent enactment of the Military Commissions Act changed the legal landscape and required the prosecutions that had begun earlier, in effect, to be started again.

In response to the Hamdan decision, Congress enacted the Military Commissions Act (MCA) of 2006, in an effort to address the issues discussed in Hamdan. Inter alia, the MCA authorized the adoption of rules and procedures by the Secretary of Defense. Under this authorization, the Secretary issued a Manual for Military Commissions. Subsequently, at the instance of the Obama administration in 2009, Congress amended the 2006 Act in a number of respects, but the basic approach remained intact. In 2010, a revised version of the Manual for Military Commissions was issued; it was revised again in 2012.

Prior to the inauguration of President Obama in January, 2009, only three commission trials, which had been initiated post-Hamdan and post 2006 MCA, had been completed. As one of his first official acts after the inauguration, President Obama requested that ongoing and impending military commission trials be suspended for 120 days. The three cases that had been completed prior to this suspension were:

David Hicks, who pleaded guilty. He had been charged with providing material support for terrorism and attempted murder in violation of the law of war. In March, 2007, he entered into a plea agreement, under the terms of which he effectively served an additional nine months (which would be served in Australia) in exchange for which he pleaded guilty.

Salim Ahmed Hamdan. Hamdan was convicted in August, 2008 on a charge of providing material support to terrorism and acquitted on a charge of conspiracy. He was sentenced to five and a half years in prison which, given time already served, meant that he only had to serve four additional months. He was subsequently released and transferred to Yemen in November, 2008 where he served the remainder of his sentence. He was released from jail in Yemen in January, 2009. After his release, he filed an appeal aimed at setting aside his conviction. Excerpts from his case on appeal are reproduced infra.

Ali Hamza al Bahlul. He was convicted on November 2, 2008 by a nine person jury of military officers for conspiracy, solicitation to commit murder and providing material support for terrorism. Bahlul refused to participate in the trial or to permit his counsel to participate. It was alleged that he had scripted videotaped wills of two of the September 11 hijackers, and he was charged with having made a two hour al Qaeda promotional video designed to recruit suicide bombers that included a portrayal and praise of the attack on the U.S.S. Cole. Bahlul was sentenced to life in prison. The case involving his appeal is reproduced infra.

A number of other cases were pending before the military commissions at the time President Obama suspended proceedings. In some instances, the government requested an additional suspension of the proceedings, while the administration sought new legislation, which it eventually obtained in the form of the 2009 revision of the Military Commissions Act. In a few instances, the government moved to dismiss some of the pending cases.

QUESTIONS AND NOTES

1.   Some of the offenses listed under the MCA have been challenged as not being offenses under the laws of war. If they are not law of war offenses, it is questioned whether they can be applied to persons who engaged in the proscribed conduct before the MCA was enacted. Among the controversial offenses are conspiracy and the crime of providing material support. Recall that Justice Stevens in Hamdan, speaking for a plurality of the Court, addressed the question of whether conspiracy was a crime under the laws of war.

2.   Two cases mentioned above, were appealed to the United States Court of Military Commission Review, that of Salim Ahmed Hamdan and Ali Hamza Ahmad Suliman Bahlul, and subsequently, to the United States Court of Appeals for the District of Columbia Circuit. The general issues described in note 1 supra, were before the reviewing court in both the Hamdan and Bahlul cases.

3.   The U.S. Court of Appeals for the D.C. Circuit reversed Hamdan's conviction, Hamdan v. United States, 696 F.3d 1238 (D.C. Cir. 2012), stating:

> We turn, then, to the question whether material support for terrorism is an international-law war crime.

> It is true that international law establishes at least some forms of terrorism, including the intentional targeting of civilian populations, as war crimes. See, e.g., Rome Statute of the International Criminal Court art. 8(2)(b), July 17, 1998, 2187 U.N.T.S. 90; Geneva Convention Relative to the Protection of Civilian Persons in Time of War (Geneva IV), art. 33, Aug. 12, 1949, 6 U.S.T. 3516, 75 U.N.T.S. 287; COMMISSION OF RESPONSIBILITIES, CONFERENCE OF PARIS 1919, VIOLATION OF THE LAWS AND CUSTOMS OF WAR 17 (Clarendon Press 1919) (the Allied Nations condemned Germany for "the execution of a system of terrorism" after World War I).

> But the issue here is whether material support for terrorism is an international-law war crime. The answer is no. International law leaves it to individual nations to proscribe material support for terrorism under their domestic laws if they so choose. There is no international-law proscription of material support for terrorism.

> To begin with, there are no relevant international treaties that make material support for terrorism a recognized international-law war crime. Neither the Hague Convention nor the Geneva Conventions—the sources that are "the major treaties on the law of war"—acknowledge material support for terrorism as a war crime. See Hamdan, 548 U.S. at 604, 126 S.Ct. 2749 (plurality); Geneva Convention Relative to the Protection of Civilian Persons in Time of War (Geneva IV), Aug. 12, 1949, 6 U.S.T. 3516, 75 U.N.T.S. 287; Hague Convention (IV) Respecting the Laws and Customs of War on Land and Its Annex, Oct. 18, 1907, 36 Stat. 2277.

> Nor does customary international law otherwise make material support for terrorism a war crime. Customary international law is a kind of common law; it is the body of international legal principles said to reflect the consistent and settled practice of nations. See

RESTATEMENT (THIRD) OF FOREIGN RELATIONS LAW OF THE UNITED STATES § 102(2) (1987).[10]

But here, the content of customary international law is quite evident. Material support for terrorism was not a recognized violation of the international law of war as of 2001 (or even today, for that matter). As we have noted, the Geneva Conventions and the Hague Convention do not prohibit material support for terrorism. The 1998 Rome Statute of the International Criminal Court, which catalogues an extensive list of international war crimes, makes no mention of material support for terrorism. See Rome Statute of the International Criminal Court, July 17, 1998, 2187 U.N.T.S. 90. . . .

Commentators on international law have similarly explained that material support for terrorism is not an international-law war crime. See, e.g., ANDREA BIANCHI & YASMIN NAQVI, INTERNATIONAL HUMANITARIAN LAW AND TERRORISM 244 (2011) ("there is little evidence" that a proscription of "material support for terrorism" is "considered to be part of the laws and customs of war"). Nor is the offense of material support for terrorism listed in the JAG handbook on the law of war. See U.S. ARMY JAG, LAW OF WAR HANDBOOK (Maj. Keith E. Puls ed., 2005); see also Jennifer K. Elsea, The Military Commissions Act of 2006: Analysis of Procedural Rules and Comparison with Previous DOD Rules and the Uniform Code of Military Justice 12 (CRS, updated Sept. 27, 2007) ("defining as a war crime the 'material support for terrorism' does not appear to be supported by historical precedent") (footnote omitted).

In short, neither the major conventions on the law of war nor prominent modern international tribunals nor leading international-law experts have identified material support for terrorism as a war crime. Perhaps most telling, before this case, no person has ever been tried by an international-law war crimes tribunal for material support for terrorism.

---

[10] Although customary international law, including the customary international law of war, contains some well-defined prohibitions at the core, the contours of customary international law are imprecise. That imprecision provides good reason for Congress and the Executive, when they want to outlaw violations of perceived international-law norms, to enact statutes outlawing specific conduct, rather than simply prohibiting violation of something as vague as "international law" or "the law of nations" or the "law of war." Congress has done so in many recent statutes, . . .

At the same time, the imprecision of customary international law calls for significant caution by U.S. courts before permitting civil or criminal liability premised on violation of such a vague prohibition. Cf. Sosa v. Alvarez-Machain, 542 U.S. 692, 124 S.Ct. 2739, 159 L.Ed.2d 718 (2004). A general prohibition against violations of "international law" or the "law of nations" or the "law of war" may fail in certain cases to provide the fair notice that is a foundation of the rule of law in the United States. Therefore, as the Supreme Court required in an analogous context in Sosa, and as the plurality suggested in Hamdan, imposing liability on the basis of a violation of "international law" or the "law of nations" or the "law of war" generally must be based on norms firmly grounded in international law. See Sosa, 542 U.S. at 724–38, 124 S.Ct. 2739; Hamdan, 548 U.S. at 602–03 & n. 34, 605, 126 S.Ct. 2749 (plurality). In this case, the asserted norm has no grounding in international law, much less firm grounding.

Not surprisingly, therefore, even the U.S. Government concedes in this case that material support for terrorism is not a recognized international-law war crime. No treaty that the Government has cited or that we are aware of identifies material support for terrorism as a war crime. And the Government further admits: The "offense of providing material support to terrorism, like spying and aiding the enemy, has not attained international recognition at this time as a violation of customary international law." Brief for the United States at 48; see also id. at 55–56 (same).

To be sure, there is a strong argument that aiding and abetting a recognized international-law war crime such as terrorism is itself an international-law war crime. And there are other similar war crimes. But Hamdan was not charged with aiding and abetting terrorism or some other similar war crime. He was charged with material support for terrorism. And as the Government acknowledges, aiding and abetting terrorism prohibits different conduct, imposes different mens rea requirements, and entails different causation standards than material support for terrorism. If the Government wanted to charge Hamdan with aiding and abetting terrorism or some other war crime that was sufficiently rooted in the international law of war (and thus covered by 10 U.S.C. § 821) at the time of Hamdan's conduct, it should have done so.

The Government latches on to a few isolated precedents from the Civil War era to prop up its assertion that material support for terrorism was a pre-existing war crime as of 2001 for purposes of 10 U.S.C. § 821. There are several independent reasons that those cases fail to support the Government's argument. First, the Civil War cases did not involve any charges of material support for terrorism. . . . The Government contends that those Civil War precedents illuminate what it calls the "U.S. common law of war"—not the international law of war. But the statutory constraint here imposed by 10 U.S.C. § 821 is the international law of war. As the Government told the Supreme Court in Quirin, "This 'common law of war' is a centuries-old body of largely unwritten rules and principles of international law which governs the behavior of both soldiers and civilians during time of war." Brief for the United States at 29, in Quirin, 317 U.S. 1, 63 S.Ct. 2. To be sure, U.S. precedents may inform the content of international law. But those Civil War precedents fail to establish material support for terrorism as a war crime under the international law of war as of 1996 to 2001. And even the Government admits that material support for terrorism was not an international-law war crime as of 1996 to 2001.

In short, material support for terrorism was not an international-law war crime under 10 U.S.C. § 821 at the time Hamdan engaged in the relevant conduct.

. . .

Because we read the Military Commissions Act not to sanction retroactive punishment for new crimes, and because material support for terrorism was not a pre-existing war crime under 10 U.S.C. § 821, Hamdan's conviction for material support for terrorism cannot stand. We reverse the decision of the Court of Military Commission Review and direct that Hamdan's conviction for material support for terrorism be vacated.

So ordered.

———————

The United States did not appeal the Hamdan decision, supra, and initially it appeared that the government was not going to challenge the Hamdan ruling. It was reported in the New York Times that the legal strategy to pursue in connection with the issues raised by the Hamdan decision was the subject of controversy within the administration. The decisions in the appeal of Al Bahlul followed soon after.

AL BAHLUL V. UNITED STATES
767 F.3d 1 (D.C. Cir. 2014) (en banc)

Before: GARLAND, CHIEF JUDGE, and HENDERSON, ROGERS, TATEL, BROWN, GRIFFITH and KAVANAUGH, CIRCUIT JUDGES.

Opinion for the court filed by CIRCUIT JUDGE HENDERSON.

Ali Hamza Ahmad Suliman al Bahlul (Bahlul) served as a personal assistant to Osama bin Laden, produced propaganda videos for al Qaeda and assisted with preparations for the attacks of September 11, 2001 that killed thousands of Americans. Three months after 9/11, Bahlul was captured in Pakistan and transferred to the United States Naval Base at Guantanamo Bay, Cuba. Military prosecutors charged him with three crimes: conspiracy to commit war crimes, providing material support for terrorism and solicitation of others to commit war crimes. A military commission convicted him of all three crimes and sentenced him to life imprisonment. The United States Court of Military Commission Review (CMCR) affirmed his conviction and sentence. Bahlul appeals. For the reasons that follow, we reject Bahlul's ex post facto challenge to his conspiracy conviction and remand that conviction to the original panel of this Court for it to dispose of several remaining issues. In addition, we vacate his material support and solicitation convictions.

I.   Background

Bahlul is a native of Yemen. In the late 1990s, he traveled to Afghanistan to join al Qaeda. He completed military-like training while staying at an al Qaeda guesthouse and eventually met and pledged an oath of loyalty ("bayat") to bin Laden. Bin Laden assigned Bahlul to work in al Qaeda's media office.

On October 12, 2000, al Qaeda suicide bombers attacked the U.S.S. Cole, killing 17 American servicemen and wounding 39 others. Bin Laden later instructed Bahlul to create a video celebrating the attack for use as a recruiting tool. The video Bahlul produced (and bin Laden edited) includes footage of the attack, calls for jihad against the United States and propaganda blaming "Western infidels" and complicit Middle Eastern regimes for Muslim suffering. Bahlul considered it one of the best propaganda videos al Qaeda had produced and it has been translated into several languages and widely distributed.

Bin Laden then appointed Bahlul as his personal assistant and secretary for public relations. Bahlul arranged the loyalty oaths of two of the 9/11 hijackers, Mohamed Atta and Ziad al Jarrah, and prepared their "martyr wills"—propaganda declarations documenting al Qaeda's role in the attacks. Bahlul claims he sought to participate in the 9/11 attacks himself but bin Laden refused because he considered his media man too important to lose. In the days preceding 9/11, Bahlul assembled al Qaeda's media equipment and evacuated al Qaeda's Kandahar headquarters with bin Laden and other senior al Qaeda leaders. They traveled to a remote region of Afghanistan where, on September 11, 2001, they heard reports of the day's attacks via a radio operated by Bahlul. Bin Laden subsequently asked Bahlul to research the economic effects of the attacks and report his findings.

In the following weeks, Bahlul fled to Pakistan. He was captured there in December 2001 and turned over to U.S. forces. In 2002, he was transferred to the U.S. Naval Base at Guantanamo Bay, Cuba, where he has since been detained as an enemy combatant pursuant to the 2001 Authorization for Use of Military Force (AUMF). Two months after 9/11, President Bush invoked the AUMF and Article 21 of the Uniform Code of Military Justice (UCMJ), 10 U.S.C. § 821 (hereinafter "section 821"), to establish military commissions to try "member[s] of . . . al Qaeda" and others who "engaged in, aided or abetted, or conspired to commit, acts of international terrorism, or acts in preparation therefor." In 2003, the President designated Bahlul eligible for trial by military commission and in 2004 military prosecutors charged him with conspiracy to commit war crimes.

. . .The Supreme Court has long recognized that unlawful enemy combatants may be prosecuted by military commission for their war crimes. There are three traditional bases for military commission jurisdiction: military government, martial law and the law of war. First, military commissions may try ordinary crimes—e.g., manslaughter or robbery-and violations of military orders committed by both soldiers and civilians in territories under U.S. military government. Second, military commissions may try ordinary crimes and violations of military orders committed by soldiers and civilians in territory under martial law-as much of our country was during the Civil War. Third, and "utterly different" from the first two categories, military commissions may try offenses against the law of war. It is undisputed that the commission that tried Bahlul is of the third type: a law-of-war military commission. A military commission convened pursuant to the 2006 MCA must be composed of at least five "members," who are qualified active duty officers of the armed forces and play a role similar to a petit jury. A military judge presides over the trial.

In 2008, military prosecutors amended the charges against Bahlul to allege three of the offenses enumerated in the 2006 MCA based on the conduct summarized above-conspiracy to commit war crimes, providing material support for terrorism and solicitation of others to commit war crimes. The conspiracy and solicitation charges alleged seven object crimes proscribed by the 2006 MCA: murder of protected persons, attacking civilians, attacking civilian objects, murder in violation of the law of war, destruction of property in violation of the law of war, terrorism and providing material support for terrorism. Bahlul admitted all of the factual allegations against him, with the exception of the allegation that he had armed himself with a suicide belt to protect bin Laden. He nevertheless pleaded not guilty to the charged offenses because he denied the legitimacy of the military commission and sought to absent himself from the proceedings as a boycott. He objected to representation by appointed defense counsel and expressed a desire to proceed pro se, although his attempts to absent himself from the proceedings at times complicated matters and forced defense counsel to stand in for Bahlul and carry out his instructions not to present a defense. Bahlul waived all pretrial motions, asked no questions during voir dire, made no objections to prosecution evidence, presented no defense and declined to make opening and closing arguments.

The military commission convicted Bahlul of all three offenses. Using a detailed findings worksheet, it found that Bahlul conspired to commit and solicited each of the seven alleged object offenses and that Bahlul committed ten of the eleven alleged overt acts. The commission sentenced him to life imprisonment and the convening authority, Susan J. Crawford, approved the findings and sentence. The CMCR affirmed Bahlul's conviction and sentence in a 112-page opinion. Bahlul then appealed to this Court.

While Bahlul's appeal was pending, this Court held that the 2006 MCA "does not authorize retroactive prosecution for conduct committed before enactment of that Act unless the conduct was already prohibited under existing U.S. law as a war crime triable by military commission." Hamdan v. United States (Hamdan II), 696 F.3d 1238, 1248 (D.C.Cir.2012). The

Court declared that providing material support for terrorism—the only charge at issue in that appeal—was not a pre-existing war crime triable by military commission; it therefore vacated Hamdan's conviction on that offense. Id. at 1248–53. The Government subsequently conceded that Hamdan II's reasoning required vacatur of all three of Bahlul's convictions. Based on that concession, a panel of this Court vacated the convictions. We subsequently granted the Government's petition for rehearing en banc.

II. Standard of Review

Bahlul argues that the 2006 MCA must be construed to make triable by military commission only those crimes that were recognized under the international law of war when committed. He further contends that, if the 2006 MCA authorizes retroactive prosecution of new law-of-war offenses by military commission, his convictions violate the Ex Post Facto Clause. Bahlul made neither of these arguments before the military commission.

"—'No procedural principle is more familiar to this Court than that a constitutional right,' or a right of any other sort, 'may be forfeited in criminal as well as civil cases by the failure to make timely assertion of the right before a tribunal having jurisdiction to determine it.' " United States v. Olano, 507 U.S. 725, 731, 113 S.Ct. 1770, 123 L.Ed.2d 508 (1993). This fundamental principle of appellate review generally bars a party who failed to preserve an argument in a lower tribunal from raising it on appeal absent plain error or exceptional circumstances.

. . .

III. Statutory Analysis

As noted, Hamdan II held that the 2006 MCA "does not authorize retroactive prosecution for conduct committed before enactment of that Act unless the conduct was already prohibited under existing U.S. law as a war crime triable by military commission." Because we conclude, for the reasons that follow, that the 2006 MCA is unambiguous in its intent to authorize retroactive prosecution for the crimes enumerated in the statute—regardless of their pre-existing law-of-war status—we now overrule Hamdan II's statutory holding.

A. The 2006 MCA is Unambiguous

The 2006 MCA confers jurisdiction on military commissions to try "any offense made punishable by this chapter or the law of war when committed by an alien unlawful enemy combatant before, on, or after September 11, 2001. " "Any," in this context, means "all." The "offense[s] made punishable by this chapter" include the charges of which Bahlul was convicted: conspiracy to commit war crimes, providing material support for terrorism and solicitation of others to commit war crimes. There could hardly be a clearer statement of the Congress's intent to confer jurisdiction on military commissions to try the enumerated crimes regardless whether they occurred "before, on, or after September 11, 2001." And the provisions of the statute enumerating the crimes triable thereunder expressly "do not preclude trial for crimes that occurred before the date of the enactment of this chapter." For good reason: If it were otherwise, section 948d's conferral of jurisdiction to prosecute the enumerated crimes occurring on or before September 11, 2001 would be inoperative. Although we presume that statutes apply only prospectively "absent clear congressional intent" to the contrary, that presumption is overcome by the clear language of the 2006 MCA.

Review of the inter-branch dialogue which brought about the 2006 MCA confirms the Congress's intent to apply all of the statute's enumerated crimes retroactively. In Hamdan v. Rumsfeld, the Supreme Court considered the President's order that a military commission try Hamdan, a Guantanamo detainee, for one of the very crimes of which Bahlul was convicted: conspiracy to commit war crimes. Hamdan challenged the President's authority to convene the military commission by petitioning for habeas corpus relief and the Supreme Court's resulting decision initiated two games of interpretive ping-pong between the judiciary and the legislature. One involves the issue presented here: whether conspiracy is triable by a law-of-war military commission. In Hamdan, four justices concluded that it was not triable under the extant statute (section 821) and three concluded that it was. Four justices also "specifically invited Congress to clarify the scope of the President's statutory authority to use military commissions to try unlawful alien enemy combatants for war crimes."

The Congress answered the Court's invitation with the 2006 MCA, which provides the President the very power he sought to exercise in Hamdan—the power to try the 9/11 perpetrators for conspiracy—by including conspiracy as an offense triable by military commission, and by conferring jurisdiction on military commissions to try alien unlawful enemy combatants for conspiracy based on conduct that occurred "before, on, or after September 11, 2001," id. § 948d(a). We must heed this inter-branch dialogue, as Boumediene instructs. . .

. . .

. . . In enacting the military commission provisions of the 2006 MCA, the Congress plainly intended to give the President the power which Hamdan held it had not previously supplied—just as the 2006 MCA clarified that in fact the Congress did intend section 7(b)'s ouster of habeas jurisdiction to apply to pending cases. The legislative history confirms this view. Supporters and opponents of the legislation alike agreed that, the 2006 MCA's purpose was to authorize the trial by military commission of the 9/11 conspirators. And because the 9/11 conspiracy took place long before 2006, the statute could accomplish its explicit purpose only if it applied to pre-enactment conduct. As the Court itself made clear, "we cannot ignore that the [2006] MCA was a direct response to Hamdan's holding."

Reading the MCA in this context and given the unequivocal nature of its jurisdictional grant, we conclude the 2006 MCA unambiguously authorizes Bahlul's prosecution for the charged offenses based on pre-2006 conduct.

IV. Bahlul's Ex Post Facto Challenge

Because the Congress's intent to authorize retroactive prosecution of the charged offenses is clear, we must address Bahlul's ex post facto argument. As noted, we may overturn Bahlul's convictions only if they constitute plain constitutional error.

The Constitution prohibits the Congress from enacting any "ex post facto Law." In Calder v. Bull, Justice Chase set forth his understanding of that meaning:

> 1st. Every law that makes an action, done before the passing of the law, and which was innocent when done, criminal; and punishes such action. 2nd. Every law that aggravates a crime, or makes it greater than it was, when committed. 3rd. Every law that changes the punishment, and inflicts a greater punishment, than the law annexed to the crime, when committed. 4th. Every law that alters the legal rules of evidence, and receives less, or different, testimony, than the law required at the time of the commission of the offence, in order to convict the offender.

In our order granting en banc review, we asked the parties to brief whether the Ex Post Facto Clause applies in cases involving aliens detained at Guantanamo. The Government has taken the position that it does. Although we are not obligated to accept the Government's concession, we will assume without deciding that the Ex Post Facto Clause applies at Guantanamo. In so doing, we are "not to be understood as remotely intimating in any degree an opinion on the question."

A. Conspiracy

We reject Bahlul's ex post facto challenge to his conspiracy conviction for two independent and alternative reasons. First, the conduct for which he was convicted was already criminalized under 18 U.S.C. § 2332(b) (section 2332(b)) when Bahlul engaged in it. It is not "plain" that it violates the Ex Post Facto Clause to try a pre-existing federal criminal offense in a military commission and any difference between the elements of that offense and the conspiracy charge in the 2006 MCA does not seriously affect the fairness, integrity or public reputation of judicial proceedings. Second, it is not "plain" that conspiracy was not already triable by law-of-war military commission under 10 U.S.C. § 821 when Bahlul's conduct occurred.

1. Section 2332(b)

Bahlul was convicted of conspiracy to commit seven war crimes enumerated in the 2006 MCA, including the murder of protected persons. Although the 2006 MCA post-dates Bahlul's conduct, section 2332(b) has long been on the books, making it a crime to, "outside the United States," "engage[ ] in a conspiracy to kill[ ] a national of the United States." 18 U.S.C. § 2332(b); Section 2332(b) is not an offense triable by military commission but, the Government argues, "[t]he fact that the MCA provides a different forum for adjudicating such conduct does not implicate ex post facto concerns."

The right to be tried in a particular forum is not the sort of right the Ex Post Facto Clause protects. . .

It is therefore not a plain ex post facto violation to transfer jurisdiction over a crime from an Article III court to a military commission because such a transfer does not have anything to do with the definition of the crime, the defenses or the punishment. That is so regardless of the different evidentiary rules that apply under the 2006 MCA.

Our inquiry is not ended, however, because the 2006 MCA conspiracy-to-murder-protected-persons charge and section 2332(b) do not have identical elements. The difference is a potential problem because the Ex Post Facto Clause prohibits "retrospectively eliminating an element of the offense" and thus "subvert[ing] the presumption of innocence by reducing the number of elements [the government] must prove to overcome that presumption." The 2006 MCA conspiracy charge is in one sense more difficult to prove than section 2332(b) because it applies only to alien unlawful enemy combatants engaged in hostilities against the United States. But the 2006 MCA charge is in two ways easier to prove than a section 2332(b) charge. It does not require that the conspiracy occur "outside the United States" or that the conspiracy be to kill a "national of the United States," as section 2332(b) does. It simply requires a conspiracy to murder "one or more protected persons."

Nevertheless, Bahlul cannot bear his burden of establishing that the elimination of the two elements "seriously affect[ed] the fairness, integrity or public reputation of judicial proceedings." He cannot satisfy the fourth prong because the charges against him and the commission's findings necessarily included those elements and the evidence supporting them was undisputed. . .

Here, the evidence of the two missing elements was not simply "overwhelming" and "essentially uncontroverted"—it was entirely uncontroverted. Bahlul was charged with committing numerous overt acts "in Afghanistan, Pakistan and elsewhere" that furthered the conspiracy's unlawful objects; those objects included the murder of protected persons. He did not dispute that his conduct occurred outside the United States nor did he dispute that the purpose of the conspiracy was to murder United States nationals. . .There is no scenario in which the commission could have found that Bahlul committed these overt acts yet rationally found that the conspiracy did not take place outside the United States and did not have as an object the murder of United States nationals. Although the commission was not specifically instructed that it had to find these two elements, the overt acts it did find Bahlul had committed necessarily included the two elements and Bahlul did not, and does not, dispute either. Therefore, although the 2006 MCA conspiracy offense, as charged here, does "eliminat[e] an element of the offense," the omission did not seriously affect the fairness, integrity, or public reputation of the proceedings.

2.　Section 821

When Bahlul committed the crimes of which he was convicted, section 821 granted—and still grants—military commissions jurisdiction "with respect to offenders or offenses that by statute or by the law of war may be tried by military commissions." 10 U.S.C. § 821. Section 821 and its predecessor statute have been on the books for nearly a century. We must therefore ascertain whether conspiracy to commit war crimes was a "law of war" offense triable by military commission under section 821 when Bahlul's conduct occurred because, if so, Bahlul's ex post facto argument fails.

. . .In Hamdan II, the Court said that "law of war" as used in section 821 is a term of art that refers to the international law of war. Language in several Supreme Court opinions supports that proposition. . .

On the other hand, section 821 might not be so limited (as two of our colleagues would hold on de novo review). Significantly, both the Hamdan plurality and dissent relied primarily on domestic precedent to ascertain whether conspiracy could be tried under section 821. Moreover, as the Supreme Court has explained, when the Congress enacted section 821 and its predecessors, it intended to preserve, not limit, the pre-existing jurisdiction of military commissions. It is therefore arguable that the Congress also intended to incorporate military commission precedents predating section 821's enactment.

Ultimately, we need not resolve de novo whether section 821 is limited to the international law of war. It is sufficient for our purpose to say that, at the time of this appeal, the answer to that question is not "obvious."

. . .Here, the Congress has positively identified conspiracy as a war crime. We need not decide the effect of the Congress's action, however, because we rely on the second difference: The Hamdan plurality's review was de novo; our review is for plain error. We think the historical practice of our wartime tribunals is sufficient to make it not "obvious" that conspiracy was not traditionally triable by law-of-war military commission under section 821.

B.	Material Support

A different result obtains, however, regarding Bahlul's conviction of providing material support for terrorism. The Government concedes that material support is not an international law-of-war offense, and we so held in Hamdan II. But, in contrast to conspiracy, the Government offers little domestic precedent to support the notion that material support or a sufficiently analogous offense has historically been triable by military commission. Although Bahlul carries the burden to establish plain error, we presume that in the unique context of the "domestic common law of war"—wherein the Executive Branch shapes the relevant precedent and individuals in its employ serve as prosecutor, judge and jury—the Government can be expected to direct us to the strongest historical precedents. What the Government puts forth is inadequate.

The Government relies solely on a number of Civil War-era field orders approving military commission convictions of various offenses that, the Government contends, are analogous to material support. Before delving into the specifics of the orders, we note our skepticism that such informal field precedent can serve as the sole basis for concluding that a particular offense is triable by a law-of-war military commission. Unlike the Lincoln conspirators' and Nazi saboteurs' cases, which attracted national attention and reflected the deliberations of highest-level Executive Branch officials, the field precedents are terse recordings of drumhead justice executed on or near the battlefield. Indeed, several precedents cited by the Government for trying material support and solicitation under the "law of war" were issued by the same 1862 military commission that tried one Henry Willing for the offense of "[b]eing a bad and dangerous man." In addition, the military commissions these orders memorialize were not always models of due process. And, as the Hamdan plurality explained, the Civil War commissions "operated as both martial law or military government tribunals and law-of-war commissions," obliging us to treat the precedents "with caution" because of their unclear jurisdictional basis.

In any event, even if the law of war can be derived from field precedents alone, none of the cited orders charges the precise offense alleged here—providing material support for terrorism. The Government nonetheless contends that the material support charge "prohibits the same conduct, under a modern label, as the traditional offense of joining with or providing aid to guerrillas and other unlawful belligerents."

First, every precedent cited by the Government involves offenses committed in Missouri, a border state; none is from a state that seceded. The difference between a border state—whose citizens owed a duty of loyalty to the United States—and a state that seceded—whose citizens did not—is significant. The crime of "aiding the enemy," which includes as an element the breach of a duty of loyalty owed to the United States, had long been triable by military commission.

Second, several of the cited field orders appear to involve offenses more akin to aiding and abetting a law-of-war violation. Aiding and abetting is a theory of criminal liability, not a stand-alone offense like material support. As the Court said in Hamdan II, "aiding and abetting terrorism prohibits different conduct, imposes different mens rea requirements, and entails different causation standards than material support for terrorism." Thus, "[i]f the Government wanted to charge [Bahlul] with aiding and abetting terrorism . . . it should have done so."

Third, other orders appear to involve the offense of unlawful belligerency—that is, directly waging guerrilla warfare.

The upshot is that the Civil War field precedent is too distinguishable and imprecise to provide the sole basis for concluding that providing material support for terrorism was triable by law-of-war military commission at the time of Bahlul's conduct. We therefore think it was a plain ex post facto violation—again, assuming without deciding that the protection of the Ex Post Facto Clause extends to Bahlul—to try Bahlul by military commission for that new offense.

C. Solicitation

We also conclude that solicitation of others to commit war crimes is plainly not an offense traditionally triable by military commission. The Government concedes it is not an international law-of-war offense. The Government contends that solicitation "possesses a venerable lineage as an offense triable by military commission," but it cites only two Civil War-era field orders involving three defendants in support thereof. It mischaracterizes one of the orders, asserting that "a military commission convicted Francis Skinner of 'counsel[ing]' and 'invit[ing]' others to destroy a railroad in violation of the law of war," when in fact Skinner was acquitted of that offense. And although the other two defendants in the cited cases were convicted on charges that resemble the 2006 MCA solicitation offense, they were also convicted of personal involvement in the crimes they solicited.

As noted, we are skeptical that field orders can be the sole basis for military commission jurisdiction over a particular offense. Moreover, the two field orders discussed fall far short of meeting any showing we would require. Because solicitation to commit war crimes was not an offense triable by law-of-war military commission when Bahlul's conduct occurred, it is a plain ex post facto violation—again, assuming without deciding that the protection of the Ex Post Facto Clause extends to Bahlul—to try him by military commission for that new offense.

V.   Remaining Issues

In his brief to the panel, Bahlul raised four challenges to his convictions that we have not addressed here. He argued that (1) the Congress exceeded its Article I, § 8 authority by defining crimes triable by military commission that are not offenses under the international law of war; (2) the Congress violated Article III by vesting military commissions with jurisdiction to try crimes that are not offenses under the international law of war; (3) his convictions violate the First Amendment; and (4) the 2006 MCA discriminates against aliens in violation of the equal protection component of the Due Process Clause. We intended neither the en banc briefing nor argument to address these four issues.

For the foregoing reasons, we reject Bahlul's ex post facto challenge to his conspiracy conviction and remand that conviction to the panel to consider his alternative challenges thereto. In addition, we vacate Bahlul's convictions of providing material support for terrorism and solicitation of others to commit war crimes, and, after panel consideration, remand to the CMCR to determine the effect, if any, of the two vacaturs on sentencing.

So ordered.

KAREN LECRAFT HENDERSON, CIRCUIT JUDGE, concurring:

I write separately to emphasize, for me, the critical nature of the Government's concession that the Ex Post Facto Clause protects Bahlul. Had the Government not conceded the point and the Court not decided to act on the concession, I would have reached a different conclusion.

. . .Bahlul points to no case from the Supreme Court or any court of appeals, nor to any other "absolutely clear" legal norm, opining that the Ex Post Facto Clause applies beyond the sovereign territory of the United States. Finding such a precedent would be a remarkable feat inasmuch as Boumediene expressly recognized that it was the first case to apply any constitutional provision to aliens located beyond our sovereign territory: "It is true that before today the Court has never held that noncitizens detained by our Government in territory over which another country maintains de jure sovereignty have any rights under our Constitution." Because there is no clear precedent establishing that the Ex Post Facto Clause applies to aliens held at Guantanamo, prosecuting Bahlul under the 2006 MCA cannot constitute plain constitutional error.

. . .Even if our review were de novo, I would conclude that the Ex Post Facto Clause does not apply to aliens detained at Guantanamo. As discussed above, only one constitutional protection applies to Guantanamo even after Boumediene. Boumediene is the law and therefore it must be followed. But before 2008, the Constitution did not apply to aliens without property or presence in the United States. After 2008, the Suspension Clause—and only the Suspension Clause—protects only those aliens detained on the southeastern tip of an island outside the sovereign United States. We have previously said that, "[a]s a novel constitutional development, we are loath to expand Boumediene's reach without specific guidance from the Supreme Court, particularly where expansion would carry us further into the realm of war and foreign policy." I see no reason to abandon that caution.

Finally, we must remember the who, what and where of this case. Bahlul is an alien unlawful enemy combatant who—like Hitler's Goebbels—led Osama bin Laden's propaganda operation and freely admitted his role in the 9/11 atrocities. He was tried outside the sovereign United States for war crimes. During the post-World War II Nuremberg trials several defendants raised ex post facto objections but they were rejected as "sheer absurdity" under international law. I cannot agree that Bahlul is entitled to domestic constitutional protections—to which he would not be entitled under international law—simply because his war crimes trial was held at an American naval base located in Cuba.

ROGERS, CIRCUIT JUDGE, concurring in the judgment in part and dissenting.

Ali Hamza Ahmad Suliman al Bahlul, a self-avowed member of al Qaeda who has been held in the Naval Base at Guantanamo Bay, Cuba since 2002, was convicted and sentenced to life imprisonment by a military commission for three offenses under the Military Commissions Act of 2006. The question before the en banc court is whether these charges support the jurisdiction of the military commission. Because Bahlul's conduct occurred prior to the enactment of the 2006 Act, and the military commission lacked jurisdiction to try these non-law-of-war offenses, Bahlul's convictions must be vacated. The court is vacating Bahlul's convictions for material support and solicitation. . .I would also vacate Bahlul's conviction for inchoate conspiracy. . .

. . .All three convictions must be vacated as violations of the Ex Post Facto Clause. It remains for the Administration to decide whether to bring other charges against Bahlul before a military commission or whether to charge him in an Article III court. To the extent that Congress has created an obstacle to bringing Bahlul to the United States, Congress can remove it. The question whether Congress has impermissibly intruded upon the President's Article II powers is not before the court. In the meantime, "[t]he laws and Constitution are designed to survive, and remain in force, in extraordinary times. Liberty and security can be reconciled; and in our system they are reconciled within the framework of the law."

BROWN, CIRCUIT JUDGE, concurring in the judgment in part and dissenting in part:

Over five years ago, Ali Hamza Ahmad Suliman al Bahlul was convicted of conspiracy, solicitation, and providing material support for terrorism. Since that time, the government has been defending the conviction, first before the Court of Military Commission Review and now before this court. In this appeal, the government seeks clarification of the prosecutorial tools it can employ in the war on terror. While I concur in the court's judgment affirming Bahlul's conspiracy conviction and vacating the solicitation and material support convictions, I cannot agree with the way the court reaches that result. By reviewing Bahlul's claims under a plain error standard, the court minimizes the value its opinion might provide to the government in future prosecutions. And by remanding residual issues to a panel, the court delays resolution of Bahlul's case.

I would definitively answer the important questions raised by Bahlul's appeal, reviewing his ex post facto arguments under a de novo standard. I would also affirm Congress's power under the Define and Punish Clause to make certain offenses, including conspiracy, triable by military commission. This legal saga has endured long enough, and we should take this opportunity to resolve important legal questions that have arisen from the war on terror.

. . .Even if the offense of conspiracy was not recognized under international law in 2001 by the same labels used by Congress in the 2006 Military Commissions Act, the substance is similar. Indeed, it is to be expected that international law, which was largely created by jurists trained in the civil law and which only more recently has begun to absorb common law ideas and institutions, differs formally from our own common law tradition. But that does not mean that when Congress decides to implement international law domestically it cannot adapt that law to fit within our common law institutions. Such adaptation is appropriate both because of the evolving nature of international law and the necessities of implementing international law in an established domestic legal system. International law recognizes analogues to conspiracy and other inchoate offenses.

. . .The Framers and subsequent courts recognized that to define the law of nations, Congress required a zone of deference. Without a measure of deference, legislative fear of second-guessing would hobble Congress's power under the Define and Punish Clause, leaving the nation subject to the fate Madison depicted for most previous democratic experiments: "short in their lives . . . [and] violent in their deaths." Contemporary international practice exhibits the same kind of practical deference to permit individual states to assess their own obligations. The principle of complementarity requires international tribunals to accord deference to state investigations and recognizes that what is mandated still leaves room for what is merely permissive

. . .Congress's determination that conspiracy is an offense against the law of nations constitutes a reasonable interpretation of international law and is fully consistent with that law. Therefore, the judiciary is bound to uphold Congress's exercise of authority under the Define and Punish Clause.

. . .The United States is engaged in a war on terrorism. As the various iterations of Hamdan and this case demonstrate, the Executive Branch needs concrete guidance as to how it can proceed with its prosecution of the September 11 conspirators and other detainees. Bahlul was first charged before a military commission ten years ago. Today, this court again leaves the government without any definitive answers. The court does not express respect to the coordinate branches of government by further delaying the executive's prosecutorial efforts and thwarting the legislative's expressed preference that detainees be tried by military commission. I would resolve now the exceedingly important questions presented in this case.

KAVANAUGH, CIRCUIT JUDGE, concurring in the judgment in part and dissenting in part:

. . .At the time of Bahlul's conduct, neither any federal statute nor the international law of war proscribed conspiracy as a war crime triable by military commission. So the question we must decide is whether U.S. military commission precedents treated conspiracy as an offense triable by military commission. In other words, we must decide the question that was addressed by seven Justices in Hamdan but not decided by the Court. The answer, in my view, is yes: U.S. military commission precedents have treated conspiracy as an offense triable by military commission.

. . .A few words in response to the majority opinion: I find the majority opinion surprising both in what it decides and in what it declines to decide.

First, I am surprised by what the majority opinion decides. After all, the majority opinion reaches the same bottom-line conclusion that this Court reached in Hamdan II: The offense of material support for terrorism may not be tried by military commission for conduct that occurred before the 2006 Act. But the majority opinion does so based on the Ex Post Facto Clause alone and "overrules" Hamdan II's statement that the 2006 Act itself incorporates ex post facto principles.

. . .Second, from the other direction, I am also surprised by what the majority opinion does not decide. We took this case en banc specifically to decide whether, consistent with the Ex Post Facto Clause, a military commission could try conspiracy for conduct that occurred before the 2006 Act. Yet the majority opinion does not actually decide that question.

. . .On top of not deciding how the ex post facto principle applies to conspiracy trials before military commissions, the majority opinion also does not decide Bahlul's Article I, jury trial, equal protection, or First Amendment challenges, but rather sends those four issues back to a three-judge panel for resolution. I also respectfully disagree with that approach.

The remaining issues are not that complicated; we have the requisite briefing; and we could request supplemental briefing if need be. Moreover, those issues are especially easy to decide on plain error review, which after all is the standard of review that the majority opinion indicates must be applied to those issues. Sending the case back to a three-judge panel will delay final resolution of this case, likely until some point in 2015, given the time it will take for a decision by the three-judge panel and then resolution of any future petitions for panel rehearing or rehearing en banc. Like Judge Brown, I believe that we should resolve the case now, not send it back to the three-judge panel.

In short, I respectfully disagree with the majority opinion's addressing the ex post facto issue in a way that does not actually decide the legal issue with respect to conspiracy and provides little clarity or guidance on that issue going forward, and also with its sending the other four issues back to a three-judge panel. There is a time to avoid and a time to decide. Now is the time to decide.

In sum, I would affirm Bahlul's conspiracy conviction, vacate the material support for terrorism and solicitation convictions as ex post facto violations, and remand to the U.S. Court of Military Commission Review for it to address the consequences, if any, for Bahlul's life sentence.

QUESTIONS AND NOTES

1.   On remand of the principal case, the original three judge panel of the U.S. Court of Appeals again ruled in favor of Al Bahlul, concluding, "The government has failed to identify a sufficiently settled historical practice for this court to conclude that the inchoate conspiracy offense of which Bahlul was convicted falls within the Article III exception for law of war military commissions." Accordingly, the court vacated Al Bahlul's conviction for conspiracy. Al Bahlul v. United States, 792 F. 3d 1 (D.C. Cir. 2015). The government again sought en banc review; its motion was granted, and the en banc court again disagreed with the three judge panel. See Al Bahlul v. United States, 840 F.3d 757 (D.C. Cir. 2016):

PER CURIAM:

Bahlul is a member of al Qaeda who assisted Osama bin Laden in planning the September 11, 2001, attacks on the United States. Bahlul was convicted by a U.S. military commission of the offense of conspiracy to commit war crimes, among other offenses. The U.S. Court of Military Commission Review affirmed Bahlul's conviction.

In a prior en banc decision, we recounted the facts and considered Bahlul's Ex Post Facto Clause objection to the conspiracy conviction. Applying plain error review, we concluded that the Ex Post Facto Clause did not preclude the conspiracy charge against

Bahlul. See Al Bahlul v. United States, 767 F.3d 1 (D.C. Cir. 2014) (en banc).

In this en banc case, Bahlul argues that Articles I and III of the Constitution bar Congress from making conspiracy an offense triable by military commission, because conspiracy is not an offense under the international law of war.

We affirm the judgment of the U.S. Court of Military Commission Review upholding Bahlul's conspiracy conviction. Six judges—Judges Henderson, Brown, Griffith, Kavanaugh, Millett, and Wilkins—have voted to affirm. Three judges—Judges Rogers, Tatel, and Pillard—dissent.

Of the six-judge majority, four judges (Judges Henderson, Brown, Griffith, and Kavanaugh) would affirm because they conclude that, consistent with Articles I and III of the Constitution, Congress may make conspiracy to commit war crimes an offense triable by military commission. They would uphold Bahlul's conspiracy conviction on that basis.

Judge Millett would apply plain error review and affirm Bahlul's conviction under that standard of review. She would not reach the question of whether Congress may make inchoate conspiracy an offense triable by military commission.

Judge Wilkins would affirm because he concludes that the particular features of Bahlul's conviction demonstrate that Bahlul was not convicted of an inchoate conspiracy offense. He further concludes that Bahlul's conviction complies with the Constitution because the particular features of Bahlul's conviction have sufficient roots in international law. He therefore would not reach the question of whether Congress may make inchoate conspiracy an offense triable by military commission.

Judges Rogers, Tatel, and Pillard have filed a Joint Dissent. They conclude that Article III of the Constitution bars Congress from making inchoate conspiracy an offense triable by a law-of-war military commission.

Bahlul has also raised First Amendment and Equal Protection challenges to his conviction. The Court rejects those challenges. . . . The Joint Dissent neither reaches those claims nor adopts the above characterization of the facts.

. . .

We affirm the judgment of the U.S. Court of Military Commission Review upholding Bahlul's conspiracy conviction. So ordered.

2.   Regarding the military commission cases that have resulted in convictions, see Al Bahlul v. United States:

TATEL, CIRCUIT JUDGE, concurring

. . .

. . .[A]though the detention camp at the U.S. naval station at Guantánamo Bay has held at least 780 individuals since opening shortly after September 11th, and although military prosecutors have brought charges against some two hundred, the commissions have convicted only eight: al Bahlul, Hamdan, Noor Uthman Muhammed, David Hicks, Omar Khadr, Majid Khan, Ibrahim al Qosi, and Ahmed al Darbi. See Miami Herald, Guantánamo: By the Numbers, http://goo.gl/SEPfV6 (last updated May 12, 2015).

3. In March, 2011, the Obama administration indicated that trials before the military commissions would resume. On April 4, 2011, Attorney General Holder, reversing a previous decision to prosecute the indicated cases in federal court in New York, announced that Sheik Mohammed and four others, accused of having planned the 9/11 attacks, would be prosecuted in a military commission trial. Those five cases are still in preliminary proceedings.

4. Of the eight cases cited by Judge Tatel, supra note 2, the sentences in two of them are worth mentioning. Noor Uthman Muhammed (Sudanese) pled guilty to conspiracy and providing material support for terrorism having served as an instructor and as the deputy commander of the Khalden terrorist training camp in Afghanistan. Although sentenced to 14 years' confinement by the tribunal, his plea agreement provided for a maximum sentence to be served of 34 months' confinement. See: http://www.mc.mil/cases/militarycommissions. aspx.

Omar Ahmed Khadr, a Canadian citizen pled guilty on Oct. 25, 2010, to terrorism-related charges. Mr. Khadr admitted to a military judge that he threw a grenade that killed an American soldier during a firefight and that he had planted 10 roadside bombs for Al Qaeda. Mr. Khadr was 15 years old when he was captured in Afghanistan. The charges to which he pled guilty included murder in violation of the law of war, supporting terrorism, and spying. Mr. Khadr was sentenced to 40 years in prison, but under the terms of a plea agreement, Mr. Khadr was to serve no more than eight years. Moreover, after one year, Mr. Khadr, a Canadian citizen, was to be transferred to a prison in Canada, where he would be eligible to apply for parole after serving two years and eight months. See: http://topics.nytimes.com/top/reference/timestopics/people/k/omar_khadr/index.html.

The Supreme Court denied certiorari review on Khadr's habeas claim. Khadr v. Obama, 131 S.Ct. 2900 (May, 2011).

5. A number of additional cases are, at the time of this writing, listed in the military commissions docket as pending and active. These include:

     a. The afore-mentioned cases involving charges against five individuals (Khalid Shaikh Mohammad; Walid Muhammad Salih Mubarek Bin Attash; Ramzi Binalshibh; Ali Abdul Aziz Ali; and Mustafa Ahmed Adam al Hawsawi) who are charged jointly, in connection with their alleged roles in the September 11, 2001 attacks against the United States. They are charged with committing the following eight offenses: conspiracy; attacking civilians; attacking civilian objects; intentionally causing serious bodily injury; murder in violation of the law of war; destruction of property in violation of the law of war; hijacking or hazarding a vessel or aircraft; and terrorism;

　　　b.　　Abd al Hadi al-Iraqi who is charged with Denying Quarter, Attacking Protected Property, Using Treachery or Perfidy, and Attempted Use of Treachery or Perfidy in a series of attacks in Afghanistan and Pakistan between about 2003 and 2004;

　　　c.　　Abd al-Rahim Hussein Muhammed Abdu Al-Nashiri who is charged with perfidy, murder in violation of the law of war, attempted murder in violation of the law of war, terrorism, conspiracy, intentionally causing serious bodily injury, attacking civilians, attacking civilian objects, and hazarding a vessel. The charges arise out of an attempted attack on the USS THE SULLIVANS in January 2000, an attack on the USS COLE in October 2000, and on the MV Limburg in October 2002;

　　　d.　　Ahmed Mohammed Ahmed Haza al Darbi who is charged with conspiracy, attacking civilian objects, hazarding a vessel, terrorism, attempt, and aiding the enemy. The charges stem from an attempt to carry out terrorist attacks against shipping vessels in the Strait of Hormuz and off the coast of Yemen, and a terrorist attack against the French oil tanker, MV Limburg;

　　　e.　　Majid Shoukat Khan who is charged with conspiracy, murder in violation of the law of war, attempted murder in violation of the law of war, providing material support for terrorism, and spying. The charges arise out of, among other things, the August 2003 bombing of the J.W. Marriot in Indonesia, and an attempted assassination of former Pakistani President Pervez Musharraf.

E. THE CHOICE OF FORUM: PROSECUTION BEFORE A MILITARY COMMISSION IN GUANTANAMO OR IN U.S. DISTRICT COURT

1. INTRODUCTION

The Military Commissions Act, like the President's November 13, 2001 Military Order, authorizes trial only of aliens before the military commissions. At the same time, the government has, in two instances thus far, the cases of Hamdi and Padilla, held U.S. citizens as unlawful enemy combatants. In the case of Hamdi, a settlement was reached and he was released to Saudi Arabia. In the case of Padilla, he was transferred back to civilian jurisdiction and prosecuted and convicted of, and sentenced for terrorism offenses. Is there a disconnect between the government's assertion of the power to hold U.S. citizens as enemy combatants and the fact that the power to try them before a military commission is lacking. That disconnect, of course, helps to account for the government's decision to shift Padilla back to civilian custody. But note how holding Padilla in military custody for years before shifting him back to prosecution in federal court enhanced the government's ability to interrogate him at length and added years to his time of confinement.

The bases, too, on which the government early on was making the decision whether to treat some individuals as normal criminal arrestees and some as enemy combatants have not been publicly articulated. Examination of what is publicly known about the persons who have been treated in one category or the other does not entirely help to explicate the criteria that have been applied. One possible speculation is that the government was more likely to use the enemy combatant approach when it believed that the individual being detained had important information and wished to be able to interrogate at length, without being restricted by the procedural protections that attach in normal civilian criminal process. A second factor might be that the enemy combatant category was more likely to be used when the government considered the person to be guilty and too dangerous to release but did not have enough admissible evidence to convict.

Some of the cases that have been prosecuted have made the choices being made seem puzzling. For example, John Walker Lindh was picked up on the battlefield, and prosecution was initiated in a United States district court in the Eastern District of Virginia. It is hard to see how his case differed from that of Hamdi, and on the face of things, the case for treating him as an enemy combatant seemed, if anything, stronger than the Padilla case. A possible explanation is that the government quickly made a decision to prosecute Walker Lindh, and did not see him as a potential source of important intelligence, so prolonged detention in a facility for military custody was not appropriate. Further, given that he is a U.S. citizen, prosecution of necessity had to be in a civilian forum.

Other cases, too, present similar questions as well. Zacarias Moussaoui, is a French citizen who was apprehended in the United States and was prosecuted in a U.S. District Court although at times, there were statements made by government officials that seemed to indicate there was a possibility that his case would be transferred to military jurisdiction. Richard Reid, a British citizen, the so-called "shoe bomber," was apprehended on an airplane bound for the United States, and he, too, was criminally charged in a civilian court in Massachusetts where the plane was diverted. One wonders whether, if somehow any of the persons who actually perpetrated the 9/11 attacks had survived and been apprehended, would they have been prosecuted in civilian federal court or in military commission trials? Regarding the choices made in prosecuting those who are alleged to have planned the 9/11 attacks, see below.

Our criminal enforcement system, of course, is rife with choices that prosecutors make regarding the forum in which to prosecute. A frequent choice-of-forum issue is between a state or a federal prosecution, and many different kinds of considerations can affect that choice, including the legal advantages of prosecuting in one or the other forum. See generally, Norman Abrams, Sara Sun Beale and Susan Riva Klein, Federal Criminal Law and Its Enforcement, ch. 4 (6th ed. 2015).

At an early stage and prior to the promulgation of any regulations establishing the procedures to be used before the military commissions, they appeared to have enormous legal and practical advantages for the government (and corresponding disadvantages for a defendant) to prosecute before a military commission in comparison with prosecution in a federal court. The gap of comparative advantage between the two kinds of procedures narrowed, however, at each successive stage of regulatory or legislative revision. What comparative advantages and disadvantages remain between military and civilian prosecution, looking only to the procedures and rules of evidence provided for in the MCA of 2009 and the Manual for Military Commissions and the comparable procedures and rules applied in federal courts?

Of course, assessing comparative advantage based on the legal documents fails to take account of how the two systems compare based on how they operate in practice, that is, in real life. For present purposes, however, it should suffice to quote a tweet from President Trump:

> "Would love to send the NYC terrorist to Guantánamo but statistically that process takes much longer than going through the Federal system,"

See Charlie Savage and Adam Goldman, Following Trump's Lead, Republicans Grow Quiet on Guantanamo, N.Y. Times, Nov. 4, 2017, https://www.nytimes.com/2017/11/04/us/politics/republicans-guantanamo-military-commissions-civilian-courts-terrorism.html.

2. ATTORNEY GENERAL HOLDER'S STATEMENT REGARDING THE CHOICE OF THE FORUM

In connection with the choice between civilian or military commission prosecution, consider the following comments, excerpted from Attorney General Holder's speech at Northwestern University on March 5, 2012:

Several practical considerations affect the choice of forum.

First of all, the commissions only have jurisdiction to prosecute individuals who are a part of al Qaeda, have engaged in hostilities against the United States or its coalition partners, or who have purposefully and materially supported such hostilities. This means that there may be members of certain terrorist groups who fall outside the jurisdiction of military commissions because, for example, they lack ties to al Qaeda and their conduct does not otherwise make them subject to prosecution in this forum. Additionally, by statute, military commissions cannot be used to try U.S. citizens.

Second, our civilian courts cover a much broader set of offenses than the military commissions, which can only prosecute specified offenses, including violations of the laws of war and other offenses traditionally triable by military commission. This means federal prosecutors have a wider range of tools that can be used to incapacitate suspected terrorists. Those charges, and the sentences they carry upon successful conviction, can provide important incentives to reach plea agreements and convince defendants to cooperate with federal authorities.

Third, there is the issue of international cooperation. A number of countries have indicated that they will not cooperate with the United States in certain counterterrorism efforts—for instance, in providing evidence or extraditing suspects—if we intend to use that cooperation in pursuit of a military commission prosecution. Although the use of military commissions in the United States can be traced back to the early days of our nation, in their present form they are less familiar to the international community than our time-tested criminal justice system and Article III courts. However, it is my hope that, with time and experience, the reformed commissions will attain similar respect in the eyes of the world.

Where cases are selected for prosecution in military commissions, Justice Department investigators and prosecutors work closely to support our Department of Defense colleagues. Today, the alleged mastermind of the bombing of the U.S.S. Cole is being prosecuted before a military commission. I am proud to say that trial attorneys from the Department of Justice are working with military prosecutors on that case, as well as others.

And we will continue to reject the false idea that we must choose between federal courts and military commissions, instead of using them both. If we were to fail to use all necessary and available tools at our disposal, we would undoubtedly fail in our fundamental duty to protect the Nation and its people. That is simply not an outcome we can accept.

3. EXERCISE OF PROSECUTORIAL DISCRETION DURING THE OBAMA ADMINISTRATION

During this same general period, Attorney General Holder announced plans to prosecute five "high value" Guantanamo detainees in federal court in New York City, while also indicating that of the remaining detainees who were going to be prosecuted, some of the prosecutions would occur in a federal district court in the U.S., and some would be prosecuted before the military commissions. The plan to prosecute the five high value detainees (who were alleged to have been involved in the planning of the 9/11 attacks) also generated significant controversy, both in the Congress and in the City of New York, and after more than a year of delay, the Attorney General announced that the five would, after all, be prosecuted before military commissions. Thus far, it appears that only one Guantanamo detainee has been prosecuted in New York City, see United States v. Ghailani, 761 F.Supp.2d 167 (S.D.N.Y 2011).

4. JUSTIFICATIONS FOR USE OF MILITARY COMMISSIONS

QUESTIONS AND NOTES

1. Numerous pragmatic justifications have been offered by the government as to why military commissions are needed. Of course, ultimately, the use of a military commission is premised on the fact that we are at war and that cases against enemy combatants can be adjudicated under the laws of war before military commissions.

2. How many of the following justifications are likely to be applicable to some cases and not to others? How many of them, if applicable in a particular case, might be grounds for using a military commission instead of a federal district court?

    a. Military handling of a matter permits more effective interrogation of the defendant and a lengthier period in which to gather evidence;

    b. It is easier to maintain the confidentiality of classified information in a military commission (in this connection, compare the protection afforded to classified information in a civilian court under the Classified Information Procedures Act);

    c. Military trials can be conducted more quickly—it is possible to avoid prolonged delays and lengthy proceedings; (this particular feature seems belied by how the military commissions have in fact been operating).

    d. It does not make sense to bring hundreds of persons captured in military encounters abroad to the United States to be tried in U.S. civil courts for being accessories to terrorism; there is even less justification for bringing such persons to the U.S. for trial when they are almost all foreign nationals;

e. It is easier to close a military commission proceeding to the press and public than to close a civilian trial. Non-public proceedings may be desirable and even necessary in some of these cases;

f. It is easier to keep the participants safe from retaliatory terrorist activity in a military setting;

g. Military commissions avoid the use of lay juries. Juries in these cases make for inefficiency, change the style of presentation of the evidence, and open up the possibility of the jurors' passions and prejudices affecting the proceeding.

3. Can you think of other pragmatic factors that might be taken into account in deciding whether to prosecute in a military commission a person who is subject to the terms of the MCA? The military commission process has proved to be a process fraught with many problems, especially, delay and other inefficiencies. Should that be a or the determinative factor?

F. LITERATURE REGARDING MILITARY COMMISSIONS

A great deal has been written in the scholarly literature about the military commissions and enemy combatant status. A selection includes: Christina M. Frohock, Military Justice as Justice: Fitting Confrontation Clause Jurisprudence into Military Commissions, 48 New Eng. L. Rev. 255 (2014); David Glazier, Destined for an Epic Fail: The Problematic Guantánamo Military Commissions, 75 Ohio State L. J. 903 (2014); Robert Bejersky, Closing Gitmo Due to the Epiphany Approach to Habeas Corpus during the Military Commission Circus, 50 Willamette L. Rev. 43 (2013); Benjamin G. Davis, The 9/11 Military Commission Motion Hearings: An Ordinary Citizen Looks at Comparative Legitimacy, 37 S. Ill. U. L. J. 599 (2013); Frank J. Williams and Nicole J. Benjamin, Military Trials of Terrorists: From the Lincoln Conspirators to the Guantanamo Inmates, 39 N. Kentucky L. Rev. 609 (2012); Stephen Vladeck, The Laws of War as a Constitutional Limit on Military Jurisdiction, 4 J. NAT'L SEC. L. & POL'Y 295 (2010); Jennifer Elsea, Cong. Res. Service, CRS Rep. for Congress, The Military Commissions Act of 2006: Analysis of Procedural Rules and Comparison with Previous DOD Rules and the Uniform Code of Military Justice (Sep. 27, 2007), http://www.fas.org/sgp/crs/natsec/RL33688.pdf; Developments Regarding the Military Commissions Act and Detentions at Guantanamo Bay, 101 AM. J. INT'L L. 659 (2007); Richard H. Fallon, Jr. & Daniel J. Meltzer, Habeas Corpus Jurisdiction, Substantive Rights, and the War on Terror, 120 HARV. L. REV. 2029 (2007); Allison M. Danner, Defining Unlawful Enemy Combatants: a Centripetal Story, 43 TEX. INT'L L.J. 1 (2007); Carl Tobias, The Process Due Indefinitely Detained Citizens,

85 N.C. L. REV. 1687 (2007); Robert J. Pushaw, Jr., The "Enemy Combatant" Cases in Historical Context: the Inevitability of Pragmatic Judicial Review, 82 NOTRE DAME L. REV. 1005 (2007); Christopher J. Schatz & Noah A. F. Horst, Will Justice Delayed be Justice Denied? Crisis Jurisprudence, the Guantanamo Detainees, and the Imperiled Role of Habeas Corpus in Curbing Abusive Government Detention, 11 LEWIS & CLARK L. REV. 539 (2007); Jennifer Van Bergen & Douglas Valentine, The Dangerous World of Indefinite Detentions: Vietnam to Abu Ghraib, 37 CASE W. RES. J. INT'L L. 449 (2006); Aya Gruber, Raising the Red Flag: the Continued Relevance of the Japanese Internment in the Post-Hamdi World, 54 U. KAN. L. REV. 307 (2006); Jennifer Elsea, Cong. Res. Service, CRS Rep. for Congress, Detention of American Citizens as Enemy Combatants 2 (Mar. 31, 2005), http://www.fas.org/sgp/crs/natsec/RL31724. pdf; Morris D. Davis, In Defense of Guantanamo Bay, 117 YALE L.J. Pocket Part 21 (2007).

CHAPTER 12

TARGETED KILLING

■ ■ ■

A. INTRODUCTION

The subject of targeted killing presents complexities and concerns different from any of the other topics addressed in this volume. Earlier, there had been difficulty in obtaining any significant official information about this subject, and internal government policy had not been available to be perused and evaluated. How the government made decisions in individual cases was entirely hidden from view. More recently, some official policy and an important memorandum have been disclosed. Another special feature of this area of anti-terrorism law is that decisions in individual cases are less likely to be the subject of litigation, civil or criminal, than other matters treated in this book.

In an unusual confluence of circumstances, however, in one recent instance, litigation was initiated challenging the alleged placing of an individual on a kill list. While the lawsuit was dismissed, it nevertheless presented a unique opportunity for a judicial airing, albeit limited, of some of the issues in this complex subject.

The topic, if anything, is recently more in the public eye. There are several reasons: The Al-Aulaqi litigation, mentioned above, initiated by his father engendered much media attention (which, of course, was part of its purpose). The U.S. policy to use drones extensively to target terrorists in the border regions of Afghanistan and Pakistan is a form of targeted killing, albeit in a clear-cut battle zone, and has contributed to keeping the general issue in the realm of public discussion.

In section B, some presidential executive orders dealing with governmental policy regarding assassination are reproduced. Section C raises a series of issues and questions regarding rationales for and policies regarding targeted killing; section D presents excerpts from an article by Professor Gregory McNeal describing in some detail the current process of decisionmaking and applicable policies for targeting killing by U.S. military authorities and intelligence agencies, and section E presents the Al-Aulaqi case.

B. EXECUTIVE ORDERS

Executive Order 11905 (United States Foreign Intelligence Activities)

February 18, 1976 [signed by President Gerald Ford].

41 FR 7703, 1976

Sec. 5. Restrictions on Intelligence Activities

. . .

(g) Prohibition of Assassination. No employee of the United States Government shall engage in, or conspire to engage in, political assassination.

. . .

Executive Order 12333 (United States Intelligence Activities)

December 4, 1981 [signed by President Ronald Reagan].

46 FR 59941, 1981 WL 76054.

Part 2

. . .

2.11 Prohibition on Assassination. No person employed by or acting on behalf of the United States Government shall engage in, or conspire to engage in, assassination.

2.12 Indirect Participation. No agency of the Intelligence Community shall participate in or request any person to undertake activities forbidden by this Order.

C. RATIONALES AND POLICY ISSUES

QUESTIONS AND NOTES

1. The Gerald Ford Executive Order prohibition on political assassination was reaffirmed by President Carter. Note that the Ford prohibition speaks of "political assassination" while the Reagan Order simply prohibits "assassination." Is this difference significant? How would you define "political assassination"? Note that during the Reagan administration the U.S. dropped bombs on the home of Libyan leader Colonel Muammar Gaddafi, the Libyan leader, in retaliation for a terrorist bombing in Germany directed against a place frequented by American soldiers. During the Clinton administration, the U.S. fired cruise missiles at suspected guerrilla camps in Afghanistan after the bombings of two U.S. embassies in Africa. See U.S. Policy on Assassination, CNN transcript, November 4, 2002, 6:38 p.m. Should these events be viewed as breaches of the policy or as a guide to how the assassination ban is being (should be?) interpreted?

2.   It was reported by CNN, supra note 1, that after the September 11 attacks, the White House said that the prohibition against assassinations would not prevent the U.S from acting in self-defense. Other administration sources have indicated that the ban on assassination does not apply in wartime. Senate Joseph Biden was quoted as saying: "These are combatants of war. And I find no difficulty with it." See Senators Support CIA Anti-Terror Effort, Reuters, December 15, 2002, 4:18 p.m.

3.   Apart from executive orders on the subject, for a long time, there was no publicly available statement of policy in this area. News reports have indicated that after September 11, the President signed a secret finding that authorizes the CIA to covertly attack al Qaeda members anywhere in the world, contains no exemption for American citizens, and does not require that the President approve specific operations. Reportedly also, the administration has prepared a list of terrorist leaders the CIA is authorized to kill, but the CIA's authority to kill is not limited to those on the list. See James Risen and David Johnston, Threats and Responses: Hunt for al Qaeda: Bush Has Widened Authority of CIA To Kill Terrorists, N.Y. Times, December 15, 2002.

4.   On November 3, 2002, a missile fired by a U.S. unmanned aerial vehicle killed a carload of suspected operatives in Yemen. The principal target of the attack was a man named Qaed Salim Sinan al-Harethi, who was allegedly an al Qaeda operative in Yemen. He was suspected of having been involved in the terrorist attack on the U.S.S. Cole. Reportedly, an American citizen was also in the car which was totally destroyed. For a news story about a failed targeted killing that killed many bystanders and an indication that there have been numerous such attacks since 9/11, see Josh Meyer, CIA Expands Use of Drones in Terror War, LA Times, July 29, 2006.

5.   Immediately after the Yemen attack described in note 4, supra, many legal commentators criticized such targeting and killing of persons suspected of terrorist acts. See Laura K. Donohue, The "Good Guy" Turns Assassin, LA Times, Nov. 17, 2002, Sunday Opinion Section. Professor Donohue argues, inter alia: 1) how can we claim to be a protector of human rights when we engage in extrajudicial killings; 2) is it better to kill individuals whose guilt is unproved than for lives of Americans to be put at risk? 3) if we are at war, it should be a just war and we must be careful in the force that we use; 4) we need to provide immunity for innocents whenever possible; 5) assassination erodes national security by undermining our image and our moral authority before the world community. Also see Daniel B. Pickard, Legalizing Assassination? Terrorism, The Central Intelligence Agency and International Law, 39 Ga. J. Int'l & Comp.L. 1 (2001); Patricia Zengel, Assassination and the Law of Armed Conflict, 45 Mercer L. Rev. 615 (1992).

6.   Is the argument that "we are at war and killing the enemy in wartime is acceptable" a sufficient answer to the kind of arguments articulated in the previous note? If you were in a position of authority in the administration, what position would you take on this issue?

D. THE PROCESS OF TARGETED KILLING

See Gregory S. McNeal, Targeted Killings and Accountability, 102 Geo. L. J. 681, 684–715 (2014):

When the United States government kills people on traditional and non-traditional battlefields—and it does so on a near daily basis—bureaucrats play a key role in the killings. Bureaucrats help create lists of people to be killed, and sometimes bureaucrats themselves carry out the killings. The process is called targeted killing, and it involves bombs and missiles dropped from Unmanned Aerial Vehicles (UAVs) by members of the military or civilians employed by the Central Intelligence Agency (CIA). Some of the killings are sanctioned directly by the President of the United States, while others are authorized at a much lower level of government, deep within the military or intelligence bureaucracies of the Executive Branch. No matter which agency pulls the trigger, bureaucrats—far removed from public scrutiny and oftentimes outside the reach of courts—are essential to the success of the program.

America's bureaucrats kill with amazing efficiency. . . . Dozens, perhaps hundreds of people make incremental contributions to a well-oiled killing machine, ensuring that by the time a target shows up in the cross-hairs of an operator, the operator can rest assured that the target is worth killing.

. . .Persons are designated for killing by being added to "kill-lists." Such persons may fall into three categories: (1) targets who fall within the AUMF and its associated forces interpretations; (2) targets who fall within the terms of a covert action finding; and (3) targets from an ally's non-international armed conflict in which the United States is a participant.

It is not surprising that the creation of kill lists is a matter of popular debate and scholarly commentary. Since World War I, military and civilian personnel have compiled target lists for bombing. And since the inception of airpower, various theorists have argued over what type of target is proper. Thus, though controversy over targeting decisions is not new, the levels of precision and accuracy possible in modern air strikes are new. New technology has created an expectation about accuracy and has led to the politicization of air delivered weapons. Concomitantly, as the accuracy of weapons has increased, the demand for intelligence and for accountability with regard to intelligence-based decisions has also increased dramatically.

...Because killing the wrong person may lead to serious consequences, these lists are vetted through an elaborate bureaucratic process that allows for verification of intelligence information before a person is added to a kill list. . . . Who specifically should be killed? If multiple people are to be killed, how can the military and the CIA sort out the key targets from the less important targets? How does the United States ensure that killing someone will have an impact on the terrorist organization? What about the political and diplomatic consequences that might flow from a targeted killing? Who approves adding names to a kill-list and by what criteria? The United States addresses these questions in a heavily bureaucratized target-development process. Obama Administration counterterrorism advisor and CIA Director John Brennan described the process as committed to:

> ensuring the individual is a legitimate target under the law; determining whether the individual poses a significant threat to U.S. interests; determining that capture is not feasible; being mindful of the important checks on our ability to act unilaterally in foreign territories; having that high degree of confidence, both in the identity of the target and that innocent civilians will not be harmed; and, of course, engaging in additional review if the al-Qaida terrorist is a U.S. citizen.

Brennan further argued that it was the rigor of the process that ensured accountability in the policy. Though he refrained from going into great detail about the bureaucratic process of reviewing individuals who are both legitimate and necessary targets of lethal force, he gave assurances that the administration would continue to "strengthen and refine these standards and processes."

The kill-list creation process for the military is more transparent than the process followed by the CIA; however, the possible distinctions between the agencies may no longer matter because recent public statements by current and former government officials suggest that targeting procedures followed by the military are also followed by the intelligence community with one unified process existing at the final levels of approval. In fact, according to at least one account, much of the work of the CIA and the military's JSOC is completely integrated: "JSOC people [work] with CIA, and CIA people with JSOC. They have access to each other's system."

The process of developing names for the list is initially delimited by the categories of individuals who may be targeted. Those limits are established by the law of armed conflict, which prohibits the targeting of civilians except those who are members of an organized armed group and those who are directly participating in hostilities. Because direct participation in hostilities is a fleeting, time-delimited categorization, the only criteria by which an individual would likely be added to a kill-list would be if they fall into the category "members of an organized armed group." The term "organized armed group" and its interpretation are the subject of international debate. . . There are some plausible circumstances under which individuals might be added to a kill list, despite their non-membership in a group. For example, consider an individual who is known to plant IEDs but does so on a per-IED basis, for pay, or on an irregular schedule. That person, a contractor of sorts, would not be a member of an organized armed group, yet one can see why the United States would want to add his name to a kill list. Moreover, because the United States likely disagrees with the temporal dimension (for instance, the definition of "for such time as") of participation as articulated in the DPH study, killing this named person under this view would also not be unlawful. Though seemingly simple, the term "members of an organized armed group" is subject to extensive debate.

First, what counts as an "organized armed group"? . . .the executive branch, relying on the Hamdan case, the AUMF, and the NDAA, asserts that the United States is involved in a non-international armed conflict with al Qaeda and associated forces. Setting aside the debate regarding the classification of the conflict does not resolve all issues because the law of armed conflict question with regard to organization (and thereby the question of what counts as associated forces) is a continuously evolving concept. This is a critical point as the legal questions flow into the policy questions about who can be added to kill lists and who should be added to lists. Thus, as a threshold matter, we must recognize that the task of saying which groups and persons should be understood as comprising the enemy likely cannot be accomplished by using anything other than broad laws, with details left to bureaucrats to flesh out and implement. Moreover, as groups evolve, associate, and disassociate with one another over time, the most operational flexibility can be maintained by keeping threats broadly defined.

. . .Second, even assuming that a group is sufficiently affiliated, as a matter of law, which members of an organized armed group are targetable? Many in the international community reject the idea that members of an organized armed group are always targetable based merely on their membership in that group. Rather, they believe that for members of an organized armed group to be always targetable requires them to have a "continuous combat function." That term, as described by the ICRC's Interpretive Guidance on the Notion of Direct Participation in Hostilities (DPH study), refers to those individuals whose "continuous function" within the group "involves the preparation, execution, or command of acts or operations amounting to direct participation in hostilities." The United States and many international law experts do not subscribe to the DPH study's continuous combat function interpretation because it creates different standards for members of regular armed forces, who are always targetable based on their membership, and members of organized armed groups, only some of whom are always targetable based on their membership. Under the American approach, all that is needed to target an individual is "sufficiently reliable information that [the person] is a member of the organized armed group," such as the Taliban, al Qaeda, or associated forces; however, under the ICRC interpretation, the United States would also need to know that person's function before attacking him. This is an important and fundamental distinction for any debate about accountability for targeted killings. The United States claims the authority to target persons who are members of organized armed groups, based merely on their membership status; in so doing, the United States is not just considering planners or commanders as potential targets, but all members of enemy groups. This may mean that an outside observer who does not interpret the law as the United States does may see the killing of a person who was placed on a kill list as an unlawful killing. Thus, any debate about accountability requires that participants clearly specify what law they are applying to any given factual circumstance.

Although law delimits the categories of persons who can be killed, in practice, developing kill lists looks far beyond law to questions about the identity of a particular target and the accuracy and currency of the supporting intelligence. After intelligence is reviewed, a validation step revisits the initial legal determination to ensure that attacking an individual is lawful under the law of armed conflict or a particular covert action finding or executive directive. In explaining the compliance steps that the CIA would follow were it to carry out a targeted killing, CIA General Counsel Stephen Preston stated:

First, we would make sure all actions taken comply with the terms dictated by the President in the applicable Finding, which would likely contain specific limitations and conditions governing the use of force. We would also make sure all actions taken comply with any applicable Executive Order provisions, such as the prohibition against assassination in Twelve-Triple-Three. Beyond Presidential directives, the National Security Act of 1947 provides, . . . "[a] Finding may not authorize any action that would violate the Constitution or any statute of the United States." This crucial provision would be strictly applied in carrying out our hypothetical program.

In addition, the Agency would have to discharge its obligation under the congressional notification provisions of the National Security Act to keep the intelligence oversight committees of Congress "fully and currently informed" of its activities. Picture a system of notifications and briefings— some verbal, others written; some periodic, others event-specific; some at a staff level, others for members.

That leaves Compliance in Execution with reference to International Law Principles. Here, the Agency would implement its authorities in a manner consistent with the four basic principles in the law of armed conflict governing the use of force: Necessity, Distinction, Proportionality, and Humanity. Great care would be taken in the planning and execution of actions to satisfy these four principles and, in the process, to minimize civilian casualties.

So there you have it: four boxes, each carefully considered with reference to the contemplated activity. That is how an Agency program involving the use of lethal force would be structured so as to ensure that it satisfies applicable U.S. and international law.

The process also includes bureaucratic analysis aimed at determining both the short- and long-term costs and benefits of striking a particular target, with an eye toward both strategic and tactical considerations.

The kill-list creation process is complex and time intensive, usually involving dozens of analysts from different agencies. The goal of the process is to ensure that any person whose name appears on a kill list has been identified, vetted, and validated. Only then may they be nominated for placement on a kill list, with approval for nominations resting at the highest levels of government—oftentimes requiring the approval of the President of the United States. The particular targets that receive presidential review are those with the most heightened levels of policy concern, such as strikes with potential negative diplomatic fall-out or a high risk of collateral casualties; these, of course, are also the targets that will generally raise the most difficult questions under the law of armed conflict.

To develop targets, bureaucrats leverage intelligence analysis from experts spread across the government's civilian and military agencies. For targeted killings, target development is a systematic examination of enemy organizations and their members. Analysts are not simply looking to create a kill list based on membership; rather, they act in accordance with a doctrine known as effects-based targeting. Roughly summarized, effects-based targeting begins with the identification of certain strategic objectives, which lead to targeting decisions based on how engaging those targets will impact the enemy's decision making process and activities. Notably, the focus is not merely on the direct and immediate military advantage that will flow from the destruction of the target, but also on longer-term impacts. The process is open-ended and recursive. After national security bureaucrats identify enemy groups and individuals within enemy groups, they examine how the killing of specific individuals will affect the enemy organization, looking beyond the immediate death of the individual to broader network effects.

. . .Despite the controversy over al Aulaqi's placement on a kill-list and subsequent killing, his case was an easier one than others because at least some facts existed to suggest he was a senior member (akin to an individual with a continuous combat function). But what about lower level "foot soldiers," couriers, or mere members of enemy groups? Though under the U.S. view all members of an organized armed group may be placed on a kill list, not all of them will be. Rather, only those individuals who are of sufficient value to the enemy organization will be placed on a list. But what low-level people are worth adding to a kill-list? Bomb makers? Couriers? As various organizations have reported, it is not just high profile individuals like al Aulaqi who may find themselves the target of an attack; other individuals, deemed low level or insignificant by outside commentators, have also found themselves the subject of attacks. This is the case because the effects sought by killing are not merely the immediate effects of eliminating a person, but also the second- and third-order effects such as pressuring, desynchronizing, and debilitating the effectiveness of terrorist networks. Although killing Anwar al-Aulaqi, Osama Bin Laden or other high-ranking individuals may be an obvious policy choice, what about the propriety of killing low level operatives?

It is the job of national security bureaucrats to ask whether killing someone will be effective at disrupting organizations. It is also their job to ask whether the right people are being killed, and whether there will be blowback or other repercussions from a targeting decision. . . . Thus, it is the procedures for deciding who is worth killing that lie at the heart of the accountability debate. When scholars wonder if the United States is achieving short term goals while losing the long war, they should recognize that to best answer that question, transparency is necessary regarding the bureaucrat's process of assessing whether the deaths of those persons on a kill list will further national strategic interests. In short, the determination of whether targeted killings are effective is an analysis performed by national security bureaucrats, and assessing how well they do so is the central issue in the accountability debate.

. . .

QUESTIONS AND NOTES

1. Assume that in fact you are employed in the administration. Your superior asks you to prepare a critique of the process of targeted killing as described by Professor McNeal in his article, reproduced, supra. Assume, too, that you have grave doubts about the morality and/or the efficacy of such a policy. What would you do?

2. Assume that you do not have any qualms about targeted killings and therefore set to work on your assignment. What position would you recommend should be taken on the following issues?

a. Does it appear that the specific determination to target an individual suspected terrorists is being made at the right level? Absent urgency, should the President be involved in each such case? Should the Secretary of Defense? Anyone else? Note: news reports have indicated that the President has issued a finding authorizing such killings, but is not consulted in the individual case.

b. What kind of terrorist involvement, al Qaeda membership, leadership role in al Qaeda, and/or specific terrorist acts should be required, before a targeting order is approved?

c. What kind of evidence of the involvements described in b. above should be required? Suppose all of the information is based on informants' reports? How would you formulate the standard of proof?

d. Should there be a kind of formal fact-finding process? What kinds of formalities, if any? Any process of review of the fact-finding determination? By whom? How many? Should an effort be made to make it an adversarial process?

e.   Under what circumstances should a targeted killing be considered an acceptable option? For example, should there be a specific determination that the option of capturing the suspect would be too dangerous or logistically impossible? Note that it is reported that Harethi was living in a remote area of Yemen that was a lawless region where the Yemeni government had little control. See N.Y. Times, December 15, 2002, infra, note 3.

f.   Targeted killings have occurred on the battlefield, that is, in Afghanistan and in Yemen. Should the policies distinguish between the kinds of settings?

g.   Should the consent of the host country's government be required, before undertaking such an action? Note that news reports indicated that unofficially the Yemeni government actually assisted in the Harethi killing by providing intelligence. Suppose the host country is one that tacitly or actively supports the terrorist organizations? Suppose there is a concern about leaks if the host government is brought into the picture?

h.   Should the policies regularly require input from U.S. law enforcement agencies involved in the anti-terrorism effort, before a determination to target an individual is made?

i.   Should the policies prohibit targeted killings on U.S. soil?

j.   What kind of assurance should be required in the policies that innocent bystanders will not be injured? What kind of "collateral damage" should be deemed acceptable?

3.   The New York Times (David Johnston and David E. Sanger, Yemen Killing Based on Rules Set Out by Bush, N.Y. Times, Nov. 6, 2002) reported that the CIA did not "seek input from or consult law enforcement officials" prior to the killing by missile of Mr. Harethi and his companions in Yemen, supra. Law enforcement officials indicated they had wanted to question Harethi about the Cole attack, but they were not unhappy that he had been killed. This would appear to be an area where coordination between the law enforcement and intelligence-military operation needs to be improved, despite post-September 11th congressional and administration efforts to improve communication and coordination between these governmental functions.

4.   For news reports and discussion of some targeted killing efforts, see:

a.   Dana Priest, Surveillance Operation in Pakistan Located and Killed Al Qaeda Official, WASH. POST, May 15, 2005, at A25, available at: http://www.washingtonpost.com/wp-dyn/content/article/2005/05/14/AR2005051401121.html;

b.   Douglas Jehl & Mohammad Khan, Top Qaeda Aide is Called Target in U.S. Air Raid, N.Y. TIMES, Jan. 14, 2006, at A1, available at: http://www.nytimes.com/2006/01/14/politics/14afghan. html;

    c.   Griff Witte & Kamran Khan, U.S. Strike On Al Qaeda Top Deputy Said to Fail: Thousands Protest After Attack In Pakistan Leaves 17 Dead, WASH. POST, Jan. 15, 2006, at A1.

    d.   Carlotta Gall & Douglas Jehl, Strike Aimed at Qaeda Figure Stirs More Pakistan Protests, N.Y. TIMES, Jan. 16, 2006, at A3, available at: http://www.nytimes.com/2006/01/16/international/ asia/16pakistan.html;

    e.   For correspondence between U.N. Special Rapporteur on Extrajudicial, Summary, or Arbitrary Executions and the U.S. government concerning the above incidents, see Project on Extrajudicial Executions, Center for Human Rights and Global Justice, N.Y.U. School of Law.

    5.   For scholarship on this subject, see Anna Goppel (2013): Killing Terrorists. A Moral and Legal Analysis. De Gruyter, Berlin;. Jason Fisher, Targeted Killing, Norms and International Law, 45 COLUM. J. TRANSNAT'L L. 711 (2007); Saad Gul & Katherine M. Royal, Burning the Barn to Roast the Pig? Proportionality Concerns in the War on Terror and the Damadola Incident, 14 WILLAMETTE J. INT'L L. & DISP. RESOL. 49 (2006); David Kretzmer, Targeted Killing of Terrorists: Extra-Judicial Executions or Legitimate Means of Defence?, 16 EUR. J. INT'L L. 171 (2005); Daniel Statman, Targeted Killing, 5 THEORETICAL INQUIRIES IN L. 179 (2004).

E. THE AL-AULAQI CASE

NASSER AL-AULAQI V. OBAMA

727 F. Supp. 2d 1 (D.D.C 2010)

JUDGE: JOHN D. BATES

MEMORANDUM OPINION

On August 30, 2010, plaintiff Nasser Al-Aulaqi ("plaintiff") filed this action, claiming that the President, the Secretary of Defense, and the Director of the CIA (collectively, "defendants") have unlawfully authorized the targeted killing of plaintiff's son, Anwar Al-Aulaqi, a dual U.S.-Yemeni citizen currently hiding in Yemen who has alleged ties to al Qaeda in the Arabian Peninsula ("AQAP"). Plaintiff seeks an injunction prohibiting defendants from intentionally killing Anwar Al-Aulaqi "unless he presents a concrete, specific, and imminent threat to life or physical safety, and there are no means other than lethal force that could reasonably be employed to neutralize the threat." Defendants have responded with a motion to dismiss plaintiff's complaint on five threshold grounds: standing, the political question doctrine, the Court's exercise of its "equitable discretion," the absence of a cause of action under the Alien Tort Statute ("ATS"), and the state secrets privilege.

This is a unique and extraordinary case. Both the threshold and merits issues present fundamental questions of separation of powers involving the proper role of the courts in our constitutional structure.... Vital considerations of national security and of military and foreign affairs (and hence potentially of state secrets) are at play.

Stark, and perplexing, questions readily come to mind, including the following: How is it that judicial approval is required when the United States decides to target a U.S. citizen overseas for electronic surveillance, but that, according to defendants, judicial scrutiny is prohibited when the United States decides to target a U.S. citizen overseas for death? Can a U.S. citizen—himself or through another—use the U.S. judicial system to vindicate his constitutional rights while simultaneously evading U.S. law enforcement authorities, calling for "jihad against the West," and engaging in operational planning for an organization that has already carried out numerous terrorist attacks against the United States? Can the Executive order the assassination of a U.S. citizen without first affording him any form of judicial process whatsoever, based on the mere assertion that he is a dangerous member of a terrorist organization? How can the courts, as plaintiff proposes, make real-time assessments of the nature and severity of alleged threats to national security, determine the imminence of those threats, weigh the benefits and costs of possible diplomatic and military responses, and ultimately decide whether, and under what circumstances, the use of military force against such threats is justified? When would it ever make sense for the United States to disclose in advance to the "target" of contemplated military action the precise standards under which it will take that military action? And how does the evolving AQAP relate to core al Qaeda for purposes of assessing the legality of targeting AQAP (or its principals) under the September 18, 2001 Authorization for the Use of Military Force?

These and other legal and policy questions posed by this case are controversial and of great public interest. "Unfortunately, however, no matter how interesting and no matter how important this case may be . . . we cannot address it unless we have jurisdiction." Before reaching the merits of plaintiff's claims, then, this Court must decide whether plaintiff is the proper person to bring the constitutional and statutory challenges he asserts, and whether plaintiff's challenges, as framed, state claims within the ambit of the Judiciary to resolve. These jurisdictional issues pose "distinct and separate limitation[s], so that either the absence of standing or the presence of a political question suffices to prevent the power of the federal judiciary from being invoked by the complaining party."

. . .Because these questions of justiciability require dismissal of this case at the outset, the serious issues regarding the merits of the alleged authorization of the targeted killing of a U.S. citizen overseas must await another day or another (non-judicial) forum.

BACKGROUND

This case arises from the United States's alleged policy of "authorizing, planning, and carrying out targeted killings, including of U.S. citizens, outside the context of armed conflict." Specifically, plaintiff, a Yemeni citizen, claims that the United States has authorized the targeted killing of plaintiff's son, Anwar Al-Aulaqi, in violation of the Constitution and international law. See id.

Anwar Al-Aulaqi is a Muslim cleric with dual U.S.-Yemeni citizenship, who is currently believed to be in hiding in Yemen. . . . Anwar Al-Aulaqi was born in New Mexico in 1971, and spent much of his early life in the United States, attending college at Colorado State University and receiving his master's degree from San Diego State University before moving to Yemen in 2004. On July 16, 2010, the U.S. Treasury Department's Office of Foreign Assets Control ("OFAC") designated Anwar Al-Aulaqi as a Specially Designated Global Terrorist ("SDGT") in light of evidence that he was "acting for or on behalf of al-Qa'ida in the Arabian Peninsula (AQAP)" and "providing financial, material or technological support for, or other services to or in support of, acts of terrorism[.]". . . . In its designation, OFAC explained that Anwar Al-Aulaqi had "taken on an increasingly operational role" in AQAP since late 2009, as he "facilitated training camps in Yemen in support of acts of terrorism" and provided "instructions" to Umar Farouk Abdulmutallab, the man accused of attempting to detonate a bomb aboard a Detroit-bound Northwest Airlines flight on Christmas Day 2009. Media sources have also reported ties between Anwar Al-Aulaqi and Nidal Malik Hasan, the U.S. Army Major suspected of killing 13 people in a November 2009 shooting at Fort Hood, Texas. According to a January 2010 Los Angeles Times article, unnamed "U.S. officials" have discovered that Anwar Al-Aulaqi and Hasan exchanged as many as eighteen e-mails prior to the Fort Hood shootings.

Recently, Anwar Al-Aulaqi has made numerous public statements calling for "jihad against the West," praising the actions of "his students" Abdulmutallab and Hasan, and asking others to "follow suit." Michael Leiter, Director of the National Counterterrorism Center, has explained that Anwar Al-Aulaqi's "familiarity with the West" is a "key concern[ ]" for the United States, and media sources have similarly cited Anwar Al-Aulaqi's ability to communicate with an English-speaking audience as a source of "particular concern" to U.S. officials. . . . But despite the United States's expressed "concern" regarding Anwar Al-Aulaqi's "familiarity with the West" and his "role in AQAP," United States has not yet publicly charged Anwar Al-Aulaqi with any crime. For his part, Anwar Al-Aulaqi has made clear that he has no intention of making himself available for criminal prosecution in U.S. courts, remarking in a May 2010 AQAP video interview that he "will never surrender" to the United States, and that "[i]f the Americans want me, [they can] come look for me." . . .Plaintiff does not deny his son's affiliation with AQAP or his designation as a SDGT. Rather, plaintiff challenges his son's alleged unlawful inclusion on so-called "kill lists" that he contends are maintained by the CIA and the Joint Special Operations Command ("JSOC"). In support of his claim that the United States has placed Anwar Al-Aulaqi on "kill lists," plaintiff cites a number of media reports, which attribute their information to anonymous U.S. military and intelligence sources. For example, in January 2010, The Washington Post reported that, according to unnamed military officials, Anwar Al-Aulaqi was on "a shortlist of U.S. citizens" that JSOC was authorized to kill or capture. A few months later, The Washington Post cited an anonymous U.S. official as stating that Anwar Al-Aulaqi had become "the first U.S. citizen added to a list of suspected terrorists the CIA is authorized to kill." And in July 2010, National Public Radio announced—on the basis of unidentified "[i]ntelligence sources"—that the United States had already ordered "almost a dozen" unsuccessful drone and air-strikes targeting Anwar Al-Aulaqi in Yemen.

Based on these news reports, plaintiff claims that the United States has placed Anwar Al-Aulaqi on the CIA and JSOC "kill lists" without "charge, trial, or conviction." Plaintiff alleges that individuals like his son are placed on "kill lists" after a "closed executive process" in which defendants and other executive officials determine that "secret criteria" have been satisfied. Plaintiff further avers "[u]pon information and belief" that once an individual is placed on a "kill list," he remains there for "months at a time." (quoting unnamed U.S. officials as stating that "kill lists" are reviewed every six months and names are removed from the list if there is no longer intelligence linking the person to "known terrorists or [terrorist] plans"). Consequently, plaintiff argues, Anwar Al-Aulaqi is "now subject to a standing order that permits the CIA and JSOC to kill him . . . without regard to whether, at the time lethal force will be used, he presents a concrete, specific, and imminent threat to life, or whether there are reasonable means short of lethal force that could be used to address any such threat."

The United States has neither confirmed nor denied the allegation that it has issued a "standing order" authorizing the CIA and JSOC to kill plaintiff's son. Additionally, the United States has neither confirmed nor denied whether—if it has, in fact, authorized the use of lethal force against plaintiff's son—the authorization was made with regard to whether Anwar Al-Aulaqi presents a concrete, specific, and imminent threat to life, or whether there were reasonable means short of lethal force that could be used to address any such threat. The United States has, however, repeatedly stated that if Anwar Al-Aulaqi "were to surrender or otherwise present himself to the proper authorities in a peaceful and appropriate manner, legal principles with which the United States has traditionally and uniformly complied would prohibit using lethal force or other violence against him in such circumstances."

Nevertheless, plaintiff alleges that due to his son's inclusion on the CIA and JSOC "kill lists," Anwar Al-Aulaqi is in "hiding under threat of death and cannot access counsel or the courts to assert his constitutional rights without disclosing his whereabouts and exposing himself to possible attack by Defendants."

Plaintiff therefore brings four claims—three constitutional, and one statutory—on his son's behalf. He asserts that the United States's alleged policy of authorizing the targeted killing of U.S. citizens, including plaintiff's son, outside of armed conflict, "in circumstances in which they do not present concrete, specific, and imminent threats to life or physical safety, and where there are means other than lethal force that could reasonably be employed to neutralize any such threat," violates (1) Anwar Al-Aulaqi's Fourth Amendment right to be free from unreasonable seizures and (2) his Fifth Amendment right not to be deprived of life without due process of law. Plaintiff further claims that (3) the United States's refusal to disclose the criteria by which it selects U.S. citizens like plaintiff's son for targeted killing independently violates the notice requirement of the Fifth Amendment Due Process Clause. Finally, plaintiff brings (4) a statutory claim under the Alien Tort Statute ("ATS"), 28 U.S.C. § 1350, alleging that the United States's "policy of targeted killings violates treaty and customary international law."

Plaintiff seeks both declaratory and injunctive relief. First, he requests a declaration that, outside of armed conflict, the Constitution prohibits defendants "from carrying out the targeted killing of U.S. citizens," including Anwar Al-Aulaqi, "except in circumstances in which they present a concrete, specific, and imminent threat to life or physical safety, and there are no means other than lethal force that could reasonably be employed to neutralize the threat.". Second, plaintiff requests a declaration that, outside of armed conflict, "treaty and customary international law" prohibit the targeted killing of all individuals—regardless of their citizenship—except in those same, limited circumstances. Third, plaintiff requests a preliminary injunction prohibiting defendants from intentionally killing Anwar Al-Aulaqi "unless he presents a concrete, specific, and imminent threat to life or physical safety, and there are no means other than lethal force that could reasonably be employed to neutralize the threat." Finally, plaintiff seeks an injunction ordering defendants to disclose the criteria that the United States uses to determine whether a U.S. citizen will be targeted for killing.

[The court proceeded in a lengthy opinion to dismiss the complaint on the grounds that the plaintiff lacks standing, there is no cause of action under the Alien Tort Statute and the issues raise a political question. The court declined to decide the defendants' state secret privilege argument. In addressing the political question issue, the court made the following comments:]

. . .

Judicial resolution of the "particular questions" posed by plaintiff in this case would require this Court to decide: (1) the precise nature and extent of Anwar Al-Aulaqi's affiliation with AQAP; (2) whether AQAP and al Qaeda are so closely linked that the defendants' targeted killing of Anwar Al-Aulaqi in Yemen would come within the United States's current armed conflict with al Qaeda; (3) whether (assuming plaintiff's proffered legal standard applies) Anwar Al-Aulaqi's alleged terrorist activity renders him a "concrete, specific, and imminent threat to life or physical safety," and (4) whether there are "means short of lethal force" that the United States could "reasonably" employ to address any threat that Anwar Al-Aulaqi poses to U.S. national security interests, Such determinations, in turn, would require this Court, in defendants' view, to understand and assess "the capabilities of the [alleged] terrorist operative to carry out a threatened attack, what response would be sufficient to address that threat, possible diplomatic considerations that may bear on such responses, the vulnerability of potential targets that the [alleged] terrorist[ ] may strike, the availability of military and non-military options, and the risks to military and nonmilitary personnel in attempting application of non-lethal force." Viewed through these prisms, it becomes clear that plaintiff's claims pose precisely the types of complex policy questions that the D.C. Circuit has historically held non-justiciable under the political question doctrine.

. . .

The type of relief that plaintiff seeks only underscores the impropriety of judicial review here. Plaintiff requests both a declaration setting forth the standard under which the United States can select individuals for targeted killing as well as an injunction prohibiting defendants from intentionally killing Anwar Al-Aulaqi unless he meets that standard—i.e., unless he "presents a concrete, specific, and imminent threat to life or physical safety, and there are no means other than lethal force that could reasonably be employed to neutralize the threat." Yet plaintiff concedes that the " 'imminence' requirement" of his proffered legal standard would render any "real-time judicial review" of targeting decisions "infeasible," and he therefore urges this Court to issue his requested preliminary injunction and then enforce the injunction "through an after-the-fact contempt motion or an after-the-fact damages action . . . [T]here is a "textually demonstrable constitutional commitment" of the United States's decision to employ military force to coordinate political departments (Congress and the Executive), and any after-the-fact judicial review of the Executive's decision to employ military force abroad would reveal a "lack of respect due coordinate branches of government" and create "the potentiality of embarrassment of multifarious pronouncements by various departments on one question."

. . .

To be sure, this Court recognizes the somewhat unsettling nature of its conclusion—that there are circumstances in which the Executive's unilateral decision to kill a U.S. citizen overseas is "constitutionally committed to the political branches" and judicially unreviewable. But this case squarely presents such a circumstance. . . .

QUESTIONS AND NOTES

1. Does the court's discussion in Al-Aulaqi affect your views about any of the policy issues in this area of terrorism law? For example, about the possible feasibility or efficacy of judicial review of these issues?

2. The court in the Al-Aulaqi makes passing reference to one of the arguments raised by plaintiffs—why should governmental intrusions on privacy abroad through electronic surveillance be subject to legislative regulation (see ch. 5, supra) while governmental targeting killings abroad are not? Are these two areas of the law different?

3. The fact that Anwar Al-Aulaqi's name was put on a kill list was leaked (it turned out to be a leak of accurate information). This may have been, like many leaks of confidential information, leaked against the wishes of government authorities, motivated by the private reasons of the leaker. There is, however, another possibility: the government may have wanted to disseminate the information. How many reasons might there be why the government would want to make this information unofficially public?

4. The Al-Aulaqi case quickly triggered a number of papers: See, e.g., Ryan Patrick Alford, The Rule of Law at the Crossroads: Consequences of Targeted Killings of Citizens, http://ssrn.com/abstract=1780584; Debate-Targeted Killing: The Case of Anwar Al-Aulaqi, 159 University of Pennsylvania Law Review 175 (2011); Robert Chesney, Who May be Killed? Anwar Al-Awlaki as a Case Study in the International Legal Regulation of Lethal Force, Yearbook of International Humanitarian Law), Vol. 13 (2010) p. 3.

5. In the wake of the Al-Aulaqi killing, the issue of the use of drones to kill individuals came to national attention and became the subject of much discussion, in the press and among members of the public. Information was leaked about memoranda spelling out the authorities relied upon by the administration for its policy regarding the use of drones and the policy relating

to the killing of U.S. citizens. The President initially resisted demands to make the memoranda public but finally, in connection with the Senate consideration of John Brennan to be the Director of the CIA, the administration was compelled to agree to share the memoranda (reportedly, 11 memoranda) with the Senate and House Intelligence committees. Earlier, Attorney General Holder had given a speech at Northwestern University, on March 5, 2012, dealing with national security matters, in which he spelled out the criteria being used by the administration to make decisions about targeted killings by drone. Relevant excerpts from his address are reproduced below:

> Now, I realize I have gone into considerable detail about tools we use to identify suspected terrorists and to bring captured terrorists to justice. It is preferable to capture suspected terrorists where feasible—among other reasons, so that we can gather valuable intelligence from them—but we must also recognize that there are instances where our government has the clear authority—and, I would argue, the responsibility—to defend the United States through the appropriate and lawful use of lethal force.

> This principle has long been established under both U.S. and international law. In response to the attacks perpetrated—and the continuing threat posed—by al Qaeda, the Taliban, and associated forces, Congress has authorized the President to use all necessary and appropriate force against those groups. Because the United States is in an armed conflict, we are authorized to take action against enemy belligerents under international law. The Constitution empowers the President to protect the nation from any imminent threat of violent attack. And international law recognizes the inherent right of national self-defense. None of this is changed by the fact that we are not in a conventional war.

> Our legal authority is not limited to the battlefields in Afghanistan. Indeed, neither Congress nor our federal courts has limited the geographic scope of our ability to use force to the current conflict in Afghanistan. We are at war with a stateless enemy, prone to shifting operations from country to country. Over the last three years alone, al Qaeda and its associates have directed several attacks—fortunately, unsuccessful—against us from countries other than Afghanistan. Our government has both a responsibility and a right to protect this nation and its people from such threats.

> This does not mean that we can use military force whenever or wherever we want. International legal principles, including respect for another nation's sovereignty, constrain our ability to act unilaterally. But the use of force in foreign territory would be consistent with these international legal principles if conducted, for example, with the consent of the nation involved—or after a determination that the nation is unable or unwilling to deal effectively with a threat to the United States.

Furthermore, it is entirely lawful—under both United States law and applicable law of war principles—to target specific senior operational leaders of al Qaeda and associated forces. This is not a novel concept. In fact, during World War II, the United States tracked the plane flying Admiral Isoroku Yamamoto—the commander of Japanese forces in the attack on Pearl Harbor and the Battle of Midway—and shot it down specifically because he was on board. As I explained to the Senate Judiciary Committee following the operation that killed Osama bin Laden, the same rules apply today.

Some have called such operations "assassinations." They are not, and the use of that loaded term is misplaced. Assassinations are unlawful killings. Here, for the reasons I have given, the U.S. government's use of lethal force in self defense against a leader of al Qaeda or an associated force who presents an imminent threat of violent attack would not be unlawful—and therefore would not violate the Executive Order banning assassination or criminal statutes.

Now, it is an unfortunate but undeniable fact that some of the threats we face come from a small number of United States citizens who have decided to commit violent attacks against their own country from abroad. Based on generations-old legal principles and Supreme Court decisions handed down during World War II, as well as during this current conflict, it's clear that United States citizenship alone does not make such individuals immune from being targeted. But it does mean that the government must take into account all relevant constitutional considerations with respect to United States citizens—even those who are leading efforts to kill innocent Americans. Of these, the most relevant is the Fifth Amendment's Due Process Clause, which says that the government may not deprive a citizen of his or her life without due process of law.

The Supreme Court has made clear that the Due Process Clause does not impose one-size-fits-all requirements, but instead mandates procedural safeguards that depend on specific circumstances. In cases arising under the Due Process Clause—including in a case involving a U.S. citizen captured in the conflict against al Qaeda—the Court has applied a balancing approach, weighing the private interest that will be affected against the interest the government is trying to protect, and the burdens the government would face in providing additional process. Where national security operations are at stake, due process takes into account the realities of combat.

Here, the interests on both sides of the scale are extraordinarily weighty. An individual's interest in making sure that the government does not target him erroneously could not be more significant. Yet it is imperative for the government to counter threats posed by senior operational leaders of al Qaeda, and to protect the innocent people whose lives could be lost in their attacks.

Any decision to use lethal force against a United States citizen—even one intent on murdering Americans and who has become an operational leader of al-Qaeda in a foreign land—is among the gravest that government leaders can face. The American people can be—and deserve to be—assured that actions taken in their defense are consistent with their values and their laws. So, although I cannot discuss or confirm any particular program or operation, I believe it is important to explain these legal principles publicly.

Let me be clear: an operation using lethal force in a foreign country, targeted against a U.S. citizen who is a senior operational leader of al Qaeda or associated forces, and who is actively engaged in planning to kill Americans, would be lawful at least in the following circumstances: First, the U.S. government has determined, after a thorough and careful review, that the individual poses an imminent threat of violent attack against the United States; second, capture is not feasible; and third, the operation would be conducted in a manner consistent with applicable law of war principles.

The evaluation of whether an individual presents an "imminent threat" incorporates considerations of the relevant window of opportunity to act, the possible harm that missing the window would cause to civilians, and the likelihood of heading off future disastrous attacks against the United States. As we learned on 9/11, al Qaeda has demonstrated the ability to strike with little or no notice—and to cause devastating casualties. Its leaders are continually planning attacks against the United States, and they do not behave like a traditional military—wearing uniforms, carrying arms openly, or massing forces in preparation for an attack. Given these facts, the Constitution does not require the President to delay action until some theoretical end-stage of planning—when the precise time, place, and manner of an attack become clear. Such a requirement would create an unacceptably high risk that our efforts would fail, and that Americans would be killed.

Whether the capture of a U.S. citizen terrorist is feasible is a fact-specific, and potentially time-sensitive, question. It may depend on, among other things, whether capture can be accomplished in the window of time available to prevent an attack and without undue risk to civilians or to U.S. personnel. Given the nature of how terrorists act and where they tend to hide, it may not always be feasible to capture a United States citizen terrorist who presents an imminent threat of violent attack. In that case, our government has the clear authority to defend the United States with lethal force.

Of course, any such use of lethal force by the United States will comply with the four fundamental law of war principles governing the use of force. The principle of necessity requires that the target have definite military value. The principle of distinction requires that only lawful targets—such as combatants, civilians directly participating in hostilities, and military objectives—may be targeted intentionally. Under the principle of proportionality, the anticipated collateral damage must not be excessive in relation to the anticipated military advantage. Finally, the principle of humanity requires us to use weapons that will not inflict unnecessary suffering.

These principles do not forbid the use of stealth or technologically advanced weapons. In fact, the use of advanced weapons may help to ensure that the best intelligence is available for planning and carrying out operations, and that the risk of civilian casualties can be minimized or avoided altogether.

Some have argued that the President is required to get permission from a federal court before taking action against a United States citizen who is a senior operational leader of al Qaeda or associated forces. This is simply not accurate. "Due process" and "judicial process" are not one and the same, particularly when it comes to national security. The Constitution guarantees due process, not judicial process.

The conduct and management of national security operations are core functions of the Executive Branch, as courts have recognized throughout our history. Military and civilian officials must often make real-time decisions that balance the need to act, the existence of alternative options, the possibility of collateral damage, and other judgments—all of which depend on expertise and immediate access to information that only the Executive Branch may possess in real time. The Constitution's guarantee of due process is ironclad, and it is essential—but, as a recent court decision makes clear, it does not require judicial approval before the President may use force abroad against a senior operational leader of a foreign terrorist organization with which the United States is at war—even if that individual happens to be a U.S. citizen.

That is not to say that the Executive Branch has—or should ever have—the ability to target any such individuals without robust oversight. Which is why, in keeping with the law and our constitutional system of checks and balances, the Executive Branch regularly informs the appropriate members of Congress about our counterterrorism activities, including the legal framework, and would of course follow the same practice where lethal force is used against United States citizens.

Now, these circumstances are sufficient under the Constitution for the United States to use lethal force against a U.S. citizen abroad—but it is important to note that the legal requirements I have described may not apply in every situation—such as operations that take place on traditional battlefields.

The unfortunate reality is that our nation will likely continue to face terrorist threats that—at times—originate with our own citizens. When such individuals take up arms against this country—and join al Qaeda in plotting attacks designed to kill their fellow Americans—there may be only one realistic and appropriate response. We must take steps to stop them—in full accordance with the Constitution. In this hour of danger, we simply cannot afford to wait until deadly plans are carried out—and we will not.

6.   In June of 2014, the Justice Department released an Office of Legal Counsel memo that authorized the targeted killing of Anwar Al-Aulaqi. The memo was released as a result of a Freedom of Information Act lawsuit brought by The New York Times and The American Civil Liberties Union. The memo which appears below is redacted in parts, and footnotes have been omitted.

U.S. Department of Justice
Office of Legal Counsel

Office of the Assistant Attorney General   Washington, D.C. 20530
July 16, 2010

MEMORANDUM FOR THE ATTORNEY GENERAL

Re: Applicability of Federal Criminal Laws and the Constitution to Contemplated Lethal Operations Against Shaykh Anwar al-Aulaqi

. . .

We begin our legal analysis with a consideration of section 1119 of title 18, entitled "Foreign murder of United States nationals." Subsection 1119(b) provides that "[a] person who, being a national of the United States, kills or attempts to kill a national of the United States while such national is outside the United States but within the jurisdiction of another conntry shall be punished as provided under sections 1111, 1112,and 1113." 18 U.S.C. § 1119(b). In light of the nature of the contemplated operations described above, and the fact that their target would be a "national of the United States" who is outside the United States, we must examine whether section 1119(b) would prohibit those operations. We first explain, in this part, the scope of section 1119 and why it must be construed to incorporate the public authority justification, which can render lethal action carried out by a governmental official lawful in some circumstances. We next explain in part III-A why that public authority justification would apply to the contemplated DoD operation. Finally, we explain in part III-B why that justification would apply to the contemplated CIA operation. As to each agency, we focus on the particular circumstances in which it would carry out the operation.

A

... It is ... clear that section 1119(b) bars only "unlawful killings."

This limitation on section 1119(1)'s scope is significant, as the legislative history to the underlying offenses that the section incorporates makes clear. The provisions section 1119(b) incorporates derive from sections 273 and 274 of the Act of March 4, 1909, ch. 321, 35 Stat. 1088, 1143. The 1909 Act codified and amended the penal laws of the United States. Section 273 of the enactment defined murder as "the unlawful killing of a human being with malice aforethought," and section 274 defined manslaughter as "the unlawful killing of a human being without malice." 35 Stat. 1143. In 1948, Congress codified the federal murder and manslaughter provisions at sections 1111 and 1112 of title 18 and retained the definitions of murder and manslaughter in nearly identical form, see Act of June 25, 1948, ch. 645, 62 Stat. 683, 756, including the references to "unlawful killing" that remain in the statutes today—references that track similar formulations in some state murder statutes.

. . .

Here, we focus on the potential application of one such recognized justification—the justification of "public authority"—to the contemplated DoD and CIA operations. Before examining whether, on these facts, the public authority justification would apply to those operations, we first explain why section 1119(b) incorporates that particular justification.

The public authority justification, generally understood, is well-accepted, and it is clear it may be available even in cases where the particular criminal statute at issue does not expressly refer to a public authority justification. Prosecutions where ... a "public authority" justification is invoked are understandably rare, see American Law Institute, Model Penal Code and Commentaries § 3.03 Comment 1, at 24 (1985); cf. VISA Fraud Investigation, 8 Op. O.L.C. 284, 285 n.2, 286 (1984), and thus there is little case law in which courts have analyzed the scope of the justification with respect to the conduct of government officials. Nonetheless, discussions in the leading treatises and in the Model Penal Code demonstrate its legitimacy. See 2 Wayne R. LaFave, Substantive Criminal Law § 10.2(b), at 135 (2d ed. 2003); Perkins & Boyce, Criminal Law at 1093 ("Deeds which otherwise would be criminal, such as taking or destroying property, taking hold of a person by force and against his will, placing him in confinement, or even taking his life, are not crimes if done with proper public authority."); see also Model Penal Code § 3.03(1)(a), (d), (e), at 22–23 (proposing codification of justification where conduct is "required or authorized by," inter alia, "the law defining the duties or functions of a public officer ...."; "the law governing the armed services or the lawful conduct of war"; or "any other provision of law imposing a public duty"); National Comm'n on Reform of Federal Criminal Laws, A Proposed New Federal Criminal Code § 602(1) ("Conduct engaged in by a public servant in the course of his official duties is justified when it is required or authorized by law."). And this Office has invoked analogous rationales in several instances in which it has analyzed whether Congress intended a particular criminal statute to prohibit specific conduct that otherwise falls within a government agency's authorities.

. . .

. . . [W]e believe the touchstone for the analysis of whether section 1119 incorporates not only justifications generally, but also the public authority justification in particular, is the legislative intent underlying this criminal statute. We conclude that the statute should be read to exclude from its prohibitory scope killings that are encompassed by traditional justifications, which include the public authority justification. There are no indications that Congress had a contrary intention. Nothing in the text or legislative history of sections 1111–1113 of title 18 suggests that Congress intended to exclude the established public authority justification from those that Congress otherwise must be understood to have imported through the use of the modifier "unlawful" in those statutes (which, as we explain above, establish the substantive scope of section 1119(b)). Nor is there anything in the text or legislative history of section 1119 itself to suggest that Congress intended to abrogate or otherwise affect the availability under that statute of this traditional justification for killings. On the contrary, the relevant legislative materials indicate that in enacting section 1119 Congress was merely closing a gap in a field dealing with entirely different kinds of conduct than that at issue here.

. . .

It is true that here the target of the contemplated operations would be a U.S. citizen. But we do not believe al-Aulaqi's citizenship provides a basis for concluding that section 1119 would fail to incorporate the established public authority justification for a killing in this case. As we have explained, section 1119 incorporates the federal murder and manslaughter statutes, and thus its prohibition extends only to "unlawful" killings, 18 U.S.C. §§ 1111, 1112, a category that was intended to include, from all of the evidence of legislative intent we can find, only those killings that may not be permissible in light of traditional justifications for such action. At the time the predecessor versions of sections 1111 and 1112 were enacted, it was understood that killings undertaken in accord with the public authority justification were not "unlawful" because they were justified. There is no indication that, because section 1119(b) proscribes the unlawful killing abroad of U.S. nationals by U.S. nationals, it silently incorporated all justifications for killings except that public authority justification.

III.

Given that section 1119 incorporates the public authority justification, we must next analyze whether the contemplated DoD and CIA operations would be encompassed by that justification. In particular, we must analyze whether that justification would apply even though the target of the contemplated operations is a United States citizen. We conclude that it would—a conclusion that depends in part on our determination that each operation would accord with any potential constitutional protections of the United States citizen in these circumstances (see infra part VI). In reaching this conclusion, we do not address other cases or circumstances, involving different facts. Instead, we emphasize the sufficiency of the facts that have been represented to us here, without determining whether such facts would be necessary to the conclusion we reach.

. . .

In applying this variant of the public authority justification to the contemplated DoD operation, we note as an initial matter that DoD would undertake the operation pursuant to Executive war powers that Congress has expressly authorized. See Youngstown Sheet & Tube Co. v. Sawyer, 343 U.S. 579, 635 (1952) (Jackson, J., concurring) ("When the President acts pursuant to an express or implied authorization of Congress, his authority is at its maximum, for it includes all that he possesses in his own right plus all that Congress can delegate."). By authorizing the use of force against "organizations" that planned, authorized, and committed the September 11th attacks, Congress clearly authorized the President's use of "necessary and appropriate" force against al-Qaida forces, because al-Qaida carried out the September 11th attacks. See Authorization for Use of Military Force ("AUMF"), Pub. L. No. 107-40, 115 Stat. 224, § 2(a) (2001) (providing that the President may "use all necessary and appropriate force against those nations, organizations, or persons he determines planned, authorized, committed or aided the terrorist attacks that occurred on September 11, 2001, or harbored such organizations or persons, in order to prevent any future acts of international terrorism against the United States by such nations, organizations, or persons."). And, as we have explained, supra at 9, a decision-maker could reasonably conclude that this leader of AQAP forces is part of al-Qaida forces. Alternatively, and as we have further explained, supra at 10 n.5, the AUMF applies with respect to forces "associated with" al-Qaida that are engaged in hostilities against the U.S. or its coalition partners, and a decision-maker could reasonably conclude that the AQAP forces of which al-Aulaqi is a leader are "associated with" al Qaida forces for purposes of the AUMF. On either view, DoD would carry out its contemplated operation against a leader of an organization that is within the scope of the AUMF, and therefore DoD would in that respect be operating in accord with a grant of statutory authority.

Based upon the facts represented to us, moreover, the target of the contemplated operation has engaged in conduct as part of that organization that brings him within the scope of the AUMF. High-level government officials have concluded, on the basis of al-Aulaqi's activities in Yemen, that al-Aulaqi is a leader of AQAP whose activities in Yemen pose a "continued and imminent threat" of violence to United States persons and interests. Indeed, the facts represented to us indicate that al-Aulaqi has been involved, through his operational and leadership roles within AQAP, in an abortive attack within the United States and continues to plot attacks intended to kill Americans from his base of operations in Yemen. The contemplated DoD operation, therefore, would be carried out against someone who is within the core of individuals against whom Congress has authorized the use of necessary and appropriate force.

. . .

In light of these precedents, we believe the AUMF's authority to use lethal force abroad also may apply in appropriate circumstances to a United States citizen who is part of the forces of an enemy organization within the scope of the force authorization. The use of lethal force against such enemy forces, like military detention, is an " 'important incident of war,' " Hamdi, 542 U.S. at 518 (plurality opinion) (quotation omitted). See, e.g., General Orders No. 100: Instructions for the Government of Armies of the Untied States in the Field ¶ 15 (Apr. 24, 1863) (the "Lieber Code") ("[m]ilitary necessity admits of all direct destruction of life or limb of armed enemies"); International Committee of the Red Cross, Commentary on the Additional Protocols of 8 June 1977 to the Geneva Conventions of 12 Aug. 1949 and Relating to the Protection of Victims of Non-International Armed Conflicts (Additional Protocol II) § 4789 (1987); Yoram Dinstein, The Conduct of Hostilities Under the Law of International Armed Conflict 94 (2004) ("Conduct of Hostilities") ("When a person takes up arms or merely dons a uniform as a member of the armed forces, he automatically exposes himself to enemy attack."). And thus, just as the AUMF authorizes the military detention of a U.S. citizen captured abroad who is part of an armed force within the scope of the AUMF, it also authorizes the use of "necessary and appropriate" lethal force against a U.S. citizen who has joined such an armed force. Moreover, as we explain further in Part VI, DoD would conduct the operation in a mariner that would not violate any possible constitutional protections that al-Aulaqi enjoys by reason of his citizenship. Accordingly, we do not believe al-Aulaqi's citizenship provides a basis for concluding that he is immune from a use of force abroad that the AUMF otherwise authorizes.

In determining whether the contemplated DoD operation would constitute the "lawful conduct of war," LaFave, Substantive Criminal Law § 10.2(c), at 136, we next consider whether that operation would comply with the international law rules to which it would be subject—a question that also bears on whether the operation would be authorized by the AUMF. See Response for Petition for Rehearing and Rehearing En Banc, Al Bihani v. Obama, No. 09-5051 at 7 (D.C. Cir.) (May 13, 2010) (AUMF " 'should be construed, if possible, as consistent with international law") (citing Murray v. Schooner Charming Betsy, 6 U.S. Cranch) 64, 118 (1804) ("an act of Congress ought never to be construed to violate the law of nations, if any other possible construction remains")); see also F Hoffman-La Roche Ltd. v. Empagran S.A., 542 U.S. 155, 164 (2004) (customary international law is "law that (we must assume) Congress ordinarily seeks to follow"). Based on the combination of facts presented to us, we conclude that DoD would carry out its operation as part of the non-international anned conflict between the United States and al-Qaida, and thus that on those facts the operation would comply with international law so long as DoD would conduct it in accord with the applicable laws of war that govern targeting in such a conflict.

. . .

In looking for such guidance, we have not come across any authority for the proposition that when one of the parties to an armed conflict plans and executes operations from a base in a new nation, an operation to engage the enemy in that location can never be part of the original armed conflict—and thus subject to the laws of war governing that conflict—unless and until the hostilities become sufficiently intensive and protracted within that new location. That does not appear to be the rule, or the historical practice, for instance, in a traditional international conflict. See John R. Stevenson, Legal Adviser, Department of State, United States Military Action in Cambodia: Questions of International Law (address before the Hammarskjold Forum of the Association of the Bar of the City of New York, May 28, 1970), in 3 The Vietnam War and international Law: The Widening Context 23, 28–30 (Richard A. Falk, ed. 1972) (arguing that in an international armed conflict, if a neutral state has been unable for any reason to prevent violations of its neutrality by the troops of one belligerent using its territory as a base of operations, the other belligerent has historically been justified in attacking those enemy forces in that state). Nor do we see any obvious reason why that more categorical, nation-specific rule should govern in analogous circumstances in this sort of non-international armed conflict.

. . .

For present purposes, in applying the more context-specific approach to determining whether an operation would take place within the scope of a particular armed conflict, it is sufficient that the facts as they have been represented to us here, in combination, support the judgment that DoD's operation in Yemen would be conducted as part of the non-international armed conflict between the United States and al-Qaida. Specifically, DoD proposes to target a leader of AQAP, an organized enemy force that is either a component of al-Qaida or that is a co-belligerent of that central party to the conflict and engaged in hostilities against the United States as part of the same comprehensive armed conflict, in league with the principal enemy. See supra at 9–10 & n.5. Moreover, DoD would conduct the operation in Yemen, where, according to the facts related to us, AQAP has a significant and organized presence, and from which AQAP is conducting terrorist training in an organized manner and has executed and is planning to execute attacks against the United States. Finally, the targeted individual himself; on behalf of that force, is continuously planning attacks from that Yemeni base of operations against the United States, as the conflict with al-Qaida continues. See supra at 7–9. Taken together, these facts support the conclusion that the DoD operation would be part of the non-international armed conflict the Court recognized in Hamdan.

. . .

DoD represents that it would conduct its operation against al-Aulaqi in compliance with these fundamental law-of-war norms. See Chairman of the Joint Chiefs of Staff, Instruction 5810.01D, Implementation of the DoD Law of

War Program ¶ 4.a, at 1 (Apr. 30, 2010) ("It is DOD policy that . . . [m]embers of the DOD Components comply with the law of war during all armed conflicts, however such conflicts are characterized, and in all other military operations."). In particular, the targeted nature of the operation would help to ensure that it would comply with the principle of distinction, and DoD has represented to us that it would make every effort to minimize civilian casualties and that the officer who launches the ordnance would be required to abort a strike if he or she concludes that civilian casualties will be disproportionate or that such a strike will in any other respect violate the laws of war. See DoD May 18 Memorandum for OLC, at 1 ("Any official in the chain of command has the authority and duty to abort" a strike "if he or she concludes that civilian casualties will be disproportionate or that such a strike will otherwise violate the laws of war.").

Moreover, although DoD would specifically target al-Aulaqi, and would do so without advance warning, such characteristics of the contemplated operation would not violate the laws of war and, in particular, would not cause the operation to violate the prohibitions on treachery and perfidy—which are addressed to conduct involving a breach of confidence by the assailant. See, e.g., Hague Convention IV, Annex, art. 23(b), 36 Stat. at 2301–02 ("Mt is especially forbidden . . . to kill or wound treacherously individuals belonging to the hostile nation or army"); cf. also Protocol Additional to the Geneva Conventions of 12 August 1949, and Relating to the Protection of Victims of International Armed Conflicts, art. 37(1) (prohibiting the killing, injuring or capture of an adversary in an international armed conflict by resort to acts "inviting the confidence of [the] adversary. . . with intent to betray that confidence," including feigning a desire to negotiate under truce or flag of surrender; feigning incapacitation; and feigning noncombatant status). Those prohibitions do not categorically preclude the use of stealth or surprise, nor forbid military attacks on identified, individual soldiers or officers, see U.S. Army Field Manual 27-10, ¶ 31 (1956) (article 23(b) of the Annex to the Hague Convention IV does not "preclude attacks on individual soldiers or officers of the enemy whether in the zone of hostilities, occupied territory, or else-where"), and we are not aware of any other law-of-war grounds precluding the use of such tactics. See Dinstein, Conduct of Hostilities at 94–95, 199; Abraham D. Sofaer, Terrorism, The Law, and the National Defense, 126 Mil. L. Rev. 89, 120–21 (1989). Relatedly, "there is no prohibition under the laws of war on the use of technologically advanced weapons systems in armed conflict—such as pilotless aircraft or so-called smart bombs-as long as they are employed in conformity with applicable laws of war." Koh, The Obama Administration and International Law. DOD also informs us that if al-Aulaqi offers to surrender, DoD would accept such an offer.

In light of all these circumstances, we believe DoD's contemplated operation against alAulaqi would comply with international law, including the laws of war applicable to this armed conflict, and would fall within Congress's authorization to use "necessary and appropriate force" against al-Qaida. In consequence, the operation should be understood to constitute the lawful conduct of war and thus to be encompassed by the public authority justification. Accordingly, the contemplated attack, if conducted by DoD in the manner described, would not result in an "unlawful" killing and thus would not violate section 1119(b).

B.

We next consider whether the CIA's contemplated operation against al-Aulaqi in Yemen would be covered by the public authority justification. We conclude that it would be; and thus that operation, too, would not result in an "unlawful" killing prohibited by section 1119. As with our analysis ofthe contemplated DoD operation, we rely on the sufficiency of the particular factual circumstances of the CIA operation as they have been represented to us, without determining that the presence of those specific circumstances would be necessary to the conclusion we reach.

* * *

. . . Specifically, we understand that the CIA, like DoD, would carry out the attack against an operational leader of an enemy force, as part of the United States's ongoing non-international armed conflict with al-Qaida.

* * *

. . . [T]he CIA—would conduct the operation in a manner that accords with the rules of international humanitarian law governing this armed conflict, ...

* * *

See also infra at 38–41 (explaining that the CIA operation under the circumstances described to us would comply with constitutional due process and the Fourth Amendment's "reasonableness" test for the use of deadly force).

Accordingly, we conclude that, just as the combination of circumstances present here supports the judgment that the public authority justification would apply to the contemplated operation by the armed forces, the combination of circumstances also supports the judgment that the CIA's operation, too, would be encompassed by that justification. The CIA's contemplated operation, therefore, would not result in an "unlawful" killing under section 1111 and thus would not violate section 1119.

IV.

For similar reasons, we conclude that the contemplated DoD and CIA operations would not violate another federal criminal statute dealing with "murder" abroad, 18 U.S.C. § 956(a). That law makes it a crime to conspire within the jurisdiction of the United States "to commit at any place outside the United States an act that would constitute the offense of murder, kidnapping, or maiming if committed in the special maritime and territorial jurisdiction of the United States" if any conspirator acts within the United States to effect any object of the conspiracy.

. . .

CHAPTER 13

USING THE MILITARY IN DOMESTIC LAW ENFORCEMENT

■ ■ ■

A. INTRODUCTION

The attacks on September 11, 2001 posed many questions for this country never before asked. Among them is whether our existing law enforcement agencies are adequate to deal with the dangers that the terrorism poses to our security on the home front. A few leaders have raised the possibility of increasing the role of the military in helping to deal with the problem of terrorism in the United States.[1] Throughout our history, we have been reluctant, however, to expand the role of the military beyond its traditional confines. Justice Douglas dissenting in Laird v. Tatum, 408 U.S. 1, 19, 23–24 (1972), considered supra in Chapter 4, described our tradition very well:

> Our tradition reflects a desire for civilian supremacy and subordination of military power. The tradition of civilian control over the Armed Forces was stated by Chief Justice Warren:
>
>> "The military establishment is, of course, a necessary organ of government; but the reach of its power must be carefully limited lest the delicate balance between freedom and order be upset. The maintenance of the balance is made more difficult by the fact that while the military serves the vital function of preserving the existence of the nation, it is, at the same time, the one element of government that exercises a type of authority not easily assimilated in a free society. . . .
>
> . . .
>
>> "In times of peace, the factors leading to an extraordinary deference to claims of military necessity have naturally not been as weighty. This has been true even in the all too

---

[1]   See Eric Schmitt, Wider Military Role in U.S. Is Urged, N.Y. Times, July 21, 2002, at A16 (reporting that the then new commanding general of the U.S. military's North America command supported an expansion of military activities against terrorism.) See also Joyce Howard Price, Biden Backs Letting Soldiers Arrest Civilians, Wash. Times, July 22, 2002 at A1. And calls, more recently, by President Trump and some Senators to place terrorists apprehended in the United States into military custody can be viewed in the same vein.

imperfect peace that has been our lot for the past fifteen years—and quite rightly so, in my judgment. It is instructive to recall that our Nation at the time of the Constitutional Convention was also faced with formidable problems. The English, the French, the Spanish, and various tribes of hostile Indians were all ready and eager to subvert or occupy the fledgling Republic. Nevertheless, in that environment, our Founding Fathers conceived a Constitution and Bill of Rights replete with provisions indicating their determination to protect human rights. There was no call for a garrison state in those times of precarious peace. We should heed no such call now. If we were to fail in these days to enforce the freedom that until now has been the American citizen's birthright, we would be abandoning for the foreseeable future the constitutional balance of powers and rights in whose name we arm."

. . .

The action in turning the "armies" loose on surveillance of civilians was a gross repudiation of our traditions. The military, though important to us, is subservient and restricted purely to military missions.

. . .

The act of turning the military loose on civilians even if sanctioned by an Act of Congress, which it has not been, would raise serious and profound constitutional questions. Standing as it does only on brute power and Pentagon policy, it must be repudiated as a usurpation dangerous to the civil liberties on which free men are dependent. For, as Senator Sam Ervin has said, "this claim of an inherent executive branch power of investigation and surveillance on the basis of people's beliefs and attitudes may be more of a threat to our internal security than any enemies beyond our borders."

The challenge to the army surveillance program in Laird was framed in constitutional First Amendment terms, but it also arguably might have posed an issue[2] under the Posse Comitatus statute, 18 U.S.C. § 1385, which provides:

Whoever, except in cases and under circumstances expressly authorized by the Constitution or Act of Congress, willfully uses

---

[2] The surveillance program challenged in Laird was begun by the U.S. Army in the wake of the urban riots in the summer of 1967 when it was thought that federal troops might be needed to quell the disturbances. Emergency situations have traditionally been viewed as basis for an exception to the Posse Comitatus prohibition, and are governed by other provisions in federal law. See, e.g., 10 U.S.C. § 331.

any part of the Army or the Air Force as a posse comitatus or otherwise to execute the laws shall be fined under this title or imprisoned not more than two years, or both.

The Posse Comitatus Act was enacted after the Civil War to bar the use of federal troops in overseeing elections and in other ways in the former Confederate States once civilian authority had reestablished itself. The Act was later amended to include the Air Force. Although the Navy and Marines are not mentioned in the Act, those services have applied the prohibition expressed in the Act to themselves. The Coast Guard, which had been in the Department of Transportation but is now in the Department of Homeland Security, has traditionally had a domestic law enforcement role in policing our shores, and thus has not been affected by the Act. The federal army reserves have always been considered subject to the Act, but the states' National Guard units have not, for historic reasons related to Federalism.

The Posse Comitatus Act has served both symbolically and in practice as a major[3] legal restriction on the domestic use of the military for law enforcement purposes. Thus when proposals for using the military against terrorism have been broached, they have sometimes been framed in terms of amending the Act.

Modifications of the prohibition also occur through the recognition of exceptions or through direct grants of authority under specific statutes. For example, Section 104 of the USA PATRIOT Act authorized the Attorney General to request the Secretary of Defense to provide assistance in support of Department of Justice activities relating to the enforcement of Federal criminal code provisions regarding the use of weapons of mass destruction during an emergency situation involving a weapon of mass destruction. This section broadened the authority of the President, Pentagon and Justice Department to use military assets for assisting law enforcement in situations involving the use of weapons of mass destruction in the United States.

In 2002, in enacting the provisions of the new Homeland Security Act, Congress addressed both the relationship between the new Department of Homeland Security and the Department of Defense, and the question of using the military in the fight against terrorism.

These provisions seemed to reflect the desire of Congress to separate the functions of the two largest departments in the government, and, at the same time, continued the policy of preventing the military from playing anything more than a supporting role in the domestic anti-terrorism effort. Section 876 of the Homeland Security Act explicitly precluded the new

---

[3]   The Act is not the only relevant statute regarding the use of the military domestically. The Insurrection Act, 10 U.S.C. § 333, deals with the use of the military in emergency situations. See section C infra.

Department from engaging in any military activity. Section 886 expressed a "sense of Congress" that the new agency not undermine the existing Posse Comitatus doctrine by using the military in more than a supporting role against terrorism.

Homeland Security Act of 2002

PL 107–296 (HR 5005; 116 Stat. 2135).

November 25, 2002.

SEC. 876. MILITARY ACTIVITIES.

Nothing in this Act shall confer upon the Secretary any authority to engage in warfighting, the military defense of the United States, or other military activities, nor shall anything in this Act limit the existing authority of the Department of Defense or the Armed Forces to engage in warfighting, the military defense of the United States, or other military activities.

SEC. 886. SENSE OF CONGRESS REAFFIRMING THE CONTINUED IMPORTANCE AND APPLICABILITY OF THE POSSE COMITATUS ACT.

(a) FINDINGS—Congress finds the following

(1) Section 1385 of title 18, United States Code (commonly known as the 'Posse Comitatus Act'), prohibits the use of the Armed Forces as a posse comitatus to execute the laws except in cases and under circumstances expressly authorized by the Constitution or Act of Congress.

(2) Enacted in 1878, the Posse Comitatus Act was expressly intended to prevent United States Marshals, on their own initiative, from calling on the Army for assistance in enforcing Federal law.

(3) The Posse Comitatus Act has served the Nation well in limiting the use of the Armed Forces to enforce the law.

(4) Nevertheless, by its express terms, the Posse Comitatus Act is not a complete barrier to the use of the Armed Forces for a range of domestic purposes, including law enforcement functions, when the use of the Armed Forces is authorized by Act of Congress or the President determines that the use of the Armed Forces is required to fulfill the President's obligations under the Constitution to respond promptly in time of war, insurrection, or other serious emergency.

(5) Existing laws, including chapter 15 of title 10, United States Code (commonly known as the 'Insurrection Act'), and the Robert T. Stafford Disaster Relief and Emergency Assistance Act

(42 U.S.C. 5121 et seq.), grant the President broad powers that may be invoked in the event of domestic emergencies, including an attack against the Nation using weapons of mass destruction, and these laws specifically authorize the President to use the Armed Forces to help restore public order.

(b) SENSE OF CONGRESS—Congress reaffirms the continued importance of section 1385 of title 18, United States Code, and it is the sense of Congress that nothing in this Act should be construed to alter the applicability of such section to any use of the Armed Forces as a posse comitatus to execute the laws.

Several years later, however, in 2006, the Insurrection Act, cited in section (a)(5) of section 886, supra, was significantly amended. The amended language is reproduced and addressed in section C below, following consideration of the legal authorities interpreting the Posse Comitatus Act.

B. INTERPRETATION AND APPLICATION OF THE POSSE COMITATUS ACT

Over the years, violations of the Posse Comitatus Act have been alleged, but most of these have not come close to a broad-based use of the military in domestic law enforcement. Typically they have involved police actions by military against civilians close to a military base; a few military personnel assisting local law enforcement, typically, in drug cases; the military being called upon to assist law enforcement in hostage or long-term stand-off cases; or the use of the Navy on the high seas in aid of anti-drug enforcement.[4] As mentioned above, the army surveillance program challenged in Laird v. Tatum was perhaps the most comprehensive nationwide military program that has surfaced that could be viewed as relating to domestic law enforcement, but that program began with a concern about civil disturbances that could justify military involvement as an exception to the Posse Comitatus Act.

The Act is framed as a criminal prohibition, but no one has ever been prosecuted for violating the Act. Questions of the interpretation of the Act, specifically, what it means "to execute the laws," have arisen, however, when persons charged with criminal violations claim, for example, that the military was involved in apprehending or interrogating them, and they argue that evidence obtained from them should be excluded because of violation of the Act. Typically, the courts reject the idea that a violation of the Act can result in the exclusion of evidence, but along the way, they

---

[4] The majority of statutory exceptions to the Posse Comitatus doctrine were enacted during the 1980s to support the "war on drugs" during the Reagan and Bush Administrations. See 10 U.S.C. §§ 371–382. See also, Major Craig T. Trebilcock, The Myth of Posse Comitatus, Journal of Homeland Security, October 2000.

discuss whether the Act has in fact been violated. The district court opinion in United States v. Yunis, reproduced below, is such a case. It provides a good summary of the various approaches taken in interpreting the Act.

UNITED STATES V. YUNIS
681 F.Supp. 891 (D.D.C.1988)

[The following statement of facts is taken from the Court of Appeals opinion in the same case, United States v. Yunis, 924 F.2d 1086 (D.C.Cir.1991):

On June 11, 1985, appellant and four other men boarded Royal Jordanian Airlines Flight 402 ("Flight 402") shortly before its scheduled departure from Beirut, Lebanon. They wore civilian clothes and carried military assault rifles, ammunition bandoleers, and hand grenades. Appellant took control of the cockpit and forced the pilot to take off immediately. The remaining hijackers tied up Jordanian air marshals assigned to the flight and held the civilian passengers, including two American citizens, captive in their seats. The hijackers explained to the crew and passengers that they wanted the plane to fly to Tunis, where a conference of the Arab League was under way. The hijackers further explained that they wanted a meeting with delegates to the conference and that their ultimate goal was removal of all Palestinians from Lebanon.

After a refueling stop in Cyprus, the airplane headed for Tunis but turned away when authorities blocked the airport runway. Following a refueling stop at Palermo, Sicily, another attempt to land in Tunis, and a second stop in Cyprus, the plane returned to Beirut, where more hijackers came aboard. These reinforcements included an official of Lebanon's Amal Militia, the group at whose direction Yunis claims he acted. The plane then took off for Syria, but was turned away and went back to Beirut. There, the hijackers released the passengers, held a press conference reiterating their demand that Palestinians leave Lebanon, blew up the plane, and fled from the airport.

An American investigation identified Yunis as the probable leader of the hijackers and prompted U.S. civilian and military agencies, led by the Federal Bureau of Investigation (FBI), to plan Yunis' arrest. After obtaining an arrest warrant, the FBI put "Operation Goldenrod" into effect in September 1987. Undercover FBI agents lured Yunis onto a yacht in the eastern Mediterranean Sea with promises of a drug deal, and arrested him once the vessel entered international waters. The agents transferred Yunis to a United States Navy munitions ship and interrogated him for several days as the vessel steamed toward a second rendezvous, this time with a Navy aircraft carrier. Yunis was flown to Andrews Air Force Base from the aircraft carrier, and taken from there to Washington, D.C. In Washington, Yunis was arraigned on an original indictment charging him with conspiracy, hostage taking, and aircraft damage. A grand jury subsequently returned a superseding indictment adding additional aircraft damage counts and a charge of air piracy.]

PRETRIAL MEMORANDUM ORDER NO. 3

(Denying Defendant's Motion to Dismiss for Violation of the Posse Comitatus Act)

BARRINGTON D. PARKER, United States District Judge:

The Posse Comitatus Act ("the Act"), 18 U.S.C. § 1385, prohibits the use of the nation's military forces as a posse comitatus[1] or otherwise to execute the laws of the United States. Counsel for Fawaz Yunis has moved to dismiss the indictment claiming that the involvement of the United States Navy in the apprehension and arrest of the defendant in the Mediterranean Sea and later, his transportation to the United States, violated the Act.

This Court concludes that the motion should be denied. The Navy's participation and involvement did not embrace nor did it extend to such regulatory, proscriptive, or compulsory military powers as contemplated under the Act. The facts in this case show that the Navy played at most, a passive role which indirectly aided the execution of United States laws. By providing military materials, supplies and equipment to the Federal Bureau of Investigation ("FBI"), the Navy did not violate the Posse Comitatus Act. Moreover, that service branch was merely aiding law enforcement efforts of FBI agents in international waters, where no civil governmental authority existed.

The Act provides that:

> Whoever, except in cases and under circumstances expressly authorized by the Constitution or Act of Congress, willfully uses any part of the Army or the Air Force as a posse comitatus or otherwise to execute the laws shall be fined not more than $10,000 or imprisoned not more than two years, or both. 18 U.S.C. § 1385 (1979).

It was originally enacted in response to the use of military personnel to enforce laws in the South during the reconstruction period following the Civil War. Legislative history indicates that the immediate objective of the Act was to end the use of federal troops in former confederate states where civil power had been reestablished. Many southerners believed the troops altered the outcome of state elections by actively supporting reconstruction candidates in disputed elections. . . . Nearly 40 years ago, our Circuit Court noted that Congress intended to preclude the military from assisting local

---

[1]   The phrase "posse comitatus" is literally translated from Latin as the "power of the county" and is defined at common law to refer to all those over the age of 15 upon whom a sheriff could call for assistance in preventing any type of civil disorder. United States v. Hartley, 796 F.2d 112, 114 (5th Cir.1986) (citing H.R. Rep. No. 97–71, Part II, 97th Cong., 1st Sess. 4 (1981)).

law enforcement officers in carrying out their duties. Gillars v. United States, 87 U.S. App. D.C. 16, 182 F.2d 962, 972 (D.C.Cir.1950). As noted in a recent appellate ruling, the Act was designed to limit "the direct active use of federal troops by civil law enforcement officers" to enforce the laws of the nation. United States v. Hartley, 796 F.2d 112, 114 (5th Cir.1986) (quoting United States v. Red Feather, 392 F.Supp. 916, 922 (D.S.D.1975)). Limiting military involvement in civilian affairs is basic to our system of government and the protection of individual constitutional rights.

Because the proscriptions of the Act have been relied upon in various situations, several tests have been articulated to determine whether an individual's rights have been infringed upon through violations of the statute. In the litigation which arose out of the standoff between Native American Indians and federal law enforcement authorities at Wounded Knee, South Dakota, in 1973, United States Marshals, FBI agents, the National Guard, as well as Army and Air Force personnel were both visible and involved. The first test was whether civilian law enforcement agents made "direct active use" of military personnel to execute the laws. Red Feather, 392 F.Supp. at 921. (The statute prohibits the "direct active use of Army or Air Force personnel and does not mean the use of Army or Air Force equipment or materiel." Id.). The second, whether "use of any part of the Army or Air Force pervaded the activities" of the civilian law enforcement agents. United States v. Jaramillo, 380 F.Supp. 1375 (D.Neb.1974), appeal dismissed, 510 F.2d 808 (8th Cir.1975) (No one questioned that substantial amounts of Army material and equipment were used. But "it is the use of military personnel, not materiel, which is proscribed by 18 U.S.C. § 1385." Id. at 1379. Since there was reasonable doubt whether military personnel were involved enough to render their actions unlawful, the defendants were acquitted. Id. at 1381). The third test is whether the military personnel subjected citizens to the exercise of military power which was regulatory, proscriptive, or compulsory in nature. United States v. McArthur, 419 F.Supp. 186 (D.N.D.1975), aff'd sub nom. United States v. Casper, 541 F.2d 1275 (8th Cir.1976), cert. denied, 430 U.S. 970, 52 L.Ed.2d 362, 97 S.Ct. 1654 (1977). (In McArthur, military personnel were used, but it was "not material enough to taint the presumption that the law enforcement officers were acting in performance of their duties." Id. at 195. "The borrowing of highly skilled personnel, like pilots and highly technical equipment like aircraft and cameras, for a specific, limited, temporary purpose is far preferable to the maintenance of such personnel and equipment by the United States Marshals' Service." Id. at 194).

It is not surprising that arguments similar to those relied upon by Yunis' counsel have been regularly advanced by a number of defendants charged with federal crimes, who resided abroad when the military was utilized to effect their arrest. In the late 1940's the First Circuit held when

United States military forces arrested a defendant overseas in an area where no civil regime exists, that there was no violation of the Act. Chandler v. United States, 171 F.2d 921 (1st Cir.1948), cert. denied, 336 U.S. 918, 93 L.Ed. 1081, 69 S.Ct. 640 (1949) ("This is the type of criminal statute which is properly presumed to have no extraterritorial application in the absence of statutory language indicating a contrary intent," particularly in an enemy territory occupied by the United States military. Id. at 936). In another situation, when military authorities in an allegedly illegal and unlawful manner brought from Japan to San Francisco, a notorious American citizen—Tokyo Rose—suspected of treason, her counsel's claim that the Posse Comitatus Act had been violated, and that the federal court lacked jurisdiction, was of no avail. Iva Ikuko Toguri D'Aquino v. United States, 192 F.2d 338, 351 (9th Cir.1951). Relying upon Chandler and Gillars, the Ninth Circuit held that the defendant's claim was without merit. Both Toguri D'Aquino and Chandler involved situations where the United States military had a substantial presence in post-war enemy territory. More than two decades later, the Ninth Circuit in United States v. Cotten, 471 F.2d 744 (9th Cir.1973), again rejected the posse comitatus argument as applied to persons abducted overseas. Two Americans living in Viet Nam were forcibly returned to the United States and later charged with federal law violations. They claimed that the use of military personnel and equipment to remove them from Viet Nam and bring them to the United States violated the Act as well as their due process rights. The Ninth Circuit recognized that defendants had been treated severely (military handcuffs, leg irons and cargo chains were used and defendants were "physically subdued" with blows to the back of the head). The government acknowledged that the military's removal was in fact a kidnapping of the defendants. Nonetheless, the Circuit Court found no violations of the Act and denied challenges to federal court jurisdiction.

At the recent February 5, 1988 argument on this motion, government counsel took the position as it had done throughout their pleadings that the Act by its express terms does not apply to the Navy. Thus Navy participation did not provide a basis for the relief sought—dismissal of the indictment. Counsel for defendant however, has steadfastly maintained that the Act applies to the Navy even though only the Army and Air Force are the services mentioned in Title 18. A canvass and review of case law shows that there may be some merit to his position. In this connection Yunis' counsel relies upon 10 U.S.C. §§ 371–378. That statute was enacted in 1981, as a part of the Department of Defense Authorization for Appropriations for Fiscal Year 1982, Pub. L. No. 97–86, 95 Stat. 1099 (1981). Title IX, § 905 of the Act, "Military Cooperation with Civilian Law Enforcement Officials," is the pertinent section and is codified at 10 U.S.C. §§ 371–378. As a part of the 1982 Defense Appropriations Act, new provisions were enacted to "clarify and reaffirm the authority of the Secretary of Defense to provide indirect assistance to civilian law enforcement officials, consistent with the principles established in the Posse Comitatus Act." S. Rep. No. 58, 97th Cong., 1st Sess. 148 (1981). The Senate Armed Services Committee further explained the rationale behind the laws:

The Department of Defense historically has provided some forms of indirect assistance to civilian law enforcement officials within the framework of the Posse Comitatus Act. . . . The Department has also loaned military equipment for use by civilian law enforcement agencies. But due to the age of the Posse Comitatus Act and its rather vague legislative history on the subject of indirect aid, court decisions have failed to outline uniformly the precise limits of permissible indirect assistance. This diverse guidance has created some uncertainties as to the authority of the Department . . . to provide such aid. Id.

Recognizing that the Department of Defense ("DoD") is primarily concerned with military preparedness, the committee stated that "where available, indirect assistance by the Department of Defense can help civilian law enforcement officials. . . . For example, the loan of equipment or access to base or research facilities, where it does not interfere with military preparedness, would avoid cost duplication in buying and maintaining such equipment and facilities." Id. The final version of the appropriations bill agreed upon by a joint conference committee contained the same provisions which "clarif[ied] the authority of the Secretary of Defense to make available certain military equipment and facilities." H.R. Conf. Rep. 311, 97th Cong., 1st Sess. 119, reprinted in 1981 U.S. Code Cong. & Admin. News 1860.

Very few cases have involved the military cooperation provisions of the Defense Authorization Act for 1982. A recent 1986 District Court opinion with facts similar to those presented here, held that the newly enacted sections 371–378, actually authorize the use of military aircraft to transport defendants when such defendants are under the direct control of civilian law enforcement officials. In United States v. Gerena, 649 F.Supp. 1179 (D.Conn.1986),[3] the use of naval helicopters and a military air base to transport civilian defendants from Puerto Rico to New York was upheld

---

[3]   Gerena was decided in December 1986, nearly twelve months after United States v. Roberts, 779 F.2d 565 (9th Cir.1986), a Ninth Circuit opinion which held that the Posse Comitatus Act did not apply to the Navy. In Roberts, the Court recognized, however, that the Navy had adopted the Act as a matter of policy. Id. at 567. In its opinion the Court declined to "defy [the] plain language by extending it [the Act] to prohibit use of the Navy." Id. Instead, the Court chose to focus on the proscriptions of 10 U.S.C. §§ 371–378, finding those provisions to be more directly applicable to the Navy. In analyzing §§ 371–378, the Court stated that "the Posse Comitatus Act and sections 371–378 of Title 10 embody similar proscriptions against military involvement in civilian law enforcement." Id. at 568.

The Gerena Court did not follow the Ninth Circuit's strict construction of the Act. It relied upon United States v. Del Prado-Montero, 740 F.2d 113 (1st Cir.), cert. denied 469 U.S. 1021, 105 S.Ct. 441, 83 L.Ed.2d 366 (1984) (the Act is "a proscription that has been extended by executive act to the Navy." 740 F.2d at 116) and the regulations promulgated under 32 C.F.R. § 213 which specifically address the Act's applicability to the Navy.

under the authority of §§ 372 and 375. Defendants were in the custody of United States Marshals at all times. The trial court in ruling that the military's involvement did not constitute a violation of either the Posse Comitatus Act or 10 U.S.C. §§ 371–378 noted:

> Among the legitimate governmental interests promoted by the use of military involvement in civilian affairs is the interest 'in improving the efficiency of civilian law enforcement by giving it the benefit of military technologies, equipment, information, and training personnel. 649 F.Supp. at 1182.

Section 372 actually empowers the Secretary of Defense to make available "any equipment, base facility, or research facility of the Army, Navy, Air Force, or Marine Corps to any Federal, State, or local civilian law enforcement purposes." 10 U.S.C. § 372 (emphasis added). This includes the assignment of military personnel, provided such assignment is done in accordance with adequate regulation and in compliance with applicable law. 10 U.S.C. § 375.

Regulations promulgated under the Appropriations Act, 32 C.F.R. §§ 213.1–213.11 (1987), also permit local DoD components to authorize the use of available military equipment for civilian law enforcement purposes. Section 210 of the federal regulations lays out the restrictions on DoD personnel participation: "The primary restriction on military participation in civilian law enforcement activities is the Posse Comitatus Act. . . ." In explanation of the connection between the DoD military cooperation statutes and the Posse Comitatus Act, the regulations provide:

> The following forms of indirect assistance activities are not restricted by the Posse Comitatus Act . . .:
>
> > (ii) Such other actions, approved in accordance with procedures established by the head of the DoD Component concerned, that do not subject civilians to the exercise of military power that is regulatory, proscriptive, or compulsory in nature.

32 C.F.R. § 213.10(a)(7). Under this regulation a court in reviewing the legality of the military involvement at issue, must decide whether the assistance in question subjected defendant Yunis "to the exercise of military power that is regulatory, proscriptive, or compulsory in nature."

In this proceeding, the Navy's activities in the apprehension of Yunis were not the type prohibited by the Posse Comitatus Act, nor were they prohibited by the DoD military cooperation laws. The FBI was in charge of the operation at all times. At most, the Navy merely provided necessary support services. Navy personnel never participated in the arrest or interrogation of the defendant. Their equipment and staff already stationed in the Mediterranean were at the disposal of the FBI for only limited purposes, involving a passive role. Their limited role included: advising the FBI crew aboard the yacht (used in the capture of the defendant) on its location in international waters; providing a launch to transport the defendant from the FBI yacht to the Navy vessel—the U.S.S. Butte, supplying the defendant with shelter, clothes, food, and toiletries while on board the Navy launch and providing required medical attention; arranging a rendezvous between the Butte and the aircraft carrier—the USS Saratoga; piloting the Navy plane with the defendant and his FBI custodians from the Saratoga to the United States.

It is clear from these facts that the Navy's activities did not constitute direct active involvement in the execution of the laws, nor did the use of military personnel pervade the activities of the civilian authorities. Rather, it was a civilian operation originating from within the FBI. By its very nature, the operation required the aid of military located in the area. Under the direction of the FBI, the Navy gave the necessary support in the form of equipment, supplies, and services. The furnishing of materials, work, and services, standing alone, is not a violation of the Posse Comitatus Act. See, e.g., Hartley, 796 F.2d at 114; Bissonette v. Haig, 776 F.2d 1384, 1390 (8th Cir.1985); Caspar, 541 F.2d at 1276, aff'g McArthur, 419 F.Supp. at 194–95; United States v. Hartley, 486 F.Supp. 1348, 1356–57 (M.D.Fla.1980); Red Feather, 392 F.Supp. at 923; Jaramillo, 380 F.Supp. at 1379.

There is further support for the position that Congress did not intend that the Posse Comitatus Act should prohibit the use of military material, supplies or equipment in the aid of executing the laws. More than fifty years ago, Congress established procedures that enable any government department (especially military departments) to furnish materials, work, and services to any other bureau or agency within the government. The Economy Act of 1932, 31 U.S.C. § 686.

Finally, the Navy personnel involved in the transportation of the defendant played passive roles. The Naval doctor gave Yunis a physical examination and later treated him for seasickness and pain to his wrist. The defendant's food was prepared by Navy personnel.

None of the Navy's activities constituted the exercise of regulatory, proscriptive, or compulsory military power. A power regulatory in nature is one which controls or directs. In this case defendant Yunis was under the exclusive control and authority (as well as the physical custody) of the FBI agents accompanying him. The military did not exercise any authority or control over the defendant, nor did the military threaten such control or authority.

Nor can it be said that the military's involvement was proscriptive. A power proscriptive in nature is one that prohibits or condemns. Again, the defendant was never confined by Navy personnel but at all times was in the custody of the FBI agents who arrested him. Yunis was in no real way ever subject to the proscriptive powers of the military or military law.

Finally, it cannot be said that the Navy's involvement was compulsory. A power compulsory in nature is one that exerts some coercive force. The military personnel involved exerted no such force over the defendant. In reality, the Navy's involvement in the operation was indifferent, passive, and subservient to the FBI's task.

Conclusion

For the above stated reasons, the Court concludes that the Navy's involvement in the apprehension, arrest and transportation of the defendant from international waters of the Mediterranean Sea, until he arrived at Andrews Air Force Base, Maryland, did not violate the Posse Comitatus Act or any other federal law.

QUESTIONS AND NOTES

1.   The defendant in Yunis moved to dismiss based on an alleged violation of the Posse Comitatus Act. If the court had found a violation of the Act, would this have been grounds to grant the motion?

2.   The court in Yunis describes three different tests that were articulated in three cases growing out of the events in 1973 at Wounded Knee, South Dakota. How do the tests differ from each other? Which do you think should be the test? Why?

3.   One learns from Yunis that qualifications and exceptions to the Act have been adopted either by statute or in regulations, and the case cites and quotes some of them. Note that the DoD regulation contained in 32 C.F.R. § 213.10(a)(7) adopts the same test for determining the applicability of the Act's prohibition that was first formulated in United States v. McArthur, supra.

4.   National Guard units trace their history back to state militias before the American Revolution. Today, National Guard officers work first for their state governor, and second for the President. This gives them a unique legal status as state officers who are not governed by the Posse Comitatus Act. This makes sense given the law's history—it was enacted to protect states' rights at the end of post-Civil War Reconstruction. In Gilbert v. United States, 165 F.3d 470 (6th Cir.1999), the 6th Circuit explained this doctrine:

> By its own terms, the [Posse Comitatus] Act applies to the Army and Air Force. United States v. Yunis, 288 U.S. App. D.C. 129, 924 F.2d 1086, 1093 (D.C.Cir.1991) (Act inapplicable to the Navy); Schowengerdt v. General Dynamics Corp., 823 F.2d 1328, 1340 (9th Cir.1987) (same). See also United States v. Roberts, 779 F.2d 565, 567 (9th Cir.1986) (Act extended by Executive Order to include the Navy.) The Act does not apply to members of the National Guard unless they have been called into "federal service." Until called into such service,

members of the National Guard remain state, rather than federal officers. Perpich v. Department of Defense, 496 U.S. 334, 345, 110 S.Ct. 2418, 110 L.Ed.2d 312 (1990) ("unless and until ordered to active duty in the Army, [Guardsmen] retained their status as members of a separate State Guard unit"). Thus, "except when employed in the service of the United States, officers of the National Guard continue to be officers of the state and not officers of the United States or of the Military Establishment of the United States." United States v. Dern, 74 F.2d 485, 487, 64 App. D.C. 81 (D.C.Cir.1934). "Guardsmen do not become part of the Army itself," as pointed out in United States v. Hutchings, 127 F.3d 1255, 1258 (10th Cir.1997), "until such time as they may be ordered into active federal duty by an official acting under a grant of statutory authority from Congress." Only when "that triggering event occurs [does] a Guardsman become[ ] a part of the Army and lose[ ] his status as a state serviceman." Id. See generally, Steven B. Rich, The National Guard, Drug Interdiction and Counterdrug Activities and Posse Comitatus: The Meaning and Implications of "in Federal Service," 1994 Army Law. 16.

The record in this case shows conclusively that the National Guardsmen who participated in appellants' arrests and ensuing searches and seizures were in state, rather than federal service when they did so. Aside from the complete absence of any proof that the Guardsmen had been called into active service with the Army, see id. at 18 (noting limited and specific ways in which Guardsmen may enter active duty), the record contains ample evidence that the Guardsmen were acting in response to directives issued by their Commander-in-Chief, the Governor of Kentucky.

The Governor issued an executive order creating a Marijuana Strike Force. The Strike Force's objective was "total eradication of marijuana in [the] Commonwealth." Command of the Strike Force was delegated to a ten member committee, one of whose members was an officer with the National Guard's Department of Military Affairs. Although federal officials were also members of the Strike Force and its governing committee, those officials were from civilian agencies, rather than the United States Army. The Guardsmen assigned to the Strike Force were unquestionably under state, rather than federal control.

Notwithstanding this proof of the Guardsmen's status, appellants contend that, because the Guardsmen were serving in a full-time capacity and were being compensated with federal, rather than state funds, they were "in federal service" and acting as members of the United States Army. These circumstances are immaterial: "the issue of status depends on command and control and not on whether: state or federal benefits apply; state or federal funds are being used; the authority for the duty lies in state or federal law;

or any combination thereof." Rich, supra, at 19. "Although National Guard members receive federal pay and allowances . . . while performing full-time National Guard Duty," they remain members of the state National Guard and not members on active duty in federal service with the United States Army. Id. Consequently, the Act, which applies only to members of the federal armed services, does not apply to the Guardsmen in this case.

Similarly, the fact that the Guardsmen looked and acted like soldiers, rather than law enforcement officers, is immaterial. "These indicia, however persuasive they may be to the eye," the court noted in Hutchings, 127 F.3d at 1258, "have never determined the character of a Guardsman's service. . . . That question depends solely on whether command of the Guardsman has been taken away from a state's governor by one authorized to do so by Congress." In this case, as in Hutchings, command remained with the state.

Alternatively, the circumstances under which the Guardsmen were acting in this case were, as permitted by the terms of the Act, authorized by an Act of Congress. Pursuant to 32 U.S.C. § 112(b), full-time National Guardsmen may be used for the "purpose of carrying out drug interdiction and counter-drug activities." Use by the Commonwealth of Kentucky of its Guardsmen in accordance with this federal statute provides another basis for exempting those officers from the Posse Comitatus Act.

We conclude, accordingly, that officers of the Kentucky National Guard did not violate the Posse Comitatus Act when they participated in the surveillance of appellants' marijuana cultivation and harvesting, arrested them for those unlawful activities, and searched them and the area in which they had been growing their contraband crop.[2]

5. Note that while the Congress in 2002 in the Homeland Security Act reaffirmed the importance of maintaining the general thrust of the Posse Comitatus prohibition, it also expressly recognized the President's responsibility to deal with any domestic emergencies, including, in his capacity as Commander-in-Chief, the possible use of the military in such circumstances. See generally, Michael Bahar, The Presidential Intervention Principle: The Domestic Use of the Military and the Power of the Several States, 5 Harv. Nat'l Sec. J. 537 (2014); William C. Banks, The Normalization of Homeland Security

---

[2] We need not reach the issue of whether, had we found the Act to have been violated, suppression should have occurred. We note, however, that every federal court to have considered the issue has held that suppression is not an appropriate remedy for a violation of the Act. United States v. Al-Talib, 55 F.3d 923, 930 (4th Cir.1995); Hayes v. Hawes, 921 F.2d 100, 103 (7th Cir.1990); United States v. Hartley, 796 F.2d 112, 115 (5th Cir.1986). Accord, United States v. Griley, 814 F.2d 967, 976 (4th Cir.1987); United States v. Wolffs, 594 F.2d 77, 85 (5th Cir.1979); United States v. Walden, 490 F.2d 372, 376–77 (4th Cir.1974). See also Note, The Posse Comitatus Act as an Exclusionary Rule: Is the Criminal to go Free Because the Soldier Has Blundered?, 61 N.D. L.Rev. 107, 129 (1985) ("There is no evidence Congress intended the Posse Comitatus Act to double as an exclusionary rule").

After September 11: The Role of the Military in Counterterrorism Preparedness and Response, 64 La. L. Rev. 735 (2004).

6. Consider the following excerpt from Major Kirk L. Davies, The Imposition of Martial Law In The United States, 49 A.F. L. Rev. 67, 80–85 (2000) regarding the use of the military in domestic emergencies:

> Determining when the military is in violation of the [Posse Comitatus] Act can be difficult. However, considering the Act's punitive provisions, commanders have an obvious interest in ensuring they do not disobey it. Over time, Congress has authorized relatively significant exceptions to the Act's sweeping prohibitions. None of the exceptions have specifically granted the military a domestic law enforcement role, but the recent pattern is to accord the military a greater role in civilian affairs than had been previously envisioned.
>
> . . .
>
> Congress has also granted the President specific statutory authority to use federal troops in a law enforcement role in the case of national emergency involving civil disturbances. This authority exists even though responsibility for quelling such rebellions lies primarily with State and local governments. These statutory exceptions to the Posse Comitatus Act include insurrections within a state (upon the Governor's request); rebellions which makes it impracticable to enforce federal laws; or any insurrection or violence which impedes the state's ability to protect citizens of their constitutional rights, and the state is unable or unwilling to protect those rights.
>
> Perhaps the President already has the authority to act in situations involving maintenance of public order, even without congressional authorization. According to the Code of Federal Regulations (CFR), "the Constitution and Acts of Congress establish six exceptions,[69] generally applicable within the entire territory of the United States, to which the Posse Comitatus Act prohibition does not apply."[70] The CFR cites two constitutional exceptions. The first is an emergency authority to prevent lost of life or property during serious disturbances or calamities.[71] The second authority allows the use of

---

[69] Besides the two constitutional exceptions, the Code of Federal Regulations lists four statutory exceptions to the Posse Comitatus Act. They include the three statutory exceptions found in 10 U.S.C. §§ 331–33, and another exception for assisting the Secret Service in providing protection to governmental officials and political candidates. 32 C.F.R. § 215.4(c)(2)(i)(a–d).

[70] Id. at § 215.4 (c)

[71] Id. at § 215.4(c)(1)(i) states:

The emergency authority. Authorizes prompt and vigorous Federal action, including use of military forces to prevent loss of life or wanton destruction of property and to restore governmental functioning and public order when sudden and unexpected civil disturbances, disasters, or calamities seriously endanger life and property and disrupt

military forces to protect Federal property and governmental functions.

Obviously, the Code of Federal Regulations is not the source of the President's emergency response authority.[73] However, when considering whether Congress has granted the President either "express or implied" authority to use military troops in a domestic crisis, evidence of a federal regulation that recognizes such a constitutional basis for authority is extremely relevant. This is especially true if Congress takes no action to modify or interpret the language of the Code.

. . .In recent years, Department of Defense personnel have acted in civilian emergency situations without any specific statutory authorization. They have done so under a theory of "immediate response authority." An example of the military acting under this immediate response authority occurred in Oklahoma City after the bombing of the Alfred P. Murrah federal building. In that case, local authorities could be assisted by the military providing support to the investigation in the form of "medevac aircraft, ambulances, bomb detection dog teams, and various military personnel." Local commanders at Fort Sill and Tinker Air Force Base provided this support under the theory of the commander's immediate response authority.

This immediate response authority is mentioned in two Department of Defense Directives, one relating to disaster relief support to civil authorities, and the other relating to support for civilian agencies during civil disturbances. According to these regulations, commanders may act to prevent human suffering, save lives, or mitigate great property damage, even without prior authorization from the President. Commanders may act in these cases if there is an emergency that "overwhelms the capabilities of local authorities."

The "most commonly cited rationale to support Immediate Response actions is the common law principle of necessity." From a

---

normal governmental functions to such an extent that duly constituted local authorities are unable to control the situations.

[73] Interestingly, the Code of Federal Regulations also defines martial law. Id. at § 501.4. Noting, in relevant part, that,

martial law depends for its justification upon public necessity. Necessity gives rise to its creation; necessity justifies its exercise; and necessity limits its duration . . . In most instances the decision to impose martial law is made by the President, who normally announces his decision by a proclamation, which usually contains his instructions concerning its exercise and any limitations thereon . . . When Federal Armed Forces have been committed in an objective area in a martial law situation, the population of the affected area will be informed of the rules of conduct and other restrictive measures the military is authorized to enforce . . . Federal Armed Forces ordinarily will exercise police powers previously inoperative in the affected area, restore and maintain order, insure the essential mechanics of distribution, transportation, and communication, and initiate necessary relief measures.

humanitarian, common sense perspective, it seems self-evident that a military commander should be able to use available resources to alleviate human suffering, without first requiring a bureaucratic permission slip. Arguably, that is why Department of Defense directives articulate this authority. Interestingly, even though Congress undoubtedly is aware of the military's actions under these Department of Defense directives, congressional leaders have not acted to limit or codify a commander's authority to act in these types of scenarios.

. . .

It appears that the traditional prejudice against military involvement in civil affairs may be on the decline. The evidence of that decline is manifest in congressional willingness to create exceptions to the Posse Comitatus rules allowing for military support during law enforcement activities, and the President's continued use of the armed forces in these roles. Whatever the reason, Congress has implicitly or explicitly given the military increased authority in the civilian domain, an authority Presidents have not hesitated to use. This trend has serious implications for the legality of a President's actions under a proclamation of martial law.

. . .

Ideally, the President will never have to declare martial law in response to a national crisis. The best scenario envisions the nation responding to such a crisis with civilian agencies in the forefront and the Department of Defense in its traditional support role. However, should civilian agencies become overwhelmed in an environment of chaos and panic, one of the President's obvious options for restoring order would be to declare martial law. Such a response is an extreme option, well beyond what is contemplated under statutes relating to disaster response actions or limited military support to civilian law enforcement authorities.

7.   In connection with the kind of terrorism-caused emergencies that might trigger military involvement on the domestic U.S. scene, consider the following excerpt from Davies, op. cit. supra, note 6 at footnote 19:

As the country pays more attention these issues, the military will likely emerge as a central player in whatever course the nation ultimately takes. For example, the DoD is "stationing 10 Rapid Assessment and Detection Teams (RADT), each composed of 22 specially trained Air Force and Army National Guard personnel, in 10 states to respond to chemical and biological weapons attacks." Jim Landers, U.S. Quietly Upgrading Homeland Defense Plan, THE DALLAS MORNING NEWS, Feb. 9, 1999 at 1A. In addition, some factors indicate that FEMA is not prepared to properly execute its statutorily authorized role to control disasters. One author stated,

In practice, nobody knows who would do what if American city-dwellers faced a lethal cloud of anthrax or nerve gas. An exercise in March, designed to test the authorities' response to a genetically engineered virus spread by terrorists on the Mexican-American border, led to bitter squabbling among rival agencies. "There is no clear demarcation line between the FEMA, and knowledge about disease and hazardous materials is spread over a broad array of institutions," says Zachary Selden, a germ-warfare boffin. "Somebody is needed to sit on top of these operations."

8. Also see N.Y. Times, Jan. 23, 2005, Pt I, p. 1 reporting that a small group of super-secret commandos, with state of the art weaponry, operating under a secret counterterrorism program code-named Power Geyser, was on standby ready to help protect the presidential inauguration; that the Command to which this unit belonged has in the past provided support to domestic law enforcement agencies for events such as the Olympics and political party conventions.

C. EXCEPTIONS TO THE POSSE COMITATUS RULE? MORE EXTENSIVE USE OF THE MILITARY IN EMERGENCIES AND FOR OTHER PURPOSES?

NOTES AND QUESTIONS

1. The following commentary was written four years before September 11, 2001, but after the Oklahoma City bombing and first World Trade Center bombing. Did September 11th change the situation?

Matthew Carlton Hammond, Note: The Posse Comitatus Act: A Principle in Need of Renewal, 75 Wash. U. L. Q. 953 (1997):

. . .

In the last fifteen years, Congress has deliberately eroded this principle by involving the military in drug interdiction at our borders. This erosion will continue unless Congress renews the PCA's (Posse Comitatus Act) principle to preserve the necessary and traditional separation of civilian and military authority.

The need for reaffirmation of the PCA's principle is increasing because in recent years, Congress and the public have seen the military as a panacea for domestic problems. Within one week of the bombing of the federal building in Oklahoma City, President Clinton proposed an exception to the PCA to allow the military to aid civilian authorities in investigations involving "weapons of mass destruction." In addition to this proposal Congress also considered legislation to directly involve federal troops in enforcing customs and immigration laws at the border. In the 1996 presidential campaign, candidate Bob Dole pledged to increase the role of the military in the drug war, and candidate Lamar Alexander even proposed replacing the Immigration and Naturalization Service and the Border Patrol with a new branch of the armed forces.

The growing haste and ease with which the military is considered a panacea for domestic problems will quickly undermine the PCA if it remains unchecked. Minor exceptions to the PCA can quickly expand to become major exceptions. For example in 1981, Congress created an exception to the PCA to allow military involvement in drug interdiction at our borders. Then in 1989, Congress designated the Department of Defense as the "single lead agency" in drug interdiction efforts.

. . .

Major and minor exceptions to the PCA, which allow the use of the military in law enforcement roles, blur the line between military and civilian roles, undermine civilian control of the military, damage military readiness, and inefficiently solve the problems that they supposedly address. Additionally, increasing the role of the military would strengthen the federal law enforcement apparatus that is currently under close scrutiny for overreaching its authority. Although it seems benign, such an increase in military authority revives fears of past overreaching during the late 1960s.

. . .

This dearth of judicial interpretation has left "the parameters of the [PCA] . . . substantially untested." Due to the resulting lack of clarity, the PCA does not actually prohibit all so-called "exceptions" to its application, and such exceptions-in-name have been enacted to clarify—or, depending upon your view, alter—its boundaries and to provide guidance to military commanders. The greatest uncertainties regarding the PCA concern what constitutes "any part of the Army or Air Force" and what actions "execute the laws."

. . .

The PCA explicitly recognizes constitutional and legislative exceptions to its application. The existence of any constitutional exceptions was contested at the time of the PCA's enactment. Some proponents of the PCA saw the exceptions as inherent in the executive powers of the President and in his position as Commander-in-Chief of the armed forces, thus making them beyond the reach of Congress to limit. Others who supported the PCA's passage recognized no such exceptions. The existence of constitutional exceptions to the PCA may only actually lie in the "twilight zone" where the President may act where Congress has not. . . .

Another "constitutional" exception to the PCA is described by the Department of Defense regulations based upon the "inherent right of the U.S. Government . . . to ensure the preservation of public order

and to carry out governmental operations . . . by force, if necessary."
The Office of Legal Counsel of the Department of Justice has
promulgated a similar view in recognition of the U.S. government's
power to protect federal functions. The power to protect federal
functions has been so broadly interpreted, however, that if accepted
it would become the exception that swallows the rule. Now-Chief
Justice William Rehnquist interpreted this power to extend to any
"uniquely federal responsibility" while he was an attorney in the
Office of Legal Counsel. However, this exception has yet to be tested
in the courts and would likely be interpreted as narrowly as the other
exceptions to the PCA.

Congress itself has recognized several exceptions to the PCA,
which this Note categorizes as exceptions-in-fact and exceptions-in-
name. The exceptions-in-fact are true exceptions that exempt
otherwise criminal actions under the PCA and alter its boundaries.
Exceptions-in-name include exceptions that are described or
perceived as exceptions to the PCA, but which authorize allowable
acts under any of the court-created tests. Exceptions-in-name do not
alter the accepted boundaries of the PCA and do not make previously
criminal acts legal. They are sometimes simply termed
"clarifications."

Exceptions-in-name allow the military to provide equipment and
supplies, technical assistance, information, and training to law
enforcement agencies. Such provisions constitute passive assistance
to civilian law enforcement, which does not subject any civilian to the
regulatory, proscriptive, or coercive power of the military.

. . .

Exceptions-in-fact . . . include the quelling of civil disturbances
and labor strife that rises to the level of civil disorder. For example,
Troops were used to put down the Whiskey Rebellion long before the
PCA was passed and to maintain order during school desegregation
in the South after the Act's passage. Troops have . . . been used to
quell riots in Detroit and other cities. More recently, they were
deployed on the streets of Los Angeles in 1992 after the Rodney King
verdict.

The courts have recognized another type of exception through
the military purpose doctrine, which is not explicitly mentioned in
the PCA. The doctrine allows the military to enforce civilian laws on
military installations, to police themselves, and to perform their
military functions even if there is an incidental benefit to civilian law
enforcement.

. . .

There are many other uses of the military which seem to
implicate the PCA, but are not within its scope because [the] law is

not being enforced. Since the passage of the PCA, the military has been used several times for domestic purposes that do not conform to its traditional role. The PCA proscribes use of the army in civilian law enforcement, but it has not prevented military assistance in what have been deemed national emergencies, such as strike replacements and disaster relief. However, these emergencies differ in character from other exceptions to the PCA by their very nature as emergencies and by the duration of the military involvement.

. . .

The PCA's exceptions-in-name and exceptions-in-fact endanger the military and the United States by blurring the traditional line between military and civilian roles, undermining civilian control of the military, damaging military readiness, and providing the wrong tool for the job.

. . .

The military's primary mission is national security, and the wisdom of all military decisions is ultimately weighed against whether national security is enhanced or damaged. Military readiness is a key to modern warfare and to the maintenance of national security. In recognition of this fact, the military can refuse a request for aid in drug interdiction and in the investigation of chemical and biological weapons if military readiness might be compromised. However, this power of refusal does not prevent injury to military readiness, because while the military still takes on these missions, their mere consideration injures readiness through the redirection of resources in the decisionmaking process by adding a nonmilitary factor to the decision.

The border duty, investigative support, and drug interdiction exceptions are double-edged swords with respect to military readiness. The military has embraced new missions like drug interdiction as a way to preserve force structure and budget levels and to improve public relations. In this respect, these new missions may aid readiness by preserving support for military strength and funding, but this benefit is outweighed by the shift of focus slightly away from the mission to fight a war. This change of focus lessens the fighting edge of the military and dampens the "warrior spirit." Additionally, these missions require equipment modifications and the reallocation of resources. For example, F-15 pilots do not hone their dogfighting skills by tracking a single-engine Cessna flying north from Mexico; in the Gulf War, there were stories of inadequately trained National Guard units that had participated more frequently in nontraditional missions, yet were incapable of fulfilling their military mission.

The three exceptions to the PCA affect military readiness in a variety of ways. Drug interdiction has injured military readiness as a result of expensive equipment modifications and the redirection of resources. The 1993 Department of Defense budget included more than $1.4 billion for drug interdiction missions. This budget allocation has resulted in a "drug command" of sorts which is entirely focussed on the domestic mission of drug interdiction. Border duty requires a different mindset and a different level of restraint than warfare, thus disrupting the optimum culture and mindset needed to maintain national security. Investigatory support by the military is also a mission differing from that which currently exists in the military. To redirect resources or to consider performing such nonmilitary missions involves considerations that lessen the importance of strictly improving military readiness, even when the only question is where to train.

Illegal immigration, drug interdiction, and investigative support relating to terrorism are all long-term problems requiring long-term solutions. These problems are not easily resolved, however, and no foreseeable end to the military's involvement appears forthcoming. Because of the significance of the problems and their continuing and chronic nature, using the military to combat these problems is like using a sledge hammer to open a locked trunk when all one needs is the key. It is better to fashion a key than to destroy the trunk.

All three exceptions to the PCA require using the wrong tool for the job. For example, border duty forces the military to alter its mindset and training. The border patrol and other law enforcement agencies already have the proper mindset and qualifications and are better able to do the job. Using an F-15 to track drug smugglers' slow planes is both excessive and expensive. A basic military soldier costs the government $82,000 a year in training and upkeep. A soldier's involvement in drug interdiction is much more expensive than a civilian counterpart's participation. Investigatory support for weapons of mass destruction to counter terrorism is more than a minor exception because terrorism is a continuing problem without end. We would best be served by developing these resources in civilian law enforcement.

The fundamental precept of maintaining the separation between the military and civilian spheres of action must be renewed, not eroded by exceptions. Both exceptions-in-name and exceptions-in-fact should be avoided because they injure that separation. To maintain the principle that animates the PCA, the PCA should be reaffirmed and strengthened. The need to fight "the war" on drugs, to combat terrorism, and to deter illegal immigration are long-term problems that are currently high on the public agenda and will not go away without long-term solutions. Tight budgets and the desire for a quick-fix do not create an emergency justifying the conversion of martial rhetoric to reality. Relegating these problems to a military solution poses dangers to our individual rights and to the history and underlying structure of the United States that should not be ignored.

. . .

Resources must be made available to create viable civilian law enforcement responses to these problems. If these resources must be redirected from the military, then Congress should do so. Declare "war," but let it be fought by civilian law enforcement with the right weapons for the job. The military should be the last resort, not the first solution. In the long run, the "war" will be more effectively fought with dedicated "soldiers" with an undivided focus.

2.   Hurricane Katrina placed enormous strains on the major exception to the Posse Comitatus Act that is carved out in the Insurrection Act, 10 U.S.C. § 333. For an excellent, detailed recounting of the dynamic that occurred at the time between the Bush administration and the governor of Louisiana, see Thaddeus Hoffmeister, "The Transformative Power of Law: An Insurrection Act for the Twenty-First Century," 39 Stetson L. Rev. 861 (2010). As a result of these strains and concerns about the ability to use the military to respond to major emergencies, 10 U.S.C. § 333 was substantially rewritten by the Congress, without significant public discussion, to read as follows:

Title 10, U.S.C.

§ 333.   Major public emergencies; interference with State and Federal law

     (a)   Use of armed forces in major public emergencies.

     (1)   The President may employ the armed forces, including the National Guard in Federal service, to—

        (A)   restore public order and enforce the laws of the United States when, as a result of a natural disaster, epidemic, or other serious public health emergency, terrorist attack or incident, or other condition in any State or possession of the United States, the President determines that—

           (i)   domestic violence has occurred to such an extent that the constituted authorities of the State or possession are incapable of maintaining public order; and

           (ii)   such violence results in a condition described in paragraph (2); or

        (B) suppress, in a State, any insurrection, domestic violence, unlawful combination, or conspiracy if such insurrection, violation, combination, or conspiracy results in a condition described in paragraph (2).

(2)   A condition described in this paragraph is a condition that—

(A)   so hinders the execution of the laws of a State or possession, as applicable, and of the United States within that State or possession, that any part or class of its people is deprived of a right, privilege, immunity, or protection named in the Constitution and secured by law, and the constituted authorities of that State or possession are unable, fail, or refuse to protect that right, privilege, or immunity, or to give that protection; or

(B)   opposes or obstructs the execution of the laws of the United States or impedes the course of justice under those laws.

(3)   In any situation covered by paragraph (1)(B), the State shall be considered to have denied the equal protection of the laws secured by the Constitution.

(b)   Notice to Congress. The President shall notify Congress of the determination to exercise the authority in subsection (a)(1)(A) as soon as practicable after the determination and every 14 days thereafter during the duration of the exercise of that authority.

3.   This amended version of the statute caused concerns, mainly among state governors, and as result, the 2006 version of 10 U.S.C. § 333 was repealed in 2008, and the prior version reinstated. The earlier and current version reads as follows:

Title 10, U.S.C.

§ 333.   Interference with State and Federal law

The President, by using the militia or the armed forces, or both, or by any other means, shall take such measures as he considers necessary to suppress, in a State, any insurrection, domestic violence, unlawful combination, or conspiracy, if it—

(1)   so hinders the execution of the laws of that State, and of the United States within the State, that any part or class of its people is deprived of a right, privilege, immunity, or protection named in the Constitution and secured by law, and the constituted authorities of that State are unable, fail, or refuse to protect that right, privilege, or immunity, or to give that protection; or

(2)   opposes or obstructs the execution of the laws of the United States or impedes the course of justice under those laws.

In any situation covered by clause (1), the State shall be considered to have denied the equal protection of the laws secured by the Constitution.

4.   The same concerns which had prompted the enactment of the revised version of § 333 persisted, however, and scholars have called for revision of the Insurrection Act. Thus, for example, Professor Hoffmeister, see note 2, supra,

argues for a revised version of the 2006 Act. Also see Ashley J. Craw, A Call to Arms: Civil Disorder Following Hurricane Katrina Warrants Attack on the Posse Comitatus Act, 14 Geo. Mason L. Rev. 829, 850–851 (2007):

> Due to the . . . inadequacies of the law enforcement component of current natural disaster response systems, Congress should pass a statutory exception to the PCA allowing the military to keep the peace and prevent chaos immediately following a large-scale natural disaster.

5. How did the 2006 amendment of the Insurrection Act change the circumstances in which the President could order the military to act on the domestic front? Was this a significant inroad on the policy underlying the Posse Comitatus Act?

6. Were there adequate safeguards in the 2006 amended language? To protect against what? Would you have added any more?

7. Suppose it is concluded that the FBI does not have adequate resources to handle the task of policing the entire country in regard to terrorism? What are our options for increasing the manpower to be thrown into the anti-terrorism effort? Should using the military be considered as one of the viable options?

8. Clearly there are exceptions even under existing law that permit the military to provide assistance to law enforcement agencies. Are there specific tasks which the military should be prohibited from performing domestically?

9. Can you imagine a scenario where the U.S. military might be used to help in the hunt for a criminal suspect, such as a serial killer? Could the statutory exceptions be employed to use military surveillance planes or intelligence assets to track down a criminal suspect without any clear nexus to terrorism? During the hunt in Oct. 2002 for the alleged "Washington DC Sniper," this is exactly what happened. Consider Phillip Carter, Why Can the Army Help Cops Catch the D.C. Sniper?, Slate, Oct. 17, 2002:

> The U.S. Army has sent aircraft to help Beltway police find the sniper who has murdered nine people. But a federal statute prohibits the military from enforcing domestic law. So, when, exactly, can soldiers help the cops?
>
> Almost always, so long as they don't directly engage in police work. The Army can offer intelligence, transportation, and logistical assistance to cops, but it can't conduct searches or make arrests.
>
> . . .
>
> No one has ever been prosecuted for violating the Posse Comitatus Act. That's partly because it has a number of exceptions—enough exceptions, it turns out, to virtually swallow the rule.
>
> . . .

In the 1980s . . . [t]he main exceptions grew out of the "War on Drugs," allowing the military to do things like fly surveillance planes on the U.S. border with Mexico, train police officers in various military specialties, or provide radar data to the U.S. Border Patrol and Customs Service. A federal law also allows the military to share intelligence with local law enforcement officers, provided the intel is collected during normal military operations. Another major exception, created in 1996 after the Oklahoma City bombing, authorizes the military to provide support to local cops in the event of a chemical or biological attack.

The Army's current plan to fly reconnaissance planes in Maryland is covered by these exceptions: Army personnel will fly the planes and operate the equipment, but civilian police will ride along to analyze any evidence gathered while in flight.

10.   Are the core values that the Posse Comitatus Act is designed to serve threatened by permitting Army personnel to get involved in a domestic criminal or terrorism investigation by flying reconnaissance planes and operating the plane's surveillance equipment? Is this a slippery slope issue?

11.   See the lead editorial in the New York Times, July, 30, 2009, The Military Is Not the Police, A 24, expressing concerns about the use of the military in a police role, specifically reacting to a news story that President Bush had considered sending troops into Buffalo in 2002 to arrest a group of terrorist suspects.

12.   Consider also the following: On January 24, 2017, four days after his inauguration, President Donald Trump tweeted that "If Chicago doesn't fix the horrible "carnage" going on, [citing the number of shootings and killings], I will send in the Feds!" This was interpreted by some as a threat to send in the military or impose martial law. See, for example, https://www.salon.com/2017/01/25/donald-trump-threatens-to-impose-martial-law-in-chicago-and-it-may-be-over-a-feud-with-rahm-emanuel/. (Of course, he might have meant that he would send in the FBI, or other federal agencies.) Would the President have the authority to send in military forces or declare martial law to deal with the problem of gang violence or a high rate of killings in Chicago?

APPENDIX

EXCERPTS FROM GENEVA CONVENTION III RELATIVE TO THE TREATMENT OF PRISONERS OF WAR, 75 U.N.T.S. 135, ENTERED INTO FORCE OCT. 21, 1950

■ ■ ■

General Provisions

Article 1

The High Contracting Parties undertake to respect and to ensure respect for the present Convention in all circumstances.

Article 2

In addition to the provisions which shall be implemented in peace time, the present Convention shall apply to all cases of declared war or of any other armed conflict which may arise between two or more of the High Contracting Parties, even if the state of war is not recognized by one of them.

The Convention shall also apply to all cases of partial or total occupation of the territory of a High Contracting Party, even if the said occupation meets with no armed resistance.

Although one of the Powers in conflict may not be a party to the present Convention, the Powers who are parties thereto shall remain bound by it in their mutual relations. They shall furthermore be bound by the Convention in relation to the said Power, if the latter accepts and applies the provisions thereof.

. . .

Article 4

A. Prisoners of war, in the sense of the present Convention, are persons belonging to one of the following categories, who have fallen into the power of the enemy:

1. Members of the armed forces of a Party to the conflict as well as members of militias or volunteer corps forming part of such armed forces.

2. Members of other militias and members of other volunteer corps, including those of organized resistance movements, belonging

to a Party to the conflict and operating in or outside their own territory, even if this territory is occupied, provided that such militias or volunteer corps, including such organized resistance movements, fulfill the following conditions:

(a) That of being commanded by a person responsible for his subordinates;

(b) That of having a fixed distinctive sign recognizable at a distance;

(c) That of carrying arms openly;

(d) That of conducting their operations in accordance with the laws and customs of war.

3. Members of regular armed forces who profess allegiance to a government or an authority not recognized by the Detaining Power.

. . .

6. Inhabitants of a non-occupied territory, who on the approach of the enemy spontaneously take up arms to resist the invading forces, without having had time to form themselves into regular armed units, provided they carry arms openly and respect the laws and customs of war.

. . .

Article 5

The present Convention shall apply to the persons referred to in Article 4 from the time they fall into the power of the enemy and until their final release and repatriation.

Should any doubt arise as to whether persons, having committed a belligerent act and having fallen into the hands of the enemy, belong to any of the categories enumerated in Article 4, such persons shall enjoy the protection of the present Convention until such time as their status has been determined by a competent tribunal.

. . .

Article 9

The provisions of the present Convention constitute no obstacle to the humanitarian activities which the International Committee of the Red Cross or any other impartial humanitarian organization may, subject to the consent of the Parties to the conflict concerned, undertake for the protection of prisoners of war and for their relief.

Article 10

. . .

When prisoners of war do not benefit or cease to benefit, no matter for what reason, by the activities of a Protecting Power or of an organization provided for in the first paragraph above, the Detaining Power shall request a neutral State, or such an organization, to undertake the functions performed under the present Convention by a Protecting Power designated by the Parties to a conflict.

If protection cannot be arranged accordingly, the Detaining Power shall request or shall accept, subject to the provisions of this Article, the offer of the services of a humanitarian organization, such as the International Committee of the Red Cross, to assume the humanitarian functions performed by Protecting Powers under the present Convention.

Any neutral Power or any organization invited by the Power concerned or offering itself for these purposes, shall be required to act with a sense of responsibility towards the Party to the conflict on which persons protected by the present Convention depend, and shall be required to furnish sufficient assurances that it is in a position to undertake the appropriate functions and to discharge them impartially.

Article 11

In cases where they deem it advisable in the interest of protected persons, particularly in cases of disagreement between the Parties to the conflict as to the application or interpretation of the provisions of the present Convention, the Protecting Powers shall lend their good offices with a view to settling the disagreement.

For this purpose, each of the Protecting Powers may, either at the invitation of one Party or on its own initiative, propose to the Parties to the conflict a meeting of their representatives, and in particular of the authorities responsible for prisoners of war, possibly on neutral territory suitably chosen. The Parties to the conflict shall be bound to give effect to the proposals made to them for this purpose. The Protecting Powers may, if necessary, propose for approval by the Parties to the conflict a person belonging to a neutral Power, or delegated by the International Committee of the Red Cross, who shall be invited to take part in such a meeting.

PART II

General Protection of Prisoners of War

. . .

Article 13

Prisoners of war must at all times be humanely treated. Any unlawful act or omission by the Detaining Power causing death or seriously endangering the health of a prisoner of war in its custody is prohibited, and will be regarded as a serious breach of the present Convention. In particular, no prisoner of war may be subjected to physical mutilation or to medical or scientific experiments of any kind which are not justified by the medical, dental or hospital treatment of the prisoner concerned and carried out in his interest.

Likewise, prisoners of war must at all times be protected, particularly against acts of violence or intimidation and against insults and public curiosity.

Measures of reprisal against prisoners of war are prohibited.

Article 14

Prisoners of war are entitled in all circumstances to respect for their persons and their honour.

Women shall be treated with all the regard due to their sex and shall in all cases benefit by treatment as favourable as that granted to men.

Prisoners of war shall retain the full civil capacity which they enjoyed at the time of their capture. The Detaining Power may not restrict the exercise, either within or without its own territory, of the rights such capacity confers except in so far as the captivity requires.

Article 15

The Power detaining prisoners of war shall be bound to provide free of charge for their maintenance and for the medical attention required by their state of health.

Article 16

Taking into consideration the provisions of the present Convention relating to rank and sex, and subject to any privileged treatment which may be accorded to them by reason of their state of health, age or professional qualifications, all prisoners of war shall be treated alike by the Detaining Power, without any adverse distinction based on race, nationality, religious belief or political opinions, or any other distinction founded on similar criteria.

Captivity

Section I

Beginning of Captivity

Article 17

Every prisoner of war, when questioned on the subject, is bound to give only his surname, first names and rank, date of birth, and army, regimental, personal or serial number, or failing this, equivalent information.

If he wilfully infringes this rule, he may render himself liable to a restriction of the privileges accorded to his rank or status.

Each Party to a conflict is required to furnish the persons under its jurisdiction who are liable to become prisoners of war, with an identity card showing the owner's surname, first names, rank, ...

No physical or mental torture, nor any other form of coercion, may be inflicted on prisoners of war to secure from them information of any kind whatever. Prisoners of war who refuse to answer may not be threatened, insulted, or exposed to any unpleasant or disadvantageous treatment of any kind.

. . .

INDEX

References are to Pages
